The Drama: Kleist

Matthias Goertz

ATROPOS PRESS
new york • dresden

To my mother.

© 2019 by Matthias Goertz

Think Media EGS Series is supported by the European Graduate School

ATROPOS PRESS
New York • Dresden

151 First Avenue # 14, New York, N.Y. 10003

Book Design by Sarah and Schooling

All rights reserved

I-S-B-N

Table of Contents

Acknowledgements		vii
Author's Note		ix
Abbreviations		xi

1.	**FOUR "LIVES" OF KLEIST**	
1.1	"was so ein Emigrant zu tun hat": *The Satirical*	2
1.2	"den sichern Weg des Glücks zu finden": *The Satyrical*	12
1.3	"Ah! Der Skorpion!": *The Syphilitical*	21
1.4	"auch das sagen, was er nicht sagt": *The Po(i)etical*	44

2.	**THE EIGHT DRAMAS**	
2.1	*Die Familie Schroffenstein*: The German Disease (A Diagnosis)	62
2.2	*Robert Guiskard*: The Usurper's Death (A Prognosis Ahead of Its Time)	107
2.3	*Der Zerbrochne Krug*: Coronation at Vienna (An Urgent Manifesto to The King)	138
2.4	*Amphitryon*: Endless Night at Königsberg (Another Urgent Manifesto to The King)	190
2.5	*Penthesilea*: The Usurper's Death: Reloaded (An Utopia)	244
2.6	*Das Käthchen von Heilbronn*: Wedding at Vienna (A Fantasy Staged Too Late)	298
2.7	*Die Hermannsschlacht*: World of Warfare version.09 (A MMORPG Wargame)	342
2.8	*Prinz Friedrich von Homburg*: Of Lordship and Bondage (A Swansong)	386

3.	**KLEIST'S PLANE OF COMPOSITION**	
3.1	Notes on Projects Not Executed or Not Extant	442
3.2	*The Berliner Abendblätter* as Poetico-Political Platform	484
3.3	Further "Lives" of Kleist: *The Priapic, The Familial, The Filial, The Orphic*	494

| 3.4 | On the Magnetic Symposium: A Fool's Journey | 551 |

List of Images of Artworks Reproduced   567
Endnotes   584

Acknowledgements

My greatest thanks are due to my wife Lamyai who endured this book's lengthy genesis. Kleist's writing is addictive, and once it has us in thrall, it does not let go, and our spouses first and foremost suffer from our intoxication.

Many thanks to Sarah and Schooling for their beautiful layout design, to Wolfgang Schirmacher for his invaluable support, and to Rachel Donald at Atropos Press for her excellent management of the book's publication.

Author's Note

The dramas represent Heinrich von Kleist's foremost poetic creations—the ones dearest to him, into which, over a period of ten years, he invested his greatest passion (desire, pathos, suffering). Chr. Martin Wieland saw Kleist "uniting the spirits of Aeschylus, Sophocles and Shakespeare," yet I maintain that Kleist above all emulated Aristophanes, grand master of the eminently political and parodistic, and often exceedingly licentious and bawdy, Attic Old Comedy. Whatever his models, Kleist's works are unprecedented, in that they comprise intricate text(ure)s woven together from multiple *covert* (not immediately evident) topical "threads" that together produce seemingly conventional *overt* narratives which, however, merely serve as vehicle and camouflage for the "threads" encrypted into them. Kleist obliquely hinted at the nature and process of his poetic production in a letter of June 1801: *"Alles liegt in mir verworren, wie die Werchfasern im Spinnerocken, durcheinander… selbst meine Wünsche wechseln, und bald tritt der eine, bald der andere ins Dunkle, wie die Gegenstände einer Landschaft, wenn die Wolken drüber ziehen"* (II:654).

Reading Kleist entails a quasi-Foulcauldian archaeology, a quasi-Freudian *"Lesetechnik"*: the unravelling, excavation, decryption of codified messages and their evaluation in relation to the discursive formations that shaped Kleist's historical and social context and his personal biography. Kleist's works, their *overt* packaging apart, comprise *nothing but* codified messages—*they are pure code*—, and the reader who ignores or rejects this fact is doomed, like the diver who refuses to don scuba gear, to float on the ocean's choppy surface, unable to fathom the wondrous world below, let alone immerse himself into it.

The Drama: Kleist traces and unravels the "threads" or "lives" Kleist encoded into his eight dramas. Part I examines four pertinent Kleistian "lives": his *political* appeals to the Hohenzollern King Fr. Wilh. III, the Habsburg Emperor Franz II/I, and their respective courtiers and ministers (*"The Satirical"*); his *erotic* fantasies of pederast, symposiac and orgiastic homosexual experiences (*"The Satyrical"*); his *personal*— psychological and physiological—battles with the harrowing symptoms and social effects of syphilis and the disease's no less gruesome therapies (*"The Syphilitical"*); his *poetical* investments in agonistic duels with the likes of Goethe and Iffland, modulated by his need to derive income and recognition from his professional work (*"The Po(i) etical"*). Part II excavates these four "threads" or "lives" from each of the eight dramas. Part III widens the exploration of Kleist's "plane of composition" to encompass select other poetic projects, beyond the dramas, as well as four additional "lives." This treatise complements my previous books, *The Emigrant, the Emperor, the King and Everybody's Favourite Queen*, in which I explore "*The Satirical*" and "*The Satyrical*" in Kleist's novellas, and *The Awakening Child*, in which I develop my instrumentarium for reading—decoding—Kleist, and begin to identify "navels"—apparent inconsistencies or incommensurabilities—from which Kleist's works can be unravelled.

Kleist, with his *covert* "threads," targeted specific audiences, as well as, with his *overt* stories, aiming for a commercial mass market; and yet, in a certain sense, he wrote above all *for himself*: for the national bard or herold, the puppeteer, magnétiseur or voodoo master that Kleist aspired to be, for whom his works provide the script, stage, channel, stage directions, sets, props, engines, score and choreography with which he lets his "puppets"—emperors, kings, queens, courtiers and ministers, intellectuals and lovers, rival poets, critics and theatre directors—dance to his tune, turn on a dime, supercharge and discharge, dither and die. It is not that Kleist never produced or pursued the "life plan" he announced in his early letters: he did, in and through his works. His dramas stage and enact his dramatic life's *Agôn* and *Erôs*, its *Kampfplätze* and *Lustgärten*, while rehearsing his theatrical death, the inevitable collapse of his body and the yearned-for release of his soul.

Kleist's works being thoroughly autobiographical, *The Drama: Kleist* chronicles a poet's *line of flight* whose vanishing point could only have entailed self-annihilation, and whose trajectory tracks the very "*Schönheitslinie*" that, in Kleist's own conception, makes for exciting drama. As Kleist hurls himself towards the abyss, like a comet towards the Sun's embrace, his poetry soars like an eagle and stands tall like a cedar—his own metaphors, bawdy ones, through which, in his happier hours, he celebrated life: health, joy, friendship, loyalty, virility, vigour, creation and procreation, the good, the true and the beautiful.

Matthias Goertz, Singapore, March 2019

Matthias Goertz is Heinrich von Kleist Fellow at the European Graduate School's Division of Philosophy, Art and Critical Thought. He is Author of *The Awakening Child: Re-reading Kleist* (Atropos Press, 2014) and *The Emigrant, the Emperor, the King and Everybody's Favourite Queen: The Satirical and Satyrical Novellas of Heinrich von Kleist* (Atropos Press, 2018). He lives in Singapore with his family.

Abbreviations

BA	*Berliner Abendblätter* (Ed. Heinr. von Kleist)
Ph	*Phöbus. Ein Journal für die Kunst* (Eds. Heinr. von Kleist, A. Müller)
I, II	Heinrich von Kleist. *Sämtliche Werke und Briefe*, Vols. 1 and 2 (Ed. Helmut Sembdner)
MA I, II, III	Heinrich von Kleist. *Sämtliche Werke und Briefe*, Münchener Ausgabe, Vols. 1, 2 and 3 (Eds. Roland Reuß, Peter Staengle)
LS*	*Kleists Lebensspuren* (Ed. Helmut Sembdner)
NR*	*Kleists Nachruhm* (Ed. Helmut Sembdner)
KJB	*Kleist Jahrbuch* (Eds. Hans Joachim Kreutzer, Günther Blamberger, et al)
KH	*Kleist Handbuch* (Ed. Ingo Breuer)
Beiträge	*Beiträge zur Kleist-Forschung* (Eds. Wolfgang Barthel, Hans-Jochen Marquardt)
AML*	*Adam Müllers Lebenszeugnisse* (Ed. Jakob Baxa)
HRR	*Heiliges Römisches Reich* (Holy Roman Empire)
RF	*République française* ([1st] French Republic)
ARF	*Armée révolutionnaire française* (the army of the 1st Republic)

Ad'A	*Armée d'Allemagne* (French imperial army)
HQ	Headquarters

A.; Alex.; Aug.; Chr.; Ferd., Fr.; Heinr.; Joh.; Max.; Wilh.; L.
Recurring given names: Adam; Alexander; August; Christoph or Christian; Ferdinand; Friedrich; Heinrich; Johann; Maximilian; Wilhelm; Ludwig

Fr. Wilh.	Prussian King Friedrich Wilhelm III
	(for King Fr. Wilh. II the Roman numeral II is always given)
M. / Mme	Monsieur / Madame
/O.; /M.; /H.; i.Br.	an der Oder; am Main; an der Havel; im Breisgau
RT	*Reichsthaler*
	(widely used silver coin, 16th-19th century)
OT; NT	Old Testament; New Testament (Bible)
AD; BC	Anno Domini; before Christ
VIP	Very important person
M&A	Mergers & acquisitions
BDSM	Bondage & discipline, dominance & submission, Sadism & Masochism
MMORPG	Massively multiplayer on-line role-playing game
VR	Virtual reality
Trans.	Translation
Vol./Vols.	Volume/volumes

Ed./Eds.   Edition; editor/editors

MS; MSS   Manuscript; manuscripts

Ger.; Fr.; Engl.; Span.; Lat.; Gr.; Hebr.
German; French; English; Spanish; Latin; Greek; Hebrew

FLTR; LHS; RHS   From left to right; left-hand side; right-hand side

n.   Note, footnote

LS, NR and *AML* are quoted by entry number, not page number

1. Four "Lives" of Kleist

1.1 "was so ein Emigrant zu tun hat": The Satirical

In *Emigrant* I maintained that Kleist throughout his poetic career pursued a decidedly political agenda—whose pursuit may have compelled him to become a poet (a bard, a rhapsode) in the first place, rather than, say, an officer or civil servant—; that with the help of a technique I term *"pescheräic"* (the exploitation of a word's multiple significations, and more generally, of language's plasticity diverse contexts) he sought to manipulate the political leaders of his day; and that in every work discus in that treatise—the eight novellas, select poems, essays and anecdotes—he betrays his political credo, as well as offering his diagnosis and prescription to political decision-makers in view of unfolding historical events. This political, activist "thread" that pervades his life and œuvre I term *"The Satirical."*[1] The *Kleist-Forschung* has largely rejected the notion of, or chosen to ignore the evidence for, a consistent political purpose informing Kleist's œuvre beyond those few works or projects, often treated as outliers, in which a political agenda is self-evident, such as *Hermannsschlacht*, *Homburg*, and *Germania*.[2] I argue that, conversely, Kleist pursued a deeply-felt calling as political bard, advisor and augur, called upon to compose and perform poetic works in response to, or in anticipation of, actual political developments, in which he analysed the situation and its complications, framed scenarios of plausible future developments, and offered recommendations for action to his target audiences, above all the Prussian King and the Holy Roman Emperor.[3]

Kleist is a master of Castiglionian *sprezzatura*—"a certain nonchalance, so as to conceal all art and make whatever one does or says appear to be without effort and almost without any thought about it"—, and of *"Raffinesse"*—a cynical "cheekiness," "deception" and "sophistication in league with ambition" Peter Sloterdijk ascribes to the rococo and enlightenment thinkers:

> Nicht nur kann man Täuschungen erleiden, man kann sie auch, ungetäuscht, gegen andere benutzen. Genau das haben die Denker des Rokoko und der Aufklärung vor Augen gehabt—von denen sich im übrigen nicht wenige mit dem antiken Kynismus befaßt hatten (z.B.

Diderot, Ch. M. Wieland). Sie benennen diese Struktur—mangels einer entwickelten Terminologie—als "Raffinesse", die im Bündnis mit dem "Ehrgeiz" steht; beides sind Qualitäten, die der Menschenkenntnis in der höfischen und städtischen Sphäre jener Zeit geläufig waren. In Wahrheit bedeutet diese Betrugstheorie eine große logische Entdeckung—einen Vorstoß der Ideologiekritik zum Konzept einer *reflexiven Ideologie*.[4]

The dramas in particular, I maintain, were meant to be recited before these rulers and their respective entourages, or to be staged at their private theatres, or else on their respective capital cities' public stages, among whose audiences members of the court and government would be expected to be present, as had been the case in antiquity among Greek amphitheatres' audiences during major festivals. Among Kleist's role models were the classical *dramatists*, whose tragedies and comedies were performed at festivals such as the Attic City Dionysia, the medieval *troubadours*, whose courtly songs combined romance with politics, as well as the ancient Greek *rhapsodes*, who performed oral recitations of Homeric epics, hymns, and cult lyrics. Greek rhapsody influenced oral narrative poetry and rhapsodic music throughout the ages, all the way to our contemporary rap, at various times paralleled by the performances of, say, Celtic bards, Germanic skalds, and medieval minstrels; the term *"rhapsōidein,"* "to sew together," perfectly denotes Kleist's methodology: like the ancient rhapsodes, he built a repertoire of dramas, epics, myths, tales, anecdotes, jokes, news reports, topical allusions, etc. he wove together to tailor messages to audience and occasion.[5] A commensurate *rhapsode,* Kleist in his poetic productions liberally mixed elements of the Old Comedy (*archaia*) of an Aristophanes and (in the Lat. tradition) Plautus, famous for his puns and wordgames, the tragedy (*tragodoi*) of an Aeschylus, Sophocles and Euripides, the oratory of a Demosthenes and Cicero, the satire of a Lucian, Horace, Ovid, Martial and Juvenal, the *grand chants* or *canzones* of the medieval troubadours, the modern drama of a Shakespeare, Cervantes and Schiller, and various popular modern genres of storytelling: "mirror for princes" literature, Rabelaisian irreverent satire, burlesque commedia dell'arte, picaresque novel, "pornographic enlightenment literature in flagranti" (Sloterdijk), Goethean *Bildungsroman*, Grimmean fairy tale, Lewisian gothic tale, Kotzebuean *Rührstück* (melodramatic romance), traditional chronicle, news report, etc.⁶

Nowhere does Kleist explicitly articulate his political credo, which I reconstruct through my *"critical and clinical"* (Deleuze) evaluation of his works, but there are occasional hints at it in letters and essays. In his famous late-1805 letter to Otto Aug. Rühle von Lilienstern, Kleist laments Fr. Wilh.'s temporising and uninspiring response to Napoleon's aggression, and wonders: *"Warum sich nur nicht einer findet, der diesem bösen Geiste der Welt die Kugel durch den Kopf jagt. Ich möchte wissen, was so ein Emigrant zu tun hat—"* (II:761).⁷ In *Emigrant* (whose title is inspired by this passage), I offered that the "emigrant" Kleist had in mind not one, but two, *"böse Geister"* whose brains he would love to blow out: Napoleon *and* Fr. Wilh.: while Napoleon's removal was obviously required for a free and unified Germany to be achieved, Kleist at times dared to think that his King's replacement by a more effective successor could also become a necessary step towards it (his loyalty was to the House of Hohenzollern, not to any specific incumbent of the throne). In the 1811 essay *Brief eines Dichters an einen anderen* Kleist offers three examples of his political concerns, which I summarised in *Emigrant* as follows:

> So what are those "great, sublime, cosmopolitan" issues Kleist cares about? He gives three examples—all paradoxes—in reference to Shakespeare's plays:
>
> - A historic battle—the *Battle of Agincourt* of 1415—in which a numerically superior army is defeated, encumbered by its very scale (*Henry V*).
> - A person of noble spirit [who] is brought down, like the oak tree in Kleist's paradox, precisely because his spirit is too noble (*Hamlet*).⁸
> - A leader who commits heinous crimes in order to secure his succession promptly perishes without having produced a successor (*Macbeth*).

These three examples, Kleist is hinting to his readers, have their concrete equivalents in his own time and work: *Agincourt = Austerlitz* and *Jena-Auerstedt*; Hamlet = Fr. Wilh. III; Macbeth = Napoleon. *Voilà*, in a nutshell we have here Kleist's main *satirical* concerns that inspire all his novellas, if not all his major works. (*Emigrant*, 384-5)

Such occasional hints in view, on the basis of my evaluation of the novellas in *Emigrant* I reconstructed Kleist's political credo as follows:

[W]e are now in a position to paraphrase his *credo*:
- [Diagnosis] Napoleon's hegemony over Germany and Europe is above all a result of the disunity and mistrust among the German princes, in particular the Habsburgs and the Hohenzollerns, as well as the mistakes made by German leaders, above all Fr. Wilh.
- [Prognosis] Unless Napoleon is overcome, he and his dynasty will eventually rule most of Europe and "*francofy*" Germany; to avoid this outcome, Napoleon must be defeated and the Holy Roman Empire reinstalled (ideally under Hohenzollern leadership).
- [Prescription] To defeat Napoleon, the German princes must put the common before their dynastic interest and put themselves at the head of a broad-based people's insurrection.
- [Treatment] Fr. Wilh. III must be replaced by a more courageous and decisive successor who can mobilise and lead the Germans; this decisive step is to be achieved with the help of the bard's advocacy. (*ibid*, 386)

In the present treatise, in exploring *"The Satirical"* in each of the eight dramas, I shall proceed on the assumption, subject to further validation, that the findings from my reading of the novellas grosso modo apply to the dramas, and that the same key personages I identified there, the *quaternary* comprising Napoleon, Fr. Wilh., Luise (*Borussia*) and Kleist, will also be prominent here.[9] I shall evaluate each drama in its political context *at the time of its genesis and publication (or staging)*, on the assumption that, like the novellas, the dramas incorporate actual events as they unfold and sketch future scenarios plausible at the time. As the dramas' geneses sometimes overlap with each other, as they do with those of other works—novellas, essays, anecdotes, poems, epigrams, album entries, letters—, political messages may in part repeat (though often from a fresh angle), in part supercede prior ones.

Dynastic Rivalry, Realpolitik and Ohnmacht. As scion of the ancient von Kleist family, which furnished a distinguished line of Prussian generals and, occasionally, poets and inventors in the loyal service of the House of Hohenzollern, Kleist was confronted with Prussian and German political and military affairs early on, as a matter of course. Having entered service in the élite Regiment Garde—since Fr. II the Great's reign the Prussian Kings' personal guard—at the tender age of 15, Kleist partook in several battles of the *War of the First Coalition*, in which German powers led by the Prussian King and the Habsburg Holy Roman Emperor confronted the *RF*, aiming to reinstall the Bourbon monarchy. During the 1793 *Siege of Mainz* and the subsequent 1793-4 *Palatine Campaign*, both part of the *Rhine Campaign* of 1792-5, Kleist gained first-hand experience with a new type of warfare, embodied by the *ARF* and its principle of *levée en masse*, that clashed with the Frederician principles under which the Prussian army still operated. While the *Siege of Mainz* and the *Palatine Campaign* were successful for the Coalition, these ultimately indecisive campaigns tied down the Prussians while further north the *ARF* overcome the Austrians in the more decicive *Flanders Campaign*. Perhaps realising that his costly campaign against France was ineffectual, and desiring to focus on a more promising war in Poland, Prussia's King Fr. Wilh. II in April 1795 entered a separate *Peace of Basel* with the *RF*, in which he and all northern German princes declared themselves neutral just as the *War of the First Coalition* was reaching its peak, leaving the Austrians to their own devices, swinging the pendulum of war in the *RF*'s favour and precipitating the Habsburg Emperor Franz II's accepting the 1797 *Treaty of Campo Formio* which explicitly confirmed key provisions of the *Basel* treaty, including a secret amendment in which Fr. Wilh. II conceded the Rhineland to the *RF*, the object of desire France had been eyeing since at least Louis XIV's reign.

These transactions left an indelible mark on Kleist's political "religion," whose "original sin" *Basel* comprised.[10] The young Kleist, who thought he was fighting on behalf of the status quo ante, the preservation of France's *ancien régime* and the *HRR*'s integrity, was forced to watch his in September 1793 delegating the command of the Rhine army, recalling his generals from strategic positions conquered along the French borders, "parking" his troops in camps in Eschborn and Osnabrück, and, after signing *Basel*, ordering their return to Prussia. Not only will Kleist, like many fellow Prussian officers and cadets, have been deeply frustrated at these developments, but he may even have anticipated that the King's decisions could precipitate the *HRR*'s demise, for if one of its leading dynasties was prepared to compromise the Empire's most important border, and relinquish its most valuable territory, to its arch-enemy, its very existence was called into question.[11] Kleist left no explicit notes on this issue, there being no extant letters from February 1795 till March 1799, but his frequent implicit allusions to the Rhine border in his writings clearly indicate that this was a matter of utmost concern to him. *Basel* and *Campo Formio* constituted Kleist's painful introduction into the world of *Realpolitik*: in a series of treaties an opportunistic Fr. Wilh. II and an ineffective Franz II sacrificed the integrity of the *HRR* on the altar of their respective dynastic self-interests.[12] It was in the wake of these momentous developments that the *political* Kleist fully formed.

His King's abandonment of the Rhine's left bank must have felt to Kleist like a personal injury: the following map superimposes the theatre of war in which he fought onto the political borders fixed by *Basel* and confirmed by *Campo Formio*, showing that the very German cities and lands he had helped defend at his life's risk, his monarch simply signed over to France. Mainz, which Kleist helped liberate, now became known as Mayance, and visiting it meant entering France.

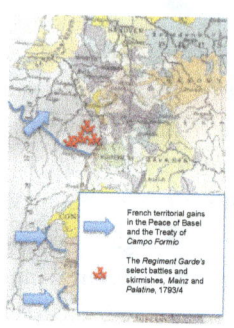

LHS: Major battles Kleist's regiment engaged in, virtually all on territory ceded to France at *Basel*; RHS: Capitulation of Mainz on 22nd July 1793 in the presence of King Fr. Wilh. II and Kleist's Regiment Garde. In the foreground the type of artillery trenches Kleist's unit dug at Marienborn (the hills on the left, in the distance) and before the Gustavsburg (left, just across the Main river).

If Kleist repeatedly laments France's rising political and cultural hegemony over Germany—a development I termed Germany's "*Francofication*"—, it was perhaps this French territorial expansion into German heartland that first sparked his alarm and disgust at those he held responsible for it: the Hohenzollern King, the Habsburg Emperor, and their respective ministers and courtiers. Kleist will have perceived that when Fr. Wilh. II at *Basel* left the *HRR* and Franz II in the lurch, the ancient rivalry between the Hohenzollerns and the Habsburgs played a major role: the jealous Prussian King would rather that the *RF* control the Rhineland and the Netherlands, than that the Habsburgs did. The ultimate victim of such self-interested machinations, Kleist correctly predicted, could only be the *HRR*, and the ultimate beneficiary, France.[13] The "*Ohnmacht*" ("swoon," also "impuissance") into which the Marquise (representing Queen Luise or *Borussia*) in Kleist's 1807 novella *Die Marquise von O....* sinks before Count F (Napoleon) mirrors not only Prussia's powerlessness after the *War of the Fourth Coalition*, but also Kleist's own during the *War of the First Coalition*, forced to observe the war's dismal ending from the imposed idleness at his Potsdam garrison, to which he and his regiment had been confined by Prussia's withdrawal. His dismay at a political—and particularist—settlement that in no way reflected the military successes he and his comrades had helped secure may have been a decisive factor in Kleist's decision to quit the army in April 1799: the arduous and bloody campaigning, the youthful idealism, the killing and maiming, were rendered vain by the single stroke of a pen at *Basel*: the signature of Fr. Wilh. II's plenipotentiary Karl Aug. von Hardenberg. Kleist, I offer, left the Prussian army neither because he dreaded the rigours of warfare, nor because he rejected its outdated Frederician principles (though he certainly did critique them), but because he disdained idly standing by while meek civilians negotiated ignominious treaties that voided the army's bravery. The King and his technocrats relegated Prussia's enthusiastic young officers to a Schopenhauerian suffering and boredom that was bound to breed discontent—it certainly did Kleist's. Thus a young officer exchanged the musket for the pen—and a political, militant poet was born. even though he liked to call them "lost," his years of military service were formative. Throughout his writing career he remained impressed by the power of the cannonades he first witnessed at *Mainz* (soon to underpin Napoleon's victories), yet during his idle years at Potsdam the idea must have solidified that he himself could yield more power with the lyre than the cannon.[14] Kleist, contrary to appearances, never turned his back on the Prussian army: he merely exchanged his "weapon." There was a compelling if audacious logic to his leaving the army: if a pen (Hardenberg's, say) could reshape the map of Europe more effectively than a hundred cannons, then Kleist, who given his personal leanings and talents perhaps expected to attain only a mediocre officer rank, as Germany's national bard could aspire to shaping Europe's destiny.[15]

Dynastic Hybris: Napoleon. Napoleon Bonaparte first appeared on the international political stage as chief French negotiator at *Campo Formio*, having already left his mark as a general during the *First Italian Campaign* of 1796-7, but it will have been with his illustrious *Campaign of Egypt and Syria* of 1798-9, his daring coup d'état in November 1799, his appointment as First Consul, his decisive victory over the *HRR* at the *Battle of Marengo* in June 1800, and the subsequent *Treaty of Lunéville* which ended the *HRR*'s involvement in the *War of the Second Coalition* and cemented the Rhine border, that this Corsican *parvenu* fully entered Kleist's consciousness. When between 1800 and 1802—a period encompassing the Würzburg journey, "Kant-crisis," Paris journey and Swiss sojourn—Kleist's political aspirations crystallised, his rise as poet echoed Napoleon's as ruler: Kleist became a *satirical* bard in the slipstream of the Corsican general becoming the dominant political figure in Europe, the eye of a storm that enthralled and uplifted Kleist as it did many a European intellectual of his day. Napoleon's rise, and the German rulers' paralysis before it, far more than the reading of philosophical treatises, precipitated Kleist's "crisis" (making the "Kant-crisis" something of a "Napoleon crisis"), journey to Paris (Napoleon's seat of power, the centre of Europe), and production of his *Erstling*: Kleist witnessed the dawn of a new era—the *Age of Napoleon*—and decided to wield his word, not his sword.[16] Napoleon, who in Kleist's work first enters the stage as *Schroffenstein*'s witch Ursula, came to loom large in all of Kleist's subsequent political tableaux.[17]

We discern in his dramas how observant and prescient Kleist was with respect to major historical movements: Napoleon's de facto seizing the Holy Roman imperial crown in 1804, and Franz's de jure abdicating it in 1806, he anticipated and articulated as early as 1801, in his first drama, in which he called on the Hohenzollern and Habsburg monarchs to unite and confront Napoleon jointly before he could cement his hegemoniac régime. Kleist never forgot the German monarchs' negligence towards the *HRR* he had witnessed in his youth, and throughout his writing career admonished them not to repeat this mistake, until in 1811 finally concluding that his battle had been in vain: it is surely no coincidence that his final novella's eponymous "*Zweikampf*" pits Franz I (as Rotbart) against Fr. Wilh. III (as Trota) and takes place in—*Basel*.[18] Its dystopian ending—Franz ignominiously pined away, Fr. Wilh. rendered impotent, Napoleon emerged all-powerful—comprises a revisiting and conclusion of a rivalry Kleist first set up, ten years earlier, in his *Erstling*. By locating the duel in Basel, Kleist at the end-point of the arc traced by his œuvre reiterates his credo that *Basel* encompassed the early nexus of the destructive twin "diseases," of German disunity and French hybris, he explores in his works; his political refrain remained unchanged, and for all their apparent diversity, every one of his works is cast in the same *satirical* mould.

The Hermit.[19]

1.2 "den sichern Weg des Glücks zu finden": *The Satyrical*

Many eminent Kleist readers, scholars and biographers have inquired into Kleist's sexuality, among them Stefan Zweig, Thomas Mann, László F. Földényi, Heinrich Detering, James M. McGlathery, Hans Dieter Zimmermann, Gerhard Schulz and Günter Blamberger.[20] My—I believe—novel and decisive insight in this respect, which I offered in *Emigrant*, is that Kleist's sexual experiences and fantasies do not merely form his works' "subtext" (Detering), but, like his *satirical* messages, are articulated as a "thread" woven everywhere into the textual fabric. While the modern Kleist reception increasingly accepts that Kleist may have been gay (or bi-), it caveats this possibility by pointing to the almost complete lack of biographical, and the inherently ambiguous and inconclusive nature of textual, evidence.[21] Such caveats, I offer, are rendered obsolete by a *"critical and clinical"* evaluation of Kleist's texts, which demonstrates conclusively that his erotic desire was directed towards the masculine, even as he adored, and repeatedly sought to harness, the maternal, life-giving and caring aspects of the feminine.[22] I term Kleist's (homo-)erotic—often licentious, bawdy, obscene and bucolic—"thread," "*The Satyrical*."

In reading Kleist in a *satyrical* vein, the risks identified by Detering and Schulz, of "over-determining" his works, of "reducing" them to his sexuality, are mitigated provided we let Kleist's works speak for themselves.[23] By tracing the French term *camouflage* to the concealment of fortresses, Blamberger hits the nail on its head: Kleist, in his depiction of the Würzburg fortress in September 1800, rehearses precisely that camouflage of eroticisms he would soon deploy in his works: "*Auch soll viel Geschütz oben sein—doch das alles soll nur sein, hinauf auf das Zitadell darf keiner. Viele Schießscharten sind da, das ist wahr, aber das sind vielleicht bloße Metonymien*" (II:558).[24] "Cannon" and "loophole" are metaphors for those erogenous features—phallus and anus—Kleist evidently cared for, and this instance establishes a metaphorical field, a digital (I/O) symbolism, he would re-iterate across his works—cf. *Marquise*'s "F" and "O," *Findling*'s "key" and "keyhole," *Zweikampf*'s "arrow" and "ring"—including, as we shall see, the dramas.

Kleist's first extant piece of writing, a c.1791 album entry for his half-sister Minette, may already entail the teenager's sensing his sexual awakening and his "queer" inclinations: *"Ich will hinein und muß hinein, u. solts auch inder Quere seyn. Dein treuer u. aufrichtiger / Bruder u. Freund / Heinrich vKlst"* (MAII:483). Does Kleist's *"inder Quere"* "out" him as *Querkopf* or *Querulant*—or as "queer"? Does the *"treue u. aufrichtige... Freund"* codify his "erect member"?[25] This only apparently harmless album entry already demonstrates that Kleist's sexual fantasies pop up in unexpected places, and that beyond the widely acknowledged *loci classici*—the letter to Ernst von Pfuel of 7th January 1805, the poem *Schrecken im Bade*—, The Satirical pervades Kleist's works as comprehensively as *The Satyrical*.[26]

Initiation. Kleist's full sexual "initiation" may have taken place in the Mainz "amphitheatre," in the spring of 1793, at the "hand" of three regiment comrades: that of Karl Adolf von Müller, in a rowing boat in the no-man's land between the Nassauian Schiersteiner Aue and Biebricher Wörth islands (today fused into the Rettbergsaue) and the Hessian Ingelheimer Aue, across from Biebrich Castle; that of Carl von Gleißenberg, in a slightly larger boat on the Rhine near Schierstein, just west of Biebrich Castle (perhaps behind the Schiersteiner Wörth, today fused with the mainland); and that of Georg von Barsse, in a hole dug into a hill near Marienborn, where their unit had been assigned to dig trenches. Kleist in July 1801 recounts all three encounters in his *"großem Bekenntnisbrief"* (Rudolf Loch) to Adolphine von Werdeck: *"Sechzehn Jahre, der Frühling, die Rheinhöhen, der erste Freund... Damals entwickelten sich meine ersten Gedanken und Gefühle... Wir standen damals in Biebrich... Vor mir blühte der Lustgarten der Natur—eine konkave Wölbung, wie von der Hand der Gottheit eingedrückt"* (II:673).[27]

 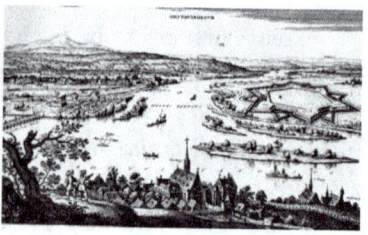

"*Wir standen... in Biebrich*" (I): the Schiersteiner Aue or Biebricher Wörth, where Kleist in late March 1793 experiences his "initiation" by Müller (left); the Mainspitze with the Gustavsburg, where Kleist in late May 1793 experiences his "baptism of fire" by French attackers.

The following plan of the 1793 *Siege of Mainz* shows the movements of Kleist's Regiment Garde during the three months from its arrival at the Mainz theatre on 25th March till its departure for the Palatine theatre on 23rd June 1793 (Mainz's siege proper lasted from 4th April until 22nd June). Thanks to Peter Michalzik's recovery of Carl von Reinhard's eyewitness report of the regiment's movements, we are able to pinpoint with some confidence where and when both Kleist's sexual "initiation" and military "baptism of fire" may have occurred:

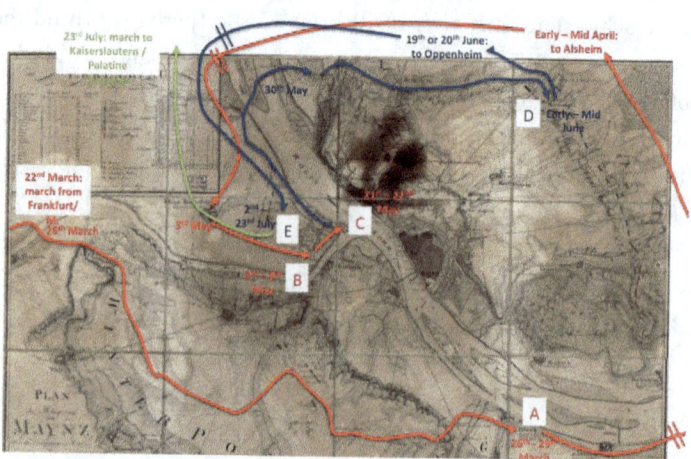

A. While his unit is stationary at Biebrich, c.26th-29th March, Kleist is twice seduced on boats in the no-man's land between the Rhine's meadow islands, first by Müller, then Gleißenberg;

B. After a march to Alsheim in the south (off-map; during a couple of weeks of idleness, Kleist enjoys the Nierenstein and Oppenheim wines of *Krug* fame), his unit during 3rd-8th May for the first time reaches the actual warfront: near the Gustavsburg they dig artillery trenches from which French positions in Kostheim, across the Main, are bombarded;

C. During 21st-22nd May, Kleist's unit directly engages French attackers on the Mainspitze's meadow islands in hand-to-hand combat—probably Kleist's "baptism of fire" as soldier;

D. During early-mid June, at the Coalition's Marienborn HQ, Kleist's unit digs trenches, in one of which he is seduced by (or seduces) Barsse;

E. By 2nd July Kleist's unit is once again at the front, rejoining the Coalition's positions on the Mainspitze, where he witnesses the relentless daily and nightly bombardment of Mainz till the city's capitulation on 22nd July; likely he witnesses, perhaps from the Main's south bank, the city's surrender to Fr. Wilh. II. before departing for Kaiserslautern the next day.

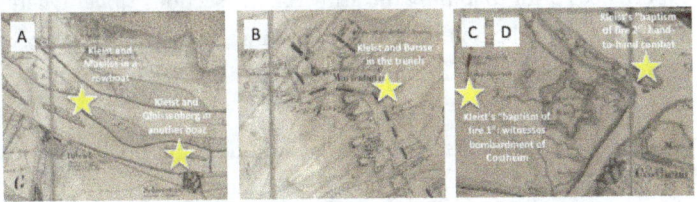

"*Wir standen… in Biebrich*" (II): Kleist circumnavigates the "amphitheatre" of Mainz in the pursuit of *Erôs* and *Agôn*.[28]

The cornfield and shady maple tree featured in Kleist's early *satirico-satyrical* poem Der Höhere Frieden imply a summer setting, suggesting that he may have composed it at the Marienborn camp, perhaps as farewell gift to a lover on the eve of being transferred, on 2nd July 1793, back into the war zone on the Mainspitze; the poem documents just how tightly in lockstep Kleist's *satirical* credo and *satyrical* longing, his initiation into the worlds of *Erôs* and *Agôn*, took shape, rendering it archetypical for his œuvre.[29] Kleist turned the "amphitheatre" of Mainz, the battlefields of the Palatine, his encampments at Biebrich (1793), Marienborn (1793), Eschborn (1794/5) and Lage (1795), and his garrison at Potsdam (1795-9), into his original *Kampfplätze*-cum-*Lustgärten*: the real-life blueprints for his poetical *loci* in which relentless violence is temporarily interrupted by intervals of idyllic peace. Do not the "cave" in *Schroffenstein*, the "verdant valley" in *Erdbeben*, recall the calm bays beween Biebrich's meadow islands, the hole in the hill near Marienborn? Did not all of these *loci* recall the anatomy of his lovers' rear—his desire's vanishing point, his member's pleasure garden, battleground and resting place?

Another piece of evidence for our claim that Kleist at this time of his life was sexually active, or at least longed for sexual fulfilment, is contained in his letter to Aunt Massow from Frankfurt/M., dated 13th-18th March 1793, i.e., only days prior to his unit's departure for the Mainz theatre, in the form of a clear example of his (I/O) symbolism hid in a passage ostensibly recalling his ascent to the Wartburg: *"Ein steiler Fußweg zeigte mir die Öffnung zum Schloß"* (II:465). This fantasy could be prospective, but sounds rather retrospective. Irrespective of whether or not he had had sexual experiences prior to joining the army (cf. my sections *"inder Quere"* and *The Priapic* below), Kleist certainly imagined, on the verge of going into war, that the campaign could offer him the opportunity.

Liaisons. Apart from his liaisons with comrades Müller, Gleißenberg and Barsse, Kleist may have encountered quite a few lovers before completing his first drama: in Frankfurt/O., *possibly* Heinr. Zschokke, whom he could have met there before 1795 and whom he rejoined in Switzerland in 1801; in Potsdam, apart from Gleißenberg, to whom he remained attached much of his life, *certainly* Hartmann von Schlotheim and Otto Aug. Rühle von Lilienstern—together with Kleist these three men formed a musical quartet and in 1797 visited the Harz mountains (cf. I:315)—, as well as Ernst von Pfuel, and *possibly* Fr. de la Motte Fouqué, who like Rühle joined the Potsdam garrison in 1795 (cf. *LS*,105), and Joh. Daniel Falk, with whom Kleist and Fouqué in 1803 were hanging out in Dresden (cf. *LS*,107a); after taking leave from the army, *certainly* L. von Brockes, whom Kleist met on the Baltic island of *Rügen* in early 1800, and Fr. Lose (*"Seine*

Rede ist etwas rauh, doch seine That ist sanft"), whom he first met in Dresden in 1801 and who joined him from Paris to Switzerland, and *possibly* Brockes' friend Alex. zur Lippe, whom he may have met during the Dresden period, if not earlier; in Bern, *possibly* the members of his poetical quartet, which apart from Zschokke included Heinr. Geßner and L. Wieland.[30] Other liasons followed later: in Königsberg, *possibly* Achim von Arnim (cf. Schulz, *Kleist*, 287); in Dresden and again in Berlin, *certainly* A. Müller, *possibly* Clemens Brentano (whom, I conjectured in *Emigrant*, Kleist could have already met during the Würzburg journey), Fr. von Gentz (cf. Rühle's evasive reminiscence, *LS*,193), Rahel Varnhagen's brother L. Robert, Otto von Loeben, Theodor Körner and others; in Bohemia, *certainly* his "Siamese twin" Fr. Chr. Dahlmann.[31] Kleist may also have been sensually attracted to senior figures in the Prussian administration, notably his mentor Karl vom Stein zum Altenstein and the famed officer and statesman Neidhardt von Gneisenau.[32]

Kleist may have had sexual experiences with women—say, playfully with Ulrike von Kleist, more seriously with Luise von Linckersdorf and Wilhelmine von Zenge—, but his *satyrical* writings clearly suggest that it was male-to-male intercourse that truly satisfied his erotic passions. I showed in *Emigrant* that the novellas are imbued with orgiastic scenes, reminiscent of bucolic satyr dances or intoxicated revels held at ancient Dionysiac festivals, or of classical private *orgia* or *symposia*, and frequently centred on a *ménage à trois* involving three male lovers, cast in the classical Greek paiderastaiac roles of *erastês* (master), *erômenos* (youthful object of desire) and *dmōs* (servant), and engaged in a sexual constellation I denote "*FFF*," with each "*F*" representing an ithyphallic male. Kleist's musical quartet in Potsdam (and similarly later his poetical quartet in Bern) may have constituted a "brotherhood" for the pursuit not only of friendship and music—the long, idle sojourn at the officers' quarters in the comfortable *Residenzstadt* would have been eminently condusive to all-male symposiac and orgiastic exploits, and the close connexion Kleist perceived between music and orgiastic sexuality is palpable in novellas such as *Erdbeben* and *Cäcilie*.[33]

Kleist's earliest extant essay, *Aufsatz, den sichern Weg des Glücks zu finden*, is addressed to Rühle, his (boy-)friend at Potsdam, and comprises Kleist's first extant experiment ("*essai*" = "attempt") with the sustained, systematic deployment of his *pescheräic* technique—exploiting polysemy, camouflage, dissimulation. If his 1810 essay *Marionettentheater* comprises the mature Kleist's reminiscences of his sexual apprenticeship in the "Babylonian" Paris of 1801, his 1798/9 *Aufsatz* encompasses the youthful Kleist's declaration of love to a dithering Rühle, whom he implores to recognise homosexuality (or homoeroticism) as the greatest "*Tugend*" ("virtue") and find it in his—Kleist's—arms, and to forfeit status, wealth, career and rank and follow his—Kleist's—example of leaving the army for the life of the artist and libertine.[34] In his letter to Pfuel of 1805, whose notorious "bathing scene" presumably harks back to actual experiences during their extended "honeymoon" in Switzerland in 1803, Kleist expresses "*wahrhaft* mädchenhafte *Gefühle*" towards his lover, admires his athletic body and masculine prowess, "*Deinen schönen Leib... ein musterhaftes Bild der Stärke,*" and implores him, "*sei Du die Frau mir, die Kinder, und die Enkel*" (II:749), thus claiming the social role of his elder brother and "husband" (like Rühle, Pfuel was two years his junior) while offering himself to him as his *erômenos*.[35] Whereas during his military campaign his lovers had tended to be his seniors—Gleissenberg and Schlotheim certainly, von Müller and Barsse presumably—, from the Potsdam period onwards they tended to be his juniors or peers—Pfuel, Rühle, Fouqué, Lose, Brentano, A. Müller, Arnim, Dahlmann—; the significantly older Brockes being an exception. Kleist's famously adolescent, effeminate facial features shown on his only unambiguously attributable portrait (of 1801, i.e., aged c.24) suggest that even in his later years he may still have looked the part of the *erômenos*.[36]

With his departure from the army, his (unofficial) engagement with Wilhelmine von Zenge, and his various journeys and projects of the early 1800s, Kleist jettisons any remaining attachment to a conventional "*Lebensplan*" in favour of his "*große Idee,*" of pursuing an alternative family model in which he seeks to reconcile his aspirations, on the one hand, of producing a heir, on the other, of dedicating himself to the twin "goddesses" of poetry and homosexual love: the years 1800-2 encompass his mysterious Würzburg journey and "honeymoon" with Brockes; his articulation, in the Würzburg letters, of his project of "*Scheidung*"—the separation-yet-co-existence of his heterosexual relationship with Wilhelmine for producing children, and his "brotherhood" with male lovers for producing poetry and *jouissance*—; his "Kant crisis" and sojourn in the "Babylonian" alleyways of Paris together with his "amphibian" half-sister Ulrike; his "emigration" to a Rousseauian island near Thun, where he hopes to put his alternative family model into practice; his final abandonment of Wilhelmine when she fails to join him there; and his first sketch of his *Erstling*.[37]

I offered in *Emigrant* that Kleist envisions his fictional characters—male and female—to be enacted on stage exclusively by male actors (a feature he borrowed from classical Greek drama), typically equipped with phallic props that combine the *satirical* and *satyrical* functionality of "igniting," "firing," "hitting a target"—guns, cannons, rifles, arrows, bullets, spears, axes, clubs, daggers, swords, sticks, torches, lamps, the Dionysiac *thyrsos*, the Hermetic *kērykeion*, the Jovian thunderbolt, etc. I argued that Kleist's works are quasi-autobiographical, that he projects himself into them as much as he generates them out of his own personal experiences, so that the erotic constellations depicted in his works hark back to, or project, his own amorous relationships and sexual experiences, and the "satyrs" appearing in them correspond to actual personages:

"Brotherhood": (top, FLTR) Kleist, Zschokke, Rühle, Pfuel, Fouqué, Falk; (bottom) Altenstein, A. Müller, Gentz, Dahlmann, L. Robert, Armin.[38]

"So... liegt über Kleists gesamter Dresdner Zeit ein Hauch von Erotik," reflects Peter Michalzik (*Kleist,* 325), correctly if much too narrowly: Kleist's *entire life* was "overlaid by eroticism"—indeed, it was enwrought by it through and through.

The Lovers.[39]

1.3 "Ah! Der Skorpion!": *The Syphilitical*

While biographical data is scarce—Kleist was notoriously guarded about his private affairs, and so were his close friends (Samuel and Brown aptly speak of a "conspiracy of silence")—, it is clear that he repeatedly fell ill, and from 1799 till 1811 on numerous occasions consulted doctors or healers, often famous ones: *certainly or very probably* the pioneer of electro-thearapy Adolf Traugott von Gersdorf in Meffersdorf (Riesengebirge), the famous surgeons Carl Caspar von Siebold and Hermann Joseph Brünninghausen in Würzburg (cf. II:561), the doctor and pharmacist Karl Wyttenbach in Bern, the prominent doctor and Jacobine Georg von Wedekind in Mainz, an unnamed Brunonian practitioner in Königsberg, his *Ph* collaborators Gotthilf Heinr. Schubert (whose lectures on animal magnetism Kleist attended) and Karl Fr. Gottlob Wetzel in Dresden, and the prominent *magnétiseur* Matthias Wilh. de Neufville in Frankfurt/M. (immortalised in *Verlobung*); *possibly* the famous vitalist Chr. Wilh. Hufeland in Würzburg, the leading German practioner of Bruonianism and disciple of Schelling's "romantic medicine" Andreas Röschlaub in Bamberg, the Puységurian mesmerist Eberhard Gmelin in Heilbronn, Anton Mesmer himself in Paris, Amand-Marie Jacques de Chastenet, Marquis de Puységur in Strasbourg or on his estate in Buzancy (en route from Reims to Paris), Joh. Lorenz Böckmann, author of the leading German compendium on Puységur magnetism, in Karlsruhe, and the *BA* collaborators Karl Chr. Wolfart (a leading Mesmerian) and Ludolph Beckedorff (cf. *LS*,343; 344; 348), as well as the pioneer of psychiatry Joh. Chr. Reil in Berlin.[40]

Kleist will furthermore have sought treatment by various unnamed doctors, at the spas he frequented—Flinsberg or Warmbrunn (Riesengebirge), Sagard (Rügen), Pillau (Ostpreußen), Töplitz (Böhmen)—, and in the cities in which he sojourned or through which he passed.[41] In Königsburg he may have met the anatomist Wilh. Gottlieb Kelch (cf. II:759) and the prominent pharmacist and founder of the scientific discipline of pharmaceutical chemistry Karl Gottfried Hagen (cf. II:753), and in Dresden in 1809 he conveniently lived upstairs from a pharmacy. And while there is no direct evidence, it is plausible that in the summer or autumn of 1811 he once more consulted Hufeland in Potsdam or Berlin: his younger brother Leopold underwent potentially life-threatening surgery with Hufeland (cf. *NR*,100), and it is hard to imagine that Kleist, who was attached to his brother and visited him repeatedly in Potsdam, would not have met, and at that occasion consulted with, Hufeland; if such a consultation took place, a pessimistic diagnosis by Hufeland could even have contributed to Kleist's resolve to end a battle against illness he could not win.

A pattern of obscure episodes in Kleist's life—his Riesengebirge and Würzburg journeys, extended periods of illness in Bern, Mainz and Königsberg, "disappearance" in Prague—and in works—the mysterious injuries or infections that waste away Colino in *Findling* and Rotbart in *Zweikampf*, and nearly Count F in *Marquise*—, gives credence to the idea that one of the "demons" (Stefan Zweig) Kleist was battling was perennial ill health, and that when Goethe termed him "*hypochondriac*" (*LS*,384), he could well have sensed an actual physiological condition lurking beneath the perceived psychological bent.

Skorpion. I maintain that Kleist's perennial health problems were caused by severe chronic infection—likely syphilis, possibly in conjunction with gonorrhoea—and compounded by the insidious and gradually accumulating side-effects of its treatment—in particular, mercury and arsenic poisoning.[42] To substantiate my "*syphilitical hypothesis,*" I shall explore an obscure yet relevant "navel" in *Schroffenstein*. In the drama's climatic *anagnorisis* the blind Sylvius and the mad Johann (only the blind man and the madman appear to be unhampered by the ambient "blind madness" of mistrust) uncover a mix-up of identities:[43]

SYLVIUS indem er die Leiche betastet.
Ein Schwert—im Busen—einer Leiche.—
JOHANN. Höre, Alter,
Das nenn ich schauerlich. Das Mädchen war
So gut, und o so schön.
SYLVIUS. Das ist nicht Agnes!
—Das wäre Agnes, Knabe? Agnes' Kleid,
Nicht Agnes! Nein bei meinem ewgen Leben,
Das ist nicht Agnes!
JOHANN die Leiche betastend.
Ah! Der Skorpion!
's ist Ottokar! (V.2644-50)

Sylvius feels out the corpse and discovers that it is not Agnes'; Johann follows Sylvius' example and identifies it as Ottokar's: *"Ah! Der Skorpion! s' ist Ottokar!"* It appears that a tactile difference unequivocally marks this corpse as Ottokar's, not Agnes'; if Agnes' body were female, the difference would be obvious, but since it is male (Kleist's female figures always being enacted by male actors), there must be another tactile difference, one that clearly distinguishes one male corpse from antoher, and I offer that Johann's curious exclamation (which certainly does not merely equate either the murderer or the victim with a venomous stinger) can be "translated" as: "Ah! I feel lesions. This is Ottokar's member!"; that what Sylvius and Johann feel out on the corpse is a *chancred penis*, indicating the presence of venereal disease, the most widespread and feared of which in Kleist's time was syphilis, among whose typical early stage symptoms are penile chancres. Kleist's stage direction, "*indem er die Leiche betastet,*" whose "*Leiche*" is an anagram of "*Eichel*" ("glans"), confirms which body part it is that Sylvius and Johann subject to tactile examination.[44]

Johann's exclamation, "*Ah! Der Skorpion!,*" furthermore entails a precise reference to syphilis, for according to astrological lore the first syphilis epidemic in Europe (in 1494) was precipitated by an inauspicious conjunction of Saturn and Mars with *Scorpio* in the ascendant.[45] Albrecht Dürer in his 1496 woodprint *Der Syphilitiker* captured this superstition, showing a syphilis sufferer underneath a zodiac featuring a prominent *Scorpio*.⁴⁶ And, intriguingly, Ferdinand Hartmann's zodiacal constellation on the frontispiece for the first issue of *Ph* corresponds closely to Dürer's, highlighting the same portion of the zodiac, with *Libra* (Kleist's zodiacal sign) in the centre and *Scorpio* next to it:

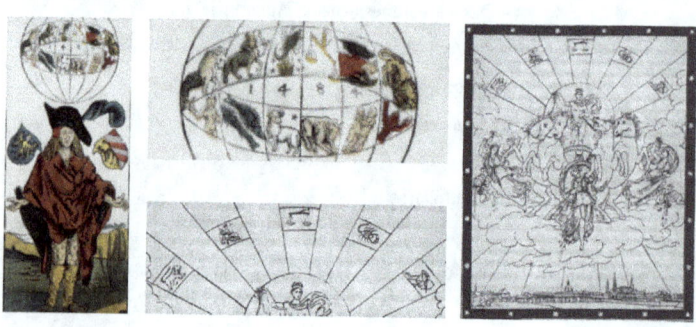

"Ah! Der Skorpion!": *Scorpio* ascendant, Dürer (1496) and Hartmann (1808).

The well-known interpretation of Harmann's imagery put forth by Katharina Mommsen, according to which Kleist put himself (*Libra*) in the centre of the sky above Phoebus Apollo—god of poetry and music—, with Goethe (*Virgo*) to his right and Schiller (*Scorpio*) to his left, is plausible, but does not exclude Kleist's also wishing to evoke the ascendant *Scorpio*. I should add that Phoebus Apollo is also god of purification and healing, and deliverer of pestilence—siding with the Trojans during the *Trojan War*, he sends arrows into the Greek camp impregnated with plague germs—, and that he also features in the story whose protagonist gave the disease its name: when in Girolamo Fracastoro's 1530 educational poem *Syphilis sive Morbus gallicus* the shepard Syphilus insults him, Apollo punishes him with the disease.⁴⁷ There can be no doubt that Kleist knew Fracastoro's story, still widely popular in Europe in his day: Fracastoro also features Scorpio hovering above Phoebus Apollo, and his ill-fated hero's name Syphilius is near-homophone with that of Kleist's blind seer Sylvius.

The first recorded outbreak of syphilis in Europe originated among Charles VIII's soldiers during their occupation of Naples (in 1494-5). In a pattern of proliferation that mimicked that of the bubonic plague 150 years earlier, by the end of 1495 the returning soldiers had spread the disease to France, Switzerland and Germany, by 1497 to England and Scotland, by 1500 to most of Europe, and by 1520 to most of the known world. Voltaire noted sarcastically: "On their flippant way through Italy, the French carelessly picked up Genoa, Naples and syphilis. Then they were thrown out and deprived of Naples and Genoa. But they did not lose everything—syphilis went with them."[48] Syphilis in most of Europe became known as "French disease" (*maladie française, Franzosenkrankheit, morbus Gallicus*), in France as "Neapolitan disease" (*mal de Naples*) or "Spanish disease." In Kleist's day the disease was widespread and feared; Goethe, in *Römische Elegien*, refers to it as "poisonous sludge" and "Amor's poison," Schopenhauer, in *Aphorismen*, as "Amor's poisoned arrows."[49] Kleist's reference, in *Marquise*, to the city of Naples (*Napoli* in Italian) is a cypher not only for *"Napoleon's polis"* (Paris), but also for *"mal de Naples,"* so that his concept of "French disease" is meaningful *satirically* as well as *syphilitically*: Napoleon = *mal de Naples* = "French disease."[50]

Syphilitical Hypotheses. I shall explore three hypotheses: (1) references to syphilis are widespread in Kleist's novellas; (2) this pattern is already present in *Schroffenstein*; and (3) Kleist's *"The Syphilitical"* is as autobiographical as *"The Satyrical."* Ad (1), in *Marquise*, Count F is nearly killed by a mysterious "bullet" on an unnamed battlefield; since *Kampfplätze* in Kleist are always also *Lustgärten*, this incidence plausibly signifies Count F's contracting syphilis during an orgiastic encounter (battle = orgy = syphiliac *"rondes d'amour"*), which would explain, firstly, the Marquise's coyness vis-à-vis the returning Count's erotic advances, whom she recognises to have transformed from "angel" (pure, immaculate lover) into "devil" (diseased, infectious lover); secondly, her attempt, with her *"Ich* will nichts *wissen"* (II:129) gesture, to recoup the paradisical, pre-lapsarian (pre-syphilitic) state of their affair; and, thirdly, the Count's Thinka vision (Katharina = "the pure") in which he recalls throwing "faeces" (diseased ejaculate) at her. The

Count's inquiries regarding the Marquise's wellbeing, then, pertain not to whether he *impregnated*, but whether he *infected* her (or both). Mercury, in the form of the solvable compounds Mercury I chloride (calomel) or Mercury II chloride (mercuric chloride) the most common anti-syphilitic in Kleist's day, is alluded to when Count F is said to be leaving *"mit Schritten, die die Freude beflügelte"* (II:118): the prolific and ithyphallic trickster Mercury (Hermes) is commonly depicted with winged feet, and Kleist arguably points not primarily to the Count's libidinal insatiability or seductiveness, but to his undergoing mercury therapy.[51] In *Verlobung*, Gustav's tale of the girl who insidiously kills her lovers by infecting them with yellow fever may refer to a syphiliac woman: yellow fever simply afforded Kleist a suitable analogy within the novella's *overt* context, for it was as common in the French colony of Saint-Domingue (today's Haiti, where the *overt* story is set) as syphilis was in Europe; like syphilis, yellow fever was commonly treated with mercury, and according to a widely-held theory, Columbus' crew brought syphilis to Europe from their journeys to Hispaniola, the island on which Haiti is located.[52] The motif of the *femme fatale* or "poison woman," who deliberately infects men with syphilis, was current in Kleist's time (cf. John Keats' 1819 poem *"La Belle Dame sans Merci"*), and the tale's theme of mistrust and suspicion can be read, in a *syphilitical* vein, as depicting a "brotherhood" of lovers doubtful of others' infectiousness. In *Findling*, a fatal epidemic disease (the plague) claims Piachi's only son; Nicolo, whom Piachi subsequently adopts, promptly carries the "disease" of discord and jealousy into his household. While in his own time no longer a relevant threat, the "plague" provides an analogy for syphilis in *Findling*'s *overt* late medieval setting that is just as suitable as is "yellow fever" in *Verlobung*'s *overt* Caribbean context (among syphilis' monikers was *"Geschlechtspest,"* "genital plague"). In *Kohlhaas*, the eponymous hero's salivating like a horse or rabid dog may imply that he is undergoing syphilis treatment: mercury therapies often entailed the induction of salivation.[53] In *Zweikampf*, the mysterious disease or poison that wastes away Rotbart after he is injured in the duel (i.e., in sexual intercourse) may refer to syphilis. Across the novellas, certain props that recur regularly—hats, caps, gloves, wigs, coats, cloths, aprons, codpieces—may allude to two common predicaments faced by syphiliacs: as condoms, to the perennial fear of infection, as accessories, to the need to conceal visible symptoms.[54]

Ad (2), the family's very name, Schroffenstein ("gruff" or "rugged stone"), alludes to the disease, invoking as it does a penis afflicted with chancres—the lesions or ulcers thanks to which a common name for the disease was "*Harter Schanker*" (*ulcus durum*), and with whose help Sylvius and Johann identify Ottokar's corpse. The drama's originally envisaged settings, France or Spain, allude to syphilis having been known as "French" or "Spanish disease"; the family's names in the earlier versions, Thierrez and Ghonorez, similarly refer to the disease: Ghonorez recalls gonorrhoea—in Kleist's day a widespread venereal disease that often went together, and was even erroneously compounded, with syphilis—, as well as Gomorrah, the city YHWH destroyed together with its twin city Sodom because of their inhabitants' impenitent sinfulness and sexual excess, Thierrez recalls *Tripper,* a colloquial German term for gonorrhoea.[55] When Kleist relocates the drama's final version to Swabia (mainly for *satirical* reasons, as I shall show later), he "translates" the family's speaking name from French- or Spanish-sounding proxies for "gonorrhoea" into a Swabian-sounding proxy for "chancred penis"—in all three cases meaning syphilis.[56] The family's artful names (Thierrez, Ghonorez, Schroffenstein), and the drama's choiceful settings (France, Spain, Catholic Swabia) suggest that Kleist's first poetic project was *syphilitical* from the core; its evident equating a "poisoned" family constellation with a diseased "brotherhood" implies that it is its very structural principle to parallel *The Satirical* (dynastic rivalry, disunity) and *The Syphilitical* (disease, infection). The drama's miasmatic atmosphere is accentuated by its serpentine symbolism (deception, temptation, venomousness): in its sixth verse the chorus of maidens chants with respect to the Rossitz infant Peter, "*Nieder trat ihn ein frecher Fuß,*" which entails a reference to YHWH's cursing serpent and woman:

> And I will put enmity
> between you and the woman,
> and between your offspring and hers;
> he will crush your head,
> and you will strike his heel. (*Genesis*, 3:15);

this symbolism continues with Rupert and Santing's comparing the rival House of Warwand with a snake's den (cf. V.68; 2514), and with Sylvester's lamenting Agnes' death in the final scene: "*Sie… / Die nun ein frecher Fußtritt mir zertreten*" (V.2591-2).[57] The family's Rossitz and Warwand branches are equally afflicted by this curse of enmity: in the Chorus' lines, Warwand corresponds to the "cheeky foot," Rossitz to the "snake"; in Rupert and Santing's speech, Warwand to the snake, in Sylvester's lament, Rossitz to the "cheeky foot." This chiastic "serpentine-ness" roots both branches' demise in the same underlying cause: the "German disease" of *dynastic rivalry*, whose presence in turn buttresses and facilitates the proliferation of the "French disease" of *dynastic hybris*: "*Das Mißtraun ist die schwarze Sucht der Seele, / Und alles, auch das Schuldlos-Reine, zieht / Fürs kranke Aug die Tracht der Hölle an*" (V.915-7).[58]

Ad (3), after an initial outbreak of primary syphilis the disease progresses to its secondary stage, during which for many years it may remain latent yet infectious, and during which its symptoms may recur irregularly, until it eventually reaches its tertiary stage, in which it is no longer infectious but may produce debilitating, and eventually fatal, symptoms such as deformations, progressive *paresis* (dementia), paralysis and *tabes dorsalis* (degeneration of the spinal cord), and blindness (both Johann's madness and Sylvius' blindness may be symptoms of tertiary syphilis). A typical cycle of syphilis therapy, sometimes administered in dedicated *Syphilis-Spitälern*, involved the application (as ointment, vapour, beverage or injection) of mercury, arsenic or extract of the guaiacum plant—poisonous substances all—in therapeutic cycles lasting three to eight weeks, during which the symptoms usually subsided, although in many cases the patient was not cured.[59] Kleist's repeated medical therapies do not prove, but are consistent with, an ongoing battle with syphilis, and so are his request for dismissal from the army in March 1799 (which was granted surprisingly quickly), his abrupt departure from Frankfurt/O. in August 1800 (which perhaps was not quite as abrupt as it appeared: *"Ich hatte über den Gedanken dieses Planes schon lange lange gebrütet"*), and his request for prolonged medical leave in 1806: it would have been difficult to hide syphilis symptoms in the army or civil service, and humiliating to be discovered by one's family, fiancée, neighbours and acquaintances. Kleist's secretiveness regarding the Würzburg journey's purpose, and his less-than-convincing pretexts for it (job interview without appointment, espionage mission without remit) are easily explained by his requiring out-of-town treatment when tell-tale signs of a socially tabooed disease becoming visible where they could not be concealed. His Würzburg sojourn was sufficiently long for a cycle of syphilis treatment, at the Julius-Hospital or in a private surgery.[60] When Kleist tells Wilhelmine and Ulrike that his journey could save a life, he is perhaps not exaggerating, and it is *his own life* that is at stake (cf. II:563; 582). Even his unusual request to Finance Minister Carl Aug. Struensee, to be permitted to join the sessions of the Technical Deputation without having formally joined the civil service, may reflect a *syphilitical* agenda: one of the two inspectors who witnessed Kleist's introduction to the Deputation's director was a medical inspector, Sigismund Fr. Hermbstädt, senior government advisor on modern chemistry and pharmaceutics (the other, a war inspector—cf. *LS*,49), and Kleist may have hoped that by joining the Deputation's sessions he could gain access to latest information on developments in the fields of medicine and pharmaceutics: one of the Deputation's branches, the *Königliche technische Deputation für das Medizinalwesen*, was in charge of maintaining the *pharmacopoeia* that informed and governed Prussia's medical professionals, pharmacies and chemical industry.[61] (Only) Kleist's desperate quest to defeat disease explains his sudden eagerness to enter a domain of trade and industry he had hitherto paid scant attention to; the reason for his asking to join a few working sessions *before* committing to this career was simply that, being unsure whether it would yield the information he required, he had to retain the option of a quick exit should he find that it did not. If he informally offered Struensee's deputies to conduct low-key espionage during his journey, which I consider probable, destinations such as Bamberg and Vienna were as relevant from the point of view of gathering information on medical developments in rival German states (respectively Wittelsbach Bavaria and Habsburg Austria) as they were from that of seeking therapy: the former hosted Germany's leading Brunonian school, the latter the famous Vienna school of medicine (to which Mesmer had belonged before seeking exile in Paris, and one of whose founders had been Gerard van Swieten, who in 1750 paved the way for the use of mercury chlorid in treating syphilis).[62] Offering to conduct informal espionage on behalf of Prussia in the field of medical developments would have correlated perfectly with a primary purpose of obtaining treatment for himself.[63]

Syphilitic journeys. Already in the summer of 1799, during his visit to the Riesengebirge, Kleist may have sought therapy at the health resorts of Flinsberg (were Gleißenberg was undergoing treatment of some sort) or Warmbrunn, as well as seeking out the pioneer of electric therapy Adolf Traugott von Gersdorf in nearby Meffersdorf (cf. *LS*,34a). In the summer of 1800, when he and Brockes chanced upon each other at the Sagard's *Gesundbrunnen* on Rügen, they may have discovered that they shared not only the same erotic passions but also the scourge associated with them, which would have made Brockes Kleist's ideal brother-in-arms for the Würzburg journey's "medical tourism"-cum-"honeymoon."[64] Already in *Emigrant* I speculated that Kleist (and perhaps Brockes) originally planned to seek Mesmerian treatment in Vienna or Brunonian treatment in Bamberg, before the English envoy Lord Elliot in Dresden redirected them to the vitalist Hufeland in Würzburg and the magnetists Gmelin in Heilbronn, de Neufville in Frankfurt/M., and Puységur in Strasbourg.[65] A hiatus of almost five weeks (23rd September-27th October) in Kleist's extant Würzburg letters, sufficient for a cycle of syphilis treatment, is interrupted by only one (extant) letter, his famous "birthday letter" of 10th/11th October, in which he concretises plans for starting a family with Wilhelmine: when half-way through his treatment his symptoms begin to recede, and his doctors assure him that he may safely beget a child, Kleist elatedly envisions himself as procreator.

During his sojourn in Thun, while working on *Schroffenstein*, Kleist in August 1802 sought medical treatment for at least two months with Wyttenbach in nearby Bern (cf. II:726-7). In 1803 he and Pfuel travelled from Switzerland to Paris via Lyon (cf. Loch, *Kleist*, 182, 523), together with Strasbourg and Paris a leading centre for magnetism.[66] From December 1803 till May 1804 Kleist sojourned in Mainz for nearly six months (possibly with brief interruptions), during which he underwent treatment with Wedekind—that Kleist nowhere mentions it (we know of this fact thanks to Wedekind's letters) only strengthens my hypothesis that the "strange undefinable illnesses that remained his companions" (Michalzik, *Kleist*, 433) were perfectly "definable," if *ineffable*.[67] In July 1804 Kleist tells Ulrike that he is hoping to join Marie von Kleist's brother Peter von Gualtieri on a trip to Landeck in Silesia, one of the oldest and most prominent health spas in Silesia: *"da ich* irgend eines Bades *schlechterdings bedarf"* (II:742)—in plain English: "I need treatment, and fast."[68]

In Königsberg, in November 1805, Kleist complained to Altenstein about "constant abdominal pain" (II:758), and in a letter mentioned treatment by an unnamed "Brunonian doctor"; in the summer of 1806 he reported to his superiors an "ongoing condition in his abdomen" (II:765), which he claimed constituted a "relapse of an earlier ailment [he] previously suffered from in France" (II:764), and a "chronic condition" (*LS*,151a). In October 1806 Kleist was again—or still—ill, telling Ulrike of his "continuously ill disposition" (II:770), encompassing constipation, attacks of sweating and fever, and a "destroyed" nervous system, and mentions a sojourn of five weeks in Pillau, a Baltic sea spa near Königsberg; his first biographer, Eduard von Bülow, reports his frequent "fevers" during late 1806 (cf. *LS*,149). How much of Kleist's ill health was real, how much entailed "storytelling" aimed at obtaining medical leave, remains indiscernible (cf. *LS*,150); certainly Kleist did seek the latter, for otherwise he would have remained mute about his health, but this does not mean that there was no material basis for his complaints. I gather that he did not feign his poor health, but exaggerated it when it suited him; in December 1806 he reaffirmed his frail condition to Ulrike (cf. II:773), towards whom he had no reason to pretend (unless he hoped it would make it easier to extract funds from her). Kleist's symptoms are unspecific, neither conclusively pointing to syphilis, nor at odds with it, and his deliberate vagueness left his contemporaries, and leaves us today, forever guessing.[69]

In Dresden, in 1808/ Kleist took opium (cf. *LS*,269), presumably palliatively or therapeutically, which may have been a life-long habit (cf. *NR*,353a); in March and April 1809 he lived four flights of stairs above Dresden's Löwen-Apotheke (cf. II:824), a choice of location which may or may not have been coincidental: this is precisely where one *would* choose to camp if one was in need of regular supply of medication, and wanted to avoid touting the fact; Kleist evidently *was* in need of regular supply of medication: according to Friedrich Laun, shortly after leaving Dresden for Bohemia on 29th April he ordered a supply of arsenic from the Löwen-Apotheke, which the pharmacies in the Bohemian spa town of Töplitz, a days' journey south of Dresden, refused to dispense without prescription (cf. *LS*,321); the lack of a prescription may imply that Kleist was self-medicating and that his pharmacist at *Löwen-Apotheke* was supplying him without prescription, presumably at a premium— Kleist, ten years into his therapeutic career, at this stage seems to have ditched mercury and resorted to arsenic, whose side-effects are less severe than mercury's if professionally administered, but far more dangerous if mishandled.[70] Töplitz offered therapeutic saline and alkaline sources, and although he stayed only a few days—on 5th May he was already in Prague (cf. *MA*III,835)—, Kleist could have sought temporary relief while meeting political interlocutors in this strategically located town en route from Berlin and Dresden to Prague and Vienna.[71] When on 3rd May he begged Ulrike for money, he may have been financially stretched to the limit by expensive medication and therapies, and when following *Wagram* in July he "disappeared" for several months, rumours that he had died in Prague's monastery of the Brothers of Mercy (cf. *LS*,345; 332b; c) were perhaps not entirely groundless.[72]

At the eve of 1810 Kleist was in Frankfurt/M. (cf. II:831), plausibly to seek treatment with Neufville; thereafter he apparently confined himself to Berlin.[73] All considered, and though much remains conjecture, I offer the following overview of Kleist's *syphilitical* events and journeys:

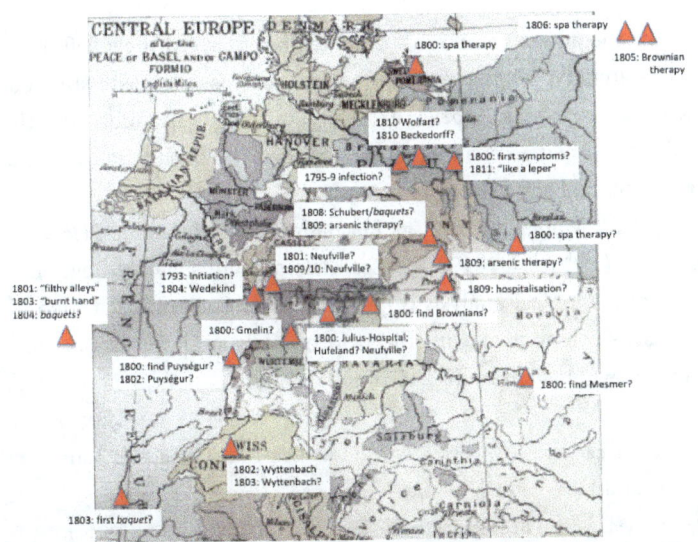

Kleist's *syphilitical* events and journeys, from the late 1790s till 1811.[74]

Syphilianum. The possibility that Kleist suffered from syphilis has been raised before, though not, as far as I am aware, in the *Kleist-Forschung*. The authors of a teaching book on homeopathy deduce Kleist's syphilis not via medical diagnosis but an assessment of behavioural traits, of which they claim that they correspond to the "*Syphilianum*" archetype:

> *Syphilianum* (Persönlichkeitsbild). Ist ein menschlicher Einzelgänger… Erst in der Agonie, wenn seine Schmerzen unerträglich geworden sind. Die typische Syphilianum-Persönlichkeit bleibt stets distanziert… Es ist, als ob diese Menschen nicht richtig am Leben teilhaben könnten. Eine treffende Beschreibung findet sich in Elias Canettis Darstellung der Persönlichkeit von Robert Musil, der mit Syphilis infiziert war… Syphilianum hat typischerweise einen klaren Verstand und

ausgezeichnete analytische Fähigkeiten. Sein Denken ist präzise und die Logik kann messerscharf sein. Ein gutes Beispiel für diese Qualität des Intellektuellen lässt sich in der Sprache des an Syphilis erkrankten und durch Suizid verstorbenen Heinrich von Kleist finden, dessen Ausdrucksweise durch große Exaktheit und Präzision besticht.[75]

While the authors could just as easily have derived their definition of the archetype *a posteriori* from Kleist's case, as their assessment of Kleist's case from an *a priori* archetype, and while I cannot judge the validity of their assessment, I take note that it yields the same results as my textual analysis.

Paul Ridder in the essay *Ein Bildnis des unbekannten Heinrich v. Kleist* (17th April 2015) deduces Kleist's syphilis via physiognomic and physiological analysis of portraits and handwriting, which he seeks to corroborate with the help of Kleist's autopsy report and textual evidence from his letters and dramas:

> Als der Dichter Heinrich v. Kleist... nach einem Besuch in Paris wieder die Grenze zu seinem Heimatland passierte, begab er sich in die medizinische Behandlung des Arztes Dr. Christian Wedekind... bei dem er November 1803 bis Juni 1804 wohnte, um sich wegen venerischer Leiden und depressiven Gemütszuständen behandeln zu lassen. Für die genannten Indikationen war nach dem Kenntnisstand der damaligen Medizin die Anwendung von Quecksilberpräparaten (Kalomel) angezeigt... Laut Obduktionsbericht: zeigte der „Denatus" Kleist zahlreiche braunrote Flecken auf dem Rücken und an den Lenden. Diese Exanthema weisen auf Symptome der Syphilis oder auf eine Vergiftung hin. Ferner fand sich eine widernatürliche große und harte Leber, wo der Körper bekanntlich die Medikamente abbaut. Auch war die Gehirn-Substanz, dem wichtigsten Zielort der Arzneimittelwirkung von Quecksilberpräparaten, viel fester als gewöhnlich. Das Metall hat die nämlich die Eigenschaft, sich bevorzugt im Gehirn und in der Leber abzulagern, in den Nieren hingegen nur selten. Dort waren denn auch keinerlei Veränderungen festzustellen. Die bei der Obduktion beobachteten Veränderungen im Körpergewebe lassen demnach Symptome einer chronischen Vergiftung durch Quecksilber erkennen.

Dazu gehören zusätzlich weitere Kennzeichen, vornehmlich eine nach ca. 5-6 Jahren erscheinende, hellgrau-rötlichbraune Verfärbung der Augeniris... Ob heutzutage noch eine Krankenakte "H .v. Kleist" existiert, konnte nicht erwiesen werden. In der Literatur werden sowohl Syphilis als auch psychische Störungen berichtet. Kleist selber betrachtete sich als "gemütskrank," zudem war er nach seinen eigenen Worten "von einem chronischen Übel" befallen... In seinen späten Stücken (Der zerbrochne Krug, Amphitryon, Hermannsschlacht) zeigte sich Kleist denn auch mit dem Quecksilber-Medikament „Kalomel" durchaus vertraut... Im engeren Sinne der psychischen Veränderungen einer Quecksilberbehandlung zeigt der Patient Heinrich v. Kleist folgende Symptome: Überhöhte Reizbarkeit, Schlaflosigkeit und Angstgefühle, Verlust des Selbstvertrauens, Unentschlossenheit und Persönlichkeitsschwund – bei im wesentlichen erhaltener intellektueller Leistungsfähigkeit... Der chronischen Vergiftung geht oft eine lange Latenzperiode mit diffusen neurasthentischen Symptomen voraus. Die unspezifischen Allgemeinsymptome können wochen-, monate- oder jahrelang anhalten, bevor weitere Vergiftungserscheinungen hinzukommen. Der Prozeß der Vergiftung beginnt also schleichend. Frühsymptome sind Appetitlosigkeit und Gewichtsabnahme, die sich in vergleichsweise eingefallenen Wangen und einer Hagerkeit der Gesichtszüge (wie auf dem neuen Porträt) ausdrückt... Hinzu kommen folgende Symptome einer Quecksilber-Vergiftung bei H. v. Kleist: Der Patient fühlt sich gehetzt, nervöse Unruhe und ein erhöhtes Tempo bei allen Tätigkeiten (auch beim Schreiben) stellen sich ein. Besonders beeindruckend aber ist: Das Zeiterleben verändert sich! H. v. Kleist leidet an Depressionen (Erethismus mercurialis), er zieht sich aus menschlicher Gesellschaft zurück, flieht menschliche Nähe, wechselt die Aufenthaltsorte. Häufige Selbstmordgedanken stellen sich symptomatisch ein. Die Suizidgefährdung gehört zum Symptombild.[76]

Whether the image on which he bases part of his analysis, and which he attributes to Gerhard von Kügelgen, authentically portrays Kleist remains indiscernible, but Ridder makes a credible effort to triangulate Kleist's syphilis from several angles, and although I am in no position to ascertain the conclusion Ridder draws from his physiognomic and physiological analysis, like the abovementioned behavioural assessment, it parallels the one I draw from my textual analysis.[77] That the youthful face depicted by Peter Friedel in a matter of eight or nine years could have become as careworn and lined as that shown on Kügelgen's painting is supported by the parallel deterioration in Kleist's *"Zitterschrift"* (Ridder). Whatever the shortcomings of such circumstantial and post-mortem analyses—psychological, physiognomical, physiological or otherwise—, none of those I have found refute, and all of them strengthen, my "syphilitical hypothesis."

The syphilitical Kleist. There is, of course, nothing unusual about an early 19th century aristocrat contracting syphilis: what *is* unusual is that Kleist systematically enacts his personal struggle with the disease in his œuvre, rendering syphilis at least as integral to his works as, say, Gustav Klimt does a century later. The proverbial prevalence of syphilis among intellectuals and artists of that period—be it because the disease stimulates creativity, as the meme of the *"geniale Syphilitiker"* suggests, because intellectuals and artists inherently pursue riskier sexual practices than average citizens, or because their cases simply obtain greater public notoriety—, makes it all the more surprising that this idea is comprehensively ignored or dismissed by the *Kleist-Forschung*, even as practitioners of homeopathy and of pathological and physiognomic analysis evidently consider it almost self-evident.[78] One plausible explanation for this recitence may be that just when the *Kleist-Forschung* gained traction around the centenary of Kleist's death, the scourge of syphilis was being overcome, thanks to Paul Ehrlich's 1910 invention of its first truly effective medication, *Salvarsan*, and its earstwhile widely recognised symptoms and symbolism may then have quickly faded from literary professionals' radar screens.

Sigmund Rahmer in his 1909 Kleist biography has a close brush with the crux of the matter (cf. *Kleist*, 395-6), yet with his peculiar knack for allowing nonsense to undermine good sense, he first surfaces, then dismisses an excellent analogy with the romantic lyricist Nikolaus Lehnau, whose creeping melancholy and progressive paralysis he has no difficulty attributing to syphilis, while rejecting the same diagnosis in Kleist's case, despite noting the parallels of their life and literature, in favour of a nebulous notion of "mental dysfunction," an evasive gesture repeated in Thomas Mann's notions, à propos of Kleist, of "melancholy" and "darkness," and Sembdner's, of "psychosis" and "mania" (cf. *In Sachen Kleist*, 372). Presumably it is such sweeping and hazy generalisations that motivate Günter Blamberger to caution against reading Klesit's entire live and work through the lens of his *death*—I add that we should instead evaluate them throught that of his *diseased life*.[79]

Kleist, his contemporaries attest, was prone to spending days on end in bed, working on MSS, and may have literally been undergoing therapy *while and through writing*: writing as therapeutic intervention against suffering and boredom, and as epiphenomenon of the disease's social stigmatisation, and of the ebb and flow of pain, exhaustion, elation during remissions, and terrified anticipation of relapse. Kleist, then, was not merely a Dionysiac poet (cf. Schulz, *Kleist*, 363), but was indeed himself physically and mentally suffering repeated *sparagmos*, like Rotbart in *Zweikampf* being slowly wasted away by disease and mercury poisoning, his life entailing not this or that crisis, but *a single, ongoing, neverending crisis*: if Kleist, as Blamberger acutely observes (*Kleist*, 493), experienced himself, in Helmut Plessner's terms, as "*Leib sein*" rather than "*Körper haben*," this was so not least because his *Leib* was in a perennial state of suffering. I paraphrase (and turn on its head) a dictum by E.M. Cioran: "*Es ist unmöglich, eine Zeile von Kleist zu lesen, ohne daran zu denken, daß er an der Lues litt. Es ist, als sei sein Leiden seinem Werk vorangegangen.*"[80] were not Kleist's lines to Wilhelmine, of 21st July 1801, written by one inflicted with a terrible and communicable disease?

> Mir war es zuweilen auf dieser Reise, als ob ich meinem Abgrund entgegen ginge—Und nur das Gefühl, auch Dich mit mir hinabzuziehen, Dich, mein gutes, treues, unschuldiges Mädchen, Dich, die sich mir ganz hingegeben hat, weil sie ihr Glück von mir erwartet—Ach, Wilhelmine, ich habe oft mit mir gekämpft, ob es nicht meine Pflicht sei, Dich zu

verlassen? Ob es nicht meine Pflicht sei, Dich von dem zu trennen, der sichtbar seinem Abgrunde entgegeneilt? (II:667-8)

Towards the end of his life, did Kleist enter the disease's tertiary and final stage? Did he choose to die not least because he, perhaps more so than his fellow suicidee Henriette Vogel, was incurably ill, and because the symptoms worsened in the autumn of 1811, or he had simply had enough of battling them?[81] When on his last visit to Frankfurt/O. his sisters treated him almost like a *leper* (cf. II:883), was it really only because he remained without career and money, or because he quite literally, visibly, *was one*? Was the unfathomable pain Kleist expressed in his final letters physiological as well as psychological? When he writes Marie on 10th November, "*meine Seele ist so wund, dass mir, ich möchte fast sagen, wenn ich die Nase aus dem Fenster stecke, das Tageslicht wehe tut, das mir darauf schimmert*" (II:883), harking back to a passage in *Schroffenstein*, "*Die Schuld liegt an der Spitze meiner Nase*" (V.809), in which Johann alludes to his syphilitic affliction (tip of the nose = glans), is not Kleist contemplating his wrecked nose (and penis, too)?[82] Is not the passage with which he so hauntingly commences his final letter, "*Meine liebe Marie, wenn Du wüßtest, wie der Tod und die Liebe sich abwechseln*" (II:887), a poetic version of the sarcastic maxim, current in his day, "One night with Venus, a lifetime with Mercury"? Does not the unpredictability of latent syphilis in and by itself explain the emotional oscillations Kleist experienced, and render superfluous any recourse to unspecific syndromes such as "melancholy" or "hypochondria"? Do not observations by his contempories—say, regarding his stuttering and stammering—indeed point to an onset of *neurosyphilis*, of progressive paralysis?[83]

If by 1811 he experienced symptoms of tertiary syphilis, whose onset typically occurs within 3-15 years (for *neurosyphilis*, 10-30 years) of the initial infection, Kleist could indeed have contracted the disease as early as 1797-9, during his Potsdam garrison, and recurring symptoms could indeed have precipitated his decision to quit the military.[84] When in his 1798/9 *Aufsatz* he maintains, "*Es waltet ein gleiches Gesetz über die moralische wie über die physische*

Welt" (II:308), is not Kleist referring to syphilis as the "law" that governs the sufferer's physical (i.e., health, sexuality, reproduction) *and* moral (i.e. social, partnership, family) life? Does not the essay's long title's dark element, "*Aufsatz, den Sichern Weg des Glücks zu Finden und Ungestört—Auch Unter den Grössten Drangsalen des Lebens—Ihn zu Geniessen!*," beg the question what "greatest tribulations" a young man, aged 22, could possibly have been confronting? Does not Kleist's linking "virtue" (male virility) to "bleak clouds of fate," the "burden of oppressive destinies," and "the nights of thunderstorms" (cf. II:306) evoke a gay lover's *syphilitical* fears, and does not Rühle's "*Menschenhaß*" (cf. II:312) suggest that he is repelled by (Kleist's) disease?[85] When Kleist in *Marionettentheater* praises the usefulness of a wooden dildo ("*Gliedermann,*" II:345) for overcoming a lover's "coyness," does not this "coyness" refer to a "virgin" *erômenos*' recoiling from a diseased *erastês*, in an age prior to reliable rubber condoms?[86] Could it be that one of the world's great poetic œurvres was born from *syphilitical* suffering much as from *satirical* determination? Do not his works comprise Kleist's desperate implorations to his lovers to stay with him in spite of it all?

"**Heimlich Kranker.**" Pathological or psychological analyses of Kleist have a long tradition—Goethe considers him hypochondriac; Stefan Zweig approaches him psychoanalytically; Th. Mann notes his "psychogenic illnesses" (*NR*,500d)—, yet typically remain vague and psychologising. If Kleist did suffer from syphilis, would not his contemporaries—not only insiders committed to silence, like Ulrike, Marie and his lovers—have noticed his symptoms?[87] When in February 1801 Kleist tells Ulrike of his "unspeakable embarrassment" which he "could hide only with the greatest effort so that it would not become conspicuous" (II:628-9), is he not referring to *visible* symptoms? Goethe is said to have had an almost paranoid fear of syphilis—that "*Gift unter den Rosen der Lust,*" of which he remarks with evident horror: "*Nirgends legt man das Haupt ruhig dem Weib in den Schoß, sicher ist nicht das Ehebett mehr, nicht sicher der Ehebruch.*"[88] One need not adhere to conspiracy theories, according to which his "*Bettschatz*" Christiane Vulpius, their joint son Karl Aug., even Goethe himself suffered from the disease, to recognise that the unease and irritation Goethe felt in Kleist's presence, *"mir erregte dieser Dichter... immer Schauder und Abscheu, wie ein von der Natur schön intentionierter Körper, der von einer unheilbaren Krankheit ergriffen wäre"* (NR,274), may reflect a (conscious or unconscious) recoiling from an actual disease, and that Goethe's clever reference to *Ph* as *"Phébus"* (*LS*,264b), i.e., *"Schwulst"* ("pomposity"), may have been *doubly* clever: *"Schwulst"* recalls *"Geschwulst"* ("blastoma," "tumor").[89]

When he grouped Kleist with Hölderlin and Nietzsche in *Der Kampf mit dem Dämon*, did Stefan Zweig not consider that Kleist, like them, could have been afflicted by syphilis? When he writes, *"Jeder will zu [Kleist], jeder scheut vor seinem Dämon zurück... Die ihn nicht kennen, halten ihn für gleichgültig und kalt. Die ihn kennen, schauern und erschrecken vor dem finsteren Feuer, das ihn verzehrt... wer ihm nahe war, hat sich versengt an seinem Feuer"* (*Dämon*, 166), is he not (consciously or unconsciously) depicting the *syphilitical* Kleist?[90] Although Zweig explicitly rejects the idea that Kleist was physically or mentally ill, *"Seine preußischen Ahnen hatten ihm eine solide, fast allzu harte Physis vererbt: sein Verhängnis stak nicht im Fleisch, zuckte nicht im Blut, sondern schwärmte und gärte unsichtbar in seiner Seele. Aber er war auch eigentlich nicht ein Seelenkranker"* (*ibid,* 169), preferring instead to ascribe his consuming fire to an excess of passion, *"Er hatte zu viel Leidenschaft, eine maßlose, zügellose, ausschweifende übertreiberische Leidenschaft des Gefühls, die beständig zum Exzeß drängte"* (*ibid*), his claim that Kleist suffered from "pathological mysophobia" merely begs the question as to its material basis, as to the precise nature of the "dirt" Kleist supposedly abhorred: could it not have been his own ravaged and infectious body? Zweig, implausibly, imputes Kleist's troubled sexuality to his inability to reconcile his (masturbatory) *"Knabenlaster"* with his moral convictions, and a lack of sexual fulfilment with Wilhelmine, while, only slightly less implausibly, linking the rich eroticism expressed in Kleist's letters to his lack of physical prowess, *"Eben weil ihm die gerade Stoßkraft des Begehrens (vielleicht auch des Könnens) im Sexuellen fehlte, war er aller Vielfältigkeiten und Zwischengefühle fähig: darum auch seine magische Kenntnis aller Kreutzwege und Seitenschliche des Eros, all der Vermengungen und Verkleidungen des Gelüsts, dies merkwürdige Wissen um das Tranvestitentum des Triebs"* (174; Zweig in the same section also rejects the notion of Kleist's homosexuality), but fails to explain how Kleist could have acquired his "magical knowledge" of sexual matters, if not by practical experience.

Written almost 20 years after *Dämon*, Zweig's essay *Die Welt von Gestern* betrays a more reflected understanding of the temptations of youth:

> Denn... ständig... überschattete damals noch ein anderes Element die Seele...: die Angst vor der Infektion... denn es darf nicht vergessen werden, daß vor vierzig Jahren die sexuellen Seuchen hundertfach mehr verbreitet waren als heute... ergab damals [c.1902] die Statistik beim Militär und in den Großstädten, daß unter zehn jungen Leuten mindestens einer oder zwei schon Infektionen zum Opfer gefallen waren... zu der Angst vor der Infektion kam noch das Grauen von der widrigen und entwürdigenden Form der damaligen Kuren, von denen gleichfalls die Welt von heute nichts mehr weiß. Durch Wochen und Wochen wurde der ganze Körper eines mit Syphilis infizierten mit Quecksilber eingerieben, was wiederum zur Folge hatte, daß die Zähne ausfielen und sonstige Gesundheitsschädigungen eintraten; das unglückliche Opfer eines schlimmen Zufalls fühlte sich also nicht nur seelisch, sondern auch physisch beschmutzt, und selbst nach einer solchen grauenhaften Kur konnte der Betroffene lebenslang nicht gewiß sein, ob nicht jeder Augenblick der tückische Virus aus seiner Verkapselung wieder erwachen könnte, vom Rückenmark aus die Glieder lähmend, hinter der Stirn das Gehirn erweichend. Kein Wunder darum, daß damals viele junge Leute sofort, wenn bei ihnen die Diagnose gestellt wurde, zum Revolver griffen, weil sie das Gefühl, sich selbst und ihren nächsten Verwandten als unheilbar verdächtig zu sein, unerträglich fanden. Dazu kamen noch die anderen Sorgen einer immer nur heimlich ausgeübten vita sexualis. Suche ich mich redlich zu erinnern, so weiß ich kaum einen Kameraden meiner Jugendjahre, der nicht einmal blaß und verstörten Blickes gekommen wäre, der eine,

weil er erkrankt war oder eine Erkrankung befürchtete, der zweite, weil er unter einer Erpressung wegen einer Abtreibung stand, der dritte, weil ihm das Geld fehlte, ohen Wissen seiner Familie eine Kur durchzumachen.[91]

Did Zweig, when he wrote these lines (in 1939-41), retroactively realise that his succinct assessment of the effects of a formerly widespread disease (the infection rate among soldiers he cites for 1902, 10-20%, may not have been much lower in 1802) could go a long way towards explaining Kleist's "demons"?[92] That syphilis therapy and its difficult-to-hide side-effects, the feeling of psychical and physical *"Beschmutzung"* ("blemish," "abjectedness"), the uncertainty as to when and how symptoms would break out, the hand on the revolver, the sense of shame vis-à-vis family and friends, the secretiveness, the need to obtain money for the treatment without asking the family for help, could apply to Kleist as well as to anyone?

If Heinr. Zschokke reflects, *"trug [Kleist] eine geheime Wunde? Ich wagte nicht sie zu berühren"* (*LS*,73), and if Christa Wolf discerns in Kleist a "never healing wound," my analysis corroborates both their intuitions: Kleist's *"tief und absichtsvoll verschleiertes Geheimnis"* (Wolf) comprised a fateful nexus of homosexuality and syphilis, and I have no doubt that one of the *"Heimlich-Kranken"* Zschokke refers to in the foreword to his 1841 tale *Alamontade* (cf. *LS*,74) is Kleist.[93] A passage from Karl Bertuch's diary entry of 18th April 1804, *"A la grande Galerie de tableaux je trouve Mr. de W. bleu de ciel et Kleist qui porte les suites de s'etre brulé,"* illuminates the stratagems by which Kleist veiled his condition: his bandages, I offer, covered not burns but syphiliac rashes.[94] His relative obscurity during his lifetime apart, the scarceness of portraits of Kleist may well have resulted from his deliberately shunning the public eye, and the perpetuation of his features.

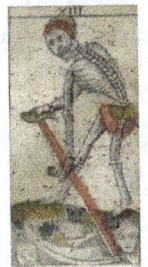

Death.[95]

1.4 "auch das sagen, was er nicht sagt": *The Po(ï)etical*

I term *"The Po(ï)etical"* (*"poïesis"* = "to create") Kleist's poetical aspirations, productions and battles. Unlike the other "lives," *"The Po(ï)etical"* is not so much woven into Kleist's text(ure)s as it comprises their totality: the œuvre as such, its genesis (conception, production, publication, dissemination, monetarisation) and contextual and intertextual relations, and his own emergence and evolution as poet, his life *of* poetry and *as* poetry, his *po(ï)etical* object and tradecraft—as he put it: *"auch das sagen, was er nicht sagt"* (II:757)—, his aesthetics and ethics, theory and practice, machinic producing and desiring.[96]

"Gesetze des Trauerspiels." Kleist's note on the margin of the *Ghonorez* MS, *"Puppen am Drahte des Schicksals,"* recalls an expression he in 1801 shared with Wilhelmine, *"und der Zufall führt uns allgewaltig an tausend feingesponnenen Fäden fort"* (II:642), and anticipates his 1802 or 1803 *Gesetze des Trauerspiels* and his 1810 essay *Marionettentheater*. In all these conceptions a target audience's *fate* is governed by an author in accordance with a set of laws, and with the aid of a *technē*, of manipulation: the dramatist manipulates his audiences via the "thousand finely spun threads" of his poetry in accordance with certain dramatic "laws," the *magnétiseur*'s manipulates his mediums via magnetic force in accordance with certain psychical mechanisms, and the *Maschinist* manipulates his marionettes via wires in accordance with gravitational and mechanic laws.[97] The poet or dramatist, then, is *magnétiseur* and *Maschinist kat' exochen*: *"Ja es ist im richtigen Sinne sogar möglich, das Schicksal selbst zu leiten,"* Kleist tells Rühle in *Aufsatz*, in a succinct statement of his *po(ï)etical* purpose and method: to *direct* (in accordance with his Stoic postulate of the equivalence of the physical and moral worlds) *the fate of real personages,* whose avatars his characters represent.[98]

The linguist Chr. Gottlieb Hölder in his travel journal jotted down an annotated diagram Kleist in 1802 or 1803 reportedly scratched on a wooden table at Interlaken to illustrate his *"Gesetze des Trauerspiels"*:[99]

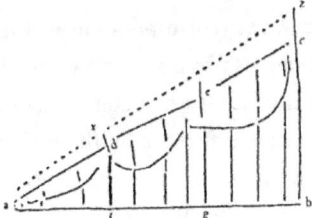

Die Linie a b ist die extensive Größe der Begebenheiten; sie liegt in der Fläche des menschlichen Lebens; auf ihr die Zwecke des Helden. Diese Linie ist in drei gleiche Teile geteilt, a f, f g, g b; Exposition, Schürzung des Knotens, und Katastrophe. Die Linie b c ist die intensive Größe der Begebenheiten, der Charakter des Helden. Der Punkt a ist der Standpunkt des Zuschauers, von welchem aus er den Gang des Helden verfolgt, den er auf dem Endpunkte c erwartet; man könnte a c die Direktionslinie der Erwartung nennen. Die Linie c b, welche den Charakter des Helden andeutet, ist grav (gravidiert gegen a b), das Schicksal, welches den Helden verfolgt, ist antigrav (erhebt den Helden über die Linie a b). Wäre der antigrave Druck von a b gleich stark mit der Gravidative von c b, d.h. kämpften das Schicksal und die intellektuelle Kraft des Helden mit gleicher Stärke gegen einander, so würde der Held notwendig auf der Linie a b fortgehen müssen. Wäre der Druck des Schicksals immer gleichmäßig wirkend, aber mächtiger als der Charakter des Helden, so müßte dieser in einer geraden Linie, etwa a c, fortgehen, und sich immer von seinem Zwecke entfernen. In diesen beiden Fällen würde nun das Interesse des Zuschauers unmöglich stark genug geweckt werden können. Der Gang des Helden muß also in parabolischen Linien fortlaufen—und auch hier beweist sichs, daß dies die Schönheitslinie ist. Das Schicksal muß den Helden erheben, ihn von seinen Zwecken entfernen; er selbst nähert sich wieder denselben durch seine eigene Kraft, bis er endlich in dem Punkte c von dem Schicksal zermalmt wird. (*LS*,77aa)

In strict accordance with these "laws of tragedy," a marionette theatre's operator ("*Maschinist*," corresponding to a drama's author) by the "*antigrav*" force of his pull moves the puppets (corresponding to the drama's heroes, avatars of real personages) above the stage (corresponding to the diagram's line a b, the trajectory of the hero's purpose) via wires (corresponding to the diagram's vertical lines); the *"grav"* puppets are pulled down to the stage by gravity (corresponding to the hero's character strength), where they are "brushed off" the stage's resistance by the operator's force, thereby producing a series of parabolic movements (corresponding to the drama's *"Schönheitslinie,"* "aesthetic path"), until the operator ends the performance and pulls them up above and behind the stage (corresponding to the diagram's *"Endpunkt"* c, denoting the hero's always already determined *fate*).[100] A marionette theatre's operator, choreography, puppets, stage, wires, gravity, and *"antigrav"* force— and correspondingly, a drama's author, script, hero, the latter's fate, purpose and character strength— comprise a Deleuzean *agencement* whose "plane of composition" is comprised by the play's—and correspondingly, the drama's—performance, and whose equivalent in the actual world is the *agencement* encompassing Kleist, his tools, methodologies, genres and channels, the imperial or royal leaders, their fate (as determined by Kleist), purpose (*raison d'état*), and character strength.[101]

As his dramas aim to manipulate the real world, in order to keep his script aligned with the actual movement of history, Kleist must continuously reconcile his scenario with the represented personages' (the King, the Emperor, the usurper) progression. Perhaps it was not least because this challenge proved to be unsolvable in the case of *Guiskard* that he aborted it: let us say, Guiskard's ultimate fate (denoted by c) is death, against which he stems himself repeatedly, only to be pulled up again towards fate's trajectory (denoted by the line a c), yet the real personage represented by Guiskard—say, Napoleon—thanks to his character strength stems himself against his fate not only temporily but permanently, so that his progression does not correspond to the parabolical *"Schönheitslinie,"* but unflinchingly follows the trajectory of his purpose (denoted by the line a b), then not only is the dramatic effect lost, but also does Kleist's manipulation fail. In this case, within the parameters set by his own "laws," Kleist has three options: firstly, adjust the character Guiskard's fate (against the audience's expectation); secondly, physically kill the actual personage represented by his hero (impractical in most cases);

thirdly, jettison the drama.[102] Suffice to say Kleist, in keeping with his own rule-book, chose the latter option.

It was perhaps not that Kleist's *Gesetze* proved too rigid, excessively limiting his options for composition, but rather that his scope for *Guiskard* was too ambitious, and his timeline for Napoleon's downfall too optimistic, and that having chosen to anchor his *satirical* story in the hero's death, he was unable to adjust in a manner that maintained the play's dramatic tension. The *Gesetze* do perhaps not comprise the "*Jahrtausenderfindung*" (Ingo Breuer) of which Kleist tells Ulrike in October 1803 (cf. II:736), but nor do they deserve to be dismissed outright, as Breuer does (cf. *KH*,17), for they illustrate important aspects of Kleist's method, including the very principle that underpins his *po(i) etical* project: that real actors, like Napoleon, Fr. Wilh., Franz, can be manipulated by a poet provided he is able to literally "pull the strings" with his performance. This latter insight, arguably, is Kleist's "*Jahrtausenderfindung*": that poetry can be a form of "magnetism," a physically and psychologically effective *technē* of manipulation. Just as the operator's "will to power" is actualised in his puppets' movements, and the *magnétiseur*'s in his medium's somnambulant, entranced actions, the dramatist's is in targeted real political actors' decisions. Hence Kleist's insistence on the equivalence of the physical and psychological (moral) realms: in the absence of such equivalence, there could be no transmission between them, and speaking in a Lacanian and Deleuzean register, the virtuality of his drama (*The Imaginary, The Symolic*) could not be actualised in *The Real*. Hence also Kleist's interest in physical phenomena such as visual, auditory, electrical or telegraphic transmission, and mental phenomena such as magnetic *rapport,* sympathy, somnambulism, hypnosis and dream-states: all of them potentially offered mechanisms by which his manipulation of fictional characters could be transmitted, transported, translated over to those real political actors he sought to manipulate. In essays such as *Über die allmähliche Verfertigung, Allerneuester Erziehungsplan, Marionettentheater* Kleist explores theoretically those techniques he puts into practice both in his works and his life: "Bringt man den unelektrischen Körper in den Schlagraum des elektrischen, so fällt, es sei nun von diesem zu jenem, oder von jenem zu diesem, der Funken" (II:330). He, Kleist was convinced, who was able to harness and unleash such modes of transmission, could *change the course of history*.[103]

Poetry as Magnetism. Kleist's poetry, then, was in the first instance *instrumental*—a tool for manipulating political and thought leaders, lovers, rivals—, and his *po(i)etical* practice found a physical-cum-psychological model in the popular medical and social practice of animal magnetism. The below quotes (interspersed with my commentary) from an influential compendium published by Kleist's BA collaborator (and possibly therapeut) Karl Chr. Wolfart, *Mesmerismus oder System der Wechselwirkungen* (Berlin, 1814), conveys principles and practices of magnetism that evidently influenced Kleist's poetry.[104]

§79. Es gibt ein festes Gesetz der Natur, das darin besteht, daß ein gegenseitiger Einfluß auf alle Körper überhaupt existiert, der folglich auch auf alle Teile, aus denen sie bestehen, und auf ihre Eigenschaften wirkt.

§80. Dieser gegenseitige Einfluß und die Beziehungen aller miteinander existierenden Körper bilden das, was man Magnetismus nennt.

This "law of magnetism" or "law of mutual bodily influence," a concretisation of Wieland's concept of "sympathy," is the basic operating principle that governs characters' interactions (*rapport*) on Kleist's "plane of composition." Upon entering each other's orbit, they mutually attract, repulse or re-polarise each other, the permutations of their *rapport* being a function of their respective electro-magnetic "charge," and of the context or "magnetic field" (*Lustgarten, Kampfplatz*) in which their encounter takes place. When Penthesilea and Achilles enter each other's orbit, the the former charged "-," the latter "+," they inescapably clash in armed battle or sodomistic ecstasy (*Erôs = Agôn, Küsse = Bisse*); when Käthchen and Strahl do, the former erotically supercharged, the latter neutral, they promptly re-polarise each other, her charge being absorbed by him, turning him into an ithyphallic *über*lover, her into a submissive puppet devoid of power or coyness. One could, in principle, reconstruct any Kleistian drama as an apparatus containing a magnetic field within which an interplay of forces and charged bodies is catalysed in accordance with the laws of physics, or as a computer simulation whose objects' interactions are governed by encoded algorithms.

> §160. Der Mensch befindet sich immerfort in allgemeinen und besonderen Strömen und wird von denselben durchdrungen.

> §161. An den am meisten hervorstehenden Teilen oder Extremitäten gehen Ströme aus und ein.

While in normal mesmeric practice the "extremities" used to manipulate and transfer magnetic *fluidum* are typically the *magnétiseur*'s hand and the mediums' afflicted body part(s), in Kleist's versions they are invariably his characters' penises or buttocks.[105] Just as the moon's gravity modulates the tides, and the *magnétiseur*'s hands the medium's *fluidum,* Kleist's poetry, or so he hoped, would modulate his target audience's bodily and mental fluids (blood and ejaculate, phlegm and bile, desire and valour, etc.).

> §184. Es ist nachweisbar... daß wir noch mit einem inneren Sinn begabt sind, der mit dem Ganzen des Weltalls in Verbindung steht.

> §238. Zwei Wesen haben den größten Einfluß aufeinander, wenn sie so gestellt sind, daß ihre gleichartigen Teile auf genaueste entgegengesetzt sind. Folglich müssen zwei Menschen, damit sie so stark als möglich aufeinander wirken, Gesicht gegen Gesicht kehren. In dieser Stellung können sie angesehen werden, als machten sie nur ein Ganzes aus.

When Adam and Eve in *Krug* for two minutes stare at each other, or when Penthesilea and Achilles engage in hand-to-hand combat, they come, magnetically speaking, *face-à-face*, and Kleist, with his works, sought to come *"Gesicht gegen Gesicht"* with his King, so as to "mesmerise" him (when in 1811 Kleist physically comes face-to-face with Fr. Wilh., to his surprise and chagrin he finds the King to be firm and not at all swayable). Kleist was fascinated by "the patient's utter dependency in the magnetic fusion" (Fr. Hufeland), and by the "devotion of the [patient's] passive aspects to the alien [*magnétiseur*'s] will" (Fichte): one need not look further than Käthchen's submissive behaviour in relation to Strahl.[106] Kleist's conception of magnetism, although in part Mesmerian, was overall more pronouncedly Puységurian—cf., e.g., Käthchen's, Homburg's, Gustav's (as August) somnambulism—; about this eminent student of Mesmer Peter Sloterdijk notes:

> Puységur... konzentrierte sich zunehmend auf einen von Mesmer beiseite gelassenen Aspekt der magnetopathischen Kuren, den sogenannten kritischen Schlaf—eine an die Präsenz des Magnetiseurs gebundene hypnotoide Tiefenregression der Patienten, die häufig in Zustände mentaler Luzidität mit erhöhter Sinneswahrnehmung und selbstdiagnostischer Einsicht mündete... Für Puységur war der von ihm so genannte künstliche Somnambulismus der Königsweg zur magnetopathischen Heilung; er setzte die luziden Trancen ein, um seinen Heilungswillen für den Patienten in diesen selbst wie einen unbewußten Imperativ zu implantieren... Von Puységur ging die Neudeutung des magnetischen Verfahrens als Willensübertragung vom Magnetiseur auf den Magnetisierten aus—eine Vorstellung, die im besonderen auf die Denker des Deutschen Idealismus Eindruck machte.[107]

To return to Wolfart:

> §309. Es gibt nur eine Krankheit und nur ein Heilmittel; in der vollkommenen Harmonie aller unserer Organe und ihrer Verrichtungen besteht die Gesundheit. Die Krankheit ist bloß die Abweichung von dieser Harmonie.

Kleist evidently accepted this proto-homeopathic theory, and leveraged it for his life and work, his eclectic choices of medical therapies for his illness, and of poetic techniques and genres for his works, paralleling each other not least because they were equally based on such esoteric teachings and practices.

§333. Keine Krankheit kann ohne Krisis geheilt werden; die Krisis ist das Streben der Natur, durch Vermehrung der Bewegung, des Tonus und der Spannung, die Hindernisse, welche die Zirkulation hemmen, zu zerstreuen.

§334. Wenn die Natur nicht hinreichend ist, Krisen hervorzubringen, so unterstützt man sie durch den Magnetismus.

The parallels between the magnetic *"krisis,"* the tragic *"peripeteia"* (in which the hero is purified or doomed), the political *"crisis point"* (at which war is triggered or averted) and the patient's *"crisis"* during the progression of an illness (in which the patient recovers or succumbs) will have intrigued Kleist, among whose chief *po(i)etical* experiments was to bring them into conjunction in his works.

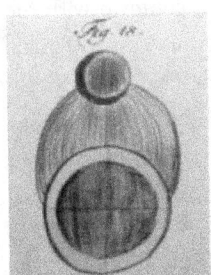

Poetry of Magnetism (FLTR): *"an tausend feingesponnenen Fäden"*: Mesmer's hand-drawing of the tides that served as analogon for his conception of the magneto-fluidal dynamic within and between human bodies; *"Gesicht gegen Gesicht"*: Kleist mesmerising Queen Luise with his birthday poem; *"Thierischer Magnetismus"*: mesmerism as a means of overcoming *"Ziererei."*

On stage. Off stage. In Attic theatre, all-male casts and largely-male audiences regularly interacted directly, most notably in the chorus' *parabasis*. Since at important festivals the political élites—

the *basileus* (king), *archons* (magistrates), curators and judges—sat in the amphitheatre's front rows, surrounded by citizens of standing (country folk and women took the back seats, if any), such interaction provided the dramatist unmatched opportunities to address his rulers in an unmediated manner (mediated only by his own script and staging). Classical theatre was eminently political—and as such, considered properly the domain of men. When Kleist tells Marie (cf. II:796) that the quality of German theatre would increase if women were not admitted, he is thinking not only of curtailing their admission to the audience, but also to the *cast*: for him politics, sex and theatre (the enactment on stage of politics and sex) were intimately bound up, and were all predominantly male domains. Kleist resented in particular the perceived involvement of Queen Luise (whom Napoleon termed "the King's best minister") in Prussian political decision-making, and her sway over her husband, and the fact that he writes his comments concerning women on stage (i.e., the political stage) to none other than Marie is suggestive, Marie being the Queen's confidante. As said, he conceived his dramas for an all-male cast, even if this conception did not conform with the theatrical praxis of his day: he *envisaged* the actors cast in female roles as males, wearing female masks and costumes. No doubt Kleist, as he posts his note to Marie, is anticipating disapproving reactions to *Penthesilea* from contemporary audiences conditioned for a light menu of sentimental and "pathetic" (Gentz) Kotzebuean and Ifflandian *Rührstücke* (popular especially with women); yet he is also expressing a genuine longing, indeed a project, for recreating the artistic and political conditions of classical Attic theatre.[108]

When Kleist, in epigram no. 2, *Komödienzettel*, "*Heute zum ersten Mal mit Vergunst: die Penthesilea, / Hundekomödie; Acteurs: Helden und Köter und Fraun*" (I:20), equates heroes, dogs and women, he not only deliberately seeks to provoke scandal, but also explicates his method: not only do his drama's "women" (the Amazons) represent male soldiers (Napoleon's *Ad'A*), but also does he envisage his "*Acteurs*" to be exclusively male, not only to those enacting "heroes" (Napoleon, Luise/*Borussia*, Fr. Wilh.) and "women" (warriors, soldiers), but even those enacting the "dogs"

(here, presumably, referring to the "doggisch" *Rheinbündler*: the actors in question would wear cartoonish dog-masks with features resembling those of, say, Fr. Aug. of Saxony and Max. Joseph of Bavaria). The "dog-comedy" the epigram defiantly and cynically (*kynikos* = dog-like) announces is an all-male, *satirico-satyrical*, erotico-agonistic, orgiastic hurly-burly—only that most of his audience does not realise it, because Kleist's recourse to Aristophanesian Old Comedy does not fit into their frame of reference with respect to a contemporary play's "look and feel." To this day, I take it, *none* of his dramas' stagings have corresponded to Kleist's *image* of how they ideally *ought to be staged*.

When Kleist writes Goethe à propos of *Penthesilea*, "*Es is übrigens ebenso wenig für die Bühne geschrieben, als jenes frühere Drama: der Zerbrochne Krug*" (II:805), he confirms that his dramas are not in the first instance written for the public stage in the manner of, say, Shakespeare's, or even Aristophanes', plays: they are written for a select audience and have their greatest effect when declaimed in the intimate setting of an audience chamber or salon, comprising a select circle of cognoscendi—say, Zschokke, Gessner and Wieland Jr. for *Schroffenstein*, Wieland Sr. for *Guiskard*, Queen Luise and her court ladies for the birthday poem, Prince Radziwill's private theatre for *Homburg*—, which is why in Leipzig Kleist took lessons in declamation, and why Wilhelmine's trait that most endeared her to him was her being a good listener.[109] With the partial exception of *Käthchen,* which Kleist produced specifically for Vienna's and Berlin's public stages, and whose concessions to "pop" tastes he subsequently regretted, Kleist's dramas indeed are "made for the *Lesekabinett*" (Fouqué, Chr. Gottfried Schütz and Tieck, à propos of *Krug*); they indeed are *"mehr zum Lesen, als für die Bühne"* (Wilh. von Schütz-Lacrimas); and they indeed comprise "*Sprechtheater*" (Goethe), "*Lesedrama*" (Sembdner, Kreutzer), or "*Erzähltheater*" (Grathoff).[110]

Kleist, as we saw, adopted key themes from Shakespeare for his *satirical* "thread," but the most important influence on his dramas was the "*ungezogene Liebling der Grazien*" (Goethe) Aristophanes, grand master of that famed Attic Old Comedy so saturated with irony, satire, polemic, innuendo, slapstick, obscenity and farcical

anti-climax: *Schroffenstein*'s ending, of which Zschokke reminisced, *"Als uns Kleist eines Tages sein Trauerspiel "Die Familie Schroffenstein" vorlas, ward im letzten Akt das allseitige Gelächter der Zuhörerschaft, wie auch des Dichters, so stürmisch und endlos, daß, bis zu seiner letzten Mordszene zu gelangen, Unmöglichkeit wurde"* (*LS*,67a), is as Aristophanesian as anything in modern drama. Alas, classical Greek formats—lyric poetry, tragedy, comedy, satyr play, epic, oration, rhapsody, etc.—and stages—the public *amphithéatrōn*, the private *andrōn*, where symposia were held—could only partially and imperfectly be mimicked by Kleist's contemporary genres—classicist drama, *Rührstück*, novel, novella, anecdote, patriotic song, etc.— and stages or channels—public theatre, audience chamber, private salon, book, magazine, etc.—, and Kleist's dramas were practically unstageable—speaking with Goethe, Kleist was watiting *"auf ein Theater [...], welches da kommen soll"* (*LS*,224) and producing *"unsichtbare[s] Theater"* (*LS*,185)—because they were not primarily *intended* for the stage, or else, because the stage they were intended for *no longer existed*. In order to fully appreciate Kleist's dramas, then, we must project ourselves into the formats and stages for which he, in an ideal world, envisaged and created them.[111]

Agôn. Kleist invested so much effort in the production of dramas because demonstrating excellence in the *Königsklasse* of poetry was necessary to credibly challenge the likes of Goethe and Schiller and emulate the likes of Aristophanes and Shakespeare. His drama production may have been informed by the formal requirements of the Attic *City Dionysia*, the most important poetical contest— *Agôn*—in antiquity (and arguably in human history)—Aeschylus, Sophocles, Euripides and Aristophanes are among the known winners—, at which contestants presented a *tetralogy* comprising three tragedies (or two tragedies and one comedy) and a satyr play, remnants of which format persisted via the Roman *Bacchanalia* into modern times: Shakespeare produced two complete *tetralogies*, and Wagner's *Ring* may be considered a *tetralogy*.[112] It appears that in line with ancient tradition, Kleist set out to produce a *tetralogy* in his imaginary competition with Goethe for the honour of being celebrated as Germany's *Nationaldichter* or *poeta laureatus*, and while he may not have considered his *Erstling* suitable material for a competitive *tetralogy*, he intended *Guiskard* as its opening shot, to be complemented by two more tragedies, or one tragedy and one comedy (say, *Amphitryon*), plus perhaps *Krug* as satyr play; with *Guiskard*, in 1803 he abandoned not only his most ambitious drama, but arguably the very project of the *tetralogy*—and thus, for the time being, his full-frontal *Agôn* with Goethe.[113]

Kleist's dramas are also imbued with the festival's cultic and therapeutic roots: according to tradition, the *City Dionysia* was established after the Eleuthereans brought a statue of Dionysos to Athens which the Athenians rejected, whereupon Dionysos punished them with a plague affecting the male genitals and only let them be cured when they adopted his cult, a tradition celebrated each year by Attic citizens carrying *phalloi* in procession, and by intoxicated young men bawdily revelling in the streets of Athens (*kōmos*).[114] Kleist, in light of his own *syphilitical* concerns, will have been intrigued by Dionysos' "plague," and like Aristophanes incorporated dionysiac rituals or practices into his works, for example repeatedly featuring gangs of young men—Penthesilea's man-eating "dogs," the cobbler's rowdy "*Rotte*" in *Erdbeben*, Count F's doggish pack of "*Scharfschützen*" in *Marquise*, the brothers' teasing and taunting "*Bilderstürmer*" in *Cäcilie*—that enact at once *kōmos* and *choros* (the latters' members, in Old Comedy, were frequently equipped with prodigious strap-on leather *phalloi*, which they used for bawdy gestures such as flinging them over their shoulders, a gesture adopted by *Marquise*'s *Scharfschützen*, who fling their "guns" over their shoulders, and by *Kohlhaas*' knacker, who does likewise with his "whip").

In his quest to reach at once a carefully targeted audience for his *covert* messages and a mass audience for his *overt* spectacles, Kleist experimented with a plethora of dramatic styles: *Schroffenstein* may be considered a proto-Gothic, quasi-Shakespearean "*Rittergeschichte ohne Gespenster*," *Guiskard* a quasi-Schillerian historical drama, *Amphitryon* a quasi-Molièrian court comedy, *Krug* a quasi-Aristophanean comedy-cum-satyr play, *Penthesilea* a quasi-

Sophoclean epic tragedy, *Käthchen* a quasi-Grimmian dramatised *Märchen*, etc. And yet he failed utterly on both fronts: neither did any of his dramas shape the politics of his day, nor did any strike gold at the box office.[115] Perhaps he was trying too hard, to do too many things at once, leaving his audiences baffled, annoyed, horrified.

Kleist and Goethe. Kleist's reported aspiration, of becoming "*der größte Dichter seiner Nation,*" necessitated that it was above all Goethe whom he "*den Kranz von der Stirn reißen wollte*" (Pfuel: LS,112). Kleist's motto in life was "*Alles oder nichts*" (again Pfuel: LS,117), and his stance towards the *Dichterfürst* was in some respects similar to that towards the French Emperor: grudging recognition of their greatness coupled with disdain and envy at the exalted position they occupied in their respective domains; Pfuel was probably spot-on when he maintained that what Kleist hated was Goethe's "primacy."[116]

In epigram no. 1, *Herr von Göthe*, "*Siehe, das nenn ich doch würdig, fürwahr, sich im Alter beschäftigen! / Er zerlegt jetzt den Strahl, den seine Jugend sonst warf*" (I:20), Kleist insinuates that the mature Goethe had become a conformist *eminence grise* of German letters who, though having lost his own creative edge, could "make or break" a younger poet's career. Kleist's term "*zerlegter*" "*Strahl*" (i.e., castrated phallus) mocks Goethe's "*Farbenlehre*," which Kleist in a letter to Marie of 1811 (cf. II:875) pits against his own "*Musiklehre*," contending that music, in particular the *basso continuo*, more than colour or light, imbues poetry, thereby placing himself in direct opposition to Goethe's "pet" theory of poetry.[117] In *Verlobung*, Kleist crafts a veritable counterfactual to Goethe's theory, depicting a world in which unreliable *visual* information—the myriad hues of skin colour present in Haiti's complex racial mix, amplified by the misleading effects of varying shades and intensities of light—breeds mistrust (an insight anticipated by his "green glasses," making the "Kant-crisis" also something of a "Goethe-crisis"). It is the *visual* image of Toni entering the room at Strömli's hand, Seppy on her arm (alluding to Raphael's *Sistine Madonna*) that momentarily turns the meek Gustav into the virile August, who kills Toni, but it is the *auditory* reverberation of his cousins' thundering voices that reverts him back to his normal self, the meek Gustav, who promptly kills himself. In *Cäcilie*, it is once again an *auditory* force, the eponymous "power of music," rather than a concurrent *visual* force, the coloured light falling through the convent church's window rose (eros, anus), that arrests the iconoclasts' onslaught (who, by virtue of their being *icono*clasts, are rebelling against the *visual*). Not having been able to emulate Goethe's popular or critical success, Kleist sniped at his conceptual edifice.[118]

Already in *Aufsatz* Kleist told Rühle: "*Wir sehen die Großen dieser Erde im Besitze der Güter dieser Welt... darum nennt man sie die Günstlinge des Glücks. Aber der Unmut trübt ihe Blicke, der Schmerz bleicht ihre Wangen, der Kummer spricht aus allen ihre Zügen... Dagegen sehen wir einen Tagelöhner, der im Schweiße seines Angesichts sein Brot erwirbt... die Freude lächelt auf seinem Antlitz, Frohsinn und Vergessenheit umschweben die ganze Gestalt*" (II:301). That Kleist's "*Günstlinge des Glücks*" included Goethe first and foremost can be gleaned not least from the fact that his passage paraphrases the master himself, as Klaus Müller-Salget points out (*Kleist*, 1111): "*Es haben die Großen dieser Welt sich der Erde bemächtigt, sie leben in Herrlichkeit und Überfluß*" (Goethe, *Wilhelm Meisters Lehrjahre*). Goethe's face, says Kleist, has become blanched by troubles and pain, while his own, the simple poet-craftsman's, radiates happiness. In his seductive entreaties to Rühle, Kleist uses Goethe as bogey—as in: "don't *go* Goethe—don't become an old, boring, conformist stick; let us remain young and wild together." Quite a pick-up line!

The line with which Kleist presents *Penthesilea* to Goethe, "*Es ist auf den 'Knieen meines Herzens' daß ich damit vor Ihnen erscheine*" (II:805), abounds in ambivalence and irony: the heart, for Kleist, never bends, only the mind does—the "heart," so to speak, has no "knees," and it does not bend but *break*. Satyrically speaking, "kneeling" in Kleist's œuvre refers to a Bill-Clintonian gesture: Kleist positions himself as *erómenos* to the *erastês* Goethe in the full consciousness that the apprentice will soon surpass the master; *Penthesilea* is precisely the *Meisterstück* with which he shall do so, and by offering it to him, Kleist once again (as previously with *Krug*), hands Goethe the very weapon with which he entices him to kill himself. Luther, whose Bible translation Kleist paraphrases here, as Goethe had himself done, in *Kohlhaas* furthermore appears as a Goethean, conformist figure whose amnesty halts Kohlhaas' momentum: it bends his mind and tames his heart.[119] *Penthesilea* comprises Kleist's attempt to rekindle his *Agôn* with Goethe; it is meant to bring *Goethe* to his knees, not Kleist.[120]

Nietzsche, an admirer of Goethe, noted: "*was Goethe bei Heinrich von Kleist empfand, war... die unheilbare Seite der Natur. Er selbst war konziliant und heilbar*" (NR,357).[121] Nietzsche's thought, which may well reflect his own "incurability" (in his last ten years he suffered from syphilis-induced paralysis), chronologically falls between his early treatise, *Die Geburt der Tragödie* (1872), in which he celebrates the *Dionysian*, a force easily discernible in Kleist (as well as in the young Goethe of the *Sturm und Drang* period), and his late writings, such as *Ecce Homo* (1888), in which he envisiones a synthesis of the *Apollonian* and the *Dionysian*, as perhaps embodied by the mature Goethe. The shift in Nietzsche's thought may suggest that had Kleist lived long enough, he himself might have *"gone Goethe,"* and us today must almost be grateful that it did not come to that.

Nietzsche: "*Goethe über Kleist: fürchtet sich.*" (NR,357)

Ricarda Huch: "*[Goethes] Abscheu vor Kleist stammt wesentlich daher, daß er an diesem Jüngling erleben mußte, wie der sich verwegen dem Dämon hingab, dem er selber immer behutsam auswich.*" (NR,378)

Hugo von Hoffmannsthal: "*Ja, wer hat denn Heinrich von Kleists Seele getötet, wer denn? Oh, ich sehe ihn, den Greis von Weimar.*"[122]

Deleuze and Guattari: "Goethe and Hegel are old men next to Kleist."[123]

Kleist and Iffland. During his final years in Berlin, Kleist's *po(i)etical* bogey was no longer Goethe but Aug. Wilh. Iffland, a leading, if controversial, stage actor—Goethe admired him; Gentz and members of his circle despised him (cf. *AML*,32; 418)—and repeatedly director of Berlin's *Staatstheater,* favoured by Luise and Fr. Wilh.

and sponsored by Kleist's arch-nemesis Hardenberg, whose signature productions were harmless family *Rührstücke* (melodramas). Iffland in 1811 became director of all royal stagings and as such controlled all presentations before the Prussian royalty, i.e., Kleist's main target audience, and in that role was instrumental in preventing Kleist's dramas from being staged in Berlin, and it was with him, a far lesser figure than Goethe, that Kleist now found himself in competition with for influence in the royal court and cabinet. When in 1810 Iffland refused to stage *Käthchen*, Kleist responded in *BA* with a punch below the belt: "*es gefiele Ihnen nicht. Es tut mir leid, die Wahrheit zu sagen, daß es ein Mädchen ist; wenn es ein Junge gewesen wäre, so würde es Ew. Wohlgeboren wahrscheinlich besser gefallen haben*" (II:836).[124] Kleist's cynical swipe at Iffland's (widely presumed) homosexuality is doubly ironic: not only was Kleist himself gay, but he also envisaged Käthchen, like all his figures of maidens, as enacted by an effeminate male youth. Kleist poked fun not only at Iffland's sexual orientation but also his ignorance as to what was going on in the drama—the latter aspect being sadly ineffective, for one cannot hurt anyone with a swipe they do not comprehend. In a *BA* entry of October 1810, *Ton des Tages* (cf. II:408), Kleist parodies Iffland's reliance on gesturing; since *hands* in Kleist's works are always phallic, he is imagining Iffland brandishing his private parts on stage rather like the members of Aristophanes' chorus their outrageous leather *phalloi*. Again, such codified innuendoes will have gone over Iffland's head and thus left him cold.

In his last year it must have dawned on Kleist that he was too clever by half, ot else not clever enough: his virtuoso sarcastic parodies did not affect those they targeted, who simply did not "get" them, or else shrugged them off. It is saddening to observe, even from the distance of two hundred years, how Kleist in his final year allowed himself to be ground down in futile trench warfare with someone as inconsequential (from today's vantage point) as Iffland. Is not Kleist's oafish character Trota, who in *Zweikampf* is vanquished when he stumbles over his own spurs, which he forgot to take off for this duel on foot, eminently autobiographic? Kleist did repeatedly shoot himself in the foot, and in the end could no longer recover from such self-inflicted injuries.[125]

The Chariot.[126]

2. The Eight Dramas

2.1 *Die Familie Schroffenstein*: The German Disease (A Diagnosis)

Genesis and Context. Kleist probably created *Die Familie Schroffenstein. Ein Trauerspiel in fünf Aufzügen* in Switzerland in 1802. Possibly he completed the drama's initial sketch, *Die Familie Thierrez*, in the autumn of 1801 in Paris, or by early 1802 in Thun, and soon thereafter commenced the drama's first version, *Die Familie Ghonorez*.[127] *Schroffenstein* was published anonymously by Geßner in Zurich in November 1802 (1803 is given as publication date). Kleist lived in Switzerland from December 1801 till October 1802, primarily on a small, idyllic island near Thun. Günter Blamberger suggests (*Kleist*, 157) that Kleist relocated from cosmopolitan Paris, where he sojourned from July till November 1801, to provincial Switzerland because of a "late reflex of the 18th century's enthusiasm with all things Swiss"; others have offered that Kleist sought peace and idleness in order to produce his first major work, the idea to which may have crystallised in Paris, if not earlier.

Apart from its idyllic charm and remoteness, which he could have found elsewhere, and its location at the threshold of the French and German cultural spheres, which he will have relished, I believe Switzerland attracted Kleist for two specific reasons linked to his poetic plans.[128] Firstly, central Switzerland is the homeland of the Habsburg dynasty which, I shall demonstrate shortly, is prominently represented in *Schroffenstein* alongside the Hohenzollern dynasty, and Kleist could have sought proximity to their ancestral castle, the Habsburg, to the national archives in Bern, and to his old friend from Frankfurt/O. days, and expert on Swiss history, Heinr. Zschokke, in order to research the Habsburgs' history in preparation of his *Erstling*. Possibly already the Würzburg journey's original destination, Vienna, had had not only a *syphilitical*, but also a *satirical* rationale, of researching the Habsburgs and soaking in the atmosphere of their capital, and the basic idea for *Schroffenstein* could have entered Kleist's mind already before his hasty depature from Frankfurt/O. in Aug. 1800, or even before taking his leave from the army in early 1799: having had ample time, at Potsdam, to study the Hohenzollerns from close up, he may have wanted to brush up his knowledge of the Habsburgs so as to be able to give a balanced account of both leading German dynasties.[129]

Secondly, Switzerland, as recently as 1799, had been a major theatre of the *War of the Second Coalition* that pitted Austria and Russia against France and saw Napoleon rise to prominence. Napoleon, fêted as hero upon his return from the *Campaign of Egypt and Syria* (September 1799), via the coup d'état of *18 Brumaire* (9th November 1799) had become First Consul for 10 years, and having thus consolidated his power at home, took up the undecided war and turned it into a resounding French victory: in June 1800 he thrashed the Austrians at the *Battle of Marengo*, in February 1801 he forced them to sign the *Treaty of Lunéville*, which confirmed "complete French sovereignty" over *HRR* territories on the Rhine's left bank (today's Belgium, Luxemburg, Limburg, Palatine and Rhineland, among the richest and most populour regions of Europe and of strategic importance), and added significant French territorial gains in northern Italy, another wealthy region long contested between France and the Habsburgs, thus cementing in a matter of months centuries' old French aspirations that not even Louis XIV had been able to accomplish—a caesura Kleist will have been painfully aware of.[130] Soon after arriving in Switzerland, Kleist furthermore was to gain first-hand experience with the scourge of national disunity and the opening for outside intrusion it entails, which were to become such central themes in *Schroffenstein*: as soon as the *ARF* evacuated Switzerland in 1802, the Swiss Unitarians and Federalists became embroiled in a civil war—the *"Stecklikrieg"*—that forced (or invited) Napoleon to intervene once more, and to re-order the country with the *Act of Mediation* (February 1803) that established the *Swiss Confederation*, whose cantons were granted extensive self-rule, fragmenting and weakening the national government in Bern and thereby strengthenign France's de facto control of the country.[131]

It was in this context that Kleist produced *Schroffenstein*, translating in "real-time" the dynamics he observed in Switzerland into a German context. Instead of fathering a *"Kind seiner Liebe"* (II:694) with Wilhelmine, Kleist in Thun fathered a first *"Kind seiner*

Feder," *Schroffenstein*, as well as conceived two further dramas, *Guiskard* and *Krug*, the latter *"Experimentierstück"* (Rühle), in particular, in the context of his Bernese literary circle's *"Werkstatt"* (Sembdner, Blamberger). Kleist's first dramas thus originated in a tenuous Swiss idyll located in the very eye of the storm named Napoleon and always already on the cusp of being swept away by world-historical events; perhaps it could not have been otherwise.

Erbvertrag. By enacting a dynastic feud fuelled by self-interest and mutual distrust, and exacerbated by an ancient *Erbvertrag* (treaty of succession) that structures the stand-off as a "winner takes all," "zero-sum" game, *Schroffenstein* depicts a two-player game that anticipates the game-theoretical constellations articulated, in the 20th century, by the likes of von Neumann, Morgenstern and Naish, and that precipitates the *state of exception* theorised, in the same century, by Carl Schmitt and Giorgio Agamben.[132] In game-theoretical terms, the family's two main branches, who throughout the stand-off remain ignorant, deluded or suspicious regarding the other's intentions, are caught up in a classical *prisoner's dilemma*: under condition of uncertainty about the other's intentions and pay-offs, their rational choice is to "pre-empt and kill," rather than to "collaborate," rendering the drama's outcome just as inevitable as the hero's fate in Kleist's *Gesetze*. The realist Kleist recognises—as he demonstrates to Chr. Gottlieb Hölder at Interlaken—, that a *prisoner's dilemma* constellation, as ingenious as it may be as an analytical concept, in its blind automatism remains devoid of dramatic potential, and consequently renders his constellation more realistic and dramatic by throwing the rivals a "lifeline," introducing the (all-too-human) twist of the two houses' heirs *falling in love* (at least so it seems), thereby rendering "collaborate" a viable choice: if both rivals *believe* that by marrying their heirs they can neutralise the effects of the *Erbvertrag*, escape the "winner takes all" trap, and pave the way for a "win-win" outcome, they may stem themselves against fate, if temporarily (which, in Kleist's *Gesetze*, produces the "Schönheitslinie" that makes the drama interesting). Alas, Kleistian fate—like Nemesis—is inevitable and inexorable: both patriarchs cling to the primordial instinct of "blood being thicker than water," refuse to "collaborate," and default back to "pre-empt and kill," thereby precipitating a "lose-lose" outcome in which both successors are annihilated.[133]

Little fingers. The plot commences with the death of the young Rossitz scion, Peter. His father Rupert, the Rossitz patriarch, by compounding a concatenation of apparently contingent events—a witch chances upon the drowned child and cuts off its *left* little finger, for use as talisman or in the pharmacopoeic production of a magic potion; Warward folk chance upon the scene, and are about to do likewise with the corpse's *right* little finger, when a member of the Rossitz branch pops up and surprises them, bloody knife in hand—and an act of self-delusion—he tortures a Warwand eyewitness to press a (unreliable) testimony—, triggers a feud with the Warwand patriarch Sylvester.[134] The vendetta culminates in the two patriarchs' killing their own heir when they confuse their respective identities because the heirs exchanged their clothes; only upon recognising their tragic error they bury the hatchet.[135] Kleist's scenario is as paradoxical as it is axiomatic: only by killing their own successors, which is made possible only by the *Kleidertausch* (i.e., by a delusion), can the patriarchs break the cycle of violence. To re-state this outcome as a general rule: a struggle among a family's two branches, or rival successors, of comparable strength can only culminate in the entire family's elimination.[136]

In Kleist's story, it soon transpires that not only young Peter, but also the young Warwand scion Philipp recently died in an unexplained manner, in an incidence that could just as easily have sparked the vendetta, had Sylvester at the time not quelled rumours to the effect that young Philipp was poisoned by the Rossitzes (cf. V.455-6). Since in the case of Peter's death both the witch's and the tortured Warwand's testimonies are uncorroborated or unreliable, the circumstances of the two scions' deaths are in fact strictly equivalent: both incidences could have sparked the vendetta, the only difference between them being that in the second incidence Ursula's and the Warwands' (contingent) interventions produce physical "clues" (bloody fingers, knives in hand), and Rupert deliberately fans the rumours, whereas in the first incidence no such "clues" were produced, and Sylvester chose to quell, rather than fan, the rumours. This strict equivalence and exchangability of the two incidences renders the vendetta at once *accidental* (triggered by contingent circumstances) and *necessary* (sooner or later, it was *bound* to be triggered by some contingent event or other). In other words, while the feud's triggers—Peter's drowning coupled with Ursual's and the Warwands' finger-cutting and the Rossitz's chancing upon them—may well have been contingent, its underlying cause—dynastic rivalry, self-interest and distrust—is structural and deterministic: in Deleuzean terms, an extant, known *virtuality* whose *actualisation* is merely a function of (contingent) forces; in the terms of Kleist's *Gesetze*, the interplay of a predetermined fate and (all-too-human) character traits; in the terms of *Marionettentheater*, the predictable interplay of the operator's movement and the puppet's "brushing" off the stage in accordance with known physical laws. The actual cause of Peter's death in Kleist's *overt* story remains as indiscernible as that of Philipp's: Ursula and Barnabe's testimony (cf. V.2186-202), according to which Peter had already drowned and they came across his lifeless corpse, remains uncorroborated, making it just as possible that *they* drowned him, or that they conspired with the Warwands in murdering him in order to share the bounty—the women taking his *left*, the Warwands his *right* little finger. It is one of Kleist's delicious ironies that the patriarchs *trust* the witch's testimony just as blindly as they *distrust* each other's.

The Schroffensteins. As has been widely noted, many of the characters' given names are of Biblical origin. For Kleist, this may have been a matter of both convenience and convention: given names in Catholic Swabia during the late medieval period, in which the drama is *overtly* set, would indeed have been predominantly of Biblical origin (they perhaps still were in Kleist's day), and they seamlessly tie in with the Biblical references—the holy sacraments of baptism and eucharist, the topos of original sin, the story of Cain and Abel, the credo of the immaculate Mary—Kleist works into the drama, be it to camouflage, be it to illuminate his *satirical, satyrical* or *syphilitical* concerns.[137] The drama's eschatological and messianic themes, for example, may refer not only to Christ, but also to the medieval *Friedenskaiser* Fr. I Barbarossa (1122-90), who according to legend will one day awaken from his slumber in the *Kyffhäuser* cave and unify the *HRR*, and who in Kleist's day became mythicised as the greatest of Holy Roman Emperors and as symbol of German unity.[138]

As I pointed out, all three versions' family names comprise artful inventions that allude, already in their respective (working) titles, to the prevalence in the drama of *The Syphilitical*.[139] Among the names Kleist assigns to the family's branches, Rossitz (literally "horse's seat") points to the Hohenzollerns, whom Kleist repeatedly parodies for their fondness of horses, Warwand (literally "was wound") to the Habsburgs and their imperial dignity (cf. Homburg winding himself a laurel), and Wyk ("ward" in Frisian or Dutch) to a leading northern German dynasty, presumably the Welfs of Hannover and England or the Wettins of Saxony.[140] The drama's basic blueprint is this: the Rossitz, Warwand and Wyk family branches correspond to the Hohenzollerns (Prussia), Habsburgs (Austria), and Welfs (Hannover) or Wettins (Saxony), and the Schroffensteins as a whole—"those of the chancred penises"—to the *HRR*, i.e., to the "family" of rivalrous German dynasties, whom Kleist mischievously equates with a "brotherhood" of syphiliac, distrusting, envious gay lovers.

"Das Stück spielt in Schwaben." Having initially planned to set the drama in France or Spain, Kleist eventually set it in medieval Swabia.[141] The Duchy of Swabia was an important principality at the heart of the medieval *HRR* (cf. left-hand map below), the ancestral land of no less than six illustrious German dynasties (cf. centre map), and topographically the location of the Gottard Massif, a major European watershed whence three major rivers—Rhine, Rhône and Ticino/Po—spring forth that together symbolise the Empire's reach across German, French and Italian lands (cf. right-hand map; the Danube, which flows to the east, furthermore originates in Swabia's Black Forest region).[142]

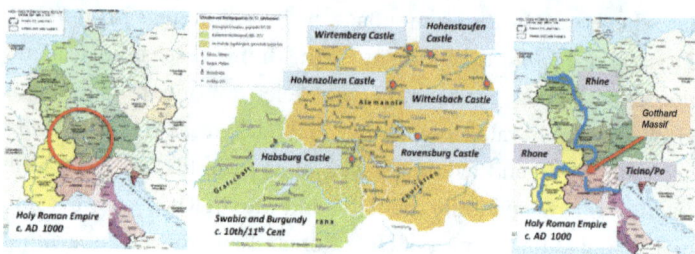

The heart of Germany.

Medieval Swabia thus constituted a heartland and a microcosm of ancient Germany, and represents at once Germany's unity during the "golden" era of the Hohenstaufen (the left-hand map depicts the *HRR*'s greatest extension under the Hohenstaufen Emperor Fr. II), and her subsequent fragmentation under the rivalrous dynasties that sprang from these ancestral lands. As such, Swabia was an exceedingly apt proxy for the geographical and historical situation Kleist was concerned with: the *HRR* in c.1802, riven by the "German disease" of *dynastic rivalry*, and in her weakened state defenceless against "infection" by the "French disease" of *dynastic hybris*, transmitted by the "pathogen" Napoleon.

Ursula and Barnabé/Barnabe. While Kleist adjusted most names with the consecutive shifts in the story's geographic setting, two names stand out for not, or only minimally, changing across the versions: Ursula (diminutive of Lat., "she-bear") and Barnabé/Barnabe (Hebr., "son of prophecy").[143] The former, who in *Thierrez* appears unnamed as "a woman," in *Ghonorez* is introduced as the witch, and gravedigger's widow, Ursula (Ursula is a Ger. name whose Span. version is Úrsula, yet in *Ghonorez* the name is given in the Ger., not Span., spelling); the latter, not mentioned in *Thierrez*, in *Ghonorez* is introduced as Ursula's daughter (Barnabé normally being a male given name suggests that s/he could just as well be Ursula's son).[144] When Kleist in the drama's final version drops Barnabé's *accent aigu*, he only apparently "Germanises" the name, for in Ger. it would properly be given as Barnabas; Barnabe (without *accent* aigu) retains the name's "French" root while making it *appear* "German."

Kleist's obscure play with versions of their names, with the inclusion or omission of accent marks, designates both Ursula and Barnabe as inherently ambiguous figures. Ursula's designation as diminutive she-bear furthermore suggests ferocity, as gravedigger's widow, ruthless nonchalance (she who, like Atë, walks over the heads of men), and she soon emerges as the drama's *movens*, as Kleist's annotation to the *Ghonorez* MS, "*Man könnte eine Hexe aufführen... als Schicksalsleiterin*" (I:833), announced, and as Rupert and Johann confirm:[145]

> RUPERT. Du hast den Knoten
> Geschürzt, du hast ihn auch gelöst. Tritt ab.
> JOHANN. Geh, alte Hexe, geh. Du spielst gut aus der Tasche,
> Ich bin zufrieden mit dem Kunststück. Geh.
> Der Vorhang fällt.   (V.2723-6)

Ursula's *Fingerzeige* and *Taschenspielertricks* define fate's trajectory (line a c in Kleist's diagram): her *cutting off* Peter's *left* little finger (a sinister, phallic *rough stone*) *triggers* the feud, her *tossing* the putrefying finger-phallus amidst the family members *ends* it.[146] Ursula in the course of the story appropriates, transforms and re-inscribes the finger, boiling it in her magic potion (whose bubbles perhaps spawn or invigorate her rather like the foam produced when Cronos throws Uranus' genitals into the sea spawns Aphrodite), before returning its emaciated remains to the family, having originally planned to keep it under her doormat to fend off the devil.[147] The scene in Ursula's *Hexenküche* (IV/3) harks back to the opening scene in *Macbeth* (Kleist replaces Shakespeare's three witches by three spells), and thereby already indicates that Ursula is set to bring upon Rupert and Sylvester what Lady Macbeth brought upon her husband: instigation to murder, and precipitation of their respective houses.

Contrary to Fr. Hebbel's verdict that the drama's "*Ausgang allerdings schwach ist,*" I consider Kleist's ending a stroke of genius: in one swift movement he cuts through the ancient rivalry's Gordian knot by confronting it, *ex machina*, with an unfathomable, incommensurable *Third*: Ursula.[148] By the time the dynastic rivals perceive the novel threat, Ursula has already usurped centre stage—as the folk saying goes: *"Wenn zwei sich streiten, freut sich der Dritte."* When the curtain falls, it is indiscernible whether Ursula leaves the stage, as Rupert and Johann entreat her to do, or simply stays put.[149] Kleist's ending is neither *tragic* nor *comic* nor *tragi-comic*—it is *dystopian*: the triumphant Ursula and Barnabe apart, all that remains when the dust settles are two ruined houses and a post-apocalyptic wasteland populated by dead bodies, castrated patriarchs, blind elders, mad youths, and putrefying members.

Move over, Mad Max and The Walking Dead. Here comes Ursula.

Peter and Philipp. If young Peter of Rossitz is that "angel" whose praises the chorus sings in the opening scene, his corpse's folded "hands" are mutilated: Kleist's finger-cutting implies that the "angel" was castrated. His drowning in a river links him to Fr. Barbarossa, who en route to Jerusalem during the *Third Crusade* drowned in the Anatolian river Saleph, whose mortal remains were interred in the Church of St. Peter (!), and whose sudden death left the crusader army under the joint command of three rivals (!)—Philipp II of France, Richard the Lionheart of England and Fr. VI of Swabia (!)—, whose discord contributed to the crusaders' defeat by Saladin. If young Philipp of Warwand's "poisoning" is but a rumour (spread by Gertrude), so is, as I showed, Peter's "drowning" (spread by Ursula and Barnabe): either of the youngsters could in fact have been murdered or succumbed to an accident or illness. Importantly, what did in fact happen is immaterial to events, since the leading protagonists are animated not by facts, but by rumours and by confessions pressed under torture; *Schroffenstein* depicts a world in which rumours and deceptions shape opinions and precipitate decisions and actions: even when murder is undoubtedly committed, as in the case of Jeronimus, the perpetrators (Rupert and Santing, in this case) immediately "recycle" the facts as rumours and false accusations, promptly broadcasted via effective channels (the chatty Eustache, in this case).[150]

Jeronimus/Jerome. Jeronimus ("sacred name") of Wyk on several occasions is referred to as Jerome, the name's Fr. spelling, Jérôme, minus the *aigu* and the *circonflexe*, marking this character as yet another liminal figure. The most famous historical bearer of this name, St. Jerome, is best known for translating the Bible into Latin (the *Vulgate*), and Jeronimus' role in Kleist's drama is indeed that of interpreter and mediator: he correctly observes that what shapes political choices is not truth but perception, "*von der Gelegenheit gereizt, / Den Erbvertrag zu seinem Glück zu lenken, / ...so sich zu bedienen, / Daß es der Welt erscheint, als hätten wirklich / Sie ihn ermordet—*" (V.1183-91), and articulates the plausible solution to the drama's "knot" (i.e., *prisoner's dilemma*), namely marital union between the rival branches: "*Denn fast kein Minnesänger / Könnt etwas Besseres ersinnen, / ...der Stämme Zwietracht ewig / Mit seiner Wurzel auszurotten, als / – Als eine Heirat*" (V.1663-8). Now, this time-honoured method of reconciliation and alliance between European dynastic houses offers far too straightforward a solution in the context of a Kleistian drama, and Jeronimus' attempt to mediate between Rupert and Sylvester from the outset is a "mission impossible": within *Schroffenstein's* rigorously Aristotelian logic, encompassing the principles of *identity* ("I am a Rossitz," "I am a Warwand"), *non-contradiction* ("I am a Rossitz, therefore I am not a Warwand"), and *excluded middle* ("If you are not a Rossitz, you must be a Warwand, and *vice versa*"), no *third term*, such as a Wyk, can mediate or encompass the incommensurable opposites; only an absolute Other, an alien intruder from outside the system, such as Ursula, can escape the system's logic, by annihilating both opposites (the witch's *modus operandi* is not *logical* but *alchemical*: it involves transformation, fusion, annihilation, compounding).

Johann. Johann's being Rupert's illegitimate son apparently puts him out of contention for Rupert's succession, though not for Agnes' attention. Johann's most illustrious name-giver, St. John the Apostle, is held to have been the only one of the Twelve Apostles not to have died a martyr's death, to have outlived all others, and to have been "the disciple whom Jesus loved" and the author of the *Gospel of*

John, which includes most eyewitness accounts of Jesus' life. If Kleist indeed had John the Apostle in view when crafting this figure, Johann should be deemed not mad but *visionary*, and his features could be effeminate—cf. St. John's depiction in Leonardo da Vinci's *The Last Supper*, or Alcibiades' in Anselm Feuerbach's *Symposium*). Johann's ironic last words, "*Ich bin zufrieden mit dem Kunststück. Geh*" (V. 2725), are indeed clairvoyant: he is the only Schroffenstein who appreciates Ursula's stunt and realises its far-reaching consequences. His Dionysiac revel "*Bringt Wein her! Lustig! Wein! Das ist ein Spaß zum / Totlachen! Wein!*" (V.2717-18) parallels Barnabe's "*Ei, was lach ich? Ich bin lustig*" (V.2161).

Rupert and Santing. Rupert embodies a tyrannical sovereign, Santing an archtetypical underling who unquestioningly executes orders, including the order to murder Jeronimus and cover up the deed: "*Was Dienen ist, das weiß / Ich auf ein Haar. Befiehl*" (V.1835-6). The "*Pfiff*" ("whistle") with which Rupert lines up Santing, his other servants, and his dogs (V.1518-24) comprises not only a "running gag" (Roland Reuß), but also, more importantly, Kleist's swipe at Prussia's *Frederician* system.[151] His personal experience here clearly comes to bear: to his erstwhile teacher Chr. Ernst Martini he wrote in March 1799, just as he was submitting his resignation from the Prussian army:

> Die größten Wunder militärischer Disziplin… wurden der Gegenstand meiner herzlichsten Verachtung; die Offiziere hielt ich für so viele Exerziermeister, die Soldaten für so viele Sklaven, und wenn das ganze Regiment seine Künste machte, schien es mir als ein lebendiges Monument der Tyrannei. (II:479)[152]

Kleist's personal experiences echoed widespread criticism of the *Frederician* army following the 1792 *Battle of Valmy*, at which the *ARF*'s loosely organised *tirailleurs* (skirmishers) fended off a nominally superior Prussian army. *Valmy*, the first victory in history of a citizen army, became as *famous* among the French, for whom it inaugurated a new, *Republican*, era, as it became *infamous* among the Prussians, for whom it put into question an old, *Frederician*, one.[153] Although Kleist's unit did not partake in this battle, one can imagine the soul-searching this unexpected defeat generated among the Prussian cadets; it was an inauspicious start to Kleist's military career: three months after he joined the famed Prussian army, it buckled before a bunch of French *tirailleurs* and was thrown into deep crisis.

Even more bewildered must Kleist have been at King Fr. Wilh. II's failure, in the years subsequent to *Valmy*, to exploit Prussian military successes when they did occur: after the successful *Siege of Mainz*, the King ordered his Field Marshal von Kalckreuth to grant 20,000 enemy troops honourable retreat, and after the *Palatine Campaign*, in which the Prussian troops occupied strategic positions along the French border, he ordered their withdrawal before relinquishing, at *Basel*, the *HRR*'s very territories in whose defence Prussian blood had been spilled. During his nearly six years of service—for the most part spent idly at the Potsdam garrison, playing music, enjoying male comraderie, observing the royal court, and debating politics—Kleist had ample time to reflect, and his letter to Martini comprises a summary *conclusio* of his reflections and experiences.[154] Yet the most succinct expression of his dismay at the once glorious, now out-dated Frederician system is encased, in a nutshell, in two simple words in his *Erstling*'s stage direction: "RUPERT *pfeift*" (V.1518).

Sylvester and Theistiner. Sylvester is Rupert's counter-draft—indecicive, defensive, unable to control his people—, while his loyal servant Theistiner is a more emancipated version of Santing. Kleist by no means endorses Sylvester's softness by contrasting it with Rupert's harshness: it is precisely Sylvester's lack of deciciveness that allows rumours spread by Gertrude to drive the Warwand people into headless action. To Rossitz' all-too-rigid system of command and control, Kleist juxtaposes Warwand's all-to-swayable system of tolerance and populism, a system prone to uncontrolled eruptions of mob power. Both leadership styles, in Kleist's analysis, fail; Sylvester's blind compliance, "*Denn weil du Rupert stets mit blinder Neigung /*

Hast freigesprochen" (V.2052-3), is merely the flip side of Rupert's mindless aggression, and it is the coincidence and interplay of both styles that fuels the feud.

Ottokar and Agnes. In his first lines, Ottokar vows revenge for his younger brother's presumed murder: "*Mein Herz / Trägt wie mit Schwingen deinen Fluch zu Gott. / Ich schwöre Rache, so wie du. [...] / Rache schwör ich, / Sylvester Schroffenstein! [...] / Rache! Schwör ich, Rache! / Dem Mörderhaus Sylvesters.* / Er empfängt das Abendmahl" (V.26-35). "Revenge..., Revenge..., Revenge!... Revenge!" is the drama's relentless *basso continuo*. Ottokar's three exclamations anticipate the three blows of the sword that in the final scene strike down himself (two blows) and Agnes (one blow). Accompanied as it is by the holy communion, his vow cannot fail but be *performative*: his and Agnes' fate is sealed in the moment of his vow; the fatal blows are already struck at the drama's onset, the final scene merely reverberates their echo.

Ottokar is repeatedly linked to venomous or voracious animals: Rupert, when he kicks his fallen body, marks him as serpent (cf. the aforementioned Biblical passage); he also calls him an otter (cf. V.2534; "*Otter*" is practically a contraction of Ottokar) and a basilisk (cf. V.2527; a mythical, highly venomous king of snakes), while Johann identifies him as scorpion (cf. V.2650; cf. my earlier discussion of this symbolism).[155] It is Ottokar who lures Rupert, Agnes and Sylvester to the cave that soon becomes not only *Minnegrotte* and church, but also crime scene and tomb. The drama's hero, in short, is something of an anti-hero.

Agnes, on her part, is by no means as innocent as her designation "*Maria*" implies: she deliberately stirs Johann's and Ottokar's desire before playing them off against each other; when she notices Ottokar stalking her (possibly she is luring him), she craftily pretends not to see him and speaks to herself, in a manner that Ottokar cannot fail to overhear, "'*s ist doch ein häßliches Geschäft: belauschen; / Und weil ein rein Gemüt es stets verschmäht, / So wird nur dieses grade stets belauscht. / Drum ist das Schlimmste noch, daß es den Lauscher, / Statt ihn zu strafen, lohnt*" (V.694-8), a *speech act* that enacts a double entendre, signalling to Ottokar that his audacity shall be rewarded, while preserving her innocent aura.

A not-so-chivalric knight (Ottokar), a not-so-innocent maiden (Agnes), a clairvoyant madman as third wheel to the cart (Johann), and a hapless messenger and scapegoat (Jeronimus): such is the *quaternary*, erotico-agonistic constellation at the drama's core, which makes *Schroffenstein* not as much a Kleistian version of, as a Kleistian counter-draft to, Shakespeare's and Ovid's triadic or dyadic love romances with which it is frequently paralleled. Agnes, like Ovid's Thisbē, leaves behind a veil, which however, in a typically Kleistian twist, falls into the hands not of Ottokar but Johann, thereby triggering a series of jealousies: Kleist's version of *Romeo and Juliet*, as it were, contains a whole lot of *Othello*.

A Murder Mystery. Kleist's cryptic text allows for the possibility that Agnes is calculatingly pursuing her suitors' destruction. When the love-struck Johann is nearly killed by the jealous Jeronimus, there is a distinct possibility that Agnes *orchestrated* this occasion to get rid of one, if not both, of them: his (near-)murder of Johann all but seals Jeronimus' own death. If someone were indeed to have been poisoned during the enigmatic "poison scene," it would not have been Agnes, who only sips a single drop of the dreaded liquid (V.1307), but Ottokar, who gulps down the rest (V.1333), and there again is a distinct possibility that Agnes deliberately took a tiny sip of the dubious liquid in order to *encourage* Ottokar to gulp down the rest. Similarly, in the *Kleidertauschszene* only Ottokar, but not Agnes, would have died had things gone according to plan (whose plan? Ottokar's? or did Agnes seed this idea in him?), and it is only thanks to Sylvester's unexpected appearance in Rupert's slipstream that Agnes is killed alongside Ottokar. Rather than a Maria-figure, Agnes is a *femme fatale*, an *erinye* (angel of revenge) who systematically drives her suitors (rivals?) into their demise: she remains firm in her conviction that the Rossitzes poisoned her beloved young brother Philipp, which furnishes her a powerful motive for revenge, and the reader all too easily forgets, not least because her lovers apotheosise her, that Agnes may have spoken precisely the same vow of revenge against the Rossitzes that Ottokar spoke against the Warwands, and only because the lecherous Ottokar soon forgets his sacred vow, we must not assume that Agnes necessarily does likewise. Consider the outcome had Jeronimo and Sylvester not appeared on the respective scenes: Agnes would have successfully eliminated all her rivals and emerged as the family's sole surviving heir, the triumphant beneficiary of the *Erbvertrag*.

Kleist keeps the audience in suspense with respect to Agnes' motives: when Ottokar hails their ostensible alliance, "*Nun wohl, s'abgetan. Wir glauben uns*" (V.1419), she remains tellingly mute, and when she falls around his neck (V:1334), this could be to *kiss* or to *kill* him.[156] This latter ambivalence (which reappears in *Penthesilea* and *Marquise*) foreshadows the fact that contrary to appearances—appearances artfully concocted by Kleist—*it is Agnes, not Rupert, who kills Ottokar*: although "*Er [Rupert] ersticht Ottokar*" (V.2514), and "*Er [Rupert] zieht das Schwert aus dem Busen Ottokars*" (V.2533), Ottokar is still alive when Agnes returns, and dies only after Agnes "falls onto him," i.e., *after Agnes deals him the fatal blow*:

> AGNES.   So wäre Ottokar noch hier?
> Ottokar! — — Ottokar!
> OTTOKAR mit matter Stimme.   Agnes!
> AGNES.   Wo bist du?—Ein Schwert—im Busen—Heiland!
> Heiland der Welt! Mein Ottokar! Sie fällt über ihn.
> OTTOKAR.   Es ist—
> Gelungen.—Flieh! Er stirbt.   (V.2555-9)

"*Sie fällt über ihn*" is an eminently Kleistian choice of words: while it may be read as Agnes' swooning over Ottokar, or as her slipping down to him to embrace him, this expression is most commonly used as part of the phrase, "*fällt über…her*," ("comes at…," "savages…"; "*Überfall*" = "attack").[157] Kleist artfully blurs readers' perceptions by having Ottokar hold on, till his final breath, to his love for Agnes and his belief that he saved her, and Rupert, to his conviction that he murdered his own son. It is Rupert who inadvertently confirms that Agnes killed Ottokar when he notices, in passing, *two* stabbing wounds in Ottokar's corpse: "*Zweimal die Brust durchbohrt! Zweimal die Brust*" (V.2678-9). Nothing in the earlier scene suggests that Rupert stabbed Ottokar *twice*; Rupert, lacking any other explanation for the double blow, assumes that in his blind rage he stabbed her repeatedly, but the reader, with the benefit of Kleist's stage directions, realises that it is Agnes who deals Ottokar the second, fatal blow when she "falls upon him."

The *Kleidertausch*, then, entails a final twist in Kleist's astounding tale of murder and revenge: had Ottokar not wrapped Agnes into his own coat, she would not have been killed by Sylvester and would have triumphed; thanks to the *Kleidertausch*, Ottokar unwittingly *avenges his own murder* at Agnes' hand, and in doing so fulfils his vow: "Revenge…, Revenge…, Revenge!... Revenge!"

Schroffenstein, Satirically

Schroffenstein depicts the *HRR*'s political situation c.1802, marked by rivalry between the major German dynasties and the appearance on the scene of Napoleon, and projects it into a near future in which the two leading dynasties', as well as the Empire's, survival is at stake as Napoleon takes advantage of their disunity to occupy Germany's centre stage.

Sorcier & Fils. Kleist's enigmatic figure Ursula—sourcière, *Taschenspielerin*, castratress—who takes advantage of the rivalry among the German dynasties to usurp their position, embodies Napoleon Bonaparte, since June 1800 First Consul, since May 1802 First Consul for Life, whose meteoric rise from obscure general to most powerful man on earth Kleist observed with increasing fascination and trepidation. Ursula's cottage, then, represents the Palais des Tuileries, Napoleon's official residence, her *Hexenküche* his throne room. Via Sylvester's speech, Kleist depicts the dawn of the Napoleonic era as an irresistible suction: "*Es zieht ein unsichtbarer Geist, gewaltig, / Nach einer Richtung alles fort, den Staub, / Die Wolken, und die Wellen.—*" (V.2021-3).

Ursula's "beautiful daughter" Barnabe possibly enacts Eugène de Beauharnais, Napoleon's stepson, *aide-de-camp* during the 1796-

7 *Italian Campaigns,* and loyal side-kick during the 1799 *Siege of Accra,* whom Napoleon in 1805 would appoint *Viceroy of Italy,* in 1806 adopt as his son (though exempting him from the imperial succession), and in 1809 appoint commander of the *Armée d'Italie*. When he has Barnabe make a wish, *"daß mich ein stattlicher Mann / Ziehe mit Kraft kühn ins hochzeitliche Bett. / Gnädiger Schmerz: daß sich [...] die liebliche Frucht / Winde vom Schoß o nicht mit Ach! mir und Weh!"* (V.2111-27), Kleist anticipates that Napoleon will seek to expand his dynastic reach by having his close relatives and associates marry into German dynasties, thereby penetrating and contaminating the German body-politic and generating an army of *monstrous* (or so Barnabe herself fears) Franco-German bastards. Kleist proved remarkably clairvoyant: Beauharnais in 1806 would marry the daughter of Napoleon's closest German ally, the Wittelsbach King of Bavaria.

The German Dynasties. At the heart of the drama's *satirical* thread is the intractable, perennial rivalry into which the two most prominent German dynasties, the Habsburgs (Warwand) and the Hohenzollerns (Rossitz), had been locked since the *War of Austrian Succession* (1742) and the *Seven-Years'-War* (1756-63).[158] When in 1785 the Habsburg Emperor Joseph II (reigned 1765-90) sought to annex Catholic Bavaria, the Protestant princes led by the Hohenzollern King Fr. II the Great (reigned 1740-1786) formed the *Fürstenbund* (Princes' Alliance) against Austria; the rivalry remained unresolved when the French Revolution intervened in 1789, and only their shared infuriation at the detention, later the execution, of Bourbon King Louis XVI, whom they considered the legitimate French monarch, and in particular of his wife Marie Antoinette, a Habsburg, daughter of the late Emperor Franz I (reigned 1745-65) and sister of the then reigning Emperor Leopold II (reigned 1790-2), compelled Leopold II and then reigning Prussian King Fr. Wilh. II to form an ad hoc alliance, formalised in the 1791 *Declaration of Pillnitz* and aimed at restoring the French king, and to launch the *War of the First Coalition* that Kleist himself partook in. The drama's "ancient" *Erbvertrag* represents this unresolved stand-off, whose perceived "winner-takes-all" pay-off—the imperial dignity, which the Habsburgs had claimed for centuries, and the Hohenzollerns now eyed for themselves—stood in the way of German unity, weakening the *HRR* against the *RF*, and fatally so once Napoleon appeared on stage.

Rupert embodies the initially revered, later reviled Fr. II the Great, Sylvester the reform-minded, yet ultimately ineffective Joseph II, whose reigns significantly overlapped, and who were indeed mortal rivals. While historians recognise them as two of the three "great enlightenment monarchs" of their era (the third being Catherine the Great of Russia), hailing Fr. II for establishing Prussia as the fifth great power on the basis of a highly effective, if authoritarian, military and political system known as *Fredericianism*, and lauding Joseph II for reforming the Austrian state, eliminating remnants of feudalism and encouraging civil liberties, including freedom of the press, in a system known as *Josephinism*, Kleist parodied both rulers and their respective systems of governance.

In *Fredericianism*, Kleist attacked in particular its rigid reliance on discipline and authoritarian command and control—cf. Rupert's whistling to lign up soldiers, servants and dogs alike (Fr. II was indeed as legendary for his devotion to his greyhounds as for his reliance on corporeal punishment in maintaining discipline among his soldiers, such as the infamous *Spießrutenlaufen*). When Kleist has Rupert reflect, "*Nicht ein Zehnteil würd / Ein Herr des Bösen tun, müßt er es selbst / Mit eignen Händen tun*" (V.1827-9), he may have in mind *Frederician* generals' habit of riding *behind* their soldiers, to strike fear in them by threatening to shoot them should they seek to defect, in contrast with *ARF* generals' approach of riding *before* their soldiers, to inspire them by putting their own lives at risk even before theirs. For a scion of the Kleist family and former member of the Regiment Garde, equating Fr. II with a cholerical tyrant and even the devil (cf. V.2228-9) was outrageous, and in itself already explains Kleist's need for camouflage and anonymity.

Fredericianism: Rupert *pfeift* (Fr. II with greyhounds, left);
instead of inspiring soldiers' *hearts*, his generals maltreat their *backs* (centre),
and instead of from the *front*, lead them from *behind* (right).

In *Josephinism*, Kleist critiqued notably its lack of decisive leadership and order, which gave rise to repeated popular revolts—frequently stoked by rumours, in some cases allegedly instigated by Prussian agents—that accompanied Joseph II's "enlightened rule" and undermined the monarch's authority: "*Dem Pöbel, diesem Starmatz—diesem / Hohlspiegel des Gerüchts—diesem Käfer / Die Kohle vorzuwerfen, die er spielend / Auf's Dach des Nachbarn trägt—*" (V.531-4). In short, Rupert's and Sylvester's rivalry re-enacts Fr. II's and Joseph II's during the 1760s-80s.

These two illustrious monarchs were succeeded by comparatively inferior figures: Fr. Wilh. II (reigned 1786-97), widely regarded as ineffective ne'er-do-well, who during the *War of the First Coalition* with *Basel* abandoned Austria and the Empire in blatant disregard of his promises made to Joseph's successor Leopold II with *Pillnitz*, and who at the age of 53 prematurely died of hydrothorax (accumulation of watery fluid in the lung), and Leopold II (reigned 1790-2), who had not yet been able to leave his mark when he suddenly died at the age of 45, his unexplained death giving rise to rumours, never substantiated, that he had been poisoned. I offer that Rupert's *rumoured-to-have-drowned* son Peter represents Fr. Wilh. II (hydrothorax's effect being akin to drowning), and Sylvester's *rumoured-to-have-been-poisoned* son Philipp, Leopold II, so that the two heirs who in Kleist's story die young and under mysterious circumstances are avatars of an interim, inconsequential generation of Hohenzollern and Habsburg rulers.[159]

The drama's action takes place during the reign of a third generation of rulers, those contemporary with Kleist: King Fr. Wilh. III of Prussia (reigned 1797-1840), represented by Ottokar, and Emperor Franz II/I (reigned 1792-1806 as Holy Roman Emperor, 1804-1835 as Austrian Emperor), enacted by Agnes. Kleist folds three successive generations of rulers into a single plot: Rupert and Sylvester as Fr. II and Joseph II, whose legacies—*Fredericianism, Josephinism,* their unresolved dynastic rivalry—still casts a major shadow on Kleist's time, Peter and Philipp as the hapless Fr. Wilh. II and the short-lived Leopold II, to whom Kleist grants no voice at all (but who help to carry on and exacerbate the rivalry), and Ottokar and Agnes as the reigning monarchs at time of writing. Jeronimus may represent Fr. Aug. III/I of Saxony (reigned 1763-1806 as Elector, 1806-27 as King), who in 1791 hosted Leopold II and Fr. Wilh. II at *Pillnitz*.[160]

Jeronimus (Fr. Aug. III, centre) mediating between Rossitz (Fr. Wilh. II, right) and Warwand (Leopold II, left); Pillnitz Castle, 27th August 1791.

When he has Rupert address Ottokar-Fr. Wilh. III (whom he mistakes for Agnes-Franz II) as "basilisk" (V.252), Kleist in a single movement designates both his monarchs as mere "little kings" ("*basiliskos*"), unable to step out of the shadows of their great forebears—says Ottokar to Agnes: "*Ich mildern? Meinen Vater? Gute Agnes, / Er trägt uns, wie die See das Schiff, wir müssen / Mit seiner Woge fort*" (V.1454-6)—and leaving in their wake a venomous trail of pettiness and mediocrity, poisoning Germany's spirit of resistance. Kleist here establishes a pattern of belittling and lampooning his King and his Emperor, while depicting them as dangerous because their weakness "infects" all around them.

The Rhine's Left Bank. Peter's left little finger is not only an obviously *satyrical* (phallic) prop but also a *satirical* symbol, namely of the Rhine's left bank territories the *RF* at *Basel* and *Lunéville* cut off the German "body"; it *had* to be the *left* little finger (cf. V.2680) that Ursula cut off, not only because her magic is *sinister*—that too—, but because the *RF* annexed the Rhine's *left* bank.¹⁶¹ When he has the Warwand folk attempt to cut off Peter's *right* little finger, Kleist may be recalling that the Habsburgs at *Campo Formio* and *Lunéville* were compensated for forfeiting the Austrian Netherlands with territories in the east, and their rule of the *HRR* was reconfirmed.¹⁶² When he has Johann exclaim, "*Papa hat es nicht gern getan, Papa / Wird es nicht mehr tun. Seid nicht böse*" (V.2710-11), Kleist either claims— ironically and correctly—that the Habsburg Emperor ("*Papa*") is bound to do it again, or oracles—too optimistically—that he won't have a chance to do it again, because the imperial dignity is bound to fall to the Hohenzollerns.

The HRR. The drama's first four acts entail a stylised account of the Habsburg-Hohenzollern rivalry, its fifth act a dystopian scenario of both their demise when Fr. Wilh. III and Franz II in a remote cave on the border delineating their respective realms annihilate their own dynastic successors, leaving the *HRR* and the imperial dignity for Napoleon to grab. The drama's mountain setting may evoke the Schneekoppe, the highest peak on the border between Silesia (the Prussian realm) and Bohemia (the Austrian realm), which Kleist ascended in 1799.¹⁶³ The Schneekoppe is situated almost precisely half-way between Berlin and Vienna, so that if Ottokar and Rupert (from Berlin) and Agnes and Sylvester (from Vienna) set off concurrently, and move towards each other at equal speed, they cannot fail to meet in its vicinity, where Kleist hilariously has the two most powerful German monarchs play a childish game of hide-and-seek (or who-is-who) in a remote cave, quite oblivious to the fact that in the meantime Napoleon, in his Parisian witch's den, is busily concocting a toxic, hegemoniacal potion.

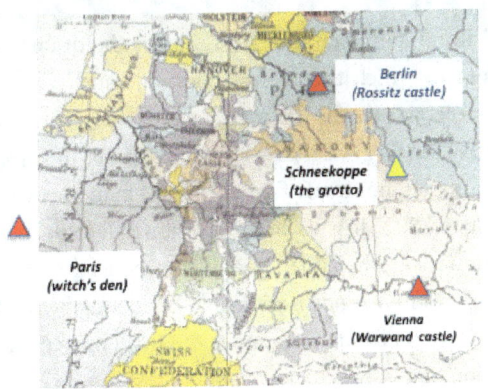

"*Gegend im Gebirge.*"

Kleist's *Kleidertausch* entails a specific *satirical* symbolism and scenaric experiment: what Ottokar-Fr. Wilh. III in the climatic moment takes off Agnes-Franz II and puts on himself is the Holy Roman imperial mantle. Kleist here explores a scenario in which a Hohenzollern pretender wrests the German imperial crown from the Habsburg incumbent, and in doing so destroys both of them, leaving the vacated imperial throne up for grabs for the incommensurable *Third* that appeared on the European stage: Ursula-Napoleon.¹⁶⁴ The dynastic patriarchs' uneasy reconciliation over their heirs' dead bodies, "Sylvester reicht ihm mit abgewandtem Gesicht die Hand" (V.2716), signifies that when the curtain falls, the *HRR* remains as stifled as before: the imperial banner's double-headed eagle, whose heads point in opposite directions, for Kleist perhaps recalled nothing as much as Buridan's ass (starving to death by stubborn of indecision), or, from our vantage point, anticipates nothing as much as Schrödinger's cat (which is simultaneously dead and alive). Whereas it originally symbolised the Empire's sway in East and West (a symbolism adopted from the Byzantines), for Kleist the double-headed eagle illustrates Germany's unresolved predicament as a single Empire headed by two monarchs looking the opposite way, turning their backs on each other in their perennial rivalry: "*Die Stämme sind zu nah gepflanzt, sie / Zerschlagen sich die Äste*" (V.1971-2).¹⁶⁵

And Napoleon? When Ursula says, with triumphant sarcasm, "*Gott sei Dank! So seid ihr nun versöhnt,*" Rupert weakly requests,

"*Tritt ab*," and Johann echoes, "*Geh.*" This is the drama's true *krisis*, the moment in which the critical question must be resolved: will Ursula-Napoleon *leave* the German stage, or will she remain put and *hold sway*? When "*Der Vorhang fällt,*" the *krisis* remains unresolved: Kleist offers no catharsis, he simply freezes the action in line with the status quo as of late 1802. It is as if Kleist knows that he must produce further dramas—perhaps he already commenced *Guiskard*—, and as if he conjures in *Schroffenstein*'s final lines, long before the advent of the Hollywood production model, the thrill of a cliff-hanger, and its invocation of a—*sequel*.

The Disciple Most Loved. So whom does Johann, the illegitimate son exempted from succession, the *disciple most loved*, represent? I conjecture that the mad or clairvoyant Johann represents Queen Luise or *Borussia* (the personification of Prussia), who in the final scene emerges as Napoleon's puppet: "*JOHANN tritt vor Ursula. / Was willst du, alte Hexe? / URSULA. 's ist abgetan, mein Püppchen*" (V.2704-5). Napoleon as *Maschinist*, dominating the stage and determining the fate of Europe; *Borussia* as his marionette, whom he can sweep across the stage at will: such is the dystopian scenario Kleist concocts in his *Erstling*.[166]

Schroffenstein, Satyrically
Their "brotherhood's" designation as "rugged stone" marks the German princes as ithyphallic satyrs afflicted with venereal disease, and the drama itself as a Dionysiac revel-cum-mercurial martyrdom.

The Dyadic. The location of Ottokar's and Agnes' first encounter is a "*Gegend im Gebirge. Im Vordergrund eine Höhle*" (V.684). Kleist's "landscape allegories" are never innocent, and it is not fallacious to read into his mountains and caves human bodies and their orifices.[167] During their second encounter, "*im Vordergrunde der Höhle*" (V.1241), the reader finds out what actually took place during the first:

AGNES.   Warum nennst du mich Maria?
OTTOKAR. Erinnnern will ich dich mit diesem Namen
An jenen schönen Tag, wo ich dich taufte.
Ich fand dich schlafend hier in diesem Tale [...]
　　　　　　—Da erwachtest du,
Und blicktest wie mein neugebornes Glück
Mich an. —Ich fragte dich nach deinem Namen;
Du seist noch nicht getauft, sprachst du, —Da schöpfte
Ich eine Hand voll Wasser aus dem Quell,
Benetzte dir die Stirn, die Brust, und sprach:
Weil du ein Ebenbild der Mutter Gottes,
Maria tauf ich dich.
　　　　　Agnes wendet sich bewegt.
　　　　　　　　　　　　Wie war es damals
Ganz anders, so ganz anders. Deine Seele
Lag offen vor mir, wie ein schönes Buch,
Das sanft zuerst den Geist ergreift, dann tief
Ihn rührt, dann unzertrennlich fest ihn hält.
Es zieht des Lebens Forderung den Leser
Zuweilen ab, denn das Gemeine will
Ein Opfer auch; doch immer kehrt er wieder
Zu dem vertrauten Geist zurück [...]
　　　　　　　　　　　Nun bist
Du ein verschloßner Brief.—
AGNES wendet sich zu ihm.　　　(V.1254-81)

Ottokar recalls how during their first encounter he, an experienced *erastês*, initiated Agnes, an ostenisbly "virgin" *erômenos*, to the mysteries of pederastic love: having "purified" her/him with his *cum*, he penetrated Agnes repeatedly, first in her/his slumber, then awakened, and laments that having been open to him on that earlier occasion, Agnes has now become coy and impenetrable.[168] I offer the following *satyrical* "trans." of this passage:

AGNES. Why do you call me Immaculate?
OTTOKAR. I wish to remind you with this name
  Of the beautiful day when I initiated you
  When I found you slumbering here in this vale […]
      —Then you awoke
  And looked at me like my new-born
  Happiness. —I demanded to know your status;
  You had not yet been initiated, you said, —Thereupon
  I generated a full load of ejaculate from my source,
  Showered your glans, and ass, and spoke:
  Because you are the image of immaculateness,
  I cover you with my cum.
  Agnes turns to offer his rear.
      How at the time it was
  Very different, so very different. Your body
  Lay open to me, like a voluptuous sheath
  That gently first receives the member, then deeply
  Stirs it, then inseparably holds it tight.
  Even when life's necessities pull the sodomiser
  Away occasionally, since the bladder demands
  Its dues as well, he nevertheless always returns
  To the familiar body […]
      But now your
  Orifice is sealed.—
AGNES turns his front to him.

Hilariously, the two lovers' repeated performance of the sexual act was interrupted only—by the *urge to pee*.

The Triadic. Agnes' coyness in the second encounter is evidently due to the intermittent interference of a *Third*, the "*Jüngling*" (V.1284) Johann. When Ottokar calling him his "friend," Agnes becomes nauseous (cf. V.1291-2), presumably because having encountered him before (cf. V.288ff), she believes Johann to be infectious. Having come into his condom—"*Ottokar kommt mit Wasser in dem Hute*" (V.1301)—, Ottokar offers Agnes his ejaculate for drink, of which she only sips one drop, evidently fearing it to be contaminated. Ottokar himself ingests the liquid's remainder, be it to die alongside Agnes, or to demonstrate its being safe. Subsequently the two lovers unite repeatedly: *"AGNES. Ottokar! / Sie fällt ihm um den Hals. / Ottokar! [...] OTTOKAR. O Agnes! Agnes!"* (V.1335, 1440). The sequences "Ottokar! Ottokar!" and "O Agnes! Agnes!" denote the order of their thrusts, first O! O!, then A! A!, with "O" marking the moment in which they change positions, Ottokar now offering Agnes his rear. Johann is conspicuous by his absence as the *third* lover, "*den dritten, der uns fehlt*" (V.1426), needed to complete the "*FFF*" constellation that maximises *jouissance* for all participants.

Satyrical triad: Ottokar, Agnes, Johann.[169]

The location of Ottokar and Agnes' third encounter is "*Das Innere einer Höhle*" (V.2370): inside a cave that is at once *Lustgarten* and *Kampfplatz*, *locus amoenus* and *Minnegrotte*, wedding chapel and tomb. Their movement into the cave—nearby => in front of => inside—corresponds *satyrically* to anal penetration, *satyrically* to the HRR's potential fate: *disunited* => *suspended* => *annihilated*.

The Orgiastic. "*Es wird Nacht. Agnes, mit einem Hute... Barnabe. Beide... schüchtern*" (V.2370): inside the cave, Agnes, condom pulled over, and Barnabe are producing "torrents of water" (cf. V.2388) while shyly awaiting, not Ottokar but "*die beiden Ritter*" (V.2399). In other words, Agnes and Barnabe are looking forward to a foursome with two well-armed, well-endowed *erastai*. When Ottokar appears instead, Agnes trembles at his "*seltsame*" appearance; "*seltsam*" ("strange") could be a contraction of "*selten*" ("rare") and "*Same*" ("seed"), which suggests that what Agnes fears is Ottokar's infectious ejaculate. As Agnes recoils, Ottokar comes before her/him, "*OTTOKAR. Ach! Agnes! Agnes! / [...] öffnet ihre Pforte! / [...] mein Weib! weißt du denn auch / Wie groß das Maß...? [...] / Ich werd es!... / [...] es kommt [...] / — Ach, Agnes!*" (V.2430-4); the Kleistian "*Ach*" marks the moment of orgasm.

Ottokar now fantasises how inside the cave's nuptial chamber Agnes will lose her/his coyness and whisper "*ich will*" (V.2444), how servants will join them with their inflamed members, "*Und eine ganze Dienerschaft mit Kerzen / Will folgen*," and how he will permit only Agnes to penetrate him: "'*Eine Kerze ist genug, Ihr Leute,' ruf ich, und die nehme ich selber.*" While Ottokar loses himself in his erotic fantasies, Agnes almost falls asleep—no wonder his friends, when Kleist recited the final act, could not stop laughing their Homeric laughter (cf. *LS*,67a).[170] Ottokar penetrates the half-asleep Agnes, "*Leise öffne ich / Die Türe, schließe leise sie, als wär / Es mir verboten... Wo blieb ich stehen? / —*" (V.2463-74), before taking off her/his condom and manually making her/him come: *Dann kühner wird die Liebe, [...] / So nehm ich dir den Hut vom Haupte* er tuts, *störe / Der Locken steife Ordnung* er tuts, *drücke kühn / Das Tuch hinweg* er tuts, *du lispelst leis: o lösche / Das Licht! [...] / [...] Nun entwallt*" (V.2474-9). While Agnes comes, Barnabe and the two "knights" (Rupert and Santing) engage in a *ménage à trois*: "*BARNABE* aus dem Hintergrunde. */ O Ritter! Ritter!,*" and again, "*Ritter! Ritter! / Geschwind!*" (V.2481; 2492). Ottokar equips Agnes and himself with condoms: "*OTTOKAR* der vor ihr steht. */ Wer würd glauben, daß der grobe Mantel / So zartes deckte, als ein Mädchenleib! / Drück ich dir noch den Helm auf deine Locken*" (V.2499-2501), and the orgy climaxes in an orgasmic firework as each of the lovers comes: "*BARNABE* kommt [...] */ Sie kommen! Ritter! Sie kommen! OTTOKAR. Mein Vater kommt.—*" (V.2503-5).

The Dionysiac. The threshold between the *erotic* and the *agonistic* becomes indiscernible as the plot veers between Dionysiac *kōmos* and Maenadic *sparagmos*. Rupert, in a single movement, sodomises and stabs Ottokar, while himself being penetrated by Santing: "RUPERT. [...] Er ersticht Ottokar. / Santing! Santing! [...] Er zieht das Schwert aus dem Busen Ottokars" (V.2514). Satirically, Rupert's stabbing Ottokar with his "sword" is an act of sodomy, and so is Agnes' "falling onto" Ottokar, only that in the latter case the act is fatal: Kleist forks *satyrical* sodomy into *satirical* severance of succession on the one hand and *syphilitical* infection on the other.

Other Dionysiac revellers soon join the scene, "*Ein Zug mit Fackeln*" (V.2536), "*Ein Leichenzug mit Kerzen [...] /Im Fieber!*" (V.2549-50), while the "knights" finish their business with Barnabe: "*Soeben gingen die zwei Ritter / Heraus*" (V.2554). Finally Sylvester, Theistiner and a torchbearer intercept Agnes, who has just finished off Ottokar and is about to flee the scene; Agnes is just readying his "sword" for "hand-to-hand" battle when Sylvester stabs him fatally:

AGNES richtet sich auf. [...]
SYLVESTER. [...]   Er ersticht sie.
AGNES.   Ach! Sie stirbt.   (V.2569)

In scenes such as the third act's "*Giftszene*" and the fifth act's "*Kleidertauschszene*," Kleist weaves together *Erôs* and *Agôn*, *Lustgarten* and *Kampfplatz*, *The Satyrical*, *The Syphilitical* and *The Satirical*, into an intricate fabric whose action culminates in a Dionysiac frenzy that encompasses, in a single movement, "little death" by sodomy, fatal infection, and death on the battlefield.[171]

Schroffenstein, Syphilitically

Having shown that the drama's *syphilitical* "thread" can be unravelled from the "navel" "*Ah! Der Skorpion!*," I investigate the interplay between *The Satirical*, *The Satyrical* and *The Syphilitical*: political rivalry, gay love and agonising suffering.

Two spiders in a box. Johann and Ottokar's relationship is as agonistic as erotic; Kleist's image, "*wie zwei Spinnen in der Schachtel*" (V.854), marks both as venomous, i.e., syphiliac. Johann's expression "*Die Schuld liegt an der Spitze meiner Nase*" (V.809) exposes his own infectiousness, his certainty that in their "duel" (sexual act) he shall die at Ottokar's "sword," Ottokar's.[172] Knowledge of the syphilis pathogen's transmission mechanism having still been rudimentary in Kleist's day, Johann's reflection regarding the "basilisk" Ottokar, *"Nicht stechen will sie, nur mit ihrem Anblick / Mich langsam töten"* (V.860-1), suggests that Kleist believed the disease to be transmittable by air, and uses "basilisk" ("he whose venomous stare is fatal") to denote a highly contagious lover: Ottokar's infectiousness is so acute that he virtually radiates it like a basilisk.

"Angel" and *"dove."* When Agnes ("the pure") enters the picture, Johann and Ottokar immediately turn their attention to this glorious apparition. Ottokar, as we saw, baptises her "Maria."[173] Johann, meanwhile, recalls how she appeared to him in her immaculate glory (*"Strahlenrein, wie eine Göttin"*), put on a condom (*"verhüllte sie sich"*), penetrated him anally (*"das Geschäft der Engel tat sie"*), while stimulating his member (*"hob... mich hingesunkenen"*) and, having herself come, pulls off her condom and uses it to gather his cum (*"löste... den Schleier, mir... das strömende, zu stillen"*) and mingle it with her own, and finally, handing this concoction to him (*"ließ sie / Den Schleier mir"*), departs:

> JOHANN. [...] Es war ein nackend Mädchen.
> OTTOKAR.
>   Wie? Nackend?
> JOHANN.   Strahlenrein, wie eine Göttin
>   Hervorgeht aus dem Bade. Zwar ich sah
>   Sie fliehend nur in ihrer Schöne—Denn
>   Als mir das Licht der Augen wiederkehrte,
>   Verhüllte sie sich.—
> OTTOKAR.   Nun?
> JOHANN.   Ach, doch ein Engel
>   Schien sie, als sie verhüllt nun zu mir trat;
>   Denn das Geschäft der Engel tat sie, hob
>   Zuerst mich Hingesunknen—löste dann
>   Von Haupt und Nacken schnell den Schleier, mir
>   Das Blut, das strömende, zu stillen.

OTTOKAR.   O
    Du Glücklicher!
JOHANN.   Still saß ich, rührte nicht ein Glied,
    Wie eine Taub in Kindeshand. (...)
    Doch hastig fördernd das Geschäft, ließ sie
    Den Schleier mir, und verschwand.   (V.288-305)

My reader can easily *satyrically* "trans." this passage in the manner I exemplified earlier. Agnes' putting on a condom before penetrating Johann may reflect a standard precaution among "brotherhood" members, or may imply that Johann's infection is well-known, or obvious. Although deemed "immaculate," Agnes is clearly no "virgin," but an experienced lover who immediately assumes the role of *erastês*. For Johann, the encounter with Agnes is a syphiliac lover's "dream come true": out of nowhere this ithyphallic, seemingly aboundingly healthy *erastês* appears and satisfies his passions, before mingling their cum and offering him the concoction as departing gift, be it as a token of love or as purifying drink.[174] Expressions such as "*Geschäft der Engel*" (an *erastês* anally penetrating an *erômenos*) and "*Wie eine Taub in Kindeshand*" (an *erastês* manually stimulating an *erômenos*) may belong to a gay vernacular, or "brotherhood code," current in Kleist's circles, with "dove" perhaps being "code" for a submissive, willing and accessible *erômenos*, "angel" and "goddess" for a healthy, well-endowed *erastês*.[175]

If *satirically* Agnes is an *erinye* who orchestrates and executes Ottokar's premeditated murder, *satyrically* and *syphilitically*, by analogy, she is a *femme fatale*—in other words, far from being a "pure," "angelic" "Maria," Agnes may in fact be a contagious "devil" (borrowing a term from *Marquise*). It is to Agnes that Kleist first applies his oak paradox (cf. V.505-7)—the strongest oak (member) being most susceptible to being brought down by the storm (syphilis) because its mighty crown (glans) offers the greatest resistance—, and Johann's frequent caveats, "*wie*," "*Schien*," "*ich sah / Sie fliehend nur*," "*hastig*," may imply that his first impressions of her—"*Strahlenrein, wie eine Göttin*," "*ein Engel*"—is delusional.[176]

Ottokar, during their second encounter, offers Agnes his own cum for drink, be it to commit double suicide with her (*pharmakon* = poison), to immunise her against his infectiousness (*pharmakon* = prophylactic), or to purify her following her risky encounter with Johann (*pharmakon* = remedy or antitode):

> OTTOKAR kommt mit Wasser in dem Hute.
> Hier ist der Trunk—fühlst du dich besser?
> AGNES.   Stärker
> Doch wenigstens. [...]
>   Ein Tropfen ist
> Genug.   Sie trinkt, wobei sie ihn unverwandt ansieht. [...]
> Hier ist übrige, ich will es leeren.
> OTTOKAR. Nein, halt!—Es ist genug für dich. Gib mirs,
> Ich sterbe mit dir. Er trinkt.   (V.1299-1302)[177]

The intricacy and intimacy with which Kleist narrates the dynamic of desire, anxiety, deception and jealousy among the three lovers suggests his account to be at least in part autobiographical.

Excursus: "Brotherhood" code. The topoi of defilement and purification are part of a gay "code," and "code of conduct" or "praxis," Kleist systematically develops in *Schroffenstein*, and applies across his œuvre, as the following table shows:[178]

"Code"	"Trans."	Examples in the Novellas
scorpion	syphilis	plague (F); poison (Z)
poisoning	infection	mysterious bullet (M); head wound (F)
duel	unprotected intercourse	ordeal *(Z)*
serpent	infectious lover	rabid dog *(K)*
basilisk	highly infectious lover	yellow-fevered girl (*femme fatale*) *(V)*
angel	healthy, ithyphallic *erastês*	Gustav (staff of god) (V); angel vs. devil = infected erastês (M)
Maria	immaculate lover	Mariane, Madonna (V)
dove	submissive, willing *erômenos*	devotion *(F)*
business of angels	anal penetration	show Roman strength (E)
in child's hand	manual satisfaction	handiwork (M, V);
baptism	immunisation or treatment	diving, spraying with holy water *(M)*; burning by fire *(M, B, K)*
water	ejaculate (a *pharmakon*)	ditto *(M)*; tears *(V)*
Corpus Christi	orgy (feast of the body)	ditto *(E, C)*; battle *(K)*; lynching *(E)*; musical performance *(C)*

(E) = Erdbeben; (M) = Marquise; (K) = Kohlhaas; (V) = Verlobung; (B) = Bettelweib;
(C) = Cäcilie; (F) = Findling; (Z) = Zweikampf.

The "German Disease." For Kleist, in a Nietzschean *revaluation of all values*, an immaculate lover, an own son and heir, and a unified HRR would assume the greatest value. In the broken world of his apocalyptic *Erstling*, however, all of these values are compromised: none of the lovers (rulers) turn out to be immaculate, even if in Agnes' case this may not be symptomatically apparent; all of the family branches' (dynasties') male lines are thoroughly diseased, including young Peter, whose "pockmark," by which Eustache recognises his "finger," is chancreatic (cf. V.2688-90), and young Philipp, whose corpse bears the same marks of the disease, "*die bösen Flecken noch am Leibe*" (V.481), as does Kleist's own, according to his autopsy report; and the entire Schroffenstein family (*HRR*) is thus corrupted through and through.[179]

This state of affairs explains why the "French disease"— "*Francofication*" or "*Bonapartisation*"—proliferates so effortlessly across Germany: the German rulers are already weakened by disease, for prior to the advent of the prolific "French disease" of *dynastic hybris* there is already a rampant "German disease" of *dynastic rivalry* (coupled with ineffective or obsolete systems of governance, *Fredericianism* and *Josephinism,* that further weaken the German body politic). While Kleist certainly detests Napoleon's propagating the "French disease" across Germany, he recognises that the "German disease" paves the way for it, and for this he blames the German princes, led by the Hohenzollern King Fr. Wilh. III, and the Habsburg Emperor Franz II. The *satirical* co-proliferation of the "German" and "French diseases" across the *HRR* parallels the *satyrico-syphilitical* co-evolution of gay love and syphilic infection across the "brotherhood":

Character/Object	*Satirical* meaning	*Satyrical/Syphilitical* meaning
Schroffenstein	HRR	"brotherhood"
Rossitz, Warwand, Wyk	Hohenzollerns, Habsburgs, Wettins	constellations of lovers, liaisons
Agnes	Emperor Franz II	diseased *erastês*
Ottokar	King Fr. Wilh. III	diseased *erastês* or *erômenos*
Johann	Queen Luise / *Borussia*	diseased *erômenos*
Ursula	Napoleon	therapist, pharmacist
magic potion	"French disease" (dynastic hybris)	*pharmakon* (poison-cum-remedy)
Erbvertrag	"German disease" (dynastic rivalry)	jealousy, distrust, deception
cut finger	annexed territory; ceased succession	castration, impotence

Kleist advocated and supported a reformed *HRR*; during the *War of the First Coalition* he may have been among those Prussians who fought with enthusiasm on its behalf, and among his favourite bogeys was Fr. Wilh. II, who so shamelessly put the interests of his dynasty and kingdom before those of the Empire.[180] Yet his *satirical* constellation suggests that he considered the Hohenzollerns somewhat less fatally "corrupted by disease" than the Habsburgs: while Agnes-Franz II succumbs to the inherent weakness of *Josephism* alone (embodied by Sylvester, who kills her), Ottokar-

Fr. Wilh. III, though immobilised by *Fredericianism* (embodied by Rupert, who injures him), succumbs only after Agnes' final blow. Because the "German disease," an amalgamation of the Prussian and Austrian "pathogens," respectively, of excessive authoritarianism and popularism (of which the latter in Kleist's view is even more "poisonous" than the former), weakens the HRR, all Ursula-Napoleon has to do is concoct his hybristic, hegemoniacal potion, throw in the Rhine's left bank as a catalyst, and apply this *pharmakon* (poison-cum-remedy) of *"Francofication"* to the German rulers. *"Francofication"* relates to "German disease" rather like mercury to syphilis: it alleviates external symptoms, while slowly poisoning the body. Just as the syphiliac becomes dependent on his doctors and pharmacists, the Germans will become hegemonised by the Bonapartes—when the curtain falls, I offer, Ursula remains centre stage, chuckling and counting her profits.[181]

Schroffenstein, Po(i)etically

Schroffenstein is *overtly* "pop" literature, and together with *Käthchen*, *Bettelweib*, and *Zweikampf* belongs to the genre of which Kleist in the autumn of 1800 playfully wrote: *"Rittergeschichten, lauter Rittergeschichten, rechts die Rittergeschichten mit Gespenstern, links ohne Gespenster, nach Belieben.—"* (II:563). Kleist, in crafting his *overt* (cover) stories, mimicked a range of popular genres—medieval romances and histories, Gothic tales and *Schauerromane*, libertine novels, Wielandian and Goethean *Bildungsromane*, Ifflandian and Kotzebuean *Familienrührstücke*—, while drawing on classical tragedies, comedies, satires, *symposia* and myths, and early modern dramas, essays, novels and novellas. Apart from practicality (it was efficient for his production, often under time pressure, to "borrow" and incorporate pre-existing materials that suited him), artistic curiosity, fun, and sheer craftsmanship (as a genuine master wordsmith, Kleist was capable of "dabbling" in any genre), one motive for his style experiments may have been that he needed to figure out what "stories" would sell: for some time he held on to the hope that he could make a living from writing.[182] Another reason for his eclectic variation of genres, styles and formats may have been that he feared, as his *covert* content and techniques remained largely unchanged across his œuvre, that excessive repetitiveness would bore his audiences (and himself) if he did not sufficiently vary the *overt* "packaging." This superficial variety, on its part, served to camouflage the consistency of his "threads"—so effectively, in fact, that to this day the *Kleist-Forschung* has not appreciated that *all of his works are essentially the same*, that there is, at bottom, but a single Kleistian work (cf. my later section, "Kleist's Plane of Composition").

Kleist has his finger on the pulse of his time, with respect not only to great power politics, but also to the functioning of the emergent "culture industry" (speaking with Horkheimer and Adorno): the politics of theatre, the psychology of "pop" literature, the economics of the publishing industry. This sensitivity allowed him, in a delicate tightrope walk, to partake in this "industry" while remaining on its margins and avoiding being assimilated by it.

A Poetry of Ecstasy and Despair. How inextricably *The Satirical, The Satyrical* and *The Syphilitical* are linked in Kleist's drama is evident already in the drama's opening lines, sung by the chorus of youths and maidens:

> CHOR DER MÄDCHEN mit Musik.
>> Niedersteigen,
>> Glanzumstrahlet,
>>> Himmelshöhen zur Erd herab,
>> Sah ein Frühling
>> Einen Engel.
>>> Nieder trat ihn ein frecher Fuß.
> CHOR DER JÜNGLINGE.
>> Dessen Thron die weiten Räume decken,
>> Dessen Reich die Sterne Grenzen stecken,
>> Dessen Willen wollen wir vollstrecken,
>> Rache! Rache! Rache! Schwören wir.   (V.1-10)

To the sound of music (French military marches? Catholic church music?), the maidens bemoan the earstwhile immaculate (Holy

Roman) "angel" now being trampled on by the (Napoleonic) boot, while the youths swear revenge on behalf of the Emperor, not realising that de facto their Emperor may soon be—*Napoleon*.

The maidens' lyrics anticipate Johann's first encounters with, respectively, the "seemingly pure" Agnes and the "obviously impure" Ottokar, as well as recalling Kleist's own sexual initiation at *Mainz*, where ecstasy—"*Hoch an dem Gewölbe des großen Schauspielhauses strahlte die Girandole der Frühlingssonne,... es war, als ob der Himmel selbst hernieder gesunken wäre auf die Erde—*" (II:673-4)—soon gave way to despair: "*Ach, das Leben des Menschen... Es fließt nur fort, indem es fällt... Wir sinken und sinken*" (II:674). Kleist keenly perceived the *nexus* of the prolific trajectories of dynastic warfare (*The Satirical*), jealous gay love (*The Satyrical*) and insidious venereal disease (*The Syphilitical*): military operations necessarily entail a "company of men," and it is in the "company of men" that homosexuality is consummated, faithfully accompanied by its scourge. I already hinted that this nexus is present in Kleist's earliest extant piece of poetry, *Der Höhere Frieden* (cf. I:9), which under the guise (anachronistically speaking) of an "anti-war" song links the sensuous side of sexuality—*Erôs*: the lush "cornfield," the "nightingale's song"—with its sinister aspect—*Agôn*: "dread," the "dark shadow" of the maple tree and its pointy leaves—, by which Kleist primarily meant not war but venereal disease. In the very moment in which Kleist fully experiences the joy and ecstasy of love, he also awakens to its dark, insidious side.[183]

(Old) Comedy. Schroffenstein's five acts approximate the classical dramatic arc comprising *prelude* (I), *protasis* (II), *epitasis* (the central act, III), *catastasis* (climax or *krisis*, IV), and *catastrophe* (V), the latter corresponding to point *c* in Kleist's diagram.[184] By assigning to the chorus the task of summing up the drama's essence via its *parabasis*, Kleist from the beginning positions his drama in the tradition of Attic Old Comedy.[185] This gesture in the very first lines of his poetic project sets the tone for his entire œuvre, setting it apart from modern and classicist drama and locating it in Aristophanes' orbit, whose techniques Kleist widely adopts:[186]

- Like Aristophanes' comedy, Kleist's drama *parodies conventional tragedy:* Romeo and Juliet's heterosexual love affair becomes a gay three-some;
- Kleist's stage is the *locus of real political action,* not mere representation: the very leaders he addresses are expected to be present in the audience, even to step onto the stage and perform real-time decisions and actions;
- As in Attic theatre, *three principal actors* appear on stage, supported by a cast of minor characters (who may be the members of the chorus); Kleist realises this convention in a series of interacting triads: Rupert-Jeronimus-Sylvester (patriarchs); Ottokar-Agnes-Johann (youths); Eustache-Agnes-Gertrude (women); Ursula-Sylvius-Johann (magicians/visionaries);
- These actors wear *masks* that depict not stereotypical characters but actual personages expected to be among the audience, who are thereby teased, taunted and mocked, and also compelled to (re-)act on the spot;
- The *chorus* frames the narrative, anticipates its outcome and, by interacting directly with the audience in the *parabasis,* shapes history;
- An eclectic *mixture of styles and means* is deployed: a hullabaloo of dialogues involving argument, burlesque, obscenity, fantasy, absurdity, word-play, pun, slander, ridicule, etc., performed within a formal, conventional structure and choreography and deploying traditional means such as stage directions, settings, *machinē,* etc.;[187]
- *Props* are in-your-face and lifelike: Ursula throws an actual putrefying children's finger, not a dummy, onto the stage
- *Obscene bawdiness,* dirty jokes, and grotesque costumes accompany *Dionysiac* revels and *Symposiac* orgies (Aristophanes' *Frogs* features goat-penises and fig-wood *phalloi* deployed in Dionysiac rituals)
- The climax is a *farcical anti-climax* (as the laughter with which Kleist's friends accompany his recital of *Schroffenstein*'s final scene confirms);

- The catastrophe is *suspended and thereby extended*; the curtain falls not on a catharsis or dénouement but on an unresolved situation, a cliff-hanger.

More even than Aristophanian Old Comedy, Kleistian drama *constitutes itself in its very enactment or declamation*; it is performed *and* performative, diagnostic *and* prescriptive, curative *and* palliative, auto- *and* hetero-poïetic. Above all, it is *authentic*: Kleist strives (*satirically*) to influence real political actors, (*satyrically*) to stage genuine personal erotic experiences and phantasies, and (*syphilitically*) to enact his actual physical and mental suffering. He offers his audiences not only critique, counsel and call to action, but also a genuine *kairotic* opportunity to make actual political choices and perform on-the-spot actions: when Ursula flings the putrefied finger (the emaciated left-bank territories) before Rupert, Kleist not only highlights a mistake made in the past, but also invites Fr. Wilh.—presumed to be present in the audience, as the *basileus* would have been during the *City Dionysia*—to *step onto the stage, pick up the finger, and in doing so reclaim the Rhine's left bank*.[188] A palpable pause is created by the *"und"* in the stage direction, "*Sie wirft einen Kindesfinger in die Mitte der Bühne und verschwindet*" (V.2680), as if Kleist is here "holding space" for Fr. Wilh., giving him the chance to step forth and act. Kleist aspired to nothing less than *eradicating the boundary between theatre and politics*, between the *Imaginary* and the *Symbolic* on the one hand, and the *Real* on the other. He envisioned his stage, his "plane of composition," not primarily as a space of representation, or even of negotiation or contention, but of *action*.[189]

Breaking the Rules. While producing *Schroffenstein* Kleist will have worked out his *Gesetze*, according to which the tension between the trajectory of the hero's *purpose* (line *a b* in his diagram), the "anti-grav" force of *fate* that pulls him away from this trajectory, and the strength or gravitas of his *character* (line *b c*) that enables him to temporarily stem himself against the pull of fate, together determine the dramatic progression (hyperbolic lines) towards the catastrophe (point *c*) in which the hero is inevitably "crushed by fate" (cf. *LS*,77aa). In *Schroffenstein,* point *c* corresponds to the *Kleidertauschszene,* which Kleist sketched as follows: "*Rodrigo (Ottokar) und Ignez (Agnes) wechseln die Kleider.— Fernando (Rupert) ersticht seinen Sohn, Alonzo (Sylvester) seine Tochter—die Frau (Ursula) erkennt das Geheimnis.—Die Greisen reichen sich über ihre Kinder die Hände*" (I:722).

Ottokar is initially the protagonist whose fate is inscribed in point *c*, and against which he repeatedly stems himself, for example when in I/1 he allies himself with Johann, when in II/1 he develops a *rapport* with Agnes, and when in III/1 he allies himself with Agnes (or so he believes). The *"anti-grav"* force of fate repeatedly pulls him back, for example when in III/2 Jeronimus (who sought to avert the catastrophe) is murdered, when in IV/1 Eustache is unable to sway Rupert, when in IV/2 Gertrude spurs on Sylvester, and when in IV/5 Ottokar escapes from prison only to hurl himself into *krisis* (point *e*). Kleist may well originally have envisioned *Thierrez* to play out in strict accordance with his *Gesetze*, but already with *Ghonorez* Kleist overstepped his own rules, positioning Agnes as insidious antagonist whose figure almost eclipses Ottokar's, undermining the principle of the single main protagonist his *Gesetze* postulate and rest upon.

"**Kleidertausch.**" The *Kleidertausch* superficially evokes a classical *harmatia*, an error to which, according to Aristotle, the tragic hero necessarily succumbs. And yet, since Sylvester's eleventh hour appearance prevents Agnes' triumph and mitigates Ottokar's error (the exchange of clothes *a posteriori* ensures that he revenges himself), Kleist's drama could at best be termed *quasi-tragic.* Furthermore, its double infanticide's (a reversal-cum-doubling of the patricide in Sophocles' *Oedipus*) paving the way for the two houses' reconciliation turns the *quasi-tragedy* into a *quasi-comedy* (cf. Kleist's Swiss fellows' Homeric laughter). The (phallic) "arrow" that *only just* misses Sylvius (cf. V.2643) indicates that Kleist's drama at most contains an *almost-harmatia* (the term's literal meaning being that of a marksman missing his mark); the *mad* Johann's saving the *blind* Sylvius from the (presumably diseased) "arrow" renders this instant *comic*, indeed bawdy, and perhaps the full stop in the middle of his obscene line, *"Ein Pfeilschuß. Beuge Dich"* (V.2643), marks the precise point at which Kleist consciously re-positions his pseudo-tragedy as (*satyrical*) burlesque and as (*satirical*) scenario: the madman saves the blind man from being sodomised by a diseased penis—will say: the clairvoyant Kleist opens Fr. Wilh.'s and Franz's eyes to the imminent danger of the twin Franco-German diseases.[190]

Reportedly the *Kleidertauschszene* was the first passage Kleist sketched, and from which he subsequently suspended the drama (cf. *LS*,66;70).[191] In so far as the *Kleiderstausch* represents the Hohenzollern challenger's ambition to wrest the imperial mantle from the Habsburg incumbent, it is worth highlighting that the idea that sparked Kleist's poetic project would have been not merely that of German *dynastic rivalry* but, more precisely, that of German *dynastic transition*. If Kleist's initial aspiration was to help the Hohenzollerns ascend the *HRR* throne, then the appearance of the "witch" Napoleon on the German stage—most notably with Marengo in June 1800 and *Lunéville* in February 1801—had the potential either to throw a spanner in his works, or conversely, to unlock a centuries-old paradigm of default Habsburg successions; Napoleon, then, could indeed become the Hohenzollerns' *pharmakon*: their remedy, or their doom.

Possibly Kleist was in part inspired to his poetical *Urszene* by his observation, at a Würzburg nature cabinet, of taxidermied birds, of which he told Wilhelmine: "*Das Gefieder der Vögel ist, ohne die Haut, auf Pergament geklebt*" (II:557), an idea that entails the inverse of that of the *Kleidertausch* (and, if one flips the latter along yet another conceptual "fold," that of real/imaginary, also of that of Hans Chr. Andersen in his 1837 tale "The Emperor's New Clothes").[192] Kleist concluded his note to Wilhelmine with an afterthought, "*Verzeihe mir diese Umständlichkeit. Ich denke einst diese Papiere für mich zu nützen*" (II:557), and evidently with the *Kleidertauschszene* he makes good on this earlier intention to "utilise these notes" (which would imply that already during the Würzburg journey the first contours of his *satirical* project emerged). The blind Sylvius' discovering the mix-up of identities may have been inspired by an incidence in Paris, where Ulrike habitually wore men's clothes to mingle in male society, and on one occasion a blind man—and only he—"saw through" her masquerade because her *voice*, towards which his attention was naturally tuned, gave her away.

In ideating this scene, Kleist could have drawn on the precedence of the Old Norse *Edda*, in which an exchange of appearances takes place between Gunnar (Gunther) and Sigurd (Siegfried) with the help of a magic helmet (*Ögishelm*), with ultimately tragic consequences.[193] The *Ögishelm* is in some accounts not a helmet but a runic sign drawn onto the forehead with the index finger of the left hand, so that when in the final scene Johann exclaims, "*Der Teufel hatt im Schlaf die beiden / Mit Kohlen die Gesichter angeschmiert, / Nun kennen sie sich wieder*" (V.2717-20), he dould be referring to the *Ögishelm* runes, as well as syphiliac *corona veneris*. Presumably it was "brotherhood" practice to mark diseased lovers in this manner.

"Eine elende Scharteke." In a letter to Ulrike of March 1803 Kleist terms his *Erstling "Eine elende Scharteke*" (II:731), before striking this note in such a manner that it remained legible. According to Duden.de, a *Scharteke* is: 1a. *ein altes und seinem Inhalt nach …*1b. *anspruchsloses Theaterstück*; 2. *eine unsympathische ältere Frau*.[194] I take it that Kleist meant to *strike* the first meaning, thereby emphasising that his drama, *au contraire*, was neither out-dated nor un-ambitious, and to *retain* the second meaning, for it corresponds to a note to Adolphine of October 1807:

> Was sagen Sie zur Welt, d.h. zur Physiognomie des Augenblicks? Ich finde, daß mitten in seiner Verzerrung etwas Komisches liegt. Es ist, als ob sie im Walzen, gleich einer alten Frau, plötzlich nachgäbe (sie wäre zu Tode getanzt worden wenn sie fest gehalten hätte); und sie wissen, was dies auf den Walzer für einen Effekt macht. Ich lache darüber, wenn ich es denke. (II:795)

This is a most apposite metaphor for the world in the Napoleonic era. The French usurper "*waltzes*" the world, or the old woman *Germania*, with so much swerve that she must let go, lest she risk collapsing alltogether. Is not Ursula's nonchalantly throwing the emaciated finger among the Schroffensteins already an analogous "physiognomic" snapshot of the state of the world? Unless Fr. Wilh. steps onto the stage immediately and reclaims the finger (which he does not), the *HRR* must let go of the Rhineland, lest it risk collapsing altogether (Kleist's 1807 note to Adolphine is, of course, in a later context, in which this collapse, with Franz II's abdication in 1806, has already taken place—cf. Kleist's "broken jug"—, but his 1803 note to Ulrike already anticipates it). In *Schroffenstein*, the *HRR* only just saves itself by letting go. "*Lustig!*" "*zum Totlachen!*" (V.2717-8). Not only his friends could not stop laughing when he recited the fifth act—neither could Kleist himself. The vanishing point of "*Totlachen's*" line of flight is, of course, "*Tod.*"

"**Generalbaß.**" Kleist compounds his *satirical* and *satyrical* action in a pattern, which he deploys throughout his œuvre, whereby utterances, syntax and interpunctation converge in a staccato rhythm that recalls artillery barrages as much as sexual orgasms, and that constitutes a veritable *basso continuo* underpinning the textual movement. Consider Johann and Agnes's encounter in II/3, in which the latter apparently recoils from the former's lusty approach:

> AGNES tritt in Hast auf.
>   Zu Hülfe! Zu Hülfe!
> JOHANN ergreift sie. [...]
>   [...] Ich vergöttre dich! [...]
>   Ich zittre vor Wollust [...]
>   [...] dich [...]
>   [...] zu umschließen.
> AGNES.   Was willst du, Rasender, von mir?
> JOHANN.   Nichts weiter.
>   Mir bist du tot, und einer Leiche gleich,
>   Mit kaltem Schauer drück ich dich ans Herz.
> AGNES. Schützt mich...!
> JOHANN. Sieh, Mädchen, morgen lieg ich in dem Grabe,
>   Ein Jüngling, ich—nicht wahr das tut dir weh?
>   Nun, einem Sterbenden schlägst du nichts ab,
>   Den Abschiedskuß gib mir. Er küßt sie.

AGNES. Errettet mich...!
JOHANN. [...]
                    —Da,
    Nimm diesen Dolch.—
AGNES.   Zu Hülfe!...
JOHANN streng. Nimm diesen Doch, sag ich.— [...]
Agnes.   Entsetzlicher!
        Sie sinkt besinnungslos zusammen.
Johann sanft.
    Nimm diesen Dolch, Geliebte—Denn mit Wollust, [...]
    Reich ich die Brust dem Stoß von deiner Hand.   (V.1031-57)

The passage contains no less than twelve phallic, thrusting *exclamation marks* (eight in Agnes' speech, four in Johann's), five buttocky, wiggly *question marks* (two in Agnes' speech, three in Johann's), and five orgasmic, ecstatic *dashes* (all in Johann's speech):

AGNES tritt in Hast auf.	! !
JOHANN ergreift sie.	! !
AGNES.	?
JOHANN.	?
AGNES.	?
JOHANN.	
AGNES.	!
JOHANN.	?
AGNES.	!
JOHANN.	—! — —
AGNES.	! ! !
JOHANN streng.	— ?
AGNES.	!
Sie sinkt besinnungslos zusammen.	
JOHANN sanft.	—

The sequence begins with the *staccato* of Agnes' thrusting and ends with the *diminuendo* of Agnes' fading and Johann's holding his lover softly. The "story" told by this non-verbal *basso continuo* is very different from that told by the text's spoken word or "melody": the punctuation marks depict a repeated thrusting and receiving on the parts of Agnes and Johann, with Agnes initiating the process, whereas the speeches suggests a wooing on Johann's part of a recoiling Agnes. This interweaving of two registers of signs, verbal and non-verbal (the latter almost onomatopoeitic, or cheironomic), allows Kleist to overlay two inverse narratives, demonstrating that not only words, but also signs can be *pescheräic*.[195]

In *Ph* epigram no. 44, *Die Gefährliche Aufmunterung*, Kleist would later equate musical intervals and fencing stabs: "*Schauet ihn an! Da steht er und ficht und stößet den Lüften / Quarten und Terzen durchs Herz, jubelt und meint, er trifft mich*" (I:25). Musical rhythm, fencing parries (cf. *Marionettentheater*'s fencing bear), electrical discharges (cf. *Über die allmähliche Verfertigung*'s twitching upper lip), artillery barrages, the thrusty and wiggly movements of sexual intercourse: all of these movements represent a play of (Deleuzean) difference, repetition and intensity that outside of Kleist's dramatic intonation, only music can mobilise.[196]

Metaphor and the Real. Anthony Stephens offers:

> Kleist's modernity is nowhere more in evidence than in his recognition of the power inherent in metaphor to supplant rational discourse. In *Die Familie Schroffenstein*, metaphorical language appears to run riot, but this is only the case if we approach the play with expectations derived from the Enlightenment or Weimar Classicism. The ultimate incoherence of the metaphorical dimension of the text is deliberate, and is a proof of the thesis that there is no criterion of objective reality by which all aberrations or distortions may ultimately be judged, but that such reality as there is, is no more than the mode in which rival subjectivities encounter one another and fail to disagree. The autonomy which the metaphorical dimension gains in the play is one of Kleist's great achievements, for all that it tends to throw the plot and characterisation out of balance and disappoint conventional expectations. The best way of reflecting the many uncertainties that beset him in this regard was abandon the Aristotelian principle of using metaphor as a series of

> projections from a stable, underlying reality and, instead, to allow it to unfold its full 'creative' powers. (*Kleist. The Dramas*, 39)

Stephens, I'm afraid, is quite wrong: far from "abandon[ing] the Aristotelian principle of using metaphor as a series of projections from a stable, underlying reality," Kleist projects his *satirical, satyrical* and *syphilitical* metaphors precisely from a rootedness in Germany's "underlying realities," as well as in his own stigmatised sexuality and debilitating disease. Far from using metaphor to produce "incoherence," "subjectivities," and "autonomy" (from underlying reality), or to reflect the "uncertainties that beset him," Kleist uses metaphor to produce *coherence, objectivity,* and *unity* (with underlying reality), and to reflect the (tough) *certainties* that beset him. For example, the metaphorical field of *poison* or *venom* (serpent, *basilisk,* scorpion, poisoned dagger) *satirically* encrypts the "venomous" rivalry of the German dynasties, and the disunity it breeds, and *satyrically* and *syphilitically* encodes the "poisonous" venereal disease that spreads among lovers, and the coyness it precipitates. I suppose Stephens discerns "incoherence" in Kleist's drama because Kleist's *pescheräic* technique, whereby a single metaphorical field encrypts *more than one* objective reality, deceives him, his interpretation being predicated on the (unfortunate) assumption that one metaphor necessarily corresponds to precisely one objective reality (or else, none)—in other words, that in relation to objective reality a metaphor assumes the binary state of either "on" or "off." Yet Kleist's metaphors are in fact "on, on, on," whereby each of the multiple "ons" Kleist interweaves in a single text(ure) are perfectly coherent, and only the surface pattern their interweaving produces generates an impression of incoherence.

2.2 Robert Guiskard: The Usurper's Death
(A Prognosis Ahead of Its Time)

Genesis and Context. While Erich Schmidt put Kleist's commencement of *Robert Guiskard, Herzog der Normänner* as early as 1801 in Paris, the Kleist reception today typically situates it in the spring of 1802 in Thun, coinciding with *Schroffenstein*'s production. Kleist will have continued working on *Guiskard* in the winter of 1802/3 in Oßmannstedt, where he famously recited passages to Wieland Sr., and in the summer of 1803 in Switzerland, before ostensibly burning the MS in October 1803 in Paris.[197] Much of the "labour of 500 days and nights" Kleist tells Ulrike about in the letter of 5th October 1803, in which he announces the project's termination, he will have spent on *Guiskard* (as well as on *Schroffenstein*'s completion and *Krug*'s commencement); if the "500 days" are fairly precise, they also provide the project's approximate commencement: mid-May 1802.

Years later, in the April/May 1808 issue of *Phöbus* (*Ph*), Kleist published a substantial *Guiskard* fragment of 524 lines. Whether he had retained this fragment from the 1803 MS, reproduced it from memory, or wrote it from scratch, remains indiscernible.[198] There is circumstantial, if inconclusive, evidence that the *Guiskard* MS had been more advanced than the *Ph* fragment's few scenes, and that Kleist had kept a copy of the 1803 MS; Heinr. Joseph von Collin he tells of 14th February 1808: *"Ich bin... im Besitz zweier Tragödien, von deren eine Sie eine Probe im dritten oder vierten Heft sehen werden... Das erste Werk, womit ich wieder auftreten werde, ist Robert Guiskard"* (II:810).[199] His repeated use, in the *Ph* fragment, of explanatory footnotes (cf. I:163; 164; 167), which occurs nowhere else in his published works, suggests that MS passages existed (or had once existed), which Kleist did not select (or recreate) for the *Ph* fragment, but which contained important contextual information, and that he filled the gaps his choicefulness created with the help of these footnotes. For all the theatricality with which he abandoned *Guiskard* in 1803, it is eminently plausible that Kleist retained a copy of the original (Paris) MS *till the very end*, just in case history "caught up" with his scenario, and that during the nights running up to his suicide (*LS*,526), he "fired the oven," among other things, with a retained *Guiskard* MS. In which case *Guiskard*, in effect, *was burned twice*.[200]

Whether it represents essentially a new production or—more likely—a part of, or a more or less faithful adaptation from, the 1803 MS: the very fact that Kleist published the *Ph* fragment proves that these passages were *satirically* relevant in the context of early 1808. Assuming that the fragment was indeed based on the original MS, the portion he selected must have been sufficiently *pescheräic* to "work" in the changed context of 1808 (by the same token, the parts of the 1803 MS he *did not* select for publication in *PH*, or elsewhere, will no longer have been relevant, or will not have been sufficiency *pescheräic*).[201] The *Ph* fragment, then, likely offers us a *sample* from Kleist's masterpiece, which, since *Ph* was meant to his platform (or at least launching pad) for his *Agôn* with Goethe, may well include some of the MS' *po(i)etically* most compelling passages, possibly including those that so excited Wieland, in addition to providing a stunning *example* of Kleist's masterful *practice of (re)production*.

"**die ganze Sippschaft.**" *Guiskard*'s cast encompasses members of an extended ducal family—"*die ganze Sippschaft*" (V.151)—, representatives of the Norman people—"*das Volk*"—, as well as (off stage) the City's ruler and traitors. If *Schroffenstein* narrates a stand-off between two branches (dynasties) of a single family (*HRR*)—a *two-player game* with a *2x2 pay-off matrix* and a *prisoner's dilemma*-type imperfect information (and with Ursula thrown in as wildcard)—, *Guiskard* depicts a more complex constellation involving a stand-off between two rival dynastic successors (Robert and Abälard) and another, concurrent, one between the ruling family (represented by Guiskard) and the people (represented by Armin)—a *four-player game* with a *4x4 pay-off matrix* and partial (but not perfect) information (and with Alexius and the traitors thrown in as wildcards). Whereas *Schroffenstein*'s outcome is predictable, *Guiskard*'s is anything but: while two players, Abälard ("noble strength," the spurned pretender) and the people (torn between fighting and withdrawing), tend towards "collaborate" (and so does Alexius), the third player, Robert ("famed," the usurper's son), who is backed by the fourth, Guiskard (the usurper who may be about to die), leans towards "kill" (and so do the traitors), making for a large number of possible permutations as well as possible asymmetries, interdependencies and sequentialities in the players' choices, rendering the drama's outcome eminently unpredictable. Whatever other complications Kleist faced in producing *Guiskard*, one of them clearly was that the complexity of its constellation far exceeded the relative simplicity of the *Gesetze* (one hero) or the *prisoner's dilemma* (two players).

The *Ph* fragment (and quite possibly the original MS) commences with the chorus of the people, whose opening lines could well be anticipating (as in *Schroffenstein*) the drama's entire storyline *in nuce*.[202] The chorus introduces the charismatic hero Guiskard ("rock"), the waivering people ("ocean"), and the lingering plague ("poisonous vapour"), as well as the imperial capital (*"jene Kaiserstadt"*) that would fall either to the people's children or to one of the two dynastic successors, so that the drama's possible *satirical* outcomes encompass modulations of power and governance: republic (the people win), tyranny (Robert wins) or constitutional monarchy (Abälard wins). The chorus:

> Auch ihn ereilt, den Furchtlos-Trotzenden,
> Zuletzt das Scheusal noch, und er erobert,
> Wenn er nicht weicht, an jener Kaiserstadt
> Sich nichts, als einen prächtigen Leichenstein!
> Und statt des Segens unsrer Kinder setzt
> Einst ihres Fluches Mißgestalt sich drauf,
> Und heul'nd aus ehrner Brust Verwünschungen
> Auf den Verderber ihrer Väter hin,
> Wühlt sie das silberne Gebein ihm frech
> Mit hörnern Klauen aus der Erd hervor!   (V.27-36)

Guiskard, the chorus anticipates, is on the brink of being infected by *"das Scheusal"* of *dynastic hybris*, so that, should he die in the course of the conquest, and the imperial throne become his tombstone, his power would default not to the people but to his dynastic successor, who, the chorus fears, might turn out to be not "*Furchtlos-Trotzend*" like his father (a conqueror), but a monstrous "*Mißgestalt*" "*mit hörnern Klauen*" (a tyrant).[203] If in *Schroffenstein* a fateful disease (the "German") fuels a dynastic rivalry that opens the door for *a foreign hegemon,* in *Guiskard* another fateful disease (the "French") destroys a popular leader and republican spirit and predicates *home-grown dynastic tyranny.*[204]

"Scheusal" *and* "Mißgestalt." *Schroffenstein*'s "German disease," "*die schwarze Sucht*" (V.515) of *dynastic rivalry,* is represented as poison or venom, *Guiskard*'s "French disease," the "*Scheusal*" ("monster"; V.28) of *dynastic hybris,* as bubonic plague.[205] The plague, an external and contingent force that infests victims indiscriminately, would not lend itself as *movens* for a tragic plot, but understood metaphorically as *dynastic hybris* lodged in the hero's *character,* it renders him a properly tragic figure, whose *harmatia* it is to succumb to the temptation of usurping the *res publica* and replacing it with dynastic rule. What sets Kleist's drama apart from Aristotelian tragedy is that Guiskard's *harmatia* is not purely personal and discreet, but *infectious,* i.e., horizontally transferable within a generation, and *genetic,* i.e., vertically inheritable to subsequent generations: it is, so to speak, not "heroic" but "prolific," and Napoleon is not a "lone wolf" but, to paraphrase Deleuze and Guattari, a "wolfing." Since it can, in principle, be *avoided, masked* (within limits), and deliberately *induced,* this "plague" is not purely transcendent and contingent but immanent and instrumental: it lodges itself inside of the players, and can be wielded by them, say, as a weapon or a means of extortion. Abälard is evidently channeling rumours about Guiskard's infection, while Robert may even have physically infected him, and Guiskard's fate is sealed not only by his personal *harmatia* and the generic mechanics of the disease's proliferation, but also by the infectiousness and choices of the other players.

Kleist in his drama furthermore deals with the inherently paradoxical nature of succession: the successor for whom the charismatic hero wishes to pave the way must remove this very hero in order to assume his place. The stronger the hero, the more pronounced his propensity to found a new dynasty, but also the greater the incentive for his successor to take recourse to treason or murder to remove him. Kleist here explores a dynamic that is no longer Aristotelian or Shakespearean, but Freudian (succession necessitates the father's death), Nietzschean (the son nevertheless cannot escape the father's shadow), and Deleuzean (the force by which he brings down the father exceeds the son himself, and will bring him down too).[206] The corollary of the "monster" of *dynastic hybris* is the *"Mißgestalt"* ("monstrosity") of the *tyranically successor*. According to this reversible logic, the successor (Robert) necessily "infects" the predecessor (Guiskard), as if by reverse inheritance, while the tragic hero (Guiskard) inevitably brings forth an unheroic, counter-tragic successor (Robert), in the manner, say, in which a Christ inevitably entails an Antichrist. *Harmatia* in Kleist, then, is a sort of *blindness* vis-à-vis the reversible logic and dynamic of the disease, which only the madman and the blind man are able to fathom can "see through." Guiskard's *Erbfolge* channels fate as surely as does Schroffenstein's *Erbvertrag*; both define Kleist's point *"c,"* and differ only in so far as *Erbfolge* modulates the vertical linkage between father and son(s), *Erbvertrag* the horizontal relationship between brothers, or brother and nephew.

"Gnadenkettlein." When the drama sets in, only a single night separates Guiskard and his people from seizing the utimate payoff: on the following day traitors will hand over the keys to the imperial city, which will surely fall to them within the day (allowing Kleist to adhere to the classical unities of place and time). When his exhausted people discover that Guiskard is infected, and thus potentially incapacitated to lead the attack and ascend the conquered throne (a commitment he made to the traitors in exchange for the keys), they bid him to call off the attack. Guiskard's death is already announced in the drama's (ostensible) working title, *Tod Guiscards des Normanns* (*LS*,89), but the dramatic tension is preserved, indeed heightend, by the uncertainty as to whether his death will materialise in the forthcoming night, i.e., before the attack, or later.

Several scenarios have been offered in the Kleist reception as to how Kleist might have unfolded the drama (none of which have found wide acceptance), and I deem it worthwhile to add to this speculation, not least since certain clues contained in the Ph fragment apparently have not been given due consideration:

- Guiskard's "broad shoulders" are enchained by a *"Gnadenkettlein"* (V.403; "chain of grace"), for Kleist a symbol and instrument of submission, suggesting that he is already no longer truly sovereign;[207]
- The true sovereign is arguably Robert, as his arrogance suggests and the people confirm: *"Du bist der Guiskardssohn, das ist genug!"* (V.313);
- Robert may have been murdering his father by infecting him during those *"drei schweißerfüllte Nächte / Auf offnem Seuchenfelde"* (V.78-9);
- Robert's use of similar idiom as Ursula's in *Schroffenstein*, *"wenn es abgetan"* (V.320), suggests that Guiskard's death is imminent;
- Guiskard's nephew Abälard, the legitimate and popular successor to the Norman throne, who could challenge Robert, is held back by none other than Guiskard himself, *"Tritt hinter mich... lautlos"* (V.412), making clear that Guiskard wishes Robert to succeed him.

When in the moment of *krisis* the *Ph* fragment breaks off, Guiskard in the eyes of the people and traitors remains *"Ewig-Unersetzlicher"* (V.472), implying that if he died before the conquest, the people might reject Robert's leadership, or the traitors might refuse to surrender the keys. To secure his bloodline, Guiskard must survive the night, achieve the conquest and ascend the imperial throne, thereby making his biological son Robert the legitimate successor to a heritary throne he *conquered*, rather than merely *usurped*. Yet such a linear outcome seems "unKleistian," as would one in which Guiskard does not survive the night, Robert claims leadership of the Normans, is challenged and overcome by Abälard and the people, whereupon Abälard assumes his legitimate title as Duke of the Normans, aborts the conquest and leads the Normans home. Excluding these uninteresting scenarios leaves two plausible (and "Kleistian") storylines:

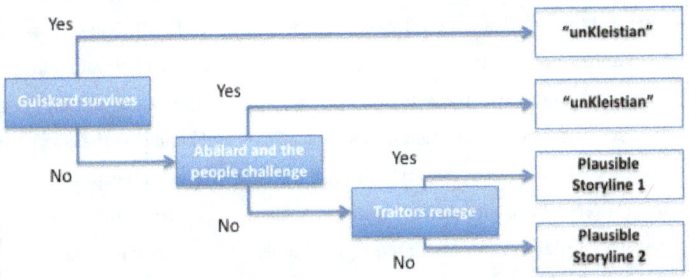

Plausible ("Kleistian") Storyline 1:
[Picking up from where the *Ph* fragment breaks off]. In the subsequent night, Guiskard and Cäcilie die and Robert assumes command unchallenged, enchaining Abälard with Guiskard's *Gnadenkette*. The traitors arrive; when they behold Guiskard dead and Robert in charge, they refuse to hand over the keys, escape and return to the city, alerting the defences and throwing in their lot with Alexius. In the early morning hours, Robert leads a futile attack in which the Norman nation, weakened by disease, perishes before the city's impenetrable walls. Robert dies in battle while Abälard and Helena are captured alive by the Greeks, who castrate Abälard (in line with his namesake Abélard) and enter Helena (like Héloïse) into a convent. Guiskard's corpse is buried in a shallow grave, whence the birds dig out his bones and disperse them.

This storyline in Kleist's eye could have had the disadvantage of not teeing off a sequel, or calling for a complement: the Napoleonic era, in this scenario, would simply have come to an end before properly taking off.

A second storyline presupposes that the Chorus' haunting lines, "*Einst ihres Fluches Mißgestalt… / Wühlt sie das silberne Gebein ihm frech / Mit hörnern Klauen aus der Erd hervor!*" (V.32; 35-6), are meant to hint that Robert himself desecrates his father's grave, thus he does not die in the conquest (because the traitors do not renege on their promise to hand over the keys), occupies the imperial throne, deposes of his rival, and establishes a tyranny:

> **Plausible ("Kleistian") Storyline 2**
>
> Robert obtains the pivotal information that the traitors' condition for handing over the keys is that Guiskard personally ascends the throne (n.b.: a *Ph* footnote states that this information surfaces later in the drama—cf. I:167). Guiskard is dead; Robert pretends to forfeit his right of succession in Abälard's favour and, when the traitors arrive, presents Abälard as Guiskard's legitimate successor, endorsed by the people. The traitors endorse Abälard and hand over the keys, whereupon Abälard leads the city's conquest. As soon as Alexius is deposed, Robert overwhelms, enchains and castrates Abälard, enters Helena into a convent, murders the traitors, orders a grand funeral for Guiskard in a bid to highlight his filial piety, and ascends the throne. Yet Robert is feared rather than loved, and the people, Normans and Greeks alike, continue commemorating Guiskard at his tomb, in defiance of Robert's orders. His inability to replace his father in his people's hearts drives Robert into madness and he defiles Guiskard's tomb.

This storyline does call for a sequel or complement (in which either the people or the usurped dynasties rise against the tyrant), and Kleist's apparent exploring or sketching, around the time when working on *Schroffenstein* and *Guiskard*, of three other dramas, *Leopold*, *Peter* and *Numantia* (cf. my later section, "Notes on Projects Not Executed or Not Extant"), may suggest that he indeed invisioned a sequel, complement, or alternative to *Guiskard*. If *Schroffenstein* could be said to encompass the *thesis* of the "German disease," and *Guiskard* the *antithesis* of the "French disease," then a *synthesis* was needed to complete a drama cycle entitled, say, *The Rise and Fall of Napoleon and the Unification of the German Empire* (adding a satyr play would have completed the *tetralogy*). Since *Schroffenstein* ends with a cliffhanger, so could have *Guiskard*.

Guiskard, Satirically

My *satirical* reading of *Guiskard* will be two-pronged: firstly, I reconstruct Kleist's political agenda in 1802/3, on the basis of the *Ph* fragment, which I assume represents a compilation or faithful reproduction of passages from the original; secondly, I explore his agenda in early 1808 when he publishes the *Ph* fragment.

***1802/3:* "Tod Napoleons des Korsen."** Napoleon's proclamation, on 2nd August 1802 (*14 Thermidor, An* X), as First Consul for Life could have triggered Kleist's conception and commencement of *Guiskard*, at a time when he was still completing *Schroffenstein*. In the latter drama, as we saw, Napoleon plays a shadowy, if decicive, role, and when the momentous event of *14 Thermidor* foregrounded the First Consul, Kleist may have concluded that his *Erstling* had progressed too far for him to re-write it such as to cast Ursula-Napoleon in a more prominent role, and instead decided to produce a sequel or companion piece that would put Napoleon centre stage from the beginning.[208] Behind Kleist's curtain, veiled by the audience, Napoleon, in his own *Kleidertausch*, morphs from popular general with a magic touch (Ursula) into dynastic ruler *in spe*, de facto usurper of the Bourbon throne and pretender to the imperial dignity. Kleist, then, conceived *Guiskard* to carry forward *Schroffenstein*'s trajectory, while shifting the focus from the German dynasties to the French ones: the Bonapartes (represented by Guiskard and Robert) and the Bourbons (enacted by Abälard).[209]

If Guiskard = Napoleon, then the Normans = the French, and the term "entire" in the chorus' expression "*ganze Heereswog*" (= all French people) that "*umschäumt*" (i.e., "encompasses") Guiskard ("*Schlaukopf*," "clever Dick," i.e., Napoleon) corresponds to a precise value: 99.76%, the percentage of votes cast in favour of Napoleon's *Life Consulate* in the 1802 plebiscite. Kleist's repeated reference to Guiskard-Napoleon's popularity is thus as much ironic as it is factual: no doubt Napoleon *was* tremendously popular, but his supporters went to such lengths to rig the plebiscite in his favour that the ballot count became farcical.[210] Given that the chorus admonishes Guiskard-Napoleon to refrain from seizing the imperial throne (not from retaining the Norman, i.e., French, throne he usurped), the writing must have been on the wall already in 1802/3 that Napoleon could be eyeing the imperial dignity (on 2nd December 1804 Napoleon would indeed crown himself Emperor, and 18 months later compel Franz II to abdicate the *HRR*'s crown, thus de facto usurping it), and the event of *14 Thermidor*, perhaps more than that of *18 Brumaire*, must have signalled to Kleist that the *parvenu*

Napoleon was inexorably bent on joining Europe's high aristocracy and turning his non-hereditary office of First Consul for Life into a dynastic monarchy by assuming the Holy Roman imperial mantle.[211] Napoleon remained childless, but when on 10th October 1802 Joséphine's grandson Napoléon Charles Bonaparte was born, he was widely considered Napoleon's designated heir, fuelling rumours that Napoleon was seeking to establish a new dynasty.

The drama's imperial city may entail up to five *satirical* references, making it a *pescherä* par excellence: *Rome*, in reference to the historical parallel of first Caesar, then Octavian and Antonius seeking control of the Eternal City; *Constantinople*, in reference to Napoleon's famous, if aborted, 1798/9 *Campaign of Egypt and Syria,* aimed at conquering the eastern capital; *Paris*, in reference to Napoleon's expected bid to establish a French Empire; *Vienna*, in reference to the fact that in order to establish a western empire, Napoleon would have to usurp the Holy Roman imperial throne; and *London*, in reference to the *Invasion of Britain* that Napoleon was beginning to prepare in early 1803.[212]

In the historical context as of late 1802/early 1803 (the time of Kleist's Oßmannstedt sojourn and Wieland Sr. declamations), we may reconstruct *Guiskard*'s original *satirical* storyline. In outline: having de facto usurped the Bourbon throne by becoming First Consul for Life, Napoleon now reaches for the imperial capital (symbolised by Constantinople, but meaning Vienna); his succumbing to the "monster" of *dynastic hybris,* in accordance with Kleist's *Gesetze*, destroys him—depending on the scenario Kleist was favouring, either before or after Vienna's conquest (in the context of Kleist *Gesetze*, these choices shape the drama's "Schönheitslinie," hence dramtic impact). Napoleon's death (in Kleist's scenario) is inevitable, as his reported working title, *Tod Guiscards des Normannen*, inscribes (cf. *LS*,89), and as a first-hand observer clearly expected (cf. *LS*,77a), and as he is fading, his chosen successor and the usurped prince jockey for his succession. Robert probably embodied Beauharnais, Napoleon's most likely successor should he die before Napoléon Charles Bonaparte reached maturity; Abälard likely enacted the executed Louis XVI's brother, Louis Stanislas Xavier, Count of

Provence and Dauphin (the heir apparent to the Throne of France, who in 1814 with the *Bourbon Restauration* indeed was to become King Louis XVIII).[213]

The critical nexus in the establishment of any dynasty is the transition from the charismatic founder, who by definition is *sui generis*, to his immediate successor, whose establishes the *repetition* that defines a dynasty *qua* dynasty. This moment of *krisis* in the Bonaparte dynasty's genesis was arguably the critical *satirical* issue at the heart of Kleist's original (1802/3) *Guiskard*: if the incumbent dynasties, the Bourbons and the Habsburgs, failed to intervene at this most vulnerable point in its creation, to eliminate Robert-Beauharnais before he could assume either the royal or the imperial throne, and to re-install Abälard-the Dauphin, as well as to re-confirm Alexius Franx II (if Napoleon had conquered Vienna), the new dynasty of the Bonapartes would inexorably establish itself *qua* dynasty in the moment it successfully transitioned its source of legitimacy, in Max Weberian terms, from the founder's *charismatic authority* to the successors' *rational-legal authority*.

1808: "Napoleon, Herzog der Normänner." Kleist in 1808 will have published the *Ph* fragment, firstly, because the issue at the heart of the original drama, of how Napoleon would secure his succession and establish a dynasty, remained topical, and secondly, because the selected passages fit in well with his agenda *du jour*. Napoleon had crowned himself Emperor and adopted Beauharnais (but excluded him from imperial succession); in May 1807 his potential heir, Napoléon Charles, died before reaching the age of five, and as of May 1808, Joséphine had continued to fail to produce him a heir. The rumours that triggered his initial work on *Käthchen* (cf. my discussion below), that Napoleon was seeking to divorce Joséphine and marry into an established imperial dynasty, could also have triggered Kleist's pulling the *Guiskard* material out of the drawer. Just as he had meant the 1802/3 version of *Guiskard* to complement *Schroffenstein*, Kleist could have meant the 1808 version to complement *Käthchen*, whose initial fragment, incidentally but probably not coincidentally, he published in the same (April/May) issue of *Ph* (the *Guiskard* fragment first, as the issue's opening item, with the *Käthchen* fragment as next-to-last entry).

The *Ph* fragment's cast comprises Guiskard, Robert, Abälard, Cäcilia, and Helena, plus, among the "*Normänner*," "the old man" Armin, a "committee of knights," and "the people." Presumably these figures were also among the original version's cast (which could have been more extensive, featuring, say, Alexius, the traitors, and others: *Schroffenstein* has a cast of 20 or so), but that does not mean that in 1808 they represent the same actual personages as in 1802/3. As of 1808, Guiskard evidently still enacts Napoleon, although his position has changed: in 1802/3 he was reaching for the *imperial dignity* as such; in 1808, having crowned himself Emperor, he is reaching for a marital alliance (today we might say: he is scouting for "M&A" opportunities) with an established *imperial dynasty*—either the Habsburgs or the Romanovs of Russia. His "conquest" of the imperial city refers to his quest to "hijack" the Vienna- or the St. Petersburg-based dynasty (any "merger of equals" with Napoleon would de facto be a take-over by him).

Cäcilia, similarly, still enacts Joséphine, but her position has also changed, even more so than Napoleon's: in 1802/3 *tous le monde* expected her to bear Napoleon a heir; by 1808 it has become widely accepted that she will not bear Napoleon a heir, and the question of whether Napoleon will divorce her and take another wife has come to the fore. I offer that in the *Ph* fragment's final passage, Kleist anticipates that she will eventually give in and permit Napoleon to remarry:

> Guiskard sieht sich um, der Greis stockt.
>
> DIE HERZOGIN leise.
>   Willst du—?
> ROBERT.   Begehrst du—?
> ABÄLARD.   Fehlt dir—?
> DIE HERZOGIN.   Gott im Himmel!
> ABÄLARD. Was ist?
> ROBERT.   Was hast du?

DIE HERZOGIN.   Guiskard! Sprich ein Wort!
Die Kaiserin zieht eine große Heerpauke herbei und schiebt sie hinter ihn
GUISKARD indem er sich sanft niederläßt, halblaut.
     Mein liebes Kind!—   (V.487-90)

The last line states succinctly what for Napoleon it is all about. Kleist's *"Paukenschlag"* (Bernhard Greiner) is the moment in which Joséphine resolves to selflessly cosset up Napoleon, to grant him the saving grace (drum-cushion) of a divorce, *so that he may have another go at producing his "dear child."* Helena in the fragment's ending confirms that *dynastic hybris* has now spread to Cäcilia-Joséphine: *"HELENA zögernd. Es scheint—"* (V.517).

Ach! Helena! Given that *Guiskard*'s original focal question was that of Napoleon's *succession*, the *Ph* fragment should still be expected to address this question, a question which in the context of 1808 had to re-cast as that of his *quest for a bride*. Helena is the *Ph* fragment's object of desire. Her position is unique in that she is liaised with almost everyone, and straddles east and west: she is Guiskard's daughter, Abälard's fiancé, and the widow of the Emperor of the east (how far east?, we wonder). Already in her most famous, Homeric, version, the Helena figure embodies a much sought-after object of desire and a principle of dynastic inter-marriage: Helena of Troy elopes with, or, depending on the version of the story, is whisked away by, *a foreign prince*. If rumours spread in the spring of 1808 that Napoleon was considering marrying either a Habsburg princess or a Romanova, *it could have been precisely its Helena figure that motivated him to pull* Guiskard *out of the drawer* and publish the fragment that had suddenly again become *satirically* pertinent. Her designation as "Guiskard's daughter" can quite easily be trans. *satirically* as "Napoleon's bride"; but were does he have to snatch Helena from? The Hofburg in Vienna or the Winter Palace in St. Petersburg? Her other two designations could point either way: towards an Orthodox (the Greek Emperor) and a Catholic aspect (Abälard). That this question cannot easily be answered may imply this: Kleist, as of May 1808, also did not know, and left it open:

Helena remains a "larval subject" (Deleuze), a virtuality who in due course may actualise either as Habsburg princess or as Romanova; "Helena" is thus a placeholder and *pescherä*, whose functioning is this: "an imperial bride, up for grabs, from (a) the Habsburgs; (b) the Romanovs (delete as applicable), named _____ (fill in as applicable)."

When Kleist published the *Ph* fragment in c.June 1808 (the April/May issue having been distributed with delay), the event at which Napoleon planned to complete his *Brautschau*, the *Congress of Erfurt* of 27th September-14th October 1808, was probably already pencilled into his calendar, and invitations to the respective "daddies," Alex. and Franz, were being diplomatically prepared.

"Tritt hinter mich." All of Kleist's *Ph* entries during the first half of 1808—the *Penthesilea* fragment, *Marquise*, the *Krug*, *Käthchen* and *Kohlhaas* fragments—deal with political scenarios whose main actors are Napoleon, Fr. Wilh. and Franz, and the *Guiskard* fragment being situated in the same context, it ought to include them in its cast. As of 1808, the association of Robert with Beauharnais and that of Abälard with the Dauphin were no longer relevant: Beauharnais was out of contention for Napoleon's imperial succession; the Dauphin was no longer a credible challenger after the end of the Enghien affair and the abdications of the Bourbon Kings of Spain and Naples. The characters Robert and Abälard were thus "freed up" and could be recast as—I offer—Fr. Wilh. and Franz. The latter being indeed an "usurpee," his Holy Roman imperial dignity having been snatched by the "clever Dick," suggests that Abälard = Franz, hence his archrival Robert = Fr. Wilh.

Napoleon, having given short thrift to Fr. Wilh. in 1806/7, whose final humiliation, at the *Convention of Paris* of 9th September 1808, will already have been on the horizon, now lines up Franz as a possible ally and contender, together with Alex. (=Alexius), as his future father-in-law:

> GUISKARD mit erhobener Hand.
> Wo ist der Prinz, mein Neffe?
> Allgemeines Stillschweigen.
> Tritt hinter mich.
> Der Prinz, der sich unter das Volk gemischt hatte, steigt auf den Hügel, und stellt sich hinter Guiskard, während dieser ihn unverwandt mit den Augen verfolgt.
> Hier bleibst du stehn und laulos.—Du verstehst mich?
> —Ich sprech nachher ein eignes Wort mit dir.   (V.411-13)

Casting Fr. Wilh. as the ambitious, defiant Robert already ancitipates the roles in which Kleist would soon cast him in *Kohlhaas* and *Hermannsschlacht*: the former's fragment he produced within weeks of publishing the *Guiskard* fragment, the latter he completed within months thereof.

"**Der Greis.**" The *Ph* fragment's title, *Robert Guiskard, Herzog der Normänner*, drops the working title's reference to Guiskard's death (which the fragment does not cover, and which as of 1808 clearly is not on the horizon), while adding Guiskard's title (*duke*) and a direct reference to the Norman *people*. The title contains a sarcastic swipe at Napoleon: for a duke, ranked below a king in the aristocratic pecking order, to reach for the imperial dignity entails a blatant *over-reaching*; originally, *dux* in republican Rome denoted a military commander without governing rank, which in Kleist's view will have been precisely the appropriate rank for Napoleon. With the Germanic term *Normänner*, Kleist may have sought to emphasise that Napoleon had come to rule not only the French people (the *Normannen*, i.e., those acculturated in Normandy) but also, de jure or de facto, the Germanic people (*Normänner*), so that *"Das Volk,"* which in the 1802/3 version will have denoted the French people, in 1808 also encompassed the Germans, Dutch, and sundry other peoples now under Napoleon's sway.[214]

When the people rise *"in unruhiger Bewegung,"* "Der Greis" Armin, who considers democracy ineffective, proposes the establishment of a representative committee of twelve knights; the people reject his proposal and instead appoint him as their speaker in urging the Duke to abort his prolific war:

> DER NORMANN. Du sollst, würdiger Greis, die Stimme führen,
> > Du einziger, und keiner sonst. Doch wenn er
> > Nicht hört, der Unerbittliche, so setze,
> > Den Jammer dieses ganzen Volks, setz ihn,
> > Gleich einem erznen Sprachrohr an, und donnre,
> > Was seine Pflicht ist, in die Ohren ihm—!
> > Wir litten, was ein Volk erdulden kann. (cf. V.48-54).[215]

Guiskard-Napoleon recognises Armin's appointment as the people's spokesman:

> GUISKARD mit erhobener Hand. […]
> > *Er wendet sich zum Greise.*
> > Du führst, Armin, das Wort für diese Schar?
> DER GREIS.
> > Ich führs, mein Feldherr! (V.411-15)

The frequency, length and weight of Armin's appearances in the *Ph* fragment is remarkable. He is the only character to remain on stage from beginning to end (in the first scene, as member of the chorus), and his interventions orchestrate and channel the fragment's plot; he is the first among the main characters to find out (cf. V.131ff.) about Guiskard's personal physician's arrival from Naples (!), and the first to articulate the word "plague" in conjunction with Guiskard (cf. V.327); he concludes the fragment with a haunting appeal to Napoleon to leave the *Normänner* in peace in their homeland (cf. V.524; "Italy" = Germany; the fleet anchored in the background symbolises not only the disease's propagation into Germany, but also the Norman (French) contingent's option— unlike the Greeks before Troy, they have not sunk their ships, i.e., torn down the Rhine bridges—of leaving Germany); and he warns Abälard-Franz not to give in to the temptation of marrying a Habsburg princess to Napoleon:

> Nun jeder Segen schütte, der in Wolken
> Die Tugenden umschwebt, sich auf dich nieder,
> Und ziehe deines Glückes Pflanze groß!
> Die Gunst des Oheims, laß sie, deine Sonne,
> Nur immer, wie bis heute, dich bestrahlen:
> Das, was der Grund vermag, auf dem sie steht,
> Das zweifle nicht, o Herr, das wird geschehn!—
> Doch eines Düngers, mißlichen Geschlechts,
> Bedarf es nicht, vergib, um sie zu treiben;
> Der Acker, wenn es sein kann, bleibe rein.
> In manchem andern Wettstreit siegest du,
> In diesem einen, Herr, stehst du ihm nach.   (V.297-308)

Let "uncle" Napoleon's Sun shine on your fiefdom if you must, says Armin, but do not allow him to contaminate your "pure" dynastic soil with his seed; confront him in the battlefield, but do not open to him your household, for you can only lose.

"*Der Greis*" Armin ("the protective"), the spokesman of the people, can only represent one person: *the people's bard Kleist*. The *Guiskard* fragment is as autobiographic as it gets: Kleist himself is an actor in his play, and not only in a cameo appearance but in a leading role. Does the *Maschinist* have to join the puppets' "dance" himself?, Kleist will later ask in *Marionettentheater*, and the *Guiskard* fragment already anticipates the answer given by Herr C. in the essay: if the situation demands it, when "*der* Weg der Seele" (II:340) is at stake, the answer is a resounding "yes!" Like Nietzsche's Zarathustra, Kleist descends from the mountain to dwell among the people and make himself heard: the *Guiskard* fragment does not comprise an appeal directed at Napoleon—the French Emperor presumably is not among the *Ph*'s subscribers (although his censors and spies probably are)—, nor in the first instance a manifesto directed at the German rulers (although it contains elements thereof), but a kind of self-advertisement on Kleist's part directed at the German people ("the people," in the *Ph* fragment, referring above all to the German people): "This is the power of my word; appoint me as your speaker, and I shall set you free." If we think of *Ph* as a precursor of today's TV casting shows—*Deutschland sucht den Superstar; Das Supertalent*—, offering poets a national platform to exhibit their skills, then *Guiskard* is Kleist's signature performance, designed to impress a German mass audience; if we think of *Ph* as a rock album, *Guiskard* is the "single" lifted from it. Having thus launched his "pop hit," Kleist soon shifts to producing "heavy metal": addressing Fr. Wilh. directly, with *Kohlhaas* and *Hermannsschlacht* he is on his *Highway to Hell*.[216]

Guiskard, Satyrically

Consider Kleist's opening tableau:

> Szene: Zypressen vor einem Hügel, auf welchem das Zelt Guiskard's steht, im Lager der Normänner vor Constantinopel. Es brennen auf dem Vorplatz einige Feuer, welche von Zeit zu Zeit mit Weihrauch, und andern starkduftenden Kräutern, genährt werden. Im Hintergrunde die Flotte.

Mediterranean cypresses, phallic plants par excellence, are also known as "mourning cypresses," and thus embody the twin Freudian registers of *Eros* and *Thanatos*. The cypresses complement the *Normänners'* "tents" and "spears," and the city's *"Kaiserzinne"* ("imperial merlon"; V.360) in establishing a sweeping erotico-agonistic horizon, at whose centre bulges Guiskard's "hill"—buttocks, command centre, sacrificial altar, tomb? Conflagration in Kleist's tableaux frequently represents libidinal energy *in the moment of its release* (viz. the burning fortress in *Marquise*'s opening scene; the burning house in Elvire's flashback in *Findling*), and the "few" fires burning down suggest that the *Normänner* are both *satirically* and *satyrically* exhausted. Row upon row of soldier-*phalloi* are lined up before a sacrificial altar, on which a ritual sacrifice may be about to take place—Helena's?—amidst a miasmatic "poison fume" descending on the camp, so pestilent that frankincense is burned day and night to neutralise it.[217] Guiskard's "tent": dell of Parnassus, witch's den, crisis room, dom's dungeon? the Chateau de Compiègne's master bedroom?

Guiskard encrypts the typical Kleistian *satyrical* "code." Consider the previously quoted passage,

> GUISKARD mit erhobener Hand.
> Wo ist der Prinz, mein Neffe?
> Allgemeines Stillschweigen.
> Tritt hinter mich.
> Der Prinz, der sich unter das Volk gemischt hatte, steigt auf den Hügel, und stellt sich hinter Guiskard, während dieser ihn unverwandt mit den Augen verfolgt.
> Hier bleibst du stehn [...]
> Er wendet sich zum Greise. (V.411-12),

which depicts a *"FFF"* constellation involving the *erastês* Guiskard-Napoleon, the *erômenos* Armin-Kleist, and the *dmôs* Abälard-Franz:[218]

> NAPOLEON with erect member.
> Where is the *dmôs*, my Habsburgian sex-slave?
> Universal silence.
> Take me from behind.
> The Austrian Emperor, who had been mingling with the orgiasts, scales Napoleon's buttocks and erects behind him, while the other follows him ceaselessly with his eyes:
> Here you stay erect [...]
> He turns towards the Prussian *erômenos*.

May the *Maschinist* engage in the dance? You bet! Kleist to Napoleon: *"baise-moi!"*

Guiskard, Syphilitically

Kleist's *"Peststück"* is *syphilitical* through and through: already the opening scene, as we saw, oozes "poison fume" (infectious disease) and "frankincense" (superficial remedy). The plague was as anachronistic to Napoleon's Europe (his troops did encounter the disease in the Levant) as it was to the historical Robert Guiscard's Byzantium (I found no recordings of major outbreaks of the bubonic plague in the 11th century; Guiscard and many of his soldiers did succumb to disease, but likely typhoid).[219] Syphilis, the most feared "plague" of Kleist's day, indeed reached epidemic proportions in the 18th and 19th centuries, and the proverbial curse of the plague is an exceedingly apt metaphor for Germany's infestation with it. The frankincense could refer to mercury vapour, in Kleist's day a common anti-syphilitic."[220] Before the gates of "sin city" (Constantinople = Sodom, Babylon, Paris), on the "open field of contagion" (cf. V.78-9), during their repeated, several-night-long orgies the German soldier-lovers risk being wasted away by the *"Scheusal"* syphilis, barely kept at bay by ambient mercury vapour.

Read in the 1808 context, Kleist's term *"Mißgestalt"* (cf. V.32; 390) refers to Napoleon, *"mißlichen Geschlechts"* (V.304), to his seed. *"Donnerkeil"* ("thunderbolt"; V.6) and its synonym *"Wetterstrahl"* (V.329) evidently denote renewed, potentially fatal, infection, paralleling *Schroffenstein*'s imagery of the scorpion's sting and the basilisk's gaze. When, in the first lines, DAS VOLK implores the cherub, "*Schickt einen Donnerkeil / Auf ihn hernieder, daß ein Pfad sich uns / Eröffne*" (V.6-8), the people are praying that a highly contagious heavenly lover will penetrate Guiskard, take him to the brink, and over the edge; when Robert curses Abälard, "*Daß dir ein Wetterstrahl aus heitrer Luft / Die Zunge lähmte, du Verräter, du!*" (V.329-30), he is invoking the same heavenly force (*"Lämung"* = "paralysis," so Robert-Fr. Wilh. curses Abälard-Franz. with final stage syphilis). In *Marionettentheater*, the cherub guards the "rear entry" to paradise with his flaming sword, and it clear from the *Guiskard* passages that this particular "angel" is not only ithyphallic but also syphiliac, and extremely contagious (hence he is such an effective a guard of the heavenly opening). Scorpion, basilisk and cherub, then, in Kleist's "code" are synonyms, and so are sting, gaze and thunderbolt.

Guiskard, Po(i)etically

Did *Guiskard* (with Samuel and Brown) "fail for technical reasons"?

"Durchlesen, verworfen und verbrannt." Kleist handed *Guiskard* over to its *auto-da-fé* not in a mad frenzy but after careful deliberation (cf. II:737). Did he perceive *Guiskard* to be suffering from the structural deficit in his *Gesetze* denoted by the line *a z* (cf. *LS*,77aa)—viz., the pull of fate being too strong for the hero to stem himself against, thereby undermining the story's dramatic tension? Such a *"po(i)etical"* (or, with Samuel and Brown, "technical") snag is not implausible: if death was too obviously inscribed in Guiskard in the form of a fatal disease lodged in his body (i.e., a quasi congenital defect inherent his dynastic designs), he did not make a credible hero. If in the summer of 1803 Kleist scratched his diagram into the restaurant table at Interlaken, he may well have done so *precisely because* he ran into this "technical" impasse with *Guiskard*, and elaborated his *Gesetze* as a last ditch attempt at analysing and resolving it; it is suggestive that he abandoned the drama within weeks of passing through Interlaken: perhaps in the very movement of scratching that line *a z* into the table he realised that *Guiskard* was doomed.

Another possibility, compossible with the above and even more plausible, is that the snag was not primarily *"po(i)etical"* but *"satirical,"* that Kleist's *Guiskard* scenario, or its key premises, as of the autumn of 1803 no longer corresponded to the political realities, thus no longer permitting Kleist to meet his self-imposed "journalistic" standard of his scenarios always having to be anchored in the actual situation at the time of publication.[221] What could have made *Guiskard satirically* untenable and irretrievable was Napoleon's broaching the idea of a *hereditary* monarchy. As said, ever since he became First Consul for Life, it will have been clear to observers, including Kleist, that Napoleon would seek to establish a dynasty. Having remained childless in his (otherwise happy) marriage with Joséphine of seven years (as of March 1803), it will have appeared as if he would content himself with appointing a successor from within his wider family— Beauharnais (Joséphine's son from her previous marriage) or, if he himself was to live long enough, Napoléon Charles (Joséphine's grandson and Louis Bonaparte's son)—and Kleist's original conception of *Guiskard* was based on this premise.

Historians put Napoleon's first openly broaching the idea of the hereditary monarchy into early 1804, at the peak or in the aftermath of the *Duke of Enghien Affair*, but rumours to this effect could already have been circulating by mid-1803, just when Kleist was struggling with his *Guiskard*. Did Kleist leave Thun *precisely because such rumours reached him there*? Let us reconstruct: Kleist and Pfuel, who over the summer leasurely explore Alpine landscapes, enjoy idyllic Thun and its lake, and savour their "honeymoon" (a all of a sudden folds up his tents and travels to Geneva; just as abruptly he suggests to Ulrike from there (5th October 1803; cf. II:736) that he has given up on *Guiskard*: he must have obtained important information there that reconfirmed his worst fears; he presses on to Paris, to the source, to be crystal-clear about the information that so rattled him, and the necessity it evidently entailed for him to abandon his masterwork, as well as to figure out what to do next.[222] *Kleist, this is to say, could only have burned Guiskard in Paris and not anywhere else.*

Given that Kleist's original conception of *Guiskard* was anchored in the premise that Beauharnais (represented by the ambitious and ruthless Robert) was his designated successor (who in Kleist's story orchestrates Napoleon's demise), everything changes with respect to his drama in the moment Napoleon insists that his heir must be *of his own blood*.[223] Kleist was clearly obsessed with *The Familial* (cf. my section below), and already in *Schroffenstein* demonstrated his faith in the veracity of the medieval proverb "blood is thicker than water," and any credible rumour to the effect that Napoleon would not appoint Beauharnais, or anyone else not of his own blood, as his successor, would have sent him scrambling for an exit. For it meant one of two things: either Napoleon had to wait and see if Joséphine delivered (let us call this move *"pray"*), or he had to divorce her (*"act"*). *"Act,"* though more in his character than *"pray,"* had its own snag: since in order to build a dynasty he needed not only a successor but also a title, and since a royal title did not satisfy his ambition he intended to reach for the imperial dignity (*"seize"*), Napoleon could not, in the foreseeable future, divorce Joséphine, since the Pope would surely refuse to crown him after divorcing his wife (both of them being Catholic), and he needed the Pope's endorsement to lend legitimacy to his imperial aspirations, both vis-à-vis the French public and establishment (especially the die-hard royalists) and the (Catholic) Habsburg incumbents. Napoleon, in other words, could either reach for the imperial dignity or divorce and remarry, but *not both at the same time*. In those fateful days in Geneva it could have become clear to Kleist that Napoleon's rational choice would be to sequence his strategies, seizing the imperial dignity first while putting on hold till later the divorce: phase 1: "*seize*" (and "*pray*"); phase 2: "*act*" (unless "*pray*" did the trick). The lucid and clairvoyant Kleist may even have reached this conclusion *before Napoleon did himself*.

Napoleon's next move, then, had to be "*seize*." Kleist's *Guiskard* scenario assumed that Napoleon would have to conquer Vienna in order to wrest the imperial dignity from the Habsburgs, or at least to force them to accept the Holy Roman title's formal division. However, just when it dawned on him that there might not be any designated successor, Kleist in the summer of 1803 must also have realised that Napoleon was making no efforts to invade Germany and conquer Vienna—instead, he was setting his sight on Britain: while Kleist was busily composing Napoleon's death before the walls of Vienna, the First Consul at Boulogne was busily assembling the *Armée des côtes de l'Océan*, the most formidable invasion force the world had ever seen. Even though the city of Constantinople in Kleist's drama could symbolise London just as well as Vienna, the conquest of Britain was *not* associated with the seizure of the imperial dignity. Holy Roman Emperor Franz II in August 1804 would proclaim himself Franz I, Emperor of Austria, paving the way for Napoleon crowning himself Emperor of France a few months later, and it is possible that in c.September 1803 the idea of such a construct was first broached (be it in Vienna or Paris), or first reached Kleist's ear, and compelled him to rush to Geneva to find out how it would affect Napoleon's strategy. The important information he obtained in Geneva, then, could have been this: Napoleon had concluded that "*seize*" did not necessarily entail conquering Vienna; if he could line up the Pope and his Curia, he could implement "*seize*" without the Habsburg Emperor intervening. With no successor in sight, no urge to "*act*" now, and no need to achieve "*seize*" via conquest, in October 1803 Kleist could only conclude that *Guiskard*'s main premises had all but collapsed.

Despite his heart-wrenching letters and his quarrels with Pfuel, Kleist appears to have pulled the plug on his "masterpiece" remarkably cold-bloodedly; considering the un-ceremonial manner in which in 1802 he had terminated his "project" with Wilhelmine, we discern here another element of Kleist's standard operating procecure: if a project ran into an insurmountable snag, he would turn on a dime, let go and move on without further ado. By discarding *Guiskard*, Kleist perhaps abandoned the entire *tetralogy*, and with it, at least for the time being, his self-declared *po(i)etical Agôn* with Goethe. As such, abandoning *Guiskard* marked a major turning point in Kleist's career, a veritable *Befreiungsschlag*: henceforth his *satirical* aspirations would take precedence over the *po(i)etical*. By no means was this an *easy* choice—but a *choice* it was nevertheless, and a devastating *failure* it was not: rather, it was a *new beginning*.

Saint-Omer et Boulogne. Having abandoned or shelved *Guiskard*, Kleist immediately set out to pursue a follow-on project: observing Napoleon in action, from close up. Whether or not he was seeking to die on the shores of England, or in the waters of the Channel (I:737; cf. *LS*,119b), Kleist was certainly aiming to observe and narrate Napoleon's audacious *Invasion of Britain*: instead of sagging on an army drum wrecked by disease, the restless First Consul was busily preparing an undertaking whose sheer scope—an invasion army of 200,000 men, the most sophisticated invasion force in the history of warfare, assembled on the French coast and to be transported over the Channel by innumerable vessels (even an aerial invasion by hot-air balloons was under consideration), set to conquer the island defended by the world's greatest fleet—cannot have failed to impress Kleist who, if nothing else, would have been attracted by the *descente*'s very spectacle.[224]

Kleist was a pioneer not only of "medical," but also "war tourism," and his journeys are as much part and parcel of his life's *Gesamtkunstwerk* as his works; he craved to partake in history *as it took place*, and moving towards the war front is a recurring aspect of his modus operandi.[225] His apparent death-wish apart—which may have been no more than a "cover story" for the unlikely case that an accident did happen: Kleist disliked accidents, preferring to direct his own fate, and should he be killed in his adventure, he would have preferred it to appear as if he had planned it—there was nothing *per se* unusual about his two attempts in late 1803, respectively at Saint-Omer and Boulogne, to observe (and perhaps join) the French invasion force. Saint-Omer and Boulogne are located a short journey from Paris and Kleist, having abandoned *Guiskard* after struggling with. It 500 days and nights, and having *been* abandoned by Pfuel after a heated quarrel, had time on his hands, no urgent matters to attend to, and probably required some fresh air and inspiration for scoping out his drama on the *Invasion*.

Perhaps the greatest pull-factor for Kleist's two stints to the shores of the English Channel was the opportunity to observe Napoleon in action—the *genie* let out of his bottle, doing his magic: the First Consul was regularly inspecting his troops being assembled there, and would surely lead the invasion in person—, and possibly to be present at his *fall*.[226] It has been suggested that Kleist sought to assassinate Napoleon, but logistical difficulties apart, this would have been rather counterproductive, from the point of view of his *Gesetze*, and from that of his aspiration, "*Dich, o Vaterland, will* [ich] *singen*" (II:376): to steer Germany's "*Draht des Schicksals*," Kleist needed Napoleon (and France) either to *fail spectacularly*—which would rally the German princes to recover the lost territories and reinstall the *HRR*—, or to *succeed spectacularly*, which would entice him to soon turn around and confront the Germans, *full frontal———Alles oder nichts!*

Mayence et Coblence. After the *Saint-Omer et Boulogne* "project" failed—the French and Prussian authorities did not play along, and the invasion turned out to be less imminent than expected—, Kleist was escorted back to the French border, where he submerged at Mayence (Mainz) to seek out the famous doctor and former Jacobin Georg Wedekind.. While he certainly sought medical consultation and treatment, Kleist may also have wished to tap into Wedekind's political connections in France, at a time when conspiracies against Napoleon reached their peak: the *Cadoudal Affair*, which in February

1804 culminated in the arrest of its two royalist ringleaders, Jean-Charles Pichegru and George Cadoudal, and the *Duke of Enghien Affair*, which in March resulted in Enghien's apprehension when he was (falsely)associated with Pichegru and Cadoudal. Possibly Wedekind was directly or indirectly connected to conspirators; certainly by locating himself in Mayence Kleist was able to stay inside France, yet ready at any moment to pop across the Rhine if necessary. Even if he was not himself associated with conspirators, Kleist will have wanted to remain as close as possible to unfolding events, ready to launch a propaganda offensive rallying the German princes and people, should an assassination attempt succeed.[227]

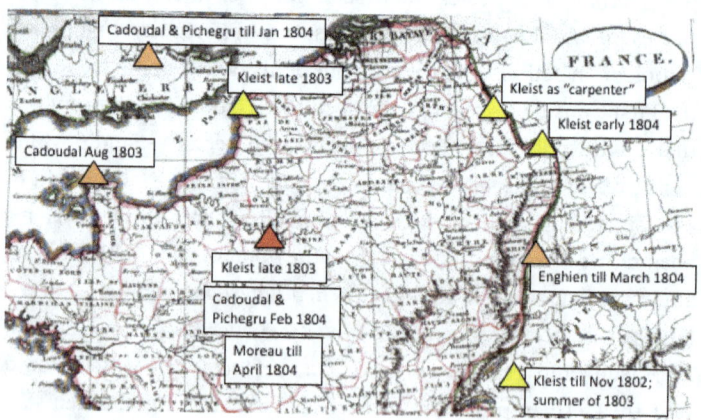

Conspirators and Suspects: Along the Edges of the Napoleonic Realm, Circling its Centre (1802-4).

Wedekind told Wieland that all his patient Kleist needed was *occupation*. While this diagnosis surely downplayed Kleist's medical condition, it provided a credible rationale for his taking on an unusual assignment whose true nature was best kept secret: Kleist was to apprentice as a carpenter in Coblence (Koblenz), like Mayence a left-bank gateway city within the French Empire. The *Kleist-Forschung* has tended to treat this apparently bizarre idea as an expression of Kleist's profound crisis (cf., e.g., Schede, *Kleist*, 74), but plausibly "carpenter in Koblenz" was simply "code" for a sensitive job Wedekind was lining up for him, most likely with his friend Charles

François Philibert Masson, Secrétaire-général of the Départment Rhin-et-Moselle in Coblence.[228] I suspect that Wedekind and Philibert Masson were both readying themselves to support a coup d'état should an attempt on Napoleon's life succeed; Wedekind would have preferred that a republican order be established in France, but may have been willing to support the restauration of the Bourbon monarchy on the basis of a modern constitution, while Philibert Masson may have been a royalist, which would explain his interest in employing Kleist, who will have sympathised with the royalists, although he would have welcomed any solution that excluded Napoleon. In the case of a coup, Kleist could serve the putschists as liaison with the Prussian legation in Paris and the court in Berlin, supporting them in garnering Prussian support or neutrality.

By March 1804 Napoleon, with the arrests of the discontented republican general Jean Moreau (14th February) and of the royalist conspirators Pichegru (28th February) and Cadoudal (3rd March), and with the execution of the scapegoat Enghiens (21st March), had checked any overt resistance to his rise to absolute power, and with the *Constitution de l'an XII* of 18th May proclaimed himself hereditary imperial monarch (cf. Loch, *Kleist*, 195; this date marks the official start of the French Empire). Kleist left Mayence for Prussia in April, soon after it became clear that the conspiracy had failed, and that Napoleon's imperial proclamation was inevitable. Kleist's "lost year" encompassed three interlinked "projects"— *Guiskard; Saint-Omer et Boulogne; Mayence et Coblence*—by which he sought to help overcome Napoleon, respectively by "writing" the First Consul's withering before the walls of Vienna, by reporting his *fall* before the cliffs of Dover, and by sealing his dynasty's ruin by stirring a German intervention following a successful royalist or republican coup. Kleist's year was "lost" only because Napoleon prevailed; had Napoleon succumbed, 1804 would have marked the zenith of Kleist's careers as *satirical* bard.

"eine gewisse Entdeckung im Gebiete der Kunst." On 3rd July 1803 Kleist wrote Ulrike that he was preparing to travel to Switzerland together with Pfuel, at the latter's expense, and stay there until *"ich* *eine gewisse Entdeckung im Gebiete der Kunst, die ihn [Pfuel] sehr interessiert, völlig ins Licht gestellt habe"* (II:733). What this ominous "discovery in the field of arts" amounted to has been subject to inconclusive debate in the *Kleist-Forschung*. Pfuel will have been important for Kleist not only as lover and financier, but also as sparring partner and "beta tester" in his production process: *"unter seinen Augen vollenden."* Like Wilhelmine's, Pfuel's foremost quality may have been his ability and willingness to give Kleist his undivided attention (Kleist during the journey also declaimed or dictated to Pfuel *Krug*'s first three scenes).

Years later, in his *BA* essay *Empfindungen vor Friedrichs Seenlandschaft,* Kleist in similar terms would attest to Caspar David Friedrich that he had *"eine ganz neue Bahn im Felde seiner Kunst gebrochen"*:

> und ich bin überzeugt, daß sich, mit seinem Geiste, eine Quadratmeile märkischen Sandes darstellen ließe, mit einem Berberitzenstrauch, worauf sich eine Krähe einsam plustert, und daß dies Bild eine wahrhaft Ossiansche oder Kosegartensche Wirkung tun müßte. Ja, wenn man diese Landschaft mit ihrer eigenen Kreide und mit ihrem eigenen Wasser malte; so, glaube ich, man könnte die Füchse und Wölfe damit zum Heulen bringen. (II:327-8)[229]

Ossian was a fictional (some would say, fake) Celtic epic poem cycle published as "authentic" by James Macpherson in c.1760; L. Gotthard Kosegarten was a poet-pastor on the island of Rügen who in the late 1790s and early 1800s held popular sermons by the shore, to which fishermen listened while fishing, in a quasi re-enactment of Jesus' early ministry on the shores of lake Galilee (Kleist probably observed Kosegarten's performance "live" in 1800). Since *Ossian* was deemed almost more "Celtic" than authentic Celtic poetry, and Kosegarten's performances almost more "Christ-like" than Jesus' own, Kleist here anticipates Jean Baudrillard's concept of the *hyperreal* (that which is *more real than the real*):

> Today abstraction is no longer that of the map, the double, the mirror, or the concept. Simulation is no longer that of a territory, a referential

being, or a substance. It is the generation by models of a real without origin or reality: a hyperreal. The territory no longer precedes the map, nor does it survive it. It is nevertheless the map that precedes the territory—precession of simulacra—, that engenders the territory.²³⁰

Is not Kleist's "discovery in the field of the arts" a *praxis of the hyperreal*: "the generation by models of a real without origin," of "maps that precede and the territory," of dramas that are not only predictive or prescriptive, but *performative*? Are not the inexorable "Laws" of *dynastic rivalry* and *dynastic hybris* inscribed into the very "algorithm" that generates Kleist's model of reality, his simulation of history? Does not Kleist's "discovery" comprise a novel, plastic *po(ï)etical* language, designed to "paint the souls" of great men, and to overcome the very limits of (ordinary) language—*"die Sprache... kann die Seele nicht malen"* (II:626)—, by being no longer merely mimetic and representative, i.e., mediating the Lacanian domains of the *Imaginary* and the *Symbolic*, but increasingly productive and performative, i.e., encompassing the *Real*?²³¹ If a *master painter* is able to bring to life a landscape by painting it with "chalk" and "water" extracted from its very ground, then, as Kleist suggests elsewhere (cf. II:766-7), a *master poet* ought to be able to bring to life erotico-agonistic tableaux by writing them with his own "tears"—the outpour and flush of bodily fluids in passion, suffering and ecstasy. Kleist aims not merely to create an *aesthetic* experience but to *write history*, to mobilise and manipulate "puppets"—leaders and lovers—who, like the targets of hypnosis or voodoo, are so mesmerised by his poetry, *"als ob einem die Augenlieder weggeschnitten wären"* (II:327), that they can not help but *act in accordance with his script*.

The realist Kleist "out-Hegels" the idealist announcer of Napoleon as "world spirit"; the aristocrat Kleist pre-empts the promoter of the proletariat as movens of history.²³² If for Hegel the "end of history" (Alexandre Kojève) entails a state of mutual recognition between master (he who is willing to risk his life for prestige and glory) and servant (he who is not), for Kleist it encompasses a state in which the ruler is cleansed of *dynastic hybris* and adopts the spiritedness (*thymos*) towards his people that Plato demands of the Republic's guardians.²³³ Into an ancient discourse on political philosophy, Kleist introduces a quasi-Shakespearean "desire for succession" that is related to, but distinct from, Hobbes' "desire for self-preservation," and Hegel's "desire for recognition." When *Napoleonic* France at *Jena-Auerstedt* demonstrates its absolute superiority over *Frederician* Prussia, for Hegel the "end of history" is nigh, whereas for Kleist, Napoleon merely turns into a Hobbesian ruler who, instead of *sublimating* the dialectic of master and servant, *exploits* it, thereby sliding into despotism. Kleist recognises that *thymos* can be a positive force when directed towards the good of the state and people ("*megalopsychia*," "magnanimity"), a negative one when accumulated by the ruler ("*magalothymia*," "exaggerated self-esteem." His faith in the emergence of a magnanimous ruler, if not in France then in Germany, if not among the Habsburgs then among the Hohenzollerns, rests on a bard who has appeared on stage, as of the summer of 1803, ready to take up the Kantian duty of educating the ruler and awakening the masses: H.v.K. ²³⁴

Towards a Pragmatics and a Praxis of Publishing. In the spring of 1808, it appears, Kleist recovered *Guiskard* from his drawer and selected, edited and published a fragment that together with other pieces ready at hand served to populate *Ph*, thereby establishing a pattern of his *publishing platforms* co-evolving with his *formats*— *Ph* with the fragment and epigram, *Germania* with the ode and poem, *BA* with the anecdote and essay (complementing the book format and the theatre stage).²³⁵ When in the summer of 1808 Kleist's contributions to *Ph* largely ceased, *Ph* had outlived its usefulness for him *as a platform*: not only had Kleist, following several months of rapid-fire publication of mostly extant pieces, exhausted his *in petto* materials, and would have needed to "rev up" the production engine to keep up with *Ph*'s monthly publication schedule, but also did a series of external events—the interception of Heinr. Fr. Karl vom und zum Stein's August 1808 letter, which advocated that Prussia join Austria in a renewed Coalition and instigate a popular insurrection against Napoleon, Prussia's subsequent punishment with debilitating war reparations at the September 1808 *Convention of Paris*, Napoleon and Alexander's reconfirmation of their alliance at the September/October *Congress of Erfurt*, Franz's boycott of the conference, the precarious situation in the *Peninsula War* in late autumn—rendered war once again imminent, compelling Kleist to produce explicit and urgent political manifestos for which an art magazine was not a suitable platform. The need to inspire his King and people directly (neither being typical readers of art magazines) rekindled Kleist's interest in the *stage* as distribution platform, to which he tailored *Hermannsschlacht*; once war broke out, the need to disseminate patriotic propaganda among soldiers and insurrectionists favoured an easy-to-produce and quick-to-distribute pamphlet: *Germania*.[236]

2.3 *Der Zerbrochne Krug*: Coronation at Vienna (An Urgent Manifesto to the King)

Genesis and Context. The idea to *Der Zerbrochne Krug, ein Lustspiel* goes back to a poetic competition—an *Agôn*—Kleist in 1802 entered with his friends Heinr. Zschokke, L. Wieland and Heinr. Gessner upon observing Jean Jacques André Le Veau's engraving *La juge, ou la cruche cassée*. In the summer of 1803 Kleist appears to have declamed or dictated *Krug*'s initial scenes to Pfuel (cf. I:924; II:769; LS,102) before resuming work on the drama in late 1804 in Berlin, or in early 1805 in Königsberg, and possibly sending an early version (not extant) to Chr. von Massenbach in April 1805, in the context of the formation of the *Third Coalition* against Napoleon.[237] In early 1806, in the aftermath of Austria's defeat in the *War of the Third Coalition*, Kleist resumed work on the drama, on 30th August 1806 sending an MS, including the lengthy twelfth scene, to Marie (cf. II:769), evidently hoping that via her and the Queen it will reach the King, then on the brink of ordering Prussia's mobilisation. In August 1807, a year after its completion, A. Müller handed a version of the MS to Goethe, who adopted it for the Weimar stage (the adaptation is not extant), where it premièred on 2nd March 1808. After the performance famously tanked, Kleist published a fragment in *Ph*'s March 1808 issue. A significantly shortened book version was published in February 1811, with a long version nearly identical with the 1806 MS version included as *Variant* in the appendix. *Krug*'s genesis thus spanned nearly nine years, the longest period of any of Kleist's works, and four versions are extant: *MS* (with foreword), *Variant* (with a slightly modified ending compared with *MS*), *Ph* fragment, and book version.

Innocence Lost. Le Veau's c.1780 engraving (below, left), which inspired Kleist and his friends to their poetic competition, is based on a lost painting by Philibert-Louis Debucourt, who may have adopted the popular topos of the broken jug representing a woman's lost innocence from other contemporary works, such as Jean-Baptiste Greuze's 1771 painting *La cruche cassée* (right):

Something's broken.

Le Veau (or already Debucourt) relocates the scene from its conventional bucolic setting—alluding to the paradisaic *Fall*—into a courtyard that marks the threshold between the bucolic and matriarchal world on the one hand, and the urban and patriarchal world on the other, perhaps alluding to the "lost innocence" not only of *woman* but also of *humanity*. Blamberger considers (cf. *Kleist*, 254) "Kleist's genial turn" to have been to "associate the broken jug not with the young couple but with the judge himself and the young woman," but fails to credit Le Veau (or Debucourt) for already effecting this "genial turn": Le Veau's central figures are not the young woman and her fiancé, or the young woman and her womb, as in Greuze's painting, but the maiden and the judge; he visually contrasts the judges on the left with the country folk on the right, with the seated judge and the maiden straddling both realms.[238] Kleist maintains this juxtaposition, but shifts his story's "centre" yet further to the left (in reference to Le Veau): the three judges' rivalry, as much as Adam, Eve and her fiancé's affairs, drive his drama's momentum.

Kleist's *Foreword* to some extent assumes the function of the opening chorus, out of place in a comedy:[239]

> Diesem Lustspiel liegt wahrscheinlich ein historisches Factum, worüber ich jedoch keine nähere Auskunft habe auffinden können, zum Grunde. Ich nahm die Veranlassung dazu aus einem Kupferstich, den ich vor mehreren Jahren in der Schweiz sah. Man bemerkte darauf—zuerst einen Richter, der gravitätisch auf dem Richterstuhl saß: vor ihm

> stand eine alte Frau, die einen zerbrochenen Krug hielt, sie schien das Unrecht, das ihm widerfahren war, zu demonstriren: Beklagter, ein junger Bauernkerl, den der Richter, als überwiesen, andonnerte, vertheidigte sich noch, aber schwach: ein Mädchen, das wahrscheinlich in dieser Sache gezeugt hatte (denn wer weiß, bei welcher Gelegenheit das Delictum geschehen war) spielte sich, in der Mitte zwischen Mutter und Bräutigam, an der Schürze; wer ein falsches Zeugniß abgelegt hätte, könnte nicht zerknirschter dastehn: und der Gerichtsschreiber sah (er hatte vielleicht kurz vorher das Mädchen angesehen) jetzt den Richter mistrauisch zur Seite an, wie Kreon, bei einer ähnlichen Gelegenheit, den Ödip. Darunter stand: der zerbrochene Krug.—Das Original war, wenn ich nicht irre, von einem niederländischen Meister. (I:176)

I offer the following comments to Kleist's *Foreword*:

- "*wahrscheinlich ein historisches Factum*": Kleist hints that *Krug* is based on a historical event;
- "*einen Richter, der gravitätisch*": Adam is introduced as less than "graceful" (in *Marionettentheater* equated with "anti-grav");
- "*das Unrecht, das ihm widerfahren*": injustice was done to the jug ("*ihm*"), not the old woman or the maiden; to calibrate the "injustice," we must understand the functional value of the "jug";
- "*Beklagter... den der Richter, als überwiesen, andonnerte*": "as if guilty" suggests that the judge knows more than he admits, or that the farmhand is innocent;
- "*ein Mädchen, das wahrscheinlich in dieser Sache gezeugt hatte*": "*zeugen*" means both "to give evidence" and "to beget"; while Eve may have became pregnant, this is not certain;
- "*(denn wer weiß, bei welcher Gelegenheit das Delictum geschehen war)*": Kleist warns the reader not to jump to conclusions;
- "*spielte sich, in der Mitte zwischen Mutter und Bräutigam, an der Schürze*": an "FFF" constellation, with Eve as *erâstes* (an experienced lover);
- "*wer ein falsches Zeugniß abgelegt hätte, könnte nicht zerknirschter dastehn*": Eve may or may not have given evidence;

- "*und der Gerichtsschreiber sah (er hatte vielleicht kurz vorher das Mädchen angesehen) jetzt…*": the scribe's glance at the girl suggests that he is not innocent in this matter, or knows more than he admits;
- "*wie Kreon, bei einer ähnlichen Gelegenheit den Ödip*": the reference to Sophocles is usually taken to imply that Adam, like Oedipus, investigates a crime he himself committed; yet it also reminds us that Licht, like Creon, is set to inherit Adam's legacy;
- "*Darunter stand: der zerbrochene Krug*": the broken jug is the drama's crux; Kleist's modification of his original title, replacing "*zerbrochene*" with "*zerbrochne*," subtly shifts the emphasis: "*zerbrochene*" refers more to a state—"something is broken"—, "*zerbrochne*," which accentuates the last syllable, more to an event: "something is being broken";
- "*Das Original war… von einem niederländischen Meister*": while Le Veau's model was not by a Dutch master, the Dutch liberation struggle against the Spanish Habsburgs depicted on the jug may be a proxy for Kleist's *satirical* concerns; his *satyrical* tableau may well have been inspired by a "Duch master," Teniers (cf. my discussion below).

The Case of Adam. Adam's biblical name obviously links him to Eve, and his case to the *Adamsfall*, i.e., "original sin" and forbidden knowledge. In German, "*Fall*" has physical, metaphorical, biblical, juridical and grammatical connotations; it may refer to Adam's physical stumble during the previous night, his demise as a public figure, his sinfulness, his legal case, and his investigation, which is proceeding along the lines of the grammatical cases: "*wer oder was?*" "*wen oder was?*" "*wessen?*" "*wem?*" ("*cui bono?*"). His clubfoot, meanwhile, links Adam to Oedipus, Satan ("accuser") and the bucolic Pan. The Kleist reception's *communis opinion* has it that Adam is himself implicated in the crimes he investigates; if his "crimes" (impregnating Eve, breaking the jug) appear to be less severe than Oedipus' (killing his father, seducing his mother), it is considered commensurate with Kleist's choice of genre: if Oedipus' *tragedy* consists in his agonising discovery of his own guilt, Adam's *comedy* consists in, it is held, his hilarious efforts to dissimulate a guilt of which he is aware from the beginning.

And yet: Kleist's *Foreword* already hints that things may not be as they appear, compelling us to question the evidence, even as Kleist appears to tighten its noose around Adam's neck (as Sophocles does around Oedipus'); Kleist's parallels with Sophocles, precisely because they are so obvious, may be spurious.[240] Kleist brilliantly veils that, firstly, there is no solid evidence against Adam with respect to either "crime" (in any regular court of justice, Adam would be declared not guilty); secondly, while our attention is focused on Adam's comical efforts to stem himself against fate, the scheming Licht actively promotes Adam's downfall, and Walter has an agenda on his own. Regarding the "evidence" against Adam, consider the following:

- While Eve apparently *was* penetrated vaginally in the previous night, and Adam *was* present at the "crime scene" and did penetrate her, it is not certain that it was him who penetrated her *vaginally*;
- Even if Eve *were* pregnant, she could have been impregnated on another occasion; the *symbolic* linkage between the shattered jug and her impregnation constitutes no proof;
- Clues that implicate Adam—his injuries, his wig found on the crime scene, the footsteps, Brigitte's claim that the perpetrator was bald—, albeit suggestive, are inconclusive: Adam could have contracted the injuries elsewhere (as he claims he did), anyone could have placed the wig (Ruprecht admits having been the last to have been in its possession), the footsteps could be fake (this could easily be done: *"Ein Fuß ist, wie der andere, ein Klumpen"*); Brigitte's claim is uncorroborated by other eye-witnesses; the possibility remains that someone is framing Adam;[241]
- Adam's fleeing the court-room is not in itself an admission of guilt; Adam never admits any wrongdoing;
- The "victims" of the two "crimes" do not articulate an accusation—Eve refuses to do so on the grounds that "no maiden's mouth would dare articulate" it; Marthe in her garbled eloquence is unable to do so;

- Eve's testimony is delivered under duress (Walter's threat to arrest her fiancé) and must be deemed unreliable.

For all his eloquence, the "crafty," "buffoonish," "Falstaffian" Adam fails to escape the tightening noose because he is unable to produce an alternative narrative, an alibi, or eyewitnesses who exonerate him. Still, he could be a hapless scapegoat rather than a criminal: Licht associates him with a lustful buck, and *"Sündenbock"* ("sinful buck") indeed means "scapegoat."[242] If one of the criticisms heaped on the play was that the plot was too transparent, we discover it to be anything but.[243]

An obscure comment by Adam, *"Die Kerle unterscheiden ein Gesicht / Von einem Hinterkopf nicht, wenn er kahl ist. / Setzt einen Hut dreieckig auf mein Rohr, / Hängt ihm den Mantel um, zwei Stiefel drunter, / So hält so'n Schubiack ihn für wen Ihr wollt"* (V.86-90), highlights a key element of the "brotherhood's" "code of conduct": in an orgiastic setting, the "satyrs" will let themselves be penetrated by any reveller's phallus, be it diseased (*"Gesicht"* = chancreatic glans) or not (*"kahler Hinterkopf"* = smooth glans), provided it is properly covered by a condom ("hat," "coat"). The maid's testimony, *"Kahlköpfig wart Ihr, als Ihr wiederkamt; [...] / Das Blut mußt ich Euch noch vom Kopfe waschen"* (V.228-30)," suggests that Adam returned from the orgy without a condom pulled over, his ejaculate ("blood") still dripping; the "crime" Adam could then be accused of is that of infringement of the "brotherhood's" "code of conduct," risking that he infects a fellow "satyr" (or accidentlly impregnates a maiden).[244]

The Case of Licht. Licht is presently only the scribe, but slated to succeed Adam in office as judge, giving him a motive to eliminate or discredit him. Licht's name is just as much associated with the devil as is Adam's clubfoot: the Latin name for Satan is *Lucifer*, "carrier of light." Licht is a commensurate schemer: already in the opening sequence it is hinted that he seeks to topple Adam and assume his position, and his repeated reference to Adam's clubfoot may suggest that he seeks to frame Adam. Adam did visit Eve in the said night, but Licht could have orchestrated their meeting: its purpose, according to Eve, was for Adam to write her a certificate exempting Ruprecht from conscription, and the—false—rumour that the conscripts were to be deployed in the East Indian colonies, not in defense of the home country, could well have been spread by Licht, and we only have Licht's uncorroborated testimony that it was Adam who spread it (cf. V.1930). Adam may be blackmailing Eve, but it could have been Licht who created the conditions for this, in order to frame Adam just as Walter's inspection is about to take place. While there is no more solid proof for my conjectures about Licht's machinations than there is for Adam's guilt, it may well have been Licht, not Adam, who has been "throwing sand into [people's] eyes" (cf. V.1003). Vis-à-vis Walter, Licht pursues a two-pronged strategy of producing "evidence" against Adam while positioning himself as credible successor.[245] Licht's scheming becomes so obnoxious that even Walter himself towards the end of the inquiry becomes weary, stops purusuing the case, appoints Licht to Adam's office only "pending further notice" (V.1963-4), and calls for Adam to be brought back.

The Case of Walter. Walter's title (*"Gerichtsrat"* = "judicial controller") and name (*"Walter"* = "ruler," "he who holds sway") mark him as the senior-most of the three judges. When his arrival is announced, Adam initially—jovially—believes that he will turn out to be just as corrupt as his predecessor Wachholder, "*der wackre Mann, der selbst / Sein Schäfchen schiert*" (V.78-9), and operating according to the same logic as do Licht and he himself: "*Der Mann hat seinen Amtseid ja geschworen, / Und praktisiert, wie wir, nach den / Bestehenden Edikten und Gebräuchen*" (V.98-100). When Licht cites evidence to the contrary—"*der Gerichtsrat Walter / Erschien in Holla unvermutet gestern, / Vis'tierte Kassen und Registraturen, / Und suspendierte Richter dort und Schreiber*" (V.101-4)—, and relates the Holla judge's suicide attempt and his successor's appointment, Adam realises that Walter represents a greater danger for both of them than they do for each other, and appeals to Licht to suspend their rivalry and jointly confront Walter.[246] When Licht remains non-committal, Adam shares with him a premonition of their common fate (offering a succinct summary of the drama's entire plot):

> ADAM.—Mir träumt', es hätt ein Kläger mich ergriffen
> Und schleppte vor den Richtstuhl mich; und ich,
> Ich säße gleichwohl auf dem Richtstuhl dort,
> Und schält' und hunzt' und schlingelte mich herunter,
> Und judiziert den Hals ins Eisen mir. [...]
> Drauf wurden beide wir zu eins, und flohn,
> Und mußten in den Fichten übernachten.   (V.269-76)[247]

Walter plays a deliberate game, curtailing Adam without eliminating him, while stoking the rivalry by appointing Licht to investigate the crime scene, giving him the opportunity to gather (or manufacture) evidence against Adam. Walter's strategy of *divide et impera*, and of *suspending* rather than *dispensing* justice, holds Adam, Licht, Ruprecht and Marthe in check: he appoints Licht temporarily to Adam's office while calling for Adam's return, and suspends Ruprecht and Eve in a Kafkaesque loop by referring them to imprenetable higher authorities. His attempt at blackmailing Eve—he offers to bail Ruprecht out of conscription in exchange for sexual favours, "Wenn du mir deine / Unschuldigen bewährst [...] / Bewähr ich auch dir meine menschlichen" (V.1755-7)—mimics Adam's. Little separates Walter in moral terms from Adam or Licht—he only carries a bigger stick.[248]

The Case of Ruprecht. In said night Eve was joined by Adam and Ruprecht in an *"FOF"* constellation:[249]

> EVE. [...] Ich führt ihn [Adam] in die Kammer ein. [...]
>   Da wir jetzt in der Stube sind—zehnmal [...]
>   [...] ich die Tür behutsam zugedrückt [...]
>   Und stoß ihm vor die Brust [...]
>   [...] Ruprecht kömmt!
>   [...] hör ich ihn donnern.
> RUPRECHT. Ei, sieh! da kam ich [...]   (V.2199-223)

In this passage it remains unclear who of the two ithyphallic "satyrs" penetrated Eve frontally, and in doing so evidently deflowered ("*Die*

Hochzeit ist es, die ein Loch bekommen" (V.440-1) refers to Hymen, the Greek god of marriage, and implies that Eve's hymen has been perforated), and possibly impregnated, her.[250]

Ruprecht testifies, *"daß ein andrer das Geschirr, / ... zerschlagen"* (V.2267-8), and Eve corroborates this testimony (cf. V.2276-7), but since we cannot simply presuppose the equivalence of the broken jug and the torn hymen—a symbolic equivalence Kleist obvious plays on as did Le Veau, Debucourt and Greuze, but which in Kleist's drama may be a decoy: the person who broke the jug may or may not be the same person who impregnated Eve—we do not accept this testimony as evidence in the question of Eve's impregnation. Ruprecht's testimony that he found Eve's "door barred," *"Und geh, und drück, und tret und donnere, / Da ich der Dirne Tür, verriegelt finde, / Gestemmt, mit Macht, auf einen Tritt, sie ein* (V.966-8), also does not clarify matters, fof he could have encountered such resistance at Eve's "front gate" or "back gate," as intact hymen or coyness. Frau Marthe's testimony, *"Als laute Männerstimmen, ein Tumult, / In meiner Tochter abgelegener Kammer, [...] / [...] der Flaps dort, / Der trotzt, wie toll, Euch in des Zimmers Mitte"* (V.746-7), confirms the double penetration, the "mayhem" in Eve's "remote chamber" confirming that Eve was sodomised (by several men, or a chain of men), Eve's being "confronted" in "her chamber's middle," that she was impregnated; however, whether the "brat" was Adam or Ruprecht remains indiscernible.[251]

Eve testifies, firstly, that Adam had come to her place to put his signature under a doctor's certificate for Ruprecht; secondly, that she invited Adam to inject his "ink" where *"in der Mitte / Ein Platz, so groß just, wie ein Tümpel, offen"* (V.2177-8), and gave him a hand in doing so, *"Ich führt ihn in die Kammer ein"*; thirdly, that Ruprecht penetrated her, needing no invitation or help, *"Ruprecht kracht ins Zimmer. [...] / Und stößt—"* (V.2237-9). Her testimony suggests that Adam penetrated her vaginally, entering "unfamiliar territory," and Ruprecht penetrated her anally, entering a well-trodden path; Eve's pushing Adam's breast, while hearing Ruprecht "thunder" (orgasm), confirms that she was facing Adam and turning her back to Ruprecht. Since we earlier established that Adam had failed to put on a condom, and we now established that he penetrated Eve vaginally we conclude, based on the above evidence, that Eve agreed to, or even offered, Adam impregnating her, in exchange for his signature (whether this is a case of coercion on the part of Adam, or of seduction on the part of Eve, remains indiscernible).

The Case of Eve. Anthony Stephens' uncaveated insistence (*Kleist. The Dramas*, 61) that "Eve is innocent" is not even affirmed by Eve herself: unlike the Marquise, whose well-timed swoon protects her "innocence," Eve does not even attempt to concoct an "alibi": "*Was hilft's, daß ich jetzt schuldlos mich erzähle?*" (V.1946). Eve is not a mere victim of circumstance, let alone of violence: her intercourse with Adam may have been consensual (if possibly coerced, but that is unclear), and her penetration by Ruprecht, even if not explicitly invited, is unlikely to constitute rape, having been witnessed by Marthe and others (if it were to have been rape, it would have to have been gang rape). Eve's admission that she previously did a "Bill Clinton" on Lebrecht, "*Und hättest du durch's Schlüsselloch mich mit / Dem Lebrecht aus dem Kruge trinken sehen*" (V.1169-70), confirms that, while she may have been a virgin, she is no wallflower.

"Sündenbock." Whereas the drama's comedy is often held to derive from Adam's knowing the truth and seeking to pre-empt its discovery, in an inversion of Sophocles' plot, we saw that this is evidently not the case: Adam, Eve, Ruprecht, Marthe and several others who appear on the scene (cf. V.2259ff.) evidently know what took place in said night, and it is eminently plausible, even probable, that *everyone present in the courtroom*, Walter exempted, already before the court hearing commences *knows exactly what happened in said night*. The plaintiffs, then, come to the courtroom not to convict a culprit and to obtain a verdict and retribution, but *to sanctify and sacrifice a scapegoat* (cf. V.1538).[252] Adam offers himself as the most suitable candidate for the sacrificial victim (a he-goat, evidently), not least because Licht has been framing him for this role, and Walter, at least initially, confirms and accepts him.

The courtroom, in this regard, is a temple or sacrificial site, and the scribe's desk (cf. Le Veau's engraving) is its altar; the plaintiffs constitute a sacrificial procession that brings the victim to Walter's altar (cf. the procession in *Erdbeben* that brings the victims to St. Iago's church), and Walter is the god they worship, as well as the chief priest and hierophant who presides over the ritual and accepts the victim. We could say that in *Krug*, Kleist posits the strict equivalence of a modern court hearing and an ancient sacrificial rite.

Krug, Satirically

Key political events during the MS' genesis, from Kleist's dictating to Pfuel its first scenes in the summer of 1803 to its completion in August 1806 included:

- 28th March 1803: Napoleon authorises the *Napoléon* gold coin; the first coins are struck in the latter part of 1803;
- 21st March 1804: *Code Napoléon* enters into force;
- 11th August: Franz II proclaims himself Franz I, Emperor of Austria;
- 2nd December: Napoleon crowns himself Napoleon I, Emperor of France;
- 17th March 1805: Napoleon proclaims Beauharnais Vice-Roy of Italy;
- April 1805: Britain, Russia an Austria form the Third Coalition against France, while Prussia abstains;
- 26th May: Napoleon crowns himself King of Italy;
- September: Hardenberg offers Napoleon's envoy a Franco-Prussian alliance against the Coalition; Austrian lobbying manages to avert the alliance;
- 25th September-30th October: Napoleon crosses the Rhine and in the *Ulm Campaign* destroys an Austrian army;
- 21st October: in the *Battle of Trafalgar* Napoleon loses the core of his fleet;
- 3rd November: Alex. I and Fr. Wilh. III sign the *Convention of Potsdam* which anticipates Prussia's joining the Coalition;
- 13th November: Chr. Haugwitz leaves for Paris to deliver Fr. Wilh.'s ultimatum to Napoleon, but deliberately delays his mission until it is overtaken by events; his *"Schaukelpolitik"* makes him widely unpopular in Prussia and Germany;

- 2nd December: in the *Battle of Austerlitz* Napoleon vanquishes a vast Austro-Russian army; he subsequently occupies Vienna, where he resides at Schönbrunn Palace; Franz, who fled to Olmütz, bids for peace;
- 15th December: with the *Treaty of Schönbrunn* Haugwitz relinquishes Cleves, Ansbach-Bayreuth and Neuchâtel to Napoleon, in exchange for a dubious promise of sovereignty over Hannover (which Britain also claims);
- 26th December: with the *Treaty of Pressburg* Austria withdraws from the Third Coalition and relinquishes territories to France and Bavaria;
- 12th January 1806: Napoleon adopts Beauharnais, who two days later marries Princess Auguste, daughter of Bavarian King Max. I Joseph;
- 5th June: Napoleon converts the Batavian Republic into the Kingdom of Holland and appoints his brother Louis King of Holland;
- 12th July: with the *Treaty of the Confederation of the Rhine* 16 German states create a confederation (*Rheinbund*) under Napoleon's tutelage;[253]
- July-August: Napoleon broaches the idea a North-German Federation under Prussia's leadership, and of the Hohenzollern King assuming a German imperial title; meanwhile Luise and the Prussian "war party" lobby Fr. Wilh. to mobilise against France;[254]
- 1st August: The *Rheinbund* members secede from the *HRR*;
- 6th August: Franz II dissolves the *HRR* and abdicates its imperial title;
- Early August: Napoleon offers Hannover to Britain;
- 9th August: Fr. Wilh. orders Prussia's mobilisation.

"Der Krüge schönster" *(I).* Kleist's main *satirical* concern in *Krug* is the *HRR*'s collapse as a result of the German dynasties' rivalry and Napoleon's intervention: *Der Zerbrochne Krug = The Shattered Empire*. For good reason the jug is described as having a clay pedestal or foot (cf. V.703-4): the fragile *HRR*, Kleist suggests, literally stood on *feet of clay*. The town of Huisum, this *"kleiner Teil der Welt"* (V.313) in which the drama's events take place, may represent Germany (and, by analogy, the province of Utrecht, the French Empire, and

Holland, Europe). For Kleist the loss of the Rhine's left bank and Napoleon's seizing the imperial dignity had marked the beginning of the end of the *HRR*, and with it the ancient order in which countless generations of von Kleists and Germans had prospered, and his evident fascination in 1802 for Le Veau's engraving will have been due not least to its depicting a similar transition from an ancient order, represented by the country folk on the right (!), to a new one, embodied by the stately figure entering the courtyard on the left (!), with the tired-looking judge caught in the middle, mediating this transition without being able to arrest or shape it.

Kleist's jug, as symbolic object, is akin to the "Shield of Achilles" in Homer's *Iliad*, which according to Agallis of Corcyra depicts the history of Attica, to the "Shield of Aeneas" in Virgil's *Aeneid*, which according to Lessing depicts an anticipation of the *Pax romana*, and to the chalice in Schiller's *Piccolomini*, which according to Gernot Müller (*Gemälde*, 130-1) depicts Ferd. II's coronation, and Frau Marthe's (Hebr.: "bitter") ekphrasis comprises her eulogy to the *HRR*:

> Der Krüge schönster ist entzwei geschlagen.
> Hier grade auf dem Loch, wo jetzo nichts,
> Sind die gesamten niederländischen Provinzen
> Dem span'schen Philipp übergeben worden.
> Hier im Ornat stand Kaiser Karl der fünfte:
> Von dem seht ihr nur noch die Beine stehen.
> Hier kniete Philipp, und empfing die Krone:
> Der liegt im Topf, bis auf den Hinterteil,
> Und auch noch der hat seinen Stoß empfangen.   (V.647-55)

The jug's breaking in two (*"entzwei"*), leaving a gaping hole where there had been a depiction of Holy Roman Emperor Karl V handing over his Dutch provinces to Philip of Spain, firmly places Marthe's (hi)story in the present moment: in early August 1806 Franz II/I permitted the secession of the *Rheinbund*, whereby the *HRR* indeed broke in two, a French-controlled part, and a remainder; his abdication of the Holy Roman crown a few days later left a void at Germany's symbolic centre, indeed leaving a gaping hole where there had been a Holy Roman Emperor, leaving intact only his "legs," Austria and Prussia.²⁵⁵

"und jungt darin." In so far as a judge's power to dispense (or suspend) justice epitomises sovereignty, the judicial controller Walter, the judge Adam, and the designated judge Licht must be *sovereigns*.²⁵⁶ It takes but little imagination to discern in the chacter Walter the actual Napoleon, in Adam, Franz II/I, and in Licht, Fr. Wilh. III. It is a little harder to perceive that already before Walter-Napoleon appears on the scene, the Bonapartean dynasty makes its presence felt, in the figure of Joséphine disguised as—*cat*.²⁵⁷ Adam-Franz's excuse for not wearing his judge's wig (the *HRR*'s crown) at the court hearing is that a cat birthed into it:

> In meine [Perücke] hätt die Katze heute morgen
> Gejungt, das Schwein! Sie läge einsäuet
> Mir unterm Bette da... [...]
> Fünf Junge, gelb und schwarz, und eins ist weiß.
> Die schwarzen will ich in der Vecht ersäufen.
> Was soll man machen? [zu Licht] Wollt Ihr eine haben? [...]
> Ich hatte die Perücke aufgehängt [...]
>   [...] sie fällt— [...]
> Ich stieß sie [Perücke] die mit dem Fuße heut hinunter,
> Als ich es sah. [...]   (V.242-57)

Franz, when his crown (wig) dropped to the floor, instead of picking it up, carelessly nudged it under the bed (!), where Joséphine (the cat) promptly birthed her litter into it. The six kittens' fur colours represent the tinctures or colours of the coats of arms or flags of the most prominent German states: the *HRR*, yellow (*or*) and black (*sable*), the Austrian Empire, equally yellow (*or*) and black (*sable*), and the Kingdom of Prussia, white (*argent*) and black (*sable*). By having her birth these thus-coloured kittens, Kleist anticipates that Joséphine will generate the imperial dynasty Napoleon craves by intermarrying and infiltrating her offspring with that of the Habsburgs and Hohenzollerns. The three black kittens Adam plans to drown in the river Rhine (the Vecht is a Rhine branch in the province of Utrecht) may represent either Joséphine's male or her female progeny: if male, Adam is (optimistically) hoping that the German dynasties can avert being taken over by Bonapartean princes, which would be the worst-case scenario, and that, instead, Bonapartean princesses will be married into them, permitting them to retain a degree of autonomy, while still being tied to the Bonapartean super-dynasty. When he offers Licht one of the kittens, it thus remains open whether he offers him a Bonapartean bride or, insidiously, a Bonapartean usurper. In the course of the hearing it transpires that Franz has a second imperial crown (wig) in reserve (namely the Austrian), which, however, he had to turn in for repair (cf. V.1500), so that in the courtroom he finds himself without any (insignia of) power.

In the eleventh act Brigitte compares the space cleared by the pestilent culprit with that cleared by the snorting Joséphine: *"ein Kreis, / Wie scheu ein Hund etwa zur Seite weicht, / Wenn sich die Katze prustend vor ihm setzt"* (V.1768-70): German doggish dogs giving way to a Bonapartean catty cat: what compellingly cartoonish image of Germany under the sway of the Bonapartes!

"ein Denkmal seiner." Following a prologue encompassing the first three scenes, in which Kleist recaps, in the form of Adam's and Licht's hilarious dialogue, the ancient dynastic rivalry that forms the core of *Schroffenstein*'s plot, *Krug* in the fourth and fifth scenes sets off precisely where *Schroffenstein* ended, with Walter-Napoleon appearing centre stage, establishing himself as master of Germany (Huisum), having already done so in neighbouring France (or Italy: Holla), and forcing Adam-Franz and Licht-Fr. Wilh. to define their respective stance towards him (as well as towards each other). Franz resolves to trying to keep Napoleon at bay, lest he depose him as he did Holla's ruler (cf. V.104); Licht instead seeks to enrol Napoleon in his bid to usurp Franz's imperial dignity.[258]

Satyrically, the court hearing (sixth to twelfth scene) entails Kleist's parodistic re-enactment of the *War of the Third Coalition,* which ended in Napoleon's crushing victory over Franz II/I and Tsar

Alex. I, and which proved devastating for the *HRR* (cf. the broken jug), while Franz himself got away severely bruised (cf. Adam's injuries).²⁵⁹ Adam's court room (or sacrificial temple) represents Vienna's Hofburg, Walter's "inn," Schönbrunn Palace, where Napoleon lodged in December 1805 while negotiating *Schönbrunn* with Prussia and *Pressburg* with Austria, and Eve's "bedroom," Bavaria, where Napoleon in the sweeping *Ulm Campaign* expelled the Austrian army from Bavaria (Eve herself, then, may represent Princess Auguste or *Bavaria*). The events of the previous nights recounted in the court hearing comprise Kleist's parody of the campaign, as follows: having invaded "Eve's bedroom" (Bavaria), Adam-Franz engages the *Ad'A* in erotico-agonistic battle (*Ulm*); he is repulsed through a "window" (the corridor formed by the Danube between the Bohemian Forest and the Alps, through which the Austrian forces retreated); the *Ad'A* advances along the "swollen brook" (Danube) and through to "the village," (towards Vienna; cf. V.893); Adam-Franz, having been ejected from "Eve's bedroom," finds himself thrust into, and caught up among, the "bushes" and "vines" below the "window" (Moravia; cf. V.1520-2; 1627), where "in the heat of the battle" (*Austerlitz*; cf. V.49) he sustains his injuries; in the dark of the night he pussyfoots his way back through the "garden" (Moravia and Lower Austria) to his courthouse (Vienna; cf. V.1779-82).²⁶⁰

Adam's nightly sneaking through the "garden" incorporates a veiled reference to an event to which we can ascribe a precise date, 6ᵗʰ August 1806: "*FRAU BRIGITTE. Nicht weit davon jetzt steht ein Denkmal seiner, / An einem Baum [...] / ADAM für sich. Verflucht mein Unterleib*" (V.1771-3). The "monument" Adam-Franz left behind after *Austerlitz* represents a digit of the Roman numeral "II," which denoted him as Holy Roman Emperor Franz II, and which on 6ᵗʰ August 1806 he abdicated, forthwidth ruling only as Franz I of Austria. If the "wig" into which the cat birthed represents the *HRR*'s Imperial Crown, the "monument" may furthermore denote its Imperial Sceptre. Which begs the question of whether there is not to be found in the drama a representation of the Imperial Orb, which would complete the *HRR*'s main Imperial Regalia. And, arguably, there is: Adam enumerates three glasses of wine he wants to pour down Walter's throat, *"Eins ist der Herr. Zwei ist das finstre Chaos. / Drei ist die Welt"* (V.1532-3), and these can indeed be identified with the three regalia: "lord" = crown, "dark chaos" = sceptre (diseased phallus), "world" = orb. In the end, when he runs away from the courthouse, Adam even drops his "mantle"—the Imperial Cope (*pluviale*; V.1902).

Adam-Franz II drops his Imperial Regalia for Napoleon to snatch—a "wig," "monument," "mantle."

Although Walter is not mentioned, he must have been present when Adam gets caught up in the vines below Eve's "window" (*Austerlitz*) and leaves his "monument" behind: it precisely in those vines—the battlefield of *Austerlitz*—that their paths first cross.[261] Conceivably the billy goat with whom Adam claims to have "fenced" so vehemently in said night (cf. V.50-1) may have been the stealthy Walter (a billy goat-Emperor and a scapegoat-Emperor playing hide and seek behind the oven—quite a goat ride, ha ha).

Krug's curious "footology" parallels this regalian symbolism in tracing the *HRR*'s disintegration and demise, embodied as Adam's extremities: his left—"club"—foot may be said to represent the unsightly remainder of his empire, i.e., Austria, his dislocated right leg, the seceded *Rheinbund*, and its bloody leg stump, the festering, unsutured wound along Austria's borders with Prussia, Saxony and Bavaria, where the rest of Germany has been ripped off his body. His armies vanquished, the enemy lounging in his summer palace, he himself *"von seinem Amt... suspendiert,"* Adam-Franz's premonition of doom (cf. V.269-76) has turned out to have been eminently clairvoyant.

Rhenish and Franconian Wine, Limburg Cheese, and Pomeranian Goose.

The drama's central court hearing encompasses Kleist's re-enactment of Napoleon's *Schönbrunn* (with Prussia) and *Pressburg* (with Austria) negotiations. Kleist continues unabatedly to add to Krug's bristling, plastic symbolism of the *HRR*'s dismantling, depicting with great comedy how Adam-Franz recklessly serves up parts of the *HRR* to satisfy Walter-Napoleon's territorial appetite, while selfishly protecting his Habsburg turf. *"Kuhkäse, Schinken, Butter, Würste, Flaschen / Aus der Registratur geschafft!"* (V.194-5): Adam, on a *satura lanx*, lines up solid traditional German fare for the spoilt conqueror. Adam begins by offering Walter a breakfast of Braunschweig sausage and Danzig liquor, which Walter declines.[262] When he requests water, Adam instead offers him *Franconian* and *Moselle* wine:

ADAM.
    Ein Glas mit Wasser!—
DIE MAGD.   Gleich! Ab.
ADAM.   Kann ich Euch gleichfalls—?
WALTER. Ich danke.
ADAM.   Franz? oder Mos'ler? Was Ihr wollt.   (V.1070-1)

After initial hesitation, Walter accepts Rhenish, Moselle and Franconian wine (the Rheinland, the Palatine and the Principality of Ansbach-Bayreuth) and Limburg cheese (the Duchy of Cleves), while passing over the Pomeranian goose:[263]

WALTER für sich. Verwünscht!
    Laut. Her Richter Adam, wißt Ihr was?
Gebt ein Glas Wein mir in der Zwischenzeit.
ADAM. Von ganzem Herzen gern. He! Margarete! [...]
    Was befehlt Ihr?—Tretet ab, ihr Leute.
    Franz?—Auf den Vorsaal draußen.—Oder Rhein?

WALTER. Von unserm Rhein. [...]
ADAM. Fort! Marsch, sag ich!—Geh, Margarete!
Und Butter, frisch gestampft, Käs auch aus Limburg,
Und von der fetten pommerschen Räuchergans. [...]
WALTER. Gut. Ein Stück Käse dann, doch weiter nichts. [...]
ADAM. [...] Hier—von dem fetten jetzt—kann ich—?
WALTER. Ein Stückchen.
Aus Limburg?
ADAM. Rect' aus Limburg, gnädiger Herr. [...]
WALTER. [...]
Er trinkt.
Niersteiner?
ADAM. Was?
WALTER. Oder guter Oppenheimer?
ADAM. Nierstein...
Adam schenkt wieder ein. [...]
WALTER. 's ist halb noch voll.
ADAM. Wills füllen.
Er schenkt ihm ein.
WALTER.—Was recht und gut und true ist, Richter Adam!
Sie trinken.
ADAM. Nun denn, zum Schluß jetzt, wenns gefällig ist.
Er schenkt ein. [...]
WALTER. Auf Euer Wohlergehen!— (V.1416-1597)

Franz's empties his imperial buttery with the same eagerness as he does his imperial treasury: to rub it all in, Kleist does not depict Napoleon as excessively voracious, but rather Franz as frivolously generous and eager to please.

"**Rhein-Inundations-Kollektenkasse**." Adam's ridiculously complicated *über*-German term (cf. V.348; it refers to a mutual fund set up to compensate adjoining owners for flood damage) alludes to another precise date, 12th-16th July 1806, during which sixteen German princes in Paris, under French tutelage, formed the *Rheinbund* (*Confédértion du Rhin*), thereby putting the nail in the

HRR's coffin. The *Rheinbund* member were compelled to commit to steep increases in their defense budgets and to putting their armies at the *Ad'A*'s disposal, forcing them to raise taxes and significantly raise public debts. Kleist here ridicules, yet also bemoans, the fact that a significant part of Germany has now become a source of recurring funds and live bodies lined up to fuel Napoleon's future wars.

"**Die ganze Sippschaft.**" Eve, caught up *"Zwischen Mutter und Bräutigam"* (cf. Kleist's foreword), i.e., between Germany and France, may prepresent Bavarian Princess Auguste, and her fiancé Ruprecht, Napoleon's step-son Eugène de Beauharnais whom she marries on 14th January 1806. Although Prussua did not formally enter the war, Napoleon forced her into negotiations: Licht-Fr. Wilh. remains absent from "Eve's bedroom," but is present at the subsequent negotiations in the court room.[264] His increasingly assertive stance vis-à-vis Walter in the course of the drama mirrors Fr. Wilh.'s increasingly belligerent stance vis-à-vis Napoleon in the summer of 1806, which precipitated Prussia's declaration of war in September.

With great dexterity Kleist links Le Veau's figures to actual personages via his drama's characters:

Le Veau's engraving	Kleist's *Krug*	Actual Personages
Presiding judge	Adam	Franz II/I / *Austria*
Scribe	Licht	Fr. Wilh. III / *Borussia*
Stately figure	Walter	Napoleon
Old woman	Marthe	The German People / *Germania*
Young girl	Eve	Princess Auguste / *Bavaria*
Young man	Ruprecht	Beauharnais

Kleist selectively adds characters to those already distinguished in Le Veau's engraving. If Ruprecht represents Beauharnais, then his "father" Veit Tümpel may enact King Max. I Joseph of Bavaria, who with his daughter Auguste's marriage to him indeed became his father-in-law. The names Veit and Ruprecht are both traditionally associated with the devil; *"Tümpel"* ("puddle") is furthermore derogatory, and so is Veit's designation as "peasant"; all of these contemptuous associations express Kleist's profound disapproval of the turn-coating, self-interested Bavarian monarch and his clan.[265] Veit's sister Brigitte (Gaelic: "strengths"), who plays a supporting role in bringing Adam down, could enact Fr. II/I of Württemberg (parts of the *Ad'A* during the *Ulm Campaign* cut through Württembergian territory); *"Ein Bedienter,"* who announces Napoleon's arrival at Schönbrunn (cf. V.163ff.), could embody Napoleon's chief diplomat Charles-Maurice de Talleyrand.

The drama's *"ganze Sippschaft"* (cf. V.499) may then comprise:

WALTER, Gerichtsrat	NAPOLEON, Emperor of France
ADAM, Dorfrichter	FRANZ II/I, Holy Roman Emperor (till 1806) / Emperor of Austria
LICHT, Schreiber	FR. WILH. III, King of Prussia
FRAU MARTHE RULL	The German People (GERMANIA)
EVE, Ihre Tochter	AUGUSTE, Princess of Bavaria (BAVARIA)
VEIT TÜMPEL, ein Bauer	MAX. IV/I JOSEPH, Elector (till 1805) / King of Bavaria
RUPRECHT, sein Sohn	EUGENE DE BEAUHARNAIS, Vice Roy of Italy
FRAU BRIGITTE	FR. II/I, Elector (till 1805) / King of Württemberg
EIN BEDIENTER	CHARLES-MAURICE DE TALLEYRAND, French Emissary
BÜTTEL, MÄGDE usw.	French, Prussian and Austrian ministers and emissaries.

The six other named people participating in the battle-cum-orgy in "Eve's bedroom"—neighbours Ralf and Hinz, aunts Sus and Lies, the "holy couple" Joseph and Maria (cf. V.2259-73)—presumably refer to prominent French and French-allied generals and rulers involved at *Ulm*; Kleist may well have had specific peronnages in mind, but these are difficult to identify retrospectively.

"mit den nächsten Mai'n blüht unser Glück." Kleist—working frantically—will have produced the long and complex twelfth scene in the days and weeks running up to 30th August 1806, when he rushed the *MS* to Marie. The scene deals with issues that he considered of vital importance to Fr. Wilh. in deciding how to deal with Napoleon. A heated debate was under way in Prussia between Francophiles on the one hand and the "war party" (tacitly supported by Queen Luise) on the other, with options discussed ranging from entering an alliance with Napoleon, on the basis of an idea he had broached, of a North-German Federation under Prussia's leadership, possibly even with a Hohenzollern Emperor, to pressurising Napoleon to re-install the *status quo ante*, while mobilising against him in order to raise the ante.[266]

To understand where Kleist stood in this debate, we shall take recourse to his important letter to Rühle of late 1805 (cf. II:760-1), in which, more explicitly than anywhere else, he unguardedly articulates his view on the situation.[267] Kleist, firstly, advocates that Prussia raise a conscription army of an additional 300,000 men, doubling the size of Prussia's standing army, and, secondly, warns that Napoleon will subjugate and occupy Austria and comprehensively reconfigure the German political landscape, specifically, Kleist anticipates, that within one year (i.e., by end-1806) he will appoint the Wittelsbach monarch as *"König von Deutschland"* (and as his *lieu-tenant* in Germany). I will revert to the first point, of the conscription army, shortly. Regarding the second point, in the 7 or 8 months elapsed since the letter, Napoleon had created facts on the ground: Austria was defeated, the Wittelsbach elevated to King—though of Bavaria, not Germany—, Beauharnais adopted and married to the Bavarian princess, the *Rheinbund* formed, the *HRR* dissolved. The comprehensive reconfiguration of Germany Kleist anticipated had indeed taken place, excepting only that Napoleon had not (yet) created a (client) German Kingdom and crowned a *"König von Deutschland."*

I believe that Kleist's premise, in writing the twelfth scene in August 1806, was that Napoleon would still seek to pursue this plan, by elevating not Max. but Beauharnais into that pan-German leadership position. As said, Napoleon had broached the idea of Fr. Wilh. assuming that role, but Kleist will either have assumed this move to be a decoy, or, if it was not a decoy, have considered it eminently undesirable, for it necessarily implied Prussia's vassalage, which was utterly unfathomable to him, worse than her destruction (this theme runs through his works all the way to *Homburg* and his suicide). Appointing anyone other than a Hohenzollern to the title, alas, necessarily required that Prussia, as the pre-eminent

North-German power, be either destroyed or sidelined. In Kleist's view, then, Prussia in August 1806 truly faced an *"Alles oder Nichts"* crossroads.

It is in the context of this fundamental premise that in *Krug*'s final lines (V.2392-3 in *Variant*; V.1953 in the book version) the "wedding" of Ruprecht and Eve is announced (in Variant by Walter, in the book version by Veit) for the following Pentecost (i.e., for 17th May 1807): Kleist remains convinced that Napoleon will crown a *"König von Deutschland,"* but shifts the anticipated date by half a year, from late 1806 in the letter to May 1807 in the drama. The announced "wedding" is not a wedding (Ruprecht-Beauharnais and Eve-Auguste are already married by now), but a coronation: *the coronation of Beauharnais and Auguste as King and Queen, Viceroy and Vice Queen, even Emperor and Empress, of Germany.*[268]

"Und die vereinten Staaten… / Die lassen trommeln." In the twelfth scene, Die vorigen ohne Adam (V.1908)—i.e., Walter-Napoleon, Ruprecht-Beauharnais, Eve-Auguste, Veit-Max., Brigitte-Fr., and Marthe-Germania—design and prepare *the future of Germany*. Adam-Franz is outside, "running through the ploughed winter fields" (cf. 2405: *"vom Acker machen"* is Ger. idiom for getting away); Licht-Fr. Wilh. is present, lingering by the window (cf. V.2403; the "window," we recall, I marks the threshold to the battlefield: Fr. Wilh. is veering between joining the gang and tossing a grenade among them). In a nutshell, *Krug*'s twelfth scene comprises Kleist's scenaric simulation as to how Napoleon will turn all of Germany into a puppet state, and his *urgent manifesto to his King* to act decicively to pre-empt Napoleon's "Project Pentecost."[269]

Napoleon appoints Auguste as his project manager for "Project Pentecost": *"Steh auf, mein Kind"* (V.1951). Auguste kicks off the project by bringing everyone gathered in the "war room" up to speed (Fr. Wilh. is listening in, but may not be a dependable team player, having his own designs): *"Ihr wißt, daß ein Edikt jüngst erschienen, / Das von je hundert Söhnen jeden Orts / Zehn für dies Frühjahr zu den Waffen ruft, / Der rüstigsten"* (V.1959-62). Wolf Kittler points out (cf. *Geburt,* 120-1) that the 10% conscription Auguste reports (she is evidently referring to Prussia) would raise precisely the additional 300,000 soldiers for Fr. Wilh. Kleist had called for in the letter (cf. II:760-1). Fr. Wilh. on 9th August had ordered Prussia's mobilisation, but only of the existing army, not of additional, conscript contingents (being weary of mob dynamics). Kleist presumes that in the near future Fr. Wilh. *will* authorise this conscription army, and his *manifesto to the King* simulates Napoleon's response to Fr. Wilh.'s mass mobilisation of 600,000 men.

Auguste articulates the overall vision for "Project Pentecost": now that Bavaria and 15 other German principalities, by forming the *Rheinbund*, have "cast the first stones," in a domino effect the other German princes will follow, and the "United States of Germany" will soon take shape; once this is achieved, the rest of Europe will fall in line with Napoleon, too: "*Folgt er einmal der Trommel, / Die Trommel folgt dem Fähndrich, der dem Hauptmann, / Der Hauptmann folgt dem Obersten, der folgt / Dem General, und der folgt den vereinten Staaten wieder, / Und die vereinten Staaten… / Die lassen trommeln, daß die Felle platzen*" (V.2035-41).[270]

Being a well-trained management consultant, Auguste shares with her team her issue analysis and hypotheses: *Situation*: Austria defeated, *Rheinbund* formed, *HRR* dissolved, *Ad'A* in ready positions along the Rhine. *Complication*: Prussia is reticent and threatens to strike. *Question*: "how can we respond to Prussia's challenge and achieve our vision?" *Answer*: "five strategies:

1. Implement conscription;
2. Coin hard currency;
3. Propagate blood relations;
4. Maximise military containment;
5. Stoke ancient rivalries.

Questions, anyone?"

"'s ist eine *Land*miliz." Beauharnais raises the concern that, as King (or Viceroy) of Germany, he would be deployed in the service of a foreign nation. Napoleon (the officer-in-charge of the project) reassures him: "*Die Miliz / Wird nach Batavia nicht eingeschifft: / Sie bleibt, bleibt in der Tat bei uns, in Holland*" (V.2308-10). Napoleon does not lie, he merely fails to clarify that with "Batavia" he is referring not to the distant Dutch colony by that name, as Beauharnais believes, but to the republican, at least notionally independent, Batavian Republic, which on 5th June 1806 Napoleon converted into the Kingdom of Holland, appointing "*[s]eine[n] Bruder*" (V.2368) Louis as King of Holland. When he affirms that Dutch conscripts will henceforth defend not "Batavia" but "Holland," what he means is that they will no longer fight on behalf of an independent Dutch republic, but of the Bonapartean Empire; that like the Suriname slaves in Kleist's 1811 essay, they will uphold the very system that enslaves them. For "Batavia," read "Germany": Napoleon is reassuring Beauharnais that in the future, German conscripts, while notionally fighting for Germany, will in fact be fighting for the Bonapartean Empire; that as German king he will remain, just like "bro" Louis, "*in der Tat bei uns*": in effect, in practice, with us, the Bonapartes.

Fr. Wilh., "*ganz unverfänglich,*" enters the discussion by confirming: "*Die Miliz / Bleibt in dem Land, 's eine Land*miliz" (V.2319-20); like the fox Napoleon, Fr. Wilh. is playing with words: by "*Land*," he evidently means Prussia, possibly Northern Germany.[271] Kleist admonishes his King to outfox the fox, and shows how to do it: "whatever Napoleon *thinks* he will get from us, and from the Germans," Kleist says, "do not let it happen: the Prussian conscripts are yours, and if you can win over the hearts and minds of the (northern) German people, so are theirs" (this is yet another theme that runs through Kleist's works).

"Das Antlitz hier." When Beauharnais remains unconvinced, Napoleon offers him another argument, one that is both material and symbolic, both "hard" and "soft"—namely, a purse with 20 "unalloyed," "freshly minted" "Guilders," with the words: "*Sieh her, das Antlitz hier des Spanierkönigs*" (V.2370). Evidently the "guilders" are not Dutch Guilders or Florins, but imperial *Napoléons*, and what Napoleon is really saying is, "look, my portrait, as your Emperor and paymaster, is on them":

"*Das Antlitz hier*" (I): 20-Franc gold *Napoléon* (1806).[272]

The *Napoléon*, first minted in 1803, became the de facto reserve currency across and beyond the lands under Napoleon's sway; for people in occupied lands it entailed the same ambiguity as would have a Dutch coin featuring the (unloved) foreign ruler Philip II of Spain.[273] Soldiers, *per definitionem*, fight for whoever pays them: Fr. *solde* and Ger. *Sold*, from Lat. *solidus*, mean "pay," and the "soldier" is, literally, "he who is paid." "I give you, Beauharnais," says Napoleon, "these *Napoléons* so that wherever I send you to fight, you will always remember who is paying you, who you are fighting for."

Fr. Wilh. does not enter the discussion, but is no doubt listening carefully in the background. With the formation of the *Rheinbund* on 12th July 1808, the *RT* ceased to be minted, and the Prussian silver Thaler, which contained only two-thirds of the *RT*'s fine silver, became the standard currency in northern Germany. Kleist here advises his King to ditch his inferior Thalers and mint a gold coin featuring his portrait in appropriately imperious posture, so as to create the hard and aspirational currency needed to mobilise, sustain and motivate a large conscription army. "This one," advises Keist, "won't do:"

"*Das Antlitz hier*" (II): 1 Prussian silver Thaler (1803), featuring a youthful Fr. Wilh. III.[274]

"**So. Das ist brav.**" Auguste "gets it" immediately, and so does, eventually, Beauharnais:

> EVE. Ob Ihr mir Wahrheit gabt? O scharfgeprägte,
> Und Gottes leuchtend Antlitz drauf! O Jesus!
> Daß ich nicht solche Münze mehr erkenne!
> WALTER. Hör, jetzt geb ich dir einen Kuß. Darf ich?
> RUPRECHT. Und einen tüchtigen. So. Das ist brav. (V.2374-8)

Ruprecht-Beauharnais accepts the money (and its significance), and endorses Eve-Auguste's rewarding Walter-Napoleon with the very same "kiss" she had previously granted Adam-Franz.[275] If this "kiss" indeed mirrors the previous one, then Ruprecht's inconspicuous "*So*" marks the very moment in which Eve is vaginally penetrated by Walter, implying, on the story's *overt* level, that both Adam (during the previous night) *and* Walter (on the following day) are possible impregnators (perhaps Kleist assumed that Napoleon—somehow—had the faster, more competitive sperm), and on the *satirical* level, that Napoleon has always already injected his own seed into the future German royal family.[276] This explains why the "wedding" is scheduled for the following year's Pentecost, and why Beauharnais must first serve "a short year of (military) duty": in order to ensure that the fruit Auguste shall bear springs indeed from his embrace, and not from Beauharnais', Napoleon must keep them separated for nine months:

> WALTER. Und ist sein kurzes Dienstjahr nun verflossen,
> So komm ich Pfingsten, die nächstfolgenden,
> Und melde mich als Hochzeitsgast. (V.2391-3)

Beauharnais' "*kurzes Dienstjahr*" has a precise duration: nine months, from mid-August 1806 till mid-May 1807, and the "wedding" is not only a *coronation*, but also a *baptism*: that of Napoleon's son, his Bonaparte-Wittelsbachian heir and future King of Germany (rendering Beauharnais a mere interim ruler and placeholder).[277] Max. and *Germania* duly give their consent to Napoleon's future German order, and welcome Beauharnais into its fold:

> WALTER. Ihr seid damit zufrieden doch, Frau Marthe?
> RUPRECHT. Ihr zürnt mir jetzo nicht mehr, Mutter—nicht?

>FRAU MARTHE. Warum soll ich dir zürnen, dummer Junge? Hast du
>   Den Krug herunter vom Gesims geschmissen?
>WALTER. Nun also.—Er auch, Vater.
>VEIT.   Von Herzen gern.   (V.2396-2400)

Fr. Wilh. observes and keeps silent. "Beware," Kleist tells his King, "of Napoleon spreading his seeds across German lands and dynasties; do not offer him a Hohenzollern princess, for you will merely be cuckolded, and his bastard will undermine your dynasty."

"**Schildwach.**" Beauharnais is now fully "pepped up" to serve; Auguste (Bavaria) offers to fund his deployment with "cured butter" (palm grease):

>WALTER. Du also gehst nach Utrecht?
>RUPRECHT.   Ich geh nach Utrecht,
>   Und stehe tapfer auf den Wällen Schildwach.
>EVE.Und ich [...]   bring ihm
>   Im Kühlen Topf von frischgekernter Butter:
>   Bis ich ihn einst mit mir zurücknehme.
>WALTER. Und ich empfehle meinem Bruder ihn,
>   Dem Hauptmann von der Landmiliz, der ihn
>   Aufnimmt, wollt ihr, in seine Kompanie? [...]
>EVE.O guter Herr! O wie beglückt ihr uns.   (V.2379-90)

Kleist evidently does not expect Napoleon to launch a pro-active war against Prussia. Having quasi annexed the *Rheinbund* to his Empire, and put Austria in her place, all he has to do is *contain* Prussia. He therefore does not command Beauharnais to prepare the *Ad'A* for attack, but to position it along the Empire's borders in ready position, to "stand guard along the walls." With the formation of the *Rheinbund* he now controlled not only the Rhine's entire *left* bank, but also its entire *right* bank, and not only the most important transport artery in Europe, but also the military deployment zones east of the river, whence he could launch attacks on Prussia (or Austria) at any time, at great speed (Napoleon in October 1806 would indeed rout the

Prusso-Saxon forces at *Jena-Auerstedt* within less than a fortnight, and occupy Berlin a mere eleven days later, and in April/May 1809 he would push the Austrians out of Bavaria and occupy Vienna with similar speed):

Left: the *Rheinbund* (as of August 1806, red outline) and the dissolved Empire (yellow outline, in the borders of 1795). Right: Napoleon's "fast track" to Berlin in 1806 and to Vienna in 1809.

The *Ad'A* amassed along the Rhine had become Prussia's (and Austria's) sword of Damocles; so superior was his strategic position that Napoleon in September 1806 reportedly refused to believe that Fr. Wilh. had ordered mobilisation.

"Napoleon," Kleist tells his King, "now militarily occupies the high ground. Unless you act urgently to pre-empt him, from his position of strength he will tighten the noose around you, until you will be forced to concede and join his "United States of Germany," or become sidelined as a minor power.

"**Sie treten ans Fenster.**" Fr. Wilh. for some time has been lingering by the "window" and the other rulers in the "war room" are now stepping towards it (cf. 2408). This is the drama's moment of *krisis*: war could break out at any moment. And what does Napoleon do? He demands that Fr. Wilh. bring Franz back, so that he can take his place in the new order. Napoleon, in other words, wishes to get every German state enrolled, especially the two main ones; which, he knows full-well, will rekindle their ancient rivalry and allow him to easily keep them in check: *divide et impera*. Fr. Wilh. appears to comply: "*Licht ab*" (V. 2422).

"Stop!" Before the curtain falls, Kleist turns to his King and looks him in the eyes. "What now? Think!" Kleist here sets up precisely the same kind of *kairotic* moment as he did in *Schroffenstein* when Ursula, shortly before the curtain falls, flings the decaying Rhineland among the German rulers to see if anyone will step forth to pick it up. "*Quo vadis*, Fr. Wilh.? Are you going to comply with Napoleon and bring Franz into the fold? If so, we will be back to square one, where we were at the beginning of *Schroffenstein*, only that now Ursula is no longer shadowy but saviour and *Übervater*, and your rivalry with Franz will be mere sand box games. Or are you thinking of fetching Franz to form a new Coalition? Think again. That crippled goat?"

Pause. Fr. Wilh. is averting his eyes, dragging his feat. "King!" thunders Kleist. "Do you hear me? Do you not see that Napoleon's five strategies can be turned against him? That whatever *he* can do, *you* can do? You *must* do?"

*   *   *   *

Epilogue. Marthe announces that she shall submit herself to the juridicial authorities in Paris to adjudicate in the case of the broken jug. Says Walter-Napoleon: "better still, take the bits and pieces that are left and sell them in the Parisian markets." The main "bit" left of the *HRR*, for her to convert into petty cash, is, of course—*Prussia*.

"This," Kleist warns his King as the curtain falls, "will be your fate, and our glorious nation's, if you do not seize the initative now. Whatever will be left of us—it will be sold in the Parisian slave market.

"*Ende.*"

An Urgent Manifesto to The King. Kleist advises Fr. Wilh. to act decisively, but not heedlessly: "do mobilise, but do it *fully*, not half-heartedly, by doubling the size of your army via conscription; mint gold coin replacing the Prussian Thaler, to pay your soldiers and fund your war; strike alliances with northern German rulers (Saxony et al), and do not hesitate to throw some pretty Hohenzollern princesses into the mix; do not wait for your containment to be complete—prepare to concentrate your army at Napoleon's weakest point and strike in the early spring, before Pentecost; by all means, do align with Franz to ensure that he will remain neutral, so that your back is covered, but do not wait for him to recover from his defeat, and do not rely on him to play an important role in your plans. All of the above, if you get going now, can be done by spring. Do it!"

Needless to say, Fr. Wilh. understood—or would have—nothing of it, and in late September 1806 issued an ultimatum that Napoleon predictably took as a declaration of war. Kleist had feared as much: the day after sending *MS* to Marie, he invited Rühle to die together with him in performing a final "good deed" (II:768), by which he may have meant either driving a bullet through Fr. Wilh.'s head (cf. II:761) or joining this ill-fated rushed mobilisation and perishing among the Prussian soldiers. In the event Rühle did join Fr. Wilh.'s army, Kleist did not, Napoleon unleashed the *Ad'A*, and the rest, as they say, is history.[278] Had the King followed his advice, Kleist with *Krug* could indeed have *written history*, possibly helping to avert Prussia's triple catastrophe of *Jena-Auerstedt, Berlin* and *Tilsit*. *MS*' twelfth scene, oft-slammed by critics, is one of the most important pieces of *satirically* writing Kleist produced and delivered. If students of literature like to dismiss it as second-rate poetry, they should pass it on to their colleagues at the history departments, for it is a *historical document of the first order*.

Version Control. We analysed in detail the context of Kleist's submission of *MS*. When Goethe in March 1808 staged *Krug* (his stage adaption is not extant), its original *satyrical* context was no longer compellingly given. Why did Kleist permit Goethe to stage it, seemingly against his own rule that any work had to be politically relevant and up-to-date as and when published? I believe there may be two parts to the answer: one, while the drama's *satirical* content was no longer urgent, it remained pertinent, not only as a *schadenfreudiges* "I told you so" after the fact, but also as a forward looking "next time, let's do it right" manual: Prussia's standing army having been curtailed, building up a militia would be all the more important; her finances being in tatters, a stable reserve currency could raise investor confidence. Two, Kleist wanted the drama to be staged because it was going to be staged by—*Goethe*. Letting Goethe, of all people, stage *Krug* may have been a typical Kleistian manoeuvre: he may have expected that Goethe's staging of this remnant of the very *tetralogy* with which he had hoped to topple him would be such an overwhelming success (not unreasonably: *Krug* probably remains Kleist's most popular drama today) that by staging it Goethe would effectively dethrone himself and lift his successor onto the pedestal. Goethe had personally advertised the play (cf. *LS*,241), but when it tanked, it was Kleist, not Goethe, who was shredded by the critics (cf. *LS*,247;248a; 249). Had Goethe had an inkling of Kleist's manoeuvres? Had he let Kleist fall on his face? Conjectures of this sort on Kleist's part could explain why he went as far as challenging Goethe to a duel (cf. *LS*,252): for Kleist, the staging was but a move in their ongoing fencing match; he had been hit; he launched a riposte. *Alles oder nichts*. At any rate, permitting the staging will have had primarily a *po(i)etical*, as opposed to *satirical*, rationale.

Exonerating the *"verunglückte"* staging (cf. II:835) may well be part of the rationale for publishing the *Ph* fragment: the fragment comprises the highly comical opening scenes and early stages of the court hearing, and Kleist could certainly hope to have fans of comedy on his side, as well as, among those who understood his *satirical* innuendos, all those who were unhappy with Napoleon's sway and the *HRR*'s demise. Apart from being choiceful in his selection of passages, Kleist used the opportunity to make subtle changes, e.g.:

> FRAU MARTHE. Ihr krugzertrümmerndes Gesindel, ihr!
> Ihr loses Pack, das an die Schranken mir,
> Und jeder Pfeiler guter Ordnung rüttelt!
> Ihr sollt mir büßen, Ihr!   (II:838)

The first and fourth lines are in *MS*; the second and third are added. They make us sit up, for their language anticipates *Kohlhaas*' (whose *Ph* fragment, published three months later, sets off with the hero being stopped at a newly erected customs *barrier* and finding the traditional *order* shaken to its foundation *pillars*). *Kohlhaas* is geared towards formenting public opinion against the new order, in which such barriers have been erected across Germany, and new masters call the shots. Compared to *Krug*'s sarcastic, spiteful, boisterous irony, its language is one of angry, aggressive, driven revengefulness. Kleist, it appears, published the *Ph* fragment to begin shifting his *satirical* language, from a cynical, analytical language towards a polemic, goading one.

In early 1811, with *BA* failing and himself in desperate need of cash, Kleist with marginal incremental effort created a marketable "pop" version of *Krug*, featuring a much shortened twelfth scene, in which *MS*' complex ending is turned into an—ostensibly— straightforward "happy end." Economic pressures apart, Kleist had a *satirical* rationale for publishing the text in this revised form, at this point in time: his core advice to his King of August 1806 remained eminently valid in early 1811, namely to avoid at all cost entering an "unholy" union with France, no matter what means of coercion or seduction Napoleon deployed. The book version retains the *MS*' announcement of the "wedding" for the forthcoming Pentecost (cf. V.1953), but whereas in August 1806 the next Pentecost was nine month away, in February 1811 it was a mere three month away, suggesting that Kleist considered the risk of Fr. Wilh. entering an alliance with France to be imminent. On 14th May 1811 Count Herzberg indeed submitted Fr. Wilh.'s offer of an alliance to Napoleon—and in 1811 Pentecost fell on the 25th May! Kleist's decision to publish the book version may well have been triggered by rumours of such an alliance: the only as-of-yet-unpublished material he had ready at hand, and that could be adopted to the situation speedily, was *Krug*. With minimal effort Kleist was thus able to send Fr. Wilh. a warning shot across the bow.

Kleist will have appended *Variant* to the book version (a gesture that has puzzled some readers) because many ideas in *MS*' original, full-length twelfth scene remained broadly relevant, and because it offered Fr. Wilh. an alternative—preparing to strike—to the book version's (un-)"happy" outcome of alliance. The 1811 book, thus, contains two alternative scenarios, and the (discerning) reader, having been sufficiently shocked and awed by the first, "worst case" scenario, will be de delighted by the *Variant*'s detailed narrative for a "best case" one. It is precisely this juxtaposition that makes the book truly impactful.

Krug, Satyrically

Krug abounds in *satyrical* scenes; having first rehearsed it in early letters and album entries, and honed it in *Schroffenstein*, Kleist arguably perfected his *satyrical* vocabulary with *Krug* (as well as *Marquise*).[279] While usually classified as a comedy, this abundance of *satyrical* scenes in combination with its bucolic setting suggests that Kleist may initially have conceived of *Krug* as satyr play in the Attic tradition, even if it ended up as a modern take on Aristophanesian Old Comedy.[280]

Adam is a prolific generator of vulgarities; already in his opening dialogue with Licht, he offers a hilarious recapitulation of the previous night's events:

- "*Erster Auftritt. Adam sitzt und verbindet sich ein Bein*": if "leg" = member, Adam is doctoring his cock;
- "*Zum Straucheln brauchts doch nichts, als Füße*": if "feet," as in *Erdbeben*, = genitals, "*Straucheln*" ("stumbling") refers to risky intercourse;
- "*Auf diesem glatten Boden…*": if this movement, as in *Bettelweib's* "*glitschte mit der Krücke auf dem glatten Boden aus*" (II:196), refers to the male members sliding into the lover's anal or vaginal channel, Adam injured himself during intercourse;
- "*denn jeder trägt / Den leidgen Stein zum Anstoß in sich selbst*": as "*Anstoß*" = "push," "hitting a resistance," and "stone" = "erect, possibly chancreatic, phallus," Adam refers to the nexus of ithyphallic virility and disease;[281]

- "*Der Klumpfuß*": a reference not only to Oedipus and Satan but, together with "*Pferdefuß*" (V.1719), also to the rustic god Pan and the satyrs that accompany him, who feature horse tails and goat hooves;
- "*Mit dem verfluchten Ziegenbock, / Am Ofen focht ich*": if, as in *Bettelweib*, "oven" refers to the rear, Adam sodomised a satyr.[282]

Franz II/I and Napoleon at *Austerlitz*: Adam *"mit dem verfluchten Ziegenbock."*

Not only Adam and the he-goat, but all of the drama's characters are "satyrs"—ithyphallic and bawdy males—, including the *overtly female* figures: Eve is said to have a bib (cf. V.915)—a feature that I argued in *Emigrant*, à propos of *Verlobung*, refers to a codpiece—, and is asked to "stand up" (cf. V.1951); Frau Marthe is shown to be endowed with a "lamp" (cf. V.1028), with which s/he enters Eve's "chamber," and to produce semen (cf. V.1575). The previous evening's battles, *satyrically*, encompassed Dionysiac revel, pederast symposium, and satyr dance.

"Für die gute Zahl." When Adam enumerates three glasses of wine he wants to pour down Walter's throat, "*Eins ist der Herr. Zwei ist das finstre Chaos. / Drei ist die Welt. Drei Gläser lob ich mir*" (V.1532-3), he not only, *satiricall,y* depicts Franz offering Napoleon supremacy over the *HRR*, but also, *satirically*, alludes to the "*FFF*" constellation: "Herr" = *erastês*; "*das finstre Chaos*" = the *erômenos*' gaping hole; "*die Welt*" = a crowd of *dmotes*.[283] The wine links Adam's (and the *HRR*'s) sacrifice not only to Christ's crucifixion (via the *Last Supper*), but also to Dionysos' sparagmus. Kleist in *Krug* juxtaposes a "*Dionysian*"— *corporeal, uninhibited*—mode of reconciliation, involving free flow of wine and seminal fluid, to the *"Apollonian"—cerebral, regulated—* mode pursued by diplomats, involving back-room arm-twisting and theatre visits. For Kleist, Napoleon and Haugwitz haggling in the loges of the *Schlosstheater,* or Metternich and Alex. I (in 1815) in the ante-chambers of Viennese ballrooms, while *"Der Kongress Tanzt,"* would have seemed anodyne in comparison with his own steamy "reconciliation scenes," which comprise not mere vulgar expressions of his personal fantasies, but profound reflections on the nature of human relationship, reconciliation and social cohesion: contemporary society, Kleist may have felt, had become atomised and alienated not least because it lacked the experience of joint male sensual ecstasy that had been such a fundamental Attic institution.

"Der Krüge schönster" *(II).* If the "most beautiful jug" *satirically* symbolises the *HRR, satyrically* it may constitute a sex toy Eve keeps in her room for erotic stimulation: *"zum Scheuern"* = "for rubbing" (V.2211). Delftware quite frequently comes in shapes similarly to that of the *girandole,* whose phallic properties Kleist praises elsewhere (cf. II:673):

Marthe's jug? FLTR: recent theatre prop; three (phallic) pieces of delftware; *girandole.*

More intriguingly still, for a scion of the Kleist family a jar (a vessel similar to a jug) entailed a *familial* reference, namely to the *Kleistian* or *Leyden jar* (*boteille de Leyden*), the world's first practical electrical condenser and proto-battery, invented in 1745 by Kleist's distant relative Ewald Georg von Kleist, and subsequently further developed at Leiden University:

Marthe's Kleistian jar?[284]

Public demonstrations of electricity condensed with the help of Kleistian jars became popular during the second half of the 18th century, involving, e.g., the application of electric shocks to a human chain connected to the device, which caused convulsions in the experiment's subjects known as "*Kleistscher Stoß*" ("Kleistian shock," "blow," or "thrust"; also known as "galvanic shock"). Georg Chr. Lichtenberg, the first German university professor of experimental physics, noted in his famously irreverent *Sudelbücher* (1764) that "a few years ago, in Paris, one believed to have discovered that the Kleistian shock invariably led to impotence." Given that his works are saturated with electro-magnetic events and metaphors, and his characters are regularly electrified, as well as castrated or otherwise rendered impotent, Kleist could well have been familiar with such stories; it is probable that he had read the *Sudelbücher*, for his teacher Martini is known to have been fond of them (cf. *LS*,34a).

Kleist's frequent references to "*Anstoß*" or "*Stoß*," including in *Krug*'s opening scene, may routinely correspond at once to the thrust of the male member, the "Kleistian shock" generated by a Kleistian jar, and the electrifying moment of *jouissance*—as well as, *satirically* speaking, to the moment at which an enemy army's centre is smashed by a concentrated cannonade: Kleist's *satirical* equivalent of the Kleistian jar was Napoleon's *Grande batterie,* the tactical concentration of artillery firepower Kleist refers to throughout his œuvre, most obviously in *Cäcilie*, where he equates the power of organ music with that of the *Grande batterie*, anticipating a similar analogy drawn by German WWII soldiers awed by Russian rocket launchers; since the events in Eve's room *satirically* depict a battle, Kleist's underlying topos of the equivalence of *Erôs* and *Agôn* here finds its succinct and plastic expression in the equivalence of a battery of Kleistian jars and a battery of cannons:

"Grande batteries" (FLTR): battery of Leyden jars (c.1750); cannonade of Mainz (1793); Katyusha rocket launchers (aka *"Stalinorgeln"*) at Stalingrad (1942).[285]

Eve's using Marthe's "jug" "for rubbing" is consistent with it being a Kleistian jar: cradling the jar's glass with one hand closes the electric circuit, while rubbing it with the other generates triboelectric charge. If Marthe's Kleistian jar serves as sex toy, the revellers are erotically stimulated at the same time by mechanical phallic thrusts and by electrical shocks.[286] Just as Lichtenberg's experimental subjects, by holding each others' hands to create a human chain connected to a Kleistian jar, each receive a Kleistian chock, Kleist's ithyphallic satyrs, by sodomising the one in front to create a "daisy chain" conntect to Marthe's "jug," each enjoy electrostimulation. If *Marionettentheater*'s puppets are recharged by their "brushing" (*"streifen"*) off the stage, *Krug*'s satyrs are electrified by the Kleistian shock generated by Eve's "rubbing" Marthe's jar, and if Ewald Georg von Kleist invented the first electrical battery, Heinrich von Kleist perhaps imagined the first electrosex machine. The *agalma*, the *objet petit a*, at the centre of the orgies/battles in Eve's bedroom is not only *everyone's favourite Empire*, but also *everyone's favourite electrostimulator*.[287]

Manoeuvres sur les derrières. The *Ulm Campaign* entered the annals of warfare not least because of Napoleon's audacious *manoeuvres sur les derrières,* the bypassing and encircling from behind of enemy units, then arrayed around the city of Ulm (a manoeuvre whose most famous replicant would be the 1905 *Schlieffen Plan*). Since the orgiastic battle in Eve's bedroom re-enacts *Ulm*, its well-armed, ithyphallic lover-soldiers are performing a concatenation of "*manoeuvres sur les derrières*" on stage. Ruprecht's "crashing into Eve's room" from behind ejects Adam from Eve's open "window," thereby pulling down the jug to which he is connected by his wig, smashing the jug precisely in the instant in which Adam, Eve and Ruprecht form a *"FOF"* constellation or "double penetration" (cf. V.1230-7), and just before in quick sucession Frau Marthe, neighbours Ralf and Hinz, aunts Sus, Lies and Brigitte, and the holy couple Joseph and Maria (cf. V.2259-73) "crash" into the one before them till they form a "daisy chain" plugged into Eve in the manner in which Lichtenberg's human chain is plugged into the Kleistian jar:

 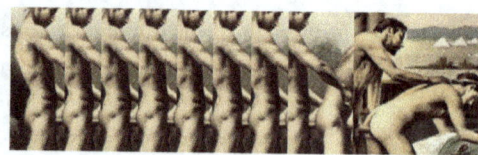

La chambre d'Ève: manoeuvres sur les derrières, style Napoléon et style Kleist.[288]

Eve's room is the quintessential Kleistian *Kampfplatz-cum-Lustgarten, satirically* representing the battlegrounds of *Ulm* littered with corpses and dropped weapons, *satyrically* a symposium's *andrōn* littered with blood, semen, dildos and electrosex gear. Later, in court, a bunch of shame-faced, sheepish German satyrs (princes, ministers, envoys, generals) appear before a hapless Emperor, a mumbling *Germania*, and a haughty conqueror to explain how in their unbridled orgiastic battle they allowed the precious "jug" to be blown to bits. No wonder they offer such muddled testimonies: everyone is dazed, everyone is implicated.

Krug, Syphilitically

Licht, who evidently "knows" Adam's "feet" just as well as *Erdbeben*'s cobbler does Josephe's, in the opening scene observes that Adam's "clubfoot" "travels the path of sinfulness," and contrasts its "bulkiness" with the "dislocated" right foot's "slithery-ness" (a feature condusive to anal intercourse). Adam evidently disposes of an entire collection of prostheses or dildos—a *"Sack voll Knochen"* (V.192)—, but his bloody leg stump prevents him from re-attaching

one of them in lieu of the "monument" he left behind and relegates him to "dancing" with his deformed, diseased "club foot." When he showcases his "clubfoot" to Walter and Licht, Walter opines that "it's a good foot" (V.1821), whereupon Adam promptly affirms that it is "good for dancing," as if in this moment making up his mind that henceforth he shall uninhibitedly fornicate with his diseased member (*satirically*, rule as Franz I of Austria).[289]

"Fiedel." The proliferation of prosthetic or strap-on phallic devices—Adam's *"Knochen"* and *"Monument,"* Ruprecht's *"Muskete"* (V.458), the corporal's *"Holzgebein"* (V.471), Eve's *"Fiedel"* (V.488)— suggests that disease and mutilation are as commonplace in Husum (Germany) as are the dionysiac revels whose inevitable corollary they constitute. Kleist, then, equates Germany with a "brotherhood" of "satyrs." For Kleist's imagery there is ample literary and artistic precedence: dildos feature, e.g., in Aristophanes' *Lysistrata* and in Shakespeare's *The Winter's Tale*, in Greek vase art and in medieval Chinese records; peglegs will have been prevalent in war-time. In male-to-male intercourse, dildos (typically made from wood, stone, clay, bone or ivory) may indeed come in handy for addressing the twin challenges of "coyness" (impenetrability due to contraction of anal sphincters) and infectiousness.[290]

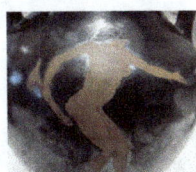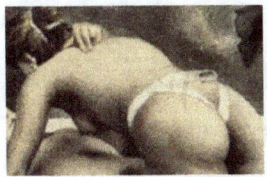

"Bones" and "Monuments": dildo (c.490 BC); strap-on dildo (c.1900); pegleg (c.1807).

"Sodom und Gomorrha." The repeated references to the sinful cities purified by YHWH with sulphur and fire add to an atmosphere as *musty* and *miasmatic* as it is *rustic*. *Krug*'s courtroom, like *Guiskard*'s camp, is pervaded by sulphurous fumes that mark the courthouse (i.e., Vienna) as *Pesthaus*, and whose main source is evidently Adam himself, who apart from a deformed member also sports

a putrefying rear: "*Ihr habt zwo Wunden, vorne ein' und hinten*" (V.1467); "*Rect' aus Limburg, gnädiger Herr*" (V.1486); "*Feu'r fällt vom Himmel auf mein sündig Haupt, [...] / Brennt sie wie Sodom und Gomorrha schon*" (V.1492-7); "*und hinter ihm / Erstinkts wie Dampf von Pech und Haar und Schwefel*" (V.1686-7); "*wo Schwefeldämpfe von sich lassend*" (V.1767); "*Die Eur' ist ja im Feuer, / Wie Sodom und Gomorrha, aufgegangen*" (V.1846-7). Kleist's Vienna encompasses a veritable Pieter Brueghel-ian, Peter Greenaway-ian, scatological *Schlaraffenland* inundated with the plasticity and foul odour of decay and decomposition: "rectal" Limburg *Stinkekäse* (V.1486), "cow's cheese" (V.194), "foul fish" (V. 773), "raven's carrion" (V.1318), "carp" (V.1613), "snorting cat" (V.1770), "rat" (V.1903).[291]

"**Pips.**" Like *Guiskard's* plague and *Schroffenstein's* poison, *Krug's* pip represents the propagation of syphilis, whose main vector of transmission is Adam. Pip (a contagious disease of birds) is explicitly equated with the plague (cf. V.839), associated with a male member deformed by syphilis (cf. "*Kloß von Nudeln*"; V.840), and said to have been transmitted by guinea fowl from "India" (as I noted, syphilis was believed to have been imported from the West Indies). Adam's seeking to "gavage" (V.560) this bird is a pretext for visiting Eve suggests that Eve *syphilitically* functions as a *healer*—not of birds (cf. V.1590-4), but of men: "*Nun, Evchen, höre, / Dreh du mir deine Pille ordentlich*" (V.1610-11; "*Pillendreher*" = "pharmacist"). The "pill" refers not only to the tale Adam wants Eve to spin in order to shield him (Eve = "spin doctor"), but also to the therapy he seeks from her for the "lumb" on his "noodle" (Eve = "quack doctor"); "gavaging a bird" may be code for both "infecting" and "ingesting a remedy," so that Adam is visiting Eve in her "bedroom" for a satyr revel-cum-therapeutic session.

"**Der Krüge schönster**" *(III).* Eve's apparent role as healer or therapist points to the "jug" located in her bedroom being a device not only for the *generation of pleasure*, but also for the *treatment of disease*, perhaps one Kleist had had personal experiences with, say, when undergoing "electrotherapy" or "electromagnetic therapy," on the basis of Mesmerian or Puységurian *magnetism*, or of Galvanian or Aldinian *bioelectricity*.[292] Kleist's jug could, e.g., represent a *Mesmerschen Kübel* or *Mesmer-Bottich* (*baquet*, Mesmerian bucket), a device in part based on a Kleistian jar, with the help of which Mesmer from c.1780 onwards conducted collective magnetic *séances* with up to twenty patients, which became popular social events known as "*baquet*" (the name applying to both the device and the event). Mesmer was working in Paris in 1801, and while we have no record of Kleist meeting him in person, it is certainly possible that he did; at any rate, Kleist could have participated in" *baquets*," whether performed by Mesmer himself or by one of his students or imitators.

A rare surviving Mesmerian bucket on display in Lyon is described by an English physician as follows:

> In a medical museum in Lyon there is a strange tub-like object constructed of oak and decorated with lengths of ornately woven rope. About six inches in from the rim, eight evenly spaced iron rods sprout up from a highly polished lid. In the eighteenth century, a group of patients would sit or stand around this device in such a way as to press the afflicted areas of their bodies against these moveable metal wishbones and, bound to the instrument by the ropes, would link fingers to complete an "electric" circuit. The atmosphere in which these sessions took place was heavy with incense and séance-like; the music of a glass harmonica (invented by Benjamin Franklin) provided a haunting soundtrack, and thick drapes, mirrors, and astrological symbols decorated the opulent, half-lit room.[293]

Marthe's bucket.

Eve's bedroom evidently represents a Parisian-style *salon* or "crisis room" quite in line with the above description, in which Marthe's Mesmerian bucket is installed, and in which the members of Huisum's *haute volée* convene for "*baquets*".[294] The same English physician reports observing a "*baquet*":

> In the middle of the room is placed a vessel of about a foot and a half high which is called here a "baquet." It is so large that twenty people can easily sit round it; near the edge of the lid which covers it, there are holes pierced corresponding to the number of persons who are to surround it; into these holes are introduced iron rods, bent at right angles outwards, and of different heights, so as to answer to the part of the body to which they are to be applied. Besides these rods, there is a rope which communicates between the baquet and one of the patients, and from him is carried to another, and so on the whole round. The most sensible effects are produced on the approach of Mesmer, who is said to convey the fluid by certain motions of his hands or eyes, without touching the person. I have talked with several who have witnessed these effects, who have convulsions occasioned and removed by a movement of the hand.[295]

Eve's bedroom.

Mesmerian magnetism postulates that the transmission of "*fluidum*," or "*fluide universel*," to a medium's body via connection with the bucket, together with the manipulation of its flow across her body by the motion of the *magnétiseur*'s hands, produces a "crisis" in the medium; Gudrun Debriacher (*Rede*, 34) adds that "*Zum mechanischen Druck und den Streichbewegungen kam noch das typische Anstarren des Patienten hinzu… Vorboten der späteren Hypnose.*"

Now, Adam ostensibly visits Eve in her room to sign Ruprecht's medical certificate in exchange for intercourse (anal, presumably); yet as soon as he completes both tasks (cf. V.2201-4) he does something else, as Eve recounts: *"Legt er [...] Dint und Feder auf den Tisch, / Und rückt den Stuhl herbei sich [...] / Und hängt [...] / [the wig] auf den Krug dort, den zum Scheuern ich / Bei mir aufs Wandgesimse hingestellt. [...] / Läßt er am Tisch jetzt auf den Stuhl sich nieder, / Und faßt mich so, bei beiden Händen, seht, / Und sieht mich an [...] / Zwei abgemessene Minuten starr mich an"* (V.2200-17). In other words, having completed their business transaction, Adam and Eve are having a *séance*, whereby Adam attaches his afflicted body part—his genitals: "ink sac" and "feather"—to the bucket, by means not of the ornately woven *robes* observed by the English physician, but of his similarly ornately woven justice's *wig*, and stares at Eve for two motionless minutes, during which she mesmerises or hypnotises him.

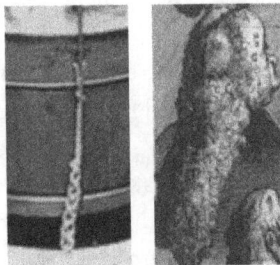

Mesmer's ornately woven bucket robe; Adam's ornately woven justice's wig.

Once entranced, he requests her to open her "window" (cf. V.2226)—which she had "closed" (cf. V.2203), and he himself had "boltet" (cf. V.2207), presumably with a chastity belt—; when she complies, he impregnates her in his somnambulant state, guiding his "ink and feather" to her window" (V.2225) and pushing up the heavenly Jacob's ladder—"stool, chair, cornice"—of her vagina. In that moment Ruprecht, from behind, "crashes into her room" (cf. V.2237), while Adam receives a Kleistian shock and "crashes out of her window," thereby pulling down from the cornice (cf. V.2235-6) the bucket to which he remains attached by his wig (cf. V.2234); the bucket crashes onto the floor and bursts into pieces just as the other participants, one after another, "enter" and "crash" into Ruprecht and each other (forming a "daisy chain"): *"die Mutter, / [...] hebt die Lamp und fällt ergrimmt, / [...] den Ruprecht / [...] an. / [...] Nachbar Ralf fällt ihn, / [...] und Nachbar Hinz ihn an, / Und Muhme Sus' und Lies und Frau Brigitte [...] / Und: Joseph, [...] und Maria"* (V. 2245-72).

Eve, presumably having continuously been rubbing the bucket, has become so electromagnetically super-charged that she turns into a greenish-phosphoric shimmering magnet, akin to the steel magnets used in some *"baquets"*: *"Jetzt steh ich noch, / Goldgrün, wie Flammen rings, umspielt es mich"* (V.2243-4).[296] In her electromagnetic "crisis," Eve's two "poles" (rear, front) exert an irresistible force on all satyrs in her vicinity: an *attractive* force on those whose polarity is opposite to that of whichever of her two poles they face in that moment—the nine ithyphallic satyrs, facing her rear pole—, and an irresistible *repulsive* force on those whose polarity is the same as that of her pole they face—Adam, facing her front pole—, such that the former are unstoppably pulled into her, and into each other, the latter, forcefully repulsed from her, the blowback being so strong that it catapults Adam out of her "window" and into the "bushes" (pubic hair) beneath.

The *physical cause* of the jug's shattering are the electromagnetic forces at play between the polarity of Eve's two "magnetic" poles (her rear, anal, or "+" pole; her front, vaginal, or "-" pole) and the respective polarities of the patients: if Adam and Ruprecht are both negatively ("-") charged, Ruprecht *can not help but* "crash into" Eve's rear or "+" pole, and Adam *can not help but* "crash out of" her vaginal or "-" pole. If we take "**+O-**" to depict the supercharged "magnet" Eve with her twin (anal and vaginal) polarities, "**F**" to represent Ruprecht and the other satyrs, crashing respectively into her and each other, and an inverted "**F**" to denote Adam in the moment of his repulsion, whereby he pulls down the bucket to which he remains attached, we can graphically depict this "crisis" as follows:

Eve-*Bavaria*, at the centre of the *Ulm Campaign*, is so *attractive* to Ruprecht-Beauharnais and the French generals invading from the west that they cannot help but be pulled into her; she is so *repulsive* to Adam-Franz approaching from the east that he cannot help but be pushed out through the "window" (the Danube valley). The battle's outcome, Kleist indicates, was a matter of *physical laws*, and as such, always already predetermined. That the *HRR* was shattered in the event, however, was due to *negligence*: Franz, unlike Kleist's old woman, who let go lest she be waltzed to death, did not let go. "*Und sie wissen, was dies auf [das HRR] für einen Effekt macht. Ich lache darüber, wenn ich es denke*" (II:795). What a compelling instance of Kleistian "*Physiognomie des Augenblicks!*"

Eve's nod, "*sie nickte mit dem Kopf bloß*," in response to Marthe's imploring her to affirm that it was Ruprecht who impregnated her, is no more than an effect of electric discharge: as her body-battery gradually reverts to neutral, its discharge materialises as a twitching of her head that, akin to the twitching of the master of ceremony's upper lip that, Kleist in *Über die allmähliche Verfertigung* claims tongue-in-cheek, triggered the French Revolution (cf. II:321). Eve's nod is a purely mechanical electro-physiognomical effect that in itself means—*nothing*. She does not lie: her head simply twitches. Eve, and the other characters, are indeed mere "*Puppen am Drahte des Schicksals.*"

Krug, Po(i̇)etically

On 25th April 1811 Kleist tells Fouqué, "*[Krug] kann auch, aber nur für einen sehr kritischen Freund, für eine Tinte meines Wesens gelten; es ist nach dem Tenier gearbeitet, und würde nichts wert sein, käme es nicht von einem, der in der Regel lieber dem göttlichen Raphael nachstrebt*" (II:862).

Teniers. In *Marionettentheater*, Kleist refers to the motif of dancing peasants found in works by David Teniers the Younger (1610-90): "*Eine Gruppe von vier Bauern, die nach einem raschen Takt die Ronde tanzte, hätte von Teniers nicht hübscher gemalt werden können*" (II:339).[297] Teniers was a prodigal producer of bawdy and irreverent paintings, and his tableaux of frivolous village feasts (e.g., *Kermis on St. George's Day*, c.1664-7, below left) are as inundated with erotic symbolism as his impressions of rustic country life (e.g., *A Barn Interior*, c.1650, below right):

"*Eine Gruppe von vier Bauern*" (II:339);
"*Im kühlen Topf von frischgekernter Butter*" (V.2384)

Teniers' thinly disguised satyr revels and voyeuristic peeps could indeed have furnished Kleist with blueprints for scenes such as that in Eve's bedroom; Veit Tümpel is introduced as "peasant," implying that his son Ruprecht and sisters Sus, Lies and Brigitte belong to the same "profession": rustic "satyrs" and *dmotes*.[298]

Teniers' irreverent motifs will have delighted Kleist, among them his prolific depictions of aristocrats disguised as costumed apes sporting phallic feather hats; Kleist's depiction of French and German aristocrats mimicks Teniers'—compare, e.g., Teniers' *Gesellschaft Kostümierter Affen* (undated, below left) with one of Adolph Menzel's sketches for *Krug* (1876-7, below right):

"*Gesellschaft Kostümierter Affen.*"

Another one of Teniers' stock motifs, the crucified Christ depicted as gutted animal—cf., e.g., *Butcher Shop* (1642, below left) and *In the Kitchen* (1669, second from left)—anticipates the Poe-esque techniques of camouflage Kleist deploys in his works: everything is in the open, and one only has to put aside one's "green glasses" to *see*, with Wittgenstein, not only *this* carcass, but also *as* Christ:

Adam in the butcher shop? (FLTR: 2x Teniers; Rubens; Scorzelli).²⁹⁹

Kleist is as irreverent as Teniers when it comes to parodying Christianity: the "saviour" announced repeatedly in *Krug* is none other than Napoleon (whom Kleist no doubt would have loved to see gutted and hung up to dry). Kleist and Teniers indeed had much in common, and while Teniers' influence pervades Kleist's entire œuvre, *Krug* could be said to be his most "Teniersian" work.³⁰⁰

Raphael. If Teniers is irreverent, Raphael (1483-1520), in Kleist's own words, is "divine," which in the context of the conventional aesthetics of his time would have implied "pure," "perfect," "august," "spiritual." Yet Kleist would not have been Kleist if he had not also meant something else, something idiosyncratic, and he offers a hint at what this might be in an album entry of 1801: *"Es gibt Menschen, wie die ersten Arabesken; man versteht sie nicht, wenn man nicht Raphael ist"* (*LS*,51d). Only Raphael, says Kleist, was able to understand *and* authentically portray the soul of even the most inscrutable subjects, and for Kleist this was indeed a "divine" skill to emulate. In a letter to Adolphine of November 1801 (cf. II:701-2) he recalls observing, at the Louvre, Raphael's *Transfiguration* (1516-20), *Saint Michael Slaying the Devil* (1518) and *Saint John the Baptist Preaching* (1505), whose subjects' "transfigured" faces for him perhaps expressed expectancy, awe, ecstasy and agony before a "divine" lover; one cannot help imagining that Kleist associated Raphael's faces with those of his lovers in moments of supreme ecstasy or agony, and that he pictured his own characters with Raphaelian faces projected onto the masks worn by the actors. If from Teniers Kleist adopted frivolously "dancing" bodies and erotic symbols, from Raphael he gleaned authentically ecstatic physiognomies.[301]

The painting by Raphael that most intrigued Kleist was the *Sistine Madonna* (1512), which he repeatedly viewed at Dresden's Gemäldegalerie, and of which he noted in a letter to Wilhelmine of 21st May 1801 (II:650-1), "*mit Umrissen, die mich zugleich an zwei geliebte Wesen erinnerten,*" suggesting that what fascinated him in Raphael's painting were the "*silhouettes*" or "*outlines*" of the figures portrayed. What stands out in Raphael's painting is Mary's prominent headscarf, which envelops her and the child, and by which Raphael indicated the presence of the (unportrayable) divine Father. Given Kleist's proto-Freudian mindset, it may be helpful for us to recall Freud's conjecture that Mary's similarly prominent drapery in Leonardo da Vinci's *The Virgin and Child with St. Anne* (c.1503) entails the outline of a vulture, a figure Freud interpreted as manifestation of da Vinci's passive homosexual childhood fantasies (cf. below, left, Freud's "vulture" outlined in blue).[302] I offer that what Kleist discerned in Raphael's painting (below, right) was, on the one hand, the presence of Wilhelmine with their baby boy and himself as *father* (the headscarf), and on the other, a "*FFF*" constellation (three male lovers, outlined in red, yellow and green):

Freudian and Kleistian "silhouettes."[303]

His superimposition of a *familial* and a *satyrical* constellation onto Raphael's painting could have triggered Kleist's idea of *the possibility of achieving both aspirations at once*, the pursuance of which became his "*Lebensplan.*"

"Zusammengetztes Lustspiel." Ernst Ribbart notes, *"Der zerbrochne Krug ist ein schwieriges Stück. Wer behauten wollte, einen Interpretationsansatz gefunden zu haben, der alle Elemente des Textes zu einer einheitlichen Bedeutung zusammenfügte, der würde sich—und andere—täuschen."*[304] Kleist himself, in his introduction to the *Ph* fragment, refers to *Krug* as *"zusammengesetzt"* (I:835), no doubt having in mind the distinct periods of the drama's genesis, and the diverse occasions of its various versions' communication or publication, which necessarily led to shifts in *satirical* content and style; this "composite" nature, to an extent, became paradigmatic for dramas with lengthy and complex geneses, most notably *Käthchen*.[305] I have sought to show that despite the complexities that come with the drama's lengthy genesis, and consequently "composite" nature, the consistency of Kleist's themes and "code," be it in the domain of *The Satirical, The Satyrical* or *The Syphilitical*, ensures that (*pace*, Ribbard) "all elements of the text" *can* be integrated "into one unitary meaning": not necessarily on the *overt* level, but on the level of each of these "threads."

"Kreuzgeflecht." Having been ejected from Eve's "window," Adam becomes entangled in a *"Spalier"* ("trellis," "lattice"; V.976; 1522; 1625), or *"Kreuzgeflecht"* ("crossed mesh"; V.1627), evidently installed to tame the vines and bushes into which he fell beneath the window. I already noted that this passage refers to Adam-Franz being badly bruised at *Austerlitz*, whose battlefield indeed was set among vinyards and their orderly patterns of rows of vines. *"Spalier stehen"* means "to form a guard of honour," and troops in attack formation can be said to form "trellis," "lattice" or "crossed mesh" patterns:

Austerlitz: The "lattice" entangles Adam-Franz II/I.

Kleist clearly respected Napoleon's ability to impose order onto a battlefield (and a political landscape) in a manner that to him may have reflected a distinctly French, *rationalist*, mind. In *Findling*, Nicolo's wife is named *Parquet*, which I argued in *Emigrant* (p.347) may refer to the orderly pattern of administrative units first envisaged by French revolutionaries and later implemented by Napoleon, not only in the French Empire, but to a significant degree also in Germany, whose historically grown patchwork of states he rationalised in a series of treaties, showcasing the rationalist order he envisioned for Europe as a whole. At the same time, Kleist recognised that what made Napoleon apparently invincible, was that in the *kairotic* moment in which it mattered, he could overturn the very order he had imposed and make a sudden, intuitive move that dealt the unsuspecting enemy the deathblow (Kleist's frequent analogy of Jupiter's thunderbolt is apt).

In how far did Kleist seek to apply similar techniques to his own works?[306] As said, the *overt* textual fabric or surface text(ure) of his works is generated by his interweaving or enmeshing multiple *covered* "threads" with the help of *"pescheräic"* words, metaphors, and codes and in an intricate interplay of mathematical precision and artistic playfulness. To encode *The Satirical, The Satyrical*, and *The Syphilitical*, Kleist required a grid or tabulation of equivalences:

	The Syphilitical	*The Satyrical*	*The Satirical*
Objective	curative/palliative	erotic	agonistic
Occasion	séance, *baquet*	orgy, revel, symposium	battle, peace negotiat
Participants	*magnétiseur*, mediums	*erastai, erómenoi, dmotes*	rulers, envoys, genera
Tools	Kleistian jar/Mesmerian bucket	electrosex gear	cannons, pens
Constellation	"FFFFFFFFO"	"FFF," "FOF," "FFO"	*sur les derrières*
Krisis	Kleistian shock/Mesmerian crisis	ecstatic orgasm, swoon	Grande batterie, cong
Outcome	brief respite/temporary idyll	satisfaction, infection	truce, peace terms

The occasions or events that fascinated Kleist most—the *baquet*, the *banquet*, the *battle*—entail an inherently chaotic, primordial, feral, Dionysiac streak, which is no doubt precisely what made them so intriguing to him, but which also called for his imposition of order:

Dionysiac chaos: *Baquet, Banquet* and *Bataille* (I).

It is, arguably, with *Krug* that Kleist became fully conscious of his role as poet being akin to that of the *magnétiseur,* puppeteer or supreme commander: he who harnesses, orchestrates and manipulates those enrolled and implicated in these events—rulers, lovers, warriors.

Apolloniac order: *Baquet, Banquet* and *Bataille* (II).

Commencing with *Krug,* Kleist in his dramas would henceforth impose an Apolloniac order onto his Dionysiac revelries and fantasies—and in doing so, *pull the strings.* Yet every now and then, he would throw in an intuitive twist, an instance of the "*Physiognomie des Augenblicks,*" allowing the Dionysiac chaos to break through the Apolloniac order and *spice it up.*

2.4 *Amphitryon*: Endless Night at Königsberg
(Another Urgent Manifesto to The King)

Genesis and Context. *Amphitryon. Ein Lustspiel nach Molière* was published by Arnold in Dresden in May 1807, with a foreword by A. Müller.[307] Two opionions prevail in the Kleist reception as to the timing of the drama's completion: in the spring of 1807, while Kleist was imprisoned at Fort de Joux and Châlons-sur-Marne, or in late 1806 in Königsberg, or even prior to that. Similarly, two views prevail regarding its commencement: in 1803, soon after Kleist met Falk, then working on his own adaptation of the material, or in 1805-6 in Königsberg.[308] As the subtitle suggests, Kleist's version is based on Molière's, from which Kleist translated and incorporated passages.[309]

"Jetzt, Freund, mußt du an deinen Anfang denken." Kleist's opening scene, featuring Sosias rehearsing the message he is to convey to Alkmene on behalf of Amphitryon, is a veritable gem. If Sosias' message was straightforward—say, along the lines of the legendary Marathon runner Pheidippides' "we have won!"—he would not have to *rehearse* it: one rehearses a sophisticated lie or deception, scarcely a simple truth. In the case of the *Battle of Marathon,* the distance to Athens was considerable (42 km, or so we assume), and apparently no horse was available, Pheidippides was presumably chosen to deliver the *breaking news* to the Athenians on account of his speed and stamina as a runner; in the case of Kleist's *Battle of Pharissa,* Sosias was evidently chosen on account not of his running, but his oratory skills ("*Rednerkunst,*" V.35). Since a horse *was* available for him (cf. V.28), why did he sneak and stagger back to Thebes through the darkness of the night, instead of waiting till daybreak and riding to Thebes triumphantly on horseback? If victory *was* his, why did Amphitryon not return in person to announce the *good news* to his wife and people, rather than sending Sosias and delaying his own return: "*so früh nicht, als er wünscht*" (V.63-4)?

These curious circumstances make us weary of Sosias' story; indeed it appears as if he not so much *rehearses*, as *invents*, it: his oddly-worded prompt to himself, "*Jetzt, Freund, mußt du an deinen*

Anfang denken" (V.32), compels us to read *"denken"* as *"ausdenken"* — in other words, it dawns on us that Sosias may be cooking up his story. Sosias, who by his own admission during the entire battle not once peeked, let alone ventured, outside his tent (cf. V.39-40), in crafting his story is following Amphitryon's instructions: the *news* he is preparing to pass to Alkmene is at best *second-hand news*, at worst *fake news*. Again by his own admission, his story is a "cumbersome," "convoluted" (cf. V.74) "rant" and "harangue" (cf. V.62)—and so it is: instead of from the Thebans', he sets out to relate the events from the opposing Athenians' perspective, which turns his account into storytelling, rather than the reporting of facts:

> [...] der Feind.
> Nachdem er ein Gelübd zum Himmel jetzt gesendet,
> Daß Euch der Wolkenkreis erzitterte,
> Stürzt, die Befehle treffend rings gegeben,
> Er gleich den Strömen brausend auf uns ein.
> Wir aber, minder tapfer nicht, wir zeigten
> Den Rückweg ihm,—und Ihr sollt gleich sehen, wie?
> Zuerst begenet' er dem Vortrab hier;
> Der wich. Dann stieß er auf die Bogenschützen dort;
> Die zogen sich zurück. Jetzt dreist gemacht, rückt er
> Den Schleudrern auf den Leib; die räumen ihm das Feld
> Und als verwegen jetzt dem Hauptkorps er sich nahte,
> Stürzt dies—halt! Mit dem Hauptkorps ists nicht richtig.
> Ich höre ein Geräusch dort, wie mir deucht.   (V.85-98)

In Sosias' account the Athenians are advancing everywhere, the Thebans retreating on all fronts; when he gets to the battle's climax, the decicive clash of the two armies' main corps, he lets slip that something was not right with the Theban corps, then—suddenly pauses. Ostensibly he is distracted by a noise; since he never picks up his thread again, the audience remains in the dark as to what happened at the battle's climax: the decisive moment remains hidden by a quintessential Kleistian ellipsis.[310] What Sosias' convoluted sophistry amounts to, I offer, is this: the Thebans in fact experienced not victory but defeat. Kleist almost imperceptively *inverts* the original story's starting point—Amphitryon returning victorious—into that of Amphitryon, defeated in battle, meekly delaying his return, and instead of facing his wife and people, sending the glib Sosias to artfully prepare them for the unpalatable *bad news*.[311] This *inversion* present in the drama's very opening sequence alerts the reader: *nothing* in Kleist's version can be assumed to simply carbon-copy or re-state Molière's, or any other, earlier version.

Sosias inadvertently informs the audience about the cause of the Thebans' defeat: while reporting that the Athenians successfully solicited the support of Jupiter, the mightiest of gods—"*der Feind. / Nachdem er ein Gelübd zum Himmel jetzt gesendet, / Daß Euch der Wolkenkreis erzitterte*" (V.85-7)—, he makes no mention of the Thebans having similarly obtained divine succour. If they did not, by classical convention their war was doomed from the start, and Amphitryon was reckless in the extreme.[312] Even before he usurps Amphitryon's bedroom, Kleist's Jupiter thus already vanquished him on the battlefield, and not Sosias' crafty story, but the *tiara* Amphitryon brings Alkmene, conveys the truth: Alkmene finds engraved therein, contrary to her expectation, but, as we now realise, appropriately, the letter "J."

"von endloser Länge." "*Es ist Nacht*"; Merkur—Jupiter's sidekick as well as his son—with the help of his proverbial winged feet has arrived at Amphitryon's palace long before Sosias, to make arrangements for the "endless night" (V.111) the victorious Jupiter will spend with Alkmene. His father already having put Phoebus into a slumber (cf. V.117-8) and delayed Aurora's rise (cf. V.507), Merkur now sets Thebes' sun dial back by five hours, so that his master shall enjoy an extended night, of seventeen hours, with Alkmene (cf. V.520), undisturbed by her household or the returning Amphitryon.[313] An "endless night" has fallen on Amphitryon's palace and kingdom—his army vanquished by a superior warrior, his palace usurped, his wife seduced by a superior lover—; yet Kleist's inversion of Amphitryon's victory into defeat also turns Jupiter's claim on Alkmene from sly opportunism into victor's justice: having vanquished his opponent in battle, Jupiter merely takes what by ancient convention is due to him, and which Amphitryon negligently gambled away by hubristically confronting an army under the tutelage of the mightiest of gods. Kleist's Amphitryon is neither mere horned husband (a *comical* figure), nor pure *tragic* hero (he who commits the *harmatia* par excellence of *hubris against the mightiest of gods*), but something of a fool: Kleist's anti-hero, instead of stemming himself against fate, digs his own grave.[314]

"Was ich empfinde." Having consummated their "endless night," Alkmene implores her divine lover, whose "arrows" penetrated her "bosom" and filled her deserted "house," to stay with her in the privacy of her palace:

> [...] Ach, wie
> So lästig ist so viel Ruhm, Geliebter!
> Wie gern gäb ich das Diadem, das du
> Erkämpft, für einen Strauß von Veilchen hin,
> Um eine niedre Hütte eingesammelt.
> Was brauchen wir, als nur uns selbst? [...]
> Doch dieser flüchtge Reiz, kann er vergelten,
> Was ich empfinde, wenn im wilden Treffen
> Der Pfeil auf diesen teuern Busen zielt?
> Wie öd ist, ohne dich, dies Haus! [...]   (V.423-37)

Kleist offers a subtle hint that despite his "perfect" guise as Amphitryon, Alkmene from the beginning recognises, perhaps initially unconsciously, Jupiter *as* Jupiter (whose guise, therefore, may be *im*perfect): the violet is the flower of Io, one of the mortal lovers of Zeus, who incurred Hera's wrath; Alkmene longs for a whole bunch of violets (nights with Zeus), knowing that she must avoid Io's fate; "*Iostephanos*," "garlanded with violets," is an epiteth of the city of Athens, Thebes' archenemy, which suggests that Alkmene is already being drawn *to the other side*, that she has entered a process of *becoming-Jupiter's*, of *becoming-the-enemy's*.

Alkmene is introduced as a woman who knows what she wants and expects to obtain it; her speech is above all about *herself*: it is *her*, she says, to whom *he* belongs, it is *her* who reflects *his* honour, it is *her* bosom that is "precious," and it is above all *her jouissance* that is at stake. She acknowledges that her night with Jupiter-in-the-guise-of-Amphitryon exceeded anything she ever experienced, with Amphitryon or any other lover, "*Das fühl ich, mein Amphitryon, erst seit heute, / Da ich zwei kurze Stunden dich besaß*" (V.441-2), as if only in the divine Jupiter's embrace she can fully come into her own *as lover* (Jupiter's guise, then, is not *im*perfect but, in Baudrillard's term, *hyper*perfect: Jupiter does not *equal* Amphitryon in prowess, but *exceeds* him). Alkmene's perception that she enjoyed Jupiter's embrace for a mere two hours is as erroneous as it is telling: she was so immersed in the divine experience that seventeen hours, for her, felt like two.

Alkmene, who in the *Kleist-Forschung* is unquestionedly held up as Amphitryon's faithful wife and Jupiter's helpless victim, is in fact a *highly sexed lover*, who arguably adores not so much Jupiter as her own *jouissance*. Naïve readings of this figure—say: "*Alkmene, die junge, groß und naiv Liebende, setzt den Geliebten, Amphitryon, absolut… So 'vergöttert' Alkmene in ihrer Liebe Amphitryon*"—are (*pace*, Jochen Schmidt) wholly misguided: the Alkmene introduced in scene I/4 has *nothing* in common with such an "ideal" spouse: her "love" is not "grand and naïve" but *libidinal*, and what she "posits as absolute" and "deifies" is not Amphitryon but those seventeen hours of *divine sex*.[315] Whether or not she already senses that not only her *jouissance*, but also her lover, is divine: it is above all the experience, not the person, she craves; in the terms of Maurice Merleau-Ponty's phenomenology, her love is *narcissistic*:

> [T]here is a fundamental narcissism in all vision… a carnal adherence of the sentient to the sensed and of the sensed to the sentient… There is a circle of the touched and the touching, the touched takes hold of the touching; there is a circle of the visible and the seeing, the seeing is not without visible existence; there is… transitivity from one body to another.[316]

That the tiara's alternating signs, "J" and "A," together make an affirmative "*Ja*" has been noted; it is a "yes" to *jouissance*, to "Jupiter and Alkmene."³¹⁷ The "*Kleinod*" ("gem," "treasure," *agalma*) lodged inside of her is an inestimable (Freudian, Lacanian) *desire for the desire of the other*. The tiara's empty box = her deserted, craving body. Alkmene, I argue, longs to repeat her encounter with Jupiter by all means; having Io's fate in mind, she must devise a scheme that allows her to do so while remaining "innocent" in Hera's, Amphitryon's and the Thebans' eyes.

"**Gelieber und Gemahl!**" Jupiter's desire is as narcissistic as Alkmene's: he desires to be loved by her *as* Jupiter, not *as* Amphitryon—in Wittgensteinian terms, he wishes that she not only see in him *this* Amphitryon, but also see him *as* Jupiter. Much of Kleist's drama's fascination derives from the tension between Jupiter's wish that she acknowledge him *as* Jupiter, and Alkmene's wish to safeguard her public aura of innocence while continuing to enjoy his embraces: she must never acknowledge her lover *as* Jupiter, for Hera, Amphitryon and the Thebens would immediately pounce on her. When Jupiter, evidently more capable of adopting others' guises than of manipulating others' feelings, puts her to the test, Alkmene vigorously defends her ostensible innocence:

> JUPITER. [...] So öffne mir dein Innres denn, und sprich,
>   Ob den Gemahl du heut, dem du verlobt bist,
>   Ob den Geliebten du empfangen hast?
> ALKMENE.
>   Gelieber und Gemahl! Was sprichst du da?
>   Ist es dies heilige Verhältnis nicht,
>   Das mich allein, dich zu empfahn, berechtigt?
>   Wie kann dich ein Gesetz der Welt nur quälen,
>   Das weit entfernt, beschränkend hier zu sein,
>   Vielmehr den kühnsten Wünschen, die sich regen,
>   Jedwede Schranke glücklich niederreißt? (V.455-64)

Before departing, Jupiter wants to own her, "*So öffne mir dein Innres denn*," in public, right before the eagle-eyed Charis. Yet in addition to being highly sexed, Alkmene is also exceedingly clever: she turns Jupiter's advance into an argument, with the help of which she rationalises the previous night's events before Charis, Thebes' rumour-monger-in-chief. Alkmene realises that since her lover looks exactly like her husband, not only for her, *but also for everyone else*, marital law is not her enemy, *but her friend*: in her husband's absence, her embracing her divine lover-in-the-guise-of-her-husband is *sanctioned* by that very law; her "*kühnsten Wünsche*" will be fulfilled precisely because the law, "*weit entfernt, beschränkend hier zu sein*," indeed "*berechtigt*" ("authorises," "empowers")—even *obliges*—her to do exactly what she desires to do: make love to the god. Far from *constituting a barrier*, she recognises, the law "*reißt jedwede Schranke glücklich nieder.*"

In Kleist's version, not Jupiter is the impostor, but Amphitryon (who disguises his defeat) and Alkmene (who disguises her affair). Kleist not only enhances Alkmene's *weight*—in Plautus', Rotrous' and Molière's versions she is largely a passive object of desire and plays no role in the later acts—, but also fundamentally changes her *character traits*. Jupiter's wish that Alkmene distinguish *amant* and *époux* already appears in Rotrous and Molière, but Kleist turns their story of a sly Jupiter imposing himself on a passive Alkmene into a crafty Alkmene's pro-actively producing her alibi. He achieves this radical shift in part by subtly altering the language; compare, for example, his Alkmene's ambiguous "*heiliges Verhältnis*," which according to her persists between "*Geliebter und Gemahl*," with Rotrous' Alkmene's unambiguous "*Je ne sépare point ce qu'unissent les dieux, / Et l'époux et l'amant me sont fort précieux.*"[318] While retaining the play's conventional title, Kleist turns Alkmene into the drama's central character, whose most characteristic line is this: "*Ich wills*" (V.866).

Kleist changes not only Alkmene's, but also Jupiter's character traits. For quite some time Jupiter does not "get" Alkmene's scheme of crafting for herself an alibi under whose cover she can continue giving herself to him without risking repercussions; in Kleist's version, if anyone is "naïve" it is not Alkmene but Jupiter, who evidently found it easier to vanquish Amphitryon than to manipulate Alkmene; he, the mightiest of gods, is nearly reduced to beseeching her: "*Was ich dir fühle, teuerste Alkmene, / Das überflügelt, sieh, um Sonnenferne, / Was ein Gemahl dir schuldig ist. Entwöhne, / Geliebte, von dem Gatten dich, Und unterscheide zwischen mir und ihm*" (V.465-9), and when he insinuates that Amphitryon married her only for dynastic reasons (cf. V.479-80), Jupiter shows himself to be as base and jealous as any mortal: only human, all too human.

"**So früh zurück—?**" Having reluctantly let Jupiter take his leave, Alkmene coolly receives Amphitryon when he appears with Sosias at the palace:[319]

> ALKMENE. [...] Da sie den Amphitryon erblickt.
> O Gott! Amphitryon!
> AMPHITRYON. Der Himmel gebe,
> Daß meine Gattin nicht vor mir erschrickt,
> Nicht fürcht ich, daß nach dieser flüchtigen Trennung
> Alkmene minder zärtlich mich empfängt,
> Als ihr Amphitryon zurückgekehrt.
> ALKMENE. So früh zurück—?
> AMPHITRYON. Was! Dieser Ausruf,
> Führwar, scheint ein zweideutig Zeichen mir,
> Ob auch die Götter jenen Wunsch erhört.
> Dies: "Schon so früh zurück!" ist der Empfang,
> Beim Himmel, nein! der heißen Liebe nicht. (V.776-86)

Alkmene's performative exclamation, "*O Gott! Amphitryon!*," demonstrates how assuredly she can tell lover and husband apart, and how instantaneously she can shift her attention from one—"*O Gott!*"—to the other—"*Amphitryon!*" Amphitryon, on his part, also has an acute intuition: that during his absence their honeymoon has ended. His despair at Alkmene's aloofness does not sway her:

ALKMENE.   [...] Ich denke gestern, als
    Du um die Abenddämmrung mir erschienst,
    Trug ich die Schuld, an welche du mich mahnst,
    Aus meinem Busen reichlich ab.
    Kannst du noch mehr dir wünschen, mehr begehren,
    So muß ich meine Dürftigkeit gestehn:
    Ich gab dir wirklich alles, was ich hatte.
AMPHITRYON. Wie?   (V.806-13)

Unlike Amphitryon, Alkmene is a consummate poker player: bluffing, she simulates indignation at Amphitryon's not "remembering" how in the previous night she "gave him all she had," while mocking him for identifying himself with Jupiter (cf. V.821-3), and humiliating him by graphically reiterating the liberties "he" took with her (cf. V.847-50).

Alkmene turns Amphitryon's fake evidence of his victory—the tiara—into fake evidence of her innocence. Her stratagem is undermined only when the purported simpleton Sosias unties the drama's "knot" (assuming the "mad" Johann's part in *Schroffenstein*) by telling Amphitryon: "*Ihr seid doppelt, / Amphitryon vom Stock ist hier gewesen, / Und glücklich schätz ich Euch, bei Gott—*" (V.901-3); Sosias' comment also confirms which part of Jupiter's body is *not* a carbon copy of Amphitryon's: his "stick."[320] Alkmene further tightens the noose around Amphitryon's neck by insinuating that all is not right with his victory tale: "*Vielleicht daß eine Sorge dir des Krieges / Den Kopf beschwert...?*" (V.922-3). The account of the battle she believes in is Jupiter's (V.944-8), not Sosias', and she plays out her knowledge against Amphitryon, who acutely feels the sting: "*Kann man, frag ich, den Dolch lebhafter fühlen?*" (V.954).[321] Alkmene puts another finger in the wound by dwelling on details of "their" amorous night:

ALKMENE. Jetzt ward das Abendessen aufgetragen,
    Doch weder du noch ich beschäftigten
    Uns mit dem Ortolan, der vor uns stand,
    Nicht mit der Flasche viel, du sagtest scherzend,

> Daß du von meiner Liebe Nektar lebtest,
> Du seist ein Gott, und was die Lust dir sonst,
> Die ausgelaßne in den Mund dir legte! [...]
> AMPHITRYON.   Hierauf jetzt—?
> ALKMENE.   Standen
>   Wir [...] auf; und nun— [...]
>   Gingen wir———nun ja!
> Warum steigt solche Röt ins Antlitz dir?
> AMPHITRYON. O dieser Dolch, er trifft das Leben mir!   (V.955-70)

The triple dash, thrice the length of *Marquise*'s more famous one, alludes at once to Jupiter's infinite ithyphallic prowess and their "endless" night auf debauchery. Alkmene, with considerable chutzpah, adds fuel to the flames by insinuating that it is not her but Amphitryon who is having a secret lover (cf. V.983-4), before issuing an unveiled threat, "*Du siehst entschlossen mich das Band zu lösen, / Das deine wankelmütge Seele drückt; / Und ehe noch der Abend sich verkündet, / Bist du befreit von allmem, was dich bindet*" (V.987-90). This is sheer bluff, for Alkmene knows full well that Jupiter makes love to, but never marries, mortal women, and that she continues to depend on Amphitryon for her livelihood and social standing in Theban society. Her bluff nevertheless pays off: Amphitryon recoils, though not without calling for eye-witnesses to help him tear apart the "fabric" of lies and deception he perceives (V.996-7). Which is interesting: it implies that he has reason to presume that eye witnesses *were* present during Alkmene's mysterious tête-à-tête—an assumption presumably informed by previous experiences.

"**Was für ein Ich?**" The game Alkmene plays, and which she demands Jupiter to play along with, mirrors an intriguing dialogue between Merkur and Sosias:

> MERKUR. Halt dort! Wer geht dort?
> SOSIAS.   Ich.
> MERKUR.   Was für ein Ich?   (V.146-8)

One has to be the appropriate *"I"* at the appropriate time, a philosophical Merkur tells Sosias, just as Alkmene tells Jupiter to be *"Jupiter-I"* in the privacy of her bedroom, and *"Amphitryon-I"* in her palace's corridors and in Thebes' squares: whether he is *"Gelieber"* or *"Gemahl,"* Alkmene insists, *must depend on the occasion*—it must be contingent not absolute, as Jupiter wants it to be: in public, he must be *"Gemahl,"* in private, *"Gelieber."* Sosias offers Merkur, who beat the living daylights out of him, the very concession Alkmene is seeking from Jupiter: *"Ach! / Ich bin jetzt, was du willst. Befiehl, was ich / Soll sein"* (V.238-40). Jupiter, of course, is a tougher nut to crack than Sosias, and Alkmene and Jupiter continue talking past each other as she insists on the *identification*, he on the *differentiation*, of lover and husband. Alkmene's shock at Charis' discovery of the *"J"* engraved in her tiara, frequently taken by the Kleist reception as proving her innocence, in fact confirms her cognizance: Alkmene immediately perceives that Charis' find threatens to blow her cover: *"Ein Zeugnis wider mich ist dieser Stein"* (V.1223).

"Mein Herr und mein Gemahl!" In the drama's famous *"scène à faire"* (Thomas Mann) we witness not an overpowering Jupiter's brutal interrogation of a helpless Alkmene, but an eye-level, tit-for-tat *fencing duel* between two formidable lovers that is as much sensual as it is verbal. While Charis and Sosias—Thebes' paparazzi—are lingering in the background, ears pricked and eyes wide open, Alkmene seeks to compel Jupiter to let her publicly treat him *as Amphitryon*, while Jupiter aims to coerce Alkmene to admit publicly that she loves him *as Jupiter*.

En Garde. Êtes-vous prêts? Allez! Alkmene thrusts by addressing Jupiter as *"Mein Herr und mein Gemahl!"* (V.1236), acknowledging him *as Jupiter* (*"Herr"*), while giving the eavesdroppers the impression that she speaks to him *as Amphitryon* (*"Gemahl"*), then lunges and goes down on her knees before him, girdled with her "tiara" (this *"diamantner Gürtel"* evidently functions as a chastity belt), conveying to the onlookers that she has remained dutifully chaste to her husband, to Jupiter, whom the letter *"J"* engraved in the belt faces, that she belongs to him.[322] Jupiter parries, then launches his own opening thrust:

> JUPITER. [...] Was sich dir nahet, ist Amphitryon.   (V.1261)

With his formulation "*What* approaches you" (not: "*Who* approaches you") Jupiter terms only his appearance (his "*what*"), not his identity (his "who"), "Amphitryon." Alkmene now seeks to impose on him the predicate "*Gemahl*" by a veritable speech act:

> ALKMENE. Oh mein Gemahl! [...]
> Warst dus, wast du es nicht? O Sprich! du warsts!   (V.1262-3);

Jupiter responds by mimicking Sosias: "*Ich wars*" (not: "*Ich, Amphitryon, wars*"). Alkmene, predictably, is not satisfied—"*Nein, mein Amphitryon, hier irrst du dich*"—, for in order to maintain her public alibi, she must get Jupiter to unambiguously identify himself as "*Amphitryon*," not merely an unspecific "*I.*"

They now exchange blow by blow. Alkmene bluffs, "*Leb wohl! Leb Wohl! [...] / Fort, fort, fort— / Geh, sag ich*" (V.1276-7); Jupiter counters by proposing to take her to Mount Olympus, (implausibly) promising that even Hera and Artemis shall welcome her. Alkmene understandably refuses; Jupiter outs himself as Jupiter. Alkmene retorts by adopting the persona of a pious woman to whom Jupiter's claim is blasphemous—turning his sally against him by offering herself to him not as his lover but his faithful; Jupiter changes tack and offers her a divine son: "*wie Tynariden.*" Alkmene warns him that he must not show himself *as* Jupiter, as she would inevitably suffer Semele's fate: "*Würd ich vor solchem Glanze nicht versinken?*" (V.1365); Jupiter becomes angry: "*Du unternimmst, Kurzsichtige, ihn zu meistern?*" (V.1372). The prudent Alkmene feints a retreat, "*Gut, gut, Amphitryon. Ich verstehe dich*" (V.1374), only to mock him again: "*Du hast dies Wort, ich weiß es, hingeworfen, / Mich zu zerstreun*" (V.1376-7); Jupiter responds by pointing to the "J" on the tiara. Alkmene admits that only the victorious Jupiter—"*Er selbst! Er!*"—could have have so boldly visited her last night, but refuses to identify the one standing before her with "*Him*"; Jupiter backs off and defaults to the conventional appeasement formula that his embrace is flattering to both the wife and her husband (Molière:

"*un partage avec Jupiter n'a rien qui déshonore*"). Alkmene concedes this point:

> ALKMENE. Nun ja. *Sie küßt ihn.*
> JUPITER. Du Himmlische!
> ALKMENE. Wie glücklich bin ich! (V.1410-2)

Alkmene may now be aiming for a "draw," but Jupiter, emboldened by having scored a point, goes on the offensive:

> JUPITER. Wie, wenn du seinen Unwillen... gereizt?
> ALKMENE. Ich? Ihn? Gereizt?
> JUPITER. Ist er dir wohl vorhanden?
> Nimmst du die Welt, sein großes Werk, wohl wahr? [...]
> Steigst du nicht in des Herzens Schacht hinab
> Und betest deinen Götzen an?
> ALKMENE. Entsetzlicher! [...] (V.1418-34)

Alkmene recoils from his onslaught, while Jupiter seizes the opportunity to turn the table on Alkmene and corner her:

> JUPITER. [...] Ists nicht Amphitryon, der Geliebte stets,
> Vor welchem du im Staube liegst?
> ALKMENE. Ach [...]
> Soll ich zur weißen Wand des Marmors beten?
> Ich brauche Züge nun, um ihn zu denken.
> JUPITER.
> Siehst du? [...]
> Abgötterei [...]
> Doch künftig wirst du immer
> Nur ihn, versteh, der dir zu Nacht erschienen,
> An seinen Altar denken, und nicht mich.
> ALKMENE. Wohlan! [...] Ich [...]
> [...] werd ihn nicht mit dir Verwechseln.

> JUPITER. Das tu. Sonst wagst du, daß er wiederkömmt.
> So oft du seinen Namenszug erblickst,
> Dem Diadem verzeichnet, wirst du seiner
> Erscheinung auf das Innigste gedenken [...]
> Erinnern, wie vor dem Unsterblichen
> Der Schreck am Rocken dich durchzuckt; wie du
> Das Kleinod von ihm eingetauscht; wer dir
> Beim Gürten hilfreich war, und was
> Beim Ortolan geschehn. Und stört dein Gatte dich,
> So bittest du ihn freundlich, daß er dich
> Auf eine Stunde selbst dir überlasse.
> ALKMENE. Gut, gut, [...]   (V.1452-86)

Jupiter extracts the promise from Alkmene to worship him every morning for one hour, by re-enacting their divine sexual encounter, with the tiara functioning as fetish or sex toy for her sensual meditation. In return, Alkmene insists on avoiding to publicly acknowledge him as being distinct from Amphitryon. Jupiter, not yet satisfied, changes tack again, appealing to her pity and sense of duty:

> JUPITER. [...]   Ach Alkmene!
> Auch der Olymp ist öde ohne Liebe. [...]
> Er will geliebt sein, nicht ihr Wahn von ihm. [...]
> Währst du vom Schicksal nun bestimmt [...]
> Ihm [...]
> In einem einzgen Lächeln auszuzahlen,
> Würdst du dich ihm wohl—ach! [...]
> Nun?—
> ALKMENE.   Läßt man die Wahl mir—
> JUPITER.   Läßt man dir—?
> ALKMENE. Die Wahl, so bliebe meine Ehrfurcht ihm,
> Und meine Liebe dir, Amphitryon.   (V.1518-32)

Alkmene resorts to clever sophistry: she (truthfully) declares the one before her (whom she knows to be Jupiter) to be the one she *loves*, while (deceptively) continuing to *address* him as Amphitryon. This move leads to a stalemate:

> JUPITER. Entscheide du. Amphitryon bin ich.
> ALKMENE. Amphitryon—
> JUPITER. Amphitryon, dir ja.
> Doch wenn ich, frag ich, dieser Gott dir wäre,
> Dir liebend from Olymp herabgestiegen,
> Wie würdest du dich dann zu fassen wissen?
> ALKMENE. Wenn du mir, Liebster, dieser Gott wärst—ja [...]
> So würd ich folgen dir, wohin du gehst [...]
> JUPITER. [...] Und jetzo dein Amphitryon sich zeigte,
> Wie würd dein Herz sich wohl erklären?
> ALKMENE. Wenn du, der Gott, mich hier umschlungen hieltest
> Und jetzo sich Amphitryon mir zeigte,
> Ja—dann so traurig würd ich sein, und wünschen,
> Daß er der Gott mir wäre, und daß du
> Amphitryon mir bliebst, wie du es bist.
> JUPITER. Mein süßes, angebetenes Geschöpf! [...]
> ALKMENE. Amphitryon! (V.1544-74)

With this stalemate, Kleist's brilliant "duel" ends in a "truce," both combatants having achieved their main objective: Jupiter has coerced Alkmene to admit that the one she desires is Jupiter *as Jupiter*; Alkmene has compelled Jupiter to accept that she shall continue calling him "Amphitryon" in public. This central scene is justly famous; without Charis' and Sosias' presence in the background, howeer, it would be meaningless: its main purpose is to manipulate public perceptions.

"dieses Helmes Feder eingeknickt." When it has become obvious that not one but two Amphitryons are making the rounds in Thebes, Amphitryon mutilates or castrates himself before the eys of his men, thereby creating an unmistakable mark of his identity: *"daß ich Amphitryon, / Ihr Bürger Thebens, bin, / Der dieses Helmes Feder eingeknickt"* (V.2123-7). Yet Amphitryon soon realises that his sacrifice was in vain, for Jupiter is able to mimic his outer appearance accurately and in "real time," so that the people still cannot distinguish them: *"Kann sich ein menschlich Auge* *hier entscheiden?*" (V.2185); with this realisation, "*Was hilft der eingeknickte Federbusch?*" (V.2190), Amphitryon faints. As a result of Amphitryon's rash move, Jupiter-in-the-guise-of-Amphitryon at suitable occasions "out-Amphitryonises" Amphitryon: while he can erect at will—"*Hier steht*"—, Amphitryon no longer can: "*Das lügst du dort!*" Cognisant of this "minimal difference," Alkmene, when asked to chose between them, naturally chooses—*Jupiter*. She does not make a *mistake*, as some readers suggest, but consciously—girls will be girls—picks the omnipotent, ithyphallic god rather than the impotent, mutilated mortal. Amphitryon takes note of her disloyalty teeth-gnashingly: "*O ihrer Worte jedes ist wahrhaftig. / [...] Daß er Amphitryon ihr ist*" (V.2281-90).

Jupiter, Alkmene and Amphitryon in the drama's ending establish a Kleistian "*gebrechliche Einrichtung*" that anticipates *Marquise*'s and involves, firstly, Jupiter revealing himself *as Jupiter*—in terms that mirror YHWH's "I am I am" (*Exodus* 3:14): "*Das was da war, was ist, und was sein wird*"; V.2300)—, secondly, Alkmene choosing Jupiter while remaining in her "*Josephsehe*" (Ortrud Gutjahr), and thirdly, Amphitryon accepting the consolation of Jupiter's promise of a divine son. As he leaves the stage, Jupiter sums up the outcome to Amphitryon: "*Sie wird dir bleiben; / Doch laß sie ruhn*" (V.2347-8)—"she may stay with you; but don't touch her." Jupiter has accomplished his mission he shared with Alkmene early on, "*Sieh, ich möchte deine Tugend / Ihm, jenem öffentlichen Gecken, lassen, / Und mir, mir deine Liebe vorbehalten*" (V.481-3); his admonition to Amphitryon to stay away from her is perhaps superfluous: when the people offer their *cum* to him in a sacrificial mass-masturbation, Amphitryon is unable to join the salvo: "*Er ists! In Staub! In Staub das Antlitz hin! / Alles wirft sich zur Erde außer Amphitryon*" (V.2315)—in *satyrical* trans.: "It's Jupiter! Ejaculate! Point your glans, ejaculate! / All ejaculate, except Amphitryon." Amphitryon, evidently, is now impotent.

Amphitryon, Satirically

Amphitryon's satirical context seamlessly pickes up where *Krug*'s *MS* left off:

- 27th September 1806: Fr. Wilh. issues his ultimatum to Napoleon;
- 8th October: the ultimatum expires without a response, triggering Prussia's declaration of war; [323]
- 14th October: the Saxo-Prussian allied forces are defeated decisively by the *Ad'A* in the *Battle of Jena-Auerstedt*; the Prussian King and Queen, and remaining Prussian units, flee eastwards;
- 27th October: Napoleon enters Berlin and resides in Schloss Charlottenburg;
- October-November: most Prussian fortresses capitulate without a fight;
- 21st November: the *Berlin Decree* establishes the Continental System;
- 11th December: with the *Treaty of Posen*, Saxony becomes a French ally and joins the *Rheinbund*;
- 20th December: Saxon Elector Fr. Aug. III is proclaimed Fr. Aug. I, King of Saxony, and in personal union rules the Duchy of Warsaw;
- December 1806-January 1807: as the *Ad'A* advances, Fr. Wilh. and Luise flee to Königsberg, temporarily the Prussian capital, and on to Memel;
- 7th-8th February: the *Battle of Eylau*, pitting a Russo-Prussian army against the *Ad'A*, ends in a tactical draw with high losses on both sides;
- February: Napoleon's envoy Bertrand at Memel offers Fr. Wilh a separate peace; following Hardenberg and Luise's advice, the King rejects;[324]
- Early April: Alex. I visits Memel to convince Fr. Wilh. not to waver;
- 26th April: Prussia and Russia renew their alliance in the *Treaty of Bartenstein*, setting the stage for the war's resumption.[325]

Our *satirical* analysis may shed light on the "cut-off" date at which Kleist, imprisoned in France, submitted the MS for its publication in May 1807.

"Mit dem Hauptkorps ists nicht richtig." Kleist's partial inversion of the original story—a *defeated*, rather than victorious, Amphitryon returns to find his bedroom usurped by Jupiter—offers a "navel" from which the *satirical* thread can be unravelled: given the probable timing of the drama's genesis, we can confidently assume that the battle whose account Sosias rehearses in the drama's opening scene is *Jena-Auerstedt*, where on 14th October 1806 the Saxo-Prussian army under Fr. Wilh. III's personal command was routed by Napoleon's *Ad'A*, leading to the almost instantaneous collapse of the Prussian state. Sosias' internal dialogue comes to an abrupt halt when he visualises the moment in which the Prussian *Hauptkorps*, commanded by Karl Wilh. Ferd. von Braunschweig, is crushed by "The Iron Marshal" Louis-Nicolas Davout's corps right beneath Fr. Wilh.'s eyes, who is directing the battle from his Auerstedt HQ.[326]

"Amphitryon vom Stock." Sosias' epithet of Jupiter (cf. V.902) is a pertinent moniker for the trained artillery officer Napoleon, master of the *Grande batterie* and wielder of the biggest (military) stick the world had ever known. That Jupiter—"the electrical god *kat exochen*" (Jürgen Schröder), among whose Greek epithets are "cloud-gatherer," "lightninger," and "thunderer"—represents Napoleon is already suggested by the obvious congruence of their main symbols, eagle, thunderbolt and sceptre, and of the typical poses in which they are shown, a congruence no doubt intended by Napoleon and the artists he commissioned:

"Es schwebt ein Adler mit dem Donnerkeil aus den Wolken nieder": Jupiter and Napoleon.[327]

His association with Napoleon explains why the god in Kleist's drama usually appears by his Lat. name, Jupiter: for Kleist, as for many Germans in the wake of Joh. Joachim Winckelmann's popular works classical Greece generally came to represent Germany (and Thebes, in Kleist's drama, Prussia), while imperial Rome came to signify Napoleonic France, so that his Lat. appelation marks Napoleon as *French*, his occasional Gr. appellation (cf. e.g., V.1336) as (de facto) *German* Emperor.[328] When Kleist uses the name Zeus, he spells the letter "u" in its Latin rendering "v" (Sembdner unfortunately "corrects" this), thereby indicating that Napoleon is *German* Emperor with a decidedly *French* hue, and that Germany's *"Francofication"* is progressing.[329] His association with Napoleon furthermore explains why Kleist's Jupiter is not all-powerful, and in many ways eminently human. Ancient tragedians refrained from presenting Jupiter/Zeus on stage, unlike other Olympian gods, whereas Kleist (as already Molière, for whom this figure also represented a powerful French monarch, Louis XIV) has no qualms showing Jupiter-Napoleon on stage: pompous, vein and moody.

"Zwei Führer." When Alkmene mentions "two leaders" who she says *are* and *are not* difficult to distinguish (V.1182-4), instead of Jupiter and Amphitryon, she may be referring to Jupiter and Merkur, his son. I presume that Merkur, like Krug's *Ruprecht*, represents Beauharnais: Kleist's occasional use of his Greek (implying: German) name Hermes, and Merkur's voracious appetite for Charis' sausages (cf. V.2027), may plausibly allude to Beauharnais' "having gone German" by marrying the Bavarian princess.[330] Beauharnais was the very archetype of the loyal and competent side-kick, supporting Napoleon in governing his increasingly far-flung empire and in expanding his dynastic reach. Beauharnais had been Napoleon's *aide-de-camp* during the *Italian Campaigns* (1796-7), before taking command of the *Armée d'Italie*, and in 1804 being appointed Viceroy of Italy. The *aide-de-camp's* badge of office was an *"aiguillette"* ("small needle"), an ornamental, braided cord with a pointed tip, to which Merkur's *"Stachel"* may allude.[331]

In 1798 Beauharnais' *Armée d'Italie* became the core of the newly formed *Armée d'Orient*; he loyally seconded Napoleon during the *Campaign of Egypt and Syria* (1798-1801), whose key milestones Kleist enumerates obliquely in his drama: the *Battle of the Pyramids* of July 1798, in which Napoleon wiped out the Mamluk army (*"Pyramide"*; V.2341); the *Battle of the Nile* of August 1798, in which the British navy defeated the French, trapping Napoleon's army in Egypt (*"Der… Katarakten Fall"*; V.1428); Napoleon's expedition to the Sinai, where he was said to have visited the so-called Fountains of Moses (*"Verkündet nicht umsonst der Berg ihn dir"*; V.1426); the *RF*'s celebration on Cairo's main square in September 1798 (the feast Sosias organises for the people). The campaign did not end in success, but its sheer daring strengthened Napoleon's political position in France: his *coup d'état* and appointment as *First Consul* followed soon after his return from Egypt.

The *Siege of Acre* of March–May 1799, at which Beauharnais was wounded and countless French soldiers succumbed to the plague, became a turning point not only of the campaign but of history, for had Napoleon taken Acre, the route to Constantinople, via Syria and Anatolia, would have been open, and his conquest of the Ottoman Empire and his crowning himself "Emperor of the East" almost inevitable: *"Had I been able to take Acre… Instead of a battle in Moravia* (Austerlitz), *I would have won a Battle of Issus* [where Alexander defeated Persia], *I would have made myself emperor of the East, and I would have returned to Paris by way of Constantinople."*[332] Napoleon imagined himself as a second Alexander or Caesar, harbouring grand ambitions of forging a new Empire of the West and the East, and dreamed of challenging the British in India by the land route; Alkmene, when anticipating that her love could soon belong to a *"Parther oder Perser"* (V.1158), already pictiures herself as future Empress of the Orient.

"jenen öffentlichen Gecken." Jupiter's opinion of Amphitryon is far from flattering: *"den eitlen Feldherrn der Thebaner / … der für ein großes Haus / Jüngst eine reiche Fürstentochter freite? / … Ihm, jenem öffentlichen Gecken"* (V.478-82). The "Theban commander" and "public fool," of course, represents King Fr. Wilh. III, supreme commander of the Coalition forces at *Jena-Auerstedt*, whose wife Luise was indeed the wealthy daughter of a prince—the Duke of

Mecklenburg-Strelitz—whom he married on behalf of a "great dynasty" (the Hohenzollern). Amphitryon-Fr. Wilh. cuts a sad figure: vanquished, cuckolded and (self-) castrated, he is reduced to humbly knocking at his own door like a beggar (cf. V.1836) and to hailing his conqueror as German Emperor: "*Vater Zeus*" (V.2330). Amphitryon's delayed return from the battlefield alludes to Fr. Wilh.'s precipitate flight to East Prussia from the battlefield of *Jena-Auerstedt*: when Napoleon entered Berlin on 27th October 1806, setting up his HQ at the Hohenzollerns' *Charlottenburg* residence, as he had done a year earlier at the Habsburgs' *Schönbrunn* residence, Fr. Wilh. and Luise escaped first to Königsberg (cf. "*Königsburg*," V.636), then, when Napoleon and the *Ad'A* in early 1807 closed in on that city, via the frozen Courland Lagoon to Memel, a Baltic port at the furthest reaches of East Prussia, where they took residence at the Danish consul's mansion. When he turns Amphitryon's "castle" into a "house," subsequently a "hut," Kleist, far from being inconsistent as some critics have maintained, accurately reflects how Fr. Wilh. and Luise are forced to trade their stately Charlottenburg Castle first for the modest Königsberg Castle, then for a mere mansion.

"**Entsetzlich**." If Amphitryon represents Fr. Wilh., the "*entsetzte*"/"*entsetzliche*" Alkmene embodies Luise (or *Borussia*), who was indeed "*entsetzt*"—literally, "un-settled," "dis-placed"— when her cozy Brandenburgian world went topsy-turvy after *Jena-Auerstedt*, and when she found herself in the remotest reaches of Eastern Prussia, at the very edge of European civilisation (or so she may have felt). Kleist assigns as much responsibility for Prussia's fall to the flirtatious Queen as to the vain King: when Merkur and Jupiter arrive at her palace (in Königsberg), they find Alkmene-Luise revelling amidst ithyphallic satyrs, on the verge of giving herself to whoever chances upon her first; having recklessly sent her blue-eyed husband into war, she amuses herself in his chambers with a bunch of courtiers, envoys and ministers.[333] Amphitryon's characterisation of his wife's conduct, "*Und unter rauschende Vergnügen sind / In diesem Schloß fünf abgezählte Monden / Wie so viel Augenblicke hingeflohn*" (V.798-801), reflects Kleist's of his Queen's: if Fr. Wilh. is a naïve *fool*,

Luise is a lusty *whore*, always at risk of melting away before the virile Napoleon or the philandering Hardenberg. An insufficiently manly, conceited King, and an only too womanly, beddable Queen: such is Kleist's portrayal of his Royals. Alkmene's melting before Jupiter anticipates the Marquise's swooning before Count F and Lisbeth's supplicating before the Brandenburg Elector:

	Alkmene-Luise	the Marquise-Luise	Lisbeth-Luise
:al context at ›f writing	Post *Jena-Auerstedt*; post *Posen*; pre *Tilsit*	Post *Jena-Auerstedt*; post *Tilsit*	Post *Jena-Auerstedt*; post *Tilsit*
ication mode	Melting	Swooning	Supplicating
Borussia's fate	Sodomised by Napoleon; impregnated by Merkur? (see below)	Sodomised by Napoleon; impregnated by the *Rheinbund* "dog"?	Raped and killed by Brandenburg (Napoleon?)
ılh.'s fate	(Self-)castration	Enslavement (social castration)	Beheading (symbolic castration)
ff for Prussia, ohenzollerns	Hohenzollern-Bonaparte succession (divine son); Prussia hegemonised	Hohenzollern-Bonaparte succession (*Ganze Reihe*); Prussia restored	Hohenzollern heirs designated future Emperors; Prussia restored
ff for any/the *HHR*	Napoleon looms large, *HRR* remains dissolved	Napoleon incorporated into a restituted *HRR*	Reinstituted *HRR* (2 blacks); Napoleon's sway unalleviated

"**Verräter.**" Sosias is not the simpleton he is often made out to be.[334] Having repeatedy turncoated back and forth, this "traitor" (cf. V.1790; 97; 1859; 65) eventually settles into his new role as Napoleon's *lieu-tenant*; having been thrashed into submission by Beauharnais, he is ennobled by Napoleon: "*er besingungswürdge Schläg erhalten… Führwahr! Solch ein Triumph—*" (V.2355; 61; the

German term for ennoblement is *Ritterschlag*). Evidently Kleist's Sosias depicts the Saxon Elector Fr. Aug. III, who at *Jena-Auerstedt* was Prussia's ally, but subsequent to the defeat switched sides in the Treaty of Posen—"*Wir schlossen Waffenstillstand*" (V.269)—, which Napoleon rewarded by elevating him, on 20th December 1806, to Fr. Aug. I, King of Saxony. Already during the battle Sosias-Fr. Aug.'s value as Prussia's ally is put into question when he hides in his tent: "*da ich / Dabei nicht war*" (V.38-9).[335] In addition to depicting him as a coward, Kleist portrays Sosias-Fr. Aug. as a lecher who has his own designs on Alkmene-Luise, "*Und stellte witzig die Laterne mir, / Als Eure Gattin, die Prinzessin, vor*" (V.646-7; "lantern"= phallus, "*vorstellen*" = "to imagine," but also "to erect"), an insinuation not entirely without historical basis, for the Saxon Wettins repeatedly aimed to replace the Prussian Hohenzollerns as the leading German dynasty bar the Habsburgs—and Fr. Aug. indeed nearly succeeded: when at *Tilsit* Napoleon awarded him the Duchy of Warsaw in personal union, the combined Saxon and Polish population under his rule exceeded that of Fr. Wilh.'s stunted Prussia.

Already in the opening scene's soliloquy Sosias-Fr. Aug. prepares to revoke his alliance with Amphitryon-Fr. Wilh.: "*Ging ich / Durch eine Höllenfinsternis, als wäre / Der Tag zehntausend Klaftern tief versunken, / Euch allen Teufeln, und den Auftrag, gebend, / Den Weg nach Theben, und die Königsburg*" (V. 632-6). In this convoluted, "*legitim kleistischen*" (Thomas Mann), sentence Fr. Aug. envisages descending into hell, where he hands Fr. Wilh. over to the devil Napoleon, before making his way towards Luise's castle and bedroom (had Jupiter and Merkur not pre-empted him, can there be any doubt that Sosias would have delivered his message in Alkmene's *bedroom*?). A ravenous, cowardly and cynical opportunist, whose "*wolfmäßger Hunger*" (V.1965) makes him a natural ally of the "*allgemeinen Wolf*" Napoleon (cf. II:718), who ogles his ally's wife and posessions while deserting him in battle and delivering him to his enemy: such is Kleist's portrayal of the despised Saxon. Fr. Aug. slyly equates his own fate with Fr. Wilh.'s, "*Und kurz ich bin entsosiatisiert / Wie man Euch entamphitryonisiert*" (V.2158-9), but Kleist will have deemed neither their respective fates nor their character traits equivalent: whereas Fr.

Wilh.'s humiliation or "*Entamphitryonisierung*" is the price he pays for his vain and reckless, but not malicious, unprepared mobilisation against a superior enemy, Fr. Aug.'s vasallage or "*Entsosiatisierung*" is the result of a cowardly and premeditated act of treason against the German nation. In his quest to "francofy" Germany, Napoleon was equally happy to vanquish or to sway.

"**in der Küche.**" Charis ("grace") is just as desirous and flirtatious as Alkmene, and as smitten by Merkur as her mistress by Jupiter. Although her tastes are more rustic—she favours farmhands over generals, sausages over ortolans, and kitchens, wash-kitchens or haystacks over lavish bedrooms—, Charis regularly joins Alkmene in her orgiastic parties and auto-erotic sacrifices before Hermes' altar. Charis evidently represents Princess Auguste, Beauharnais' "dearest wife" (V.564), and thereby embodies *Bavaria* and the Wittelsbachs as Sosias does *Saxonia* and the Wettins, and Alkmene, *Borussia* and the Hohenzollerns. Kleist's naming this figure Charis (in Molière's version she is named Cleanthis, in Plautus', Bromia) entails a sarcastic swipe at the Bavarian princess who so "gracefully" gave herself to the arch-enemy: in *Marionettentheater,* "graceful" denotes the devoted *erômenos* selflessly submitting to the *erâstes*' sodomy.

The Theban commanders, "*Hunde, die... Knie umwedeln*" (V.882), who vacillate between their loyalty to Amphitryon and their awe of Jupiter, could represent the Prussian generals who shared the responsibility for Prussia's defeat: Hohenlohe, Rüchel, Kalckreuth in the main; perhaps a von Kleist.[336] Amphitryon rescinds these tepid "friends" who one after another lay down their arms, "*Geht, ihr Schwachherzgen! Huldigt dem Verräter! / Mir bleiben noch der Freunde mehr, als ihr*" (V.1925; 1930-1), while Jupiter woos them, "*Auf denn, ihr Herrn, gefällts euch! Ehrt dies Haus / Mit eurem Eintritt,*" eagerly supported by his new sidekick Sosias: "*und tischt, und pokuliert bis morgen*" (V.1955-9).

Endless Night at Königsberg. The *dramatis personae* could be as follows:

JUPITER, in der Gestalt des Amphitryon	NAPOLEON, Emperor of France
MERKUR, in der Gestalt des Sosias	EUGENE DE BEAUHARNAIS, Viceroy of Italy (possibly also HENRI GATIEN BERTRAND, Aide-de-camp, and LOUIS-ALEX. BERTHIER, Chief-of-staff)
AMPHITRYON, Feldherr der Thebaner	FR. WILH. III, King of Prussia
SOSIAS, sein Diener	FR. AUG. I/III, Elector, then King, of Saxony
ALKMENE, Gemahlin des Amphitryon	LUISE, Queen of Prussia (or *BORUSSIA*)
CHARIS, Gemahlin des Sosias	AUGUSTE, Vice Queen of Italy (or *BAVARIA*)
FELDHERREN	Prussian generals.
(Die Szene ist in Theben vor dem Schlosse des Amphitryon)	(The set is in East Prussia, before Fr. Wilh.'s Königsberg Castle)[337]

The limited cast reflects that, Saxony apart, Prussia in the War of the Fourth Coalition faced Napoleon alone. Kleist's subtitle, "*Ein Lustspiel nach Molière*," may *satirically* be "trans." as: "*Preußens Trauerspiel nachdem der Franzose kam.*" If Kleist pictured *Krug's* "wedding at Vienna" as a village kermis à la Teniers the Younger, he imagined *Amphitryon's* "endless night at Königsberg" as a scatological feast à la Peter Greenaway; cartographically, the feast can be depicted as follows:

 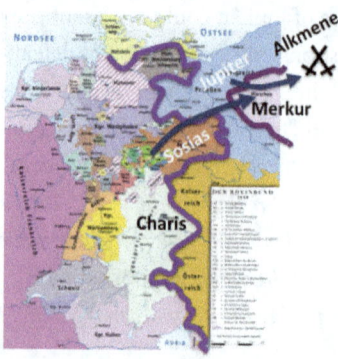

Prussia's "endless night" of *Agôn* and *Erôs* (left: October 1806; right: February 1807).

"**die Pyramide jetzt, vollendet.**" Sosias and Charis, having observed Jupiter and Alkmene's "duel," in the ensuing scene (II/6) debate the pros and cons of their *satirico-satyrical* "marriage" (cf. V.1607). Sosias compares their union with that of a stallion and a jenny (cf. V.1610), whose hybrid offspring, a hinny, is sterile, implying that a union of Napoleon and Luise/*Borussia* would not only produce a bastard or "monstrosity" (cf. *Guiskard*), but also fail to secure Napoleon's succession.[338] Charis, in contrast, likens their union to a match made in heaven: "*Ein Gott und eine Fürstin*" (V.1612). I do not suppose that Kleist literally anticipated Luise divorcing Fr. Wilh. in order to marry Napoleon, but he may well have considered the possibility of Napoleon marrying a Hohenzollern princess.

"The beds of the immortals," Burkert quotes Homer (*Greek Religion*, 183), "are never barren," and with *Amphitryon* Kleist once again addresses *Guiskard's* unresolved snag, of Napoleon's bed *having* remained barren. The Amphitryon myth will have struck Kleist as suitable material for a drama not least because it allowed him to design a scenario in which Napoleon appoints, as it were, a *surrogate father*—Fr. Wilh.—to produce for himself a "divine" (i.e., Bonapartean) son: Napoléon Hercule (Heracles' foster father, in ancient myth, is Amphitryon; his mortal twin brother, Iphicles, is Amphitryon's son). Napoleon's ideal scheme, Kleist suggests, is modelled on Tyndarus', who impregnated Leda in the same night as Zeus, whereupon Leda gave birth to two *pairs of twins*, one pair fathered by Zeus, the other by Tyndarus, in a sort of "double-double": "*ich neide Tyndarus, / Und wünsche Söhne mir, wie Tyndariden*" (V.1354-5).[339] Sosias' opinion, that any offspring of Napoleon's union with a Hohenzollern will be sterile, introduces an ambivalence into Kleist's solution: Alkmene's "divine" sons (or pair of twin sons), if Sosias is right, would comprise a dynastic "dead end" for Napoleon (unlike Heracles, that ideal stud), as well as posing a threat to him (as Heracles did for Jupiter).[340] Fr. Wilh. may not be quite the fool after all: perhaps he accepts Napoleon's bribe because he anticipates that the egg(s) Napoleon is laying into his nest will be sterile, while his own will be fertile and sire legitimate imperial successors in the following generation. However, Kleist leaves it open whether Sosias is right, or Charis, who evidently believes that the "divine" son(s) will precipitate a truly Herculean dynasty.

As Sosias and Charis debate the merits of the French stallion's and the Prussian jenny's union, Jupiter proclaims that with the birth of Herkules his "pyramid shall be complete" (V.2341). The "pyramid" symbolises the construct Kleist introduced in *Schroffenstein*, *Guiskard* and *Krug*, and whose equivalent today is the extended family enterprise, Ponzi scheme or multi-layer-marketing firm: the *dynastic empire*, constructed by the twin mechanisms of *succession*, or vertical replication (production of legitimate heirs), and *supplementation* or horizontal replication (intermarriages, family appointments, vassalages):

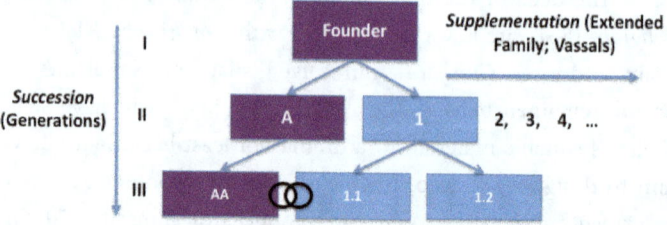

Napoleon's dynastic *"pyramid"* (violet: sons, grandsons; blue: wives, brothers, vassals).

When Goethe in 1807 suggested to A. Müller that Kleist's *Amphitryon* "contorted" the opposition of antiquity and modernity (which Goethe strove to synthesise), and "divided more than uniting" them (cf. *LS*,185), he read Kleist through the "green glasses" of his own concerns. Kleist was primarily concerned not with an aesthetic theory but a political praxis, one sketched not by Goethe's (Christian) *cathedral* (below, left) but by the (pagan) *pyramid*, symbol of an ancient *dynastic principle* that the Pharaohs already knew (below, right):

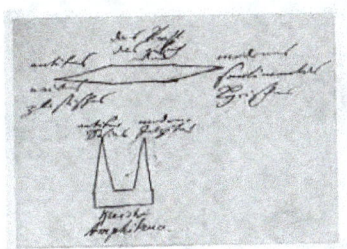 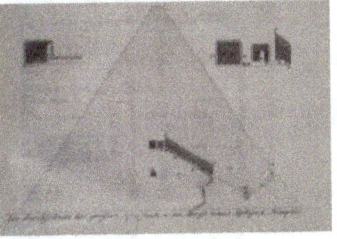

"Cathedral" vs. "pyramid": Goethe's sketch re Kleist's *Amphitryon* (left); the Great Pyramid of Khufu (right), the King's Chamber shown at the centre.

It could have been during his visit of the King's Chamber of the Great Pyramid of Khufu in 1798 that Napoleon first had a vision of dynastic empire; it could have been in Egypt that he became infected with the "French disease":[341]

Napoleon solves the riddle of the Sphinx: "How to build an empire?" "As a pyramid, stupid!"

In *Amphitryon* Kleist explores how in Napoleon's "pyramid" *succession,* via adoption (Merkur-Beauharnais) and siring (Herkules-Napoleon Jr.), is complemented by *supplementation,* via intermarriage (Charis-Auguste) and vassalage (Sosias-Fr. Aug.). Napoleon succeeded in appointing numerous *supplements,* but as of 1807 had failed to produce a *successor,* having been, unlike Jupiter, rather less successful in the marital bed than on the battlefield, so that his work-in-progress "pyramid," although "far-flung," remained "flat":

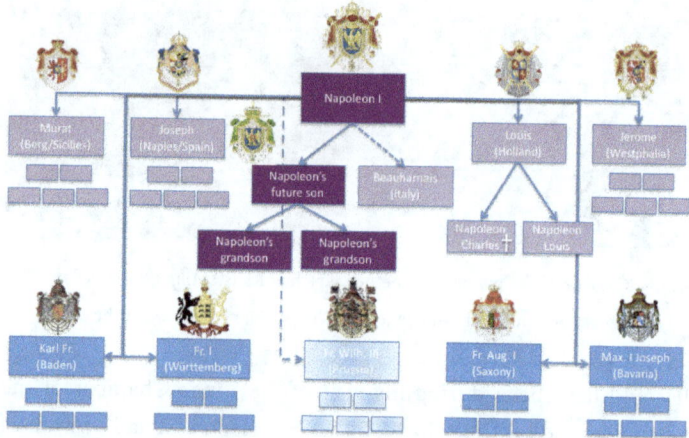

Napoleon's work-in-progress "pyramid" (c.1808);
violet: successors (strictly speaking, Beauharnais does not count);
blue: supplements (family members, vassals).

Founder/ Patriarch:
- Napoleon, Emperor of France (December 1804), King of Italy (May 1805)

Successors (vertical replication):
- None (Beauharnais is excluded from imperial succession; Napoléon Charles dies on 5th May 1807)

Supplements (horizontal replication):
- Eugène de Beauharnais (adopted son), Viceroy of Italy (May 1805)
- Max. I Joseph (vassal), King of Bavaria (January 1806)
- Fr. I (vassal), King of Württemberg (January 1806)
- Karl Fr. (vassal), Grand Duke of Baden (January 1806)
- Joseph Bonaparte (brother), King of Naples (March 1806); King of Spain (June 1808)
- Louis Bonaparte (brother), King of Holland (June 1806)
- Fr. Aug. I (vassal), King of Saxony (December 1806)
- Jérôme Bonaparte (brother), King of Westphalia (July 1807)
- Joachim Murat (brother-in-law), Grand Duke of Berg (March 1808); King of the Two Sicilies (June 1808)

- Napoléon Louis Bonaparte (nephew), Grand Duke of Berg (1809)

Kleist saw Napoleon's *horizontal replication* coming—in late 1805 he told Rühle, "*Es wird sich aus dem ganzen kultivierten Teil von Europa ein einziges, großes System von Reichen bilden, und die Throne mit neuen, von Frankreich abhängigen, Fürstendynastien besetzt werden*" (II:761)—, and a glance at the map of Europe in 1812 proves him right: Russia and the Ottoman Empire apart, which Kleist evidently did not consider part of "civilised" Europe, only Britain, Sweden and Portugal remained outside of Napoleon's "extended family enterprise":

"*ein einziges, großes System von Reichen*": Napoleon baking many new little kings, firing his oven with the old ones (left); Napoleon's sway, 1812 (right).

Kleist also firmly believed that Napoleon would produce a son, one way or the other—and he was correct in this, too: in 1811, Napoleon did. Yet after the *Guiskard* debacle, Kleist in *Amphitryon* hedges his bets, merely *promising* the son, and blurring the father's identity. Kleist would remain obsessed with the question of Napoleon's succession till the end; Napoléon Franz's birth, to a Habsburg mother, in March 1811 may well have helped precipitate his suicide.

Amphitryon, Satyrically

Among the dramas, *Amphitryon* epitomises *"The Satyrical"* just as *Marquise*, clearly derivative of *Amphitryon* in this respect, does among the novellas.

"was / Beim Ortolan geschehn." Among the decadent delicacies Jupiter consummated with Alkmene during their "endless night," one mimicks the consumption of ortolans: a French (!) delicacy, these small birds—which Roman Emperors reportedly had fattened by stabbing their eyes out, making them feed incessantly—are served drowned in liquor and swallowed whole, from the tail-end, the diner throwing a napkin over his head to trap their aroma. Alkmene here offers Amphitryon (and Kleist's audience) a fairly unexpurgated view of these pleasures they enjoyed during their "endless night": Jupiter, having blindfolded her (protecting her from Selene's fate), "drowned" her in alcohol, before "consuming" her from behind, underneath the bedsheet.[342] Kleist's *satyrical* scene has an analogous *satirical* meaning: Fr. Wilh., "fattened" by overconfidence, "blinded" by vanity, and "drunken" with recklessness, was "swallowed hole" by Napoleon "from behind" (moving rapidly from the Rhine via Jena and Berlin, in early 1807 Napoleon invaded East Prussia via Warsaw).

"Von welchem Stand bist du?" Jupiter and Alkmene's "duel" is mimicked by Merkur and Sosias' more rustic one. Like two fencers they face each other and begin by parading their "weapon" and sizing up the other:

> MERKUR. Halt! […]
>   Von welchem Stand bist du?
> SOSIAS.   Von welchem Stande?
>   Von einem auf zwei Füßen, wie Ihr seht.   (V.152-3)

"*Von welchem Stande?*: Merkur and Sosias
(Temple of Dionysos, Delos; cf. also *Krug*, V.86-9).

Merkur, "*das Ich vom Stocke*" (V.746), is extremely well equipped for their bout: his "arm" demands "respect" (V.121), his "stick" is well-versed in "dancing" (V.129), and his "sausage" or "iron eater" is "stiff" and specialised in "back-sides" (V.133-4). Their unequal combat parodies *Jena-Auerstedt*: Merkur attacks like a Jovian thunderbolt, "*Wetter! / Ihr schlagt mir eine gute Faust*," whereupon Sosias immediately seeks retreat, "*Er will gehn*," but Merkur unleashes a staccato of blows on him, "*Ihr Bürger! Ihr Thebaner! Mörder! Diebe!*" (V.213), i.e., !—!—!—!, and Sosias quickly concedes. Like Jupiter of Amphitryon, Merkur is not a faithful copy, but a hyperreal simulacrum, of Sosias, equipped with a far "bigger stick" (V.220). When he has Merkur parade his "beater" before Amphitryon (V.1734-6), Kleist alludes to the *East Prussian Campaign*, during which in early February 1807 Napoleon pulled the *Ad'A* together at Allenstein, in striking distance from Königsberg and quasi right before Fr. Wilh.'s eyes.

Kleist recovers the topos of male sizing-up in the final scene, when Alkmene must choose between the divine and the human lover—which she does, naturally, on the basis of their *phalloi*. By light of day, there *is no comparison* between Amphitryon's pathetic (or severed) piece of equipment, and Jupiter's magnificent member: "*Jetzt erst was für ein Wahn mich täuscht', erblick ich. / Der Sonne heller Lichtglanz war mir nötig, / Solch einen feilen Bau gemeiner Knechte, / Vom Prachtwuchs dieser königlichen Glieder, / [...] zu unterscheiden?*" (V.2247-51).[343] The choice is clear for her—as I said, girls will be girls.

"**Bei dem Geräusch der Spindel.**" Like *Krug's satyrical Urszene* in Eve's bedroom, *Amphitryon's* in Alkmene's chambers entails a battle-cum-banquet-cum-*baquet*. Unlike Walter-Napoleon at *Ulm*, Jupiter-Napoleon in *East Prussia* himself joins in.

> ALKMENE. [...] Der Abend dämmerte,
> Ich saß in meiner Klause und spann, und träumte
> Bei dem Geräusch der Spindel mich ins Feld,
> Mich unter Krieger, Waffen hin, als ich
> Ein Jauchzen an der fernen Pforte hörte.

AMPHITRYON. Wer jauchzte?

ALKMENE.　　　　　　Unsere Leute.　　(V.930-5)

It is dusk; Alkmene sits at her "spindle" and "spins"—let us say: via a twisted yarn she attaches herself to an influence machine or Mesmerian bucket, enters into a trance, and dreams of "warriors" and their "weapons." While entranced, she is penetrated *"an der fernen Pforte"* by a lover who presently *comes* "in exhultation."

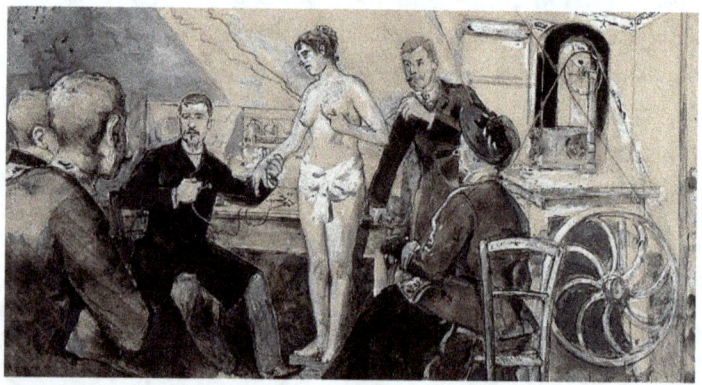

"und spann, und träumte / bei dem Geräusch der Spindel": Alkmene in her chambers.

AMPHITRYON.　　　　　Nun?

ALKMENE.　　　　　　　　　Es fiel
　Mir wieder aus dem Sinn, auch nicht im Traume
　Gedacht ich noch, welch eine Freude mir
　Die guten Götter aufgespart, und eben
　Nahm ich den Faden wieder auf, als es
　Jetzt zuckend mir durch alle Glieder fuhr.

AMPHITRYON. Ich weiß.

ALKMENE.　　　　　Du weißt es schon.

AMPHITRYON.　　　　　　　　Darauf?

ALKMENE.　　　　　　　　　　　Darauf
　Ward viel geplaudert, viel gescherzt, und stets
　Verfolgten sich und kreuzten sich die Fragen.
　Wir setzten uns— […]　　　　　(V.936-44)

Re-attaching herself to the eroticising machine, Alkmene is again penetrated, this time apparently by Jupiter, for a "thunderbolt" gives her a Kleistian shock, "*und eben / Nahm ich den Faden wieder auf, als es / Jetzt zuckend mir durch alle Glieder fuhr*" (V.938-40), and Jupiter recounts this moment in similar terms: "*wie vor dem Unsterblichen / Der Schreck am Rocken dich durchzuckt*" (V.1479-80).

"**Tiara.**" Jupiter's gift to Alkmene is variously denoted as "tiara," "diamond belt," "jewel" ("*Kleinod*") and "stone."[344] Jupiter, "*bei dem Schein der Kerze*," attaches the "tiara" to Alkmene's body, "*— Und einem Gürtel gleich verband ich es, / Den deine Hand mir um den Busen schlang*" (V.951-3); I already noted that this implement evidently represents a chastity belt she is to wear whenever he is absent, but it could also incorporate a strap-on dildo harness she is to wear whenever he is *present*—Jupiter's instructions, "*Du bist, du Heilige, vor jedem Zutritt / Mit diamantnem Gürtel angetan*" (V.1259-60), are ambivalent in this respect. The "diamond" or "stone" could well correspond to a dildo or butt plug attached to the harness (dildos in "brotherhood" banquets widen or facilitate the range of maneuvres available for impotent, coy, or diseased men, as well as women).

"**Glockenspiel**" *(I).* The theme of "plugging into" a *baquet* or similar magneto-electric device pervades the drama; Amphitryon longs for it, so as to temporarily escape the misery of his existence: "*—Fänd nur Gelegenheit sich, anzuknüpfen*" (V.1696).[345] In a trance (Kleist may reflect his experiences with opium), Amphitryon hallucinates about his body fragmenting and dispersing, "*Augen, / Aus ihren Höhlen auf den Tisch gelegt, / Von Leib getrennte Glieder, Ohren, Finger, / Gepackt in Schachteln*" (V.1683-6), and anticipates being subjected to BDSM-esque practices such as branding and subjugation with slave collars or bondage harnesses: "*Jetzo wird man / Die Ehemänner brennen, Glocken ihnen, / Gleich Hämmeln um die Hälse hängen*" (V.1687-9; cf. Réage's *Histoire d'O*).[346]

The terms "*Glocke*" ("bell") or "*Glockenspiel*" ("carillon") occur thrice in the drama (cf. V.1166; 1398; 1688). In the first instance,

Alkmene experiences a similar hallucinatory fantasy as Amphitryon does in the second, "*Nimm mir / Das Aug, so hör ich ihn; das Ohr, ich fühl ihn; / Mir das Gefühl hinweg, ich atm' ihn noch; / Nimm Aug und Ohr, Gefühl mir und Geruch / Mir alle Sinn und gönne mir das Herz: / So läßt du mir die Glocke, die ich brauche, / Aus einer Welt noch find ich ihn heraus*" (V.1161-7); it is as if the orgiasts gathered in the dim, candle-lit crisis room identify each other by the unique sounds of their bells. In the third instance, Jupiter recalls that when joining the orgy, he beheld Alkmene in thrall of a powerful ecstasy, "*So wie das Glockenspiel der Brust umgehn*" (V.1398), her galvanised and impaled body evidently convulsed so heftily that the bells of her slave collar or bondage harness jingled like a carillon.[347]

"Meerrettich." Sosias and Charis' reference—during their reminiscenses of the previous night's orgy—to horseradish root (cf. V.1082-5) also belongs into the field of BDSM.[348] A traditional remedy against muscle pain and infection, horseradish root, whose smell is pungent and whose acidity is extremely irritating to the mucosae, in ancient Greece was deployed in a disciplinary punishment meted out to adulterers and homosexuals known as *rhaphanidosis* and involving the root being shoved up a convict's rectum, where it generates a severely burning sensation.[349] In BDSM this practice, known as *figging*, more commonly deploys ginger roots and may be among the "punishments" a "top" metes out to a "bottom." Given the root's medical properties, Kleist may refer to the root both *syphilitically* as remedy and *satyrically* as torture device.

Horseradish root: the "brotherhood's" erotico-therapeutic *pharmakon*.

In short, Kleist insinuates that in Amphitryon-Fr. Wilh.'s absence, Alkmene-Luise and her entourage engage in psychedelic, hypnotico-magnetic, sado-masochistic orgies. For Kleist's audiences familiar with his *satirical* and *satyrical* code, all of this would have come across as a hilarious insider joke.[350]

"So dreist, wie dieser Fremdling." The divine Jupiter's descent onto the lascivious Alkmene during the orgy in her chambers mirrors the "angelic" Count F's descent onto the agitated Marquise during the conquest of the fortress; Alkmene's being penetrated from behind by an unidentified "warrior" just as Jupiter arrives parallels the Marquise's being "attacked" by the "last of the Russian dogs" just as Count F appears on the scene.[351] As in *Marquise*'s *"Hier—traf er, da"* moment, in which the "doctor" and "women" join the fray, in *Amphitryon*'s *"gingen wir———nun ja!"* moment yet another stealthy gate-crasher appears, for Jupiter mentions that just when Alkmene heared "an exultation at her remote gate" (cf. V.934) he sensed the presence of a "almighty" (i.e., divine) *other*: *"Nur die Allmächtigen mögen / So dreist, wie dieser Fremdling, dich besuchen, Und solcher Nebenbuhler triumphier ich!"* (V.1401-3). This divine *other*, I offer, could only have been *Merkur*, who sneaked up behind Alkmene just prior to his father.

Kleist would have been intrigued by the ancient figure of Merkur (Hermes), known as messenger of the gods, as patron of sexual intercourse and of thieves, as trickster, and as conveyor of souls. Considered quick-witted, sly, furtive, ambiguous, cunning, crafty, scheming, thieving, persuasive, diabolical and amoral, Merkur is just as much *dieu à femmes* as Jupiter: famous for his nocturnal escapades, the list of his divine and human conquests rivals Jupiter's. In Aeschylus' *Eumenides* he helps Orestes kill Clytemnestra by means of deception; in Hermetic literature he is associated with Satan.[352] Merkur's unique features include his herald's staff (*kērykeion*)—entwined by two copulating serpents, it is ascribed magical powers, and Kleist elsewhere writes of it that it opens all locks (cf. *MA*II:485)—and his winged feet, which make him the swiftest of all gods and enables him to be first on the scene whenever it matters.

First on the scene (FLTR): The quick-footed, quick-witted Merkur carries a big, magical stick; ithyphallic *hermai*; woman "sacrificing" before a *hermai*.

It slowly dawns on Alkmene that that *other*, whose presence Jupiter sensed and she herself enjoyed, was not Jupiter but Merkur:

> JUPITER. [...] Wer könnte dir die Augenblickliche
> Goldwaage der Empfindungen betrügen?
> Wer so die Seele dir, die weibliche,
> Die so vielgliedrig fühlend um sich greift,
> So wie das Glockenspiel der Brust umgehn,
> Das von dem Atem lispelnd schon erklingt.
> ALKMENE. Er selber! Er!   (V.1394-1400)

Jupiter's terms "*Lispeln*" and "*vielgliedrig*" allude to the *kērykeion*'s fork-tongued serpents (and its bearer), suggesting that he knows (but prefers not to admit) that before his "thunderbolt" struck her, Alkmene was impaled by Merkur's "staff": sent ahead to make preparations, the swift Merkur arrived on site before his "*alter Vater Jupiter*" (V.1698), found the entranced Alkmene open to whoever arrived at her "gate," and usurped his father's *droit du seigneur*. Alkmene now realises that the mysterious "*Er!*" was no ordinary warrior-lover: the "features" she hazily discerned in her trance seemed so "familiar" to her not because they were Jupiter's in the guise of Amphitryon, but because they were those of the *hermai* before which she regularly worships. Her recollection, *"Es fiel / Mir wieder aus dem Sinn... / ...als es / Jetzt zuckend mir durch alle Glieder fuhr"* (V.935-41), confirms how she puzzled about the stealthy, spectral appearance that vanished as speedily as it appeared, leaving behind nothing but a fuzzy sense of "pleasure," "granted" by the "good gods." When she experienced, re-attached to the *baquet*, the thrust of another *"es,"* namely the Kleistian shock induced by Jupiter's "thunderbolt," in her somnambulant state the two penetrations blurred into a single event.[353]

An intriguing possibility arises from this intricate scene, namely that it was *"das Ich vom Stocke"* Merkur—denoted *"Es"*—, not *"Amphitryon vom Stock"* Jupiter—denoted *"es"*—, who impregnated Alkmene: that not only Amphitryon, but also Jupiter was horned and cuckolded. Another possibility is that *both* Merkur and Jupiter impregnated Alkmene successively, who may then bear two *divine* sons (or two pairs of *divine* twins), leaving Amphitryon empty-handed.[354]

"Ich glaubs—daß mir—ein anderer—erschienen." Alkmene, then, with her searching rethoric would not only *not* be indicating to Amphitryon that Jupiter appeared to her, which some readers like to think, but would also *not* be indicating to Jupiter that she recognises him *as Jupiter*, which I suggested previously. Instead, she would be pleading with Jupiter to tell her whether an unsolicited Third, a "son of a god" (V.1200), usurped her "chamber."[355] Rather than taunting and teasing Jupiter, Alkmene during the "duel" would be desperately seeking to confirm that it was Jupiter who impregnated her: *"Warst dus, warst du es nicht? O sprich! du warsts!"* (V.1265). Like the Marquise, Alkmene *must identify* the father—not because she needs to appoint a *social father*, as the widowed Marquise, for Amphitryon will play that role, but because she needs to ascertain her offspring's *blood line*. Jupiter's response is evasive: *"Ich wars. Seis wer es wolle. Sei—sei ruhig"* (V.1266); perhaps he is about to say, *"Seis wer es wolle. Sei es Merkur,"* but in the moment he has his son's name on his tongue, hesitates, before finishing his sentence with the incongruous *"sei ruhig."* Nevertheless, in seeking to assuage her,

"*Wer deine Schwelle auch betreten hat,* / *Mich immer hast du, Teuerste, empfangen*" (V.1269-70), Jupiter may inadvertently be giving Merkur away: Merkur was also known as the god of *thresholds*. Ultimately, *pater semper incertus est*: Alkmene shall never know who fathered her divine child. "*Ach!*"

"**Böse Kunst.**" Jupiter's relaxed attitude regarding Merkur's intervention suggests that he does not mind Merkur pre-empting him: "Er *war* / *Der Hintergangene, mein Abgott!*" (V.1287-9).[356] Merkur's carefree admission that he merely followed his father on a "love-struck earth adventure" (V.1697-8) furthermore implies that, far from being rivals, father and son were in it together from the start; perhaps they appeared not successively but concurrently, double-penetrating Alkmene:

F O ꟻ

Ménage à trois à Königsberg: Merkur-Alkmene-Jupiter
(or Jupiter-Alkmene-Merkur).[357]

If in their triadic encounter—as related by Alkmene: "*als ich* / *Ein Jauchzen an der fernen Pforte hörte [...] Nun? / Es fiel [...] als es / Jetzt zuckend mir durch alle Glieder fuhr*" (V.934-41)—Merkur's orgasm is marked by "*Ein Jauchzen... Es fiel*" ("a moan... Merkur flagged"), Jupiter's by "*es / Jetzt*" ("Jupiter, now"), and Alkmene's by "*Jetzt zuckend mir*" ("now flashing through me"), then all three lovers *came virtually at once*.

As in *Krug*, Kleist again experiments with incorporating a female figure into a "brotherhood" constellation—as *erômenos* (below, left), as *dmōs* or *erastês*, with the aid of a dildo harness (centre left and centre right), or as *woman* (right):

F F O   O̶F F   F O̶F   F O ꟻ

Ménage à trois constellations incorporating a female lover (red bar = strap-on dildo).

It falls to Sosias to announce publicly the triadic union forged in the "endless night": *"Doch seht! Da kommt er selbst schon. Er und sie"* (V.2166); *"er selbst"* = Jupiter, *"Er"* = Merkur, *"sie"* = Alkmene. Amphitryon takes his cue from Sosias and grudgingly acknowledges the constellation: *"Blitz, Höll und Teufel"* (V.2179); *"Blitz"* = Jupiter, *"Teufel"* = Merkur, *"Höll"* = Alkmene. Alkmene, Amphitryon thus acknowledges, has now become his—*hell*.

Amphitryon, Syphilitically

"One night with Venus, a lifetime with Mercury," as the saying went: Venus, of course, lent her name to venereal disease (*morbus venerus*), and Mercury his to its most common—and scarcely less gruesome— remedy. Merkur's presence in *Amphitryon* is stealthy but pervasive— as is Venus', for in Kleist's character Alkmene the two deities unite: Alkmene is *hermaphrodite* in the precise sense that in her *Mercury* (Hermes) and *Venus* (Aphrodite), gruesome therapeutic poisoning, insidious venereal disease, and passionate erotic love, coincide. Alkmene is more than the central character of Kleist's drama: she embodies the very paradigm of his œuvre—her body and soul is the very *Lustgarten*-cum-*Kampfplatsz*, the very *plane of composition*, on which all Kleistian forces and intensities clash: *"Ach!"*

"Stachel." Since Sosias' member features a *"Klotz"* or "chunk" (V.516; cf. Adam's *"Klumpen"*), given his perfect guise as Sosias, *"Zwei Tropfen Wasser sind nicht ähnlicher"* (V.715), Merkur's must be "chunky," too—which a quick self-check of his Sosian body confirms: *"Da unten ist ein ungeschliffener Riegel"* (V.1722; *"ungeschliffen"* = "course," *"Riegel"* = "latch," "bolt"; cf. *Schroffenstein*'s "rugged stone"). This does not mean that Merkur *as Merkur* is diseased: only Merkur-in-the-guise-of-Sosias is, for he assumes Sosias' bodily appearance precicesly, including its symptoms. Markur *as Sosias* carries and transmits the disease, without himself, as immortal god, being infected (the same applies to Jupiter *as Amphitryon*). Apart from acting as vector of the disease, Merkur also functions as its *pharmakon*, so that Alkmene's worshipping before his *hermai* implies that she is undergoing mercury treatment. Merkur's "well-known feature"—his "staff"—is also referred to as "sting"—"*O einen Stachel trägt er, glaub es ihm / Den aus dem liebeglühnden Busen ihm / Die ganze Götterkunst nicht reißen kann*" (V.1295-8)—, thus symbolising not only a mighty member but also a gargantuan syringe.

Like the other characters, Merkur regularly plugs into a *baquet* or Kleistian jar to recharge—"to feed on the bottle's nourishment," as he puts it. His entwined staff/sting, which he conveniently carries with him at all times, is the perfect body part for connecting to the device: "*Denn aus dem Flaschenfutter trinkt man nicht, / Wenn man, wie ich, zufällig nicht im Sacke / Den Schlüssel, der gepaßt, gefunden hätte*" (V.365-7).[358] Alongside Alkmene's "spindle," Merkur's "sting" or "staff"—Beauharnais' *aiguillette*, Hermes' *kērykeion*—enriches Kleist's ingenious typology of *baquet*-strings:

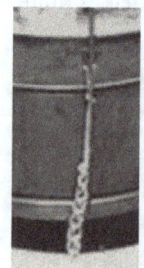    

Baquet-strings: Mesmer's cord, Adam's wig; Alkmene's spindle, Merkur's staff (*aiguillette*, *kērykeion*).

The "preparations" Jupiter sent Merkur to orchestrate thus involved not only resetting the sun dial to keep the citizens in their extended slumber, but also injecting Alkmene with mercury as a prophylactic, so as to protect her from infection while Jupiter makes love to her in Amphitryon's diseased body. Since an injection by Merkur is always also a penetration, Merkur's pre-empting Jupiter comprised the inoculation and immunisation of Jupiter's objet of desire authorised and prescribed by Jupiter himself. Alkmene, during her fantastical "endless night," experiences the full gamut of *satyrico-syphilitical* interventions: inoculation, double penetration, infection, therapy.

"**wie ein Maienwurm.**" Despite Merkur's inoculation, Alkmene on the morning after suffers an outbreak of syphilis symptoms. She promptly blames Amphitryon for her condition: "*Du Ungeheuer! Mir scheußlicher, / Als es geschwollen in Morästen nistet! / Was tat ich dir, daß du mir nahen mußtes, / Von einer Höllennacht bedeckt, / Dein Gift mir auf den Fittich hinzugeifern? / Was mehr, als daß ich, o du Böser, dir / Still, wie ein Maienwurm, ins Auge glänzte?*" (V.2240-6). Alkmene's *syphilitical* "code" covers familiar ground: "monster" appears in a similar context in *Guiskard*, "poison" in *Schroffenstein*, and "morass" (as "mud") in *Marquise*; "*Maienwurm*" ("oil beetle") may belong into the same metaphorical field as "angel," "dove," and "swan," denoting the immaculate, symptom-free lover.[359] Alkmene's blaming Amphitryon after having enjoyed Jupiter's embrace may suggest, *satirically*, that she considers "German disease" to have preceded, and precipitated, the advent of "French disease" (cf. also *Schroffenstein*).

"**Opferdampf.**" Alkmene and Charis are repeatedly shown sacrificing "fervently" and "glowingly" before an "altar" (probably a *hermai*) installed in the vestibule of Amphitryon's house (cf. V.773-4; 830).[360] Alkmene's reflection before the altar, "*Ich bin bewegt, den Göttern will ich opfern*" (V.829), implies that "being stirred" is part and parcel of the sacrificial act, and that her "offering" consists in fresh *cum*, which she produces *in loco* and uses as therapeutic purifier (say, of solvable mercury compounds).[361] Alkmene's ritual before the *hermai*—"*Anbetung, glühnd, wie Opferdampf, gen Himmel / Aus dem Gebrodel des Gefühls...?*" (V.1440-2)—may furthermore suggest that her "worshipping" involves mercury steam baths:

> Patients would be shut up in a 'stew', a small steam room, often for twenty or thirty days at a time. Wrapped in blankets, they were left to sweat in a hot tub or by a fire and given mercury, either as a drink or as an ointment for their suppurating sores. One of the more curious methods was fumigation, in which the patient was placed in a closed box with his or her head sticking out. Mercury was placed in the box and a fire was started under the box that caused the mercury to vaporise—a gruelling process of breathing in the fumes for the patient.

These methods induced sweating and salivation. It was said that the patient needed to produce at least three pints of saliva for the poison to be expelled from the body.³⁶²

In addition to electro-shock and magnetic therapy, Alkmene's treatment apparently involves purification with *cum* (ointment), worshipping Merkur's "sting" (injections), and exposure to "sacrificial vapour" (mercury fumigation):

  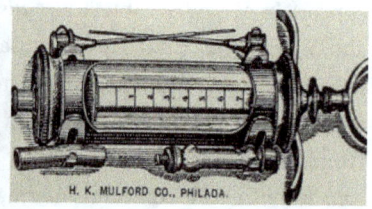

"Martyrdom of Mercury" (John Sintelaer, 1709):
Mercury fumigation, pills or ointment, syringe.³⁶³

When she insists that prior to the "endless night" she was a "*Maienwurm*," i.e., immaculate, Alkmene is not necessarily lying: her sacrifices before Hermes could have been prophylactic, aiming at protecting her from infection, a rational choice given her husband's evident diseasedness and her own promiscuity.

"Glockenspiel" *(II).* Jupiter's associating the carillion with Alkmene's *feminine soul*, "*die Seele dir, die weibliche, / Die so vielgliedrig fühlend um sich greift, / So wie das Glockenspiel der Brust umgehn*" (V.1396-8), recalls Johann's associating an asphyxiating serpent with his *life in madness*, "*Es hat das Leben mich wie eine Schlange, / Mit Gliedern, zahnlos, ekelhaft, umwunden*" (V.1048-9), and Marthe's equating a boa constrictor with *the contortion of speech*: "*Daß die Rede sich, / Herr Richter, wie die Reisenschlange aufbäumt, / Und Wahrheit, mit geschmeid'gem Gliederbau / Geknäuelt wie in blökend Lamm, erdrückt.*"³⁶⁴ Plausibly Kleist's carillon, like his serpent, refers to symptoms of syphilis that cover, and itchingly entwine, the entire body—say, papules or nodules.

"**In Staub.**" The Germans' collective spraying of *cum*, "*Er ists! In Staub! In Staub das Antlitz hin!* / *Alles wirft sich zur Erde außer Amphitryon*" (V.2315) may suggest that in the drama's grand finale, the Germans undergo group-therapy involving a combination of electroshock delivered by Jupiter-Napoleon and mercury fumigation applied by Merkur-Beauharnais. Fr. Wilh., excluded from the session, is doomed to suffer a fate of slow deformation, madness, and death.[365]

Amphitryon adds to our understanding of the *state of knowledge* concerning the progression and characteristics of syphilis on which Kleist based his *syphilitical* "threads:

- Some lovers are more contagious than others (presumably in proportion to the severity to the symptoms they exhibit—cf. *Schroffenstein*'s "scorpion" and "basilisk"); lovers whose disease is in a latent stage are uninfectious;[366]
- Renewed intercourse with (highly) contagious lovers boosts or restores one's own symptoms and increases the virulence of one's own infection, and may even induce instant death;[367]
- Conversely, infectiousness can be suppressed by mercury treatment, which is therefore applied not only therapeutically but also prophylactically, as part of "initiation" or "purification" rituals (hence the euphorical reception, in Kleist's works, of lovers emerging "purified" from mercury baths, and Kleist's own tireless quest for therapies despite their side-effects);
- Intercourse with a "pure," "immaculate" lover, and ingestion of, or bathing in, his ejaculate, are themselves remedial—ejaculate is a *pharmakon*: remedy if "pure," poison if "contaminated"—, and pure ejaculate is a valued commodity gathered and circulated among "brothers."

Amphitryon, Po(ï)etically

Why did Kleist, who admittedly never shied away from adopting elements from extant works, his own or others', with *Amphitryon* take this palimpsestic approach to an extreme? How does *Amphitryon*'s genesis relate to his personal adventures between December 1806 and July 1807, which took him on foot from Königsberg to Berlin, and thence, as French prisoner, to Fort de Joux in the French Jura and Châlons-sur-Marne in the Champagne?

"Ein Lustspiel nach Molière." Concerning the first question, the drama's subtitle's ambiguous term, "*nach*"—i.e., "after," "adopted from"—, alerts the reader to expect a decidedly *un*Molièrean (namely, Kleistian) text that is only *overtly* situated within the "genealogy of texts" (Franz M. Eybl) that includes, apart from Molière's, most notably Hesiod's, Sophocles', Plautus', Rotrous', and Falk's versions.[368] What Kleist's drama owes to this "genealogy of texts," apart from "raw materials" and "intermediate products" that helped accelerate his assembly, is this very situatedness *as such*, which adds an extra layer of camouflage especially towards a certain type of educated but naïve reader (and censor) who "reads" the text precisely through the lens of this "genealogy," the lens then becoming akin to "green glasses" that preclude her from appreciating Kleist's drama as entirely *sui generis*.[369]

By crediting Molière in the subtitle, and painstakingly translating entire passages from him verbatim, Kleist positions his drama not as latest contribution to a "genealogy," but as adaptation of *one particular instance* within it, specifically, a French (!) one, thereby rendering his drama less conspicuous and suspicious to censors than any other work he could possibly have written, in German, during wartime, while imprisoned in France. At its limit, Eybl's insistence on the literary concept of "genealogy" can become counter-productive in understanding Kleist's manoeuvre, for it veils that which is most essential, namely Kleist's *specific context*, by subsuming his drama under a generic series. Kleist's copying entire passages from Molière was not only a matter of *practicality*, allowing him to produce a full-length drama faster than otherwise, but above all one of *strategy*: by making it *appear* as an adaptation from Molière, he packages his highly inflammatory anti-French political pamphlet as a deferential hommage to a French cultural icon. Molière's text, as it were, serves Kleist as *pescherä* upon which he constructs a "*Gewebe*" (V.996) that is entirely "*Trugnetz*" (V.1831).[370] I have no doubt that Kleist held Molière in high regard, but desperate times call for desperate measures, and Kleist had no qualms deploying the French master against an unhinged France that Molière himself, would have inundated with massive doses of his trademark satire.

"*Die Unsrigen / In Schlachtordnung auf einem Hügel hier.*" Concerning the second question, at first sight the drama's evident references to historical events that took place between mid-October and late December 1806—*Jena-Auerstedt* (14th October; cf. Sosias' soliloquy), the *Treaty of Posen* (11th December; "*Wir schlossen Waffenstillstand*"; V.269), Fr. Aug.'s proclamation as King of Saxony (20th December; "*er besingungswürdge Schläg erhalten*"; V.2355) and Fr. Wilh.'s exile in East Prussia (from late December 1806; "*so früh nicht, als er wünscht*"; V.63-4)—suggest that these ten weeks comprised its *main stage* of production. It is, however, possible and plausible that an *initial stage* of production took place *before* that period, not as early as 1803 or 1804, as some commentators have suggested, but in the first half of 1806, because all the above-mentioned references could originally have been designed to cover historical events of late 1805: *Austerlitz* instead of *Jena-Auerstedt*, *Schönbrunn* and *Pressburg* instead of *Posen*, the Bavarian Elector's instead of the Saxon Elector's elevation, Franz II's exile in Bohemia instead of Fr. Wilh.'s in East Prussia. In certain details *Amphitryon*'s text squares even better with the events of 1805/6 than with those of 1806/7: for example, in Sosias' account of the battle, *"Die Unsrigen / In Schlachtordnung auf einem Hügel hier"* (V.83-4) evokes the Austro-Russian positions on the famous Pratzen Hill near Austerlitz rather more readily than the Saxo-Prussian positions near Auerstedt or Jena; Beauharnais' marriage to Auguste, alluded to by Merkur's encounter with Charis, took place in January 1806; the transfer of the imperial dignity from Franz II to Napoleon, symbolised by the tiara's "A" becoming "J," was completed with Franz's abdication as Holy Roman Emperor in August 1806. Kleist could have worked on *Amphitryon* alongside *Krug*, and at some point in the early summer decided to prioritise the latter as the more suitable platform for his urgent manifesto to Fr. Wilh. Three months later, Prussia's debacle at *Jena-Auerstedt* suddenly rendered his *Amphitryon* draft more pertinent and timely than ever, Prussia's plight in late 1806 indeed entailing a déjà vu of Austria's in late 1805, and Kleist could have pulled *Amphitryon* out of the drawer and turned it into his response to Prussia's catastrophe.

"daß der Postenkurs gestört ist." It is, furthermore, possible and plausible that a *third stage* of production took place *after* the October-December 1806 period. This remains conjecture, and if Kleist did revise the MS in early 1807, the revisions may have been focused on a few passages, but possible and plausible it is. The Kleist reception generally assumes that Kleist had completed *Amphitryon* by late December 1806, a reasonable assumption given that he told Ulrike on 31st December 1806 of MSS he had sent to Berlin (presumably to Rühle—cf. II:775; 781), that Chr. G. Körner's on 17th February 1807 offered Göschen an *Amphitryon* MS he received from A. Müller (cf. LS,169), and that in March 1807 from Fort de Joux twice requested Wieland's help in finding a publisher for MSS, of which Kleist in December 1807 recalled—caveated *"wenn ich mich nicht irre"*—that they included *Amphitryon* (cf. II:799).[371] It is indeed plausible that from late December 1806 onward Kleist sought to publish (a version of) *Amphitryon*: the war was far from over—Russia remained undefeated, 120,000 Russian troops under the command of Levin August von Benningsen were gathered along the East Prussian border and the river Vistula, several fortresses remained in Prussian hands, and up to 75,000 Prussian soldiers were re-grouping in Farther Pomerania, Silesia, and East Prussia, and several Prussian *Freikorps* were launching partisan action against the *Ad'A*—and the 1806/7 turn of the year would indeed have been a *kairotic* moment for Kleist's war propaganda.[372] As Napoleon was drawing together 200,000 men near Warsaw in preparation for a spring campaign in East Prussia, and the French were consolidating control of occupied Prussia, *Amphitryon*'s unique camouflage made it the most suitable vehicle for Kleist's messages, be they addressed to the King in East Prussia or to the wider Prussian resistance. Yet people who obtained copies of an *Amphitryon* MS—Rühle in Berlin, A. Müller and Körner in Dresden, Gentz in Prague (cf. LS,172b; 173)—evidently did not find a publisher, while Kleist himself, having posted his MSS from Königsberg, hit the road. *Amphitryon*'s message of Prussia's "endless night"—her humiliation in battle and interminable occupation and vassalage—remained pertinent, but events continued to develop unabatedly, while a publisher remained evasive.

Kleist's mailing his MSS to Berlin on 30th December, and leaving Königsberg south-westwards for Berlin a few days later, virtually on the same day on which the royal household left the city north-eastwards for Memel, are clearly connected. While Königsberg was at risk of being completely encircled and put under siege, Prussian troops remained operational in some areas to the west, e.g., in Farther Pomerania; Prussia's political élite largely remained in Berlin, which, despite its occupation, Kleist may have expected to become the hub of Prussian political resistance: Napoleon's imminent *East Prussian Campaign*, and the Royals' flight to Memel, would take the spotlight away from Berlin. Such considerations enticed him to set off in the direction diametrical to that the Royals were taking, motivated by the same objective that would trigger his similarly precipitous departure from Dresden for Vienna and Prague in April 1809: *to help fuel the German resistance*. The MSS he mailed to Berlin could have served as agitatorial propaganda, in purpose if not in style anticipating his 1809 *Germania* project. Since the French controlled all postal corridors to Berlin—"the postal connections were interrupted" (cf. II:775)—, Kleist could not expect his documents to reach their destination uncensored, if at all. To mitigate the risk of losing his work, he backed up mailing his parcel with personally couriering a second copy to Berlin. There were thus (at least) *two* copies of these MSS: one in the mail (which evidently did reach its addressee), the other in his rucksack.[373] Upon reaching Berlin in January 1807, he may have found French control too tight to allow resistance to incubate, and decided to press on to unoccupied Dresden, which he may have anticipated could become a hotspot of resistence, as Prague would in 1809.[374] Had he not, in late January, been apprehended at Berlin's southern city gate, evidently en route to Dresden (cf. Rahmer, *Kleist*, 102), Kleist in 1807 might have churned out the type of quick-fire patriotic propaganda he would notoriously produce two years later; perhaps the idea of the *Germania* journal already fermented in his mind.

"daselbst meine litterarischen Projecte eben so gut ausführen."
Kleist and his two fellow travellers, Carl Franz von Gauvain and Fr. Ehrenberg, were arrested as spies and transported across Germany to Joux, where they were imprisoned from 5th March till early April 1807, when they were transferred to Châlons, where they remained under less severe conditions until released on 12th July, following *Tilsit* (which settled the mutual release of prisoners of war). Kleist took his capture with equanimity: on 17th February, en route to Joux, he tells Ulrike: "*so kann ich daselbst meine litterarischen Projecte eben so gut ausführen als anderswo*" (II:777). Where better to write anti-French propaganda than in French retention, provided one was furnished with the necessary writing materials and one's captors remained in the dark about one's true intentions? Whichever "literary projects" Kleist was looking to advance—*Amphitryon, Penthesilea, Käthchen, Kohlhaas, Marquise*, items not extant —, he presumably carried all his MSS and works-in-process with him when he was arrested, since he could not have expected to return to Königsberg or Berlin in the foreseeable future. He may have introduced himself to the French military police as a poet sustaining himself with his literary work, including trans. from the French; the *Amphitryon* MS with its long passages of verbatim trans. of Molière, which every French military policemen would recognise, could virtually have been his passport and life insurance; it would be oh-so-Kleistian if the anti-French propaganda he encrypted into a famous work of French literature saved him and his friends from a fate worse than imprisonment.

On 31st March, a few days before his transfer to Châlons, Kleist wrote to the *Commandant du fort de Joux* to thank him for furnishing him a French dictionary and grammar (cf. II:777), perhaps fashioning an excuse for misappropriating these materials and taking them with him to Châlons: his note, "*nous en fons le meilleur usage que possible*," is as assuaging as it is ironic. Assuming he was permitted to keep the MSS he carried with him upon being arrested, which is likely given his lighthearted letter to Ulrike, Kleist could have continued revising

Amphitryon in captivity, thus adding a *third stage* of its production during the spring of 1807, so that the version published in May by Arnold in Dresden *could have been distinct* from the earlier version, now lost, that had found its way to Körner.[375]

The voice from Joux. The two key *satirical* events of early 1807 were *Eylau* (7/8th February) and Napoleon's subsequent peace overtures to Fr. Wilh., culminating in his envoy Bertrands' visit to Memel within days or weeks of the battle. Fr. Wilh. remained undecided, when Alex. in early April visited Memel to press for a renewal of their alliance (which he accomplished with the signing of *Bartenstein* on 26th April). During his transport to Joux, Kleist will have been kept abreast of developments by his loyal friend Schlotheim who followed his caravan (cf. Rahmer, *Kleist*, 94), but upon arriving in Joux on 5th March, he will have depended on information provided by his French captors, who may have conveyed an unshaken belief that a separate peace between France and Prussia was imminent. It is, in other words, possible that Kleist's *memorandum* was based on the false premise, in part misconstrued by his guards, in part by Kleist himself, that Fr. Wilh. was about to enter a peace with Napoleon, and that Luise and Hardenberg were advocating such a move, which in fact they were opposing (in this *third stage* of the drama's genesis Sosias could have come to represent Hardenberg).[376]

The drama's central "duel," in which Alkmene-*Borussia* forces Jupiter-Napoleon into a draw, may already have existed in the earlier version, but may have undergone careful edits in my conjectured *third stage* of projection: on the one hand, it may be said to comprise Kleist's stylised rendering of *Eylau*, an epic but inconclusive battle in which a Coalition army for the first time shook Napoleon's nimbus of invincibility, inflicting heavy losses on the *Ad'A* (up to 30,000 French casualties, roughly matched on the Prusso-Russian side), halted Napoleon's advance on Königsberg, and bolstered Alex.'s, and to some degree Fr. Wilh.'s, resolve to fight to the end.[377] On the other hand, the scene may be said to encompass the subsequent diplomatic exchanges between Napoleon (via his envoy Bertrand) and Fr. Wilh. (advised by Luise and Hardenberg), in which *Borussia* signals that she is prepared to submit to Napoleon's de facto sway, provided she is permitted to remain de jure independent: *Borussia* agrees to a secret alliance with Napoleon, in exchange for his evacuating her and promising Fr. Wilh. a notional imperial title for his successor (divine child).

Upon arriving in Joux, Kleist may immediately have set to work to fashion *Amphitryon*, mostly with subtle edits, into a manifesto to his King. The *terminus ante quem* for completing the revised *Amphitryon*, allowing for sufficient time for mailing it to Dresden and preparing its publication in May, would have been early-mid April—incidentally, precisely the time when Alex. visited Fr. Wilh. in Memel! Kleist urges his King to resist the temptation of entering a Faustian pact with a Mephistophelian Napoleon (i.e., self-castrate, as he has Amphitryon do with poor results) that could only lead to Prussia's utter submission: *"Doch laß sie ruhn, wenn sie dir bleiben soll!—"* (V.2347) is the key warning: whatever his promises, in any alliance with Napoleon, you will lose de facto control of your country!

Possibly Kleist posted the revised *Amphitryon* MS from Joux on the very day—say 1ˢᵗ April—before was to be transferred to Châlons (the transfer involved an easing of the conditions of his retention, possibly including permission to post mail). His guards certainly screened his mail, but a "trans." of a famous French comedy posted to a Dresden publisher (Saxony being a French ally) had a better chance of leaving Joux and reaching Dresden than just about any other document he could have requested to post. Perhaps Kleist's assurance to the *Commandant du fort de Joux* of 31ˢᵗ March, *"nous en fons le meilleur usage que possible,"* was doubly ironic: "thank you very much indeed, Sire, for equipping me to write anti-French propaganda, and for now letting me post it to my Dresden publisher." The drama's subtitle and verbatim trans. from Molière will have been *essential* for it to pass the censors and become published; and had *Amphitryon* not been published in May 1807, it might never have been, and we might know no more about it today than we do about other projects not executed or not extant. When he dispatched it on 1ˢᵗ April 1807, *Amphitryon* "fell into the middle of time" just as precisely as *Krug* did on 30th August 1806, and *Hermannsschlacht* on 1st January 1808. By the time the drama was published, *Bartenstein* had been signed and Kleist's manifesto came ever so slightly too late (and, as it turned out, would not have been required); but from France, Kleist at this point had no more control over the publication.

"wenn ich nicht irre." Should we take at face value Kleist's assertion to Wieland that he had produced the abovementioned MSS (which we assume included *Amphitryon*) had been produced already in the summer of 1806 (cf. II:1049)? As we saw, while there may have been an initial version of *Amphitryon* at that time, Kleist will have significantly revised it in October-December 1806, and again in early 1807, and his assertion probably served as decoy: anything produced by a Prussian writer *after* Fr. Wilh.'s ultimatum to Napoleon of 26th September 1806 would have been treated with greater suspicion by the French authorities than anything produced *before* it, and Kleist may have deliberately inserted a fake date to mislead the censors in case his letter was intercepted; an unsuspecting Wieland might furthermore share the fake information with publishers—*et voilà*, Kleist would have created a fictional genesis that made the drama appear harmless. Kleist's *"wenn ich nicht irre"* (V.799) caveat to Wieland may have sought to alert Wieland that the MS referred to in the letter was not identical with the published version that he by now would be familiar with, and to establish whether Wieland was still in possession of a *Amphitryon* MS. Kleist routinely destroyed interim versions of his works and requested interlocutors to return drafts to him.

Kohlberg. "*Was überhaupt bewog Heinrich von Kleist, sich im Januar 1807 von Königsberg auf den Weg nach Berlin zu machen?*," asks Gerhard Schulz (*Kleist*, 303-6), and conjectures that Kleist left for Dresden to meet his publishers. Günter Blamberger offers (*Kleist*, 246) that Kleist was motivated primarily by financial problems and hoped to beg Ulrike for cash (on 31st December he indeed told her that he was running dry—cf. II:775), who at the time was staying in Schorin in Pomerania, halfway between Danzig and Kolberg near the Baltic coast, which would explain Kleist's choice of route—which, Michalzik points out (*Kleist*, 284), is furthermore explained by the fact that Farther Pomerania remained under Prussian control. Most commentators also agree that Kleist dreaded being immobilised in Königsberg when Napoleon was closing in on the city, and decided to leave before all exit routes were shut. While all of these propositions are plausible—and compossible—, they betray a lack of appreciation of what motivated Kleist above all else: *his political agenda*.

Beyond the need to escape from Königsberg's looming encirclement, and to address financial and publishing issues (all of which may have played a role), I conjecture that Kleist prepared to foster a *"Grande Riposte"* against Napoleon. If Napoleon was to be pinned down by the Russian and Prussian forces in East Prussia, Kleist, together with leaders such as Gneisenau and Ferd. von Schill, could orchestrate counterstrikes in Napoleon's rear, disconnecting him from supplies. If Britain and Sweden were to join the Coalition and to launch an invasion of Pomerania from the Baltic Sea, as in early January 1807 they were negotiating, they could march on Berlin and the *Ad'A* off.[378] When he left Königsberg for Pomerania, Kleist could well have anticipated that the fortunes of war were about to turn, and that Pomerania would become the main theatre of Prussia's liberation. The Baltic fortress of Kolberg, with a garrison of 6,000 Prussian troops, and the entire coast of Farther Pomerania, between Diegenow on the Oder's outlet in the west, and Köslin in the east (the ancestral lands of the von Kleist family), remained under Prussian control, and the illustrious Major Schill's *Freikorps* operated in the western part of Farther Pomerania, from a base in Greifenberg (which Kleist would pass en route to Berlin). With Silesia also still largely under Prussian control, a Prussian pincer movement from Pomerania and Silesia, supported by a British-Swedish landing near Stettin, could liberate Berlin and isolate the *Ad'A* in Eastern Prussia and Poland, wedged between the Russians advancing from the east, and the consolidating Coalition forces in the west:

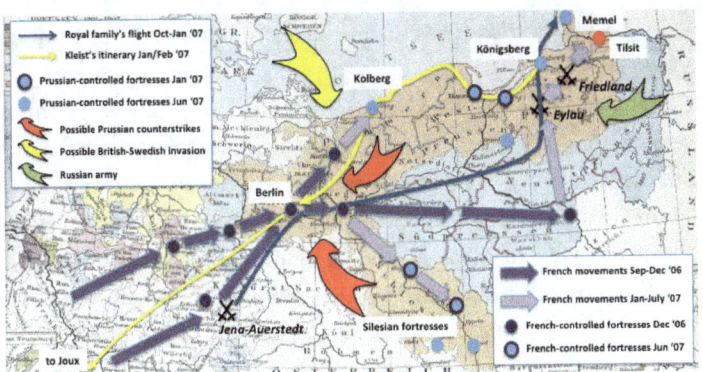

"Grande Riposte": Kleist vs. Napoleon.

The real question, then, is not why Kleist went to Pomerania, but why he *did not stay there*, soon moving on to Berlin and, had he not been arrested, Dresden. In so far as he and his comrades had hoped to "embed" themselves with the defenders of Kolberg, they arrived *too early*, for the *Siege of Kolberg* would commence only on 14th March, and Gneisenau was only to arrive in late April to lead the defence. In so far as they had expected to join Schill—Kleist, Pfuel, Gauvain and Ehrenberg were all decommissioned officers and could have hoped to offer their services to the *Freikorps*—this may have proven impractical. Perhaps aalready before arriving in Kolberg, they learned that three major Silesian fortresses had capitulated, so that the pincer movement Kleist envisioned became unfeasible, or that the British-Swedish invasion had been called off. At this juncture, rallying a nothern German insurrection in Napoleon's rear became the final straw—and this was best done from Berlin or Dresden.[379] It would make for a fascinating "alternative history" to play through what Kleist might have done had he not been seized.[380] In the event, Kleist was locked up during the decisive months running up to *Tilsit*, relegated to composing dramas; if his retention provided the occasion for *Amphitryon*'s completion and *Penthesilea*'s conception, we shall even be grateful for it.

Ach!

2.5 *Penthesilea*: The Usurper's Death: Reloaded (An Utopia)

Genesis and Context. *Penthesilea. Ein Trauerspiel* survives in three versions: an MS (M), extant in copy produced by another hand but corrected by Kleist himself, which Sembdner (cf. II:960) terms "more blatant" than the other versions, and whose completion Kleist reported to Marie in the late autumn of 1807 (cf. II:796), to Ulrike and Wieland on 17th December 1807 (cf. II:798-9); an *Organisches Fragment aus dem Trauerspiel: Penthesilea* (Ph), published in the January 1808 issue of *Ph*, and a book version (P), published by Cotta between June and October 1808, on which my analysis primarily rests.[381]

In February 1808 Kleist requested Joh. Gottlieb Gärtner to publish *Penthesilea,* which was prevented by the publisher's financial difficulties (cf. II:810; *KH*,50); the drama's "complete reading" in Körner's house in April 1808 (cf. Schulz, *Kleist*, 323) likely involved (P)'s MS. While the differences between the three versions, in terms of style, wording, syntax, orthography, punctuation, etc., are not trivial, I focus on exploring intricacies of their genesis and publication history. For example, January's (Ph) does not include Penthesilea's death, cutting off as it does with the "breaking news" of her vanquishing Achilles (cf. V.2584), while February's MS offered to publishers certainly included this ending; having *privately* "pronounced her dead" already in December 1807 (cf. II:796), what were the *satirical* circumstances that in February 1808 compelled Kleist to *publicly* announce or predict Penthesilea's death?

On 31st August 1806, the day after sending the *Krug* MS to Marie, Kleist told Rühle that he had commenced a *"Trauerspiel"*—usually held to be *Penthesilea* (cf. *KH*,50)—which he expected to complete within 3-4 months; having been granted leave of absence by Altenstein (cf. II:769), he hoped to henceforth produce *"Trauerspiele und Lustspiele"* at a rate that would enable him to make a living from writing. When Prussia's crushing defeat in October, and Napoleon's swift campaign across northern Germany, rendered Kleist's situation in Königsberg precarious, he responded by experimenting with a different genre altogether, one optimally suited for generating rapid output and conveying news: *the novella*. Kleist probably completed *Erdbeben* by December 1806 and commenced *Kohlhaas* soon after, progressing it during his retention alongside *Marquise*, while also revising *Amphitryon* and commencing *Penthesilea*.[382]

Released from retention and arrived in Dresden in August 1807, Kleist and his new friend A. Müller begin preparing the *Ph* project, Kleist's designated platform for the serial publication of his works (the friends also hoped to set up a publishing company, but failed to obtain the necessary license). The autumn of 1807 was a busy period for Kleist: while putting in place the commercial and legal aspects of *Ph*, he worked intensely on lining up publishable materials—his own and others'—to be able to "feed" (in Goethe's pejorative, yet apposite, term) a monthly publication of not insubstantial volume, on average encompassing c.50 pages per issue. Kleist tried, but failed, to recover the *Erdbeben* MS from Cotta, yet in addition to the as-of-yet unpublished *Krug* and *Marquise*, managed to line up *Penthesilea*, *Guiskard*, *Kohlhaas* and *Käthchen* fragments, with his work on *Penthesilea* (M) and (Ph), the commencement of *Käthchen* (cf. II:797), and the completion of *Marquise* overlapping. Instead of publishing a drama every 3-4 months, as he announced to Rühle in August 1806, Kleist in 1807 commenced, without necessarily completing, a more diverse set of works, his "publication channel" to some extent shaping his output: had he succeeded in setting up a publishing company, he might have executed his original plan communicated to Rühle, for dramas would have lent themselves for book publication, but when *Ph* became his main channel, he focused on churning out shorter, faster-to-market pieces: novellas, epigrams, poems, fragments. This interdependency of channel and genre establishes a pattern that prevails throughout his writing career: for Kleist *writing* is always *delivered writing*, delivered to a *target audience*, within a *precise context*; he never pursued his art purely for art's sake.

Kleist, his letters to Ulrike suggest, during the autumn of 1807 was in reasonably good health and full of optimism. On the political front things have quieted down after *Tilsit*, and while much of Prussia remained French-controlled, the Saxon capital was relatively open and liberal and attracted many Prussian intellectuals and political refuges. Kleist experiences a period of calm, during which he systematically pursued his projects, and once more foregrounded his *Agôn* with Goethe, notably centred on *Penthesilea*. That he invested great energy into that drama is suggested by its MS' many iterations (cf. II:797), by its repeated recitations in Dresden salons, and by the tears he (and Pfuel) shed when in late 1807 he announced: *"jetzt ist sie tot"* (II:796; cf. *LS*,198). *Penthesilea*'s designation, *"Ein Trauerspiel,"* links it to *Schroffenstein* (*"Ein Trauerspiel in Fünf Aufzügen"*) and *Guiskard* (*"Fragment aus dem Trauerspiel"*), and even if by this time he is no longer thought along these lines, it could be said that *Penthesilea* capped a *tetralogy* of sorts, comprising the two tragedies (*Schroffenstein*, *Penthesilea*), the comedy (*Amphitryon*), and the satyr play (*Krug*) he had by now completed.

"Scene: Schlachtfeld bei Troja" *(I)*. This is how the drama's setting is introduced in (P) and (Ph); (M) has *"Scene: Schlachtfeld in der Gegend bei Troja"* (*PStAg*: 7). Although dropped in the later versions, (M)'s apparently redundant wording *"in der Gegend"* is of interest, for it puts the emphasis on *"Gegend"* ("region," "vicinity") rather than *"Schlachtfeld,"* indicating that the drama's subject is not the siege of a single city, but the developments across a wider geography. The setting *overtly* links Kleist's drama to Homer's *Iliad* and its associated myths narrating the Greeks' siege of Troy following Helena's abduction by, or elopement with, the Trojan prince Paris (like *Amphitryon, Penthesilea* is part of a "genealogy of texts"). In the *Iliad*, the drama's title character, the Amazon queen Penthesilea, appears only in a single episode, one quite tangential to Homer's overall story, in which the Amazons appear before Troy to relieve the Trojans, but are defeated by the Greeks. Kleist inflates Homer's few lines into a full-blown drama centred on *"Griechen und Amazonen"* rather than Homer's "Greeks and Trojans" (not a single Trojan character appears on stage, although a few, including Deiphobus, Priamus and Hektor, are referred to). Kleist incorporates another episode from the *Illiad*, that of Hektor's death at the hands of Achilles, which in Homer occurs *after* the Amazons' intervention and is unrelated to it, whereas Kleist situates it *before* the Amazons' arrival, thereby inventing a causal link between Achilles' outrageous deed and Penthesilea's passion for him. Kleist also draws on soures other than the *Iliad* covering Penthesilea and the Amazons, using bits and pieces of information to flesh out his drama and provide granular accounts of the Amazon state and of selected characters. Whereas in the majority of the extant myths Penthesilea is killed by Achilles, in at least one of them Penthesilea kills Achilles, and Kleist (speaking with Philip K. Dick) draws on this "minority report."

"Griechen und Amazonen" (I). The Greek leader Odysseus at first assumes that the Amazons have come, in line with Homer's episode, "*Troja zu entsetzen*" (V.21), but the Amazons, instead of siding with the Trojans, promptly pounce on them when the opportunity arises (Kleist's crafty term "*entsetzen*" can mean "to relieve" as well as "to horrify"). The audience, though not the Greeks and Trojans, soon finds out that Kleist's Amazons have not come to relieve the Trojans, but to capture men for themselves for the purpose of reproduction. As such, Greeks and Trojans are for them perfectly interchangeable, except that the Greeks, who are camping in the open, are easier prey than the Trojans, who for the most part remain behind their city walls. When the Amazons in quick succession rout Deiphobus' Trojan detachment sent to welcome them and a Greek detachment carelessly venturing from their camp, capturing countless prisoners (cf. V.153), Odysseus realises that their "war machine" (Deleuze and Guattari) comprises an incommensurable *third force* (cf. V.125-6) that is a danger to Greeks and Trojans alike, and that they may be able to fend off only by putting their rivalry on hold and uniting against it: "*Doch hier / Zeigt ein ergrimmter Feind von beiden sich, [...] / Und Griech' und Trojer müssen jetzt sich fast, / Dem Raub der Helena zu Trotz, vereinen, / Um dem gemeinen Feinde zu begegnen*" (V.128-38).[383] Odysseus' *orthodoxy*, "my enemies' friends are my enemies, and my enemies' enemies are my friends," is invalidated by the Amazons' *unorthodox* purpose, and his attempt to force Penthesilea into declaring which side she is on, "*Sie muß, wem sie Freundin sei, erklären; / Und wir dann, sie erwähle, was sie wolle, / Wir werden wissen mindestens, was zu tun*" (V.573-9), is bound to fail.

"Kentaurin" *(I)*. Penthesilea is an eminently martial appearance, *"Geschürzt, der Helmbusch wallt ihr von der Scheitel"* (V.60), and her phallus promptly inflames when s/he encounters the handsome Achilles: *"Bis jetzt ihr Aug auf den Peliden trifft: / Und Glut ihr plötzlich, bis zum Hals hinab, / Das Antliz färbt"* (V.68-70). Her palfrey (a horse trained and saddled for use by women), *"Und seine Gold- und Purpurtroddeln regend, / Zerstampft ihr Zelter unter ihr den Grund"* (V.61-2), cormprises the pivot on which her androgyne, masculine, and feminine aspects swivel: *"Verwirrt und stolz und wild zugleich"* (V.99). While no match for Achilles in hand-to-hand combat (cf. V.89-90), her designations—*"Kentaurin"* (V.118), *"Wölfin"* (V.163), *"Hyäne"* (V.331)—suggest that she is more at home on the *Kampfplatz* than in the *Lustgarten*; her oscillating between *blushing* (being shot by Eros' arrows) and *bloodying* (piercing her prey with arrows) prefigures her failure, in the climatic scene, to distinguish *Erôs* and *Agôn*, *"Küsse"* and *"Bisse."* Penthesilea faces an intractable dilemma that will turn out to be her undoing: her *personal* desire for Achilles—as *targeted*, as opposed to *random*, prey—puts her in direct conflict with her *public* role as chief defender of the Amazon Law (which proscribes such selectiveness). Her response to her dilemma is to rise above the Law, to become Law onto herself, in a gesture reminiscent of a Cixousian *rire de la Méduse*, a Lacanian *devenir-Autre*, or a Fichtean *autopoïesis*.

"stahlumglänzt" *(I)*. Achilles is *"stahlumglänzt"* (V.360) because as an infant his mother Thetis dipped him into the waters of the river Styx, whereby his skin became steeled and imprenetrable except at the (proverbial) heel by which she held him.[384] The (very Kleistian) *minimal difference* Kleist introduces is that his version of Achilles is vulnerable not at the heel but at the (phallic) *arm* (cf. V.493), implying that Thetis held the infant not by the heel but the *genitals*. This makes it possible for Penthesilea to *castrate* Achilles: *"Die Glieder des Achills reißt sie in Stücken!"* (V.2597; *"Glied"* = "penis"). Kleist, in *Ph* epigram no. 11 confirms, tongue-in-cheek, that Penthesilea could only have consumed Achilles' *genitals*, since the rest of his body was steeled, and in epigram no. 12 adds, again tongue-in-cheek, that it is known whether she afterwards spat out his testicles ("boots").³⁸⁵

Apart from being vulnerable to castration, Achilles is *penetrable anally*. This is suggested by Penthesilea's shape-shifting into a giant phallus, "*Die Königin [...] / [...] dem gestreckten Parder gleich, folgt sie*" (V.342-6), and entering Achilles' "grounds": "*er, der Pelide, / [...] rückwärts strebend; / [...] in den Gründen bald verschwand er*" (V.347-9). Achilles' admitting Penthesilea's thrust here must be voluntary: when the two clash in battle (cf. V.1077-80), he is well capable of fending off to her "lance's" thrust.³⁸⁶ Achilles, then, is vulnerable not only at his genitals, but also his rectum's inner linings and tissues, and the abdominal and thoracic organs accessible through it: when in the decisive scene he opens himself to her, but she turns into a raging fury, he desperately seeks to reattach his "armour" (evidently a codpiece-type equipment protecting his genitals and anus), which Penthesilea effortlessly tears off before penetrating his "white chest" with her "tooth," in her unbridled passion ravaging his inner organs (cf. V.2265-70); like the Prussian drummer in *Anekdote aus dem Letzten Kriege* (*BA*, October 1810), Achilles is destroyed through his *a...hole!*³⁸⁷

"wo den Leib der golden Gurt umschließt" (I). Achilles' fate is from the beginning tied to Penthesilea's by Otrere's bequest that Penthesilea conquer only Achilles, the most desirable of Greek heroes.³⁸⁸ When Achilles is attacked by Deiphobus (cf. V.174-86), and when his *quadriga* falls into a precipice (cf. V.272), Penthesilea does not hesitate to risk her life to save his. Following their amorous encounter "in the grounds," she lays her exclusive claim on Achilles by enclosing his vulnerable soft parts in a golden harness or chastity belt, "*Seht! [...] / [...] wo den Leib der golden Gurt umschließt? / [...] Ha! Wessen!*" (V.357-63), a gesture she later repeats when she enchains him in rose garlands (cf. V.1773).³⁸⁹ Vis-à-vis the ithyphallic (cf. V.2393) *erastês* Penthesilea, highly "weaponised" with the "annihilator" Mars' fearsome *dagger* (cf. V.2428-38), Achilles assumes the role of effeminate, submissive *erômenos*. When he "disarms" before her (cf. V.1158-9) and goes down before her doggy-style (cf. V.1750), he re-enacts the manner in which he earlier offered himself to her "in the grounds," as well as anticipating the manner of his death. Both their *lines of flight* follow a trajectory whose vanishing point is annihilation in the manner of Hektor: "*Als bis ich sie zu meiner Braut gemacht, / Und sie, die Stirn bekränzt mit Todeswunden, / Kann durch die Straßen häuptlings mit mir schleifen*" (V.612-15); "*Ich will zu meiner Füße Staub ihn sehen. [...] ihn / Mir überwinden, oder leben nicht!*" (V.638; 54-6).[390]

"ihr geliebten, kleinen Rosenjungfrauen" *(I)*. The High Priestess' role, of sustaining the foundations of the Amazon social order—the cults of Mars, Diana, Aphrodite, the constitution encoded in the "*Law of Tanaïs*," and the festivals of reproduction: "*Jungfraun Fest*" (V.2041), "*Rosenfest*" (V.2076), "*Fest der reifen Mütter*" (V.2081)—at once complements and opposes the Queen's, whose primary business is to lead the Amazon warrioresses in warfare, i.e., in the acquisition of men.[391] In the Amazon capital Themiscyra the High Priestess oversees the nation's main temples and festivals: at the Temple of Diana, she nominates the virgins chosen each year to propagate the nation (cf. V.703; 2037-8) and hosts the annual *Rosenfest* (cf. V.2074-5; at the Temple of Mars, she interprets Mars' orders regarding the selection of virgins and of the nation from which men are to be captured (cf. V.2044-53), and proclaims new queens (cf. V.1968).[392]

The Amazons worship three powerful gods and goddesses (all of whom children of Zeus/Jupiter): Ares/Mars, god of war, untamed violence, destruction and extermination, also known as "*Vertilgergott*" ("annihilator"); Artemis/Diana, goddess of the hunt, virginity and childbirth, and mistress of cruel and bloody sacrifices; and Aphrodite/Venus, goddess of beauty, love and procreation, mistress of venereal disease and Ares' consort. In maintaining their social order and reproductive economy, the Amazons thus must "attune" (Heidegger) to three very different gods, suggesting that conflicts of interest between the gods inexorably shape their lives—for example, having fulfilled Diana's demand to *hunt down* a man, Penthesilea is torn between Mars' order to *annihilate*, and Venus' enticement to *love* her victim (Venus' power is circumscribed by the *Law of Tanaïs*, but her prolific envoy Eros can never be fully contained).[393]

"**Mars [...] vollzog die Ehe.**" Although two of the Amazons' three national gods are female, the High Priestess' seeking shelter beneath a pine tree (cf. V.884; pines being an anagram of penis) as well as an obelisk (cf. V.1003; a decidedly phallic object), and the Queen's doing likewise beneath an oak tree (a no less phallic symbol of Diana, whose temple is set within a grove of oak trees; cf. V.984), suggests that the Amazons' cult is *phallic*; in (M) the *Rosenfest* is held at the Temple of Aphrodite, but in (P) it is held at the Temple of Diana, and Venus' sanctuary is no longer mentioned. As important as Diana (childbirth) is to its *propagation*, the Amazon state's *foundation* was laid by Mars (war) in an act of unbridled violence, when on his command the Amazons during their "nuptials" slaughtered the invading Ethiopians by sodomising them ("consummating the marriage") with their Martian "daggers" till it rent them apart: "*Mars [...] vollzog die Ehe, / Und das gesamte Mordgeschlecht [the Ethiopians], mit Dolchen, / In einer Nacht, ward es zu Tod gekitzelt*" (V.1949-51). As a consequence of this foundational act, the Amazon reproductive economy is grounded in violence: the Amazons must self-mutilate (amputate their right breast), defeat and capture their men in battle, destroy all sons born conceived in the subsequent union, and once a daughter has been produced, immediately destroy the father, whose fate thereby re-enacts that of the Ethopians' during the Amazons' primordial "nuptials."

The virgins selected by Mars for each forthcoming reproductive cycle are equipped to capture as well as kill their prey: "*Beschenkt mit Waffen, von der Mütter Hand, / Mit Pfeil' und Dolch, und allen Gliedern*" (V.2057-8; bow and arrow are Diana's hunting weapons, the dagger is Mars' killing tool, which the virgins attach to their bodies with harnesses—"*Glieder*" = "members"). There is no indication that the virgins, upon returning to Themiscyra with their booty, hand back their weapons: the "*Arestöchter*" have now become "*Marsbräute*," mature warrioresses permitted to carry the weapons of Diana and Mars. Since they use Diana's weapon for *hunting*, why would they need Mars' weapon, if not for—*killing*? I have no doubt that the *"Fest der reifen Mütter"* is held at the Temple of Mars, where it re-enacts the original founding act of the Amazon state, the pregnant Amazons ramming their "daggers" into the fastened-down victims' rears, thus sacrificing them to the *"Vertilgergott."* The *"Rosenfeste"* comprise rampant "orgies" (V.1217) at which the virgins experience *"Entzücken ohne Maß und Ordnung"* (V.985) and behave *"wie losgelaßne Hunde"* (V.1219), and Penthesilea's ambivalent account of the *"Fest der reifen Mütter"* suggests that it is equally rampant:

> Beschenken sie, wie Könige zusamt;
> Und schicken sie, am Fest der reifen Mütter,
> Auf stolzen Prachtgeschirren wieder heim.
> Dies Fest dann freilich ist das frohste nicht,
> Neridensohn—denn viele Tränen fließen,
> Und manches Herz, von düstrem Gram ergriffen,
> Begreift nicht, wie die große Tanaïs
> In jedem ersten Wort zu preisen sei.— (V.2080-7)

The prisoners—treated as property of their captresses, and known only by their owner's name (cf. V.1806-8; say, Achilles would be known, with Margaret Atwood, as *"Ofpenthesilea"*)— are purportedly sent away *"auf stolzen Prachtgeschirren,"* but we note that this mode of departure rather closely recalls the manner in which Achilles dragged Hektor into his death: headlong through the dust, tied to a chariot (cf. V.1516). If the Amazons drag their victims to the point at which their bodies are utterly rent, it explains Penthesilea's fascination with Achilles' rending of Hector's body, as it establishes Achilles as worthy of the first daughter of Mars (while also anticipating both their fates).[394] It also explain why Mars is called *"Vertilgergott"*—*"vertilgen"* ("to devour," "to annihilate") being precisely the sacrificial rite he demands—, why the Greeks do not know of anyone who ever returned from the *"Rosenfest"*—*no one ever did*—, and why the virgins are forbidden to be choiceful regarding the men they capture: falling in love with their victim could impede their readiness to commit the subsequent sacrificial act. Penthesilea admits to Achilles that not only are the sons destroyed, but so are the fathers: "*Der Mann, des Auge diesen Staat erschaut, / Der soll das Auge gleich auf ewig schließen; / Und wo ein Knabe noch geboren wird, / Von der Tyrannen Kuß, da folgt er gleich / Zum Orkus noch den wilden Vätern nach*" (V.1963-7).

Penthesilea (like Alkmene) wears a "diamond belt" (cf. V.1083), with the help of which in her final encounter with Achilles, in which she mixes up "kisses and bites," she turns their nuptials into a bloodbath. The blood trickling from her mouth (cf. V.2674), in conjunction with Kleist's note to Marie (cf. II:796), *Ph* epigram no. 5 (cf. I:20), and the name of one of her dogs, Lycaon (a mythical king who fed his guests human flesh), has been interpreted as implying that she devours Achilles; however, epigrams No. 11 and 12 suggest that she is merely biting or tearing off his genitals (or his testicles, if the penis was already cut off),; the blook trickling from her mouth suggests that she drinks Achilles' blood, mimicking her earlier consumption of a sacrificial bull's blood.

"**Warum just vor der Dianapriestrin Füßen?**" In the context of Amazon norms, Penthesilea's ripping Achilles apart is neither unique nor outrageous: it is in line with the standard practice of rending the victims after impregnation. The decicive difference is, that she and Achilles undertook, as it were, a *"Kleidertausch"*: it is Achilles who was impregnated in their encounter in the "grounds," and not Penthesilea. Penthesilea, in other words, destroys not only her lover but also her child. The High Priestess dreads Penthesilea's deed because by being an act of passion, and taking place in the open, it undermines the *Law of Tanaïs*, and the useful illusion that after discharging their reproductive duty the prisoners are released. When the news breaks that Penthesilea annilhilated Achilles (cf. V.2585), the High Priestess reacts *"freudebeklemmt"*—a Kleistian neologism compounding delight and anxiety. Penthesilea's request that Achilles' corpse be laid at the feet of the High Priestess in her function as Diana's priestess (cf. V.2724-40), i.e., in supplication to the *goddess of childbirth*, suggests that she believes Achilles to be pregnant with her seed. The High Priestess' *"entferne sie"* grammatically could refer to either the corpse, or the supplicant, or even the seed presumed to be lodged in Achilles' womb ("*sie*" can be plural or singular); she evidently seeks to preclude Penthesilea's supplication to the goddess, for once delivered, a sincere supplication obliges a godhead to accommodate it.

The High Priestess rejects any responsibility: "*Diana ruf ich an: / Ich bin an dieser Greueltat nicht schuldig!*" (V.2711-12). Yet provided her statement's emphasis is on "*dieser,*" she in fact anticipates that there will be a *second* such deed, one that she *will be* implicated in—namely, Penthesilea's own annihilation, for the High Priestess actively seeks to drive Penthesilea into self-destruction. When she realises, "*indem sie zu überlegen scheint,*" that Penthesilea is not yet aware of Achilles' ravagement—his intact steely skin entombs and thus veils his shredded inner organs—, she calls out the "elephant in the room," ensuring that Penthesilea cannot escape *anagnorisis*: "*Sonst müßte man die Leiche des Achills— / PENTHESILEA blickt die Oberpriesterin blitzend an*" (V.2815).[395] Prothoe attempts to save Penthesilea from turning against herself by instructing the porters to quietly take the corpse away, but Penthesilea, *prompted by the High Priestess' words*, looks for the corpse, before which the cunning High Priestess demonstratively positioned herself in a tell-tale gesture that cannot fail to direct Penthesilea's gaze:

> DIE OBERPRIESTERIN sich dicht mit den übrigen Frauen zusammendrängend.
> Geliebte Königin!
> PENTHESILEA indem sie aufsteht.
> [...] Halt dort!
> Was tragt ihr dort? Ich will es wissen. Steht!
> Sie macht sich Platz unter den Frauen und dringt bis zur Leiche vor. [...]
> Ich will ihn sehn!
> Sie hebt den Teppich auf. [...]
> O Artemis! Du Heilige!
> Jetzt ist es um dein Kind geschehn! (V.2876-88)

Penthesilea's line, "*Jetzt ist es um dein Kind geschehn!,*" confirms that she believes Achilles to have been pregnant with her child, a child dedicated to the goddess of the hunt, and makes clear that the extent of Achilles' destruction—"*so entstellt, / Daß Leben und Verwesung sich nicht streiten*" (V.2930-1)—now dawns on her. The High Priestess, meanwhile, gradually imparts to her *who* did it:

> PENTHESILEA. [...]
>> Wer mir den Toten tötete, frag ich [...]
>>> [...] wer ihn so zugerichtet, [...]
>> Den will ich meiner Rache opfern. [...]
>> Geb acht, sie sagen noch, daß ich es war. [...]
> DIE OBERPRIESTERIN. [...]
>> [...] Dein Pfeil wars der ihn traf,
>> Und Himmel! wär es nur ein Pfeil gewesen!
>> Doch, als er niedersank, warfst du dich noch,
>> In der Verwirrung deiner wilden Sinne,
>> Mit allen Hunden über ihn und schlugst—   (V.2919-51)

As Penthesilea's oath of revenge against whoever ravaged her lover and child encompasses her own death warrant, and the High Priestess now subtly indicates to her her fate—Hades—; Penthesilea lightheartedly submits to it:

> PENTHESILEA. —Wie kam es denn, daß er sich nicht gewehrt?
> DIE OPERPRIESTERIN. Er liebte dich, Unselige! [...]
>> Doch du—
> PENTHESILEA. So, so—
> DIE OBERPRIESTERIN. Du trafst ihn—
> PENTHESILEA.   Ich zerriß ihn. [...]
>> Oder war es anders? [...]
>> Küßt ich ihn tot? [...]
>> Nicht? Küßt ich nicht? Zerrrissen wirklich? sprecht? [...]
> DIE OBERPRIESTERIN. Weh! Wehe! ruf ich dir. Verberge dich!
>> Laß fürdar ewge Mitternacht dich decken!

> PENTHESILEA. —So war es ein Versehen. Küsse, Bisse,³⁹⁶
> Das reimt sich, und wer recht von Herzen liebt,
> Kann schon das eine für das andre greifen. [...]
> Sie wickelt sich los, und läßt sich auf Knieen vor der Leiche nieder. [...]
> Dies, du Geliebter, wars, und weiter nichts.
> Sie küßt ihn.
> DIE OBERPRIESTERIN.
> Schafft sie hinweg! (V.2969-89)³⁹⁷

"**Sie läßt den Bogen fallen**" *(I)*. The Scythian bow, Diana's weapon and symbol of Amazon reproductive power, comes to signify the structural fissure between the two rival institutions of power, the priesthood and the monarchy: during Tanaïs' coronation as the first Amazon queen, the High Priestess clankingly dropped the bow, "*Er stürzt', der große, goldene, des Reichs, / Und klirrte von der Marmorstufe dreimal, / Mit dem Gedröhn der Glocken, auf, und legte, / Stumm wie der Tod, zu ihren Füßen sich.—*" (V.1998-2001), as if to highlight that the very institution she was about to inaugurate is empowerd only by the grace of those gods with whom she alone is authorised to communicate.³⁹⁸ By now dropping the bow before the High Priestess, reversing the latter's earlier gesture, Penthesilea frees herself from the Amazon Law:

> PENTHESILEA. Ein Schauer schüttelt sie zusammen; sie läßt den Bogen fallen.
> DIE ERSTE AMAZONE.
> Der Bogen stürzt' ihr aus der Hand danieder!
> DIE ZWEITE.
> Seht, wie er taumelt—
> DIE VIERTE.
> Klirrt, und wankt, und fällt—!
> DIE ZWEITE. Und noch einmal am Boden zuckt—
> DIE DRITTE. Und stirbt,
> Wie er der Tanaïs geboren ward.
> Pause. (V.2767-72)

The High Priestess, not having forseen this hybristic challenge to the gods and her own position, seeks to avert disaster by soothing Penthesilea:

> DIE OBERPRIESTERIN sich plötzlich zu ihr wendend.
> Du, meine große Herrscherin, vergib mir!
> Diana ist, die Göttin, dir zufrieden [...]   (V.2773-4)

Diana, she admits, is satisfied with Achilles' sacrifice; but Mars, she implies by failing to mention him, *is not*: he requires another sacrifice—Penthesilea's.

> PENTHESLIEA. Sie sieht sich um, wie nach einem Sessel.
> PROTHOE. Schafft einen Sitz herbei! Ihr seht, sie wills.
> Die Amazonen wälzen einen Stein herbei. Penthesilea läßt sich an Prothoes Hand darauf nieder.   (V.2797)

Penthesilea's storyline here ties back to *Guiskard*'s:

> PENTHESLIEA. Sie sieht sich um, wie nach einem Sessel. [...] Die Amazonen wälzen einen Stein herbei. Penthesilea läßt sich an Prothoes Hand darauf nieder. (V.2797)
>
> Die Kaiserin zieht eine große Heerpauke herbei and schiebt sie hinter ihn. GUISKARD indem er sich sanft niederläßt, halblaut. (V.488)

When Penthesilea announces not only her own death, but also that of the very institution she embodies, "*Und— — —im Vertraun ein Wort, das niemand höre, / Der Tanaïs Asche, streut sie in die Luft!* [...] */ Ich sage vom Gesetz der Fraun mich los, / Und folge diesem Jüngling hier*" (V.3008-13), her triple-hyphened "*Und— — —*" marks the end of an era. It is as if here, in *Penthesilea*'s final scene, Kleist realises the ending he had intended for *Guiskard*. If in the letter to Collin of 14th February 1808, just as he prepared *Penthesilea*'s publication, Kleist hinted that he was considering publishing *Guiskard* in full, the two dramas' respective endings could only have narrated the same historical event, or alternative scenarios that at this point in time remained, or had once again become, *compossible*.

Penthesilea, Satirically

Given Penthesilea's probable period of genesis, Kleist had to account for events such as *Jena-Auerstedt*, the royal family's flight to East Prussia, Napoleon's *Prussian Campaign*, and *Tilsit*. On the other hand, since he had already covered these events in *Amphitryon*, *Erdbeben* and *Marquise*, and since the period from mid-1807 till mid-1808 saw few significant political developments, *Penthesilea* afforded him an opportunity to indulge in *satirical* experimentation (and *po(i)etical* exuberance).

"**Scene: Schlachtfeld bei Troja**" *(II)*. In Kleist's reframing of Homer's epos, the many decades-long dynastic rivalry between the Habsburgs and Hohenzollerns corresponds to the almost 10-year long *Siege of Troy* by the Greeks, the German imperial dignity to the abducted Helena, and Napoleonic France to the Amazons, that incommensurable *third force* that intervenes in the intra-German rivalry. Kleist's "scene," then, is clearly delineated: the Amazon lands in the Pontus correspond to France, their capital Themiscyra to Paris, the river Skamandros to the Rhine, the "vicinity of Troy" to Germany, the city of Troy to Vienna, the Trojans to the Austrians and the Greeks to the Prussians.[399]

"**Griechen und Amazonen**" *(II)*. The battle in which the Amazons rout Deiphobus' Trojan army, while the Greeks stay on the sidelines (cf. V.33-8), refers to *Austerlitz*, and the subsequent battle in which the Amazons "so easily" (V.764) rout Odysseus' Greeks, and capture countless Greek prisoners (cf. V.122-52), and in which Penthesilea and Achilles first come face-to-face (cf. V.172-92), to *Jena-Auerstedt*. Kleist's brevity in covering the latter battle suggests that by the time he began to work on *Penthesilea* in earnest, his focus had already shifted to the battle's aftermath (which supports the hypothesis that he worked on the drama during his captivity, completing it in Dresden).

Kleist in *Penthesilea* fleshes out a constellation he had first sketched in one of the Würzburg letters:

> Im Westen stand das nächtliche Gewitter und wütete, wie ein Tyrann, und von Osten her stieg die Sonne herauf, ruhig und schweigend wie ein Held. Und seine Blitze warf ihm das Ungewitter zischend zu und schalt ihn laut mit der Stimme des Donners—er aber schwieg der göttliche Stern, und stieg herauf, und blickte mit Hoheit herab... und bestieg den Thron des Himmels——und blaß, wie vor Schreck, entfärbte sich die Nacht des Gewölks, und zerstob wie dünner Rauch, und sank unter den Horizont, wenige schwache Flüche murmelnd—— (II:581)[400]

In 1806/7, the conflict Kleist allegorically anticipated in the 1800 letter was actualising on the German stage, only that the outcome shaped up to to be the inverse of Kleist's earlier scenario: instead of being dispersed by the Sun (Germany, Prussia, the House of Hohenzollern) the Thunderstorm (Napoleonic France) is on the cusp of eclipsing her; this is precisely the state of affairs with which the (Ph) fragment cuts off (cf. V.2584). In (P), Kleist with the 23rd and 24th scene adds an utopian scenario in which the Thunderstorm, having eclipsed the Sun, dissolves itself, thereby bringing the drama's ending back in line with the allegory's: having rent *Borussia* and his unborn heir, Napoleon self-destructs, putting an end to his dynastic amibitions and giving way to the German (or Hohenzollern) Sun: while the French (Amazons) have not been defeated (Penthesilea hands over the reigns to the competent Prothoe), neither have the Germans (Greeks and Trojans), and with the swayable Achilles (Luise) and the hybristic Penthesilea (Napoleon) annihilated, the way is paved for German recovery. In the *Iliad* the Greeks vanquish the Trojans and recoup Helena, and Kleist's implicit end-game similarly entails the Hohenzollerns' overcoming the Habsburgs and seizing the *HRR* dignity.

"Kentaurin" (II). Penthesilea is portrayed in eminently Jovian terms—"*wie vom Himmel*" (V.51); "*mit einer zuckenden Bewegung*" (V.72); "*schlug sie mit Donnerkrachen eben ein*" (V.145);

"*wetterstrahlend*" (V.184); "*wie der Blitz*" (V.389); "*wie ein Donnerkeil aus Wetterwolken*" (V.2437)—, and like *Amphitryon*'s Jupiter, she evidently represents Napoleon.[401] It takes no great stretch of the imagination to visualise in the Deleuzean *agencement* of Penthesilea, saddle, stirrups and dapple grey, "*Geschürtzt, der Helmbusch wallt ihr von der Scheitel, / Und seine Gold-und Purpurtroddeln regend, / Zerstampft ihr Zelter unter ihr den Grund*," that same "world spirit on horseback" that Hegel observed, or imagined, at Jena in 1806: "*den Kaiser—diese Weltseele—durch die Stadt zum Rekognisziren hinausreiten [...] auf einem Pferde sitzend, über die Welt greift und sie beherrscht*," nor to recognise in Penthesilea's dapple grey the famous Arabian grey Marengo said to have carried Napoleon at *Austerlitz, Jena-Auerstedt, Wagram, Waterloo*.[402]

Napoleon was indeed known for the small hands and feet Kleist attributes to Penthesilea, "*ihre beiden kleinen Hände*" (V.291); "*zu ihren kleinen Füssen*" (V.2495), and Kleist's depiction of Penthesilea's countenance, "*Sieht sie in unsre Schar, von Ausdruck leer, / Als ob in Stein gehaun wir vor ihr stünden; / Hier diese flache Hand, versichr' ich dich, / Ist ausdrucksvoller als ihr Angesicht*" (V.63-7); "*Das Angesicht, das funkelnde, gekehrt, / Mißt sie, auf einen Augenblick, die Wand*" (V.284-5); "*Und blicket starr [...] / In das Unendliche hinaus, und schweigt*" (V.2696-9), recalls Horace Vernet's of Napoleon before *les immortels*:

"*Pferdebändigerin*"; the "*Weltseele*" monunted on Marengo; Napoleon and "*les immortels.*"[403]

The most harrowing suicide in German literary history is, quite appropriately, performed by the dominant political figure of one of history's (and literature's) most convulsive eras, and fittingly the "invincible" Napoleon is overcome not by Achilles, but by the sheer power of his own (self-) destructive Schopenhauerian *will*, or Nietzschean *will to power*. As in Achilles' steely armor, there is a chink in Napoleon's aura of invincibility: the "French disease" of *dynastic hybris*.

Penthesilea's mother's name, Otrere, is near-homophone with *Autre*, which in turn recalls *Autriche*, and we could perhaps see this figure, whose bequest in effect seals Penthesilea-Napoleon's fate, as a manifestation not only of Napoleon's actual mother, who indeed had significant influence over her son, but also of the imperial dignity the Austrian Habsburgs relinquished to him, which would eventually spell his end, by shifting the basis of his régime's legitimation from charismatic (personal) to dynastic (institutional) authority. Kleist evidently held Napoleon in high regard as brilliant general, but not as self-aggrandising dynastic ruler, and Otrere's bequest—in fact: curse—propagates the "French disease" of dynastic hybris just as inexorably as does Guiskard's plague. By destroying his maternal vessel Achilles-*Borussia*, Penthesilea-Napoleon precipitates his own demise, having already lost the ability to prosper apart from a dynastic "pyramid."

"stahlumglänzt" *(II)*. If the *overtly* female Penthesilea represents Napoleon, the *overtly* male Achilles represents Queen Luise or Borussia.[404] Achilles' overconfidence in his steely armour mirrors Luise's in her Frederician army; it spells their doom. The "bathed-in-steel," yet effeminate, Achilles is a perfect avatar of a Prussia succumbing to Napoleon due to not lack of exterior strength but interior weakness: her body politic's infestation with the "German disease" of *dynastic rivalry*. In the drama's early scenes Achilles-Luise is in constant flight (retold in breath-taking teichoscopy): having scarcely escaped her clash with Penthesilea-Napoleon (*Jena-Auerstedt*), her quadriga (Berlin) shattered along the way, she briefly disappears "in the grounds"—the lowlands, moors and forests—of East Prussia (cf. V.347-9), where she is "girdled" (encircled) by Penthesilea-Napoleon (cf. V.362), before once more escaping, by the skin of her teeth, across the frozen Curonian Lagoon to Memel—as the irreverent "*Berliner Schnauze*" ("Berlin street-lip") joked: "*Unser*

Dämel ist in Memel."[405] The no less irreverent Kleist never tires of parodying Luise's fondness of horses, "*sie, deren Seele bis vor kurzem mit nichts beschäftigt schien, als wie sie beim Tanzen, oder beim Reiten, gefalle*" (II:773), which the Queen indulged during her exile near the Trakehnen stud farm, and which made her something of an Amazon herself:

Lover of horses: Queen Luise in riding habit.

As in *Marquise*, Kleist in *Penthesilea* explores a scenario of Napoleon and *Borussia*'s marital union and of the formation of a Bonapartean-Hohenzollern dynasty and Franco-German empire. Penthesilea and Achilles' debate (cf. V.2281-90) regarding where they shall consummate their union—at Themiscyra (Paris) or Phtya (Berlin)—is as poignant as it is hilarious. Penthesilea and her dogs' tearing apart Achilles (cf. V.2595-7; 2669-71; I:20) corresponds to Napoleon and his *Rheinbund* vassals' tearing apart *Borussia*; Penthesilea's nine named dogs (cf. V.2421-6; 2655-6), like Count F's "Russian dogs," may refer to the treacherous *Rheinbündler* or to Napoleon's pack of generals, and Kleist will have associated specific personages with them. Penthesilea-Napoleon is so forcefully drawn towards the magnetic Achilles-*Borussia* not least because it was her refusal to join the *War of the Third Coalition* that precipitated *Austerlitz, Pressburg,* and Franz II's abdication—a causal chain encapsulated by the episode of the Greek (Hohenzollern) hero Achilles rending the Trojan (Habsburg) hero Hektor (i.e., Franz II). Because of her ancient rivalry with *Austria, Borussia* was a natural ally for Napoleon, whom he repeatedly sought to embrace.

"Ihn häuptlings um die Vaterstadt geschleift":
Borussia rides roughshod over Franz II and the *HRR*.

"Bravo, *Borussia*"—says Napoleon—"for rending Franz II and with him the *HRR*!"

"wo den Leib der golden Gurt umschließt" *(II)*. *Penthesilea* entails a fast-paced, Hollywoodesque re-enactment of the historical events from *Jena-Auerstedt* till *Friedland* and *Tilsit*, of Napoleon's tightening his "golden" noose around *Borussia*'s body and Fr. Wilh.'s neck. Penthesilea's standing at the edge of the precipice, Achilles, below her, hanging on by a thread, his quadriga shattered and his legs entangled (cf. V.270-81), depicts Napoleon's occupation of Berlin on 27th October and his claiming the Brandenburg Gate *Quadriga* as war booty, her ripping a chain of white and red pearls from Achilles' neck (cf. V.1313), his conquest of a string of Brandenburgian fortresses (the colours of whose flag are white and red): Erfurt (16th October 1806), Spandau (25th October), Prenzlau (28th October), Stettin (30th October), Küstrin (1st November), Schwerin (3rd November), Lübeck (6th November), Magdeburg (11th November). Penthesilea and Achilles' brief idyll "in the grounds" (cf. V.349) may refer to Fr. Wilh.'s desperate peace offer in late November 1806, which came to nothing due to unacceptable French demands.

Penthesilea's clash with Achilles in scenes 8 and 9, "*Begegnen beide sich, zween Donnerkeile, / Die aus Gewölken in einander fahren; / Die Lanzen, schwächer als die Brüste, splittern*" (V.1123-5), evidently depicts the *Battle of Preußisch-Eylau* of 7th/8th February 1807, during which Napoleon faced defeat and was about to retreat, "*Kommt hinweg.* [...] */ So will ich euch zurück zur Heimat führen*" (V.1200-1), only to change his mind while preparing to cross the river Alle: "*PENTHESILEA indem sie plötzlich, auf eine Brücke* gekommen, stehen bleibt. Doch höre: / Eins eh ich weiche, bleibt mir übrig noch" (V.1364-5). Achilles' unexpectedly appearing before the Amazons in the 10th scene, "Der Peleïd, ihr Jungfraun, ich beschwör euch, / Im Schuß der Pfeile naht er schon heran!" (V.1233-4), the may refer to General L'Estocq's Prussian reserve corps' eleventh hour intervention that may have saved the Russian army from destruction. Kleist's terse lines, "So sendet / Zehntausend Pfeile über ihn!" (V.1399-1400), encompasses as succinct a summary of *Eylau* as any: 700 cannons were deployed, more than twice as many as at *Austerlitz*, *Jena-Auerstedt* or *Friedland*, and probably the largest number ever deployed in a land battle at that point in time.[406]

Penthesilea's and Achilles' tête-à-tête in scenes 11 to 17 depicts Napoleon's diplomatic efforts, after *Eylau*, to lure Prussia over to his side, sending his aide-de-camp Henri Gatien Bertrand (Beauharnais' successor in this role) to Fr. Wilh. to convince him to abandon the Coalition, offering lenient terms including restoration of Prussia's pre-war borders, apart from possessions west of the river Elbe. Fr. Wilh. rejected the offer, and on 26th April reconfirmed Prussia's alliance with Russia with the *Treaty of Bartenstein*—Achilles' nonchalance reflects the King's optimism to yet be able to turn the war around. Penthesilea's defeat and destruction of Achilles in scenes 21 to 23 depicts the decisive *Battle of Friedland* of 14th June: "DER HEROLD. Sie stellt sich, ja, Neridensohn, sie naht schon; / Jedoch mit Hunden auch und Elefanten, / Und einem ganzen wilden Reutertroß" (V.2536-9); DAS HEER DER AMAZONEN *außerhalb der Szene*. / Triumph! Triumph! Triumph! Achilles stürzt!" (V.2582). If at *Friedland* Napoleon broke *Borussia*'s resistance, at *Tilsit* he "rent" her body: "Den Zahn schlägt sie in seine weiße Brust… Troff Blut von Mund und Händen ihr herab" (V.2670-4). Kleist's gory rendering of *Borussia*'s fate at *Tilsit*—suitably bloodily reproduced in Michael Thalheimer's early 21st century staging of *Penthesilea* (below right)—will have been diametrically opposite to the Prussian public's perception of the event, which is probably quite fittingly represented by Gustav Eberlein's idealised, late 19th century work *Königin Luise und Napoleon in Tilsit* (below left):

Perceptions of *Tilsit*: the Prussian public's (Eberlein's 1899 sculpture) vs. Kleist's (Michael Thalheimer's 2015 staging).⁴⁰⁷

"ihr geliebten, kleinen Rosenjungfrauen (II)." Penthesilea-Napoleon's most formidable antagonist in Kleist's drama is not Achilles-*Borussia* but the High Priestess, that *"Höllenfürstin, im Gewand des Lichts"* (V.2944) who could represent Pope Pius VII and the Catholic church. The Priestess-Pius is so shocked at the Catholic Emperor's pursuit of the Protestant Queen (both of them already married) that s/he seeks to restrain Napoleon, and even threatens to send him "on the Way of the Cross" (V.2576). The conflict between Napoleon and the Papacy indeed reached a new peak just as Kleist was finishing *Penthesilea:* in February 1808 French troops occupied Rome and Beauharnais' Kingdom of Italy annexed most provinces still under Papal control; in 1809 the curse Kleist's High Priestess-Pius pronounces on Penthesilea would prove to have been clairvoyant: Pius excommunicated Napoleon. Although in his scenario Pius helps drive Napoleon into self-destruction, Kleist shows little sympathy for the Pope: with much sarcasm he portrays the High-Priestess surrounding herself with virgin maidens, *"Rosenjungfraun"* (V.881), like so many Papal altar boys.⁴⁰⁸

"wie ein Kinderspiel." Among the leaders of the Greek Coalition, Odysseus could represent King Fr. Wilh. III, Diomedes Tsar Alex. I, Antilochus the Elector Fr. Aug. III of Saxony, and the absent Agamemnon, the supreme Greek leader, the Holy Roman Emperor *absconditus*. Odysseus-Fr. Wilh. holds on to the "senseless" rivalry with the Habsburgs ("*Helenenstreit*") and rejects Achilles-Luise's suggestion of a union with the "colourful" Bonapartes: "*Und unser Helenenstreit, / Vor der Dardanerburg, der Sinnentblößte, / Den will er, wie ein Kinderspiel, weil sich / Was anders Buntes zeigt, im Stiche lassen?*" (V.2507-10).[409] Diomedes-Alex.'s Ätolians-Russians are absent from the earlier battle (*Jena-Auerstedt*); in the later battle (*Eylau*) they enter the stage (battlefield) from the side opposite to that from which Odysseus-Fr. Wilh.'s Prussians enter, which is historically correct; so is that Diomedes-Alex. becomes the Amazon's main interlocutor and, unlike Odysseus-Fr. Wilh., has real bargaining power.[410] Among the Trojan-Austrian leaders, Priam could represent Franz I, and Deiphobus possibly the Austrian Chief of Staff Franz von Weyrother, whose battle plan was widely held responsible for the débâcle at *Austerlitz*; among the Amazon princesses, the loyal Prothoe could represent Beauharnais, the less effective Meroe, Max. I Joseph of Bavaria, and Asteria, who arrives late to reinforce the Amazons (cf. V.757-8), without taking a major role in the ensuing action, King Fr. Aug. I *after* his elevation, replacing Antilochus-Elector Fr. Aug. III, who appears only in the first four scenes (*Jena-Auerstedt* and its aftermath); Tanaïs, mythical founder of the Amazons state, could signify Charlemagne, Napoleon's self-declared predecessor.[411]

"Sie läßt den Bogen fallen" *(II).* The fascinating parallels between the symbols of the Amazon state and those of the *RF* may be coincidental, yet such coincidences scarcely escaped Kleist. The *RF*'s emblem (below, left) is composed of a crescent shield tapering off in a lion's and an eagle's head and inscribed with the monogram "*RF*," a bundle of *fasces* enclosing an axe (representing justice), an olive branch (peace), and an oak branch (wisdom). Weapons commonly attributed to the Amazons include the crescent shield (*peltae*; cf. "*ihren goldnen Halbmond*," V.2269) and the double axe (*labrys*):

Fragile polities: the *RF* and the Amazon state.

Penthesilea's recounting the history of the Amazon state thus entails Kleist's recounting the history of the *RF*, the Amazons' liberation from slavery (cf. V.1954), formation of an egalitarian state (cf. V.1958), and establishment of a *sorority* (cf. V.1989) reflecting the French revolutionary principles *liberté, egalité et fraternité*.[412] From its inception, the Amazon state suffers a congenital defect, the exclusion of men, and incorporates remnants of an earlier monarchical system symbolised by the Scythian bow.[413] The Amazons soon reinstate a monarchy, the High Priestess' presenting the golden bow to the newly appointed Queen harking back to the Archbishops of Reims' presenting the royal crown to the French Kings, as well as anticipating the Pope's chairing Napoleon's coronation. The revolution chokes on the children it devours, and Penthesilea-Napoleon becomes its gravedigger by precipitating a hereditary empire: "Den Kranz, der mir die Stirn umrauscht'" (V.715).

Inaugurated with a congenital defect, and propagated by acts of violence, the Amazons' survival furthermore depends on an act of self-mutilation, the burning off of their right breast so that it may not interfere in their drawing the Scythian bow's string in battle, the "wonder weapon" on which their power rests. Goethe makes a bit of a fool of himself when he considers the passage in which Kleist refers to this self-mutilation "highly comical... a motif, that on a Napolitanian folk theatre put in the mouth of a Colombina facing a boisterous Pulcinella, perhaps would trigger a decent effect on the audience" (*LS*,281):[414]

>ACHILLES *indem er sein Gesicht an ihre Brust drückt.*
>   O Königin!
>   Der Sitz der jungen, lieblichen Gefühle,
>   Um eines Wahns, barbarisch—
>PENTHESILEA.   Sei ganz ruhig.
>   Sie retten in diese Linke sich,
>   Wo sie dem Herzen um so näher wohnen.
>   Du wirst mir, hoff ich, deren keins vermissen.—   (V.2012-17)

Satirically speaking, Kleist's passage is anything but comical: Penthesilea-Napoleon conveys to Achilles-Borussia that Germany (the right breast = the lands on the Rhine's right bank) must be burned off so that France (the left breast = the lands on the Rhine's left bank) may prosper, that one head of the German double-headed eagle must be chopped off so that Napoleon's single-headed eagle may triumph, and that the "charming feelings" of French military and administrative sway, Bonapartean dynastic rule, and French cultural hegemony shall be lodged in this new super-state's "heart": Paris. "I trust, my dear Borussia," Napoleon tells Luise, "that you will not miss your fatherland, nor the eagle's head and territories I had to chop off, so as to erect my Empire on the ruins of the HRR, and that you will henceforth devote yourself to my, and France's heart." On this self-serving appeal Penthesilea's exposé of Amazon history ends.

"**Bei der Eiche, unter der sie fiel.**" Penthesilea-Napoleon repeatedly rests below, and draws strength from, oak trees (cf. V.449; 561; 1471)—Jupiter's symbol, as well as the supreme Asgardian god Wotan's. When Diomedes laments that the entire Greek "*Stamm*" ("trunk," as well as "tribe") is burst into pieces by the Amazons' thunderbolts, "*Die Schlacht, [...] / Schlug sie mit Donnerkrachen eben ein, / Als wollte sie den ganzen Griechenstamm / Bis auf den Grund, die Wütende, zerspalten. / Der Krone ganze Blüte liegt [...] / [...] von Sturm herabgerüttelt*" (V.144-9), the closeness of his imagery to Kleist's oak paradox leaves no doubt that the "trunk" belongs to an oak. Diana's temple's towering over a grove of oak trees, then, symbolises French hegemony over the German tribes. Kleist's oak symbolism encapsulates in a nutshell the drama's narrative, and thereby his sweeping history of the Napoleonic era and scenario of its dramatic end: Napoleon's thunderbolts (artillery) subdue the Germans, until he towers over them and draws strength from their very oppression, yet in the end he succumbs to the sheer weight of his own hybris, his imperial "crown" seized by the "storm" of the German resistance:

> PROTHOE. Sie sank, weil sie zu stolz und kräftig blühte!
> Die abgestorbne Eiche steht im Sturm,
> Doch die gesunde stürzt er schmetternd nieder,
> Weil er in die Krone greifen kann.   (V.3040-4)

Genesis revisited. In line with ancient principles of unity, the drama's entire action takes place in a single day, the 24 scenes corresponding to 24 hours, and in a single location, the "region of Troy" (Germany). Kleist's (hi)story covers historical events (H) from December 1805 till July 1807, interspersed with fictional ones (F):

1. Habsburg Austria (Troy) and Hohenzollern Prussia (Greece) are locked in an ancient rivalry over the Holy Roman imperial dignity (Helena); the *Ad'A* (the Amazons) intervenes, defeating Austro-Russian (Trojan) forces at *Austerlitz* and Saxo-Prussian (Greek) forces at *Jena-Auerstedt* (H);
2. Napoleon (Penthesilea) enters Berlin and seizes the quadriga; Luise (Achilles) barely escapes (H);
3. Luise flees to East Prussia, hotly pursued by Napoleon, where she unsuccessfully sues for peace (H);
4. Luise falls into a trance and admits her passion for Napoleon (F);
5. Napoleon falls into a trance and admits his passion for Luise (F);
6. Pope Pius VII (the High Priestess) admonishes Napoleon to abandon the war and his pursuit of Luise (F/H);
7. Disregarding the Pope, Napoleon readies himself to pursue Luise (F/H);
8. Napoleon is nearly defeated at *Eylau* (H);

9. Napoleon is about to abandon the campaign but changes his mind and renews his assault (F/H);
10. In an eleventh hour intervention, L'Estocq's Prussian reserve corps (Achilles) attacks Davout's right wing (Amazon archers) (H);
11. The Prussian corps advances and kills many French (Amazon) soldiers (H);
12. Prussian (Odysseus) and Russian (Diomedes) forces in a pincer movement almost trap and annihilate Napoleon (F/H);
13. Luise regards the lifeless Napoleon (F; Kleist insinuates that the Prusso-Russian forces could have annihilitated Napoleon but failed to do so);
14. Napoleon awakens (F);
15. Napoleon recounts to Luise the history of the *RF*, his rise to power, and the prophecy that he shall unite with her (F);
16. The enemy armies once more march against each other (H);
17. Following *Eylau*, Napoleon (through his envoy General Bertrand) makes a last-ditch effort to sway Luise to join his side (F/H);
18. Luise seeks to deter Napoleon from going into the final battle (F);
19. The Pope makes a last-ditch effort to avert the final battle (F);
20. Luise (*Borussia*) challenges Napoleon to a duel (F/H; with *Bartenstein*, Fr. Wilh. once again throws down the gauntlet to Napoleon);
21. Luise seeks to deter the Prusso-Russian army from going into battle (F);
22. Napoleon vanquishes *Borussia* at *Friedland*, rends her at *Tilsit* (F/H)
23. Even the French soldiers are shocked at *Borussia*'s annihilation (F);
24. Napoleon realises the enormity of his deed and, prompted by Pius, commits suicide, handing the French imperial crown to Beauharnais (Prothoe) (F).

The drama's first scene alludes to *Jena-Auerstedt*, and Kleist may not have worked on the drama in earnest before late 1806 or early 1807; when he tells Rühle on 31st August of a "*Trauerspiel unter der Feder*" (II:769), he is perhaps only beginning to research or sketch it. The majority of the drama's scenes, 8-22, cover historical events coinciding with Kleist's retention, and he may well have worked extensively on *Penthesilea* at Joux and Châlons, filling information gaps with fictional scenes (had Kleist not been detained, and thereby insulated to some degree from reliable and up-to-date information, *Penthesilea* as we know it might not have come into existence). Once returned to Berlin and settled in Dresden in late August 1807, he will have gotten up to speed on events, especially *Tilsit*, reworked the "*von kassierten Varianten strotzende Manuskript*" (II:797), and completed the final two scenes: "*Jetzt ist sie tot*" (II:796), he reports to Marie in late autumn.

Kleist's selections for (Ph) are instructive: he spares his readers the final two scenes' outrageous climax and dénouement, but subtly prepares them for it by selecting passages and adding notes that emphasise Penthesilea's madness: in a note to the 14th scene he adds, "*(Zur Nachricht: Penthesilea ist, in einem Anfall von Wahnsinn...)*," and in a note to the 19th scene, "*(Zur Erklärung: Penthesilea... steht... jetzt beschämt und zitternd... vor ihrem Volke da...)*," and from the 19th scene onwards he selects passages in which Penthesilea appears to be in a mad rage, before cutting off the fragment with the High Priestess' exclamation "*Seht, die Wahnsinnige!*," as if to lodge that statement firmly in his readers' minds. Kleist thus uses (Ph) to manipulate his readers into expecting an outrageous yet plausible, even inevitable, ending, paving the way for (P). In a letter to Goethe of 24th January 1808, Kleist explains his technique of leading the reader towards a given solution, "*So, wie es hier steht, wird man vielleicht die Prämissen, als möglich, zugeben müssen, und nachher nicht erschrecken, wenn die Folgerung gezogen wird*" (II:805). Kleist understood the power not only of the *sequel*, but also the *teaser*, and his staggering of *fragments*, *stagings* and *publications* betrays a deliberate marketing plan that takes into account reader psychology and market dynamics.

Scenario Narratives. *Penthesilea*'s scenic ending, in which Napoleon destroys *Borussia*, his seed, and finally himself, rescinding his dream of an imperial dynasty by dropping the bow and appointing a successor who is not a blood relation (Beauharnais), complements *Amphitryon*'s, in which Napoleon rules supreme and impregnates

Borussia with a divine son, and *Marquise*'s, in which he is subdued by *Germania* and incorporated into the House of Hohenzollern. Kleist's scenarios of Napoleon's fate in these three works of the 1807/8 period being so diverse suggests that he deemed the *satirical* "end-game" eminently undecided. As utopian or dystopian as Kleist's scenarios may appear, each of them was plausible at time of writing: in 1814, vanquished in the *War of the Sixth Coalition* and exiled to Elba, Napoleon would indeed attempt suicide (*Penthesilea*'s scenario); had his *Invasion of Russia* of 1812 been successful, he would indeed have dominated Europe (*Amphitryon*'s); and had he overcome the antagonism of Franz and the Germans, his marriage to Marie-Louise in 1810 could indeed have inaugurated a Franco-German empire (*Marquise*'s, if with a Bonapartean-Habsburgian, not a Bonapartean-Hohenzollern, dynasty).[415] *Penthesilea*'s scenario is the most optimistic among these three: although *Borussia* is destroyed, she pulls Napoleon with her into the abyss (*Marquise*'s is much more ambivalent: while Napoleon is harnessed, a wolf remains a wolf, and is never fully domesticated).

Penthesilea: Satyrically

Penthesilea's *satyrical* metaphorical field is even more highly charged than *Amphitryon*'s; perhaps his relative isolation during retention further incited Kleist to incorporate his sexual fantasies into his works. *Erôs* = *Agôn*: nowhere else does Kleist's fundamental equation become more explicit than in *Phenthesilea*: "*heißer Kamfplust voll*" (V.19); "*Küsse heiß von Erz*" (V.606); "*des Kampfes Inbrunst*" (V.851); "*mit Eisen umarmen*" (V.859); etc.[416] The erotic "landscape allegories" of Kleist's Würzburg letters have here become orgiastic "battle vignettes," from the very first scene—"*Wie zwei erboste Wölfe sich umkämpfen: [...] / Des einen Zahn im Schlund des anderen.—*" (V.5; 11; "tooth and gullet" belong into Kleist's I/O symbolism)—all the way to the end: "*Staub ringsum, / Vom Glanz der Rüstungen durchzuckt und Waffen: / Das Aug erkennt nicht mehr, wie scharf es sieht. / Ein Knäuel, ein verworrener, von Jungfraun, / Durchwebt von Rossen bunt*" (V.433-7); "*Es läßt kein Federbusch sich unterscheiden. / Ein Schatten überfleucht von Wetterwolken / Das weite Feld ringsher, das Drängen nur / Verwirrter Kriegerhaufen nimmt sich wahr* (V.1101-4), etc. In Kleistian *satyrical* code, "*Staub*" = seminal fluid, "*Jungfraun*" = male youths (*erômenoi*), "*Rosse*" = noble lovers (*erastai*), "*Federbusch*" = phallus, "*durchzucken*" = electro-magnetic orgasmic ecstasy, etc.[417] The imagery of the "golden and purple tassels" (V.61)—repeated in the bird's "purple dust" (V.868), Penthesilea's "is it dust, is it blood" (V.453), and the "string of pearls, white and red" (V.1313)—alludes to the mingling of blood and ejaculate during unbridled sodomy; the battle's ebb and flow, "*Jetzt hier, in glühender Begier, jetzt dort*" (V.308), mimicking *Marquise*'s "*hier—traf er, da*" (I:106) and *Prolog*'s "*Hier jetzt..., jetzt dort*" (I:9), denotes the prolific promiscuity among the "brotherhood's" members.

"**wie von der Nachtigall geboren.**" In her monologue in the 23rd scene the First Priestess recalls that Penthesilea, prior to being selected for this year's batch of designated "virgins," had been a model Amazon "maiden" whose "grace" (the virtue of the *erômenos*) and excellence as "flutist" (the virtue of the *erastês* or *dmōs*) were in equal measure admired by the priestesses of Diana's temple and the members of Themiscyra's "sisterhood": "*sittsam,*" "*in jeder Kunst der Hände so geschickt,*" "*so reizend, wenn sie tanzte,*" "*so voll Grazie,*" "*von der Nachtigall geboren,*" "*flötete, und schmetterte, und flötete*"—in brief: Penthesilea was a model male homosexual lover.[418] Yet when she beholds Achilles, Penthesilea's desire to sire a heir overcomes her and she becomes infatuated with the hermaphroditic Achilles and confused about her own sexuality. It is above all this confusion between homosexual ecstatic desire and heterosexual dynastic aspiration that the High Priestess denotes as "madness," and that spells Penthesilea's doom.

"**In Staub.**" Penthesilea and Achilles are both fascinated by the production and application of *dust* (ejaculate). Achilles fantasises about dragging Penthesilea headlong through the dust in the manner he did Hektor: "*den Wagen dort / Nicht her zu meinen Freunden will ich lenken, [...] / Als bis ich sie zu meiner Braut gemacht, / Und sie, die Stirn bekränzt mit Todeswunden, / Kann durch die Straßen häuptlings* *mit mir schleifen*" (V.610-15)—in my "translation": "this tool of mine / I shall not steer to any of my lovers, [...] / Till I have made Penthesileus mine, / And he, his glans garlanded with fatal wounds, / Has ground his member through my passages"; Penthesilea fantasises about showering Achilles, kneeling before her in the dust (cf. V.638), with a "perl necklace," and offering his rear to her as unconditionally as he previously did to Hektor: "*Wie du, entflammt [...] / Das Antlitz wandtest, während er die Scheitel, / Die blutigen, auf nackter Erde schleifte; [...] / Daß ein Gefühl [...] / Den marmorharten Busen dir durchzuckt*" (V.2197-202)—in my "translation": "How you, aroused [...] / Turned your back to him, while his glans, / The bloody one, ground your naked rear [...] / Till ecstasy [...] / Jerked your marble bottom." Penthesilea's and Achilles' "desire for the desire of the other" are perfectly complementary: Achilles desires to be *erômenos* to Penthesilea, Penthesilea *erastês* to Achilles.

"**mit Eisen... umarmen**" *(I)*. Another recurring erotico-agonistic topos is that of Penthesilea and Achilles longing to "embrace" each other "with iron"—a metaphor that is no more incommensurate than that of Eros' deadly-yet-impassioning arrows, or Jupiter's deadly-yet-electrifying thunderbolts. Achilles longs, "*Auf Küssen heiß von Erz im Arm zu nehmen*" (V.606); Penthesilea insists, "*Weil ich mit Eisen ihn umarmen muß!*" (V.859). Iron and steel, of course, conduct electric current, and the armour they both wear in "battle," forms part of an *agencement de jouissance* that also comprises Achilles' "steely" skin, their lances, arrows, daggers, saddles, stirrups, and "leaden" horses' necks (cf. V.537), all of which generate, amplify and dissipate ecstatic, orgasmic electric currents across their bodies, creating a *champ électromagnétique* in which *jouissance* is maximised.

"**Im Kampf, Penthesilea und Achill, / Einander trafen.**" Penthesilea and Achilles' first encounter, like *Amphitryon*'s *Urszene*, takes place at dusk (cf. V.172-93); in addition to them, it involves the Trojan warrior Deophobus and a skewbald horse.[419] Gabriele Debriacher (*Rede*, 65) points out that "electricity is a central thematic and structural element of Kleist's overall conception," and already in this initial encounter this central element comes to the fore. The erotic potential of *Amazonomachy*—a battle involving Amazon and Greek warriors—has fascinated artists long before Kleist, and so has the electrifying aspect of the sexed human body on horseback—cf., e.g., John Collier's *Lady Godiva* of c.1807, which features an *agencement* of horse, mane, saddle, bridle and reins, human body and locks—, yet in Kleist's scene we discern the characteristic signs not only of the Dionysiac orgy, but also of the Mesmerian *baquet*: Penthesilea's "*entfärbt, läßt zwei Minuten / Die Arme sinken*" mirrors Adam's "*Und sieht (...) / Zwei abgemessene Minuten starr mich an*" (*Krug*, V.2216-7). In her séance with Achilles and Deophobus, Penthesilea experiences a Kleistian shock ("*Schlag*") when she closes the bio-electric circuit by penetrating Deophobus with her "sword" while his own "sword" is rammed into Achilles' steeled body.

Penthesilea is referred to as *centaur* because she is virtually one with her *horse*, to which she is tied like the Mongolian warriors in Deleuze and Guattari's iconic "man-horse-stirrup constellation" (*Thousand Plateaus*, 399), and whose *bio-power* affords Penthesilea a maximum level of "charge" every time she penetrates an enemy or victim: "*Hebt sie vom Pferdesrücken hoch sich auf, / Und senkt, wie aus dem Firmament geholt, / Das Schwert ihm wetterstrahlend in den Hals*" (V.182-4).[420] The "battle," which *satirically* constitutes a fight to the death, *satyrically* comprises an orgiastic *baquet*, the battlefield becoming the crisis room, the horse and saddle the Mesmerian bucket, and the warriors the magnétiseur and mediums. In the same manner in which Amphitryon immediately understands Alkmene when she alludes to her séance, "*Ich weiß.*" / "*Du weißt es schon*" (V.941), Antilochus does Penthesilea: "*Ganz wunderbar!*" Perhaps *all* Kleistian characters are "in the know" about such magneto-orgiastic séances—events that (speaking with Deleuze and Guattari), from the *stratified space* of states, estates, and armies, isolate and carve out a temporary *smooth space* in which Amazons, Greeks and Trojans, kings, queens and priestesses, warriors, maidens and horses mingle in a Kleistian idyll, an ideal society in which the principles of *liberté*, *egalité* and *fraternité* are actualised as libertarian exchange and fraternal cohabitation of lovers (cf. *Erdbeben*'s dark valley).

"**Sie läßt den Bogen fallen**" *(III)*. The golden bow is at once symbol of state power and generator of electro-magnetic *puissance*. It is metallic—when it drops it "clanks" or "chinks"—, and the tension generated by its two "kissing ends" propels arrows like thunderbolts: "*Und spannt mit Kraft der Rasenden, sogleich / an, daß sich die Enden küssen, / Und habt den Bogen auf und zielt und schießt, / Und jagt den Pfeil ihm durch den Hals*" (V.2646-9); Penthesilea's shot with her Scythian bow (below, left) thus mimicks Jupiter's unleashing his thunderbolt:

"*daß sich die Enden küssen*": Scythian bows,
electric arc effect, Jupiter, natural thunderbolt.[421]

Upon accepting Achilles' challenge, Penthesilea immediately *re*charges herself, so as to maximise her potential to *di*scharge her viritility during their encounter:

> PENTHESILEA mit einer fliegenden Blässe.
>> Laß dir vom Wetterstrahl die Zunge lösen […]
> PENTHESILEA glühend.   Nun denn,
>> So ward die Kraft mir jetzo, ihm zu stehen: […]
>>> Der Donner rollt. […]
> PENTHESILEA mit zuckender Wildheit. […]
>>> Sie ergreift den großen Bogen […]
>>> Der Donner rollt heftig. […]
> PENTHESILEA […].
>> Und wie ein Donnerkeil aus Wetterwolken,
>> Auf dieses Griechen Scheitel niederfalle! […]
> PENTHESILEA indem sie den Bogen spannt.
> PENTHESILEA. […]
>>> Ab […] unter heftigen Gewitterschlägen. […]
>>> Alle ab.   (V.2370-2447)

Depending on context, "*Spannung*" can mean "excitement," "tension," or "voltage," and Kleist plays on the analogy between the metallic bow's tensing culminating in the discharge of an arrow, the clouds' gathering, in the discharge of a thunderbolt, Penthesilea's "glowing" arousal, in *jouissance,* and her electric charging-up, in its release as Kleistian shock. The Amazons' joint ejaculation, with which the scene ends, *satyrically* signifies an orgasmic crescendo, *satirically* the concentrated fire of the *Grande batterie*.

"aus dem Monde nieder." When Achilles tells Penthesilea, "*Ich dachte eben, / Ob du mir aus dem Monde niederstiegst?—*" (V.2031-2), we are reminded that in Aristophanes' satire, narrated in Plato's *Symposion* (189e-191e), the primordial spherical creatures—whose bodies faced in opposite directions and were welded together back-to-back, implying that they were equipped with two sets of genitals but lacked rear orifices—, existed in three distinct genders—*males, females* and *androgynes*—, with the *males* being descendants of the Sun, the *females* of Earth, and the *androgynes* of the Moon. Once Jupiter split these creatures with his thunderbolts, the two halves of the *males* became homosexual men, those of the *females*, lesbian women, and those of the *androgynes*, respectively a heterosexual man and a heterosexual woman.[422] According to Aristophanes' scheme, Penthesilea, as a descendant of the Moon (cf. V.2032), is in the first instance a heterosexual man or woman, Achilles, as a descendant of the Sun (cf. V.356-62; 1034-43; 2207; 2212), a homosexual man.

Throughout the text, Kleist alludes to a series of transformations required for Penthesilea to become both Amazon and begetter, and for Achilles to become both Greek warrior and expectant mother.[423] When he comes down to Earth, Achilles (cf. V.1385; 2031-2) turns into a woman, enabling Penthesilea to impregnate him. Penthesilea, who also came down to Earth (cf. V.2031-2), in order to become Amazon, in her encounter with Achilles swings herself up into heaven to become his Sun (cf. V.1755), thus turning into male begetter. In *Penthesilea* the drama of the production of a son comes to a head, and nowhere else in his works is it more apparent that Kleist sympathised with Napoleon's struggle to produce a heir, a struggle *that was also his own*, and that he turned his Napoleon figures into "lab rats" for experimenting with a problem *that was eminently autobiographical*.

Penthesilea: Syphilitically

Kleist in *Penthesilea* once more moves centre state the general principle of Napoleon's demise he had first postulated in *Guiskard*—the "French disease" of *dynastic hybris*—, and in doing so perhaps comes as close as ever to completing that earlier project. In *Guiskard*, the hero succumbs to the temptation of favouring a less qualified candidate for succession who is a family relation (Robert) rather than a more popular and legitimate one who is not (Abälard). In *Penthesilea*, Napoleon's temptation of *choosing the son* is reframed as that of *choosing the mother*. Kleist, as it were, shifts the dynastic principle's leverage point "upstream," from the offspring to its incubator: since Joséphine failed to bear him a son, Napoleon must *find a suitable mother* (whereas *overtly* Penthesilea captures herself a father so as to produce daughters, *satirically* Napoleon acquires himself a mother so as to produce sons). In both dramas Napoleon acts on the basis of a *hybristic presumption*: in *Guiskard*, that his (or Joséphine's) charisma is inheritable, in *Penthesilea*, that Otrere's (private) bequest takes precedence over Tanaïs' (public) law. If in *Penthesilea* Napoleon's *dynastic hybris* destroys his heir as well as himself, on the assumption that the later project completes the earlier, abandoned one, we may conjecture that Kleist's intended outcome for *Guiskard* was analogous: both Guiskard and Robert were to be wrecked by the disease.

"Schmerzen, Schmerzen." Guiskard and Penthesilea alike suffer from the disease that is Kleist's physical corollary of the moral "disease" of *dynastic hybris*, and that always already poisons Eros' arrows (cf. V.1075; 1085):

PROTHOE.   [...] die Hand versagt ihr,
  Nach einem andern noch sich auzustrecken.—
  Komm, magst dus jetzt an meiner Brust vollenden.
  —Was fehlt dir? Warum weinst du?
PENTHESILEA.   Schmerzen, Schmerzen—
PROTHOE.
  Wo?
PENTHESILEA.
       Hier.
PROTHOE.   Kann ich dir Linderung—?
PENTHESILEA.   Nichts, nichts, nichts.
                                           (V.1288-93)

Penthesilea's "hand" fails her and she feels nothing but excruciating pain; to the question "Where?" she can only respond with an indeterminate "Here": her pain is ambient and pervasive.

"**einen Helm voll Wasser.**" Kleistian jars that animate slackening members and relieve diseased lovers in the drama feature in the form of water-filled battle-helmets that Greeks and Amazons alike wear in battle, thus carrying their personal electrical condenser and battery with them as part of their standard war equipment. In his first few lines Odysseus demands, "*Schafft einen Helm mit Wasser!*" (V.12), and upon receiving it affirms, "*Dank! Meine Zunge lechzt*" (V.139; we have an inkling which body part his "tongue" refers to). Later the wounded and exhausted Penthesilea is re-animated with the help of Kleistian jars in the shape of helmets and cups: "*Schafft einen Helm voll Wasser, sag ich! / Hier!*" (V.1402-3); "*Sie zuckte—sahst du es? [...] / So hat sie noch den Kelch nicht ausgeleert? / Seht [...] / Sie atmet*" (V.1487-9). Kleist's suitably antiquising term for a Kleistian shock, "spark of Prometheus" (V.2923), anticipates Mary Shelley's 1818 novel *Frankenstein*'s subtitle—*or, The Modern Prometheus*—, as well as reflecting the state of the art of electro-medical technology in his day. Following Luigi Galvani's bio-electric experiments with frogs in the 1780s, and his nephew Giovanni Aldini's with animal and human corpses in the early 18001, electrotherapy had come to fascinate the medical and literary professions in equal measure:[424]

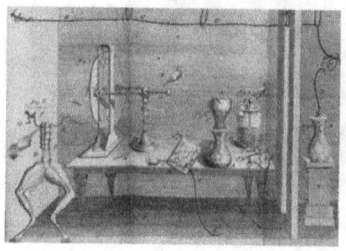 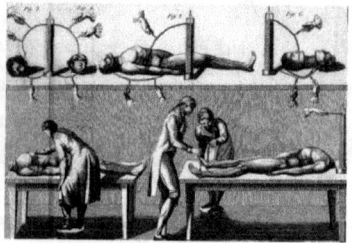

Galvani's late 1700s (left) and Aldini's early 1800s (right) bio-electricity experiments (in Galvani's set-up, electricity is generated from the frog's muscles and condensed in a Kleistian Jar).

"Man bringt die Schläuche schon." When Achilles is "injured" at his "arm" (cf. V.493; 504), he seeks electro-therapy by connecting not to a helmet or cup, but, via hoses, to his—*horse*:

> AUTOMEDON indem er ihre Hälse mit der Hand prüft.
> Wie Blei.
> ACHILLES.   Gut. Führe sie.
> Und wenn die Luft sie abgekühlt, so wasche
> Brüst ihnen und der Schenkel Paar mit Wein.
> AUTOMEDON.
> Man bringt die Schläuche schon.   (V.537-40)

In Kleist's equine electrotherapy set-up, the (living) horse's thigh and crop muscles ("*Schenkel*") serve as influence machine or electrostatic generator, generating electricity subsequently stored in its "leaden" neck, which functions as Kleistian jar, i.e., as condenser and battery (lead was indeed commonly used for the metal foil with which the inside and outside of a Kleistian jar was coated). Connected to the horse's body via hoses, Achilles' member functions as Franklin rod that channels the Kleistian shocks, their impact perhaps potentiated by his body's encasement in "steely" skin and by the severity of his injuries.[425] While undergoing therapy, Achilles observes a "seething" Penthesilea (cf. V.562) experiencing her own electromagnetic session under an oak tree: *"An ihres Pferdes Nacken [...]/ [...] seht ihr den Helm am Boden?"* (V.450-1).[426] Kleist thus explores a variety of electromagnetic therapeutic set-ups: Achilles' equine engine incorporates generator (thigh and crop muscles), condenser and battery (leaden neck), and hoses for connecting to them; Penthesilea's consists in a condenser and battery in the form of the helmet placed on the ground (cf. Aldini's set-up below), and a generator in the shape of a magnetising tree reminiscent of Puységur's elm at his Buzancy estate, to which he connected mediums via ropes or hoses.⁴²⁷

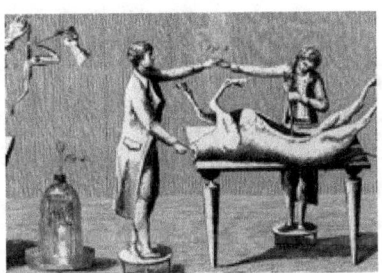

"*seht ihr den Helm am Boden?*": Aldini's bio-electrical apparatus (with Keistian Jar).

Penthesilea's characters take recourse to Aldinian bio-electrotherapy or Puységurian magnetism with similar frequency as *Amphitryon*'s do to the Mesmerian *baquet*: "*O, wie er mit der Linken / Vor, über seiner Rosse Rücken geht! / Wie sie [...] erregt, / Der Erde Grund [...] zerstampfen! / [...] ziehn sie [...] / Mir ihrer Schlünde Dampf, das Fahrzeug*" (V.376-83); "*Seht! wie sie mit den Schenkeln / Des Tigers [dapple grey] Leib inbrünstig umarmt!*" (V.395-6); "*Bestieg sie schon den Perser wieder? [...] / Wohlhan! So schafft mir auch ein Roß*" (V.616-20); "*schafft mir ein Pferd*" (V.1205); "*Die Pferde vor!*" (V.2265). Both Penthesilea and Achilles are "lovers of horses," and Penthesilea is furthermore fond of dogs, "*Sie liegt, den grimmigen Hunden beigesellt*" (V.2595), as if perennially dwelling in a nexus of bestial orgy, animal magnetism and bio-electricity.

Braided *baquet*-strings (cont'd)

It is after their synchronous therapy in sight of each other (patients undergoing treatment in the same clinic—cf. Kleist and Brockes in Rügen) that Achilles and Penthesilea declare their morbid mutual passion, solemnly vowing their martial "I do"—"*Als bis ich sie zu meiner Braut gemacht*" (V.612); "*ihn / Mir überwinden, oder leben nicht!*" (V.655-6)—, to be joined forever in pleasure and pain, "till death do them part," exchanging "*Staub*" (ejaculate and/or calomel) in place of rings. Yet a "minimal difference" seeps into this solemn wedding ceremony at a distance: Achilles awakes from his somnambulistic trance *before* making his vow, "*Mir vorgestellt? / Nein, nichts. Was wars? Was wollt ihr?*" (V.565-6), whereas Penthesilea does so only *after* performing hers, "*Warum? Weshalb? Was ist geschehen? Was sagt ich? / Hab ich?—Was habe ich denn—?*" (V.665-6). Thus, while Achilles delivers his vow in full consciousness, Penthesilea does not, and consequently goes on to confuse *Bisse* and *Küsse*, as if she never fully awakens from her somnambulant stance.

"in diesem Strom der Lust." Penthesilea—anticipating Georges Bataille: "the nature of eroticism is defilement"—considers herself a "defiled child" (V.1676) that must purify itself by bathing in, and digesting, a sacrificed bull's blood, in accordance with the maxim, "blood is purified through blood" (Burkert):[428]

> Zuerst den Stier, den feisten, kurzgehörnten,
> Mir and den Altar hin; das Eisen stürz ihn, [...]
> Das Blut [...]
> Ihr goldenen Pokale, füllt euch an [...]
> Oh laß mich, Prothoe! O laß dies Herz

> Zwei Augenblick in diesem Strom der Lust,
> Wie ein besudelt Kind, sich untertauchen;
> Mit jedem Schlag in seine üppgen Wellen
> Wäscht sich ein Makel mir vom Busen weg.
> Die Eumeniden fliehn, die schrecklichen [...]
> Zum Tode war ich nie so reif als jetzt. (V.1645-82)

Penthesilea's fantasy of her sacrifice and self-purification on Diana's altar foreshadows her sacrifice, first of Achilles, then of herself, as well as her *hamartia* of confusing or compounding *Küsse* and *Bisse*, sacrifice to Diana (childbirth) and to Mars (annihilation): the bull is the sacrificial animal to the latter but not the former. The blood that trickles from her mouth during her sacrifice of Achilles implies not that Penthesilea devours him, but that she drinks his blood and perhaps smears herself with it; her sacrifice of Achilles is already sketched in Kleist's letter to Pfuel of January 1805: "*Ich habe Deinen schönen Leib oft, wenn Du in Thun vor meinen Augen in den See stiegest, mit wahrhaft mädchenhaften Gefühlen betrachtet... als ob Du dem schönsten jungen Stier, der jemals dem Zeus geblutet, nachgebildet wärest*" (II:749; the bull is also Jupiter's sacrificial animal). The Athenian sacrifice to Zeus Polieus (the city protector) entailed the burning of a piglet followed by the slaughter of a bull, and Penthesilea's sequential sacrifices of Achilles and herself could allude to this Maussian escalation (Achilles = piglet; herself = bull).[429]

The "short-horned bull's" blood may furthermore represent mercury chloride solutions in which Penthesilea bathes and which she drinks, for Mercury's symbol looks very much like a "short-horned bull" (cf. image below left), and Kleist's sacrificial set-up encompassing altar, bull, mercury solution (bull's blood), gold cups, electric current ("*Strom*"), and iron rods ("*Eisen*") recalls Giovanni Aldini's bio-batteries deploying severed ox heads as generators:

"*in diesem Strom der Lust*": Mercury symbol; sacred bull rhyton; Aldini's bio-battery set-up.

Do not Kleist's *"Eumenides"* (the euphemistic name for the dreaded *Erinyes* or Furies, the angels of revenge) embody the Janus-faced aspect of mercury as *pharmakon*—as remedy *and* poison? Does not Diana's temple represent a physicist's lab, and is not Kleist in his (self-)sacrificial fantasies re-enacting his therapeutic experiences? Is not the bull another bio-electro-magnetic device powering his *satyrical* orgiastic séances, and *syphilitical* therapeutic sessions?

"wenn du dich jetzo reinigtest." Purification rituals pervade the drama, depicting syphilis therapy involving mercury ointments, drinks, or steam baths. With Penthesilea's purification by her sisters Kleist offers a detailed account of a course of syphilis treatment. The therapist Prothoe begins by inspecting (kissing) Penthesilea's member (hand) and diagnosing its syphiliac symptomatology:

> PROTHOE. [...] Ach, wie man dir dein Handwerk ansieht, Liebe. [...]
>   Doch wie, wenn du dich jetzo reinigtest,
>   Händ und Gesicht?—Soll ich dir Wasser schaffen?
>   — —Geliebte Königin!
> PENTHESILEA. Sie besieht sich und nickt.
> PROTHOE.   Nun ja. Sie wills.
>   Sie winkt den Amazonen; diese gehen Wasser zu schöpfen. [...]
> DIE ERSTE PRIESTERIN.
>   Wenn man mit Wasser sie besprengt, gebt acht,
>   Besinnt sie sich. [...]

PROTHOE. Nimm dir den Lorbeer ab, den dornigen, [...]
   Und auch den Hals befreie dir—So, so!
   Schau! Eine Wund und das recht tief! [...]
Zwei Amazonen bringen ein großes flaches Marmorbecken, gefüllt mit Wasser.
PROTHOE.   Hier setzt das Becken her.—
   Soll ich dir jetzt die jungen Scheitel netzen?
   Und wirst du auch erschrecken nicht— —? Was machst du?
PENTHESILEA läßt sich von ihrem Sitz auf Knien vor das Becken nieder-
   fallen, und begießt sich das Haupt mit Wasser.
PROTHOE. Sieh da! Du bist ja traun recht rüstig, Königin!
   —Das tut dir wohl recht wohl?
PENTHESILEA sie sieht sich um.   Ach Prothoe!
         Sie begießt sich von neuem mit Wasser. [...]
PROTHOE.   Vortrefflich!
   Das Haupt ganz unter Wasser, Liebe! So!
   Und wieder! So, so! Wie ein junger Schwan!— [...]
DIE ERSTE PRIESTERIN. Wie sie das Köpfchen hängt!
MEROE. Wie sie das Wasser niederträufeln läßt. [...]
PENTHESILEA.   Ach!—Wie wunderbar.
PROTHOE. Nun denn, so komm mir auf den Sitz zurück!—
   Rasch eure Schleier mir, ihr Priesterinnen,
   Daß ich ihr die durchweichten Locken trockne! [...]
   Laßt uns ihr Haupt und Nacken ganz verhüllen!
   So, so!—Und jetzo auf den Sitz zurück!
Sie verhüllt die Königin, hebt sie auf den Sitz, und drückt sie fest an ihre Brust. [...]
PENTHESILEA nach einer Pause, mit einer Art von Verzückung.
   Ich bin so selig, Schwester! Überselig!
   Ganz reif zum Tod [...]   (V.2802-65)

This passage could well be autobiographical: Prothoe could represent Wedekind or another of Kleist's doctors (maybe even in Chalôns), the "sisters," nurses who attended him ("*Schwester*" is a common address for a female nurse), Penthesilea's "*Händ und Gesicht,*" "*Scheitel,*" and "*Haupt*" his own member and glans being repeatedly dipped into mercury solution and finally wrapped into (mercury-impegnated?) cloths, the "thorny laurel" *corona veneris*, which Prothoe promises her treatment will tackle, and the rock on which Penthesilea sits (in a nod to *Guiskard*), a hot oven for sweating or a hot seat in a mercury fumigation box.[430]

Purity—the absence of syphiliac symptoms—is the Amazons' "Elysium"; in Themiscyra they operate a grotto (clinic) where they undertake purifications (therapies). Says the ailing Penthesilea to her nymph (therapist) Prothoe:

> O sagt mir!—Bin ich in Elysium?
> Bist du der ewig jungen Nymphen eine,
> Die unsre hehre Königin bedienen,
> Wenn sie von Eichenwipfeln still umrauscht,
> In die kristallne Grotte niedersteigt? (V.2844-8)[431]

"Wenn seine Lippe schäumt." Epigram no. 14, *Robert Guiskard* (cf. I:21), in which Kleist pokes fun at those *Ph* readers who booed *Penthesilea*, and seeks to pre-empt their booing *Guiskard* as well, suggests that when she tears Achilles apart, Penthesilea *is rabid* (as are the fang-baring Guiskard, cf. V.513, and the foaming Kohlhaas, cf. II:31). Penthesilea-Napoleons transmits the canine disease among her Rheinbund "dogs", "*Jetzt unter ihren Hunden wütet sie, / Mit schaumbedeckter Lipp*" (V.2568-9); Achilles is afflicted too: "*Wenn seine Lippe schäumt*" (V.226).[432] Rabies can of course simply be "code" for syphilis, similar to *Guiskard*'s plague and *Krug*'s pip, but it is noteworthy that among the side-effects of mercury therapy was excessive salivation, sweating and emission of body odours, which were considered part of the remedial process: the disease was to be flushed out with the bodily fluids (cf. in this context also Kleist's obsession with ejaculation). A typical Kleistian *satyrico-syphilitical* set of equivalences would be: erotic passion = rabid madness = infectious disease = purification ritual.

"diese rätselhafte Sphinx." The Sphinx, archetype of mysteriousness; in Sophocles, harbinger of the plague, at Gizeh has lost her—*nose*. Sustained mercury poisoning had a destructive effect on bones and cartilages, nowhere rendered more visibe than at the olefactory organ; some syphiliacs lost their nose entirely.[433] Odysseus' portrayal of Penthesilea, "*Hier diese flache Hand, versichr' ich dich, / Ist ausdrucksvoller als ihr Angesicht*" (V. 66-7), suggests that Penthesilea is already suffering this fate. Between them, Penthesilea and Achilles thus exhibit a wide range of symptoms associated with the progression of syphilis and the side-effects of mercury treatment: rabid madness, chancred penises, blemished foreheads, crushed noses, bloated lips (cf. V.2958), blemished bodies (cf. V.2750), rashes on the forehead (see below).

"**Den Kranz, der mir die Stirn umrauscht.**" The perverse image of being laurelled—*satirically* alluding to Napoleon's empire-building, *po(ï)etically* to Kleist's *Agôn*—*syphilitically* refers to rashes on the forehead (*corona verneris*), a typical symptom of advanced syphilis much feared by syphiliacs because difficult to hide. Like Christ's crown of thorns, *corona veneris* inscribes his predicament onto the condemned's forehead, for all to see. Syphilitic infection is the inexorable corollary of the Amazons' custom of capturing men as sex objects and reproduction machines—as Prothoe's formula, "*Verfolgt, gesucht, gegriffen und bekränzt*" (V.1329), makes clear, and as Achilles' reflection, "*Als bis ich sie zu meiner Braut gemacht, / Und sie, die Stirn bekränzt mit Todeswunden*" (V.611-12), and Penthesilea's longing, "*Rosen für die Scheitel unsrer Helden*" (V.880), confirm. Her "desire for the *disease* of the other" explains why Penthesilea parades her disease with pride: "*Da schreitet sie heran, / Bekränzt mit Nesseln, die Entsetzliche, / Dem dürren Reif des Hag'dorns eingewebt, / An Lorbeerschmuckes Statt*" (V.2704-8); disease becomes the ultimate token of love; it falls to Prothoe to articulate this inexorable nexus between *satyrical* passion and *syphilitical* suffering: "*Und doch war es die Liebe, die ihn kränzte?*" (V.2911).[434]

"**—O Aphrodite!**" A Dr J. Sintelaer noted in 1709:

> after these unfortunate creatures [syphilis sufferers] see themselves thus infected by the poisonous fruits Venus bestows upon them, [...] they should have the additional misfortune, to be entangled also in the most

deceitful snares of Mercury, whose lash being so severe, as not only to tear the flesh, but also to strike to the very bones, their case instead of becoming better, is thus rendered much worse, to the accomplishment of their destruction.[435]

The theme of "being entangled" in mercury's "most deceitful snares" is as prevalent in *Penthesilea* as is that of mercury's "lash being so severe" in *Amphitryon*. Penthesilea and Achilles are both "entangled" and "ensnared" by the slow but relentless progression of mercury poisoning and the accompanying cauterisation of flesh and bones. Penthesilea's harrowing *cri de cœur*, "*Daß ich den ganzen Kranz der Welten so, / Wie dies Geflecht der Blumen, lösen könnte! / —O Aphrodite!*" (V.1229-31), is a desperate appeal to Venus to take away those thorny, syphilitic rose garlands that "adorn" her. But Aphrodite's temple (syphilis clinic?) having disappeared, her appeal to the goddess of love and beauty is bound to remain unanswered.

The related topos of being enwound—"*mit Eisen umarmen*" (V.859), "*umstrickt an allen Gliedern*" (V.1565)—recalls *Schroffenstein*'s "*Mit Gliedern, zahnlos, ekelhaft, umwunden,*" and *Krug*'s "*mit geschmeid'gem Gliederbau... erdrückt,*" and anticipates *Marionettentheater*'s "*unsichtbare und unbegreifliche Gewalt [die] sich, wie ein eisernes Netz, um das freie Spiel seiner Gebärden zu legen [schien]*" (II:344). The serpent's asphyxiating embrace may *satirically* recall the Roman legions' dragon-shaped military standards (*Draco*) and scale armor (*Lorica squamata*), and the *Ad'A*'s encirclement tactics, and *syphilitically,* as I suggested previously, depicts the papules, nodules and blemishes that symptomise secondary syphilis. If Penthesilea's dapple-grey is "spotted," so is she! (and so is Kleist: cf. his obduction report).

"**Gleich einem Schacht.**" Having relinquished her conventional *satyrical-syphilitical* "weapons" (daggers, arrows), Penthesilea autodestructs by forging inside her body's cavities a sharp-pointed, phallic steel blade, dipped in vitriolic poison, with which she rips apart and dissolves herself:

> Denn jetzt steig ich in meinen Busen nieder,
> Gleich einem Schacht, und grabe, kalt wie Erz,
> Mir ein vernichtendes Gefühl hervor.
> Dies Erz, dies läutr' ich in der Glut des Jammers
> Hart mir zu Stahl; tränk es mit Gift sodann,
> Heißätzendem, der Reue, durch und durch;
> Trag es der Hoffnung ewgem Amboß zu,
> Und schärf und spitz es mir zu einem Dolch;
> Und diesem Dolch jetzt reich ich meine Brust:
> So! So! So! So! Und wieder!—Nun ist es gut.
>
> Sie fällt und stirbt. (V.3025-34)[436]

The most extraordinary suicide in German literature, I offer, depicts not only Napoleon's self-destruction by an excess of *dynastic hybris*, but also Kleist's by a relentless pursuit of *mercury therapy*. The defiling, disintegrating, wounding, grinding and rending of bodies pervading *Penthesilea* depicts not only the destructive forces unleashed on Germany by Napoleon's expansionism, but also those at work in Kleist's own body, the "embers of sorrow," "hot-vitriolic poison of remorse," and "eternal anvil of hope" not only the suffering of the oppressed German people, but also that of the diseased lover.[437] *Penthesilea*'s "*So! So! So! So! Und wieder!—*" reflects that horror of *repeatability*, of Nietzschean *eternal recurrence*, that Jean Baudrillard discussed à propos of al-Qaeda's attack on the New York World Trade Center's twin towers, whereby the attack on the *second* tower heightened the terror by demonstrating the discretionary repeatability, *in principle,* of any terrorist attack, and that Pauline Réage inscribed in Sir Stephen's branding O's *second* buttock, thereby manifesting the perfect unconditionality of her submission.[438] It is precisely the predictable unpredictability of the recurrence, and the progressive worsening, of its symptoms, and the inevitable inexorabilty of the unintended side-effects associated with its therapy, that make syphilis so horrific. Is not Kleist himself that "defiled child"? Does not Penthesilea embody *"Den ganzen* (satyrical, syphilitical) *Schmutz seines Körpers und den ganzen* (satirical, po(ï)etical) *Glanz seiner Seele"*? If Kleist shed tears when he "killed" Penthesilea, were those not tears of joy, for he rehearsed the redemption not only of Germany, but also of himself? *"Jetzt ist sie tot,"* he told Marie and Pfuel, and was thereby, in that very moment, himself *"zum Tode ganz reif"* (cf. V.1682; 2865).

Penthesilea: Po(ï)etically

Penthesilea's genesis' overlapping with *Ph*'s invites a juxtaposition of the two projects. Regarding Kleist's *Prolog* to the latter, Blamberger notes (*Kleist*, 313):

> Kleists Prologheld hat mit Harmanns Phöbus wenig gemein. Er erscheint eher als donnernder Jupiter oder umhertanzender Dionysos den als friedlicher und maßvoller Apoll. Ihn kennzeichnet eine alle Grenzen sprengende, ins Offene, Zukünftige, Unendliche zielende schöpferische Kraft, die an Moralität nicht gebunden, also jenseits von Gut und Böse ist.

The evident discrepancy between Hartmann's "Apollonian" quest for *measure* (and A. Müller's for *synthesis*), and Kleist's "Dionysiac" tendency to perturb it, begs the question: why did Kleist pack his unconventional poetry between Hartmann's conventional images and Müller's no less conventional theories?[439] Apart from practical and commercial considerations, the most plausible answer is once again: for *camouflage*. Where to hide a purloined letter? In the open, among ordinary letters. For this to work, however, the *defiled* child must not stand out from the *pure* ones, and this is where Kleist may have miscalculated: his texts stood out like sore thumbs, incommensurate in style and content. Though Kleist treated *Ph* as his personal fiefdom, this discrepancy he could ultimately resolve only by withdrawing, which spelled the project's doom.

Hartmann's frontispiece—Phoebus Apollo in his *quadriga* surrounded by *Horai*, the Dresden cityscape beneath, the astrological symbols above (positing Kleist between and above Goethe and Schiller)—, and the journal's subtitle—"*Ein Journal für die Kunst,*" positing a monolithic "*die Kunst,*" covered by a single "*Ein Journal*"—were perhaps sufficiently subtle not to get people up in arms right away, but the *Prolog* is not, and although the *Epilog* seeks to dampen the havoc the *Prolog* is bound to wreak among conventional audiences, Kleist's choice of *Penthesilea* as "opening shot" leaves readers in no doubt that they are about to embark on an extraordinary, unfathomable journey. *Ph* was a Kleistian invitation of "love it or hate it"; for the most part, they *hated it*.[440]

"den Kranz von der Stirne reißen." Kleist really hoped to gain Goethe and other big names as contributors, though probably expecting only minor contributions from them, which would benefit *Ph* commercially by generating credibility and "pull," but would not rival his own contributions.[441] Kleist presumably chose or condoned the journal's title because Phoebus Apollo symbolised *all that which he sought to top or topple*: he was going to pull down and unhinge from its lofty position within German letters the entire edifice of Weimar Classicism and its flagbearer Jena Romanticism, and he would do so, as it were, *from within*; therefore his chosen arena had to be "the one journal" for "the one art." *Alles oder Nichts*. The frontispiece's Phoebus is always already a Phaidon, an Achilles about to tumble into the crevice, his quadriga smashed; Kleist's *"Prologheld"* (Blamberger) is a guerrilla fighter, his magazine, dynamite. Just as Guiskard (with the help of traitors) the imperial city, Kleist (with the help of collaborators) was to gut the Weimar machine-gun nest by sneaking in his magazine's explosive content, *Penthesilea* first of all, so as to *blow up Goethe's foxhole from within*.

That Kleist published (Ph) at the earliest occasion, in the first *Ph* issue of January/February 1808, while also urgently seeking to publish (P), is suggestive. Did he anticipate that *Faust. Eine Tragödie*, whose publication was announced for the 1808 Leipzig Easter fair, was set to immortalise Goethe? Was this the *kairotic* moment to preempt *Faust*?[442] Did Kleist plan for the two acmes of German drama to appear in print alongside each other (quite literally: at the same Leipzig fair), so that like two giant enemy ships-of-the-line they could fire broadsides at each other?

"**auf den 'Knieen meines Herzens'.**" Kleist's much-quoted line, in his letter to Goethe accompanying the first issue of *Ph* (containting *Penthesilea*), "*Es ist auf den 'Knieen meines Herzens' daß ich damit vor Ihnen erscheine*" (II:805), has a distinguished genealogy: it paraphrases Luther, Goethe himself, as well as *Penthesilea*.[443] Whereas *Penthesilea*'s (and *Marquise*'s) critique of *Borussia*'s actual *Kniefall* before Napoleon at *Tilsit* is *cynical*, Kleist's virtual *Kniefall* before Goethe is blatantly *kynical*.[444] It is also *satyrical*, for the act Prothoe performs on Penthesilea in the lines Kleist paraphrases in his letter, "*O du, / Vor der mein Herz auf Knieen niederfällt, / Wie rührst du mich! / Sie küßt die Hand der Königin*" (V.2799-2801), is evidently Bill-Clintonian: Prothoe, on her knees before Penthesilea, gives her a blowjob (this scene, in E.A. Poe's term, is "X-ed" from the *Ph* fragment).

Picture Kleist, in his armchair enjoying a pipe, imagining Goethe reading *Penthesilea*, tracing his own demise, and, arriving at the climatic scene, frantically auto-sodomising till he collapses. Kleist's letter to Goethe is not a letter—it's a *letter bomb*; his Phoebus is not a guardian of the arts—he's a *suicide bomber*: he will crash his quadriga, loaded with explosive poetry, into Goethe's study and blow it to bits; Goethe, electrified, hands over his laurel to Kleist, before, like the Marchese in *Bettelweib* (another quintessentially Kleistian Napoleon/Goethe figure), auto-destructing in an auto-erotic frenzy.[445]

"**Ebenso wenig für die Bühne geschrieben.**" *Penthesilea*, Kleist tells Goethe in the same letter, "*ist übrigens ebenso wenig für die Bühne geschrieben, als [...] der Zerbrochne Krug [...] und so sehr ich auch sonst in jedem Sinne gern dem Augenblick angehörte, so muß ich doch in diesem Fall auf die Zukunft hinaussehen*" (II:805-6). The drama's *stageability* must have been questionable not least from a logistical point of view: the nine main characters apart, Kleist casts minors and extras in numbers that far exceed those of his previous dramas: among the Greeks feature, in order of appearance, a captain, a Myrmidonian, an Aetolian and another, a Dolopian, various Greeks, various voices, a Greek prince, a first Greek, a second, and another, later several more, a herald; among the Amazons, a princess, an Amazon and another, later several more, four young girls, a first Amazon, a second, a third, later a fourth, fifth, sixth, seventh, and eighth, a captain, a first priestess, a second and another, later three more, a colonel, later a second and a third, another Amazon princess, a maiden and another, an entire chorus of maidens, an entire Amazon army, several women, a porter and another; from the animal kingdom, Penthesilea's nine named dogs, assorted other dogs, horses, elephants.[446] Even assuming that each actor would play multiple roles, as was typical in Attic theatre—chorus apart, three actors played all roles by repeatedly changing costumes and masks—, staging *Penthesilea* would have required a stage and troupe of a scale no working theatre in Kleist's time could furbish; only in the 20th century would a performance as scripted and cast by Kleist become feasible, on film rather than on stage.[447]

The prominent critic Karl Aug. Böttiger concluded that Kleist's "*Scharen von Griechen und Amazonen, Mädchen und Müttern*" entailed "mere spectacle" (as opposed to, I suppose, "proper theatre"), yet for all its spectacle Kleist's drama features a remarkably conventional structure, the 24 scenes (cf. the 24 hours of the day, the 24 books of the *Iliad*) in accordance with classical conventions being conveniently divisible into five "acts," and its frequent messenger reports and teichoscopies (techniques introduced in classical plays in order to comply with conventions such as the *three-actor-rule* and the *three unities*) demonstrate that Kleist did not abandon classical conventions but merely adapted them.[448]

"aus einem so wunderbaren Geschlecht." Böttiger got one thing quite wrong: as always in Kleist, no "girls" or "mothers" are involved at all, only men wearing female masks and costumes, in line with Attic convention: "*niemals hätte sich das Wesen des griechischen Theaters entwickelt, wenn sie [die Frauen] nicht ganz davon ausgeschlossen gewesen wären*" (II:796). Goethe, on the the other hand, correctly perceived something *off-centre* in *Penthesilea*, concerning its "wondrous" "*Geschlecht*" ("genus," "gender," "lineage"—he was presumably thinking of the drama, its protagonist and its author).

The main female personage Kleist is concerned with, Queen Luise, is not only enacted by a male *actor*, but also represented by a male *character* (Achilles). Taking his critique of Luise's influence over Prussian politics to its limit, he eliminates gender altogether, not only from politics and war, but also from sex and even succession, reducing incubation and its machinery to an androgyne aspect of the male. Kleist is not concerned with a sociology of gender wars but with an alchemy of gender fusion, a performative *po(i) etical* production whose end-product is the *ideal statesman-lover-begetter*. Perhaps Goethe, the old fox, had an inkling of all this. And instinctively recoiled.

"**Der Blickt drängt unzerknickt sich durch die Räder…nicht hin!**" *Penthesilea* at times feels more like a script for a cinematic film than a screenplay for theatre.[449] Kleist's *Amazonomachy*, even if much of it is told in tychoscopies, anticipates the lavish epic historical drama films of the 1950s (think William Wyler's *Ben-Hur*, with its wide-aspect-ratio cinematography and chariot race) and the equally lavish space operas popular since the 1970s (think George Lucas' *Star Wars* franchise, with its proliferation of weird creatures, galactic battles and laser-sword duels).[450]

The drama's characteristic tychoscopies add an immediacy that anticipates live radio—cf. the following example, in which three Greeks comment the battle action in real time, rather like radio hosts a live football match:

> An seiner Seite fliegt sie schon!
> Doch jetzt urplötzlich reißt er—
> Zur Seit' herum!
> Zu uns her fliegt er wieder!
> Ha! Der Verschlagne! Er betrog sie—
> Hui!
> Wie sie, die Unaufhaltsme, vorbei
> Schießt an dem Fuhrwerk—
> Prellt, im Sattle fliegt,
> Und stolpert—

>   Stürzt!
>   Was?
>   Stürzt, die Königin!
> Und eine Jungfrau [...]
>   Und eine noch—
>   Und wieder—
>   Und noch eine—
> Ha!   (V.419-30)

Kleist's depiction of "live" action by means of stretched or arrested time, motion-blurred objects, and fragmented vision in some cases—e.g., "*Gehetzter Hirsche Flug ist schneller nicht! / Der Blickt drängt unzerknickt sich durch die Räder, / Zur Scheibe fliegend eingedreht, nicht hin!*" (V.384-6); "*Staub ringsum, / Vom Glanz der Rüstungen durchzuckt und Waffen: / Das Aug erkennt nicht mehr, wie scharf es sieht*" (V.433-5)—anticipates techniques of 20th century comics, in others—e.g., "*Und dem gestreckten Parder gleich, folgt sie / Dem Blick auch auf dem Fuß*" (V. 346-7); "*Wie sie, bis auf die Mähn' herabgebeugt, / Hinweg die Luft trinkt lechzend, die sie hemmt! / Sie fliegt, wie von der Sehne abgeschossen: / Numidische Pfeile sind nicht hurtiger! / Das Heer bleibt keuchend, hinter ihr, wie Köter, / Wenn sich ganz aus die Dogge streckt, zurück!*" (V.397-402)—those of film, such as that of "bullet time" in the Wachovskis' 1999 sci-fi classic *The Matrix*.[451]

The excessive number and rapid turnover of characters, dialogues, perspectives and scenes, the excess of rushes and catatonias, the exuberant variety and plasticity of costumes and props, and the superabundance of theatrical or filmic techniques (close-up, slow motion, hypotyposis, etc.), if actualised on stage, would provoke massive audio-visual overburdening; this overwhelming, shell-shock experience not only anticipates the effect on the audience of surround sound and 3D in 21st century multiplexes, but also mimicks that of the *Grande batterie*'s sustained barrages on enemy forces, and that of the Coalition's siege artillery on the citizens of Mainz. A pounding. Relentless. Kleist transports his theatre audience straight into the theatre of war, as if by live VR simulation.

"die Welt, nahm ich, ihr wißts, wie sie steht." *Penthesilea* is spectacle and kaleidoscope of orgiastic war and raptuous sex, of *Erôs* and *Agôn*, with all their associated exuberant gestures, movements, voices, noises and mayhem.[452] It is not that Kleist *did not succeed* in making the drama playable: *he did not intend to*. The *Napoleonic Wars* and his personal *satyrical* and *syphilitical* battles were perhaps *too real* to be reduced to into imaginary or symbolic stage-play; the only stage that could authentically accommodate them was *life itself*. "I took the world as it stands," Kleist tells his readers in epigram no. 6., *Verwahrung*: "Scheltet, ich bitte, mich nicht! Ich machte, beim delphischen Gotte, / Nur die Verse; die Welt, nahm ich, ihr wißts, wie sie steht" (I:21)—not: "as it *is*," but: "as it *stands*," "as it *erects*": Kleist's world is a world *as artillery barrage*, as "Stahlgewitter" (Ernst Jünger); it is a world *as ithyphallic revel, as pederastaic jouissance*; it is a world *as syphiliac sting, as mercurial syringe*.

Kleist's drama, in Lacanian terms, is the *"sinthome"* that ties together the domains of meaning—the *imaginary*, the *symbolic*, the *real*—without itself conveying meaning. I repeat: Kleist's *overt* drama *conveys no meaning*. It is mere bombastic surface, the crumbled, discarded newspaper or pulp fiction into which the "rotten fish" of the *Real*, the perversity of the *Imaginary*, and the insidiousness of the *Symbolic* are wrapped. Its *overt* function is not *semantic* or *hermeneutic* but *pragmatic*: as packaging, transport, storage, camouflage for Kleist's "threads." The drama, therefore cannot be *interpreted*, only *evaluated* in its functioning and *unravelled* into its threads (each of which carries meaning). If Shakespeare reinvented theatre as *show business*, Kleist reinvented it as *terrorism*.

"Sie läßt den Bogen fallen" *(IV)*. I showed the polyvalent functioning of Penthesilea's golden bow as symbol of archaic (Amazon, pre-revolutionary French) state power, as wonder weapon (Napoleon's *Grande batterie*, Jupiter's thunderbolts), and as electromagnetic generator, influence machine, electro-stimulator. This auspicious symbol parallels, and even visually recalls, other symbols dear to Kleist: the laurel and the lyre. A good year after publishing the *Penthesilea* fragment in *Ph* (whose back cover features precisely the lyre, bow and laurel, the attributes of Apollo—cf. *LS*,222b), Kleist ends his lament *Das Letzte Lied* with the following lines, dedicated to himself: "*Schließt er sein Lied, er wünscht mit ihm zu enden, / Und legt die Leier weinend aus den Händen*" (I:32). Penthesilea puts down her golden bow, Napoleon his imperial laurel, the national bard, his lyre: in death Penthesilea, Napoleon and Kleist are united.[453]

2.6 Das Käthchen von Heilbronn: Wedding at Vienna
(A Fantasy Staged Too Late)

Genesis and Context. Two initial fragments (Ph I) and (Ph II) of *Das Käthchen von Heilbronn oder Die Feuerprobe. Ein Grosses Historisches Ritterschauspiel* appeared in *Ph* in 1808; the play premièred at the Theater an der Wien on 17th March 1810 and was published in book format (P) in September 1810. Kleist commenced work on *Käthchen* more or less seamlessly upon completing *Penthesilea*; the genesis of several novellas overlapped with *Käthchen*'s, and *Hermannsschlacht*'s fell in the middle of *Käthchen*'s, which spanned at least three years, with these milestones:

- Late autumn 1807: Kleist first mentions the drama to Marie, as *Penthesilea*'s "opposite pole" (cf. II:797);
- April/May 1808: (Ph I) appears (scenes I/1-II/1);
- June 1808: Kleist promises Joh. Fr. Cotta a MS by end of 1808, hoping it will be published as pocket book and staged in Vienna (cf. II:813-4);
- October 1808: Kleist sends Heinr. Joseph Collin a draft stage adaptation, which in December he authorises him to shorten (cf. II:817-8);
- September/October 1808: (Ph II) appears (scenes II/2-13), distributed to subscribers with substantial delay in February 1809;
- 1st January 1809: Kleist sends *Hermannsschlacht* to Collin, asking him to prioritise it over *Käthchen*; the outbreak of the *War of the Fifth Coalition* delays both stagings; Kleist shifts his focus to the *Germania* project;
- 12th January 1810: Kleist submits a *Käthchen* MS to Cotta (cf. II:830), who does not publish it (cf. II:832);
- 28th January 1810: Kleist requests Collin to stage *Käthchen* or restore the MS to him (cf. II:831);
- 17th-19th March 1810: the play premières in Vienna in Collin's stage adaptation (cf. II:831);
- 12th August 1810: Kleist submits a *Käthchen* MS to Georg Reimer (cf. II:837), possibly an edited version of the Cotta MS;

- 8th September 1810: Kleist submits revisions to Reimer (cf. II:839; *KH*,71);
- Late September 1810: (P) is published at the Leipzig autumn fair.

Extant versions of the drama include (Ph I), (Ph II), and (P); the Cotta and initial Reimer MSS and stage adaptation(s) are lost; an extant 1842 prompt book (cf. I:905-7; 961) is of interest and to be discussed later.

"Die Handlung spielt in Schwaben." So did *Schroffenstein*'s, and the associations in *Käthchen* are similar, though the atmosphere is different: fairy tale-ish, rather than gothic. Like Kleist's *Erstling*, *Käthchen*, entails a constellation of rivalling princes—Count vom Strahl, Burggrave von Freiburg, Rhinegrave vom Stein—squabbling over a disintegrating empire, physically represented by Kunigunde and symbolically by Der Kaiser. Names of characters and locations— e.g., Thurneck, Stauffen, Wart, Freiburg, Straßburg, Heilbronn, Swabian Mountains, Alps, Hundsrück, Worms, Neckar, Rhine—are located in or adjacent to, or associated with, medieval Swabia; only the family name Friedeborn, which Käthchen shares with her suitor Gottfried, is not Swabian but Brandenburgian.[454]

The speaking name Wetter, Graf vom Strahl associates this knight with Jupiter (*"Wetterstrahl"* = "thunderbolt"), hence Napoleon. The no less speaking name Das Käthchen von Heilbronn, literally "The Little Pure One of the Healing Well" (variations of which we observe repeatedly in Kleist's works: Thinka, Katharina), associates the maiden with health and wholesomeness, and, Heilbronn being home to the famous practitioner of Puységurian magnetism Eberhard Gmelin, magnetic therapy. Yet another speaking name, Kunigunde ("clan wars" in old Germanic), links this matron with that very "German disease" that is the "poodle's kernel" of Kleist's œuvre, and contrasts her starkly with the *über*wholesome Käthchen.[455]

"mit den Insignien des Vehmgerichts." The first act depicts a session of a vehmic court—a tribunal of the late medieval and early modern era that operated in secret, under the direct authority of the emperor, to deal with serious *"in flagranti"* cases of murder, heresy, occultism or witchcraft. A defendant pronounced guilty by a vehmic court almost invariably faced the death sentence, typically executed on the spot by hanging from the nearest tree. Members of vehmic courts were carefully chosen, ceremonially initiated, and distinguished by the widely recognised—and feared—vehmic insignia of stone (*Stein*), rope (*Strick*), grass (*Grass*) and green (*Grün*), or "*S.S.G.G.*" for short. Judge Count Otto articulates a vehmic court's mission thus: "*den Frevel aufsuchen, da, wo er, in der Höhle der Brust, gleich einem Molche verkrochen, vom Arm weltlicher Gerechtigkeit nicht aufgefunden werden kann*" (V.3-6).

The vehmic court convenes to hear Theobald Friedeborn's complaint that Count Strahl used black magic or witchcraft to seduce his 15-year old foster-daughter Käthchen. Theobald's complaint is not without risk, for should the court find his foster-daughter complicit in the crime, her own life might be forfeited, together with that of the convinct. In the event, the judges conclude that the only "magic" at play between Strahl and Käthchen was romantic love and erotic attraction, that Käthchen fell, as teenagers do, head over heels for a dapper knight (the medieval equivalent of a rock star), and are about to dismiss the case when the accused, apparently dissatisfied with the hearing, by subtle rhetoric and Käthchen's relentless cross-examination turns himself into the accuser, the maiden into the defendant: his sophistical "*Hier steh ich, ein Verklagter, wie du*" (V.367), if one drops two consonants, becomes "*ich,... Verklager*" ("I, the accuser"), "*Verklagte,... du*" ("the accused, you"). The judges surprisingly condone Strahl's turning himself into de facto presiding judge: "*Ihr zeigtet / Von der Gewalt, die Ihr hier übt, so manche / Besondre Probe uns*" (V.637-9). Käthchen shows herself quite incapable of rationalising why she has been following the Count like a dog.[456]

"**eurem stolzen Reigen will ich mich anschließen.**" In (Ph I), Strahl states his aspiration of appending himself to a long and illustrious genealogy of emperors (the first of whom, Winfried, direct descendant of a part-Romanised *Zevs*, presumably referring to Charlemagne). Strahl categorically rejects marrying Käthchen, though he confesses desiring her erotically (cf. V.707-8), because the only way for him to fulfil his aspiration is to marry an emperor's daughter. Strahl admits that the ancestral emperor Winfried might well have chosen Käthchen as his bride, on account of her vigorous health, and irrespective of her ancestry, expecting her to be fertile and produce him heirs, but prefers himself to marry into an imperial dynasty.[457] *Käthchen* is not a story of romantic love (a domain Kleist happily leaves to the Kotzebues and Ifflands of the world) but of dynastic politics, of an ambitious parvenu's quest to marry into an imperial dynasty; Strahl is so adamant to absolve himself before the vehmic court, not only from the accusation of having used black magic, but from the suspicion that he laid his hands on Käthchen, because if he was to be declared the legal father to her (a commoner's) offspring, or to be forced to marry her, it would ruin his plan.

"dies wesenlose Bild." In (Ph II), Strahl encounters an *eligible* bride, Kunigunde von Thurneck, whom he "saves" from one of her suitors. The fragment does not contain the information, imparted to the audience in (P), of her imperial lineage (cf. V.1141-2; 1378), but her claim to the lands of the "*Stauffen*" hints at her imperial status, the Hohenstauffen having been a medieval imperial dynasty. Kunigunde, on her part, sets her sight firmly on Strahl, in the tenth scene fantasising about entrapping him like a bird. Although her many suitors suggest that she may once have been attractive, her false teeth (cf. V.822) put her into stark relief against the youthful Käthchen. Yet lineage matters more than youth to Strahl, and when Kunigunde, before his and his mother's eyes, tears apart the papers that enshrine her claim to the Stauffen lands, he embraces her as his bride: "*die begehr ich / Zur Frau!*" (V.1372-3). A widely-held view that Strahl mindlessly falls for Kunigunde's artificial charms is untenable: only his boundless ambition compels him to chose her as his future wife: "*Ihr kleines verwünschenes Gesicht ist der letzte Grund aller dieser Kriege wider mich*" (V.791-2).

Strahl's veering between the desirable, but ineligible, Käthchen and the eligible, but undesirable, Kunigunde in (Ph II) remains unresolved; perhaps Kleist put his story on hold to await actual developments that would provide the template for its continuation, or he sought to kindle readers' anticipation of a sequel with this cliffhanger. That he published (Ph II) at all, given that *Ph* was, for Kleist, already beyond repair, will have had a *satirical* reason.

"einen Hahn… rupft' er." This detail, which Kleist mentions obliquely in (Ph II) and more explicitly in (P), refers to the ancient anecdote of the Cynic philosopher Diogenes of Sinope—Plato's "*Sokrates mainomenos*" ("frenzied Socrates")—throwing a plucked chicken amidst the students of the Athenian Academy in response to Socrates' definition of man as featherless bird. Kleist thus associates Kunigunde with a plucked bird, Strahl with the great Cynic who disdained all established authorities and conventions.[458] Elsewhere in (Ph II), Kunigunde recalls a single, prominent feather with which her waiting-maid Rosalie adorned her, "*Hier diese Feder, sieh, die du mir stolz / Hast aufgepflanzt, die andern überragend*" (I:901), as if positing herself as *primus inter pares* among "plucked birds." Kleist's sustained avarian imagery—elsewhere one of her suitors compares Kunigunde with a leprous chick (cf. V.931-2)—, together with his hint at her imperial lineage, associates Kunigunde with the most illustrious of heraldic birds, the *HRR*'s double-headed Quaternion Eagle. Similarly, her mosaic, artificial, plucked and dishevelled physical appearance alludes to the *HRR*'s chaotic composition and advanced state of disintegration:

> Sie ist eine mosaische Arbeit, aus allen drei Reichen der Natur zusammengetzt. Ihre Zähne gehören einem Mädchen aus München, ihre Haare sind aus Frankreich verschrieben, ihrer Wangen Gesundheit kommt aus den Bergwerken in Ungarn, und der Wuchs, den ihr an ihr bewundert, hat sie einem Hemde zu danken, das ihr der Schmied, aus schwedischem Eisen verfertigt hat.—" (V.2446-53)[459]

 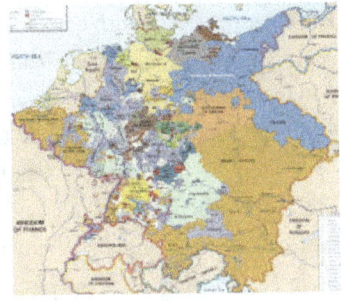

Kunigunde ("clan wars"): Quaternion Eagle with its "mosaic" coats of arms representing its constituent principalities (left); the *HRR* (1793) and its "mosaic" state-scape (right).

The faded object of desire, embodied by Kunigunde, is once more the *HRR*'s imperial dignity, or what is left of it after the confluence of the "German disease" of *dynastic rivalry* and the "French disease" of *dynastic hybris* dilapidated it to the point of disintegration.[460] If the "pure" Käthchen embodies a wholesome, but merely royal, *Borussia*, and the "mosaic" Kunigunde a dilapidated, but imperial, *Germania* (or her self-appointed successor, *Austria*), then Kleist's *Grosses Historisches Ritterschauspiel* depicts Strahl-Napoleon veering between bedding an erotically desirable Hohenzollern maiden and marrying a dynastically desirable Habsburgian matron.

"Unter den Holunderstrauch" *(I)*. Like the pomegranate tree in Greek mythology, the elder (*Sambucus*; cf. V.1458; 2023; 2615) in Celtic folklore marks the border between the subterranean and terranean worlds; in Christian folklore Judas Iscariot hanged himself on an elder, which is therefore also known as "devil's tree." In Germany (where it is called *Holunder* or *Holler*), the elder is associated with Frau Holle, a mythical figure which the Grimm Brothers popularised in the first vol. of their *Kinder- und Hausmärchen* (1812/13).[461] While published only after Kleist's death, Jacob Grimm on 17th October 1810 sent a MS of *Märchen* to Brentano, which could have circulated and been read in Berlin salons. In the Grimms' version of the story, two unequal sisters, the fair and industrious *Goldmarie* and the ugly and lazy *Pechmarie*, end up being showered by Frau

Holle, respectively, with gold and pitch. Jochen Schmidt (*Kleist*, 139) sees "Kunigunde as evil witch and Käthchen as good fairy," and while it may be convenient to discern in Kunigunde a version of *Pechmarie* and in Käthchen an avatar of *Goldmarie*, the radical reversibility of his female protagonists sets the Kleistian *Käthchen* apart from the Grimmean fairy-tale: as we shall see, in the drama's ending it is Käthchen who marries the usurper, which in Kleist's eyes makes her a *Pechmarie* ("*Pech*" = "pitch," "bad luck"), while Kunigunde, in the eleventh hour, like a phoenix from the ashes, re-emerges as a *Goldmarie* figure.

The mythical Frau Holle may be derivative of Holla, Germanic goddess of fertility, particularly revered in Swabia (!), and associated with Odin's wife Frigge, the goddess of childbearing (!). Sacred or sacrificial sites dedicated to Holla were often located below elder bushes growing near sources—cf. "Heilbronn"—, and Kleist's "*unter dem Holunderstrauch*" could well represent such a site: "Szene: Schloß Wetterstrahl. Platz, dicht mit Bäumen bewachsen, am äußeren zerfallenen Mauerring der Burg. Vorn ein Holunderstrauch, er eine Art von natürlicher Laube bildet, worunter von Feldsteinen, mit einer Strohmatte bedeck, ein Sitz. An den Zweigen sieht man ein Hemdchen und ein Paar Strümpfe usw. zum Trocknen aufgehängt" (V.2019). The "bower" in Kleist's Würzburg letters and in *Amphitryon* is associated with sexual intercourse. With all her clothes hung up for drying: "shirt, socks, etc." ("etc." presumably refers to the piece of clothing worn half way between shirt and socks), Käthchen is evidently *stark naked*. The "seat" of "fieldstones covered with a straw mat" could serve as bed (cf. the "straw" in *Bettelweib* and *Zweikampf*) and/or sacrificial table. Did Strahl appear on the scene *to make love* to Käthchen, or *to sacrifice* her? His "sheath" or "case" ("*Futteral*") could hide his ithyphallic member or his sacrificial knife (or both in one).

"zur Rechten, im Vordergrund, ein Portal." The drama's settings alternate between bucolic (caves, grottoes, huts, hermitages, inns) and urban spaces (castles, squares, churches, chambers, gardens):

I/1-I/2:	An underground cave. Vehmic court.
II/1-II/3:	The forest before the cave.
II/4-II/8:	A charcoal maker's hut in the mountains. Thunderstorm.
II/9-II/13	Wetterstrahl Castle. A chamber.
III/1:	An hermitage in a mountain forest.
III/2-III/4:	An inn.
III/5-III/6:	Thurneck Castle. A chamber.
III/7-III/15:	Square before the castle. The castle burns.
IV/1-IV/3:	Mountain area with waterfalls and a bridge.
IV/4-IV/8:	Garden. A gothic grotto in the background.
V/1:	Worms. Open square before the imperial castle. Ordeal court.
V/2-V/3:	Worms. Chamber in the imperial castle.
V/4-V/9:	Wetterstrahl Castle. Kunigunde's chamber.
V/10-V/12:	Inside a cave. View onto a landscape.
V/13:	Castle square.

These settings may appear conventional, yet at least the final scene's castle square is portrayed with a precision that suggests an *actual location*—namely, I offer, the Schloßplatz before Vienna's Hofburg, until 1806 seat of the Holy Roman, since 1804 of the Austrian, Emperor, whose aspect in Kleist's day is approximately rendered by these mid-19th century paintings:

"Szene: Schloßplatz, zur Rechten, im Vordergrund, ein Portal. Zur Linken, mehr in der Tiefe, das Schloß mit einer Rampe. Im Hintergrund die Kirche." (V.2644)

The viewpoint to which Kleist's V/13 scene description corresponds is marked by the red dot on below's *LHS* base-map: atop a bastion of the city's Burgwall, from which the observer beholds, *to his left*, the Leopoldinischer Trakt ("*Schloß*") and its ramp ("*Rampe*"), leading up to the main entrance of the imperial apartments located on the second floor, by which the imperial carriages entered; *to his right*, the Altes Burgtor ("*Portal*"); *in the foreground*, the castle square ("*Schloßplatz*"; in the base-map shown as Volksgarten and Hofgarten); *in the background*, the slim spire of the Augustinerkirche ("*Kirche*"). The viewpoint to which the *LHS* painting corresponds is marked on thee base-map by the green dot: inside of, and below, the Burgwall, from which angle the Altes Burgtor is on the far right, outside the painting's visual field; that to which the *RHS* painting corresponds, by the blue dot: outside the Burgwall and Burgtor:

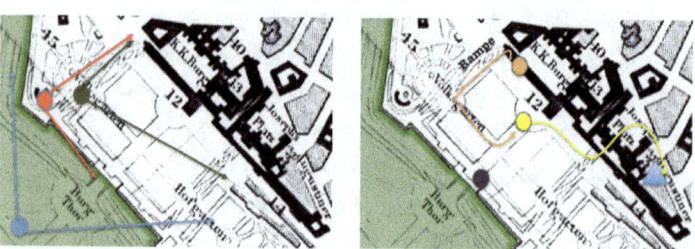

"*Glockenklang*": Locating Käthchen's wedding (No. 12 = Leopoldinischer Trakt; blue triangle: Augustinerkirche; green area: glacis between Burgwall and suburbs.

We can now locate *Käthchen*'s wedding scene with precision: Strahl, together with the Emperor and his retinue (yellow dot), is waiting at the centre of the Schloßplatz (cf. V.2655) as Kunigunde (violet dot) is watching the proceedings from the Burgtor; Käthchen (orange dot) is led by Strahl's mother Helena down the ramp (cf. V.2667; orange path) and united with Strahl under the baldachin; she swoons but is revived by Helena, and together with Strahl proceeds to the Augustinerkirche (cf. V.2680; yellow path), whose wedding bells soon toll.[462]

If we can so precisely locate the drama's "castle square," how about its "Thurneck Castle" and "Wetterstrahl Castle"? A Thurneck Castle once existed in Swabia, whose name Kleist could have borrowed, but which was ruined in the 17th century and had no historical relevance; no Wetterstrahl Castle appears to have existed, neither in Swabia nor elsewhere. However, if Kunigunde represents the imperial eagle then her "castle" could refer to the Hofburg's Swiss Wing, which houses the Imperial Treasury in which the Holy Roman insignia and banners are kept and in which in 1525 a fire broke out that destroyed the wing, much of the Hofburg, and parts of old Vienna. Der Kaiser's "Wormser Schloss" may refer to the Leopold Wing; the "*Innere der Höhle mit Aussicht*" (V.2527), to the chambers of the *Reichshofrat* (Aulic Council—cf. Kleist's "*Reichsräte*") located at the Hofburg until the *HRR*'s dissolution. "Wetterstrahl Castle" could refer to three different locations: in (Ph I), to the Palais des Tuileries, Napoleon's *pied-à-terre* in the capital (cf. V.665); in (Ph II), to the Statthalterei in Erfurt, a fortified city that with *Tilsit* had become Napoleon's personal domain (*domaine réservé à l'empereur*), and where in September/October 1808 he hosted Alex. I and the *Rheinbund* princes for the *Congress of Erfurt* (on which occasion he also received Goethe and Wieland); and in (P), to Schloss Schönbrunn, the Habsburg summer residence outside Vienna, where Napoleon resided from May till September 1809:

"Wetterstrahl Castle": *Kaiserliches Lustschloss Schönbrunn* (In the distance: Vienna).

The elder bush (IV/2), as well as the "*Grotte im gotischen Stil*" (V.2179) in which Käthchen encounters Kunigunde, are then located in the latter's Schlosspark (the grotto may allude to the eponymous castle's "*Schöner Brunnen*").

(P)'s urban settings evidently being in and near Vienna suggests that its rural settings could be in the city's environs—e.g., the "bridge by the waterfalls" (cf. V.1937) could refer to the Tabor bridges that connected Vienna, via the forests and swamps on the Danube's left bank, to Prague and Pressssburg (alternative means of crossing the Danube were indeed ferryboats—cf. V.2013):

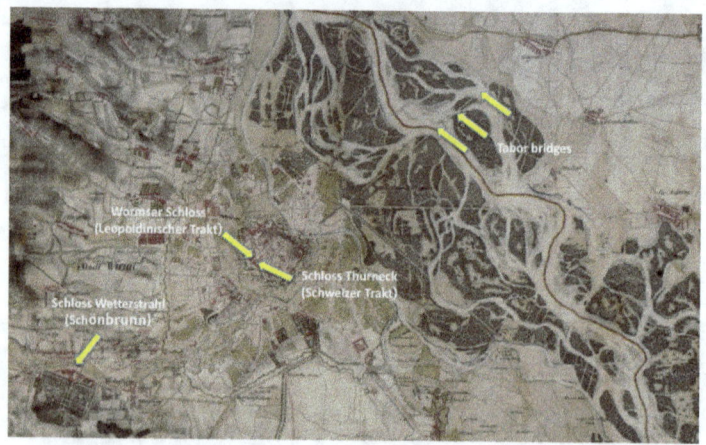

Käthchen: The urban and rural setting (Vienna and environs, c. 1800).

When Strahl-Napoleon appears at "Thurneck Castle" (III/5), i.e., in the heart of Vienna, Kleist's writing catches up with historical events: we find ourselves in the middle of the *War of the Fifth Coalition*, Napoleon has occupied Vienna (10th May 1809) and prepares to confront the Austrian army on the Danube's left bank.

Käthchen, Satirically

When Kleist commenced *Käthchen*, in the late summer or autumn of 1807, his depiction of Käthchen as doggishly following Strahl will have harked back at Luise's supplication to Napoleon at *Tilsit*, suggesting that his initial conception for the drama entailed a scenario in which Käthchen-*Borussia*'s supplication precipitates her union with Strahl-Napoleon, inaugurating a Hohenzollern-Bonapartean dynasty. When he published (Ph I) in early 1808, he evidently no longer considered this scenario plausible, for Strahl announces that a union with Käthchen is infeasible because he will only consider a bride of imperial lineage (cf. V.681-2). When he followed through with (Ph II), Kleist introduced the figure of Kunigunde as an eligible bride for Strahl. From late 1808, with Europe again on the brink of war, until the negotiations of the *Treaty of Schönbrunn* in October 1809, *Käthchen*'s focal question of Napoleon's quest for a bride remained on the back burner, and

Kleist turned his attention to *Hermannsschlacht* and *Germania*. When in late 1809 or early 1810 Kleist picked *Käthchen* up again, the final (P) version had to account for a number of intervening political events, in addition to those already relevant for (Ph I) and (Ph II). Events relevant for (Ph I) include:

- On 5th May 1807 Napoleon's designated heir, Joséphine's grandson Napoléon Charles Bonaparte, dies, triggering speculation that he could divorce Joséphine and remarry in order to produce an heir;
- The *Battle of Friedland* of 14th June ends the *War of the Fourth Coalition*;
- On 6th July Queen Luise supplicates to Napoleon at Tilsit; three days later the *Franco-Prussian Treaty* halves Prussia's territory and population; Napoleon returns to Paris, Prussia remains occupied by the *Ad'A,* and Fr. Wilh. and Luise remain in East Prussias exile;
- On Napoleon's request, on 10th July Heinr. Fr. Karl vom und zum Stein is appointed Prussian Minister of State;
- On 9th March 1808 Napoleon's chief of staff, Louis-Alexandre Berthier, marries Max. I Joseph's nice, Maria Elisabeth;

Additional events relevant for (Ph II) include:

- In June/July 1808 reports of the Spanish *guerrilleros'* successes reach Germany; Franz I authorises a *Landwehr* (militia), but Fr. Wilh. III desists;
- In August French agents seize a letter by Stein advocating a people's uprising in northern Germany ("Stein Affair"); Napoleon confiscates Stein's personal properties in Westphalia, declares him "enemy of France and of the *Rheinbund*," and pressures Fr. Wilh. to dismiss him from office;
- At the *Convention of Paris* in September, Napoleon imposes crippling war reparations on Prussia and curtails her army to 42,000 men, 1/5th of its pre-war strength; by 3rd December the French occupation forces evacuate Prussia, with the exception of three strategic fortresses;

- At the *Congress of Erfurt* in September/October, Napoleon reconfirms his alliances with Alex. I (to whom he possibly broaches the idea of marriaging his younger sister Katharina), and the *Rheinbund* princes (4 German kings and 34 princes attend); when Franz I abstains, an angry Napoleon writes to him: *"In meiner Macht hat es gestanden, die österreichische Monarchie zu vernichten. Was Eure Majestät sind, sind Sie durch Unseren Willen"*;[463]
- From October till December 1808 Napoleon personally takes command of the *Armée de l'Espagne* fighting the guerrilleros in Spain;
- On 24th November 1808 Fr. Wilh. dismisses Stein;

Lastly, additional events relevant for (P):

- On 10th April 1809 Austrian troops under Archduke Karl's command invade Bavaria, triggering the *War of the Fifth Coalition*;
- Following the *Battle of Regensburg* of 19th-23rd April, the *Ad'A* pushes into Austria; Fr. Wilh., contrary to earlier promises, refuses to join the war and succour the distressed Austrians;
- On 10th May Napoleon occupies Vienna and puts up at Schönbrunn Palace where his mistress Maria Walewska becomes pregnant, indicating that he is fertile; after years of hesitation, he resolves to divorce Joséphine and find an eligible bride, initially focusing his quest on Katharina, until her mother refuses to endorse the marriage;
- On 17th May Napoleon decrees, from Schönbrunn, France's annexation of the Papal State; when Pope Pius VII excommunicates Napoleon, he is kidnapped by French soldiers;
- On 21st/22nd May Archduke Karl repulses Napoleon at *Aspern*;
- On 5th/6th July Napoleon vanquishes Karl at *Wagram*;
- On 8th July Klemens von Metternich is appointed Austrian Minister of State, replacing Foreign Minister Stadion; having previously supported the war, following *Wagram* Metternich advocates that Austria sue for peace;[464]
- On 12th July Austria signs the *Armistice of Znaim*;

- On 12th October German patriot Friedrich Staps' assassination attempt on Napoleon at Schönbrunn fails;
- On 14th October the *Treaty of Schönbrunn* is signed, in which Austria and France renew the *Austro-French Alliance* of 1756, directed against Prussia and Britain; Metternich proposes, and negotiates with Napoleon's envoy Louis, comte de Narbonne-Lara, the marriage with Marie-Louise of Austria;
- On 14th December Napoleon divorces Joséphine;
- On 23rd December 1809 Fr. Wilh. and Luise return to Berlin after three years of exile in East Prussia;
- On 7th February 1810 Napoleon officially agrees to marry Marie-Louise;[465]
- On 11th March Napoleon and Marie-Louise are married by proxy in Vienna's Augustinerkirche; she is then brought to France, where Napoleon receives her at Compiègne and consummates their marriage (mimicking the precise procedure the Dauphin and Marie Antoinette had followed in 1769);
- On 2st April their Catholic wedding ceremony is officiated by Cardinal Fesch at the Louvre (Napoleon distancing himself from the Dauphin in so far as the latter's wedding ceremony was held at Versailles);
- On 4th June Hardenberg is appointed Prussian Chancellor, having forced the resignation of Kleist's friend and mentor Altenstein's cabinet;
- On 19th July Queen Luise dies "of a broken heart."

"und räumt ihm diesen." The opening scene's judge's chair is evidently a *curule chair* (cf. also I:666, V.779), symbol of magisterial power since Etruscan and Roman times and a furniture Napoleon was clearly fond of: he symbolically seated himself on the 7th century Merovingian curule "Throne of Dagobert" and had his favourite *chateaux*—Malmaison, Fontainebleau, Compiègne—furnished with curule seats, thrones and beds; even his sarcophagus is modelled on its design:

Napoleonic curule chairology.[466]

Otto's vacating the curule seat for Strahl (at Käthchen's request: "*Ihr würdgen Herrn,…/ Steht gleich vom Richtstuhl auf und räumt ihn diesem!*"; V.395-6), reflects Napoleon's having de facto ascended the HRR's vacated imperial throne.[467]

Among Napoleon's entourage, Strahl's mother may refer to Letizia Bonaparte, *M*^{me} *Mère de l'Empereur*, a resolute woman with considerable influence over Napoleon: "*Eurer Mutter, der Gräfin, Gebot*" (V.737); Flammberg (the name refers to a double-edged, wave-bladed sword), to Eugène de Beauharnais, who guards Napoleon's empire as stubbornly as *Marionettentheater*'s cherub does paradise; Gottschalk ("servant of God"), to Napoleon's chief of staff Louis-Alexandre Berthier.[468] Kunigunde, introduced in (Ph II), enacts imperial brides: initially Katharina, later Marie-Louise.

"**Ich bringe dir die Waffen.**" Käthchen in (Ph I) and (Ph II) represents Queen Luise or *Borussia*, for whose "doggishness" Kleist in the opening scene reserves his most scathing parody. Käthchen is a thoroughly ambiguous creature: an elf—in German, *Elfe* or *Alb*—that is at once a dream and a nightmare (*Albtraum*). Käthchen's swoon before Strahl mirrors the Marquise's before Count F, suggesting that in Kleist's initial conception, "*Das Käthchen von Heilbronn*" = "The submissive Queen of Tilsit." Käthchen's ridiculous leap out of the window when Strahl mounts his grey (cf. V.181-5; 2060) re-enacts Fr. Wilh.'s rash mobilisation in 1806, and subsequent disaster at *Jena-Auerstedt*, which Kleist here compares with the a heedless leap of faith of a love-struck teenage girl. Her breaking both her "legs" refers to Prussia's being curtailed and crippled at *Tilsit*, her "weaponising" Strahl (cf. V.1786) to Prussia's being forced to give up most of her armies, and to fund Napoleon's with her war reparations, at *Paris*.

Käthchen's foster-father Theobald ("bold people") Friedeborn ("born-for-peace") could represent Prussia's Minister of State zum Stein, her "fiancé" Gottfried Friedeborn, whose ridiculously redundant name literally means "god's-peace born-for-peace," the exiled Fr. Wilh. III. The topographical detail of her ancestral lands being "bounded" (V.100-1) by Gottfried's is accurate: Luise was a born Dutchess of Mecklenburg-Strelitz, whose family's ancestral lands were indeed largely enclosed by the Hohenzollerns' territories (below, in orange):

"umgrenzen": Käthchen-Luise's ancestral lands "bounded" by Gottfried-Fr. Wilh.'s Prussia.

"Krieg! Ein Aufgebot zu neurer Fehde." When Kleist produced (Ph II), in the autumn of 1808, the interception of Stein's letter, Prussia's renewed humiliation at *Paris*, and Franz's refusal to join *Erfurt*, had once again raised the prospect of war. Accordingly, (Ph II) kicks off with Flammberg-Beauharnais warning Strahl-Napoleon of impending war, *"Krieg! Ein Aufgebot zu neurer Fehde"* (V.741-2), and of the smoldering German resistance, *"Wenn Ihr den kleinen griechischen Feuerfunken nicht austretet, der diese Kriege veranlaßt, so sollt Ihr noch das ganze Schwabengebirge wider Euch auflodern sehen"* (V.752-5); his reference to the "herald's message" may allude to Stein's intercepted letter, whose content for Napoleon was almost tantamount to a declaration of war.

Among the three German knights united in their pusuit of the imperial bride Kunigunde, Burggrave von Freiburg (whom Strahl hilariously calls *"Afterbräutigam,"* V.1058; literally "anus' groom") could represent Fr. Wilh.'s younger brother Prince Wilh. von

Preußen, Prussia's envoy at *Paris* and *Erfurt*, Rhinegrave von Stein, Austria's Foreign Minister Count Stadion, who tirelessly sought to forge a new Coalition against Napoleon, and Georg von Waldstätten, Aug. Fr. von der Goltz, Prussian plenipotentiary at *Tilsit* and *Erfurt*: (Ph II) depicts Austro-Prussian diplomatic *mélange* in face of Franco-Russian *entente*.

"Köhlerhütte im Gebirg" *(I)*. (Ph II) includes a curious scene (II/5-9) in which Freiburg and Waldstätten kidnapped Kunigunde and hid her in a charcoal burner's hut, where Strahl chances upon them, liberates (or appropriates) her, and whisks her to Wetterstein Castle. Charcoal burner's huts were typical features of German *Mittelgebirge* (several of which Kleist had visited on his journeys), and I offer that this scene comprises Kleist's re-staging of *Erfurt*, which took place at the foot of a *Mittelgebirge*: the Thüringer Wald. The charcoal burner's boy—*"Des Kaisers Hunden... Isaak"* (V.874-5)—, who hands over Kunigunde to Strahl, then represents Tsar Alex. I, who at *Erfurt* offers Katharina to Napoleon:

"*Erfurter Köhlerhütte im Thüringer Wald*": Germany submits to Napoleon's hegemony, while Alex. (far right) has an ace up his sleeve.[469]

Kleist's *satirical* motivation for publishing (Ph II), then, was that the Napoleon's marrying Katharina Pavlovna suddenly seemed imminent; a *Käthchen* fragment in *Ph* was his vehicle of choice for promptly commenting on this development.[470] The transfer, in scene II/5-9, of the imperial bride Kunigunde from Freiburg to Strahl, mediated by Isaak, signifies that no longer a German, but a Russian princess is now the front-runner: inside the charcoal burner's kiln, in an alchemical *Magnum Opus*, the German bride, whom Prince Wilh. had kidnapped in order to prevent Napoleon laying his hands on her, is transmuted into a Russian bride, whom Alex. now presents to Napoleon.[471] Kleist, in this transmutation, does not even have to change Kunigunde's appearance: the coats of arms of the *HRR*, the Austrian, and the Russian Empire all share the double-headed eagle, as well as a mosaic marshalling of their shields.

When Kleist later incorporates passages from (Ph II) into (P), in scene II/9, in line with developments of late 1809 and early 1810, he inserts another transmutation devices, *Brigitte's speech*, to "pass the baton" back to a Habsburg princess (who, thanks to yet another transmutation mechanism, *Käthchen's ordeal by fire*, is henceforth enacted by Käthchen and no longer Kunigunde). Napoleon's zig-zagging quest for a bride *was* confusing, and Kleist, with the help of a few *po(ï)etical* sleights of hand, dexteriously if fantastically handled its tacks and turns, thereby avoiding having to abandon Käthchen altogether.

"FRÄULEIN KUNIGUNDE VON THURNECK (am Putztisch, beschäftigt) *(I)*." (Ph II)'s scene II/10, featuring a less-than-graceful Kunigunde at her vanity table, pokes fun at a Russian princess who, marked as the usurper's bride by an oversized feather in her cap, is about to be sacrificed for an unholy Bonapartean-Romanovan union. In (P) Kleist strikes most of this scene: the Russian princess is no longer in play, and Kunigunde, as we shall see, is assigned a new role, one no longer consistent with the exotic, colourful (and hollow?) bird depicted in (Ph II).

The mother's scepticism regarding the union (II/13) is historical, except that in Kleist's version it is Napoleon's mother who becomes the transaction's stumbling block, wheras in reality it was Alex.'s.[472] Kleist could have added this short scene in the last moment before *Ph* no. 9/10 went to the printers, to ensure that his storyline remained up-to-date; alas, already before the New Year of 1809 it may have become public knowledge that the marriage with Katharina was called off, in which case by the time (Ph II) was distributed to readers in early 1809, Kleist's fragment would already have been obsolete, or was about to become so. In fast moving times, such delays in distribution were antithetical to Kleist's *satirical* project, and they will have put him off the *Ph* project even more thoroughly. The magazine's chief advantage, of hiding and camouflaging his inflammatory, agitatorial texts between harmless ones, was outweighed by the disadvantage of its encompassing too many moving parts (two editors, many contributors, several financiers and distribution partners, etc). Lesson learned: Kleist was going to be adamant to be sole editor of *BA*, retaining full control over content, process and timeline, and to contribute much of its content himself; ditto, I'm certain, with *Germania*, had it taken off.

"Weder auf die Strahlburg, noch ins Kloster!" In III/1, presumably the first scene Kleist produced when picking up the drama again in late 1809, Käthchen-*Borussia* goes into a forest seeking to join a hermitage of Augustines (a Catholic order promoting chastity and obedience); her "going chaste and Catholic" may allude to Prussia's initial promise to join the war on Austria's side. When the Augustine prior, Hatto, offers to instead introduce her into an Ursuline monastery (a community of cloistered nuns, also under the rule of St. Augustine; in *Schroffenstein*, Ursula = Napoleon), she hesitates, before eventually deciding to join neither the Augustines (Austria) nor the Ursulines (Napoleon), reflecting Prussia's decision to stay neutral and on the sidelines during the *War of the Fifth Coalition*.[473] Hatto could embody Napoleon's half-uncle Joseph Cardinal Fesch, then Prince-Archbishop of Regensburg (the "forest hermitage" could be that Bavarian city).[474]

"es ist ein Schweinstall." In III/2, the Rhinegrave (Archduke Karl?) and Herrnstadt (Joh. I Joseph Prince of Liechtenstein?) invade Bavaria, mischievously depicted by Kleist as a—*pigsty*. The swineherd Jakob Pech ("*Pech*" = "bad luck," "pitch") evidently represents King Max. I Joseph; the "sow and its litter" (V.1522), then, his daughter Auguste, Beauharnais' wife, and their offspring. In April 1809, the *Ad'A* in the *Landshut Manoeuvre* the pushed the Austrian army back, allowing Napoleon to quickly move in on Vienna and occupy the

Austrian capital without resistance. By the time the Rhinegrave-Archduke Karl is able to muster his troops on the Danube's left bank across from Vienna (cf. V.1774), Strahl-Napoleon has put up his HQ at Wetterstrahl Castle-Schönbrunn and pulled together his army in Vienna's vicinity. The episode of the mixed-up letters (cf. V.1674-80), in which Käthchen-*Borussia* saves Strahl-*Napoleon* by channelling to him Hatto's intelligence, may again refer to the *Stein Affair*, which contributed to Fr. Wilh.'s decision to abstain from the war, thereby, in Kleist's eyes, "saving" Napoleon.

"Szene: Gegend im Gebirg, mit Wasserfällen und einer Brücke."
IV/1's opening corresponds to the actual situation on the eve of the *Battle of Aspern*: the Austrians having torn down the Tabor bridges, Berthier requisitioned materials—"*Schafft Balken und Bretter her!*" (V.1958)—to build pontoon bridges at Lobau island in preparation of the *Ad'A*'s attack the Austrian positions on the Danube's left bank. In a daring sally, Napoleon then set across these ponton bridges with 70,000 men, confronting Archduke Karl's 90,000 troops at *Aspern*:

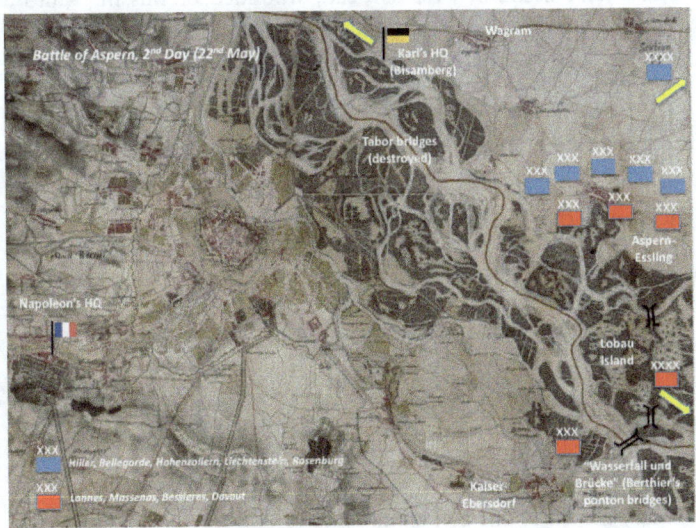

"*mit Wasserfällen und einer Brücke*": the strategic situation on the eve of *Aspern*.

Karl at *Aspern* won a tactical victory, but was unable to expel Napoleon from Vienna and the Danube's right bank, or to prevent his occupying the strategically located Lobau island, which Berthier soon connected to the mainland with firmer bridges, secured with strong batteries, and turned into the bridgehead from which, only a few weeks later, the regrouped *Ad'A* would launched another sally, confronting Karl's army at *Wagram*, 15km north-west of Aspern.

Kleist depicts Napoleon's epic push across the Danube, to confront the Austrians near Wagram, as childs' play, "*Folgt! Folgt! Es ist ein Forellenbach, / weder breit noch tief!*" (V.1961), and his massive pounding of the Austrian army, by now grown to 170,000 men (deriled by Kleist as mere "riff-raff"), as slapstick comedy: "*So recht! So recht! Laßt und das Gesindel / völlig in die Pfanne hauen!*" (V.1962-3). "*Völlig in die Pfanne hauen!*" means "to blow away completely," and *Wagram* indeed saw the intensive deployment of the *Grande batterie* yet, with nearly 900 cannons deployed on the battlefield (compared with 700 at *Eylau*). Kleist telescopes the mayhem of this bloody, and decicive, battle—of 300,000 men involved on both sides, 80,000 were accounted for as dead, wounded or missing—into a single word: "*Getümmel*" (V.1966), "hurly-burly."

"**Es ist der rechte Schlüssel nicht.**" While thus parodying the demise of the grandest of Austrian armies, Kleist crafts an episode that allows him to bring Käthchen, and Strahl's quest for a bride, back into the picture: Käthchen's "ordeal by fire," announced prominently on (P)'s title leaf, in the second part of the drama's title: "*Die Feuerprobe*." The "key" that Strahl-Napoleon seeks to retrieve, with Käthchen's help, from the burning Turneck Castle may refer to the key to the imperial city Vienna, synecdochally, the key to world domination. To lay his hands on this "key," Strahl instrumentalises Käthchen-*Borussia* as his truffle-dog: "*DER GRAF VOM STRAHL* [standing before Käthchen] erblickt die Peitsche. / ...ergrimmt. / Hab ich hier Hunde, die zu schmeißen sind?" (V.1743-4); [to Käthchen] "*Such! / ...Such, sag ich! / ...Ich sage, such!— / Verflucht die hündische Dienstfertigkeit!*" (V.1864-6). Käthchen-*Borussia* dutifully retrieves the key, which she finds suspended above Kunigunde's washstand (the key to world domination, apparently, is a woman's toiletry), and hands it over to him, thereby establishing her "credentials" with him. "*Die Feuerprobe*," then, comprises the "cauldron" in which Käthchen is "forged" into Strahl's "key" to dynastic empire: into an eligible imperial bride.

"**Und der Jupiter ging eben im Osten auf.**" "Jupiter" = Napoleon; if "East" = Germany, this celestial occurrence during *Der Kaiser's* fling with Käthchen's mother Gertrud (cf. V.2410) suggests that their *tête-à-tête*, nearly 16 years ago, already paved the way for Napoleon's triumph over Germany.[475] Counting backwards from early 1810, when the drama's *satirical* plot culminates, Kleist could be alluding to the epic *Battle of Fleurus* of 26th June 1794, in which during Franz II's *Flanders Campaign* the ARF routed the Austrian-led Coalition forces, a defeat that precipitated the loss of the Austrian Netherlands, the end of the Dutch Republic, and the French occupation of the Rhineland.

Jupiter (the reconnaissance balloon *l'Entreprenant*) rises in the East: *Battle of Fleurus*.[476]

The Prussians, including Kleist's Regiment Garde, rather than succour the Austrians, dragged their feet in the inconsequential *Palatine Campaign*, before withdrawing to winter quarters in Eschborn and awaiting Hardenberg's negotiation of *Basel*. The connection Kleist may be pointing to is if Prussia's absence from *Fleurus* marked the beginning of the end of the *HRR*, her absence from *Wagram* sealed the end of Germany as a power.

If *Der Kaiser* = Franz II, and Käthchen's mother = Fr. Wilh. II, then the oh-so-pure Käthchen is the spawn of an ill-fated alliance among rivals, a *"Mißgestalt"* (*Guiskard*) born of the débâcles of *Fleurus* and *Basel* that was bound to destroy Germany. *Der Kaiser*'s ineffable *"Geheimnis"* (V.2431) is that his defeat at *Fleurus*, and the *HRR*'s demise, were precipitated by *Borussia*'s absence, an absence now repeated at *Wagram*, that "The Pure of the Healing Well" embodies precisely the "German disease," and that the impending marriage of a Habsburg princess to Napoleon is but the vanishing point of an inexorable line of flight whose trajectory was determined 16 years earlier, when with the Prussian King's assistance the stars began to align for Napoleon's rise in Germany.[477]

"Freier Platz vor der kaiserlichen Burg." The fifth act covers the negotiation of *Schönbrunn*, involving *Der Kaiser*-Franz and Strahl-Napoleon, followed by the marriage of Strahl-Napoleon and Käthchen-Marie-Louise. Napoleon was recorded as telling the Austrian negotiator, "Your master and I are like two bulls who wish to mate with Germany and Italy," confirming that for him the game was one of territorial and dynastic expansion, primarily at the expense of the Habsburgs.[478] The final scene compounds Napoleon and Marie-Louise's marriage by proxy in Vienna's Augustinerkirche together with their subsequent marriage ceremony at Paris' Louvre. The intervention by Gebhardt ("brave gift"), Erzbischof von Worms, may allude to Pius VII's last-ditch effort to avert the marriage, the challenge by Theobald, to the German nobility's futile rejection of the marriage.[479] Marie-Louise's wedding vow consists in a very Kleistian version of "in good times and bad": *"einem Hunde gleich, durch Feuer und Wasser"* (V.2034). Despite her initial misgivings, Marie-Louise would indeed become Napoleon's loyal wife.

"Käthchen, in einer Verkleidung." During *Käthchen*'s protracted genesis Kleist once again encountered the problem he had faced during *Guiskard*'s and *Krug*'s: history overtook the initial premises upon which he had begun to construct his experiment. In *Guiskard*'s case, Kleist despaired of this challenge; in *Krug*'s, he succeeded in evolving his *satirical* plot and cast in tandem with the changing political context; yet arguably it was *Käthchen*'s case that forced him to pull all registers in this respect. And so he did, resorting to the sleight of hand of chiastically switching Käthchen and Kunigunde's respective roles mid-way through the story, transmuting the former from wholly ineligible into perfectly eligible bride, the latter from chosen bride into toxic nemesis. The "ordeal by fire" marks this swivel's "pivot," buttressed by several carefully choreographed poetic devices: the parallel dreams, *Der Kaiser*'s sudden recollection of his role in Käthchen's conception, the Aulic Council's affirmative verdict, the imperial princess' reddish mark, popping up not on Kunigunde's but on Käthchen's neck.[480] When Käthchen's imperial descent is solemnly declared, her anointment entails a degradation: from the sacred product of a *hieros gamos*, "*als ob der Himmel von Schwaben sie erzeugt*" (V.78) she is reduced to the profane product of a ruler's one night stand. The stage direction highlights that she henceforth appears "*in einer Verkleidung*" (V.2527): the actor enacting Käthchen has changed his mask, from one portraying Luise (or Friederike?) to one depicting Marie-Louise (the switch may be taking place when the cherub touches her head with a palm branch; cf. V.1888).

Kleist reproduces a device he previously deployed in *Marquise* (cf. II:140), of having not one, but two women show up at the ceremony, dressed in wedding gown. The "minimal difference" he introduces, of Käthchen appearing "*im kaiserlichen Brautschmuck,*" Kunigunde merely "*im Brautschmuck,*" is decicive: the former's "imperial wedding gown" may be nothing more than that flimsy "chemise" that on many occasions evidently comprises her sole piece of clothing (cf. V.1222; 2127), whereas the latter's "wedding gown," I offer, consists in *steely armour*: Kunigunde in the final scene comes to embody not a monstrous cyborgan artifice or a soulless insignia of a decayed empire, but a *Valkyrie*, a Germanic Nemesis, a *spirit of resistance*. Did not perhaps Kleist distill a quantum of the recently deceased Luise's spirit into this figure?[481] Kunigunde's veins once again fill with life, her spine straightens, her chest bursts the Swedish corset, her cheeks flush with blood, her dazzling white teeth bare, and her German hair, her French wig cast off, shines golden in the sun:

"Heil dir, o Jungfrau!": The *Valkyrie* Kunigunde-Germania *"im Brautschmuck."*

Count Otto's salute, *"Heil dir, o Jungfrau!,"* hails not Käthchen but Kunigunde: "Hail Kunigunde, *Germania* reborn!" A new *Germania* rises, she *"quillt... wieder unterm Stein hervor"* (*LS*,272) and steps through the *Gewölbe* of the Hofburg's Altes Portal to inaugurate a new era of German resistance. Napoleon's (and the drama's) last ejaculation, *"Giftmischerin!,"* marks not the German drama's *"Ende,"* not even the beginning of its end, but perhaps the end of the beginning of German resistance: *Germania* rise!

And Käthchen? <small>"Sie sinkt; die Gräfin empfängt sie"</small> (V.2679); rather like Toni in *Verlobung*, *"hauchte sie ihre schöne Seele aus"* (II:193): the Marie-Louise whom Napoleon takes with him to Malmaison and Fontainebleau, in Kleist's utopian ending, *no longer has a soul*, and has herself become *"wesenlose[s] Bild."*

"Ein Grosses Historisches Ritterschauspiel." Kleist's second subtitle is now easily explained and located:

"Grosses historisches Ritterschauspiel": "Grand imperial wedding at Vienna and Paris."

When Klaus Müller-Salget insists, *"Auch gibt es keinen Hinweis darauf, dass irgendeine Figur des Stücks einer historischen Person nachgebildet wäre,*" he is certainly wrong: every one of the drama's main characters is likely to be "modelled on a historical person," even if some associations are difficult for us to reconstruct retrospectively. Tentatively, I offer:

Der Kaiser	Franz II / I
Gebhardt, Erzbischof von Worms	Pope Pius VII or Cardinal Fesch
Friedrich Wetter, Graf vom Strahl	Napoleon
Ritter Flammberg, des Grafen Vasall	Eugène de Beauharnais
Gottschalk, sein Knecht	Louis-Alexandre Berthier, Napoleon's chief of staff, or Henri Gatien Bertrand, his aide-de-camp
Kunigunde von Thurneck	Katharina (Ph II); the tattered *HRR*, *Germania* re-born (P)
Theobald Friedeborn, Waffenschmied	Heinr. Fr. Karl Freiherr vom und zum Stein
Käthchen, seine Tochter	Luise (*Borussia*) (Ph I, II); Marie-Louise (*Austria*) (P)
Gottfried Friedeborn, ihr Bräutigam	Fr. Wilh. III
Maximilian, Burggraf von Freiburg	Prince Wilh. von Preußen, Prussian envoy
Georg von Waldstätten, sein Freund	Aug. Fr. Ferd. von der Goltz, Prussian envoy
Rheingraf vom Stein	Joh. Philipp von Stadion, Austrian diplomat / Archduke Karl, Austrian field marshal
Friedrich von Herrnstadt, sein Freund	Karl von Vincent, Austrian envoy / Joh. I Joseph Prince of Liechtenstein, Austrian general
Eginhardt von der Wart	Klemens von Metternich, Austrian foreign minister
Jakob Pech, ein Gastwirt	Max. I Joseph
Ein Köhlerjunge	Alex. I

Käthchen premièred on 17th March 1810, two weeks before Napoleon and Marie-Louise's wedding ceremony in Paris, at the Theater an der Wien, in walking distance of the Augustinerkirche where six days previously the wedding by proxy had taken place. Despite Kleist's and Collin's best efforts, the drama was *staged too late* to prevent Napoleon's completing his quest (if a drama could ever have done so). Still, Kleist could not refrain from advertising, on (P)'s cover, "*Aufgeführt auf dem Theater an der Wien den 17. 18. und 19. März 1810*": his drama had been staged *in the right place*, and *almost in time*.

Genesis revisited. Kleist had learned his lessons from the aborted *Guiskard*, henceforth avoiding committing to scenaric outcomes too soon, and if necessary pausing production to allow history to catch up with him. Still, on two occasions during *Käthchen*'s genesis he may have overshoot, if by the narrowest of margins: in October 1808, with (Ph II), which by the time it was distributed to readers will have been overtaken by events, and his stage adaptation for Collin, which will have suffered the same fate, and in January 1810, with the MS he sent to Cotta for pubication, which by February will similarly have been overtaken by events.

The trigger for *Käthchen*'s initial conception will have been *Tilsit*: in the late summer or early autumn of 1807, while preparing the *Ph* project, Kleist may have commenced the first act of a drama narrating how Luise (*Borussia*) fell under Napoleon's spell, and exploring the question whether a union between them was in the cards, and how it might come about (complementing *Marquise*'s scenario). Rumours in the wake of the death, on 5th May 1807, of Napoleon's designated heir, Joséphine's grandson Napoléon Charles Bonaparte, to the effect that he was exploring alternatives, will have increased in plausibility when Napoleon in the second half of 1807 spent several months by Joséphine's side without her becoming pregnant. Since he considered Austria and Russia his main rivals on the Continent, marrying a Hohenzollern could have been a plausible option. Luise's younger sister Friederike, then unhappily married to Prince Fr. Wilh. zu Solms-Braunfels, could have been under consideration (the prince would indeed later agree to a divorce, and Friederike in 1814 would remarry the Duke of Cumberland, thereby in 1837 becoming Queen of Hannover). Kleist will have been constantly running through a list of plausible candidates (as will Napoleon): when he has the Marquise review all potential *fathers* to her son—*"durchlief… alle Momente des verflossenen Jahres"* (II:120)—Kleist simply ironically inverts Napoleon's doing likewise with potential *mothers* to his heir. Friederike, in 1808 only 30 years of age, but already a "tried and tested" mother of five surviving children, though tainted by scandal (the "lioness," as she was known, was famously coquette and had given birth out of wedlock), may well have been Kleist's model for his *attractive-yet-ineligible* Käthchen:

Käthchen? Friederike von Preußen,
"die schönste Frau, de je mein Auge gesehen" (Gentz).

When prior to publishing (Ph I) Kleist appended scene II/1, having Strahl-Napoleon preclude any candidate withough imperial lineage, he may have reacted to an actual statement by Napoleon or his inner circles.[482]

When at *Erfurt* Napoleon explored with Alex. the possibility of marrying Katharina, Kleist urgently drafted the stage adaption he submitted to Collin on 2nd October 1808 (cf. II:817), uncharacteristically permitting him to edit the draft, which underlines the urgency (cf. II:818; 831).[483] The (Ph I) and (Ph II) fragments' unusual extensive prose monologues suggests that they may have been taken from stage scripts Kleist had not fully developed stylistically (cf. the *Thierrez* sketch, and the suggestion that Kleist initially produced *Schroffenstein* in prose). Kleist may have added scene II/13, in which Strahl's mother intervenes in the eleventh hour, when rumours spread that either the Tsar's mother or *Mme Mère de l'Empereur* (or both) raised objections to the proposed the marriage.

When on 1st January 1809 Kleist urged Collin to prioritise *Hermannsschlach* over *Käthchen*, it must have been clear to him that the marriage had been called off, while France and Austria were rapidly steering into war; when he told Collin that the former drama *"ist um nichts besser, und doch scheint es mir seines Erfolges sichrer zu sein"* (II:819), he meant not popularity with audiences, but impact with political decision makers (a year later Kleist explained to Collin that the events that took place soon after he had sent him the stage adaption had made it impossible to stage *Käthchen*—cf. II:831).

When in May 1809 Napoleon's mistress became pregnant at Schönbrunn, rumours of Napoleon's impending divorce of Joséphine re-ignited, though Kleist appears to have resumed *Käthchen* only when in October 1809 Metternich broached the idea of Napoleon's marriage with Marie-Louise; when on 14th December 1809 the divorce became effective, Kleist was already well advanced with reworking Käthchen; on 12th January 1810 he sent Cotta a MS to be published as pocket book. Following Napoleon's formal confirmation of the marriage on 7th February, Kleist appears to have sent Cotta a revised version of this MS, about whose status he inquired on 4th March (cf. II:832). Possibly the January 1810 MS contained a warning against the marriage, which following Napoleon's announcement Kleist revised into a scenario of its consequences. Kleist made every effort to keep his text "in the middle of time," but he may have "blown" an opportunity to seize a *kairotic* moment when he asked Cotta for up-front payment, which may have been one step too far for Cotta, who evidently did not respond. Given Cotta's reticence, Kleist may then have decided to parallel-process the play's staging, and on 28th January 1810 reconnected with Collin to inquire about the stage adaption he had sent him 15 months earlier. When ten days later Napoleon announced the wedding, Kleist may have pressured Collin to go ahead with the staging, and presumably sent him a revised adaptation (neither a letter in this respect nor a revised stage adaption are extant).

Whereas Collin's staging in March came too late, Reimer's publication in August 1810 once again fell in the middle of time: by adding the last few lines, Kleist with a single masterly stroke turned his now obsolete polemic against Napoleon's wedding to a Habsburg into his obituary to his recently deceased Queen, and into his prophecy of—and call for—*Germania*'s insurrection.

Käthchen, Satyrically

Käthchen, wrote Kleist, "veered towards the romantic" (II:813); the drama's erotic passages are certain as prolific as, if less violent than, *Penthesilea*'s.[484]

"**GRAF OTTO** steht auf." Count Otto, with his erection, kicks off an orgiastic symposium or séance whose participants—Strahl, Käthchen,

Theobald, a dozen or so "judges" or "knights"—are gathered in an underground dungeon, perhaps decorated as a Gothic vault or Romantic cave, the air perhaps heavy with opium. In their role-play, Strahl is introduced as virile erastês: *"mit Schwert und Dolch"* (V.22); *"hervorglühend"* (V.42); *"den Zauberstab in der Hand"* (V.49); *"aus dem Staub"* (V.52); *"mit Hörnern, Schwänzen und Klauen"* (V.54-5); Käthchen, as erômenos and everybody's toy-boy and object of desire: *"ein Kind recht nach der Lust Gottes"* (V.66); *"ein Wesen von zarterer... Art"* (V.69); *"der ganze Markt... wetteiferte, sie zu beschenken"* (V.84-6); *"den Strohhut auf"* (V.74); *"das schwarzsamtene Leibchen, das ihre Brust umschloß, mit feinen Silberkettlein behängt"* (V.75-6); the "judges," as dmōtes: *"ihr irdischen Schergen Gottes"* (V.30); *"Scharen, die... ihre glutroten Spieße schwenken"* (V.32); *"Vermummt von Kopf zu Füßen"* (V.380); and Theobald, *"indeem er sich die Augen trocknet"* (V.137), as prostitute or everybody's plaything.[485]

Käthchen is no more "innocent" than Alkmene or the Marquise: Theobald notes her habit of receiving suitors—in my "director's cut": *"Hat er sie am Brunnen getroffen, wenn sie Wasser schöpfte... den Pfeiler gestellt,... an ihr Fenster geschlichen, und, indem er ihr einen Halsschmuck umgehängt... Nicht mit Augen... hat sie ihn gesehen..., wenn er sie verführt hat"* (V.114-26)—, a habit that may perhaps be termed repetitive-compulsive.[486] An erômenos is always a *Jüngling*, and we can take it at face value, *"daß sie kein Fräulein war"* (V.95-6): her "well" yields "water," her "neck" is wrapped into a "*Halsschmuck*" (bib or condom), her "feature" is "inflaming" (erecting), and we may assume that her "window" that is so attractive for her suitors is her *rear* window (she never gets to see her lovers, always turning her back to them).

"O du———." Strahl's and Theobald's soliloquies before the vehmic court (I/1) echo the *encomiums* delivered at Plato's *Symposion*. Strahl fantasises:

> Alles, was die Wehmut Rührendes hat, will ich aufbieten, Lust und in den Tod gehende Betrübnis sollen sich abwechseln, und meine Stimme, wie einen schönen Tänzer, durch alle Beugungen hindurch führen,

> die die Seele bezaubern; und wenn die Bäume nicht in der Tat bewegt werden, und ihren milden Tau, als ob es geregnet hätte, herabträufeln lassen, so sind sie von Holz, und alles, was uns die Dichter von ihnen sagen, ein bloßes liebliches Märchen. O du———wie nenn ich dich? Käthchen! Warum kann ich dich nicht mein nennen? Käthchen, Mädchen, Käthchen! (V.678-87)

Strahl imagines himself as Pan-like shepherd in a bucolic setting, in which even the horses are transformed into sheep and goats (*satyrical* animals *par excellence*), indulging in a Rousseauist reverie of "*Rührendes*," "*Lust*," and "*bewegt werden*," encountering a "dancer" with a wooden "trunk," and being exposed to "*Bäume [die] in der Tat bewegt werden, und ihren milden Tau, als ob es geregnet hätte, herabträufeln lassen*" (V.682-4), until covered with bloody *cum*: "*ein leichtes weißes linnenes Zeug bedeckte mich, mit roten Bändern*" (V.669-70). *Märchen* is distinct from *Mädchen* by only one consonant, and from *Käthchen* by one diagraph, and Strahl's ultimate "fairy tale," like Kleist's own, is to cohabit with both a youthful lover and a mother to his heir; "O du———[...] Käthchen, Mädchen, Käthchen" may be "translated" as: "O let me '—' you lovely *erômenos*, and here '—' you fertile mother, and once more here '—' you delectable youth!"

Theobald in his soliloquy recounts a *baquet* (cf. V.156-10), featuring a Mesmerian bucket ("silverware": the bucket's highly polished lid), a battery of Kleistian jars ("bottles"), wine ("glasses," "cups") and food ("snacks," "dishes," "cups"), and involving the "armoured" Strahl electro-shocking Käthchen, "*als ob sie ein Blitz nieder geschmettert hätte*," as well as assorted "servants" and "maidens" (cf. V.169-70).[487] Käthchen's "*wie ein Taschenmesser zusammenfallen*" (V.166), before the "chivalrous" Strahl mirrors the Marquise's "*völlig bewußtlos niedersank*" (II:106) before the "angelic" Count, and Alkmene's "*fällt in Amphitryons Arme*" (II:319) before the "divine" Jupiter. Strahl recalls the "twenty days" he spent with Käthchen (cf. the "dash" in Count F's "*Hier—traf er*" encounter with the Marquise and Jupiter's artifully extended "endless night" with Alkmene), before being joined by Theobald in a *ménage à trois* (in my "director's cut):

> Drauf, da [Theobald] am zwanstigsten Tage… bei mir erscheint, und ich ihn in meiner Väter Saal führe: erschau ich mit Befremden, daß er, beim Eintritt in die Tür, die Hand in den Weihkessel steckt, und mich mit dem Wasser… besprengt. Ich… nötige ihn auf einen Stuhl nieder… mit Offenherzigkeit… eröffne ihm… wieder ins Geleis… und führ ihn… in den Stall hinunter, wo sie steht, und mir eine Waffe… säubert. So wie er in die Tür tritt, und die Arme mit tränenvollen Augen öffnet, sie zu empfangen, stürzt mir das Mädchen. Leichenblaß zu Füßen… Gleich einer Salzsäule steht er… das… Antlitz auf mich gerichtet… schmeißt mir den Hut… ins Gesicht… und läuft. (V.301-20)

Strahl lets himself be sodomised by Theobald, "*ich ihn in meiner Väter Saal führe,*" who, "*die Hand in den Weihkessel,*" promptly ejaculates, "*Wasser besprengt*"; Strahl then stimulates Theobald, "*auf einen Stuhl… wieder ins Geleis rücken,*" till he is ready to penetrate him again, "*führ ihn in den Stall,*" while Käthchen concurrently performs fellatio on Strahl, "*mir eine Waffe… säubert*"; Theobald soon *comes* again, "*So wie er in die Tür tritt… mit tränenvollen Augen… Gleich einer Salzsäule steht er,*" and so does Strahl with Käthchen's help, "*stürzt mir… zu Füßen*"; finally Theobald purifies Strahl with *cum* he gathered in his condom: "*den Hut… Gesicht… und läuft.*"

"**Er erhebt sie.**" Following Strahl and Theobald's *encomiums*, the orgy gathers momentum (I/2). In *Käthchen*, Kleist perfects the use of apparently innocuous stage directions for articulating *satyrical* action, quite literally "between the lines."[488] The following extended passage exemplifies this technique:

> Käthchen mit verbundenen Augen, geführt von zwei Häschern.—Die Häscher nehmen ihr das Tuch ab, und gehen wieder fort.—Die Vorigen.
> KÄTHCHEN sieht sich in der Versammlung um, und beugt, da sie den Grafen erblickt, ein Knie vor ihm. […]
> Er erhebt sie. […]
> KÄTHCHEN stellt sich neben den Grafen vom Strahl, und sieht die Ritter an. […]
> KÄTHCHEN für sich. […]
> GRAFF OTTO befremdet. […]
> Sie sehen sich an. […]

KÄTHCHEN für sich. [...]
DER GRAF VOM STRAHL sie aufweckend. [...]
KÄTHCHEN sieht in an und legt ihre Hände auf die Brust. [...]
GRAFF OTTO ungeduldig. [...]
DER GRAF VOM STRAHL mit noch milder Strenge. [...]
KÄTHCHEN zur Schranke tretend. [...]
KÄTHCHEN da sie den Vater erblickt, auf ihn zugehend. [...]
                        Sie will seine Hand ergreifen. [...]
                        Sie ergreift seine Hand und küßt sie. [...]
KÄTHCHEN zu den Richtern, da sich ihr die Häscher nähern. [...]
GRAFF OTTO da sie vor der Schranke steht. [...]
KÄTHCHEN hochrot zum Grafen. [...]
KÄTHCHEN in den Staub niederfallend. [...]
DER GRAF VOM STRAHL zu den Richtern. [...]
GRAFF OTTO ihn forschend ansehend. [...]
DER GRAF VOM STRAHL
    wendet sich zu Käthchen, die noch immer auf den Knieen liegt. [...]
                        Er hält inne. [...]
KÄTHCHEN sieht vor sich nieder. [...]
KÄTHCHEN errötend. [...]
KÄTHCHEN besinnt sich. [...]
DER GRAF VOM STRAHL kalt. [...]
KÄTHCHEN im Affekt. [...]
DER GRAF VOM STRAHL mit dem Schein der Heftigkeit. [...]
                        Käthchen weint.
                        Pause. [...]
THEOBALD nähert sich ihr gerührt. [...]
                        Er will sie an seine Brust heben. [...]
DER GRAF VOM STRAHL sieht sie an. [...]
DER GRAF VOM STRAHL erhebt das Käthchen vom Boden. [...]
                        —Auf den Boden hinzeigend. [...]
WENZEL mit Bedeutung. [...]
DER GRAF VOM STRAHL glutrot, indem er sich an Käthchen wendet. [...]
        Käthchen läßt sich auf Knieen vor ihm nieder.
DER GRAF VOM STRAHL zum Käthchen. [...]
DER GRAF VOM STRAHL ebenso. [...]

DER GRAF VOM STRAHL mit unterdrückter Heftigkeit. [...]
HANS auffahrend. [...]
GRAFF OTTO halblaut. [...]
GRAFF OTTO zu Grafen vom Strahl. [...]
DER GRAF VOM STRAHL zum Käthchen. [...]
DER GRAF VOM STRAHL erhebt das Käthchen. [...]
      Pause. [...]
GRAFF OTTO unwillig. [...]
 Vehmherold sammelt die Kugeln und bringt den Helm, worin sie liegen, dem Grafen.
GRAFF OTTO steht auf. [...]
     Zu den Richtern. [...]
     Die Richter erheben sich. [...]
      Sie fällt in Ohnmacht. [...]
THEOBALD empfängt sie. [...]
DER GRAF VOM STRAHL wendet sich. [...]
    Er verbindet sich die Augen.
GRAFF OTTO vom Richtstuhl herabsteigend. [...]
    Sie betrachten sie.
DER GRAF VOM STRAHL zu den Häschern. [...]
THEOBALD weint. [...]
WENZEL freudig. [...]
    Alle ab. [...] (V.364-659)

Kleist in this passage combines aspects of a BDSM dungeon, a symposium, a Mesmerian *baquet* or Puységurian séance, and a mercury therapy session. The "cloth" the henchmen take off Käthchen apparently refers not to her blindfold but to her "chemise"—in other words, Käthchen is stripped stark naked before the "judges," while remaining blindfolded.[489] The courtroom's "bar" (*"Schranke"*) to which Käthchen steps, like the gable's "bar" (*"Balken"*) onto which Elvire is lowered in *Findling* (cf. II:202), clearly represents an erect penis or phallic device; *"erröten," "glutrot," "gerührt," "mit Affekt," "weinen," "Ohnmacht"* denote arousal, orgasm and ejaculation; *"sich erheben," "stellen," "niederfallen," "innehalten," "heben,"* phallorhythmic action; and *"im Stall besuchen," "aus der Grotte schöpfen,"* "*am Harnsisch wirken*," anal penetration. When they are face-to-face, the participants are offering each other their genitals, when they are not, their rears. They close the session by together ejaculating in an orgasmic rescendo ("*Alle ab*").

The BDSM theme continues at the "charcoal burner's hut": upon their arrival, Strahl and Gottschalk are told that *"drinnen wäre ein geharnischter Mann, / der ein Fräulein bewachte: das läge geknebelt und mit verstopftem / Munde da, wie ein Kalb, das man zur Schlachtbank bringen will"* (V.977-9). In BDSM role-play, strap-on vaginal and butt plugs—separately or in combination—are used to either stimulate or lock up the wearer, and Kleist's redundancy, "*geknebelt und mit verstopftem Munde*" ("gagged and with plugged mouth"), may suggest that a double plug/gag has been applied to Kunigunde (or even a triple: oral gag plus vaginal and butt plugs). Strahl, not amused to find his object of desire held in a rival "dom's" dungeon, in precisely that position of bondage into which he himself had previously vowed to subdue her, makes short shrift of Freiburg and takes possession of his "sub."

"Unter den Holunderstrauch" *(II)*. The elder bush scene (IV/2) comprises not Strahl and Käthchen's *anagnorisis*, but the re-enactment of their previous encounter on New Year's eve, of which their "dreams" are recollections:

> Pause.—Er rasselt mit seiner Rüstung. […]
>
> Er faßt ihre Hand. […]
>
> KÄTHCHEN lächelnd. […]
>
> DER GRAF VOM STRAHL mit einem Seufzer. […]
>
> Pause.
>
> DER GRAF VOM STRAHL gerührt. […]
>
> Pause.—Sie seufzt, betwegt sich, und lispelt etwas.   (V.2071-111)

Reduced to the bare essentials: "*Pause.—Er rasselt mit seiner Rüstung. / Pause.—Sie seufzt*" ("*Rüstung*" = "male equipment").

Two clarifications regarding this much-discussed scene. Firstly, there is no reason to read an attempted rape into it (something of a default reflex in the Kleist reception): Käthchen is evidently conscious and makes no attempt at screaming "*zeter mordio*. Secondly, Strahl is by no means the first lover to embrace her in this *locus amoenus*: Kleist's terms "again" and "always" in the passages, "*Gottschalk... hat mir gesagt, das Käthchen wäre wieder da*" (V.2020-1), and, "*Dreierlei hat er mir gesagt: einmal, daß sie einen Schlaf hat, wie ein Murmeltier, zweitens, daß sie, wie ein Jagdhund, immer träumt, und drittens, daß sie im Schlaf spricht*" (V.2048-53), imply both seriality and intimacy. Before Strahl, Käthchen had already received Gottschalk in her lovenest, and probably many others.

Käthchen, Syphilitically

The drama's main geographic coordinates, Heilbronn and Straßburg, suggest that Kleist is experimenting with Puységurian magnetism, whose technique of artificial somnambulism (today known as hypnotic induction) could be the means by which the *magnétiseur* Strahl "enchants" or "bewitches" Käthchen: Strahl's "magic" plausibly consists in *hypnosis*, establishing him as *magnétiseur*, the maiden as his medium. The curule seat Otto vacates for Strahl may function as the "brothers'" Mesmerian bucket or electrostimulator.

"**gleich einem Molche.**" The scourge of syphilis is introduced in the most hideous terms—"*Frevel... in der Höhle der Brust, gleich einem Molche verkrochen*"—, as well as in familiar "code": "*Stachel*" (V.26); "*Skorpion*" (V.28); "*Basiliskengeist*" (V.649). It was in order to confront this "newt" that the judges convene the vehmic court session, a mercury therapy ritual in which each participant gives up one of their "balls," gathered by a "*herald*" (an avatar of Hermes-Mercury) in a "helmet," from which "balls" is drawn and applied to the diseased.[490]

"Vehmherold sammelt die Kugeln": mercury droplets.

"Graf von der stinkenden Pfütze." When Theobald appears at Strahl's castle to snatch Käthchen from his clutches, his first act is to purify the Count with ejaculate (V.304-5). This may have been superfluous, for Strahl appears as "gleaming cherub," suggesting that he only just undertook a mercury bath or ointment (cf. V.330), perhaps in preparation for Theobald's visit.

When it suits, the "Count of the stinking puddle" wields his disease like a weapon, with which he menaces and curses, e.g., Kunigunde: *"Daß sie die Pocken kriegte! Ich wollte, ich könnte den Nachttau in Eimern auffassen, und über ihren weißen Hals ausgießen!... und so lange ich den Märzschnee nicht vergiften kann, mit welchem sie sich wäscht, hab ich... keine Ruhe"* (V.788-94); *"würd ich ihr einen Possen zu spielen wissen, daß sie es ewig in einer Scheide tragen sollte"* (V.807-8).[491]

"Gesund an Leib und Seele." Theobald emphasises Käthchen's health (cf. V.64) and insists that her body is protected from the the "newt" by a "black velvet bodice" and a "fine silver chain" (V.75-6), yet later admits that her body does have one "blemish," the "mole" on her "neck" that *satirically* marks her as imperial daughter (cf. V.123; 1231; 2137), and that she has been undergoing therapy with the help of Kleistian jars (*"Flaschen"*; V.353), thereby casting doubt on her "purity." Käthchen's "ordeal by fire," as very term hints (Gr. $\pi\tilde{\upsilon}\rho$ = fire), encompasses purification ritual as much as alchemical purgatory. Strahl, whose cross-examination of Käthchen (I/2) reveals that they previously repeatedly had sexual intercourse, also insists, in terms almost identical to Theobald's, on the purity of her body and soul (cf. V.713). Both Strahl and Theobald hold on to the same ideal (or illusion), of the immaculate *erómenos*.

"**sie, vom Aussatz zerfressen.**" Kunigunde is "eroded from leprosy" (V.934), her loose teeth being typical symptoms of syphilis. Like Eve in her bedroom and Alkmene in her palace, Kunigunde keeps a *baquet*-type device in her castle, of which the visiting Strahl and Gottschalk do not hesitate to avail themselves: *"Der Graf vom Strahl sitzt gedankenvoll an einem Tisch, auf welchem zwei Lichter stehen. / Er hält eine Laute in der Hand, und tut einige Griffe darauf. / Im Hintergrunde, bei seinen Kleidern und Waffen beschäftigt, Gottschalk."* The two lights on the table (cf. *Bettelweib*) may serve as phallic props, the lute (an instrument associated with Venus and Amor), as magnetic apparatus to which Strahl's "finger" is stringed, while Gottschalk hangs on to his "back" with his "weapon." The vehmic insignia, whip, and lute add to Kleist's arsenal of *baquet*-strings:

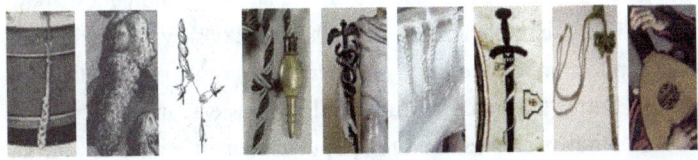

Braided *baquet*-strings (cont'd).

When Käthchen joins their séance, "*Macht auf! Macht auf! Macht auf!*" (V.1626), Strahl and Gottschalk disconnect from the *baquet*, the former erecting, the latter offering his rear, and engage her in a "*FFF*" constellation, with Käthchen as *dmōs*:

> DER GRAF VOM STRAHL legt die Laute weg. [...]
> DER GRAF VOM STRAHL steht auf. [...]
> GOTTSCHALK legt alles aus der Hand. [...]
>   Er öffnet die Tür. [...]
> KÄTHCHEN indem sie eintritt.   (V.1629-36)

"**Kuvert**"/"**Futteral.**" In scene III/6, Käthchen hands Strahl not only a letter but, significantly, also an envelope ("*Kuvert*"; cf. V.1738); and in scene III/15, it is not Strahl's image that Kunigunde wants salvaged from the burning castle, but its cover ("*Futteral*"; cf. V.1911—*satirically*, it contains the property titles to the German lands). "Envelope" and "cover" presumably signify condoms or similar containers in which ejaculate is gathered and kept. Is not the ultimate gesture of selfless, unconditional love among "brothers" the gift of *cum*, the ultimate *pharmakon*? Käthchen acts as *pharmacist* for Strahl-Napoleon: on at least two occasions she delivers *ejaculate* to him (cf. Eve promising to regularly deliver "cured butter" to Ruprecht while on service, and Kleist in April 1809 receiving a delivery of arsenic in in Töplitz from his Dresden pharmacist).

"Unter den Holunderstrauch" (III). In the drama's primordial scene, Strahl lays his hands on Käthchen's body (cf. V.2053), "rattles with his armour" (V.2071), and "grabs her hand": clearly we are witnessing a Mesmerian séance, with Strahl as therapist and Käthchen as patient. The practice of *"Bleigiessen"* ("molybdomancy," divination with molten metal; cf. V.2089-90; 2898) evidently involves the application of mercury ointment, presumably to Käthchen's naked body. In medieval times, Elder flowers and leaves were indeed known as *pharmakons*: popular remedies against various ailments, but poisonous in strong doses and, in the case of black elder, hallucigogenic.[492] Possibly Strahl's and Käthchen's magnetic séance-cum-mercury therapy session also involves a joint "acid trip," which would explain their parallel dreams. "Under the elder bush" is a quintessentially Kleistian *locus amoenus*, its significance *satirical, satyrical, syphilitical* and *po(ï)etical*.

"eine Grotte, im gotischen Stil." Käthchen's encountering the naked Kunigunde in a "grotto" (IV/4-5) enacts their bumping into each other at a health spa or syphilic clinic (cf. Kleist's encountering Brockes at a Rügen spa):

> Ei Käthchen! Bist du schon im Bad gewesen?
> Schaut, wie das Mädchen funkelt, wie es glänzet!
> Dem Schwane gleich, der in die Brust geworfen,
> Aus des Kristallsees blauen Fluten steigt! (V.2209-10)

The shiny mercury solution covering Käthchen's body makes her appear swan-like; the parallels with *Marquise*'s Thinka are obvious, down to the name (Thinka = Katharina = Käthchen); for our expanding *satyrico-syphilitical* "dictionary" we define "swan" as *"maculate* (infected) lover emerging from the purifying bath outwardly *immaculate* (symptom-free). The intertextual juxtaposition of *"Kot"* (*Marquise*) and *"Glanz"* (*Käthchen*) traces the disease's progression from the outbreak of symptoms (*"Kot"*) to their abating in the course of a cycle of treatment (*"Glanz"*). Kleist's famous "*der ganze Schmutz zugleich und Glanz meiner Seele*" (II:797) has a precise physical corollary: the *eternal recurrence* of the disease and of its temporary relief, a rhythm or oscillation that haunted Kleist's entire adult life till his death—a death that entailed, among other things, *escape* from the relentless physical and mental suffering brought about by the disease.

Käthchen (perhaps an early-stage syphiliac whose only visible symptom are chancres on her member—the "mole" on her "neck"), is so shocked by the aspect of the naked Kunigunde (presumably a late-stage syphiliac, whose entire body is *"vom Aussatz zerfressen"*) because *Kunigunde projects Käthchen's own, inescapable, fate*. Kunigunde seeks to compel Käthchen to join her gruesome therapy: the (presumably white) powder in her black box, mixable with wine, water or milk, and sufficient to corrode the entire castle (cf. V.2261-2; 2277), is probably *calomel*. Käthchen is soon afterwards depicted as *"sitzt auf einem Stein"* (V.2527; cf. Guiskard, Penthesilea): she's back in her mercury bath box. Kleist's poem *Der Schrecken im Bade* may be a "spin-off" from, or a model for, this scene: Margarete is the equivalent of Kunigunde, Johanna of Käthchen, and Fritz, of Strahl. Cf. also Marital (*Epigrams*, 4.22): "Cleopatra had sunk herself deep in the glittering waters, hiding from his embraces."

"in die romantische Gattung schlägt." In scene V/12, a tender *tête-à-tête* ensues between *erastês* and *erômenos*:

> Der Graf vom Strahl und das Käthchen.
> DER GRAF VOM STRAHL indem er sie bei der Hand nimmt, und sich setzt. [...]
> KÄTHCHEN schamrot. [...]
>
> Er weint.
>
> KÄTHCHEN ängstlich. [...]
>
> Sie will seine Hand küssen.
> DER GRAF VOM STRAHL zieht sie zurück. [...]
>
> Er küßt ihre Stirn. [...]
> Er wischt sich die Tränen ab. [...]
> KÄTHCHEN kleinlaut. [...]
>
> Pause. [...]
> KÄTHCHEN hält ihre Schürze vor die Augen. [...]
> Er küßt ihr die Tränen aus den Augen. [...]
> Er führt sie ab. (V.2583-644)

This passage is as "romantic" as any in Kleist; and yet, it conveys the heartrending predicament of "Love in the Time of Syphilis" (to paraphrase Gabriel Garcia Márquez): the lovers behave in accordance with a precise code of conduct, corresponding to their disease's progression: the Count (probably a late-stage syphiliac) retracts his member ("*Hand*") when Käthchen (an early-stage syphiliac) seeks to kiss it; she covers herself with a condom ("*Schürze*") when Strahl wants to swallow her cum ("*Tränen*") and kiss her glans ("*Kopf*"), and does not bestow these favours on him in return. As in the case of Agnes and Ottokar, their intercourse involves complex rituals of purification and a strict code of conduct.

Käthchen: Po(i)etically

When noting that *Käthchen* "veered towards the romantic" (II:813), Kleist not only meant, "associated with Medieval chivalry"—as in: "*die Schwärmerei der alten Chevalerie, Traumgestalten*" (II:701)—, but also, "tailored to popular taste": "*nur die Absicht,* [Käthchen] *für die Bühne passend zu machen, hat mich zu Mißgriffen verführt, die ich jetzt beweinen mögte*" (II:874).[493] Blamberger's contention (*Kleist*, 184), à propos of *Schroffenstein*, that "*Kleist codiert das Stück sozusagen doppelt, als ernsthafte Literatur und als Unterhaltungsliteratur,*" is true à propos of all of Kleist's works, and *Käthchen* first of all.

"zu Mißgriffen verführt." The one concrete information available to us regarding a change Kleist made to the text stems from Tieck, who told Bülow that when he and Kleist debated a scene, and he opined that it was unduly veering towards the "fantasy-esque," Kleist promptly struck it (to Tieck's regret):

> Dieser Szene gemäß wandelte Käthchen im vierten Akt auf dem Felsen und erschien ihr untern im Wasser eine Nixe, die sie mit Gesang und Rede lockte. Käthchen wollte sich herabstürzen, und wurde nur durch eine Begleiterin gerettet. Vorher belauschte sie Kunigundens badende Häßlichkeit und war außer sich vor Angst, wie sie den Ritter vor dem Ungeheuer errette. Und dieser Schilderung des Bildes erinnerte sich Tieck noch des schönen Verses: "Da quillt es wieder unterm Stein hervor." (LS,272)[494]

Though he jettisoned this passage, Kleist with the grotto scene kept the topos of Käthchen observing Kunigunde's "ugliness," so that perhaps little of the text's *syphilitical* substance was lost. Yet the "monster" that eerily "wells out" from "beneath the rock," and from which Käthchen seeks to "rescue" Strahl-Napoleon, could *satirically* refer to the seething German resistance, so that this passage contained a veiled accusation against either Luise or Marie-Louise: *treason*.

"eine mosaische Arbeit." Wilh. Grimm considered *Käthchen* "entirely of one piece" (LS,369), but we are compelled to qualify that it *is* and it *is not*. The drama is testament to Kleist's ingenuity and resourcefulness in stitching together and evolving a storyline whose underlying topos—Napoleon's quest for a bride—remained intact, but whose option space kept shape-shifting in the course of its genesis. Some of Kleist's sleights of hand—*der Kaiser's* fling with Käthchen's mother and his 15-year long amnesia thereof, Käthchen and Strahl's improbable parallel dreams—have given rise to criticism; yet, as we saw, they became necessary lest Kleist was to abandon the work altogether.[495] In Kleist's *chronique d'un marriage annoncé*, the front-runners—a Protestant Hohenzollern, an Orthodox Romanova, a Catholic Habsburg—remained caught up in a prolonged game of musical chairs, whose outcome remained unpredictable for some time.

"**daß er sie trennt.**" In the autumn of 1807 Kleist repeatedly linked Käthchen to Penthesilea: "*das [Käthchen] ist die Kehrseite der Penthesilea, ihr andrer Pol, ein Wesen, das ebenso mächtig ist durch gänzliche Hingebung, als jene durch Handeln*" (to Marie; II:797); "*Zweierlei ist das Geschlecht der Fraun; vielfältig ersprießlich / Jedem, daß er sie trennt: Dichtern vor allen. Merkt auf!*" (epigram no. 23; I:22); "*sie gehören ja wie das + und − der Algebra zusammen, und sind ein und dasselbe Wesen, nur unter entgegengesetzten Beziehungen gedacht*" (to Collin; II:818).[496] Given the "law" he established, in *Über die allmähliche Verfertigung...*, according to which "*in einem Körper, der von dem elektrischen Zustand Null ist, wenn er in eines elektrisierten Körpers Atmosphäre kommt, plötzlich die entgegengesetzte Elektrizität erweckt wird*" (II:321), Penthesilea and Käthchen—initially devoid of charge, i.e., persisting in the "0" (neutral) state—become charged in the presence of an electrified body, say, Achilles' or Strahl's: let Achilles be charged "+" (say, effeminate), then Penthesilea upon entering his "atmosphere" assumes the "-"(say, masculine) charge; let Strahl be charged "-" (say, ithyphallic), then Käthchen upon entering his "orbit" assumes the "+" (say, submissive) state.[497] Penthesilea and Käthchen are equivalent in so far as, firstly, for both of them the default state is "0"; secondly, they both become charged upon entering the orbit of an erotically or agonistically charged body; thirdly, for both of them the intensity ("*mächtig*") of their "+" charge ("*Hingebung*") is inversely proportional to that of their "-" charge ("*Handeln*").

We can take these characteristics and patterns to be archetypical for Kleistian characters, permitting for some variation. Instead of the transistor's two (0,1) states, Kleist's electro-magnetic code has three (n,+,-) states, of which two (+,-) are dynamically determined by the influence of third bodies; and whereas a transistor exists only in an *actualised* state (i.e., in either the $0 = off$ or the $1 = on$ state), a Kleistian character can persist as a *virtuality* (i.e., in neutral state), actualised either in the presence of a third body, or sometimes spontaneously.[498]

"er scheide gern." The drama contains an explicit depiction of Kleist's process of *"Scheidung,"* whereby a homosexual lover temporarily becomes a heterosexual procreator in order to produce an heir. In a no doubt autobiographical passage Strahl (i.e., Kleist) describes this process: first, he puts himself into a "strange melancholy" (V.1154), in which he conceives of the separation of his twin desires—*boys* and *sons*—, and mentally prepares himself for vaginal penetration—*"er scheide gerne"* (*Scheide* = vagina; *scheiden* = to separate, to die)—, before in "three subsequent nights" being initiated by a "mother" (plausibly an experienced female prostitute) into the mysteries of heterosexual love (cf. V.1163-75), which he subsequently rehearses—*"streckt alle Glieder von sich"*; *"So! So! So!"*—until the sight of *phalloi* ("lights") no longer excites him (cf. V.1178-99); in the end, he becomes once again "healthy as before" (V.1216), i.e., properly homosexual, having completed his heterosexual apprenticeship. The trick in executing this necessary, if (for him) repulsive, operation, Strahl-Kleist imparts, is, firstly, to imagine the bride as *erômenos*, and her vagina ("chamber") as anus (cf. V.1228; 1231); secondly, to have a *dmōs* enter one's rear immediately upon completing the reproductive act (*"Eintritt"*; V.1233-5), so as to swiftly be brought back into the "brotherhood" mode.[499]

"FRÄULEIN KUNIGUNDE VON THURNECK (am Putztisch, beschäftigt) *(II)."* Did Kleist in (Ph II) include the hilarious but tangential scene II/10, depicting Kunigunde before her vanity table, to take a swipe at Goethe, whom Napoleon at Erfurt received with the words: *"Voilà un homme!"*? Does Kunigunde's (Goethe's?) lecture to Rosalie (Schiller?), concerning the art of vanity ironise Goethe's *"Farbenpsychologie"* theory? *"Die Kunst, die du an meinem Putztisch übst, /Ist mehr, als blos ein sinnereizendes / Verbinden von Gestalten und von Farben. / Das unsichtbare Ding, das Seele heißt, / Mögt' ich an Allem gern erscheinen machen, / Dem Todten selbst, das mir verbunden ist"* (I:901): Goethe, Kleist may be joking, would even attempt to raise the dead with the help of his colour-psychology; yet it is his own psychedelic magnetism that makes puppets "dance." As said, Kleist struck most of this scene in (P): not only the Russian princess, also Goethe was no longer a prime target.

2.7 *Die Hermannsschlacht*: World of Warfare version.09
(A MMORPG Wargame)

Genesis and Context. Kleist reiterated repeatedly that he wrote *Hermannsschlacht* "for the moment" (cf. II:820; 821; 824), and the drama indeed had a particularly laser-sharp focus on a precise situation: *Hermannsschlacht* comprises Kleist's detailed recommendations to his King as to *what* to do in the context of late 1808 and early 1809, and *how* to do it. Kleist probably wrote *Hermannsschlacht* in one creative burst in the autumn of 1808 (cf. *KH*,76), effectively as a sequel to *Ph*'s *Kohlhaas* fragment, to which it is thematically connected, and in response to the *Stein affair, Paris* and *Erfurt*, in whose wake war appeared to be imminent and Fr. Wilh. once again faced a critical decision, a *kairotic* moment or *krisis*. Kleist executed this drama with unembellished simplicity, without the extensive camouflage that had warped, say, the *Krug* MS's twelfth scene, and no doubt with great speed and urgency.

Regarding the *what*, Kleist advises Fr. Wilh. to unleash an "unfettered war" on the *Ad'A* (cf. V.1484); concerning the *how*, he advises him to gain Franz's trust by putting his own children's lives at his disposal and openly renounce any claim to the imperial dignity, to attack the *Ad'A* without delay, while Napoleon remains tied up in Spain, to unite the German princes, including those allied with Napoleon, and to unleash a people's insurrection.[500] Blamberger (*Kleist*, 370), appositely, terms the drama a "manual for the Prussian *guerrillero*" and an adaptation of Machiavelli's *Il principe*, but it is important to highlight that for Kleist, the chief Prussian *guerrillero* was to be none other than Fr. Wilh. himself. Rather than a mere manual or manifesto *Krug*, *Hermannsschlacht* comprises a veritable *strategic wargame*, a war simulation tool Kleist puts at his King's disposal, with which he may "play out" the winning strategy for Prussia. Nowhere in his œuvre is Kleist more authentically a scion of the Kleist family as here: shoulder-to-shoulder, he stands by his monarch in his poetical equivalent of a "war room":

"War rooms" (FLTR): Fr. Wilh. IV and Bismarck (1848); Wilh. II and Hindenburg (c.1914); Hitler and Goebbels (1934).

From a letter by Chr. G. Körner of 19th December 1808 (cf. *LS*,304a), we glean that, while Kleist did not deem *Hermannsschlacht*'s highly classified content *publishable*, he did consider it *stageable*. On 1st January 1809 he sent Collin the MS, and subsequently repeatedly urged him to stage it (cf. II:819-21; 824), even offering to waive his author's fees. For reasons unknown, Collin failed to bring the drama to the stage (it was published in full only in 1821, by Tieck, presumably based of the MS Kleist had sent to Collin). Once Fr. Wilh., by April 1809, reneged on his promise to join the war, *Hermannsschlacht*'s thinly veiled *satirical* message became a potential embarrassment for the King, and a liability for Kleist, which explains why Kleist insisted so stubbornly that he wrote the drama for a precise moment only, and did everything in his power to prevent its publication, probably destroying any remaining MSS in his possession, while seeking to recoup those he had circulated (thankfully, he did not fully succeed in his self-censoring *auto-da-fé*). Already in his letter to Collin of 22nd February, Kleist acknowledged, if obliquely, the possibility of Fr. Wilh. reneging on his promise to join the war; by the time of his letter to Ulrike of 8th April, in which he informed her of his plan to travel to Vienna, Kleist has already shifted his focus towards Franz and Archduke Karl, and on 29th April left Dresden, with Dahlmann, for Prague and Vienna.[501]

"Ausrutscher." To this day, *Hermannsschlacht* is occasionally held in the Kleist reception to be an outlier in Kleist's dramatic œuvre, a nationalistic, militaristic diatribe, whose *"fesselloser Krieg"* uncomfortably closely resembles the *"totaler Krieg"* the Nazis unleashed in WWII, and which therefore ought to be attributed a *"Sonderstellung"* (Klaus Müller-Salget), and to be considered an *"Ausrutscher"* (Walter Müller-Seidel).[502] That *Hermannsschlacht* contains gruesome violence is not in question—but no more so than, say, *Penthesilea*: the tearing apart of the helpless Ventidius by Hermann's she-bear is no more gruesome than that of the disarmed Achilles by Penthesilea and her dogs, and the dismemberment of Hally's corpse is no more horrific than the rending of Achilles'. That its being based on Germanic history (or folklore) made *Hermannsschlacht* particularly susceptible to misappropriation by German nationalists and Nazi propagandists, and that its *pescheräism* invited abuse even more readily than did Nietzsche's *perspectivism*, should not be held against Kleist.[503]

Hermannsschlacht's patriotism is not an *end*, but a *means* to an end—the end of rallying the Germans to unite and liberate Europe, and the only thing that does set it apart from the other dramas, is that Kleist applied a much thinner veneer of camouflage to its *satirical* messages, a choice *necessitated* by the urgency of the situation and by his experience that his previous, heavily encrypted, attempts had been ineffective, and *made possible* by a general relaxation of censorship following the French withdrawal (had the French not evacuated Prussia in early December 1808, *Hermannsschlacht* as we know it would not have come into existence). Kleist dropped his usual guard, and let his trousers down, to address his core audience— the Prussian King, the Austrian Emperor, their courtiers and ministers, the leaders of the German resistance—as unequivocally and forcefully as possible, disguising the real personages represented by his characters so thinly that his audiences could scarcely fail to identify them. *Hermannsschlacht* is the product of poetic license taken in the face of political expedience; as such, it is no more or less "Kleistian" than any other of the bard's works, and no more or less purposeful, authentic, succinct or forceful; it is merely, together with a few other so-called "political works" of 1809, *less camouflaged*.[504]

"**Und alle Greul des fessellosen Krieges!**" Napoleon's hegemony, for Kleist, constituted a "state of exception" that called for exceptional measures—measures legitimised by this "state of exception" alone.[505] Kleist in this, as in other "political works" of this period, pursues a political logic and ethic that would be theorised succinctly only in the 20th century, by Carl Schmitt (who coined the term "*Ausnahmezustand*," "state of exception") and Giorgio Agamben. Simply put, once a state of liberty and justice is established, all political acts must be lawful and sanctioned by the state's axioms; but in a situation in which liberty and justice are not yet established, or have been undermined or suspended, unlawful acts may be legitimate if—and only if—they serve to re-establish that very state of liberty and justice. Hermann understands this logic: his ruthlessness and sheer "will to power" transgress all normal limits, because only on the far side of any limits can a Law re-establish itself that delimits and contains this ruthlessness.[506] He instigates his "unfettered war" because in a situation in which Napoleon's armies control most of the Continent, "total war" is the only feasible means of achieving "total peace."

Hermann transgresses the Romans' deceptions by unleashing an avalanche of deceptions that "out-deceive" them: "*So kann man blondes Haar und blaue Augen haben, / Und doch so falsch sein als ein Punier?*" (V.2097-8); he transgresses his wife's transgressive infatuation with the Roman general by orchestrating an injury that in the decicive moment turns her burning love into blazing hate, the caring mother into a bestial she-bear; he neutralises the German princes' treason not by counter-treason but by disregard, rendering them so utterly irrelevant that their treason simply fizzles out; he overpowers the enemy's *extensive* propaganda by unleashing a new kind of *intensive* propaganda: there could have been no more effective call for unity than distributing to the fifteen German tribes the dismembered body parts of a German maiden purportedly violated by Roman aggressors (It is immaterial for the efficacy of Hermann's propaganda whether Hally was indeed violated, and by whom, for his claim is credible by virtue of its echoing what everybody already believes).

Hermann masters the art of *leading by example*: he is prepared to give up everything that is most precious to him—wife, children, home, community, friends, fellow warriors, even the Teutoburg itself—, because only by doing so can he demand the same level of commitment from others; if he is ruthless and relentless, he is so first of all against himself. He also understands Occam's "law of parsimony": he sets precisely *one* example—no less, but also no more—for every important point he needs to convey, in each case picking the most prominent and compelling case possible: in order to eradicate any lingering pro-enemy feelings among the Germans, he picks on his own wife's errant feelings; in order to eradicate the idea that individual tribes may pursue their own independent agendas, he picks on the one chief, Aristan, who is the most prominent proponent of this view. Hermann does not kill blindly: equipped with Occam's razor, he conducts precision surgery, and applying Ann Radcliffe's *theory of the gothic*, he sows *terror* in his people's minds, and *horror* in his enemies'.

Kleist, in repeatedly emphasising that he produced this drama for a specific context only, sought to pre-empt any notion that his prescriptions were generalisable, that the exceptional means Hermann deploys—(total) war, insurrection, deception, murder, etc.—could become the norm, or that any end other then that of re-installing the norm (i.e., peace, liberty, egality and fraternity) could sanctify such means. He insists that a "state of exception" is precisely *that,* and that it is expedient to end it with as much speed and determination as possible, and as much ruthlessness as necessary.[507]

"ins Gleichgewicht gestellt." Hermann's endgame is not "total war," but "total peace": a new "equilibrium" (*"Gleichgewicht"*) in which "all mankind unites":

> Wenn sich der Barden Lied erfüllt,
> Und unter *einem* Königszepter,
> Jemals die ganze Menschheit sich vereint,
> So läßt, daß es ein Deutscher führt, sich denken,
> Ein Britt', ein Gallier, oder wer ihr wollt;

Doch nimmer jener Latier, beim Himmel!
Der keine andre Volksnatur
Verstehen kann und ehren, als nur seine.
Dazu am Schluß der Ding auch kommt es noch;
Doch bis die Völker sich, die diese Erd umwogen,
Noch jetzt vom Sturm der Zeit gepeitscht,
Gleich einer See, ins Gleichgewicht gestellt,
Kann es leicht sein, der Habicht rupft
Die Brut des Aars, die, noch nicht flügg,
Im stillen Wipfel einer Eiche ruht.   (V.307-21)

Kleist's endgame entails a pan-national confederation, perhaps modelled on the *HRR*—a sort of proto-European Union (whose motto, *in varietate concordia*, could well have been Kleist's). His vision was cosmopolitan, rather than nationalistic: the envisioned super-state would be chaired by a monarch, probably elected (cf. V.2595), who could hail from any of the leading (European) nations, including the French—*"ein Gallier"*—, a feature many Kleist scholars have found convenient to overlook, because it does not correspond to their conviction that Kleist's stance was irredeemably *anti-French*—which it was patently not: rather, it was *anti-Bonapartean* (nor was it decidedly *pro-German*: it was *cosmopolitan*). Only the "falcon" Napoleon—*"jener Latier"*—had to be excluded from the conferation's leadership, for he would always put the interests of his family or clan before that of the citizens, or of other clans or nations. Kleist's distinction between *"Gallier"* and *"Latier"* is precise: *Gallier* = the French in general; *Latier* = a particular Corsican, i.e., Napoleon. Kleist was deliberate and consistent in referring to Napoleon *as Roman, Latin* (hailing from Latium) or *Corsican* (cf. his *Katechismus*), but never as *French*, precisely because he did not consider him representative of the French people, or state.[508]

Even the thoughtful and circumspect Dirk Grathoff quotes Kleist (*Kleist und Napoleon*, 31) without properly *reading* him: *"Eine antifranzösische [Einstellung] kann... wohl nur mit Einschränkungen unterstellt werden. Freilich hat [Kleist] blutrünstige Befreiungskriegslieder gegen "diese Franken" geschrieben (so:*

I:26)." The "*Franks,*" patently not the same people as the "*French,*" were a collection of Germanic peoples that in the course of their migrations in late antiquity came to settle in lands that straddled what only in medieval times became known as, respectively, France and Germany; in 800 their leader Charlemagne founded a western European empire, in which the Franks formed an aristocratic upper class ruling numerous peoples, into which they gradually became absorbed.[509] When thundering against "*those* Franks" (my italics), Kleist is evidently referring not to the Frankish *nation,* but to their *mode of governance:* "clannish," and detached from the people. "*Those* Franks," then, include not only the Bonapartes in France, but also, say, the Wittelsbachs in Bavaria, and the Wettins in Saxony—even the Habsburgs and Hohenzollerns, if they put their own dynastic interests before those of the people and nations they governed.[510] In this view, when in 1807 Luise makes her "*Kniefall*" before Napoleon, she is at risk of "going Frankish," and when in 1810 Franz marries his daughter to Napoleon, he has "gone Frankish" *tout court.*

Kleist hated not any nation; he hated individuals who, irrespective of their nationality, committed what he considered treason against their own people. As long as we keep in mind Kleist's subtle but vital differentiations— "*Gallier*" ≠ "*Latier*"; "*Franke*" ≠ "*Franzose*"; "Napoleon" or "the Bonapartes" ≠ "the *RF*" or "the French people"—, we remain on safe grounds in evaluating the drama's martial language, including Hermann's notorious rants: "*Rom, / Das Drachennest, vom Erdenrund vertilgen*" (V.1601-2); "*Die ganze Brut, die in den Leib Germaniens / Sich eingefilzt, wie ein Insektenschwarm*" (V.1681-2); "*die höhnische Dämonenbrut*" (V.1732); "*Vor dieser Mordbrut keine Ruhe, / Als bis das Raubnest ganz zerstört*" (V.2633-4). Whatever misgivings one may have regarding Kleist's choice of words, one must not ignore the fact that these statements refer to Napoleon and the Bonaparte clan, not to France and the French people.

Kleist clearly understood the *complication* that stood between the world as it was and as he envisioned it: the "falcon" Napoleon, whose hegemony stymied the emergence of an "eagle" who would unify the Germans. Kleist was "nationalist" in so far that, in his view, the nation fated to overcome the hegemon war Germany: Britain ruled the sea, but had limited scope on the Continent; Ruissia was large, but remained quasi-feudal and underdeveloped. Yet the Germans could only succeed if they united under a single leader—most plausibly, in Kleist's opinion (and in this he was not a German, or Prussian, nationalist but simply a scion of the Kleist family), a *Hohenzollern ruler*. If Kleist's propaganda showed a patriotic bend, this was so because he was seeking to rally a German resistance, addressing a German audience, in German, using conventional German symbols (eagle, oak, etc.). Had the political situation been the reverse—a German tyrant hegemonising a divided French people—, the cosmopolitan Kleist might just as well have written propaganda in support of a legitimate French monarch, addressing a French audience, in French, using French symbols.

Hermannsschlacht, Satirically

Hermannsschlacht's political agenda, unlike that of other works, has been widely recognised and requires no further demonstration—I refer the reader to Jochen Schmidt's coverage of this drama, to Peter Michalzik's account of Kleist's biographical circumstances, and to Jeffrey Sammons' summary of Kleist's agenda: "Hermann *symbolises* what the play attempts to do, namely to articulate the claim of the *Dichter* in his representative capacity to function as the king's advisor and partner."[511] As in *Krug*, Kleist advocates the use of deception, namely entering a *"Scheinbündnis"* with France (Rome), under cover of which Prussia (Cheruska) and the other northern German principalities (Germanic tribes) shall ally themselves with the most powerful southern German state, Austria (Suevia), confront the Ad'A (Roman legions) and instigate a guerrilla insurrection across northern Germany.[512]

"…und der Freiherr vom Stein." Richard Samuel's seminal work on the *political* Kleist to this day stands within the *Kleist-Forschung* as a monument to insightful (con)textual analysis, and his 1961 essay *Kleists "Hermannsschlacht" und der Freiherr vom Stein* remains one of the more authoritative explorations of the drama's political context.[513] Yet my *satirical* evaluation differs from Samuel's in three important respects: firstly, it suggests that the key themes Kleist espoused in this drama are already discernible in earlier works, and are therefore not, or not substantially or primarily, based on Stein's intercepted letter of 15 August 1808, as Samuel argues:[514]

> Kleist fand in dem Brief die folgenden Einzelheiten, die er in sein Drama verweben konnte:
> 1. Den Gedanken der Insurrektion und der Aufreizung der Bevölkerung durch heimlich zu verbreitende Propaganda.
> 2. Den Gedanken eines Bündnisses mit Österreich in einem Krieg gegen Frankreich und der Verbindung desselben mit der Insurrektion.
> 3. Den Einfluß des spanischen Aufstands.
> 4. Die diplomatische Doppelzüngigkeit, die in dem Kommentar [by the French publishers of Stein's letter] geschickt erhellt worden war.
> 5. Die Unschlüssigkeit am Königsberger Hofe.
> 6. Die Drohung der Enteignung des Briefschreibers.   (*Stein*, 445-6)

Kleist and Stein (and other reformers) worked in the same context, drew on similar information, and often (but not always) arrived at similar conclusions, and Kleist will have considered the *Stein affair* important in that it helped shape the onerous provisions of *Paris* and fuel Fr. Wilh.'s reluctance to openly confront Napoleon, but the issues Samuel enumerates, apart from the last one, which relates directly to the *Stein affair*, Kleist had been working on long before the affair. Samuel is correct in arguing that letters play an important role in the drama (cf. *ibid*, 427), yet Kleist will have been intrigued not only by the *Stein affair*, but more generally by the proliferation of letters and memoranda then taking place across a veritable "axis of resistance," or *"Kette der Intriganten,"* in which Kleist himself partook, not least as courier.[515]

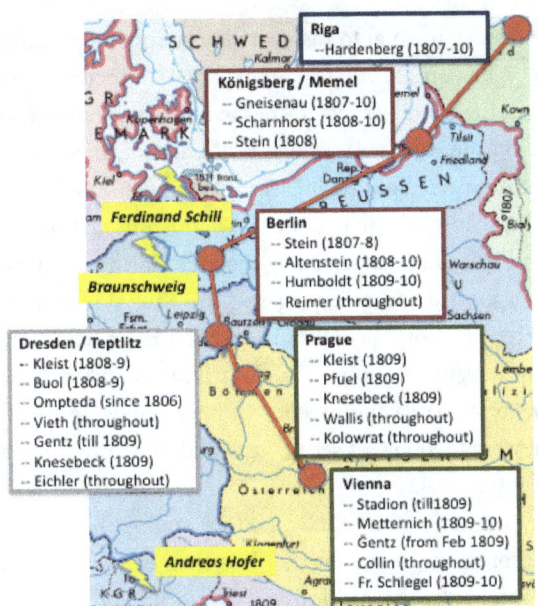

"Kette der Intriganten" (1808-10); sample political actors, local rebellions and *Freikorps* operations (1809).

Kleist could not have learned much he did not already know from Stein's letter, or from the memoranda the members of the "Triumvirate"— Stein, Gneisenau, Scharnhorst—submitted to the King in the course of the summer and autumn of 1808, except that Prussian *politics* was (finally) catching up with his *poetics*, and that his *satirical* vision was shared and articulated by people with political influence, who could potentially nudge the King in the direction Kleist hoped for. Although Samuel's assumption that Kleist took his political ideas from Stein is probably misguided, Stein's letter, in conjunction with the various memoranda, will nevertheless have influenced *Hermannsschlacht*'s production: not by shaping Kleist's political views, which preceded these events, but by alerting him that the *kairotic* moment had come to push his agenda: his drama "fell into the times" because "the times" had caught up with his vision, and might even overtake it.

Secondly, my reading suggests that Kleist, although he concurred with many of the reformers' ideas, came to consider their activities as detrimental to his own plans in one important respect: when Fr. Wilh., on 23rd August, in the Royal Council openly rejected their plans, the triumvirs secretly began preparing a *coup d'état* aimed at replacing the King with Prince Wilh., whom they deemed to be more enthusiastic about their ideas (cf. Samuel, *Stein*, 443, n.53). I believe that Kleist, who in later works would himself devise scenarios in which Fr. Wilh. is sidelined or replaced, in the autumn of 1808 did not support a conspiracy against the King, for it contradicted his *doctrine* that, for a people's insurrection to be palatable, it must be led by a *legitimate monarch*; the triumvirs' subversive agenda, however, exacerbated the urgency of his completing his drama: if Fr. Wilh. were to follow its script, he would pre-empt the conspiracy *and* defeat the *Ad'A*.[516]

For the monarchist Kleist, politics and warfare remained, as it were, more akin to a game of *Chess* than of *Go*: the "figures" in play are inherently hierarchical and *a priori* differentiated by their (absolute) capabilities, and not inherently uniform and only *a posteriori* differentiated by their (relative) position on the board: as in a game of Chess, in Kleist's wargame it is above all the figures of "King" and "Queen" that determine the outcome:

Stratified (*Chess*: state, aristocratic) and
smooth (*Go*: nomadic, insurrectional) spaces of war.

Although innovatinos such as *levée en masse* and guerrilla warfare modulate and complement the *stratified space* of conventional aristocratic warfare, they do not, in Kleist's view, replace it outright: they re-architect the "Chess board" of modern warfare, so that it accommodates a greater number and variety of "pawns" (people's armies, *Landwehren, tirailleurs,* guerrilla fighters) and supports novel multi-player configurations or alliances, but do not turn it into a "Go board":

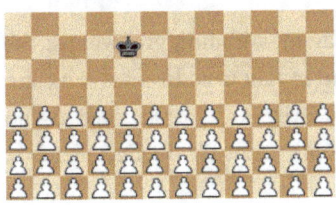

Napoleon facing a German insurrection;
Prusso-Austrian pincer movement against the *Ad'A*.

I concur with Samuel that a specific event in the late summer of 1808 may have triggered Kleist's production of *Hermannsschlacht*, but this event would have been not the publication of Stein's intercepted letter, but rumours concerning the impending *coup d'état*; and although these two events may have taken place within a few week of each other, this differentiation is important, for it highlights that Kleist, far from being a mere follower of the reformists' policies, as Samuel believes, pursued his own agenda, which in part corresponded to the reformers' (e.g., with respect to their enthusiasm for people's insurrection), and in part contradicted it (e.g., regarding the King's role). Samuel's relegating the *coup d'état* to a footnote, presumably because it did not take place (and thus, for him, literally remained a mere footnote of history), suggests that he did not fully appreciate Kleist's method: since he aimed to *shape* events, Kleist did not simply respond to actual events as they occurred, but sought to *anticipate* them, on the basis of conjectures or rumours, which, if he deemed them credible, could trigger his work. "*Credo tibi, uerum dicere, Fama, soles*" (Martial, *Epigrams*, 7.6).

Thirdly, my evaluation suggests that Kleist's Hermann represents not Stein, as Samuel believes, but Fr. Wilh., as most Kleist scholars nowadays suspect. Samuel's unnecessary leap of faith, "*dann kann Hermann nur ein Porträt des Freiherrn vom Stein darstellen*" (p. 449), is surprising, given his otherwise circumspect approach, though it may be explained by his perhaps never having completed a comprehensive evaluation of Kleist's works, and thus having been unable to appreciate its *patterns*, including Kleist's consistency in casting Fr. Wilh., Franz and Napoleon as his leading male protagonists. Kleist would never have cast a mere technocrat, no matter how prominent, as his drama's leading protagonist: the self-appointed German national bard sought to address his King and his Emperor, and a few others secondarily. Any correlation between his Hermann and Stein is spurious: Hermann's ideas reflect Stein's in so far as Stein's mirror Kleist's.

"der gegenwärtige Zeitpunkt." Fr. Gentz's reflections in an essay of the summer of 1808, "*Gedanken über die Frage: Was würde das Haus Österreich unter den jetzigen Umständen zu beschließen haben, um Deutschland auf dauerhafte Weise von fremder Gewalt zu befreien,*" may closely parallel Kleist's own political thought at that time (replace "Austria" with "Prussia"). Notes Michalzik:

> Gentz stellte fest, dass "eine unbestimmte Fortdauer des jetzigen Zustandes von Deutschland—mit dem unmittelbaren Lebensinteresse der deutschen Nation—mit der Erhaltung und Sicherheit der österreichischen Monarchie—mit der Wohlfahrt, der Freiheit und den Wünschen der gesamten europäischen Völker-Masse—unter keiner Bedingung verträglich sei." Daraus entwickelte er die Vorstellung eines neuen deutschen Bundes unter Führung Österreichs und die Möglichkeiten und Aussichten eines Aufstandes gegen Frankreich. Der Moment sei günstig wie nie: "der gegenwärtige Zeitpunkt, wo der größte Teil des deutschen Gebietes von den französischen Truppen geräumt werden mußte, und diese auf einem weit entfernten Schauplatz, und allem Vermuten nach langwierigen Krieg verwickelt sind, mehr als irgendein vorhergehender, und…mehr als irgendein später zu erwartender, für ein solches Unternehmen geeignet sein würde." Die Rivalität und das Misstrauen zwischen Deutschland und Österreich, "der alte verdächtige Kaltsinn, die unruhige Eifersucht, die argwöhnische Besorgnis, jene ganze unselige Spannung," waren für den Moment "einem fast unbeschränkten Vertrauen, der entschiedensten Vorliebe" gewichen, wie Gentz schrieb. (*Kleist*, 352)

Michalzik's assumption (*ibid.*, 353) that Kleist knew Gentz' text is plausible; who influenced whom, and in what way, is impossible to discner today, but Gentz' essay could have further heightened Kleist's sense of urgency: if this clear-sighted and level-headed political thinker was openly calling upon the (in Kleist's opinion) "second-best" candidate for German leadership, it was all the more urgent for Kleist to nudge Fr. Wilh. into assuming this role. The bard's window of opportunity, then, was delimited not only by Napoleon's being tied-up in Spain, and the triumvirs' progression towards a *coup d'état*, but also Franz's propensity to assume this role. Kleist took Gentz' views seriously: in a letter to A. Müller Gentz notes the "excessive weight Kleist placed on my judgment" (cf. *ALM*,322).

We once again observe the *Realpolitiker* Kleist at work: while missing no opportunity for decrying the rivalry between the leading German dynasties, this scion of the Kleist family instinctively favoured one—the Hohenzollerns—over the others. As long as there remained a chance of the Hohenzollern King joining the war—that is, at least till early April 1809—, he worked tirelessly to buttress Fr. Wilh; as soon as it became clear that Austria faced Napoleon alone, he threw in his lot with the Habsburg Emperor, on 28th April leaving Dresden for Austria, on 25th May visiting the battlefield of Aspern, and on 13th June announcing his *Germania* project to Fr. Schlegel (who in Archduke Karl's HQ published the *Oesterreichische Zeitung*, which Kleist's more pamphletic *Germania* could have complemented). Nonetheless, even though in his "political works" of 1809 Kleist endorses Franz as Germany's wartime leader, he no longer addresses him as legitimate Holy Roman Emperor, only as (temporary) "guardian" of the Germans, leaving open the question of leadership in the post-war order. Kleist's primary aim with *Germania* was to stoke a northern German resistance, which would help defeat Napoleon, but would also ensure that Habsburg Austria would not emerge as the sole liberator of Germany. Kleist "hedged his bets" in line with historical realities, but never lost sight of his twin loyalties: to the *HRR* (or a suitable successor enity) and to the Hohenzollern family.[517]

"Die Geburt des Partisanen." Apart from Richard Samuel and Jeffrey Sammons, the Kleist scholar who contributed most to exposing *Hermannsschlacht*'s political fabric is Wolf Kittler, who traced Kleist's endorsement of partisan, insurrectionist warfare not only in this drama, but also in *Krug*, thereby demonstrating that Kleist's "military-political tendency" extended well beyond the works traditionally denoted in the *Kleist-Forschung* as "political":

> Die Pamphlete und Kriegslieder, die Kleist im Frühjahr und Sommer 1809 verfaßte... sprechen die Ideen der "Hermannsschlacht" im Klartext aus. Und das einzige Rätsel, das ist die Frage, wie es möglich war, das dichterische Werk ihres Verfassers so weit von diesen propagandistischen Texten abzuspalten, daß man die eindeutig wehrpolitische Tendenz seiner Dramen und Novellen übersehen konnte. (*Geburt*, 254)

My own analysis expands on Kittler's, whose focus on partisan war, while touching on one important aspect, does not do justice to the full scope and force of Kleist's simultation: among the learnings Kleist drew from Spain was that, while partisans could tie down regular armies of disproportionally larger size, they could scarcely in and by themselves decide a war—the decisive blow still had to be struck by a regular army. Kleist would later elaborate this argument in *Kohlhaas*, his post-facto critique of the limits of a partisan war lacking legitimacy and broad support (exemplified by the rapid collapse of Schill's *Freikorps* in 1809). In *Hermannsschlacht*, which is proscriptive and simulative, rather than descriptive and analytic, he assigns a key role to Brunhold's regular army (cf. V.2452). Kittler's single-minded focus on partisan war prevents him from perceiving Kleist's key insight, that only a propitious nexus of three mutually reinforcing factors would allow Germany to overcome the *Ad'A*: a broad-based people's insurrection under legitimate command (preferably Fr. Wilh.'s); a concurrent strike by a fully-fledged regular army (which could only be Franz's); and *kairotic* timing (Napoleon's being tied up in Spain).[518]

Kittler, to his credit, does recognise the role intellectuals like Kleist could play in unleashing the energy of a people's insurrection:

> Auf die bange Frage ihres Königs: Wer wird den Tumult des Volkes bändigen, antworten Kleist und Gneisenau also übereinstimmend mit dem Hinweis auf die deutsche Poesie. Der Autor der "Hermannsschlacht" gab diese Antwort schon im Jahre 1808, gleizeitig mit seinem Vorgesetzten Altenstein, der andere formulierte sie im Jahr 1811. Und es ist keine Frage, wer die Idee als erster ausgesprochen hat, der deutsche Dichter oder der preußische Offizier. (*Geburt*, 252)

However, Kleist defined his task not in the first instance as mobilising the masses, but as *guiding his King*; his concern, unlike Kittler's or Clausewitz', was not *military theory* (the theory of orchestrating large bodies of men) but *political praxis* (the praxis of manipulating the minds of their leaders), and he appreciated, even endorsed, that in his day politics remained "top-down."[519] Kittler remains noncommittal concerning whom he thinks Kleist addresses, and whom his characters represent: while he acknowledges that Hermann and Marbod could represent Fr. Wilh. and Franz (cf. *ibid*, 242), he hedges that Hermann could also represent Stein, Scharnhorst, or Gneisenau (cf. *ibid*, 229). Like Samuel, Kittler lacks a coherent theory of Kleist's agenda and method, and hence is unable to come to a precise conclusion; when he insists that the drama is *"agitatorisch"* (*ibid*, 229, n.37) he is not *wrong*, but neither is he *succinct*: Kleist's drama is not a "song" (Kittler) performed for all and sundry, but a finely tuned address to his King.

Kittler misses an opportunity when he states, *"Aber es geht ja gar nicht darum, das Drama als Schlüsseltext zu lesen, sondern vielmehr um die Erkenntnis einer historischen Konstellation"*: *Hermannsschlacht* is precisely a *"Schlüsseltext"* (and it matters not whether Kittler means "cypher text" or *"roman-à-clef,"* for Kleist's texts are always both), and Kittler, even while correctly stating that *"das Drama ist eine klare und eindeutige Aufforderung zur Aktion"* (p.240), fails to ask: *"injunction to whom? to do what?"*[520] Even Kittler ultimately recoils from the idea that Kleist was a consummate *zoon politikon*, and that his works were, above all, means of wielding political influence.

"Verwirre das Gefühl mir nicht!" Hermann does not "embody the ideal German man" (Barbara Vinken, *Bestien*, 17)—rather, he is the "right man for the job," who in a *kairotic* moment taps into the *"Nachtseite seiner Natur"* (to mis-appropriate Gottfried Heinr. Schubert's title). Hermann experiences doubt (cf. V.2285) and vulnerability—when he picks up his "sword" he is promptly wounded or castrated (cf. V.2514)—; he is vain and decadent—his tent is "splendid" (V.396-7), his seat cushioned with tiger pelts (cf. V. 865-6), his lifestyle "sybarite" (V.962)—, and cunning and ruthless, acting in accordance with situational exigencies not universal principles—he enlists Roman experts to help organise his forces so as to vanquish the Romans by their own tactics (cf. V.2249-50), pretends to be corruptible by accepting Augustus' gift of a quadriga, and declares the enemy *"vogelfrei"* (i.e., outside of the law, *homo sacer*) so that anyone may hunt him down scot-free.[521] Hermann exhibits the full spectrum of human feelings, ranging from wholesome love of his family and nation—*"Dem Weib das mir vermählt, der Gatte, / Ein Vater meinen süßen Kindern, / Und meinem Volk ein guter Fürst zu sein"* (V.436-8; cf. II:683; 725)—to merciless fury towards the enemy: his diatribe calling for "unfettered war" (cf. V.1482-9) is as vehement as any of the notorious passages Kleist prepared for *Germania*.

There can be no doubt that this *furor teutonicus*, who has been facing an overwhelming enemy for a draining twelve years (cf. V.2505), represents Fr. Wilh. (1809 marks his 12th year on the throne).[522] Hermann is not Fr. Wilh.'s "*Gegenbild*," as Jochen Schmidt puts it (*Kleist*, 145), but his "*Vorbild*." That Hermann-Fr. Wilh. misses the very battle to which he lends his name, is in keeping with Kleist's actual context: following *Tilsit* and *Paris*, Prussia barely had any regular troops or financial means at her disposal, and the role Kleist ascribes to Fr. Wilh. is that of mobilising a people's insurrection in northern Germany, while lining up the Austrians to muster the regular forces required to overcome the *Ad'A*. In this situation, Fr. Wilh. must act not as military commander but as charismatic leader and masterful propagandist, able to rally and manipulate people and pull the strings—a master *Maschinist* à la *Marionettentheater*. Kleist's Hermann shows himself to be up to the task when he:

- executes Septimius with a club of double weight (cf. V.2219);[523]
- makes Thusnelda the first "convert" to his ideology (cf. V.1862);
- offers Marbod his two sons as pledge;[524]
- distributes Hally's body parts to the disunited German chiefs;
- absents himself from the battlefield, thereby putting himself on the same level as the absent Augustus;
- safeguards his own honour, while testing Fust's loyalty, by leaving Varus' necessary but dishonourable execution to him;
- turns Aristan's execution into the founding act of a new Germany.

Kleist's Hermann does not recoil from murder if he deems it necessary, but ensures that such acts remain highly surgical and symbolic—far more so, say, than the so-called "surgical strikes" that produce such unacceptable "collateral damage" in our day: he requires no more than *four* carefully staged deaths— Septimius', Ventidius', Varus' and Aristan's—to achieve his purposes (Hally is already dead when he demands her dismemberment). His scorched-earth tactics may seem morally objectionable, but when in 1812 the Russians would apply the same tactic against the *Grande Armée*, they would be celebrated across Europe.

"Um, wie ein Krebs, zurückzugehn." When he has Dagobert poignantly say of Hermann, *"Gleich einem Löwen grimmig steht er auf, / Warum? Um, wie ein Krebs, zurückzugehn"* (V.363-4), Kleist reminds his audience that Hermann-Fr. Wilh. is not self-evidently heroic and charismatic; in the tropical Zodiac the constellation *Cancer* (22nd June-22nd July) appears at the zenith right before that of *Leo* (23rd July-22nd August), and by setting the drama in mid-August, Kleist admonishes Fr. Wilh. to seize the *kairotic* moment marked by *Leo*, and not to fall back to an earlier pattern, marked by *Cancer*, of foot dragging. When he assuages Dagobert that he is looking only forward—*"Nach Rom…!"* (V.366)—the heroic Hermann is born. We recall Thucydides' maxim: "men are bold through ignorance, whereas reflection makes them cautious" (as given in Lucian, *Nigrinus*).

"Wie steht die Schlacht, sag an?" Franz I is represented by Marbod, a historical Germanic chieftain who in Arminius' day consolidated a powerful kingdom of the Suevi and Markommani centred on modern-day Bohemia, in Kleist's day part of the Austrian Empire; Kleist explicitly refers to this fortuitous equivalence of historical and contemporary geography when he has Marbod's army descend from the *"Sudeten"* and *"Riesenbergen"* (V.425), the Bohemian mountain ranges that in his day indeed marked the boundaries between Austria and the rest of Germany. Kleist's Marbod-Franz is no charismatic leader in the mould of Hermann: cautious and circumspect, he enters the war only at Hermann's instigation, and leaves the command of his army in the capable hands of his general Brunold. In Kleist's wargame, the Austrian (Suevi) army bears the brunt of the conventional military action, while the Prussians (Cheruskans) play a subsidiary role, falling into the enemy's back, disrupting their supply lines and obstructing their retreat routes, while a broad-based insurrection of northern Germanic tribes (cf. V.2447) grinds down the Roman legions. Brunold, whose timely intervention decides the battle in the Germanic alliance's favour (cf. V.2452), probably represents Archduke Karl, Commander in Chief of the Austrian army and future victor of *Aspern*, to whom Kleist dedicated two enthusiastic poems (cf. I:29-31).

Marbold-Franz and Hermann-Fr. Wilh. complement one another: the latter leverages his *charismatic authority* to rally a broad-based resistance, the former brings to bear his *traditional authority*, as last Holy Roman Emperor,M and his formidable army and resources base.[525] In the drama's eminently Kleistian ending Hermann-Fr. Wilh. bends his knee before Marbod-Franz, who promptly raises him up and in turn bends before him: Hohenzollern *charisma*, in Kleist's scenario, trumps Habsburg *tradition*.

"Er hat zur Bärin mich gemacht!" *(I).* Hermann's wife Thusnelda represents Queen Luise, whose weakness for bric-a-brac and swayability by *charmeurs* Kleist once again parodies. Having Hermann-Fr. Wilh. address her disparagingly as "Thuschen" is irreverent in the extreme, yet entirely in keeping with Kleist's previous portrayals of his Queen. Dahlmann's recollection of Kleist's description of Thusnelda may well convey Kleist's view of Luise with precision: "*Meine Thusnelda ist brav, aber ein wenig einfältig und eitel, wie heute die Mädchen sind, denen die Franzosen imponieren; wenn solche Naturen zu sich zurückkehren, so bedürfen sie einer grimmigen Rache*" (*LS*,319). Thusnelda-Luise's object of desire, the Roman legate Ventidius, could represent Kleist's favourite bogey Hardenberg, who in late 1808, while officially in exile in Riga, once again sought to shape Prussian politics, on 10th November meeting Fr. Wilh. and two days later publishing his *Braunsberger Denkschrift*, in which he advocated Stein's dismissal; of Hardenberg's relationship with the Queen one observer reported:

> Königin Luise und Hardenberg verstanden sich auf Anhieb. Das Verhältnis war geprägt von Vertrauen und Sympathie. Mit keinem Staatsmann hat Königin Luise so ausgezeichnet zusammengearbeitet, wie mit Hardenberg, für den sie sich persönlich mehrfach einsetzte. Unmittelbar vor dem Treffen mit Napoleon am 6. Juli 1807 beriet sie sich mit ihm mehrere Stunden lang, um die Strategie des Gesprächs abzustimmen.[526]

Among the King's ministers and courtiers, Hardenberg was certainly closest to the Queen (who disliked Stein), and Kleist's enacting their relationship as erotic flirt is perhaps not entirely off the mark: "Hardenberg" was purportedly among the dying Queen's last words. It will have been with considerable glee that Kleist had his figure Thusnelda-Luise orchestrate Ventidius-Hardenberg's gruesome death.[527]

Kleist could have been inspired to his hilarious sub-plot, of Ventidius eyeing Thusnelda's blonde locks, by a number of sources: historical acccounts of Roman matrons adorning themselves with wigs made of blonde human hair, a major Germanic export commodity; ancient myths according to which appropriating someone's lock of hair confers power over that individual; reports of Caesar having the long hair of noble Gallic captives cut off as a sign of submission; tales of Germanic hunters cutting off the locks of caught aurochs to fashion them into fertility belts for their women; the conventional imagery of grasping Fortuna by her locks; the common habit of keeping a loved one's lock as a token; Alex. Pope's burlesque *The Rape of the Lock* (1712/14) in which the proverbial "storm in a teacup" is triggered by the theft of a desirable woman's lock (cf. also II:756). Important to us is Hermann's prerogative of manipulation: he shapes Thusnelda's interpretation of Ventidius' intentions and thereby her response.[528] Just like the "Hally" subplot, the subplot of the "locks" conveys the effectiveness of Hermann's "truth-making."

"Tyrannenknecht." The absent Augustus represents Napoleon, who at the time of writing remained tied up in the *Armée d'Espagne*'s bitter war against the Spanish guerilleros. One of the key premises of Kleist's simulation was that Fr. Wilh. and Franz had to act quickly, to push the *Ad'A* out of Germany before Napoleon could intervene personally. The *"Tyrannenknecht"* (V.2482) Varus may represent Maréchal Louis-Alexandre Berthier, Napoleon's chief of staff and designated supreme commander of the *Ad'A* (Berthier officially assumed the position in March 1809). That Varus does not cut a dashing figure in battle accurately reflects that Maréchal Berthier was better known for organising the French forces than for commanding them in battle. Berthier could well have been among Kleist's bogeys: as Napoleon's chief negotiator at *Tilsit,* he arm-twisted the Prussian negotiator Kalckreuth into accepting harsh terms, and was rewarded by Napoleon with the Hohenzollern principality of Neuchâtel. Varus' clumsiness in his attempted suicide, and the degrading manner in which the Germanic chieftains quarrel over the right to finish him off, suggest that Kleist cared little for Berthier.

"Zum Verräter mich gemacht." Fust, Aristan and Gueltar represent *Rheinbund* princes, probably the three German Electors Napoleon had elevated to Kings, thereby turning them into his staunches allies: Fust likely represents Fr. Aug. I, King of Saxony; Aristan, Max. I Joseph, King of Bavaria; and Gueltar, Fr. I, King of Württemberg.[529] Of Fr. Aug., whom he permits to redeem himself by killing Varus,

Kleist in late 1808 indeed still hoped that he could be brought back into the German fold: in his essay *Über die Abreise des Königs von Sachsen*, which covers events of March/April 1809, Kleist offers his rationale for hoping that Fr. Aug. would rejoin the Coalition, including his family ties with the Habsburgs and the public mood in Saxony. Only after Fr. Aug.'s precipitate departure from Dresden on 16th April 1809, under Napoleon's pressure, did Kleist write off the Wettin completely, predicting that if Austria failed to win the war, Fr. Aug.'s departure will become his "Bayonne."[530] Aristan-Max. Joseph, "*Der ungroßmütigste von allen deutschen Fürsten*" (V.12), whom Hermann condems to death, for Kleist was beyond redemption.[531]

"**Die schreiben, Deutschland zu befreien.**" Kleist parodies the "*mißvergnügten*" (cf. I:534) Prussian reformers-cum-conspirators (Loch refers to them as "*Enragés*," Blamberger as "*Verschwörergruppe*") by having Hermann say dismissively:

> Die Schwätzer, die! Ich bitte dich;
> Laß sie zu Hause gehn.—
> Die schreiben, Deutschland zu befreien,
> Mit Chiffern, schicken, mit Gefahr des Lebens,
> Einander Boten, die die Römer hängen,
> Versammeln sich um Zwielicht—essen, trinken,
> Und schlafen, kommt die Nacht, bei ihren Frauen.—
> Wolf ist der einzge, der es redlich meint.   (V.1446-53)

Parody is a form of flattery, and being parsimonious in his writing, Kleist only included personages he deemed sufficiently important. In the above passage he advises his King not to ignore these "dissatisfied" "chatterers," and that among them only Wolf—"the only one who means well" (cf. V.1503)—deserves his trust. "Wolf" is the word with which the drama opens, and probably Wolf embodies Gneisenau, whom Kleist admired.[532] Thuiskomar, Dagobert and Selgar could then represent, respectively, Stein, Scharnhorst, and Clausewitz; Thuiskomar's identification with Stein is suggested by his first line, which links him to letters: "*Er muß hier diese Briefe lesen!"* (V.21). Stein, for Kleist, will indeed have been merely one among several "chatterers," and while he is clearly referring to the *Stein affair* in the drama, it is unlikely that he considered Stein, a late convert to the cause of German resistance, a major inspiration for his work. Gneisenau's (and Scharnhorst's) memoranda were closer in content and tone to Kleist's stance, and if any of these statesmen inspired the poet, then Gneisenau.[533]

"Verharrt bei eurem Entschluß nicht zu fechten!" Among the Cherusci (Prussians), the cautioning Egbert could represent Prince Wilh., who with *Paris* accepted punishing conditions in order to secure the end of the occupation. Samuel suggests (cf. *Stein*, 438) that in Stein's plans, *Paris* was merely part of a duplicitous game of deceiving France while preparing an insurrection, but while such a stratagem would have been eminently Kleistian, Kleist may have considered the price too high. The three clueless Cheruscan commanders ("*Die deutschen Uren*"; V.937) could refer to Prussian generals Kleist did not hold in high regard; Thusnelda's two ladies, to Luise's close confidantes Marie von Kleist and Sophie Marie von Voß. Among Fr. Wilh.'s courtiers, Eginhardt could represent Prussian Foreign Minister Goltz, Prussian signatory at *Tilsit* and representative at *Erfurt*, and his three sons the envoys Götzen, Lucey and Tiedemann, whose secret missions in July 1808 Samuel discusses (cf. *ibid*, 441-2; the latter three could also be enacted by the three Cheruscan messengers). The *Alraune*—a Germanic fairy—could be Kleist himself, in a cameo appearance as soothsayer.

Among the Suevi (Austrians), Marbod's counsellor Attarin could represent Foreign Minister Philipp von Stadion, who supported the war and actively sought to foster an alliance with Prussia, and whose representative in Dresden, Joseph von Buol-Mühlingen, Kleist befriended. Komar, a Suevan captain, could embody Austrian Chief of Staff Max. von Wimpffen (who would significantly contribute to Austria's victory at *Aspern*). If Hally embodies the Quaternion Eagle, her father, the armourer Teuthold ("true German"), who prefers to kill her rather than see her live in dishonour, could refer to Franz's earlier incarnation Franz II, who preferred to dissolve the *HRR* rather than see it survive as a violated rump, and his "cousins," who assist in Hally's dismemberment, to Princes who helped dismember the *HRR* by joining the *Rheinbund*.

The she-bear may be an avatar of *Germania*, the bear-keeper Childerich ("king," "ruler") of Fr. Barbarossa, and the auerochs of the German people. Our tentative casting list is as follows (Augustus-Napoleon, Brunold-Archduke Karl, Hally-*HRR*, and She-bear-Germania do not appear on stage):

ERMANN, Fürst der Cherusker	FR. WILH. III, King of Prussia
HUSNELDA, seine Gemahlin	LUISE, Queen of Prussia
NOLD and ADELHART, seine Knaben	FR. WILH. and WILH., Crown Princes
GINHARD, sein Rat	GOLTZ, Prussian Foreign Minister
JITGAR, ASTOLF, WINFRIED, dessen Söhne	GÖTZEN, LUCEY, THIEDEMANN, Pr. envoys
GBERT, ein anderer cheruskischer Anführer	PRINCE WILH., Fr. Wilh.'s younger brother
ERTRUD and BERTHA, Frauen der Thusnelda	MARIE VON KLEIST and COUNTESS VOSS, Luise's confidantes
ARBOD, Fürst der Sueven	FRANZ I, Emperor of Austria
TTARIN, sein Rat	STADION, Austrian Foreign Minister
OMAR, ein Suevischer Hauptmann	WIMPFFEN, Austrian Chief of Staff
OLF, THUISKOMAR, DAGOBERT, SELGAR:	GNEISENAU, STEIN, SCHARNHORST,
ißvergnügte	CLAUSEWITZ: Prussian reformers/conspirators
JST, GUELTAR, ARISTAN: Verbündete des Varus	FR. AUG. I, King of Saxony; FR. I, King of Württemberg; MAX. I JOSEPH, King of Bavaria: Napoleon's German vassals
UINTILIUS VARUS, römischer Feldherr	MARÉCHAL BARTHIER, French commander
ENTIDIUS, Legat von Rom	HARDENBERG, advisor to Fr. Wilh. and Luise
ÄPIO, sein Geheimschreiber	JORDAN, Hardenberg's secretary
PTIMUS and CRASSUS, römische Anführer	French Commanders of Prussian fortresses
UTHOLD, ein Waffenschmied	FRANZ II, formerly Holy Roman Emperor
HILDERICH, ein Zwingerwärter	FR. BARBAROSSA, mythical German liberator
NE ALRAUNE	KLEIST, German national bard and soothsayer
LTESTE, FELDHERRN, HAUPTLEUTE, BOTEN, RIEGER, VOLK.	French and German statesmen, generals and envoys, soldiers, the German people.

"wie ein dummer Streich." *Hermannsschlacht* simulates a "goldilocks" scenario in which for a brief *kairotic* moment several conditions for German success coincide (the "moment," for which Kleist repeatedly emphasises he conceived the drama, corresponds precisely to this coincidence of conditions):

1. Napoleon remains tied up in Spain, leaving Berthier, not a proven battle commander, in command of the *Ad'A*
2. Fr. Wilh. inspires a people's insurrection across northern Germany;
3. Franz allies himself with Fr. Wilh. and puts his brother, the competent Archduke Karl, in command of the Austrian forces;

Under these conditions, Kleist's wargame plays out in Germany's favour:

1. The *Rheinbund* princes allied with France are neutralised by Fr. Wilh.'s manoeuvring and fail to succour the *Ad'A*;
2. Karl leads the Austrian army to victory against Berthier;
3. The *Rheinbund* princes join a pan-German confederation;
4. Coalition troops sweep across Germany and drive the remaining *Ad'A* contingents across the Rhine;
5. Once the Rhine border has been secured, giving Germany time to rebuild her strength and rear a new generation of leadership, the stage is set for the final conquest of Paris and of the Bonapartean Empire (this final stage is beyond the drama's scope, but anticipated in Hermann's speech).

Kleist expected it would take up to two generations to overcome the Bonapartes, and *Hermannsschlacht* offers a simulation only of Germany's liberation, not of Napoleon's, or his dynasty's, final defeat. The caveat, *"Und dann – nach Rom selbst mutig aufzubrechen! Wir oder unsere Enkel"* (V.2630-1), may imply that despite the mercurial charisma he ascribes to him in his drama, Kleist did not expect Fr. Wilh. to overcome Napoleon: his Hermann-Fr. Wilh. is a purely *kairotic* figure, in the decisive moment super-charged by Kleist's *"Griffel"* (II:263) to achieve a precise task: liberating Germany east of the Rhine. This task achieved, Kleist advocates that Germany bide her time till a new generation of Hohenzollern leaders—Fr. Wilh.'s sons or even grandsons—are groomed, capable of attacking Paris (Rome) and completing Europe's liberation; Prussia in the course of her history *had* produced leaders who would have been a match for Napoleon—Fr. II the Great, the Great Elector—, but only once every few gerations.[534]

History did not play out according to Kleist's script: Fr. Wilh. refused to join the war, and to endorse, let alone lead, a people's insurrection; Archduke Karl on 10th April 1809 did launch a preemptive strike against the *Ad'A* in Bavaria, but by this time Napoleon had already returned from Spain, arrived in the Bavarian theatre within a matter of days, personally took charge of the *Ad'A*, reversed the Austrian army's momentum, and following *Landshut*'s audacious *manoeuvre sur les derrières*, occupied Vienna; and although Karl subsequently achieved a tactical and highly symbolic victory at *Aspern*, he failed to turn the temporary advantage into a decicive victory and allowed Napoleon to regroup and vanquish the Austrian army at *Wagram*, thereby deciding the war in his favour. Of Kleist's three key success factors, only one materialised: Franz did provide the regular army Kleist had called for; Fr. Wilh. utterly failed to play his part, and the window of opportunity of Napoleon's absence was missed. The disastrous outcome was entirely in line with the logic of Kleist's wargame, demonstrating that it was well-constructed: had all three mutually reinforcing factors materialised, the Germans might well have succeeded; when two out of three of did not, they stood no chance.

"**im Morast des Teutoburger Walds.**" The Teutoburg, which Hermann-Fr. Wilh. in an apocalyptic vision turns into a battleground, "*EGINHARDT.* [...] */ Ganz Teutoburg siehst du in Schutt und Asche! / HERMANN. Mag sein! Wir bauen und ein schönres auf*" (V.2564-5), refers to Berlin (as Rühle already noted). Kleist had no qualms about sacrificing the capital, and neither, he felt, should his King—cf. his poem for the King's return, "*Und müßt auch selbst noch, auf der Hauptstadt Türmen, / Der Kampf sich, für das heilge Recht, erneun: / Sie sind gebaut, o Herr, wie hell sie blinken, / Für bessre Güter, in* *den Staub zu sinken!"* (I:33). Augustus' "empty" (cf. V.75) gift of the quadriga—the Brandenburg Gate quadriga, which Napoleon in 1806 had claimed as war booty and transported to Paris—alludes to the French withdrawal after *Paris* as an "empty" gesture because the French retained control of three strategic Prussian fortresses, "Trojan horses" from which they could re-occupy Prussia at any time.

The drama's town names are necessarily fictional—little is known to this day about Germanic settlements of the 1st century AD—, but its topographical markers are not, and Kleist's account of how the rivers Rhine (to the west), Weser (to the north and east) and Main (to the south) delineate a corridor through which the Romans invade Germany, using the Lippe as transport axis for their advance towards the Teutoburg Forest, is as accurate in reference to the situation in AD 9 as it is relevant and acute for Kleist's simulation of AD 1809:

The Roman legions invading along the Lippe in AD 9 (left); the same axis superimposed on the formerly Prussian territories of Cleves (violet/green), Mark (light blue), and Münster (pink), captured by France since 1795 (centre); the French-controlled corridors towards Prussia and Austria in 1808/9 (right).[535]

In Kleist's simulation, Merbod's soldiers confront the eastward-moving Roman legions early on, with Hermann's guerrilleros falling into their backs:

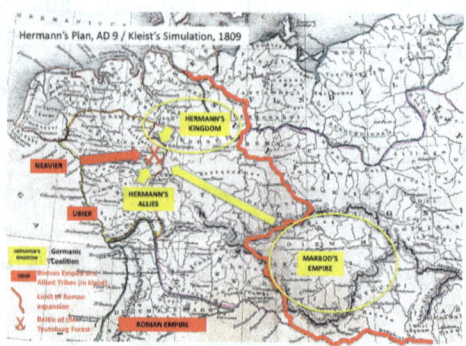

Pincer movement, AD 9/ AD 1809 (Kleist's simulation).

For all the apparent parallels with the historical events of AD 9, Kleist's wargame is designed not to reconstruct these events (of which most details remain obscure to this day), but to simulate those of AD 1809; I offer that his relevant *contemporary* point of reference was a plan proposed by Prussian War Minister Gerhard von Scharnhorst in August/ September 1808, envisioning Prussia and Austria engaging the *Ad'A* in a decisive battle in the spring of 1809, involving a pincer movement of the Austrians pushing from Bohemia northwards towards Breslau, and the Prussians concurrently from Pomerania and East Prussia southwards towards Posen, converging on a corridor-shaped theatre of war delineated by the rivers Oder to the west and south-west, and Weichsel to the north and north-east, in which the *Ad'A* would be crushed:

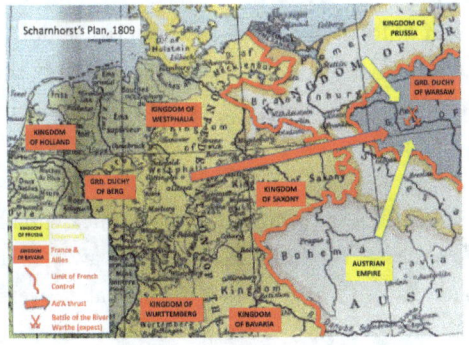

Pincer movement, AD 1809 (Scharnhorst's plan).

I maintain that *Hermannsschlacht* comprises Kleist's immediate response to Scharnhorst's plan, compared to which it offers two significant modifications (Scharnhorst's plan was drawn up *before*, Kleist's *after, Paris*): firstly, by capitalising on Napoleon's absence, the Coalition is able to confront the *Ad'A* much further in the west, compared to Scharnhorst's plan of luring it eastwards, away from its secure supply lines; secondly, the pincer movement is completed not by regular Prussian forces, but by insurrectionists, for whose guerrilla warfare the marshy plains and forested hills of north-western Germany is ideally suited.[536]

"**Rom, / Das Drachennest.**" Rome, of course, represents Paris. I consider it implausible that Kleist would have advocated a "nihilistic" (Gerhard Kluge) "annihilation" (Anthony Stephens) of that great metropolis, as his drama's final lines may seem to suggest: the highly cultured intellectual Kleist would probably have sooner fathomed parochial Berlin going to ashes than cosmopolitan Paris. His monikers, "*Raubnest*" ("robber's den") and "*Drachennest*" ("dragon's den"), refer not to the city of Paris but to Napoleon's seat of power located therein, and in Hermann's apocalyptic vision, "*Und nichts, als eine schwarze Fahne, / Von seinem öden Trümmerhaufen weht!*" (V.2635-6), Napoleon's imperial standard burns atop the shambles not of the entire metropolis, but merly of the Palais des Tuileries.[537]

Hermannsschlacht, Satyrically

Hermannsschlacht focused on *satirical* concerns, and Kleist was in a rush to get it staged before the window of opportunity closed. While his *satyrical* vocabulary is as present here as anywhere, elaborate orgiastic scenes are less common.[538]

"**Bewegung.**" The drama commences in a quintessentially Kleistian *symposiac* love nest—a hunting lodge tugged away in a forest (an assembly of *phalloi*), in which a group of ithyphallic lovers (equipped with "bows" and "arrows") discuss the political situation while enjoying each other's favours:

> WOLF indem er sich auf den Boden wirft. [...]
> THUISKOMAR zu Dagobert und Selgar, die im Hintergrund auf und nieder gehen. [...]
>   Wolf und Thuiskomar machen eine Bewegung. [...]
> THUISKOMAR dazwischen tretend. [...]
> EIN FÜRST ebenso. [...]
>   Man hört Hörner in der Ferne. [...]
> WOLF indem er sich erhebt.   (V.1-73)

The *erômenos* Wolf goes down on his knees before the *erastês* Thuiskomar, while the *dmōtes* Dagobert and Selgar "work" in the background; others join the fray with their "horns." By largely relegating the *satyrical* action to stage directions (as already in *Käthchen*) Kleist focuses the speech sequences on the *satirical* messages and avoids complex *pescherä*, thus short-cycling production.

"Den Strich mir…/ An…der Lippe überlassen." One of the drama's iconic terms is *"Lippe"* ("lip"), which appears at least a dozen times.[539] We saw that the river Lippe is an important topographical feature, and evidently Kleist plays on its polyvalent bodily (erotic) meanings (*"Lippen"* = "lips"; *"Schamlippen"* = "labia," and, by analogy, pectinate line or anal sphincters). Dagobert's demand to Selgar, *"Den Strich mir, der mein Eigentum, / An dem Gestad der Lippe [zu] überlassen"* (V.52-3), implies competing territorial claims on a geographical (*"Landstrich"* = "region," "area"), as well as a bodily, region (two *dmōtes* quarrelling over preferential access to their *erastês*). *"Strich,"* furthermore, colloquially denotes a location where prostitutes gather, and Kleist may be insinuating that whoever seeks to territorialise this region, risks being prostituted by the French, for whom the corridor along the Lippe is the vital attack route into Germany. A *"Strich"* ("line," "dash") is also *phallic*, and in so far as the "lips" are *anal*, this pairing (*line and lips*) belongs to the (I/O) symbolism (cf. also Hermann's *"Donnerkeil"* and Marbod's *"Ring"*; Lat. *"anus"* = "ring," "circle").

"mit pfeildurchbohrtem Nacken." In I/2, Thusnelda relates her breathless encounter with Ventidius during the hunt: *"Ventidius! Römerritter! Ur! Heil! Heil! Was! Ihn? Freunde! herbei! mir! zu!"* (V.75-81)—in short, *"!—!—!—!—!—!—?—!—!—!—!,"* or *"bam—bam—bam—bam—bam—bam—wiggle—bam—bam—bam—bam."* Scäpio, and probably other "hunters," being present, the encounter is orgiastic; the aurochs, like the horses in *Penthesilea*, may serve as Kleistian jar or Mesmerian bucket. Ventidius' and Thusnelda's intimate conversations are far more peppered with eroticised vocabulary—*Fuß, Lippe, Herz, Pfeil, Hand, Glieder, Busen, Mund, Brust, Locke, Scheitel, Weib, Schäferpaare, Milch, Honig, Seele*—than are Hermann's and Thusnelda's, an ironic take on the asymmetry in someone's relationship, respectively, with lover and spouse we already encountered in *Amphitryon*, and which is inherent in Kleist's concept of *"Scheidung."* It has been suggested in the Kleist reception that Ventidius exemplifies Kleist's disdain for superficial—"French"—gallantry, but arguably Kleist is as dismissive of the naïve and swayable Thusnelda as of her gallant seducer: a Queen must be able to channel her passions to the benefit of her people, failing which her husband the King has every right, indeed *duty*, to intervene. Thusnelda may consider her passion for Ventidius a private affair, but for Hermann (and Kleist), a Queen's affections are a public good.⁵⁴⁰ Kleist does not hesitate to seize the opportunity to teach his Queen a lesson she will not forget.

"Er hat zur Bärin mich gemacht!" *(II).* The venue of his death, which Kleist mischievously permits Ventidius-Hardenberg to choose himself (cf. V.2364; 2375; 2382), resembles an anal channel: "Im Hintergrund ein eisernes Gitter, das in einen, von Felsen eingeschlossenen, öden Eichwald führt" (V.2287-8). Moving deeper into this dark valley, while Thusnelda stands (!) behind him, lock and key in hand (!), Ventidius finds himself "stuck"; in vein he pushes forward: "*! O...! ! O...!*" (V.2421). The "barren" orifice he penetrated turns out to belong to a ferocious she-bear, who promptly turns around and and attacks him. Ventidius (indicated below by the red letter "F"), who came to the idyllic "park" to enjoy himself as *erâstes* in a *"FFF"* constellation with a cute, blond Germanic *erômenos* before him and his favourite *dmos* Tuschen behind him, finds himself crushed in a pincer movement, and simultaneously gored by ravenous ithyphallic lovers before and behind:

This *satyrical* scene simulates the *satirical* battle Kleist does not *overtly* depict: Ventidius = Varus; she-bear = Herrmann; Thusnelda = Marbold; *"Der stille Park, von Bergen eingeschlossen"* (V.2354) = the Lippe's swampy plain, enclosed by the crescent-shaped Teutoburg Forest. Varus carelessly pushes into this impassable terrain in pursuit of the yielding Herrmann before him, not realising that Herrmann is drawing him ever deeper into the morass, and that Marbold has appeared in his back, blocking his only retreat route. Deep into the barren valley, Herrmann suddenly turns around and strikes at him like a berserk; as Varus is thrown off balance by this sudden thrust, Marbold crushes into him from behind. Kleist with this scene metes out a double punishment at his Queen: he has her gallant lover die an agonising death, and he has her live in the consciousness that she let herself be instrumentalised as the decoy that lured him into the fatal trap.

Hermannsschlacht, Syphilitically

Hermansschlacht's syphilitical passages are similarly scant, and frequently draw on imagery already present in earlier works.

"**Brich auf!**" Hally's being "broken up" ("*Aufbrechen*," a huntsman's term for gutting a kill) by her father and cousins' "daggers," *satirically* her sacrifice as scapegoat and propaganda tool, *satirically* signifies her gang bang as *erômenos*, *syphilitically* her purifying inundation with *cum*: "*Stirb! Werde Staub!*" (V.1573). Her death is a *coup de grâce*: her "*elend,*" "*schmachbedeckt,*" "*fußzertreten,*" "*kotgewälzt,*" "*zertrümmert*" (V.1545-7) body, so unsightly that, like Achilles' mutilated corpse, it must be veiled, suggests that it exhibits symptoms associated with the disease's final stage.

Terms such as "*abbrechend*" and "*bricht auf*" already feature in the stage directions for scene (I/3), in which Hermann and his "*Mißvergnügten*" recline on grass benches around a stone table and circulate a cup in which they gather, mingle and share their cum. Their symposiac orgy encompasses "*Abbrechen*" ("to abort"), "*Aufstehen*" ("to erect"), "*Aufbrechen*" ("to force,") notably a coy initiate, possibly with a "horn"), thrusting, "! ! ! ! !," and "*Abgehen*" ("to go off," "to discharge"), and culminates in their collective ejaculation (*bukkake*):

HERMANN abbrechend. [...]

                    [...] Er steht auf. [...]

DAGOBERT bricht auf. [...]
HERMANN in die Szene rufend. [...] ! [...] !

SELGAR ebenso. [...] ! [...] ! [...] !

   Die Fürsten brechen sämtlich auf.

HERMANN. [...]

   Er geht ab; Hörnermusik.

WOLF. [...] ! [...] ! [...] !

   Alle ab. (V.388-96)

"Und seine Hand war—." Thusnelda magnetises herself with a lute (cf. V.593-605), while Ventidius connects to her via her locks, which serve as *baquet*-string; by cutting off her locks, Vintidius thus severs his own connection to the source of energy and healing (and thus already precipitates his death):

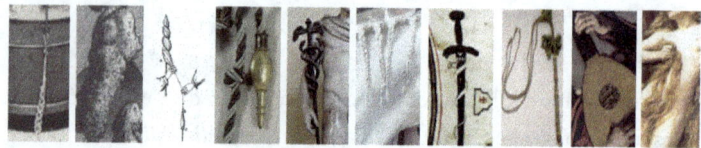

Braided *baquet*-strings (cont'd).

Thusnelda, in her song, recalls her syphilitic infection: as a youth, s/he inserts her member ("*Hand*") into a lover's muddy orifice ("*Becken*" = "basin," "pelvis"); when s/he pulls out, her member is infected: "*Und seine Hand war—*" (V.599). Lawrence Ryan has correctly identified the missing word marked by the dash as "*drecken*" ("dirty"), but cannot make head or tail of the passage, for only in the *syphilitical* framework do Kleistian terms such as "*drecken*," "*Schmutz*," "*Kot*" take on a definite meaning.

"Er hat zur Bärin mich gemacht!" *(III)*. When Thusnelda claims that Ventidius turned her into a rabid she-bear (cf. V.2321), she *satirically* implies that he "francofied" her, *syphilitically* that he infected her. Sacrificing him, then, for her is an act not only of revenge, but also of *purification*. The she-bear, whose "bristles, black and stiff" (cf. V.2406) recall the scorpion's sting and the basilisk's fangs, and whom Gertrud calls "*das Ungeheu'r*" (V.2417), is, however, an avatar not of Thusnelda but of Herrmann, who infects "*de[n] Unglücksel'ge[n]*"

(V.2353) Ventidius with a massive dose of "German disease," against which he has no antidote or immunisation.

Hermannsschlacht, po(i)etically
Kleist's usually fastidious wordsmithing in the case of *Hermannsschlacht* may occasionally have fallen victim to exigency, and his choice of words may at times seem unfortunate, but his no-holds-barred agitation reflects the general atmosphere in which he wrote, as Dahlmann confirms, and the need for his message to be as bold and straightforward as possible.

"eines Wilden Witz." It has been noted that the drama borders on the comical and farcical; already Clemens Brentano found it "bizarre" and "immensely funny" (*NR*,76). If the drama had such a serious purpose, how does this "bizarre" element fit in? Jeffrey Sammons and Anthony Stephens point out the prevalence of the motif of play in Kleist's drama, characterising Hermann variously as *"Schauspieler," "Puppenspieler"* and *"Glücksspieler."*[541] In fact, the "player" is not Hermann-Fr. Wilh. but Kleist, and *Hermannsschlacht*'s computer-game-ish timbre, which echoes *Penthesilea*'s filmic and cartoonish, and *Käthchen*'s fantasy-esque hues, has a material basis: Kleist with it recreates the *Taktisches Kriegsspiel* of a Georg Leopold von Reiswitz or Ernst von Pfuel in a narrated space, an immersive "scape" (Arjan Appadurai), across which he moves his avatars of real political actors in the manner in which the *Maschinist* "brushes" his marionettes across the stage, and the video gamer moves his characters across the MMORPG's screen.

"wie ein spielendes Kind" (I): *Taktisches Kriegsspiel*, early 1800s and early 2000s.[542]

Already in his 1805 letter to Rühle (cf. II:761) Kleist had mused about how he, the "emigrant," with his poetry, would drive a "bullet" through Napoleon's head, and in *Hermannsschlacht* in particular he plays out this scenario, hoping that it will become *performative*: that when his play is staged, Fr. Wilh. and Franz, sitting in the audience, respectively, at Berlin's Nationaltheater and Vienna's Burgtheater, will actualise it in accordance with his script, anticipating Orson Scott Card's 1985 science fiction novel *Ender's Game*, in which the title hero, made to believe that he is being trained in a VR simulation, unwittingly commands an actual army that annihilates an enemy civilisation. Kleist's concept, *"allgewaltig an tausend feingesponnenen Fäden"* (II:642), is remarkably similar to Card's; we may term it *"voodoo warfare"*: if he can directly communicate with the actual political leaders via suitable audio-visual or hypnotic "tethers," they will actualise his virtuality in real time; in Lacanian terms, he anticipates that *The Imaginary* (scenario) will be translated via *The Symbolic* (stage performance, wargame) into the *The Real*.[543]

"wie ein spielendes Kind" (II): War Rooms, 1898, 1940, 1964, 2005.

With the theatre stage as his "interface" (in contrast to Ender's computer screens and VR goggle), Kleist, from his "war room" or "strategic command centre" (his study, his armchair), by subtle shifts of his "joystick" (pen, stage directions) manipulates an entranced Fr. Wilh. into rallying a pan-German insurrection.

In their somnambulistic state, Fr. Wilh. and Franz are Kleist's puppets, their minds functioning as projection screens through which the theatre performances are externalised into the real world, as if via *Marionettentheater*'s "*Hohlspiegel*": the moves on stage, passing through the "eternity" of their (un)consciousness (cf. II:345), materialise as action on the battlefields. Kleist's fascination with the "power of music" (cf. *Erdbeben* and *Cäcilie*) can easily be explained along the same lines, for what is music if not a controlled orchestration of invisible "tethers," by which the conductor, flutist or organist (cf. Sister Antonia) animates and manipulates an audience or medium? Be it by musical, theatrical, magnetic-hypnotic or wargaming performance: the *musicien et magnétiseur extraordinaire* Kleist lets the king-puppets and soldier-puppets dance, and at the end of the performance, having won his victory, he *"lacht und geht ab"* (V.2539). The *"Witz"* ("wit," "cunning") Kleist attributes to the "brute" Hermann-Fr. Wilh.—cf. the dying Varus' last words, *"Da sinkt die große Weltherrschaft von Rom / Vor eines Wilden Witz zusammen, / Und kommt.../ Mir wie ein dummer Streich der Knaben vor!"* (V.2464-7)—implies this: the wittiness and cunning Kleist had previously attributed exclusively to the French—*"Der Deutsche spricht mit Verstand, der Franzose mit Witz"* (II:687; cf. also II:662)—he now also grants to the Germans. Fr. Wilh. can out-wit—"out-French"—the French. For standing above and behind the "witty savage," pulling the strings, is none other than the "operator" Kleist himself.

"Der geschnittne Stein." Thusnelda obtains "end-to-end visibility" into the "endgame" when inspecting a carved gem Hermann brought her from Rome:

> HERMANN. So? Der geschnittne Stein, gefaßt in Perlen?
> Ein Pferd war, dünkt mich, drauf?
> THUSNELDA.   Ein wildes, ja,
> Das seinen Reiter abwirft.—Er betrachtet das Diadem.   (V.993-5)

Napoleon's predicted fall from his battlehorse mirrors and inverts Achilles' (*Borussia*'s) 1806/7 fall from his chariot.[544] Not only is Thusnelda prescient (as we know, Napoleon *would* fall, faster than Kleist dared to hope), but also is she furnished with Kleist's *po(ï)etical* equivalent of a "crystal ball": for what is her "cut stone" if not an optical lens, a *"Hohlspiegel"* ("parbolic mirror," cf. *Marionettentheater*) that projects an image into the distance (into the future)? The artful "lens" stemming from Rome (Paris) implies that the place of origin of the dreaded "Francofication" already encompasses, and projects, its own fall. Q: What is the "wild horse's" name? A: *Marengo*. Q: What does it baulk at? A: *Kleist*.

"des Vaterlandes grauses Sinnbild, / Zerstückt." The consternation and disdain with which the *Kleist-Forschung* has frequently reacted to Hally's gruesome fate appears misplaced once one accepts that Kleist's drama comprises a simulation, and that the violated and dismembered maiden Hally is simply the simulation's avatar of the dishevelled Quaternion Eagle and the dissolved *HRR*, as were, say, the shatterd jug in *Krug*, the tattered old woman in *Erdbeben*, and the emasculated blacks in *Kohlhaas*. Hermann's "wake-up call" to the German chieftains is not an "absurdity" (Klaus Müller-Salget) but a striking case of *Realpolitik*: although he knows full well that the Germans' own disunity and myopia precipitated their pitiful situation, he appreciates that in order to restore their unity and ignite their fervour against the enemy, it is opportune not to quell the meme that French aggression caused it, but to accentuate and exaggerate it.[545] Its being "broken up" and dismembered turns Hally's corpse into a *sign* that can be multiplied and disseminated: in a reversal of John the Evangelist's gesture, not the word becomes flesh but the flesh becomes sign (whose efficacy is potentiated by the circulated body parts having belonged to a desirable *erômenos*).[546] Hally's *Zerteilung, Aufteilung* and *Verteilung* entails Hermann's *Verurteilung* of the traitors who precipitated the *HRR*'s *Teilung*, and his *Mitteilung* to his fellow chieftains to jointly re-constitute it.

Kleist's scheme of using a dismembered Germanic maiden as medium and message (the medium here *really is* the message: McLuhan), as war tactics and propaganda message (the promise of liberation, rejuvenation), has a distinguished "genealogy" in literature and the visual arts:

"Brich auf!" (FLTR): Medea; the Peliades; Judith.[547]

Kleist anticipates 20th century war propaganda's common scheme of representing the enemy as inhuman, and as violating the sanctity of one's nation:

Plus ça change: Wilh. II as "mad brute," with German *"Kultur"*
as his cudgel, abducting the Allied maiden (c.1917);
Hitler and Hiroito as double-headed monster, knifing Lady Liberty (c.1944).

Hally is homophone with *Halley*, the famous comet whose periodic return every 75-76 years was calculated by Edmond Halley in 1705 (whose name rhymes with *valley*) and whose next appearance would be in 1834/5. Given his fondness for astronomical and astrological metaphors, in particular those involving comets, *Halley*'s return for Kleist may have served as harbinger of a new era, and as proxy for the timeline required to eliminate the Bonapartean *"Dämonenbrut"*: a further 25 years after Hermann's victory. The imagery of the comet is intimately connected to Kleist's propaganda war: among the participants in the *"Kette der Integranten,"* "comet" denoted "secret message." This convention could even have inspired the Hally episode, for what does Hermann's dissemination of Hally's body parts signify if not the communication of codified messages to the

German princes?[548] As such, the figure Hally is also autobiographic: not only did Kleist think of himself as "comet," but also was he evidently involved in relaying secret messages ("comets") between Brandenburg (Fürstenwalde, Baruth/Mark, Wormlage) and Bohemia (Töplitz) (cf. Michalzik, *Kleist*, 351-7).

The parcelled-out and multiplied Hally, finally, also advertises Kleist's forthcoming programme: his "coughing up," rapid-fire, patriotic works that "fall in the middle of time" and aim to kindle Germany's "*Volkssturm.*"[549] Hally represents, *in nuce*, the entire nexus—of the divided nation (violated *Germania*), the dissolved *HRR* (dishevelled Quaternion Eagle), the guerrilla and propaganda war (killing on the "open street," *sparagmos*) and the network of secret communications ("comets")—at whose very centre stands: *Kleist.*

"lyrische Entgleisungen." A few lines from Kleist's 1809 ode *Germania an Ihre Kinder* (§4, 5-8), which Kleist scholars have variously termed "a lyrical *faux pas,*" "grotesque," "shocking," and "unworthy of Kleist," shall serve to exemplify how readily Kleist is misunderstood:

> Dämmt den Rhein mit ihren Leichen;
> Laßt, gestäuft von ihrem Bein,
> Schäumend um die Pfalz ihn weichen,
> Und ihn dann die Grenze sein!" (I:26-7)

Kleist's admittedly martial language should not preclude his readers from appreciating that Kleist's proposition to redirect the Rhine around the Palatine is not meant literally: one need not have campaigned extensively in this region, as Kleist had in 1793/4, to know that in such mountainous terrain this "proposition" is physically impossible. Perhaps slightly less obvious is that Kleist, with his fantastic imagery, makes a perfectly serious point, namely that the French and German territorial claims are *structurally* irreconcilable *qua* being based on *categorically* different premises, one topographical, the other cultural: the French insist that the Rhine must be the *physical* border between the two realms, the

Germans that the German-speaking regions on the river's left bank must remain German. The only way to reconcile these irreconcilable claims, Kleist points out, would be to *physically shift the course of the Rhine*, say by damming the river before it enters the Palatine, redirecting it westwards (cf. the hypothetical dashed blue line in the two *LHS* maps below), which would make it run along the linguistic border (cf. the second map; pink marks Germanic, blue, Romance languages), a limit Napoleon's expansionism had significantly overstepped (cf. the yellow line in the second map, marking the French Empire's border in 1809).[550]

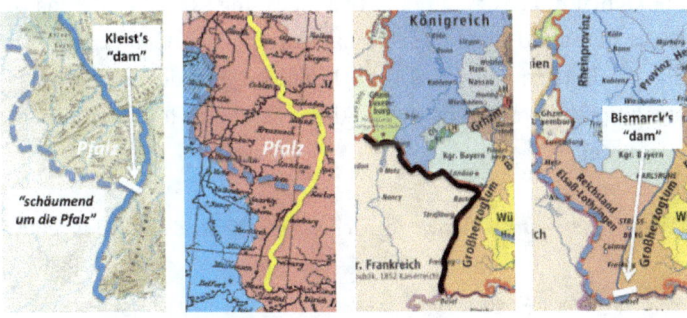

"schäumend um die Pfalz": the Franco-German border, topographically, linguistically and politically.

Kleist's imagery of a heap of soldiers' corpses precipitating peace by damming and redirecting the Rhine is topographically impossible, but realpolitically astute: given Napoleon's unquenchable voracity, only by pushing the *Ad'A* beyond the Rhine—at the expense of many fatalities, on both sides—can Germany create the conditions for a compromise—say, one along the lines of that reached at the *Congress of Vienna* in 1815, of France relinquishing the Rhineland but retaining the Alsace, thus a partial Rhine border, delineating a border (cf. the black line in the third map) that would prove durable (it persists today, three Franco-German wars later), and that was practically identical to the one Kleist proposed.

It is remarkable that Kleist's solution allocates to France the largely German-speaking Alsace, including the city of Straßburg / Strasbourg he repeatedly visited on his journeys: he could just as easily have had the soldiers' corpses "damming" the Rhine not at the Palatine but further upstream, at Basel, thereby redirecting the river in a way that not only the Rheinland but also the Alsace would be on the German side (cf. the dashed blue line in the fourth map). Yet to his credit, unlike Bismarck in 1871, Kleist did not demand the Alsace's annexation by Germany; his supposedly so "shocking" proposal seeks no *retribution* on the part of Germany, solely *restoration* of the *status quo ante*, of the borders at the time of Louis XVI's deposition.[551] In Kleist's view, the Bourbon's deposition had been illegitimate (the *War of the First Coalition*, in which he fought, aimed at restituting the French monarchy, an objective the young as well as the mature Kleist supported), and the *Directoire* and Bonapartean régime were historical aberrations, and once Napoleon was deposed, the pre-revolutionary borders (with the Alsace belonging to France) should be restored.[552]

"**Wehe**." *Hermannsschlacht*'s distich is a rare feature in Kleist's œuvre:

> Wehe, mein Vaterland, dir! Die Leier, zum Ruhm dir, zu schlagen,
> Ist, getreu dir im Schoß, mir, deinem Dichter, verwehrt. (I:533)

While we do not know whether Kleist or Tieck added it to the drama (cf. I:944), the distich could shed further light on the precise "moment" for which Kleist "calculated" *Hermannsschlacht*: if we strike the syllable "land," the distich's *"Dir"* refers to the drama's main addressee, Fr. Wilh., and Kleist laments having been denied the opportunity to "strike his lyre" *for his King*. This suggests that he "calculated" the drama towards an event *that did not take place*: Fr. Wilh.'s hoped-for return from exile in early 1809, for which Kleist also wrote his poem *An den König von Preussen zur Feier seines Einzuges in Berlin im Frühjahr 1809* (cf. I:32-3). In a letter to his friend and mentor Altenstein (who had succeeded Stein as Prussia's finance minister), Kleist on 1st January 1809—the same day on which he sent the drama's MS to Collin—expresses his hope that Altenstein's impending return to Berlin from Königsberg foreshadows the King's:

> Ew. Exzellenz Ankunft in Berlin erwarte ich bloß... um Denenselben die Abschrift einer Hermannsschlacht zuzustellen... Und wenn der Tag uns nur völlig erscheint, von welchem Sie uns die Morgenröte heraufführen, so will ich lauter Werke schreiben, die in die Mitte der Zeit hineinfallen. (II:820)

The "many works that fall into the middle of time" that Kleist here alongside his drama announces to Altenstein, whom he quasi already lines up as his communication channel to the King, would probably have been Prusso-centric versions of his later Austro-centric *Germania* pieces: had the King returned, *Hermannsschlacht* would have been but his "opening shot" in what could have become the world's first sustained propaganda "*Grande batterie*."[553]

On 24th April 1809 Kleist's request for permission to publish his poem to the King, with the added caveat "*(wenn sie stattgefunden hätte)*," is rejected by Berlin's police president and chief censor Gruner (cf. *LS*,315b). Only days earlier, on 21st/22nd April, Archduke Karl had suffered a major defeat at the *Battle of Eckmühl*, the climax of Napoleon's *Landshut Manoeuvre*, and was forced to evacuate Bavaria and retreat to Bohemia, opening the way for Napoleon's march on Vienna. Kleist's attempt to publish the poem-cum-caveat could have been triggered by Karl's defeat, for which he will have made his King's absence at least partially responsible: it could have served as a veritable "*J'accuse...!*" against his King, as Gruner apparently did not fail to notice. If Kleist on the very day on which he requested to publish the poem had received the *breaking news* of Karl's defeat, say, on the 23rd if the news could be conveyed between Landshut and Berlin, a distance of nearly 500km, by *télégraphe Chappe* (semaphore) or homing pigeon, or the 24th if part of the distance had to be covered by horse relay, and if with this *bad news* he gave up any residual hope that Fr. Wilh. would join the war, then we have pinpointed with precision the date on which he accepted that *Hermannsschlacht* had become obsolete, and on which he may have penned not only the caveat to his poem, but also the distich to his drama: 23rd or 24th April 1809.[554] The distich, as it were, comprises the drama's *obituary*. If by *theatrically burning* it Kleist had branded *Guiskard* as misconceived, by *quietly burying* it he marked *Hermannsschlacht* as *well-conceived but obsolete*; if he abandoned *Guiskard* in a fury, he laid to rest *Hermannsschlacht* with a lament.

In the middle of time. Kleist's physical movements once again reflected the shifting political situation: whereas in late 1808 he expected that from his base in Dresden, mid-way between Berlin and Vienna, he would travel to Berlin to welcome the returning King and subsequently join his march westwards to the theatre of war his simulation located in the vicinity of the historical *Battle of the Teutoburg Forest*, Kleist on 29th April instead left Dresden in the opposite direction, south-eastwards towards the Danube's left bank across from Vienna, whereto Karl had retreated after *Eckmühl*, and where he expected to confront Napoleon (cf. II:825; *LS*,316).[555] His attempt, on 24th April, to publish his poem to the King thus marked his farewell to Berlin as well as to *Hermannsschlacht*.

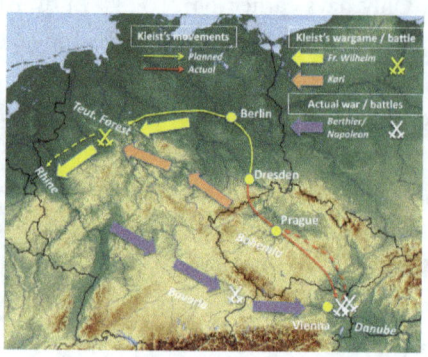

Kleist's wargame (yellow/orange arrows) and the actual French attack of April/May 1809 (violet arrows); correspondingly, Kleist's anticipated (yellow) and actual (red) movements.

Aspern briefly invigorated Kleist, who after their visit to the battlefield with Dahlmann settled in Prague, alongside many leaders of the resistance, to work on *Germania* while performing courier or other missions on behalf of the Austrian authorities. *Germania* became *Hermannsschlacht*'s replacement: in the now Austro-centric context, Kleist's main objective remained to rally resistance in northern

Germany (cf. *LS*,328a; 328b), the same task that in his Prusso-centric simulation he had ascribed to Fr. Wilh., whose charismatic leadership he now sought to replace with broadsides of patriotic songs. *Schönbrunn* in the autumn of 1809 buried his propaganda project, and instead of on 24th April, it is also plausible that he added the distich, and laid to rest *Hermannsschlacht,* only on 14th October, when *Schönbrunn* was signed: that he had kept the MS with him throughout the Prague hitatus, *just in case his King belatedly woke up.*

2.8 *Prinz Friedrich von Homburg*: Of Lordship and Bondage
(A Swansong)

Genesis. Kleist's main historical source for his last completed drama was probably Karl Heinr. Krause's *Geschichte der hohenzollerischen Regenten* (1803), which Kleist borrowed from Dresden library on 9th January 1809 alongside Fr. II's memoirs (cf. *LS*,307), a choice of reading materials that suggests that, having completed *Hermannsschlacht* and put *Käthchen* on hold pending further developments on the marriage front, and having announced in his letter to Collin of 1st January 1809 "many works that fall into the middle of time" (II:820), Kleist set about producing a series of works, possibly including one or several drama(s), as sequel(s) to *Hermannsschlacht*.[556]

Whether Kleist sketched first passages of a *Homburg* in 1809 is unknown; plausibly he could have explored a scenario in which The Elector = Franz, the Swedes = the French, Homburg = Fr. Wilh., who in the eleventh hour succours Franz. Kleist first refers to what appears to be an early version of *Homburg* more than a year after borrowing the source materials from the library, in a letter to Ulrike of 19th March 1810 in which he announces a private performance, for Princess Luise von Preußen's husband Prince Radziwill, of "a piece of mine taken from Brandenburgian history" (cf. II:833). We have no record of such a performance, but it is possible that Kleist had completed a first version or substantial fragment of a *Homburg* by this time; in the wake of the Royals' return to Berlin in December 1809, plausibly he could have conceived a scenario in which The Elector = Alex. I, the Swedes = the French, Homburg = Fr. Wilh., aimed at nudging the King into an alliance with the Tsar.[557] If a private staging took place, it would have comprised but a milestone in Kleist's production process, similar to his small-circle readings of drafts on various other occasions, allowing him to co-create his works in interaction with select audiences (the Prince and Princess, as members of the Hohenzollern family, would have been an eminently relevant "focus group"). Kleist next mentions the drama 15 months later, when on 21st June 1811 he offered it to Reimer, though not yet in fair copy; this timing suggests that Kleist could have intended it for the anniversary of Luise's death. Reimer evidently did not accept the commission. Eventually, on 3rd September 1811, Marie submitted a handwritten quality copy, later to become the basis of Tieck's 1821 publication (cf. *NR*,126; 127a ;b; c), to Prince Wilh.'s wife Princess Amalie Marie Anne, a born Hessen-Homburg, to whom Kleist dedicated the drama.

Two and a half years thus elapsed between Kleist's accessing the source material and completing the drama, during which *Homburg*'s genesis may have progressed in three distinct stages: firstly, in 1809, as sequel or alternative to *Hermannsschlacht*, of which no record is extant, and which would have become obsolete with *Znaim* and *Schönbrunn*; secondly, in 1810, as dedication to Queen Luise (cf. II:833), (parts of) which may (or may not) have been performed before members of the Hohenzollern family, of which no record is extant, and which could have become inopportune when in July 1810 the Queen passed away; thirdly, in 1811, as (extant) dedication to Princess Amalie Marie Anne, situated, together with *Zweikampf*, in the twilight of Kleist's career and life and comprising his *swansong* to the Hohenzollerns as well as himself.

"ein Drama, ein *vaterländisches* (mit mancherlei Beziehungen)."
In the wake of *Wagram* and *Znaim*, between July and November 1809, Kleist "disappeared" in Prague; no single letter from this period is extant, and A. Müller originated or relayed the rumour that Kleist had passed away (cf. *LS*,332a; c; d). While he obviously did not pass away, Kleist during this period may well have been ill, as accounts by Schütz and Körner suggest (cf. *LS*,322; 341), and may have undergone medical treatment while also resuming work on *Käthchen* and producing *Verlobung* as quick-fire sarcastic commentary on *Aspern, Wagram* and *Schönbrunn* (= "*Sainte Lüze*"). In November 1809 Kleist popped up in Frankfurt/O., where he arranged financial and family matters (cf. II:830); on 12th January 1809 he was in Frankfurt/M., whence he sent Cotta the *Käthchen* MS, and where he may have undergone treatment with the *magnétiseur* Mathias Wilh. de Neufville (*Verlobung*'s Guillaume von Villeneuve).558

A key event of this period was Fr. Wilh. and Luise's return, on 23rd December 1809, to Berlin, after three years of exile in Memel and

Königsberg. While we do not know Kleist's whereabouts between his last letter from Frankfurt/O. dated 23rd November and the one from Frankfurt/M. dated 12th January, I find it hard to believe that he could have missed this much-awaited event. It is certainly *possible* that he was in Berlin just before Christmas, and I deem it *probable*: since he must have travelled from Frankfurt/O. to Frankfurt/M. at some point between late November and early January, and will almost inevitably have passed through Berlin, located on the directest route, it would seem extremely unlikely that he did *not* time this passage to coincide with the royals' return. Joseph von Eichendorff noted that on 15th December he met a "Major von Kleist" at A. Müller's house (cf. *LS*,340), and although Kleist left the army with the rank of second lieutenant, and there could have been several von Kleists in Berlin, this is suggestive, there being no indication that Müller welcomed another von Kleist into his circle; meanwhile Arndt noted that he "saw Kleist frequently [at Reimer's] in the winter of 1809" (cf. *LS*,337), and although he could have been referring to the period after Kleist's known return to Berlin on 4th February (winter officially ending on 21st March), this is suggestive as well.[559] We may conjecture Kleist's movements between late November 1809 and early February 1810, his last major journeys before settling in Berlin, as follows: a fast traveller—Michalzik (*Kleist*, 377-80) shows that by renting his own carriage, he could have covered 80-100km per day for several consecutive days—, Kleist could have spent the bulk of December in Berlin, been seen by Eichendorff at Müller's on the 15th, and by Arndt at Reimer's throughout the month, observed Fr. Wilh. and Luise's return on 23rd, and, provided he left within days after that event, reached Frankfurt/M. around New Year's day, where he could have undertaken a course of therapy of, say, 2-3 weeks with Neufville in Frankfurt/M. before returning to Berlin in early February.[560]

The rigours of travel he would have taken upon himself to see that famous healer—the round trip Berlin-Frankfurt/M.-Berlin amounts to approx. 1,000 km, and travel in a carriage was anything but comfortable—suggests that the *"Ungeheuer,"* perhaps its final-stage symptoms, once more reared its ugly head, and that he avoided therapy closer to home, lest it compromise his plans for Berlin. The trip to Frankfurt/M. smacks of desperation: a finally sally in a losing battle of which the Würzburg journey, ten years prior, had been the opening shot.

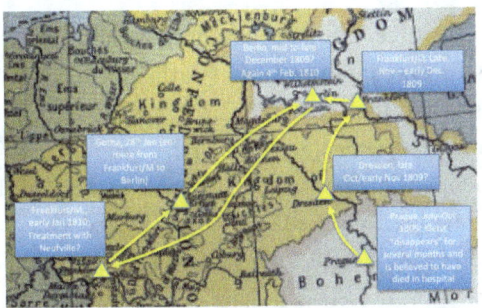

Kleist's Last Journeys: "Return of the King" and "Return of the Monster"?

On 4th February 1810 Kleist settled in Berlin for good, not to leave the city again, brief excursions to nearby places like Potsdam and Frankfurt/O. apart. No doubt his choice of location was tied to the return of the Royals and the political situation: with Vienna in political hibernation following *Schönbrunn*, Berlin became the centre of German politics and even culture, a place where Kleist could hope to find renewed patronage by the court, commercial success (cf. *BA*), and opportunities to exert influence over the King.[561] *Homburg* as we know it squarely belongs into this context: the heart of Prussia once again beat in Berlin, whose vicinity was imbued with Prussian history and memories of Kleist's adolescence (Potsdam is 30 km from Berlin; Fehrbellin, 70 km; Brandenburg/H., 80 km; Frankfurt/O., 90 km). After years of journeying across German and enemy territories, Kleist joined the Prussian Royals, intellectuals and politicians in this pulsating, fermenting "youngest European metropolis," from which Napoleon's demise could perhaps finally be orchestrated.

From Berlin, Kleist writes Ulrike on 19th March:

> Ich habe der Königin, an ihrem Geburtstag, ein Gedicht überreicht, das sie, vor den Augen des ganzen Hofes, zu Tränen gerührt hat; ich kann ihrer Gnade, und ihres guten Willens, etwas für mich zu tun, gewiß sein. Jetzt wird ein Stück von mir, das aus der Brandenburgischen

> Geschichte genommen ist, auf dem Privattheater des Prinzen Radziwil gegeben, und soll nachher auf die Nationalbühne kommen, und, wenn es gedruckt ist, der Königin übergeben werden. (II:833)

Kleist, one last time, throws in his lot with the Prussian King and Queen. As I showed, in my *Emigrant*, the poem to the Queen, to which Kleist refers in the letter (cf. I:33-5), is anything but innocent, and far from complementary towards her, and since in the above letter he mentions the poem and the drama in the same breath, the same may have been true for the drama he looked to dedicate to her. Kleist loved playing a duplicitous game, biting the hand he expected to feed him: this, he seems to have felt, was his poetic licence, a licence that had incented him to become a poet in the first place (there is no such license for an army officer or civil servant). The announced private performance before the Radziwills may suggest that Kleist originally hoped to stage the drama on the occasion of the Queen's 33rd birthday, and when this plan did not materialise, submitted the poem in lieu, while seeking the Radziwills' patronage for the drama's staging.⁵⁶²

If Kleist in March 1810 had a *Homburg* in hand, or under his pen, why did he not turn it into Luise's obituary when she passed away in July? Did he feel that her depiction in the drama (as Natalie) was no longer palatable following her death, or that the drama was no longer timely or pertinent? When in October 1810 he published, in *BA*, the *poem to the King* that police chief Grunder had rejected 18 months earlier (cf. I:32-3; presumably censors considered it less risky now that the King *had* returned), he did he not publish his *poem to the Queen* alongside, and since we have the poem (in three versions), we may conjecture that he did not do so because its insinuation that Fr. Wilh.'s had recklessly left Prussia's fate in Luise's hands would have been extremely inflammatory, offending precisely those members of the broader public he sought to mobilise with his *BA* project, and who were then busily mythifying their Queen. If the 1810 version of *Homburg* contained similar insinuations—say, Nathalie being depicted as unduly influencing Homburg—, he could have withheld it for the same reason.

In the works he published in the immediate aftermath of Luise's death—*Käthchen, Kohlhaas, Bettelweib*—, Kleist cast the Queen in a positive light, perhaps expecting the *dead* Queen to play a more constructive role in the war against Napoleon than the *living* had done, in his view. In *Käthchen* and *Kohlhaas,* he incorporated her "purified" spirit or soul at the eleventh hour, respectively as the reborn Kunigunde (a *Valkyrie*), who spearheads the German insurrection, and as the revenant gypsy (a sibyl), who paves the way for Hohenzollern imperial succession; in *Bettelweib*, he conceived her as *movens* from inception, as the apparition (a Nemesis) that drives the Marchese-Napoleon into self-immolation.

Luise's "purified" spirit: Kunigunde (*Valkyrie*), gypsy (*sibyl*); apparition (Nemesis).

Yet already in the *BA* version of *Cäcilie*, in November 1810, Kleist once again cast Luise's spirit as a destructive force, in the form of the spectral Antonia and her seductive *Catholic* organ music (the *Salve Regina*) that halts the Protestant iconoclasts' (i.e., the northern German insurrectionists') momentum and sways them into surrendering to the Catholic order (i.e., to Napoleon and the Habsburg-Bonapartean dynasty in the process of establishing itself).[563] Kleist's conception of *Cäcilie* could well have coincided with news breaking of Empress Marie-Louise's pregnancy, a connexion that would render the novella's *overt* occasion, the Protestant baptism of the Catholic convert A. Müller's daughter, especially auspicious. His ironic *BA* report, of 23rd December, on Luise's funeral (cf. II:402-3) reinforces the impression that, after a brief interval of perhaps three months in the immediate aftermath of her death, Kleist reverted back to "Queen-bashing"; the extant *Homburg*, including Nathalie's embodiment of Luise's spirit, will have to be read in this context.

When *BA* folded in early 1811, Kleist re-ignated two projects that had been on the back burner during *BA*'s heyday: the second volume of *Erzählungen* and *Homburg*. For the former, he had *Verlobung, Bettelweib*, and the first version of *Cäcilie* in hand, which, however, did not suffice to fill a book; for the latter, he will have been able to draw on earlier research and version(s). Given that on 21st June 1811 Kleist offered Reimer what must have been a substantially revised version of *Homburg*, and on 15th August offered Fouqué another, probably further revised one, while completing the materials for the second vol. of *Erzählungen* in time for its publication at the autumn book fair in August, the period between February and August 1811 was one of the most productive in Kleist's career, generating or completing the revised *Homburg*, the extended *Cäcilie, Findling*, and *Zweikampf*.

During this period Kleist veered back and forth between renewed hope—spurred on by Gneisenau's agitations—that Fr. Wilh. would mobilise and lead a German insurrection, and dread that his King would instead enter an alliance with Napoleon. *Homburg*'s completion, presumably just before 3rd September, essentially coincided with *Zweikampf*'s and came only shortly after *Findling*'s, and we shall evaluate whether Kleist ended his final drama with a scenario more akin to *Findling*'s utopian, or *Zweikampf*'s dystopian one. The King's oscillation in part explains why Kleist had to create such a diverse portfolio of scenarios: the future, even the near-term future, remained wide open as long as Fr. Wilh. procrastinated. This also implies that the *Homburg* Kleist was then working on must have been sufficiently *pescheräic* to permit Kleist, with limited effort, to shape it towards one future or another, to cast and recast its figures as one actual person or another. We thus have the Prussian King to thank for Kleist's extraordinary prolificacy during this period (conversely, then, we also have the King to blame for Kleist's eventual collapse when he believed that the King had decided, and chosen the "wrong" option).

For the *"Reichspatriot"* Kleist, *"vaterländisch"* (II:871) referred to Germany, the *HRR*, as well as Prussia. The drama's patriotic designation, as well as Kleist's bracketed note *"(mit mancherlei Beziehungen),"* aimed at tantalising Reimer, whom he wanted to publish the drama urgently; his ambiguous term *"mancherlei"* ("various") also hinted that those "connections" were complicated, that what *actually* takes place could be at variance with what readers are bound to *assume*. Actual *"connections"* that need to be obscured are best hid among *spurious "connections" that seem obvious*: as a general principle, then, the more obvious a Kleistian "connection," the more likely it is either trivial or fake—a red herring or decoy. Precisely because 17th century Brandenburg's "connection" to 19th century Prussia *is obvious*, we must be prepared for *it representing something else altogether*.[564] *Caveat lector*!

"**Erster Akt. Szene: Fehrbellin.** Ein Garten im altfranzösischen Stil. Im Hintergrund ein Schloß, von welchem eine Rampe herabführt.—Es ist Nacht." In the famous *Battle of Fehrbellin*, in June 1675 a Brandenburgian army under the command of Fr. Wilh. von Brandenburg (aka "The Great Elector") defeated a Swedish army—Sweden was then a major power allied with Louis XIV's France—and thereby laid the foundation for Prussia's rise as great power: only a quarter century later, in 1701, Fr. Wilh.'s son would crown himself King Fr. I of Prussia. Situated 70 km north-west of Berlin and 60 km north of Brandenburg/H., amidst the moors and forests of the Margraviate of Brandenburg, Fehrbellin marks the Brandenburgian heartland of Prussia—"Prussia's guts" (Peter Michalzik).

Alas, Kleist immediately introduces a dissonance or incommensurability into his ur-*"vaterländische"* setting: a "garden in old-French style," in the middle of the barren "markian sands" of Brandenburg? A castle with a "ramp"? In 1750 (i.e., after the period in which Kleist's *overt* story is set) a "castle" of sorts was indeed erected in Fehrbelling, *Schloss Wustrau* (really only a manor), which even has a "ramp" of sorts (really only a staircase), though scarcely one of which it could be said that it *"dehnt sich... / Endlos, bis an das Tor des Himmels aus"* (V.181-2), or that it is made of marble (cf. V.143).

Kleist's grandiose feature is far more commensurate with, say, the Hofburg's massive ramp (though not of marble) or the Château de Fountainebleau's impressive staircase (indeed of marble).[565] I cannot exclude the possibility that *Schloss Wustrau* once featured a "garden in old French style" (it does not today), but at any rate this was irrelevant for Kleist, for even if *he* knew this to have been the case (if he had visited the location), he could scarcely expect that his audience did—leaving them puzzling: *Where are we?*

"**Erster Auftritt. Der Prinz von Homburg** sitzt mit bloßem Haupt und offner Brust, halb wachend halb schlafend, unter einer Eiche und windet sich einen Kranz.—" The first scene's stage direction adds further dissonance and incommensurability: the hero of *Fehrbellin* sits somnambulate underneath a (quintessentially German) oak tree and winds himself an (archetypically Roman) laurel wreath, symbol of victory and glory, of imperial dignity and power, and of poetic achievement. The historical Landgrave Fr. II von Hessen-Homburg had indeed been an ally of Brandenburg's Great Elector during the *Swedish Invasion of Brandenburg* (1674-5); yet by 1806 his small landraviate had been incorporated, as a consequence of Napoleon's mediatisation, into the Grand Duchy of Hesse, a member of the *Rheinbund* and loyal ally not of Brandenburg's successor state, Prussia, but of—France! *Where are we, and who is who?*[566]

The stage direction introduces an extensive cast of characters: *"Der Kurfürst, seine Gemahlin, Prinzessin Natalie, der Graf von Hohenzollern, Rittmeister Golz und andere treten heimlich aus dem Schloß, und schauen, vom Geländer der Rampe, auf ihn nieder.— Pagen mit Fackeln."* The Elector, his wife, his nice Princess Natalie, Count Hohenzollern, and the cavalry captain on top of the "ramp," as if in a theatre's loge, are the audience observing the somnambulate Homburg acting his part on the virtual stage in the garden below, an ensemble that recalls the natural amphitheatres Kleist described repeatedly in earlier letters as well as *Käthchen*'s vehmic court, in which Käthchen is observed by the judges before or above her, from whom she is separated, not by a "ramp," but a "bar," and whose concave cave ceiling, illuminated by "lamps," anticipates *Homburg*'s oak tree's concave crown, illuminated by "torches."

"**in meinem märkschen Sand.**" The wreath's laurel, a mediterranean plant that would scarcely have prospered in the sandy soil of Brandenburg, seems as decidedly out of place as the "endless ramp" and the "garden in old-French style":

> DER KURFÜRST über ihn gebeugt.
> Was für ein Laub denn flicht er?—Laub der Weide?
> HOHENZOLLERN.
> Was Laub der Weid, o Herr!—Der Lorbeer ists,
> Wie ers gesehn hat, an der Helden Bildern,
> Die zu Berlin im Rüstsaal aufgehängt.
> DER KURFÜRST.—Wo fand er den in meinem märkschen Sand?
> HOHENZOLLERN. Das mögen die gerechten Götter wissen!
> DER HOFKAVALIER. Vielleicht im Garten hinten, wo der Gärtner
> Mehr noch der fremden Pflanzen auferzieht. (V.46-53)

It is unlikely that Homburg could have encountered images of Brandenburg Electors featuring laurel wreaths in a Berlin armoury, for since ancient Roman times the laurel wreath was for emperors, and in modern times only Napoleon is depicted thus adorned, so that Homburg plausibly could have seen such imagery only in an armoury in Paris or Rome. His braiding himself a laurel implies not only that he anticipates victory, but also that he aspires to the imperial dignity—a dignity not within the purview of a mere landgrave.

The "garden in the rear, in which the gardener is cultivating further alien plants," could allude to the Hofburg's extensive gardens, in which case the "gardener" represents Franz I, who, having handed over his daughter to Napoleon, is now "cultivating" "further alien plants," i.e., Habsburg-Bonapartean heirs; in March 1811 the first of these "alien plants," Napoléon-Franz, is born, and Kleist may be anticipating more being on their way.[567] Homburg himself, in relation to the audience on top of the ramp, appears like an "alien plant," a displaced figure, mirrored by the German oak amidst the "garden in old-French style," and the Mediterranean laurel transplanted into the Brandenburgian sands (or the Viennese soil). *Where are we, who is who, and who belongs to whose side?*

"**hängt ihm die Kette um.**" The cypher created by The Elector's winding his chain around Homburg's laurel recalls the harnesses, belts, rose garlands, *Gnadenketten*, *Sklavenkettern* and similar props with which elsewhere in Kleist's works characters are tied down, locked up, enchained and enslaved. While the symbolism of the laurel is invariably noted in the Kleist reception, that of the chain is just as invariably ignored or passed over; yet it is the symbolism of the Deleuzean *agencement* of laurel, chain, The Elector's hand, Natalie's hand, and Homburg's head and neck that is eminently Kleistian, not that of the laurel by itself, which is merely conventional.[568] Homburg, Kleist's symbolism suggests, is a tale of misplaced ambition that culminates in enslavement and abjection—a tale of *how The Elector's chain, wrapped around the laurel and conferred by Natalie's hand, ends up around Homburg's neck*. We can see at once that this *po(i)etical* cypher entails *satirical*, *satyrical* and *syphilitical* connotations: laurel = the *promises* of victory and imperial dignity, of erotic *jouissance* and poetic fame; chain = the *banes* of political submission, syphilitic symptoms and mercury poisoning.

The first scene's setting, together with its repetition in the final scene, frames the storyline and its sub-plots as a *mise en abîme*: "*Szene: Schloß, mit der Rampe, die in den Garten hinabführt; wie im ersten Akt.—Es ist wieder Nacht*" (V.1830). In the drama's ending, darkness has once again fallen across the land, and Homburg is once again sitting beneath the oak tree, this time not in a trance but blindfolded, so that the darkness for him appears even starker than in the opening scene: "*Der Prinz von Homburg wird... mit verbundenen Augen durch das untere Gartengitter aufgeführt*" (V.1830); only the shine of the torches still dimly penetrates his pupils. Kleist's final drama thus ends with its protagonist descending into perpetual darkness and "seeing" only shadows he, like the prisoners in Plato's cave to whom Kleist no doubt alludes, takes as representing *The Real*. It is in this state that Homburg speaks his famous lines, "*Nun, o Unsterblichkeit, bist du ganz mein! / Du strahlst mir, durch die Binde meiner Augen, / Mit Glanz der tausendfachen Sonne zu!*" (V.1830-2). Homburg apparently envisions himself passing, through death, into a life on another planet. Only when Stranz tells him, "*Die Augen bloß will ich dir wieder öffnen*" (V.1849), but instead of removing his blindfold, merely "opens" his *mind* to his enslavement, does Homburg realise that he is still on this Earth—and promptly swoons. The correct answer to Homburg's famous question, "*Ist es ein Traum?*" (V.1856), can only be: "*Ein Albtraum, was sonst?*" Horst Häker's "*preußischer Sommernachtstraum*" is really Prussia's "*Winternachtsalbtraum*": the nightmare of her perpetual winter, to which Homburg here awakens.[569] *Heil! Heil! Heil!*

As already in *Zweikampf*, we encounter in *Homburg* an all-powerful patriarch—there The Emperor, here The Elector—who, with an exceptional gesture, sets in motion a development that inescapably fulfils itself in the course of the story: The Emperor's issuance of an ad-hoc *act* ("*Legitimationsakte*"; II:229); The Elector's issuance of an ad-hoc *cypher*: as Homburg sits beneath the oak tree in his trance, braiding himself his wreath, The Elector, having stepped down the ramp, "*nimmt ihm den Kranz aus der Hand; der Prinz errötet und sieht ihn an. Der Kurfürst schlingt seine Halskette um den Kranz und gibt ihn der Prinzessin; der Prinz steht lebhaft auf. Der Kurfürst weicht mit der Prinzessin, welche den Kranz erhebt, zurück; der Prinz mit ausgestreckten Armen, folgt ihr*" (V.65). The Elector's gesture of intertwining his chain with Homburg's laurel inexorably ties the victory Homburg shall attain in the impending battle to his, The Elector's, grace. His handing this thoroughly overdetermined cypher to Natalie turns the princess into the transformation's conduit: her erotic desirability makes her at once the bone of contention and the connective tissue between Homburg and the Elector, whose joint fate is henceforth mediated by her, her structural role mirroring Littegarde's in *Zweikampf*.[570]

In the final scene, "*Der Kurfürst gibt den Kranz, an welchem die Kette hängt, der Prinzessin, nimmt sie bei der Hand und führt sie die Rampe herab. Herren und Damen folgen. Die Prinzessin tritt, umgeben von Fackeln, vor den Prinzen, welcher erstaunt aufsteht; setzt ihm den Kranz auf, hängt ihm die Kette um, und drückt seine Hand an ihr Herz. Der Prinz fällt in Ohnmacht*" (V.1851). *Homburg* consists in a concatenation of *hand-overs*: Homburg's *hand* braids the laurel wreath, passes it into The Elector's *hand*, which winds the chain around it and passes the assembly into Natalie's *hand*; via its exchange with the *glove* as pledge and shibboleth (cf. V.70), which Homburg's *hand* drops before everyone's eyes and which The Elector's *hand* picks up (cf. V.347) and leaves on Natalie's "table" (cf. V.1279), presumably in exchange for it, the cypher finds its way back into the Elector's *hand* (cf. V.1845), and thence into Natalie's *hand*, which completes the circulation by disassembling the intertwined items and by putting the wreath on Homburg's *head*, and the chain around his *neck*:

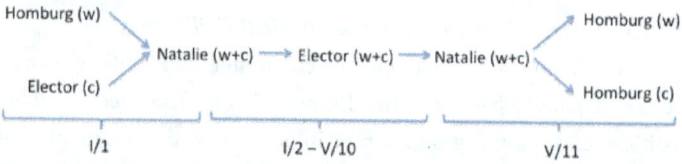

The drama's underlying movement is thus crystallised in the two stage directions I quoted: in I/1, Homburg's wreath (w) and the Elector's chain (c) are *assembled* and put into Natalie's *hand*, whence they pass to the Elector's *hand*; in V/11, they revert into Natalie's *hand* where they are *disassembled*, the "minimal difference" compared to the starting configuration being that the chain is not returned to the Elector's *hand*, but put around Homburg's *neck*. The drama's plot, at its most essential level, can be represented thus:

$$\begin{array}{cc} \text{Elector (c)} \longrightarrow & \text{Homburg (c)} \\ \text{I/1} & \text{V/11} \end{array}$$

The laurel merely serves as vehicle or substrate onto which The Elector hitches the chain; while the laurel's placement on Homburg's *head* suggests that he is overtly granted the glory of victory, the chain's concurrent placement around his *neck* makes clear that he is thus decorated as The Elector's vassal.

We already know what Kleist's *Gnadenkette* oder *Sklavenkette* signifies—cf. *Zweikampf*, *Amphitryon*: Homburg is *enslaved* by The Elector, as is Trota by The Emperor, and Amphitryon by Jupiter. In all cases the object of desire—Natalie, Littegarde, Alkmene (i.e., *Borussia* or *Germania*)—is *promised* to a hero who is *castrated*, disabled from effectively "owning" it. Trota is castrated in his duel with Rotbart, while Homburg, like Amphitryon, self-castrates, for in the final scene he fails to recover the "sword" he previously unbuckled (cf. V.788). His self-castration explains why he exhorts

Natalie to enter a convent and adopt a son (or "buy" a lover—cf. V.1045-7).[571] Homburg is reduced to serving as eunuch, or *"bottom,"* in the Elector's harem, or *"dungeon"*: perhaps the worst fate Kleist could imagine, worse than death.[572]

Homburg may be thought of as an *essaie* on Hegel's *master-slave* dialectic, according to which *the master constitutes himself as master by the same movement by which the slave constitutes himself as slave*.[573] Only Homburg's *insistence* that he be condemned to death, confirming that he considers the *Law of the Master* (Kleist: *"Kriegsrecht"*) to be absolute, allows The Elector to fulfil his destiny of *becoming-master*, and thereby Homburg to fulfil his destiny of *becoming-slave*. Hegel's twin poles of *becoming-master* and *becoming-slave* are as intimately and inexorably bound up with each other as are Kleist's "+" and "-," whose interplay anticipates Hegel's dialectical movement. Had Homburg reneged against the law, or the Elector complied with the soldiers' request to pardon Homburg, their relationship would have remained non-dialectical and contingent; only by Homburg's *voluntarily* submitting to the Elector's *Law* are both of them, in Hegelian terms, *"aufgehoben"* ("sublimated").

Kleist's *Über den Zustand der Schwarzen in Amerika* (*BA*, January 1811) provided the template for *Homburg*'s Hegelian movement: the slaves in Suriname are so embedded into, and corrupted by, the very *system* of slavery, that instead of seeking to break free, they strive to uphold the very rules and mechanisms that perpetuate their bondage and render the colonialists' lordship absolute. In the same vein, Homburg is now so utterly under the Elector's sway that instead of rebelling against his *system* of hegemony, he embraces the very law that perpetuates it. Whether or not Kleist in *Penthesilea* parodied the "world spirit on horseback" that Hegel pictured seeing Napoleon pass beneath his window at Jena, in *Homburg* he evidently adopts a Hegelian dialectical movement that culminates in Homburg's complete sublimation under the Elector's sway.[574] Nietzsche: *"Wer mit Ungeheuern kämpft, mag zusehn, dass er nicht dabei zum Ungeheuer wird. Und wenn du lange in einen Abgrund blickst, blickt der Abgrund auch in dich hinein."*[575]

"**Scene: Berlin. Lustgarten.**" In *Zweikampf* the action moves from the Emperor's seat at Worms via several knightly castles to the Schlossplatz at Basel, where the duel takes place, before retracing the same route back to Worms—a zooming in and out that recalls *Marionettentheater*'s "*das Bild des Hohlspiegels, nachdem es sich in das Unendliche entfernt hat, plötzlich wieder dicht vor uns tritt*" (II:345):

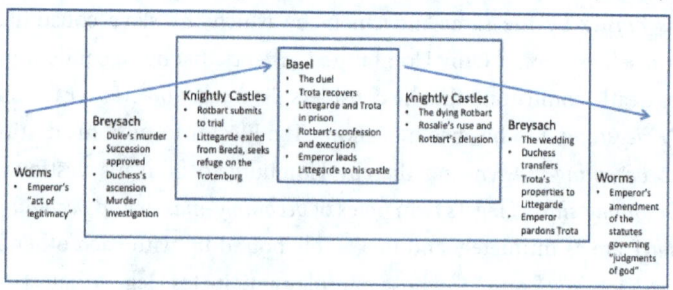

Plot structures I: Zooming in and out, *Zweikampf* [source: my *Emigrant*].

In *Homburg*, the action similarly reverts to its origin, this time by tracing a figure 8, whose start- and end-point is Fehrbellin Castle's ramp:

> [START] Fehrbellin Castle's ramp (I/1-4)
> => hall within the castle (I/5-6) (H)
> => battlefield near Fehrbellin (II/1-2) (B)
> => room in a village ((II/3-8) (R)
> => *Lustgarten* before Berlin Castle (II/9-10) (L)
> => Fehrbellin prison (III/1-2) (P)
> => The Electress'; The Elector's; Natalie's room (III/3- IV/2) (E); (E); (N)
> => Fehrbellin prison (IV/3-4) (P)
> => hall within the castle (V/1-9) (H)
> => Fehrbellin Castle's ramp (V/10-11) [END]

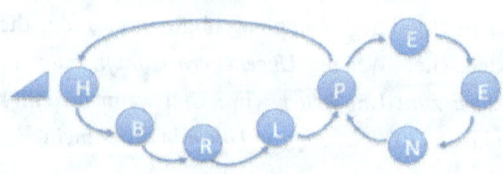

Plot structures II: Figure 8, *Homburg*.[576]

Both plot structures are anchored in two locations, the patriarch's seat of power (Fehrbellin Castle, Worms Castle) and the public space where his law is administered (Berlin's Lustgarten, Basel's Schlossplatz). The extant *Homburg*'s carefully designed plot structure suggests that it was produced in one piece, probably reasonably quickly (at 1858 lines it is among Kleist's shorter dramas); its close parallels with *Zweikampf*'s imply that Kleist's two final works were produced alongside each other, as if in an intimate dialogue with each other.

Homburg, satirically

The parallels between *Homburg* and *Zweikampf* extend to their respective character line-ups. *Zweikampf*'s The Emperor and *Homburg*'s The Elector are quasi interchangeable with respect to their structural roles as master and mastermind; the latter is more directly involved in the action, while the former, for the most part, remains back-stage, intervening only in critical moments.[577] This exchangeability suggests that The Elector represents none other than Napoleon—a daring hypothesis that turns the drama's "consensus reading" on its head: if The Elector = Napoleon, then Brandenburg = French Empire ≠ Prussia, and the "all-too-obvious" association of Brandenburg with Prussia is, then, *precisely wrong*. Brandenburg, in Kleist's drama, represents not Prussia but France; Brandenburg's most illustrious ruler, not the Prussian King, but the French Emperor.

"Das F; sein Zeichen!—" Homburg acknowledges The Elector's *imperial* majesty: *"Friedrich! Mein Fürst! Mein Vater!"* (V.67); *"der Kurfürst, mit der Stirn des Zeus"* (V.158); *"O Cäsar Divus!"* (V.713). The drama's references to oriental or Roman despots—the Dei of Algier, the Dei of Tunis, Sardanapalus, the *"Altrömische Tyrannenreihe"*—, frequently noted in the Kleist reception with bewilderment, is intelligible in reference to Napoleon; the *"Mamluks"* (cf. V.98) were an elite cavalry squadron of Napoleon's Imperial Guard.[578] The subplot of The Elector escaping death by swapping his horse—a grey, naturally (cf. V.540)—, while taken from Kleist's historical sources (cf. I:950-1), could well have been one of the many myths about

Napoleon and his mount that circulated in Kleist's day; Kleist's much-discussed associating The Elector with Lucius Junius Brutus, usurper (!) of the royal throne, and first ever consul (!) of Rome, who famously condemned his own sons to death when they joined the *Tarquinian Conspiracy*, of 509 BC, that sought to re-install the monarchy, clearly points to Napoleon, First Consul of the *RF*, who made short thrift of conspirators, and whose penchant for the "*kurulsche Stuhl*" (V.779), seated on which Brutus is frequently depicted, I already discussed.[579] The Elector is not "mythically elevated" (Franz M. Eybl, *Kleist-Lektüren*, 231), but simply represents the world's most powerful man, whose monogram, appropriately, is not *FW* or *FrW* (which it would be if it was in line with his namesakes', Fr. Wilh. II and Fr. Wilh. III), but *F* (cf. V.1318): *F* as in France, *F* as in ithyphallic *erastês* (cf. *Marquise*'s Count F).

"im Garten hinten." Napoleon's favourite residence was Fontainebleau, 55 km south-east of Paris, and Kleist's "*Lustgarten*" denotes not the Hofburg's Burggarten, nor Berlin's Lustgarten, but the gardens of the Château de Fontainebleau, which indeed features not only a prominent marble staircase, but also extensive "gardens in the old French style":

"*Die Rampe dehnt sich... / Endlos, bis an das Tor des Himmels aus...!*"

The courier's conjecture concerning the laurel's provenance, "*Vielleicht im Garten hinten, wo der Gärtner / Mehr noch der fremden Pflanzen auferzieht*" (V.52-3), is plausible: not only would *laurus nobilis* prosper more readily in Fontainebleau's gardens than in Vienna's, but also does the "gardener" Franz, who "cultivates further foreign plants" (presumably trans-planted from Spanish, Italian, Illyrian, Dutch and German soils), grow a Bonaparte-Habsurgian dynasty, and a neo-Carolingian Empire, centred on Paris, not Vienna.⁵⁸⁰ The stark choice The Elector-Napoleon offers Homburg before his castle's gate, "*Ins Nichts, mit dir zurück, Herr Prinz von Homburg, / Ins Nichts, ins Nichts!*" (V.74-5), in this light is eminently apposite: outside of his rapidly expanding "garden," there will soon be—*nothing*.

"In Staub mit allen Feinden Brandenburgs!" *Homburg* is Kleist's most daring, surprising and shocking work: everyone is compelled to read it as the bard's *hymn* to his fatherland, whereas in fact it is its *swansong* or *requiescat in pace*: "*DER PRINZ VON HOMBURG faltet, in ihrem Anschaun verloren, die Hände*" (V.1062). If The Elector = Napoleon, then Brandenburg's enemies = the French Empire's enemies, and the drama's famous final line must be "*trans.*" *satirically* as: "*In Staub mit allen Feinden Frankreichs!*" Kleist's *Fehrbellin* marks not the beginning of Prussia's and Germany's liberation, but the completion of their subjugation, and in the final scene, Napoleon's German vassals are singing the anthem, not of their *old* fatherland, but of their *new* one: the *Chant du depart*, the seventh line of whose first stanza goes: "*Tremblez ennemis de la France!*"

Delicious ironies abound with respect to *Homburg*'s reception: in the later 19th century, Kleist's The Elector—embodying Napoleon!—came to be celebrated as the most patriotic of depictions of the Prussian hero; already in 1828 L. Robert, discussing *Homburg* in a newspaper article, knows of "*keine vaterländische Hymne, die sich mit dem einfachen und erhabenen Monolog des großen Churfürsten messen könnte*" (if Kleist did *read* passages of the drama to him, as Robert claims, he evidently did not *explain* them to him (cf. *LS*,159a).⁵⁸¹ Little did the German nationalists of the 1870s, or the Nazi propagandists of the 1930s, realise that by appropriating the oh-so-fatherlandish *Homburg*, they were adopting for their propaganda purposes the story of a wretched Germany's subjugation, and of the "French disease"'s proliferation, dished up by a cosmopolitan homosexual. Ha! Ha!

"**Der Prinz von Homburg... halb schlafend.**" The prince, who so somnambulately walks straight into his enslavement, is of course the same Fr. Wilh. whom Kleist in his previous drama called upon to "out-falcon" Napoleon, merely differently "charged": as Hermann, "supercharged," as Homburg, "discharged." Homburg-Fr. Wilh.'s *potential*—typical for Kleistian "larval subjects"—to reverse his polarity by re- or dis-charging (cf. Gustav's momentarily turning into August, and Kohlhaas into an avatar of the archangel Michael), is demonstrated when he is triggered into attack-mode by an artillery salvo (cf. II/2), and once again when he momentarily transforms, during the hiatus opened up by the *canard* of the Elector's death, into a fiery archangel who, flaming sword-penis in hand, claims the vacated throne (cf. II/6). "Homburg" is near-homophone with "*Humbug*" ("hokum"), and a mere eighteen months after depicting his King as hero and true souvereign ("*Herr-Mann*": Barbara Vinken), an evidently resigned Kleist portrays him as lowliest of subordinates ("*Cavalleriehauptmann*": Dirk Grathoff). Homburg-Fr. Wilh.'s "*Friedrich! Mein Fürst! Mein Vater*" (V.67)—"Hail Napoleon! Hail my Emperor! Hail my Master!"—in the first scene is merely echoed by the German vassalls' "*Heil! Heil! Heil!*" in final scene.[582]

Homburg's autonomous decision-making in battle may well reference broadly similar situations the historical Fr. II von Hessen-Homburg and Prince Louis Ferd. von Preußen found themselves in (references frequently cited in the *Kleist-Forschung*); yet it belongs to those "*mancherlei Beziehungen*" that are spurious: what Kleist is really insinuating is Fr. Wilh.'s rapidly advancing "Francofication," for autonomous decision-making is a hallmark, not of the *Frederician,* but of the *Napoleonic* officer. If prior to the battle Homburg-Fr. Wilh. still clung to *Frederician* principles, as his obscure comment "*Diktieren in die Feder macht mich irr*" indicates (V.421; written dispatches on the battlefield were among Napoleon's innovations), in the heat of the battle he acts in accordance with *Napoleonic* principles, and in doing so decides the battle in The Elector-Napoleon's favour.[583] The battle is the cauldron or kiln in which the vassal Homburg is forged.

The Elector-Napoleon on his part hesitates whether to judge Homburg-Fr. Wilh.'s insubordination in accordance with the *Frederician* system hitherto "proper" to him (*"auf märkische Weise"*; V.1419), or in accordance with his own, *Napoleonic* principles. In the first case he would have to condemn Fr. Wilh. to death; in the second, decorate him for his courage. By offering Homburg the choice between requesting pardon and accepting the verdict, he puts him to the test: does his new apprentice still cling to the *Frederician* system, whose enlightened absolute ruler (*"oberste Gnadeninstanz"*: Alex. von Bornmann) may grant pardon, or does he grasp the *Napoleonic* one, based on rule of law and due process, in which pardon by fiat is abolished as a matter of principle?[584] Having observed Homburg's "Francofication" in relation to his *system of warfare*, The Elector's "test drive" (Avital Ronell) now investigates his "conversion" in relation to his *system of governance*—and thus his overall readiness for enslavement. Homburg passes the test: by choosing acceptance over pardon he graduates as the Emperor's favourite apprentice, and the French Empire's most faithful servant. His "conversion" is mirrored by his mount's colour changing from black (cf. V.380; the Prussian and Holy Roman eagles) to golden chestnut (cf. V.744; Napoleon's eagle).

"Das Vaterland, das du uns gründetest." Whereas Kleist lets the reader witness the "coversions," respectively, of *Cäcilie*'s Mother and *Zweikampf*'s Littegarde, that of *Homburg*'s Natalie is already effected in the opening scene, when she appears on the ramp as member of The Elector's entourage. When Homburg renounces her, *"Nataliens... / Begehr ich gar nicht mehr, in meinem Busen / Ist alle Zärtlichkeit für sie verlöscht"* (V.1024-6), he does so in the recognition that she has already been lured to the "dark side:" the *"Vaterland... Mit Zinnen, üppig,"* whose founding Natalie praises, and whose destiny she glorifies (cf. V.1131-8), refers not to the German or Austrian, but to the French Empire. Horst Häker's conclusion regarding Natalie's much-debated association with Luise (*Kleist*, 84), *"Aber so sympathisch der Gedanke ist, Natalie trage die Züge der Königin, wird man doch nicht annehmen dürfen, Kleist habe die*

Unklugheit begangen, sie bewußt so auszustatten—weder zu Lebzeiten der Königin noch nach ihrem Tode hätte ihm derartiges in den Sinn kommen können," is misguided in so far as Kleist represented the Queen in such a way repeatedly, both before and after her death.[585] Still, by the summer of 1811 Queen Luise had been dead for a year, and all the submissive, instrumentalised female figures in his late works no longer embody pure Luise-figures but compounds of *Borussia* (Luise's spirit), *Austria* (Marie-Louise and her son), and *Germania* (the German people, the *HRR*'s legacy): handmaids of Napoleon, known to their peers, with Margaret Atwood, simply as "*Ofbonaparte*."

"**Stallmeister.**" Not only is Homburg's *black* replaced by a *golden chestnut*, but also is The Elector's *grey* by Froben's *sorrel*. Hans Jürgen Scheuer (*KH*,191) has shown that Kleist's equine coat colours correspond to heraldic tinctures:[586]

Mount (equine coat colour):	Corresponding heraldic tincture:
Homburg's *Rappe* (black)	*Sable* (black)
Homburg's *Goldfuchs* (golden chestnut)	*Or* (gold)
Elector's *Schimmel* (white or grey)	*Argent* (silver or white)
Stallmeister/Elector's *Fuchs* (sorrel)	*Gules* (red) and *Or* (gold)

If the replacement of Homburg's *black* by a *golden chestnut* reflects his conversion to Napoleon's vasall, then what is symbolised by The Elector's *grey*'s "red-shift"? I offer that Kleist's equine transformations symbolise the twin movements of *consolidation* of the French Empire and *legitimisation* of Napoleon's dynastic rule: the *Sable* of the German and Prussian eagles becomes the *Or* of Napoleon's eagle, the Bourbons' *Agent* becomes the Habsburgs '*Gules* and the Bonapartes' *Or*. Kleist may well have anticipated that Napoleon would create himself a composite coat of arms, akin to those adopted by other Bonapartean rulers, integrating the blazons of their acquired kingdoms with Napoleon's standard:

FLTR: Joseph, King of Spain; Louis, King of Holland; Jérôme, King of Westphalia, Eugène, Vice-Roy of Italy, Murat, Grand-Duke of Berg (till 1808), Murat, King of Naples (from 1808).

A hypothetical composite of Napoleon's personal standard and the Habsburg's coat of arms ("*Or*, a lion rampant *gules* armed langued and crowned *azure*") could perhaps be, in a layman's conception, as follows:

FLTR: the arms of Napoleon I; those of the House of Habsburg; a hypothetical composite standard of a Habsburg-Bonapartean emperor.

Stallmeister Froben (whose hobby is evidently gardening) represents Franz, his handing over his horse to the Elector (cf. V.664-5), his marrying his daughter to Napoleon.[587] The curious transaction by which Froben "bought" the Elector's *grey* with much *gold* in London (cf. V.657-8) becomes intelligible if London = Vienna, where with *Schönbrunn* Napoleon's "red-shift" began, culminating in Napoléon Franz's birth in March 1811. Kleist, in his final drama, no longer casts the Austrian Emperor (whom in *Zweikampf* he lets die, as Rotbart, an agonising death); only his *voice* still appears. The *master of horses* Napoleon reigns supreme, while the Austrian "*Stallmeister*" ("equerry") is reduced to helping him onto his mount (cf. the German idiom "*jemandem den Steigbügel halten*," literally "to hold the stirrup for someone," which means "to aid someone in their career progression").[588]

"Was ergriff er da?" Count Hohenzollern's ambivalent role in the unfolding drama has been recognised in the Kleist reception.[589] He speaks the drama's first, and, jointly with others, its final verses, and orchestrates Homburg's fateful encounter with The Elector that sets in motion the drama's events: as the reader finds out in passing (cf. V.1714-15), it was Count H who invited the Elector to descend the ramp into the garden where Homburg is sitting underneath the oak, and who called to The Elector's attention that Homburg failed to join the cavalry detachment as ordered (cf. V.21). While aparently seeking to excuse him, Count H insinuates Homburg's confusion (cf. V.39) and intoxication with ambition (cf. V.28), in relation to the forthcoming battle (cf. V.56), thereby overdetermining Homburg's first impression on The Elector (and on the audience). Count H claims the drama's *Meinungshoheit*: his "*Traumdeutung*" (Freud) becomes the "régime of truth" (Foucault) that shapes the Elector's course of action. Critically, his oblique references to "*Mädchen*" and "*Haube*" ("bonnet"; "*Unter die Haube kommen*," colloquially "to get married") incite The Elector to assemble the *agencement* of laurel, chain and hands, creating the cypher whose acquisition Count H then artfully couples with Homburg's joining the Elector's side (cf. V.75). Although Kleist leaves this open, it could well have been Count H who orchestrated the entire opening scene, compelled Homburg to take his seat underneath the oak, furnished him with the laurel from the castle's garden, and, under a suitable pretext, enticed the Elector to step onto the ramp where he could not fail to behold Homburg, thus catalysing the entire movement that culminates in Homburg-Fr. Wilh.'s enslavement.

William C. Reeve deserves credit for clearly articulating Count H's role:

> Hohenzollern, a unique dramatic catalyst, not only initiates *all* the major actions, hence governing more of the story line than any other single individual, but manipulates consciously or unconsciously both the Prince and the Elector without ostensibly becoming directly involved himself. (*Power*, 113)

Count H remains the drama's *éminence grise*, whose subtle interventions progress his agenda of bringing Homburg into the Elector's fold; he:

- conspires with The Elector in drawing Homburg into the battle (I/3);
- distracts Homburg when he beholds Natalie's glove, a tell-tale sign that could objectify Homburg's dream and "awaken" him (cf. V.1669) (I/4);
- placates The Elector when Homburg ignores his orders (cf. V.495), knowing that it will play into The Elector's hands (I/5);
- informs Homburg that The Elector is about to sign his death sentence,   links the sentence to Natalie, and proposes the conversation with The Electress that precipitates Homburg's beholding his grave, encountering Natalie and submitting to the Elector (III/1);
- in the decicive moment softens The Elector's intransigence by producing a second memo in Homburg's favour (cf. V.1622) (V/5).

Colonel Kottwitz is almost Count H's counterdraft: unwaveringly loyal to Homburg, he evidently pursues no agenda on his own; his memorandum in Homburg's defence, although dismissed by Homburg (cf. V.1740-5), ultimately convinces The Elector to let the Prince live, saving his life, but also inadvertently precipitating his enslavement. I offer that Count H represents Hardenberg, whose diplomatic shenenigans precipitate Prussia's demise; that the loyal Kottwitz enacts Gneisenau (in a typical Kleistian aside, Kottwitz curses the plague not with the German exclamation "*uff,*" but the French "*ouf,*" V.368, denoting the "disease" as "French"); and that The Elector's loyal aide, Dörfling, embodies Berthier.[590]

"Frei ist sie, wie das Reh auf Heiden." At the time of writing, the last battles with Napoleon—*Aspern* and *Wagram*—lay almost two years in the past. *Homburg*'s battle, therefore, is scenaric, set in the (near) future. As of early September 1811, Napoleon's only remaining rivals were Britain and Russia, and since after *Trafalgar* he could no longer invade Britain, while Britain, though managing to defend Portugal, could seriously challenge him on the Continent, Russia became his main rival. The alliance he had established with Tsar Alex. at *Tilsit*, and cemented at *Erfurt*, in the course of 1810 became increasingly strained: the *Continental System* economically affected France and her allies, including Russia, at least as much as it did Britain, who could redirect trade towards her colonies, and when Napoleon annexed Holland and the northern German port cities against the Tsar's wishes, Alex. withdraw Russia from the system.[591] Gerhard Schulz, referring to the spring and summer of 1811, notes perceptively (*Kleist*, 511-2), "*Die Spannungen zwischen Frankreich und Rußland hatten in diesen Monaten zugenommen, und ein neuer Krieg drohte, in dem Napoleon Preußen entweder annihilieren oder für den er es auf seine Seite ziehen konnte,*" but fails to link his succinct analysis of the political context to *Homburg*, for which it is eminently pertinent. Throughout the summer of 1811 Europe was on the brink of a war, and Prussia found herself between the "rock" of putting herself under Napoleon's command and the "hard place" of siding with Russia, either way risking annihilation. Kleist describes her predicament thus: *"Frei ist sie, wie das Reh auf Heiden"* (V.1026). Reduced, since *Tilsit* and *Paris*, to a modest kingdom of five million citizens, with a nominal standing army, Prussia is that nominally "*frei*" ("free") but effectively "*vogelfrei*" ("fair game") and "*todgeweiht*" ("fey") a deer on the heath (cf. below map, yellow: Prussia) on the cusp of being crushed between the Napoleonic wolf (blue: French Empire and client states) and the Russian bear:

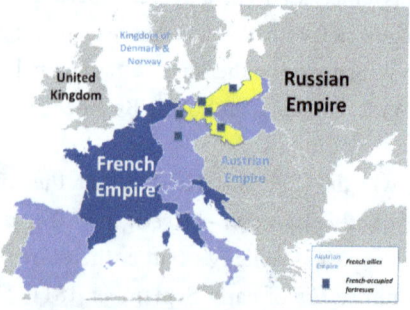

"Frei ist sie, wie das Reh auf Heiden": Prussia's Strategic Situation, September 1811.

This is the context in which *Homburg* narrates the scenario of a somnambulant Fr. Wilh. (Homburg), edged on by Hardenberg (Count F), joins Napoleon (The Elector) in his war against Russia (Sweden), thereby saving Prussia from annihilation, but submitting her to perennial servitude.[592]

"der Brückenkopf am Rhyn." In the historical *Battle of Fehrbellin* (1675), the Swedes crossed the river Rhyn, a modest tributary to the river Havel that traverses the Brandenburgian landscape of moors, carrs and forests in east-westerly direction. The Brandenburgians confronted them on the river's south bank and, due in part to Homburg's intervention, managed to push them back across the river; the heavy casualties they sustained in their disorderly retreat into the moors straddling the river's north bank compelled the Swedes to abandon their invasion of Brandenburg. As he had done with the AD 9 battle in *Hermannsschlacht*, Kleist in *Homburg* uses the AD 1675 battle as model for his simulation of a future battle pitting Napoleon's *Grande Armée* (The Elector's Brandenburgians) and his Prussian allies (Homburg's Hessians) against Alex.'s Russians (the Swedes).[593]

A hindsight view of Napoleon's *Invasion of Russia* of 1812 (the turning point in the *Napoleonic Wars*, which Kleist sadly did not live to compose paeans for) shows Kleist's 1811 simulation to have been clairvoyant: it correctly anticipates Prussia becoming the key deployment zone for the *Grande Armée*'s mobilisation against Russia (in the same manner in which, in 1809, Bavaria was for the *Ad'A*'s advance against Austria). Although in 1812 the Russians, instead of launching a pre-emptive sally into East Prussian territory, as Kleist's scenario predicts, yield and drew the *Grande Armée* deep into Russian territory, Kleist's scenario of the Russians (the Swedes in his simulation) advancing first, was eminently plausible (the Prussians had done so in the *War of the Fourth Coalition*, and the Austrians in the *War of the Fifth Coalition*).[594]

The following map shows the point, near Kovno, at which on 24th/25th June 1812 Napoleon and the bulk of the *Grande Armée*, the greatest army ever assembled (estimates range between 420,000 and 600,000 men, of which perhaps half provided by German, Polish and other allies), crossed the Neman (Memel) river, the boundary between the French client state, Duchy of Warsaw, and Russia:

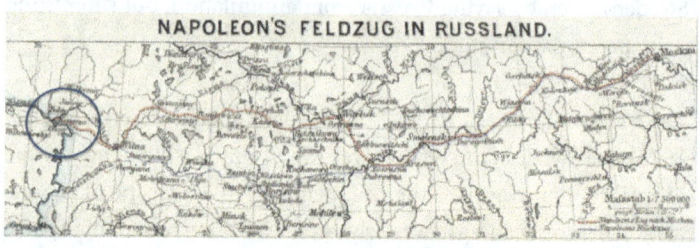

"*der Brückenkopf am Rhyn*" (I): the *Grande Armée* on
24th/25th June 1812 crosses the Neman.

Charles Minard's famous graph of the advancing *Grande Armée*'s rapid shrinkeage en route to Moscow between June and September 1812, among other things conveys the massive *scale* of the invasion force assembled along the Neman, 2-3 times the size of the British invasion force at Boulogne in 1803/4:

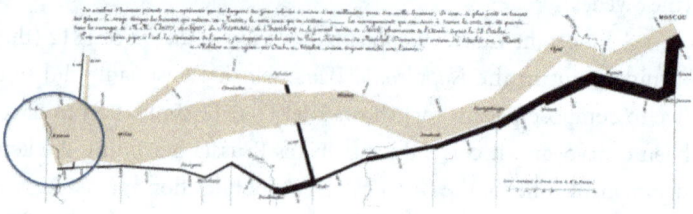

"*der Brückenkopf am Rhyn*" (II): the *Grande Armée,* from Prussia to Russia.

As Kleist predicted, the chief deployment zone for this massive invasion army was East Prussia (light blue):

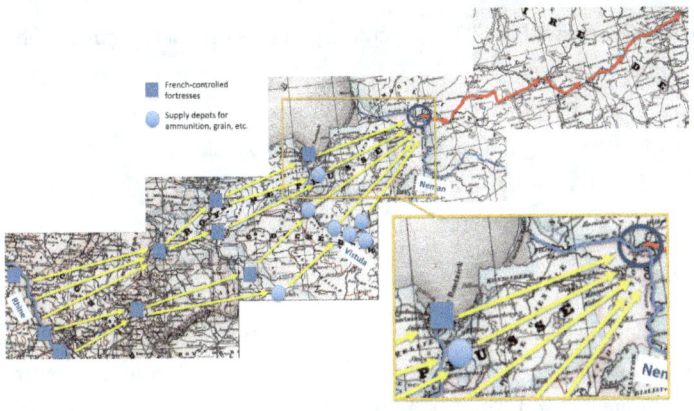

"*der Brückenkopf am Rhyn*" (III): East Prussia as the
Grande Armée's chief deployment zone.⁵⁹⁵

No doubt the topographical detail of the river crossing was among the items that made the historical *Battle of Fehrbellin* so compelling a model for Kleist's simulation: in the Swedish invasion of 1675, the Rhyn was of similar strategic importance as the Neman was to be in the expected Russian attack.⁵⁹⁶

Instead of a protracted and costly French *Invasion of Russia*, Kleist anticipates a Russian advance into East Prussia that is soon arrested by the *Grande Armée* and turned into a quasi-repetition of *Friedland*, only that this time Prussia fights on the side of France, not Russia. As I noted before, Kleist appears to have systematically underestimated Tsar Alex. and Russia: it could have been clearer to him that Alex. was a smart operator—after defeat at *Austerlitz*, he safely withdrew and left it to Franz II to negotiate a peace with Napoleon, and after defeat at *Friedland*, he negotiated terms at *Tilsit* that were much more damaging to Prussia than Russia—, and that for all her backwardness (and in part *because* of it), Russia was extremely difficult to conquer. Alas, neither Kleist nor Napoleon fathomed that the Russians would simply evade major battles and let topography, climate, a large and hardy population, scorched-earth and *rasputitsa* defeat the grandest of armies—a miscalculation that may have been as fatal for Kleist as it would turn out to be for Napoleon: had Kleist in the autumn of 1811 anticipated that Napoleon would fail in Russia, he might have chosen to live.⁵⁹⁷

"das Gesetz will ich." The Elector articulates the basic premise of his military strategy:

> Den Sieg nicht mag ich, der, ein Kind des Zufalls,
> Mir von der Bank fällt; das Gesetz will ich,
> Die Mutter meiner Krone, aufrecht halten,
> Die ein Geschlecht von Siegen mir erzeugt! (V.1566-9)

Miltary success, for Napoleon, is the function of a system or "law" that automates a "genealogy of victories" by eliminating every contingency and foreclosing any interference by "glacial erratics" such as Fr. Wilh.[598] When Homburg cheers him on, *"Geh und bekrieg, o Herr, und überwinde / Den Weltkreis"* (V.1798-9), he signals that he has understood, and come to accept, the superiority of Napoleon's *scientific warfare*, acknowledging that erratic heroes like himself no longer play a role in the future of warfare, unless they become incorporated into the *war machine*.

With his third monologue (cf. V.1830-9), the blindfolded Fr. Wilh., under the illusion that his soul is about to depart for a new life, is in fact initiated into the *Grande Armée*, on the brink of war with Russia: he who is immortal and glares like a thousandfold sun is, of course, Napoleon, and Homburg's famous line, *"Nun, o Unsterblichkeit, bist du ganz mein!"* (V.1830), marks the moment in which Fr. Wilh. applies to join his *Garde Impériale*, widely known as *"Les Immortels."*[599] The staccato of the final cannon salvo (cf. V.1853), and of the officers' *"Heil! Heil! Heil!"* (V.1854), hammers *"Napoleon's Law"* into his sedated brain, until he becomes pure puppet, akin to Ken Kesey's McMurphy following his lobotomy and George Orwell's Winston Smith following his re-education in "Room 101." Thus "cured" of his erratic behaviour, Fr. Wilh. joins Napoleon's ranks:

> ALLE.   In Staub mit allen Feinden Frankreichs!
> *Ende.*

"Ende" marks not only the end of this (hi)story: it marks *the end of history as such*—and with it, *of Kleist's poetry.*

Napoleon expands his territory deep into Russia, introducing the Asiatic gillyflower (*matthiola*; cf. V.1841-2) into his "garden" of French violas and German carnations, turning his Empire into an Eurasian one. The "girl" said to have planted this exotic flower into his garden—is her name not Borussia?[600] Stranz cuts a carnation for Homburg, which he vows to "put in water at home" (cf. V.1845). It is a *cut* flower: it is not the seed of a future Germany, but the souvenir of the past one. Fr. Wilh. returns home to a Germany that has now become *a French still life*.

"nicht ein einziger Lichtpunkt in der Zukunft." Our *satirical* analysis demonstrates that the extant *Homburg*'s production, together with that of *Findling*, the extended *Cäcilie* and *Zweikampf*, fell into the spring and summer of 1811, during which Kleist veered between hope for a German insurrection (*Findling*) and despair at the prospect of Fr. Wilh. submitting to Napoleon (*Cäcilie, Zweikampf, Homburg*).[601] Kleist's seesawing mirrors Fr. Wilh.'s, who via his envoy Count Harzberg on 14th May offered Napoleon an alliance (Napoleon rejected), on 21st July appointed Gneisenau privy councillor and instructed him to oversee Prussia's re-armament, but on 8th August rejected Gneisenau's recommendation that he spearhead a people's insurrection (Cf. Kittler, *Geburt*, 365).

Kleist's letters of this period suggest that his oscillation between hope and resignation, together with other challenges—his bankruptcy after *BA* folded, his feuds with Hardenberg and Iffland, the depatures of Müller and Marie—, are wearing him down: "*Das Leben, mit seinen zudringlichen, immer wiederkehrenden Ansprüchen*" (II:873); "*Das Leben, das vor mir ganz öde liegt*" (II:874); "*[die] widerwärtigen Verhältnisse, in denen ich lebe*" (II:874). When in June 1811 he offers *Homburg* to Reimer (cf. II:871), he is still "writing it down"; when in late July he sends a reminder to Reimer, he is still working on it, for otherwise he would have included the MS; and when on 15th August he offers the drama to Fouqué "*in kurzem*" (cf. II:876), he is evidently still not done with it. We know that Kleist always edited his works till the eleventh hour (cf. *LS*,273a; 346; 347), and *Homburg* was surely no exception, especially as its *satirical* context clearly suggests that he was waiting to see whether Gneisenau could sway the King into standing up to Napoleon (if he had, *Homburg* as we know it would no longer have been pertinent and been rewritten or replaced by another drama, possibly one already in progress—cf. below section on works not extant). When Marie on 3rd September submits *Homburg* to Prince Wilh. and Princess Amalie, Kleist has probably just written off a clean copy, so that *Homburg* as we know it will have been completed more or less precisely on 1st or 2nd September 1811. By this time Kleist must already have submitted the novellas for publication, making *Homburg* almost certainly his last completed extant work.

As with *Krug*, Kleist orchestrated and timed his submission of *Homburg* with great precision: in September, the debate between the supporters of armed confrontation with Napoleon, led by Gneisenau, and the advocates of an alliance with him, led by Hardenberg, came to a head. Prince Wilh. may have been siding with Gneisenau, which would explain why Kleist looked to him as communication channel (via Marie, as with *Krug*). *Homburg* was but one building block of Kleist's final propaganda assault on his King, and the two weeks following its submission were arguably the most important two weeks in the life of the *satirical* Kleist: *he now is where he had wanted to be*, what he had settled in Berlin for, what he had been striving for all along: in direct communication with the King, in a *kairotic* moment in Prussia's existence. Raising the bar, on 7th September he submits a request for his re-activation as officer to his King (not extant)—which Marie on the 9th endorses with a submission of her own (cf. *LS*,507a)—, and within days, possibly on the morning of the 11th, is invited to a private audience with the King; on the same day a cabinet order acknowledges his in-principle eligibility to re-join the army *if war brakes out*, briefly rekindle his hopes (cf. II:879).[602] Kleist's conversation with the King is the stuff for a novel, not for our speculation here. We must wait and see what happens next. Pause. No letters extant till the 17th. Pause. Then, on the 17th, he writes to Marie, with palpable resignation:[603]

(M)an erwartet den Kaiser Napoleon zum Besuch... es ist mir ganz stumpf und dumpf vor der Seele, und es ist auch nicht ein einziger Lichtpunkt in der Zukunft, auf den ich mit einiger Freudigkeit und Hoffnung hinaussähe. Vor einigen Tagen war ich noch bei G[neisenau] und überreichte ihm, nach Ihrem Rat, ein paar Aufsätze, die ich ausgearbeitet hatte; aber das alles scheint nur, wie der Franzose sagt, moutarde après diner. Wirklich, es ist sonderbar, wie mir in dieser Zeit alles, was ich unternehme, zugrunde geht; wie sich mir immer, wenn ich mich einmal entschließen kann, einen festen Schritt zu tun, der Boden unter meinen Füßen entzieht. G ist ein herrlicher Mann... Ich bin gewiß, daß wenn er den Platz fände, für den er sich geschaffen und bestimmt fühlt, ich, irgendwo in seiner Umringung, den meinigen gefunden haben würde... Soll ich, wenn ich das Geld von Ulriken erhalte, nach Wien gehen?... Der Brief an R[ex] ist besorgt und zwar, wie Sie mir befohlen haben, eigenhändig. Ich habe dabei in einer sehr langen Unterredung auch ihn Gelegenheit gehabt, näher kennen zu lernen... mich dünkt er hat Herz und Verstand. (II:877-9)

Here are the *breaking news* that are so heartbreaking for Kleist, and that he evidently just receieved: on the 12th, i.e., *one day after his private audience with the King* (!), Fr. Wilh. sent an appeasing letter to Napoleon, and on the 15th, Privy Counsellor Fr. Aug. von Staegemann, whose house Kleist frequented, reported to Königsberg (where part of the government remains) that war had been averted (cf. Loch, *Kleist*, 405). For Kleist, *bad news* indeed! Kleist's letter also suggests: Gneisenau has been sidelined; and: Napoleon is expected to visit Berlin in person , presumably to sign an alliance with Fr. Wilh. *Bad, bad news.*

We have to be clear about this: the *bad news* from Berlin does not simply *invalidate* the Cabinet order that declares Kleist fit to serve in the army if war breaks out. No, it is much worse than that: it means that he would have to serve in a Franco-Prussian war against Russia! He would be serving Napoleon in consolidating his Empire! Not only his King would be exactly in the position of Homburg that Kleist anticipated—but he himself would be—*as a lowly lieutenant, perishing in the mud of Russia on behalf of the French Emperor.*

PICTURE THAT!

Kleist says he is considering going to Vienna, evidently to turn his back on his King, join Gentz and Müller, and help orchestrate the Austrian resistance. Kleist is unsure what to do: this is rare! His King, he admits, has "heart and mind," and deep inside, his loyalty to him is strong. His King heared him out, and acted upon what he heard, with his letter to Napoleon the following day. Good! But his King clearly not *accept* his advice! If anything, Kleist's personal intervention appears to have backfired, it urged the King to act, but in the opposite way he had hoped. It's bad, it's really, really bad. He asks Marie to chose for him: "Should I Stay or Should I Go?" (The Clash).

Having sent his letter to Marie, Kleist immediately sets of for Frankfurt/O., evidently to obtain money from Ulrike for going to Vienna. She does not comply. On the 18th he is on the Marwitzes' Friedersdorf estate, a few hours from Frankfurt/O. en route back to Berlin, where he engages L. von der Marwitz in a "tactical wargame," presumably of the type I depicted above, which Marwitz could well have put up in his salon or library. As if to design a counterdraft to the *bad news* he had just received, Kleist, develops a wargame scenario (cf. II:880) in which (1st "stake") Prussia declares war on France, precipitated by a French ultimatum (2nd "stake") that forces Fr. Wilh.'s hand: *"Die Franzosen... setzen den König so, daß er den Frieden brechen muß."* The King's army corps attempts to cross the Oder river eastwards near Frankfurt/O. (3rd "stake"); failing to accomplish it (presumably because of the significant Ad'A garrison in Küstrin), he falls back to Berlin's Spandau fortress. Knowing that the Ad'A will rapidly march on Spandau from Magdeburg, Kleist offers two plausible "endgames." "E1" (4th "stake"): the King retreats to Kolberg on the Baltic Sea, whence he could escape to London or St. Petersburg, leaving Berlin undefended, for the Ad'A to occupy a second time. "E2" (5th "stake"): the King and his corps manage to cross the Oder and engage the Ad'A in battle, in which, on 14th October, they are crushed.

Kleist terms "E2" "unexpected," but clearly *favours* it, thought he does not necessarily want his conservative host to recognise that. "E2" may at first sight seem the far bleaker scenario, but from Kleist's perspective encompasses an opportunity, however slight, that the King's defeat could trigger a people's insurrection (Kleist offers precisely this scenario in *Findling*, published only a few weeks earlier, reminding us just how tightly his works of this period are tied to developments). "E1" may at first sight seem preferable, but for Kleist it is not, for it could well entail the end of the Prussian Kingdom and its royal dynasty: there might be no second *Tilsit* (where Napoleon had spared Prussia).⁶⁰⁴ "In "E2," Kleist's "*Chess*-like" game plan becomes "*Go*-like": the sacrifice of the King marks the end of war-making according to the "aristocratic" rules of *Chess*, and its beginning according to the "insurrectionist" principles of *Go*: the war is no longer won by preserving one's own King, but by surrounding and immobilising the enemy army with the people's masses. Kleist's wargaming is never "tactical," but always "strategic," indeed "transformational": he does not merely seek to *optimise tactical moves* within a given set of rules, but to *change those very rules*.⁶⁰⁵ In response to his own lament to Marie on the day before, *"es ist auch nicht ein einziger Lichtpunkt in der Zukunft,"* here he points to the one and only "point of light" left: transform warfare in a fashion never seen before—*sacrifice the King!*

On the very day of the wargame, the 18ᵗʰ, Fr. Wilh. sends a response to Marie, in which he tells her that war is by no means as imminent as various persons, including herself assume—very likely using her to convey this message to Kleist (*LS*,507c). On the 21ˢᵗ Hardenberg talks the King out of oing to Kolberg, as the "magnificent" Gneisenau had recommended, arguing that Napoleon would consider such a move tantamount to a declaration of war. On the 26ᵗʰ Fr. Wilh. informs Alex. that he is de-mobilising, and urges him to do likewise.⁶⁰⁶

"zum Tode ganz reif." On 10ᵗʰ October Fr. Wilh., in a gesture of appeasement towards Napoleon, dismisses Gebhard Leberecht von Blücher, who is overlooking upgrades to Kolberg's fortifications; soon after he rejects Scharnhorst's last-ditch effort, in a secret mission to Saint Petersburg on 17ᵗʰ October, to forge an alliance with Russia (cf. Loch, *Kleist*, 403-5); and on 29ᵗʰ October he commences formal negotiations with Napoleon for an alliance. On 2ⁿᵈ November

Napoleon, together with Marie-Louise, arrives in Düsseldorf, the right-bank capital of the Grand Duchy of Berg, equidistant between Paris and Berlin, whose ruler Napoleon is in personal union, Joachim Murat having become King of Naples. With his move Napoleon raises the heat on Fr. Wilh., signalling his readiness to "visit" Berlin, be it to ink a Franco-Prussian alliance or to "squash" Fr. Wilh.: from Düsseldorf, Napoleon could take personal command of the French forces at Magdeburg, on the Prussian border, within 2-3 days.[607] Napoleon casts his long shadow, and Fr. Wilh. and Alex. budge: on 6th November Fr. Wilh. makes further concessions to the French ambassador St. Marsan; Tsar Alex. signals that he is keen to avert war.

On 10th November Kleist sends Marie his *satirical testament*:

> Die Allianz, die der König jetzt mit den Franzosen schließt, ist auch nicht eben gemacht, mich im Leben festzuhalten. Mir waren die Gesichter der Menschen schon jetzt, wenn ich ihnen begegnete, zuwider, nun würde mich gar, wenn sie mir auf der Straße begegneten, eine körperliche Empfindung anwandeln, die ich hier nicht nennen mag. Es ist zwar wahr, es fehlte mir sowohl als ihnen an Kraft, die Zeit wieder einzurücken; ich fühle aber zu wohl, daß der Wille, der in meiner Brust lebt, etwas anderes ist, als der Wille derer, die diese witzige Bemerkung machen: dergestalt, daß ich mit ihnen nichts mehr zu schaffen haben mag. Was soll man doch, wenn der König diese Allianz abschließt, länger bei ihm machen? Die Zeit ist ja vor der Tür, wo man wegen der Treue gegen ihn, der Aufopferung und Standhaftigkeit und aller andern bürgerlichen Tugenden, von ihm selbst gerichtet, an den Galgen kommt. (II:884)[608]

"Time" (with *Hamlet*) is "out of joint," and no one can now "clinch" it. At the centre of his life's work had been his service to his King and country, and Kleist is now forced to acknowledge that his King will not heed his advice, that his final *cri de cœur*, *Homburg*, failed to reach his ear, and that he has nothing left to offer to him: "*Was soll man doch, wenn der König diese Allianz abschließt, länger bei ihm machen?*"; "*Jetzt trösten, jetzt verletzen seine Klänge.*"

Kleist's firm belief that his *Homburg* scenario is about to play out precipitates his suicide: the King's imminent alliance with France seals his fate—a fate inscribed in *Homburg*. Kleist's haunting line, *"meine Seele ist so wund, daß mir, ich möchte fast sagen, wenn ich die Nase aus dem Fenster stecke, das Tageslicht wehe tut, das mir darauf schimmert"* (II:883), suggests that on this day he readies his soul to spread its wings, as his avatar Homburg had foretold: *"Durch stille Ätherräume schwingt mein Geist; / [...] / Und jetzt liegt Nebel alles unter mir."*

On 19th (*MA* II: 9th) November Kleist is *"zum Tode ganz reif"* (II:885); two days (or weeks) later, he is—*dead*.[609]

Homburg, satyrically

"Müllers Abreise hat mich in große Einsamkeit versenkt. Er war es eigentlich, um dessentwillen ich mich vor nun ohngefähr einem Jahr in Berlin niederließ" (to Marie, July 1811; II:872); *"Das Leben, das ich führe, ist seit Ihrer und A. Müllers Abreise gar zu öde und traurig. Auch bin ich mit den zwei oder drei Häusern, die ich hier besuche, seit der letzten Zeit ein wenig außer Verbindung gekommen"* (to Marie, summer 1811; II:873). Had the now-departed A. Müller been his only remaining lover in town? As Michalzik put it (*Kleist*, 386), "in Berlin, they were considered a couple." As we saw, Kleist considered, half-heartedly, to follow Müller to Vienna. Perhaps what had become "bleak" and "dull" was above all his *love-life*, the members of his "brotherhood" having married, moved away, or distanced themselves from him.[610] Eroticisms still abound in *Findling* and *Zweikampf*; in *Homburg* they do not—did Kleist lose his sexual mojo?[611] The *"Perserbraut"* who bedded Homburg (cf. V.122) before joining The Elector's entourage may alludes to Hardenberg and, by analogy, A. Müller before he left Berlin for Vienna. Does not Müller's "treason" against Kleist mirror Hardenberg's against his King?

"schauen, vom Geländer der Rampe, auf ihn nieder." *Käthchen's* eponymous object of desire in the opening scene is separated from, or fixated before, the "judges" by the "bar"; in *Homburg's*, the protagonist is similarly separated from The Elector's entourage by the "endless" ramp, at

whose bottom he sits, while the entourage repeatedly descends and ascends (cf. V.41; 66), "*Endlos, bis an das Tor des Himmels*" (V.182). In *Marquise*, Count F's "ascending the rear ramp" (cf. II:128) implies sodomy, and so it does, arguably, in *Homburg*: Homburg, it appears, is an *erômenos*, tied to a *baquet* underneat the oak tree and in a permanent trance, whom the members of the entourage take turns to sodomise. In the final scene, Homburg is admitted into The Elector's entourage, but degraded to *dmōs*: a permanently blindfolded "bottom" of an all-powerful, ithyphallic "top" and his gang of "brothers." The oak's crown's concavity, that earlier comprised a "crisis room," has now become a *dungeon*, in which, at the bottom of the "ramp," blindfolded and enchained, Homburg endures his "dom's" exquisite tortures.

"**Heftige Kanonade.**" The orgiastic *Grande batterie* in II/2 lacks the rivetting energy of Kleist's earlier battle scenes and appears anaemic, stale and mechanic:

Ein Kanonenschuß fällt.
Sie besteigen sämtlich einen Hügel.

GOLZ auf dem Hügel.
DER PRINZ VON HOMBURG hält sich die Hand vors Auge.

Kanonenschüsse in der Ferne.
Schüsse in der Nacht.
Heftige Kanonade.
Musketenfeuer.
Pause.—Ein Siegesschrei in der Ferne.

DER PRINZ VON HOMBURG steigt vom Hügel herab.
DER PRINZ VON HOMBURG wild.
OBRIST KOTTWITZ beleidigt.
GOLZ zu Kottwitz.

Er stößt ihn zurück.
Er reißt ihm das Schwert samt dem Gürtel ab.

DER PRINZ VON HOMBURG auf ihn einschreitend.
HOHENZOLLERN zu dem Offizier.

> DER PRINZ VON HOMBURG indem er den Degen abgibt.
>> Zu Kottwitz und den übrigen Offizieren.
> HOHENZOLLERN beilegend.
> DER PRINZ VON HOMBURG beruhigt.
>> Alle ab. (V.429-97)

The repetitive "pounding," and even the officer's castration at the hand of Fr. Wilh., *"Er reißt ihm das Schwert samt dem Gürtel ab,"* leave the reader cold, and so does Fr. Wilh's auto-castration, *"DER PRINZ VON HOMBURG nachdem er sich den Degen abgeschnallt. / [...] Er gibt den Degen an den Offizier und geht ab"* (V.777; 789).[612] Some Kleist scholars consider *Homburg* Kleist's most mature work—which, *po(i)etically*, it may well be, but more obviously, it is, *satirically*, his most *resigned* one. Even the appearance on stage of a half-naked Napoleon, with the (presumably equally half-naked) Hardenberg and other courtiers in tow, fails to excite:

> Der Kurfürst kommt halbentkleidet aus dem Nebenkabinett; ihm folgen Graf Truchß, Graf Hohenzollern, und der Rittmeister Golz.—Pagen mit Lichtern.
> GRAF TRUCHSS öffnet das Fenster.
> DER KURFÜRST nach einer kurzen Pause.
>> Die Offiziere ab.
>> (V. 1395-1411)

The officers jointly ejaculate. The audience yawns.

Homburg, syphilitically

"*Wer heut sein Haupt noch auf der Schulter trägt, / Hängt es schon morgen zitternd auf den Leib, / Und übermorgen liegts bei seiner Ferse*" (V.1290-2): *satyrically* the most *flaccid*, *Homburg* is *syphilitically* Kleist's most *morbid* work; his erotic passions may have been waning in synch with the waxing of his syphilitic symptoms. If *Schroffenstein* reflected Kleist's early exposure to the interplay of pleasure and agony, *Homburg* relates the final stage in the syphilitic lover's journey, in which the latter all but extinguishes the former.

"der Demant, den er am Finger trägt." Early on Homburg is marked as diseased: *"Flecken"* (V.43); "mit einem Schwarzen Band um die linke Hand" (V.401); *"um das Schwert... / Schlingt sich vielleicht ein Schmuck der Gnade noch"* (V.825-6); *"Ein Stein ist er, den Bleistift in der Hand"* (V.1693). Syphilitic symptoms—encrusted ulcerations, skin blotches, *corona veneris*, on-set of impotence and mental illness, death wishes—appear so frequently and acutely in *Homburg* that we may infer that Kleist in mid-1811 was experiencing many of them himself.

"und windet sich einen Kranz." The Elector's entourage on top of the "ramp" is evidently engrossed in a *baquet*, the ramp serving as bucket, and its railing as *baquet*-strings; Homburg, the odd man out, experiences his personal séance underneath the Puységurian oak-elm, where he is recharging his *"Glieder"* (V.17) by attaching them to the tree, the laurel wreath perhaps serving as *baquet*-string.

The circulation of the drama's cipher or *agencement* is as *syphilitical* as it is *satirical*: the Mediterranean *laurel* (syphilis appeared first in Naples or Spain) growing in the "garden in the old French style" (French soldiers brought the disease to France) is plucked by the Francophile Count H who *hands* (sexually transmits) it to Homburg (thus reaching the less "fertile" German "soil"), who winds it into a *wreath*, which his *hand* passes to The Elector's hand, who—himself already diseased: *"der Kurfürst, mit der Stirn des Zeus"* (V.158); *"In dem Demanten, den er jüngst empfing"* (V.900); *"gleich dem Schwerte, / Das tot in deinem goldnen Gürtel ruht"* (V. 1580-1)—adds his *chain* (mercury droplets), before passing the *agencement* to Natalie's *hand*, whence the *wreath* passes to Homburg's *forehead* (as *corona veneris*), the *chain* to his *neck* (as chancre), completing the circulation:

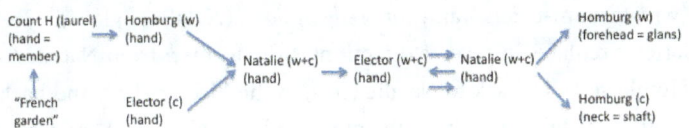

Simplified:

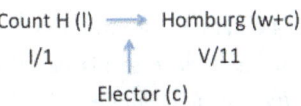

"*One night with Hardenberg, a lifetime with Napoleon,*" is how we could re-state this *satirical-syphilitical* movement. *Homburg* introduces the laurel wreath (shown below), reiling and chain to Kleist's inventory of *baquet*-strings:

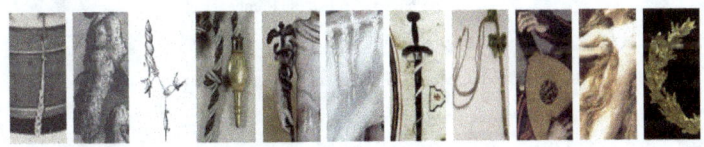

Braided *baquet*-strings (cont'd).

As the disease proliferates among lovers, its virulence appears to augment. The "brothers" may well have believed—wrongly, as we today know—, that sudden symptomatic outbreaks after periods of recession and latency can be triggered by intercourse with lovers who showing visible symptoms, as if their libidinal economy was one of ruinous economy of excess, a constant potlach of Batailléan *parts maudites,* of Maussian *dons.*

"Er erhascht einen Handschuh von der Prinzessin Hand." Condoms (here: Natalie's glove) in the "brotherhood" appear to have served a triple purpose: *protection* against venereal disease, *token* of love and trust, and *container* for gathered ejaculate, valued as purifier or *pharmakon,* if produced by lovers deemed "pure" (here: Natalie). Such resorting to "alternative medicine" is perhaps not surprising, given the toxicity of what "school medicine" had to offer in Kleist's day: mercury and arsenic, in the main. *Homburg* is the story of not one, but two, related, circulations: of *infection* (wreath-cum-chain) and of *redemption* (Natalie's glove). The latter circulates in reverse direction as the former: from Natalie to Homburg (I/1), back to Natalie (I/5), to the Elector (I/5), and back again to Natalie, who finds the glove on her table (IV/2), evidently left behind by The Elector.

When Homburg obtains the glove-condom from Natalie's *hand* and subsequently carries it close to his *heart*, it has already been filled—"*der Handschuh in den Händen klebt*" (V.198)—, possibly during their early encounter:

> der Prinz steht lebhaft auf. Der Kurfürst weicht mit der Prinzessin, welche den Kranz erhebt, zurück; der Prinz, mit ausgestreckten Armen, folgt ihr. [...]
>
> Sie besteigen sämtlich die Rampe. [...]
>
> DER KURFÜRST rückwärts ausweichend. [...]
>
> DER PRINZ VON HOMBURG nach dem Kranz greifend.
>
> O! Liebste! Was entweichst du mir? Natalie!
>
> Er erhascht einen Handschuh von der Prinzessin Hand. (V.65-70)

The ejaculate-*pharmakon* making the rounds, gathered in the condom, is "enriched" by every contributor it passes, before being applied to those in need, in a movement that mimicks that of the voting ball-*pharmakon* making the rounds, gathered in a helmet, in *Käthchen*'s vehmic court.[613]

"**Ach!... / Sah ich das Grab, beim Schein der Fackeln, öffnen.**" Kleist's torches are always phallic (in classical Greece nocturnal processions involving torches were closely associated with Dionysiac festivals), and the gaping "tomb" or "abyss" Homburg gazes into is as much *anal* as it is *fatal*.[614] The nexus of the glowing pleasure-instrument and the gaping pleasure-hole was Kleist's destiny, the vanishing point of his life's line of flight; if I previously held that Kleist invested more of himself into Hermann than into other characters, I correct: even more so into Homburg. *Homburg* is Kleist's most unguardedly autobiographic drama.[615]

The "*Todesfurchtszene*"—or, in Emperor Wilh. II's memorable, if misguided, term, "*Feigheitszene*"—has puzzled or irritated audiences, including, but not limited to, the Hohenzollern monarchs, but as soon as one accepts that the extant *Homburg*'s production substantially fell into the summer of 1811, it is easy enough to correlate Homburg's predicament with Kleist's: "*Wenn dich der Tod umschauerte, wie mich!*" (V.972); "*Nur ich allein, auf Gottes weiter Erdem, / Bin hülflos, ein Verlaßner, und kann nichts!*" (V.978-9); "*Ach! Auf dem Wege, der mich zu dir führte, / Sah ich das Grab, beim Schein der Fackeln, öffnen, / Das morgen mein Gebein empfangen soll*" (V.981-3). Müller having left Berlin, a lonely and destitude Kleist associates death with his "*Gebein*" (= "*Glied*" = "member"), one more time, penetrating a "tomb": "*das Grabgewölb wünscht' er zu sehen*" (V.1729).

Homburg's enchained laurel wreath symbolises Kleist's failure to become Germany's poet laureate just as decidedly as it does Fr. Wilh.'s to overcome Napoleon and seize the imperial laurel; the fatal *gun-shot* into his *mouth* (gun = phallus; mouth = anus; bullet = ejaculate) Kleist would soon enact on the shores of the Kl. Wannsee mimicks the final ecstatic orgasm Homburg dreads and desires: Homburg's "*Todesfurchtszene*" is Kleist's "*Todeswunschszene.*" That Kleist in early September still recoiled from the "tomb" may have had more do with with the absence of Müller or another suitable brother-in-death than with a glimmer of *Lebenswille* that may still have animated him: Kleist simply had no "tomb" into which to "sink"; he was not ready to *die*, because he was not *ready* to die. His "final solution" involving the sister-in-death Henriette was perhaps not yet on the horizon, or not yet palatable: perhaps he preferred a *male* fellow-traveller for the final journey, if he could find one.

Homburg, po(i)etically
Homburg epitomises some of Kleist's most intriguing *po(i)etical* techniques—notably those which I term, respectively, *the panoramic* and *the telescopic*, the former referring to the poet's taking up an ideal vantage point vis-à-vis the world, the latter to his seeking effectively move across space-time by way of foresight (scenaric thinking) and hindsight (evaluation). By being systematically constructed "panoramically" and "telescopically," Kleist's works create a *virtual*

space—a scenario, a simulation, a (pre-digital) cyberspace—into which the audience is drawn and immersed, to a point wehre fiction and reality become indiscernible, where the virtuality of Kleist's fiction becomes actualised in the audiences' experience, in a *"Physiognomie des Augenblicks"* (II:795).

"von allen Seiten, ringsherum... sehen." Kleist in *Homburg* crafts poetical manifestations of the ideas for a "perfect" panorama he outlined to Wilhelmine in August 1800, after seeing, in Berlin, Joh. A. Breysig's *Panorama of the City of Rome*:

> Panorama ist ein griechisches Wort... Die erste Hälfte des Wortes heißt ohngefähr so viel wie: *von allen Seiten, ringsherum*; die andere Hälfte heißt ohngefähr: *sehen, zu Sehendes, Gesehenes*... Ich sage, es ist die erste Ahnung eines Panoramas, und selbst die bloße Idee ist einer weit größeren Vollkommenheit fähig. Denn da es nun einmal darauf ankommt, den Zuschauer ganz in den Wahn zu setzen, er sei in der offnen Natur, so daß er durch nichts an den Betrug erinnert wird, so müßten ganz andere Anstalten getroffen werden. Keine Form des Gebäudes kann nach meiner Einsicht diesen Zweck erfüllen, als allein die kugelrunde. Man müßte auf dem Gemälde selbst stehen, und nach allen Seiten zu keinen Punkt finden, der nicht Gemälde wäre. Weil aber das Licht von oben hinein fallen und folglich oben eine Öffnung sein muß, so müßte um diese zu verdecken, etwa ein Baumstamm aus der Mitte sich erheben, der dick belaubte Zweige ausbreitet und unter dessen Schatten man gleichsam stünde. (II:518-9)

A "perfect" panoramic illusion (Kleist's term is "*Betrug*," "deception"), he argues, is attained by the observer's "standing within the painting and in any direction observing no point that is not part of the painting"—in other word, the "perfect" panorama must be perfectly spherical: "*Keine Form... als allein die kugelrunde.*"[616] It is precisely this "perfect" illusion that Kleist seeks to produce in *Homburg*—not only for Fr. Wilh. and other members of the audience, but for himself: he immerses himself so entirely into his *auto- po(ï)etic* panaroma—"*Ein Traum, was sonst?*"—that he, like Homburg, face-to-face with the gaping hole that confronts him, beholds the "truth" of his fate.[617]

Already in the above-quoted letter passage, posted during the first leg of the Würzburg journey, Kleist defines his *po(i)etical* project as *panoramic*, as comprising a *"von allen Seiten, ringsherum... sehen,"* as production of a *perfect illusion or simulation* into which he immerses himself and his audience. I have variously termed Kleist's works *scenaric, perspectivist* and *experimental*, and Kleist's concept, *panoramic*, complements these techniques: in taking a *panoramic* position, the poet situates himself at the scene's focal point and looks outwards into all directions, towards the objects that surround him, whereas in taking a *perspectivist* stance (narrated, e.g., teichoscopically), he situates himself at the periphery and looks inwards from various directions onto the object situated at the focal point; in crafting a *scenario*, the poet projects a present situation into the future, or multiple compossible futures, whereas in crafting a *panorama*, he transports a distant or absent situation into the present moment; in performing an *experiment*, the poet explores multiple possible outcomes, or tests their premises, in displaying a *panorama*, he presents to his audience an specific—typically manipulative—outcome. Kleist, with his panoramic project, seeks to occupy the Eleatic "ecstatic concentric," "amphiscopic" position that (says Slotderdijk) Renaissance thinkers sought to obtain, and that in 20th century philosophy is echoed in Heidegger's *"In-der Welt-Sein"* and, in a manner, also in Deleuze's *"pure immanence"* and *"virtuality"*:

Parmenidean Eye: All-seeing Eye (1766); Eye of Providence (1782); The Shield of Achilles, at its centre Phoebus Apollo, surrounded by the zodiac, scenes of city and country life, and *Okeanus*.[618]

The 360° *artificial* panoramas that became popular spectacles in European cities from the late 18th century were early approximations

(Kleist: *"die erste Ahnung"*) at his "perfect" panorama, whose realisation to this day remains elusive. A different technology that seeks to approximate a "perfect" panorama is the VR simulation, whereby the visual data is projected not onto a spherical screen, but into an observer's individual goggle. The *Guckkasten* apparatus Kleist refers to in a letter, only days after visiting the Berlin panorama (he is reminiscing about the rapidly changing landscapes he observed traversing Saxony from his postal carriage), is perhaps the earliest version of this technology (a *Kaiserpanorama*, a late 19th century version). The MMORPG simulation I discussed earlier differs from VR devices in that the player maintains an *eccentric*, rather than *concentric* and immersed, position relative to the objects he manipulates.

Artificial panoramas (FLTR, top): *Pantheon*, Rome (110 AD); Vasari's *Last Judgment,* Florence (1597); Bentham's *Panopticon* (1791); *Rotunda*, London (1801); (bottom): *Guckkasten* (1835); (*Cinéorama*, Paris (1900); La Géode IMAX, Paris (1985); VR headset (2018).

The equivalent of VR in visual arts is the attempt to visually draw the observer into the image: C.D. Friedrich's *Mönch am Meer* (1810) precipitates and augments the monk's (and the observer's) sense of disorientation and forlornness in a boundless landscape—"*als ob einem die Augenlieder weggeschnitten wären*"—by dispensing with perspective and depth, while Gustave Doré's *The Empyrean*, conversely, uses perspective and depth to precipitate and augment Dante's and Beatrice's (and the observer's) awe of the infinite and eternal.

Friedrich's *Mönch* (1810); Doré's *Dante and Beatrice visiting The Empyrean* (c.1870s).

Homburg's tomb entails Kleist's (inverted) counterdraft to C.D. Friedrich's boundless desert: an abyss as frightfully *claustrophobic* for the condemned as is the seascape *kenophobic* for the monk.[619]

Among the most perfect *natural* panoramas are those experienced from prominent mountain peaks, from capes jutting into bodies of water, or from boats floating on them. Having grown up in the flat, featureless landscapes of Brandenburg, Kleist may first have conciously encountered natural panoramas in early 1793, when en route to his military engagement he climbed the Rudelsburg near Naumburg and the Wartburg near Eisenach, and during the *Siege of Mainz*, observed the "live" spectacle of the city's bombardments from exposed locations: the allied HQ on Marienborn hill, the Mainzpitze promontory.[620]

Natural panorama: 360° View from the Schneekoppe (mid-1800s).

Kleist continued to experience natural panoramas during his travels: in 1797, on the Stubenberg, Regenstein and Brocken peaks in the Harz mountains, in 1799, on the Schneekoppe peak in the Riesengegirge, one of the highest peaks in Europe then accessible to travellers without alpine equipment, in 1800, on Cape Arkona on the island of Rügen, in 1802, on Lake Thun's Scherzligen pensinsula, where he imagined scaling the 4000m peaks of the Bernese Oberland visible in the distance;[621]

Panoramic viewpoints: mountaintops (Brocken/Harz, Schneekoppe); capes and promontories (Kap Arkona/Rügen; Scherzligen/Thun).

In addition to tracing Kleist's *experiencing* artificial and natural panoramas, we may trace his *producing* poetic panoramas throughout his writings—e.g.:

- his recollection of his 1793 sexual "initiation" during the *Siege of Mainz*, as narrated to Adolphine;[622]
- his fantasy of listening to spherical music on the Rhine, probably in the same year, as narrated to Wilhelmine;[623]
- his 1797 reflections atop the Brocken, as retold in *Aufsatz*;[624] a panoramic landscape description near Brockes' home at Coblentz;[625]
- his enthusiastic note, en route to Würzburg, of a Tharandt valley vista;[626]
- his 1800 attempt to "re-skill" Wilhelmine into becoming "virtuous," deploying as analogy the climing of a hill;[627]
- his early 1801 alarm at his "unbearable lucidity" (Sloterdijk);[628]
- his late 1801, existential, impressions upon entering Switzerland;[629]
- his "scaling the Schreckhorn" while sipping a coffee;[630]

"*ich besteige das Schreckhorn*": Kleist from his house on the Inseli (left) sets over to Scherzligen with his Jüngli, drops him at the village church, and "scales the Schreckhorn" (not visible, covered by Kleist's house) while sipping a coffee at Scherzigen's promontory (in the centre, left of the church).

- his depiction of a panoramic scene within a drama: *Penthesilea*, 3rd scene;[631]
- and another: *Käthchen*, 13th scene;[632]
- his depiction of himself, as prophet, addressing the Germans from • the top of the Harz, that most "German" of mountains;[633]
- his agenda for *BA*, as outlined in *Gebet des Zoroaster*;[634]
- his conception, in *BA*, of a panoramic *text* (a grammar, a syntax);[635]
- *Bettelweib*'s famous opening of the same period;[636]
- his discussion, two weeks later in *BA*, of C.D. Friedrich's *Mönch*;[637]
- his reflections, in *Marionettentheater*, on the soul's transportation;[638]
- his reporting to Marie, in the spring or summer of 1811, his po(i)etical powers' final rearing;[639]
- further depictions of panoramic scenes in a drama: *Homburg*, 1st act, 1st scene; 5th act, 10th and 11th scenes;[640]
- his vision of his soul taking off like an aeronaut, in his letter to Sophie Müller on the eve of his death.[641]

Experiencing, imagining and creating *the panoramic* pervades Kleist's life and œuvre; its significance is twofold: on the one hand, his evident ability to *see* more lucidly and clairvoyantly than most of his contemporaries predestined (or doomed) him to becoming the nation's *seer and bard*—we term this gift, or bane, *vision*; on the other hand, it opened his mind to the possibility of *fate* transcending the horizon of existence on this Earth, offering solace in the here and now, but perhaps also kindling an inclination to let go—we term this solace, or illusion, *faith*. Vision and *faith* are the twin corollaries of Kleist's *panoramic* outlook, shaping his poetic *technē* and *aisthetikos*, and his life choices.[642]

"**Die Terrassen… dienten statt der Logen, Wesen aller Art blickten… herab.**" A *technē* prominent in Kleist's writings, comprising the architectural complement or counterpart of the panorama, is the *amphitheatre*, whose *natural* archetype Kleist may have encountered in the summer of 1800 while observing, at Cape Arkona, Kosegarten's performances from the beach, or from a boat by the beach, and whose *artificial* archetype, in the autumn of 1800 at the Julius-Hospital in Würzburg (cf. II:559), whose *theatrum anatomicum* and *auditorium* he visited within a month of observing Kosegarten's performance and Breysig's panorama (cf. II:559).[643] In man-made amphitheatres, the actor occupies the equivalent position, at the physical centre, as the observer, but he does not only look out, but also speak out, addressing a "live" audience that itself observes, listens, gestures, and occasionally shouts back or claps. The amphitheatre architects a *perspectivist* stance from the point of view of the spectators, each of whom have a unique, for slightly shifted, position relative to the stage (if one could link up the brains of a hundred spectators, each equipped with stereoscopic vision, and intergrate their respective visual sensations, one would obtain a highly immersive experience).[644]

Already the ancient Greeks took advantage of the physical properties of concave amphitheatrical structures, whose seating arrangement brought all spectators as equidistant as possible to the stage, situated at its focal point, while acoustically augmenting and disseminating sound originating from it. To maximise attendance, under the constraint of maintaining attendants' approximate equidistance to the stage, a perfectly spherical structure would indeed be required, as Kleist envisaged, with the stage, or rather the performers, suspended at its centre. The Greeks constructed amphitheatres comprising a quarter sphere to hemisphere, the Romans, fully enclosed, oval, arenas. Apart from the anatomical theatre and auditorium, the amphitheatrical structure Kleist would have been most familiar was probably the Renaissance theatre.

Artificial amphitheatres (FLTR, top): Theatre of Dionysos, Athens (4th Cent. BC); Colosseum, Rome (80 AD); Theatrum anatomicum, Leyden University (1609); Berlin Veterinarian Anatomical Theatre (1790);

(bottom): Teatro La Fenice, Venice (1792); Debating Chamber, European Parliament, Strasbourg (1999), Pierre-Boulez-Saal, Berlin (2017).[645]

Kleist's amphitheatrical impressions of Mainz (cf. II:673), Dresden (cf. II:544) and Würzburg (cf. II:579) are as *repetitive*—repetition being part and parcel of his poetic technique—as they are *apt*. In the panoramic vista of Würzburg from the Steinberg (a vista this author himself enjoyed) the cascading vinyards in the foreground indeed resemble a Greek amphitheatre's horseshoe rows of seats: *"In der Tiefe... liegt die Stadt, wie in der Mitte eines Amphitheaters. Die Terassen der umschließenden Berge dienten statt der Logen"* (II:579):

"In der Tiefe... wie in der Mitte eines Amphitheaters": Mainz and Würzburg.

Leveraging these complementary "augmented reality" techniques, Kleist carved out for himself three distinct roles vis-à-vis his audiences: firstly, that of the *observer* (akin to that of the "participant observer" or "embedded reporter"), who positions himself *at the centre of a situation* to explore it inside-out, for example, when in 1803 he sought to join the *Armée des côtes de l'Océan* at Saint-Omer, or when in 1801 he immersed himself into the Parisian gay scene; secondly, that of the *producer* and *publisher*, who locates himself *in the background* to produce his manifestos, scenarios or simulations, for example, when in 1802 and 1803 he exiled himself in Switzerland in order to produce his first dramas; thirdly, that of the *broadcaster* (bard, conductor, director) who positions himself *at the margins of a situation*, whence he communicates inside-out, into enemy or occupied territory, for example when in 1807 he sought to locate in Dresden, in order to incite the Prusssian resistance behind the eastward advancing *Ad'A*, or when in 1809 he "networked," as courier, the northern German people and the Austrian resistance, while seeking to "broadcast" to them via *Germania*, from his hiding place in Prague. Kleist's medial repertoire and analytic range are extraordinary, encompassing the *descriptive* (panorama, perspective reportage), *predictive* (scenario, experiment), *analytic* (game theory), *prescriptive* (manifesto, user manual) and *simulative* (wargame, simulation), all of them codified in a poetry that is at once *pescheräic*, cryptographic and musical.

"Durchgang durch das Unendliche." Related to the *panorama* is Kleist's concept of the *Hohlspiegel*, or parabolic mirror (cf. II:345), with whose aid an observer may, for example, obtain a close-up image of a distant object. The *panorama* brings the observer's surroundings into view all at once, in an instance (*"Augenblick"*), lending itself for gathering immersive impressions; it entails a *technē of immanence*. The *parabolic* mirror, in contrast, transcends space-time: depending on how waves—light, sound, radio, radar, the soul's vibrations—fall onto it, it transports or zooms a distant (or, by analogy, future) object into the near (or the present), or a near (or present) object into the distance (or the future); it entails a *technē of transcendence*.

Homburg's dream, or somnambulant trance, adds a *Hohlspiegel* effect to his panoramic amphiscopy; in addition to *outward*, from underneath the oak tree, it directs his gaze *inward*, into his soul, making his vision at once *con*centric and *epi*centric, and allowing him to reflect his external reality through his pneumatic "lens."[646]

Hohlspiegel (FLTR): Archimedes' mirror (214-12 BC);
Borel's head mirror (mid-17th cent.); Tschirnhaus' spherical reflector (1686),
which Kleist could have seen in Dresden—cf. II:379.

Like that of the *Pescherä*, the *technē* of *Hohlspiegel* is at the heart of Kleist's *po(ï)etical* production machine. The poet himself—Kleist—*is* that *Hohlspiegel*: he bundles and takes in sensual and chronological data, via zooming-in or immersion, re-assembles and codifies them—*pescheräically*—into poetic productions, and reflects and broadcasts them back into the world, via their publication or staging. The "eternal" (*"Unendliche"*) through which an image or word makes its passage (*"Durchgang"*), so as to reconstitute itself on its other side is Kleist's soul—the *soul* as mirror and *mirrored*, transporter and *transported*.[647]

"den Zuschauer ganz in den Wahn zu setzen, er sei in der offnen Natur." A passage in Kleist's BA essay *Empfindungen vor Friedrichs Seelandschaft* (1810), in which he imagines himself in the monk's place at the centre of the indeterminate "scape" (it lacks *"Abbruch,"* he says, "abrupt termination"), expresses the same idea of *perfect immersion* as did his reflection, ten years earlier, on the Berlin panorama, *"Man müßte auf dem Gemälde selbst stehen, und nach allen Seiten zu keinen Punkt finden, der nicht Gemälde wäre"*:

> Nichts kann trauriger und unbehaglicher sein, als diese Stellung in der Welt: der einzige Lebensfunke im weiten Reiche des Todes, der einsame

> Mittelpunkt im einsamen Kreis... so ist es, wenn man es betrachtet, als ob einem die Augenlider weggeschnitten wären. (II:327)[648]

The essay then moves from a *description of the experience of perfect immersion* (the monk, the observer) to the creation of perfect illusion:

> Ja, wenn man diese Landschaft mit ihrer eignen Kreide und mit ihrem eignen Wasser malte; so, glaube ich, man könnte die Füchse und Wölfe damit zum Heulen bringen. (II:328)

In the first scene, Homburg uses laurel (equivalent to the essay's chalk and water) to wreathe (paint) himself an imperial crown, or poet's laurel, that is as *real* to him as Kleist's landscape is to the essay's foxes and wolves (or as Zeuxis' grapes are to the birds). The illusion remains "perfect" as long as he is seated underneath the tree, whose canopy, in accordance with Kleist's reflections on the Berlin panorama, screens him—"*unter dessen Schatten*" (II:519)— from the sunlight that would illuminate, and thereby disillusion, him.[649] In the final scene, Homburg finds himself once more immersed in an illusion, of metempsychosis (the blindfold has assumed the canopy's screening function), from which he is awakened, by the Jovian glare of a thousand Suns, to the "Desert of the Real" (Baudrillard).

Is Homburg-Fr. Wilh.-Kleist doomed to a life of perennial enslavement, or did he leave an escape route? The final act's resounding *"Alle"* (V.1855; 1858), Bernd Hamacher points out (cf. *KH*,85), may not include Homburg. Does Kleist leave the door open for a *final final* act to his drama? An act he finally enacts on the 21st of November? One he calls on his King to enact as well?

Zwölfter Auftritt (inszeniert am 21. November 1811)

Offene Fläche nahe einem See. Kühler Novembernachmittag. In der Ferne grölen siegestrunkene Soldaten. Ein Mann und eine Frau trinken, in ausgelassener und heiterer Stimmung in einer kleinen Versenkung sitzend, Rum. Drei Pistolen in einer Satteltasche. Ein Bote ist dabei, zum Hauptquartier zurückzukehren, als ein Schuss hallt, gefolgt, ein paar Schritte später, von einem zweiten.

BOTE verwirrt.
    Was denn. Ist der Sieg schon erungen—? [Etc.]

Does not this *final final* act call for an epilogue?

Epilog (nachgetragen am 15. Juni 2018)

Auf einem anderen Stern, in einer Galaxie weit weit entfernt.
Drei junge Leute in einem idyllischen Tal, umgeben von Weinbergen.

HOMBURG erregt.   Natalie!
BARDE nimmt die Leier auf.   Regt Euch. Ein Lied!
NATALIE.   Ach!
    Alle ab.

3. Kleist's Plane of Composition

3.1 Notes on Projects Not Executed or Not Extant

Kleist's plane of composition is *consistent*: the same concerns configure, the same techniques shape, all his works, from the first to the last. Kleist's œuvre is a *Gesamtkunstwerk*, whose individual pieces and choices are tightly linked. In Kleist's first published lines, *Schroffenstein*'s chorus of Swabian (German) maidens and youths articulates a dystopian prophecy of a mutilated *HRR* usurped by Napoleon, a prophecy fulfilled in his final published lines, in which *Homburg*'s chorus of Brandenburgian (French) soldiers salutes the glorious Napoleonic era. Kleist's *satyrical* and *syphilitical* threads are as consistent, (autobiographically) tracing the ebb and flow of his confrontations with Venus and Mercury. Given this consistency, it is not idle to conjecture about works Kleist planned, commenced, or completed and destroyed, if evidence of their existence is compelling, even if such evidence may be limited to a single reference by him, or people close to him.[650]

Kleist probably destroyed work-in-progress on several occasions, most notoriously during the "*Guiskard* crisis" of 1803, and during the nights before his suicide, when he "fired the oven with MSS (cf. *LS*,526); the summer of 1811 saw a flurry of publications, as if Kleist was "clearing his desk," and works in progress he deemed not ready or timely for puplication at that point, unless copies persisted with friends, are forever lost to the flames.

Leopold von Österreich

This drama appears to have crystallised during Kleist's sojourn in Thun in 1802. Notes Erich Schmidt (*Kleist als Dramatiker*, 5; 13):

> Es folgt Kleists glücklichste Zeit, der Schweizer Aufenthalt…Die "Schroffensteiner" werden fertig; sein Lustspiel, der "Guiskard," der "Leopold von Österreich" keimen… [D]er Plan zu einem 'Leopold von Österreich' sagt uns, daß… Kleist in der Schweiz einen Hauch eidgenössischen Heldenthums gespürt hat. Und wenn Pfuel einer Scene sich entsann, wo die übermüthigen österreichischen Ritter am Vorabend das Schlachtenglück im Zelt auswürfeln und einer nach

dem andern schwarz wirft, so hat Kleist gewiß selbst in jungen Jahren lebenslustige Leutnants heute roth, morgen todt gesehn.

Similarly Adolf Wilbrandt (*LS*,78):

Einen andern größeren Stoff fand er in der Schweizer Geschichte auf: ein Trauerspiel 'Leopold von Österreich'... Kleist ließ sich zunächst an seinen schweizerischen Quellen genügen; und Pfuel erzählt, daß er diesen Quellen viele picante Züge entnahm, die er mit gewaltiger Wirkung verwertete. Die Hauptszene aber es ersten Aktes war, wie die Ritter Leopolds vor der Sempacher Schlacht würfeln, wer mit dem Leben davonkommen wird, wer nicht... Man muß nach allem vermuten, daß Kleist diesen ersten Akt schon auf seiner Insel in der Aare schrieb; er hat überhaupt (wie Pfuel versichert) nur den einen vollendet.

Sembdner notes (cf. *LS*,78) that Paul Hoffmann traced this remarkable scene to Joh. Jakob Hottinger's drama *Arnold von Winkelried*, published in 1812, alongside Kleist's *Krug*, in the antology *Deutsche Schaubühne*, and concludes that Pfuel will have come across Hottinger's passage there and, his faculties diminished by age, erroneously associated it with Kleist because it appeared alongside *Krug*. I find Sembdner's conclusion unconvincing, for Pfuel knew Kleist far too well to confuse his work with another's. I can think of several plausible explanations how Kleist and Hottinger could both have produced this scene, be it independently of each other or not: firstly, Hottinger, a philologist and author of Swiss patriotic dramas, could have drawn on the same "Swiss sources" as did Kleist (Hoffmann's failure to trace a common source does not prove that none existed); secondly, Hottinger could have gleaned the scene from Kleist, for example via Zschokke, as Michalzik suggests, or via Chr. Martin Wieland, with whom Hottinger co-edited *Neues Attisches Museum* (Zürich, 1802–10), and whom Kleist visited at Oßmannstedt upon his return from Switzerland, on which occasion he could have shared passages from *Leopold*, as he did from *Guiskard*, which Wieland could have passed on to Hottinger who, when he published his drama in 1812, with Kleist dead and

Leopold unpublished, ran little risk of being accused of plagiarising; thirdly, Kleist could have met Hottinger in Switzerland and heard the anecdote from him.[651]

There is no reason to doubt Pfuel's account that Kleist had written down this scene, and the drama's first act, in Thun in 1802. Rühle even suggested that Kleist had completed the entire drama, "in the Shakespearean style" (Bülow; cf. *LS*,118), and although Tieck doubts this (cf. *ibid*), it is not implausible: *Leopold* is repeatedly mentioned in the same breath with *Guiskard* (cf. *LS*,503c), and its genesis may have closely mirrored *Guiskard*'s. Wilh. von Schütz noted, also leaning on Pfuel, that Kleist later, in Dresden in 1807/8, produced or reproduced at least one scene (cf. *LS*,190; 503c), possibly the one he wrote in Thun, and it appears plausible that Kleist had written a *Leopold* fragment or version in 1802, burned it in Paris in 1803 together with *Guiskard*, and rewrote it from memory or surviving notes in late 1807 or early 1808 when lining up publishable materials for *Ph*.

As said, Kleist will have used his extended Swiss sojourn to research the history of the Habsburg dynasty, whose eponymous ancestral castle is located only a few hours upriver from Kleist's island hideaway on the river Aare. In Switzerland Kleist could have drawn on official records accessible in Bern, as well as sources made available to him by friends, notably Zschokke, to prepare both *Schroffenstein* and *Leopold,* and it is not far-fetched to surmise that researching the Habsburgs was one of the main reasons for Kleist's having been drawn to Switzerland in the first place. His moves and location choices were always purposeful, and Switzerand will have been no exception.

The (hi)story of Leopold III "the Just," Duke of Austria (1351-1386), will have intrigued Kleist, as he could draw on this important figure in the Habsburgs' illustrious history for no less than three *satirical* themes he looked to tackle. Firstly, the Habsburgs' complex house rules (*Hausordnungen*) and succession treaties (*Erbverträge*), which provided a prominent example for the complexities and vagaries of dynastic rule and succession: Leopold's father, Albrecht II "the Wise," in 1355 promulgated a *Hausordnung* establishing that his three sons should jointly rule the Habsburg domains, to which his eldest son, Rudolf IV "the Founder," in 1364 added the *Rudolfinische Hausordnung*, which declared all Habsburg lands the brothers' joint property, whereupon in 1365, when Rudolf died prematurely, his teenage brothers Leopold III and Albrecht III came to rule the Habsburg realms jointly in an uneasy duumvirate, before in 1379 splitting it between them in a treaty of separation, thereby establishing the dynasty's Leopoldinian and Albertinian lines that would prevail into the 15th century. Secondly, the Habsburgs' said split into two competing lines, which weakened them in their a drawn-out and bitter conflict with the rising Swiss Confederacy, and furbished Kleist historical precedence for his *topos* of the rivalrous German dynasties having to face the rising *RF*: the fraternal rivalry was widely considered a major reason for Leopold's disastrous defeat at the hands of the Confederated army in the epic 1386 *Battle of Sempach* (in which the Habsburg army outnumbered the Swiss 3:1), in which he and many Habsburg nobles perished, in which the Habsburgs' lands on the Rhine's left bank (!) were lost, and in whose wake the Confederacy consolidated its power, increasingly squeezing the Habsburgs out of their ancestral lands, a development that culminated in the complete loss of those lands in Kleist's own time.[652] Thirdly, Leopold's personal travails and death, which offered Kleist a stark case study of a powerful ruler's loss, not only of his life, but also his succession: when at *Sempach* the Swiss closed in on the Austrian banner, "*Der Herzog* [Leopold] *eilte herbei zur Verteidigung seines Banners; hier, mitten unter seinen Feinden stürzte er, seine schwere Rüstung hinderte ihn sich aufzurichten. Ein Mann, der ihn, so sagt man, nicht kannte, tötete ihn mit grosser Mühe*"; his sons having been underage at the time of his premature death, Leopold was succeeded by none other than his brother and bitter rival Albrecht (only after Albrechts death in 1395 did Leopold's sons manage to regain the rule of their line).[653] These three *topoi*, which Kleist could draw from Leopold's (hi)story, correspond closely to the "Shakespearean" themes he in *Brief eines Dichters an einen anderen* highlights as most deserving of a poet's attention: in a decisive battle a spirited people's army overcomes a numerically far superior enemy

(*Agincourt, Sempach*); a ruler fails to to secure his succession, despite directing all his striving towards it (Macbeth, Leopold); a noble leader falls because he stumbles over his very nobility (Hamlet, Leopold). Already in 1801/2 Kleist was researching several of the *satirical* themes that would shape his œuvre.

Just as he wove certain themes from Habsburg dynastic history—the risk of succumbing to an external force in times of internal dynastic discord; the risk of usurpation—into *Schroffenstein*, Kleist may well have intended to work others—the game-changing battle (*Sempach*); the tragic ruler (Leopold)—into its sequel or companion drama *Leopold,* narrating *Sempach* as a model for an epic battle he anticipated for the near future, in which a large German army weakened by dynastic rivalry (in *Leopold*, the rival Habsburg lines) is routed by a smaller, more nimble French citizen army (the Confederacy), and in which Holy Roman Emperor Franz II (Leopold) succumbs to his own chivalrous bravery and the weight of his (outdated) armour, whereupon his imperial dignity falls to his fellow-German Fr. Wilh. III (Leopold's fellow Habsburg Albrecht). If Napoleon was to be embodied in the drama by the Swiss mythical hero Arnold von Winkelried, who decided *Sempach* in the Swiss' favour when he threw himself against the Habsburg phalanx of pikes, like a human *Grande batterie* opening a breach in their centre through which the Swiss pushed and killed Leopold, then *Leopold*'s scenario entailed not only Franz's heroic death, but also Napoleon's (as did, evidently, *Guiskard*'s).

Presumably Kleist prioritised *Guiskard* over *Leopold* when Napoleon's proclamation as *First Consul for Life* in August 1802 rendered a scenario in which he dies a heroic death in the battle's frontline implausible; instead, it became plausible that he would establish a dynastic rule and even reach for the imperial dignity. *Leopold* thus may have suffered the same fate as *Guiskard*—only earlier in its progression, and therefore less spectacularly and painfully—of being overtaken by historical developments and ending up in the drawer (or, together with *Guiskard*, in the fire). If Kleist in late 1807 or early 1808 indeed resurfaced or reproduced a *Leopold* fragment, it will have been in the same context as his recovery of the *Guiskard* fragment: with *Ph* he now had a suitable platform for their publication (and required materials to feed it), and parts of its original text could once again have become *satirically* pertinent, hence publishable. Why, then, did no *Leopold* fragment appear in *Ph*? Presumably, when the situation rapidly grew more acute after news of the Spanish guerrilla war broke in mid-1808, it called for a *Kohlhaas* and a *Hermannsschlacht*, and Kleist once again shelved any *Leopold* fragment he may have been working on, as he soon did *Ph* as a whole. Finally, when in early 1809 Fr. Wilh. reneged on his promise to side with Austria, and Franz alone stood up to Napoleon, the bard required material suitable for *Germania*: not a dystopian *Leopold* warning against the perils of aristocratic disunity, but utopian patriotic songs conjuring the power of a unified people. For *Leopold*'s theme and configuration, no auspicious moment ever recurred, and the MSS Kleist destroyed during the nights before his death could well have included a fragment, even a more or less complete version, of *Leopold*.

Leopold is of interest not only *satirically*, but also *po(i)etically* (of its *satyrical* and *syphilitical* potential we remain ignorant, except that we know the historical Leopold to have been popular and attached to his people, which for Kleist could have made him an orgiastic figure *par excellence*). *Sempach* for a long time lingered in the Swiss' collective consciousness, as a turning point in their history, the climax of their centuries-long confrontation with the Habsburgs in which their nation was born, as legends such as those retold in Schiller's *Wilhelm Tell* (1804) and Hottinger's *Arnold von Winkelried* (1812) relate. Whereas the likes of a Schiller or a Hottinger sought to inspire the German resistance against Napoleon by retelling stories of the Swiss resistance against the Habsburgs, Kleist turned the conventional symbolism on its head: in his rendering, the victorious Swiss will have represented not the Germans but the French! As such, *Leopold* would have been a precursor to *Homburg*, with its similarly unconventional twist (the Brandenburgians = the French), indicating that Kleist's technique of *Umpolung* coincided with the beginning of his career as writer, making *Leopold* a worthy companion piece to *Schroffenstein*, with its ingenious *Kleidertausch* (the Hohenzollern's

447

attempt to wrest the imperial mantle from the Habsburg). Only in juxtaposition with *Leopold* can we fully fathom *Schroffenstein*'s poetic concern, perhaps even the impetus for Kleist's career choice: while in both dramas a third force (the Swiss, Ursula) takes advantage of the German weakness induced by dynastic rivalry, in *Schroffenstein*, Ottokar-Fr. Wilh.'s attempt at forcing a *Kleidertausch* fails, whereas in *Leopold*, Albrecht-Fr. Wilh.'s usurpation of the imperial throne succeeds (assuming that Kleist in this respect followed historical precedence), so that *Leopold* and *Schroffenstein* comprise alternative scenarios for *a specific focal question*, one not concerned primarily with the *weakness* that comes from dynastic rivalry, and the opening it provides for a third party's inroads, but with *the conditions for a transfer of imperial power from the Habsburgs to the Hohenzollerns*. From the very beginning of his poetic career, Kleist's approach would then have consisted in producing *alternative scenarios* exploring diverse outcomes for *a specific focal question* (anticipating modern scenario planning).

Kleist moved to Switzerland not primarily to seek rest and recreation, or to orchestrate his filial reproduction with Wilhelmine (which he could have done elsewhere), but *to launch a poetry propelled by a precise dynastic dialectic,* and deploying a price, scenaric, technique.[654] Given his core *topos* of German *dynastic rivalry*, he arguably could not have commenced his poetic career in cosmopolitan Paris, but only before the ancient ruin of the Habsburg, on the tranquil river Aare.

Peter der Einsiedler
This drama is referred to only by the aging Rühle, who mentions it to Bülow in the same breath with *Leopold*, recalling that Kleist shared the general plan for this second drama "in the Shakespearean style" with Pfuel in Paris in 1803 (cf. *LS*,118). Since there is no other reference to it, and the old Rühle is not universally taken as reliable witness, some commentators have expressed doubt whether *Peter* ever existed, even in concept. Yet I see no reason to doubt Rühle's account, not only because I do consider him a reliable source, but also because his contention is plausible: the historical Peter the Hermit is

the type of figure that could well have attracted Kleist's attention, and inspired a Kleistian drama. Erich Schmidt's assertion (*Kleist als Dramatiker*, 13), "*Wir wissen gar nichts über 'Peter den Einsiedler'*," is somewhat misguided, for assuming that we can trust Rühle, we know that Kleist conceived of *Peter* within the same *satirical* context as *Guiskard* and *Leopold* (and, I might add, may have abandoned it for similar reasons). From this context we can conjecture *something* about Kleist's drama (or its concept).

Peter the Hermit (c.1050-1115), aka Cucupeter, Little Peter, or Peter of Amiens, in the late 11th century galvanised faithful commoners across Europe with his harrowing sermons, inspiring them to march towards the Holy Land even before Pope Urban II's "official" First Crusade got under way. Of the 40,000 faithful he in April 1096 gathered at Cologne, and led into what came to be known as the *Paupers' Crusade,* 30,000 in July 1096 reached Constantinople, where they received scant support from Emperor Alexius I Comnenus, who had originally called for Christian support against the Seljuk Turks, but beholding the disorderly Christian masses, became as weary of them as he was of the Muslim invaders. While Peter was tied up trying to solicit Alexius' support, the impatient Paupers set over to Anatolia without him, where they were routed by a Seljuk army in the *Battle of Civetot*, in which perhaps as many as 17,000 of them were slaughtered, with the survivors fleeing back to the Capital of the East. When the main contingents of the "official" *Knights' Crusade* arrived in Constantinople in late 1096, they united with the remaining *Paupers* and proceeded towards Jerusalem, whose Fatimid governor, Iftikhar al-Dawla, surrendered to them in July 1099, after a brief siege. Iftikhar was escorted out of the city and vanished into obscurity (implying that *Peter*'s scenario could have paralleled *Leopold*'s and *Guiskard*'s in that Kleist at this stage still expected Napoleon to remain a transitory figure).[655]

Peter's ability to inspire the masses and rally a people's movement against a seemingly overwhelming enemy would have intrigued Kleist (and perhaps reminded him of Kosegarten's harrowing sermons on the shores of Rügen). If *Guiskard* addresses the issue of Napoleon's hybris and succession, and *Leopold* that of

German weakness from disunity, *Peter* could have inquired into the conditions for a charismatic German leader rallying a broad-based people's movement. In which case Kleist as early as 1803 explored all key success factors of a successful resistance he would later elaborate in *Hermannsschlacht*: a charismatic German leader (Peter, a proto-Hermann) inspiring a pan-German people's army (the Paupers) supported by a full-fledged army led German princes (the Knights) to reconquer the Rhine's left bank (the Holy Land) from the Seljuk and Fatimid intruders (the *RF*, Napoleon). *Hermannsschlacht* would then be a "Germanised" version of *Peter*, with the main difference being that in the 1803 scenario, Kleist anticipated Franz II (Alexius) to be unsupportive, whereas in the 1808/9 scenario, he expected Franz I to play a significant role.

The figure of Peter could also have intrigued Kleist *satyrically*. For the fervent Christian faithful this preacher must have been an object of desire *par excellence*; in other words, for the *erastai*-Knights and *dmotes*-Paupers in his drama, Peter would have been the perfect *erômenos* for their mass orgies consummated first before, then inside, the walls of Jerusalem. The nicknames "Cucupeter" and "Little Peter" could have fired Kleist's vulgar fantasies, and inspired *Schroffenstein*'s young Peter and his cut-off little "finger," as well as *Marionettentheater*'s small but "graceful" male member. *Peter* could furthermore have served as blueprint for *po(i)etical* themes Kleist later explored in *Erdbeben* and *Cäcilie*: long before the "Catholic" *power of music* animates the Catholic congregation into mob lynchings (*Erdbeben*), or reduces the Protestant iconoclasts into devout submissiveness (*Cäcilie*), Peter's "Protestant" *power of the sermon* triggers the Christian faithful into liberating their "Holy Land" (that the preacher and hermit Peter is a suitable avatar of the bard and emigrant Kleist almost goes without saying). Thanks to the consistency of Kleist's *plane of composition*, if we were to feed a computer with a set of Kleistian *po(i)etical* "algorithms" (concerns, metaphors, encryption codes, *pescherä*, other poetic techniques), the computer could probably construct a version of *Peter* with an eminently Kleistian touch and feel, and even though Kleist himself may never have evolved this drama beyond an initial plan or concept, far from knowing "nothing" (Erich Schmidt) about it, we would almost know it *intimately*.

Die Numantia

On 13th August 1803 Adolphine von Werdeck, having on the previous day visited the *Reichenbachfälle* in the Bernese Oberland (of Sherlock Holmes fame) with her husband, Kleist and Pfuel, penned down: *"Der unschlüssige Kleist... beschloß... nach Thun zurückzukehren, um sein Peststück (ein Trauerspiel, das dünkt mich "Die Numantia" heißen sollte) zu vollenden"* (*LS*,114a). Note Samuel and Brown:

> in 1809 or 1810 Adolphine von Werdeck concocted from earlier notes... a "Diary"... of her travels in 1803 and 1804, during which, so Hoffmann says, she enjoyed the company of Heinrich von Kleist. Hoffmann [who assembled parts of Adolphine's legacy]... show[s] that Adolphine believed that the title of Kleist's "Peststück" (i.e. *Robert Guiskard*) was "Die Numantia." Hoffmann uses this obvious misunderstanding to accuse Adolphine of being ignorant of Kleist's talents and works. (*Lost Year*, 5)

Kleist was certainly working on *Guiskard* at the time of his and Pfuel's joint travels with the Werdecks (cf. II:735), but the MMS he burned in Paris could nevertheless ahve included a sketch of a drama entitled *Die Numantia*. "*Peststück*" almost certainly refers to *Guiskard*, but it is plausible that Adolphine, when compiling her "diary" from earlier notes, compounded two pieces of information, one concerning the "*Peststück*," *Guiskard*, and another concerning a separate drama Kleist was working on at the same time, *Numantia*, so that her "misunderstanding" would have consisted in compounding *two actual, different projects*: she could have assumed that the latter was the (working) title of the former. Had Adolphine read the *Guiskard* fragment in *Phöbus*, she could have become aware of her error, but perhaps she did not, in which case Hoffmann would not be entirely unfair when admonishing her ignorance of Kleist's work; still, he is not entirely fair either, since for his contemporaries, Kleist's works did not line up as neatly as they do for us today, thanks to the work of Sembdner *et al*, and the prolific Kleist will have repeatedly conceived of, and subsequently abandoned, projects, and talked to his acquaintances about them, and his works-in-progress will have been difficult to track for all but his closest friends. In short, it is eminently plausible that Kleist in the summer of 1803 was working on, or envisioned, "*Die Numantia*."[656]

The tragic fate of the people of Numantia would have intrigued Kleist: the remnants of the once powerful Celtiberian people, who in the course of the *Celtiberian Wars* (181-133 BC) had been reduced by the Roman legions to their last stronghold, the city of Numantia, in the *Siege of Numantia* (134-133 BC), under the command of chief Avarus, held out for many months against the Consul Scipio Aemilianus' (aka the Younger, to distinguish him from the illustrious Scipio Africanus) siege, till until starvation and mass suicides of entire families decimated the populace and, a last ditch attempt by their general Rhetogenes at rallying neighbouring tribes to succour the city having failed, a few hundred survivors set fire to their city and submitted to slavery. Roman historians commended the Numantians for their resilience and enthusiasm for liberty, but noted that they succumbed to the Romans not least because they failed to rally other Celtiberian tribes, notably the neighboring Arevaci and Lutia, to their cause.

Kleist would have had little difficulty turning this (hi)story—of a divided people's heroic but futile resistance to a superior enemy under the command of a charismatic general—into a scenario of a divided Germany, led by Franz II (Avarus) and Fr. Wilh. (Rhetogenes), succumbing to Napoleon's (Scipio's) siege of Vienna on the Danube (Numantia on the Duero), having failed to rally the other Celtiberian tribes (German peoples) to their succour.[657] A number of details of the historical siege would have fascinated Kleist: the mass suicides (which already fascinated Cervantes, who turned the material into a drama), the instances of cannibalism among the starving population, and especially a tragic episode of Rhetogenes convincing 500 Lutian youths to join his ranks, only for the Lutian elders, concerned about repercussions for their tribe, to warn Scipio of the youths' designs, who rounds them up and summarily has their hands (for Kleist: penises) chopped off.[658]

* * * *

By the summer or autumn of 1803, Kleist could thus have assembled the plans or sketches for four "historical" dramas—*Leopold, Peter, Guiskard, Numantia*—, all constructed around his two main *satirical* concerns, the *dyadic* rivalry between Franz and Fr. Wilh., and their *triadic* rivalry with Napoleon. If we include *Schroffenstein* and the first three scenes of *Krug*, which Kleist reportedly dictated to Pfuel also in the summer of 1803, the scenarios Kleist explored in the compact period between spring 1802 and autumn 1803 were as follows:

	Fr. Wilh. and Franz figures	Their outcomes	Napoleon figure	His outcomes
Commenced or conceived before Napoleon's proclamation as 1st Consul for Life (August 1802)				
Schroffenstein	Ottokar & Agnes	Both die when Fr. Wilh. tries to seize the imperial mantle	Ursula	Default beneficiary when Franz and Fr. Wilh. self-destruct
Leopold	Albrecht & Leopold	Franz dies; the imperial mantle falls to Fr. Wilh.	Arnold von Winkelried?	Winner in battle
Peter	Peter & Alexius	Franz retains the imperial throne	Iftikhar al-Dawla?	Forced to retreat, but not vanquished
Commenced or conceived following Napoleon's proclamation as 1st Consul for Life				
Guiskard	Äbelard & Robert	The imperial mantle falls to Fr. Wilh. (B)	Guiskard	Dies before or after conquering Vienna; succeeded by his designated heir (A)
Numantia	Rhetogenes & Avarus	Both die or are enslaved/castrated	Scipio	Conquers Germany
Krug	Licht & Adam	Franz damaged; Licht scheming to usurp his position; outcome open	Walter (appears in scene 4)	Outcome open

453

Taken together, the four "historical" drama projects of 1803 encompass all *satirical* scenarios Kleist appears to have deemed plausible and potentially imminent at that time; *Krug*'s satirical scenario remained open, thus fungible, which goes a long way towards explaining why this drama "survived" Kleist's 1803 *auto-da-fé*, was eventually completed, and published.

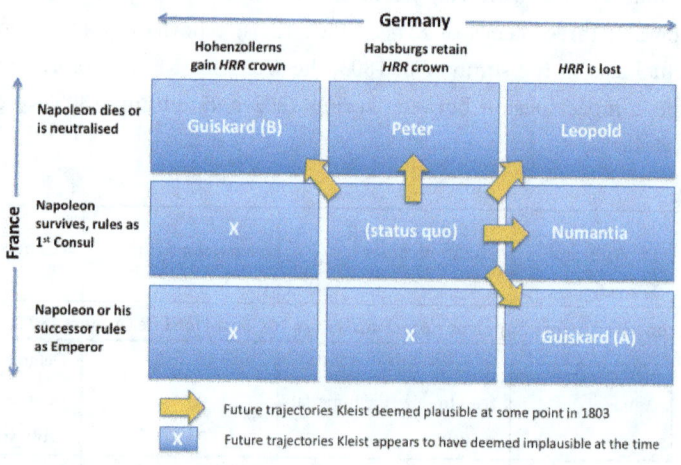

The matrix pinpoints Kleist's conundrum: following Britain's declaration of war in April 1803, Napoleon soon began assembling the British invasion force at Boulogne, and by the summer of 1803 it will have become apparent to Kleist that none of these four "historical" dramas, with their focus on Germany, fit the emerging realities; this recognition could have triggered the second Swiss journey with Pfuel and caused his "indecision," and eventual decision to return to Thun, which Adolfine recorded in her "diary." Kleist during the Swiss journey may have toyed with a number of ideas for how to proceed, including turning *Numantia*, rather than *Guiskard*, into a Britain-centric scenario (*Siege of Numantia* = siege of London)—which could have caused Adolphine's compounding the two dramas. Having earlier put *Peter* and *Leopold* on the back-burner, Kleist in October 1803 abandoned or shelved *Guiskard* and *Numantia*, and in view of the speed with which the Napoleonic juggernaut was moving, instead of writing scenarios that had a short shelf-life, decided to throw himself *medias in res* at Saint-Omer.

Die Zerstörung Jerusalems

Among the books Kleist borrowed from the Dresden library in late 1808 and early 1809 (cf. *LS*,307) were Joh. David Michaelis' *Mosaic Law* and Flavius Josephus' *Works*. The latter chronicles the *First Jewish-Roman War* of AD 66-72, during which the future Roman Emperor Titus suppressed a Zealot revolt and, aided by disunity among the Jewish factions, after a siege of six-months, in AD 70 conquered Jerusalem, razed the Second Temple, and killed, enslaved or exiled hundreds of thousands of Jews.[659] Kleist borrowed the works by Josephus and Michaelis *before* those by Fr. II and Krause that were to inform *Homburg*, and kept Krause's book longer, suggesting that he seriously prepared for a drama named *Die Zerstörung Jerusalems* or *Titus von Jerusalem* (cf. *LS*,503a; b; c; *NR*,198b).

For or all their differences, the two historical periods Kleist immersed himself into concurrently—the Brandenburgian resistance against the Swedes in the 17th, the Israeli revolt against the Romans in the 1st century—shared certain characteristics, including the *topoi* of disunity and rebelliousness (the Jewish factions; Homburg's insubordination). Kleist could initially have conceived *Jerusalem* as another sequel to *Hermannsschlacht*, and an alternative scenario for *Homburg*: it's engame could have been one not of submission, but of utter destruction and exile (a scenario similar to *Numantia*'s, but featuring a conqueror, Titus, who had credentials not only as general, as did Scipio, but also as emperor, as the son and designated heir of the Emperor Vespasian).

During the *Germania* period Kleist jotted down a brief note on Ernst Moritz Arndt's 1806 *Geist der Zeit*, in which he evidently draws on Josephus' history:

> O du, der du so sprichst, du kömmst mir vor, wie etwa ein Grieche, aus dem Zeitalter des Sülla, oder, aus jenem des Titus, ein Israelit.

> Was! Dieser mächtige Staat der Juden soll untergehen? Jerusalem, diese Stadt Gottes, von seinen leibhaftigen Cherubimen beschützt, sie sollte, mit Zinnen und Mauern, zu Asche versinken? Eulen und Adler sollten in den Trümmern dieses salomonischen Tempels wohnen? Der Tod sollte die ganze Bevölkerung hinwegraffen, Weiber und Kinder in Fesseln hinweggeführt werden, und die Nachkommenschaft, in alle Länder der Welt zerstreut, durch Jahrtausende und wieder Jahrtausende, auf ewig elend, verworfen, wie dieser Ananias prophezeit, das Leben der Sklaven führen?
> Was!
>
> (II:377; 937)

Is this not as succinct a summary as any of *Jerusalem*'s plot? Kleist explicitly equates the Israelis' uprising against Titus with the Greeks' against Sulla (in Kleistian code, Greeks = Prussians or Germans).[660]

When *Wagram* and *Znaim* had ended the war, Austria's fate hung in the balance at *Schönbrunn*, and Kleist "disappeared" in Prague, he could well have resumed work on Jerusalem: had Napoleon at *Schönbrunn* chosen to dismantle the Habsburg Empire, he could have led the call for a final stand. When Napoleon spared Austria, and rumours of his proposed marriage with Marie-Louise spread, Kleist will have stashed his work-in-progress *Jerusalem* into his *Ideenmagazin* and pulled out his work-in-progress *Käthchen*, which he rushed to complete. Whereas during the Prague hiatus Kleist appears to have remained mute about Jerusalem, in Berlin he mentions the drama repeatedly, and in the summer of 1811, when he still nourished hopes that Fr. Wilh. would confront Napoleon, *Jerusalem* once again became pertinent, and he may even have resumed working on it. When in early November Fr. Wilh. entered into negotions for an alliance with Napoleon, it had become clear that the hoped-for German revolt of 1811 would not take place, and that the story of the heroic, if futile, revolt of AD 66-72 was again obsolete. At that point in time, Kleist ran out of *anything* to write altogether: he had become a poet in order to help propel Germany's resistance and unification, and with Prussia's impending alliance with Napoleon, *there was nothing left for him to say* (as said, the idea that Russia might defeat the *Grande Armée* did not occur to him). This is, above all, why he could die, and *did die*: King and Fatherland no longer needed the bard. Among the MSS Kleist burned in his final nights, there will have been a *Jerusalem* MS. *Alles oder Nichts? Nichts! Red or Black? Black, Black, Black.*

Onkels Neue Scheune
We revert to the beginnings. We shall take as given that the 10-year old Kleist (*"in seinem elften Jahre"*; LS,9) in late 1787 or 1788 wrote and recited a poem on the subject of his uncle's new barn, in a contest with his younger brother Leopold held at their uncle's Tschernowitz estate; while Kleist's poem is not extant, Leopold's, who won their poetic *agôn*, is. Uncle Aug. Wilh. von Kleist, who presumably initiated and chaired their contest as presiding judge, was the Royal Prussian Chamberlain, and it does not take a huge leap of faith to conjecture that his new barn, whose praises he challenges the boys to sing—in Leopold's verses, "*Stehe denn, du fest Gebäude, / Hundert Jahre noch*"—, for him represented a rejuvenated Prussia under his new master, the initially popular Fr. Wilh. II, who in August 1786 had ascended the throne upon the death of the—by then—deeply unloved Fr. II: in Leopold's rendering, a more "pastoral" incarnation of *Fredericianism*, the cows (subjects) still demurely lined up in orderly rows, but more content with their pastures and homely barn.

We have no record of the contest's exact date. As Kleist was "in his eleventh year," it certainly took place after Fr. Wilh. II's invasion of Holland in September-October 1787, which led to the re-instatement of his brother in law, Dutch Stadtholder Wilh. V, and to the creation of a Protestant alliance between Holland, Great Britain, and Prussia (which, in conjunction with his support for anti-Habsburg revolts during the *Russo-Austrian War against the Turks*, exacerbated Prussia's rift with Austria)—events which Fr. Wilh. II celebrated with the commission of the triumphal Brandenburg Gate, whose architecture owes a great debt to the Propylaea of Pericles, founder of a golden age, whom Fr. Wilh. II evidently sought to emulate. In particular Leopold's line, *"Deine schöne Symmetrie,"* apparently out of place in reference to a mere barn, even a well-proportioned one, suggests that it was part of the rules of the contest that the "barn" was to represent not only the new Prussia in general, but specifically this new architectural symbol—whose symmetry is indeed striking—that was to synecdochally represented Prussia's stately grandeur and her King's proud magnificence:

Uncle Fr. Wilh. II's new "barn":
"Und ein Brand verwüste nie / Deine schöne Symmetrie."[661]

Although the monumental gate's construction commenced only in 1789, i.e., after the contest's presumed date (it was completed in 1793), the architect Carl Gotthard Langhans may well have produced initial sketches already in 1788, and as the King's chamberlain, the uncle may have been involved in the design stage and obtained a copy of the sketches, which he may have shown his nephews. The reported, and at first sight surprising, fact that the then barely 8-year old Leopold, not the three years older (and surely more talented) Heinrich, won the contest tells us something else: already Kleist's first poem must have been—or must have appeared to the uncle—

irreverent, queer, or otherwise reprehensive. If Leopold's poem celebrated a Prussia that in its newest incarnation was to be firm, durable, handsome, healthy, straight and orderly, and glorious in its eventual demise, Heinrich's presumably *did nothing of that sort.*

We shall take into account another contextual factor that may well have been relevant for the contest: their father's death on 18th June 1788. Joachim Fr. von Kleist had suffered from a protracted illness and prepared for this event, in his final months doing his utmost to alleviate economic hardship for his family following his imminent departure; alas, four days after his death the King refused his widow a pension, and to make matters worse, his testament's execution was stalled by a court on formal grounds.[662] While it is possible that the visit on the uncle's estate took place *before* the father's death—say, over Easter or Pentecoast 1788—, it is much more probable that it took place *soon after* the father's death, i.e., during the summer of 1788: *that,* following the father's burial, the mother, Juliane Ulrike, née von Pannwitz, distressed and having to cope with seven children while pursuing her entreaties to the King and her inheritance case in court, and unable to continue paying Kleist's tutor Catel (which would explain why Kleist's private eduction with Catel in Berlin evidently came to an abrupt halt at this time), asked the uncle to afford her two sons a carefree summer on his estate, away from the troubles of Frankfurt/O; *that* the uncle at Tschernowitz entertained the two boys with various activities, including showing them the sketches for the Brandenburger Tor and orchestrating their poetic contest; *that* the barely 8-year old Leopold, appropriately for his age, remained blissfuly unperturbed by the peril that had befallen the family, got over the father's death fairly easily and, as his poem suggests, in his childish exuberance soon adopted the uncle's enthusiasm for his King's reign—an enthusiasm the late father may not have shared, and that the uncle now seized the opportunity to instill in the boys; finally, *that* Heinrich, at almost 11 years of age quite able to make up his own mind, fond of his mother and cogniscent of her distress, and perhaps also fond of Catel and dismayed at his education having been disrupted by the King's intransigence, adopted an altogether more sombre, dark and brooding attitude towards the state of affairs, and addressed it in his poem.[663]

From all that we can infer from his later writings and actions, it is probably safe to assume that Kleist:

- blamed Fr. Wilh. II's vein self-agrandisement for his mother's distress and his education's abortion (Fr. Wilh. II's court responded to Fr. II's unpopular niggardliness with an extravagant lavishness, while refusing the modest pension to Mme Kleist on the grounds that the state treasury was depleted);
- deemed Fr. Wilh. II's grandiose plans for the Brandenburg Gate altogether misplaced, in relation to the purportedly empty state coffers, as well as the King's foreign policies' questionable achievements;
- sided with his father's dispassionate, but genuine, loyalty to the Hohenzollern dynasty, not with his uncle's doggish veneration for the present King, and may have been dismayed at his uncle's blatant attempt at brain-washing him and his brother, within days or weeks of the father's passing away and irrespective of the mother's troubles with the King.

460 Whereas Leopold in the Brandenburger Tor evidently saw but the King's glory and Prussia's grandeur, Heinrich may have seen in it but the King's vanity and carelessness, and a harbinger of Prussia's impending catastrophe. Given the consistency of his plane of composition, Kleist's later, often apocalyptic and dystopian, depictions of combusting or decaying structures convey an idea regarding, not the precise lines of his last poem, but the idiosyncratic poetic style and force that the—presumably horrified—uncle may have been treated to by his brooding, irreverent older nephew:[664]

> Der Palast des Vizekönigs war versunken, der Gerichtshof... stand in Flammen, und an die Stelle, wo sich ihr väterliches Haus befunden hatte, war ein See getreten, und kochte rötliche Dämpfe aus. (II:149)

> Feuer! Feuer! Feuer! Erwacht ihr Männer von Thurneck, ihr Weiber und Kinder des Fleckens erwacht!... Feuer! Der Frevel zog auf Socken durchs Tor! Der Mord steht, mit Pfeil und Bogen, mitten unter euch, und die Verheerung, um ihm zu leuchten, schlägt ihre Fackel an alle Ecken der Burg! Feuer! Feuer! (I:491)

> Denn eh doch, seh ich ein, erschwingt der Kreis der Welt
> Vor dieser Mordbrut keine Ruhe,
> Als bis das Raubnest ganz zerstört,
> Und nichts, als eine schwarze Fahne,
> Von seinem öden Trümmerhaufen weht! (I:628)

> Gleichwohl, als der Knecht schreckenblaß, wenige Momente nachdem der Schuppen hinter ihm zusammenstürzte, mit den Pferden, die er an der Hand hielt, daraus hervortrat,… und…fragte: was er mit den Tieren nun anfangen solle? (II:33)

> Am Fuße der Alpen, bei Locarno im oberen Italien, befand sich ein altes, einem Marchese gehöriges Schloß, das man jetzt, wenn man vom St. Gotthard kommt, in Schutt und Trümmern liegen sieht… (II:196)

We know nothing of Kleist's early poem but this: it caused Uncle Aug. Wilh. consternation, gained young Leopold a default Louis d'or, and gave Kleist *an inkling of the power—and, given he lost the contest, also of the futility—of his word.* At the tender age of 10, on a summer evening, the *satyrical* bard Kleist was born.

"inder Quere."
I include in this section an exploration of Kleist's first extant piece of writing, a c.1791 album entry for Minette:

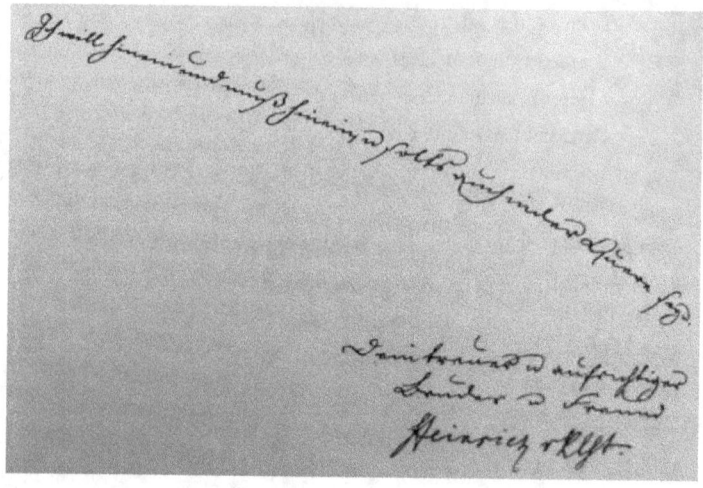

Ich will hinein und muß hinein, u. sollts auch inder Quere seyn.

Dein treuer u. aufrichtiger

Bruder u. Freund

Heinrich vKlst.   (MAII:483)

Minette presumably not having been among Kleist's most important interlocutors, this album entry may well have been but one of a *series* of early poetical attempts, whose other specimens are not extant, perhaps because they were sensitive in the eyes of the recipient(s) and deliberately destroyed (the album entrymay be extant because Minette did not "get" any of it, and saw no need to destroy it).

The movement indicated by Kleist's "*hinein,*" in conjunction its implicit corollary "*hinaus,*" anticipates canonical *satyrical* passages in Kleist's works—e.g., "*hier/da*" in *Marquise*; "*hier/dort*" in *Prolog*—, and his dedication "*Dein... aufrichtiger* (literally: erect) *Bruder*" is explicit. Kleist's signing his entry "*vKlst,*" omitting the vowals *o, e* and *i*, may have been common shorthand (*v.* instead of *von* certainly was; Beethoven signed some of his scores "*Bthvn*"), but could also have entailed the first extant example of his pervasive I/O symbolism ("i" = phallus, "o" = anus, "e" = cavum oris). If Kleist in c.1791, at approx. 14 years of age, provided these succinct articulations of his homosexual desires (*"Ich will hinein... inder Quere"*) and physical prowess (*"treu u. aufrichtig"*), he could have had first intimate experiences during which he became conscious of them.⁶⁶⁵ If so, his "brother-in-arms" in his sensual explorations could have been his cousin Carl von Pannwitz, his senior by one year, who in 1795, apparently either on, or on the eve of, Kleist's 18ᵗʰ birthday committed suicide by shooting himself, and with whom Kleist had entered a suicide pact in which they promised each other to die by their own hand—a promise both of them honoured (cf. *LS*,6; 5a).⁶⁶⁶

Kleist and Pannwitz will have spent significant time together in Frankfurt/O. in 1787, when the two youngsters—Heinrich aged 10, Carl, 11—were jointly educated by the private tutor Chr. Ernst Martini, and perhaps again from mid-1788 till 1791, where there is a gaping whole in Kleist's biography (apart from the 1788 summer holiday on the uncle's estate I reconstructed), when they may again have been jointly being taught by Martini, until Pannwitz in 1791 joined the army.⁶⁶⁷ Their undocumented period of puberty—Heinrich aged 12-14, Carl, 13-15—will naturally have been highly formative for both teenagers, and if they did spent much of it together, they could well have discovered their emerging sexuality jointly (as well as more generally exerting tremendous influence on each other)—a fascinating possibility whose comprehensive side-lining by the *Kleist-Forschung* is only partially excused by the lack of biographical data. Kleist's ominous album entry could have coincided with, or closely followed, Pannwitz's departure for military service: it betrays a Lacanian *manque*, as well as the same kind of obstinacy as the suicide pact.

Kleist's appearance during this time could be represented well by a portrait whose attribution to Kleist is uncertain, but plausible (below, centre left): its soft, almost girlish, features situate it on the trajectory defined by those at age 7 (left; attribution uncertain but probable), age 18 (centre right; attribution uncertain) and 24 (right, attribution accepted):

Sweet object of desire: Kleist (?) at age 7, 12, 18 and 24.[668]

An effeminate-yet-ithyphallic teenager with a taste for his own gender: like his half-sister Ulrike, that *"Wesen... das... gleich wie eine Amphibie zwischen zwei Gattungen schwankt"* (II:676)—indeed, arguably more than her—Kleist deserved the epithet *"amphibion."* I have found no image of Pannwitz's, but let us assume for the sake of this argument that he was a more masculine type, that they were drawn to each other sensuously, and that together they explored their nascent homoeroticism, without necessarily fully consummating it yet (as said, Kleist's full initiation may have taken place during the *Siege of Mainz*; Pannwitz's similarly may have during his military service).

While the above is speculative, what *is* known is that Pannwitz's father (Kleist's uncle) Karl Wilh. von Pannwitz, in a very personal, letter entitled *Lehren eines Vaters an seinen Sohn, der sich dem Soldaten Standt widmete*, expressly warned his son of the dangers of homosexuality, which is not something a father does without reason; admittedly, the father's admonition could reflect a non-specific concern, homosexuality being an obvious corollary of army life, yet it could also have been fuelled by a concrete suspicion. This letter kindles, with Blamberger, "speculation about the motive for Pannwitz's suicide on the homeward march from battle in Poland"— namely: *"Selbstmord seines Vetters und Freundes Carl von Pannwitz, 1795, vermutlich zur Verdeckung homosexueller Erfahrungen während des Militär- und Kriegsdienstes"* (KH,369).[669] My own conjecture is that Carl and Heinrich jointly explored their homosexuality already *before* they were separated by the duty of war, and that when in 1791 Carl departed for his military service—it will have been already clear at that time that Kleist in 1792 would follow suit—, they entered their suicide pact, which they may have reconfirmed in writing in subsequent letters.[670] Within roughly a year of each other, both young men were deployed in military campaigns at opposite ends of Prussia's geographical reach: first Heinrich, from April 1793, in the *Rhine Campaign* in the west, then Carl, from the summer of 1794, in the *Polish Campaign* in the east; in the same year, 1795, both were marched homewards after their campaigns concluded, respectively, with *Basel* (5th April 1795) and the *Third Partition* (24th October 1795), Heinrich arriving safely in Potsdam in early July, Carl shooting himself on the way back in October (aged 19). We do not know why Pannwitz took his life (no farewell letter is extant), but we may speculate that he dreaded confronting his father, either because his homosexuality had become an open secret, or because he had contracted syphilis or another venereal disease whose symptoms were becoming obvious, or else that he had reason to believe that Heinrich's desire for him had cooled—Kleist could have written him as much: we know how brutally direct he could be—, or that he feared that their reunion would be marred by his his disease. If his suicide indeed coincided with Kleist's birthday, it must have been meant as a deliberate message for Heinrich—either: "this is for you," or, in line with the suicide pact: "now it's your turn."

In October 1789 Pannwitz produced the following album entry, signed "Karl von Pannwitz Gulben d 15. Oktober 1789":

> Noch rauscht der schwarze Flügel des Todes nicht,
> Drum hasch die Freuden, eh sie der Sturm verweht
> Die Gott, wie Sonnenschein und Regen,
> Aus der vergeudenden Urne schüttet.
>
> (quoted in Loch, *Kleist*, 424, n.26)

Do not "the joys poured forth from the urn" evoke *ejaculation*? Are not the "black wings of death" those associated with a frightening *venereal disease*? If Carl during this period produced such eroticopoetical attempts (as youths do everywhere, if not necessarily in such a refined manner), would not have Heinrich done likewise?

Did Kleist not, during these youthful exploits together with cousin Pannwitz, begin to hone his poetical language? Did he not, within a year or so of his proto-*satirical* attempt in the contest with Leopold, at the tender age of 12 or 13, and in an intimate erotico-poetical exchange with Pannwitz, produce his first proto-*satyrical* poetry? And does not his album entry for Minette comprise the sole extant trace of an "inaugural *satyrico-po(i)etical* project," a project entailing Kleist's discovery, and exploration in poetry, of the inexorable link between *Erôs* and *Thanatos*? Did Kleist and Panwitz both carry a bundle of poems with them into battle they had written for each other? Did Heinrich ditch his bundle when he cooled to Carl following his initiations near Mainz? Did Carl burn his when he despaired of Heinrich? Did Carl von Pannwitz burn Kleist's collected juvenile poems on the day of his death?

Geschichte meiner Seele

Kleist ostensibly wrote the legendary, or lost, autobiographical *Geschichte meiner Seele* in the wake of his "Kant-crisis" in 1801 (cf. *LS*,51b). Given the autobiographic nature of *all* his writings, and his suicidal tendency (the "Kant-crisis" may well have encompassed a "suicide project"), I consider it plausible that Kleist did write such an essay or memoir, which could indeed have been "lost in the turmoil of those years," as Johanna von Haza put it to Tieck in 1816 (cf. *NR*,134), or more precisely, *destroyed*—by Kleist himself and, if he had entrusted it to close friends, by them, possibly only after his death.[671] *Geschichte* could have served Kleist as "evangelium" for friends whom he sought to "convert" to his "religion," "life plan" and "death plan"; his *Aufsatz* to Rühle could have been a precursor. Alternatively (or concurrently), it could have been his farewell letter-cum-apology which, when he decided to live, had to be ditched.

For Kleist, "*Seele*" was separate from, but intimately connected and correlated with, "*Leib*"—in his own terms, "moral" and "physical" life are governed by the same "laws."[672] When Ottokar tells Agnes, "*Deine Seele / Lag offen vor mir, wie ein schönes Buch*" (V.1269-70), it was evidently her *body* that was "open" to him at their earlier rendezvous, which however could only have been the case if her *soul*, too, had been "open." *Geschichte* would have been a *Geschichte meiner Seele und meines Leibes,* just as his famous phrase à propos of *Penthesilea* would have meant, precisely, *"der ganze Schmutz zugleich und Glanz meiner Seele und meines Leibes,"* and would have covered the intricately enmeshed complex of his *satyrical* and *syphilitical,* his *familial* and *filial,* "lives."

The concept of metempsychosis—the human soul (*psyche*) as an immortal entity that has its own essence independent of the body—was at the core of Kleist's "religion" (his own term—cf., e.g., II:496; 633).[673] Kleist may have first been exposed to concepts of the afterlife by his tutor Chr. Ernst Martini, a student of theology and disciple of the rationalist Lutheran theologian Josias Fr. Chr. Löffler at the Viadrina, who may again have been tutoring Kleist following his father's death in June 1788, during which period Martini could have imparted to the 11-year old the idea of metempsychosis as a means of consolation. During the same period Löffler, like Martini a neighbour of the Kleist family, may have paid visits to Mme *Mère du Poète* to provide solace, and Kleist (and Carl von Pannwitz, presumably then also living in the Kleistian home), may have been listening to his teachings.[674] During *Mainz* Kleist read Chr. M. Wieland's *Sympathien,* steeped in Pythagorean metempsychosis (and, relatedly, Platonic spiritual kinship): *"Seelen, die vielleicht schon unter einem andern Himmel sich liebten"*; *"Wie süß ist es ihnen, ihr Innerstes einander aufzuschließen."*[675]

In his "Kant-crisis" letter of March 1801 Kleist explains how his "religion," or "principle of action," was modulated by his reading of Kantian treatises:

> Ich habe schon als Knabe (mich dünkt am Rhein durch eine Schrift von Wieland) mir den Gedanken angeeignet, daß die Vervollkomnung der Zweck der Schöpfung wäre. Ich glaubte, daß wir einst nach dem Tode von der Stufe der Vervollkomnung, die wir auf diesem Sterne erreichten, auf einem andern weiter fortschreiten würden, und daß wir den Schatz von Wahrheiten, den wir hier sammelten, auch dort einst brauchen könnten. Aus diesen Gedanken bildete sich so nach und nach eine eigne Religion, und das Bestreben... unaufhörlich einem höhern Grade von

> Bildung entgegenzuschreiten, ward bald das Prinzip meiner Tätigkeit. Bildung schein mir das einzige Ziel, das des Bestrebens, Wahrheit der einzige Reichtum, der des Besitzes würdig ist. [...]
>
>> Wenn alle Menschen statt der Augen grüne Gläser hätten, so würden sie urteilen müssen, die Gegenstände, welche sie dadurch erblicken, *sind* grün... So ist es mit dem Verstande. Wir können nicht entscheiden, ob das was wir Wahrheit nennen, wahrhaft Wahrheit ist, oder ob es nur so scheint. Ist das letzte, so *ist* die Wahrheit, die wir hier sammeln, nach dem Tode nicht mehr—und alles Bestreben, ein Eigentum sich zu erwerben, das uns auch in das Grab folgt, ist vergeblich—
>>
>> Ach, Wilhelmine, ... Mein einziges, mein höchstes Ziel ist gesunken, und ich habe nun keines mehr.— [...]
>
>> Liebe Wilhelmine, laß mich reisen. (II:633-5)

If the truth-content of any knowledge is *subjective* and *relative*, has no meaning or value apart from its subject and context—if, say, intelligent beings on another "star," instead of through human eyes (or minds), *see this* knowledge through "green glasses" (or differently structured minds), thus *seeing* it *as* something quite different, then it is futile to accumulate knowledge in this life in the hope that the immortal soul will carry it forward to another "star," for it is profoundly *un*transportable, *un*transplantable and *un*translatable.[676]

I argued in *Emigrant* that his so-called "Kant-crisis" entailed Kleist's *liberation*, his unburdening himself from the *consumption* of stale, generic, second-hand, theoretical *book-knowledge* and his unleashing of his creative *production* of plastic, idiosyncratic, first-hand, practical *life-knowledge*: the only "knowledge" of genuine value was that which one *produced* oneself, for a specific situation and purpose *in this world*, and whose utility consists, not in *grasping*, but in *shaping*, the world. With the "Kant-crisis," then, Kleist fully came into his own *as poet* ("ποιητής" = "maker"). Henceforth he prioritised *action in this life* over *accumulation of knowledge for a future life*, and let his body and soul pursue the immutable Platonic objects— the good, the true, the beautiful (cf. II:309)—, not by a "cool acknowledgment of fact" but in passionate pursuit of action:

"*Liebe Wilhelmine, laß mich reisen.*" The "Kant-crisis" recast Kleist's goal and plan for the present life, not his faith in reason, nor that in metempsychosis, *per se*—the latter he re-affirmed in July 1801, soon after the "Kant-crisis," to Caroline von Schlieben: "*Wenn Sie auf diesem Sterne keinen Platz finden können, der Ihrer würdig ist, so finden Sie vielleicht auf einem andern einen um so bessern*" (II:665).[677]

Kleist's imagery of the "comet," which appears early in his writings—he could have gleaned it from Wieland's *Sympathien* (cf. Schrader, *KJb* 1988/9, 165)—and recurs throughout, may serve as conceptual proxy and shorthand for "his soul's history."[678] A comet is a small body that is ejected from its origin, at the fringes of the solar system (the Oort Cloud or Kuiper Belt), and that in the course of eons wanders around the Sun in excentric (relative to the main planets' orbits) and increasingly tighter orbits, until eventually flaring up in her corona. This *aionic* and excentric movement properly constitutes the comet's "origin," "history" and "fate." In *Aufsatz* Kleist tells Rühle precisely what is at stake:

> Jetzt freilich wanken wir noch auf regellosen Bahnen umher, aber, mein Freund, das ist uns als Jünglinge zu verzeihen... Wir kennen die Beschwörungsformel noch nicht, die Zeit allein führt sie mit sich, um die wunderbar ungleichartigen Gestalten, die in unserem Inneren wühlen und durcheinander treiben, zu besäftigen und zu beruhigen. Und alle Jünglinge, die wir um und neben uns sehen, teilen ja mit uns dieses Schicksal... Sie erscheinen mir wie Kometen, die in regellosen Kreisen das Weltall durchschweigen, bis sie endlich eine Bahn und ein Gesetz der Bewegung finden. (II:309)

"Comets" = "*Jünglinge, die wir um und neben uns sehen*" = members of the "brotherhood"; "*Bahn*," "*Beschwörungsformel*," "*Gesetz der Bewegung*" = a life plan that allows to reconcile the pursuit of homosexual desire with that of producing successors; "*Schicksal*" = the eventual embrace by, and flaring up in, the Sun. In the letter to Caroline von Schlieben of July 1801 Kleist compares this ideal "Sun" or "fate" with the "heavenly kindness" of a woman:

> Ja, es gibt eine gewisse himmlische Güte, womit die Natur das Weib gezeichnet hat, und die ihm allein eigen ist, alles, was sich ihr mit einem Herzen nähert, an sich zu schließen mit Innigkeit und Liebe: so wie die Sonne, die wir darum auch Königin, nicht König nennen, alle Weltkörper, die in ihrem Wirkungsraum schweben, an sich zieht mit sanften unsichtbaren Banden, und in frohen Kreisen um sich führt, Licht und Wärme und Leben ihnen gebend, bis sie am Ende ihrer spiralförmigen Bahn an ihrem glühenden Busen liegen— (II:660)

"Comet" is "brotherhood" code for a *homosexual man* who must break out of the rigid context of his home, and, after some youthful erratic meandering, find a regular "orbit"—"happy circles"—and an "incantation," "law of motion" or life plan—say, one involving "*Scheidung*" and "*Einrichtung*"—that allows him to pursue a "*Mittelpfad*," a "*Mittelstraße*" (II:477; 309) distinct from, but alongside, conventional society (the planets), pursuing his homosexual and, in Kleist's case, poetical, passions while remaining tethered to a woman as the "Sun" who will be the mother to his children and, when the time comes, his sister-in-death. The "comet's" protracted but finite journey in ever tighter excentric orbits around the "Sun" sums up the "history of his soul."

Kleist's letters, from the beginning of the Würzburg journey till the "Kant-crisis," chronicle his "ejection" from the "Oort Cloud" of provincial Frankfurt/O., and from the "Kuiper Belt" of his family's conventional expectations, and his quest for a stable "orbit" around a "Sun" (Wilhelmine, at that time, being his designated fixed star). Kleist's portrayal of his "ejection" from his "origin," and his acceleration towards a "solar orbit," is among his earliest poetic masterpieces:

> Als ich im Halbdunkel des Morgens abfuhr... Der Wagen rollte weiter, indessen mein Auge immer noch mit rückwärtsgewandtem Körper an das geliebte Haus hing. (II:515).

When he sets off, his eyes (the windows of the soul, as they say) are still attached to his origin (his family home), while, in a momentary contortion, his body (his vehicle) already accelerates towards its destination, rather like a projectile hurled towards a target by a catapult's torsion spring's release. A staccato of *"adieus"* accompanies his progressive acceleration, from posting house to posting house *en route* to Würzburg: *"ich werde abgerufen... Adieu"* (21st Aug.; II:531); *"Adieu. Ich muß zusiegeln"* (1st Sept.; II:538); *"Lebe wohl... In 5 Minuten reise ich von hier ab"* (4th Sept., 5 am; II:546); *"Adieu. Der Postillion bläst"* (5th Sept., 8 am; II:548); *"Adieu, in der nächsten Station noch ein Wort"* (5th Sept., 10:30 am; II:550); *"Adieu. Schlafe wohl"* (5th Sept., 8 pm; II:553); *"Ich bleibe hier.... Adieu"* (9th/10th Sept.; II:554). Every *"Adieu,"* a firing of his rocket engine.

Würzburg inaugurated a *series* of journeys, whose every station provided Kleist a temporary abode, a planet along his path through the galaxy whose gravitational field slows him down for a while, redirects his trajectory, and accelerates him again towards the next stage, slingshotting and planet-hopping him around central Europe, *"Wie die alten Ritter, von Burg zu Burg"* (II:656), "like the medieval knights" (with their chivalrous, jousting lances), "like the courtly troubadours" (with their romantic *grand chants*), "from anus to anus."[679] The "Kant-crisis" letter's conclusion, *"Liebe Wilhelmine, laß mich reisen,"* simply put, means this: "let me pick up my excentric wanderings again; I have not yet found the magic formula, which time alone can supply, but I am going for it, and I shall find it, trust me." *"Vertrauen auf uns, Einigkeit unter uns." Adieu, Adieu, Adieu!*

"Ein Roman"
A fine line separates Kleistian projects "extant" and "*not* extant," as the case of *Homburg* demonstrates. Horst Häker shows that Fouqué had reason—namely, jealousy of a superior rival—to suppress *Homburg*'s publication, and may have actively sought to do so, if unsuccessfully; sighs Häker, with Fouqué in view: *"an was für Menschen und Verhänissen ein Dichter wie Kleist gescheitert ist."*[680] Häker traces how Fouqué was working on the *Fehrbellin* topos in parallel with Kleist, how in 1812 his resulting dramatic poem, *"Die Heimkehr des großen Kurfürsten"* (cf. *NR*,549), enjoyed considerable success with the Prussian public and royal family, and how, following Kleist's death, he eagerly sought to put his hands on any copy of

Homburg in circulation, presumably aiming to withhold them from the public, and how, as late as 1830, he still relativised the merits of Kleist's drama (cf. *NR*,559), which following its publication in 1821 by Tieck, could not fail to overshadow his own work.[681]

For all its brilliance, I maintain that Häker's analysis of this episode misses several important considerations: firstly, that it may have been Fouqué in the first place who pointed out to Kleist the source materials for *Homburg* (as Falk did for *Amphitryon*, Pfuel for *Kohlhaas*), which would not excuse Fouqué's jealousy and scheming, but explain it: he may have felt that Kleist appropriated his idea; secondly, that Kleist in the summer of 1811 was evidently aware that Fouqué was also working on *Fehrbellin* material: on 15th August he announces that he is "stepping into the ring" with him (cf. II:876; "*In die Schranken treten*" = "entering the lists") and immediately offers him a "deal" (a truce of some sort); thirdly, that Kleist may well have been desperate not to loose "my beloved Fouqué" (cf. II:860; 876; 1051), possibly his only remaining lover following Müller's departure: "*inzwischen kommt es mir vor, als ob eine Verwandtschaft zweischen uns prästabillisiert wäre, die sich in kurzer Zeit gar wunderbar entwickeln müßte, und es gehört zu meinen liebsten Wünschen, dies noch im Lauf dieses Herbstes zu versuchen*" (II:876). Is not the "deal" he offers Fouqué a *bribe*, or a *bridal gift*?[682]

Fouqué's response to Kleist's offer is not extant; nor do we have evidence that Kleist made good on his promise to visit him at his Nennhausen estate. Yet we may trace or conjecture the contours of their erotico-agonistic, desirous-rivalrous, tit-for-tat relationship during the summer of 1811:

- Fouqué's romantic, fantastic tale *Undine*, today the work he is chiefly remembered for, was published in June 1811; its ending—Undine forfaits the opportunity to aquire a soul; her lover, Huldbrand, his life (by Undine's deadly kiss; cf. Achilles' death by Penthesilea's deadly kiss)—may entail a veiled reference at his risky (Fouqué being married) relationship with Kleist: Kleist = Undine; Fouqué = Huldbrand; Caroline = Bertalda; having reportedly written the tale in 1809, the timing of its publication, June 1811, suggests that it comprised Fouqué's opening shot at Kleist: when push comes to shove, he would have to forfeit, not his wife, *but him*; when Kleist, shortly before his death, admitted to Marie that it had been "in several ways dangerous" to be associated with him (II:883), he may have had, *inter alia*, Fouqué and his marriage in mind;[683]

- The timing of Kleist's note to Marie regarding his regret at the nods to popular romantic taste he had let seep into *Käthchen*, spring or summer of 1811, suggests that he had his "duel" with Fouqué firmly in view: Fouqué may well have inspired parts of *Käthchen*, at least stylistically; for example, the episode, struck by Kleist after Tieck termed it "fantasy-esque" (cf. LS,272), in which Käthchen ponders how to rescue the knight from his abdominable bethrothed, and encounters a mermaid who tries to lure her into the depths, could have been inspired by (or, conversely, could have inspired) *Undine*, the *"Mißgriffe"* Kleist later regretted suggest that he did not think highly of *Undine* (and perhaps of Fouqué's poetry in general);

- *Zweikampf*, published in August 1811, may entail a riposte to *Undine*: the duel leaves the exalted but vain Rotbart (Kleist, Undine) wasted, his "black soul" "exhaled" into the ether, and the jealous and mediocre Trota (Fouqué, Huldbrand) impotent, doomed to live alongside a desirable woman he cannot possess; Kleist sends Fouqué the 2nd vol. of *Erzählungen* (cf. II:876);

- Finally, it may well have been as part of his erotico-agonistic "duel" with Fouqué that Kleist in the summer of 1811 undertook to explore a genre he had not previously worked in: that of the novel; when he tells Marie in the spring or summer of 1811 that he "wishes to once more undertake something quite fantastical," and links this wish to a sense of rejuvenation and youthful love (cf. II:874), Kleist may be referring to this project, as well as to his relationship with Fouqué.

In late July 1811 Kleist told Reimer that he was *"mit einem Roman ziemlich weit vorgerückt… der wohl 2 Bände betragen dürfte"* (II:872), and (apparently) in August he told Arnim, *"er habe Lust ein Buch nach der Art wie die Manon Lecoult zu schreiben"* (*LS*,71b). That these two notes are not entirely congruent should not bother us unduly, for not only were Kleist's statements regarding work-in-progress not always reliable (vis-à-vis Reimer he may have exaggerated somewhat to keep him interested), but also is the date of his mentioning the novel to Arnim uncertain (it could have been earlier). Ferd. Grimm later noted that Kleist's lost novel was "supposed to have been very good" (cf. *NR*,130a), which suggests that a draft existed and was read; Grimm was in Reimer's employment and—had Kleist sent Reimer a draft—could have obtained this appraisal from one of the editors.[684] Kleist's indicating that the novel would come in two volumes suggests that he had at least a plan or outline (though possibly he simply anticipated it because his model, Antoine-François Prévost's 1731 novel *Histoire du Chevalier des Grieux et de Manon Lescaut*, has two parts). That Kleist sought to add a novel to his œuvre is not surprising: so did Rousseau, Goethe, Novalis, Brentano and many others; it was a genre *du jour*. Why did Prévost's novel inspire Kleist? A few observations:

- In Prévost's novel, the antagonism between passion and reason is decided in favour of the former, not the latter; his "bad case" serving as "good example" anticipates Kleist's Allerneuerster Erziehungsplan: like Kleist's Erzählungen, Prévost's immoral tale is, in a manner, a moral tale;
- Prévost's ground-breaking style features one first-person narrative nested within another, a thrilling roller-coaster ride of emotions (think today's action movies), a tension that stretches the reader to breaking point, a cruel realism, and a rhythmicity that anticipates Kleist's basso continuo; As if to comply with Kleist's Gesetze, Prévost's protagonist Des Grieux ceaselessly stems himself against an inexorable fate: from their first encounter he is Manon Lescaut's thrall, "The sweetness of her glance... my evil star already in its ascendant and drawing me to my ruin" (his "evil star in its ascendant" evidently refers to Scorpio or Venus); if Manon is as femme fatale, the one whom she drives into death is in the first instance not Des Grieux but herself; it is Des Grieux who suffers most: whereas Manon dies quickly, he is fated to die a slow, mournful death, and to tell their tale;[685] Prévost's characters may represent real personages, as his spiteful portrait of the elder G...M... suggests (like Kleist's, Prévost's abbreviations may have been as revealing to cognoscendi as dissembling to others);

- Prévost's biography parallels Kleist's: hailing from an ancient family in loyal service to the royal dynasty, as a young man he enlisted in the army and fought in war (the War of the Spanish Succession of 1712 and the Franco-Spanish War of 1718-19); later he was forced into exile abroad and faced bankruptcy as his illicit love affairs ruined his career prospects; his novel may be just as autobiographical as, no doubt, Kleist's would have been.

The Ger. word *Roman* (from the Fr.), is of course related to *romance*; as Kleist was choiceful regarding the genre, format and style he adopted in relation to his purpose and audience, *Ein Roman* could well have comprised a romance dedicated to Fouqué: a riposte to his thrust, *Undine*, with an opposite outcome: Kleist (Manon, Undine) dies, Fouqué (Des Grieux, Huldbrand) lives and suffers. Like *Jerusalem*, *Ein Roman* may well have been among the MSS Kleist burned in his last nights; *perhaps it was the last document he threw into the fire at Stimmings.*[686]

When Hitzig before the end of 1811 published a second edition of *Undine*, in book format, Fouqué added a dedication which, I offer, was his epitaph to Kleist, of whose suicide he will have only just learned:

Zueignung.

Undine, liebes Bildchen Du,
    Seit ich zuerst aus alten Kunden
    Dein seltsam Leuchten aufgefunden,
    Wie sangst Du oft mein Herz in Ruh!
Wie schmiegtest Du Dich an mich lind,
    Und wolltest alle Deine Klagen
    Ganz sacht nur in das Ohr mir sagen,
    Ein halb verwöhnt, halb scheues Kind.
Doch meine Zither tönte nach
    Aus ihrer goldbezognen Pforte
    Jedwedes Deiner leisen Worte,
    Bis fern man davon hört' und sprach.

> Und manch ein Herz gewann Dich lieb,
> Trotz Deinem launisch dunklen Wesen,
> Und Viele mochten gerne lesen
> Ein Büchlein, das von Dir ich schrieb.[687]

Can there be any doubt that the *"halb verwöhnt, halb scheues Kind,"* the *"launisch dunkles Wesen"* Fouqué addresses here is Kleist? That Fouqué's *"Zither"* and *"goldbezogne Pforte"* belong into the same metaphorical field as Kleist's arrow and ring, key and keyhole, F and O? As well as referring to Fouqué's aspiration to succeed and outshine him as poet, with *Undine* merely his first step in a comprehensive future programme to out-Kleist Kleist? Having in the dedication's first four verses (quoted above) mourned the loss of his lover, Fouqué in its remaining three verses looks forward, inviting Undine-Kleist's soul to change tack and accompany him on his journey into his *"Einrichtung"* (rather like Beatrice replacing Vergil to accompany Dante into Paradise), during which he shall "morally" "greet" the "noble men," while paying due attention to the "beautiful women"—*"er ist ein treuer Ritter, / Und dient den Frau'n mit Schwerdt und Zither."* If I am correct, Fouqué's *Undine* was not only inspired by, but also *written for* Kleist (cf. the last verse quoted above), which makes it all the more likely that Kleist's *Ein Roman* was not only inspired by, but also *written for* Fouqué. Its popularity apart, the reason why Fouqué got Hitzig to publish *Undine* in book format before the end of 1811, then, was *to dedicate the tale to his deceased lover-rival*. Had Kleist not died when he did, *Undine* might never have been published in book format, and might well be practically forgotten today.

What Kleist announces with his "stepping into the ring" (cf. II:876), then, is his *romantic novel* as ripost to Fouqué's *romantic tale*, and the "deal" he offers Fouqué is this: "if you insist on challenging me on my turf (modern drama), I offer to do likewise on yours (romantic tale), so as to level the playing field." Fouqué's later "fears" (Häker) regarding the surfacing of a *Homburg* MS will have been tinged with genuine sadness at the loss of his friend, lover, and rival.

"Käthchen, *reloaded*"

Sembdner notes (cf. I:905-7; 961) that an extant 1842 prompt book of Detmold's Hoftheater could have been based on as separate *Käthchen* MS by Kleist, and that its text differs from the book version (P) mainly in that all passages referring to Kunigunde's monstrosity were struck. The striking could, of course, have been done by someone other than Kleist, after his death, but my reading of the drama's ending—in the final lines, Kunigunde, as *Germania* and as *Valkyrie*, rises to spearhead a German insurrection—certainly opens up the *possibility* that Kleist later, after (P)'s publication in September 1810, created another MS—the one underpinning the prompt book—with the intention of bringing the drama back to stage, with an insurrectionist agenda, which would have required the figure of Kunigunde to be shown in a far more positive light than in (P), and without her association with a disheveled, mosaic, *HRR*. Such a project, say in the summer of 1811, would be consistent with his letter to Marie of that period (cf. II:874), in which he laments those "blunders" he had allowed to creep into (P)—a reflection that is untypical, for Kleist rarely looked back, and that may suggest that right there and then he was pulling (P) out of the drawer preparing to write a revised stage adaptation. There could have been two good reasons for him to do so. *Satirically,* his worry about Fr. Wilh. entering an alliance with Napoleon: a theatre staging could easily be framed to emphasise the insurrectional potential of the drama's final lines. Po*(i)etically,* his rivalry with Fouqué: if he was to "undertake something quite fantastical" (cf. *ibid*) in their "duel," a *Käthchen* adaptation could fit right into his arsenal of pieces with which to give Fouqué a bit of a hammering: quick to produce, quick to fire ("fire and forget," perhaps). That *Käthchen*, this *"wunderbare[...] Gemisch von Sinn und Unsinn"* (Goethe), had the required "pop appeal," its popularity throughout the 19th century would confirm.

"Projekt Orpheus"

In the spring or summer of 1811 Kleist expressed his wish, to Marie, to focus his attention, for a year or so, on nothing but music: *"mit nichts als der Musik beschäftigen"* (cf. II:874-5; MAII:969-70). This undertaking would have to be considered a "project not executed," if there was not extant evidence demonstrating that it *was* executed, if only rudimentarily: firstly, the duodrama *Die Liebe und die Freude*, which according to Bülow (*Kleist*, X), was found in Henriette Vogel's legacy, among her papers related to Kleist, and which she and Kleist may have performed at Henriette's house, where they reportedly spent entire evenings together, *"in der grünen oder roten Stube beisammen"* (II:885), making music (cf. *LS*,522; 524).[688] Henriette was considered highly musical (cf. *NR*,39), an accomplished pianist and singer, and the master flutist Kleist a competent pianist (as well as having been, of course, an exceptional lyricist), and it is eminently plausible that the duodrama was among pieces they, not only enjoyed together, but *composed* together, during those musical evenings: the fact that it was found among Henriette's Kleist papers, while not *proving* that Kleist *composed* its lyrics, is certainly suggestive.

Secondly, seen in this light, the so-called *Todeslitaneien* Kleist and Henriette composed for each other, taken together and accompanied by music, *amount to a duodrama*, which Kleist and Henriette could have composed and performed together at her piano (unlike that of *Liebe*, *Todeslitaneien*'s attribution is not in serious doubt), in a joint *"Allmähliche Verfertigung der Poesie beim Musizieren"* that would have comprised but a logical continuation of Kleist's habit of *composing* his works while *declaming* them, or having them *read to* him (cf. *LS*,305).[689]

"*Projekt Orpheus*" (I): towards an *"Allmähliche Verfertigung der Poesie beim Musizieren."*[690]

Kleist's collaboration with Henriette may have comprised no mere pastime, or mere indulgence towards his fellow suicidee, but Kleist's *Orphic project of integrating poetry and music*, of composing and performing lyrics underpinned by a *basso continuo* produced on the piano.[691] This *"Projekt Orpheus,"* as I shall call it, into which he roped Henriette in the same manner in which he had roped Carl von Pannwitz into his "inaugural *satyrico-po(i)etical* project," Müller into *Ph*, Dahlmann, provisionally, into *Germania*, and Fouqué into their erotico-agonistic "duel," would have to be considered Kleist's *final project*, extending, beyond Kleist's exchange with Fouqué, right up to their deaths, of which *Liebe* and *Todeslitaneien* comprise extant outputs. Did the *"G e s a n g b u c h"* Kleist sent to Sophie Sander in October 1811 (cf. II:882) comprise a compilation of his and Henriette's compositions—an initial output of *"Projekt Orpheus"*?[692] Has the *Kleist-Forschung* searched Sophie's legacy for this "s o n g b o o k"?

Did Kleist die because *BA*, his "duel" with Fouqué, and his Orphic project with Henriette all failed to live up to his expectations? Or was it the other way around: did he pursue these collaborations as vehicles towards death, especially towards acquiring a brother- or sister-in-death? Were his pursuits of Müller (till his departure), Fouqué, and Henriette all part of a scheme of developing and maintaining a "portfolio of options" for *whom to die with*? *"Projekt Orpheus"* at any rate comprised a logical conclusion to his development as a bard, and a stepping stone for his transition to another life: in Greek mythology Ixion's punishment of spinning across the heavens for all eternity, bound to the burning solar wheel, was halted, temporarily, only once, when Orpheus played his lyre during his descent into Hades, and Kleist, tied to his own "burning wheel" of endless suffering, may have sought similar consolation before terminating the present cycle. If *"Projekt Orpheus"* comprised his preparation for death—*"Tod, als das ewige Refrain des Lebens"*—, Kleist's note to Marie announced not one but two, related, "projects," one musical, one suicidal: *"Liebe Marie, laß mich sterben."*

Kleist may have considered pieces such as *Liebe* and *Todeslitaneien* primarily as *musical*, rather than *poetical*, works, which together with their collaborative origin and their private character would explain why he permitted them to fall short of his usual exacting standards. It is unclear whether Kleist learned to write or read "standard" musical notes (cf. *LS*,17), yet already in Potsdam he reportedly composed dances, and he was surely equipped with an exquisite memory, so that the duodrama's apparently having been found without accompanying musical notes (at least Bülow does not mention any) by no means suggests that it did not comprise the lyrics to a song.[693] Henriette probably did write and read musical notes, and could have jotted down the lytrics and musical scores to *Liebe, Todeslitaneien* and other pieces they composed together; both lyrics and score of such pieces are probably best considered their co-productions. Has the *Kleist-Forschung* searched Henriette's legacy for further lyrics and scores?

*   *   *   *

Kleist's final *po(ï)etical* endeavours, *Ein Roman* and *"Projekt Orpheus,"* shed an important light on his final months, for they share a notable characteristic: they are of an intensely private nature and no longer encompass *satirical* advice or agitation directed at a public audience, as if Kleist had all but given up on his core purpose (had Princess Amalie endorsed *Homburg*, and released it to be staged, things might well have been different; alas, she ignored or dismissed it, and in doing drove another nail into his coffin). With Kleist's *final final* project, "Projekt Wannsee," taking shape, in his final months Kleist's focus shifted towards roping in a suitable partner-in-death, with Fouqué (*"wieder etwas recht Phantastisches vornehmen"*) and Henriette (*"mit nichts als der Musik beschäftigen"*) emerging as the front runners. Kleist may have been drawn to Henriette not least because she was keen, and competent, to serve as Sappho to his Alcaeus, making her a swayable candidate (Fouqué could have played the part, too, but presumably was not prepared to die; Kleist may have abandoned *Ein Roman* for that reason). "Projekt Orpheus," then, was Kleist's final masterpiece as *magnétiseur*-cum-*Maschinist*: a hypnosis-in-music séance, spanning a number of evenings, *"in der grünen oder roten*

Stube beisammen," during which he entranced Henriette to play her minor but necessary part in his *final final project*. Duodramas such as *Liebe* and *Todeslitaneien*, then, functioned as "battle chant" for their joint march into death. Did Kleist in October 1811 send "s o n g b o o k" to Sophie Sander because he still considered her a suitable sister-in-death, and till the end kept his options open? "S o n g b o o k" as an invitation for a *rendezvous with death*? It would have been oh-so-Kleistian.

"Projekt Wannsee"

It has frequently been noted that the double suicide (in legal terms, the murder-cum-suicide) by the Kl. Wannsee had the quality of a performance, an enactment or *mis en scène*, and it indeed was, in the precise sense of a *cultic ritual*: it re-enacts the blood-sacrifice of a *victim* (Henriette) followed by the self-sacrifice of the *hierophant* (Kleist). The strict separation of the sexes prior to the rite (her doorknob is found in his pocket), the joint performance of litanies for each other, the joint procession to the small mount by the lake, the frantic dancing and playful marrymaking, the carrying of the basket containing, hidden beneath a cloth, the sacrificial weapon (gun) and libations (wine, rum), the initiates' communion by sharing drink, the victims' kneeling position before a hollow in the ground, into which the blood is spilled to be received by the chthonic gods: all of these gestures evoke or mimic the sacrificial rites of an ancient Orphic or Bacchic mystery cult. They also combine, symbolically, to resolve the dilemma Kleist faced throughout his life: that of the seemless integration of impregnation (succession), homosexual love, political impact, and the liberation of the soul: two shots (= ejaculations), delivered by two guns (= *phalloi*), one penetrating the woman's chest (= womb), another the man's mouth (= anus), the third gun reserved for Fr. Wilh. or Napoleon.

The deaths by the Kl. Wannsee could be considered a "project executed but not extant": no "script" is extant (none may have existed). There are, however, many passages in Kleist's œuvre that anticipate and rehearse this *final final* drama, and may be considered its "proto-scripts": *Schroffenstein's Kleidertauschzene* recalls

Dionysiac initiation rites, in which youths and maidens exchanged roles—the youths dressing in womens' clothes, the maidens sporting fake beards and *phalloi*—in order to reinforce traditional societal structures by their temporary negation and grotesque inversion; its chiasmic killings of two youthful victims—at the hands of their respective patriarchs-hierophants—in the consecrated setting of the cave mimics an archaic ritual of blood sacrifice.[694] *Erdbeben*'s mob lynching on the stairs of the cathedral represents a ritualistic sacrifice of scapegoats (*pharmakoi*) mirroring the human sacrifices of the Aztecs—who on the stairs of their pyramids tore out their victims' hearts with obsidian knives—, the Incas—who on the top of their mountains smashed the skulls of children against rocks, and of YHWH—who on Mount Golgatah sacrificed his son by the sheer force of his voice—; its chief hierophant, Don F, leads the procession of victims and spectators (*pompe*) from the valley of the pines (the consecrated grove) to the cathedral stairs (the sacrificial altar), where he points out the victims to the executioners (*hieropoioi*), whose sacrificial act purifies St. Iago's community thrown into disarray by catastrophe.[695] Penthesilea's sacrifice of Achilles combines elements of Dionysiac *sparagmos* and *omophagia* with those of *sphagia* (blood sacrifice): drinking the victim's blood reinforces the communion of the faithful, and of the living and the dead (concepts that survive in the Christian sacrament of communion, and its concept of transubstantiation); having communed with Achilles by drinking his blood, Penthesilea lets herself be lowered onto the altar (rock) and purified with water, before self-sacrificing. Hally is yet another *pharmakos*, whose being "broken up" by her male family members' "daggers" mimics the ritual dissecting of the victim's corpse, and followed by the dishing out of the edible and valuable parts to the members of the community.

The scene in Kleist's works that most closely anticipates the actual enactment by the Kl. Wannsee is, of course, Toni and Gustav's death in *Verlobung*. The novella, with the help of subplots, serialises Kleist's experimentation with various set-ups for the enactment of (self-)sacrifice: the yellow-feverish girl's killing her suitors by infecting them with a deadly disease combines elements of the divine marriage of Heaven and Earth (*hieros gamos*) and the ritual poisoning of victims; Mariane's death entails a self-sacrifice of one lover on behalf of another, Gustav, who is purified by this act; Toni's spread-eagling Gustav onto the bed (altar) prepares him for ritual rape (akin to that performed by the Amazons on their victims at the *Rosenfest*), crucifixion, or both. In these three set-ups the victims' (self-)sacrifice is assisted by a lover who does not join the victim in death, and Kleist thus crafted a fourth set-up, which was to become the prototype for his own death: Gustav, in adopting the sanctified name August, assumes the role of the *hierophant* who sacrifices first the victim, Toni, then himself. Toni's wiggling body is bathed in her own blood, before it oozes into the ground, where it serves as libation to the chthonic gods (Hades, Hecate, the chthonic Dionysos, the chthonic Zeus); Gustav splatters his brain through the window, into the air, where it serves as libation to the heavenly gods (the thundering cloud-god Zeus, the rising sun-god Apollo); their "beautiful souls" are released into the ether, freed so that they may journey to, and perhaps reunite on, another star.

Kleist continued rehearding alternative set-ups for his death: in *Findling*, both lovers die a sacrificial death—Nicolo by splashed brain, Elvire by pierced heart—, but *fail to die together*; in *Zweikampf,* one of the two duellists *fails to die*: while Rotbart duly succumbs to the poisoned "sword," Trota unexpectedly recovers from his injury, his soul, instead of being released, thus remaining chained to his body; in *Homburg*, Natalie *reneges on her suicide pact* with Homburg (a "pact" that perhaps was only ever *imagined* by Homburg, who mistook her glove as token of her complicity), and instead of sending him off into Hades, she pulls him back from the brink, so that, like Trota, he remains suspended between the "Earth" of eternal enchainment and the "Heaven" of liberating death, like Siptimius suffering Ixion's and Tantalus' punishments rolled into one.[696]

483

3.2 The *Berliner Abendblätter* as Poetico-Political Platform

On 1st October 1810 Kleist became the founder and editor of Berlin's first daily newspaper, *Berliner Abendblätter* (*BA*). That Kleist, following an art journal and a (planned) patriotic pamphlet, published a daily newspaper, has puzzled Kleist scholars, who for the most part explain it with Kleist's financial situation—aged 33, he had no regular income, having lost the modest stipend the now deceased Queen (or Marie) had paid him—; I shall argue that, while income was a factor, *BA* in the first instance, just as previously *Ph* and *Germania*, for the *"Projektemacher"* (Blamberger) Kleist comprised yet another *"Werkstatt"* (Häker) and *poetico-political platform*. Kleist's *Gebet des Zoroaster,* in the first issue, makes this quite clear, furnishing *BA*'s preamble and user manual:

> Nun lässt du es, von Zeit zu Zeit, niederfallen, wie Schuppen, von dem Auge eines deiner Knechte, den du dir erwählt, daß er die Torheiten und Irrtümer seiner Gattung überschaue; ihn rüstest du mit dem Köcher der Rede, daß er, furchtlos und liebreich, mitten unter sie trete, und sie mit Pfeilen, bald schärfer, bald leiser, aus der wunderlichen Schlafsucht, in welcher sie befangen liegen, wecke. (II:325-6)

The "elected servant," Kleist, takes on the mantle of Apollo—the divinatory archer whose arrows convey truth—called upon by God and King—*"du"*—to awaken his people from their somnambulant slumber:

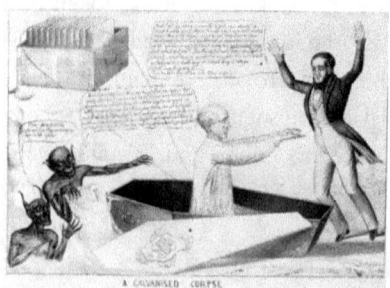

"*sie...aus der...Schlafsucht...wecke*": The "elected servant" Kleist (right) galvanises the Prussian citizens' corpse (centre), which Napoleon and Hardenberg (left) are about to clutch.[697]

Wilh. Grimm called *BA* an "ideal sausage paper," Peter Michalzik, "*eine geistreiche Boulevard-Zeitung. Man könnte das auch Feuilleton nennen.*"⁶⁹⁸ *BA* is indeed *overtly* a "*Boulevard-Zeitung*" and "*Feuilleton*," just as *Ph* is overtly an art magazine, and *Homburg*, a drama about a 17th century historical episode—but only *overtly*: its feuilletonistic appearance merely comprises Kleist's vehicle and for the dynamite wrapped into it, with which he now infiltrates bourgeois Berlin living rooms on a daily basis: the "sausage" is a hand grenade. As of late 1810, Kleist's *satirical* agenda had not changed one iota, only his target, and therefore his chosen "war engine" had: if a drama performance on a public stage may be likened to a pounding by a *Grande batterie* of 12-pounder cannons (the standard artillery weapon of the *Napoleonic Wars*), the publication of a volume of novellas, to a barrage by 6- or 8-pounder howitzers, and the distribution of an art magazine, to select precision shots by hidden snipers, then the mass-circulation of a daily newspaper may be said to correspond to an *unceasing release of canister shots*. With *BA*, Kleist adopted his battle tactics to the level of street fight and gang war, showering Berlin's somnambulant citizens with a daily hail of bite-sized propaganda-shrapnel. *BA* was just as fitting a propaganda "war engine" for aiming at Berlin's bourgeois intelligentsia as *Ph* had been for aiming at Dresden's patriotic intellectuals, and *Germania*, at Bohemia's and northern Germany's resistance leaders; its creation once again demonstrates Kleist's extraordinary sensibility for timing, occasion, audience, and genre, and his creativity in designing suitable media, and orchestrating propaganda campaigns.⁶⁹⁹

Gesamtpropagandakunstwerk. Gerhard Schulz (*Kleist*, 481) admits that *BA* was not "harmless," but denies that it comprised a "composed," "unitary" project: "*Daß die 153 Berliner Abendblätter jedoch angeblich in ihrer Gesamtheit ein von Kleist regelrecht komponiertes Kunstwerk seien,... suggeriert eine Einheitlichkeit, die sie nicht besitzen.*" I beg to differ: *BA* was precisely a "composed," "unitary" "work of art"—the art of *propaganda*—, and Kleist himself implied its "unitary" character when on 25th September he announced to his readers that he would share "a comprehensive plan" for *BA* before the end of the year (cf. II:451); that he never got around to publishing such a "plan" does not mean that he did not have one in mind. As *BA*'s "cook-general" (Peter Staengle), Kleist carefully selected, edited and word-smithed *everything* published in *BA*, "composing" it as a "tightly connected complex of texts" (Gernot Müller) with the same meticulousness with which he composed his more obviously poetic works. All *BA* entries, not limited to his novellas, essays, and anecdotes, and including entries provided by others—had a *satirical* (and sometimes *satyrical*) intent, and what *BA* shows is that Kleist was in the first place not a poet but a propagandist and polemicist, a troubadour, rhapsode, *magnétiseur*, *Maschinist*, *Taschenspieler*, juggler whose trade-craft happened to be writing, yet for whom poetry was merely part of a practice of *poïesis*: a creativity geared towards, not only depicting, but *changing the world*.

As sole editor, Kleist was fully responsible for *BA*'s content. While A. Müller *wrote* the article on taxation that so exasperated Hardenberg that he tightened the paper's censorship until it folded (with the King's backing, in fact, under the King's order), Kleist *accepted*, and almost certainly *edited* it—cf. the controversy with Brentano and Arnim after he edited their *BA* article on Friedrich's *Mönch* so thoroughly that it *de facto* became his own work. Including Müller's article in *BA* was certainly a *calculated* move on Kleist's part, if perhaps a *mis*calculated one: presumably Kleist aimed at undermining public support for Hardenberg's appeasement policy, among whose corollaries were Prussia's crippling annual war reparation payments to France; instead of challenging Hardenberg's (and the King's) foreign policy outright, which might have been considered treasonous, Kleist leaned on Müller to lead an apparently "technical" challenge to the fiscal policy that underpinned it.[700] If he could instigate the general public to resist the taxes, the government would soon be incapacitated to fulfil its contractual commitments, and find itself in open conflict with France; alternatively, if the citizens gudgingly accepted stifling taxes, he would ensure that they made France's dictat, as well as Hardenberg's accommodating policies, responsible for their burden. Either way, the debate Kleist instigated in *BA*, of which Müller's article comprised the opening shot, could nudge Prussia towards revolt and war: tax resistance, as the ancient example of the Jewish Zealots demonstrates (an example Kleist was familiar with from Josephus' and Michaelis' works), and more recent ones, of the North-American colonists and of the French revolutionaries, confirm, can *incite a general revolt*. At a minimum, Kleist could expect bumper sales for his paper, fuelled by the controversy slugged out in it. Hardenberg, though, may well have seen through Kleist's stratagems, and understood the importance of *media platforms* in the ongoing war for the hearts and minds of the citizens, which would explain the vehemence with which he cracked down on *BA*, rather than on the article's author, A. Müller.[701]

When he published entries with *overtly* political content, Kleist presented them in sober and factual language. Entries such as, for example, "*Im Russischen Reiche wird nächstens eine außerordentliche Rekrutenaushebung statt finden*," will have appeared neutral and detached, drawing as they did on official sources, and appearing in other newspapers as well; yet terms such as "*nächstens*" and "*außerordentlich*" will have subtly aroused attention: while not "fake news," and hence probably not alarming to censors, "read correctly" this entry urges readers to push for Prussia to follow Russia's example and *recruit a milita*.

A typical feature of *BA* were—apparently trivial—daily news headlines and police reports (precursers of today's "breaking news"), whose popularity contributed *BA*'s early commercial success, and compelled Wilh. Grimm to tell Brentano, "*die Polizeianzeigen nehmen sich oft lächerlich aus*" (*KH*,167). Upon closer inspection, every one of them is potentially incinerating and subversive. For example, a *BA* report on 9th October, concerning an apparently rabid alien dog triggering the emergency slaughter of countless domesticated animals in Charlottenburg, can easily be "decoded" if one recognises "rabid alien dog" as Kleistian chiffre for Napoleon, and remembers that Charlottenburg was the Hohenzollerns' favourite residence: Kleist accuses the Hohenzollerns of having performed a futile pre-emptive self-sacrifice out of sheer awe of Napoleon.[702] This simple example in mind, consider the following "police report":

> Auf dem Markte ist einem fremden Müller eine abgenutzte Metze zerschlagen und eine ungestempelte nach Erlegung von 2 Rthlr. Strafe konfisziert. Einem hiesigen Einwohner, ist ein silberner Vorlegelöffel und ein Esslöffel gestohlen. (*BA*, 13th October)[703]

"*Metze*" denotes both a traditional dry measure for grain and (colloquially) a prostitute; the term "*abgenutzte Metze*" is thus, as one would say in the street, "*eindeutig zweideutig*"; and so is "*ungestempelte Metze*": has the "alien miller" forfeited one overused and one tempered-with *dry measure*, or instead one worn-out and one illicit *harlot*? In the latter case, the report "translates" into this: the "alien miller" Napoleon dumped the "worn-out," but legitimate, Joséphine in favour of the "illicit," but fertile, Marie-Louise, and the latter, together with the imperial dignity (the two *RT* = the double-headed Quaternion Eagle), must urgently be recouped from him.[704] Meanwhile, the "local resident," Fr. Wilh., has been passively looking on as the Hohenzollerns' family silver, and the Prussian treasury, have been plundered by the French. Consider another "police report":

> Ein hiesiger Eigentümer hat sich am 20sten früh um 9 Uhr mit einem Barbiermesser den Hals abgeschnitten. Er ist 20 Monate hindurch krank gewesen, und wahrscheinlich haben ihn heftige Schmerzen zu dem Entschluß gebracht, sich zu entleiben. (*BA*, 20th October)

20 months prior to the article, i.e., in April 1809, the "sick man" Fr. Wilh. had refused to join the *War of the Fifth Coalition*, and Kleist here accuses him of self-castration ("neck" = "shaft"), and perhaps entices him to commit suicide.

That such entries were based on *actual* police reports was critical for Kleist's ability to get them past the censors, but otherwise immaterial for his intentions: by selecting, editing and publishing them, Kleist turned quotidian police reports into works of (propaganda) art, rather as Braque does quotidian objects in his collages, and Beuys, in his installations. Consider the following "police report" concerning a gang of incendiaries haunting Berlin:

Der Schreiber Seidler, Friedrichstraße Nr. 56, hat gestern in der letzten Straße einen sogenannten Brandbrief gefunden, nach dessen Inhalt Berlin binnen wenigen Tagen an 8 Ecken angezündet werden soll. Das Publikum braucht gleichwohl, bei der Wachsamkeit der obersten Polizei-Behörde, keinen unzweckmäßigen Besorgnissen Raum zu geben. Im vorigen Monat sind, durch die Wachsamkeit der Polizei-Commissarien 18 Concubinate in gesetzmäßige Ehen verwandelt worden." (*BA*, 3rd October)[705]

Whereas Kohlhaas set fire to Leipzig at *three* corners (affording the citizens a safe exit), and Hermann imagines setting fire to the Teutoburg (Berlin) at *all four* corners (after the citizens' evacuation), Kleist's gang leader Schwarz (Napoleon) ups the ante by threatening to set fire to Berlin at no less than eight corners.[706] Friedrichstraße is named after the "Great" Fr. II, and the *auto da fé* is announced from the centre of Prussia's government, whose "highest police authority" is, of course, King Fr. Wilh. III. The latter's competence in keeping Berlin safe and sound is immediately cast into doubt by the observation that under his watch, 18 concubinages (northern German vassals) were converted into legal marriages (annexed by France and converted into *Départements*, effective 1st January 1811).

Kleist's *satirical* innuendos are often not much less trivial than the reports into which they are wrapped, and not all of them hit home equally powerfully. But it is the very nature of canister shots to maximise terror by randomly scattering makeshift pellets, compensating an excess of quantity for a lack of quality; and Kleist's single-handedly churning these out on a daily basis, working with whatever raw materials official sources made available to him, was an astounding *tour de force,* showcasing his versatility, dexterity and wit.[707]

"**französische Journalistik.**" Kleist's *BA* journalism can be evaluated in the context of his 1809 essay *Lehrbuch der französischen Journalistik*, whose introduction states:

> Die Journalistik überhaupt, ist die treuherzige und unverfängliche Kunst, das Volk von dem zu unterrichten, was in der Welt vorfällt. Sie ist eine gänzliche Privatsache, und alle Zwecke der Regierung, sie mögen heißen, wie man wolle, sind ihr fremd. (II:361)

Kleist then contrasts "French journalism" with this "journalism as such," claiming that unlike the latter, the former is neither "naïve" or "innocuous," nor "entirely a private matter," but a deliberate, artful means of manipulating the public. His own journalism, by this definition, is of course every bit as "French" as the "French journalism" he (apparently) derides. Once again we encounter Kleist seeking to "out-French" the French. Kleist in the essay offers a brilliant review of "French" techniques of manipulation, as if rehearsing them for his own use, and the 1809 essay clearly paves the way for *BA*, which merely amounts to Kleist's putting in practice the principles he had already laid out in the essay.

Given his limited choices in relation to subject matter, especially following the tightening of *BA*'s censorship in the wake of the taxation debate, and given the constraints with respect to style and language imposed by the genre, one of the key manipulative choices available to Kleist was *layout*—e.g., *sequencing*: the simple choice of having two apparently unrelated entries follow each other, without break, *satirically* links them. Kleist's remarkable sequencing choices have been commented on in the Kleist reception—e.g., Gerhard Schulz:

> "Aus Travancore meldet man folgende tragische Begebenheit: Am 2ten März war des Nachts in dasiger Gegend ein Erdbeben," wobei im ersten Schrecken aus dem Harem des "Rahjah" einige Frauenzimmer "halb nackend" entweichen mußten, die der "eifersüchtige Tyrann" dann enthaupten ließ, weil sie sich den Blicken der Männer ausgesetzt hätten."… Nur acht Zeilen unter der Meldung aus Indien und noch auf derselben Seite beginnt eine andere Nachricht mit den folgenden Worten: "Gestern früh um 4 Uhr wurde der Leichnahm ihrer Majestät der verewigten Königinn, ganz in der Stille,…" Ernsthaft subversive Absichten dürften ihm allerdings gerade bei dieser von ihm verehrten Königin kaum zu unterstellen sein (*Kleist*, 468-9),

Contrary to Schulz, I insist that the reader ought *precisely* to ascribe "seriously subversive intentions" to Kleist: "jealous tyrant" = Napoleon; "half-naked courtesans escaping from his harem" = *Borussia, Austria, Germania*. Only by interpreting the two entries in their juxtaposition do they assume their full meaning: namely, Luise = Napoleon's courtesan. Klaus Müller-Salget (*Kleist*, 281) offers a pertinent analysis of how Kleist uses such juxtaposition to weaken the credibility of one article simply by having it follow another, doubtful one; Günter Blamberger, on the other hand, thoroughly misunderstands Kleist, whose "mistaken sequencing" of a parodist attack on Iffland, followed by *Ode auf den Wiedereinzug des Königs im Winter 1809*, makes him "doubt Kleist's sanity" (*Kleist*, 406); yet, I say the effect of parodying the King is precisely intended.[708]

"**Unwahrscheinliche Wahrhaftigkeiten.**" Kleist's anecdotes, for which BA was his primary vehicle (as *Ph* had been for his epigrams, *Germania* for his patriotic odes), are just as *satirically* subversive as the "police reports." Take *Unwahrscheinliche Wahrhaftigkeiten*, a framing story containing three anecdotes, of which the first tells of a soldier hit by a bullet, which, instead of penetrating his body, underneath his skin skids along a rib half-way around his body before passing out through the garment covering his back; the second, of a rowboat on the river Elbe set dry by the air pressure caused by a dropping rock; the third, of a *Junker* who with all his belongings is transported from one riverbank to the other when a nearby bridge blows up. Ingo Breuer (*KH*,156-9) discusses this text at length, but fails to address the vital questions: *quid enim? cui bono?* I offer that these curious anecdotes have precise *satirical* meanings, the first telling of Prussia in 1806 being hit by Napoleon at *Jena-Auerstedt*, who then skids around the Prussian fortresses and through Poland before popping up, in early 1807, in her "back," i.e., in East Prussia; the second, of the Prussian ships stranded on the river Elbe when Napoleon in late 1810 annexes Northern Germany, including the mouth of the river Elbe, Prussia's only access to the North Sea; the third, of the former Prusssian territories west of the Elbe lost at *Basel, Schönbrunn*, and *Tilsit*. Kleist's anecdotes entailed a relentless barrage of reminders to his readers of Prussia's continued humiliation.

Trench Warfare. Among *BA*'s targets were Hardenberg and his "*Theaterpabst*" Iffland, and alongside the notorious debate about Hardenberg's fiscal policies, more than twenty *BA* entries dealt with that other political stage: Berlin's theatre scene. Hardenberg's then being Fr. Wilh.'s most powerful minister and most intimate advisor, Iffland's, his de-facto propaganda minister, and both of their "hanging together," as Arnim put it (cf. *LS*,457), "like wheel and cart grease," made for explosive (theatre) wars, and by late 1810 Hardenberg and Iffland, rather than Napoleon and Goethe, had become Kleist's best-loved nemeses. This "turn of two unfriendly cards" overcast his final year.[709]

"Turn of two unfriendly cards": Kleist vs. Iffland and Hardenberg.

While his prolonged trench warfare with Hardenberg and Iffland will have been tidious for Kleist, I do not concur with Michalzik's view (*Kleist*, 442-6) that in his bid to save *BA*, Kleist during this stand-off was forced into "lamblike," "self-humiliating," and "complient" behaviour. Kleist had abandoned projects before, and if after definitely giving up on *BA* he repeatedly (on 4th April, 6th June, and 19th September) pestered Hardenberg with petty requests for employment and money, this was arguably all part of an ongoing "game of chicken" Kleist himself was imposing on the Chancellor: either Hardenberg would cave in, in which case he would effectively buttress Kleist in his continued quest to undermine him and his government, or he would stand firm, in which case Kleist would have created a pretext for escalating the conflict—which he promptly did: first to Prince Wilh., on 20th May, then to the King himself, in writing on 17th June, and in person on 11th September.[710] The one move by the "clever fox" (Jakob Baxa) Hardenberg that perhaps did contribute to taking Kleist to the brink was his expatriating (or exiling) the *"halbverwiesenen"* A. Müller to Vienna (cf. *AML*,514): Kleist's attachment to one of his few remaining lover became an Achilles' heel, even though, as we saw, he still had Fouqué to content with, and others, such as Armin, in the "pipeline." While Iffland was a buffoon, Hardenberg was a formidable opponent, and Kleist did not like being outmaneuvered.[711]

3.3 Further "Lives" of Kleist: *The Priapic, The Familial, The Filial, The Orphic*

The commonplace, that Kleist's writing is *"doppeldeutig"* ("ambiguous," *"doppel"* implying *two* possible meanings), remains misleading even if we replace that term with *"mehrdeutig"* ("ambiguous," *"mehr"* implying *multiple* possible meanings), for each "thread" from which Kleist's textual fabrics is woven, is, in and by itself, perfectly *un*ambiguous. Ambiguity arises only on the text(ure)'s *surface*, on which the "threads" intermesh in a complicated, sometimes seemingly "bumpy" and irregular manner. The upshot of Kleist's technique of interweaving is this: the more "threads" or "lives" we are able to identify, unravel and isolate, the fewer "ambiguities" remain. Our working assumption is that *everything* in Kleist is *per se* unambiguous and has a precise meaning in a given context—making Kleist a most *un*ambiguous writer and inviting us to continue uncovering and evaluating further "lives" as long as unexplained surface phenomena remain (one does not *have* to do this, of course: one can always choose to enjoy Kleist's poetry *as poetry*). Given the consistency of Kleist's *plane of composition*, intertextuality can serve as "Rosetta stone" for identifying "threads" and "navels": any textual pattern unwound, or code deciphered, in one text invariably becomes easily discoverable and decipherable in others. With this in mind, I shall proceed to explore four additional Kleistian "lives," complementing the four "lives" I explored so far.

The Priapic

The "graceful" figure of the *Dornauszieher* (*La Spinario*)—a copy of which sculpture Kleist will have first encountered as a young man in a Berlin gallery, and which, he suggests in *Marionettentheater*, depicts a youth losing his "innocence" and discovering his "coyness"—invites a *syphilitical* as well as a *satyrical* evaluation, for by the very same movement by which he is "initiated" by the *erastês*, the *erômenos* may also be "stung" by the "scorpion," so that his "coyness" is explained not only by his awe of initiation, but also by his fear of infection. Does not this figure, for Kleist, "freeze" the precise moment in which he himself lost his "grace" to a dreadful disease that would govern his life?

"Dornauszieher": *'Stachel im Fleisch'* and end of Grace?[712]

Now, *La Spinario* is described, in a 12th century MS, as "*simulacrum valde ridiculosum, quot priapum dicunt*," Priapos being the rustic Greek fertility god whose permanent erection led to his lending his name to the medical afflication of *priapism*.[713] Was Kleist, during the Würzburg journey, seeking medical treatment for *priapism*? Such an affliction would explain why so many of Kleist's characters are ithyphallic—Count F and Don F's priapism is even inscribed into the horizontal bar of their names' capital letter—: *they are autobiographic*. As a corollary of such an affliction, Kleist would at once have been a much sought-after object of desire—which evidently he was: "*sehr beliebt unter seinen Kameraden*" (*LS*,22)—, and highly vulnerable to infection; this dilemma is precisely what his favourite paradox, of the unyielding oak tree (a priapic penis) all-too-easily being pulled down by the storm (of syphilis), suggests.

Ironically, my speculation that Kleist may have been afflicted with *priapism* inverts the *Kleist-Forschung*'s long-standing hypothesis that he suffered from *phimosis*, in that the former dysfunction is one of, as it were, *penile excess*, the latter, one of *penile constraint* (notably during erection); in a rare, but possible, "double whammy," Kleist could even have been afflicted with both dysfunctions, the one exacerbating the pain and inconvenience caused by the other. Either of these afflictions, separately, and even more so in combination, facilitates venereal infection—phimosis increases the risk of inflammation, priapism that of injury—, as well as complicating its treatment. Did Kleist travel all the way to Würzburg because his was an unusually complicated case? This would explain his mentioning two famous surgeons—*"praktische Ärzte"* (II:561)—practicing at Julius-Hospital, Carl Caspar von Siebold and Hermann Joseph Brünninghausen: whereas phimosis could have easily been addressed by a minor surgical intervention any local surgeon could have undertaken, priapism surgery was complicated and risky and called for expert handling.

Ought we not re-read Kleist's 1791 album entry, *"Ich will hinein und muß hinein, und sollts auch inder Quere sein. Dein treuer u. aufrichtiger / Bruder u. Freund / Heinrich vKlst"* (*MA*II:483), as a *cri de cœur* on the part of a teenager for whom it was as difficult to stow away his intractable member as it was to pull back its foreskin? *"Treuer u. aufrichtiger... Freund"* = "permanently erect member"—*priapism*? *"vKlst"* = "a constricted member, representable only by consants"—*phimosis*?[714] In which case, are we not already here encountering Kleist's early experimentation with the codifications, plays of words, and letter games he would so extensively deploy in his œuvre?

As Kleist became a smash hit with male lovers—first as plaything for more senior comrades, then as *erômenos* for more experienced gentlemen, such as Brockes, finally as *erastês* to younger lovers—the moment inevitably came in wich his "fool's journey" truly began, a journey as much propelled by passion and desirousness as hampered by afflictions and suffering. *Der Dornauszieher*: a priapic-cum-phimotic, physically endowed-cum-constrained, ithyphallic-yet-effeminate Kleist, who, in his becoming-conscious of both his desirability and his vulnerability, suddenly realises that he has been—*stung*?   *Ah! Der Skorpion!"*

Albrecht Schaeffer: *"Sieh sein Knabengesicht, es ist ewig."* (NR,456)

The Fool.[715]

The Familial

Kleist's relationship with his family was thoroughly complicated. On the one hand, there can be no doubt that he was a proud scion of this ancient Pomeranian noble family, to whose repute he aspired to contribute, and whose close and long-standing affiliation with the ruling Hohenzollerns he sought to buttress, as well as leverage, be it for job opportunities or access to people in high office, all the way up to, and including, the King.[716] On the other hand, it is also clear that he dreaded the constant pressure, exerted on him by his (in his view) conservative, provincial and narrow-minded relatives, to pursue a career and "life plan" they considered appropriate. Kleist expresses his ambivalent stance towards his family, veering between love and nausea, in a letter to Wilhelmine while *en route* to Paris in 1801:

> Gestern endlich habe ich zum erstenmale an meine Familie nach Pommern geschrieben—sollte man wohl glauben, daß ein Mensch, der in seiner Familie *alles* fand, was ein Herz binden kann, Liebe, Vertrauen, Schonung, Unterstützung mit Rat und Tat, sein Vaterland verlassen kann, ohne selbst einmal schriftlich Abschied zu nehmen von seinen Verwandten?—Und doch sind sie mir die liebsten und teuersten Menschen auf der Welt! So widersprechen sich in mir Handlung und Gefühl—Ach, es ist ekelhaft zu leben— (II:655)

Squaring his aspiration for poetic glory with his family's expectations remained one of Kleist's life challenges—hence his interest in his distant relative, the noted poet and officer Ewald Chr. von Kleist: here was one von Kleist who had been able to produce, as Joh. Wilh. Gleim affirmed to him in 1801 (cf. II:656-7), both a "beautiful work" (of art) and a "great deed" (for Prussia: Ewald in 1759 fought and died in the *Battle of Kunersdorf*), and whom Kleist could emulate.

The "Lausitz Clan." When Kleist's mother passed away in 1793, his aunt, the childless widow Auguste Helene von Massow, née Pannwitz, and her brother, his uncle Karl Wilh. von Pannwitz auf Gut Gulben (Carl's father, who had written that admonishing letter to his son), became his custodians and foster parents. They belonged to the core of what I term the "Lausitz Clan," a complex of noble families centred on the *von Kleists* (first documented in 1289), the *von Pannwitzes* (1276), and the *von Schönfelds* (1216), clannishly connected through intermarriages and closely acquainted due to the neighbourhood of their Spreewald (Niederlausitz) estates, who together with other, more losely connected, families—the *von Kitzlings* (first recorded in 1265), the *von Massows* (1232), the *von Massenbachs* (1160), the *von Loebens* (1253), and the *von Einsiedels* (1299)—represent the quintessential Prussian *Junker* class of aristocratic, landowning, conversative, Protestant royalists who provided the traditional backbone of the Hohenzollerns' rule.[717] Perhaps the sandy Brandenburgian marshes, at which he occasionally wrinkled his nose, for Kleist symbolised the "Lausitz Clan" in its *"Wille zur Provinz"* (Sloterdijk) and, in the bigger scheme of things, its irrelevance: if Germany's leading dynasties suffered from the "German disease" of *dynastic rivalry*, and the Bonapartes from the "French disease" of *dynastic hybris*, then the "Lausitz Clan" families did from the "Spreewald disease" of *dynastic pettiness*. He felt ensnared by it *"wie eine Schlange, / Mit Gliedern, zahnlos, ekelhaft, umwunden"* (I:87):

"wie eine Schlange, / Mit Gliedern, zahnlos, ekelhaft, umwunden":
the Kleist—Pannwitz—Schönfeld—Klitzing—Massow—Massenbach—
Loeben—Einsiedel complex.

Where, Kleist may have wondered, had the wolves displayed on the Kleist's coat of arms (far left) gone? Himself, like Napoleon, a "wolfing," a prolific and intense force, among his family members, with the partial exception of Ulrike, he discerned no wolves, only so many bleating sheep.

It is in this context that we shall evaluate Kleist's lengthy explanation, to Martini, of his decision to quit the military service, and of his difficulties with conveying it to his custodians and, Ulrike apart, other family members:

> Allen, die um meinen Entschluss wissen, meiner Familie, mit Ausschluß meiner Schwester Ulrike, meinem Vormunde, habe ich meinen neuen Lebensplan nur zum Teil mitgeteilt, und daher trafen auch alle Einwürfe von ihrer Seite denselben nur halb. Mich ihnen ganz zu eröffnen, war aus Gründen, deren Richtigkeit Sie nach vollendeter Durchlesung dieses Briefes einsehen werden, nicht ratsam. Alle diese Leute schiffen ins hohe Meer und verlieren nach und nach die Küste mit ihren Gegenständen aus den Augen. Gefühle, die sie selbst nicht mehr haben, halten sie auch gar nicht für vorhanden. Dieser Vorwurf trifft besonders meine sonst sehr ehrwürdige Tante, die nichts mehr liebt, als Ruhe und Einförmigkeit, und jede Art von Wechsel scheut, wäre es auch die Wanderung aus einer Wohnstube in die andere. (II:473)

The contrast Kleist depicts between aunt Massow's character and his own could not have been starker. Rudolf Loch, in the course of his valuable investigation (cf. *Beiträge*, 95) of the "Lausitz Clan" (my term, not his), uncovered an entry by Massow into Ulrike von Loeben's album, in which the stern aunt admonishes her younger relation not to let "youthful fantasies" get in the way of her "felicity": *"Ohne jugendliche fantasien / Wird alsdann dein Glücke blühen."* Anyone still wondering why Kleist had to leave his homeland need look no further than this album entry: the impossibility of his most imaginative of scions making himself understood by such most unimaginative of relatives became a bane of his life.

Later in his rambling letter to Martini, Kleist reports his family's reaction to his resolution to quit the military (his forceful staccato of sentences commencing with *"Man..."* is an early example of his emerging poetic craftmanship):

> Man machte mir Einwürfe, fragte mich, welche Brotwissenschaft ich ergreifen wolle, denn daß dies meine Absicht sein müsse, fiel niemanden ein, zu bezweifeln... Man ließ mir die Wahl zwischen Jurisprudenz und der Kameralwissenschaft... Man fragte mich, ob ich auf Konnexionen bei Hofe rechnen könne?... Man lächelte... Man sagte, ich sei zu alt, zu studieren.... Man stellte mir mein geringes Vermögen vor; man zeigte mir die zweifelhafte Aussicht auf Brot auf meinem neuen Lebenswege... Man malte mir mein bevorstehendes Schicksal... mit so barocken Farben aus, daß... ich mich den unsinnigsten Toren hätte schelten müssen... Aber alle diese Einwürfe trafen meinen Entschluß nicht. (II:482-3)

Kleist's youthful spirit of defiance expressed in this letter would—could—not last: while the example of Ewald von Kleist, as related by Gleim, the positive reviews of Schroffenstein, and the endorsement by Wieland, may have kindled his optimism, in April 1804, following his abortion of *Guiskard* and Saint-Omer, he was forced to return into aunt Masslow's den, pennyless and discredited, his hopes for recognition and employment dashed—a humbling setback Rudolf Loch (*Kleist*, 196) captures well: *"Welche Überwindung muß Kleist die Rückkehr... gekostet haben. In Potsdam, in Frankfurt an der Oder, Gulben und Werben schrieb man das Unglück seinem Faible fürs Schreiben zu. Und was sollte man mit anfangen mit einem, der alle gutgemeinten Warnungen... eigensinnig in den Wing geschlagen und den guten Kleistschen Namen auch noch durch einen Disziplinverstoß...*

geschändet hatte? When he had nowhere else to turn, Kleist turned to his family, despite the humiliation this entailed. In 1811 his suicide became possible not least because he felt he could no longer entrust himself even to Ulrike.

It is in equal measure ironic and fitting that Kleist's first extant letter is addressed to his unloved, but all-important, guardian, aunt Massow. The letter is a formal and polite, cool and distant affair by an "obedient" (II:469) dependent, whose legal maturity still lay in the distant future. The only passage in the long letter that conveys genuine warmth is his reminiscence of his recently deceased mother—suggestively, Kleist brackets this passage, as if acknowledging that it does not really belong into this letter to "aunty," that the bracketed lines reflected his genuine feelings, while everything else was calculated compliance.[718] Kleist seems to have written to aunt Massow on at least one other occasion, in late August or early September 1800, in the context of his precipitate departure from Frankfurt/O. (cf. II:538), but in the main seems to have communicated with her indirectly, usually via Ulrike. The short messages and references to Massow he conveys to Ulrike in the following years veer between the polite (he still depended on Massow's support), the condescending, and the sarcastic. Kleist admonishes Ulrike not to let his aunt access his drawers in which he keeps his MSS (cf. II:583) and forbids Wilhelmine to join her tea party (cf. II:617), let alone settle in with her (cf. II:599). A dig of his, in a letter to Ulrike, at the physiognomy of his aunt's hands is naughty: he demands that Ulrike, on his behalf, kiss "aunty"'s long fingers—which he compares to (phallic) organ pipes—one-by-one, in order, from the longest to theshortest (cf. II:731), as if he were imagining giving a blow job to male lovers lined up according to the size of their manhood. For all its amusing theatricality, this state of affairs was rather tragic: the one relationship that should have bolstered and buttressed Kleist in times of duress, that with his guardian, was one of—apparently mutual—dislike.

Lack of understanding and empathy for Kleist probably pervaded the family, and vice versa: cousin Wilh. von Pannwitz's 1808 note to his brother-in-law Philipp von Stojentin, in response

to Kleist's soliciting seed funding for the *Ph* project, is probably quite representative:[719]

> wenn [Kleist] nur ein Gran Vernunft und Überlegung hätte, so konnte er bei seinem glücklichen Genie längst in einer guten Lage sein. Warum verläßt er seine Anstellung, die ihm wenigstens die Aussicht auf ein gewisses Brot gab, und wenn er den Drang zum Dichten in sich fühlt, so konnte er ihn nebenher immer befriedigen. (*LS*,288)

Wilh. von Pannwitz appreciated Kleist's prodigious talent, but not his failure to turn it into profit: poetry for him (and no doubt many other family members) was a *brotlose* Kunst: at best a hobby, not a professional pursuit. As time went by, Kleist's family did not remain entirely unmoved by his insistence and persistence, but when they grudgingly came to accept that he could not be weaned of his poetic addiction, they encouraged him to produce *Homburg*, in the pragmatic and self-serving hope that a patriotic play, in addition to generating royal goodwill for the family, would qualify for a public stipend (cf. *LS*,505a).

Even Ulrike, whom in his letter to Martini Kleist quasi nominated as his de-facto custodian, eventually allowed herself to be taken in by the clan's narrow-mindedness.[720] The spinster enjoyed extended stays at several of the Spreewald estates, and perhaps Kleist termed her "amphibian" not least because she was both outsider *and* insider, independent- *and* family-minded. Over time, she was increasingly sucked from her relative independence in Frankfurt/O. into the family's Spreewald orbit; when in November 1799 he wrote her, "*Was in aller Welt macht du denn in Werben* [the Schönfelds' estate]. *Niemand von uns, ich selbst nicht, kann begreifen, was dir den Aufenthalt dort auf viele Monate so angenehm machen kann*" (II:499), Kleist evidently feared that Ulrike's spirit of independence would prove less resilient than his own. Ulrike's final "conversion" to the family credo probably took place in 1807/8, when she spent considerable time at Gulben (the Pannwitz' estate), under Masssow's wings; by the time "aunty" passed away in 1809, the "damage" had been done.

Perhaps *Cäcilie*'s Abbess, ponderously seated on a chair adorned with dragon feet while insidiously converting the Protestant Mother to her Catholic faith, comprised not only one of Kleist's more memorable references to Napoleon and his "conversion" of *Borussia*, but also his obituary to his aunt, including his admission that she had managed to "convert" Ulrike.[721]

Dragon feet: "Abess" and "Aunty."

In *Cäcilie*, the convent is eventually secularised, but only 50 years later (cf. II:298; 219). Did Kleist in 1810 predict that not only Napoleon's régime would outlast its founder, but also "aunty'"s? Did he deem the "converted" Ulrike aunty's to have become his aunt's annointed "successor"? Ulrike was 36 when he wrote the BA version of *Cäcilie*, and it was indeed possible that she turned 86 (in fact she died in 1849, aged 74). Was *Cäcilie, familially* speaking, a swipe at Ulrike? In 1811, when he published the extended *Cäcilie*, Kleist saw no reason to remove this passage.

Reinventing the Family (I): Life Practice. In May 1802 Kleist writes Wilhelmine from Thun: "*ich habe keinen andern Wunsch, als zu sterben, wenn mir drei Dinge gelungen sind: ein Kind, ein schön Gedicht, und eine große Tat.*" A successor ("child" here means "son": girls did not count in relation to lineage) produced for his family, a poem for satisfying both his *Erôs* and *Agôn*, and a great deed for his King and nation: such were Kleist's life aspirations.[722] The fact that he put the production of a successor first reminds us that Kleist never questioned the relevance of the (aristocratic) family as such (nor, for that matter, that of the dynastic monarchy). Three years earlier, Kleist had sought to adopt a *"Lebensplan,"* in part to mollify his guardian Karl Wilh. von Pannwitz, who, as Kleist told Martini, *"mir schon erklärt hat, ein Mündel müsse sich für einen festen Lebenplan, für ein festes Ziel bestimmen"* (II:484); Pannwitz, we imagine, had taken his charge aside, as guardians do, to "talk sense into him." As is frequently the case with Kleist, he adopted an "alien" concept, then made it his own by inverting it: when two months later he tells Ulrike, *"Ein freier, denkender Mensch… entwirft sich einen Lebensplan, und strebt seinem Ziele… mit allen seinen Kräften entgegen"* (II:488-9), the "life plan" and "goal," which in the letter to Martini, in reference to Pannwitz, appeared conventional and fixed (*"fest"*), here become autopoïetic (*"entwirft sich"*) and bespoke (*"seinem"*): unlike Pannwitz's, Kleist's "life plan" is *plastic* (but not arbitrary: it must encompass solid principles of consistency, coherence and unity—cf. II:489). What for aunt and uncle is a means of aligning their charge's development with conventional family expectations, for Kleist is a tool for liberation: *"So lange ein Mensch noch nicht im Stande ist, sich selbst einen Lebensplan zu bilden, so lange ist und bleibt er unmündig… Die erste Handlung der Selbstständigkeit eines Menschen ist der Entwurf eines solchen Lebensplans"* (*ibid*); his "life plan" is one designed for "thinking" people (such as, he implies, Ulrike and himself), not for "unthinking" ones (such as, say, their siblings and cousins). In a matter of months, Kleist turns the idea of a "Pannwitzian *Lebensplan*" into that of an alternative "Kleistian *Lebensplan*," which he fleshes out in the Würzburg letters to Wilhelmine, and seeks to put into practice first in Berlin, then Paris, then Thun.

What does this "Kleistian *Lebensplan*" entail? On 3rd September 1800, from the "delightful valley of Tharandt," near Dresden, Kleist writes Wilhelmine:

> Da hangt an dem Einschnitt des Tales, zwischen Felsen und Strom, ein Haus, eng und einfältig gebaut, wie für einen Weisen. Der hintere Felsen gibt dem Örtchen Sicherheit, Schatten winken ihm die überhangenen Zweige zu, Kühlung führt ihm die Welle der Weißritz entgegen. Höher

hinauf in das Tal ist die Aussicht schauerlich, tiefer hinab in die Ebene von Dresden heiter. Die Weißritz trennt die Welt von diesem Örtchen und nur ein schmaler Steg führt in seinen Eingang.—Eng, sagte ich, wäre das Häuschen? Ja freilich, für Assemblen und Redouten. Aber für 2 Menschen und die Liebe weit genug, weit hinlänglich genug. Ich verlor mich in Träumereien. Ich sah mir das Zimmer aus, wo ich wohnen würde, ein anderes, wo jemand Anderes wohnen würde, ein drittes, wo wir beide wohnen würden. Ich sah eine Mutter auf der Treppe sitzen, ein Kind schlummernd an ihrem Busen. Im Hintergrunde kletterten Knaben auf dem Felsen, und sprangen von Stein zu Stein, und jauchzten laut— (II:545).[723]

Many members of Kleist's "brotherhood" would eventually "go legit" and "give themselves a constitution," i.e., bow to the social convention according to which their two realms of desire—the *satyrical* and the *familial*—were incompatible, and resorted to *sequencing* them: having lived out their homosexual passions in their youth, in their maturity they pursued conventional married life and career (perhaps entailing the occasional homosexual fling). Kleist, evidently would not resign himself to such a compromise, and instead of *sequencing*, sought to *parallel* the two realms in an altogether new, alternative family model, designed not merely to "camouflage his homosexuality with a marriage" (Blamberger) but enable the cohabitation, in a single household, of himself, his male lover(s), his wife, and their children. In his quest to reconcile "fatherhood," "brotherhood" and "poethood," this irreverent *Junker* scion conjured—for lack of a better term—the *post-modern family*.[724]

Having fleshed it out during the Würzburg journey in numerous letters to Wilhelmine (especially in the "birthday letter" of 10th/11th October), Kleist in November 1800 confidently announced his *bios Kleistikos* as *"Liebe, Bildung und Freiheit"* (II:586), i.e., homosexual "love" for himself and his "brother(s)," "formation" for Wilhelmine, as mother to his children, and "freedom" for himself as poet. The outline to this model Kleist perhaps had first ideated when observing the *Sistine Madonna*'s composition of immaculate mother, divine son, *erastês*-cum-patriarch (the headscarf) and at their feet, two playful cherubim (*erômenoi*): "*Dich, Wilhelmine, und zu Deinen Füßen zwei Kinder, und auf Deinem Schoße ein drittes*" (II:577).[725] Cherubim/children, for Kleist, can always be both lovers and infants (cf. *Marquise's "Eine ganze Reihe von jungen…"*). Mary, Mother of God, virgin and immaculate mother, for Kleist represented the archetype *par excellence* of the bride he was seeking to marry, the ideal complement to his archetype of the homosexual youth who effortlessly "flies from flower to flower," "jumps from rock to rock" and "travels from castle to castle," while nimbly climbing up and down between the Heaven of homosexual love and the Earth of reproductive family life. What made Raphael's painting so exceedingly compelling for Kleist were those two puttos he had added, if only to balance his composition.[726]

When Kleist on 20th September 1800 unabashedly tells Wilhelmine that when embracing her to produce a son, he will simply "close the eyes and imagine whatever he wants" (cf. II:570), this "whatever he wants" no doubt encompasses those "*FFO*" or "*FOF*" constellations he busily rehearses while traversing Saxony together with Brockes—for example, when on 1st September he fantasises about Wilhelmine joining them for a threesome in the back of their bassinet (cf. II:537).[727] A few days later he shares with her further details of his designs, specifically the attitude he requires of her, and the tools he seeks to deploy:

> und wäre ein Mädchen auch noch so vollkommen, ist sie fertig, so ist es nichts für mich. Ich selbst muß es mir formen und ausbilden, sonst fürchte ich, geht es mir, wie mit dem Mundstück an meiner Klarinette. Die kann man zu Dutzenden auf der Messe kaufen, aber wenn man sie braucht, so ist kein Ton rein. Da gab mir einst der Musikus Baer in Potsdam ein Stück, mit der Versicherung, das sei gut… Da schnitt ich mir von einem gesunden Rohre ein Stück ab, formte es nach meinen Lippen… bis es in jeden Einschnitt meines Mundes paßte——und das ging herrlich. Ich spielte nach Herzenslust.— (II:549)

"*Fertig*," "finished" = "settled in conventional behaviours," "unwilling to submit to unorthodox demands": Kleist hopes that Wilhelmine, unlike most women in the marriage market, will be, so to speak, "*unfertig*," will let herself be "shaped and educated" by him. The clarinet is obviously phallic, the mouthpiece, glans-like, and his "cutting off a piece of healthy reed," "shaping it for his lips" "till it fits into every corner of his mouth," and thereupon "playing it to his heart's content" depicts his tailoring to his atanomy a wooden dildo that Wilhelmine will use to satisfy him anally.[728] The "*diamantene Schild*" (II:577) with which Kleist imagines equipping Wilhelmine is no mere metaphor: he envisions that she shall not only condone, in their household, the presence of his lover(s), but also partake in their orgies, her vagina remaining reserved for him and off-limits to everyone else: the implement would at once serve as chastity belt ("shield") and dildo harness ("diamond").[729]

It appears that, to a not insignificant degree, Wilhelmine complied with Kleist's demands; to her new fiancé Wilh. Traugott Krug she later admitted (proving that she had adopted a fair amount of Kleistian doublespeak): "*ich strengte alle meine Kräfte an, meine Talente auszubilden, um ihn recht vielseitig zu interessieren*" (*LS*,38). In January 1801, in a long letter, Kleist acknowledges her progress in her "education" (cf. II:617), although caveating his commendation by complementing it with a veritable hymn to Brockes, whom he uses as "strawman" to raise the bar for her, challenging her to become "*unter den Mädchen..., was dieser unter den Männern*" (II:619). Brockes' most commendable "*Tugend*" and "*Vortrefflichkeit*," in Kleist's view, was his willingness to "utterly unselfishly" submit himself (for Kleist the "*most difficult* of all virtues"; II:621)—in effect, to let go of all "coyness" and be as uncompromisingly "open" to him as, say, Réage's O is for Sir Stephen.[730] Although clearly self-serving, Kleist's scheme hinged on Wilhelmine consciously submitting to her role. If Kleist was indeed something of a *sadist* (cf. *NR*,508b), then Wilhelmine must have been something of a *masochist*: drawn, like O, into a strange, scary, fascinating world, from which she could have escaped, but for a long time chose not to, and when she eventually did, only reluctantly. If Kleist, as of January 1801, remained hopeful that Wilhelmine would rise to the challenge and join him in entering a "new epoch" (cf. II:625), she must have given him reason for such optimism.

In the "crisis" letter of 22nd March 1801 Kleist informs Wilhelmine that he dismissed Berlin as the selected site for their *satyrico-familial* experiment; this decision may have had a lot to do with Brocke's departure in early 1801, whom he had earmarked as the second *"F"* in the *"FFO"/"FOF"* constellation (Brockes' departure in January, to pursue a career in Mecklenburg—cf. II:618—, rather than the reading of any Kantian treatises, could have precipitated Kleist's "crisis"). Kleist does not drop his experimental objective or change its basic "set-up," but reconsiders the "test-site" and "laboratory" for putting it into practice: "*Liebe Wilhelmine, laß mich reisen*" (II:635) opens a new chapter in his *familial* pursuit, with his sight now firmly set on a different location, far from Prussian society (and its most *ur*Prussian of thinkers, Kant), and more cosmopolitan, progressive and anomymous than Berlin: Paris.[731]

His reminiscences in *Marionettentheater* may suggest that Kleist in Paris rehearsed the envisaged *satyrico-familial* constellation with the help of a female prostitute: the "experienced dancer" *"Herr C..."* could have been a *"Mme C...,"* whom he hired for the purpose of rehearsal (cf. Strahl's rehearsal; V.1154ff), and the *"Gliedermann"* a dildo harness for her participation in the "puppets' dance," i.e., the "brothers'" orgiastic intercourse.[732] Paris may have turned out to be more suitable for rehearsing than for implementing his scheme, and Kleist soon animated Lose, who had replaced Brockes, to relocate their experiments to Switzerland, a location suitable for *satyrico-familial*, as well as for *satirical* and *syphilitical* purposes; indeed the isolated house on the tip of the Rousseauian "Inseli" suited perfectly, and a local "Mädeli" soon replaced Lose (or Zschokke) for the "triad" with Wilhelmine.[733] Alas, unlike O, who bravely joins Sir Stephen on his estate at Samois-sur-Seine, Wilhelmine ultimately recoiled from joining him in his idyll; in putting distance between them and Prussia, Kleist had solved one problem by creating another: for his chosen "lab rat," this particular "lab" was, in every respect, one step too far.[734]

Reinventing the Family (II): Poetic Practice. Alongside his real-life experiments, Kleist explored various scenarios and constellations regarding *The Familial* in his dramas. In *Schroffenstein* he investigates the complex relationships between rivalrous, yet closely related, family lines. Notes Hans Dieter Zimmermann (*Kleist*, 53): *"insofern ist das Thema 'Die Familie Schroffenstein' wörtlich zu nehmen: die nächsten Angehörigen sind die am stärksten bedrängenden Feinde."* Ottokar and Agnes, *"Stammhalter"* of their respective lines, are caught up in the incommensurability of their duties towards their family on the one hand, and their individual longings on the other, a dilemma the former seeks to overcome by forbidden love, the latter by premediated murder of *"brothers."* Perhaps the Rossitzes represent the Pannwitzes, the Warwands, the Schönfelds, and the lesser Wyks, the Kleists (his parents having passed away, these have the least influence on Kleist's affairs), and Ottokar and Agnes two prominent dimensions of Kleist's existence, *Erôs* and *Agôn*, whose A. Müllerian dialectic Kleist explicates in a Feburary 1811 BA entry: *"Schaffen und Erhalten ist der Gegensatz von Zerstören. Und doch ist beides sehr nahe mit dem Zerstören verwandt. Denn oft ist Erhaltung nur durch Zerstörung möglich, so wie oft Leben nur aus dem Tode hervorgeht."*[735] Kleist also explores that most disturbing of *familial* scenarios, later elaborated in *Penthesilea*, of the filicide of the unborn son: if Agnes is pregnant, as her baptism as Maria (Mother of God) suggests, her father, by killing her, destroys his own seed.

In *Guiskard*, the relationship between Robert and Abälard, the former being next in line, the latter more popular among the clan members, resembles that between Heinrich and Leopold (cf. Zimmermann, *Kleist*, 197). Abälard's being Guiskard's nephew opens up the possibility of adoptions within the wider family; for Kleist, if he were to fail in his quest to find a suitable bride, this could have been a real option. In *Krug*, irrespective of who impregnated Eve, legal fatherhood of her son-to-be-born is adjudicated to Adam by due legal process: Kleist explores a procedure by which a suitable patriarch is declared legal father to a son he may or may not have fathered.[736] In *Amphitryon* Kleist repeats this experiment: husband—Amphitryon/Kleist—and begetter—Jupiter or Merkur—are separated; Alkmene remains uncertain who impregnated her, demonstrating that under certain circumstances—orgy, trance, swoon—the mother may not know who is the biological father. Legal, rather than biological, fatherhood was evidently most important for Kleist, who above all desired a *successor*, which is a legal, social construct; *NT*'s mode of delivering a son, which he paraphrases in *Amphitryon*, "*Dir wird ein Sohn geboren werden, / Deß Name Herkules*" (V.2335-6), would have suited him: could he find, like YHWH and Jupiter, a surrogate father for his son?[737]

Penthesilea's Amazon society, which excludes the opposite sex, except during ritually sanctified holidays dedicated to reproduction, obviously simulates exactly the alternative family model Kleist had first developed with Wilhelmine in mind: the leader of a male-only "brotherhood," Penthesileus/Kleist, seeks to produce a heir with the help of Achillea, who, in addition to delivering and educating his children, equipped with a "spear" (dildo) joins the brothers' orgies. The experiment fails when Penthesileus/Kleist confuses Achillea's two roles (*Küsse, Bisse*) and penetrates her so forcefully that her inner organs, including their seed lodged therein, are destroyed and she bleeds to death, an outcome that may have suggested to Kleist that in the implementation of "*Scheidung*," mother and lovers are best kept apart, at least while she is pregnant.

In *Käthchen* Kleist envestigates the challenge of acquiring a suitable bride—*satirically*, for Napoleon, autobiographically, for himself. During *Käthchen*'s lengthy genesis several plausible brides may have presented themselves to him, as well as to Napoleon, and he may well have modelled the drama's lead female characters on his own actual candidates. Fascinatingly, he even seems to be exploring the possibility of treating infected sperm, and of artificially inseminating a woman with the "purified" seed: Strahl/Kleist's sperm, which is expressly represented in its *genetic* functioning—as his "picture" or "likeness"—is gathered in a case or envelope and undergoes purification via the ordeal by fire (i.e., mercury treatment).[738] Käthchen, in salvaging Strahl's purified reproductive "assets," qualifies herself as suitable mother to his children.[739]

Death in the Spreewald. Apparently Kleist and Henriette initially planned to perform their *final final* project in the "Lausitz clan's" backyard, where their mutual friend Ernst L. Hoffmeister, who resided in Auras near Drebkau, could have attended to their mortal remains (cf. *LS*,528). Auras is close to the road from Gulben to Wormlage, on which Kleist and Ulrike had travelled together in October 1807, during which trip Ulrike definitely rejected Kleist's renewed request for her to cohabitate with him (cf. II:794).[740] Apart from "shocking" (Paul Hoffmann) and "shaming" (Rudolf Loch) his family by committing suicide in close vicinity of their estates, Kleist could have picked this location to convey to Ulrike how deeply her "conversion" and rejection had hurt him, in particular during their last get-together in Frankfurt/O. Puportedly a mere coincidence—Hoffmann being in Berlin, not Auras, at the time—made them select the Kl. Wannsee location instead (cf. *LS*,528).[741] Two of the texts found with their corpses or baggage (cf. *NR*,39) may have been meant as messages for Kleist's family: Cervante's *Don Quixote*, perhaps hinting at the futility of confronting the windmills of family expectations, and Klopstock's *Die tote Clarissa* (based on Richardson's novel), pointing to family pressure as a cause of his death.[742]

Like Napoleon (cf. *The Elector* in Homburg), Kleist did not like to depend on accidents, and I am inclined to believe that he made a positive decision in favour of the Kl. Wannsee location, rather than going there merely by default. Sending a strong signal to Ulrike, then, was not a sufficiently compelling reason for him for favouring the Spreewald location. Let us look at the ominous get-together that evidently so rattled Kleist. I put in firmly on the 18th September, the day on which he nonchalantly invites himself to lunch with Ulrike (cf. II:880), at a time when he is certainly broke, possibly starved, and above all devastated by the *bad news* he just received, of Fr. Wilh. edging towards an alliance with Napoleon. Kleist swings by Ulrike's place at lunchtime, as announced, and finds her, Auguste and *die alte Wackern* at Ulrike's "*Mittagstafel*" (II:883 cf. MAIII:694).[743] Ulrike is utterly shocked at his appearance, be it because he is starved, sickly, moribund, depressed, or all of the above. The get-together is short but hefty (the wargame with Marwitz takes place in the afternoon or evening of the same day, 20km from Frankfurt/O.). Kleist asks Ulrike for money, ostensibly to fund his equipage (he is lying: there is no way he would join the army if it is to fight for Napoleon; but he doesn't say that, so that he can use the cabinet order of 11th September as pretext—cf. II:879), but perhaps he does admit that he really needs to money to travel to Vienna, unite with Gentz and Müller, and see if an Austrian resistance can be launched. From Ulrike's vantage point, neither purpose warrants her investment: the cabinet order is contingent on war actually breaking out (which she does not believe will be the case), and the proposed journey to Vienna to her makes no sense at all (if Kleist can't even find a job in Berlin, how on earth will he be able to do so in Vienna?). She vaguely promises to contribute to funding his equipment in case war breaks out, and gives him no money, save a couple of *RT* for his return trip. Kleist, frustrated, takes his leave and seeks consolation with the Marwitzes. Back in Berlin the next day, his letter to Hardenberg betrays optimism, and Marie later tells the King that in late September, Kleist was still in good spirits (cf. *LS*,509a).[744]

Let us look at the matter from the point of view of Ulrike and other family members: as of the late summer of 1811, Juliane having married Gustav von Weiher in 1809, and Leopold having recently been appointed post-master in Stolp, *Kleist is the only member of his family who*—by conventional expectations—*is a "failure."* His "little sister" Juliane's marriage befitted their family's rank; his "little brother" Leopold's appointment to a respectable and lucrative civil service position was in line with expectations (thus secured, he would go on to produce five sons and five daughters); and Kleist? He, the most talented of them all, in whom Ulrike had invested so much, had nothing whatsoever to show for it! Having finally produced a patriotic play that could at least bestow honour, if not riches, on the family, his *Homburg* was not even acknowledged, let alone performed, by the Hohenzollerns! And the King only needed him *in case of war*, but scarcely anybody (other than Kleist) hoped or expected that war was imminent! Today, when he is easily the Kleist clan's most celebrated scion, we chuckle about such "misjudgments of history," yet in his own day, this will have been no laughing matter—not for his sisters and family members, and least of all, for Kleist himself.

And Kleist? Possibly his frustration about Ulrike did not abate in the weeks following the get-together, and peaked around the time he shared his frustration about it with Marie on 10th November. Possibly he was so deeply hurt because without money, there was simply nothing he could do. He hated being condemned to inactivity. Apart from the partially conciliatory letter to her of the morning of his death, no letter to her dated after 18th September is extant, and while letters may have been lost, it is quite possible that the sulking Kleist did not write to Ulrike for two months, and that only in that final letter to her of 21st November he came to regret things he told Marie about her on 19th November (9th in *MA*). If there were indeed two months of sulky silence between Ulrike and Kleist, it will not have helped him at all: a single encouraging letter from Ulrike— better still, a single visit—*could have saved his life*.

Johannes R. Becher: "*Er Sank. Rang im Aufschrei / der letzten menschlichen Möglichkeit: / 'Schwester——————'*" (NR,393b)

The Hanged Man.745

The Filial
Although his family did not own a sufficiently sizeable estate for him to live off, and his status came with few material benefits, it will have mattered to Kleist that upon reaching maturity in 1801, as oldest son

and *"Stammhalter,"* he became head of family.[746] Together with the fact that all his siblings managed to pursue careers or marriages that met family expectations, his status as *Stammhalter* piled pressure on him to pursue a befitting and lucrative career, as well as to produce a heir. *The Filial*, i.e., the quest for a suitable bride to produce a son, became as defining a part of his life as of Napoleon's; in this respect, some of his characters representing Napoleon—say, Strahl, Count F—may be more autobiographical then some of those enacting Fr. Wilh., who had already fathered several heirs. Kleist's *"chercher la femme"* amounted to a race against time: would a *"femme fertile,"* a suitable mother to his son appear first, or instead a *"femme fatale,"* a suitable sister-in-death? The latter turned out to be the case, yet before his final turn to Henriette, Kleist explored an entire "panorama" of plausible brides:

"ringsherum... sehen": (top, FLTR) Ulrike von Kleist, Adolphine von Werdeck, Marie von Kleist, Wilhelmine von Zenge, Karoline von Günderrode; (bottom, FLTR) Emma Körner, Dora Stock, Rahel Levin, Elisabeth von Staegemann, Henriette Hendel-Schütz.[747]

Ulrike von Kleist. Kleist's "amphibian" half-sister, an Artemis to his Apollo, a Sappho to his Alcaeus, was the most sustained relationship of his life.[748] Ulrike was his earliest, and for a long time his most loyal and trusted, friend; a few intimate "brothers" apart, she was probably the only "*cognoscente*" of (most of) his life's quests and secrets, who would support and fund his exploits, without spilling the beans.[749] In his 1799 letter to Martini he nominates her, in place of the unloved aunt, as his guardian, and until they drift apart in his last years, they remain close, on two occasions living together for extended periods, 1801 in Paris and 1805/6 in Königsberg (in 1803 he apparently considered joining her on the estate where she was staying—cf. *LS*,110; in 1806 Ulrike invited him to join her in Pomerania).

It could have been during intimate moments with Ulrike, in addition to those with Carl, that the teenager Kleist first discovered erotic desire: in his May 1799 letter he attests to her that she is the only person in Frankfurt/O. "who understands him fully" (II:487), lamenting, "*Wärst Du ein Mann oder nicht meine Schwester, ich würde stolz sein, das Schicksal meines ganzen Lebens an das Deinige zu knüpfen*" (II:488): were Ulrike a man, he would chose her as his *lover*; were she not his sister, as his *bride*; in any case he recognises her as kindred spirit. In the same letter he entreats her to drop her resolve not to marry (cf. II:493), a demand he repeats in his turn-of-the-century New Year's greeting, "*Amphibion... / ...verlasse das Wasser, / Versuch es mal in der Luft*" (I:44), urging her to leave the (feminine, lesbian) "waters" and explore the (masculine, heterosexual) "skies." To no avail: Ulrike never married, perhaps not only because "going legit" was just as anathema to her as it was to her brother, but also because she remained faithful to him, whom she deeply loved, but could not own, and whom she eventually lost, but could not forget.[750] Perhaps in addition to that of Apollo and Artemis, and of Alcaeus and Sappho, their relationship also bore a resemblance to that of Abélard and Héloïse, two lovers prevented by social conventions (and castration) from consummating their love: when in 1805/6 Ulrike stayed with him for almost a year in Königsberg, Kleist went out of his way to convince Pfuel to join them (cf. Michalzik, *Kleist*, 252-3; 263), which suggests that she condoned his gay friendships, and even that Kleist considered her a suitable partner in his *filial* project: legal constraints could have been circumvented by her declaring the biological father unknown, and Kleist subsequently adopting the child—cf. his scenarios rehearsed in *Krug* and *Erdbeben*).⁷⁵¹

Kleist and Ulrike (left to right): Apollo and Artemis,
Alcaeus and Sappho, Abélard and Héloïse.

What hurt Kleist most in the wake of their ominuous final get-together in Frankfurt/O. was perhaps not that Ulrike refused to support him financially, but that she *refused to die with him*: when in 1802 he had fallen seriously ill, she had gone out of her way to come to his rescue (cf. II:725), and in the autumn of 1811 he may have expected her to either do likewise, or *to go with him all the way*. Instead he found that his guardian angel would neither guard his exit nor join him through it; perhaps it was only upon this bitter realization that Henriette fully came into the picture, quasi as Ulrike's replacement. Ulrike may have been the very first person, even preceding Carl, to whom he proposed the ultimate joint sacrifice, and in the end, Kleist was disappointed that Ulrike did "not understand the art of sacrificing oneself fully, of entirely sinking into the ground for that which one loves" (cf. II:885); by acknowledging, in his final letter to her, that she supported him *"on Earth"* as much as *"humanly"* possible (cf. II:887), he indirectly chides her for not doing so on his final journey to the beyond. It is to Ulrike that he writes his penultimate letter; the ultimate one he reserves for Marie.

Ulrike, on her part, remained attached to Kleist till her death: Hans Joachim Kreuzer, tracing the 37 years of her vita after Kleist's death, discerns *"die Spuren einer geisterhaften Zwiesprache der Schwester mit dem toten Bruder"* (*KJb* 1981, 82-3), during which she jealously guarded their secrets, burning many of his letters (cf. *NR*,113), although, luckily, some were saved.⁷⁵²

Adolphine von Werdeck. Adolphine, née von Klitzing, sprang from one of the ancient families connected to the "Lausitz clan," and the Werdecks' Spreewald estates were close to those of the Kleists, Pannwitzes and Schönfelds. Kleist apparently first met Adolphine, five years his senior, in Potsdam in 1795 (cf. II:671), or even during their youth—her family's Schorbus estate neighboured that of the Pannwitzes—, and may have communicated with her in writing for a number of years thereafter (cf. Loch, *Kleist*, 30), before meeting her again in the Bernese Oberland in the summer of 1803, in Paris in the autumn (cf. *LS*, 120), again in Paris in the spring of 1804 (unlike Sembdner, I assume that the Kleist whom Bertuch notes meeting there together with Adolphine was indeed our Kleist), in December 1809 in Berlin (cf. *LS*, 340) and perhaps elsewhere in the interim.

It is Adolphine to whom Kleist in July 1801 writes the famous letter in which he recalls, only moderately camouflaged, his sexual initiation on the Rhine during the *Siege of Mainz* (plausibly he wrote similar passages to, say, Ulrike or Marie, who burned them). Kleist's lament in the same letter, *"Ach, die Liebe entwöhnt uns von ihren Freuden, wie die Mutter das Kind von der Milch, indem sie sich Wermut auf die Brust legt"* (II:672), may intimate that he has been having "wet dreams" of her, but feels rejected by her, and perhaps suggests that they had been intimate during the Potsdam period; Sembdner notes that the "flirtatious" Adolphine "enjoyed being courted by young people" (*LS*, p.9), and Kleist on his part was repeatedly drawn to mature women, especially if caught up in unhappy relationships (Adolphine would divorce her husband in 1813), and it possible that at some point he took her into consideration as candidate for his *filial* project.[753]

Marie von Kleist. As with Adolphine, Kleist first encountered Marie, née von Gualtieri and married into the Kleist family, during his Potsdam years. Marie came to care deeply for Kleist—whose final letter is addressed to her—, procuring him a putative royal stipend (which she herself may have funded), orchestrating a last-ditch effort in late summer of 1811 to land him a job in the military, and submitting to the King an apology for Kleist's murder-cum-suicide, which Fr. Wilh. had condemned publicly in no uncertain terms, in which she put the blame squarely on "that she-devil" Henriette Vogel (*NR*,91), about whom she writes with the spite of a woman deprived of her lover (cf. *NR*,90; 91; she was not alone in blaming Henriette: so did Pfuel, *NR*,63, Arnim, *NR*,71b, and Varnhagen, *NR*,53). Most notably, she is clearly lying outright—lying to her King!—when she claims that Kleist at the end of September was still in good spirits— "*voller Pläne, voller Eifer*" (*NR*,91)—Ha! *Todespläne*, yes. She is lying to her King because she wants to shield Kleist, whom she loves more than anyone: she wants to defray any impression on the part of her King that Kleist's suicide had anything to do with the King's policy towards Napoleon (which *of course* it did, totally, utterly). Her entire letter to the King is a contrivance. It is a labour of love, her love letter to the deceased. Not one year after Kleist's death she divorced her husband, and two decades later she still mourned Kleist, "the only friend who had known her through and through" (*NR*,95a, her claim that he "know her through and through" being every bit as ambiguous as Kleist's contention, 12 years earlier, that Ulrike "knew him fully").

With Marie Kleist shared his most memorable extant commentaries on his works. In his note, "*Sie hat ihn wirklich aufgegessen, den Achill, vor Liebe. Erschrecken Sie nicht, es läßt sich lesen; wie leicht hätten Sie es unter ähnlichen Umständen vielleicht eben so gemacht*" (*MA*II:886), the passage "*wie leicht…*," struck in the extant letter, deserves our attention: what are these "circumstances" under which he presumes Marie would have "acted likewise," i.e., ingesting him? I say: in the context of a joint death, and presupposing her faith in metempsychosis. The famous passage in his follow-up letter, "*Es ist wahr, mein innerstes Wesen liegt darin, und Sie haben es wie eine Seherin aufgefaßt: der ganze Schmutz zugleich und Glanz meiner Seele*" (II:797), acknowledges her empathy with his soul; another famous passage, "*Jetzt bin ich nur neugierig, was Sie zu dem Käthchen von Heilbronn sagen werden, denn das ist die Kehrseite der Penthesilea, ihr andrer Pol, ein Wesen, das ebenso mächtig ist durch gänzliche Hingebung, als jene durch Handeln*" (*ibid*), implores her to be both "Käthchen" and "Penthesilea" for him, to abandon herself to him in life, and to guide him into death. When she refuses to play the role of sister-in-death, his admonitions, compared to those to Ulrike, are more defiant than accusatory: *"Ja, es ist war, ich habe Dich hintergangen...; wie ich Dir aber tausendmal gesagt habe, daß ich dies nicht überleben würde, so gebe ich Dir jetzt, indem ich von Dir Abschied nehme, davon den Beweis"* (II:884-5).

Marie burned many of Kleist's letters, and cut or struck passages from some of those she kept. In 1830 she noted: *"Was ist alle Liebe der Sterblichen hier auf Erden, was sind alle Romane, alle Gedichte im Vergleich mit seiner Liebe und seinen Briefen... Aber eben daher mußte ich sie verbrennen"* (*NR*,95a). What she did not burn herself, her son, in accordance with her will, destroyed after her death (cf. *NR*,95b). Luckily thirteen of Kleist's letters to Marie survived, including the above quoted one, from which she struck that unpalatable sub-sentence, be it out of denial or regret, or as a riposte: in her own "ghostly dialogue" with Kleist's soul, Marie's strike-through expressed, in a single stroke, grief, anger, jealousy, and melancholy.

Luise von Linckersdorf. This general's daughter was yet another woman whose acquaintance Kleist made during his Potsdam years—in 1798, or earlier. Kleist left behind at least two extant traces of their liaison: firstly, a passage from Wieland's *Gesicht unschuldiger Menschen*, which he wrote into her album (cf. I:43), in which he alludes to metempsychosis, *"in der Zukunft Himmel über Himmel in unbegrenzter Aussicht entdecken,"* while seducing her to abandon herself to him and submit to his educational programme: *"Menschen... deren Glück durch das Glück ihrer Nebengeschöpfe vervielfacht wird, die in der Vollkommenheit unaufhörlich wachsen,—o wie selig sind sie!"*; secondly, the passage in a letter to Wilhelmine (cf. II:535), in which he uses Luise as example for Wilhelmine to emulate: the passage's ominous triple hyphen suggests that Luise had repeatedly granted him those favours he now sought from Wilhelmine; thirdly, plausibly if indirectly, in the passage from the same period pertaining to Potsdam's *"Musikus Baer"*'s "mouthpieces."[754]

Reportedly their liaison's abrupt end left Kleist in a crisis (cf. *LS*,21). In c.1798 Kleist perhaps had not yet figured out his concept of "*Scheidung*," or was not yet ready to put it into practice; or else, Luise had had enough of his unorthodox demands, despite her apparent concessions to his whims. Ulrike apart, Luise may have been Kleist's first female sexual "lab rat," and her memory evidently lingered on, continuing to shape his expectations as to which concessions he could extract from Wilhelmine, and perhaps other women.

The Zenge Girls. Between November 1799 and April 1800 in Frankfurt/O. Kleist orchestrated a series of private lectures by Chr. Ernst Wünsch, his favourite professor at the Viadrina, to "a closed group of 12 illiterati" (*LS*,37b; cf. II:500), mostly women, among them the Kleist and the neighbouring Zenge sisters. It was during this period that Kleist slipped his "engagement" letter into Wilhelmine's purse. Not only did the private sessions generate rare, sanctioned occasions for young people of both sexes to meet, but also did Wünsch's esoteric deliberations likely inspire his eager audience's imagination—consider Kleist's concept of "*Scheidung*": if in the *physical* world elements could be separated, manipulated and re-combined in (al)chemical processes, should not the same be possible, in the *moral* world, with human relationships? Did not Kleist's asking for Wilhelmine's "hand" (cf. *LS*,39) comprise an experiment in *moral* (social, psychological) engineering, rather than a rash youthful act (or merely a bad joke)?

Kleist certainly instrumentalised Wilhelmine for his *familial-filial* project, but as I argued before, she was at least to some extent willing to go along: no wallflower herself, and probably of Sapphic leanings—for is this not what she meant when she told him, not that she *did* not, but that she *could* not love him?—, she became his "lab rat" because she showed herself pliable and ready to adopt the roles into which he sought to cast her: as dedicated mother and housewife, loyal friend and partner, patient listener to his declamations, and selfless sex object for him and his "brothers." Wilhelmine's 1803 account to Krug (cf. *LS*,38) is instructive, for it demonstrates that she internalised some of Kleist's *satyrical* code, "[Kleist] hatte einen *erhabenen Begriff von Sittlichkeit, und mich wollte er zum Ideal umschaffen, welches mich oft bekümmerte,"* and endeavoured to meet his demands: *"Ich fürchtete ihm nicht zu genügen, und strengte alle meine Kräfte an, meine Talente auszubilden, um ihn echt vielseitig zu interessieren."* What troubled her in their relationship was evidently not Kleist's "seeking to shape her to his ideal," but her fear of falling short of his "exalted notion of morals"; her account is hardly that of an exploited or humiliated woman—if anything, a certain nostalgia resonates in it, and possibly a certain regret that she did not push her "talent" for "making herself interesting [to him] in varied ways" even further than she did: *"Ich kannte seine Wünsche und wußte mich so gut in seinem sonderbaren Wesen zu schicken, daß ich überzeugt war, es könne außer mir kein weibliches Wesen mit ihm fertig werden"* (*LS*,62a).⁷⁵⁵ Perhaps more than any woman he met before or after her, Wilhelmine was able to meet Kleist's unorthodox needs.

Michalzik's note (cf. *Kleist*, 105), that Kleist pursued Wilhelmine *despite* her telling him that she did not love him, ignores the possibilty that Kleist pursued her *because of* it: conventional love was not what he was after—indeed, it would have been in the way of his designs. Was not a lesbian woman a most promising candidate for his scheme, as her social dilemma was precisely inversely equivalent to his own? What more pragmatic solution could there be, in his day, than for a gay man to marry a lesbian woman, so as to conform to social norms, and produce children, while consenting to let each other pursue his or her homosexual passions? Kleist and Wilhelmine clearly cared for each other, and felt that they had much to offer to each other; at least for Wilhelmine, the few months they spent together in Frankfurt/O., before Kleist embarked on the Würzburg journey, seem to have been happy ones—*"So lebte er ganz für mich... ich gewann ihn recht lieb und machte mir es zur Pflicht auch ganz für ihn zu leben"* (*LS*,38)—, and her assurance to Krug, that she never loved Kleist "from all my heart, as I love Thou" (*LS*,62a), only confirms that the nature of her relationship with these two different men was radically different, the former comprising her youthful experimentation with a budding genius, the latter her "going legit" with a tenured professor.

That Kleist and Wilhelmine "knew" each other is suggested by the "*Gartenlaube*" episode Kleist repeatedly refers to in his letters (cf., e.g., II:545; 548); since love's "fatherland" for him was the *anus*, its "bower" could have referred to the *vagina*, and it appears that on that occasion he unsuccessfully demanded access to the former of her orifices (or requested that she access his, with the help of a dildo—cf. his reference to *"Musikus Baer"*'s instruments; II:549): *"Wenn Du nur an jenem Abend in der Gartenlaube nicht geweint hättest, als ich Dir einen doppelsinnigen Gedanken mitteilte, von dem Du gleich den übelsten Sinn auffaßtest"* (II:552-3). He did extract from her the promise to give in to his demand on another occasion, *"Aber Du versprachst mir Besserung, und wirst Dein Wort halten und vernünftig sein"* (II:553), which he now artfully reminds her of in his musings about the Saxon girls (or boys), emphasising that he is constantly in "ready" mode, *"Deinen Tobaksbeutel* [male genitals] *der... hangt, oder auf Deine Handschuh* [condom], *die ich selten ausziehe"* (II:546), and threatening to find another bride should she remain intransigent: *"Ich durchreiste die Gebirge, besonders die dunkeln Täler, spräche ein von Haus zu Haus... und sähe zu ob das Mädchen auch im Innern so schön sei, wie von außen"* (II:549). His letter from 1st September 1800—which Michalzik terms a "true love letter" (*Kleist*, 123)—abounds in extortionate threats and cheeky allusions. Kleist uses Brockes as "strawman" to coerce Wilhelmine, by recalling the sublime sexual pleasures he experiences with him— *"Brockes und ich, wir suchten beide und fanden... Formen* (exploring their respective bodily regions)... *den feinen Regen* (ejaculate)... *der oben herab* (sprayed on the lover)... *ich deckte mir den Mantel* (condom) *über den Kopf* (glans). *Da stand die geliebte Form* (rear part)... *ganz deutlich, mit allen Umrissen* (rounded) *und Farben* (pink?) *im engen Dunkel* (anal channel) *vor mir"*—, before shifting the perspective to Wilhelmine (Michalzik quotes the passage only from this point onwards, thus missing Kleist's pivot from Brockes to Wilhelmine): *"Ich habe mir Dich* (Wilhelmine) *in diesem Augenblick* (of orgasm) *ganz lebhaft und gewiß vollkommen wahr, vorgestellt, und bin überzeugt, daß an dieser Vorstellung nichts fehlte, nichts an Dir selbst, nichts an Deinem Anzuge* (black leather corset?), *nicht das goldene Kreuz* (anal orifice), *und seine Lage, nicht der harte Reifen, der mich so oft erzürnte* (your tight anal sphincters that so often failed to open up to me), *selbst nicht das bräunliche Mal in der weichen Mitte* (clitoris?)... *Tausendmal habe ich es geküßt"* (II:537). There are other such hectoring passages in the Würzburg and post-Würzburg letters, including Kleist's attempts to cajole Wilhelmine by recalling Luise's "many lit-up windows" and Brockes's "immaculate unselfishness," but there are also his patient efforts to explain to her his scheme, such as the comprehensive depiction of *"Scheidung"* in the "birthday letter," and his ongoing efforts to warm up to the female physique (Kleist expresses surprise and delight at the beautiful—hilly—Saxon landscapes, acknowledging that he does not like his landscapes too plump). For all the cheekiness of his designs, his journeys of 1800-2, and their accompanying letters, document a sincere wish to make their unorthodox union work. And for all the trouble it will have caused her, Wilhelmine's endeavour to comply will have been as sincere.

In 1806, in Königsberg, Kleist became a "daily visitor" in Wilhelmine's, now Frau Professorin Krug's, house (cf. *LS*,144); already in 1805, with Marie's help, they re-established contact by letter (cf. Schulz, *Kleist,* 285). Kleist was never shy to approach married women, Wilhelmine by now had given birth to a healthy son, proving her "worth" in this respect, and her husband was perhaps not wrong when he suggested that Kleist's 1808 fable *Die beiden Tauben* comprised "a song to her" (cf. *LS*,147). Wilhelmine appears to have been content with married life, and there was probably little chance of their relaunching their earlier project, yet they were still drawn to each other. Like Ulrike and Marie, Wilhelmine after Kleist's death took great pains to control the circulation of personal information relating to their relationship (cf. *NR*,164b; 165), contributing to the *auto da fé* of letters, "all written with the greatest passion" (*NR*,167), and carefully curating those letters that she did pass on to Tieck. Given that the extant letters contain intensely private passages, the destroyed one will have, emphatically.

Wilhelmine's younger sister Luise—Kleist's "goldnes *Louischen*" (II:685ff; *LS*,39; 144)—probably attracted Kleist's attention around

523

the same time as did she: Wilhelmine was surprised at Kleist's "engagement" letter not least because she assumed that it was Luise he was interested in (cf. *LS*,38). Whereas Wilhelmine was (probably) *homo* and a patient *listener* (i.e., pliable but passive), Luise was (probably) *hetero* and an accomplished *dancer* (i.e., erotically charged and pro-active), and Kleist's letter to Luise from Paris, a response to a letter from her, suggests that Luise kept her "eyes on the ball" even after his engagement to Wilhelmine, and Kleist, on his part, "kept her warm," telling Wilhelmine in December 1801: "*Sage [Luise], daß wenn mir keine Jugendfreundin zur Gattin würde, ich nie eine besitzen würde. Das wird sie bewegen—*" (II:706). When in 1805 in Königsberg he bumped into the Krugs at a grand ball (inadvertently or by design), Kleist asked not Wilhelmine, but Luise, to the dance, who had tugged along unattached. While Kleist could have instrumentalised Luise to pressurise Wilhelmine, he was a juggler and trickster, and understood "option value," and it is safest to assume that, as with his male liaisons, he was apt at keeping multiple female candidates in play. Luise probably remained a "wildcard" for him throughout: she apparently still met him as late as 1809 (cf. *LS*,334), and it was she who in 1831, in Thun, recovered his only extant portrait (cf. *LS*,553b)—and presumably not only because of *her sister's* liaison with him.

There could have been yet another angle to the Zenge saga: during 1800 and 1801 Kleist, in his letters, mentioned their brother Carl at least a dozen times, and we cannot exclude the possibility that the von Zenge he was most attracted to was actually—*Carl*. In Berlin the two men shared a room, and had not Wilhelmine's letter of 10th April 1802, in which she informs him of Carl's sudden death, remained unopened (cf. Sembdner's note; II:723), one would almost want to believe that it was *Carl's death* that made Kleist finally break with Wilhelmine.[756]

Brockes' Girls. At the time Kleist met him in Rügen in the summer of 1800, Brockes, like Kleist in search of a suitable life-plan, was courting Cäcilie von Werthern; Varnhagen later opined (cf. *LS*,44) that their relationship comprised "a rich novel" (which ended tragically: days before their scheduled wedding in 1815 Brockes suddenly passed away, as if his mind and body recoiled from the event).[757] In early June 1801 in Göttingen, en route to Paris, Kleist met Julie Westfeld (cf. Sembdner's note; *LS*,65), who apparently had set her eyes on Brockes (cf. Rahmer, *Kleist*, 77) and now took an interest in Kleist: in 1802, she begged Brockes to send her news on Wyttenbach and Kleist (cf. *ibid*). Her interest in not one, but two gay men suggests a leaning that could have intrigued Kleist, who may conceivably have toyed with the idea of locating his *familial-satyrico-filial* experiment, casting Brockes, Cäcilie, Julie and himself, in that liberal university town, where he had once aspired to study (cf. II:483); a few month after Brockes' departure, Kleist may still have hoped that if he could conjure an attractive *familial* constellation for both of them, he could lure him back.

Kleist's Paris journey was voyage of discovery and a scouting expedition; though he had Ulrike in tow, it lent itself to broadening his horizon, conceptually and practically, with respect to his *familial* project, including to lining up options along the way: "*Liebe Wilhelmine, laß mich reisen*" (II:635) entailed the (admittedly cynical) twin demands on Wilhelmine, to let him *explore options* while *staying put*. When Lose agreed to join him to Switzerland, Kleist ditched Brockes from his roster, as his final letter to him from Paris in November 1801 makes clear (cf. II:698), and with him perhaps any constellation involving his girls.[758]

The Schlieben Girls. Kleist first met the charming and impoverished sisters, who carved out a living selling handicraft such as copper engravings, alongside Fr. Lose in early May 1801 in Dresden, i.e., already before meeting Julie Westfield in Göttingen.[759] "*Das* echte deutsche Mädchen" (II:662) Henriette, like Kleist born in 1777, according to a caption by her seven years younger sister Caroline was "Kleist's bride" (*LS*,109a), and Kleist's entry into her album of 17th May 1801,"*Tue recht und scheue niemand*," is ominous in the context of "*Grazie*" and "*Ziererei*."[760] Yet Caroline herself, then aged 17 and engaged to Lose, could have attracted Kleist's attention (and vice versa): of the extant letter he addressed to each of the sisters, the far longer one is to Caroline, in which in July 1801 from Paris he recalls how they repeatedly stood together before Raffael's *Sistine Madonna* (cf. II:659) and reiterates his concept of the "Sun" (in relation to the "comet"; cf. II:660), both of which passages suggest that he considered her "motherhood material" (Lose he does not mention in this context; a later note from Caroline suggests jealousy may have been at play—cf. *LS*,109b).⁷⁶¹ To Henriette, in July 1804 from Berlin, Kleist rather unapologetically apologises for "promises," made in Dresden, "left unfulfilled" (II:744), and while leaving the door open for "repeating their beautiful days of their past" (II:745), his letter's main purpose is to retrieve a suitcase he left with her in 1803, and which, as Michalzik notes (*Kleist*, 242), may have contained important work-in-progress. The tone and content of the two letters suggests that Kleist considered Caroline the more fertile, Henriette the more competent companion—taken together, they were a strong "package."

    Kleist reunited with Lose in Frankfurt/M., whence they jointly progressed to Paris, and on to Switzerland, where Lose hoped to establish himself as painter alongside Kleist's poet, in a proto-*Künstlerkolonie*. Kleist may have hoped to orchestrate a *ménage-à-cinque* involving Lose and Caroline, himself and Wilhelmine, plus Henriette who, apart from managing the household and selling handicraft, could serve as fall-back option should Wilhelmine fail to join: in the latter case, a *double wedding* involving two artists and two sisters could have been a practical solution, not least since in their Swiss exile the sisters would have had each other for company.⁷⁶² Perhaps involving also additional "brothers" who might join on an *ad hoc* basis, Kleist evidently dreamed of staging symposiastic orgies, in which song, wine and limbs would entangle in an animated *Gesamtkunstwerk*:

 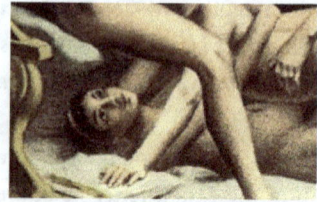

"*Und legt die Leier weinend aus den Händen*" (I): In the Kleistian *Künstlerkolonie*.

Their quarrel, and Lose's abrupt departure at Liestal, may have had something to do with Kleist's unorthodox designs; they reconciled later in 1801, after Kleist, in a highly symbolic, potlachian gift exchange, sent Lose a (phallic) key in an (anal) case, requesting him to keep the "key" and return the "case" (II:708-9).[763]

Once he arrived in Bern and united with Zschokke, L. Wieland and Heinr. Geßner, Kleist's priorities will have shifted, but when following his brief sojourn in Wieland's household at Oßmannstedt, late 1802 till early 1803, he once again spent time in Dresden, during April to July 1803, the Schlieben sisters were temporarily back on his radar screen, and he may have considered establishing his *Künstlerkolonie* in Dresden instead of Thun; Lose was in Milan, and Kleist appears to have actively tried to entice Caroline to ditch him (*"seine öfteren Entmutigungen gegen Dich," LS,*109b)—evidently to no avail—, before setting off for Switzerland with Pfuel, claiming that his sole purpose was to visit Lose in Milan (cf. *LS,*110). Although they did meet Lose in Varese (cf. II:744), the Werdecks were also there, and any "brotherly" reunion will have been hampered by the presence, if not of Adolphine, certainly of her "straight" husband: *"hatte ich, bei der Gesellschaft, die uns immer umgab, nur selten Gelegenheit, mich ihm vertraulich zu nähern."* Kleist may have had designs on Adolphine, but this would not have been welcomed by Lose, nor perhaps by Pfuel. The second Swiss sojourn was thoroughly complicated by overlapping option spaces; it ended in Paris, in the autumn of 1803, as unsuccessfully from the *familial* or *filial* point of view, as from the *po(i)etical*.

The Wieland Girls. Wedged between Kleist's explorations involving Wilhelmine and his Bernese boys' club on the one hand, the Schlieben sisters and Lose (with Pfuel and Adolphine thrown in) on the other, Kleist spent two months or so, in late 1802 and early 1803, at Chr. M. Wieland's Oßmannstedt estate, from which in February he departed with haste. Wieland's 13-year old daughter Luise is generally held to have been the reason for his flight, although it could have been more complicated than that. Having been able to line up her father as his *po(i)etical* sponsor, in addition to, already in Bern, her brother

Ludwig as his friend and possibly lover, Kleist's relationship with the Wieland household, which at that time also contained three of the widowed Wieland's daughters, became thoroughly complicated. Kleist may well have sought to compel Luise—who considered Kleist her "first love" (cf. *LS*,512)—to grant him the type of favours he had previously elicited from Luise von Linckersdorf, and perhaps from Wilhelmine. Kleist's designs on the teenager triggered Ludwig, who will have known Kleist's sexual preferences, as well as Luise's older sister Amalie, who vehemently disapproved of their liaison (cf. *LS*,94a). To complicate things further, another older sister of Luise's residing there, the widowed Caroline, apparently set her eyes on Kleist (cf. *ibid*).

Perhaps the old Wieland was only partially aware of the hubbub in his henhouse, and perhaps Kleist's sister Friederike's assertion that he approved of Kleist's and Luise's liaison is correct (cf. *LS*,92a).[764] But from Kleist's point of view the situation became explosive, and he evacuated Oßmannstedt head over heels, though not without leaving a lasting impression on Luise: when in April 1804 he visited Oßmannstedt again, she still found him "magical" (*LS*,127); in April 1811, in a letter to yet another sister, Charlotte, who was married to Heinr. Geßner and will have known Kleist well from his days in Bern, Luise ambiguously refers to "trivialities" (*LS*,94a) passing between her and Kleist—which presumably were anything but trivial, for she admits that Kleist "did not belong to the most noble of people"; finally, in September 1811, in another letter to Charlotte, she laments the "great difficulties" that "interfered with their liaison" (*LS*,94b). Only in 1814 did Luise eventually marry.

Karoline von Günderrode. During his "lost year" in Mainz and Berlin (1804), and his subsequent 18 months of civil service in Königsberg (1805-6), Kleist appears to have primarily invested in re-establishing or deepening pre-existing relationships: Marie, Ulrike, Wilhelmine (and/or Luise?), Pfuel, Rühle, Lippe (and possibly Brockes; cf. *LS*,132), Schlotheim, Gleißenberg, Altenstein. Yet we cannot exclude the possibility that he also pursued new liaisons: e.g., he may already then have befriended Finance Inspector Fr. Aug. von Staegemann's wife Elisabeth (cf. Michalzik, *Kleist*, 261), and may have *personally* made the experience that Mme von Auerswald, his boss's wife, was indeed as *"vortrefflich"* (II:767) as he praised her to be, and may have met women in War Inspector Joh. Georg Scheffner's beautiful suburban gardens *of whom we know nothing*. Most notably, I shall take seriously the information imparted by Bülow (nor corroborated by any other evidence, hence largely ignored by Kleist biographers), that Kleist during his Mainz sojourn became acquainted with Karoline von Günderrode, and had an affair with an unnamed preacher's daughter near Wiesbaden (cf, *LS*,124).[765]

Although apart from Bülow's note we know *nothing* of Karoline purported acquaintance with Kleist, we know *something* about her character and circumstances, and these, on the face of it, were highly *condusive* to such a liaison (which proves nothing, but is suggestive). Karoline, poetress—later to be known as *"die Sappho der Romantik"*—, apparently bisexual—reportedly she was wildly in love with both Bettine Brentano and Fr. Creutzer—, independent- and open-minded—no doubt she found it as difficult as Kleist to reconcile her personal aspirations with conventional social expectations—, and perennially *todessehnsüchtig*—in 1806 she committed suicide when Creutzer terminated their liaison—, was precisely the type of woman who would have suited Kleist (and perhaps *vice versa*). 1804 was a turbulent year for Karoline: she enjoyed her first poetic breakthrough—her first book, published in Frankfurt/M. under the psydonym "Tian," made waves with the likes of Goethe and Clemens Brentano—; her first significant (male) lover, Fr. Carl von Savigny, married Kunigunde Brentano (17th April); and she met Creutzer, on 4th April appointed professor in Heidelberg, and his wife, during an excursion to the Neuburg convent.[766] As Kleist probably left Mainz in May (he was registered arriving in Berlin on 3rd June— cf. *MA*III:830; Loch, *Kleist*, 197), all three of these events may fall *after* their putative meeting, but certainly the first two could already have coloured it, and the third, if it took place right after Creutzer's appointment, or even before it (if, say, he came to Heidelberg early, to settle in and perhaps explore its sights), could even have triggered Kleist's departure.[767] If they first met in early spring, it could have been at a time when Karoline was without male companion, while her relationship with Bettine remained active (Bettine then lived in Offenbach, near Franfurt/M.), and Kleist could have seen an opportunity to engineer a constellation involving the two women similar to the one he had earlier conceived involving the Schlieben sisters; if shortly thereafter she met, and fell for, the married Creuzer, Kleist may have given up his plans and left.

Finally, the circumstances of Karoline's enactment of her suicide, elements of which anticipate Keist's projects for the Spreewald and the Kl. Wannsee, are remarkable: she stabbed herself in the heart—presumably as symbolic response to Creuzer's rejection—, and she did so *on the bank of the Rhine*, in the town of Winkel (Rheingau). The location, as in Kleist's projects, is symbolic: in Winkel, very near the Rhine's embankment on which she killed herself, stands the prominent Brentanohaus, in which Clemens and Bettine, as well as many of their friends, including Karoline, will have spent time; after Clemens, in the spring of 1801, introduced Savigny to his family (i.e., to Kunigunde, his later wife, and probably to Karoline as well), they together undertook a journey along the Rhine, most likely taking in Winkel and other picturesque Rheingau towns up- and down-river. Karoline could have chosen the location of her death for yet another reason: she wanted to ensure that she was buried exactly where she *was* buried, at Winkel's (Catholic) St. Walburga church, with which she may have had a connection.[768]

Which, I dare conjecture, is where Kleist's other liaison Bülow reports could have come in: Karoline, from 1797 till c.1800, lived as *Stiftsfräulein* (canoness) in a protestant chapter of nuns in Frankfurt/M., catering for destitute aristocratic daughters, and could have been acquainted since those days with a (possibly Catholic) "preacher's daughter near Wiesbaden"; Karoline apparently thought little of "any religion whatsoever" and sought out like-minded women irrespective of religious faith.[769] What if such a friend of hers existed, and was the daughter of St. Walburga's parish priest or pastor? Winkel is located only 20km from Wiesbaden. What if she introduced Kleist to her friend, possibly because she had just fallen for Creuzer? If Kleist and Karoline undertook walks together, perhaps joined by the "preacher's daughter," it could well have been on the Rhine's embankment at Winkel or, if privacy was needed, in the Rhine meadows before the town, or in a boat in the no-man's land between Winkler Aue and Fulder Aue—which would have encompassed a precise re-enactment of Kleist's initiation on the Rhine before Biebrich, a mere 10km upriver from Winkel.

The Körner Girls. In Dresden, from the autumn of 1807 till the spring of 1808, Kleist spent much time in the house of Chr. Gottfried Körner, a well-known writer (and one-time contributor to *Ph*) and jurist who had mentored Schiller and hosted Goethe, Novalis and the painter Anton Graff, and who regularly invited artists and intellectuals to his house, including Kleist, Pfuel and Rühle. Körner's 19-year old daughter Emma, "slim," "doe-eyed, demure and graceful," received Kleist "with open arms" (Michalzik, *Kleist*, 304-5): *"Kleist sehen wir ziemlich oft, und seine Gesellschaft gewährt uns recht viel Vergnügen"* (*LS*,262).[770] So, apparently, did Körner's similarly youthful charge Juliane (Julie) Kunze, "cute and girlish" (Michalzik, *Kleist*, 329), whose evident interest in him Kleist may have reciprocated (cf. *LS*,263c; 270b). Even Körner's sister-in-law, Dora Stock, may have eyed Kleist; according to one source (cf. *LS*,269), Kleist modeled the "mosaic" Kunigunde on her (and Käthchen, on Julie). Körner's house (like Zenge's and Wieland's) was a veritable henhouse, and no doubt this was one, if not *the*, reason for the fox Kleist to frequent it, and to seek to remain "in good standing with the family" (cf. *LS*,263c): the larger the flock, the likelier he would find a suitable hen; here, (more or less) eligible women paraded themselves before him, as if in a casting show *avant la lettre*.[771] Kleist and Julie reportedly came close to becoming engaged (cf. *LS*,270b), but in July 1808 she married Alex. von Einsiedel (cf. *LS*,270c), suggesting that she was in a rush, and made a move when something did not work out with Kleist.[772] There are parallels between Kleist's relationships, respectively, with the Körner girls and the Wieland sisters: as with Wieland Sr., Kleist needed Körner as his sponsor, and may have considered it imprudent to aggressively pursue his girls, especially when *Ph* entered rough waters and his finances looked shaky. Körner remained interested in Kleist's fortunes, but the frequency of his visits soon abated.[773]

Sophie von Haza. Michalzik notes (*Kleist*, 330) that Kleist, during the Körner period, got into a rivalry with A. Müller over the latter's future wife Sophie von Haza, two years Kleist's senior and about to divorce her husband, Müller's former boss. Ulrike later maintained that Kleist had sought to prevent the Hazas' divorce (cf. *LS*,308a), while Tieck and others report that he tried to murder Müller by pushing him into the Elbe (cf. *LS*,271; 285a; 309).[774] Whether Kleist's rage was owed to genuine interest in Sophie, or to anger at Müller's neglecting him, is unclear, as is the true reason for his "eight days of raging and mindless jealousy" Pfuel observed on another occasion during this period (cf. *LS*,270a).[775] According to one of Bülow's sources, Kleist during this time attempted to take his life with an overdose of opium (cf. *LS*,269); I consider this unlikely, for such a prosaic death is utterly "unKleistian" (more plausibly, Kleist was using opium as pain killer or stimulant, and inadvertently took an overdose). His apparent pursuit of Sophie von Haza during this period was, if a pun is permitted, *hazardous* for Kleist. Curiously, it was to Sophie that he addressed his third from last letter—even if it was primarily meant for A. Müller, co-authored by Henriette, and posted, unlike the final two, on the 20th from Berlin, as opposed to on the 21st from Stimming's, this meant *something*. But what? A dying Kleist pointing his finger at the woman who had estranged one of his last remaining lover from him, and effectively dismantled his "brotherhood"? Or at a woman who should have chosen to go with him, not the other? Go where? Into reproduction mode, or into death?[776]

Rahel Levin. Certain *BA* entries suggest that Kleist's remained attached to his *filial* project during the Berlin period, possibly almost till his end: *Marionettentheater*'s rehash of his rehearsals with *"Mme C..."* in Paris; *Brief eines Mahlers an seinen Sohn*'s homage to the young man who, oscillating between male-male jouissance ("Heaven") and male-female reproduction ("Earth"), in a "lighthearted summer night" (II:329) effortlessly impregnates a woman. Kleist took stock and perhaps came to realise that his 10-year long quest for a bride, and an alternative family model, had been over-engineered, that at several occasions he could simply have "given it a shot, and that perhaps it was not too late for him to produce a son. Having settled into Berlin, in February 1810, and become a regular guest in leading salons that were again flourishing following the Royals' return from exile, he gave his quest for a bride one more push, until it increasingly turned into a quest for a sister-in-death in the course of 1811.

The well-known Jewish writer and salonnière Rahel Levin, Kleist's senior by six years, later to marry his acquaintance from the 1804 Berlin period, Karl Aug. Varnhagen, insisted that she "loved" Kleist and found him "very charming" (*LS*,357; 358a), that they had "amused themselves with each other" (*LS*,359), and that he was her "only friend" (cf. Schulz, *Kleist*, 75). Rahel could have suited Kleist as bride, as sister-in-death, and as sympathetic and thoughtful friend.[777] To Alex. von der Marwitz she wrote one day after Kleist's death:

> von Kleist befremdete mich die Tat nicht, es ging streng in ihm her, er war wahrhaftig und litt viel... Und niemals hör ich dergleichen, ohne mich der Tat zu freuen. Ich mag es nicht, daß die Unglückseligen, die Menschen, bis auf den Hefen leiden... Ich freue mich, daß mein edler Freund... das Unwürdige nicht duldete; gelitten hat er genug. Sehen sie mich! Keiner von denen, die ihn etwa tadeln, hätten ihm zehn Rtl. gereicht, Nächte gewidmet, Nachsicht mit ihm gehabt. (*LS*,51)

The "undeserving," "ignoble" conditions that in her opinion drove Kleist into death entailed, firstly, few people, bar herself, having been willing to support him, with money or otherwise—herself, she stresses, also devoted her "nights" to him!—; secondly, Kleist's unspecified debilitating physical and mental suffering.

Mother and daughter Staegemann. The influential Finance Inspector, and occasional poet, Fr. Aug. von Staegemann, whose boss was Kleist's earstwhile mentor Altenstein, became Kleist's friend and supporter in 1805 in Königsberg, and again in 1810/11 in Berlin; in both cities his wife, the divorcée Elisabeth—*"eine der edelsten Frauengestalten der Zeit"*—, ran a leading salon, in Berlin picking up the baton from her friend Rahel Levin, whose salon had ceased in 1806.[778] The glamorous salonnière's circle of friends read like a who's who of Prussia's royalty, intelligentsia, generality and administration—Kant had belonged to her circle in Königsberg; in Berlin it included the likes of Hardenberg, Stein, Gneisenau.[779] Their daughter Hedwig acknowledgd her parents as outstanding figures: *"Es ist eigentümlich, dass ein armer, im Waisenhause erzogener Knabe, dessen missgestaltete Füße ihn fast vollständig am Gehen hinderten, nicht nur eine der höchsten Stellen im Staat erreichte, sondern sich auch die Liebe einer der schönsten, umworbensten und reich begabtesten Frauen errang."*[780] Elisabeth was present at Cäcilie Müller's baptism, which is unsurprising: her and A. Müller's circles significantly overlapped.[781]

On the day before his suicide Kleist went to Elisabeth's house, who, because of an indisposition, did not receive him, for which she would subsequently blame herself bitterly: *"wenn ich ihn angenommen hätte damals—wenn—"* (cf. *LS*,521a;b); the last women he wrote to were Ulrike and Marie, but *the last woman he went to see in person*, Ulrike and Marie not being in Berlin, *was Elisabeth*, whom, 16 years his senior, he may have sought out, in the absent Marie's stead, as the mother-figure he longed to see as he stared death in its face. She was past the age in which Kleist could hav had *filial* designs on her, not to be his as sister-in-death; but it was most likely as experience, caring mother figure that he sought out Elisabeth.

Then there was her daughter. In 1811 Hedwig turned twelve, read *Käthchen* (cf. *LS*,388), and attended Kleist's declamations of *Penthesilea* and *Homburg* (cf. *LS*,504). *Käthchen* was bound to be Kleist's work of most interest to a girl in puberty, and given that her mother's salon was held in their family home, Hedwig was bound to listen to performances given by attendees, including, evidently, Kleist. Hedwig's comments on *Käthchen*, and on Kleist, betray unusual precociousness (Sembdner may have a point when he suggests that these comments reflected the mother's, rather than the daughter's, judgment), and while Kleist may have considered her similarly untouchable as earstwhile the 13-year old Luise Wieland, from her point of view Kleist could have been a welcome target for honing her skills of coquetry.

Müller's Girls. Having in Dresden been his rival for Sophie, in Berlin A. Müller established himself as Kleist's match-maker, "passing on" to him flirtatious ladies he could, or would, not longer entertain himself: Henriette Hendel-Schütz, Sophie Sander (an eleven years older cousin of his), and Henriette Vogel (cf. *NR*,14; 73a; 184; II:882; *AML*,35; 198). The urbane and dapper Müller will have attracted women more easily than the brooding and awkward Kleist— although it is the latter of whom it was said that, once they got to know him, *"Männer und Frauen hingen mit Leidenschaft an ihm"* (*LS*,43)—, and by passing on to him his lesser female conquests—as distraction from his "prize trophy" Sophie or as consolation prize— he perhaps also sought to salvage their "brotherly" relationship.

The celebrated actress Henriette Hendel-Schütz— "incomparable female Proteus" (Goethe); "personified eternity" (Schiller)—, who, as of 1811, was onto her fourth husband, gave a pantomime performance of *Penthesilea* on 24th or 25th April 1811, which Kleist politely, if unenthusiastically, commended.[782] Körner notes (cf. *NR*,14) that shortly before Kleist's death, rumour had it that he had shown interest in her; a hilarious anecdote related by Peguilhen (cf. *LS*,490a) suggests otherwise: when Henriette H.-S. found herself seated next to Kleist at Hitzig's dinner table, she inundated him with drivel before inviting him to her house to "initiate him" into her "harmonic society"; Kleist took flight, hid at Peguilhen's house, and refused to see her when she came to look for him.[783] Kleist may have been keen to maintain the principled façade he had established for himself in Berlin's polite society (cf. *LS*,490b), or simply had no interest in her: already twice before he had taken great pains to avoid her (cf. II:860; 862). Peguilhen portrayed the actress as a talkative, obtrusive, and uninhibited *"Sensitiva"* (the precise opposite of, say, a Wilhelmine), and Henriette H.-S. may have represented precisely the type of woman Kleist recoiled from: self-centred and monopolising, the accolades from the likes of Goethe and Schiller evidently having gone to her head.[784]

The beautiful and quick-witted Sophie Sander, hostess of another Berlin salon, was A. Müller's cousin (cf. Michalzik, *Kleist*, 387), whom, according to Varnhagen, Müller courted before "passing her on" to Kleist (cf. *NR*,184). Kleist certainly frequented her salon—as did Fichte, Wilh. von Humboldt, Fouqué, Brentano, Arnim, Müller, et al—, and in one of his last letters apologises to her for not being able to join her table on that day (cf. II:882), and with the letter sends her the "s o n g b o o k" whose potential relevance I discussed previously. The letter suggests intimacy, but not necessarily of an erotic kind; Kleist at this point—in October 1811, within weeks of his suicide—had probably all but scrapped his *filial* project and was focused entirely on recruiting a suitable sister-in-death.

Kleist certainly met Henriette Vogel in October 1810 at Cäcilie Müller's baptism, and possibly as early as 1804/5 in Berlin.[785] Kleist does not seem to have considered here a suitable bride: among the epithets with which he adorns her in his *"Todeslinanei"* is *"die Taufe meiner Kinder"* (I:46), but not *"die Geburt meiner Kinder."*[786] The Berlin public initially assumed that the double suicide was the result of a love affair, but people close to Kleist knew better—e.g., Körner: *"Von Kleists Tode schreibt die Chodowiecka an die Piattoli, Kleist habe nicht die Vogel, sondern eine andere Frau (auch nicht die Hendel) geliebt"* (*NR*,14)—and sought to dispel the notion: Müller, on Christmas Eve in Vienna, publicly denied that their relationship had been passionate (cf. *NR*,23), and already earlier, before that denial, when rumours spread that Henriette had suffered from cervical cancer, the public began looking for other explanations for their act—such as, for example, "mysticism."[787] The magazine *Morgenblatt* came closest to the truth: *"auf gewaltsame Weise von dieser Erde getrennt,... aus Liebe zu einem geistigen Verein in jener besseren Welt"* (*NR*,6).

Kleist's Satyrico-Filial Familial Scheme. For eleven years, mid 1800-mid 1811, in parallel with his poetic career, Kleist sustained his *filial* project, his quest for a suitable bride and mother to his son and heir. In this quest, his pragmatics in the main encompassed the following two-pronged strategy:

- "fox in the henhouse": frequent households that include multiple addressable targets—cf. the Zenge, Wieland, Schlieben, Körner households—; single out a suitable "hen," hedge your bets with her sisters, and explore the potential of a "mixed double";
- "soft targets": pursue women who stand to benefit most from a liaison with an unconventional aristocrat, are most swayable, or previously demonstrated openness to unorthodox liaisons: (1) lesbians, or social outsiders looking to "go legit" (Ulrike, Wilhelmine, Karoline, the Jewess Rahel); (2) unhappily married, or widowed, matrons (Adolphine, Marie, Sophie, perhaps the Marchese Piatolli and the Chodowiecka); (3) young, swayable girls (Luise Wieland, Hedwig Staegemann); (4) women already connected to members of his "brotherhood" (Brockes' girls, the Schlieben girls, Müller's girls).[788]

The "ideal" Kleistian "mixed double," or *ménage-à-quattre*, household, which he perhaps first ideated in conversation with Brockes in Rügen, comprised two gay men (Kleist as *erastês*, another as *erômenos*), each married to a lesbian woman, both of whom in turn sexually liaised with each other, whereby all four would engage in orgiastic sex (with additional male lovers brought in *ad hoc*), but access to the women's vaginas was reserved for their respective husband, so that offspring could unequivocally be assigned a father, but otherwise co-parented:

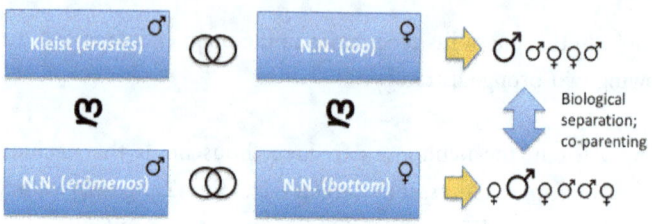

The "ideal" Kleistian household.

Unsurprisingly, Kleist's "ideal" *familial* constellation, and with it his *filial* project, failed to materialise: it required no less than *four* individuals to commit to a lifestyle that, if discovered, would have been socially ostracised. Even less "ideal" versions (say, a three-some, or a conventional parental household with male lovers coming and going) would have been difficult to realise in practice. Kleist pursued many partners for this scheme—boys and girls—, explored many angles and versions, on countless diplomatic missions, *unterwegs in Sachen Familie*, seducing, cajoling, begging, threatening, sanctioning, bribing his way through Dresden and Berlin salons, bourgeois households, "brotherhoods," "sororities," and widowhoods, but in the end was left empty-handed: even for the most progressive and independent-minded of his targets, his scheme was perhaps simply too far ahead of its time.

It is in this context that Kleist's July 1811 note to Marie, "Derjenige, mit dem ich jetzt am liebsten... in ein näheres Verhältnis treten mögte ist der gute, sonst nur zu sehr von mir vernachlässigte Achim Arnim" (II:872), is noteworthy: not so much because it comes across as a desperate, last-ditch attempt to re-connect with one of the few members of his "brotherhood" still remaining in Berlin, but because of the circumstance that Arnim and Bettine Brentano, Karoline von Günderrode's eastwhile (sapphic?) liaison, had married in March and now spent their honeymoon, withdrawn from Berlin society, as Kleist puts it, "buried alive in a pavilion in [Berlin's] Vossian Garden" (*ibid,* cf. II:1011). Kleist, in his extant letters, does not mention Bettine once until she is liaised with Arnim in Berlin in 1810 (cf. II:840), but if our conjecture concerning his acquaintance with Karoline von Günderrode is correct, he may have met her much earlier than that, and been aware of her earlier, lesbian exploits.⁷⁸⁹ Which invites a second conjecture: that in the summer of 1811 Kleist rememberd the hitherto "much neglected" Arnim not *despite*, but *because of* his marriage to Bettine; that by roping in the Arnims, and perhaps one of "Müller's girls," Kleist only a few months before his suicide, one last time braced himself to *engineer his "ideal" household and produce a son*.⁷⁹⁰

Nietzsche: *"Der Exzeß des Denkens wirkungslos. Kleist."* (NR,357)

The Sun.⁷⁹¹

The Orphic

Günter Blamberger suggests (*KH*,370; *Kleist*, 461-3) that the pertinent question is not, why Kleist *had* to die—i.e., a "banal" enumeration of reasons for his suicide—, but, why he *was able* to die, in Blamberger's words, "calmly, soberly, cheerfully and lacking religious consolation."⁷⁹² Blamberger begs his own refutation: Kleist's *savoir mourir*, I say, at least in part derived precisely from the fact that he *did not* lack "religious consolation." "*Auf irgendeine Weise muß ihn religiöse Problematik beschåftigt haben*," notes Hans Joachim Kreutzer, and I already noted that the development of Kleist's "religion" ("in pianissimo": Max Weber), notably his faith in metempsychosis, can be traced to his youth, and came increasingly to the fore in late writings.⁷⁹³ *Marionettentheater*'s metaphors of the *Hohlspiegel* that facilitates our *Durchgang durch das Unendliche*, of the *Reise um die Welt* that lets us to see if the gates of paradise are still open "from behind," and of the renewed eating the fruit of the *Baum der Erkenntnis* that promises to revert us to the state of pre-lapsarian innocence, all invoke a passage through death into a beyond, and thus prepare the faithful for death *as passage*: by passing through the "eternity" of death, the soul enters a new embodied life (*Hohlspiegel*); entry into paradise lies on "the other side of life," i.e., beyond death (*Reise um die Welt*); and since by eating from the "tree of knowledge" we became mortals, eating from it again will restore our immortality.[794] Karl Muth, on the occasion of the centenary of Kleist's death, succinctly summed up his "religion": *"So nährte [Kleist] sich denn einen kosmisch-mystischen Glauben an ein besseres Jenseits auf anderen Welten, einen Sternenglauben"* (*NR*,408).

At the Viadrina, in 1799-1800, and in Paris, in 1801, Kleist studied philosophy and classical languages—presumably Latin and Greek (cf. *LS*,30; 59)—, and will have been exposed to Pythagorean, Platonic, Stoic, Epicurean, Neo-Platonic, and perhaps Gnostic cosmogonies and doctrines of metempsychosis, most notably via Chr. Ernst Wünsch's lectures; Ulrike (and Wilhelmine), who attended Wünsch's private lectures in the winter of 1799/1800 Kleist had organised, could also have been influenced by him.[795] In October 1803, when he hit a wall with *Guiskard*, Kleist told Ulrike, *"jetzt ruft mir unsere heilige Schutzgöttin zu, daß es genug sei"* (II:735). According to Anthony Stephens referring to Melpomene, the muse of tragedy, but there are other possibilities, e.g.:[796]

- Urania, the muse of astronomy, dedicated to the Pythagorean celestial spheres and the fixed stars, and associated with universal love;[797]
- Calliope, the muse of eloquence and epic poetry, mother of Orpheus and Linus (the master of eloquent speech), embodiment of ecstatic harmony;
- Persephone (Kore), the queen of the underworld, condemned to a "grievous cycle" of iterating between the underworld and surface world;
- Aphrodite Urania, the aspect of Venus representing celestial or spiritual love (as opposed to Aphrodite Pandemos, representing sensual love);[798]
- Artemis (Diana), the *"vortreffliche"* goddess of the hunt and of virginity, and protectress of girls and childbirth.

While we cannot conclusively decide which guardian goddess Kleist took recourse to during those 500 days and nights hed struggle with *Guiskard*, his term *"unsere"* may imply that Ulrike understood, and possibly shared, aspects of his "religion."

So, apparently, did Rühle, whom Kleist in August 1806 exhorts: *"Komm, laß uns etwas Gutes tun, und dabei sterben! Einen der Millionen Tode, die wir schon gestorben sind, und noch sterben werden. Es ist, als ob wir aus einem Zimmer in das andere gehen"* (II:768). In *Krug*, which Kleist completed just as he wrote this letter to Rühle, Eve espouses her Phythagorean faith in a future life to Ruprecht, who adheres to a Stoic focus on the present life:

> EVE. [...] Ev ist brav,
> Es wird sich alles ihr zum Ruhme lösen,
> Und ists im Leben nicht, so ist es jenseits,
> Und wenn wir auferstehn ist auch ein Tag.
> RUPRECHT. Mein Seel, das dauert mir zu lange, Evchen.
> Was ich mit Händen greife, glaub ich gern. (V.1171-6)

Possibly this dialogue mirrors a conversation Kleist (=Eve) maintained with Rühle (=Ruprecht), regarding how to reconcile Pythagorean faith and Stoic life.

Others with whom Kleist may have debated "religion" include the physician, natural philosopher and mystic Gotthilf Heinr. Schubert, A. Müller (both Schubert and Müller were also *Ph* collaborators), perhaps the philosopher, mathematician and freemason Karl Chr. Fr. Krause, all of whom Kleist first met in Dresden in 1807, and possibly Fr. Schlegel, whom he likely first met in 1801. Kleist may have considered *Ph* a suitable vehicle for "religious" discourse: among its contributors, Schubert, Müller, Novalis, Karl F. Gottlob Wetzel and Otto von Loeben were invested in religious and mystical questions; Schubert, in his Dresden lectures of 1807 and 1808, explained phenomena such as dreams, animal magnetism, somnambulism, hypnosis and hallucination as symptoms of the continued existence of the soul in the beyond, from which he derived the possibility of a return to a lost paradise; Kleist will have attended his lectures alongside members of his Dresden "brotherhood": Rühle, Pfuel, Müller, et al.⁷⁹⁹

Phythagoras. Pythagoras of Samos (c.570-495 BC) taught the concepts of the soul and of metempsychosis, of cosmic harmony, eternal recurrence and the great chain of being; he and his sect practiced a proto-mesmerism and communication with occult powers of fate (*daimones*), and exerted great influence on Plato, and through him western philosophy as a whole.⁸⁰⁰ According to Pythagoras, the soul has three aspects or "vehicles": the *ethereal*, which wanders among the stars in a state of bliss; the *luminous*, which assumes all punishment for sins after death; and the *terrestrial*, which inhabits the body on this earth.⁸⁰¹ Pythagoras' tripartite concept could explain not only why Kleist readily discarded his earthly body so as to free his celestial soul, but also why he was enamoured of the imagery of the comet, which after its long journey hurls into the Sun and flares up: by such a *luminous* annihilation or fusion his earthly sins would be expurgated (*"der ganze Schmutz…"*), leaving behind only his pure *ethereal* soul (*"…und Glanz"*).⁸⁰² He so adamantly sought a brother- or sister-in-death because s/he would enact that "Sun" into whose final embrace he would melt: *"Mein Jettchen… o Sonne meines Lebens,… meine Vergangenheit und Zukunft"* (I:46). As their bodies flared up in "black-looking" death (cf. II:520), together with their mortal remains they would relinquish their disease, freeing up their purified souls to seek new, immaculate bodies. In Helmut Sembdner's perceptive remark (*In Sachen Kleist*, 268), *"Es ist, als ob er mit dem Todeserlebnis eine Tür öffnen wollte, um zu einem Neuen, Unzerstörbaren zu gelangen, und in der Wahl seiner Mittel fehlte,"* only the last part calls for clarification: metempsychosis, for Kleist, was this "means," and death entailed not "lack of choice," but precisely choice of this "means."⁸⁰³

Not only Pythagoreanism's teachings would have intrigued Kleist, but also its instituions: Pythagoras founded a sect, the "Pythagorean Brotherhood," that could have been an inspiration for Kleist's "brotherhood":

The school apparently founded by Pythagoras at Croton in southern Italy seems to have been primarily a religious brotherhood centred around Pythagoras and the cults of Apollo and of the Muses, ancient patron goddesses of poetry and culture... The rigorism of the ritual and ethical observances demanded of the members is unparalleled in early Greece; in addition to the rules of life mentioned above [loyalty, modesty, self-discipline, piety, abstinence], ...secrecy and a long silence during the novitiate were required. The exoteric associates, however, were politically active and established a Crotonian hegemony in southern Italy.[804]

Kleist's ideal community encompasses a similar mixture of *satyrical* ritual, *po(i)etical* expression, and *satirical* activism, and several of the Pythagoreans' practices could have influenced Kleist:

- Stress is put on intuitive truths revealed only to the initiated;
- Teachings involve a master's cryptic *akousmata* (Gr.: "something heard," i.e., esoteric teachings), and also mathematical *symbola* and science;
- Strict loyalty and secrecy among members;
- Admission of women to the school (unusually in ancient Greece);
- Support of a state combining elements of monarchy, oligarchy and democracy into a harmonic whole.

Although in Kleist's "brotherhood" the Pythagorean principle of *abstinence* is exchanged for one of *excess*, his concepts of *"Tugend,"* first espoused in *Aufsatz*, and of *"Ziererei,"* explored in *Marionettentheater*, celebrate modesty and self-discipline, especially on the part of the novice/*erômenos*.

Orpheus. Orphism denotes a set of religious beliefs and practices influential in classical Greece and the Hellenistic world from the 6th century BC (or earlier) till the 1st century AD, whose origins predate Pythagoras and incorporated Pythagoranean concepts, including metempsychosis, as well as Dionysiac rites. In the

Orphic conception, human souls are immortal and indestructible, but must endure embodied life in a "grivious cycle" of rebirths, a recurring cycle of suffering that is alleviated only by Orphic rites of purification, initiation, communion with the gods ("*unio mystica*") and asceticism.[805] Among the chief followers of Orphism were the socially marginalised—women, slaves, homosexuals, foreigners, vagabonds—or, in Kleist's term, "emigrants." The mythical Thracian poet and prophet Orpheus, son of the Muse Callipoe, initiator of the mysteries of Dionysos, and legendary poet whose song animated even stones and trees into dance, was said to have been one of a select few humans to have descended into Hades and returned alive (in some myths, Orpheus is considered Dionysos' reincarnation). As the archetypical inspired singer, Orpheus remained popular in Western culture to this day, and Kleist could well have aspired to the status of a modern-day Orpheus: the national bard who with his song would inspire even the most wooden leader to dance to his tune.

Myths relating to Orpheus would have intrigued Kleist. Orpheus' purported import, from Thracia, of the practice of *paiderastaia*—according to Ovid, he "abstained from the love of women" and "was the first of the Thracian people to transfer his affection to young boys and enjoy their brief springtime and early flowering this side of manhood" (*Metamorphoses,* X); his descent into the underworld to retrieve Eurydice, which failed when against Hades and Persephone's instructions he turned back at her before she reached the surface; his *sparagmos* at the hands of (depending on the version) Dionysos' maenads, when he refused to worship any god other than Apollo, enraged women, whom he had spurned in favour of men, or entranced audiences, who could no longer bear his celestial music.[806] Upon his death, Orpheus' lyre was said to have been carried to heaven by the Muses and placed among the stars, and his soul to have been reunited with that of his beloved Euridyce, and Kleist, when he in his haunting lament, *Das Letzte Lied*, puts down his lyre, "*Schließt er sein Lied, er wünscht mit ihm zu enden, / Und legt die Leier weinend aus den Händen*" (I:32), and when he has the dying Penthesilea drop her golden bow, emulates Orpheus: like Orpheus' lyre, *his* lyre shall be returned to the Muses, and like Orpheus' soul, *his* soul shall be reunited with his lovers'.

That Kleist, as a poet and as a person, had a decidedly Orphic aspect was not lost on those close to him: Fouqué reminisces in 1824 (cf. Sembdner, *In Sachen Kleist*, 290), on the occasion of the death of the famous actress and Käthchen-performer Luise von Holtei, "Heinrich, mein tönender Freund! *Du tönest noch, ob im Jenseit / Dunkel verlor sich die Spur deiner cometischen Bahn.*— / [...] *glühender Sänger* [...] */ Heinrich, du Sängergemüth* [...] */ [...] Wir—wir singen hienieden*"; Rahel, in 1810, lucidly says of him: "*Er ist wahr und sieht wahr*" (*LS*,357). Kleist may in equal measure have suffered from his Orphic vision and talent, and drawn hope and nourishment from it. His lucid, penetrating vision before C.D. Friedrich's *Mönch*, "*Nichts kann trauriger und unbehaglicher sein als diese Stellung in der Welt... der einsame Mittelpunkt in dem einsamen Kreis*," is paralleled by Homburg's before the gaping tomb, Strahl's during his feverish vision (cf. V.1153-63), and Johann's in the face of madness and clairvoyance, "*Es hat das Leben mich wie eine Schlange, / Mit Gliedern, zahnlos, ekelhaft, umwunden. Es schauert mich, es zu berühren*" (II:87). Orpheus cast his spell on Kleist, and he cast it well. Which reminds me of a few lines from a favourite song: "I will cast the spell, be sure I cast it well. / I will light a fire, kindled with desire. / I'll fill you with fear, so you'll know I'm here / and I won't be treated like a fool. / [...] You will never break the spell" (Uriah Heep, *Paradise/The Spell*, 1972).

The Great Comet. It may be coincidence that the year of Kleist's death saw the passing of "The Great Comet of 1811" (scientifically: C/1811F), visible to the naked eye for a record 260 days, studied by many scientists and depicted by many artists, and so popular that the excellent 1811 vintage came to be marketed as "Comet wine."[807] And yet, this coincidence is oh-so-Kleistian: did Kleist take the comet as an auspicuous sign that his time had come? He died within weeks of the comet's reaching its most conspicuous aspect; when he and Henriette on 21st November were frolicking along Kl. Wannsee's shore, it could have been visible. In their delirium, were they—*comet gazing*?

Death as Simulation. Kleist's "religion" explains why he so lightheartedly embraced death, and thus answers Blamberger's question. However, it does not explain the timing and circumstances of its actualisation. As to its timing, several factors appear to have conspired: *orphically,* Henriette's turning up as suitable sister-in-death; *satirically,* the birth of Napoleon's son in March 1811 (establishing the Bonapartean dynasty *as* dynasty) and especially, since mid-September 1811, the King's negotiating an alliance with Napoleon; *familially* and *filially,* Ulrike's intransingence, Marie's departure, the failure of various *filial* approaches; *satirically,* the disintegration of Kleist's "brotherhood" (Müller's departure, Fouqué's jealousy); *syphilitically,* possibly the onset of tertiary syphilis symptoms ("one hand on the gun": Stefan Zweig).[808]

As to Henriette's role, Pythagoreanism or Orphism do not explain why for Kleist it had to be *two* "cheerful aeronauts" to elevate "above the world" (cf. II:885). For this Kleistian idiosyncracy—Homburg's horror in the so-called "*Todesfurchtszene*" is not one of *Todesfurcht* (*thanatophobia*) but one of *fear of dying alone* (*monophobia, horror* vacui)—we have to take recourse to Wieland's *Symphatien,* to Aristophanes' *symbolon,* and to Simon Vouet's *Marie-Madelaine portée par les anges,* in which Mary Magdalene's dying body is gently held by angels as her soul is released: Kleist and Henriette die precisely in this kneeling, backward-leaning position.[809]

 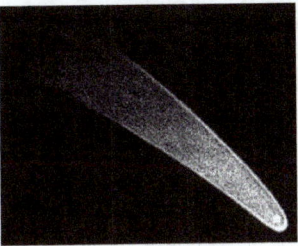 

Henri de Kleist portée par les anges (FLTR): Orpheus, "*Und legt die Leier weinend aus den Händen*"; the Great Comet of 1811; "*Ach, den Tod, als das ewige Refrain des Lebens... geflügelte Engel niederschweben, um eine Seele zu empfangen. Sie liegt, mit Blässe des Todes übergossen, auf den Knien... das liebliche Und einen Blick aus sterbenden Augen wirft sie*" (II:783).

Had Henriette not turned up, Kleist *could not have killed himself* on that chilly November day. This is not to blame Henriette: she merely—contingently— embodies the angel of death Kleist had been looking for ever since observing Vouet's painting in Châlons in 1807: "*Mein Jettchen... mein Schutzengel, mein Cherubim und Seraph*" (I:46).[810] When in the earthquake's aftermath Josephe, "*als ob alle Engel des Himmels sie umschirmten,... mit [Philipp] unbeschädigt wieder aus dem Portal hervor [tritt]*" (II:148), when during the ordeal by fire "*Käthchen..., durch ein großes Portal, das stehen geblieben ist, auf[tritt]; hinter ihr ein Cherub*" (V.1888), the time evidently has not yet come for these avatars of Kleist: their *Gewölbe* is still erect. In November 1811, in contrast, Kleist's time *had* come, his *Gewölbe had* collapsed—and an "angel," Henriette, was there to assist.

As to location, I offer that Kleist, if in the eleventh hour, decided to aim his final performance not at Ulrike and his family, but *at his King*.[811] Was it not his *destiny* to die on the Potsdam Chaussee, next to the bridge that linked the Hohenzollern residences Berlin, Charlottenburg and Potsdam?[812] Let us recall Kleist's two scenarios in the wargame with Marwitz: ONE: *Der König, für seine Person, geht nach Kolberg*; TWO: *Für den (nicht erwarteten) Fall, daß der König mit dem Korps über die Oder käme ist am 14. Okt. Eine Schlacht, in welcher er erdrückt wird*" (II:880). Having rejected the option of digging himself in at Kolberg, and thus rendered Kleist's first scenario void, in accordance with Kleist's wargame, the King now has no alternative but to confront the enemy in battle, in which the Prussian army would inevitably be crushed, and the King encircled, leaving him the sole honourable choice of suicide. What Kleist enacts on the Potsdam Chaussee, in other words, is *the simulation, using his own body, of the King's fate*: his death comprises his ultimate voodoo-esque attempt to shape his King's destiny via a theatrical happening. Its script is this:

LETZTER AKT

Szene: Offene Fläche nahe einem See. Kühler Novembernachmittag.

In der Ferne entflammt eine Stadt.

Erster Auftritt

Der König und der Staatskanzler Hardenberg trinken, in ausgelassener und heiterer Stimmung in einer kleinen Versenkung sitzend, Kaffee. Zahllose leere Weinflaschen und kleine Rumfäßchen. Drei Pistolen in in einer Satteltasche. Der Kgl. Adjutant Kleist-Noellendorf ist dabei, zum Hauptquartier zurückzukehren, als ein Schuss hallt, gefolgt, ein paar Schritte weiter, von einem zweiten.

KGL. ADJUJANT KLEIST-NOELLENDORF irritiert.

Was denn. Ist der Feind genaht—?

Zweiter Auftritt

Stube im Kommandeurszelt. Der Kgl. Adjujant und sein Sekretär schleppen zwei Leichen ins Haus. Zwei Wachsoldaten sind zur Hand. Der Kgl.

Chirurgus Hufeland tritt auf.

KGL. ADJUJANT KLEIST-NOELLENDORF ausser Atem. Hier—
Auf diesen Tisch.

Zu einem Wachsoldaten gewandt.

Du, bring die Lampe her—

KGL. CHIRURGUS HUFELAND mit zerbrochener Kopfsäge in der Hand, notierend.
Kgl. denatus weist zahlreiche braunrothe Flecken
Auf Rücken und Lenden auf.

Dritter Auftritt

Ein Königreich, dessen Schauplatz vom Süden in den Norden zurückverlegt worden ist.
Verschiedene öffentliche und private Stimmen.

STAATSKANZLER ALTENSTEIN fürsorglich. Das Publikum ist angehalten, nicht zwei Wesen lieblos zu verdammen, welche die Liebe und die Reinheit selbst waren.
KAISER NAPOLEON verstimmt. Der Mißbrauch öffentlicher Blätter zur Verbreitung der Immoralität ist bei Strafe auf das Strengste untersagt.
KGL. CHIRUGUS HUFELAND im Abschlussprotokoll zusammenfassend. Syphilianum et phlegmaticus in summo gradu.

Vierter Auftritt

Auf einem anderen Stern, in einer Galaxie weit, weit entfernt.
Drei Avatare in einem idyllischen Tal.

FR. WILH. erregt. Luise!
KGL. BARDE KLEIST nimmt die Leier auf. Regt Euch. Ein Lied!
LUISE legt den Dildoharness an. Ach!

Alle ab.

Es folgen zehn Jahre Funkstille und zweihundert Jahre Unverständnis. An einer vernünftigen Radioverbindung wird weiter gearbeitet. Während dieser Pause ist das werte Publikum angehalten, die Sitzplätze nicht zu verlassen.

Ende.

Nietzsche: *"Der Seufzer Kleists über die schließliche Unerkennbarkeit."* (NR,357)

The World. [813]

3.4 On the Magnetic Symposium: A Fool's Journey

Marionettentheater comprises Kleist's answer to Plato's *Symposion*, relating a Socratic dialogue between two symposiasts, the I-narrator, an apprentice lover (= Kleist), and a Master C..., an experienced *erastês* (or, as I suggested earlier, a Mme C..., an experienced female prostitute).[814]

ÜBER DAS MARIONETTENTHEATER	ON THE MAGNETIC SYMPOSIUM
Als ich den Winter 1801 in M... zubrachte, traf ich daselbst eines Abends, in einem öffentlichen Garten, den Herrn C. an, der seit kurzem, in dieser Stadt, als erster Tänzer der Oper, angestellt war, und bei dem Publiko außerordentliches Gück machte.	When I spent the winter of 1801 in Paris, one evening in the park near the Champs-Elysées I met Master C., who had recently been hired as leading *erastês* in this city's premier gay sauna, and who brought much happiness to its customers.
Ich sagte ihm, daß ich erstaunt gewesen wäre, ihn schon mehrere Mal in einem Marionettentheater zu finden, das auf dem Markte zusammengezimmert worden war, und den Pöbel, durch kleine dramatische Burlesken, mit Gesang und Tanz durchwebt, belustigte.	I told him that I had been surprised to behold him several times in a makeshift *baquet* that had been knocked together on the market to entertain the rabble with little homo-erotic burlesques and orgies, intervowen with oral and anal pleasures.
Er versicherte mir, daß ihm die Pantomimik die-ser Puppen viel Vergnügen machte, und ließ nicht undeutlich merken, daß ein Tänzer, der sich ausbilden wollte, mancherlei von ihnen lernen könne.	He affirmed to me that the convulsions of the mediums delighted him, and made it quite plain that any aspiring *erastês*, anxious to further senhance his skills, could learn much from them.
Da diese Äußerung mir, durch die Art, wie er sie vorbrachte, mehr, als ein bloßer Einfall schien, so ließ ich mich bei ihm nieder, um ihn über die Gründe, auf die er seine so sonderbare Behauptung stützen könne, näher zu vernehmen.	As this utterance, given the manner in which he delivered it, appeared to be as more profound than a fleeting thought, I opened myself to him, so as to experience more directly the material basis on which he grounded his curious claim.

551

Er fragte mich, ob ich nicht, in der Tat, einige Bewegungen der Puppen, besonders der kleineren, im Tanz sehr graziös gefunden hatte.

Diesen Umstand konnt ich nicht leugnen. Eine Gruppe von vier Bauern, die nach einem raschen Takt die Ronde tanzte, hätte von Teniers nicht hübscher gemalt werden können.

Ich erkundigte mich nach dem Mechanismus dieser Figuren, und wie es möglich wäre, die einzelnen Glieder derselben und ihre Punkte, ohne Myriaden von Fäden an den Fingern zu haben, so zu regieren, als es der Rhythmus der Bewegungen, oder der Tanz, erfordere?

Er antwortete, daß ich mir nicht vorstellen müsse, als ob jedes Glied einzeln, während der verschiedenen Momente des Tanzes, von dem Maschinisten gestellt und gezogen würde.

Jede Bewegung, sagte er, hätte einen Schwerpunkt; es wäre genug, diesen, in dem Innern der Figur, zu regieren; die Glieder, welche nichts als Pendel wären, folgten, ohne irgend ein Zutun, auf eine mechanische Weise von selbst.

Er setzte hinzu, daß diese Bewegung sehr einfach wäre; daß jedesmal, wenn der Schwerpunkt in einer *graden Linie* bewegt wird, die Glieder schon *Kurven* beschrieben; und daß oft, auf

He asked me if I had not found, as we were joining the *baquet*, some of the mediums' movements, especially of the younger ones, eminently arousing.

This circumstance I could not deny. One group of four rustic mediums, which in a swift rhythm took turns in performing the act, even Teniers could not have portrayed in a sexier manner.

I inquired about the mechanical properties of these entranced mediums' fluidum, and how it was possible to manipulate their members and their stoppage points in accordance with the rhythm of their movements and the *baquet*, without manipulating them via myriads of tethers?

He responded that I should not imagine that every single member, in the various stages of the orgy, had to be individually roused and steered by the magnétiseur.

Every movement, he showed, has a centre of gravity; it suffices to manipulate this centre inside the mediums; their penises, which are nothing but pendulums, then followed, without any further effort, mechanically.

He pushed home the point that this movement is a simple one; that whenever the magnétiseur performs his passes in a *straight line,* the penis immediately *curves* upward; and that often, aroused in

eine bloß zufällige Weise erschüttert, das Ganze schon in eine Art von rhythmische Bewegung käme, die dem Tanz ähnlich wäre.

Diese Bemerkung schien mir zuerst einiges Licht über das Vergnügen zu werfen, das er in dem Theater der Marionetten zu finden vorgegeben hatte. Inzwischen ahndete ich bei weitem die Folgerungen noch nicht, die er späterhin ziehen würde.

Ich fragte ihn, ob er glaubte, daß der Maschinist, dier diese Puppen regierte, selbst ein Tänzer sein, oder wenigstens einen Begriff vom Schönen im Tanz haben müsse?

Er erwiderte, daß wenn ein Geschäft, von seiner mechanischen Seite, leicht sei, daraus noch nicht folge, daß es ganz ohne Empfindung betrieben werden könne.

Die Linie, die der Schwerpunkt zu beschreiben hat, wäre zwar sehr einfach, und, wie er glaube, in den meisten Fällen, gerad. In Fällen, wo sie krumm sei, scheine das Gesetz ihrer Krümmung wenigstens von der ersten oder höchstens zweiten Ordnung; und auch in diesem Fall nur elliptisch, welche Form der Bewegung den Spitzen des menschlichen Körpers (wegen der Gelenke) überhaupt die natürliche sei, und also dem Maschinisten keine große Kunst koste, zu verzeichnen.

Dagegen wäre diese Linie wieder, von einer anderen Seite, etwas sehr Geheimnisvolles. Denn sie wäre nichts

a mere accidental manner, the body will enter into a kind of rhythmic movement that mimics sodomy.

His demonstration appeared to shed some initial light on the pleasures he claimed to have experienced in the makeshift *baquet*. Nevertheless, at this point I scarcely divined the consequences he would soon draw from it.

I asked him whether he believed that the magnétiseur, who ruled over these mediums, himself had to be an experienced sodomist, or at least had to have a notion of pederast jouissance?

He responded that even if the mechanics of a séance are simple, it does not follow that it can therefore necessarily be pursued entirely without passion.

The passage which the centre of gravity had to follow was indeed very simple and, in his experience, in most cases straight. In cases where it was curved, the law governing its curvature was only of the first or at most the second order; and even in this case merely elliptical, a trajectory that was for the glans (because of their stoppage points) is at any rate the most natural, so that it did not take much artfulness on the part of the magnétiseur to prescribe it with his passes.

And yet this passage, seen from another angle, was something very mysterious. For it is nothing less than the *Path of the*

anders, als der *Weg der Seele des Tänzers*; und er zweifle, daß sie anders gefunden werden könne, als dadurch, daß sich der Maschinist in den Schwerpunkt der Marionette versetzte, d.h. mit andern Worten, *tanzt*.

Ich erwiderte, daß man mir das Geschäft dessel-ben als etwas ziemlich Geistloses vorgestellt hätte: etwa was das Drehen einer Kurbel sei, die eine Leier spielt.

Keineswegs, antwortete er. Vielmehr verhalten sich die Bewegungen seiner Finger zur Bewegung der daran befestigten Puppen ziemlich künstlich, etwa wie Zahlen zu ihren Logarithmen oder die Asymptote zur Hyperbel.

Inzwischen glaube er, daß auch dieser letzte Bruch von Geist, von dem er gesprochen, aus den Marionetten entfernt werden, daß ihr Tanz gänzlich ins Reich mechanischer Kräfte hinübergespielt, und vermittest einer Kurbel, so wie ich es mir gedacht, hervorgebracht werden könne.

Ich äußerte meine Verwunderung zu sehen, welcher Aufmerksamkeit er diese, für den Haufen erfundene, Spielart einer schönen Kunst würdigte. Nicht bloß, daß er sie einer höheren Entwickelung für fähig halte: er scheine sich sogar selbst damit zu beschäftigen.

Er lächelte, und sagte, er getraue sich zu behaupten, daß wenn ihm ein

Lover's Fluidum; and he doubted that it could be explored in any other way than by the magnétiseur projecting himself into the mediums's centre of gravity, i.e., in other words, by *sodomising* him..

I replied that the magnétiseur's task had been described to me as rather mindless: akin to the cranking of the handle that operates a barrel organ.

Not at all, he responded. Rather, the movements of his fingers relate to the movement of the mediums tethered to them in a rather artful manner, like numbers relate to their logarithms or the asymptote to the hyperbel.

By now he believed that even the last remnants of volition of which he spoke earlier could be removed from these mediums, so that their performance would become wholly mechanical and could indeed be produced with the electric generator's crank-handle, just as I had imagined.

I expressed my astonishment at the amount of attention with which he graced this particular technique, invented for the masses, of a beautiful art. Not only did he seem to consider it capable of further development, but he even appeared to be engaging in it himself.

He smiled, and said that he dared contend that if he had an engineer

Mechanikus, nach den Forderungen, die er an ihn zu machen dächte, eine Marionette bauen wollte, er vermittelst derselben einen Tanz darstellen würde, den weder er, noch irgend ein anderer geschickter Tänzer seiner Zeit, Vestris selbst nicht ausgenommen, zu erreichen imstande wäre.

Haben Sie, fragte er, da ich den Blick schweigend zur Erde schlug: haben Sie von jenen mechanischen Beinen gehört, welche englische Künstler für Unglückliche verfertigen, die ihre Schenkel verloren haben?

Ich sagte, nein: dergleichen wäre mir nie zu Augen gekommen.

Es tut mir leid, erwiderte er; denn wenn ich Ihnen sage, daß diese Unglücklichen damit tanzen, so fürchte ich fast, Sie werden es mir nicht glauben.— Was sag ich, tanzen? Der Kreis ihrer Bewegung ist zwar beschränkt; doch diejenigen, die ihnen zu Gebote stehen, vollziehen sich mit einer Ruhe, Leichtigkeit und Anmut, die jedes denkende Gemüt in Erstaunen setzen.

Ich äußerte, scherzend, daß er ja, auf diese Weise, seinen Mann gefunden habe. Denn derjenige Künstler, der einen so merkwürdigen Schenkel zu bauen imstande sei, würde ihm unzweifelhaft auch eine ganze Marionette, seinen Forderungen gemäß, zusammensetzen können.

Wie, fragte ich, da er seinerseits ein wenig betreten zur Erde sah: wie sind

build him a mechanical medium in accordance with the specifications he would submit to him, he would be able to produce orgiastic performances with it that neither he himself, nor any other master *erastês* of his generation, excluding not even Vestris, would be able to realise.

Have you, he inquired, as my member slackened: have you heard of those mechanical dildos which English craftsmen design for those unhappy lovers whose members have been wrecked by syphilis?

I answered, no: such a thing I had never beheld before.

I am sorry for that, he responded; for if I tell you that these unhappy individuals perform sodomy with it, I almost fear that you will not believe me.— What do I say, perform sodomy? While the range of their movements is limited, within the range available to them their movements proceed with a calmness, nimbleness and grace that astonishes any passionate lover.

I suggested, jokingly, that in this way he had already found his man. For that craftsman who was able to build such a remarkable dildo would no doubt also be capable of putting together an entire mechanical lover in accordance with his specifications.

What, I pressed, as his member on its part now became flaccid: what is, then,

denn die Forder-ungen, die Sie an die Kunstfertigkeit desselben zu machen gedenken, bestellt?

Nichts, antwortete er, was sich nicht auch schon hier fände; Ebenmaß, Beweglichkeit, Leichtigkeit—nur alles in einem höheren Grade; und besonders eine naturgemäßere Anordnung der Schwerpunkte.

Und der Vorteil, den diese Puppe vor lebendigen Tänzern voraus haben würde?

Der Vorteil? Zuvörderst ein negativer, mein vortrefflicher Freund, nämlich dieser, daß sie sich niemals *zierte*.— Denn Ziererei erscheint, wie Sie wissen, wenn sich die Seele (vis motrix) in irgend einem Punkt befindet, als in dem Schwerpunkt der Bewegung. Da der Maschinist nun schlechthin, vermittelst des Drahtes oder Fadens, keinen andern Punkt in seiner Gewalt hat, als diesen: so sind alle übrigen Glieder, was sie sein sollen, tot, reine Pendel, und folgen dem bloßen Gesetz der Schwere; eine vortreffliche Eigenschaft, die man vergebens bei dem größeren Teil unserer Tänzer sucht.

Sehe Sie nur die P... an, fuhr er fort, wenn sie die Daphne spielt, und sich, verfolgt vom Apoll, nach ihm umsieht; die Seele sitzt ihr in den Wirbeln des Kreuzes; sie beugt sich, als ob sie brechen wollte, wie eine Najade aus der Schule Bernins. Sehen Sie den jungen F... an, wenn er, als Paris, unter den drei Göttinnen steht, und der Venus

the nature of the demands you expect to make on this man's craft skills?

Nothing, he responded, that was not already to be found here; regularity, agility, lightness—only all of them to a higher degree; and above all, a more natural arrangement of the centres of gravity.

And the advantage that this mechanical lover would have over living mediums?

The advantage? Foremost a negative one, my excellent friend, namely that it will never *act coyly*.—For coyness occurs, as you know, when the magnetic fluidum (vis motrix) is channelled to any point other than the movement's centre of gravity. Since the magnétiseur, to all intents and purposes, by means of his metal rods and ropes, has no other point in his power than the glans: the remainders of the members remain as they should be, stiff, pure pendulums that simply follow the law of gravity; an excellent characteristic, which one will scarcely find in most lovers.

Just look at the *erômenos* P..., he thrust, when he plays the role of Daphne and, pursued by the *erastês* Apollo, offers his rear to him; his fluidum jams in his spine; he bends forward, as if he was about to break, like a Naiad from Bernini's school. Look at the *erômenos* F... when he, as Paris, stands before the three *erastai*, and offers his anus to the most virile of them:

den Apfel überreicht: die Seele sitzt ihm gar (es ist ein Schrecken, es zu sehen) im Ellenbogen.

Solche Mißgriffe, setzte er abbrechend hinzu, sind unvermeidlich, seitdem wir von dem Baum der Erkenntnis gegessen haben. Doch das Paradies ist verriegelt und der Cherub hinter uns; wir müssen die Reise um die Welt machen und sehen, ob es vielleicht von hinten irgndwo wieder offen ist.

Ich lachte.—Allderdings, dachte ich, kann der Geist nicht irren, da, wo keiner vorhanden ist. Doch ich bemerkte, daß er noch mehr auf dem Herzen hatte, und bat ihn, fortzufahren.

Zudem, sprach er, haben diese Puppen den Vor-teil, daß sie *antigrav* sind. Von der Trägheit der Materie, dieser dem Tanze entgegenstrebendsten aller Eigenschaften, wissen sie nichts: weil die Kraft, die sie in die Lüfte erhebt, größer ist, als jene, die sie an der Erde fesselt. Was würde unsre gute G... darum geben, wenn sie sechzig Pfund leichter wäre, oder ein Gewicht von dieser Größe ihr bei ihren Entrechats und Pirouetten, zu Hülfe käme? Die Puppen brauchen den Boden nur, wie die Elfen, um ihn zu *streifen*, und den Schwung der Glieder, durch die augenblickliche Hemmung neu zu beleben; wir brauchen ihn, um darauf zu *ruhen*, und uns von der Anstrengung des Tanzes zu erholen: ein Moment, der

his fluidum has even passed (it is horrible to behold) into his elbow.

Such blunders, he pushed before interrupting coitus, have become inevitable since we have been corrupted by disease. Now the immaculate anus is locked and the infected penis erects behind us; and we must undergo excrutiating therapies to see if somewhere there is still a rear opening for us.

I moaned.—Indeed, I thought, the mind cannot err, where there is none. However, I sensed that he still had more in him, and begged that he con-tinue driving me.

Furthermore, he replied, thrusting, these mechanical lovers have the advantage that they *defy gravity*. Of the inertia of mass, the quality that most forcefully counteracts anal penetration, they know nothing: for the force that lifts them up exceeds that which ties them to the ground. What would our dear G... give up if his member were a good bit lighter, or if an equivalent weight would support it by pulling it up during the performance of its various manoeuvres? Mechanical lovers, like elves, require the lover's buttocks only in order to *brush against* them and gain fresh impetus for their members; we require it to *rest* on it, and to recover from the exertion of sodomy: a moment which clearly in itself does not count as coitus, and with

offenbar selber kein Tanz ist, und mit dem sich weiter nichts anfangen läßt, als ihn möglichst verschwinden zu machen.

Ich sagte, daß, so geschickt er auch die Sache seiner Paradoxe führe, er mich doch nimmermehr glauben machen würde, daß in einem mechanischen Gliedermann mehr Anmut enthalten sein könne, als in dem Bau des menschlichen Körpers.

Er versetzte, daß es dem Menschen schlechthin unmöglich wäre, den Gliedermann darin auch nur zu erreichen. Nur ein Gott könne sich, auf diesem Felde, mit der Materie messen; und hier sei der Punkt, wo die beiden Enden der ringförmigen Welt in einander grifen.

Ich erstaunte immer mehr, und wußte nicht, was ich zu so sonderbaren Behauptungen sagen sollte.

Es scheine, versetzte er, indem er eine Prise Tabak nahm, daß ich das dritte Kapitel vom ersten Buch Moses nicht mit Aufmerksamkeit gelesen; und wer diese erste Periode aller menschlichen Bildung nicht kennt, mit dem könne man nicht füglich über die folgenden, um wie viel weniger über die letzte, sprechen.

Ich sagte, daß ich gar wohl wüßte, welche Unordnungen, in der natürlichen Grazie des Menschen, das Bewußtsein anrichtet. Ein junger Mann von meiner Bekanntschaft hätte, durch eine bloße Bemerkung, gleichsam vor

which we can do nothing but seek to make it disappear.

I said that no matter how eloquently he defended his paradox, he would never be able to convince me that the mechanical lover could entail greater potency and pleasure than the human instrument.

He pushed back that it was simply impossible for the human tool to equal that of the mechanical lover. Only a divine member, in this respect, could measure up to such unanimated matter; and this was the point at which the two epitomes of orgiastic love merged.

I became ever more aroused, and did not know what to say to such tillitating assertions.

It appeared, he changed positon as I came inside of him, that I had not attentively read the third chapter of the Book of Genesis; and with a lover who did not know this first phase in a gay man's development, one could not have a proper conversation about the following ones, let alone the final one.

I said that I knew full well the havoc that consciousness could wreak with a man's natural potency. A young lover of mine had lost, by a mere freak incidence, as it were right before my erect member, his innocence, and had never been

meinen Augen seine Unschuld verloren, und das Paradies derselben, trotz aller ersinnlichen Bemühungen, nachher niemals wieder gefunden.—Doch, welche Folgerungen, setzte ich hinzu, können Sie daraus ziehen? Er fragte mich, welch einen Vorfall ich meine?

Ich badete mich, erzählte ich, vor etwa drei Jahren, mit einem jungen Mann, über dessen Bildung damals eine wunderbare Anmut verbreitet war. Er mochte ohngefähr in seinem sechszehnten Jahre stehn, und nur ganz von fern ließen sich, von der Gunst der Frauen herbeigerufen, die ersten Spuren von Eitelkeit erblicken. Es traf sich, daß wir grade kurz zuvor in Paris den Jüngling gesehen hatten, der sich einen Splitter aus dem Fuße zieht; der Abguß der Statue ist bekannt und befindet sich in den meisten deutschen Sammlungen. Ein Blick, den er in dem Augenblick, da er den Fuß auf den Schemel setzte, um ihn abzutrocknen, in einen großen Spiegel warf, erinnerte ihn daran; er lächelte und sagte mir, welch eine Entdeckung er gemacht habe. In der Tat hatte ich, in eben diesem Augenblick, dieselbe gemacht; doch sei es, um die Sicherheit der Grazie, die ihm beiwohnte, zu prüfen, sei es, um seiner Eitelkeit ein wenig heilsam zu begegnen: ich lachte und erwiderte—er sähe wohl Geister! Er er-rötete, und hob den Fuß zum zweitenmal, um es mir zu zeigen;

able to recover, despite all manner of sensuous attempts, the lost paradise thereof.—But, what inferences, I pushed further, are you able to draw from this?

He inquired, which incidence I had in mind?

About three years ago, I recounted, I took a mercury bath together with my *erômenos*, whose ithyphallic member exuded a wondrous potency. He may have been approximately in his sixteens year, and only from a distance could one discern the first traces of corruption, caused by the favours granted him by infected prostitutes. It so happened that only a short time prior to this we had seen in Berlin the youth who treats the chancres on his member; the cast of the statue is well known and copies of it are to be found in most German brotherhood houses. A glance he cast into a large mirror just in the moment when he put his member rubbed with ointment on a stool to dry it, reminded him of it; he groaned and told me what discovery he had just made. Indeed, I had made the same discovery just then; but be it to test the resilience of his erection, be it to heal his vanity: I groaned and replied—that he must have been imagining things! His penis flushed and erected for a second time, to show off to me; yet that attempt, as might easily have been anticipated, failed. Bewildered, he sought to lift his

doch der Versuch, wie sich leicht hätte voraussehn lassen, mißglückte. Er hob ver-wirrt den Fuß zum dritten und vierten, er hob ihn wohl noch zehnmal: umsonst! er war außerstand, dieselbe Bewegung wieder hervorzubringen— was sag ich? die Bewegungen, die er machte, hatten ein so komisches Element, daß ich Mühe hatte, das Gelächter zurückzuhalten:—

Von diesem Tage, gleichsam von diesem Augenblick an, ging eine unbegreifliche Veränderung mit dem jungen Menschen vor. Er fing an, tagelang vor dem Spiegel zu stehen; und immer ein Reiz nach dem anderen verließ ihn. Eine unsichtbare und unbegreifliche Gewalt schien sich, wie ein eisernes Netz, um das freie Spiel seiner Gebärden zu legen, und als ein Jahr verflossen war, war keine Spur mehr von der Lieblichkeit in ihm zu entdecken, die die Augen der Menschen sonst, die ihn umringten, ergötzt hatte. Noch jetzt lebt jemand, der ein Zeuge jenes sonderbaren und unglücklichen Vorfalls war, und ihn Wort für Wort, wie ich ihn erzählt, bestätigen könnte.—

Bei dieser Gelegenheit, sagte Herr C.... freundlich, muß ich Ihnen eine andere Geschichte erzählen, von der Sie leicht begreifen werden, wie sie hier-her gehört.

Ich befand mich, auf meiner Reise nach Rußland, auf einem Landgut des Herrn v. G..., eines livländischen Edelmanns,

member a third and a forth time, and went on attempting to do so probably another ten times: in vain! he was unable to reproduce the same erection again— what do I say? the erections he attempted to make were so pathetic, that I found it difficult to hold back my laughter:—

From this day, as it were from this moment onward, an incomprehensible transformation took place with my *erômenos*. He attempted to erect before the mirror for days on end; and bit by bit his potency disappeared. An invisible and inconceivable force appeared to confine, like an iron net, the free play of his members' erection, and within one year no trace remained of the manliness that had previously aroused the symposiac lovers who gathered around him. To this day a member of the brotherhood survives who eye-witnessed that strange and unhappy incidence and who could affirm it word by word, just as I have told it.—

At this point, Master C.... said while caressing me, I have to relate to you another story, of which you will easily comprehend how it fits into the context of ouir conversation.

I found myself, during my journey to Pasewalk in 1800, on the estate of the *erâstes* v. E..., a Pomeranian Junker

dessen Söhne sich eben damals stark im Fechten übten. Besonders der ältere, der eben von der Universität zurückgekommen war, machte den Virtuosen, und bot mir, da ich eines Morgens auf seinem Zimmer war, ein Rapier an. Wir fochten; doch es traf sich, daß ich ihm überlegen war; Leidenschaft kam dazu, ihn zu verwirren; fast jeder Stoß, den ich führte, traf, und sein Rapier flog zuletzt in den Winkel. Halb scher-zend, halb empfindlich, sagte er, indem er das Rapier aufhob, daß er seinen Meister gefunden habe: doch alles auf der Welt finde den seinen, und fortan wolle er mich zu dem meinigen führen. Die Brüder lachten laut auf, und riefen: Fort! fort! In den Holzstall herab! und damit nahmen sie mich bei der Hand und führten mich zu einem Bären, den Herr v. G..., ihr Vater, auf dem Hofe auferziehen ließ.

Der Bär stand, als ich erstaunt vor ihn trat, auf den Hinterfüßen, mit dem Rücken an einem Pfahl gelehnt, an welchem er angeschlossen war, die rechte Tatze schlagfertig erhoben, und sah mir ins Auge: das war seine Fechterpositur. Ich wußte nicht, ob ich träumte, da ich mich einem solchen Gegner gegenüber sah; doch stoßen Sie! stoßen Sie! sagte Herr v. G..., und versuchen Sie, ob Sie ihm eins beibringen können! Ich fiel, da ich mich ein wenig von meinem Erstaunen erholt hatte, mit dem Rapier auf ihn aus; der Bär machte eine ganz

whose sons just at that time were training to become *erastai*. Especially the older one, who had just returned from a brotherhood house, was playing the ithyphallic virtuoso, and offered me, when I joined him one morning in his chamber, his member. We had intercourse; it so happened, that I was more experienced; his passion got the better of him and confused him; almost every thrust of mine hit the target, and at the end his member slackened. Partly in jest, partly from hurt feelings, he admitted, while once more erecting his member, that he had found his master: but that everyone at all find theirs, and that now he would lead me to mine. The brothers moaned and cried: Lets go! lets go! Down into the dungeon! and with that took me by my member and led me to a hulk of a *dmōs*, whom the erâstes v. E. was keeping on the estate.

The *dmōs* erected, as I stood up before him, his giant penis straight up from his testicles, his anus impaled on a pole behind him, to which he was chained, ready to strike, and looked into my eye: this was his position for intercourse. I did not know, in confronting this awesome lover, whether a dream had come true; but thrust! thrust! said the *erâstes* v. E..., and try, whether you can find a way to penetrate him! I thrust, when I had recovered a little from my astonishment, my weapon towards him; the hulk made a swift movement with his giant penis

kurze Bewegung mit der Tatze und parierte den Stoß. Ich versuchte ihn durch Finten zu verführen; der Bär rührte sich nicht. Ich fiel wieder, mit einer augenblicklichen Gewandtheit, auf ihn aus, eines Menschen Brust würde ich unfehlbar getroffen haben: der Bär machte eine ganz kurze Bewegung mit der Tatze und parierte den Stoß. Jetzt war ich fast in dem Fall des jungen Herrn v. G... Der Ernst des Bären kam hinzu, mir die Fassung zu rauben, Stöße und Finten wechselten sich, mir triefte der Schweiß: umsonst! Nicht bloß, daß der Bär, wie der erste Fechter der Welt, alle meine Stöße parierte; auf Finten (was ihm kein Fechter der Welt nachmacht) ging er gar nicht einmal ein: Aug in Auge, als ob er meine Seele darin lesen könnte, stand er, die Tatze schlagfertig erhoben, und wenn meine Stöße nicht ernsthaft gemeint waren, so rührte er sich nicht.

Glauben Sie dies Geschichte?

Vollkommen! rief ich, mit freudigem Beifall; jedwedem Fremden, so wahrscheinlich ist sie: um wie viel mehr bei Ihnen!

Nun, mein vortrefflicher Freund, sagte Herr C..., so sind Sie im Besitz von allem, was nötig ist, um mich zu begreifen. Wir sehen, daß in dem Maße, als, in der organischen Welt, die Reflexion dunkler und schwächer wird, die Grazie darin immer strahlender und herrschender hervortritt.—

and parried my thrust. I tried to tempt him with feints; the hulk did not move at all. Once again I sallied, with a sudden adroitness, towards him; a normal lover's anus I could not have failed to penetrate: the hulk made a swift movement with his giant penis and once again parried my thrust. Now I was almost in the same situation as had earlier been the young *erâstes* v. E.... The *dmōtes*' seriousness added to my losing my composure, thrusts and feints alternated, my sweat gushed: in vain! Not only that the *dmōs*, like a world champion *erâstes*, parried all my thrusts, but to my feints he did not even react at all (something no lover in the world could imitate): penis to penis, as if he could discern my fluidum in it, he stood erect, his giant penis lifted, and whenever my thrusts were not serious, he did not move a muscle.

Can you believe this story?

Totally! I cried, with delighted applause; any stranger I would believe it, so probable is it: how much more so in your case!

Now, my excellent fellow, said Master C..., you are in possession of everything necessary to join me in consummating our symposiac love. We can see that by the same measure by which, during the symposium, reflection diminishes, potency and passion emerges ever more radiantly

Doch so, wie sich der Durchschnitt zweier Linien, auf der einen Seite eines Punkts, nach dem Durchgang durch das Unendliche, plötzlich wieder auf der andern Seite einfindet, oder das Bild des Hohlspiegels, nachdem es sich in das Unendliche entfernt hat, plötzlich wieder dicht vor uns tritt: so findet sich auch, wenn die Erkenntnis gleichsam durch ein Unendliches gegangen ist, die Grazie wieder ein; so daß sie, zu gleicher Zeit, in demjenigen menschlichen Körperbau am reinsten erscheint, der entweder gar keins, oder ein unendliches Bewußtsein hat, d.h. in dem Gliedermann, oder in dem Gott.

Mithin, sagte ich ein wenig zerstreut, müßten wir wieder von dem Baum der Erkenntnis essen, um in den Stand der Unschuld zurückzufallen?

Allerndings, antwortet er; das ist das letzte Kapitel von der Geschichte der Welt.   H.v.K.

and prevalently.—And yet, just as our consummation of intercourse prior to our symposiac dialogue, having passed through its Socrato-Bacchic infinitude, suddenly once more materialises, or our rapturous ecstasy, having dissipated into infinitude, suddenly rekindles in us: so does also our ithyphallic potency, as our consciousness has passed, thanks to our excellent wine, once more through infinitude, recur; so that this potency appears, in its purest form, in that human anatomy that has either no, or infinite, consciousness, i.e., either in the mechanical, or the divine, phallus.

Consequently, I said, scattering my cum, we would have to perform another symposiac discourse-cum-orgy to fall backinto innocence?

Indeed, he answered; that is the final chapter in the history of our brotherhood.   H.v.K

Kleist's essay is evidently autobiographical: it is eminently plausible that Kleist was infected with syphilis in late 1798, into which period he places the story of the Spinario, and within months of which he requested dismissal from the army.[815]

*   *   *   *

I aimed to show that for a text to be considered "*Kleistian*," it must be composed on a consistent *plane of composition* on which "lives" or "threads"—my examples include *The Satirical, The Satyrical, The Syphilitical, The Po(ï)etical, The Priapic, The Familial, The Filial* and *The Orphic*, but there may be others—are co-inscribed and co-encrypted into a single textual fabric, whose "surface" comprises an *overt* story that adds cohesion, camouflage and commercial potential to the encrypted "threads." Kleist fully expected that his "mass market" audiences would be unable to dive below the "surface," which he endeavoured to make as attractive as possible, without compromising the integrity of the "aristocratic" and "kynical/cynical" "threads" woven into it. However, he was frustrated by the extent to which the *cognoscendi* he targeted—King and Emperor, courtiers and ministers, members of his "brotherhood," like-minded intellectuals—failed to *understand* or, when they did understand, *appreciate* his messages; his camouflage worked only too well, his chosen vehicles and channels did not always reach the target audience, and his code was perhaps too intricate for most to bother uncoding.[816] Is not Kafka's *"Landvermesser" K.*, forever caught up in the infinite loop of his approaching the castle, an avatar of Kleist?

Where's the audience? The throne of the *Archon* (King)
in the Theatre of Dionysos, Athens.

As we begin to unravel Kleist's "threads," we discover them to be thoroughly autobiographical. Linkages between œuvre and author are always problematic, yet they are very strong indeed in Kleist's case, and they begin to give us a sense of *who he was*, of *who he was becoming.*

Pindar: "Become who you are."

A fool's journey: Kleist's "lives."

List of Images of Artworks Reproduced (in order of appearance).

Nicolas Marie-Gatteaux, *French Portrait card deck, King of Clubs; Queen of Hearts; Jack of Clubs* (1827). Playing cards, commons.wikipedia.org.

Peter Friedel, *Heinrich von Kleist* (1801). Minature, opaque colour on porcelain [detail, modified]. Staatsbibliothek Berlin.

[Unknown artist], *Friedrich Wilhelm III, König von Preußen* (19th Cent.). Oil on canvas [detail, modified, rotated]. Location unknown.

Henri Félix Emmanuel Philippoteaux, *Napoléon en 1792*. (1835) Oil on canvas [detail, modified, rotated]. Palais de Versailles.

Josef Grassi, *Portrait of Louise of Mecklenburg-Strelitz* (1802). Oil on canvas [detail, modified, rotated]. Schloss Charlottenburg, Berlin.

Gerhard von Kügelen, *Johann Wolfgang von Goethe* (1808/9). Oil on canvas (detail, modified, rotated). Tartu University Library, Tartu.

[Unknown artist], *Central Europe after the Peace of Basel and of Campo Formio* (1912). Cambridge Modern History Atlas, Map 84 [detail, modified]. commons.wikipedia.org.

[Unknown artist], *Vorstellung der, unter Höchster Anführung Se. Kö. Majestät Fr. Wilh. von Preussen durch die kombinierten Armeen belagerten... den 22. Juli 1793 wieder eroberten Stadt und Festung Mainz*. Drawing, in: Joh. Georg Bullmann, *Gründliche und wahrhafte Relation von der Belagerung*, etc. (Augsburg, 1793).

Renault, *Tarot de Besançon: L'Ermite (Le Capouche), L'Amoureux, La Mort (L'Arcane sans Nom), Le Chariot, Le Fou, Le Pendu, Le Soleil, Le Monde* (1820-30). Location unknown.

Friedrich Foltz, *Schloss Biebrich*. Steel engraving, in: *Rheinalbum* (1865). Location unknown.

Martin Zeiller, *Gustavsburg*. Engraving, in Matthäus Merian, *Topographia Archiepiscoatuum Moguntinensis* (Frankfurt: 1646). Location unknown.

C.J. Humbert, Carl Jäck, Millard Fillmore, *Plan der Belagerung von Meynz* (1793). Drawing on cloth [modified]. Library of Congress, Washington D.C.

L. Albert von Montmorillon, *Heinrich Zschokke* (1817). Lithography. Stadtmuseum, Aarau.

[Unknown artist], *Otto Aug. Rühle von Lilienstern* (19th Cent.). Lithography. Location unknown.

David Sulzer (?). *Ernst von Pfuel* (c.1830). Oil on canvas.
Musée d'art et d'histoire, Neuchâtel.

[Unknown artist], *Portrait von Fr. de la Motte Fouqué in Husarenuniform* (c.1815). Oil on canvas. Location unknown.

[Unknown artist], *Joh. Daniel Falk* (c.1800). Oil on canvas.
Gleimhaus, Halberstadt.

[Unknown artist], *Karl Freiherr vom Stein zum Altenstein* (19th Cent.) Painting. Location unknown.

Gerhard von Kügelen, *Adam Müller* (1807). Oil on canvas. Private collection.

[Unknown artist], *Friedrich von Gentz* (undated). Drawing, in: Hans Wahl, Anton Kippenberg, *Goethe und seine Welt* (Leipzig: Insel, 1932).

Nikolaus Gatter, *Ludwig Roberts* (c.1828). Drawing. Location unknown.

[Unknown artist], *Fr. Christoph Dahlmann* (19th Cent.). Steel engraving. Location unknown.

Peter Eduard Ströhling, *Achim von Arnim* (1803/4). Oil on canvas.
Freies Deutsches Hochstift, Frankfurt/M.

Albrecht Dürer, *Der Syphilitiker* (1496). Coloured woodprint.
Wellcome Images, commons.wikipedia.org.

Ferdinand Hartmann, *Phöbus über Dresden* (1808). Woodcut (frontispiece for the art journal *Phöbus*). Location unknown.

Anton Mesmer, *Darstellung der Entstehung von Ebbe und Flut* (late 18th Cent.). Drawing. Location unknown.

Ebenezer Sibly, *Mesmerism: The Operator Inducing a Hypnotic Trance* (1794). Engraving. Plate from *A Key to Physics*, 1794. Wellcome Library, London.

Michael Volz (?), *Thierischer Magnetismus. Eine ernste Beschäftigung für Denker und gläubige Gemüther* (1815). Etching. Wellcome Library, London.

Sémhur, *Map of the Holy Roman Empire near year 1000* (2011). Coloured map, commons.wikipedia.org [modified].

Marco Zanboli, *Map of Swabia and Burgundy, 10th/11th Cent.* (2005). Coloured map, commons.wikipedia.org [modified].

[Unknown artist], *Fr. II der Grosse mit Windhunden* (undated). Engraving [detail]. Location unknown.

Daniel Nikolaus Chodowiecki, *Spießrutenlauf* (1776). Engraving [detail]. Location unknown.

[Unknown artist], *Prussian Infantry* (undated). Engraving (?). Location unknown.
http://mapswar2.x10host.com/Prussian_army_of_Frederick_the_Great.htm.

Johann Heinrich Schmidt, *Zusammenkunft der Monarchen von Sachsen, Preußen und Österreich in Pillnitz im August 1791* (1791). Oil on canvas. Location unknown.

[Unknown artist], *Three Satyrs* (undated). Bronze tripod. Archaeological Museum, Napoli.

[Unknown artist], *Antichrist predigt im Tempel* (c.1360-70). Lead glass. Marienkirche, Frankfurt/O.

J. Pinkerton, *Map IV of the Atlas of J. Pinkerton*, trans. by C.A.Walckenaer (1804) [detail, modified]. commons.wikipedia.org

Jean Jacques André Le Veau, *Le juge, ou la cruche cassée* (c.1780). Copper engraving [detail], after a painting by Louis-Philibert Debucourt. Location unknown.

Jean-Baptiste Greuze, *La cruche cassée* (1771). Oil on canvas [detail]. Louvre.

L. Streitenfeld, *Der röm.-dt. Kaiser Franz II im Krönungsornat* (1874). Oil on canvas. Hofburg, Vienna.

Ziegelbrenner, *Karte des Rheinbundes 1806* (2010). Coloured map, based on Putzger—Historischer Weltatlas, 89. Aufl. 1965, et al [detail, modified], commons.wikipedia.org

Pierre-Joseph Tiolier (engraver), *Pièce de 20 francs émise sous Napoléon Ier en or* (1808). Gold coin. commons.wikipedia.org

[Unknown artist], *Napoleon Reviews Captured Prussian Battle Standards at Jena-Auerstedt* (undated). Oil on canvas. Location unknown.

Charles Meynier, *Napoleon in Berlin* (1810). Oil on canvas, Palais de Versailles.

[Unknown artist], *Badenweiler Gemälde der Königin Luise von Preußen und Napoleon in Tilsit* (c.1807). Landesarchiv Baden-Württemberg, Karlsruhe.

[Unknown artist], *Satyr and Goat* (c.520 BC). Attic ceramic. Location unknown.

Edouard-Henri Avril, *Ancient Greek sodomising a Goat* (1900). Colour illustration (Plate XVII) for Friedrich Karl Forberg, *De Figuris Veneris* (1st Ed. 1824) [detail]. Stapleton Collection, London.

[Unknown artist], *Der schöne Krug ist angeschlagen* (2015). Theaterrequisite. Photograph: Wolfgang-Borchert-Theater, https://www.wn.de/Welt/Kultur/2015/03/1925328-Meinhard-Zanger-spielt-den-Dorfrichter-Adam-in-Kleists-Lustspiel-Der-zerbrochne-Krug-Dem-Richter-daemmert-etwas.

[Unknown artist], *Delftware* (undated). Ceramic. Pushkin Museum, Moscow. Photograph: Shakko, commons.widipedia.org.

[Unknown artist], *Delft Schoonhoven scent bottle* (undated). Ceramic. Location unknown. Photograph: Charles J Sharpe, commons.widipedia.org.

A. Grieske (pottery), *Delft doré* (c. 1700-20). Imari-style ceramic vase. Museum Geelvinck-Hinlopen Huis, Amsterdam.

[Unknown artist], *Girandole* (19th Cent.). Ormolu and cut glass. Location unknown. Photograph: John Jason Jr. (2001), commons.wikipedia.org.

[Unknown artist], *Leyden Jar* (undated). Drawing. Location unknown. Wikiwand.com.

[Unknown artist], *Leydener Flasche* (c.1800). Drawing. Location unknown. commons.wikipedia.org.

Edwin J. Houston, *Von Kleist and the Leyden Jar*. Drawing. In: *Electricity in Everyday Life* (Collier, 1905). commons.wikipedia.org.

[Unknown artist], *Andreas Cunaeus attempts to "condense"electricity in a glass of water*). Drawing. In: Augustin Privat Deschanel, *Elementary Treatise on Natural Philosophy*, Part 3 (New York: Appleton, 1876), 570, fig. 382. commons.wikipedia.org.

[Unknown artist], *A battery of four water-filled Leyden jars* (late 18th or early 19th century). Exihibit. Museum Boerhaave, Leiden.

[Unknown artist], *Die Beschießung von Mainz von den Hochheimer Höhen aus* (c.1793). Copper engraving. http://www.festung-mainz.de/bibliothek/aufsaetze/festungsgeschichte/belagerung.html.

Zelma, *A battery of Katyusha rocket launchers firing during the Battle of Stalingrad*, 6th October 1942. Photograph. RIA Novosti Archive, image# 303890/Zelma/CC-BY-SA 3.0.

[Unknown artist], *Ulm Campaign, 26th September-19th October 1805* (undated). The Department of History, United States Military Academy [detail]. commons.wikipedia.org.

Edouard-Henri Avril, *Hadrian and Antinous; Threesome (1906)*. (1906). Colour illustrations (Plates VII and XVIII) for Friedrich Karl Forberg, *De Figuris Veneris* (1st Ed. 1824) [details, two images overlayed and replicated]. Bibliotèque nationale de France, Paris.

The Flying-Angel Painter, *Woman with Dildo* (c.490 BC). Red figure amphora. Petit Palais, Paris.

Edouard-Henri Avril, *Dildo being used by Women* (1906). Colour illustrations for Friedrich Karl Forberg, *De Figuris Veneris* (1st Ed. 1824) [detail]. Bibliotèque nationale de France, Paris.

[Unknown artist], *The Pegleg of Józef Sowiński* (c. 1807). Photograph.
Location unknown.

[Unknown artist], *Tina de Mesmer (Mesmer-Bottich, Baquet Mesmer)* (c.1784).
Metal, wood, robe. Musée d'Histoire de la Medicine et de la Pharmacie, Université Claude Bernard, Lyon.

[Unknown artist], *Baquet* (c.1780). Engraving.
Bibliotèque nationale de France, Paris.

William Hogarth, *The Five Orders of Perriwigs* (1761). Engraving. In: *The Genius of William Hogarth*.

David Teniers the Younger, *Kermis on St. George's Day* (1664-7). Oil on canvas.
Royal Collection, London.

David Teniers the Younger, *A Barn Interior* (c.1650). Oil on canvas.
Private Collection.

David Teniers the Younger, *Gesellschaft Kostumierter Affen* (undated). Oil on canvas.
Schloss Johannisburg, Aschaffenburg.

Adolph Menzel, *Sechster Auftritt* (1876-7). Woodcut-illustration for the anniversary edition of Heinrich von Kleist's *Der zerbrochne Krug*, published in Berlin by Hofmann & Co., 1877. Location unknown.

David Teniers the Younger, *Butcher Shop* (1642). Oil on canvas.
Museum of Fine Arts, Boston.

David Teniers the Younger, *In the Kitchen* (1669). Oil on canvas. Location unknown.

Peter Paul Rubens, *The Crucified Christ* (1610/11). Oil on canvas.
Royal Museum of Fine Arts, Antwerp.

Lello Scorzelli, *Papal Ferula* (1963). Photograph. Forums.catholic.com

Leonardo da Vinci, *The Virgin and Child with St. Anne* (c.1503). Oil on canvas.
Louvre, Paris.

Raphael, *Sistine Madonna* (1512). Oil on canvas. Gemäldegalerie Alte Meister, Dresden.

François Gérard, *La bataille d'Austerlitz. 2 decembre 1805* (1810). Oil on canvas (detail). Musée de Trianon, Versailles.

[Unknown artist], *Battle of Austerlitz* (undated). Coloured drawing.
Location unknown.

[Unknown artist], *Le Baquet de Mesmer* (late 18th / early 19th Cent.). Coloured engraving. Published in Physique et Chimie Populaires (magazine).
Location unknown.

[Unknown artist], *City Dionysia* (c.5th Cent. BC). Vase painting. Location unknown.

[Unknown artist], *Battle of Austerlitz* (undated). Oil on canvas.

© The Bridgeman Art Library.

[Unknown artist], *Mesmerisation* (undated). Drawing. Location unknown.

Horace Vernet, *Napoleon reviewing the Imperial Guard* (early 19th Cent.). Oil on canvas. La galerie des Batailles, Versailles.

Joh. A. Delsenbach, *Statue des Zeus in Olympia* (1725). Engraving for *Entwurff einer historischen* Architectur by Johann Bernhard Fischer von Erlach. Location unknown.

[Unknown artist], *Zeus' Eagle and Thunderbolt* (undated). Ancient Greek metal coin. Location unknown.

Berlin Painter (attributed), *Zeus* (c. 470-60 BC). Attic red figure amphora (montage of two aspects of the vase). Louvre, Paris.

Vicomte A. Reverend, *Armorial du Premier Empire* (1804). Heraldic design. Reprint. Location unknown.

Jean-Bertrand Andrieu and Louis Jaley, *Battaille D'Austerlitz* (1806). Commemorative bronze coin. Location unknown.

Jean-Auguste Dominique Ingres, *Napoleon I on his Imperial Throne* (1806). Oil on canvas. Musée de l'Armée, Paris.

Ziegelbrenner, *Karte des Rheinbundes 1808* (2007). Drawing based on Putzger—Historischer Weltatlas, 89. Aufl. 1965, et al [detail, modified]. commons.wikipedia.org

Wolfgang von Goethe, *Skizze zu Kleist's Amphitryon* (1808). Hand drawing. Location unknown.

Richard Pococke, *Sketch of the Pyramid of Cheops* (1754). Drawing. Location unknown.

Jean-Léon Gérôme, *Bonaparte devant le Sphinx* (1668). Oil on canvas. Herast Castle, San Simeon.

Antoine-Jean Gros, *Battle of the Pyramids* (1810). Oil on canvas. Palais de Versailles.

[Unknown artist], *The New French Oven* (c.1806). Coloured cartoon. Location unknown.

Alexander Altenhof, *Europe in 1812* (2012). Coloured map. commons.wikipedia.org.

[Unknown artist], *Phallic pillars* (c.300 BC). Marble. Temple of Dionysos (*Stoibadeion*), Delos. Photograph: Wikipedia, Zde (2014). commons.wikiedia.org.

D. Urrabieta Ortiz y Vierge, *Doctor Demonstrating Electrotherapy on Young Seminude Woman* (undated). Coloured pencil drawing. commons.wikipedia.org.

Ted Huntington, *Horseradish Root* (2005). Photograph. commons.wikipedia.org.

[Unknown artist], *Statue of Hermes* (undated). Roman marble after a Greek original. Vatican Museums.

[Unknown artist[, *Hermes ithyphallicos (Herm from Sifnos)* (c.520 BC). Marble. Nartional Archaeological Museum, Athens. Photograph: Wikipedia, Zde (2014). commons.wikipedia.org.

Edouard-Henri Avril, *Orgy* (1906). Colour illustrations for Friedrich Karl Forberg, *De Figuris Veneris* (1st Ed. 1824) [detail]. Bibliotèque nationale de France, Paris.

[Unknown artist], Cover art for Joh. Lorenz Böckmann, *Archiv für Magnetismus und Somnambulismus* (1787). Plate on the basis of drawing. Published in Straßburg by Akadem. Buchhandlung. Location unknown.

[Unknown artist], *Abbildung des Spinnvorgangs mit Spinnwirtel* (undated). Drawing from Meyer's Conversationslexikon. commons.wikipedia.org.

[Unknown artist], *Aiguillette* (Italian, early 19th Cent.). Silk, metal. Metropolitan Museum of Art, New York.

Pierre Lalouette, *Treatment of Syphilis by Fumigation* (1778). Drawing. Wellcome Images, commons.wikipedia.org.

[Unknown artist], *Drug Jar for Mercury Pills* (Italian, 1731-70). Earthenware Science Museum, London. Wellcome Library. commons.wikipedia.org.

[Unknown artist], *Syringe for Injection of Mercury*. Drawing. In: Henry R. Wharton, *Minor Surgery and* Bandaging (Philadelphia: Lea Bros., 1902). commons.wikipedia.org.

O. Meinke, Preußen, *Gebietsverluste zwischen 1801 and 1807*. Print. In: G. Droysens Historischer Handatlas, 1886. commons.wikipedia.org.

Franz von Stuck, *Amazone zu Pferde* (1897). Bronze. Niedersächsisches Landesmuseum, Hannover.

Jacques-Louis David, *Napoleon beim Überschreiten der Alpen am Großen Sankt Bernard* (1800). Oil on canvas. Schloss Charlottenburg, Berlin.

[Unknown artist], *Queen Luise in riding dress* (c.1810) Oil on canvas. Location unknown.

[Unknown artist], *Achilles dragging Hector's Corpse* (Greek, 160 AD). Marble sarcophagus. Archaelogical Museum, Ostia.

Franz von Matsch, *The Triumph of Achilles* (undated). Painted fresco. Achilleion, Corfu.

Gustav Eberlein, *Königin Luise und Napoleon in Tilsit* (1899). Plaster model for a statue. Restored, Welfenschloss, Münden.

Constanze Becker and Felix Rech, *Penthesilea* (2015), Dir. Michael Thalheimer, Schauspiel Frankfurt.

Jérôme Blum, *Armoiries de la République française* (2007). Colour graphic. commons.wikipedia.org.

[Unknown artist], *Amazon Warrior armed with a Labrys is seized by her Phrygian Cap* (4th Cent. AD). Mosaic. Louvre, Paris. Photograph: Jacques Mossot, commons.wikipedia.org.

Gabriel-Vital Dubray, *Penthesilea* (1862). Stone sculpture. East façade, Cour Carrée, Louvre, Paris. Photograph: Jastrow (2007). commons.wikipedia.org.

[Unknown artist], *Scythisans shooting with bows* (475-450 BC). Gold. Louvre, Paris. Photograph: PHGCOM (2007), commons.wikipedia.org.

Achim Grochowski, *Lichtbogen 3000 Volt* (2008). Photograph. commons.wikipedia.org.

[Unknown artist], *Jupiter de Smyrne* (c.250 BC). Marble [detail]. Louvre, Paris.

C. Clark, *Multiple Cloud-to-ground and Cloud-to-cloud Lightning Strokes during Night-time* (undated). Photograph. NOAA Central Library.

[Unknown artist], *De viribus electricitatis in motu musculari / Luigi Galvanis Froschschenkel-Experiment, Versuchsanordnung* (c.late 18th Cent). Engraving. Location unknown. commons.wikipedia.org.

[Unknown artist], *Giovanni Aldini, Essai theorique sur le Galvanisms* (c.late 18th or early 19th Cent.). Engravings. Wellcome Collection, #L0007024; #L0007025 [detail]; #L0029559. commons.wikipedia.org.

[Unknown artist], *White Horse with Braided Mane* (undated). Photograph. https://www.publicdomainpictures.net/en/view-imagephp?image=229043&picture=the-horse.

[Unknown artist], *Bulls-head Rhyton used for Libations* (Knossos, 1600-1400 BC). Stone (partially restored). Archaeological Museum, Heraklion. Photograph: Zde, commons.wikipedia.org.

Hans Burgkmair d.Ä. / Jost de Negker, *Das Heilige Römische Reich mit seinen Reichsständen (Quaternionenadler)* (c.1510). Hand-coloured woodcut. Published by David de Necker, Augsburg.

Robert Alfers, *Map of the Holy Roman Empire* (1789), trans. from a German original, in: Putzger-Historischer Weltatlas, 89. Aufl., 1965: kgberger. commons.wikipedia.org.

Rudolf von Alt, *Die Alte Hofburg mit Zufahrtrampe und dem Vorbau "Bellaria"* (mid 19th Cent.). Facsimile of original painting. commons.wikipedia.org.

Carl Wenzel Zajizek, *Rundpanorama Befestigungsanlagen Wiens* (c.1900). Panoramic painting [detail] commons.wikipedia.org.

John Murray, *Wiener Glacis, Basiskarte* (London, 1858) [detail, modified]. Graphic designed by Gugerell, commons.wikipedia.org [for comparison, cf. also Joseph Daniel von Huber, *Wiener Glacis 1773* (1778), by the same graphic designer).

Bernardo Belletto, *Kaiserliches Lustschloss Schönbrunn, Gartenfassade* (c. 1758-61). Oil on canvas. Kunsthistorisches Museum, Wien.

[Unknown artist] *Historische Landkarte BIXa 242 sectio 071, Josephinische Landaufnahme—Stadt Wien* (c.1775-80). Coloured map. Österr. Staatsarchiv, Kriegsarchiv, Wien (for comparison, cf. also Huber's contemporaneous map *Wiener Glacis*.

[Unknown artist], *Le Trône de Dagobert* (7th/9th Cent.). Bronze. Cabinet des Medailles, Bibliotèque nationale de France, Paris. Photograph: GFreihalter (2016, at an exhibition at Musée Cluny, Paris), commons.wikipedia.org.

[Unknown artist], *Chair in Joséphine's boudoir* (1800), Various materials. Château de Malmaison, Ruil-Malmaison. Photograph: Moonik, commons.wikipedia.org [detail].

François-Honoré-Georges Jacob-Desmalter, *Le Trône de Napoléon 1er aux Tuileries* (1804). Guilded wood, gold-thread embroidery, etc. Louvre, Paris. Photograph: P. Aleandro Diaz (2005), commons.wikipedia.org. [detail].

François-Honoré-Georges Jacob-Desmalter, *Chambre de liimpératice Marie-Louise* (1811). Guilded wood, etc. Château de Compiègne, Photograph: Andreas Praefcke (2008), commons.wikipedia.org [detail].

François-Honoré-Georges Jacob-Desmalter, *Cradle of the King of Rome* (1811). Mahogany, ormolu, etc. Château de Fountainebleau, Fontainebleau. Photograph: Basvb, commons.wikipedia.org [detail].

[Unknown artist], *Napoleon's Tomb* (undated). Mahogany, marble. Les Invalides, Paris. Photograph: Navin75 (2014), commons.wikipedia.org [detail].

Nicolas Grosse, *L'entrevue d'Erfurt, 27 septembre-14 octobre 1808* (2nd half of 19th Cent.). Oil on canvas. Palais de Versailles.

Jean-Baptiste Mauzaisse, *Bataille de Fleurus* (1837). Oil on canvas [detail]. Galerie des Batailles, Palais de Versailles.

Friedrich August von Kaulbach, *Germania* (1914). Oil on canvas. Deutsches Historisches Museum, Berlin.

George Rouget, *The Marriage of Napoleon and Marie-Louise on 2nd April 1810* (1810). Oil on canvas [detail]. Palais de Versailles.

Etienne-Barthélémy Garnier, *Le Cortège du mariage de Napoléon Ier et de l'archiduchesse Marie-Louise traversant le Jardin des Tuileries, le 2 avril 1810* (1810). Oil on canvas [detail]. Location unknown.

Johann Gottfried Schadow, *Friederike von Preußen* (1795). Gypsum. Alte Nationalgalerie, Berlin.

Tavo Romann, *Mercury escaped from broken Thermometer* (2017). Photographic image taken from video "Mercury—an alien metal," *chemicum channel* [detail]. commons.wikipedia.org.

[Unknown artist], *Verhandlung vor dem Femgericht* (c.1375). Miniature. In: Herforder Rechtsbuch. Kommunalarchiv Herford, Herford. Scan from: Wolfgang Schild, *Die Geschichte der Gerichtsbarkeit* (Hamburg: Nikol, 1997), 151 [detail, rotated].

[Unknown artist], *Geißel* (17th Cent.). Silk, wire, brass. Schatzkammer des Deutschen Ordens, Wien. Photograph: Wolfgang Sauber (2011), commons, Wikipedia.org. [detail].

Frans Hals, *Luitspelende Nar* (c.1623-4). Oil on canvas. Louvre, Paris. [detail, rotated].

Hermann Lüders, *Otto von Bismarck und Friedrich Wilhelm IV* (1848). Drawing. Location unknown.

Robert Sennecke, *Hindenburg, Kaiser, Ludendorff* (1917). Photograph [detail]. Location unknown.

[Unknown artist]. *Besuch von Hitler und Goebbels bei der UFA* (1935). Photograph [detail]. Bundesarchiv, Koblenz.

[Unknown artist], *Starting Position of a Chessgame* (2008). Wood. House of Staunton Collector Set. Photograph: Bubba73 (talk)/Jud McCranie, commons.wikipedia.org.

[Unknown artist], *Floor Goban with a game in progress* (2007). Wood. Photograph: Goban1, commons.wikipedia.org.

Jacek Filek, *Hexagonal Board for Three-handed Chess* (2010). Wood. commons.wikipedia.org.

Andreas Kaufmann, *Glinski Chess Setup* (2006). Graphic [Modified using *Experimental Standard Chess Board*, DOSGuy (2011), Commons.wikipedia.org.

Christiano64, *Le campagne di Druso in Germania, 12-9 a.C.* (2007). commons.wikipedia.org [detail, modified].

Alexander G. Findlay, *Germania* (1849). In: A Classical Atlas of Ancient Geography (New York: Harper, 1849). commons.widipedia.org.

Sir Adolphus William Ward et al, *French Empire and Central Europe in 1811* (1812). In: Cambridge Modern History Atlas, 1912. Perry-Castañeda Map Collection. commons.wikipedia.org.

Charles William Mitchel, *Hypatia* (1885). Oil on canvas. Laing Art Gallery, Newcastle upon Tyne.

Georg Heinrich Rudolf Johann von Reiswitz, *Kriegsspiel* (1824). Printed paper, wood. Reconstruction by Matthew Kirschenbaum (2016), commons.wikipedia.org.

Georg Heinrich Rudolf Johann von Reiswitz, *Table used to track Casulties*, in: Anleitung zur Darstellung militärischer Manöver mit dem Apparat des Kriegsspiels (1824). commons.wikipedia.org.

Ryzom, *An Event in he MMORPG Ryzom* (2014). Screenshot. commons.wikipedia.org.

[Unknown artist], *19ᵗʰ Century War Room of the U.S. Navy*. Drawing. In: Charles Morris, *From 1800 to 1900* (Chicago: A.B. Kuhlmann, 1899), commons.wikipedia.org.

[Unknown artist], *The Map Room of the Cabinet War Rooms* (c.1940), Replica. Churchill War Rooms Museum, London. Photograph: Kaihsu Tai/Silk Tork (derivative work), commons.wikipedia.org.

China Crisis, *Model of the War Room in Stanley Kubrik's* [1964 film] *Dr. Strangelove* (2012). Various materials. commons.wikipedia.org.

U.S. Air Force, *NORAD Command Center, Cheyenne Mountain*, Colorado. (c.2005). Photograph. commons.wikipedia.org.

Martin Didier Pape, *Medea's Murder of Abyrtus* (French, c.1580-1600). Painted enamel on copper plaque [detail]. Walters Art Museum, Baltimore.

Georges Moreau de Tours, *The Murder of Pelias by His Daughters* (1878). Oil on Canvas [detail]. Location unknown.

Cristofano Allori, *Judith with the Head of Holophernes* (1613). Oil on Canvas [detail]. Royal Collection, London.

H.R. Hopps, *Destroy this mad Brute—Enlist U.S. Army* (c.1917). Printed poster [detail]. commons.wikipedia.org.

[Unknown artist], *Stop this Monster at Stops at Nothing—Produce to the Limit. This is your War* (c.1941-5). Printed poster [detail]. National Archives, College Park.

NordNordWest, *Karte der Landschaften von Deutschland* (2008). Coloured map, based on Nationalatlas Bundesrepublik Deutschland, Bd.1 (Leipzig: Spektrum, 1999) et al.; shading by Lencer [detail, modified], commons.wikipedia.org.

[Unknown artist], *Sprachenkarte Deutschland 1880*. Scan (colours touched up) of a coloured drawing in Andree's Hausatlas, 1881 [detail, modified], commons.wikipedia.org.

Ziegelbrenner, *Karte des Deutschen Reiches 1871-1918* (2008). Coloured map, based on Putzger—Historischer Weltatlas, 89. Aufl. 1965, et al [detail, modified], commons.wikipedia.org

Ziegelbrenner, *Karte des Deutschen Bundes 1815-66* (2008). Coloured map, based on Putzger—Historischer Weltatlas, 89. Aufl. 1965, et al [detail, modified], commons.wikipedia.org

Hans Braxmeier, *Central Europe Relief Map with Waterbodies and Borders* (2012). Coloured map [detail, modified], commons.wikipedia.org.

Dorothy Hardy, *The Dises*. Illustration, in H.A. Guerber, Myths of the Norsemen. London: Harrap, 1909.

John Collier, *Priestess of Delphi* (1891). Oil on canvas. Art Gallery of South Australia, Adelaide.

Pierre-Paul Prud'hon, *Justice and Divine Vangeance* (1808). Oil on canvas. Louvre, Paris.

Carolus, *Grand Escalier en double fer-à-cheval, Cour du cheval blanc, Château de Fontainebleau* (2006). Photograph [detail]. commons.wikipedia.org.

Nemanja Stijak, *The Château de Fontainebleau, south-eastern Aspect* (2005). Photograph [detail]. commons.wikipedia.org.

Heralder, *Grand Coat of Arms of Joseph Napoléon Bonaparte as Spanish Monarch* (2010). Colour graphic, commons.wikipedia.org.

Tom Lemmens, *Coat of Arms of Kingdom of Holland* (2013). Colour graphic, commons.wikipedia.org.

Mathieu Chaine, *Grande armes de Jérôme Bonaparte* (2012). Colour graphic, commons.wikipedia.org.

Mathieu Chaine, *Grand Coat of Arms of Eugène de Beauharnais as Viceroy of Italy* (2012). Colour graphic, commons.wikipedia.org.

Jimmy 44, Sodacan, *Coat of Arms of Joachim Murat as Grand-Duke of Cleves and Berg* (2011). Colour graphic, commons.wikipedia.org.

Jimmy 44 et al, *Great Coat of Arms of Joachim Murat as King of Naples* (2010). Colour graphics, commons.wikipedia.org.

Spedona, Sodacan, *Greater Arms of the First French Empire, Heralic Crown Variant* (2012), Colour graphic based on Vicomte A. Reverend, *Amorial du Premier Empire* (1804), ommons.wikipedia.org.

Hugo Gerhard Ströhl, *Familienwappen Habsburg*. Lithography, in: *Wappenrolle Österreich-Ungarns*, 1. Aufl. (Wien: Anton Schroll & Co, 1890), Tafel II.

Alphathon, *Carte du Premier Empire en 1812* (2012). Based on maix, Blank map of Europe. Commons.wikipedia.org [detail, modified].

Karl Spruner von Merz, Heinrich Theodor Menke, *Napoleons Feldzug in Russland*. Drawing. In: Hand-Atlas für die Geschichte des Mittelalters und der neueren Zeit, 3. Aufl. (Gotha: Justus Perthes, 1880) [modified].

Charles Minard, *La Campagne de Russie 1812-1813* (1869). Lithography [detail, modified]. Location unknown.

Auguste-Henri Dufour, *Carte de l'Empire Français 1812* (1865). Engraving by Ch. Dyonnet, Paris. David Ramsey Map Collection [detail, modified].

[Unknown artist], *Golden Laurel Wreath* (Hellenistic era). Goldleaf. Kerameikos Archaeological Museum, Athens. Photograph: Jebulon (2016) [detail].

[Unknown artist], *All-seeing eye* (1766). Entrance of the Baptistery, Aachen Cathedral. Photograph: Trexer (2005) [detail], commons.wikipedia.org.

[Unknown artist], *Pyramid with the all-seeing eye, back side of the 1 US dollar bill.* Graphic: Verwüstung (2009), commons.wikipedia.org.

Angelo Monticelli, *The Shield of Achilles* (c.1820). Colour illustration in *Le Costume Ancien ou Moderne*.

[Unknown artist], *Querschnitt des Pantheons in Rom*, i: Wilhelm Lübke, Max Semrau: *Grundriß der Kunstgeschichte* (14th Ed.).
Esslingen: Paul Neff Verlag, 1908.

Giorgio Vasari/Federico Zucari, *Juicio Final* (1597-9). Fresco. Santa Maria del Fiore, Firenze. Photograph: LIvioandronico2013 (2016), commons.wikipedia.org.

Jeremy Bentham, Willey Reveley (architect), E*levation, Section and Plan for the Panopticon* (1791). Architectural drawing, in: The Works of Jeremy Bentham, Vol. IV, 172-3 (1843).

Robert Mitchell, *Section of the Rotunda, Leicester Sqare, in which is exhibited the Panorama* (1801). Colour drawing. Location unknown.

Theodor Hosemann, *Kinder an einem Guckkasten*. Illustration for Adolph Glasbrenner, 'Guckkästen,' in *Berlin: wie es ist und—trinkt* (Leipzig: Vetter und Rostosky, 1835).

Louis Poyel, *Cinéorama Balloon Simulation at the 1900 Paris Exposition* (1900). Illustration, in: Scientific American Supplement #1287.

Zaiton, *La Géode, Park de la Vilette, Paris* (2017). Photograph. commons.wikipedia.org.

Maintechuser, *VR headset* (2018). Photograph. commons.wikipedia.org.

Caspar David Friedrich, *Der Mönch am Meer* (1810). Oil on canvas. Alte Nationalgalerie, Dresden.

Gustave Doré, *Dante and Beatrice gaze upon the highest Heaven, The Empyrean*. Engraving, in: Dante Alighieri, *Canto XXXI, The Divine Comedy*, Henry Francis (Ed.), London: Cassell & Co. 1892.

Carl Gustav Carus, *Die Teufelskanzel auf dem Brocken* (1811). Drawing. Nationalgalerie von Norwegen, Oslo.

Ernst Wilhelm Knippel, *Aussicht von der Schneekoppe nach Norden, Osten, Süden, Westen* (c.1840-55). Lithographies, retouched. Muzeum Karkonoskie, Jelenia Góra (Hirschberg im Riesengebirge).

Carl Theodor Matthis, *Die Schneekoppe, von den Grenzbauden gesehen* (1815). Etching. Location unknown.

Emil Neumann, *Wrack eines Segelbootes bei der Insel Rügen* (1885-90). Painting on paper. Museumslandschaft Hessen, Kassel.

Malthe-Brun, *Thoun* (1856). Engraving. British Library, London.

Hubert Berberich, *Rheinpanorama, Blick vom Niederwalddenkmal by Rüdesheim* (2004). Composite photograph, commons.wikipedia.org.

Johann Jakob Wetzel, Conrad Caspar Rordorf, *Scherzligen bei Thun, von Nordwesten* (undated). Engraving. Swiss National Library, Bern.

Armin Kübelbeck, *Das Amphitheater von Nîmes (Innenraum)* (2008). Composite photograph. commons.wikipedia.org.

[Unknown artist], *Thun, Blick on der Burg Richtung Thunersee* (c.1900). Coloured lithograph [detail, modified]. Library of Congress, Washington D.C.

[Unknown artist], *Dionysostheater* (undated). Etching. In: Joseph Kürschner, *Pierers Konversationslexikon*, 7th Ed., Stuttgart: Deutsche Verlagsgesellschaft, 1891. commons.wikipedia.org.

Giovanni Battista Piranesi, *Veduta dell'Anfiteatro Flavio detto il Colosseo* (c.1760s-70s). Etching. Location unknown.

Willem Swanenurgh (engraver), *Theatrum anatomicum van Leidse Academie*, 1609 (1644). Engraving. Reijksmuseum, Amsterdam.

Carl Gotthard Langhans (architect), *Tieranatomisches Theater* (1789/90, reconstruction 2012), Humboldt-Universität Berlin. Photograph by Matthias Heyde (2012), commons.wikipedia.org.

[Unknown artist], *Interior of La Fenice* (1837). Coloured drawing. Museo Correr, Venezia.

Marco Ammon, *Debating Chamber, European Parliament* (2015). Photograph, commons.wikipedia.org

Frank Gehry (architect), *Pierre-Boulez-Saal* (2017), Barenboim-Said-Akademie, Berlin. Photograph: Jroepsdorff (2017) [detail], commons.wikipedia.org.

Joh. Conrad Felsing, *Stadt und Festung Mainz* (1815). Engraving. Stadtarchiv Mainz.

Matthäus Merian, *Panorama von Würzburg* (1642). Engraving. Peace Palace Library, The Hague.

Giulio Parigi, *Archimedes' Mirror* (c.1600). Wall painting. Uffizi, Firenze.

Ray Vaughn Pierce, *A Doctor using a Head Mirror* (19th Cent.). In: *The People's Common Sense Medical Advisor in Plain English* (Project Gutenberg), commons.wikipedia.org.

Ehrenfried Walther von Tschirnhaus, *Sphärischer Brennspiegel* (1686). Metal, wood. Zwinger, Dresden. Photograph: Derbrauni (2013), commons.wikipedia.org.

Johann Carl Richter, *Die Athener Propyläen und das Brandenburger Tor* (c.1795). Engraving. Berlin Museum, Berlin.

Franz L. Close, *Juliane Ulrike von Kleist mit dem siebenjährigen Heinrich* (?) (c.1784). Miniatur. Location unknown. In: Hans-Georg Schede, *Heinrich von Kleist* (Reinbeck: Rowolt, 2008), 13. http://www.heinrich-von-kleist.org/kleist_stammbaum_portal/en/juliane_en.html.

Jacob Wilhelm Mechau, *Portrait of the young Heinrich von Kleist* (?) (c.1792). Pastel on canvas. Location unknown. In: Hans-Georg Schede, *Heinrich von Kleist* (Reinbeck: Rowolt, 2008), 17. Cf. also http://www.pastellists.com/Articles/Mechau.pdf.

[Unknown artist], *Bildnis des etwa achzehnjährigen Kleist* (?) (c.1795). Painting. Staatsbibliothek zu Berlin—Preußischer Kulturbesitz, Berlin. In: Hans-Georg Schede, *Heinrich von Kleist* (Reinbeck: Rowolt, 2008), 3.

Giomo2, *Im Wieland-Museum in Oßmannstedt* (2007). Photograph [detail], commons.wikipedia.org.

Henry H. Robinson, *A Galvanized Corpse* (1836). Drawing. Library of Congress, Washington D.C.

Johann Heinrich Schröder, *August Wilhelm Iffland* (early 19th Cent.). Pastell on carton (detail, modified, rotated). Schloss Wahn, Köln.

Johann Heinrich Wihelm Tischbein, *Karl August von Hardenberg* (early 19th Cent.). Oil on canvas (detail, modified). Location unknown.

[Unknown artist], *Dornauszieher* (Roman, AD 150, after a Greek original.3rd Cent. BC). Marble. Altes Museum, Berlin. Photograph: Anagoria, commons.wikipedia.org.

[Unknown artist], *Wappen derer von Kleist, von Pannwitz, von Schönfeld, von Klitzing, von Massow, von Massenbach, von Loeben, von Einsiedel*, in: *Genealogisches Handbuch des Adels* (Bad Salzdetfurth: Stark Verlag, 1960-2002).

François-Honoré-Georges Jacob-Desmalter, *Le Trône de Napoléon 1er pour le Sénat* (1804). Guilded wood, gold-thread embroidery, etc. [detail]. Palais du Luxembourg, Paris.

[Unknown artist], *Ulrike von Kleist* (early 19th Cent.). Copy from a Miniature. Location unknown.

[Unknown artist), *Adolphine von Werdeck* (c.1840). Painting. Location unknown.

Lulu Gräfin von Stosch, *Marie von Kleist auf dem Sterbebett* (1832). Drawing. Location unknown.

[Unknown artist], *Wilhelmine von Zenge* (c.1800). Drawing based on a miniature. Location unknown.

[Unknown artist], Karoline von Günderrode (c.1800). Painting. Location unknown.

Emma Körner, *Selbstbildnis* (1813). Painting. Städtische Galerie, Dresden.

Johann Heinrich Wilh. Tischbein, *Sophie Kunze* (early 19th Cent.). Oil on canvas. Location unknown.

Dora Stock, *Selbstbildnis* (1795). Painting. Kügelgenhaus, Dresden.

Moritz Daffinger, *Rahel Levin* (c.1800). Painting. Location unknown.

Elisabeth von Staegemann, *Selbstportrait* (1808). Painting, in: Margarete von Olfers, *Elisabeth von Staegemann* (Leipzig, 1937).

Joseph Nicolaus Peroux, *Henriette Hendel-Schütz* (1809). Engraving. Museumserver
Schleswig-Holstein.

Briseis Painter, *Apollon et Artémis* (Attic, c.470 BC). Red-figure cup. Louvre.

Byrgos Painter, *Alkaios und Sappho* (Sicilian, c.470 BC). Red-figure kalathos.
Staatliche Antikensammlung, München.

Alexandre Lenoir, *Tombeau de Abélard et Héloïse* (1817). Stonework. Cemetière Père
Lachaise, Paris. Photograph: Pierre-Yves Beaudouin (2012),
commons.wikipedia.org.

Édouard-Henri Avril, *Foursome* and *Orgy* (1906). Colour illustrations for Friedrich
Karl Forberg, *De Figuris Veneris* (1st Ed. 1824) [details].
Bibliotèque nationale de France, Paris.

[Unknown artist], *Ithyphallic Man with a Harp* (3rd-4th Cent. AD). Terracotta.
Brooklyn Museum, New York.

William Henry Smith, *The Great Comet of 1811* (1811). Drawing, in: Amedee
Guillemin, *The Heavens* (London: 1886).

Simon Vouet, *Marie-Madelaine portée par les anges* (first half 17th Cent.). Oil on
canvas (reproduction) [detail]. Musée des Beaux-Arts et d'archéologie,
Besançon. Photograph: G. Garitan (2019), commons.wikipedia.org.

[Unknown artist], *Throne of the Archon* (3rd. Cent. AD). Marble. Theatre of
Dionysos, Athens. Photograph: DerHexer, 2008, commons.wikipedia.org.

Endnotes

1   Cf. Matthias Goertz, *The Emigrant, the Emperor, the King and Everybody's Favourite Queen: The Satirical and Satyrical Novellas of Heinrich von Kleist* (New York: Atropos, 2018), *passim*. In ancient Greece before the emergence of the philosophers *theologia*, "speaking about gods," was the privilege of the poets, and so was public parody of political leaders. Kleist claimed for himself this "poetic license," this aristocratic "birthright," to irreverently "speak truth to power." With his "Kant-crisis" he shifted his focus from the "study of philosophy" (aiming at making sense of the world) to the "practice of poetry" (aiming at manipulating it). Among Kleist's forerunners in recognising the phenomenon of a single word's multiple significations was the scholastic philosopher Pierre Abélard (whose urn Kleist visited in Paris), who in his early 12th Cent. treatise *Sic et Non* exploits it as a means of reconciling apparently contradictory statements by the Church Fathers. I took the term *"pescherä"* from Kleist's April 1809 *Brief eines politischen Pescherä* (which could have been meant as preamble or user manual to *Germania* in the manner of *Prolog* for *Phöbus* and *Gebet des Zoroaster* for *BA*, with the "political *Pescherä*" who authored it being Kleist himself), in which he relates a story of indigenous people living at the southern tip of Tierra del Fuego, upon sighting French explorers landing on their shores, repeatedly shout *"pescherä,"* a word they subsequently repeatedly use during attempts at socialising, whereupon the French explorers take the word to have multiple meanings depending on the context, and name these people Pescheré (today they are known to have been the Haush people, who became extinct c.1920; the term *"pescheré"* is believed to mean "peace" or "friend"). Kleist, who, Sembdner notes, could have come across this anecdote in C.E. Wünsch's treatise *Unterhaltungen über den Menschen*, Vol.1 (1796), 141ff. (cf. II:936), or his lectures based on it, deduced from it a general theory of the *plasticity of the word*, and I adopt his Germanised term *"pescherä"* to signify his systematic use of polysemies in constructing his multi-threaded texts. On this matter Kleist himself wrote that *"die ganze Finesse, die den Dichter ausmacht"* is that he *"auch das sagen [kann], was er nicht sagt"* (II:757), Chr. Martin Wieland noted, *"Unter mehreren Sonderlichkeiten, die an ihm auffallen mußten, war eine seltsame Art der Zerstreuung, wenn man mit ihm sprach, so daß* zum Beispiel *ein einziges Wort eine ganze Reihe von Ideen in seinem Gehirn, wie ein Glockenspiel anzuziehen schien"* (*LS*,89), and L. Tieck recalled, *"Dann fiel ein unbedeutendes Wort, auf welches niemand Wert legte, aber ihn berührte es in unbegreiflicher Weise"* (quoted in Hans Dieter Zimmermann, *Kleist, die Liebe und der Tod,* Frankfurt/M.: Athenäum, 1989, 168);

more recently, Heinz Ide states, *"daß wir uns hüten müssen, die von Kleist gebrauchten Worte so zu verstehen, wie seine Zeit sie meinte,"* a stuggestion Hans Joachim Kreutzer, who quotes Ide in *Die Dichterische Entwicklung Heinrich von Kleists* (Berlin: Erich Schmidt, 1968), 47, dismisses as "absurdity," while acknowledging a "terminological fuzziness" in Kleist's writing. Ide in fact hits on something eminently important: that Kleist's terms are not (only) to be read in their generally accepted meaning. Kreutzer's error in warning his readers not to fasten a "logical coherent system of precise notions" onto Kleist is that while there is indeed not *one* such "system" in Kleist, I argue that there are *several* of them, each of them individually coherent, yet their interwovenness into a complex texture conveying a superficial impression of "terminological fuzziness." Bernd Hamacher anticipates some of my own findings, *"Bei Goethe muss zwischen einer 'offiziellen' und einer 'verdeckten' Semantik unterschieden werden. Seine 'offiziellen' Konzepte sind relative klar und zwar complex, aber vergleichsweise einfach zu identifizieren. Bei Kleist ist die 'offizielle' Semantik aufgrund der gezielt herbeigeführten Mehrdeutigkeiten gewissermassen verrätselt und verborgen, seine 'verdeckte' Semantik aber keine andere als die 'offizielle'. Beide sind ineinandergeschoben und verschmolzen, nicht eine hinter der anderen versteckt wie bei Goethe"* (*KH*,218), making the important distinction between Goethe *saying things "between the lines,"* Kleist *saying several things within a single line*. Hamacher's terms *"offiziell"* and *"verdeckt"* anticipate my terms *"overt"* and *"covered,"* and although he was not my inspiration, I acknowledge that he arrived at them before me; his terms *"ineinandergeschoben"* ("blended") and *"verschmolzen"* ("fused") are furthermore similar to my term "interwoven," although I consider my term more apt, as it emphasises that Kleist's individual "threads" remain intact within his textual fabric and can therefore be "unraveled," which is typically not possible with the product of a process of fusion or blending, a process that often is irreversible, or reversible only with complex procedures. If Hamacher does not seem to systematically apply his profound discovery regarding Kleist's *technique* to his works—he finds the barrow, gets himself a shovel, but does not dig—then this may be so precisely because he perceives in them the result of a process of fusion or blending, reversing which would require not a (Foucauldian) archaeology but a chemical dialysis. Luckily for us Kleist does not *fuse*, but *interweaves*, and the textual fabric produced by his interveawing of multiple "threads" can always in principle, and often in practice, be "unravelled" (in *Emigrant* I refer to Freud's "navel" in *Traumdeutung*, the "navel" being an auspicious or awkward term or incident, commencing from which a dream's veiled meaning can be unravelled). Kleist encrypts but does not mystify; everything in his writings follows traceable patterns and rules, nothing is lost or deferred to random effects; he camouflages, but apparent indiscernibilities and incommensurabilities generated by this process of encryption in preinciple always remai discernible and reversible.

2   Cf. e.g., Beda Allemann, "Der Nationalismus Heinrich von Kleists," in: Walter Müller-Salget (Ed.), *Kleists Aktualität* (Darmstadt: Wissenschaftliche, 1981), 51: *"darf nicht zu der Annahme verleiten, daß es Kleist beim Schreiben in erster Linie um Inhalte und Gesinnungen tendenziöser Art, um bestimmte Überzeugungen und eine ausformulierte Weltanschauung gegangen sei. Kleist nimmt in seinem Werk relative selten persönlich Stellung zu dem, was geschieht oder erzählt wird."* Allemann is correct in so far as Kleist's narrators rarely comment on the *overt* plot; to deduce from this that Kleist's writing *tout court* does not reflect his "tendentious convictions" and "world view" is misguided: Kleist's work is a "personal statement" through and through. Similarly misguided is Gerhard Schulz when he claims, in *Kleist. Eine Biographie* (München: C.H. Beck, 2011), 317-18, that *"Kleist [war] kein politischer Mensch. So leidenschaftlich ihn politisches Geschehen zuweilen ergreifen und zur Parteinahme locken mochte, so interessierte es ihn letztlich doch nur in dem Maße, in dem es seine Arbeit, seine Selbstentfaltung als Dichter förderte oder behinderte... Das Reservoir an Stoffen, Themen und Gestalten, das er mit seinen Werken im Kopf und auf dem Papier nach Dresden mitbrachte, hatte mit Politik im engeren Sinne nichts zu tun und schon gar nichts mit der Tagespolitik... Als leidenschaftlicher deutscher Patriot hatte Kleist sich bisher durchaus nicht gezeigt, aber diese gewaltsame Störung seiner Lebenspläne ["die Franzosen, die ihm seine Pläne durcheinander-gebracht... hatten"]... legte das Fundament dafür, daß im Laufe seiner Dresdner Tage allmählich ein bedingunsloser Haß gegen Napoleon zum Ausdruck drängte. Nur gab es dafür zunächst weder Anlaß noch unmittelbares Bedürfnis im friedlichen Dresden, ganz abgesehen davon, daß die politischen Treuepflichten und Anhänglichkeiten in dieser schwankenden Zeit ohnehin mitschwankten und zumeist eher dem Land als dem Reich galten."* Au contraire, Kleist chose to become a poet not least *because* of his interest in politics, and the practical considerations Schulz emphasises, while not irrelevant, were secondary to Kleist, whose works concern world politics, not mundane *"Tagespolitik."* Kleist was a passionate *Reichspatriot*, did not hate the French, and was also a cosmopolitan European; he did not feel "unconditional hatred" for Napoleon, some of whose achievements he could not help but admire—if anything, he hatred those German leaders most, who forfaited *Reichs*-territories, switched sides, and allowed the *HRR* to implode. Though perhaps more a Reichs- than a Prussian patriot, he remained loyal

to the House of Hohenzollern, whose scions he considered the most suitable leaders of a united Germany.

3   Already in early 1798 Kleist composed a letter to his King in which he layed out reasons for a young officer to quit the service. He did not post the letter because he was not sufficiently confident that his argument was watertight or his delivery effective (cf. II:478); nevertheless, this letter marked a first step in Kleist's development as *satirical* writer, as political bard and advisor to this King. The letter to Martini of March 1799 (in which he mentions the letter to the King) may serve as proxy for the argument and language he deployed in the uposted letter. Formal and measured, almost pedantic, it is carefully constructed to lead the reader to the inexorable conclusion, and while it underweights the *pescheräic* technique Kleist had already explored in the letter to Ulrike of 1795 (*"die Zeit, die wir hier so umoralisch töten"*, cf. my discussion further below) and fully brought to bear in his *Aufsatz* for Rühle, it already includes *po(i)etic* innovations such as the staccato sentence *"Man fragte... Man lächelte... Man sagte... Man stellte...; man zeigte... Man malte..."* (II:482) that vividly conveys his exasperation at his family. Kleist's letter to his King, and later his *satirical* manifestos and scenarios, rest on a long tradition in literature, notably the genre of *specula principum* or "mirror for princes," in which (self-appointed) commentators or courtiers offer advise or self-help manuals to an often young, inexperienced prince who is about to ascend, or recently ascended, the throne (as did Fr. Wilh. III in November 1797, i.e., only briefly before Kleist's unposted letter); prominent examples include Cicero's *De Officiis* (44 BC), John of Salisbury's *Policraticus* (c.1159), Machiavelli's *Il Principe* (c.1513), Castiglione's *Il Cortegio* (1528) (Kleist's manifestos also parallel the *Denkschriften* (memoranda) addressed to the King by courtiers and reformers, the likes of Stein, Hardenberg and Gneisenau).

4   Peter Sloterdijk, *Kritik der zynischen Vernunft* (Frankfurt/M.: Suhrkamp, 1983), 76-7. Sloterdijk juxtaposes (*ibid*, 203-5; 246; 278) classical cynicism (*"Kynismus"*) and its modern corruption (*"Zynismus"*), and I offer that antique *"kynicism"* thus delineated from "cynicism" can be ascribed to Kleist almost without reserve: *"Der antike Kynismus ist... prinzipiell frech. In seiner Frechheit liegt... Methode. Zu Unrecht wird [er] als bloßes Satyrspiel, als halb lustige, halb schmutzige Episode betrachtet... So kreiert [Diogenes] eine grobianische Aufklärung. Er eröffnet den nicht-platonischen Dialog. Hier zeigt Apollon, der Gott der Erleuchtung, sein anderes Gesicht, das Nietzsche entging: als denkender Satyr, als Schinder, als Komödiant. Die*

tödlichen Pfeile schlagen ein, wo sich die Lügen hinter Autoritäten in Sicherheit wiegen... Kynismus... ist die Lebensphilosophie der Krise... Der kynische Blick versteht sich als Durchblicken eines lächerlichen und hohlen Scheins. Er möchte die Gesellschaft vor einen natürlichen Spiegel stellen, in dem sich die Menschen unverhüllt und ohne Maske erkennen." Diogenes of Sinpope (412 or 404-323 BC) was the most famous exponent of the classical philosophical school of the Cynics. Sloterdijk points out (*ibid*, 206) that *"Frechheit"* ("cheekiness") in Old High German had a positive connotation, *"eine produktive Aggressivität, Rangehen an den Feind: 'tapfer, kühn, lebhaft, keck, ungezähmt, begierig'."* The English idiom "to have the cheek to do s.th." may reflect this earlier use. When Achim calls Kleist "den unbefangensten, fast cynischen Menschen" (*LS*,347) he is in my view wrong on both accounts.

5   What, if anything, Kleist's *"Ideenmagazin"* entailed remains debated; cf. Helmut Sembdner (Ed.), *Kleist. Geschichte meiner Seele. Das Lebenszeugnis der Briefe* (Frankfurt/M.: Insel, 1980), XIII. I imagine that Kleist kept a carton box or file with items for future use—letters, documents, notes, sketches, snippets, reminders, etc. One could also consider his œuvre as such as his *"Ideenmagazin,"* for he constantly recycles and adopts ideas, themes and passages from one palimpsestic work to another.

6   A figure like Honoré Gabriel Riqueti, comte de Mirabeau fascinated Kleist on various fronts: a hugely popular orator, at one point leader of the revolution, and presumed syphiliac, he also wrote *"Literatur in flagranti"* and *"pornographische Aufklärungsbücher"* (cf. Sloterdiijk, *Kritik*, 101-2). Kleist's mentor Chr. M. Wieland was one of Germany's foremost Shakespeare translators, as well as a translator of Aristophanes, Lucian, and other classic satirists, and Kleist will have learned much about the master of Old Comedy and the great English bard during conversations with him at Oßmannstedt in the winter of 1802/3. Kleist had already read Shakespeare in 1800/1 (cf. Loch, *Kleist*, 521) and possibly earlier (presumably in German trans.), borrowed works by Aristophanes, Sophokles and Euripides from the Dresden library in June 1803, including Aristophanes' *Clouds* in the 1798 trans. by Chr. Gottfried Schütz (cf. *LS*,103b; *MA*III, 829), and will have encountered many of the classics already during his secondary education. Adam Müller publishes the essay *"Ironie, Lustspiel, Aristophanes"* In the April/May 1808 issue of *Ph*; in 1809 Kleist traverses Bohemia with Fr. Chr. Dahlmann, who had furnished a new trans. of *Clouds*, a fragment of which had been slated for publication in *Ph* (cf. *AML*,376). Aristophanes having obviously been "in the air" makes it all the more surprising that

Kleist scholars have largely overlooked or ignored his influence on Kleist, merely mentioning him as one among many classical influences, or not at all. As a minor but telling example of Aristphanes' pervasive and multi-faceted influence on Kleist, consider the famous subtitle for *Marquise*, "*vom Norden in den Süden verlegt worden*," in light of the following lines in *Clouds* (213-15): "STREPSIADES. But where [on the map] is Sparta? / PUPIL. Where it is? Ah, over here! / STREPSIADES. So close? You'd better think about that some more, and move them a whole lot farther away from us." Helmut Sembdner, exceptionally, in *In Sachen Kleist*, Heilbronn: Kleist-Archiv Sembdner, 2014, 68, traces a slew of Kleistian expressions to *Clouds*; still, by adding (*ibid*, 69-75) that the satirical letters and essays by the then popular 18th century writer Gottlieb Wilhelm Raberner likely influenced on Kleist, who could have been introduced to these works by his friend Joh. Daniel Falk, who himself was editor of the *Taschenbuch für Freunde des Scherzes und der Satyre* (1797–1803) and known for his snappy humour, Sembdner somewhat dilutes his discovery of Aristophanes' importance for Kleist—which, I argue, cannot be emphasise enough. Eberhard Siebert, in *Kleistiana Collecta* (Heilbronn: Kleist-Archiv Sembdner, 2011), 103-111 and 240-50, investigates Kleist's possible debt to Mozart, especially parallels between *Käthchen* and *Zauberflöte*, suggesting that Kleist could have observed the opera in 1795 in Potsdam (*ibid*, 103) or in 1801 as private performance in the Körners' or Schliebens' house (*ibid*, 243-4). Sloterdijk's quotation (*Kritik*, 320) of Otto Seel is instructive regarding Lucian: "*wurde Lukian (geb. ca. 120 n. Chr.) Rhetor, ein Metier, wofür unsere Zeit kaum eine Parallele bietet und das man nicht unpassend mit 'Konzertredner' wiedergegeben hat. So zog er... durch die Lande,... hielt Schau- und Prunkreden.*" Fr. Aug. Laun in his memoires terms A. Müller's speeches "rhapsodic" (*AML*,35) and notes paradoxes as a Müllerian passion (which he evidently shared with Kleist). The following Wikipedia explores the motivations of medieval troubadours: "The messenger was commonplace in troubadour poetry; many songs reference a messenger who will bring it to its intended ear. A troubadour often stayed with a noble patron of his own and entertained his court with his songs. Court songs could be used not only as entertainment but also as propaganda, praising the patron, mocking his enemies, encouraging his wars, teaching ethics and etiquette, and maintaining religious unity"—cf. https://en.wikipedia.org/wiki/Troubadour#Genres; one could scarcely come up with a more succinct description of Kleist's own project!

7   For simplicity, I omit the *accent aigu* in the case of Napoléon Bonaparte's name. Regarding Kleist's stance towards Fr. Wilh's temporising, I offer that it was more

nuanced and situational than that of certain fellow observers who labelled the King *"Zauderer"* ("cunctator") and joked that his favourite time was deliberation time: for Kleist, what defined a leader was an ability to seize a *kairotic* moment, i.e, the moment most opportune for a strike, even if this meant to wait until it arrived: he may well have had his King in mind when in a letter to Zschokke of 1st February 1802 he referred to the "famous cuncator" Quintus Fabius Maximus whose delay and guerrilla tactics wore down the great Hannibal.

8   Kleist's oak paradox appears in slight variations in several letters and dramas, e.g., *Schroffenstein* V.505-7 and *Penthesilea* V.144-9 and V.3040-3, the latter perhaps being its most famous version: *"Sie sank, weil sie zu stolz und kräftig blühte! / Die abgestorbne Eiche steht im Sturm, / Doch die gesunde stürzt er schmetternd nieder, / Weil er in ihre Krone greifen kann."* Satirically, the paradox conveys Kleist's hope that the "proud and strong" Napoleon will eventually succumb to the "storm" of the German resistance, while the "necrotic" Prussian King will prevail. Joh. von Müller, in a letter to Adam Müller of June 1805, deploys a similar oak metaphor, *"lassen Sie hundert Stämme der Deutschen… in Einen Pfeiler des Weltreichs schwinden,—es ist aus mit Europa… nie wieder sproßte die ungeheure Eiche, zu der im Sturm die Völker flüchteten"* (AML,113; *"Stamm"* = "tribe" as well as "trunk"; *"Weltreich"* = Napoleon's empire; *"Eiche"* = "Germany"; *"Sturm"* = "war"), suggesting that this metaphorical field was current and not unique to Kleist. Kleist elsewhere (cf. II:820) deploys an analogous metaphor, of the giant Antäus who is reinvigorated each time he is thrown to the ground in a wrestling match and touches Mother Earth: Antäus = Fr. Wilh. or Germany; his opponent = Napoleon.

9   Other prominent political figures who make appearances include, e.g., Franz II/I, Alex. I, the Saxon and Bavarian Electors/Kings, Eugène de Beauharnais, Berthier, Prince Wilh. of Prussia, Archduke Carl, Hardenberg, Marie-Louise of Austria. My reading of the political Kleist has affninities with Horst Häker's (cf. *Emigrant*, n.487), while being at odds with Gerhard Schulz's, who vehemently opposes the idea of there being any "key" to Kleist's works, a stance that in my view severely hampers him—cf. Schulz, "Heinrich von Kleist, oder Die Reise um die Welt," in Yixu Lü et al (Ed.), *Wissensfiguren im Werk Heinrich von Kleists* (Freiburg i. Br.: Rombach, 2012), 13: *"scheint es für mich eine nützliche, ja nötige Aufgabe der Literaturwissenschaft zu sein, Kleist nicht "entschlüsseln" zu wollen, sondern ihn vielmehr vor Missbrauch durch oft recht grobhändige Schlosser in Schutz zu nehmen,*

also vor allem vor den Mystagogen, die überall und immer bereitstehen, jedermann und der Welt den rechten Weg zu weisen, so, wie sie ihn selbst verstehen." The *"grobhändige Schlosser"* presumably is Diethelm Brüggemann, who in *Kleist. Die Magie* (Würzburg: Königshausen & Neumann, 2004), *passim*, elaborates an alchemical "key" to Kleist's works. Although I consider Brüggemann's idea of an alchemical "key" a red herring (in brief, I maintain that alchemical and Masonic vocabulary comprises useful *po(i) etical* raw material to depict the transformations Kleist's characters undergo, but does not constitute a "thread" in itself), it inspired me to seek "keys" on my own—of which, as said, I found several. Schulz's defeatism, *"Die scheue Frage bleibt für die Vorsichtigen im Lande, ob das Kleist'sche Werk sich womöglich aller Erschließung sogar letztlich entziehen könnte"* (ibid, 17), and concludes, *"Der Weg zu Kleist über seine Biographie jedenfalls scheint wenig zu versprechen... Weder vom Prinzen von Homburg, von Achilles oder Penthesilea, dem Grafen Wetter vom Strahl oder dem Heilbronner Käthchen... lassen sich irgendwelche Brücken unmittelbar zu den Lebenstatsachen Heinrich von Kleists schlagen"* (ibid, 17), instead of exploring the intimate connections between Kleist's biography and œuvre, clips them. Ilse Graham, in *Heinrich von Kleist. Word into Flesh: A Poet's Quest for the Symbol* (Berlin: De Gruyter, 1977), 47, claims that she "forged for [herself] something of a master key which... seems to enable me to unlock a good many critical doors" (ibid, 1); unfortunately, in my view, her "master key" relates much more to her own—spiritual, Christian—concerns than to Kleist's and results in her shaping Kleist towards herself, rather than the reverse. One of the eminent Kleist readers who do explore codification in Kleist's work is Klaus Kanzog: in "Geschichtlicher Stoff und Geschichtlicher Code. Heinrich von Kleists *Prinz Friedrich von Homburg*," in *Heinrich von Kleist. Spurensuche, Textzugänge, Aneignungen. Gesammelte Schriften 1968-2011* (Heilbronn: Kleist-Archiv Sembdner, 2012), 127-43, he recognises that *Penthesilea*, as *Guiskard* and *Hermannsschlacht*, "always deal with Prussia" (129), that Kleist's "message" requires to be "decoded" (ibid.), that episodes such as Homburg's insubordination entail "daring codification" that fail to "reach its addressee" (130; 141), and that Kleist applies the timeless "Aesopian trick" of "veiling but keeping discernible" "tabooed themes" (131). Kantor even—correctly—singles out King Fr. Wilh. III as one of Kleist's addressees (134; 139).

10   When Kleist in February 1795 writes Ulrike, *"Gebe uns der Himmel nur Frieden,"* he welcomes peace as such, not necessarily the price Fr. Wilh. II paid for it at *Basel*, a crucial distinction Hans-Georg Schede, in *Heinrich von Kleist* (Hamburg: Rowohlt, 2008), 20, fails to make: *"Seine Hoffnung bezog sich auf die Verhandlungen*

über einen Separatfrieden, die Preußen inzwischen mit Frankreich aufgenommen hatte." Kleist, in my view, would have favoured not a *separate* agreement entered by Prussia alone, but a *comprehensive* agreement entered by Prussia and Austria jointly, and would not have supported any agreement, irrespective of which German power signed it, that delivered the Rhineland to France.

11   Re Fr. Wilh. II's departure and subsequent campaign, cf. Peter Michalzik, *Kleist. Dichter, Krieger, Seelensucher* (Berlin: Ullstein, 2011), 55-7: "Der Oberkommandierende Herzog von Braunschweig war so unzufrieden mit dem Verlauf des Feldzugs, dass er den König um Enthebung von seinen Aufgaben bat. Bei entschiedenem Vorgehen wäre ein Sieg wohl möglich gewesen" *(ibid,* 57). Re the impact of Prussia's withdrawal from the Coalition, cf. Max Plassmann, 'Die preußische Reichspolitik und der Friede von Basel 1795,' in *Jahrb. Stiftung Preuß. Schlösser und Gärten, Berlin-Brandenburg,* Band 4, 2001/2002, 147: "Damit war ein Wendepunkt erreicht, von dem aus ein gerader und unumkehrbarer Weg zur Auflösung des Alten Reiches führte."

12   Re the evolution of European civilization since the early 1500s, Carroll Quigley notes in *The Evolution of Civilizations* (Indianapolis: Liberty Fund, 1979), 357: "The next step forward in the development of the political level reduced the number of European political units from hundreds to scores and gave us a new stage in political development to which we apply the name 'dynastic monarchy'. The military factor that contributed to it is the rise of artillery that made the private stone castle obsolete," an evoluation culminating in the early 1800s with the *Napoleonic Wars* (cf. *ibid,* 379).

13   History was soon to repeat itself: in 1805 Prussia failed to succour Austria at *Austerlitz,* in 1806 Austria, tit-for-tat, failed to come to Prussia's at *Jena-Auerstedt,* and in 1809 Fr. Wilh. III reneged on his promise to join Austria, who promptly collapsed at *Wagram.* Just as Fr. Wilh. II had abandoned Franz in the *War of the First Coalition,* Fr. Wilh. III did in the *War of the Fifth* Coalition; in both cases, in Kleist's view, the Prussian Kings' negligence precipitated a French victory. Having been forced as a young man to watch *Basel* and *Campo Formio* from the sidelines, to the mature Kleist *Schönbrunn* and *Pressburg* (1805), *Tilsit* (1807) and *Schönbrunn* (1809) will have appeared as one *déjà vu* after another.

14   What Günter Blamberger misses when in *Heinrich von Kleist* (Frankfurt/M.: Fischer, 2011), 37, he muses, *"Es sind die Kinder- und die Kriegsjahre, in denen man*

besonders intensive lebt," "deshalb kehren sie in Briefen und biographischen Notizen so häufig wieder. Nichts davon bei Kleist," is that with Kleist such recurrences take place not only in letters and biographical notes, but most importantly also in his *works*. In July 1801 Kleist reminds Adolphine von Werdeck that six years prior he had introduced himself to her as "writer," which suggests that he brought some poetic pieces with him when in 1795 he returned to Potsdam from the *Rhine Campaign* (*Der Höhere Frieden* perhaps among them). There is nothing unusual about a young officer writing poems during wartime and sharing them with family and friends upon his return; what is remarkable is that Kleist in 1801 suggests that already in 1795 he had referred to himself as a "writer." Possibly this is a spurious backward projection: now that he is much clearer about his calling he seeks to re-establish contact with Adolphine as a potential sponsor, and to endorse his poetic credentials by reminding her of an encounter six years prior which she may recall positively (say, it could have been memorable for her because the "flirtatious" Adolphine "enjoyed being courted by young people"—Sembdner, *LS*, p.9).

Much of the ensuing letter is indeed poetical, and clearly Kleist is pursuing an agenda, and whether or not in 1795 he had introduced himself as a "writer" (Rudolf Loch believes he may have—cf. *Beiträge* 1997, 90), as of 1801 he clearly seeks to establish himself as one. Peter Staengle in *Kleist. Sein Leben* (Heilbronn: Kleist-Archiv Sembdner, 2013), 108, compares Kleist's staccato writing style to "machine-gun fire," a comparison that is anachronistic and by a hair's breadth misses the effect Kleist *does* seek to reproduce with words, metaphorically and rythmically: that of *cannon fire* (as an aside, the author of the present treatise in 1984-6 served as surveyor in the German artillery and like Kleist attained the rank of 2nd Lieutenant).

15   When he tells Wilhelmine on 10th October 1800 that his goal is *"mich zu einem Staatsbürger zu bilden"* (II:578), Kleist has no mundane civil office in mind, but something grander, with a *"große[m] Wirkungskreis."* A month later he clarifies, *"Ich will kein Amt nehmen... Ich soll tun was der Staat von mir verlangt, und doch soll ich nicht untersuchen, ob das, was er von mir verlangt, gut ist. Zu seinen unbekannten Zwecken soll ich ein bloßes Werkzeug sein—ich kann es nicht. Ein eigner Zweck steht mir vor Augen... ich passe nicht für ein Amt"* (II:584-5), and *"Ich bilde mir ein, daß ich Fähigkeiten habe, seltnere Fähigkeiten... Da stünde mir nun für die Zukunft das ganze schriftstellerische Fach offen. Darin fühle ich, daß ich sehr gern arbeiten würde"* (II:587): having during his military service endured being a mere cog in a machine, his efforts in a two-year campaign having been nullified by the mere stroke of a diplomat's pen, and having discovered his talent for writing, Kleist is now merely being consequential:

it is as national bard that he will be best positioned to serve his country, not as a low-ranking officer.

16   Without seeking to dive into the unresolved debate as to what precisely comprised Kleist's "Kant-crisis," and the reading of what text(s) triggered it, I note that the upshot of the rather theatrical "crisis" Kleist conjured in his letters to Wilhelmine and Ulrike was plainly his resolution to replace a *vita contemplativa* centred on academic study with a *vita activa* that entailed being present at the places in which historical events were taking place, or could be expected to take place, and actively involving himself in the historical process by producing and disseminating *satirical poetry*. The "Kant-crisis," it could be said in relation to philosophical schools, signified a shift from an *academic* to a *peripatetic*, or from a *stoic* to a *cynic*, stance, at any rate one in which *praxis* supersedes *theory*. To put it yet more simply: the young Kleist had enough of book-learning and itched to see the world and get involved; an earthquake was shaking Europe, a storm was brewing in the West, the World as it had been known was blowing up in everyone's face; at this historical (dis)juncture, what could books still teach? Screw them! Go west, young man! *Medias in res*! The world is *your* oyster, too—not only that Corsican's!

17   Günter Blamberger (*Kleist*, 292-3) terms Napoleon Kleist's *"deus absconditus,"* but in Kleist's works Napoleon is very much *"deus revelatus."* Perhaps Kleist's first indubitable reference to Napoleon is contained in a passage in his letter to Wilhelmine of 10th October (!) 1801: *"Ist nicht oft ein Mann, der einem Volke nützlich ist, verderblich für zehn andere?"* (II:693). Kleist is in Paris, where he experiences the 14th July celebrations, which Napoleon (ab)used to cement his popularity, and by the time October comes he sees the writing on the wall which on 28th July, in his letter to Adolfine, he still hesitated to admit: *"Ach, wenn ein* einziger *Mensch so viele Frevel auf seinem Gewissen tragen sollte, er müßte niedersinken... Aber eine ganze Nation... dividiert die Schuld mit 30 000 000"* (II:675). Kleist is now fully convinced that Napoleon would shape the fate of France and Europe, and as soon as he reaches this conviction, he turns his back on Paris and sets off for Switzerland, where he shall forge his first iron for his battle with the First Consul: *Schroffenstein* (in *Thierrez* he refers to Napoleon simply as *"Frau"* (I:720; 721); possibly the sketch coincides with his 10th October 1800 "birthday letter" to Wilhelmine, in which he announces himself as newborn, with 10th October as his new birthday).

18   Horst Häker, in a profoundly *satirical* reading of the novella, already makes the connection between the duel's location and the 1794 *Peace of Basel* in 'Wessen Recht und Ehre? Parabolische Hinweise in Kleists Erzählung 'Der Zweikampf', in: Häker, *Überwiegend Kleist* (Heilbronn: Heilbronner Kleist-Studien, No. 1, 287-300). While I do not concur that Rotbart represents France—in my reading: Franz/Austria—this is a mere detail (to make this clear right away: many of my attributions, in the following sections, of real personages to Kleist's characters remain debatable).

19   *Divinatory Meanings*: prudence, circumspection, policy; *but also*: treason, dissimulation, roguery, concealment, disguise—cf. http://www.tarotlore.com/tarot-cards/the-hermit/. The term "hermit" is derived not from a living person but from the terms *Hermétique*, *Hermès*, which the Tarot is concerned with—cf. https://fr.wikipedia.org/wiki/L%27Ermite). I am not aware that Kleist ever refers to the Tarot, though he does mention card games in general (no doubt a common pasttime in his military service), and divination plays a significant role in his works, and so do astrology and esoteric, including hermeneutic, teatchings and freemasonry, all of which are connected with tarot. Nevertheless, my using select Tarot arcana (trumps) to symbolise the "lives" interwoven in his works is mere playfulness on my part and not meant to imply that Kleist had such symbolism in mind.

20   Heinr. Detering writes in *Das offene Geheimnis. Zur literarischen Produktivität eines Tabus von Winckelmann bis zu Thomas Mann* (Göttingen: Wallstein 1994), 10 and 30: "Ein Schriftsteller, der A sagen will, aber nur B sagen darf, muß entweder verstummen oder das B so sagen, daß alle, die es angeht, das A heraushören können—und so, daß alle übrigen keinen Anstoß nehmen müssen... darum geht es in dieser Arbeit... die literarische Camouflage in Texten homosexueller Autoren [...] Literarische 'Camouflage' heißt: intentionale Differenz zwischen (unanstößigem) Oberflächentext und (hier: homoerotischem) Subtext... Mit diesem Zwang zur Kombination eines Oberflächen- und eines Subtextes aber erzielt die Camouflage zugleich, und zwar notwendig, das, was ich ihre produktiven Effekte nennen will. Je nachdem, wie der einmal gewählte 'Oberflächentext' beschaffen ist und wie er sich zum homoerotischen Subtext verhält, ergibt sich eine Art literarischen Mehrwerts, die in der homoerorischen Aussageabsicht zwar begründet und aus ihr abgeleitet ist, nicht aber in ihr aufgeht." Detering's "*Oberflächentext*" and "*Subtext*" correspond to my "*overt story*" and "*covert story*," and while I do not owe my concepts to Detering, I acknowledge that he arrived at them first. He is on the right track, but fails to systematically

595

apply his insights to Kleist's works. Blamberger notes (*Kleist*, 42-3): *"War Kleist nun homosexuell und oder gar ein missbrauchter Kindersoldat? Oder bisexuell—schließlich betrachtete Kleist in Thun 1802 nicht nur Pfuel, sondern auch ein Schweizer "Mädeli" mit Wohlgefallen, das mit ihm das Haus auf der Aare-Insel teilte, was er nur seiner Schwester, nicht aber der Verlobten Wilhelmine von Zenge verriet? Oder androgyn— man schaue sich nur die von Peter Friedel im April 1801 gemalte Miniatur an..., ein Geschenk für Wilhelmine von Zenge, oder denke an den Kleidertausch der Kinder von Kleists... Schroffenstein oder an die Amazonenkönigin Penthesilea, die sich ihres Geschlechtes nicht sicher ist? Die Frage nach der Natur von Kleists Begehren ist nicht zu entscheiden. Die These von Kleists Homosexualität macht vor allem Sinn, wenn man nach ihrer Wahrheit nicht fragt, sondern an der "Hebammenkunst der Gedanken" interessiert ist, also neue Lesarten von Kleists Werken erproben will. Behauptet wurde z.B., dass bei Kleist wie bei Thomas Mann und anderen homosexuellen Autoren der Zwang zur Umschreibung, zur Camouflage des tabuisierten sexuellen Begehrens die Kreativität fördere. Das französische Wort Camouflage bezeichnet ursprünglich die Tarnung von Befestigungsanlagen, es ist also eine militärische Vokabel mit zweistelliger Bedeutung, es meint sowohl das Sich-Wappnen wie das Sich-Verbergen, im Falle Kleists also, dass er seine Literatur zu einer Festung ausbaut, in der die eigene Homosexualität zugleich bewahrt wie ummauert ist. Interessant ist weniger der defensive als der offensive, produktive Character der Camouflage. Das Sprechverbot, das über Tabus verhängt ist, könnte ja zu grandiosen Verschiebungen geführt haben. Man darf rätseln, ob aus der Geschlechter- die Rassenmischung wird, ob sich das Mann-Weib Kleist in die Mestizin Toni in der Verlobung in St. Domingo verwandelt, welche in ihrer Liebe zu dem Schweizer Offizier Gustav, der an den "Ufern der Aar" zu Hause ist, die "Verlobung" Kleists mit Ernst von Pfuel in Thun nachvollzieht. Es versteht sich dann, warum der Preis dafür der Tod ist. Der Spaß, den der Interpret gewinnen kann, ist der des Detektivs, der Camouflage-Techniken enthüllt, die Beziehungen von Text und Subtext herstellt, nicht um der rettenden Anerkennung oder gar Brandmarkung Kleists als Homosexuellen willen, sondern wegen der—freilich immer hypothetischen —Erkenntnis des Inspirationsaktes selbst. Das kann auch zu Lesarten führen, die "heilige" Texte wie... Marionettentheater einmal nicht ganz so ernst nehmen. Ist es denn nicht sonderbar, wenn zwei Männer an einem Winterabend in einem dunklen Park zusammenstehen, um sich über so delikate Fragen zu unterhalten wie die Betrachtung der Grazie eines nackten Sechzehnjährigen im Bade?"* Blamberger posits interesting questions, but refuses to answer them—for one *can* answer them, because all the issues Blamberger lists, in Kleist's case not only generate some indeterminate "creativity" and" inspiration" or other, but *constitute his texts*. Peter Michalzik rejects (*Kleist*, 147) the notion of Kleist's homosexuality, despite quoting evidence such as Kleist having cohabitated with Brockes for two and a half months in Berlin, and having found that experience *"beglückend"*; such reticence renders his book, strictly speaking, not biographical but fictional: his *"zurechtgelegter"* (paraphrasing Vinken and Haverkamp) Kleist surely has little to do with the actual one, whose life and work cannot be understood separately from his homosexuality. Re Kleistian ominous utterances to Wilhelmine of the type, *"Ja wenn Du unter den Mädchen wärest, was dieser [Brockes] unter den Männern"* (II:619), or *"Dabei war er von einer ganz reinen, ganz unbefleckten Sittlichkeit"* (*ibid*.), Michalzik insists that, *"Mit Sicherheit hätte der Sittlichkeitsapostel Kleist solche Sätze nicht geschrieben, wenn es zu einer Andeutung sexueller Handlung zwischen ihnen beiden* [Kleist and Brockes] *gekommen wäre"* (*Kleist*, 148), before relegating the whole matter to "so called Queer Studies" (149) and concluding, *"Liest man Kleists Briefe genau, ging es nicht um Sexualität, sondern um Metamorphose und seelische Verschmelzung,"* which solves precisely nothing at all.

21   Kleist's lovers largely remained mute about their erotic affairs, which is unsurprising, given that they themselves were implicated and could have been stigmatised and even criminalised for homosexual leanings, and given that most of them went on to marry and lead (at least *overtly*) "conventional" lives. For example, when Dahlmann maintains, *"Kleist erlag seiner düster nagenden Hoffnungslosigkeit, seiner Verzweiflung am Vaterlande, soviel ich irgend weiß, keiner anderen Leidenschaft"* (*LS*,519a, b), he may be merely shielding his dead friend (and himself) by emulating Kleistian camouflage. One exception is Kleist's fellow "cheerful young soldier" (cf. *LS*,105a) Fouqué, who in 1812 reminisces: *"jünglingshell,-- / ...mein Heinrich, / So standen wir, nun fest im Männerbund / Die treue Hand uns drückend, unsere Lieder / Einander... / Entgegen sendend in die freud'ge Brust"* (*NR*,252).

22   For Gille Deleuze's *"critical and clinical"* methodology of reading, and my usage thereof, cf. my *Emigrant*, 163ff. The early 20th century Kleist biographer Sigismund Rahmer, in *Heinrich von Kleist als Mensch und Dichter* (Berlin: Georg Reimer, 1909), 348, went as far as quoting a letter addressed to him by a homosexual reader who recognised in Kleist's life and writing all the difficulties and resistances he himself faced as a homosexual, before rejecting the parallels pointed out in the letter, which appear to me eminently perceptive and plausible, but evidently did not fit in with Rahmer's preconceived notions. Kleist's plan to publish a German edition

of the *Code Napoléon* (cf. II:793), apart from commercial objectives could have reflected a personal agenda: "sodomy" (in those days usually defined as encompassing homosexuality as well as any anal intercourse) in Kleist's day remained a punishable crime under Prussian law (the earlier death penalty for this "crime" had been replaced by exile or prison), but not under Napoleon's more progressive codex—cf. Michalzik (*Kleist*, 255) and Schutz (*Kleist*, 79-80). Apart from decriminalising sodomy, the *Code Napoléon* made it easier for women to seek divorce (cf. Schulz, *Kleist*, 70), which could also have motivated Kleist, several of whose female acquaintances were unhappily married women and could be suitable mothers for his production of a son (cf. my sections *The Familial* and *The Filial* below). That publishing the codex had more than economic importance to Kleist is suggested by his curious note to Ulrike that he *"über dessen eigentliche Bedeutung... mich hier nicht weitläufiger auslassen kann"* (II:793). Apart from his personal agenda and commercial pressures, Kleist could have considered it *satirically* useful to publish the codes in Saxony and elsewhere in Germany, for its imposition would highlight German enslavement by the French, who could even impose their foreign legal codes on them—cf. how in *Krug* Walter (Napoleon) imposes his foreign jurisdiction on Huisum (Germany). His publishing the codex would have entailed a similar sleight-of-hand as his translation and publication in *BA* of the essay *Über den Zustand der Schwarzen*, which had the potential to turn the public mood against the oppressors by exposing their insidious infiltration of the German body politic. Kleist was not inconsistent or treacherous, but subtle and many-faceted, and was looking to kill three birds with one stone: make a profit, agitate against the French, and increase the liberties of the German citizens, including himself (the codex, Kleist understood, ironically comprised at once a means of oppression and of liberation).

23   Cf. Heinr. Detering (*Geheimnis*, 20): *"das 'wirkliche' Begehren der Autoren besser kennen zu wollen, als diese selbst erklären, ihnen womöglich eine andere Geschichte zurückzugeben als die von ihnen erzählte"*; Gerhard Schulz (*Kleist*, 262): *"Schon früh sind homosexuelle Neigungen bei Kleist diagnostiziert worden, zuerst 1909 von Sigismund Rahmer und im Jahr darauf von Isidor Sadger, einem Wiener Nervenarzt... Nach sexueller Identität im Sinne des 20. oder 21. Jahrhunderts zu suchen, wäre jedoch unhistorisch und reduzierte Kleists Verständnis menschlichen Verhaltens und Empfindens, wie es sich in seinen Werken und Briefen darbietet, auf geschlechtliche Aspekte"* (Rahmer, as we saw, considered but rejected Kleist's homosexuality). The respective risks Detering and Schulz point to, of over-determination and of reduction,

deserve to be taken seriously, but in my view most Kleist scholars are more at risk of *underdetermining* Kleist's homosexuality than of the reverse, of *dismissing it* more than of reducing his writings to it.

24   Cf. Fr. Nietzsche: *"Was ist daher Wahrheit? Eine mobile Armee der Metaphern."* In: *Über Wahrheit und Lüge im außermoralischen Sinne.* http://gutenberg.spiegel.de/buch/-3243/1.

25   Rudolf Loch's suggestion, in *Kleist. Eine Biographie* (Göttingen: Wallstein, 2003), 24, that Kleist's entry marks his becoming aware of his being a *"Quertreiber"* ("troublemaker") or black sheep of the family, is not inconsistent with my hunch that it could also mark his sensing his homoerotic leanings. Cf. in this context Fr. Weisser in his (defamatory) article of December 1811: *"Man kannte Heinrich von Kleist... als den Verfasser einiger poetischen Produkte,... in welchen... vernünftige Leute beinahe nichts als Symptome der entschiedensten* Querköpfigkeit *warhrnahmen"* (NR,24; emphasis in the original).

26   Cf. Kleist's love letter to Pfuel of 5th January 1805: *"Du stelltest das Zeitalter der Griechen in meinem Herzen wieder her, ich hätte bei dir schlafen können, Du lieber Junge; so umarmte Dich meine ganze Seele!"* (II:749). Fritz Wittels was perhaps the first to infer Kleist's homosexuality from this letter—cf. Wittels, "Heinrich von Kleist: Prussian Junker and Creative Genius," in: Henrik M. Ruitenbeek (Ed.), *The Literary Imagination: Psychoanalysis and the Genius of the Writer* (Chicago: Quadrange, 1965), 32-3. The Spartan lawgiver Lycurgus (fl. c.820 BC) established a state-sponsored education system (*agōgē*) channelling all Spartan youths through military and educational training involving rigourous physical exercise and proverbial spartan lifestyle, and encouraging pederasty. F. Földényi in *Die Inszenierung des Erotischen. Heinrich von Kleist, "Über das Marionettentheater,"* in Günter Blamberger (Ed.), *KJB 2001* (Stuttgart: Metzler, 2001), 135-47, situates *Marionettentheater* in the context of Kleist's erotic exploits during his 1801 Paris sojourn. Földényi mentions the square before the Halle au bléd (today the Bourse de Commerce, featuring the phallic Colonne Médicis), which Kleist himself refers to as a place "in which the last restraints are let go off" (II:678), and the park near the Champs-Elysées—both well-known meeting places for gay men. Földényi offers a perceptive reading of the essay's eroticism, but with a recitience approaching Detering's fails to acknowledge the blatant sexual symbolism and physicality of Kleist's puppets and their moves. Rudolf Loch's (*Kleist,*

468) terming the Pfuel letter the *"wichtigste Dokument Kleist Sexualität betreffend"* is understandable but misguided: the most important documents regarding Kleist's sexuality are his poetic works.

27 We observe Kleist's (I/O) symbolism at work: *"Stand"* / *"konkave Wölbung."* Has there ever been a more divine depiction of the human anus than *"wie von der Hand der Gottheit eingedrückt"*? A poetical rendering that is at the same time eminently concrete: *"Hand"* = member; *"Gottheit"* = erástes, *"eingedrückt"* = initiated). Kleist had a habit of recycling entire letter passages, and it is possible that he sent similar reminiscenses to Ulrike or Marie who, unlike Adolphine, felt compelled to burn them together with other revealing letters. Hans Dieter Zimmermann (*Kleist*, 47) deserves credit for recognising Kleist's "first friendship by the Rhine" as his sexual *"Urszene"*; so does Michalzik, for noting (*Kleist*, 48): *"Auf dem einen Rheinufer wurde eine Stadt in Schutt und Asche gelegt, auf dem anderen erlebte ein junger Soldat seinen ersten Frühling."* Blamberger's question, whether Kleist was an "abused child soldier" (*Kleist*, 42), is clearly answered in the negative by the textual evidence of his reminiscence, which suggests that he rather welcomed his early sexual experiences (nor could he strictly speaking be considered a "child soldier": not only is this an anachronistic term, but his age was considered normal for an officer cadet). For the identities of "Barße" (Georg von Barsse) and "Müller" (Karl Adolf von Müller) I rely on Sembdner (II:1080;1095). Sembdner does not provide Müller's and Barsse's birth dates, but since Gleißenberg was Kleist's senior by six years (cf. II:1086), it is probable that Müller and Barsse were also his seniors—and probably experienced in sexual matters. The *Kleist-Forschung*'s "consensus view" that Kleist's work is not significantly autobiographical—e.g., Schulz (*Kleist*, 16-17): "his work appears to exist wholly independently from its author"—is correct only as long as "autobiographical" is very narrowly defined; at the same time it risks being highly restrictive and counter-productive in evaluating Kleist's texts, for this notion forecloses or veils that Kleist put his *entire body and soul* into his œuvre, which expresses and unfolds his life "expressionistically" (in the Deleuzean sense). He wished, Kleist once told Ulrike, instead of being forced to put his "unspeakable" soul into words, that he could simply extract his heart from his body, put it into an envelope, and send it to her (cf. II:729-30). This gesture for him would have constituted *authentic communication*, and short of cutting his heart out, he invests his entire being into his works as much as possible, which in this sense are eminently autobiographical. Robert E. Helbling, in *The Major Works of Heinrich von Kleist* (New York: New Directions, 1975), 183, terms Kleist's works a "spiritual

autobiography," which I directionally concur with, while adding that they just as much comprise his "embodied autobiography." Michalzik's cautious position with regard to this question (*Kleist*, 187-8), "*Briefe gelten als verlässliche Grundlage für Biographen. Bei Dichtungen ist man dagegen mit guten Gründen vorsichtig. Man kann nicht vom Werk auf den Author schließen. Bei Kleist ist das möglicherweise anders. Die Briefe von 1799 bis 1801 haben einen fiktiven Kern, für die entscheidenden Dinge liefern sie keine biographischen Fakten. Sie sind der Literatur verwandt. In der Literatur, die Kleist nun schreiben wird, steckt das Eigentliche seiner selbst*," directionally aligns with my reading, although I believe Kleist's early letters encompass more biographical facts than is generally recognised. I side with Rudolf Loch when he notes (*Kleist*, 234-5) regarding Kleist's re-establishing contact with Wilhelmine in Königsberg while working on *Amphitryon*: "*Oft stehen Leben und Werk in einem ganz unmittelbaren Verhältnis zueinander, ein heute kaum noch beachteter Tatbestand... In Kleist's Amphitryon-Dichtung... tritt uns Kleists Ich, so scheint es, gleichsam aufgespalten in drei voneinander unterschiedene dramatis personae engegen.*" I am also d'accord with Felix Bamberg's insight, "*An Kleist ist das Eigentümlichste, daß sein Leben mit seinem Schaffen in weit unmittelbarerem Zusammenhang steht als bei irgendeinem anderen deutschen Dichter*" (*NR*,352). Among the biographers, Wilbrandt is most inclined towards a quasi-biographical reading of Kleist's œuvre, at least with respect to certain characters or instances—cf. *Kleist*, 246, 250, re Penthesilea's suffering and death; 373, re Homburg's fate; 416, re the "subjectivity" of Kleist's poetry: "*so springt überall sein Ich... hervor.*" Among Kleist's contemporaries, Fr. Chr. Dahlmann noted that in *Kohlhaas* "the poet's character portrays itself precisely" (*LS*,317), and Peguilhen opined that "His Käthchen von Heilbronn is a precise portrait of himself" (*LS*,394).

28   In sketching the movements of Kleist's unit during the *Siege of Mainz*, I am greatly indepted to Peter Michalzik (*Kleist*, 44-53), who on the basis of Carl von Reinhard's *Geschichte des königlich Preußischen Ersten Garderegiments zu Fuß* reconstructs the itinerary—a contribution of great importance, illuminating what may well have been the most formative months in Kleist's live, whose erotico-agonistic nexus reverberates throughout his œuvre—indeed, encompasses its *very heart*. Michalzik also helpfully traces Kleist's subsequent movements during the *Palatine Campaign* and via Lage (near Osnabrück) back to Potsdam (*ibid*, 53-65).

29   Despite Kleist's vocabulary of war and peace, the poem is in the first instance not only *satirical* but especially also *satyrical*: it comprises his first *po(i)*

etical statement of the nexus of *Erôs* and *Agôn*—as such, the earliest blueprint for his entire œuvre. The "war" Kleist is primarily concerned with is that of "brotherly" love and erotic intercourse: "weapons" = members; "hatred" = jealousy; "higher peace" = *jouissance*. Blamberger's reading (*Kleist*, 36) the poem as *"Jugendgedicht, das in seiner ganzen Harmlosigkeit wohl noch vor Kriegbeginn verfasst sein dürfte,"* and as *"Friedenswunsch,"* is thus misguided. Although it is possible that the poem dates before Kleist's involvement in the war—Kleist himself in *Ph* dates it, somewhat vaguely, "1792 or 1793" (cf. I:909; *MA*III:585), which is a form of camouflage—I consider it most likely that it is situated in the context of his "initiation" at Biebrich and Marienborn. Clearly the poem is neither "harmless" nor does it comprise a "peace-wish" in a conventional sense. By publishing it in *Ph*, Kleist marks it as relevant to him as of 1808, and even if chronologically it is a *"Jugendgedicht,"* it does not deserve the label, as it meets the standards and reflects the concerns of the mature poet, who may furthermore have edited or recreated it from an earlier version, as Sembdner correctly points out (cf. I:909); Reuß and Staengle's grouping the poem together with others from the *Ph* period is, in this sense, appropriate. The idea of the erotico-agonistic nexus goes back to Heraclitus: *"Das Gegensätzliche strebt zur Vereinigung, aus dem Unterschiedlichen entsteht die schönste Harmonie, und alles entsteht auf Grund der Zwietracht"* (quoted in Sloterdijk, *Spären II*, 690). Sloterdijk elaborates (*ibid*, 691), *"Der Denker, vielmehr 'Seher' bezieht keine 'eigene' Stellung… in letzter Konsequenz müßte man eine solche Polaritätslehre eine Philosophie ohne Subjekt nennen. Wo diese Sicht herrscht, gibt es im Grunde genommen nur die Rhythmen, nur das Hin und Her der Energien und Gegenpole, für das Separat-Ich des Menschen bleibt keine eigene Sphäre. Im Verhältnis zu diesen Rhythmen gibt es für den Menschen nur eine gültige Haltung: Hingabe,"* in which we discover a grounding of Kleist's concept of *"Grazie"* understood as *"Hingabe"* to the lover. Kleist would later have the opportunity to refine his personal experiences at *Mainz* with A. Müller's *Lehre vom Gegensatz*—cf. the latter in a letter to Gentz of 27th May 1805: *"daß hier und im ganzen Leben der Weg von Liebe zur Liebe immer durch eine Art von Tod führe"* (*AML*,111).

30   Kleist and Pfuel's friendship may have gone back as far as to their early childhood: his branch of the Kleist family had long-established ties with the even more ancient Pfuel family. The Pfuels' Lebus estate was located a mere 10km north of Frankfurt/O.; according to Rahmer (*Kleist*, 4-8), Major Otto von Kleist in Berlin had orchestrated Pfuel's entry into Kleist's regiment; and at Potsdam, together with Kleist and the members of his musical quartet, Pfuel was on intimate terms with Chr.

and Marie von Kleist (*ibid*, 10-11; how much did Marie already then know about their "brotherhood"?). von Müller was among the cadets who joined Kleist at the Kassel *Gemäldegalerie* in 1795 (cf. *LS*,20a), thereafter his name no longer appears; Barsse remained Kleist's comrade after the Regiment's return to Potsdam—in 1798 he was one of the three friends who joined Kleist on his second Harz journey (cf. *LS*,20b); Schlotheim and Gleißenberg remained among Kleist's most duarable friends, and together with Kleist and Rühle formed the Potsdam musical quartet which in 1797 undertook a memorable journey to the Harz: Rühle in his memoires speaks of *"das ausgezeichnete Quartett"* and recalls that *"so genossen die Freunde auch mit dem leichten Fluge dieser Stimmungen die vergängliche Zeit"* (*LS*,18). Schlotheim in June 1799 visits Kleist in Frankfurt/O. and seeks to entice him to join him on a journey to the Riesengebirge, an offer Kleist declines citing his ongoing university studies—yet only a few weeks later, during the summer break, Kleist, Ulrike and Leopold together journey to the Riesengebirge, where they meet up with Gleißenberg (cf. *LS*,34a), but apparently not Schlotheim (one is tempted to imagine this episode conveying one of those not infrequent instances of jealousy and ostracisation among the "brothers"). In 1804 in Potsdam Kleist and Gleißenberg once more unite (cf. Michalzik, *Kleist*, 236), Gleißenberg delivering Kleist's suitcase he had left with the Schlieben sisters in Dresden, and which may have contained important MSS (cf. II:747), and picking up another suitcase for Pannwitz in Gulben. In 1805 Kleist rushes to Schlotheim's bedsite after his suicide attempt (cf. *LS*,137a; b), in 1807 Schlotheim and Gleißenberg both come to Kleist's assistance when he is taken prisoner by the French authorities (cf. Rahmer, *Kleist*, 94; 103), and as late as January 1810 Kleist passes through Gotha, where Schlotheim is based. Did Kleist in Potsdam maintain an extensive "brotherhood" whose "variable geometry" involved one *quaternary* (his musical quartet) and two *triads*, one with Pfuel and Rühle, the other with Schlotheim and Gleissenberg, all of which could occasionally disintegrate into *dyads*, only to be reconstituted into larger constellations? Kleist's liaison with Heinr. Zschokke, his senior by six years, may have been among his earliest—Zschokke studied and taught at the Viadrina between 1790 and 1795, and they could have met there before Kleist joined the military; in his letter to Zschokke of 1st February 1802 Kleist terms their encounter in Bern a reunion (cf. II:718)—and appears to have endured well beyond Kleist's Swiss sojourn (cf. Rahmer, *Kleist*, 79); Zschokke in 1846 would write in his memoirs: *"Kleist war eine der schönen Erscheinungen im Leben für mich, die man um ihres Selbstes Willen liebt und nie zu lieben aufhört"* (quoted in Loch, *Kleist*, 155). With Brockes Kleist will have been in contact by mail between their first encounter in Rügen in the summer of 1800 (Schulz, in *Kleist,* 548 n.17, refutes Rahmer's contention that Kleist and Brockes met as early as in 1796) and their joint departure for Würzburg from Koblentz (cf. my discussion in a later footnote of a letter by Brockes to "Heinrich" Zimmermann has unearthed). Re Kleist's relationship with Alex. zur Lippe, records are patchy, yet it could have spanned a lengthy period, from as early as 1801 onwards (cf. Rahmer, *Kleist,* 63), or else from 1804/5 onwards, and until 1810/11: Karl Aug. Varnhagen's notes and report to Bülow (cf. *LS,*44; 132; *NR,*184; 185) suggest that Kleist's relationship with Lippe outlasted that with Brockes and was reinforced by Lippe's and Kleist's relationships with Cohen and Rahel in Berlin (cf. also Rahmer, *ibid,* 61); Rahmer (*Kleist,* 59-63) usually refers to Lippe in the context of a *triad* Kleist-Brockes-Lippe, with Brockes as lynchpin, terming it *"das Freundestrio, das in den schöngeistigen Kreisen Berlins gemeinsam verkehrte,"* and noting that their relationship must have been "very intimate"; as with Pfuel and Rühle, and possibly Schlotheim and Gleissenberg, Kleist may have sustained a *triad* with Brockes and Lippe for an extended period. Rahmer's suggesting (*ibid,* 62) that Brockes at one point sought to extricate Kleist from his intimacy with Lippe suggests a reason for Brockes' and Kleist's break-up, namely jealousy on Brockes' part when Kleist leaned towards Lippe, to whom Brockes perhaps had once introduced him. The Bern constellation may have been *quaternary*; the three friends' gaiety at Kleist's declamation of *Schroffenstein*'s final scene suggests that they understood his *satyrical* innuendos and "brotherhood code" perfectly well.

31   Achim von Arnim lived in Königsberg in late 1806, where he was possibly "together" with Kleist (cf. Schulz, *Kleist,* 287 n.35); in July 1811, following A. Müller's departure, Kleist tells Marie that he hopes for a "closer relationship" with the "overly neglected" (II:872) Arnim. In *Emigrant* I speculated that Kleist could have met Clemens Brentano as early as 1800 during the Würzburg journey; Brentano's swipe during the Dresden period, "*Wenn* Adam malt *und* Eva kleistert" (*LS,*234) betrays the spurned lover, those from the Berlin period confirm that he knew Kleist's genitals just as well the cobbler does the "feet" of St. Jago's "Donnas," and Teuthold those of Hally (cf. V.1565): "a gentle, earnest man,…, roughly my size" (*LS,*345); "a good, rough… magnificiently equipped man" (*LS,*420a). Re A. Müller's sexuality, Schulz notes (*Kleist,* 327-8) his intimate relationship with Fr. von Gentz, whose letters he terms "penetrated with verbal eros": *"Ein ausgiebiger, in den Rollen zwischen Vater, Sohn, Meister, Schüler, Freund und Geliebtem changierer Briefwechsel… feierte wahre Orgien des gegenseitigen Lobes"* (cf. my later extensive footnote on this matter); Wilbrandt implies that A. Müller was gay when he notes, sarcastically, that he applied for the

post of chancellor of the University of Frankfurt "in order to preoccupy himself with the convivial education of youths" (*Kleist*, 387). Re Sembdner notes (*In Sachen Kleist*, 302) that "in Kleist's final years a special friendship must have persisted between him and Robert"; that no testimony from Kleist's hand survives of a relationship with Rahel Levin's brother, as Dirk Grathoff points out (cf. Sembdner, *ibid*), does not refute the conjecture.

32 With respect to both of these prominent men Kleist uses versions of his "comet" imagery to express the relationship he aspires to: to Altenstein he writes in August 1806, "*Wie doch der kleine Stern heißen mag, den man auf dem Sirius, wenn der Himmel klar ist, sieht?... O mein edler Freund, ist dies ein Traum?*" (II:766), certainly an unusual address to one's superior (a few weeks later he writes virtually the same to his lover Rühle—cf. II:768), and re the "magnificient" Gneisenau he tells Marie in September 1811, "*Ich bin gewiß, daß wenn er den Platz fände, für den er sich geschaffen und bestimmt fühlt, ich, irgendwo in seiner Umringung, den meinigen gefunden haben würde*" (II:878). In *A True History* (Book 1) Lucian's space traveler quips that on the comets long-haired men are admired [Gr. *kometes* = long-haired, in reference to the comet's tail].

605

33 The term "brotherhood," which appears in *Käthchen* as "*treue Brüderschaft*" (V.1557) and as Strahl's "*Verbrüderung mit dem Satan*" (an accusation Theobald rescinds), and in a slightly different form in Rühle's remiscence of their "*Vereinigung der Freunde*" (cf. *LS*,18), is to be understood primarily, if not exclusively, *satyrically*. "*Unverbrüchliche Freundschaft*" was considered, as Rudolf Loch shows (*Beiträge* 1997, 105), the highest virtue among aristocrats, as it already head been for the Epicureans and the ancient propagators of aristocratic education, or *paidaia*. Friendship ties ran deep between Kleist and various members of his "brotherhood," and will have been just as important to him as erotic attraction. In Greek mythology gods are frequently accompanied by followers, often in groups of three: maenads, satyrs, Kouretes, nymphs, Centaurs, Cyclopes, Gorgons, Erinyes/Eumenides, Charites, Muses, Nereides, Korbyantes, Titans, Horai, Moira, etc. Walter Burkert notes in *Greek Religion*. Trans. John Raffan (Malden, MA: Blackwell, 1985), 173-4: "In poetry, of course, these groups are presented as belonging to the world of gods: the satyrs and maenads dance around Dionysos, the nymphs dance with Artemis, and the Kouretes or Korybantes dance about the new-born Zeus child or the enthroned Dionysos child. The Muses surround Apollo, the Oceanides accompany Persephone on her fateful meadow, and

the Cyclopes forge the thunderbolt for Zeus." The most famous *symposion* was the one hosted by the poet Agathon on the occasion of his victory in the 416BC *City Dionysia*, immortalised by Plato's and Xenophon's separate (and rather different) accounts; there can be no doubt that Plato's rendering of Agathon's *symposion* provided Kleist a blueprint for expressing his own symposiac fantasies.

34   The ancient concept of homoeroticism is much older than that of homosexuality, the latter having been coined by Karl-Maria Kertbeny only in 1869, in an argument against the Prussian anti-sodomy law, to denote a more permanent state of identity. As the boundaries are fluid and the definitions contextual, I use these terms interchangeably, notwithstanding the fact that most of Kleist's presumed lovers, after a youthful, experimental homoerotic phase, entered durable heterosexual relationships and marriages, and notwithstanding the fact that Foucault criticised as anachronistic the retroactive application of the more recent concept to historical figures that precede it. While many of his presumed lovers, for all their homoerotic leanings, by today's terminology may have been essentially heterosexuals, I assume that Kleist himself was indeed homosexual, which goes some way towards explaining why his attempts at producing a heir—which his conventional aristocratic *familial* context called for, and which he genuinely aspired to—evidently remained unsuccessful. In *Aufsatz*, Kleist's *pescheräic* terms include *"Tugend"* = (homo-)sexual/(homo-) erotic virility; *"Glück"* = *jouissance*; *"Weg des Glücks"* = *"Weg der Seele des Tänzers"* (cf. my discussion of *Marionettentheater* in *Emigrant*); *"Unschuld"* = unconscious surrender; *"moralisch"* = *"tugendhaft"* = virile, desirous; *"Bildung"* = *"Üben"* = practicing sexual intercourse; *"Mensch"* = *"Mann"* = lover; *"Liebe für das Geschlecht"* = homoerotic desire. Later, in the *BA* essay *Allerneuester Erziehungsplan*, Kleist explicitly links *"Tugend"* to *"Laster,"* as well as proposing an educational strategy of *"Tugend durch Laster"* (II:334). Kleist was repeatedly confronted with lovers "going legit"—in Thomas Mann's terms, "giving themselves a constitution"—, i.e., leaving the "brotherhood" to marry a woman and start a family: cf. his frequent appeals to them to maintain their *"Gefühlssicherheit"* (i.e., to remain loyal to their homoerotic desires) and to avoid *"Verwirrung des Gefühls"* (i.e., veer towards heterosexual relationships). Re Pfuel, Kleist indignantly writes Rühle in late 1805 (II:760): *"Wie sehr hat mich die Nachricht erfreut, die Du mir von unserm Freund Pfuël gibst, die Nachricht, daß das Korps, bei welchem er steht, vor die Stadt rückt, in welcher zugleich der Feind und sein Mädchen wohnt!"* Perhaps no poet before or since has put *"Feind"* and *"Mädchen"* quite in such a stark connexion as does Kleist! Rühle, on his part, in 1808 followed Pfuel's example and married Henriette von Frankenberg.

35   Pfuel will have been an excellent swimmer and his body will have shown it; he is considered the inventor of the breast stroke and the founder of the world's first military swimming academy (Prague, 1810). When Kleist says that Pfuel "reignited the Greek era in his heart," he means the physical rigour and athleticism that came with rigorous exercise as well as the regime of pederasty that Lycurgus institutionalised. Kleist's *"Dein kleiner, krauser Kopf, einem feisten Halse aufgesetzt, zwei Breite Schultern"* (II:749) refers to the part of Pfuel's body—the *genitals*—he was particularly fond of: "head" = glans; "neck" = shaft; "shoulders" = testicles; cf. Adam's depiction of the "peasants" in *Krug* (V.88-9): *"Setzt einen Hut dreieckig auf mein Rohr, / ...zwei Stiefel drunter,"* Kleist's of Brockes: *"seine [..] Gestalt, die nicht schön war, aber edel. Er ist groß, nicht sehr stark, hat ein gelbbräunliches Haar, ein blaues Auge, viel Ruhe und Sanftmut im Gesicht, und ebenso im Betragen"* (II:619), and Brentano's of Kleist, quoted previously.

36   Clemens Brentano's trenchant swipe, *"Wenn* Adam malt *und* Eva kleistert" (*LS*,234), puts Kleist into the position of (effeminate) *erômenos*, even though Müller was two years his junior. In *Mädchenrätsel* (I:14) Kleist assumes the viewpoint of the *erastês*: *"wen meint er?"* answer: the *erômenos* (*"Mädchen"* = effeminate lover, "youth"); *"was weint er?"* answer: ejaculate; *"was erschrickt ihn?"* answer: the *erômenos'* coynesss; *"was beglückt ihn?"* answer: anal *jouissance*. The poem could have originated much earlier: it is the kind of riddle young cadets would have come up with during campaigns' lengthy periods of forced leisure. The accompanying poem *Jünglingsklage* (*ibid*) points to that period.

607

37   Re Kleist's *"große Idee," "Hauptgegenstand,"*or *"Hauptgedanke"* (II:575-6) of pursuing an alternative household and lifestyle model in which "under one roof" women, as mother(s) and housewife(s), and men, as friends and lovers, cohabit, cf. the "birthday letter" to Wilhelmine of 10^(th)/11^(th) October 1800 and my discussion thereof in *Emigrant* and further below. Kleist could have acquired the concept of *"Scheidung"* from Brockes, who may have become Kleist's mentor in *saytrical* matters when they met on Rügen: 10 years Kleist's senior, he had taken a "young man" along when he attended university; Kleist approvingly cites his maxim, *"Handeln ist besser als Wissen."*

38   Heinr. Detering (*Geheimnis*, 137-40) suggests that Penthesilea's relationship with Achilles echoes Kleist's with Pfuel. This may be so, but I disagree with Detering's contention, *"Ginge es Kleist lediglich um verschlüsselte Hinweise auf*

ein bestimmtes Verhältnis zwischen ihm selbst und einem bestimmten Freund zu einem bestimmten Zeitpunkt, so wäre diese Mitteilung allenfalls für Kleist-Biographen von Interesse; es bliebe bei einer Einsicht in durchaus private Details. Begreift man dagegen die homoerotischen Züge des Dramas als Teil der Kleistschen Bemühungen, homerotische "Natur" sprachlich zu erfassen, Handlungsmuster und Erfahrungsmöglichkeiten zu bestimmen, so erweist sich der Text als Bestandteil eines Reflexionszusammenhangs, der von Anfang an auf eine das Privat-Kontingente transzendierende poetische Gestaltung aus ist": it sets up false alternatives, for neither is Kleist's depiction mere "private detail" "of interest only for Kleist-biographers," nor it is "transcendent poetic composition" in the service of the "representation in language of homoerotic nature." I am unable to find images of von Müller, Gleißenberg, Barsse, Schlotheim, Lippe, and Lose. I could have included Brentano, with a question mark. I do not iclude the image of Brockes reproduced by biographers (e.g., Schulz, 120; Blamberger, 135), and those of the younger Zschokke, Rühle, Altenstein variously reproduced by Loch, Schulz, Michalzik, Blamberger or Schede, which show Kleist's lovers around the time when they knew each other, but of which it is unclear if they are in the public domain.

39   *Divinatory meanings*: attraction, love, beauty, trials overcome; *but also*: failure, foolish designs—cf. http://www.tarotlore.com/tarot-cards/the-lovers/.

40   The Brunonian system of medicine developed by the Scottish physician John Brown in the 1780s gained widespread popularity in Germany. Gmelin visited Mainz in 1787 to observe the experiments of the mesmerist Chr. L. Hoffmann, and Wedekind came to Mainz in the same year (cf. *KH*,244), so that Gmelin, Wedekind and Hoffmann could all have influenced each other. Gmelin actively practiced magnetic therapy only for a few years, 1787-90, but by 1797 had published 10 books on it, constituting its most extensive treatment in German—cf. https://de.wikipedia.org/wiki/Eberhard_Gmelin. It appears unlikely that Kleist sought treatment with Gmelin in Heilbronn during his Würzburg sojourn (as I suggested in *Emigrant* he could have done); more likely he was influenced by his writings, notably his patient cases, which he could have been explosed to during Schubert's lectures, *"über den animalischen Magnetismus und die von ihm hervorgerufenen Erscheinungen"* (cf. Schede, *Kleist*, 95; also *LS*,196), or during his personal meetings with Schubert in Dresden—cf. Schulz (*Kleist*, 385). There nevertheless remains the possibility that Kleist visited Heilbronn, and Gmelin, in 1802, when he passed through Swabia with Pfuel en route to Switzerland. Hufeland was not initially inclined towards Mesmerism, but in view of

his younder brother Fr. Hufeland exploring the field (cf. his treatise on the topic, *Ueber Sympathie*, Weimar, 1811—cf. Peter Sloterdijk, *Sphären I*, Frankfurt/M.: Suhrkamp, 1998, 244; 249-51), thawed to it and aligned it with his own concept of vitalism. Fichte shortly before his death in 1813 undertook mangetic therapy with Karl Chr. Wolfart (cf. Sloterdijik, *Sphären I*, 257), who soon published, with Mesmer's authorisation, the influential compendium *Mesmerismus oder System der Wechselwirkungen* (Berlin, 1814), and assumed one of the first German professorships for animal magnetism (*ibid*, 240). Re Kleist's connection with Wolfart, cf. Hans-Jakob Wilhelm, "Der Magnetismus und die Metaphysik des Krieges," in Gerhard Neumann (Ed.), *Heinrich von Kleist. Kriegsfall—Rechtsfall—Sündenfall* (Freiburg i.Br.: Rombach, 1994), 87, and Michalzik, *Kleist*, 430. Klaus Kanzog, leaning on Maria M. Tatar, discerns (*Kleist*, 137-8) "multiple striking parallels" between *Homburg*'s plot and Joh. Chr. Reil's method of psychological healing laid out in *Rhapsodieen zur Anwendung der psychischen Curmethode auf Geisteszerrüttungen* (1803). Reil was also a spa doctor at Halle, a 2-day journey from Berlin, which Kleist passed repeatedly on his journeys, and from 1810 the decan of Berlin's Charité (cf. II:395) and the head of Prussia's *Königliche technische Deputation für das Medizinalwesen* (which Kleist in 1800 sought to attach himself to—cf. my discussion further below).

41   In the 18th century, for the well-to-do spas replaced the public bathhouses that had been popular in German cities in earlier centuries and—ironically—had been key loci of transmission of infectious diseases—cf. Ernst Bäumler, *Amors vergifteter Pfeil. Kulturgeschichte einer verschwiegenen Krankheit* (Frankfurt/M.: Edition Wötzel, 1997), 23-4. Spa towns offered leisure, cure, convalescence, socialising and romance. If Kleist in 1800 fell in love with Brockes at a spa on the island of Rügen, presumably during their treatment for the same disease, this would have been not untypical: I already mentioned that in July 1799 Kleist visited Gleißenberg at the spa town of Flinsberg in the Riesengebirge. When in June their mutual friend Schlotheim sought to entice Kleist to join him on a journey there, Gleißenberg was presumably already there, and will have been the main reason for Schlotheim, and a month later Kleist, to pick this destination, and suggesting that Gleißenberg was afflicted by the same disease as Kleist, and could even have been the source of Kleist's infection (in which case he would be the most important person in Kleist's life who is almost wholly ignored by his biographers). Martini reports (cf. *LS*,34a) that from Flinsberg the friends visited the nearby Meffersdorf to meet Adolf Traugott von Gersdorf, who since 1788 had been experimenting with medical applications of electricity, making it quite

clear that already a year prior to the Würzburg journey and the Rügen spa sojourn, Kleist's Riesengebirge journey comprised what is nowadays called "medical tourism." In 1801, during his escape-cum-study trip, together with Ulrike, across Germany to Paris, Kleist met a number of leading medical researchers and practitioners, among them the physiologist Ernst Platner in Leipzig (whose lecture he attended), the physician Joh. Fr. Blumenbach in Göttingen, and the anatomist Heinr. Aug. Wrisberg in Göttingen. Through Platner Kleist may have become familiar with the work of the famous Dutch physician Boerhaave, "father of physiology" and founder of the modern academic hospital: Platner's father had been a student of Boerhaave, two of whose students founded the famous Vienna School, to which Mesmer belonged and which could explain why Vienna was the original destination for what became the "Würzburg journey." Alex. Košenina notes (*KH*,243) that *"Ernst Platner... ist lediglich eine Leitfigur der neuen Bewegung 'philosophischer Ärzte', die den Menschen in seiner Doppelnatur von Leib und Seele erfassen. Kleist nennt Platner—wie auch den Göttinger Anthropologen Joh. Fr. Blumenbach—einen "Lehrer der Menschheit"* (II:656)," but does not explore that Kleist could have been interested in "doctors" not because of their teachings, but because he needed treatment (to Košenina's excuse, this is not his topic in *KH*, which however exemplifies a problematic of encyclopedical formats, of artificially carving up a field into disjunct items covered by different authors; "illness" is furthermore not a headword selected for coverage in *KH*—nor is, for that matter, "sexuality," so that we obtain a *"Kleist Handbuch. Leben—Werk—Wirkung"* that skirts precisely those topics that are arguably most decicive for Kleist's life and work, "politics" being furthermore included as merely one among 15 "context" headwords (out of several dozens in total), as if they were all of equal weight.

42   The side effects of mercury or arsenic therapy could be nearly as terrible as the symptoms of syphilis. The ancient Greeks were aware of this ambivalence: the term *pharmakon* means both remedy and poison; the German *Gift* (poison), derived from *Gabe* (the given), also reflects this ambivalence.

43   Walter Burkert notes (*Greek Religion*, 80) that the ancient Greeks considered illness and madness as sent by a god and requiring purification so as to "conduct the abnormal over into normality." Madness and intoxication are associated with Dionysos and Pythia, the high priestess of the Temple of Apollo at Delphi (aka the Oracle of Delphi), whose inspirations were said to derive from her intoxication with fumes or vapours. Burkert adds (*ibid*, 111), "Plato distinguishes the prophetic

madness of Apollo from the telestic [mystical] madness of Dionysos," so that the mad or clairvoyant Johann—"*Bringt Wein her! Lustig! Wein!*"—may represent the Dionysiac variety, complementing Sylvius' Apolloniac clairvoyance (Sylviius may refer to Tiresias, the blind prophet of Apollo in Thebes).

44   "*Eichel*" means both "glans" and "acorn," and Kleist repeatedly produces wordplays involving "*Eiche*" ("oak tree"), whose shape (root, trunk and crown) is reminiscent of an erect penis, or "Leiche" ("corpse"—cf. my discussion in *Emigrant* of Kleist's *BA* report on Luise's funeral). Cf. also Heinz Schott, "Erotik und Sexualität im Mesmerismus. Anmerkungen zum *Käthchen von Heilbronn*," in Günther Emig (Ed.), *Erotik und Sexualität im Werk Heinrich von Kleists*. Heilbronner Kleist-Kolloquien II (Heilbronn: Kleist-Archiv Sembdner, 2000), 152.

45   Cf. Ernst Bäumler, *Amors vergifteter Pfeil*, 23; Nora Crook and Derek Guilton, *Shelley's Venomed Melody* (Cambridge: CUP, 1986), 127. Today's reader is at once advantaged and disadvantaged relative to Kleist's contemporaries in deciphering Kleist's messages: advantaged because us today can openly articulate what in Kleist's time was ineffable, disadvantaged because vernacular references current in Kleist's time have since been lost. Unlike readers in Kleist's time, when syphilis was widespread, readers today do not recognise that the constellation *Scorpio* was widely associated with syphilis. Scholars only recently rediscovered that codpieces (cf. *Verlobung*) were fashion items associated with syphilis; in Kleist's time this could still have been common knowledge. Kleist will have assumed that anyone with an educational background and life context similar to his own—i.e., aristocrats and certain privileged bourgeois—could understand such references. "Language conveys not only referential information but information about group-membership," writes Manuel DeLanda in *A Thousand Years of Nonlinear History* (New York: Swerve, 2000), 192, and Kleist was deliberately using *group speak* or *minor language* (Deleuze) to address target readers (while keeping non-target audiences in the dark).

46   The reference to 1484 in Dürer's print must be erroneous. Following the French invasion of Naples in 1494, which led to decade-long struggle over the southern Italian peninsula, and a destabilisation of norms and political constellations in Italy and beyond, a new breed of political and social thinkers emerged, led by Baldassare Castiglione and Niccolò Machiavelli and referred to as "the 1494ers." Castiglione in his celebrated *Il libro del cortegiano* (The Book of the Courtier) distinguishes the

behaviours of *grazia* (grace) and *affettazione* (affectation), using elegant and clumsy dance movements as examples to illustrate the difference, of which the successful courtier would exhibit the former consistently and the latter never (cf. Blamberger, *Kleist*, 352-3). No doubt *Marionettentheater*'s analogous terminology—*Grazie* and *Ziererei*—and imagery of the dance was influenced by Castiglione's, whose book remained influencial among aristocrats in Kleist's day; both Castiglione and Kleist therefore write in a context of proliferating syphilis. That Kleist was fascinated by astrological and astronomical symbolism is obvious: his re-dating his birthday to 10th October may entail astrological references (so may his timing of his suicide—cf. my later section *The Orphic*). Kleist's recorded date and hour of birth, 18th October 1777, 01:00 hrs, may have been too close for comfort to the 24th October, on which the sun enters the sign of *Scorpio* in the Ptolemaic tropical zodiac: Kleist's natal chart, accessible on www.astro.com, shows how close the position of the sun will have been to *Scorpio*. Astrological considerations apart, Kleist chose 10th October as his birthday after experiencing, on 10th October 1800, "the most important day of my life in Würzburg" (II:593), which he subsequently celebrated as his *"rebirth,"* as Hans-Jürgen Schrader and Hans Dieter Zimmermann already conjectured in the context of their phimosis hypothesis (cf. Blamberger, *Kleist*, 127-8; Loch, *Kleist*, 419 n.1). Horst Häker has offered a compelling case in favour of accepting Kleist's own dating, which Eberhard Siebert endorses (cf. *Kleistiana Collecta*, Heilbronn: Kleist-Archiv Sembdner, 2011, 11-15). As for myself, I see no reason why we cannot accept both dates: Kleist's registered birthday was the 18th October, the day of his "rebirth," 10th October. When his cousin Carl von Pannwitz killed himself on the eve of Kleist's official birthday, he evidently considered the 18th to be properly Kleist's birthday (the biographers disagree with respect to the date of Carl's suicide: Schulz (*Kleist*, 67) has the 17th, but does not provide a source; Blamberger (*Kleist*, 27), Michalzik (*Kleist*, 78) and Zimmermann (*Kleist*, 31) have the 10th, drawing on Joh. Heinr. Ernst von Schönfeldt's reminiscence (*LS*,6), who however apparently did not spell out the date, presumably added only retroactively by Sembdner). Kleist in his "birthday letter" to Wilhelmine of 10th October 1801 establishes a *new timeline*, rather as the French Revolutionary Calendar does: 10th October 1801 completes "Year 1" of his new life, on which he promptly announces to Wilhelmine his decision to become "a farmer" (cf. II:695); upon completing "Year 7," he receives his poet's laurel from Buol (cf. II:794); whether he celebrates "Year 11" by producing musical poems together with Henriette Vogel we do not know (cf. my section *"Projekt Orpheus"* below)—we do know that he saw Sophie Sander and Rahel Levin during the month of October 1811 (cf. II:882).

47   Cf. Katharina Mommsen, *Kleists Kampf mit Goethe* (Berlin: Suhrkamp, 1979), *passim*. Cf. also https://www.vocabulary.com/dictionary/Phoebus%20Apollo. Kleist will have had these as well as other attributes of Apollo in view when he chose the name for the journal: as sun-god Phoebus, obviously, but also as god of prophecy, which Kleist's own *satirical* scenarios amount to, and as god of archers, *satirically* representing cannoniers, *satyrically*, ithyphallic lovers, *syphilitically*, contagious syphiliacs (Phoebus Apollo thus lent himself perfectly to representing Kleist's *satirical, satyrical, syphilitical* and *po(i)etical* concerns all in one). Cf. furthermore Burkert, *Greek Religion*, 145: "Youthfully pure renewal at the annual gathering, the banishment of disease in song and dance, and the image of the arrow-bearing Guardian God [Apollo] are brought together in one vision; that a unified figure emerged from these elements is due probably more than in the case of other gods to the power of poetry."

48   Quoted in: http://jmvh.org/article/syphilis-its-early-history-and-treatment-until-penicillin-and-the-debate-on-its-origins/.

49   Cf. Joh. Wolfgang von Goethe, *Römische Elegien* (1795) V.8; 16; Arthur Schopenhauer, "Aphorismen zur Lebensweisheit. Chapter 4: Von dem, was einer vorstellt," in *Parerga und Paralipomena*, Vol. 1 (1851). Bäumler (*Amors vergifteter Pfeil*, 21) traces Schopenhauer's metaphor to Jean Lemaire de Belges' 1525 tale *Cupido and Atropos*. Kleist's gesture, in *Marquise*, of "shifting the location from the north to the south," is usually interpreted as reflecting a widely-held view of southern Europeans as being more *sensuous*, but it may just as much allude to the—related—prejudice of syphilis having been most prevalent in the south: "*Der Süden Europas war der prävalirendste Entstehungspunkt der Syphilis*" (Ditterich, *Syphilis*, 95). Goethe also locates his *syphilitical* elegies in the south—in Rome. Müller's note to Gentz of 25th June 1803, *"Ihres sonderbar aus Süden und Norden, oder vielmehr aus Orient und Norden gemischten Temperaments"* (*AML*,60), perhaps suggests that Gentz's sexual drive hails from the (lascivious) "south" or "orient," his political acumen from the (rational) "north."

50   Goethe's Mephistopheles pronounces a similarly thinly veiled reference to syphilis: *"Ein schönes Fräulein nahm sich seiner an, / als er in Neapel fremd herumspazierte, / Sie hat an ihm viel Liebs und Treus getan, / daß er's bis an sein selig Ende spürte"* (*Faust. Eine Tragödie*, 13).

51 Goethe links Hermes to therapeutic mercury: *"Doch wir sind nicht so ganz, wir alte Heiden, verlassen, / Immer schwebet ein Gott über der Erde noch hin, / Eilig und geschäftig, ihr kennt ihn alle, verehrt ihn! / Ihn, den Boten des Zeus, Hermes, den heilenden Gott"* (*Römische Elegien*, III).

52 The question of whether syphilis was imported from the New World by Columbus' men, or existed in the Old World before (without being recognised as a distinct disease) remains unresolved to this day; according to some evidence the disease may have evolved from a similar spirochetal disease traceable to Central Africa—cf., e.g., *Clinical Microbiology Reviews*, Jan. 2005, 205–216. Ernst Bäumler reports (*Amors vergifteter Pfeil*, 32-3) that in Kleist's day doctors still vehemently argued this point, and offers an anecdote that may be reflected in *Kohlhaas*: *"Zeitweilig erreichte der Streit geradezu gigantische Ausmaße. Erich Hoffmann, einer der beiden Entdecker des Erregers der Lues, der Spirochaeta pallida, berichtet darüber: "In Leipzig nahm die Fehde zwischen zwei Professoren, von dene der eine der Leibarzt des sächsischen, der andere der des brandenburgischen Kurfürsten war, unter Teilnahme der Studierenden solche Formen an, daß eine Trennung der beiden Kampfhähne nötig schien und deshalb die Universitäten Wittenberg und Frankfurt an der Oder neugegründet wurden."* It may be coincidence that in *Kohlhaas* the Saxon and Brandenburg Electors confront each other, that Kleist studied in Frankfurt/O. (his home-town, after all), and that during the Würzburg journey he immatriculated as a student at Leipzig U.—still, it is possible that he knew this anecdote. In his 23rd/24th January 1811 *BA* article, "*Kurze Geschichte des gelben Fiebers in Europa*," he terms *fièvre jaune* an "occidental plague," thereby *covertly* pointing to both syphilis (the premise of its import from the Western Hemisphere) and "French disease" (France being west of Germany). The "dirt" ("*Kot*") Count F throws at the swan Thinka (the immaculate *erômenos* named "Marquise") may reference Goethe's "poisonous sludge." In Chapter X of Edgar Allan Poe's novel *The Narrative of Arthur Gordon Pym of Nantucket*, in *Complete Stories and Poems* (New York: Doubleday, 1984), 666-9, the three shipwrecked men encounter a (fata morgana of) a floating brothel; a *femme fatale* appears to lure them in; as they draw closer, they perceive with horror that she, as well as all others in the brothel, many men and a few whores, are dead: purtrifying corpses, wrecked by, as the narrator puts it, "yellow fever, or some other virulent disease of the same fearful kind." Syphilis, no doubt. The woman's smile turns out to have been the fleshless grin of a decomposing skull. The moment when the sailor realises the true aspect of the sirene would no doubt have met with Kleist's approval:

The eyes were gone, and the whole flesh around the mouth, leaving the teeth utterly naked. This, then, was the smile which had cheered us on to hope! this the—but I forbear (668).

Picture Penthesilea, mixing up bites and kisses! Poe's narrator claims having been "blinded" by "the intense excitement of the moment," yet also admits to later having tried to trace the woman. Poe was as enamoured of numerology and symbolism as was Kleist: this sub-plot could only ever have comprised the novel's Chapter X: "The Cruxified." The cause of Poe's death remains a mystery; I'd put syphilis top of the list of hypotheses. His narrator introduces poisoned food and venomous species of fish or bird as rational causes, then closes the chapter admonishing his readers: "—but it is utterly useless to form conjectures where all is involved, and will, no doubt, remain for ever involved, in the most appalling and unfathomable mistery." If this is not an ending on Poe's own account, then I don't know what is. Nevertheless, I shall heed his advice—or plea—and leave it at that.

53   Ernst Bäumler imparts (*Amors vergifteter Pfeil*, 47) the following 1510 report by Ulrich von Hutten: "*Von solcher Kraft war die Salbe, daß sie aus dem entferntesten Teil des Körpers das Krankhafte in den Mund zusammentrieb... Daher floß durch Rachen und Mund die Krankheit ab... der Speichel floß ohne Unterlaß aus dem Mund, gleich von Anfang so furchtbar stinkend und so ansteckend, daß er alles sofort verunreinigte und besudelte.*"

54   Italian physician Gabrielle Falloppio (1523-62), in a treatise on syphilis, mentions condoms, made of linen sheaths soaked in a chemical solution and dried before use, and sized to cover the glans and held on with a ribbon, as proven protection against syphilis. The term "condom" may derive from the Italian *"guanto,"* "glove." In the late 16th century condoms appeared that covered the entire penis, made of linen treated with chemicals, animal bladder or intestines, or fine leather. Yet even in Kleist's day condoms remained unreliable, often riddled with holes and susceptible to sliding off or breaking—cf. https://en.wikipedia.org/wiki/Condom#Before_the_19th_century. Syphiliacs used ingenious means to cover up their ulcers, scars, and side effects of mercury poisoning; Bäumler enumerates (*Amor's vergifteter Pfeil*, 84) wigs to cover loss of hair (cf. Adam's wig in *Krug*), lace jabots to cover *corona veneris*, gloves to cover weals on the hands (cf. Nathalie's glove in *Homburg*, which I argue also represents a condom), and powder to cover facial pustules. "*Im frühen Barock*

kam die Perücke wieder in Mode. Sie diente vor allem dazu, den krankheitsbedingten Haarausfall bei der Syphilis, Alopecia syphilitica und die Folgen der Behandlung mit Quecksilber zu kaschieren"—cf. https://de.wikipedia.org/wiki/Perücke. All of this explains why Kleist sought treatment away from his family and friends, and why in his texts he so frequently and explicitly features hats, caps, gloves, wigs, coats, etc: they may at once represent condoms and accessories for covering symptoms. Other artificial means to counteract syphilis' or mercury's side-effects included nose and penis prostheses (cf. Adam's wooden prosthesis in *Krug* and *Marionettentheater*'s *Gliedermann*) and fashion accessories such as codpieces, which offered space for sufferers' genital bandages.

55   Like AIDS in the late 20th century, Syphilis from the beginning was linked to sodomy—cf. Bäumler, *Amors vergifteter Pfeil*, 23; 376. In both cases the perception soon had to be revised, but nevertheless lingered on (as a matter of fact, for anatomical reasons the passive lover during anal sex is particularly vulnerable to infection). Bäumler notes (*ibid*, 97) that syphilis and gonorrhoea frequently were compounded, and that the Parisian doctor Jean Astruc in his seminal 1736 treatise *De morbis venereis* considered gonorrhoea an early stage of syphilis, advocated the Columbus-theory of the importation of syphilis into Europe, and therapied syphilis with mercury and guaiacum.

56   Neither Thierrez nor Ghonorez appear to have been current names, whereas Schroffenstein, incidentally, was (to this day there is a castle by that name in South Tyrol), but neither the family nor the castle by this name were of historical significance, and Kleist could scarcely have known of them; instead, he could have been inspired to the name by the formerly Habsburgian Biberstein Castle near Aarau, which Zschokke in 1801 rented and lived in. Thierrez could be an artificially "Frenchified" contraction of Gutiérrez, the Spanish form of Walter (Old High German for ruler; cf. *Krug*'s Walter and Kleist's repeated usage of the related terms *Gewalt, walten* and *gewaltig* to denote a pervasive power or sway—fate is also commonly said to *"walten,"* and so are, sometimes, death, illness and misery), and the German colloquial term *"Tripper"* (i.e., gonorrhoea). Ghonorez could refer to syphilis, since in these days gonorrhoea and syphilis were still frequently compounded into a single disease. Syphilis in Germany was also known as *Lues*, which is near-homophone with the Prussian Queen's name, *Luise*; as well as Napoleon's bro's *Louis*; while conincidental, such parallels were never lost on Kleist.

57   The Greek term *choros* derives from *choreuo*, "I am dancing," and the members of ancient choruses were above all dancers, who may or may not also sing to music; *poietes,* poets, are those who produce these dances and hymns, tragedy, the play in which these dances are deployed (*tragoidia* = "goat song," *tragodoi* = "goat singers," originally the processions that led goats to their sacrifice—cf. Burkert, *Greek Religion*, 102). For Aug. Wilh. Schlegel the chorus comprises the "ideal spectator" that conveys to the audience how to interpret or react to the drama, articulates those hidden motives or emotions the actors themselves can not express, and convey information to the play's characters which they would not otherwise be able to obtain, thus playing an active part in moving the plot forward. Kleist's choruses of boys, maidens, women, or warriors, accordingly, combine several functions: as *dancers,* they enact satyr dances and erotic going-ons; as *messangers,* they succinctly put into a nutshell the play's storyline; as *processions leaders,* they usher or herd on the characters towards their fate.

58   Ilse Graham writes (*Word into Flesh*, 47) *à propos* of these lines: "Yet a diseased eye can be cured. Distrust can be overcome; and the question arises whether the cognitive and human condition, however radically it is articulated in *Die Familie Schroffenstein*, is ultimately a curable condition... The true, and worst, defect of human vision is much harder to eradicate. We may approach its definition by saying that we are constrained to see with and through our eyes, but cannot turn our gaze onto the instruments with which we see." Kleist would perhaps have concurred—cf. his "fog" riddle to Wilhelmine (cf. II:613)—that mistrust, be it among male lovers in the age of syphilis, be it among German dynasties in the age of Napoleon, *was curable*—namely, by means of his poetry. Alas, over the course of a decade of poetic production, Kleist was increasingly forced to admit that neither was either type of mistrust eradicated, nor did his poetry have a measurable effect: the former was more tenacious, the latter less effective, than he had hoped.

59   The three stages of syphilis and their typical symptoms were first described systematically by Philippe Ricord in his 1837 treatise *Monographie du chancre* and in subsequent treatises, and were not yet clearly delineated in Kleist's day, although some doctors may well have recognised the general outline of the disease's progression (Ricord was also the first to conclusively prove that gonorrhoea and syphilis were two different venereal diseases). In recent (late 20th century) treatises, *neurosyphilis*—i.e., progressive paralysis, often in conjunction with *tabes dorsalis*—is sometimes

delineated as fouth stage—cf. https://de.wikipedia.org/wiki/Neurolues; cf. also Alfons Labisch and Reinhard Spree (Eds.), *"Einem jeden Kranken in einem Hospitale sein eigenes Bett": Zur Sozialgeschichte des allgemeinen Krankenhauses in Deutschland im 19. Jahrhundert* (Frankfurt/M.: Campus, 1996), 35.

60   Kleist's note to Ulrike, "*Wärst Du ein Mann gewesen—denn eine Frau konnte meine Vertraute nicht werden,--so hätte ich diesen Freund [i.e., Brockes] nicht so weit zu suchen gebraucht, als jetzt. Ergründe nicht den Zweck meiner Reise, selbst wenn Du es könntest. Denke, daß die Erreichung desselben zum Teil an die Verheimlichung vor allen,* allen *Menschen beruht. Für jetzt wenigstens, Denn einst wird es mein Stolz und meine Freude sein, ihn mitzuteilen*" (II:514), is consistent with the notion that his purpose related to his male reproductive capacity, and his secrecy may indeed have been necessary for "success"—especially vis-à-vis Wilhelmine, who lived next door from Ulrike—, in so far as he had to avoid putting her off from the joint *"Lebensplan"* he was in the process of conjuring forth for them. His emphatic *"allen"* probably meant Wilhelmine as well as his family; perhaps he would have confided to Ulrike had she not lived amidst the Kleists and Zenges in Frankfurt/O. Rudolf Loch, in reviewing the hypothesis that Kleist in Würzburg sought treatment for a phimosis, maintains (*Kleist*, 444) that "*die graduierten Ärzte der medizinischen Klinik Würzburg, organisatorisch vereinigt mit dem ebenfalls weithin bekannten Julius-Hospital, [...] grundsätzlich, wie* [Hans-Jürgen] *Schrader belegen kann, zu einer Therapie venerisch Kranker nicht bereit waren, habe* [Kleists] *Versorgung einem der zwanzig Zunft-Wundärzte oblegen.*" Schrader's assessment, even if correct, would nullify neither my hypothesis that the young madman Kleist observed at the Julius-Hospital was syphiliac—tertiary syphilis is no longer infectious, and progressive paralysis being a late effect of syphilis was confirmed only in the second half of the 19th century, so that a patient might be admitted, knowingly or unknowingly, as a *mental* rather than a *venereal* case—, nor that Kleist in Würzburg consulted Hufeland or Neufville, neither of whom was assigned to Würzburg University's medical clinic or Julius-Hospital, so that either of them could have treated private patients as they pleased, and even doctors who *were* assigned to a clinic may have treated private patients outside their normal duties, if clandestinely (possibly Kleist stayed with the *Stadtchirurgus* Josef Wirth precisely to make it feasible for more prominent doctors from Julius-Hospital to treat him in circumvention of such restrictions, Wirth offering a private space with the necessary medical equipment for operations—the city authority's reprimand of Wirth suggests as much, cf. *LS*,42). Earlier suggestions in the Kleist reception to

the effect that the patient's madness was due to an excess of masturbation and that Kleist was so rattled by this encounter because it reminded him of his own practice are of course entirely implausible and outdated; a more plausible explanation for his vehement reaction is that he did fear that the madman could in fact be a late-stage syphiliac, and thus a harbinger of what might yet be in store for him.

61   Carl Aug. on Struensee was the older brother of Joh. Fr. Struensee, personal physician of King Fr. VII of Denmark, who is believed to have suffered of late stage syphilis (cf. Bäumler, *Amors vergifteter Pfeil*, 78), and Kleist could have had reason to assume that under Struensee's leadership the combat of venereal disease would be a priority for Prussia's medical deputation.

62   Cf. Ernst Bäumler, *Amors vergifteter Pfeil*, 92.

63   The intended or actual destinations of Kleist's journey were so saturated with famous medical institutuations—the Bruonian school in Bamberg, the Vienna School at the famed General Hospital, Puységur's school in Strasbourg, Gmelin's practice in Heilbronn en route to Strasbourg, the Julius-Hospital with its famous pharmacy and prominent doctors, many of whom were also teaching at Würzburg University's well-known medical school—that it is surprising that neither the adherents of the "medical thesis" (whether entailing treatment for phimosis, impotence or speech disorder) nor those of the "industrial espionage thesis" have considered the possibility that Kleist was trying to kill two birds with one stone by seeking to find a remedy for his own affliction while at the same time supplying the Prussian deputation with information about medical and pharmaceutical advances in foreign territories, his twin purposes providing cover and camouflage for each other: towards the Prussian officials he could position the journey as a service in the national interest (and thereby recommend himself for future employment), thereby hiding his personal agenda of seeking consultation and treatment; towards the doctors, pharmacists and hospital administrators he could foreground his personal need for treatment, thereby hiding his data gathering on behalf of a foreign state. Would this not have comprised an exceedingly elegant—and eminently Kleistian—solution to his conundrum of requiring both secrecy and official support? While installed at the city surgeon Josef Wirth's house, Kleist (so he tells Wilhelmine) spends much time reading and writing—reading and writing *what*? Could he have been *recording medical information* provided by Wirth and other sources, or gathered during his visits to the

Julius-Hospital and Würzburg University's medical school (where the surgeons Carl Caspar von Siebold and Hermann Joseph Brünninghausen, whom Kleist mentions in this letters, headed major departments)? Eberhard Siebert (*Kleistiana Collecta*, 23-46) constructs an interesting, if unconvincing, case that Kleist sought to spy out trade secrets pertaining to the production of a novel textile colour known as Pickel-green, invented and at the time fabricated only in Würzburg by Joh. Georg Pickel, professor of chemistry and pharmaceutics at Würzburg University's medical faculty, who also ran a lab at Julius-Hospital furnished for his research. Siebert's theory is unconvincing because at the time when Kleist offers Struensee's team in Berlin to provide them with classified information, Würzburg is evidently not yet on his itinerary (it apparently only pops up during or following his conversation with Lord Elliot in Dresden), whereas Siebert's case must necessarily rest on the premise that Pickel-green was of particular interest to Struensee's department (cf. *ibid*, 36-8). Siebert even suggests (*ibid*, 301-2) that Kleist's and Chr. Wilh. Hufeland's coinciding sojourns in Würzburg in the autumn of 1800 pursued the same object, namely the person of Joh. Goerg Pickel—Kleist to extract secrets about the manufacture of Pickel-green, Hufeland due to Pickel's involvement in establishing the healing springs at Bocklet and Kissingen—, but even if he wer correct regarding Hufeland's purpose, he is quite definitely wrong regarding Kleist's.

64 Zimmermann quotes (*Kleist*, 48-9) from a letter by Brockes to "Heinrich," which he dates sometime in 1800, of which he notes that we cannot be certain that the addressee is indeed Kleist, and for which he fails to provide his source): *"Nie war ich imstande, so ganz die unverdorbene Empfindung deines Herzens in all seinen Trieben zu durchschauen, als seit Du mich selbst durch die Geschichte Deiner ersten Jügnlingsjahre damit bekanntgemacht hast... Jetzt, da Du mich Deines Vertrauens gewürdigt hast, darf ich Dir wohl sagen, daß ich's ahndete, was in Deiner Seele vorging... Du hast also von mir, der ich selbst so sehr wie irgend einer diese Schwachheit an mir erfahre, gewiß kein hartes Urteil zu befürchten... Du hast es an Dir selbst erfahren, wie mannigfaltig die Sophistereien sind, wodurch die aufgeregte Sinnlichkeit der Jugend ihre Befriedigung mit der Vermeidung der gefährlichen Folgen derselben zu vereinigen hofft, und wenn sie nicht hinreichend über alles, was dahin gehört, unterrichtet wird, fast immer ein Opfer ihres Irrtums und der Verführung sein muß. Nimm ferner Deine besondere Lage... eine so mächtige Neigung...; Deine äußeren Vorzüge, welche die Verführung reizen mußten, wie Du so oft es erfuhrst; Dein Temperament, die Weichheit und Zärtlichkeit Deines Herzens... Trage nun mit ruhiger Erhebung und ohne Klage die freilich oft drückenden*

Folgen Deiner ehemaligen Handlungen... Du sagst, wie sehr es Dich noch kränken müsse, anderen, die ohne eigenes Verdienst der Verführung entgangen sind, in der Fülle der Gesundheit und des eigenen Friedens ihre Jahre genießen zu sehn, die Dir durch ihr Glück wie auch ihren verachtenden Blick Hohn zu sprechen scheinen... Physischer und moralischer Schmerz führt... macht oft den Leidenden zum Weisen und diesen zum Wohltäter seiner Brüder." It does appear highly improbable that the letter is *not* addressed to Kleist: it aligns perfectly with their "honeymoon," his early "initiation" during the *Siege of Mainz*, his physical attributes and youthful coquetry that made him irresistible to other men, the health issues that accompanied his seductiveness, his confiding in Brocke. We may conjecture what took place on Rügen: Kleist meets Brockes at the spa, finds him open- and like-minded, and opens his heart to him his symptoms and his worry whether he would ever be able to lead a "normal" life. The experienced Brockes, suffering from the same or a similar affliction, shares his knowledge about treatment options and his perspective on finding an *"Einrichtung"* between homosexual desire and heterosexual family life, possibly inspiring both the Würzburg journey as well as Kleist's concept of *"Scheidung."* Kleist's, not Brockes', health issues are the central purpose of the Würzburg journey—as Kleist implies in a letter to Wilhelmine, *"Er [Brockes] sollte damals ein Amt nehmen, er hing innig an seiner Schwester [etc.]... Um mir den Verdacht zu ersparen, als sei* ich *der eigentliche Zweck der Reise, und als hätte* ich *ihn nur bewegt mir zu folgen, welches meiner Absicht schaden konnte, gab er bei seiner Familie der ganzen Reise den Anstrich, als geschehe sie nur um seinetwillen"* (II:622)—and Brockes, genuinely enamoured of Kleist and as devoted to him as Carl von Zenge's Pomeranian is to Brockes himself, unhesitatingly accompanies him.

65   As I pointed out in *Emigrant*, Elliot's intervention likely explains the change in Kleist and Brockes' itinerary—instead of aiming for Vienna (via Regensburg), they now aim for Strasbourg (via Würzburg; in the event, they complete their mission in Würzburg and do not proceed further). Not only does Elliot not issue passports to them (which, travelling as Swedish nationals from Rügen, they require to enter Austrian territory), but he also informs them that they are more likely to find what they are looking for in Würzburg or Strasbourg. En route to Würzburg they pass through Bamberg, but it is not clear that they linger there: travelling by stagecoach, on 5th September they cover the 60km distance from Chemnitz via Zwickau to Reichenbach im Vogtland in 12 hours; taking this distance as a typical day's journey, they would have reached Hof on the 6th, Bayreuth on the 7th, and Bamberg on the

8th. From Bamberg to Würzburg the distance is almost 90km and only with the stagecoach travelling through the night could they have arrived on the morning of the 10th (re the uncertain date of the first Würzburg letter, cf. II:553). Kleist mentions to Wilhelmine that he spent some time Bayreuth (cf. II:580: *"alles, was mir... in Bayreuth... begegnet ist"*), which suggests that they may have travelled at night not only the Bamberg-Würzburg leg but also others (it is possible: in October Kleist would rush from Würzburg to Berlin during five consecutive days and nights—cf. II:582). It is thus possible that Kleist visited the leading German practitioner of Bruonianism Andreas Röschlaub at the Bamberg General Hospital (with whom Schelling's wife also underwent treatment), but it is just as possible that Elliot dissuaded him from seeking out the Brunonians and recommended he go straight to Würzburg.

66   The direct route from Bern to Paris would have been via Neuchâtel and Besançon, and travelling via Lyon encompassed a significant detour for which there must have been a reason. Already in 1801 Kleist and Ulrike planned to reach Paris via Switzerland and southern France, but in Strasbourg changed their mind and went straight to Paris in order to arrive in time for the 14th July celebrations (cf. II:658).

67   As Richard Samuel and Hilda M. Brown show in *Kleist's Lost Year and the Quest for 'Robert Guiskard'* (Leamington Spa: James Hall, 1981), in the spring of 1804 Kleist could have travelled back and forth between Mainz and Paris several times (cf. also Schulz, *Kleist*, 266-7). This is not implausible: there will have been excellent transport links between Mainz, a key fortress on the Rhine's left bank and then French territory, and Paris, and between cycles of syphilis treatment Kleist would have enjoyed periods of convalescence during which he was able to travel. It has been speculated that Kleist acted as a courier on behalf of Wedekind or was involved in an anti-Napoleonic plot organised by Freemasons around Count Schlabrendorf. Even if correct, such activities would not contradict my *syphilitical* hypothesis—on the contrary, *especially* someone battling a deadly disease would have had the audacity to undertake such daredevil missions. Thomas Wichmann suggests in *Heinrich von Kleist*, (Stuttgart: J.B. Metzler, 1988), 79, that Kleist avoided mentioning Wedekind—a known Jacobine—to maintain discretion towards the Prussian authorities, but it seems more plausible that he simply avoided any reference to his illness altogether: he rarely mentioned any of his doctors.

68   Sulphurous water was sometimes used in combating venereal diseases—cf. Bäumler, *Amors vergifteter Pfeil*, 83. Kleist could have been pursuing a triple—*syphilitical/satytical/satirical*—agenda: Gualtieri was to introduce him to Prussian cabinet councillor Joh. Wilh. Lombard, at the time spa-ing in Landeck, who was well-connected at court and "special friend" with Gualtieri—possibly code for "lover"—; Kleist in Landeck thus at the same time could have undergone treatment, enhanced his access to the court, and brefriended a "brother."

69   Syphilis is a systemic disease, affecting any part of the body, and was called "the great imitator" for its symptoms are similar to those of other diseases. Bäumler (*Amors giftiger Pfeil*, 207-8) notes that sudden severe abdominal pain coupled with vomiting may be a sign of onsetting *tabes dorsalis*. The organ most affected by mercury poisoning is the liver, and residual mercury also tends to accumulate in the area of the pubic bone, so Kleist's abdominal pain could also have been a side-effect of therapy.

70   Opium was used as pain-killer and a more benign alternative to mercury and arsenic in alleviating a wide range of symptoms—to Thomas Sydenham, the "English Hippocrates", is attributed the quote, "Among the remedies which it has pleased Almighty God to give to man to relieve his sufferings, none is so universal and so efficacious as opium"; only after Kleist's death was opium gradually superseded as a pain killer by purified and synthetic opioids such as morphine (first isolated in 1804 but not commercially available till 1817). Kleist refers to Wyttenbach in Bern as "doctor and pharmacist" (cf. II:727), which serves as a useful reminder that *access to supply* of compounds—mercury solutions, arsenic, opium, etc.—will have been just as important as *expertise* in their application. The owner of *Löwen-Apotheke* was evidently at the same time Kleist's landlord, suggesting that Kleist struck a "package deal" with him, encompassing accommodation and medical supplies, so as to benefit from discounts and/or priority status as high-value customer. It has been speculated in the Kleist reception that Kleist ordered the arsenic to poison Napoleon, and although it is not out of the question (cf. my later argument that it is possible that Kleist in 1809 entered Vienna while it was under Napoleon's personal command), I consider it far more plausible that he simply required the substance for his own use: although it became widespread as medication for syphilis only in the early 20th century, some doctors already in the early 19th century turned to arsenic to complement or replace mercury. Analyses of Napoleon's hair samples taken between 1805 and 1821 showed significantly heightened levels of arsenic (up to 38 times

normal levels), prompting numerous conspiracy theories—that Napoleon was slowly being poisoned; that he suffered from syphilis and was self-medicating with arsenic; that he used arsenic as an aphrodisiac—which could have inspired Kleist readers; cf. William R. Cullen, *Is Arsenic an Aphrodisiac? The Sociochemistry of an Element* (London: RSC Publishing, 2008).

71 Goethe spent lengthy periods in Töplitz, and in 1812 met Beethoven there; the regular guest Fr. von Gentz in the summer of 1803 notes 8,000 guests, which in those days was quite a crowd for a sleepy if famous spa town. A syphilis cure will more typically have involved sulphurous water, but alkaline or saline waters may ahve soothed certain syphilic symptoms or side-effects of arsenic therapy. Kleist had been in Töplitz before, in early September 1807, right after arriving in Dresden (cf. II:790; *MA*III, 832), when together with the Austrian envoy Joseph von Buol he visited Fr. von Gentz, then exiled in Töplitz following the Prussian defeat (in 1808/9 Gentz would relocate to Prague, as did many other members of the resistance; cf. II:819). This visit to Töplitz must have been among Kleist's very first undertakings upon arriving in Dresden, and illustrates that Dresden was a logical choice of abode between the wars, in terms of furthering his *po(i)etical, satirical* and *syphilitical* agendas: many German patriots were gathering along the "axis" Leipzig-Dresden-Töplitz-Prague—straddling Saxony and Bohemia, and only a couple days' journey end-to-end—, and Töplitz offered Kleist spa and "retreat centre" right at his doorsteps, equipped with world-class medical infrastructure and services (for those who could afford it). The prominent political writer and diplomat Fr. von Gentz was a close friend of A. Müller (cf. my discussion of their relationship further below), and of Austrian ambassador Count Stadion, and subsided on a stipend from the British crown granted for his services in the Wars against Napoleon; in September 1806 he drafted Fr. Wilh.'s ultimatum to Napoleon that precipitated the *War of the Fourth Coalition*; like Kleist he believed that Germany held the key to overcoming Napoleon's hegemony, especially Austria and Prussia acting in union—cf. https://en.wikipedia.org/wiki/Friedrich_von_Gentz.

72 Kleist's therapies must have been expensive, which goes some way towards explaining his perennial financial problems. Mercury and arsenic were relatively expensive substances, and doctors' fees will have been substantial, not least since he repeatedly sought out the most famous doctors of his day. It appears that Kleist spent 300 *Reichstaler* (RT) during the Würzburg journey, a far from insignificant amount scarcely accounted for by travel expenses alone. Kleist's salary as second lieutenant

had been 13 RT per month, so the two-months-long journey's cost were equivalent to more than two annual salaries (cf. Michalzik, *Kleist*, 290). Medical expenses comprise the most plausible explanation for such expenditures: Kleist himself links medical expenses to his financial needs when he asked Ulrike in August 1802 (cf. II:727) to send money directly to Wyttenbach, having earlier requested money from Urlike for the Würzburg journey to cover expenses linked specifically to his mysterious "purpose" (cf. also *Schulz*, Kleist, 116). Rudolf Loch maintains (cf. *Kleist*, 425) that Kleist's share of the parental inheritance amounted to 6,000-8,500 RT, and that by the autumn of 1803, two years after coming into his inheritance, Kleist had spent 3,000 RT, which, Loch notes somewhat inconsistently, corresponded to "the remainder of his small fortune (not counting his share of the family home)" (cf. *ibid*, 182). Lack of funds and borrowing requests comprise a consistent theme in Kleist's life, and since his lifestyle otherwise does not appear to have been extravagant—the flats he rented were modest, his travel was often on foot, whenever possible he would cadge meals, etc.—, only expenditures about which he remained mute, such as medical bills, account for it. Roland Reuß et al (Eds.) note in *Brandenburger Ausgabe* (quoted in Gudrun Debriacher, *Rede der Seele*, 84): "Wie ernsthaft ihn... solche [somnambulism] und ähnliche Dinge beschäftigen, ging daraus hervor, daß er auch auf einem andern Gebiet, dem der wunderbaren Erfindungen, sich derselben Neigung hingab und den betreffenden Vorkommnissen nicht bloß eine große Aufmerkamkeit widmete, sondern häufig genug nicht unbeträchtliche Summen zuwendete." At his rate of expenditure, the 500 RT loan Kleist raised in November 1809 against his share of the family house's valuation (cf. II:830) will have covered his expenses for one year at best. He did generate income from his poetic productions, especially in 1810 with the publication of the *Erzählungen* and *Käthchen*, but with the forced closure of *BA* in early 1811, into which he had presumably invested that capital, he will once again have been completely broke. His publication of *Krug* in early 1811 does not seem to have generated much revenue, and if the second volume of *Erzählungen* did not, either, his situation in the autumn of 1811 may well have become desperate: his symptoms may have worsened just at a time when he had absolutely no money left for their treatment, or even their palliation with opium. When on his infamous last visit to Frankfurt/O. Ulrike refused to offer any further financial support (cf. II:883), this may have been the last straw. Arnim's assertion re Kleist's decease may be ironic, "brothers of mercy" being rather too close to "brotherhood" not to be taken with a grain of salt. Kleist was feared dead by friends on at least three occasions, in late 1803 in Paris (by Pfuel), in the spring of 1804 when receiving treatment in Mainz (again by Pfuel), and in the autumn of

1809 in Prague (by Müller et al), a pattern that may have jad as much to do with his suicidal fantasies as with his syphiliac symptoms. The friends who feared for him knew him well psychologically and physically, and had good reason for presupposing the profound fragility of his existence. As with the Mainz sojourn, the near-complete absence of records covering the Prague sojourn suggests, the possibility that they were lost apart, that Kleist engaged in activities he wished to keep secret, including but not necessarily limited to medical treatment. He submitted, via Buol, a report concerning *Aspern* to the Austrian commander in Prague, Count Franz Kolowrat-Liebsteinsky, and it is possible that he submitted a similar report covering *Wagram*: the only Austrian report on these battles, first published in Rühle's magazine *Pallas*, covers both battles together, and Rahmer makes a plausible case (*Kleist*, 166-7) that Kleist's reports could have filtered into that publication; the Regiment Garde in Potsdam was deemed the "cradle of Prussian tactics," and Kleist was well-qualified to supply such reports. Kleist could even have been present at *Wagram*, and the rumour circulated by Scheffner, that he had succumbed to wounds contracted on the battlefield, may not have been entirely baseless (cf. *LS*,332b). He did not succumb, obviously, but he may still have been wounded, if not fatally, and may even have used injury—real or invented—as cover for a stay in hospital to treat his syphilis.

73   Cf. Klaus Müller-Salget, *Heinrich von Kleist* (Stuttgart: Reclam, 2011), 103. Wilh. von Neufville's Franco-Germanic name likely inspired that of *Verlobung*'s Guillaume von Villeneuve (cf. II:160).

74   No doubt one could trace an intimate correlation between Kleist's physical pathology and his poetic pathos by mapping his texts against these events and journeys, his experiences with the therapies of his day—mercury and arsenic therapy, Hufelandian vitalism, Brunonianism, Mesmerian and Puységurian magnetism, somnambulism and hypnosis, Gersdorfian and Aldinian electro-therapy—, and his physiological and psychological sufferings and convalescences, all of which collectively could be said to constitute his life's and œuvre's very "*Generalbaß*."

75   Gerhard Bleul (Ed.), *Weiterbildung Homöopathie*. Band F (Stuttgart: Sonntag, 2005), 123-4. Samuel Hahnemann, discoverer (or inventor) of homeopathy, was a friend of Hufeland, in whose *Journal* he published repeatedly, including the 1796 article that laid out the basic principles of homeopathy (without yet using the term, which first appears in another of Hahnemann's articles in *Journal*, in 1807).

Hahnemann became a leading expert on syphilis and gonorrhoea and was among the first to treat them as separate diseases. His approach of applying mercury in small, "homeopathic" doses could have appealed to Kleist; it was also consistent with Hufelandian vitalist principles. Unlike Hahnemann but apparently like Kleist, Hufeland remained convinced that gonorrhoea and syphilis were the same disease—cf. Philippe Ricord, *Beobachtungen über Syphilis und Tripper*. Trans. Dr. Eisenmann (Erlangen, Palm und Enke, 1836), 114. Kleist's doctor in Mainz, Georg Wedekind, would later also publish on the treatment of syphilis in Hufeland's *Journal* (No. 58, 1824)—cf. H.F. Bonorden, *Die Syphilis, pathologisch, diagnostisch und therapeutisch* (Berlin: Enslin, 1834), §81, 130. Reportedly Wedekind treated syphilis patients with roots and bark of the South American guaiacum tree—cf. Georg L. Ditterich, *Die Krankheits-Familie Syphilis: Allgemeiner Theil, Erster Band* (Landshut: Vogel'sche, 1842), 306. Both Hufeland and Wedekind were thus leading practitioners of syphilis therapy, and Kleist's doctor in Bern, Wyttenbach, is mentioned in the medical literature in conjunction with a compound used to treat symptoms of syphilis—cf. L. Griesselich, *Hygea: Centralorgan für die homöopathische oder specifische Heilkunst* (Karlsruhe: Ch. Th. Gross, 1840), 337; cf. also Blamberger, *Kleist*, 200. While the medical profession has taken an interest in Kleist's health issues, the literary profession has largely neglected it, with Sigmund Rahmer and Wolf Kittler among the exceptions. The latter notes in *Die Geburt des Partisanen* (Heilbronn: Kleist-Archiv Sembdner, 2011), 215-16: *"Um auf Kleist zurückzukommen, so bleibt zu bemerken, daß sich etwa zu der Zeit, als Freud und Breuer ihre 'Studien über Hysterie' veröffentlichen, weniger die Literaturwissenschaft als vielmehr die Medizin für seine Person und sein Werk interessierten. Die 'Penthesilea' erscheint im Sadismuskapitel von [Richard von] Krafft-Ebings Psychopathologia sexualis. Und [Cesare] Lombroso führt Kleist als Beispiel für einen typischen Melancholiker an. Andere Diagnosen von anderen Medizinern hat Sigmund Rahmer aufgelistet: "Man hat nämlich diagnostiziert: schwere Neurasthenie und Hysterie; erbliche Belastung (Hereditarier) und psychopathische Minderwertigkeit—sit venia verbo—; Kleist präsentiert sich uns als Paranoiker mit Verfolgungswahn, Größenwahn etc., als chronischer Melancholiker mit Selbstmordtrieb und schweren Depressionszuständen, die seine gelegentliche Internierung notwendig machten, er bietet das ausgesprochene Krankheitsbild der Dementia praecox mit allmähligem geistigen Zerfall bis zu ausgesprochenem Blödsinn, er leidet an sexuellen Abnormitäten—Sadismus; Päderastie wird vermutet—und schließlich ist er Alkholist und Opiophage."* Rahmer's 1903 diagnoses may not hold up to early 21st century knowledge, but they remain instructive and consistent with our reading.

76   http://bilddetek.hypotheses.org/498. For the relevant excerpt from Kleist's autopsy report, cf. *LS*,534 and Dirk Grathoff, *Kleist: Geschichte, Politik, Sprache* (Heilbronn: Kleist-Achiv Sembdner, 2008), 225. Ridder refers to another source, Anja Schonlau, *Syphilis in der Literatur* (Würzburg: Königshausen u. Neumann, 2005), not available to me and whose focus appears to be the period after 1880. I have not been able to trace other "literary sources" Ridder claims refer to Kleist's syphilis.

77   If Kleist sat for Kügelgen, this would likely have taken place in 1808/9 in Dresden. Kügelgen's son Wilhelm in his memoirs does not mention Kleist among his father's sitters, of which there were many (he does mention Rühle), but his list is of 1806, before Kleist's arrival in Dresden, and is not meant to be complete (cf. *AML*,144). Rühle counts Kügelgen among their circle in Dresden (cf. *LS*,193).

78   Cf. Martin Gayford, in *Gustav Klimt: a life devoted to women*: "To Klimt, it seems, the hostile powers [depicted in his *Beethoven Frieze*]—naked temptresses and a huge snarling ape—above all symbolised the disease syphilis of which he was terrified—and understandably, since he had contracted it at an early age"—cf. https://www.telegraph.co.uk/culture/art/3673232/Gustav-Klimt-a-life-devoted-to-women.html. Beethoven's late symphonies may have been affected by his, possibly syphilis-induced, loss of hearing, and Nietzsche's late treatises by his, also possibly syphilis-induced, onset of madness. Bruce Everiss, in *Great Artists and Syphilis,* lists Manet, Gauguin, van Gogh, Goya, Dürer and Toulouse-Lautrec—cf. https://www.bruceonarthistory.com/2017/04/27/great-artists-and-syphilis/. Ernst Bäumler (*Amors vergifteter Pfeil,* 234) dedicates an entire section in his cultural history of syphilis to famous, presumed or plausible, syphiliacs of the European cultural sphere—Nietzsche, Heine, Schopenhauer, Lenau, Grabbe, Beethoven, Maupassant, Baudelaire, Manet and Mirabeau—and points out that the onset of paralysis may indeed initially encompass a temporary increase in mental productivity because it lowers mental and emotional barriers; that he does not mention Kleist, whose œuvre has *The Syphilitical* written all over it, must in equal measure be credited to Kleist's mastery of the art of camouflage and to his timely suicide, which perhaps whisked him away before his disease reached its third and most destructive phase.

79   Bäumler, in *Amors vergifteter Pfeil,* 251-4, lists Lenau among his "famous syphiliacs." Rahmer (*Kleist,* 403) has it that Kleist's *"Vita sexualis"* provided a "substrate" for his "mental ills" (*"seelische Verstimmungen"*). Following the suicide,

conjectures regarding Kleist's "mental illness" were, perhaps inevitably, widespread; Tieck in his foreword to the first (1821) edition of Kleist's works gave some credence to the notion, which prevailed into the late 19th and early 20th centuries, when in line with the prevailing *Zeitgeist* Kleist became subjected to psychological and psychoanalytical explorations. However, since the authors of the article *Adele Bloch-Bauer (1881-1925): Possible diagnoses for Gustav Klimt's Lady in Gold* (Journal of Medical Biography, June 2014) highlight that in those days insanity was frequently used as an euphemism for syphilis, it is quite possible that the early Kleist commentators, including Rahmer, in fact did entertain the possibility that Kleist had been syphiliac, and expressed their conjecture via the euphemism, thereby protecting both Kleist's and their own honour, while still hinting at possibilities. Blamberger notes (*Kleist*, 14), *"Fast jeder Biograph schreibt seine Geschichte von ihrem monströsen Ende her und versucht in den Brandzeichen des Körpers die der Seele zu lesen... Aufgrund des rätselhaften Todes stellen die Biographen Kleist ganzes Leben im Nachhinein unter Melancholieverdacht, und seine Werke gelten ihnen somit als Dokumente des Leidens,"* adding (*ibid*, 452) that Kleist's suicide and farewell letters can be understood *"als Teil einer grandiosen Inszenierung..., mit der Kleist seine Rezeptionsgeschichte selbst präformiert hat... Die Regeln also, mit denen man das Bild seiner Autorschaft konstruiert,"* implying that Kleist readers are falling into precisely that trap he set for them with his "grandiose staging."

80   The proper quote: *"Es ist unmöglich, eine Zeile von Kleist zu lesen, ohne daran zu denken, daß er sich das Leben genommen hat. Es ist, als sei sein Selbstmord seinem Werk vorangegangen."* E.M. Cioran, "Vom Nachteil, geboren zu sein," Trans. François Bondy. In: *Werke* (Frankfurt/M.: Suhrkamp, 2008), 1513.

81   Marie denied that Henriette was terminally ill, citing Henriette's former doctor (cf. *LS*,523d), but her statement cannot be considered as disinterested. Another former doctor, Joh. Erhard, pronounced Henriette sexually incapable (cf. Eduard von Bülow, *Heinrich von Kleist's Leben und Briefe*. Berlin: Wilhelm Vesser, 1848, 73), but did not consider her condition critical; however, his last consultation with her appears to have been three years before her death (cf. *LS*,523e), so this report is also of limited validity. Her obduction report states that she suffered from "incurable uterine cancer" (*LS*,534), but as Blamberger noted (*Kleist*, 458), the Prussian officials cannot be considered disinterested either: given the King's vehement and public reaction, they will have been keen to line up "scientific" causes for the suicides, so as to pre-empt their being mystified.

82   Hypersensitivity and burning sensation on the body's extremeties can be early signs of *tabes dorsalis* (degeneration of the spinal cord), and during the tertiary stage nasal cartilage and tissue may dissolve; nose prostheses were sold across Europe and in England reportedly "no-nose clubs" sprang up.

83   Kleist's stuttering or stammering was first remarked on in 1805 and apparently became significantly more pronounced in 1810/11—cf. Michalzik (*Kleist*, 86). Bäumler notes (*Amors vergifteter Pfeil*, 201-2) speech disorders and tripping over one's tongue as typical signs of the onset of paralysis, alongside shaky handwriting, reduced facials expression, nervousness and depressiveness, and anxiety and seclusiveness. The (presumed) syphiliac Robert Schumann's medical records report "*sein Husten, das Rasseln in seiner Lunge, sein Stammeln und Stottern, seine Wutausbrüche, sein Zittern*"—cf. https://www.welt.de/print-wams/article145293/Syphilis-oder-schlicht-verrueckt.html .

84   Re the onset of tertiary syphilis, cf. https://en.wikipedia.org/wiki/Syphilis#Tertiary, and that of neuro- or quaternary syphilis, cf. https://en.wikipedia.org/wiki/General_paresis_of_the_insane. The latter wikipedia entry lists the following signs and symptoms of early and progressing paralysis: "neurasthenic difficulties such as fatigue, headaches, insomnia, dizziness, etc… mental deterioration and personality changes… loss of social inhibitions, asocial behavior, gradual impairment of judgment, concentration and short-term memory, euphoria, mania, depression, or apathy… subtle shivering, minor defects in speech… delusions, common as the illness progresses, …can be grandiose, melancholic, or paranoid… [and may] include ideas of great wealth, immortality, thousands of lovers, unfathomable power, apocalypsis, nihilism, self-blame, or bizarre hypochondriacal complaints." Michalzik (*Kleist*, 35) notes, "towards the end of the Potsdam period [Kleist] began to feel uneasy in society," and we may conjecture that Kleist was beginning to exhibit symptoms of a disease that was as widespread as it was ostracised in polite society.

85   Kleist's essay abounds in erotic symbolism: the phallus is represented as tool, property ("*Eigentum*"), spirit ("*Geist*"), man (manhood), cross, object ("*Gegenstand*"; "*Stand*" = something erect"), torch, and gallows, the anus by the "parts of the world" into which the "property" is carried, Christ's hands, the *Regenstein* mountain (whose castle witnessed a legend in which a *ring* plays a prominent part), the "vestibule of Mt. Olympus," the "ring of Polykrates," "the great all-powerful

wheel," the "great cycle of things," the "*Wirkungskreis*," and the "Earth's perimeter." In Mohammed's paradise virtuous men are attended to by 72 *houris* (virgin girls) and 28 prepubescent boys.

86   When in Shakespeare's c.1606 play *Pericles, Prince of Tyre* the abducted maiden refuses to prostitute herself, the bordello queen proposes to overcome her coyness by getting her infected with syphilis. By comparison, Kleist's proposition to use a wooden dildo for the uninitiated is a more humane solution. Already on 17th May 1801 Kleist writes into Henriette von Schlieben's album: *"Tue recht und scheue niemand,"* whereby *"Scheu"* may refer to the same phenomenon as *"Ziererei"* in *Marionettentheater*.

87   Ulrike passed away in 1849, Marie in 1831, Fouqué in 1843, Rühle in 1847, Pfuel in 1866. They all appear to have been loyal to Kleist's (and their own) secrets. When Ulrike in her memoires notes that, according to Wedekind, Kleist in early 1804 lacked nothing but employment, she (or Wedekind) may simply be complicit in Kleist's camouflage (cf. Wichmann, *Kleist*, 77).

88   Cf. http://www.spiegel.de/spiegel/print/d-13502870.html. Cf. also Sander L. Gilman, *Inscribing the Other* (Lincoln: University of Nebraska Press, 1991), 45.

89   Bäumler (*Amors vergifteter Pfeil*, 136 and 293-300) reviews and dismisses the notion that Goethe himself was syphiliac, a notion propagated, for example, by the discoverer of the syphilis bacterium Erich Hoffmann. *"Phébus"* (*LS*, 223a; 228a; 237; 286b) as well as *"Phaeton"* (*LS*,212; 217c; 263b; 286b) became popular sarcastic monikers for *Phöbus* (Phaethon snatched his father Helios' sun chariot for a day but was unable to control it; to prevent disaster, Zeus struck it down, killing Phaeton).

90   There certainly is something obsessive, almost pathological, demonic, about Kleist's poetry—cf. Stefan Zweig's "demon"—which to some degree may explain Goethe and others' vehement reactions to it. One of the men Kleist recognises as "truly great" is Socrates, and it is instructive to recall Walter Burkert's musings about the philosopher: "What drove him into isolation was a unique experience which, from our point of view, verged on the pathological, a kind of voice which in the most various situations commanded him to halt, unexpectedly and compellingly. He said that 'something daemonic', *daimonion*, had happened to him; it was probably too

mysterious even for himself for him to be able to call it divine" (*Greek Religion*, 317). Kleist may also have heard such an inner voice, such a personal *daimon* that made him suddenly halt and stutter and become irritated or withdrawn—behviours his contemporaries observed in him—; it is to Joh. George Scheffner that we owe one of the more compelling observations about Kleist: *"Wie ein der Meerestiefe entsteigender Taucher sich wenigstens in den ersten Augenblicken nicht auf alles Große und Schöne besinnt, was er in der Wasserwelt gesehen, und es nicht zu erzählen vermag, so schien es bisweilen bei Heinrich von Kleist der Fall zu sein"* (*LS*,142). The term *daimon* in ancient Greek took on a variety of meanings, positive and negative, for there were "good" *eudaimones* and "evil" *daimones*: as occult power, as unexplained force or fate, as guardian of mortals, as imaginary apparition or spirit. Writes Walter Burkert (*Greek Religion*, 181): "When Socrates sought to find a word for that unique inner experience which would compel him in all kinds of situations to stop, say no, and turn about, rather than speak of something divine, he preferred to speak of something daimoinly, the *daimonion* that encountered him. This was open to misinterpretation as dealings with spirits, as a secret cult. It cost Socrates his life." Already Joseph von Eichendorff noted regarding Kleist, *"Hier lauert auch schon der Dämon"* (quoted in Staegle, *Kleist. Sein Leben*, 127), and Adolf Wilbrandt, in *Heinrich von Kleist* (Nördlingen: Beck'sche Buchhandlung, 1863), 36 and 111, in relation to his suicidal tendencies and exaggerated ambition posited Kleist's "demon," which he paralleled with Werther's: *"Es kann keine erschreckendere Aehnlichkeit... geben, wie die zwischen Werther und Kleist... Derselbe mörderische Dämon lebt, wüthet und zerstört in ihnen beiden: der unbezwingliche Trieb, Alles an Alles zu setzen."*

91   Stefan Zweig, *Die Welt von Gestern. Erinnerungen eines Europäers* (Frankfurt/M.: Fischer, 2010), 109-10. Syphilis is caused by bacteria, not viruses, but otherwise Zweig's account is observant.

92   Bäumler (*Amors vergifteter Pfeil*, 133) quotes syphilis infection rates for male tradesmen aged 18-28 in German cities around the year 1900, ranging between 1.5% and 7.7%.

93   Cf. Christa Wolf, "Kleists 'Penthesilea,'" in Heinrich von Kleist, *Penthesilea* (Wiesbaden: Fourier: Der Morgen, undated; *GW*, Berlin: Aufbau-Verlag, 1955), 162.

94   Cf. Thomas Wichmann, *Kleist*, 80; Samuel and Brown, *Kleist's Lost Year*, 111-12. Opinions in the *Kleist-Forschung* are divided as to whether it was indeed "our" Kleist whom Bertuch met in Paris in early 1804—Sembdner, for one, doubts it (cf. *LS*,120 footnote; *In Sachen Kleist*, 370). I think it very likely *was* "our" Kleist, for Bertuch notes in his diary that he met his Kleist in early 1804 in the company of Adolphine von Werdeck, in whose company in Paris we know him for certain to have met "our" Kleist a few month earlier, on 18th November 1803 (cf. *LS*,120), yet does not note the coincidence of meeting her again, in the same city, with *another* Kleist, which he would surely have done if the second Kleist was not identical with the first.

95   *Divinatory meanings*: end, mortality, destruction, corruption, failure of projects; *but also:* inertia, lethargy, petrifaction, somnambulism, hope destroyed—cf. http://www.tarotlore.com/tarot-cards/death/.

96   Cf. Gilles Deleuze and Félix Guattari: "There is no such thing as either man or nature now, only a process that produces the one within the other and couples the machines together. Producing-machines, desiring-machines everywhere, schizophrenic machines, all of species life: the self and the non-self, outside and inside, no longer have any meaning whatsoever." *Anti-Oedipus: Capitalism and Schizophrenia.* Trans. Robert Hurley et al (Minneapolis: University of Minnesota Press, 1983), 2. Apart from the Kleist quote in my *Author's Note* (cf. II:654), I point the reader to the intriguing descriptions of Kleist's creative method offered by Pfuel (cf. *LS*,70) and Wieland Sr. (cf. *LS*,89, espec. p.81).

97   Klaus Kanzog points out (*Kleist*, 202-3) that already Plato in *Nomoi* (1, 644d-645c) compares man with a mechanical doll (Gr. *"tauma"* = "Wunderwerk," "artificial marvel"), and that in *Parmenides* (156) he describes the instance (*"Nu"*; "singularity") at which the animated turns into the arrested and the arrested into the animated. Cf. Walter Burkert (*Greek Religion*, 181): "Tragedy has ample occasion for portraying the dreadful blows of fate which strike the individual, and here, in Aeschylus especially, the *daimon* becomes an independent, individual fiend that 'falls hard upon the house.'" Kleist's metaphor of men moved by the invisible tethers of fate links a man's fate not only to his *daimon* but also to Tyche (Fortuna), who with her capriciousness turns the accidental into the fateful or necessary, or inversely, the fateful or necessary into the accidental. The much-discussed term *"zufällig"* (II:196) in *Bettelweib* means not *"accidental"* but *"fateful"*: the Marchese, upon returning

633

from the hunt, *always* returns his "weapons" to said "room," so his encountering the beggar woman lodged there is not accidental but *necessary*—their encounter is *fated* to happen (the "weapon," of course, relates to the "room" as does the "F" to the "O," the "key" to the "hole," etc.); the Marchesa, who orchestrates the encounter and certainly knows her husband's pattern, plays the role of Moira or Tyche, deliberately pulling the strings and turning the wheel of fate. Fortuna, who is often depicted with a ball (*rota fortunae*) and a ship's rudder (*gubernaculum*), and as veiled or blindfolded, explicitly appears in Homburg: "*Nun denn, auf deiner Kugel, Ungeheures, / Du, der der Windeshauch den Schleier heut, / Gleich einem Segel lüftet, roll heran!*" (V.355-7). In Lucian's dialogue *Charon or the Observers* (trans. C.D.N. Costa) Hermes affords Charon, the ferryman of the dead, a birds-eye view of the world, explaining: "And if you look closely you will also see the Fates above, working a spindle for each man, from which it happens that everyone is suspended by a slender thread."

98   Kleist's letting the theatre stage represent the actual world, his dramatic texts its script or blueprint, and his fictional characters its prominent inhabitants, goes back to at least Aristophanes' Old Comedy, and even Pythagoras—cf. Richard Edward, in *Damon and Pythias* (c.1564): "Pythagoras said that this world was like a stage / Whereon many play their parts; the lookers-on, the sage." To Petronius is attributed the quote "*quod fere totus mundus exercet histrionem*" ("because almost the whole world are actors"; cf. his Menippean satires, 1st cent. AD); Juvenal in *Satire 3* (early 2nd cent. AD) has: "All of Greece is a stage, and every Greek's an actor"; John of Salisbury (who coined the term *theatrum mundi*) writes in *Policarticus* (c.1159): "the life of man on earth is a comedy, where each forgetting his own plays another's role"; Erasmus in *The Praise of Folly* (1511), "For what else is the life of man but a kind of play in which men in various costumes perform until the director motions them off the stage"; finally Shakespeare in *The Merchant of Venice* (1596-9) has, "I hold the world but as the world, Gratiano; / A stage where every man must play a part," and in *As You Like It* (1599), "All the world's a stage." Kleist in this "world theatre" assumes the role of director or *Maschinist* who hovers *above* the stage like Pythagoras' "sage," and from his lofty vantage point *manipulates it*, like the *magnétiseur* manipulates his somnambulant medium. Sloterdijk traces (*Sphären I*, 229; 234) traces the psychological aspect of magnetism's becoming influential in the late 18th century, "*Mesmers Bedeutung für die... romantische[...] Psychotherapeutik liegt vor allem darin, daß sein... mangnetopathischer Praxisansatz eine Flut von Nachfolgeversuchen auslöste, in denen neuartige Anordnungen von Nah-Begegnungen zwischen Heiler und Patient,*

Künstler und Publikum, schließlich auch Führer und Masse durchgespielt wurden, so war das romantische Zeitalter von 1780 an bis in die Mitte des 19. Jahrhunderts eine Epoche des wilden Magnetismus...Kaum fünfundzwanzig Jahre nach Mesmers Hervortreten... hatten sich seine Anregungen zu einer turbulenten und komplexen Subkultur entaftet. Sie wurde im Zeitalter der romantischen Medizin zu einer literarischen und klinischen Großmacht ausgebaut" (Mesmer himself, Sloterdijk notes, "till the end, considered himself a physician, not a psychologist"—*ibid*, 230). Elsewhere (*Kritik*, 495) Sloterdijk discusses the influence of princely physicians: *"Ihren Gipfel erreichte die Macht des Arztes am Körper des Fürsten. Erkrankte der König, so regierte de facto für einen Augenblick der Leibarzt über den 'Körper der Macht'. Die Fähigkeit, Fürsten zu kurieren, erhob die Heilkunst erst ganz auf das Niveau der Herrenmedizin. Die herrschende Medizin ist darum die Medizin der Herrschenden. Wer die Mächtigen heilt, wird selbst zentraler Träger der Macht."* Already Wilbrandt notes that Kleist's text was not designed primarily towards the masses but an inner circle, a "state within the state" (*Kleist*, 363). An unnamed critic in the *Allgemeine Literaturzeitung Halle* in 1805 grasps the nature of Kleist's dramatic method rather well, considering it *opposed* to the idea of tragedy; à propos of *Schroffenstein* he writes (*LS*,136): *"Dies ist gegen die Idee der alten und neuen Tragödie... Eine Reihe bloß schrecklicher Auftritte, wo das Schicksal mit den Menschen, wie mit Puppen spielt—mag wohl in der wirklichen Welt nachzuweisen sein,—eignet sich indes nicht für die Kunst... Und welche Wirkung kann und mag ein solches Stück auf den Zuschauer hervorbringen? Steht er vor der Bühne, um sich vor einer rohen Wirklichkeit zu entsetzen, oder erfordert es nicht vielmehr das Wesen der Kunst, eine Handlung... in ein harmonisches Ganzes zu bringen...?"* It is as if the critic studied Kleist's *Gesetze des Trauerspiels* and now uses the example of his *Erstling* to refute them. Most strikingly, the critic notes that Kleist's style, while purportedly unsuitable for the stage, effectively mimics or parallels the "real world— "raw reality"—, which is precisely Kleist's project.

99   While the theory's attribution to Kleist has been questioned, and the date of Hölder's encounter with Kleist remains uncertain—Kleist visited the Bernese Oberland in both 1802 and 1803—, I have no doubt that it is Kleist's, for he repeatedly applies this very theory in his works, and its vocabulary is eminently Kleistian: "grav" and "antigrav" appear in *Marionettentheater*, "Schürzung des Knotens" in *Schroffenstein* (V.2722). Hilda M. Brown, in investigating the provenance of Kleist's *Gesetze*, plausibly offers that Hölder in his travelogue could have confounded several journeys—cf. Brown, "Theorie der Tragödie," in Dirk Grathoff (Ed.), *Heinrich von*

Kleist. Studien zu Werk und Wirkung (Opladen: Westdeutscher, 1990), 120 n.6—and argues in favour of Kleist's authorship (*ibid*, 117-32). Kleist could have been inspired to the diagram by the panorama of 4,000 m peaks—Schreckhorn, Eiger, Mönch, Jungfrau—visible from the shores of Lake Thun, in the same manner in which Nietzsche's intuition of the *eternal recurrence* may have been inspired by the panorama of successive layers of mountain peaks visible from the shores of Lake Silvaplana, both panoramas exhibiting a pattern akin to a *Generalbaß* hewn into stone. When he tells Ulrike on 1st May 1802 that he "scales the Schreckhorn" while his "Mädeli" attends service at Scherzligen church, Kleist evidently is not referring to an actual ascent (the first ascent of the Schreckhorn was achieved only in 1861, and an expedition even to the glaciers surrounding the peak would have taken several days, and would have been undertaken not in spring but in summer), but to "scaling" it in his imagination while sipping a coffee on the promontory today called Schadaupark, immersing himself into a natural version of the artificial panorama he observed in Berlin in August 1800. A few months earlier he alludes to a view of the Jungrau when he jokes to Zschokke: *"Die Leute glauben hier durchgängig, daß ich verliebt sei. Bis jetzt aber bin ich es noch in keiner Jungfrau, als etwa höchstens die, deren Stirne mir den Abendstrahl der Sonne zurückwirft, wenn ich am Ufer des Thuner Sees stehe"* (II:717), his allusion being doubly ironic since a desireable "virgin" for him would have been a (male) *kouros*, as Zschokke would have known, and his *"Jungfrau"* is decidedly phallic ("forehead," "ray"). The impossibility of climbing the Schreckhorn in the course of a Sunday morning has led some Kleist scholars to question the existence of "Mädeli," whom Kleist mentions in the same breath. I have no doubt that Kleist enjoyed the company of a young male lover on his Inseli—one only has to visit the site, as I did in 2017, to see what likely took place: a gentle 20 minute walk from Kleist's house, via the wooden footbridge connecting Inseli with the shore to its south, or a leisurely 10 minute crossing by rowing boat, is the fishing village of Scherzligen's beautiful ancient church, which remains extant today, and "Mädeli," being the daughter (son) of a neighbouring fisherman (cf. II:724), on Sunday mornings will have attended mass there, rather than at the grander Stadtkirche Thun, far less convenient to reach and frequented by the city's *haute* volée; Kleist would have joined his young lover to Scherzligen, dropped him at the church, taken a stroll along the nearby waterfront promenade before Schadau Castle (the castle's present structure is from the mid-19th century, but there was a previous building), which perhaps already then, as today, offered the option of sitting down for a cup of coffee while enjoying the stunning panorama; cf. my reproduction in a later section of a picture showing this precise location. In his satire *How to Write History* (trans. C.D.N. Costa) Lucian makes fun of would-be historians who tell tall stories of events and places they never got near to, such as one who had never set foot out of Corinth but claimed that "he encountered many dangers and was wounded at Sura [in Syria]—no doubt [adds Lucian ironically], while taking a stroll from Craneion to Lerna" [two neighbourhoods in Corinth].

100   Hélène Cixous in "Grace and Innocense: Heinrich von Kleist," in *Readings: The Poetrics of Blanchot, Joyce, Kafka, Kleist, Lispector, and Tsvetayeva*. Trans. Verena Andermatt Conley (Minneapolis: U of Minnesota Press, 1991), 35-42; 71, discusses Kleist's gesture of "brushing" (*"streifen,"* which she renders as *"frôlement"*—cf. *Marionettentheater*, II:342), noting the "lightness" of this gesture.

101   For my reading and use of Deleuze and Guattari's concept of "plane of composition," cf. *Emigrant*, footnotes 52; 128. For their concept of *agencement* (in Engl., typically rendered as "assemblage," cf. especially their treatise *A Thousand Plateaus*, passim.

102   If one thought of Kleist's parabolical *"Schönheitslinie"* as representing the rolled-out sections of a circle, specifically of a *vicious circle* in which his *dramatic hero* is always already caught up, one could say that Kleist underestimated a real-life hero's (notably: Napoleon's) capacity or potentiality to "break the vicious circle." His main addressee Fr. Wilh. III posed the opposite problem: if we adopt Sloterdijk's categorisation (*Kritik*, 404) of "fighting types"—"hero," "cunctator," "coward"—, by his office Fr. Wilh. would be required, and by his nobility destined, to be a "hero," but he turns out to be a "cunctator," i.e., he does not conform with Kleist's basic "tragic" movement of the hero heroically confronting fate. Already Rahmer noted (*Kleist*, 229) the *"starr einseitige Auffassung seines Schicksalsgedankens."*

103   Mirabau's twitching upper lip in *Über die allmähliche Verfertigung* is the paradigmatic case of such a "spark" changing the course of history; the fox's sudden inspiration in Lafontaine's fable, retold by Kleist in the same essay, is another: not only does the "spark" save the fox's life, but it forever establishes in western folklore the fox *qua* quintessential fox, and the donkey *qua* quintessential ass.

104   Quoted in Emil Schneider, *Der Animale Magnetismus. Seine Geschichte und seine Beziehungen zur Heilkunst*. Zürich, 1950, 338-47. Wolfart could have

been working on this compendium while working with Kleist on *BA* in 1810/11. In applying magnetism as *po(i)etical* principle, Kleist will have been influenced not only by Gotthilf Heinr. Schubert but also by A. Müller, who already in 1803 repeatedly convened with the Mesmerian Franz Joseph Schelver (cf. *AML*,81). Peguilhen, in his 1854 reflections, *Aus dem Leben H. v. Kleists*, uses metaphorical language clearly influenced by magnetism: *"Nicht schneller durchzuckt der elektrische Funke den durch die Kette verbundenen Kreis, als er..."* (*LS*,490a).

105   Ewald Georg von Kleist, the mid-18th century inventor of the Kleistian jar, the first functioning condenser, assumed that electricity consisted in a fluid, a theory not fully refuted until well into the 19th century. The "magnetisation" of *fluidum* thus paralleled electrical phenomena, and Kleist in his works deploys them as roughly equivalent.

106   Fr. Hufeland and Fichte are cited in Sloterdijk, *Sphären I*, 258-9. Sloterdijik concludes (*ibid*, 261): *"Unsere Ideengeschichtlichen Exkursionen in die beiden großen Formationen tiefenpsychologischer Diskurse und Praktiken vor dem 20. Jahrhundert, die frühneuzeitliche Intersubjektivitätsmagie und die Welt des animalischen Magnetismus, hat drei... Modelle von dyadischen interpersonalen Unionen ans Licht gehoben: die magische Hingerissenheit im erotischen Gegenseitszauber; die hypnotoide Reproduktion der Mutter-Fötus-Relation in den magnetopathischen Kuren; die Ekstase der selbstlosen Aufmerksamkeit bei Fichtes rhetorischen Gottesselbstbeweisen. Jede dieser Konfigurationen: Liebender-Geliebter, Magnetiseur-Magnetisierter, Lehrer-Hörer, kann beschrieben werden, als realisiere sie eine zeitweilig geschlossene bipolare Blase, in der sich eine einzige gemeinsame Subjektivität über zwei Partner resonierend verteilt. Der Übergang... hängt in jedem Fall von der Fähigkeit der passive Seite ab, sich ganz in die Beziehung zum aktiven Pol zu entäußern."* Kleist is right "in the middle" of these budding discourses.

107   Cf. Sloterdijk, *Sphären I*, 237. Sloterdijk does not mention Kleist in this context, but discerns the influence of Puységurian magnetism in Kant, Schelling, Fichte, Hegel and Schopenhauer (*ibid*, 237-42), and offers that *"Schellings Naturphilosophie bietet eine umfassende Rationalisierung des animalischen Magnetismus"* (*ibid*, 238): magnetism may have been as influential on Idealism as on Romanticism; interestingly, Sloterdijik also mentions Hardenberg among those leaning towards mesmeric ideas. Kleist's investment of Puységurian somnambulism in such hapless characters suggests

that by the time he produced these works he no longer had faith in the *syphilitical* efficacy of Puységurian therapy, while continuing to exploit its *po(ï)etical* potential. In Berlin, Wolfart's Mesmerism may have intrigued Kleist: Fichte, who received treatment in Wolfart's practice in 1813, notes that according to Wolfart, *"das Magnetisieren gebe Belebung, und dadurch Heilung, auch ohne Somnambulismus. Dieser letztere sei nur Eine der Krisen... die* clairvoyance, *Darstellung des vollkommenen Bewußtseins, [ist] die vollkommenste, tief erschütternste Krise"* (quoted in Sloterdijk, *Sphären I*, 257-8).

108   According to Rahmer (*Kleist*, 33) the prominent critic Karl Aug. Böttiger publicly espoused the view that women were excluded from Attic theatre; Kleist could have taken his cue from him. When he says wants to ban women from the stage, no doubt he also, and especially, means the *political* stage, and in particular has in mind Queen Luise, who in his view wields too much influence over the King while herself being too swayable by the likes of Hardenberg; it is thus no coincidence that it is Marie, the Queen's confidante, to whom he imparts his view. Juvenal, in *Satire III* (94-5), writes of homosexuals and Greeks: "Who can beat them in any performance of female parts, as courtesan, matron or slave-girl?" Meanwhile, Martial refers to his epigrams as *"libelli,"* meaning "petitions," and indeed many of them comprise flattering addresses to his Emperor (whom he appeals to for glory and patronage); he artfully wraps his rascalities into his niceties, which provide a level of camouflage for them (albeit a deliberately transparent one).

109   To Ulrike, 13th/14th March 1803, from Leipzig: "*Ich lerne meine eigne Tragödie bei ihm [Wieland] deklamieren. Sie müßte, gut deklamiert, eine bessere Wirkung tun, als schlecht vorgestellt*" (II:730).

110   Cf. Helmut Sembdner (*In Sachen Kleist*, 51); cf. also Dirk Grathoff (*Kleist: Geschichte*, 56): "*Stücke wie der Zerbrochne Krug sind mehr fürs Ohr, weniger fürs Auge geschrieben... Das Hören eines dramatischen Geschehens löst beim Zuschauer eine Form von Phantasie-produktion aus, die deutlich von der unterschieden ist, welche sich beim Anschaun von Bildern oder agierenden Körpern auf der Bühne entwickelt. Die im Anhören von Worten ausgelösten Assoziationen entfalten selbst eine Bildwelt, während im Anschaun von Bildern die Sinne entfesselt werden, um assoziativ weitäugleiten. In Kleists Theater laufen diese beiden Formen der Phantasieproduktion gewissermaßen nicht synchron, wie Goethe es wünschte... Bei Kleist ist beides asynchrony, gegenläufig angeordnet, um dadurch die Sprache in ihrer höchsten Geltungs- und Wirkungsform zu*

inthronisieren... Kleists Theater... ist ein Erzähltheater," and (*ibid,* 208): *"Penthesilea wurde 1876, sieben Jahrzehnte nach der Entstehung, uraufgeführt—und gelungene oder halbwegs gelungene Inszenierungen gibt es erst seit 1976."*

111   Kleist went to great lengths to have his dramas published in print—more so than to have them staged—because he needed to a mass audience to generate income and because enacting the polysemic, multivalent intricacies of his multi-threaded text(ure)s proved exceedingly difficult, as Goethe's staging of *Krug* demonstrated; one of the differences between 17th/18th century AD German theatre and 5th/4th century BC Attic theatre (or Shakespearean theatre) was that the dramatist did not stage his own plays, but depended on a stage director to adapt them—a process in which Kleist's codifications were inevitably "lost in translation." Bernd Hamacher (*KH*,85) correctly observes that in staging a Kleistian drama the script's ambivalences necessarily have to be "monosemitised," but fails to note that not only stage directors, but also Kleist scholars have been "monosemitising" Kleist's polysemies, which in the latters' case is not only unnecessary but counterproductive. Robert E. Helbling points (*Major Works,* 84) to another important aspect of Kleist's nuanced stagecraft: "dramatic highlights consist of silent gestures," which is exemplified by Helena's furtive moving of the drum, and Guiskard's barely audible sigh of relief. Kleist's drama does involve instances of brusque physical action and props (e.g., Ursula's tossing the severed, putrefying finger amongst the *Schroffensteins*), but much of the plot is contained in speech—e.g., *Schroffenstein*'s instance of *Fensterschau* in which Rupert's wife steps to the window and relates how Jeronimo is being murdered before her eyes, while Rupert remains frozen, *Krug*'s court dialogues, and *Penthesilea*'s pervasive *Mauerschauen* (teichoscopies).

112   Shakespeare's first tetralogy comprises the three *Henry VI* plays and *Richard III,* the second, *Richard II,* the two *Henry IV* plays and *Henry V.* Wagner's tetralogy *Der Ring des Nibelungen* comprises *Das Rheingold, Die Walküre, Siegfried* and *Götterdämmerung.*

113   The formal designation of *poeta laureatus,* existing in the *HRR* since the 13th century, in Kleist's day had become largely neglected; Voltaire and Goethe even rejected it. Kleist's quest for the laurel harked back to the ancient Greek and Roman custom more then the Holy Roman one, although he may have appreciated Gunther von Pairis' obtaining the laurel from the hands of Fr. Barbarossa in recognition of

his panegyrical epos *Ligurinus* celebrating Barbarossa's victories: Kleist was surely prepared to produce a similar panegryrical work celebrating the leader of Germany's liberation from Napoleon's hegemony, and in return expected to receive the laurel from that leader, re-installed as Holy Roman Emperor. Kleist's being honoured by Joseph von Buol with the poet's laurel on his 30th birthday was decidedly premature.

The vain, in the early Dresden period exhuberant, Kleist accepted the honour, perhaps as advance praise (*Vorschusslorbeeren*) for the "*Agôn*" with Goethe he hoped to re-ignite, and kept the laurel (cf. Schede, *Kleist*, 98). Kleist's works may have been influenced more by Schiller's than Goethe's (cf. *KH*,219-26), but Goethe, as the paragon of German letters, was the ultimate measure for a poet, and in so far as the Phoebus of the *Ph* frontispiece and the *Prolog* represents Kleist, he was not so much traversing Dresden's cityscape as he was looking to ride roughshod across Weimar's.

114   Cf. https://en.wikipedia.org/wiki/Dionysia.

115   In *Brief eines Dichters an einen anderen* Kleist exhorts his readers to put greater value on his poetry's content, not its form, on its "fruits," not its "bowl," *"dem Durstigen kommt es, als solchem, auf die Schale nicht an, sondern auf die Früchte, die man ihm darin bringt... Wenn du mir daher... die Form... lobst: so erweckst du in mir... die Besorgnis,... daß dein Gemüt, durch den Wortklang oder den Versbau, ganz und gar von dem, worauf es mir eigentlich ankam, abgezogen worden ist"* (II:347-9), his dramas being merely the most elaborate of the varied "bowls" he dishes up to serve his audiences his *satirical* and *satyrical* fruits. Kleist's exhortion may entail a swipe at Goethe and Schiller, of whose post-*Sturm und Drang* emphasis on aesthetics of form S.F. Aug. Stjernstedt writes: *"den Inhalt sollte man vergessen und als eine Nebensache der reinen Form ansehen, Shakespeares lebende und individuelle Figuren verschwanden, um typischen Charaktermasken Raum zu geben, und schließlich verlor man sich in Symbolen und Allegorien"* ("Über Heinrich von Kleist und seine Poesie," 180). Kleist, one could perhaps say, exhorts his readers to take him as a Shakespearean, not a Goethean or a Schillerian, poet, his characters as "living individual beings," and his works not as mere accumulations of ideal "symbols and allegories" but as explorations of real human and political issues. Stjernstedt in his otherwise (from today's vantage point) unproductive dissertation insightfully opposes Kleist to the Romantics: *"Die übertriebene Subjektivität finden wir auf beiden Seiten, aber Kleist ist so sehr viel wahrer und aufrichtiger in seiner subjektiven Sicht auf die anderen. Die Figuren, die er hervorrruft, sind für ihn völlig lebendig, ihre Leidenschaften und*

Bewegungen hat er selbst erfahren" (*ibid*, 182). Unsurprisingly, Kleist's dramas are difficult to categorise: in his subtitles Kleist designates *Hermannsschlacht* as *"Drama," Schroffenstein, Guiskard* and *Penthesilea* as *"Trauerspiel," Krug* and *Amphitryon* as *"Lustspiel,"* and *Käthchen* and *Homburg* as *"Schauspiel,"* and the term *"Spiel"* reminds us that all of Kleist's qualifiers *Trauer-, Lust-* and *Schau-* are only indicative, as all his dramas contain elements of satyr play—cf. Georg Lukács in "Die Tragödie H. v. Kleists," in *Deutsche Realisten des 19. Jahrhunderts* (Berlin, 1951), 43: " *in allen Dramen Kleists [ist] etwas Lustspielhaftes in Aufbau und Handlungsführung.*" Klaus Kanzog's insistence (*Kleist*, 95) that any such classification must be done from within the terminological context of the play's genesis is apposite, though his term "terminological" is unnecessarily limiting.

116   Wildbrandt argues (*Kleist*, 146-7) that in Berlin in 1801 a battle waged between Romantic Goethe-followers and "old men" (Tieck) who opposed this new aesthetic movement, and that Kleist had no choice but side with the former (n.b.: Goethe himself is already on his way towards becoming an "old man"). I agree that Kleist concurred with Fr. Schlegel and the Romantics that Goethe had become "top gun" on the German literary Parnassus, but not that he therefore had no choice but to join the ranks of the Goethe-followers: precisely because Goethe now occupied the "curule chair" of German letters, and in the most "*gravitätische*" (pompous) manner, Kleist sought to topple him. Wildbrandt misunderstands Kleist's character and aspirations when he asks, in reference to Schiller's relationship with Goethe, *"Konnte nicht auch Kleist... eine freundliche und rühmliche Stätte wenigstens neben dem Meister finden?"* (*Kleist*, 299):   Kleist was never going to remain apprentice to another master, or side-kick to another superhero: for him life and poetry really was about "all or nothing."

117   Goethe's xenion argued against Newton's theory that white light is composed of the prism colours: *"Triumph der Schule. / Welch erhabner Gedanke! Uns lehrt der unsterbliche Meister / Künstlich zu teilen den Strahl, den wir nur einfach erkannt"* (Joh. Wolfgang Goethe, in: Friedrich Schiller (Ed.), *Musenalmanach für das Jahr 1797*, quoted in Blamberger, *Kleist*, 324); cf. also A. Müller: *"Goethe ist dahin gelangt, daß er den Gegensatz das Urphänomen nennt, und tausende von gegensätzlichen Erfahrungen dem Newton entgegenstellt"* (*AML*, 435). Kleist's poetry, in my layman's terms, encompasses a polyphonic texture overlayed or underpinned by a homophonic *basso continuo* that structures his composition of the multiple "threads"

and the *overt* story, their "melody," "rhythm" and "harmony" ("*Die Mathematik des Ohrs ist der Generalbaß*": Walter Hinderer, *KJb* 2005,29). Kleist's engagement with music, as with many other domains, was unorthodox, eclectic and syncretic, combining ancient Pythgorean concepts of mathematics and universal harmony ("*Spärenmusik,*" II:569; *KH*,264) and modern, romantic ones of music as sentimental language ("*Empfindungssprache,*" *KH*,263). Kleist in the course of his career was forced to recognise that his compositions sounded harsh, shrill and jerky to his audiences, and that their intricate polyphonies did not always resonate.

118   Cf. also the section "*Aion*" in my diss., *The Awakening Child: Re-reading Kleist* (New York: Atropos, 2014), 390-7. *Cäcilie* comprises an inversion of the interplay of the same forces Kleist previously explored in *Erdbeben*: in the former, the *visual* (coloured light falling through the rose window, *rose* being an anagram of *eros*) *charges up* the iconoclasts (the Protestants), whereas the *auditory* (organ music) triggers their *discharge* (they *lower* their "weapons" and submit); in the latter, the *auditory* (organ music, the organ pipes being phalllic) *charges up* the congregation (the Catholics), whereas the *visual* (coloured light falling through the rose window) triggers their *discharge* (they *raise* their "weapons" and pursue the orgiastic massacre). In other words, the Protestants (Prussians) are *charged up* by the *visual* and *discharged* by the *auditory*, whereas the Catholics (French) are *charged up* by the *auditory* and *discharged* by the *visual*. The main difference between the two camps lies in the nature of their *discharge*: among the Prussians, *discharge* leads to flaccidness and submission, among the French, to ithyphallic prowess and hegemony. Since the Prussians are triggered into submission by the *auditory*, and the French into hegemony by the *visual*, both the (Goethean) *visual* and the (Kleistian) *auditory* are powerful forces, but in the direct comparison the latter is the more powerful one, as it precipitates death, hence liberation, whereas the former induces hegemony, hence enslavement. In how far Kleist may have dismissed the visual because he suffered from syphilis-induced poor eyesight is speculative; as an accomplished flutist he will have possessed subtle hearing—Nietzschean "small" (keen) ears. His argument was about more than just poetic theory—namely, about a life ethic: for Kleist the most important value was trust, which, he may have felt, is established and maintained more effectively by *vibrational tuning-in* than by *visual correspondence* (cf. Wieland's *Sympathie*). Not only is "rose" an anagram of "eros," but also does "*Rosette*" (i.e., window rose) in German colloquially refer to "anus."

119   Kleist may have held Luther partially responsible for the disunity among the German dynasties, by piling a *religious* divide on top of *political* ones. The proper quote is: *"Nun aber beuge ich die Knie meines Herzens und bitte dich, Herr, um Gnade"* (*Menasse*; quoted in Blamberger, *Kleist*, 322). Bernhard Blume notes that Goethe used this expression in a letter to Herder of May 1775: *"Deine Art... legt mich immer auf die Knie meines Herzens"*—cf. Blume, "Kleist und Goethe," in: Walter Müller-Seidel (Ed.), *Heinrich von Kleist. Aufsätze und Essays* (Darmstadt: Wissenschaftliche, 1967), 130; cf. also Grathoff, *Kleist: Geschichte*, 207. Blume notes this coincidence only in passing, since Kleist could not have known that Goethe had used it, yet it may still help explain why Goethe rejected *Penthesilea* (and its author) so mercilessly: the coincidence of Kleist's using the metaphor he himself had used could have reminded him of his own exuberance during the *Sturm und Drang* period, and his subsequent "getting old" and joining the establishment; Sembdner (*In Sachen Kleist*, 269) makes a similar point, leaning on Egbert Krispyn's work. If Goethe represents for Kleist that which he loathes, Kleist reflects for Goethe that which he mourns nostalgically; if Goethe represents Kleist's *horror-scenario of his own future*, Kleist comprises Goethe's *demon of his own past*. Wildbrandt argues similarly (*Kleist*, 173-4): *"Und wie wir wissen, daß Schiller in jenem harten Gericht über Bürger seine eigene Vergangenheit bekämpft hat, so begreifen wir auch, wie Goethe vor der Erscheinung Kleists wie vor einer unheimlichen Erinnerung zurückwich."*

120   When Kleist quotes or paraphrases Goethe, he typically does so to express an ambivalent character or behaviour. The famous passage in *Findling*, *"Von Zeit zu Zeit holte er sich... eine Handvoll Nüsse aus der Tasche,... und knackte sie auf"* (II:200-1), which paraphrases *Wilhelm Meisters Lehrjahre* (Stuttgart: Reclam, 2007, 241), is frequently taken to indicate Nicolo's callousness; however, since the expression *"aus der Tasche"* also appears in Johann's characterisation of Ursula (i.e., Napoleon) in *Schroffenstein* (V.2725), where it reflects Kleist's admiration for the art of *sleight of hand*, Nicolo is evidently not merely callous but also cunning (cf. Kleist's Hermann); furthermore, since he *satirically* represents Fr. Wilh., his propensity to crack nuts nonchalantly in the eye of the storm may signify his mastering the art of cunctation, which, I argued earlier, for Kleist under certain circumstances is a strength.

121   Sembdner (*In Sachen Kleist*, 277) quotes Goethe's 1799 comment on Schiller's *Wallenstein*, *"Der Schluß des Ganzen... erschreckt,"* noting that for Goethe every drama's Aristotelian catharsis should entail *"aussöhnende Abrundung,"*

"conciliatory rounding off." Perhaps Goethe sensed that, like Schiller (who suffered from tuberculosis), Kleist suffered from a slowly progressing ailment—a more sinister one, perhaps—, and was prepared to "take into account pathological causes" for unpalatable passages.

122   Quoted in Gerhard Mahr, "Katharina Mommsen: Kleists Kampf mit Goethe," in: *Die Tat*, No. 69, 25 (Zürich, 1975).

123   Gilles Deleuze and Félix Guattari, *A Thousand Plateaus: Capitalism and Schizophrenia*. Trans. Brian Massumi (Minneapolis: University of Minnesota Press, 1987), 356. Cf. also Peter Sloterdijk (*Kritik*, 215), "*Der junge Goethe hat... das vitale Geheimnis des bürgerlichen Neokynismus erahnt und als Kunst ausgelebt... in seiner hinreißend launigen, aggressiven und im wahrsten Sinn des Wortes frechen Rede zum Shakespeare-Tag 1771*," and Stephan Aug. Winkelmann to Fr. Karl von Savigny on July 1803, "*eine wichtige poetische Neuigkeit: Die Familie Schroffenstein... [Der] Verfasser... ist jung, das sieht man, aber wahrhaftig eine Jugend wie einst Goethe*" (*LS*,98c).

124   A. Müller in his Dresden lectures in 1806 already points in this direction: "*In Iffland möchte ich einige weibliche Züge entdecken*" (quoted by Jakob Baxa, *AML*,174 note)

125   Since the chiseled or jagged spur evidently *syphilitically* represents a chancred glans, Kleist could be imagining some sort of *autoinfection*; cf. also Penthesilea's death.

126   *Divinatory meanings*: succour, providence, triumph, presumption, vengeance, war; *but also:* trouble, riot, quarrel, defeat—cf. http://www.tarotlore.com/tarot-cards/the-chariot/.

127   Sembdner points out (I:919) that Kleist used the same type of writing paper for the sketch as for letters produced during the January-April 1802 period. Roland Reuß and Peter Staengle (*MAIII*:455) put the genesis of *Thierrez, Ghonorez*, and *Schroffenstein* into February to November 1802; Loch (cf. *Kleist*, 522) puts that of *Thierrez* into the summer or autumn of 1801, Louis Gerrekens (*KH*,27) into early 1802, Thomas Wichmann, on the basis of an elaborate assessment (*Kleist*, 52-4), into the summer or autumn of 1801.

128   Already in November 1800 Kleist told Wilhelmine that he wished to relocate to the *Suisse romande*, "*dem schönsten Erdstriche Europas*" (II:587), where he hoped to make a living by teaching German while writing poetry. Kleist may have had in mind *Vaud* or *Genève*, or perhaps *Neuchâtel*, then ruled in personal union by the Hohenzollern King, thus for a Prussian effectively a home away from home.

129   Zschokke from 5th April 1802 rented Burg Biberstein (cf. *LS*,75b), formerly a Habsburg possession, located just north of Aarau and 12km from the Habsburg, and Kleist could have spent time there—what more authentic location to inspire a Habsburgian drama? Biberstein's imposing gothic aspect, perched on top of a sheer cliff, could have inspired Kleist to the name Schroffenstein ("rough rock"). Kreutzer, in *Dichterische Entwicklung*, 199, furthermore discerns in Zschokke's 1801/2 novel *Alamontade* inspirations for *Schroffenstein*. Kleist's Paris sojourn of 1801 may have had a similar *satirical* rationale, of studying the Napoleonic regime close-up. When his situation in Switzerland became untenable later in 1802, Kleist again planned to go to Vienna (cf. *LS*,81c), and perhaps only L. Wieland's invitation to his father's estate at Oßmannstedt prevented him from doing so.

130   The *Treaty of Lunéville* not only spelled the beginning of the end of the *HRR*, which was dissolved only a few years later, but also defined a tit-for-tat pattern for the next 150 years: the Germans would reverse *Lunéville* at the *Congress of Vienna*, exceed it with the humiliating *Treaty of Versailles* of 1871, which the French would respond to with the equally humiliating *Treaty of Versailles* of 1919. Hitler held on to the pattern, if unenthusiastically: although he followed Bismarck's example and "brought back" Alsace and Lorraine into the *Reich*, he cared less about expanding Germany's western border than about acquiring "*Lebensraum*" in the east. His vision of the future Germany, which harked back not to the 16th-18th century aspiration of containing and catching up with and containing France but to the 11th-13th century German *Ostsiedlung* and even the 3rd-6th century migrations of Goths and other Germanic tribes to the lands of the Scythians and Sarmataeans in and around the Crimea, put Germany in conflict primarily not with France but the Soviet Union. Following WWII France recovered Alsace and Lorraine; her centralised francophone education system has since ensured that the region's German dialects are rapidly declining. Kleist's frustration at the loss of the Rhine's left bank was not unique—cf., e.g., Fr. von Gentz to Adam Müller on 20th/23rd October 1802 from Brussels (*AML*,32): "Ich habe das linke Rheinufer—und die Niederlande gesehen, mein lieber Müller! und

das Herz schlägt mir, und die Hände zittern mir, und ich halte mit Mühe meine Feder zurück,—daß ich Ihnen nicht von hier aus sagen kann, was in diesen Worten liegt. Das linke Rheinufer! Wie gleichgültig ich dies Wort in Berlin, und Dresden, und Wien, und zum Teil noch in Frankfurt aussprach. Und was ich jetzt über den Zustand dieser Länder, und über die Gemütsstimmung ihrer Einwohner sagen könnte, und—gottlob—bald, bald sagen werde... Diese acht Tage haben in meinem Kopfe eine allgemeine Gärung, eine große und wichtige Revolution gestiftet... Nicht bloß die Greuel der Revolution..., nicht bloß die... Rückbesinnung an das Vergangene bildet jenen finstern Schleier, der von Maynz bis Antwerpen *über alle diese blühenden Provinzen ausgebreitet liegt. Nein! die Gegenwart ist fast noch schrecklicher, als die Vergangenheit. Vor dem 18. Brumaire war der Gedanke, daß die Schrecknisse... notwendig vorübergehend sein müßten... eine Art von Gegengewicht gegen das Übermaß der Leiden. Aber jetzt fühlen die Unterjochten nichts mehr, als... grenzenlosen, kalten, eisernen, barbarischen, insultierenden Despotismus. Besonders hat seit einem Jahre, seitdem sich der regierende Sultan auf seinem Throne befestigt glaubte,... die Tyrannei der willkürlichen Impositionen, in einem Grade überhand genommen, von dem man sich keine Vorstellung machen kann. Es gibt kein Maß, keine Proportion, keine Regel in den Forderungen mehr."*

647

131   Kleist was personally affected by the civil war that followed the French withdrawal from Switzerland when his openly partisan friend Wieland Jr. was forced to evict the country and extended an invitation to Kleist to join him to his father's Oßmannstedt estate. Kleist remained exposed to the waxing and waning tides of war: in 1803 he was rejected by the British Invasion force and got himself in conflict with the Prussian authorities (having earlier promised not to join a foreign army); in 1807 he was forced to evict Königsberg when the French forces closed in, and passing through Berlin was imprisoned as a presumed spy; soon thereafter *Tilsit* rendered void his aspiration for a posting in Prussian Franconia; in both 1804 and 1809 he may have worked as a spy or informant; in 1809 he came close to being arrested by Austrian military police on the battlefield of *Aspern*, and possibly was wounded on that of *Wagram* two months later. He would not have wanted it otherwise: he was a keen observer of, and aspired to being a key actor in, the *great game*. What would Kleist's poetry have been without the *Napolenonic Wars*? It might not even have come into existence.

132   Anthony Stephens notes in *Heinrich von Kleist: The Dramas and Stories* (Oxford: Berg, 1994), 28, that the *Erbvertrag* is not the primary cause of the standoff

between the two family branches, but merely its "emblem," "pretext," or "cipher." The *Erbvertrag* is nevertheless an important structuring device, as are, say, the gipsy's prophecy in *Kohlhaas* and Piachi's adoption of Nicolo in *Findling*.

133   Kleist indeed here anticipates game theory's famous "prisoner's dilemma" (in the following I draw on https://en.wikipedia.org/wiki/Prisoner%27s_dilemma): Rupert (blue) and Sylvester (red) each face two choices, namely to either "Collaborate by Marrying" or "Pre-empt and Kill" their respective children, Ottokar and Agnes. If both fathers *marry* their children, they receive the payoff *Joint Continuation* for their combined Houses. If both *kill* each other's child, they receive the payoff *Joint Termination* of their respective lines. If Rupert kills Agnes while Sylvester seeks to marry her, Rupert receives the temptation payoff *Sole Continuation*, while Sylvester receives *Sole Termination*. Inversely, if Rupert seeks to marry Ottokar while Sylvester kills him, Rupert receives *Sole Termination* and Sylvester *Sole Continuation*. Rupert's and Sylvester's payoff matrix is thus as follows:

	Collaborate (Marry)	Pre-empt and Kill
Collaborate (Marry)	*Joint Continuation, Joint Continuation*	*Sole Termination Sole Continuation*
Pre-empt and Kill	*Sole Continuation, Sole Termination*	*Joint Termination Joint Termination*

Assuming the following condition holds for the values of the payoffs: *Sole Continuation* > *Joint Continuation* > *Joint Termination* > *Sole Termination*; then while *Joint Continuation* > *Joint Termination* implies that *marrying* is a strategy that is superior to *killing* each others' children, *Sole Continuation* > *Joint Continuation* and *Joint Termination* > *Sole Termination* imply that *killing* is the "dominant strategy" for both fathers (i.e., it is better than any other strategy for each of them, irrespective of the other's strategy). In technical terms, mutual killing is the only "Nash equilibrium" in this game, i.e. the only outcome compared to which each player could only do worse by unilaterally changing strategy. An optimal payoff can only be reached via communication and trust-building efforts, which the fathers, in their blind hate, fail to undertake. Kleist's set-up precisely anticipates that of the "prisoner's dilemma," in which the two prisoners cannot communicate with each other, by stipulating that both fathers kill the other's child *exactly at the same time*, and *in the same feverish haste*, so that no communication takes place in the decicive moment. Had John Nash Jr. read *Schroffenstein*, he might have chosen to dedicate his 1994 Nobel Memorial Prize in Economics to Kleist, although, to be fair, James Waldegrave in 1713 had already discussed a two-player game, in the context of the French card game *Le Her*, and Jean-Jacques Rousseau had described a two-player coordination situation, known as "stag hunt," that is similar to a *prionser's dilemma*. Kleist in turn would have empathised with Nash, who was dismissed from the (clearly un-thinking) "think-tank" RAND Corporation on the grounds of alleged homosexual leanings.

134   Hanna Hellmann (cf. Wichmann, *Kleist*, 55) shows that Kleist could have borrowed the theme of family disunion inflamed by the accidental death of a child from Friedrich Maximilian von Klinger's novel *Der Kettenträger* (1796), to which Kleist refers in his *"Kant-Krise"* letter of March 1801. The tortured Warwand's fuzzy and forced pronuncing the name "Sylvester" is as unreliable as is, in *Zweikampf*, Katharina's eleventh hour "recollection" of her dying husband's having allegedly coughed up the name *"Rotbart"* (or was it *"Trota"*? *"Rtbrt"* or *"Trt"*—who is to say?). The severed finger becomes the drama's *"Falke"* (i.e., the *Dingsymbol* or objective symbol of the story's core problematic that, according to Paul Heyse, is one of the two fundamental characteristics of the novella form), as do, e.g., the jar in *Krug*, the diadem in *Amphitryon,* and the glove in *Homburg*. *Schroffenstein* also exhibits the second of the two characteristics Heyse attributes to the novella form, that of *"Silhouette"* (i.e., the plot's concentration on a single *Leitmotiv*)—namely dynastic rivalry, objectified as *Erbvertrag*—, a fact that begs the questions whether Heyse's theory ought to be discarded because the characteristics he uniquely attributes to novellas can also apply to dramas, or conversely, whether Kleist's dramas are in fact constructed along similar lines as novellas. I offer the latter to be the case: that despite their formal differences, Kleist's dramas and novellas share the same, Heysean, characteristics (as well as Goethe's third characteristic of the novella, *"eine sich ereignete unerhörte Begebenheit"*), because the core or kernel of Kleist's dramas consist in a novellistic material he re-formats into dramatic form, to render it stageable and admissible as competitive entry into his self-imposed *Agôn*. From this perspective, the meme of Kleist having developed *Schroffenstein* out of the *Kleidertauschszene*, which he reportedly wrote in prose, gains traction, while that of his having found the shift from dramas to tales degrading is to be taken with a grain of salt: Kleist's *satirical* agenda is very much in synch with the novella format (*"novello"* = "new"), and his dramas, as accomplished as they are, betray this fact. The upshot is that any Kleistian novella could have served as kernel for a drama; indeed, they could initially have been sketches for future dramas that Kleist subsequently decided not to develop into full-fledged dramas but into faster-to-produce novellas instead.

135   Kleist's experimental set-up exceeds that of the "prisoner's dilemma": while in the latter, the prevalence of distrust and lack of communication ensures that in every iteration the (Nash-)equilibrium choice of *killing* recurs, the former introduces an *irrational* element that has the potential to sublimate the cycle of violence perpetuated by *rational* behaviour, if at a price: the *Kleidertausch,* thanks to which the fathers erroneously kill not the others' but their own child. Only his *irrational* gesture breaks the "rational" cycle of killing. As such Kleist not only anticipates von Neumann, Morgenstern and Nash's game theory but also Herbert Simon's concept of bounded rationality, thus perhaps deserving that *not one, but two* Nobel Memorial Prizes in Economics be dedicated to him: Nash's and Simon's.

136   Kleist's scheme of the *Kleidertausch* (crossdressing) may draw on ancient precedence. Plutarch records several such incidences, as Burkert reports (*Greek Religion,* 258-9): "in mummery and festivals of license, and also in connection with marriage, which upsets the familiar status: clothes and hairstyles are taken over from the opposite sex, and we find youths in girls' clothing and girls with beards, *phalloi,* and satyr costumes." If Sylvius embodies Tiresias, the blind prophet of Apollo in Thebes, he also represents gender change, for Tiresias was transformed into a woman for seven years.

137   For an overview of Kleist's biblical references, cf. Franz M. Eybl, *Kleist-Lektüren* (Vienna: WUV, 2007), 50-3.

138   Kleist refers to Fr. Barbarossa repeatedly, e.g., with *Zweikampf*'s character Rotbart (= *Barbarossa*) and the novella's *topos* of the legitimation of a son before one's death, which parallels the historical Fr. Barbarossa's actual succession management: in order to legitimise his son Manfred and safeguard the Hohenstaufen line, Fr. Barbarossa married Manfred's mother on his death-bed. The Florentine historian Giovanni Villani in *Nuova Cronica* created the legend that Manfred killed his ill father, fearing that he might yet recover from his illness; Horace Walpole's *The Castle of Otranto* may allude to the same story, its protagonist being named Manfred and its main theme being that of succession.

139   In composing his *satirical/satyrical/syphilical Erstling,* Kleist could draw on prominent literary precedence: the writer and doctor (!) Rabelais' 1532-4 book *The Histories of Gargantua and Pantagruel,* which he dedicates to sphiliacs and in whose

foreword he jokingly refers to a book titled *On the Dignity of Codpieces*; Shakespeare's 1605/6 play *Timon of Athens*, whose eponymous hero warns Alkibiades in no uncertain terms to beware his courtesan's venereal destructiveness (Bäumler cites Joh. Heinr. Rille, who in *Die Syphilis in der Dichtkunst* counts 25 instances of "pox," i.e., syphilis, in Shakesepeare's works); Hans Jacob Chr. Von Grimmelshausen's 1668 picaresque novel *Simplicissimus*, whose hero contracts syphilis in Paris, Voltaire's 1759 philosophical novel *Candide*, whose character Pangloss traces his syphilitic genealogy to Columbus, and Goethe's 1795 *Römische Elegien*. Incidentally, the chambermaid from whom Voltaire's Pangloss contracts syphilis and who later turns to prostitution is named Paquette, a name that could have inspired Kleist's figure Parquet, *"eine junge liebenswürdige Genueserin, Elvirens Nichte, die unter ihrer Aufsicht in Rom erzogen wurde"* (II:201), who, assuming that Elvire's recurring fevers are syphiliac, could have been infected by her aunt during her "education in Rome," and whose unborn child, presumably fathered by Nicolo, which dies together with her during her pregnancy (cf. II:205), could have suffered from congenital syphilis. I showed in *Emigrant* that *Parquet* has a precise *satyrical* meaning (i.e., the departementalisation of German territories that have come under French control), and in connection with Voltaire's story it may also have a *syphilitical* one.

140   Arnold Zweig is therefore precisely wrong when he contends, in "Versuch über Kleist" (1923), quoted in Streller, *Dramen 1*, 568, that *"Die streitenden Rossitz und Warwand aber haben keinerlei tragende Funktion in irgendeinem Gemeinwesen... sie existieren nirgends als auf der Bühne."* The Habsburgs trace their origins to the 10th century, the Hohenzollerns the 11th, the Wettins the 10th, the Wittelsbachs the 10th, and the Welfs the 9th. Of these five families three—the Habsburgs, the Wittelsbachs and the Welfs—furnished Holy Roman emperors: the Habsburgs 20, the Wittelsbachs 3, the Welfs 1. Ottokar's "initiation" reportedly having taken place at the "imperial court" suggests that the Rossitzes represent the Habsburgs, and the Warwands therefore the Hohenzollerns, though most other evidence suggests the reverse. Wolf Kittler highlights (*Geburt*, 41-2) certain parallels between the configuration of the Schroffenstein family and Kleist's own, and notes that one of the ancestral castles of the Kleist family was named Ruschitz. I add that the configuration of Kohlhaas' children also mirrors that of Kleist and his siblings, and that such parallels are not coincidental but underline Kleist's pragmatism: he freely recycles patterns familiar to him, as a matter of convenience and economy. Kleist appears to have had a good command of the Spanish language: Rahmer notes (*Kleist*, 66-7) that in Dahlmann's

legacy a Spanish translation by Kleist's hand was found (if so, this document should enter the canon, for we know what Kleist can do with "translations"!), that Cervantes was the "idol" of the young poets in the circles Kleist frequented from 1801 onwards, that the Spanish language and literature was particularly cultivated among them—which could explain Kleist's taking up the novella genre (as Cervantes had done), and that Arno Eichhorn's 1906 inquiry into Kleists *Katechismus* (which was based on a Spanish source) confirms this finding.

141   Jochen Schmidt suggests, in *Heinrich von Kleist. Die Dramen und Erzählungen in ihrer Epoche* (Darmstadt: Wiss. Buchgesellsch., 2011), 49, that Spain in Kleist's time was stereotyped as a country of despotism and religious bigotry. This may be so, but neither topic was particularly relevant to Kleist, and Spain's (and France's) traditional association with both sensuality and syphilis provides a more relevant rationale for Kleist's settings. The Spanish Kingdom in 1808 indeed fell to the Bonapartes not least due to discord within the ruling Bourbon family.

142   Among the six powerful dynasties that originated in medieval Swabia, the Staufen or Hohenstaufen furbished the Holy Roman Emperors from the 11th to 13th century, and were also Dukes of Swabia, the Habsburgs supplied almost all Emperors from the 15th century until Kleist's day, the Hohenzollerns provided the Electors of Brandenburg (from 1701, the Kings of Prussia), the Wittelsbachs, the Electors of Bavaria, the Welfs (of the Ravensburg), the Electors of Hanover (from 1714, the Kings of Great Britain), and the Württembergs, the Electors of the eponymous electorate. Of the most powerful German dynasties, all but one—the Wettins of Saxony—originated in medieval Swabia, and while this may be a historical coincidence, such coincidences were never lost on Kleist.

143   Fred Bridham, who traces Kleist and M.G. Lewis' mutual influence (via L. Wieland and/or Zschokke), plausibly suggests that Kleist borrowed the names Ursula and Agnes from Lewis' *The Monk* (cf. "Kleist's *Familie Schroffenstein* and "Monk" Lewis's *Mistrust:* Give and Take," in Susanne Stark (Ed.), *The Novel in Anglo-German Context,* Amsterdam: Rodopi, 2000, 75-7). I previously discussed the Gothic elements in Kleist's works in *Emigrant,* in the context of *Bettelweib.*

144   Barnabe commences an entire series of ambiguously gendered given names in Kleist's works: Josephe, Toni, Babekan, Elvire. Kleist could have gleaned this

technique from Martial, who blurs identities by deploying feminine forms of male names, e.g., Thestylis for Thestylus (*Epigrams*, 8.55, 8.63).

145   Ursula's occupation similarly commences a series, one of prefessions at once at the centre and margin of society: the cobbler in *Erdbeben*, the knacker in *Kohlhaas*, the beggar-woman in *Bettelweib*. In *Emigrant* I offer that the cobbler and knacker represent Napoleon, the beggar-woman Pope Pius VII. (In hindsight I would revise the latter association: I now believe that the beggar-woman represents Joséphine; the ruined castle is France, the opening passage recalls how Joséphine was ditched by Napoleon, the remainder of the story narrates a scenario c.20 years in the future, in which a heir—Kleist has obviously become aware that Marie-Louise has become pregnant and his story anticipates the birth of Napoléon Franz—appears to claim the Empire but is spooked and discouraged by Joséphine's spirit, whereupon Napoleon, seeking to exorcise her spirit, combusts his Empire and himself). Juvenal, in his *Satires*, deploys the same technique of denigrating actual figures by associating them with looked-down-upon professions: the Greek *parvenu* Crispinus he denotes as "fishmonger," the unscrupulous Athenian general Kleon as "tanner," etc.

653

146   Barnabe, as conduit between Ursula and the Schroffensteins, and between the play and the audience, also has a significant impact: her testimony to Ottokar conveys to all (including the audience) how the feud was triggered (cf. V.2186-2202), and her leading Rupert to the cave, and her aiding Ottokar in luring Agnes there, catalyses the drama's dénouement.

147   Ursula planned to put the little finger under her doormat to fend of the devil. I have found no evidence for such a tradition; instead, a cut children finger was held to open any lock—cf. Hinrich C. Seeba, "Der Sündenfall des Verdachts," in: Müller-Seidel, *Aktualität*, 146, n. 68. In so far as it signifies the Rhineland, the finger indeed encompasses the "key" to the Empire and the "threshold" to France. The finger is clearly phallic, implying that Peter was castrated; it's being from the *left*—i.e., *sinister*—hand suggests that it is chancreatig, as well as representing the Rhine's *left* bank.

148   From Friedrich Hebbel's diary, quoted in Siegfried Streller et al (Eds.), *Heinrich von Kleist. Dramen 1* (Frankfurt/M.: Insel, 1986), 566.

149   There is admiration in Kleist's depiction of Ursula-Napoleon's *"gut aus der Tasche spielen,"* her/his skill at conjuring sleights of hand. I argued in *Emigrant* that Kleist's perception of Napoleon was complex, combining rejection with admiration (though not fear, as Peter Stangle has it in *Kleist. Sein Leben*, 121), and that Kleist considered himself a master of sleight of hand as well—his *œurvre* and life are as much *Taschenspielertrick* as *Gesamtkunstwerk*, his trickeries and ruses during the Würzburg journey setting the tone. As such, his note to Zschokke of 2nd March 1802, *"Mich erschreckt die bloße Möglichkeit, statt eines Schweizerbürgers durch einen Taschenspielerskunstgriff ein Franzose zu werden"* (II:719), displays as much admiration as dismay: his imagined duel with Napoleon mirrors his *Agôn* with Goethe—hence my cover image—, and the First Consul here nearly outflanks him by turning Switzerland into a French province just when he is about to settle there.

150   That the rumours are spread by female characters, and that poisoning and drowning may be considered "female" modes of killing (Kleist's "male" modes of killing involves shooting bullets or smashing victims' heads against a wall or pillar—cf. *Erdbeben, Kohlhaas*), does not signifying misogyny on Kleist's part: all his characters are to be enacted by male actors adopting female and male roles, and he is simply taking recourse to "conventional" gender roles or prejudices current in his day.

151   Cf. Roland Reuß, "Heinrich von Kleist. Die Familie Schroffenstein. Ein Trauerspiel in Fünf Aufzügen (1803)," in: Günther Emig and Peter Staengle (Eds.), *Erstlinge* (Heilbronn: Kleist-Archiv Sembdner, 2004), 54. Johannes Kunisch writes, in "Von der gezähmten zur entfesselten Bellona," in: Hans-Joachim Kreutzer (Ed.), *Kleist-Jahrbuch 1988/89* (Berlin: Erich Schmidt, 1989), 50: *"Furcht vor Strafe und ein hoher Grad an Abgestumpftheit als Folge jahrelangen und jedes Sinnbezugs entbehrenden Drills waren die Grundlage der Heeresverfassung."* *"Ich pfeife drauf"* is a colloquial dismissal of something as irrelevant, and Kleist here *"pfeift auf"* the Frederician régime that treats men like dogs and that he himself endured for six years. Sembdner is misguided when he terms Kleist *"schon füh ein Verächter des Krieges und des Kriegshandwerks"* (*In Sachen Kleist*, 251): it is not war or warcraft as such that Kleist disdains, but its outmoded means, such as the Frederician—he positively *adores* Napoleon's *grande batterie* and Palafox's guerrilla warfare, and his favourite games are *war games* (see my discussion further below). A reference to the Frederician whistle recurs In *Hermannsschlacht*, when Cheruscan scouts lead Varus to *"Pfiffikon"* (cf. V.1908-11), "the estate of the whistle," i.e., Fr. II's

land, i.e., Prussia ("*-ikon,*" from Alemanic "*-ighof*" = "-estate," "-yard," "-court," is a component of several Swiss town names). The paradox Santing's speech entails echoes Epimenides' "All Cretans are liars."

152   Kleist's *overt* explications to Martini of 18th/19th March 1799 are complimented by his *Aufsatz* to Rühle, which hints at his *covert* motives for leaving the military (Kleist seeks to convince his lover to follow suit, so that they may continue enjoying each other's company). Kleist does not lie outright, but shares the truth selectively, depending on addressee and objective: *"zum Teil wahr"* (II:514); *"Du sollst alles erfahren, was ich sagen* kann*"* (*ibid*); *"habe ich Dir... nichts, auch das mindeste nicht vorgelogen, nur verschwiegen, was ich verschweigen mußte"* (II:524). Eberhard Siebert recently (2014) argued that Kleist's private teacher was not Martini but Samuel Marot. I did not follow up on that line of thought.

153   Michel Houellebecq notes in *Submission*, 128: "You could say that [French patriotism] was born at the Battle of Valmy, in 1792, and that it began to die in 1917, in the trenches of Verdun." Goethe, who was present at *Valmy,* in his report *Kampagne in Frankreich* claims that on the evening of the main cannonade he told the Prussian officers, *"Von hier und heute geht eine neue Epoche der Weltgeschichte aus, und ihr könnt sagen, ihr seid dabei gewesen."*

154   Peter Michalzik (*Kleist*, 62) notes à propos of the Prussian soldiers who partook in the *Palatine Campaign*: *"Viele empfanden es als bitter, dass man sich nach den siegreichen Schlachten von Primasens und Kaiserslautern wieder an den Rhein zurückziehen musste. Der Sieg wurde damals verschenkt, glaubte man."* Kleist and his comrades marched 1,500 kilometres and fought several battles, only for Hardenberg to sign away the fruits of that labour with a single stroke of the pen.

155   Representations of basilisks apparently abounded in the city of Basel, where Kleist could have observed them when passing through in late 1801; they symbolise sinfulness, in particular lust.

156   This ambivalent gesture anticipates Penthesilea's famous swaying between *Bisse* and *Küsse* and the Marquise's ominous falling around the Count's neck in *Marquise*'s final scene.

157   Louis Gerrekens (*KH*,32) erroneously equates apparent inconsistencies with errors on Kleist's part, instead of recognising them as "navels" from which the text can be unravelled: " *Sogar der Höhepunkt in der Handlung ist mit Inkohärenzen durchwirkt... So ist Agnes' bereits erwähnter Aufschrei, als die den tödlich verwundeten Ottokar erblickt, "—Ein Schwert—im Busen"... unvereinbar mit der Regieanweisung kurz davor: Rupert "zieht das Schwert aus dem Busen Ottokar's"...: hier wird etwas gesehen, was es gar nicht gibt.*" If Rupert pulled his sword out of Ottokar's body, and Agnes subsequently beholds a sword in it, instead of presuming that Kleist made an error, Gerrekens should recognise that *there is a second sword*—namely, Agnes'. The *Kleist-Forschung* has entirely overlooked that *Schroffenstein* is a story of premeditated murder (as are *Findling* and *Zweikampf*, cf. my *Emigrant*).

158   This rivalry is referred to by historians as "German dualism." Under Elector Fr. Aug. I "the Strong" (reigned 1694-1733), Saxony came close to becoming a great power; his successor Fr. Aug. II squandered the opportunity when he found himself on the losing side in the *War of Austrian Succession* (1742) and the *Seven Years' War* (1756-63): had Austria and Saxony jointly vanquished Prussia, Saxony would have become Germany's second power instead of Prussia.

159   Fr. Wilh. II died on 16th November 1797 in the Marmorpalais in Potsdam and was entombed on 11th December in a sarcophagus in Berlin Cathedral. Kleist, as a 2nd Lieutenant in Fr.II's own Regiment Garde, and as a member of the von Kleist family, may well have payed his last respects to the King, of which the drama's opening scene, "*Rossitz. Das Innere einer Kapelle. Es steht ein Sarg in der Mitte*," could be a reminiscence.

160   Jeronimus' being sometimes addressed as Jerome may allude to Fr. Aug. III's becoming successor to the Polish throne, his kingdom thus straddling Protestant and Catholic realms.

161   As said, the "*Schwelle*" ("threshold") is the Rhine, threshold between France and Germany. Kleist may be hinting at the cursed *Rheingold* hoard that in the medieval epic *Nibelungenlied* Hagen sinks into the Rhine near Worms after perfidiously murdering Siegfried, and thus may be implicitly equating Napoleon with the villainous Hagen, a suitable hate-figure in German folklore. The Burgundians in the 5th century settled around the city of Worms, on the Rhine's left bank, where Kleist

in *Zweikampf* locates the Emperor's (i.e., Napoleon's) seat of power; following their defeat by the Huns in AD 437, which is the epic's main topic, they were resettled by the Romans in the region around Lyon and became Romanised; in AD 534 the kingdom they established along the Rhône river was defeated by, and incorporated into, the kingdom of the Franks, which contributed to the Germanic Franks themselves becoming Gallicised. Sabine Doering in "Kinderwissen—Über einige Erkenntnisprozesse," in: Yixu Lü et al (Eds.), *Wissensfiguren*, 241-4, explores the finger's role in Kleist's drama, but remains hampered by her lack of a *satirical* and *satyrical* framework. Sembdner (*In Sachen Kleist*, 336) notes Kleist's propensity to emphasise the left side of the body (Peter's left finger, Adam's left club foot, Strahl's and Homburg's injuries to the left hand, the victim of an accident's left-side injuries— cf. II:266), but his suggestion that Kleist was left-handed explains nothing; in my reading, these incidences all refer to the same *satirical-cum-syphilitical* symbolism: *syphilitically*, the "sinister" phallus is chancreatic, *satirically*, the *HRR* has been "injured" or "amputated" on the Rhine's left bank.

162   Kleist's imagery of Ursula-Napoleon and the Warwand-Habsburg cutting off pieces of the *HRR* anticipates James Gillroy's famous 1805 cartoon of Napoleon and British prime minster William Pitt carving up the world between them, Napoleon taking Europe and Pitt the oceans. Kleist's works and Gillroy's cartoon showcase different prevailing perspectives on the Napoleonic era: in Kleist's works Britain scarcely features as a relevant player until the *BA* period, and the *Coalition Wars* are depicted as primarily a Franco-German conflict; in Gillroy's cartoon, the conflict is depicted as primarily an Anglo-French one, the German powers not even sitting at the table; both ignore Russia, whose resilience in 1812 would prove decisive in defeating Napoleon.

657

163   The Schneekoppe (1,603m) in Silesia's Riesengebirge was Germany's hightest *Mittelgebirge* (as opposed to Alpine) peak, and combining significant height and commanding views with convenient access, from the second half of the 18th century onwards became one of the world's first peaks to regularly receive tourists. According to Martini's recollections of Kleist's travel reports (cf. *LS*,34a), Kleist, Ulrike, Leopold and Gleißenberg hiked up to the Schlesierbaude at 1,400m, then westwards along a ridge to the Elbegrund formed below the source of the river Elbe. They may have stayed overnight at Spindlermühle in Bohemia, the first town on the river Elbe (Martini recalls that they stayed at Friedrichstal, but this is implausible as

it is too far to the west to enable the party to reach the Schneekoppe on the following day, as he says they did). The weather having been poor on the evening, Kleist's party will have taken shelter at the Hampelbaude at 1,258m, before climbing up to the peak early in the morning, on which they enjoyed breathtaking views, as Kleist's *Hymne an die Sonne* (I:43-4) and Leopold's and Gleißenberg respective entries into the hut's visitor book (cf. *LS*,34b) show. Kleist was clearly drawn to mountain peaks: he visited the Harz Mountains, a *Mittelgebirge* in central Germany, thrice, in 1797 with his Potsdam musical quartet, when they hiked up the Stubenberg near Gernrode (cf. II:568; Sembdner misspells it Stufenberg), already then a popular destination for tourists, in 1798 together with three other acquaintances, when they descended into the Bielshöhle, a stalactite cave that only recently had been made accessible to visitors, and hiked up to the range's highest peak, the Brocken or Blocksberg (1,141m), where according to tradition the witches in the Walpurgis Night celebrate the Witches' Sabbath (cf. Ursula's *Hexenküche* and Goethe's *Faust II*), and in 1801 with Ulrike, when they visited the Kaiserpfalz at Goslar, descended into the Rammelsberg mine, one of the world's first mines made accessible to tourists, and once again scaled the Brocken (Eberhard Siebert has plausibly argued in *Kleistiana Collecta*, 80-1, that *Schroffenstein* could incorporate elements of the history of the ancient Stolberg family in Wernigerode, at the foot of the Harz mountains, whom Kleist and Ulrike visited in 1801. Apart from mountain peaks and vistas, Kleist was fascinated by caves and grottoes, river valleys (the gentle Oderaue behind his family house, the quintessentially romantic Rhine valley between Koblenz and Mainz, the Elbgrund in the Riesengebirge, the Elbdurchbruch between Erzgebirge and the Bohemian Mittelgebirge, the Tharandt valley near Dresden, the Danube valley at Würzburg), alpine landscapes (the Bernese Oberland, the Valais, the Ticinio), the sources of great rivers (Lippspringe in Westafalen, the Elbaue in Bohemia, Donaueschingen in Württemberg, the Haslital in the Bernese Oberland in which the the Aare originates, the Rhône glacier, the Gottard Massiv on whose eastern flank the Rhine originates), waterfalls (the Elbfall, the Rheinfall near Schaffhausen, the Reichenbachfall of Sherlock Holmes fame). Perhaps his flat and sandy homeland of Brandenburg was uninspiring in comparison (cf. Michalzik, *Kleist*, 90; 124-5): I argued in *Emigrant* that his so-called "landscape allegories" are virtually always *satyrical*, and that mountain-and-valley-scapes that resemble bodily shapes and movements appealed to his *Gefühl* (cf. II:541) far more than featureless plains, whose aspect may ignite *Verstand*, philosophical thought, but not sensual fantasy. While excursions of the type Kleist undertook were fast becoming conventional in his day (Goethe had already been pretty much everywhere where Kleist went), they inspired him in unconventional ways—cf. my later discussion on *the panoramic*. As an aside, when Kleist and Ulrike in 1801 undertook a boat trip from Mainz to Cologne, a storm forced their ship had to emergency-land in a village belonging to the Bishopric of Treves (cf. II:670), which after the French occupation of the Rhine's left bank encompassed only a small area on the right bank centred around Ehrenbreitstein; while Kleist does not report the name of that village, this episode is of personal interest to this author, who in 1986-90 was a student in Vallendar, a small town a few miles downriver from Ehrenbreitstein on what was then the Bishopric's territory, where he lived for a while on the Rhenish island of Niederwerth; it so happens that the narrow straight between Vallendar and Niederwerth would have been the most ideal site for an emergency-landing—who knows, perhaps Kleist set foot on the banks of Niederwerth or Vallendar.

164   In *Marquise*, when on that "dreaded Third" the Marquise (*Borussia*) and the Mother (*Austria*), both dressed in bridal gown, await the arrival of the pretender (Napoleon), Kleist introduces a moment of uncertainty regaring whether Count F (the castrated, domesticated Napoleon) or the hunter Leopardo (the virile, voracious Napoleon) will show up. In the event, both show up, and they welcome the former, whom they incorporate into the German family in a *"gebrechliche Einrichtung"* (a version of Kleist's *"Gewölbe,"* which collapses if a single stone is removed). Incidentally, if Leopardo represents the earlier, virile Napoleon, then the Marquise's recollection of his having violated her in her slumber corresponds precisely to Count F's recollection, in his "Thinka vision," of having "thrown mud at her"—in other words, the two recollections refer to the same historical event, namely *Jena-Auerstedt*, and their parallel recollections anticipate Käthchen and Strahl's parallel dreams. *Marquise's* sequence of events is, then, as follows: the Marquise's *Kniefall* before Count F in the opening scene corresponds to *Tilsit* (cf. my *Emigrant*), their parallel recollection to *Jena-Auerstedt*, and the mysterious battle on an unnamed battlefield in which Count F is injured, to a forthcoming battle, perhaps on an Austrian or Russian battlefield, in which Napoleon is checked, whereupon the Marquise (*Borussia*) in Kleist's utopian scenario nourishes and marries him, incorporating him into the German "family." Kleist could have modeled his brides—Mother and Marquise—on Demeter and and "sacred-pure" Kore (Persephone), the abstinence of whose priestesses was considered an antithetic, dialectical preparation to procreation and birth (cf. Burkert, *Greek Religion*, 244). It is on the Third day that the saviour resurrects, and the biblical topos of the resurrection offers Kleist a means to camouflage erotic scenarios, as we can

glean from his poem *Der Engel am Grabe des Herrn* (cf. I:10-11): the two quivering Marias are awaiting their redemption before the gaping hole as the savior re-sur-*rects* or e-*rects*.

165   "*Stamm*" = "trunk" as well as "tribe," "clan." Kleist's travel companion of 1809, Fr. Chr. Dahlmann, later noted: "*Unser Vorsatz war [in 1809], von Böhmen aus nach allen Kräften dahin zu wirken, daß aus dem österreichischen Kriege ein deutscher werde... wir verlangten von Österreich nur Ausharren trotz der Niederlagen...so werde auch Preußen sich aufraffen..., das übrige Deutschland aber werde den vereinigten Adlern Österreichs und Preußens folgen*" (*LS*,316). The eagle motif was thus current among the friends, even if Dahlmann here is not referring to the Holy Roman coat of arms; the sum of Austria's and Prussia's eagle heads is three, not two, but any successor entity to the *HRR* would have been expected to adopt the two-headed eagle, as the *Deutscher Bund* did in 1815.

166   In *Emigrant* I sought to dispel the ("consenus") view that Kleist unequivocally admired Queen Luise, arguing that he considered her to have had a negative influence over the King and that his reference to her "great men" (cf. II:773; I:35; Zimmermann, *Kleist*, 177) was *satyrically* and *satirically* demining: first among the men around her was Hardenberg, whom Kleist evidently thought anything but "great." Kleist held traditional views onn gender and leadershiop: he wanted his King to lead and the Queen, to put it bluntly (if "politically incorrectly"), to look after the children and stay clear of politics. Kleist's works do feature female characters who shape the course of events, but typically in an indirect or "behind the scenes" fashion—*Schroffenstein*'s women spreading rumours, *Marquise*'s Mother quietly engineering the "*Einrichtung*," *Penthesilea*'s High Priestess subtly staging Penthesilea's encounter with Achilles' disfigured corpse, *Kohlhaas*' Lisbeth circulating her game-chaning oracle.

167   Blamberger merely fails to discern Kleist's "systematic" when he claims (*Kleist*, 132): "*Jegliche Systematik in der Schilderung von Landschaften, Städten und Menschen ist [Kleist] fremd... Kontingenz scheint das Prinzip zu sein, dem Kleist sich anvertraut, als Schreibender wie als Reisender.*" Are not Saxony's "*Täler, eng und heimlich*" (II:545) and Paris' "*enge, krumme, stinkende Straßen*" (II:685) related to each other in the same manner as, say, "*der ganze Schmutz zugleich und Glanz*" of Kleist's body and soul? The Kleist reception never tires of emphasising that Kleist

systematically exlored A. Müller's *Lehre vom Gegensatz*, but rarely explicates the *tertium comparationis* that underpins Kleistian opposites: Saxony's idyllic narrow passages and Paris' unsavoury ones refer to the same *bodily channel*, tantalising at once and scary. Functioning as code, Kleist's "landscape allegories" are necessarily as systematic as can be: otherwise en- or de-cryption would be impossible.

168   Johann depicts both Ottokar and Agnes as ithyphallic when he exclaims, "Agnes!... Ottokar!" (V.2707). This purification and initiation scene anticipates several others in *Marquise* and elsewhere, e.g., Count F's liberally spreading his semen (*"Löschwasser"*) among the fortress' inhabitants, Thinka's diving into semen (*"Fluten"*) after having been dirtied with mud (*"Kot"*), and the Marquise's sprinkling the Count's semen (*"Weihwasser"*) over the heads of her family members. Like Agnes, the Marquise is associated with the immaculately conceived Maria; Ottokar's rhythmic *"Ich... hier...—Da du"* anticipates *Marquise's "Hier—traf er, da,"* and *Prolog's "Hier jetzt lenke, jetzt dort,"* his *"Deine Seele / Lag offen vor mir, wie ein schönes Buch / [...] / Nun bist / Du ein verschloßner Brief.—",* Marionettentheater's motif of *"Ziererei"* ("coyness"). Cf. Martial, *Epigrams*, 4.7 (trans. Gideon Nisbet): "What yesterday you gave me, today you refuse: Hyllus, my boy, why? Why are you suddenly stony-faced, when lately you were soft and yielding?"

661

169   The antique bronze depicting three satyrs is from Napoli, which Kleist did not visit, but he could have seen similar images in the gardens of Kassel's Schloss Wilhelmshöhe or in the Louvre. The medieval lead glass windows in the Marienkirche in Frankfurt/O he will certainly have observed during his childhood, as the Mardienkirche is right next door to his family home (Eberhard Siebert argues plausibly in *Kleistiana Collecta*, 97, that Theobald's *"Verbrüderung mit dem Satan"* references the Marienkirche, not any actual church in Heilbronn); Kleist could easily have seen a *satyrical* triad in it. Notes Sloterdijk (*Sphären III*, 405-6): *"Das erotische Feld wird unter Spannung gesetzt... Daraus entsteht ein Eifersuchtsfluidum, das durch prüfende Blicke, humoristische Kommentare, herabsetzende Nachreden und ritualisierte Konkurrenzspiele in Zirkulation und Fluss gehalten wird. In dieser Dimension manifestiert sich der Eros nicht als dual-libidinöse Spannung zwischen Ego und Alter, sondern als trianguläre Provokation. Ich liebe dich, mich reizt deine schöne Gestalt, sobald ich annehmen darf, dass ein anderer dich liebt und deine schöne Gestalt ihn genügend reizt, um dich in Besitz nehmen zu wollen."*

170   When Hephaistos catches his wife Aphrodite and her lover Ares *in flagranti* with a net, the gods gather around them and laugh their unceasing *Homeric laughter* at this precious sight (*Odyssey VIII*, 266-366; cf. also *Odyssey XX*, 346, *Iliad I*, 599, and Burkert, *Greek Religion*, 154; 220). Re "*kynical* laughter," cf. Sloterdijk (*ibid*, 275-6): *"es [ist] für den Kyniker bezeichnend, so laut und ungeniert zu lachen, daß die feinen Leute den Kopf schütteln. Ihr Gelächter kommt aus den Eingeweiden, es ist animalisch fundiert und gibt sich hemmungslos... Im positivien ekstatischen Lachen... spielt die Energie einer fassungslosen Bejahung."*

171   Kleist uses the term *"Gewebe"* ("fabric," "tissue") in reference to a web of lies or deception—cf. I:277); he also uses a number of remarkably similar terms, in a variety of contexts: *"Teppich"* ("carpet"; II:551), *"gewirkter Fußteppich"* ("knitted rug"; II:580), *"Spalier"* ("trellis"; I:210; 228), *"Kreuzgeflecht"* ("crossed mesh"; I:232), *"Musternetz"* ("patterned network"; I:395); *"Parquet"* ("parquet"; II:201), and *"Mosaische Arbeit"* ("mosaic work"; I:520). Pfuel uses the terms "threads" and "fabric" ("*Stoff*") when he recounts—quite succinctly—to Bülow how Kleist created Schroffenstein: "[Kleist] *war eines Tages die seltsame Auskleideszene des letzten Aktes... in den Sinn gekommen, und... er [hatte] sie wie eine zusemmenhanglose Phantasie niedergeschrieben. Dann erst fiel ihm ein, sie mit andern Fäden der Erfindung, vielleicht auch mit einem zufällig entdeckten Stoff zusamenzuspinnen"* (*LS*,70).

172   This passage anticipates the duel in *Zweikampf*, during which a small scratch with Trota's infested "sword" suffices to agonisingly carry off the apparently healthy and robust Rotbart. Cf. Sloterdijk, *Sphären III*, 877: *"Besingt Sappho den doppelsinnigen Eros, so gebrauchte sie das aus* glýkos, *süss, und* píkros, *scharf, pikant, zusammengesetzte Pradikat* glykýpikros, *um auszusagen, dass die Liebe auf Lesbos, wie vermutlich anderswo, ein Glücksend, eine entzückende Tortur ist."* Cf. also Catullus, *Carmen*, 85: "I love and I hate, and I am in torment," and Martial, *Epigrams*, 10.38: "What bouts, what battles your lucky bed has witnessed."

173   Ottokar's "baptising" Agnes precedes his fall just as the act of naming— "She shall be called Woman"— in *Genesis 3* does man's. Kleist freely mixes Christian and pagan symbolism—e.g., baptism and libation—, his purification scenes owing as much to Christian rites—e.g., Bogomil or Cathar practices of purging, fasting, celebrating and dancing as means of self-cleansing—as they do to ancient Greek rituals. Re the latter, cf. Burkert (*Greek Religion*, 76): "Purification is a social process.

To belong to a group is to confirm to its standard of purity; the reprobate, the outsider, and the rebel are unclean... By celebrating the elimination of irritating matter, these rituals delimit a more highly valued realm, either the community itself in relation to a chaotic outside, or an esoteric circle within society... Purification rituals are therefore involved in all intercourse with the sacred and in all forms of initiation; but they are also employed in crisis situations of madness, illness, and guilt. Insofar as in this case the ritual is placed in the service of a clearly identifiable end, it assumes a magical character." Whereas purification rituals in pre-modern times thus primarily entailed magic and shamanism, in Kleist's day they also mimicked medico-institutional and (pseudo-) scientific techniques such as diagnosis, quarantine, systematic treatment, inoculation and vaccination. In a philosophical register, Kleist's scene anticipates Saul A. Kripke's *baptismal ceremony* (a social act of labeling the referent), J.L. Austin's *speech act*, Wittgenstein's *language game* and Foucault's *discourse formation*.

174   This passage ancitipates Gustav and Toni in *Verlobung* mingling their "tears." A meme may have been circulating in Kleist's "brotherhood" to the effect that mingling a healthy lover's "pure" with a syphiliac's "impure" ejaculate yields a *pharmakon* with healing or at least protective properties, or that intercourse with a "virgin" (immaculate lover) heals a syphiliac—cf. Bäumler (*Amors vergifteter Pfeil*, 62): *"Nun herrschte jedoch der Aberglaube, daß die Liebeskrankheit nur von einer Jungfrau hinweggenommen warden könne. Joachim Fernau... schreibt dazu: 'Die abergläubige Vorstellung von der Erlösung durch eine reine Jungfrau klang dem Menschen des 16. Jahrhunderts wunderbar und einleuchtend. Sie erinnerte an die Jungfrau Maria, und zugleich knüpfte sie wieder an die Sinnlichkeit an. Mit einem Wort: Es war eine Medizin, die nicht nur homöopathisch, sondern sympathisch war.'"* It was common in ancient Greece for the *erastês* to offer gifts to the *erômenos* upon his departure.

663

175   According to Pjotr Tchaikovsky's biographer Philipp Bullock, the composer and his brother Modest devised a "gay code" unintelligible to the uninitiated, and Kleist's *satirical* vocabulary may similarly entail "code" used for communication among "brotherhood" members. Parallels between Kleist's vocabulary and that of the likes of Brentano and Fouqué hints at such a "code": Brentano's unkind joke about Kleist and Müller, *"Wenn Adam malt und Eva kleistert"* (LS,234), mimics *Krug*'s characters in a manner that suggests that both he and his "implicit audience" understand Kleist's categories of lovers (Adam = *erastês*, Eva = *erômenos*), and the terms in which he portrays Kleist to Wilh. Grimm, *"frisch und gesund unser Mitesser,*

ein untersetzter Zweiunddreißiger, mit einem erlebten runden, stumpfen Kopf, gemischt launig, kindergut, arm und fest," parallel Kleist's when reminiscing about Pfuel's genitals (cf. II:749): "fresh and healthy" = "free from symptoms (of venereal disease)"; "fellow traveller" = "member of the brotherhood"; "stubbed 32-ish" = "his member short and of average length"; "with an experienced round, stubbed head" = "with a much-used, round, stubbed glans"; "of mixed disposition" = "effective in any roles in a *"FFF"* constellation"; "innocent as a child" = "excels in the role of *erômenos*"; "impoverished" = "constantly short of condoms and other accessories"; "firm" = "unwaivering in his sexuality, unlikely to go legit" (Brentano must have assumed Grimm to be fluent in "code"—cf. also Ueli Leuthold's claim that the Grimmean fairy tales are inundated with homosexual symbolism and that the Grimm brothers were both gay, in *Von Coming Out, Gay Pride und Stiefkind-Adoption - Männliche Homosexualität in den Märchen der Brüder Grimm: Interpretationen von 31 Grimm'schen Märchen und die Schlussfolgerungen daraus* (Hamburg: tredition, 2017). Fouqué uses "code" in his 1812 reminiscence about his and Kleist's first encounter: *"jünglingshell,-- / ...mein Heinrich, / So standen wir, nun fest im Männerbund / Die treue Hand uns drückend, unsere Lieder / Einander... / Entgegen sendend in die freud'ge Brust"* (NR,252). Gentz's and A. Müller's extensive correspondence, which from time to time ropes in other members of their "brotherhood" (Sigismund Kurnatowski, Baron Brinkmann, Joh. von Müller, scarcely Kleist), and which commences with a diary entry by Gentz on 7th June 1800, *"Den angenehmen Besuch eines meiner liebsten Freunde, des jungen Adam Müller, aus Göttingen"* (*AML*,7), extensively deploys "code." In 1802 he mentions spending a *"nuit céleste"* with the actress Christel Eigensatz (21), but having settled in Vienna in August 1802, his letters to Müller become ever more saturated with declarations of love and desirous urgency: Müller, "officially" liaised with the salonière Sophie Sander and at the heart of a major circle of intellectuals, boys and girls, responds nonchalantly, clealry skilled at driving this older lover crazy (Gentz is almost 40, Müller 24). When Müller in March 1803 joins Kurnatowski to South Prussia, the jealous Gentz inundates his *"guten Bösen"* lover with letters—6, 10, 20 at a time—and complains about the lack of responses (cf. 41; 49; 50; 73; 116)—his Adam, meanwhile, keeps him on tenterhooks. The "brothers'" correspondence is extensive, but not least because Kleist's own is so sparse (be it because he was recitent, or because correspondence was destroyed), I reproduce pertinent passages extensively, with my clarifications and occasional commentary on "code" in square brackets:

- "*ich sah ihn* [A. Müller] *sehr oft*" (9);
- "*Eine unbegreifliche Reise nach Freienwalde* [a spa town near Berlin] *—mit Müller!*" (12);
- "*Ich gäbe zwei Jahre meines Lebens drum, Müller, wenn ich Sie jetzt einen einzigen Abend bei mir haben könnte*" (24; cf. similarly 52);
- "*daß wir* [Müller and Kurnatowski] *uns täglich, vielmehr nächtlich, sehen und Ihrer erinnern. Ich habe mich recht innig an ihn attachirt*" [!] (26);
- "*so muß ich doch nun immer tiefer mit Ihnen hinein*" [cf. Kleist: "*ich muß hinein...*"] (41);
- "*In Dresden... fand ich* Adam Müller *und* Kurnatowski... *ich selbst war in tiefbewegter Stimmung, kräftig, lebendig religiös, und doch auch zu Ausschweifungen sehr geneigt und sehr fähig*" [!] (42; cf. also 43; 52; 60; 65; 82; 84);
- "*von den unvergeßlichsten Tagen meines Lebens die ich mit meinen Freunden zubrachte*" (43);
- "*Müller—den Sie doch wohl für einen ganzen Kerl gelten lassen* [cf. Kleist: Römergröße]*—wird Ihnen sagen, daß ich... ebenso jugendlich bin*" (44);
- "*Ich gehöre Ihnen und Sie mir, mein liebster, liebster Gentz... Immer möchte ich Sie auf die kleine befriedigende Stelle zurückführen* [!]... *ich ruhe nicht, wir* [Müller, Kurnatowski] *müssen Sie bald wieder sehen...; noch besser, noch zuversichtsvoller will ich Ihnen erscheinen... je m'y plongerai avec lui... in der Liebe..., da, dächte ich doch, wären wir beide flott*" (45).
- "*Keine Briefe!... während beßre Mittel dazu offenstehen* [...] *die göttlichen Nächte... die wir in Dresden verlebten* [...] *solche, wie wir, sind nicht auf immer voneinander getrennt*" (52);
- "*In unserer Dresdner Nacht ließen Sie sich fest halten*" (60)
- "*Jetzt bin ich wieder einmal im* Goldnen Engel, *und da es mir so rasend lebhaft wird, wie glückliche Stunden ich hier im Februar mit Ihnen verlebte... was ich nicht erreiche, doch umfasse, und gewissermaßen in mich aufnehme* [!]... *so konnte doch Ihre Größe* [cf. Kleist: Römergröße] *nie drückend für mich werden*" (65);
- "*Sie interessieren mich von so vielen Seiten* [!] *zugleich*" (73);
- "*unsre Berlinischen Theenächte... ob unser Genz wirklich in dem Meere seiner Genüsse, seiner ewigen Jugend* [cum?]*... sitzen geblieben ist*" (78);
- "*Er darf... keinen Menschen als mich sehen... Mein Zweck ist eigentlich, mit ihm in dieser Zeit zu leben*" [cf. Kleist's "*Zweck*" of going on a honeymoon with Brockes] (79);

- *"die Sommernächte des vergangenen Jahres"* (81);
- *"Ich kann diesen Menschen nicht aufgeben; wenige haben so mein Innerstes berührt und erschüttert"* (82);
- *"die großen [!] und heiligen Stunden, die ich mit Ihnen verlebte"* (89);
- *"sich mit mir einlassen [!] wollen... für so viel Genuß... stehe ich mit Leib und Leben"* (89);
- *"wenn Sie sich nur stellen wollen [!]... Wir freuten uns im Geiste auf die Zeit, wo Sie... unser Dritter seyn würden"* (89);
- *"gegen mich sind Sie... so tugendhaft* [cf. Kleist's concept of *"Tugend"*]... *die persönliche Nähe tut viel bei Ihnen... Sie können schmeicheln... es kömmt uns aufeinander an! Mir glüht das Herz, wenn ich an die bevorstehenden Tage denke... Wenn Sie sich nur gehörig einlassen!"* [!] (91);
- *"die ganze schlaflose Nacht hindurch... allein mit Ihnen beschäftigt; die... beständige Verjüngung, die immer steigende Regsamkeit"* ["rejuvenation" appears to have been Gentz's chief concern in his relationship with his youthful lovers; cf. Kleist's concern for "purification"] (92);
- *"Mich interessirt der heutige Wind* [cf. Kleist: *"Sturm"*] *in so fern sehr lebhaft, als ich durch ihn in der vorgefaßten Meinung von meiner Wohnung* [cf. Kleist: *"Zimmer"*] *für immer befestigt bin"* [this passage can also be read *satirically*: "Wind" = Napoleon; "Wohnung" = Germany] (94);
- *"die von Ihnen gestern erfahrene Anmuth und Milde* [cf. Kleist: *"Grazie"* and *"Tugend"*] *... Was den Wind angeht, sind dies die ersten Zimmer* [!] *der Welt"* (95);
- *"Good night, sweet boys"* (98; in Engl. in the original);
- *"Nicht alles, was Sie gestern Agend begeisterte, ging von mir aus, vieles, und offenbar das Beste, trugen Sie auf mich über. Ich gab die Permanenz...; das andere kam entschieden von Ihnen, zog mich aber wieder so an, daß wir zuletzt recht eigentlich Alle Drei Eins wurden"* [a hilarious confounding of Müller's dialectic method and the pleasures of the *"FFF"* constellation] (100);
- *"ich werde mich trösten, Sie zu verlieren, weil das Beste von Ihnen mir doch immer bleibt. Allerdings gibt es tausend Bande zwischen uns... so reizend"* [after a period of cohabitation in Vienna, Gentz frees himself intellectually, not emotionally, from Müller, whose imminent conversion to Catholicism he is unable to accept—cf. also 106] (103);
- *"Ich liebe Sie übrigens... mehr den jemals"* (108);

- *"seitdem ich die Süßigkeit... wieder recht gekostet hatte, fühlte ich mich einsamer... Denn die wenigen Reinen* ["pure" = homo] *die ich außer Ihnen noch finde, sind für mich nicht genialisch genug, und die übrigen Genialischen sind alle unrein* ["impure" = hetero]*"* (109)
- *"Sie, mit Ihrem Organ der Gutmüthigkeit!"* (111);
- *"Nicht ganz befriedigt mich der Gedanke, die Erinnerung Ihrer Vortrefflichkeit* [male vigour]*, der Majestät und wollüstigen Weichheit Ihres Charakters* [male member—cf. Kleist's *"Antlitz," "Zug"*] *und Ihres Gesprächs* [intercourse]*"* (115)
- *"mein Wunsch, mit Ihnen wieder vereinigt zu seyn"* (118);
- *"woher dieser Enthusiasmus für Sie, den er doch niemals sah... Woher also diese seltsame Zärtlichkeit?"* [Gentz is jealous of Joh. von Müller's correspondence with A. Müller] (121);
- *"Ich kenne an ihm* [A. Müller] *nur den einzigen Fehler, daß er zu wenig einseitig ist"* [Müller is veering off to women and disloyal to the "brotherhood"] (122);
- *"wenn dieser junge Mann* [A. Müller] *mit Ihnen und mir ein Jahr lang zusammenleben könnte, wir drei vielleicht im Stand wären"* [Gentz is trying to forge a new *ménage à trois*; *"Stand"* = erection, but also part of the word *"Ehestand,"* "wedlock"] (122);
- *"Hier, meine Hand, teurer Freund"* [cf. Kleist to Altenstein: *"Ich möchte Ihre Hand ergreifen, mein großer und erhabener Freund, und heißen Kuß darauf drücken"*—cf. II:819]*... "eben über diesen Punkt* [religion; here: sexual orientation] *fühlte ich mein Herz mit so* brüderlicher Symphathie *entgegen klopfen"* (142);
- *"Müller... war mir in den Abendstunden oft willkommen"* (147);
- *"Aber auf welchem Wege werde ich Sie treffen?"* [cf. Kleist, Marquise: *"hier—traf er"*] (148);
- *"Ihr furchtbares Einverständniß mit Wiesel* [Privy councillor Wilh. Wiesel]*—er hatte ja... den Gegensatz in der That auch erfunden—ist eine der schrecklichsten Entdeckungen, die ich je gemacht. Das, womit Wiesel so harmonirt, wird mir immer verdächtig sein; ich gäbe ein Jahr meines Lebens, wenn ich diese Coalition, die ich nun leider schon eine Allianz nennen muß, nie entdeckt hätte. Und wie Sie, der nichts fürchtet, den Teufel fürchten!!!* [Gentz is jealous of Müller's affair; Tieck notes that Wiesel, *"eine Art von dämonischer Philosophie der Sinnlichkeit entwickelte... Zuweilen ließ er sich in orakelhaftem Ton vernehmen, welcher tiefe Sinn in diesen Orgien sei... einer mystischen Geheimhaltung,*

die schwache Köpfe vollends in Verwirrung brachte" (quoted by Jakob Baxa, *AML*,33 notes). *"Gegensatz"* evidently refers not only to Müller's pet theory but also a "brother's" ability to reconcile homoerotic affairs and married life, a question also preoccupying Kleist—cf. my section *The Familial* below; Wiesel was married to the promiscuous Berlin socialite Pauline César, close friend of Rahel Levin (*"Ralle und Schwan"*), who later become Prince Louis Ferd.'s lover (*"Pölle und Loulou"*); cf. Kleist's similar usage of *"in der That"* (i.e., in the sexual act) and *"Teufel"* (disloyal or diseased man)]" (152);

- *"daß der Jünger [erômenos] dem Meister [erastês] über den Kopf wuchs"* (158);
- "[Müller's] *Genie* [member] *ist groß, schön und edel. (In einigen Tagen habe ich eine besondere Gelgenheit. Auch wird Metternicht über Dresden gehen.) Daß Sie auf diesen Sohn Ihrer Liebe nicht eifersüchtig sind, begreift niemand besser als ich, der ich meine Geliebten vergöttere* [Joh. von Müller's Freudian free association of A. Müller and Metternich suggests that the latter was part of the "brotherhood"; apart from A. Müller and Gentz, Metternich is the most frequently occurring name in *AML*. Gentz was Metternich's closest advisor; but as in Kleist's circles, in Gentz's *The Satirical* and T*he Satyrical* are closely intertwined (n.b.: the German resistance against Napoleon should perhaps be labelled *libidinal* rather than *romantic*)]" (161);
- *"Es verlautet, Sie hätten das glückliche, das göttliche Projekt, Gr. M(etternich) nach Dresden zu begleiten. Engel! Führen Sie es aus.. Kommen müssen Sie. Und Müller! Und Ihr Frend—Wiesel! Und alle Kunstsammlungen!* [an enthusiastic Gentz imagines orchestrating an orgy involving himself, Brinkmann, Metternich, A. Müller, Wiesel and assorted "pieces of art" (male or female)— i.e., he is seeking to re-stage that "divine night" in Dresden in early 1803] (168);
- *"Ich bin nur einseitig etwas nütze; aber ich will wenigstens in meiner Einseitigkeit das Beste werden versuchen, was ich vermag... Ihres Ganzen würdiges Glied* [member; Gentz offers himself as *dmōs*]" (170);
- "*Herr von Peterson... Mitglied des A. Müller'schen Kreises* ["brotherhood"; *"Glied"* = member, so in Ger. *"Mitglied"* can have the same double meaning as "member" in Engl.]" (173);
- *"liebster Adam! mit innigem Genuß bey der Erinnerung der schnell verflossenen Augenblike"* (187; similiarly Müller's response, 189);
- *"erwachte in mir die letzte Leidenschaft, die mich an ein Weib gefesselt hat. Die Herzogin von Acerenza... Ich schrieb selbst an Adam Müller: 'Die Reize dieser*

Frau machten mich ganz vergessen, daß es jenseits der Anhöhen um Prag eine Sonne und Sterne gebe [Gentz veers between homo- and heterosexual desire; "Sun" = Müller; "stars" = "brothers"]" (204);

- "*Ich kann darum noch nicht von Ihnen lassen, und heute will ich Ihnen sogar eine Gelgenheit an die Hand geben* [!], *mir zu dienen* [!]" (211);
- "*Sie sind ein eweiger Weigerax* [cf. Kleist's "*Ziererei*"]" (214);
- "*Es fehlt* [Schubert] *der irdische Kern... die objektive Erkenntniß des Gegensatzes ist noch kein Leben des Gegensatzes..., wo im Erkennen das Erkannte geübt und im Ausüben die Ausübung erkannt wird*—Dialektik [for Müller, sexual and political *praxis* are in a dialectical relationship with *theory*; Gentz refer to his holistic approach to life as "*Totalität*"—cf. 250]" (220);
- "*der ich weder Fisch noch Fleisch, weder Gelehrter noch Gesellschafter, noch beides zugleich bin* [he admits to being bi- or ambivalent, cf. Kleist's "*Amphibion*"]" (321);
- "*Ich hätte... gerne Ihr kochendes, gährendes Leben gedämpft... Man hat Sie dann sicherer und auch frommer* [more loyal to the "brotherhood" and to Müller]" (431);

Conspicuous in many of these passages is the writers' italicisation of key words, evidently to facilitate *satyrical* decipherment. Most explicit of all *satyrical* passages gathered in *AML* is Gentz's colourful retelling to fellow "brotherhood" member Baron Brinkmann of that celebrated "divine night" of 30th January 1803 in Dresden (cf. 42; 43; 52; 60; 65; 84), in a report suitably written in French:

"— — — *à 10 heures (du soir) j'ai pris le thé avec mes deux amis* [Müller and Kurnatowski]; *la petite avec laquelle nous nous étions amuses tous ces jours* [!] *y a assisté, mais elle n'a pu ni interrompre ni gêner notre conversation. Celle-ci est devenue infiniment animée et intéressante; à 1 heure j'ai passé avec la petite dans mon cabinet* [!], *et après y avoir fait des prodiges de valeur, je suis rentré chez Müller* [!] *vers le 2 heures. Alors a commence une des scenes plus étonnantes de ma vie; entraîné alternativement à la gaieté la plus extravagante, et à la plus profonde tristesse j'ai ri et pleuré comme un enfant; mais j'ai su m'en rendre compte comme un homme* [!]. *Depuis longtemps je n'avais senti aussi vivement l'étendue et la force de mon âme et*—*j'ose l'ajouter puisque la conscience me le dicte*—*ses grâces natives* [!] *et son incorruptible pureté* [!]. *Tout en jouissant de moimême* [!] *j'ai cependant admire plus que jamais le génie et la profondeur* [cf. Kleist: *Römergröße*] *de Müller; je me suis prosterné devant lui* [!]; *lorsqu'il m'a exposé ses ideés sur l'immortalité avec un enthousiasme que je ne lui avais jamais connue, je luis ai avoué avec un torrent de larmes* [ejaculate], *que pour la première fois je me sentais véritablement* avoir vaincu la mort [orgasm = *petite mort*]; *enfin vers 4 heures du matin* [after an "endless night" of six hours involving three male lovers and one female prostitute] *je me suis arraché dans un état absolument indescriptible... etc."* (82; Jakob Baxa's annotation, "*Hier findet sich eine ausführliche und ungeschminkte Darstellung der berühmten Nacht im 'Goldenen Engel' zu Dresden, in der Adam Müller seinen beiden Freunden Gentz und Kurnatowski mit hinreißender Beredsamkeit die Lehre vom Gegensatze vortrug,*" is either hopelessly naïve or, if it is itself *satyrical*, brilliant).

"Brotherhood" get-togethers were as much intellectual as erotic, as much *satirical* as *satyrical* (Gentz speaks of "*moralisch vs. physisch*"; 105), and so are these letters. Müller, Gentz, Brinkmann, Joh. von Müller, etc. were all politically as well as sexually active, and at times their political allegiance belonged to different masters: in one passage Müller exhorts Brinkmann to share with him all communication by Gentz, offering to do likewise "according to the terms previously agreed," clearly seeking intelligence on political developments *and* erotic liaisons: "*Sagen Sie mir, wer ist jetzt Ihr Theegenosse bey Nacht?... Gentz soll in Wien als roué so fort leben..., an die Prinzeß Luise politische Memoires einschicken*" (86). For Kleist's imagery of "dove" and "angel," compare Juvenal, *Satire II*, 63: "You censure the dove, yet absolve the perverted raven." Cf. also Kleist's "birthday letter" of 1800: "*Ich werde von der Lilie nicht verlangen, dass sie in die Höhe schiessen soll, wie die Zeder, und der Taube kein Ziel stecken, wie dem Adler*" (cf. II:576).

176   In addition to its *satirical* connotation I discussed earlier (oak's crown = royal or imperial crown or laurel), Kleist's oak paradox has a *syphilitical* one: the stronger and sustained the erection, the more exposed is the member to infection (oak = phallus, crown = glans). Johann's line, "*Hervorgeht aus dem Bade,*" parallels Kleist's reminiscence of Pfuel stepping out of Lake Thun, anticipates other bathing scenes in his works, e.g. in *Der Schrecken im Bade,* and suggests a merely superficial purity (cf. my later discussion on the mercury bath that alleviates syphiliac symptoms without curing the disease).

177   Peter Sloterdijk notes (*Sphären I*, 219-20), *"Der... Verliebte wäre von nun an über den mechanischen Grund seines überschwenglichen Wunsches nach Vereinigung mit dem anderen ins Bild gesetzt... das die Liebenden dazu bewegt, ihren Samen in das Gegenüber entsenden zu wollen oder darauf zu brennen, den Erguß des anderen in sich aufzunehmen,"* and, quoting Marsilio Ficino (*De amore*, 335), *"Daß die Liebenden... das Verlangen tragen, die geliebte Person ganz in sich aufzunehmen, bewies Artemisia, die Gattin des Mausolos... welche... seinen Leichnam in Staub verwandelte, diesen in Wasser schüttete und hinuntertrank."* Cf. the Christian sacrament of the Eucharist, Achilles' rending Hektor in the dust, Penthesilea's incorporating Achilles' body or blood, *Homburg*'s prolific meme *"in Staub."* According to a report cited by Jaques Attali in *L'Ordre cannibale* (1979; quoted in Sloterdijk, *Kritik*, 475-6), a 4th Cent. Gnostic sect, at designated "Barbelo festivals," by means of coitus interruptus generated and gathered ejaculate which they ingested with the words "this is the Body of Christ," and with which they besmirch their bodies, expecting this to facilitate their access to God.

178   Brüggemann, Siebert and others repeatedly uncover apparent references to the first step of the alchemical process, *nigredo* (blackening) or *putrefactio* (putrefication), because defilement and contamination are a key elements Kleist's *The Syphilitical*.

179   Well into the 19th century syphilis was widely held to be inheritable (cf. Bäumler, *Amors vergifteter Pfeil*, 111). It is not, as we know today, but since it is transferable from mother to child during pregnancy or birth, it could easily be mistaken to be inheritable, and although Sylvester is said to be free of the disease— *"Rein, wie die Sonne, ist Sylvester"* (V.2350)—, young Philipp acquiring it from his mother is possible. Already in Kleist's day the disease's inheritability from father to child may have been contested, and Kleist's evident elation on "the most important day of my life in Würzburg" (10th October 1800), *"Jetzt, Wilhelmine, werde auch ich Dir mitteilen, was ich mir von dem Glücke einer künftigen Ehe verspreche. Ehemals durfte ich das nicht, aber jetzt—o Gott!"* (II:576), becomes fully intelligible if on that day he was told by Hufeland, or another leading medical expert, that even though he was infected, he could still produce a healthy heir provided the mother was immaculate. This hypothesis regarding "the most important day" squares well with Kleist's ensuing letters to Wilhelmine, his almost pathological concern with the purity of his female figures (potential mothers), and his muted reaction to Raphael's *Sistinische Madonna* on his first visit to Dresden's *Gemäldegalerie*, whose depiction of divine succession

671

he will then, before "the most important day," have observed with trepidation; in his tortured state of mind, the aspect of the two gorgeous angelic puttos at the painting's bottom will have been ineffably painful for him. "The most important day" changes all this: on this day Kleist's quest for a son, which he launched with his "engagement" letter to Wilhelmine and his Würzburg journey, gathers pace and reaches escape velocity (cf. my section *The Filial*).

180   The name *"Schroffenstein,"* "rough stone" or "rough gem," suggests that for Kleist the Empire was precious, and only its surface, in its present state of disunity, was "rough" (cf. also *Marquise*, II:127).

181   In so far as Ursula *syphilitically* embodies a therapist, Kleist ironises another source of frustration for syphilis sufferers: the only ones who gained from syphilis were the doctors and pharmacists who charged exorbitant fees for largely futile, even harmful, therapies.

182   Wilbrandt already notes (*Kleist*, 188-9) that Kleist only arbitrarily and loosely adopted pre-existing materials to his purposes: *"Nie hat er aus der Geschichte mehr als die äußere Anknüpfung und nach Willkür einzelne farbige Züge entnommen; mit ihren Daten wie mit ihren Personen schaltet er souverain, ja auch von dem Geist der Zeit sucht er nur eine allgemeine Empfindung zu erregen, ohne ihm je seine individuelle und nationale Behandlungsart zu opfern: und in alledem schließt er sich offenbar an das Vorbild Shakespeares an"*; cf. also Kreutzer (*Dichterische Entwicklung*, 213): *"Daß es eine historische Quelle* [for *Guiskard*] *gibt, ist von ganz ephemerer Bedeutung."* In Roman satire adaptation from unacknowledged sources had always been fair game; Martial was particularly fond of this practice.

183   The Lat. term for maple, *"acer,"* means "sharp," "pointed," and I maintain that this poem marks Kleist's first expression of his recognition that a phallus is always also—*syphilitically*—a "sting" (cf. *Schroffenstein*'s scorpion and basilisk), that the shadow cast by the maple tree's (or the oak tree's) crown is always at once "refreshing" and "dark." The poem is, then, not only *satyrical* but also eminently *syphilitical*: erotic intercourse is always already overshadowed by the "dread" of venereal disease, and the "higher peace" he seeks to defend for himself in view of the onslaught of his passions is that of innocent, immaculate *jouissance*. Alkmene's (V.1006) or the Marquise's (II:129) insistent *"Ich will nichts wissen"* becomes Kleist's default formula for this

desire to preserve or recover a youthful pursuit of love and joy unimpeded by the shadows of suffering and death—cf. also the equivalent idea, in *Marionettentheater*, that we may have to eat from the tree of knowledge a second time, so as to transport outselves back into a pre-lapsarian state of blissful innocence (Kleist anticipates Nietzsche, *Jenseits von Gut und Böse*, 230: "*Diesem selben Willen dient ein… plötzlich herausbrechender Entschluss zur Unwissenheit… ein Zumachen seiner Fenster,… ein Ja-sagen und Gutheissen der Unwissenheit*").

184   In his diagram Kleist has three, not five, sections: "*Exposition*" (segment *a f* on the line *a b*), "*Schürzung des Knotes*" (segment *f g*) and "*Katastrophe*" (segment *g b*). Yet *Schroffenstein*'s five acts are easily reconciled with the diagram's three parts: acts I and II comprise the *Exposition*, acts III and IV the *Schürzung des Knotes*, act V the *Katastrophe*. The diagram's point *d*, at which the audience anticipates the drama's solution, in *Schroffenstein* is arguably marked by the poisoned dagger in the final lines of Act II (cf. V.1236), which *satirically* and *syphilitically* announces death; its point *e*, the point of crisis, by Ottokar's leap from the prison tower (cf. V.2368).

185   A *parabasis* usually consists of three songs (S) alternating with three speeches (s): S-s-S-s-S-s—cf. https://en.wikipedia.org/wiki/Parabasis. Since for the chorus of the maidens the stage direction is given as "*mit Musik*" (V.1), i.e., it comprises *song* (S), whereas for the chorus of the youths no such stage direction is given, i.e., it comprises *speech* (s), Kleist's pattern is precisely S-s-S-s-S-s. As in Aristophanes' *Lysistrata*, the chorus is initially divided (in Kleist's example, into boys and girls); unlike in Aristophanes' comedy, however, it is not shown to be unified and reconciled in the ending.

186   Cf. https://en.wikipedia.org/wiki/Aristophanes. Cf. Sloterdijk (Kritik, 324): "*dem Kyniker kommt, literarisch gesprochen, das komische, nicht das tragische Fach zu, die Satire, nicht der ernste Mythos… Die Existenz des Diogenes inspirierte sich aus dem Bezug zur athenaischen Komödie. Sie wurzelte in einer städtischen Lachkultur, genährt von einer Mentalität, die für Witz, Schlagfertigkeit, Spott und gesunde Verachtung der Dummheit offen ist. Ihr Existentialismus steht auf einer satirischen Grundlage.*"

187   Kleist's stage directions not only orchestrate the action on stage but also structure the storyline and produce meaning in their own right. For example, in the

fifth act the spoken word implies that Ottokar is killed by his father while trying to save Agnes, yet the stage directions make it evident that Ottokar killed by Agnes. Such instances confirm that Kleist's dramas are best understood when read, or listened to when recited or declaimed, rather than when watched on stage. That Kleist's *Erstling* comprises an idiosyncratic mix of tragedy and comedy has been widely discussed, as has its debt to Rousseauist reverie and Dionysiac revel (cf. Anthony Stephens and Bernhard Greiner, *KH*,15-27; for the drama's references to burlesque and *commedia dell'arte*, cf. James M. McGlathery, *Desire's Sway: The Plays and Stories of Heinrich von Kleist* (Detroit: Wayne State UP, 1983), 13 and passim). Greiner's notions, *"[in] dionysisch-karnevalistischer Komödientradition"* (*KH*,22-3), *"Komödien-Spiele[n]"* (*KH*,25), are imprecise: more precisely, Kleist's drama enacts a modern version of *Old Comedy* and *Satyr Play*.

188   The hero in Aristophanes' *The Acharnians* demanding that the *archon basileus* (king, ruler), who is sitting in the front row, award him first prize in a drinking competition, comprises a less than subtle hint on Aristophanes' part that he expects first prize in the drama competition (the *archon* being the most senior judge)—cf. https://en.wikipedia.org/wiki/Aristophanes. Comedies and tragedies were generally staged during the festivals of *Lenaia* and *City Dionysia*, sponsored by the state, and presided over by the *basileus* and other senior officals, so that Greek amphitheatres were literally political stages, and Aristophanes' plays were political discourses with those in power—as are Kleist's.

189   In picturing to onself Ursula-Napoleon's tossing the tattered leftovers of the Rhineland-finger, like a bone, but in the shape of a disfigured, putrifying phallus, among the tail-wagging, rabidly salivating German monarch-dogs, one cannot help but think of the cruel Magistrate in Pasolino's *Salò* throwing food spiked with nails to the tortured dog-victims. Perhaps there *was* a sadistic streak in Kleist.

190   Sylvius could *satirically* represent Fr. Barbarossa, said to be destined to return on day, from his slumber in the *Kyffhäuser* cave, to unify Germany. Picture how this passage would be *staged*: an arrow-like phallus, suspended by the theatre's *machinē*, approaches Sylvius at high speed; Sylvius bends down and points his rear towards the approaching projectile which, set to penetrate his backside, just misses him. Here tragedy becomes comedy; cf. the similarly hilarious gesture in *Anekdote aus dem Letzten Kriege*, where a Prussian tambour, as French soldiers get ready to

execute him, "*zog... sich die Hosen ab, und sprach: sie möchten ihn in den... schießen, damit das F... kein L... bekäme*" (II:268).

191   Bülow's claim (*Kleist*, 29) that Kleist built his *Erstling* from this *Urszene*, initially produced it in prose, and was convinced by L. Wieland to relocate the Spanish setting to Swabia appears unproblematic. Less so that L. Wieland and Heinr. Geßner, not Kleist himself, versified the fifth act. My general tenet is that Kleist always maintained editorial control of his works, with very few exceptions—e.g., he had no control over the foreword A. Müller added to his published *Amphitryon*. L. Wieland in late 1802 was in no privileged position vis-à-vis Kleist to perform final edits, for they left the country together; Geßner *was* in such a position, as he stayed behind, and the publication was completed, by his father's publishing company even, after Kleist's departure, but I still doubt that Kleist had so little respect for his *Erstling* that he did not even bother to complete it; the fact that he published it anonymously does not alter my view, for he had other reasons to do so, and I consider the final act qualitatively on par with the remainder of the play; for a different view, cf., e.g., Peter Stangle, *Kleist. Sein Leben*, 65. I do take seriously the idea that Kleist sought input from his fellow poets, especially in this first attempt at a dramatic production, that he took them seriously not least because of their respective fathers' importance for him, Wieland Sr. as potential mentor, Geßner Sr. as publisher, that he treated their joint session as an artisan workshop in which experimentation was encouraged, and that parts of *Schroffenstein* could have been produced collaboratively (below I shall explore the possibilities that his final productions were collaborative, with Henriette Vogel, and it is not out of the question that at the very end of his career he reverted to an approach he had explored at its very beginning).

192   With the taxidermied bird, only the outer appearance—skin and feathers—remains unchanged; with the *Kleidertausch,* conversely, only the outer appearance—the clothes—is changed; with the Emperor's New Clothes, the same exchange takes place as with the *Kleidertausch*, with the additional twist that the exchanged clothes are imagined rather than real ones. Although Ottokar's scheme fails, had they not exchanged their clothes, both youths would still have been slain, only at the hand of the other's father, not at that of their own. In which case the feud would have carried on: It is only thanks to the *Kleidertausch* that the fathers awaken from their blind hatred and make peace, if over their children's dead bodies. Paradoxically, deception is necessary for the cycle of violence to be broken, an outcome that furthermore bears

the price of termination of both houses' lines of succession: *Schroffenstein*'s plot, then, entails the *double bind* also symbolised by the taxidermied bird, whose appearance can be maintained only at the expense of its substance. In *Findling*, Nicolo's appearing before Elvire in Colino's Genoese costumer comprises another version of *Kleidertausch*, also fatal for both. In crafting such passages, Kleist may have had in mind erotic crossdressing scenarios and roleplay.

193   When Gunnar in his pursuit of Brynhild (Brunhilde) is unable to penetrate the ring of fire (*Waberlohe*) that surrounds his object of desire, he asks his friend Sigurd to take on his appearance with the help of the *Ögishelm*, penetrate the *Waberlohe*, and win Brynhild's love on his behalf. Sigurd complies and succeeds, stays with Brynhild for three days (courteously putting his sword between them during the nights), and brings her to Gunnar who, having reversed their appearances, makes her his wife. The exchange of appearances thus fulfills its purpose, until one day Sigurd's wife Gudrun, while bathing together with Brynhild, boasts to her that it had been Sigurd, not Gunnar, who had swayed her, whereupon the horrified Brynhild incites her brother to stab Sigurd to death, before, having thus stilled her thirst for revenge, killing herself, if not without requesting that her body be burned next to Sigurd's.

194   A. Müller in 1804 uses this expression in a letter to Karl Gustav Baron von Brinkmann (cf. *AML*,86), referring to an essay by Hegel on Kant, Jacob and Fichte in the following terms: *"die elende Scharteke K. Fichte, und Jakobi von [Hegel]… über deren… Niedrigkeit, Schlechtigkeit und Pöbelhaftigkeit wir… einig waren."* A critic in *Der Freimüthige* terms Ph *"eine nichtsbedeutende Charteke"* (*LS*,238a).

195   Johann gesture before Agnes, "*Mir bist du tot, und einer Leiche gleich, / Mit kaltem Schauer drück ich dich ans Herz*," anticipates Count F's before the swooning Marquise. Moments later Agnes indeed swoons, presumably when Johann enters her. Subsequently the same event that in *Marquise* is telescoped into a single conjunctive-disjunctive *dash* n *Schroffenstein* is fanned out across 30 lines of verse and 22 punctuation marks. Kleist's first editors, Tieck and Julian Schmidt, extensively "corrected" his interpunction; Reinhold Köhler, who calls Kleist's interpunctation "exceedingly unkempt" (*Zu H. v. Kleists Werken*, Weimar, 1862, foreword p.VIII), noted but did not vehemently oppose this clean-up. As we can see here, Kleist's interpunctation is so unorthodox and irregular precisely because he uses it artistically rather than mechanically. Never is his interpunctation careless

or "unkempt." Sembdner quotes (*In Sachen Kleist*, 149) Ernst Grumach calling Goethe's interpunction "rhythmic or arcoustic interpunction, or perhaps better still, as declamatory interpunction," adding, correctly, that the same could be said, even more emphatically, about Kleist. Even though the Zenge sisters tell Bülow that *"[Kleist] hegte… den Gedanken, ob man nicht, wei bei der Musik, durch Zeichen auch einem Gedichte den Vortrag andeuten könne. Er machte sogar selbst den Versuch, schrieb einzelne Strophen eines Gedichtes auf, unter welche er die Zeichen setzte, die das Heben, Tragen, Sinkenlassen der Stimme usw. Andeuteten, und ließ es also von den Damen lessen"* (*LS*,145), Kleist's innovation is not the invention of novel signs but the repurposing of common ones: his turning interpunction marks into sign language, metalanguage even, that not only regulates rhythm and tonality but conveys meaning. The famous dash in *Marquise* is only the most prominent case. Just as he uses stage directions to convey meaning that exceeds, clarifies, modifies or even negates that conveyed by the spoken text, Kleist also uses interpunctation marks to the same effect: in the abvove-quoted passage in *Schroffenstein*, only the exclamation marks, not the spoken text, convey its *satyrical* meaning.

196   *Terz* (tierce) and *Quart* are at the same time musical and fencing terms: in music they refer to, respectively, "a third" and "a forth" interval; in fencing, to the third and the fourth of eight permitted parrying positions. Notes Burkert in *Greek Religion*, 112: "Any occurrence which is not entirely a matter of course and which cannot be manipulated may become a sign: a sudden sneeze, a stumble, a twitch; a chance encounter or the sound of a name caught in passing; celestial phenomena such as lightning, comets, shooting stars, eclipses of sun and moon, even a drop of rain… Then of course there are dreams." For the musings of a kindred spirit, cf. Edgar Allan Poe: "Shadows of Shadows passing… It is now 1831… and as always, I am absorbed with a delicate thought. It is how poetry has indefinite sensations to which end, music is an essential, since the comprehension of sweet sound is our most indefinite conception. Music, when combined with a pleasurable idea, is poetry. Music without the idea is simply music. Without music or an intriguing idea, color becomes pallour, man becomes carcass, home becomes catacomb, and the dead are but for a moment motionless" (read by Orson Welles, Prelude of Alan Parsons' *The Fall of the House of Usher*).

677

197   Cf. Schmidt, *Kleist als Dramatiker*, 13; Reuß and Staengle, *Kleist*, 458; Anthony Stephens, *KH*,62. Samuel and Brown in *Kleist's Lost Year*, 28, provide a

well-reasoned, well-researched account of the drama's genesis. Wieland Sr. had trans. the satirists Horace and Lucian (the latter the author of several *symposia*) and will have been an inspirational cornucopia for Kleist. Kleist's sources for his *overt* story may have included Karl Wilh. Ferd. von Funck's "Robert Guiskard, Herzog von Apulien und Calabrien," published in 1797 in Schiller's *Horen*, and Schiller's ed. of Anna Komnena's *Alexiad*, published in 1790. The historical Robert Guiskard in 1061 captured Messina, and as Duke of Sicily founded a Norman kingdom in Italy. In 1081 he mounted a campaign against the Byzantine Empire, aiming to reinstall the dethroned Emperor Michael VII Doukas to whose son Guiskard's daughter was betrothed. While progressing towards Constantinople, Guiskard was halted not by the plague but by the need to return to Rome to help defend his ally Pope Gregory VII against the Holy Roman Emperor Heinr. IV. In 1084, having forced Heinr. to withdraw from Rome, Guiskard once more turned against the Byzantines, and in alliance with Ragusa took Corfu before together with 500 of his knights being carried off by a fever on the Ionian island of Kefalonia. Kleist's imagery of the bubonic plague may in part have been inspired by Napoleon's *Armée d'Orient* in May 1799 having been halted before Acre by an outbreak of the disease. He never reached Constantinople; Kleist's story may be compounding Funck's narratives of Guiskard's death (in 1085) and of his *Siege of Durazzo* (in 1081-2)—cf. Helbling, *Major Works*, 85 n.4-5.

198   Richard Samuel ("Heinrich von Kleists 'Robert Guiskard' und seine Wiederbelebung 1807/8," *KJb* 1981/82, 326) shows numerous stylistic parallels between *Guiskard* and *Penthesilea*, Schulz (Kleist, 383) similarly between *Guiskard* and *Krug*. Such findings seem to suggest that the *Guiskard* fragment originated during, or in the run-up to, the *Ph* period. However, as such parallels can be found right across Kleist's œuvre, the case for closeness of genesis being their necessary condition is weak. Kleist certainly edited the Guiskard fragment for *Ph*, and could have inserted stylistic items he was prone to using during that period. While I cannot refute Anthony Stephens' suggestion (cf. *KH*,63) that the *Ph* fragment could comprise a *condensation* of the MS, I consider it more plausible that he simply made a *selection* from the MS and edited it for *Ph*.

199   Kleist announces to Chr. M. Wieland in December 1807 that with *Penthesilea* complete, *Guiskard* will follow suit (II:800), as if it is near-complete: *"und ich überlasse es Ihnen, mir alsdann zu sagen, welches von beiden besser sei; denn ich weiß es nicht."* To Collin he wries in February 1808 that in addition to *Penthesilea*,

he is "in possession of two further tragedies" (II:810), by which he could only mean *Guiskard* and *Käthchen;* clearly this is to be taken with a grain of salt, for we know that of *Käthchen* at this point only a fragment existed, so the same could have been the case with *Guiskard.* Still, on 7th June 1807 Kleist offers *Guiskard* to Cotta "ready at hand" (II:813: *"stehen... zu Diensten"*). A. Müller in a letter to Goethe of 17th December 1807 refers to Kleist's "two tragedies, Penthesilea and Robert Guiskard" as if they are about to be published (*LS*,200b), and to Gentz on 25th December he enumerates *Guiskard* among the materials for *Ph* (cf. *LS*,205). Kreutzer correctly conludes (*Dichterische Entwicklung,* 156-7) that we cannot exclude the possibility that Kleist completed *Guiskard* in 1807/8.

200 Pfuel reports (cf. *LS*,102) that even before Paris Kleist had destroyed two drafts of *Guiskard.*

201 Kleist's January 1811 *BA* entry *Über den Zustand der Schwarzen in Amerika,* a trans. into German of a French trans. of an English original, extends the *pescheräic principle* to an entire text, whose meaning, despite faithful trans., reverses when transposed into a different context. Simply by publishing *Über den Zustand...* in German, in a German newspaper. targeting a German audience, Kleist reframes the message the French translator had sought to convey to his French audience by publishing the text in a French magazine. Since the French translator had already inverted the English original's intention, Kleist here *serialises* a *pescherä,* each trans. and transportation turning the meaning upside down: the English author, writing for an English audience, probably intended to laud the English administration in the colonies for being so enlightened that even the slaves themselves endorsed it; the French translator turned this meaning on its head, conveying to his French audience that the English colonialists insidiously brainwashed the slaves into blind submission; Kleist, by re-positioning the story (by virtue of publishing it in German, in a German paper) for a German audience largely disinterested in colonial affairs but suffering under French hegemony, without saying so implies that it is the French who have been doing the brainwashing. The very "uprooted-ness" of trans., which Brentano laments in his novel *Godwi,* for Kleist thus becomes a mechanism of *satirical* production.

202 The Chorus' opening (V.12-23) references the lament by the Chorus in Sophocles' *Oedipus Rex* concerning the people's suffering under the plague: "children dead in the womb / and life on life goes down / you can watch them go / like seabirds

winging west... / generations strewn on the ground / unburied...the dead spreading death" (198-208).

203   Cf. also Gentz to A. Müller, 23rd October 1802: *"die Klauen des Ungeheuers [Napoleon]."* There is no indication that Kleist was in communication with Gentz or Müller at that time, but such terminology may simply have been current, or Kleist could have introduced it only in 1808, in the *Ph* fragment, in which case he could have borrowed the term from Gentz or Müller.

204   Claire Elisabeth de Rémusat, Joséphine's *dame du palais*, noted that "men worn out by the turmoil of the Revolution... looked for the domination of an able ruler," and that "people believed quite sincerely that Bonaparte, whether as consul or emperor, would exert his authority and save [them] from the perils of anarchy" (*Memoirs of Madame De Rémusat, 1802–1808 Vol. 1*, HardPress Publishing, 2012, 542). Kleist may have modelled *Guiskard*'s constellation in part on the death of Julius Caesar and the subsequent wars of succession, accessible to him in Plutarch's *Parallel Lives* and Shakespeare's works: two eligible successors, Octavian and Antonius, competing for the succession, the republican party comprising the third player, in Kleist's play represented by the Chorus of the people.

205   The topographical nexus for the spread of the bubonic plague across Europe in 1347-51 was Constantinople, where the disease spread from the Crimea in autumn 1347, and whence by October 1347 it was carried to Messina in Sicily, and by January 1348 to Naples and Genoa on the Italian, and to Ragusa on the Illyrian mainland. From these gateways it rapidly spread across Europe along major trade routes. When *Guiskard*'s wanderer arrives from Naples as harbinger of the future (cf. I:159), this may be a reference to Naples' role as the plague's gateway as much as to the danger of Napoleon's sway (Napoli = Napoleon's polis). In *Marquise*, Count F goes on a "business trip" to Napoli and promptly returns infected; in *Findling*, Ragusa replaces Napoli as the gateway for the disease.

206   Kleist here anticipates Freud's hypothesis of the "primordial patricide" by which a clan's social structure is established—cf. Sigmund Freud, *Totem and Taboo* (Digigreads.com, 2008), 89. Kleist's "Guiskard hypothesis" exceeds Freud's "totemic hypothesis" in so far as for Kleist the primordial father must not only be killed by the son, but must play an active role in hoisting his son into

his position before relinquishing it to him, so that the patricide is at the same time self-sacrifice and suicide.

207   *Gnadenkettlein* is diminutive of *Gnadenkette* (chain of mercy) and implies that the ostensibly mighty Guiskard is so weakened by disease that he requires no more than a small chain to be harnessed. In *Zweikampf*, the Emperor enchains Trota with a similar chain, and since in *Brief eines rheinbündischen Offiziers an seinen Freund* Kleist refers to the *Kreuz der Ehrenlegion* (II: 367), actually the *Ordre national de la Légion d'honneur* established by Napoleon in 1802 and featuring his image, it is conceivable that Kleist has this enemy order in mind with his *Gnadenkette*. Napoleon explained the new order to his state council as follows: "*Ich wette, … daß man mir keine alte und neue Republik nennen kann, die keine Auszeichnungen vergeben hat. Und das nennt man Spielzeug und Flitterkram! Sehr gut! Aber mit solchem Flitterkram leitet man die Menschen. Ich würde das vom Rednerpult herab nicht aussprechen, aber in einem Rat von weisen Staatsmännern kann man alles sagen. Ich glaube nicht, daß das französische Volk Freiheit und Gleichheit liebt. Die Franzosen haben sich in den letzten Jahren der Revolution nicht geändert. Sie haben nur eine Leidenschaft, und diese nennt sich ‚Ehre'. Man muß aber diese Leidenschaft hegen und pflegen und Auszeichnungen verleihen!*"—cf. Kircheisen, *Napoleon I.*, V 272, quoted at http://www.dhm.de/archiv/magazine/orden/ueber_ehrenleg.htm.

208   *Schroffenstein*'s ending could have been shaped by the events of *14 Thermidor*, notably Johann's last ditch appeal to Ursula-Napoleon to leave the stage before an automatism of dynastic succession precipitates the *RF*'s and the *HRR*'s ruin. Thomas Wichmann (*Kleist*, 74) suggests that Napoleon's dynastic aspirations could already have become evident in the aftermath of the *Battle of Marengo* of June 1800; certainly it was evident by June 1802: Chr. M. Wieland on 10th June 1802 writes to his son, Kleist's buddy, that Napoleon's appointment as *First Consul for Life* is a "wrong step" (*ibid*,76).

209   Louis XVI was executed in 1793, and his son died in 1795, but his brother Louis Stanislav, as Louis XVIII the titular king, survived, and so did the Bourbon rulers of other lands, notably the Kings of Spain and Naples. The royalist Kleist may for some time have expected that the Bourbons could rid themselves of the parvenu Napoleon and regain their throne—reinstalling the Bourbon monarchy was the Coalitions's main objective in the *War of the First Coalition* in which Kleist fought,

and in 1814/15 Louis XVIII would indeed regain the throne—, but in the course of *Guiskard*'s genesis, evidently already before the notorious *Duke of Enghien Affair* of early 1804, he must have come to acknowledge that not only was no Bonaparte heir in sight, but also no plausible challenger among the remaining Bourbon princes. Gentz was in close contact with Louis XVIII throughout this period—which Louis XVIII primarily spent in exile in Latvia—and actively supported a Bourbon restauration (cf. *AML*,128).

210   Cf. https://en.wikipedia.org/wiki/French_constitutional_referendum,_1802. There was no secret ballot and few dared to openly defy Napoleon's régime; in January 1800 Napoleon had been appointed *First Consul* by a similarly decisive (and no doubt similarly rigged) plebiscite.

211   Kleist would have considered his own family rather more illustrious than the Bonapartes, and perhaps treated Napoleon, whose talent as a general he acknowledged but whose legitimacy as a ruler he denied, as no more than equal in rank to himself.

212   The fleet featured in Kleist's scene description, the adjective *"meerumgeben"* (V.335), the timing of the drama's genesis, and Kleist's subsequent attempts to join the French invasion force at Saint-Omer and Boulogne point to the latter city.

213   That Kleist's idea of a people's insurrection in Germany was not entirely far-fetched is suggested by observations Gentz made during a trip to Brussels and shared with A. Müller in a letter of October 1802: "*Von* Coblenz *bis* Brüssel *haben wir auf unserm ganzen Wege... nicht ein einziges Individuum gefunden, welches nicht von gleichem Hasse, von gleichen Wünschen, und von gleichen Erwartungen beseelt wäre. Es kann nicht dauern, es* wird *nicht dauern; das war der ewige Refrain aller, aller unsrer Gespräche; und wenn wir fragten: aber wie wird es endigen?—so war—ein allgemeiner Aufstand—die Antwort, die uns aus jedem Munde, ohne Ausnahme, entgegenkam.*"

214   *Normänner* is a possible but rare term for the Normans, who in German are typically referred to as *Normannen*, as they are in Kleist's working title. The historical Normans, setting out from Scandinavia, during the 10th to 12th century conquered distant territories—Normandy (911), where they became acculturated; the Italian *Mezzogiorno* (1046); England (1066); and in the course of the *Crusades*,

Levantine Antiochia (1098). The subtle changes to the title may give us a hint as to the kinds of edits Kleist may have performed on the *Ph* fragment.

215   Hans-Georg Schede (*Kleist*, 67-8) links Kleist's exploration of governance models to Schillerian dramas. Kleist's "committee of knights" as of 1808 may entail a swipe at the *Rheinbund*; in the 1802/3 *Guiskard*, if it was present, it could have been a swipe at the various short-lived systems of governance of the Revolution, especially the last one: the *Estates-General* and the *National Assembly* of 1789; Mirabeau's *National Convention* and *National Constituent Assembly* of 1789-91; the *Legislative Assembly* of 1791-2; the *National Convention* of 1792-5, the *Directorat* of 1795-9; finally the *Consulate* of 1799-1804. Kleist was neither a die-hard supporter of an *ancien régime* nor a progressive democrat: he was an enlightened monarchist and advocate of a voluntary empire of autonomous principalities and nations, of a government not *by*, but *for* the people: despite the German monarchs' blunders at *Basel* and *Lunéville*, he held on to his faith in the efficacy of the system of monarchy, while recognising that an effective monarch must govern, in a Hobbesian vein, with the interest of his people, not his dynasty foremost on his mind. Government *for* the people does not entail participation of the masses (an option his figure Armin dismisses out of hand), nor blatant populism (cf. Kleist's critique of *Josephinism*), but a monarch's rule with heart (courage) and mind (wisdom).

216   The title of AC/DC's 1979 hit single (and album) "reflects the incredibly arduous nature of touring constantly and life on the road" (https://en.wikipedia.org/wiki/Highway_to_Hell_(song)).

217   Burning frankincense to neutralise the disease's stench was an actual practice during the "Black Death." Ulrich Fülleborn previously analysed the opening scene in a similar vein as do I (cf. *KJB* 2003, 269). Burkert notes (*Greek Religion*, 76-7) that in addition to water, the ancient Greeks used fumication for purification: "Odysseus suphurates the hall after the blood bath he has caused. He also notes that "Homer mentions... the purification of the entire army after the plague" and refers to instances of purifications from madness and blood guilt, as well as to purification as atonement. The plague or pestilence was a conventional monicker for Napoleon's régime in Kleist's day—cf., e.g., Gentz to Müller, 23rd October 1802 (*AML*,32): "*Der verpestete Hauch der französischen Regierung hat alle die Länder, welche die Schwäche unsrer Zeitgenossen in die Klauen des Ungeheuers fallen ließ, versengt, ausgezehrt und besudelt*" (the terms "monster's claws" and "defiled" we also find in Kleist).

218   *"Neffe"* ("nephew") clearly denotes Abälard-Franz as servant or subordinate: the term derives from Old High German *"nevo"* = *"unmündiger"* ("underage," "minor," "dependent"). In 1802 Franz was 34 of age, Napoleon 33, Kleist 25, making for a perfectly balanced *ménage à trois*.

219   Anachronisms abound in Kleist's *overt* stories, unsurprisingly given that his historical contexts comprise mere packaging and that the contemporary concerns he *covertly* embedded in them were often quite disconnected from the *overt* stories; Kreutzer already pointed out that *Hermannschlacht*'s and *Käthchen*'s "historical drapery merely entailed a bringing to life of the present."

220   Had he known Engl., Kleist might have been intrigued by folk etymology's linking frankincense to the Franks, which would have permitted him the pun: frankincense = remidial aspect of *"Francofication."* As a matter of fact, the Engl. word frankincense derives not from the Franks but from the Old Fr. *franc encens, franc* meaning "noble," "pure."

221   Cf. Klaus Kanzog, in 'Alternativer Journalismus. Heinrich von Kleist als Herausgeber und Redakteur der 'Berliner Abendblätter" (*Kleist*, 205-16) lists five aspects of Kleist's "alternative journalism":

1. *Kleist ergriff die Initiative zum richtigen Zeitpunkt...*
2. *Kleist hat das richtige Gespür für verwertbares Material...*
3. *Kleist war sich bewußt, welche enorme Macht von der Presse für die Bildung der öffentlichen Meinung ausging und daß sie durch Manipulationen gesteuert warden konnten...*
4. *Kleist setzte im Freiheitskampf auf die Volkssouveränität...*
5. *Kleist stellte die Macht der Dynastien in Frage.*

I agree with the first three, which speak to Kleist's *po(i)etical* praxis, not the remaining two, which speak to his *satirical* credo: in my reading, Kleist viewed the masses as instrumental, rather than souveregn, and the—German—dynasties as too selfish and disunited, rather than as too powerful.

222   From Thun, Geneva was the closest major city in the French Empire, and although annexed to France in 1798, will have retained a certain degree of freedom

of speech, and been a key hub for information exchange. I wondered earlier why Kleist travelled to Paris via Lyon and not Neuchâtel or Basel, which would have been significantly shorter, and speculated that he went via Lyon for therapeutic reasons (Lyon having been a renowned centre of magnetism), but it now seems much more plausible, given the circumstances, that he was not targeting Lyon but Geneva, and not for *syphilitical* but for *satirical* reasons: he went to Geneva to gobble up the latest rumours and news on Napoleon's movements, and then decided to push on to Paris (of which he informs Ulrike on 5th October), which from Geneva was most speedily done via Lyon.

223   Did Napoleon acquire his *dynastic hybris* from his wife, who clearly had a knack for dynasty-building on her own, having married her daughter to a Bonaparte and her son to a Bavarian princess? Or could these two imigrants from the French periphery—a French Creole hailing from one island (Martinique), a Corsican from another, simply have been kindred spirits with respect to clannish behaviour? The fact that Joséphine was a Creole, coupled with the timing of her divorce from Napoleon in early 1810 (broached to her by Napoleon in late 1809), suggests that the yellow-feverish *femme fatale* featured in *Verlobung,* a work Kleist probably produced during the late-1809 to early 1810 period, could represent the Empress: if so, the unkind portrayal implies that Kleist did not forgive her for consenting to the divorce and thereby making Napoleon's marriage with Marie-Louise possible.

224   Cf. Samuel and Brown (*Kleist's Lost Year,* 100): "Having failed [with *Guiskard*], largely we must suppose for technical reasons, to give poetic substance to this very topical material [Napoleon's rise to power] during the greater part of 1803, Kleist was now [in the spring of 1804] in a position for a successful enactment of a similar theme to that of his tragedy. And that he should not be content to allow the barriers separating art and life to remain distinct, that he should attempt with such determination to involve himself in the grandiose venture of the Descente, is a vivid example of the obverse of a characteristic which has rightly been seen as typifying his literary utterances, namely his obsession with concretising poetic experience" (Samuel and Brown's term "concretising poetic experience" quotes Ilse Graham). In July 1805 Kleist and Pfuel are still debating submarine designs (cf. I:755-6), obviously relevant for an invasion (or defence) of Britain, yet in August 1805 Napoleon is forced to redirect the English invasion force against Austria, to turn the *Armée des côtes de l'Océan* into the *Ad'A,* and in October 1805 his fleet's defeat at *Trafalgar* renders an

invasion all but impossible. Zimmermann (*Kleist*, 186) dismisses Samuel and Brown's idea that Kleist at Saint-Omer sought to gather materials for his works: "Kleist did *not* write poetry derived from life, at least not in the sense that he studied milieux or investigated like reporters." Samuel and Brown are much closer to the mark in this respect than is Zimmermann.

225   In 1800 Kleist travels to Würzburg just as the city's defences are being readied against the advancing French (this may have been coincidental, or it may have been on reason for him to chose that city as his destination); in 1801 he abruptly sets off for Paris from Strasbourg so as to immerse himself into the 14th July celebrations; in 1802 he is in Switzerland when internal strive precipitates a second intervention by the French; in early 1804 he undertakes secret missions from Mainz (where he may be locating as a "sleeper") to Paris at a time the Enghien affair comes to a head and Napoleon prepares his coronation; in late 1806 he practically eye-witnesses Fr. Wilh. and Luise's precipitous flight via Königsberg to Memel; in early 1807 he passes through Kolberg, one of the last resisting Prussian fortresses, in whose neighbourhood Schill's *Freikorps* continues to operate; in early 1809 he surveys the battlefield of *Aspern*, sojourns in Prague, the centre of German resistance (once more as a "sleeper"?), possibly eye-witnesses *Wagram*, and maybe is present in Vienna when *Schönbrunn* is signed; in 1809 he eye-witnesses the return to Berlin from exile of Fr. Wilh. and Luise. His youthful experience of partaking in the *Siege of Mainz* and the *Palatine Campaign* thus defined a pattern: be it as war-tourist or -voyeur, as "embedded" war-correspondent, or even as under-cover agent, messenger or spy, the *satirical* poet required sensual stimulation and inspiration to produce his works.

226   Wichmann believes (*Kleist*, 77) Kleist met Napoleon, leaning on Hermann F. Weiss' "Ein unbekannter Brief Heinrich von Kleists an Marie von Kleist," in: *JdS* 22 (1978), 79-109. I deem this to be improbable.

227   Numerous assassination plots against Napoleon were contrived between 1800 and 1804, primarily by French monarchists, which Napoleon skilfully used as pretexts to buttress his regime, cultminating in the *Duke of Enghien Affair* in May 1804, with which all aspirations by Bourbons and their supporters to overthrow the usurper ended. The Duke of Enghien at that time lived in exile in Baden, just across the Rhine from France, and Pichegru and Cadoudal in England, just across the Channel, and Kleist's going underground in Mayence may well have followed a similar logic.

Enghien was accused, among other things, of having undertaken secret journeys into France in support of the conspiracy (there is no evidence to this day that Enghien was in fact involved in the conspiracy), and Kleist's presumed journeys to Paris from Mayence followed a similar pattern, even if merely as observer or messenger.

228   Philibert Masson apprenticed as watchmaker in Prussian-administered Neuchâtel and was subsequently private secretary to the future Tsar Alex. I in St. Petersburg. Whether or not he symphathised with the Jacobins or the Royalists, his biography suggests that he could have been critical of Napoleon's rise to power, which disturbed the balance of power the likes of Fr. Wilh. III and Alex. I sought to preserve. Cf. *LS*,126; Samuel & Brown, *Lost Year*, 73; Loch, *Kleist*, 193-5.

229   Peter Michalzik notes (*Kleist*, 335) that when Hartmann in *Ph* no. 11/12 launches a notorious diatribe against Ramdohr's critique of Friedrich's *Tetschener Altar*, Kleist remains mute: *"Das ist bemerkenswert. Er bekam hautnah eine der brisantesten Kunstdebatten seiner Zeit mit, sie wurde zum Teil in seiner Zeitschrift geführt, aber es scheint ihn nicht berührt zu haben."* Yet Kleist's "muteness" is easily explained: by the time its last issue is finally distributed in February 1809, *Ph* has long outlived its usefulness for him as a *satirical* platform, and his interest in art is primarily as a means of articulating and explicating his own project and techniques—cf. his contemplations of Raphael's *Madonna* and his essay on Friedrich's *Mönch*—, not as discursive object in its own right.

230   Cf. Jean Baudrillard, *Simulacra and Simulation*. Trans. Sheila Faria Glaser (Ann Arbor: University of Michigan Press, 1994), 1. Baudrillard reviews how Plato in *Sophist* illustrates the concept of simulacrum with the help of a statue intentionally distorted such that the upper part is crafted larger than life, so that from the perspective of a viewer standing below and looking up to it on its pedestral, its proportions appear to be true to nature—cf. also https://en.wikipedia.org/wiki/Simulacrum. The related idea of the *trompe-l'œil*—a hyperealistic, seemingly three-dimensional, painting—appears in Pliny the Elder's story of the 5th century BC Greek painters Zeuxis and Parrhasius, who enter a painting contest in which Zeuxis paints grapes so realistically that birds come to peck them, whereupon Parrhasius asks Zeuxis to pull aside the curtain that supposedly conceals his painting, and when Zeuxis sets out to do so, he finds that the curtain itself is his rival's painting; Parrhasius wins the contest—cf. Gaius Plinius Secundus d.Ä., *Naturalis Historia*, München, 1978, 65ff. The poet

Aug. Thieme, Kleist's and Kosegarten's contemporary, rhymed: *"Und Kosegarten, Dithyrambensausen / Und düstern Sterngemälden hold, / Der in des Nachtgewitters schwülen Pausen / Sein Auge wild durch Wasserwüsten rollt; / Dem der Abysse Schaum, der Brandung Brausen, / Melodisch hocherhabne Psalmen grollt; / Der uns in Ruhe lullet, wenn er flötet, /Mit Graun betäubt, wenn er im Sturm drommetet"*—cf. https://de.wikipedia.org/wiki/Ludwig_Gotthard_Kosegarten.

231   Kleist anticipates aspects of the theory of performative language and speech acts developed by J.L. Austin in the 1950s, whose fundamental insight that language not only *asserts* but *performs* is summed up by the title of his best-known book, *How to do Things with Words* (1955).

232   *"Die Philosophen haben die Welt nur verschieden interpretiert; es kommt aber darauf an, sie zu verändern"* (Marx, *Thesen über Feuerbach*, 11; http://www.mlwerke.de/me/me03/me03_533.htm). How much of Hegel's thought Kleist was aware of is not clear; any Hegelian influence on him could have been mediated by A. Müller, who convened with Hegel in Jena in 1803 (cf. *AML*,81) and whose "theory of opposites" resembles Hegel's dialectic; Müller uses the term *"Dialektik"* (*AML*,220) and posits *"Die gegensätzische Identität von Handeln und Behandeltem"* (quoted by Jakob Baxa, *AML*,97, notes, from *Lehre vom Gegensatz*, Vol. 2), as well as *"daß Kunstbetrachtung (Kunstproduktion) und Naturbetrachtung (Naturproduktion) nicht eine ohne die andere, und beide nur durcheinander möglich sind, daß sie auseinander entstehen"* (*AML*,101, notes; quoted from *ibid*, Vol. 1).

233   Cf. Francis Fukuyama, *The End of History and the Last Man* (New York: Avon, 1992), 183: "Socrates also believes that *thymos* has the capability to destroy political communities as well as to cement them together… for instance when he compares the *thymotic* guardian to a ferocious watchdog who can bite his master as a stranger if not properly trained. Construction of a just political order therefore requires both the cultivation and the taming of a *thymos*."

234   For Hegel, in my reading of Kojève's interpretation, "the Battle of Jena [comprised] the end of history" in so far as the "world Spirit on horseback" Napoleon's France represented precisely that state, which at *Jena-Auerstedt* overcame the enlightened state of which *Frederician* Prussia represented the epitome, in which the mutual recognition of master and servant materialises—cf. Alexandre

Kojève, *Introduction à la lecture de Hegel* (Paris: Gallimard, 1947), 436. If Karl Marx's critique of Hegel centres on a premise that not abstract forces but concrete actors—notably classes, especially the proletariat—shape history, Kleist could be termed a proto-Marxian, only that the "class" that must spearhead change in his view is not the proletariat but the high aristocracy (Kleist is something of a proto-Nietzschean as well). Blamberger's assertion (*Kleist*, 359-60) re Kleist's *"Kriegspropaganda," "Heroisch-Pathetische Verse könnten eine anonyme Masse steuern, bei den alten Haudegen schlagen solche Schreibtischtaten fehl,"* is misguided in that Kleist sought to address Franz I himself, whom in turn he looked to for rallying the "anomymous masses," and not, or not primarily, those "old warhorses" he chanced upon at Aspern. Blamberger, a page later, quotes Franz von Hager telling Joseph Graf von Wallis, *"streuen Eure Excellenz... Flugschriften unter das Volk aus, damit es... für die gute Sache elektrisirt werde,"* and while in the first instance Kleist sought to "electrify" the rulers, with *Germania* he did also very much have in view the need for the ruler to "electrify" the masses, therefore writing its patriotic songs in a manner that could appeal to Franz or Archduke Karl personally, as well as to the (North-) German masses (*Hermannsschlacht* displays similar characteristics).

235   Kleist may well have taken his cue from Schlegel and recognised that this format was *à jour*, but in the first instance he was probably simply being pragmatic: the fragment fit the *Ph* format and allowed him to publish materials he had not completed or was not ready to publish in their entirety.

236   Kleist's selection of platforms was inspired: *Ph* fit into the languid, cultured atmosphere of Dresden in 1808 just as well as *Germania* did into the heated, martial cauldron of Prague in 1809 and *BA* into the politicised, bourgeois milieu of Berlin in 1810. For *Hermannsschlacht* and *Käthchen* the stage was the ideal platform, combining immediacy with replicability in the decision hubs, Berlin and Vienna.

237   Kleist's job in the Prussian administration in Königsberg involved working through large amounts of court papers, and possibly attending court sessions, and this experience no doubt filters through in the court scenes making up much of *Krug*'s middle part, which may suggest that he produced them during, or soon after, this period. Kleist ends a letter to Massenbach of 23rd April 1805, *"Schließlich erfolgt der Krug"* (II:751), and while it has been speculated that Kleist referred to an economic treatise by Leopold Krug (cf. Loch, *Kleist*, 215), I consider it more plausible that he sent

Massenbach a MS of his drama: Massenbach, a leading member of the "War Party," was an outspoken critic of Fr. Wilh.'s unsteady politics and hence Kleist's natural ally, apart from being Marie's brother-in-law and Kleist's sponsor for a government job (cf. Loch, *Kleist*, 31). Massenbach would later be made responsible for the debacle of *Jena-Auerstedt*—had he only followed Kleist's prescriptions! In April 1805 Britain and Russia signed an alliance against France, and British PM William Pitt tried to pull Prussia and Austria into the nascent Coalition; Austria joined, Prussia abstained. There was thus a timely—and urgent—reason for Kleist to intervene, and I consider it unlikely that Kleist did not prepare a *satirical* message at this critical historical juncture, even if it remained work-in-progress. *Guiskard* no longer suitable, *Krug* was the only vehicle he had (more or less) ready-at-hand to address the King in the face of this pressing situation, and he could have used Massenbach as sounding board. *Krug*'s story of an unreliable Licht letting a helpless Adam run into Walter's open knife would in fact have been even more relevant in April 1805 than in August 1806, and his advocacy of conscription just as topical in 1805 as in 1806 (cf. also Kleist's late 1805 letter to Rühle, in which he advocates that Prussia aise 300,000 men via conscription). The hilarious court proceedings in which Adam dishes out the *HRR* to Napoleon were perhaps not as embellished in the earlier version, but the writing was on the wall, and Kleist could have constructed the court proceeding as a scenario rather than a retroactive ironisation of actual events at *Pressburg*. The most significant difference between the 1806 MS and a 1805 version would have been the twelfth scene: whereas in 1806 Kleist's *Krug* manifesto urges the King to create readiness first, Prussia standing alone against France, in 1805 it would have urged the King to join the Coalition immediately, Prussia standing together with other great powers. Rudolf Loch deserves credit for raising the possibility that an early version of *Krug* existed, already towards the end of 1804 (cf. *Kleist*, 524). Whether everything possible has been undertaken to dig through Massenbach's legacy for an early version of *Krug* I do not know.

238   Le Veau's (or Debucourt's) triangular composition divides his scene into two parts, the left side dominated by the judge and the court scribe, the right side by the young woman and the old woman whose jug has been broken. The door to the left leads into the enclosed, labyrinthine machinery of paternalistic institutions, the vista to the right opens into the maternalistic world of reproduction and bucolic life. Ernst Theodor Voss has plausibly suggested that the enclosure to the left represents a brothel—*"unter einem Dach mit dem Gericht, das in geheimer Komplizenschaft durch*

die Finger sieht" (quoted in Gernot Müller, *Man müßte auf dem Gemälde selbst stehen. Kleist und die bildende Kunst.* Tübingen: Francke, 1995, 126)—which would have intrigued Kleist, in whose *satirical* scheme the left half of the image corresponded to a decadent France, the right half to an innocent but naïve Germany. The judge's seat and the scribe's desk form the threshold between these two realms, the point at which the conflicts between them are negotiated. The two women, one perhaps having lost her innocence, the other her pottery, appear at this threshold that *sarically* separates the decadent and the innocent realms, *syphilitically* the polluted and the pure. The fiancé is backgrounded and depicted in an awkward pose; not so the two claimant women: in the manner proper to them—respectively as beautiful girl and drooling spinster—they both appear assertive and assured of their place. The presiding judge appears weary, reserved and unsure as to what to make of the situation, while the younger scribe appears keen, agile and scheming. In Le Veau's image an ancient patriarchal order (the weary judge) confronts a new, bourgeois one (the assertive woman, the young professional), while a third force enters through the door). There is much in Le Veau's scenario to have intrigued Kleist.

239   Kleist deployed a variety of means of framing his works: scene settings (various dramas), opening chorus (*Schroffenstein, Guiskard*), foreword (*Krug*), subtitles (*Käthchen, Marquise*), prologue and epilogue (*Phöbus*), introductory sentence (*Kohlhaas*), introductory poem (*BA*), dedication (*Homburg*).

240   The "evidence" Kleist offers for Adam's "guilt" consist in dubious "clues," hearsay, uncorroborated or contradictory testimonies, testimonies under duress, premonitions and innuendos:

- Adam, sitting in his courtroom bandaging his leg, tells the enter Licht that when he got out of bed this morning he stumbled or tripped, dislocating his right foot (I:177);
- Licht points out that Adam's face has been maltreated in the accident and shows him the damage in a mirror; Adam claims that he injured his face when losing his balance (I:178-9);
- The maids report that Adam returned at 11pm without his wig and that they had to wash blood off his wounded head; Adam denies the maids' report and offers his own (I:185-6);

- Adam shares with Licht a lucid premonition of the forthcoming court-hearing, whose outcome could spell death or exile for both of them (I:187);
- When he sees Eve and her entourage arrive at he courtroom, Adam immediately realises that they came to accuse him (I:195);
- Adam blackmails Eve with a certificate protecting Ruprecht from conscription (I:196);
- Adam reflects that he could possibly have toppled the jug (I:196);
- Marthe reports that at 11 pm she heard male voices and tumultuous noises in Eve's chamber, found the door forcefully broken, the shards of the broken jug spread across the room, and Ruprecht and (presumably) Adam in a fight (I:203);
- Ruprecht (apparently) admits to having broke the jug and reports hitting his opponent over the head with a door handle (I:212);
- When Eve prepares to testify, Adam once more attempts to blackmail her (I:214-5);
- Eve testifies that it was not Rupert who shattered the jug (I:217; 219);
- Brigitte appears and testifies that she found (one of) Adam's wig(s) at the crime scene (I:232);
- Ruprecht admits to having brought (one of) the wig(s) to a repair-shop in Utrecht (I:233);
- Brigitte testifies that the culprit could not have been Ruprecht because he was bald and left behind tracks made by one human and one hoof-like foot (I: 234);
- Adam retorts that the culprit could have appeared in the devil's disguise (I:235);
- Licht, who investigated the crime scene at Walter's request, without taking an eye-witness along, confirms the presence of the tracks as described by Brigitte (I:236);
- Brigitte testifies—and Licht corroborates—that the tracks lead into the back door of Adam's court-house, but cannot be traced through the front door, where all tracks have been smudged (I:237);
- When Adam sentences Ruprecht and prepares to throw him into jail, a terrified Eve testifies that Adam broke the jug (I:241);
- Adam runs away (I:241);
- Eve, with Walter's and Licht's help, uncovers Adam's blackmailing scheme, by which she claims he obtained favours from her that "no maiden's mouth would dare articulate" (I:243).

241   As with the arrow from Rotbart's workshop in *Zweikampf*, the facile and unequivocal traceability of the judge's wig to its owner begs the question whether he is being framed; Ruprecht testifies that he brought (one of) the wig(s) to a repair-shop, but nobody checks with the repair shop to corroborate it. Blamberger's claim (*Kleist*, 268) that *"Im Zerbrochnen Krug weisen des Richters Blessuren die Wahrheit, auf die Körperzeichen ist Verlass"* is tenable only if one accepts that the "truth" may not be what it pertains to be, and that one requires the "key" to decrypt the meaning of these "signs."

242   In the opening scene Adam relates to Licht how he injured himself by clashing with a goat-figure behind the oven. While *satycially* Adam alludes to sodomy (cf. the equivalent scene in *Bettelweib*), Eberhard Siebert's suggestion that Kleist had an actual goat-figure in mind that he had seen as decorative item on an oven remains plausible; Siebert tracks down (*Kleistiana Collecta*, 95-6) such ovens in the Würzburg Residence and in Neuhardenberg Castle, which Kleist could have seen. What is most interesting in Siebert's account, however, is his mentioning, in passing (*ibid*, 88), that the *Krug* MS has *"Cherubim"* instead of *"Ziegenbock,"* an exchangability that suggests that these two terms have the same functional value in Kleist's "code"—and indeed they do: in *Marionettentheater*, the figure of the cherub, standing before paradise's "rear gate flaming "sword" in hand," is as much ann avatar of an ithyphallic satyr as is, by ancient tradition, the goat-figure. "Behind the oven" may simply refer to the body's rear, but also rings to mind the proverb *"damit lockt man keinen Hund hinterm Ofen hervor"* ("it's nothing to write home about"), which suggests that behind the oven is the place for—*dogs*. "Dog" is a derogatory term Kleist *satirically* applies to his King (cf. *Bettelweib*), his Queen (cf. *Käthchen*), the *Rheinbund* princes (cf. *Marquise*) and here, it appears, his Emperor.

243   Wilh. Grimm mused that the play's *"Gegenstand so einfach ist, daß er durch zu genaues Auseinanderlegen leicht einförmig werden kann"* (LS,497). Yet if there were any simplicity in Kleist's drama, then only "that," to paraphrase Alfred North Whitehead, "which lies beyond complexity."

244   Adam's club foot's being "sinister" implies that it is diseased. This is corroborated by evidence: when he grabs Adam's member and notes, *"Doch auf dem Griffe lag ein Klumpen / Blei"* (V.991-2), Ruprecht implies that Adam's shaft is chancred, and when Brigitte says of Adam's member, *"Und seh, [...] / Die Glatz [...] / Wie faules Holz"* (V.1689-91), she suggests that his glans is chancred, too.

245   William C. Reeve, in *In Pursuit of Power: Heinrich von Kleist's Machiavellian Protagonists* (Toronto: University of Toronto Press, 1987) points to Licht's duplicitous game.

246   *Wacholder* (juniper) is the main flavouring in *gin*, an English derivative of the Dutch term for juniper, *genever*—in other words, Walter's predecessor was partial to drink. While the names Adam and Licht could be Dutch or German, the names Walter and Wacholder are clearly German (in Dutch they would be rendered, respectively, as Wouter and Genever), so that Kleist's *satirical* setting is clearly Germany.

247   "*Fichten*" ("spruces") could refer to the forests into which Adam and Licht flee or to the coffins into which they will be interred, made of spruce timber (the latter idea we owe to Blamberger, *Kleist*, 263); they are furthermore phallic (tall and erect, as the pines and cedars Kleist refers to elsewhere), so that *satyrically* Adam and Licht escape not into a forest but into the embrace of their "brotherhood" (cf. Josephe in *Erdbeben* evacuating to the "dark valley" of pine trees, "pines" being an anagram of "penis," Gustav in *Verlobung*'s Mariane sub-plot fleeing into the arms of his "friend" on the other side of the Rhine, and Piachi in *Findling* escaping into the bed of his "legal friend" Valerio). When Adam sends the women away and tells Walter, "*'s ist heute Holztag, / ... Die Weiber... / sind in den Fichten*" (V.1438-9), he implies that the "women" (effeminate lovers) are having an orgy.

248   Re the Kleist reception's naïve portrayals of Walter, one cannot help wondering whether Kleist anticipated such readings and considered them part and parcel of the very "comedy" he was writing. Consider Jochen Schmidt (*Kleist*, 68): "*Es macht den besonderen Reiz dieses Lustspiels aus, daß es gerade bis an die Grenze des Tragischen reicht, ja das Tragische als Möglichkeit spüren läßt, um es dann noch rechtzeitig abzuwenden. Und von vornherein ist eine Sicherheit eingebaut, die garantiert, daß alles gut ausgehen wird: Der Inspektor Walter verhindert die Rechtsbeugung*"; or Anthony Stephens (*Kleist. The Dramas*, 78): "[T]he high moral ground in the play is fully occupied by Gerichtsrat Walter." Dirk Grathoff (*Kleist: Geschichte*, 47) at least recognises that "[Walters] *Handlungsweise unterscheidet sich in ihrem Kern nicht von der vorherigen Handlungsweise Adams*," but unfortunately adds: "*er wiederholt mit selbstloser Absicht, as Adam zuvor aus Eigennutz tat.*" Blamberger (*Kleist*, 266) is slightly more circumspect: "*Walter schützt das die abstrakte Verwaltung, nicht das konkrete Recht.*"

249 "*FOF*" denotes a version of the "*FFF*" constellation in which the central figure is female (denoted "*O*"), in a double (anal and vaginal) penetration, allowing impregnation to take place alongside sodomy (if *MS World* permitted it, I would flip the second "F" along its vertical axis, so that its ithyphallic horizontal bar would be pointing to the left). The actor enacting "*O*" on stage could be a man, dressed as woman and not overtly carrying a phallus, unlike the actors enacting the "*Fs*." The symbolism of "F" and "O" is Kleist's own: in naming *Marquise*'s protagonists respectively *Graf F* and *Marquise von O....*, Kleist denotes the former as ithyphallic sodomiser and impregnator, the latter as receptive lover ("O" = anus) and potential mother ("O" = vagina, womb).

250 Re the reference to the god *Hymen*, cf. David E. Wellbery, *Geschlechterdifferenz*, 26.

251 *Marquise* encompasses a similar indiscernibility: when Count F leads the Marquise into the "wing of the palace not yet encompassed by the flames" (in contradistinction to her "other" wing, already "enflamed"), it remains indiscernible which of her "wings" refers to her front and which to her rear, so that in the famous "dash" event, it could be either Count F or the last of the Russian "dogs" who impregnates her. The novella's famous subtitle "*vom Norden in den Süden verlegt worden*" could imply that Kleist not only flipped the *satirical* setting geographically along the horizontal axis (swapping Italy for Prussia), but also the *satyrical* action topographically along the vertical axis (swapping the Marquise's vagina for her anus).

252 Kleist's court hearing comprises a *mise-en-abime* similar to the stage performance in L. Tieck's 1797 *Der Gestiefelte Kater*. According to Zschokke, apart from Goethe and Fr. Schlegel, Kleist "idolised" Tieck (cf. *LS*,67a); passages of Tieck's novel *William Lovell* may have found their way into Kleist's depictions of Paris—cf. Ingrid Oesterle, "Briefe über Paris," in Dirk Grathoff (Ed.), *Kleist: Studien*, 108.

253 The idea of the *Rheinbund* was circulated already in February 1807 by none other than Gentz's and Müller's "brother" Joh. von Müller, who by that time was in Napoleon's service—cf. *AML*,212.

254 Cf. Hermann Müller-Bohn, *Die deutschen Befreiungskriege*. 1st Vol. (Berlin: Paul Kittel/Histor. Verlag, 1901), 32 ff. Müller-Bohn leans on Paul Baillen,

Diplom. Korrespondenzen (Berlin: Publik. aus den königl. preuß. Staatsarchiven), who questions the seriousness of Napoleon's intentions, and on Veit Valentin, *Illustrierte Weltgeschichte* 3rd Vol., 925, who offers: *"Es ist sehr gut möglich, dass Napoleon eine solche Gründung geduldet haben würde, wenn sich Preußen auf ein Vasallenverhältnis eingelassen hätte."* Kleist also played with the idea of the Hohenzollern assuming the imperial dignity, which in his eyes the Habsburg had frivously gambled away, but he would have opposed the Hohenzollern accepting it by Napoleon's grace, in exchange for de facto vassalage.

255   Marthe commences the *HRR*'s history with Childerich I (c.AD 440-82), first king of the Salian Franks, whose kingdom was centred on Tournai in today's Belgium and whose son Clovis I would unite all Franks, conquer significant parts of Gaul as well as Swabia and other Germanic lands, and found the Merovingian dynasty and a Frankish kingdom spanning significant territories on both sides of the Rhine. By commencing his historical sketch with Childerich I, Kleist conveys that the *HRR* from its very beginning spanned French, German, and other nations (n.b., Marthe could also refer to Childerich III, the last of the Merovingian kings, during whose reign in AD 751 the Carolingians acquired the crown, under whom the Frankish Empire would reach its peak). *"Maximilian: der Schlingel"* (V.664) may refer to Karl V's nephew, Emperor Max. II, and may also entail a swipe at K Max. I Joseph of Bavaria, the staunches of Napoleon's German allies. Marthe parallels the 16th Century's rebellious *Wassergeusen* with Childerich, who she says *"den Spanier von hinten niederwarf, den Krug ergriff, ihn leert und weiterging"* (V.685-6; possibly a reference to Childerich I's defeat of the Visigoths in AD 463). Dirk Grathoff recognises (*Kleist: Geschichte*, 52) *Krug*'s sweeping historical horizon, but fails to trace it precisely. Anthony Stephens critiques (*Kleist*, 67-8) *Krug*'s "inconsistencies," "for example, at the beginning of her long account of the jug, Frau Marthe presents it as being 'entzwei geschlagen,' with a convenient hole in the middle... When she comes... to the events of the night before, the jug has suddenly become a heap of fragments: 'Den Krug find ich zerscherbt im Zimmer liegen, / In jedem Winkel liege in Stück' (I:203)," but fails to see that this "inconsistency" resolves itself once one accepts that Marthe's eulogy pertains to the *HRR*, first cut into "halves" by France's annexation of the Rhine's left bank, then on 1st August 1806 dissolved entirely, its members disseminated like the jug's shards (the jug's "shards," as it were, can be assigned a precise number and shape). Ilse Graham is evidently wrong when she terms Marthe's description of the broken jug "simply nonsensical"—cf. "Der Zerbrochne Krug—Titelheld von Kleist Kommödie,"

in Walter Müller-Seidel (Ed.), *Heinrich von Kleist. Aufsätze und Essays*, Darmstadt: Wiss. Buchgesesellschaft, 1967, 278. Far from veering from the "naïve into the absurd," as Graham has it (*ibid*), Marthe (Kleist) succinctly depicts the *HRR*'s precarious state before, and the utter irreversibility of its disintegration after its collapse. Her depiction of the broken jug—a yawning hole at its centre, its edges precariously hanging together—offers a vivid example of Kleist's paradoxical *"Gewölbe,"* which remain stable as long as all arch stones press against each other, and collapses immediately when a single arch stone is pulled out, only the arch's sides remaining erect because they are not subject to lateral forces. The liberation of the Netherlands from Spanish rule was a popular topic in literature in Kleist's time: Schiller covered it in *Abfall der Vereinigten Niederlande*, and Goethe did in Egmont; Wolf Kittler reviews (*Geburt*, 92-4 and 98-101) several references to Dutch history in Kleist's works and shows that Kleist had read Schiller's treatise. The scene painted on the jug depicts events during the reign of the Holy Roman Emperor Karl V (1500-58), when the Empire one last time experienced greatness before commencing its inexorable decline. It will not have been lost on Kleist that Karl V's pursuit of Habsburg dynastic interests, encompassing the territories of the Spanish and the Austrian Habsburgs, including the former's colonies, taken together indeed an "empire on which the sun never sets," did not undermine but strengthen the Empire, in particular against France, demonstrating that dynastic and imperial interests do not have to be diametrical, and can be complementary. Karl V was the last Emperor before Napoleon to be crowned in the presence of the Pope, and to be crowned King of Italy with the Iron Crown (in 1521 he forced Luther to defend himself before the Imperial Diet at Worms and in 1532 promulgated the *Constitutio Criminalis Carolina*, the first comprehensive penal code). Karl V plays a similar role in *Krug* as does Fr. II Barbarossa in *Schroffenstein*, symbolising both the Empire's greatness and vulnerability to dynastic disintegration: Barbarossa's untimely death by drowning precipitated dynastic rivalries, while Karl himself divided his empire when in 1555 he abdicated his rule of the Netherlands in favour of his son Philipp II of Spain, triggering a rivalry between the Spanish and the Austrian lines of his dynasty that following his death began driving the Empire apart, creating the conditions for France's rise—and ultimately, Napoleon's.

256   All three judges have speaking names: Adam's links him to Eve and to the Christian concept of original sin; Licht's similarly has a Biblical connotation: God before Adam created *light*, and Lucifer (bringer of light) is a name of Satan; Walter's literally means "he who holds sway" and derives from a Proto-Germanic

name for "ruler of the army"; terms such as *walten* (to preside, prevail), *Gewalt* (power, violence), *verwalten* (to administrate) are related to it, and *Gerechtigkeit* (justice) is said to be *"walten"* (to "hold sway"). Judges in days past had executive as well as judiciary powers, not always clearly separated: cf. Ernst Ribbat, "Babylon in Huisum oder der Schein des Scheins," in Dirk Grathoff (Ed.), *Kleist: Studien*, 142-3, and Peter Horn, "Das erschrockene Gelächter über die Entlarvung einer korrupten Obrigkeit," in *ibid*, 154 and *passim*.

257   Joséphine was a cat lover, keeping several about the house (Napoleon did not much care for them, thinking them lazy). Tieck, himself a cat lover, claimed that Kleist hated cats and ridiculed a passage in *Schroffenstein* (II/3), in which a cat nibbles on preserved pineapples, which to him was nonsense, cats being strict carnivores (cf. *LS*,275a). Yet Its fondness for pineapple merely marks the cat as an avatar of Joséphine: "Motifs of pineapples and other exotic articles associated with the tropics became popular because of the influence of Napoleon Bonaparte's wife Joséphine, the then fashion leader, who was from the Island of Martinique"— cf. https://www.pinterest.co.uk/pin/388576274090228051/ (n.b., Kleist having the Warwands munch on preserved fruits may furthermore entail a swipe at the Habsburgs: having lost their Italian possessions, including their orchards, as well as their only major harbour, Antwerp, they now have to make do with preserved fruit—"cat food," in Kleist's estimation).

258   Kleist's biting sarcasm at his King's efforts to please Napoleon was not altogether unwarranted: Fr. Wilh. in December 1804 became the first incumbent monarch to officially recognise Napoleon's imperial dignity. Holla could obviously refer to Bourbon France, whose throne Napoleon de facto usurped, but could also refer to Italy, in which case the deposed monarch could be Ferd. III, Grand Duke of Tuscany, a Habsburg whom Napoleon deposed in the *Treaty of Aranjuez* (1801). In this case Kleist may be insinuating that Franz II, himself born in Florence, is merely the next Habsburg in line to be toppled by Napoleon. Holla (France or Italy) and Huisum (Germany) appear as mere milestones on Napoleon's inexorable progress across Holland (Europe): Hussahe, which is next in line (cf. V.169), could be Russia, Spain or England. The names of these villages are fictional, and we may conjecture possible meanings: *"Huisum"* (V.75) may derive from *huis* (house; brothels in Germany were known as *"offen hus,"* cf. Toni's "open house" in *Verlobung*); *"Holla"* (V.73) recalls the fairytale figure *Frau Holle*, who rather like the mistress of a BDSM

dungeon dishes out generous rewards to the industrious and cruel punishment to the lazy (cf. my discussion below in the context of *Käthchen*'s *Hollunder*); *"Hussahe"* (V.169) may be derived from *hussar* (Hungarian cavalryman). It has been pointed out that these names appear to mimic coachmen's cheers (cf. Wichmann, *Kleist*, 143; Marie Leis et al (Ed.), *Heinrich von Kleist. Der zerbrochne Krug*. Stuttgart: Reclam, 2014, 102), though they may just as well mimic prostitutes' siren calls. As the town of Huissen in the Gelderland had been part of the Prussian Duchy of Cleves until 1795, Kleist may also again be taking a swipe at *Basel* by having two of his town names resemble Huissen's. Walter's stated aim,*"die Rechtspfleg' auf dem platten Land verbessern,"* may refer to Napoleon's promulgation of the *Code Napoléon*, in France since 1804, in "model" *Rheinbund* states such as the Grand Duchy of Berg since 1806.

259   Napoleon's losses at *Austerlitz* were modest, 9,000 men dead or wounded, in comparison with the Coalition's 36,000 men (and 180 guns) lost: "never have victories been so complete and less costly," is how the *Ad'A*'s 8th bulletin proclaimed the victory, quite accurately (quoted in David G. Chandler, *The Campaigns of Napoleon*. New York: Simon & Schuster, 1995, 402). Walter having merely sprained his "hand" in an "accident," while Adam received a major thrashing, is thus historically accurate.

699

260   Kleist's repeated reference to the wines in which Adam is caught up (cf. V.977; 1520; 1627) clearly points to *Austerlitz*: Moravia south of Brünn and Olmütz, where Austerlitz is located, is a traditional wine-growing area, and parts of the epic battle indeed took place amidst vinyards. Adam's fall into the vine trellises, then, refers to Austria's defeat by the *Ad'A* at *Austerlitz*. Kleist traces Adam-Franz's return route from *Austerlitz* to Vienna in detail (cf. V.1779-82): from the *"Lindengang"* ("lime alley"; the lime leaf is a traditional symbol of Bohemia and Moravia, and there may have been a lime alley in Olmütz) to the *"Schulzenfeld"* ("Bailiff's Field"; perhaps a feature along the road from Olmütz to Pressburg); "den Karpfenteich entlang" ("along the carp pond"; the Morava river, which meanders from Olmütz to Pressburg and creates many floodplains traditionally known to be rich in carp; the country road to this day runs along the river); *"den Steg"* ("the footbridge"; probably the Danube crossing at Pressburg); *"quer über den Gottesacker"* ("straight across the cemetary"; probably the Sankt Marzer Friedhof—famous for Mozart's tomb—which the country road from Pressburg to Vienna—today: Simmeringer Hauptstrasse/Brucker Bundesstrasse—passes); *"zum Herrn Dorfrichter Adam"* (straight to the Hofburg). Kleist's detailed geographical knowledge of the route, which for all we know he had not travelled,

suggests that he had access to quality maps and travel reports (cf. also my discussion below in the context of his similarly impeccable depiction of Vienna's Hofburg).

261   Napoleon during the early stages of the *Ulm Campaign* remained stationary on the Rhine's right bank while his generals fanned out across central Swabia, but by 7th-9th November he established his HQ south of Ansbach, and by 11th-14th moved it east of Ulm, at the heart of the theatre of war; at *Austerlitz* he deliberately dissimulated his presence in order to lull the enemy, while orchestrating his field marshals—the likes of Bressières, Lannes, Murat, Soult, Bernadotte, Davout, Saint-Hilaire, famous names all in the annals of warfare—from behind the lines with the aid of dispatches. At *Ulm* Napoleon initially stayed behind and let his general unfold their armies, allowing him to wait and see where the decicive action was about to occur, and then throw himself right there; at *Austerlitz* he deliberately feigned absence from the battlefield, thereby precipitating an Austro-Russian attack on the *Ad'A*'s purportedly weak right flank and diverting the Coalition army's core away from his own centre, before launching a surprise counter-attack on the famous Pratzen Hill commanding the battle theatre's topographical centre: "one sharp blow and the war is over," Napoleon was quoted as saying to Marshal Soult, and so it was. Napoleon at *Austerlitz* thus won the battle precisely because his presence was visible to his own generals, but not to the enemy's. Conversely, during the subsequent peace confernece at *Schönbrunn* and *Pressburg* he took centre stage, imposing his charismatic presence on the negotiations, while his imperial and royal counterparts hid behind their envoys. When in *Marionettentheater* Kleist explores the question of whether the *Maschinist* must himself participate in his puppets' "dance," and concludes that in a situation that calls for merely a mechanical execution of standard movements the *Maschinist* may choreograph proceedings at a distance, whereas in a constellation that requires psychological finesse he must be present in person, he may well offer his assessment of Napoleon's choices, implying that Napoleon understood, and Franz and Fr. Wilh. did not, that peace negotiations, more than battlefield tactics, required psychological finesse and charismatic presence (move over, Clausewitz!), and that it was in the theatre loges and backrooms, more than on the battlefields, that the future of Europe was decided (his youthful experience of Hardenberg in 1795 at *Basel* with a single stroke of the pen nullifying his years of campaigning is no doubt reflected here; nevertheless, especially for a scion of a family of generals, his giving precedence to the art of making peace—a game of orchestrating psychological moves—over that of making war—a game of harnessing physical forces— is remarkable). In *Krug* Napoleon's choices are depicated accurately:

during the orgy or séance in "Eve's bedroom" (*Ulm*) Walter-Napoleon remains in the background; in the trellis and vines below Eve's "window" he is present, but stealthy; during the hearing in Adam's courtroom (*Schönbrunn, Pressburg*) he foregrounds himself, presiding over proceedings, manipulating the participants, and exploiting the rivalry between Licht-Fr. Wilh. and Adam-Franz to his advantage. *Walter* is an exceedingly apt monicker for Napoleon: he who holds sway, on-stage and back-stage.

262   Braunschweiger Mettwurst was first recorded in the 1830s, but was obviously already famous in Kleist's day. Danziger Goldwasser is a herbal liqueur first distilled in the 16th century, to which occasionally gold leaf was added for its alchemical and symbolical value, making it a suitable means for bribing Walter (incidentally, today the *Goldwasser* brand is owned by the Hardenberg family). The Duchy of Brunswick-Lüneburg was a mid-sized Guelph duchy, so that what Adam initially offers to Walter-Napoleon is a modest, Protestant German territory associated with the British crown. Danzig was a major Baltic Sea port and ancient free Hanse city that in 1793 had fallen to Prussia, so that Adam "spices up" his offer with a small but strategically important Prussian territory, indicating his readiness to risk the Habsburg-Hohenzollern truce in his quest to pacify Napoleon. Martial (*Epigrams*, 4.46) has a similarly hilarious enumeration of regional dishes.

263   Nierstein and Oppenheim are neighbouring vinegrowing towns in Rheinhessen, on the Rhine's left bank and on the main country road from Mainz to Worms (today's B9), which Kleist passed repeatedly, first during his unit's circumnavigation of Mainz in 1793 and its subsequent movements in the 1793/4 *Palatine Campaign*, and most likely again during the 1801 Paris journey and the 1801 and 1803 Swiss journeys. Napoleon indeed on this occasion did not acquire Pomerania, although Swedish Pomerania was occupied by French troops in August 1807. Kleist's territorial references are precise and astute.

264   Fr. Wilh. and Alex.'s *Convention of Potsdam* and Haugwitz' subsequent diplomatic mission to Paris to deliver Prussia's ultimatum no doubt irritated Napoleon, who will have enjoyed arm-twisting Haugwitz into major concessions at *Schönbrunn*. Kleist was by no means alone in blaming the "catastrophe" of *Austerlitz* on Prussia's absence—Gentz, for one, was convinced that a Coalition involving Russia, Austria and Prussia could not have failed to vanquish Napoleon (cf. *AML*,127), and as late as 13th November 1805, i.e., one month after *Ulm* and in the wake of the

Convention of Potsdam, he was still hopeful that Fr. Wilh. would lead Prussia into war: "*Der König von Preußen ist nun—ich wette mein Leben darauf—mit Leib und Seele unser... Ja! Er wird negociren; aber geben Sie nur Achtung, wie. Ein Friede, wie wir ihn wünschen... oder—Krieg mit der ganzen preußischen Macht... Wir sind gerettet. Wer hätte je geglaubt, daß dieser König eine solche glorreiche Rolle spielen sollte: Er ist jetzt das Haupt der Christenheit wider den Erbfeind geworden*" (*AML*,132; cf. also 133). Gentz would have forfeited his life had Müller redeemed the wager! Gentz was not alone in overestimating Prussia's military might: so did Fr. Wilh. with his impetuous ultimatum to Napoleon (he would do it again nine months later!). Already on 20th December 1805, 5 days after *Schönbrunn* was signed, Müller expressed the hope that a *Fourth Coalition*, led by Prussia, would soon form (cf. *AML*,139); Gentz rejected this possibility, given the lopsidedness of Napoleon's victory (cf. *AML*,141); Müller would be proven right.

265   With *Schönbrunn*—Loch: an "*erbärmliche[r] Länderschacher*" (*Kleist*, 243)—Prussia forfeits Cleves, Ansbach-Bayreuth, where Kleist was slated to be employed as Prussian civil servant, and Neuchâtel in exchange for a dubious claim to Hannover that only serves to put her in confrontation with Britain. Kleist, like many others, blames this loss on Fr. Wilh.'s tarrying and on the "*Schaukelpolitik*" pursued by the Prussian foreign ministry's double act, Karl Aug. von Hardenberg and Chr. von Haugwitz, both of whom Kleist met in personal audiences in the summer of 1804 (cf. *MA* III,830), and against both of whom he may have borne a grudge ever since the former signed, and the latter drafted, the 1795 *Peace of Basel*. In the court scene (i.e., treaty negotiations), at least in an earlier concept or version, Veit could have represented Hardenberg and Ruprecht, Haugwitz; Veit's admission "*Ich war daheim, als sich der Krug zerschlug*" (V.1378) may allude to Prussia's absence from the *War of the Third Coalition*, and Ruprech's earlier mission Veit mentions, to Haugwitz' mission to Paris in September 1805 to submit Fr. Wilh.'s ultimatum to Napoleon, a task the envoy deliberately delayed until it became obsolete with *Austerlitz*, thereby keeping Prussia out of the war, though not the treaty negotiations. Haugwitz and Hardenberg took turns heading the Prussian foreign ministry; the former had been active in the foreign service since 1792, the latter since 1803. When Kleist met them in the summer of 1804, Haugwitz was Foreign Minister, Hardenberg his deputy; shortly thereafter, in August, Haugwitz retired following disagreements with Fr. Wilh., Hardenberg replaced him. Haugwitz in 1805 returned to the diplomatic service as chief emissary, now under Hardenberg, in December 1805 representing

Prussia at the negotiations of the *Treaty of Schönbrunn* (between Prussia and France, not to be confused with the treaty by the same name, of 1809, between Austria and France), in February 1806 at further secret meetings in which Prussia agreed to break with England, isolating herself completely. Hardenberg stepped down in mid-1806 when Fr. Wilh. veered towards all-out confrontation with Napoleon; in April 1807 he returned to office and was appointed First Minister, his portfolio covering both external and internal affairs; following *Tilsit* he was dismissed on Napoleon's request and exiled himself to Riga. In 1810 he engineered the dismissal of Kleist's mentor Altenstein's entire cabinet and replaced him as Chancellor, this time with Napoleon's endorsement, in which role in 1811 he brought down BA, ruining Kleist. Kleist appears to have hated Hardenberg with a passion that was perhaps not entirely warranted: it appears that Hardenberg helped Kleist, on Marie's and Massenbach's instigation, to obtain his job with Altenstein, for many years Hardenberg's protégé, and personally recommended Kleist's transfer to Königsberg (cf. Schede, *Kleist*, 77-8); forfaiting Ansbach will furthermore not have been easy for Hardenberg himself, who until 1798 was that province's governor, and his politics were by no means always geared towards appeasement: he could be a hardliner and a thorn in Napoleon's side; on the whole, he appears to have been a sophisticated, thoughtful operator, a complex and forceful poliitican whose competence is not represented in Kleist's polemical caricatures. Many men, including the King, were trying to do the right thing for Prussia under taxing circumstances, and Kleist, in the comfortable position of the bystander, observing and pointing fingers from the sidelines without himself having to make the tough decisions, was happy to accept help while taking it for granted and expressing no gratefulness; the "harshness" his interlocutors perceived in his conversation, and tended to rationalise as a speech disorder, is also discernible in his writings, thus not reducible to a physical impairment.

266 Re the political situation in the summer of 1806, Blamberger notes (*Kleist*, 242): "*Friedrich Wilhelm III., accompagniert von mutlosen Beratern wie Köckeritz und Haugwitz, verhält sich gegenüber Napoleon geradezu unterwürfig und handelt erst, als dieser im August 1806 Hannover um eines Friedensschlusses mit England heimlich wieder den Briten anbietet und in Preußen die anti-französische, patriotische Opposition um Karl Aug. von Hardenberg und dem Freiherrn vom und zum Stein, zu der Kleist, Rühle und Pfuel gehören, die öffentliche Meinung zu beherrschen beginnt. Er mobilisiert die Armee und verlangt den Rückzug der französischen Truppen aus Süddeutschland. Daraufhin erklärt Napoleon Preußen den Krieg.*"

267 Sembdner dates the letter "late September" (cf. II:759), Reuß and Staengle, "early December" (cf. *MA*II, 844). While the latter dating is possible but vague, the former is likely too early: while Kleist's reference to the *"Durchbruch[s] der Franzosen durch das Fränkische"* (II:760), i.e., Bernadotte's march through Prussia's territory of Ansbach in the early stage of the *Ulm Campaign* (25th September-20th October), a series of engagements between French and Astrian armies that were an important prelude to the *War of the Third Coalition*'s decisive *Battle of Austerlitz* (2nd December), appears to mark the *terminus post quem* for dating the letter (this may have informed Sembdner's dating), his warning that Napoleon will turn on Prussia once Austria has been finished off suggests that at time of writing the campaign was significantly more advanced—notably that the surrender of major parts of the Austrian army following the momentous *Battle of Ulm* (16th-19th October) had already taken place. This would shift the *terminus post quem* to late October. Kleist's failure to mention *Austerlitz*, and his reference to the defensive measures Prussia was undertaking (fortifications, winter camp), point to his expectation of a drawn-out conflict into which Prussia could yet be drawn, not to the rapid end to the war *Austerlitz* would precipitate, imply that the "earthquake" had not yet taken place, or at least that the news of its outcome has not yet reached him—which, considering that his alarmed reaction to *Jena-Auerstedt* in a letter to Ulrike (cf. II:770) came 10 days after that battle, suggests a *terminus ante quem* for the letter's dating of ca. 12th December (this may have informed Reuß and Staengle's dating). Now, what neither Sembdner nor Reuß and Staengle seem to have explored, is that Kleist's letter could have been a reaction to a specific event that falls between these termini of late October and early December, namely Tsar Alex. I's visit to Potsdam to sign the Prusso-Russian *Treaty of Potsdam* (3rd November), in which Fr. Wilh. promises "armed mediation" and pledges that Prussia will join the Coalition if mediation fails (cf. Hans-Georg Schede, *Kleist*, 80-1). The King's stance expressed in this treaty could certainly be said to correspond to Kleist's accusation of the King's "beligerent wait and see," which leads me to offer that Kleist wrote his letter in response to this treaty, i.e., that the letter must be dated somewhere between *Potsdam* (3rd November) and *Austerlitz* (2nd December). Kleist's next extant letter is dated February 1806, and while there could have been earlier, not extant, letters, it suggests that when the news of the "catastrophe" broke in early December, Kleist chose to process it *not in letters but in poetry*, that this is how *Erdbeben*—and with it the German novella—was born: a novel mode of *news breaking and processing* was needed in response to the "earthquake" of Napoleon's unfathomable victory, to that day one of the most incredible and momentous pieces of *news* ever having been

broken to the European public, and Kleist evidently could think of no more suitable format for his response than a short, crisp, hard-hitting novella (his *overt* story may have taken into account that the Molise earthquake of July 1805 in the Kingdom of Naples, and its aftermath, still reverberated among the European public when the "earthquake" of *Austerlitz* hit—cf. *AML*,124).

268   The precedence of Italy suggests that Napoleon could have aimed to crown himself "King of Germany," and Beauharnais, Viceroy. Walter-Napoleon invites himself merely as *"Hochzeitsgast"* (V.2393), but that could be ironic. He would, however, have been hard pressed to find a German equivalent of Italy's Iron Crown of Lombardy. The wedding is a common ending in Greek comedy, marked in Aristophanes by the chorus' exodus, singing wedding songs and hymns to the god Hymen (cf. *KH*,21); Kleist's "wedding" is, however, not comic but apocalyptic (or comico-apocalyptic).

269   Pentecost marks the saviour's descend from heaven and the unity of all nations, making it a perfect moniker for Napoleon's project: "saviour" = Napoleon; unity of all nations = a pan-European Bonapartean Empire. Kleist's equating Napoleon with Christ explains why *Krug* abounds in references to the coming of the savior—*"Joseph und Maria"* (V.776; 792; 794; 803; 813; 2272); *"die Jungfer"* (V.814; 1097; 1125; 1135; etc.); *"der Esel, wie ein Ochse"* (V.866); *"Jesus"* or *"Jesus Christus"* (V.1131; 1132; 1133; 2221; 2375); *"Heiland der Welt"* (V.2248)—, and why Adam repeatedly dishes up traditional Christmas dishes (guinea fowl, carp, goose): he expects that they will please Napoleon.

270   The *overt* story's United Netherlands of 1581 serve Kleist as proxy for the future "United States of Germany." Kleist's imagery perhaps recalls the machinic obedience he experienced during military service. The *Rheinbund* indeed saw its membership grow from the original 16 states in 1806 to 39 by 1809, including almost every German state bar Prussia, Austria and Bonapartean Hannover; it was, however, never consolidated into a single kingdom or empire. "Casting the first stone" is from the *Gospel of John* (7:53-8:11), where Jesus challenges the scribes and Pharisees set to lynch a victim to "cast the first stone." When Ilse Graham states (*Titelheld*, 291), *"Wie das zerstückte Bild auf dem zerbrochenen Krug sendet die Trommel geistlos ihre Botschaft aus; aber die Zeichen sind, wie jene, fragwürdig geworden. Der Sinnzusammenhang des Ganzen ist verlorengegangen,"* she misses Kleist's point entirely: the jug's image is a

705

symbol of disintegration, the drum's beating one of integration; the latter is not the equivalent of the former, but its reversal (only now under different leadership).

271   Kleist's ruminations on militias remained topical: to Ulrike he enthused on 25th October 1807 in reference to *Krug*: *"Den 10. Okt. bin ich bei dem östr. Gesandten an der Tafel mit einem Lorbeer gekrönt worden; und das von zwei niedlichsten kleinen Händen, die in Dreßden sind. Den Kranz habe ich noch bei mir. In solchen Aubenblicken denke ich immer an Dich"* (II:794-5). Why should the Austrian emissary praise Kleist so lavishly? Because, I offer, at the beginning of 1807 Franz established a committee under Archduke John to consult on the establishment of a militia (*Landwehr*), and on 9th June 1808 issued the decree establishing the militia. The "cute little hands" will have been Buol's.

272   Grathoff (*Kleist, Geschichte*, 51-3) already surmises that Kleist could refer to the *Napoléon*. Wolf Kittler interprets (*Geburt*, 101) Kleist's coin not as currency but shibboleth, on the grounds that there never was a "Guilder" or Dutch Florin featuring a Spanish king, but apart from overlooking the fact that a *gold* coin *always* comprises currency, he ignores that for Kleist it was of no consequence whether there had been an actual Dutch coin featuring Philipp, for there plausibly *could have been*, and it made a perfect placeholder for the *Napoléon* within his *overt* story. As recently as 2013 Helmut Schneider (*KH*,39) cites Klaus Müller-Salget: *"Der Anachronismus bzw. die historische Unmöglichkeit, dass das niederländische Geld den Prägestempel des Landesfeinds trägt, konnte bisher nicht gelöst werden."* Well, it is now: there is neither "anachronismus" nor "impossibility" in play, only Kleistian analogies.

273   The coin itself, in the version of c.1806, incorporated an oxymoron: on its obverse the legend reads *"NAPOLEON EMPEREUR,"* on its reverse, *"REPUBLIQUE FRANÇAISE,"* thus celebrating on the obverse the very usurper who abolished the Republic it invokes on the reverse. France's *res publica* had become a *res privata* or *res familia*, and the republican *ARF* had morphed into the imperial *Grande Armée* whose purpose was no longer to defend the *RF* but to expand the Bonapartean *dynastic empire*. There is historical precedence for such eyewash: the *imperial* Roman legions continued to carry before them the *republican* standard *SPQR* long after the Republic had de facto ceased to exist. On *Napoléons* minted before 1805, the legend on the obverse reads *"NAPOLEON PREMIER CONSUL,"* on those minted from 1809 onwards, the legend on its reverse, *"EMPIRE FRANÇAIS,"* so that this oxymoron only prevailed for a few years, which, however, *Krug*'s action falls into precisely.

274   Kleist in October 1807 in a letter to Ulrike makes crystal clear what he thinks of this Prussian currency: "*Übrigens muß es* Konventionsgeld *sein, d.h. der* Wert *davon, gleichviel in welcher Münzart, wenn nur* nicht preußisch." Wolf Kittler's musings about the *Geusenpfennig* miss Kleist's point entirely: this short-lived revolutionary *silver* currency typically featured the image of a pauper's bag or cup, scarcely a symbol soldiers anywhere risk their lives for; psychologically is was far more effective to pay them in *gold* coin featuring a Jovian Napoleon—a *proven winner*. Kleist evidently knew of the *Geusen* (cf. V.682-7), and presumably of their penney—perhaps from Schiller's *Geschichte des Abfalls der Niederlande*—, but he advocates a currency issued by a legitimate, powerful souverain, not a bunch of revolutionaries, featuring his portrait, not a pauper's bag, and minted in gold, not silver.

275   In view of the gold, Auguste offers Napoleon her allegiance and her body: "*ich... erkenne!*" ("I recognise") is distinct by a single syllable from "*ich... anerkenne!*" ("I acknowledge," namely Napoleon as legitimate ruler), as well as from "*ich... kenne!*" ("I know," in the biblical sense, i.e., she signals her readiness to be penetrated by him). David E. Wellbery, in "Das Spiel der Geschlechterdifferenz," in Walter Hinderer (Ed.), *Interpretationen. Kleists Dramen* (Stuttgart: Reclam, 1997), 28, accuses Adam of trying to take advantage, in seeking Eve's favours, of the *droit du seigneur*, but fails to extend his accusation to Walter, who here obtains from Eve those very same "favours."

276   Jochen Schmidt's assertion (*Kleist*, 77), that in the *Variant*'s ending Eve merely relates facts everyone already knows, is untenable, for she here furbishes details not present in the book version; as such the *Variant* provides a "key" for decrypting the book version.

277   Before in *Käthchen* and elsewhere exploring scenarios involving Habsburg, Hohenzollern and Romanov brides, Kleist here alludes to a scenario in which Napoleon seeks a Wittelsbach solution to his succession problem, though not by marrying a Wittelsbach princess outright, but by foisting his seed on Beauharnais' wife. Kleist became increasingly adventurous, not to say fantastical, in his scenarios for both Napoleon's and his own *filial* quests. "*Ich will ein' Klein', und krieg ein' Klein', und sollts auch durch die Hint'tür sein.*" An obstinate artist of life—what do you say to that?

278   Eberhard Siebert notes (*Kleistiana Collecta*, 120) in the context of *Homburg*, not realising that what he has to say is far more relevant in that of *Krug*,

that on 2nd September 1806 (three days after Kleist urgently seeks to communicate his *Krug* manifesto to Fr. Wilh. via Marie and Luise—if the MS ever reached the King, then presumably not before 2nd September), a memorandum inspired by Prince Louis Ferd., written by Joh. von Müller, and signed by prominent members of the "war party" (tacitly endorsed by Queen Luise—cf. Siebert, *ibid*, 126), including several Hohenzollern princes, the minister Stein, and the generals Rüchel, Schmettau and Pfull, urged the King to dismiss his cabinet (considered excessively Francophile) and to mobilise. Siebert suggests that the King was exasperated at this memorandum because, himself "of mediocre talent," he disdained the competition from the "more richly gifted" Louis Ferd. The King nevertheless relented, and on 27th September issued the ultimatum to Napoleon that precipitated the war. Kleist may have felt that Luise, rather than Louis Ferd., had a lot to do with this fateful decision. Kleist's advice to his King was always nuanced and tailored to circumstances, never ideological or generic—e.g., *Krug*: "create readiness first—600,000 men, appropriate funding, allies lined up—, then strike"; *Hermannsschlacht*: "strike immediately, while Napoleon is tied up in Spain," by combining conventional and guerrilla warfare; *Homburg*: "do not side with Napoleon, for the French wolf will not hesitate to sacrifice the Prussian deer to the Russian bear." Incidentally, Joh. von Müller, having in September 1806 written the bellicose memorandum to Fr. Wilh., by early January 1807 had changed sides and become a Bonapartean lackey, to Gentz immense chagrin (cf. *AML*, 207; 208; 212); A. Müller and Kleist appear to have been pragmatic about his turncoating (cf. *AML*,259 and Jakob Baxa's note thereto).

279   Parallels between *Krug* and *Marquise* include, e.g., the topoi of lost innocence and possible violation, the question of who is the father, the inquisitional or juridicial method of inquiry, and phrases and figures of speech such as *"einen Fehltritt... verzeihen"*; *"Ich will nichts... wissen"*; *"gleich der Mutter / eröffnet"*; *"der Garten bei dir offen?"*; *"laß er die Hand mir weg"*; etc. *Krug*'s *satyrical* passages include:

- *"Der dem Stock / Jetzt seinen Rücken bieten wird"* (V.473-4);
- *"Nehmt meine ganze / Sparbüchse hin"* (V.482-3);
- [Frau Marthe to Adam] *"Ihr guckt / Mir alle Sonntag in die Fenster ja"* (V.580-1);
- [Frau Marthe] *"am Abend / Und schon die Lamp im Bette wollt ich löschen"* (V.745-6);
- *"Als... ein Tumult, / In meiner Tochter abgelegnen Kammer"* (V.747);
- *"Der [Ruprecht] trotzt, wie toll, Euch in des Zimmers Mitte"* (V.757);

- *"Am Fenster... bleibst du auch draußen...?"* (V.885-6);
- [Ruprecht] *"und drück... / Da ich der Dirne Tür, verriegelt finde, / Gestemmt, mit Macht, auf einen Tritt, sie ein"* (V.967-8);
- *"Denn da Frau Marthe jetzt ins Zimmer tritt, die Lampe hebt"* (V.1027-8);
- *"In meine Kammer / ließ ich den Schuster, oder einen dritten"* (V.1156-7);
- *"Zu Kist' und Kasten hast du [Eve] ja die Schlüssel—"* (V.1313);
- *"Wer außer Ruprecht, geht [bei Frau Marthe] aus und ein?"* (V.1560);
- [Frau Marthe] *"Daß ich oft in meinem Haus ihn [Adam] sähe"* (V.1570);
- [Frau Marthe] *"In meinem Hause, das ihn [Adam] lockt"* (V.1605);
- [Walter to Eve] *"Steh auf, mein Kind"* (V.1951);
- *"Und Dint und Feder führ ich in der Tasche"* (V.2185);
- *"Ruprecht kracht ins Zimmer... und stößt mir vor die Brust—"* (V.2237-41);
- *"Die Mutter...hebt die Lamp und fällt... den Ruprecht /...an"* (V.2254-7);
- *"Wollt Ihr gefälligst Euch...— Sie treten alle ans Fenster"* (V.2407);
- *"Auf die Woche stell ich dort mich ein. Ende"* (V.2429).

Much of Kleist's *satyrical* vocabulary deployed in these passages I "translated" previously—e.g., stick, backside, window, lamp, chamber, door, the Third, box, key, in and out, house, stand, chest. Novel or noteworthy items include: the agglomeration *"Sparbüchse"* ("money box"), which may be decomposed into *"Büchse"* ("tin can," but pertinently also "rifle") and *"sparen"* ("to save," "to accumulate") to expliate its *satyrical* meaning, of a phallus about to ejaculate; Mathe's expression, *"die Lamp im Bette wollt ich löschen,"* which suggests that she prepared to masturbate; and the phrase, *"Dint und Feder führ ich in der Tasche"* ("ink and feather I keep in the pocket"), which depicts pulling on a condom.

280   Blamberger (*Kleist*, 253-67) elaborates the drama's comical and tragical (e.g., Sophoclean) elements. Yet the classical Aristotelian or modern conventional categories of "comedy" and "tragedy" fail to capture its essence, which, as said, owes its greatest debt to Aristophanean Old Comedy and to satyr play: Adam-Franz commits not so much a *tragic* error (the Aristotelian *harmatia*) as a *criminal* offense: the manner in which he liberally dishes out Braunschweig sausage (Hannover), Danzig liqueur (West Prussia), Rhenish (Rhineland) and Frankish (Ansbach and Bayreuth) wine and Limburg (Limburg and Cleves) cheese to Walter-Napoleon to protect his own turf is at best wantonly negligent. Underpinning his comical feast (*Schönbrunn, Pressburg*) is a Dionysiac-Maenadic *sparagmos*: Adam-Franz dishing out German lands to the

French conqueror is inversely equivalent to Hermann-Fr. Wilh. dishing out Hally's bodyparts to the German princes: Franz exploits *the German body* to appease the enemy, Fr. Wilh. *the German corpse* to rally his allies. Fr. Wilh.'s gesture both *inverses* and promises to *reverse* Franz's, symbolically returning to the German princes what Franz gave away, offering restitution and healing (*heile machen*: making whole); not only Penthesilea and Käthchen represent opposite poles on the same continuum—so arguably do Adam and Hermann. Kleist's poetic manipulation and camouflage, and his ironic disposition, make it possible that to this day the same audiences *laugh* at Adam's *sparagmos* of a living, still largely intact German body, while *balking in horror* at Hermann's *sparagmos* of an already dead, violated German corpse, where they obviously *ought* to be doing precisely the opposite: disdain Adam's liberal gifts to the enemy and cheer Hermann's hopeful promises to his people. The topos of the *HRR*'s *sparagmos* or emaciation pervades Kleist's œuvre (*Erdbeben*'s two exchangeable sons, *Kohlhaas*' two emaciated blacks, *Verlobung*'s spread-eagled Gustav) as much as that of *Borussia*'s or *Germania*'s rape by, or blind submission to, Napoleon (Alkmene, the Marquise, Achilles, Käthchen) and that of the rivalry and mutual laceration or castration of the two leading German dynasties (in *Schroffenstein, Guiskard, Krug, Zweikampf*). Klaus Kanzog notes (*Kleist*, 87-8) with respect to Kleist's *Lustspiele*: "Für A.W. Schlegel ist die *"Komödie"die höhere, das "Lustspiel"* die niedere Form, und beide sind, historisch gesehen, das Ergebnis einer Entwicklung, die in der Klassischen Philologie zur Unterscheidung zwischen *"Alter"* und *"Neuer Komödie"* führte. Repräsentant der *"Alten Komödie"* ist Aristophanes und ihr Kennzeichen die durch die *"athenische Freiheit"* ermöglichte *"demokratische Phantasie."* Die *"Neue Komödie"* dagegen ist Ausdruck einer zunehmenden Privatisierung und Verbürgerlichung... Im Hinblick auf die Lustspiel-Praxis Kleists verdienen zwei Kernsätze der Lustspiel-Theorie A.W. Schlegels besonders hervorgehoben zu werden: 1. Das Lustspiel... ist eine Mischung von Scherz und Ernst. 2. Das Lustspiel muß ein treues Gemählde gegenwärtiger Sitten, es muß local und national bestimmt sein." Kanzog does not appear to realise just how closely Kleist's *satirico-po(i)etical* project is associated with Aristophanes and "Athenian liberty."

281   In Luther's Bible translation (*Isaiah* 8,14) YHWH refers to himself as "*Stein des Anstoßes,*" "*Heiligtum,*" and "*Fels des Ärgernisses*" for the two houses of Israel. Fichte defines "*Anstoß*" as a resistance to the free activity of the I, a limit which the I encounters and in confrontation with which it recognises its finitude and becomes self-concious, but Kleist has in mind not so much a metaphorical or spiritual repulse as a physical impulse or compulsion. Kleist's "oak paradox" alludes to the same nexus.

282   In *Marquise* Count F "mounts" a horse. *Bettelweib*'s *"hinter den Ofen"* (II:196) is even more explicit than Krug's *"Am Ofen,"* and can easily be decodified as *"den offenen Hintern."*

283   In the lines *"Im dritten trinkt man mit den Tropfen Sonnen, / Und Firmamente mit den übrigen"* (V.1534-5), "Sun" may refer to ecstatic *jouissance* and "Milky Way" to seminal production. Pythagoras taught that everything in the universe has a three-part structure and that every problem in the universe is reducible diagrammatically to a triangle or the number three.

284   Ewald Georg (Jürgen) von Kleist (1700-1748) accumulated electricity in an alcohol-filled bottle with a nail inserted in the cork (far left image), but did not realise that his hand holding the bottle comprised a key part of the set-up, functioning as electrode. Researchers at Leiden University discovered the latter principle and improved Kleist's design, with metal plating replacing the conductive function of the hand (second from left image). Further improvements incorporate a simple generator (right and far right images): "The static electricity produced by the rotating glass sphere electrostatic generator was conducted by the chain through the suspended bar to the water in the glass held by assistant Andreas Cuneus. A large charge accumulated in the water and an opposite charge in Cuneus' hand on the glass. When he touched the wire dipping in the water, he received a powerful shock"—cf. https://en.wikipedia.org/wiki/Leyden_jar. Chr. Ernst Wünsch's description of the Kleistian or Leyden jar in *Kosmologische Unterhaltungen* could have been Kleist's source (cf. Debriacher, *Rede*, 67; *KH*,266). Kleist himself mentions a Kleistan jar once, in the essay *Allmähliche Verfertigung...* (1805/6; cf. II:925), in the context of Mirabeau's twitching upper lip triggering the French Revolution: *"dadurch, daß er sich, einer Kleistischen Flasche gleich, entladen hatte, war er nun wieder neutral geworden, und gab, von der Verwegenheit zurückgekehrt, plötzlich der Furcht vor dem Chatelet, und der Vorsicht, Raum"* (II:321); Mirabeau's twitching exemplifies a pattern of Kleistian characters suddenly supercharging into action before just as suddenly falling back into lethargy or complacency.

285   Benjamin Franklin, who reportedly first coined the term "battery" for an arrangement of Leyden jars (cf. left-hand image) indeed likened it to an artillery battery, i.e., an arrangement of cannons. Re Napoleon's *Grande batterie*, cf. Sloterdijk (*Kritik*, 413-4): *"je verheerender eine Waffe schon auf Distanz wirkt, desto feiger dürfen im Prinzip ihre Träger sein... Hieraus resultierte der*

strategische Primat der Artillerie,... die... aus gedeckter Stellung und großer Distanz die schlimmsten Wirkungen hervorbringt... Napoleon war nicht umsonst ein Repräsentant dieser 'denkenden' Gattung."

286   The ancient Greeks already observed the phenomenon of triboelectric charge (Gr. *"tribo"* = "rub"), which Otto von Guerike in the 16th century first generated artificially, though lacking a device to store the electricity produced, which the Kleistian jar provided a century later. All four Kleist biographers I regularly consult—Blamberger, Loch, Michalzik, Schulz—fail to list Ewald Georg (Jürgen) von Kleist in their respective register of names, even if they mention the inventor in their text, as does Blamberger, or in a footnote, as does Michalzik, and even though they list a host of other Kleist family members. Jürgen Daiber in his *KH* entry about natural sciences mentions the inventor (cf. 266) alongside other inventors in the field of electricity, but *KH*'s editor Ingo Breuer, presumably responsible for *KH*'s register of names, confounds the inventor with the poet Ewald Christian von Kleist (cf. 489): of the six references to "Ewald Georg von Kleist" he lists, only Daiber's refers to the inventor (the others to the poet). Blamberger (*Kleist*, 60) on a single page mentions the inventor twice, but under two slightly different names, Ewald Jürgen von Kleist and Ewald von Kleist (the most commonly used name for the inventor is Ewald Georg von Kleist). All this confusion and negligence is due to the simple fact that the importance of the Kleistian jar for Kleist's works in general, and for *Krug* in particular, has been very largely overlooked (Gudrun Debriacher's essay being a partial exception). Kleist's Eve could in part have been inspired by Martial's favourite "slut" (*Epigrams*, trans. Gideon Nisbet, 4.4) Leda, who is equipped with a "guttering lamp" (*ibid.*) and a "broken wine-jug" (3.82) from which the lovers "drink." Martial's Leda is unequivocally an effeminate youth, whereas Kleist's Eve has to be "amphibian," since his story incorporates the topos of impregnation.

287   Kleist in *Marionettentheater* equates "puppet" and *"Gliedermann"* (dildo, penile prosthesis), and across his works, "hands" and members. *Krug*'s *"scheuern"* ("rubbing"), *Marionettentheater*'s *"streifen"* ("brushing"), and *Bettelweib*'s *"glitschen"* ("skidding," "slithering") all depict movements produced by (organic or inorganic) phalloi, and as such are closely related to *Marquise*'s *"Hier—traf er, da"* and *Prolog*'s *"Hier jetzt lenke, jetzt dort"* movements, which depict erections and penetrations, as a passage in *Marionettentheater* makes clear: *"die Glieder, welche nichts als Pendel wären, folgten, ohne irgend ein Zutun, auf eine mechanische Weise von selbst"* (II:339).

"Brushing" even in today's usage may denote penile rubbing against a partner's prostrate (the "male G-spot") through the anal wall, and although the term "G-spot" (after the physician Ernst Gräfenberg who first described it) came into usage only in the 1950s, and today's usage of the term "brushing" is probably only coincidentally linked with Kleist's, Kleist's understanding of the anal and abdominal atanomy, gained in practical observation, was perhaps not inferior to Gräfenberg's. The terms *"Scheuern," "streifen," "glitschen"* exemplify Kleist's uncanny ability to re-function everyday terms for the most plastic, expressionistic scenes. The erotic device he invents in *Krug* has its 20th Century correlates in the "excessive machine" in Roger Vladim's *Barbarella* (1968), the futuristic sexploitation instruments in Just Jaecklin's *Gwendoline* (1984), and the pleasure chamber in Russel Hoban's *Fremder* (1996).

288   Gentz, in a letter to A. Müller probably dated late October 1805, represents the *Ulm Campaign's* staccato of battles in a—curiously Kleistian—rhythmical vein: *"Am 8., 9., 12., 13., 14., 15., 16., 17., jeden Tag eine Schlacht. Aber der 14. War der dies nefandus! Da ging Ulm, Memmingen und mehr als 24 Bataillons verloren! O Gott! Und wir* [the Prussians] *konnten es hindern!"* (*AML*,130).

289   Adam's "club foot" and "monument" mirror Kleist's oak paradox (cf. *Penthesilea*, V.3040-3), with the prosthesis corresponding to the died off oak, the club foot to the healthy oak ravaged by the storm (disease). Adam-Franz's *satyrical* "foot issue"—henceforce he may partake in satyr dances (orgies) only with his diseased member, being unable to reattach a wooden prosthesis to his injured leg stump—mirrors his *satirical* conundrum: henceforce he may appear in the ballrooms and on the battlefields of Europe only as the diminished ruler of Austria. Kleist misses no opportunity to deride this "sinister," "devilish," "deformed" political entity (a hundred years later, in WWI, Austria would indeed become a veritable *Klotz am Bein*, albatross around the neck, for Germany) and ironises Franz's conviction that his diseased "left foot" is still "good for dancing" (*satirically* and *satyrically*). In *A True History* (Book 1) Lucian's space traveler refers to a race of "Tree-men" who are equipped with artificial genitals, of ivory or of wood, which serve them in having intercourse with their mates.

290   In *Marionettentheater*, which Kleist may have composed just as he prepared *Krug* for publication, to which it relates almost like a companion essay, Kleist praises the superiority of inorganic prosthetic members or dildos specifically in overcoming a lover's *"Ziererei"*: *"jenen mechanischen Beinen... Der Kreis ihrer Bewegungen ist zwar*

beschränkt; doch diejenigen, die ihnen zu Gebote stehen, vollziehen sich mit einer Ruhe, Leichtigkeit und Anmut, die jedes denkende Gemüt in Erstaunen setzen" (II:341).

291   In picturing his courtroom scene, Kleist may have drawn on still lifes and vanitas paintings he observed in the Kassel and Dresden galleries. Re the "snorting cat," cf. Bäumler (*Amors vergifteter Pfeil*, 47): *"der Speichel floß ohne Unterlaß aus dem Mund, gleich von Anfang so furchtbar stinkend und so ansteckend, daß er alles sofort verunreinigte und besudelte."* The visual, auditory, olfactory and haptic "special effects" Kleist incorporated into his script could have been inspired by *phantasmagoria*, a type of horror theatre that deployed magic lanterns projecting frightening images such as skeletons, demons, and ghosts onto walls, smoke or screens, as well as spooky decorations, light and sound effects, sensory stimulations such as smells and electric shocks, and even fasting, fatigue (late shows) and drugs in order to manipulate spectators. The shows started under the guise of séances in Germany in the late 18th century and gained popularity through most of Europe throughout the 19th century (cf. https://en.wikipedia.org/wiki/Phantasmagoria).

292   The first medical treatment involving electricity was recorded at Middlesex Hospital in London in 1767; in 1790 Luigi Galvani inaugurated systematic therapies based on "animal electricity"; in 1803 his nephew Giovanni Aldini in London publicly demonstrated electro-stimulation or "galvanisation." Gudrun Debriacher in her helpful overview of Kleist's context with respect to medical techniques, electricity, magnetism and anthropology (*Die Rede der Seele*, 66-7) notes that both Kleistian jars and influence machines (*Elektrisiermaschinen*) were used for medical therapy in Kleist's day.

293   Cf. http://www.cabinetmagazine.org/issues/21/turner.php. Kleist and Pfuel passed through Lyon in the autumn of 1803 en route to Paris; possibly Kleist experienced his first *baquet* there, Lyon together with Strasbourg then being the leading centre of magnetism (which may explain their detour: the route via Neuchâtel would have been significantly shorter than that via Geneva and Lyon).

294   In *Kohlhaas*, Count Kallheim refers to the situation as a *"Zauberkreis[e], in dem man befangen"* (II:51); in *Emigrant* I argued that *satirically* the "Zauberkreis" may refer to Austria's encirclement by France; here I add that *syphilitically* it may imply that The Elector and his courtège are undertaking a *baquet* session.

295   Cf. https://en.wikipedia.org/wiki/Franz_Mesmer.

296   Copper may tinge ordinary light green, and if copper wires are used in electro-magnetic apparatuses, green light or vapour may be observed. Mercury-vapour lamps, whose functioning is based on electric discharge in mercury vapour, also produce a greenish light, an effect first recorded in 1835 (cf. https://en.wikipedia.org/wiki/Mercury-vapor_lamp), but possibly observed earlier. The phenomena of fluorescence and phosphorescence were known, respectively, since the 16th and the early 17th century. Cf. Gotthilf Heinr. Schubert in *Ansichten von der Nachtseite der Naturwissenschaft* (1808): *"Auch für das menschliche Daseyn scheint sich zuletzt die Befreyung von dem Planeten auf eine ähnliche Weise nach Außen kund zu geben, und vielleicht ist die Geschichte unserer letzten Verwandlung, schon mit dem Erscheinen des Phosphors geendet."* In so far as Kleist had Schubert in mind, he may have envisaged the magnetised, electrified Eve momentarily entering a supra-natural state akin to that of a goddess or apparition.

297   Teniers Jr. was prolific—c.800 of his paintings are extant—and Kleist could have encountered his (and other) notorious works in 1795 in Kassel's Gemäldegalerie, in 1800 and 1801 in Dresden's Gemäldegalerie, and in 1801 and 1803 in the Louvre. Gernot Müller, in *Man müßte auf dem Gemälde selbst stehen. Kleist und die bildende Kunst* (Tübingen: Franke, 1995). 124, n.44, notes: *"In zahlreichen Kasseler Niederländern scheint Kleists sich heranbildender Dorfrichter als Pan, Satyr und Bacchus vorgebildet. An den schuldig-unschuldigen Satyr in Gestalt des klump- bzw. bocksfüßigen Adam erinnern Jacob Jordaens 'Bacchus mit Gefolge', 'Die Kindheit des Jupiter', 'Der Satyr beim Bauern', sowief Gérard Lairesse, 'Bacchus mit Gefolge'."*

298   When Kleist tells Wilhelmine in 1801, *"Ich will im eigentlichsten Verstande ein Bauer werden"* (II:695), he means in the first instance "satyr" (member of a "brotherhood"), yet since *"Bauer"* ("peasant," "farmer") encompasses the notion of "builder," ""creator," he evidently also means that he will seek to fulfill his *familial* and *po(i)etical* aspirations alongside the *satyrical*: the Kleistian *"Bauer"* is to be satyr, patriarch and bard, he who "cultivates" lovers, children and dramas.

299   In *Butcher Shop* it is the strategically placed white loincloth that gives the allusion away, in *In the Kitchen* it is the carcass' aspect, which recalls famous depictions of Christ on the cross (cf. prominent examples by Rubens and Scorzelli). I argue in

Emigrant (67-8 and *passim*) that two ways of seeing, later theorised by Wittgenstein's as *"seeing this"* and *"seeing as"* and exemplified by the famous "duck-rabbit illusion," underpins the compossibility of Kleist's *overt* and *covert* stories.

300   Arnd Beise (*KH*,254) suggests that Teniers' *Fête flamande oder die lustige Hahnreyschaft*, displayed in Dresden, could have influenced *Amphitryon*; this is possible, but Teniers' influence on Kleist may have been much more far-ranging.

301   In addition to the Teniersian and Raphaelian aspects, Zschokke's recollection (cf. *LS*,67a), that the friends, in observing Le Veau's engraving at his apartment, discerned a "sad pair of lovers, a nagging mother with a broken majolica-jug and a big-nosed judge," suggests that Kleist's characters feature aspects of stock characters found in *commedia dell'arte*: the *innamorati*, the *ruffiana*, the *pulcinella*, the *pantalone*; James M. McGlathery's suggestion (*Desire's Sway*, 51-62) that Kleist in *Krug* applied style elements and vocabulary from *commedia dell'arte* and its derivatives—*burlesque, opera buffa, comédie lamoyante* and *opéra comique*—is plausible. The fact that Napoleon upon his conquest of Italy in 1797 outlawed *commedia dell'arte*, evidently fearing that the irreverent comedy, like the carnival he also outlawed, could become a platform for dissent against his régime, would have intrigued Kleist, who may have sought to take a swipe at the Prussian authorities for approving only harmless *Rührstücke* for Berlin's stages. David E. Wellbery parallels (*Geschlechterdifferenz*, 21) Adam and Licht with stock characters in the comedy of late antiquity: *alazon* (boaster) and *eiron* (ironic-clever). Adam has also been compared with the German comedy's stock character *Hanswurst*, a coarse, half-cunning, half-doltish figure originally found in Sebastian Brant's *Ship of Fools* (1519).

302   Cf. Sigmund Freud, "Leonardo da Vinci and a Memory of his Childhood," in: *The Uncanny*. Trans. David McLintock (New York: Penguin, 2003), 72.

303   Kleist visited Dresden's Gemäldegalerie repeatedly, including with Brockes in September 1800, with Ulrike and Karoline (and Henriette?) von Schlieben in May 1801, with Fouqué in the spring of 1803, and again during 1808/9, on each occasion adapting his relationship with Raphael's masterpiece. In 1800, just weeks prior to "the most important day of my life in Würzburg," its immaculate aspect merely exacerbated his pain; in 1801 the same aspect fortified him in his "alternative family model" with Wilhelmine or one of the Schlieben sisters (cf. II:650-1; 659; cf

below's section *The Familial*); in 1803, according to Joh. Daniel Falk's recollection, he downplayed Raphael's *Madonna* in favour of another (unnamed) master's (cf. Michalzik, *Kleist*, 223); his comments à propos of *Krug* suggest that in Dresden he renewed his appreciation for Raphael's painting. What these oscillations in Kleist's reception of the painting show is that he experienced objects through the lens of his subjective state at the given moment, making them, as it were, mirrors of his soul. Kleist reproduces his Raphael fantasy with *Erdbeben*'s "holy family"—Jeronimo, Josephe and the infant Philipp—underneath the pomegranate tree, with *Der Engel am Grabe des Herrn*'s angel and two Marias before Christ's tomb, and perhaps with many of the triadic or quaternary constellations that recur throughoug his œuvre. The Kleist reception has paralleled *Erdbeben*'s scene with popular depictions of the holy family resting on their flight to Egypt, and not only is this analogy valid, but also does it give credence to Falk's recollection that Kleist during a certain period favoured another Madonna which could have been Leonardo's, as Kleist could have seen in at the Louvre in 1801. Ilse Graham's suggestion (*Titelheld*, 294) that Kleist was seduced by "*die leidenschaftliche Beschäftigung mit jener transzendenten Anmut, die durch Raphaels Namen bezeichnet ist*" is unKleistian.

304   Ernst Ribbart, "Babylon in Huisum oder der Schein des Scheins. Sprach- und Rechtsprobleme in Heinrich von Kleists Lustspiel 'Der zerbrochne Krug,'" in Grathoff (Ed.), *Kleist*, 133-48.

305   *Krug*'s genesis, spanning nine years, can be divided into five distinct stages: firstly, an initial period of several years which perhaps entailed his production of a first sketch in 1802, his dictation of the first three scenes to Pfuel in the summer of 1803, and his crafting the forth and fifth scenes in early 1805 in response to Napoleon's coronation; secondly, the first half of 1806, covering the aftermath of *Austerlitz*, the *Rheinbund*'s secession and the *HRR*'s dissolution, during which Kleist may have produced the seven central scenes that comprise almost two-thirds of the drama's length; thirdly, the month of August 1806, when he may have been frantically reworking the twelfth scene in view of Fr. Wilh.'s mobilisation; fourthly, early 1808 in which he published *Ph* fragment in the wake of the Weimar débâcle; and finally, early 1811, when he published of the final version together with the *Variant*.

306   Cf. Kleist's well-known statements in this respect about himself: *"Ich kann ein Differentiale finden, und einen Vers machen"* (1805; II:750); *"Man könnte*

die Menschen in zwei Klassen abteilen; in solche, die sich auf eine Metapher und 2) in solche, die sich auf eine Formel verstehen. Deren, die sich auf beides verstehn, sind zu wenige, sie Machen keine Klasse aus" (1810; II:338).

307   Of A. Müller Hans-Jochen Marquardt writes in his introduction to *AML*: "[Müller] gelangte, auch unter dem Eindruck der napoleonischen Fremdherrschaft, zu einer Auffassung, welche die Literatur, historisch begründet, in den gesamten Lebenskontext einer Nation einbettete... Sein Ideal bestand in der lebendigen Vermittlung der Gegensätze in einer realitätsbezogenen, organischen literarischen Kommunikationssphäre, innerhalb derer dem Publikum als historisch-konkretem, schöpferischen Subjekt der Rezeption die gleiche Bedeutung wie dem Werk selbst zukomme... So definierte Müller 'Poesie' als 'geschlossene Kunstdarstellung des Lebens durch das Wort'... er ging den Schritt zur Auffassung von Dichtung als einem historischen Kommunikations- und Wirkungszusammenhang... in bewusster Abgrenzung vom vorgefundenen Mythos der Kunstproduktion als eines Schöpferaktes sui generis. Müllers deutliche Aufwertung des Rezipienten... war wesentlich auch der geschichtlichen Situation Deutschlands... geschuldet. So bemaß er die Wirkung der Kunst... daran, inwieweit sie für die historisch besondere Situation des Individuums unter konreten gegebenen Umständen als Triebkraft wirken solle und müsse... Hervorgehoben wurden von ihm vor allem solche Werke... welche die angestrebte Versöhnung von 'Ökonomie', hier verstanden als Topos der bürgerlichen Alltagsphäre und des politisch-realen Lebens, und 'Poesie' beförderten, so die Funktion des Narren oder der Monologe in Shakespeares Dramen, die Bedeutung des Chors, der Masken und des Satyrspiels für die antike Bühne, das Extemporieren in der italienischen Volkskomödie oder das Werk des Hans Sachs als Beispiel für die Einheit von Dichtkunst und nationaler Emanzipation." Clearly, Müller's and Kleist's interests significantly overlapped and there will have been a fair amount of mutual influence, Kleist's praxis shaping Müller's theory and vice versa; no wonder Müller was excited about *Amphitryon* even before meeting Kleist in person, and they became close collaborators in the *Ph* project.

308   Regarding the drama's completion, the first hypothesis is supported by Samuel and Brown (*Kleist's Lost Year*, 90), who assume that Kleist completed *Amphitryon* in March 1807, the second by Blamberger (*Kleist*, 250), Loch, (*Kleist*, 524), Schmidt (*Kleist*, 95), and Stephens (*Kleist. The Dramas*, 72), The latter hypothesis resting primarily on the fact that Kleist wrote to Ulrike on 31st December 1806 that he had sent MSS to Berlin (likely to Rühle), among them probably *Erdbeben*

and *Krug*, as well as possibly *Amphitryon* or *Marquise* (cf. *LS*,148; 152). Anne Fleig (*KH*,41) considers it "proven" that Kleist sent the *Amphitryon* MS to Rühle, insisting that Kleist must have completed the drama by the beginning of 1807 because on 10th March, in a letter from Joux (cf. II:1049), he requested Chr. M. Wieland to bring a few MSS to print, and while Kleist does not name *Amphitryon*, he does so in another letter to Wieland, of 17th December 1807 (cf. II:799), in which he tells him that he had written to him twice from Joux (only one of the two letters he says he wrote is extant) requesting this service from him. Regarding the drama's commencement, Kleist may have first encountered the Amphitryon topos in 1803 in conversation with Joh. Daniel Falk, whose *Amphitruon* was published in 1804 (cf. Blamberger, *Kleist*, 272), which however does not necessarily mean, as Sembdner (cf. I:928; also *In Sachen Kleist*, 23-52) and Loch (cf. *Kleist*, 225; 523) assume, that he commenced his drama at that time (Sembdner may nevertheless be correct saying that Falk could have had a significant influence on Kleist—cf. *ibid*, 46). Loch (*Kleist*, 150) plausibly suggests that Kleist could have already encountered Molière's comedy in 1801/2 when Zschokke was preparing a translation of several of Molière's works, though not *Amphitryon* (cf. also Rahmer, *Kleist*, 92)—I consider Loch's aside (*ibid*, 154),"*Die Schweizer Verhältnisse und die Persönlichkeit Zschokkes haben vermutlich mehr in Kleist, in seiner Entwicklung und in seiner Dichtung, ausgelöst, als bislang erkannt worden ist*," as noteworthy as Sembdner's regarding Falk's influence.

309   Peter Szondi showed that Kleist eliminated Molière's societal concerns, which referred to the France of Louis XIV, and upgraded Sosias' role, as well as Alkmene's (cf. Jochen Schmidt, *Kleist*, 91; 101).

310   Cf. the section "*Nabel* and *Auslassung*" in my *Awakening Child* (331-50) for a discussion of Kleist's use of ellipses as a means to at once hide-cum-highlight key developments.

311   Astonishingly, the Kleist reception does not appear to have noticed that Amphitryon suffers *defeat* in battle, even though on close reading this is patently the case, and Kleist scholars such as Bernard Greiner have correctly discerned Jena-Auerstedt in Sosias' description—cf. his *Eine Art Wahnsinn. Dichtung im Horizont Kants* (Berlin: E. Schmidt, 1994), 167. Günter Blamberger (*Kleist*, 279-80) comes close to perceiving it, but cannot convince himself to accept its plausibility: "*[A.] Müllers Interpretation, dass Amphitryon nicht nur als Liebhaber vor Alkmene, sondern*

"*ebenso wohl*" *als Heerführer vor seinem Volk* "*zu schanden werde*," *ist vom Text her kaum begründbar, sie verleiht dem Stück vielmehr erst ein zeitgeschichtliches Potential, insofern sie den Leser nicht mehr an die Dreierkonstellation Amphitryon, Jupiter, Alkmene denken läßt, sondern an eine gänzlich andere: an den schwachen Heerführer Friedrich Wilhelm III., an seine Gattin Luise, die Napoleon wie Zar Alexander I. als Unterhändlerin zu faszinieren weiß. In jeder Hinsicht zweideutig wären dann Jupiters Abschiedsworte an Alkmene nach der Liebesnacht:* "*Und besser wird es ein Geheimnis bleiben [...] Die Welt könnt ihn mißdeuten, diesen Raub*" [Blamberger quotes V.416-20]. *Ob Kleist selbst eine solche Parallele von Alkmene und Luise wirklich* "*gewollt*" *hätte, darf man angesichts seiner Verehrung Luises füglich bezweifeln.*" Blamberger even quotes a passage that clearly supports Müller's assertion, yet his unflinching faith in the widely-held myth of "Kleist's veneration for Luise" prevents him from accepting the textual evidence. As recently as 2013 Anne Fleig (*KH*,44) still refers to Sosia's "message of victory."

312   Cf. Burkert, *Greek Religion*, 128: "Here, too [in the *Gigantes*' battle against the Olympian gods], it is Zeus with his thunderbolt who decides the day… it is Zeus who gives victory. Every tropaion, that monument draped with booty on the battle field, can be called an image of Zeus… The power of the strongest of gods is manifest not only in battle and victory, but also in inexhaustible sexual potency." In antiquity, proper war preparations encompassed above all securing divine support—cf. the impressive line-up of gods on both sides in Homer's *Iliad*.

313   Sosias leaves the battlefield at midnight (cf. V.18). Unlike Pheidippides, the famed runner of Marathon, he walks the distance slowly and hesitantly (cf. V.639) and arrives at Amphitryon's palais, still bathed in moonlight (cf. V.6), at about 5 o'clock according to the tower clock (cf. V.112). Jupiter soon emerges from the palace and prepares to leave, cogniscent that Aurora will appear soon (cf. V.507; 824), which suggests that sunrise is at about 6 o'clock. According to Merkur, the "endless" night encompassed seventeen hours (cf. V.520; for the passionate Alkmene these felt like two—cf. V.442), so that Jupiter, aided by Phoebus, Aurora and Selene ("*die gute Göttin Kupplerin*"; V.519), added five hours to the regular twelve hours between dusk and dawn, while putting the Thebans into prolonged sleep (cf. V.216; 520); Merkur, accordingly, set the clock back by five hours, in case someone woke up and checked the clock. Sosias walks for ten hours, and having left the battlefield at midnight, expects to arrive at the palace at 10 o'clock—hence his amazement that it is still dark

(cf. V.111). According to Alkmene, Jupiter arrived at the palais at dusk, i.e., at 6 o'clock on the previous evening (cf. V.807), so that, assuming that he transports himself near-instantaneously, Jupiter will have set off from the battlefield six hours prior to Sosias. In Greek mythology Hermes (Merkur) is ascribed the power to put men to sleep with his magic staff; Kleist adds a comical element by letting him manipulate the tower clock instead, which is of course anachronistic: in ancient Greece it should have been a sun dial.

314   In this respect Amphitryon anticipates *Zweikampf*'s Trota (*Trottel* = oaf), defeated in the duel when he stumbles over his own spores, which in a combat on foot he shouldn't have put on in the first place.

315   Jochen Schmidt, *Kleist*, 95. There is a veritable "school of apologists" for Kleist's female characters, including but not limited to Alkmene. Ricarda Schmidt, in "Manipulation, Liebe und Gewalt," in Ricarda Schmidt et al (Ed.), *Unverhoffte Wirkungen*, 208, makes the unhedged claim, *"Denn Alkmene ist eine treue Ehefrau, der Ehebruch nicht im Traume einfallen würde. Für Alkmene ist vielmehr die Ehe die Sittliche Grundlage dafür, daß der Leidenschaft freier Lauf gelassen werden kann. Sie erwidert Jupiters List mit der ihr zur zweiten Natur gewordenen Haltung der Gattenliebe,"* and Lawrence Ryan, in "in der Götter Namen teilnehmend fühlen," in Yixu Lü et al, *Wissensfiguren im Werk Heinrich von Kleists* (Freiburg i.Br.: Rombach, 2012), 61, jumps to a similar conclusion: *"'Lästig' ist ihr nämlich der 'Ruhm' Amphitryons, der ihr 'so viel Fremdes' aufdrängt, während sie iherseits nur für ihn lebt: 'Was brauchen wir, als nur uns selbst?'"* (V.423-41). There is, however, no evidence that Alkmene "lives only for (Amphitryon)," and her words are addressed not to Amphitryon but to Jupiter in the guise of Amphitryon, so that the issue comes down to whether one believes her to be ignorant of her lover's divine identity or not (I have sought to show that she is not). Even Wolf Kittler, so rigorous in his analysis of Kleist's political agendas, is plainly naïve regarding Kleist's female characters: à propos of the central scene II/5 he claims (*Geburt*, 75-6): *"Was sich hier vor dem allwissenden Jupiter enthüllt, ist das große Geheimnis namens Frau. Die Szene ist eines der vielen inquisitorischen Rituale, in denen Kleist das Absolutum der weiblichen Unschuld demonstriert."* Among Kleist's biographers the same pattern commenced with Wilbrandt (cf. his notes re the Marquise and Alkmene in *Kleist*, 226 and 232-3) and culminated with Michalzik: *"[Alkmene] liebt ihren Amphitryon so sehr, wie wenn er ein Gott wäre"* (*Kleist*, 244). As I seek to show, the textual evidence suggests

that Alkmene is anything but "innocent," "ignorant" or "blameless," and that Kittler's claim (*Geburt*, 80) that "*Die Schuld haben die Männer, den Schmerz aber hat Alkmene*" is plainly untenable ("guilt" is distributed across several characters, and "pain" accrues above all to Amphitryon). Not Kleist's female characters are "naïve" (Helbling, *Major Works*, 123), but some Kleist scholars are, who appear to be unable or unwilling to entertain the possibility that Kleistian women are no mere "*Damen ohne Unterleib*" (Jürgen Schröder), nor Fichtean supplements to their husbands. Kleist evidently was *more* "modern" than some of his readers are two centuries later. At least Peter Stangele (*Kleist. Sein Leben*, 91) admits that not only Jupiter, but also Alkmene may have enjoyed that endless night. And why not?

316   Merleau-Ponty, "The Visible and the Invisible," in: Thomas Baldwin (Ed.), *Maurice Merleau-Ponty: Basic Writings* (London: Routledge, 2004), 256; 259.

317   Cf. Ortrud Gutjahr, "Unheimliche Heimkehr. Der Schauplatz des Anderen in Heinrich von Kleists Amphitryon," in Gutjahr (Ed.), *Heinrich von Kleist. Freiburger Literaturpsychologische Gespräche*, Vol. 27 (Würzburg: Königshausen & Neumann, 2008), 105. What apparently has not been noted is that "*i-ah*" (in German) is the ass' bray, and that later in the drama Kleist equates Alkmene with a jenny.

318   Jean Rotrous, *Les Sosies* (1638), quoted in Karlheinz Stierle, "Amphitryon. Die Komödie des Absoluten," in: Walter Hinderer (Ed.), *Interpretationen*, 43.

319   It is now nearly 12 o'clock noon regular time. Amphitryon and his entourage arrived before Thebes hard on the heels of Sosias, i.e., just after 5 o'clock (10 o'clock regular time), immediately setting up their camp outside the walls, where Sosias spends much of the two hours following his arrival (cf. V.1818) and where his conversation with Amphitryon takes place at 6 o'clock (11 o'clock regular time), just as Aurora awakens, Jupiter departs (perhaps lifted off the stage by a *machine*— cf. V.509), and Merkur sets the tower clock back to regular time. The time elapsed between the delayed sunrise and the back-to-normal noon is only one hour, which Sosias uses to prepare a luncheon banquet requested by Jupiter in the guise of Amphitryon before his departure (cf. V.1920). Cf. also Sloterdijk, *Sphären III*, 716 (my trans.): "The theatre machines of the Baroque, too, had discovered the dimension of height, and let Mercury with his winged feet, or Fortuna on her sphere, hover through the air above the heads of the audience."

320   "*Amphitryon vom Stock*" is a pertinent monicker for the ithyphallic, thunderbolt-wielding Jupiter, whose escapades with women—mortals and immortals—are legendary. Sosias must be cleverer than he seems: he not only unties the drama's "knot," but also wisely proposes to Amphitryon a face-saving solution, namely to take it as an honour that his wife was chosen by the mightiest of gods (this gesture already appears in the myth's earlier versions); Amphitryon initially rejects Sosias' proposition (cf. V.904), but relents when Jupiter's promises him a divine son.

321   Alkmene exclusively addresses Jupiter, never Amphitryon, with the terms *Geliebter* and *Gemahl*: ALKMENE [to Jupiter]: *Geliebter und Gemahl!* (V.488); *Mein Herr und Gemahl!* (V.1236); *O mein Gemahl!* (V.1264); *du Geliebter* (V.1271). Amphitryon, upon his return, she addresses thus: ALKMENE [To Amphitryon]: *So früh zurück—?* (V.782); *Ich weiß nicht— (V.793); Ich habe Müh, mein teurer Freund, zu fassen* (V.802); *Und du fragst noch!* (V.813); *Was das für Fragen sind!* (V.818). In short, she addresses Jupiter as lover, Amphitryon as "hubby" and gate crasher. Jupiter, on his part, equally addresses Alkmene far more passionately than does Amphitryon: *meine teuerste Alkmene* (V.410); *Geliebte!* (V.443); *teuerste Alkmene* (V.465); *Süßes Kind!* (V.507); *Mein schönes Weib!* (V.1245); *Mein großes Weib!* (V.1254); *Geliebte* (V.1268); *Teuerste* (V.1270); *Mein Augenstern!* (V.1277). However ambiguous the content of what is said may be: the language used is unambiguous, and it speaks volumes.

322   A "diamond harness" first appears in Kleist's "birthday letter" to Wilhelmine of 10th/11th October 1800 (cf. II:577) and similar implements recur in his dramas from time to time. Kleist could have gleaned the idea from Chr. M. Wieland's *Sympathien*: "*Mach dich stark, und lege um diese allzu zarte Brust, wie einen diamantenen Schild, den großen Gedanken: Ich bin für die Ewigkeit geschaffen*" (quoted in Sembdner, *Geschichte*, 409, n.116). A similar verbal duel (*agon*), between a philosopher and a sophist, takes place in the 3rd act of Aristophanes' *Clouds*; the sophist wins the duel. Kleist may also have had in mind a myth regarding the nymph Egeria, who supports Numa, King of Rome, in a battle of wits with Jupiter in which he seeks to gain protection from his thunderbolts.

323   The King's manifesto of 9th October explaining the declaration of war makes for fascinating reading, providing context for his decision to rush into war: http://www.documentarchiv.de/nzjh/preussen/1806/preussisches-manifest-gegen-frankreich.html

324   Gentz vehemently advocated that Prussia seek peace with Napoleon after *Eylau*—cf. *AML*,228.

325   The *Treaty of Bartenstein* set out joint Prusso-Russian war-goals, including the replacement of the *Rheinbund* by a German confederation under joint Austro-Prussian leadership, a construct that would indeed be adopted at the *Congress of Vienna* (1815). On the Prussian side, Hardenberg was the treaty's signatory, which gave Kleist yet more ammunition for his polemics against him (and against Luise, whom he will have assumed to have sided with Hardenberg and to have swayed the King). Having thus renewed the alliance with Russia, Hardenberg nevertheless until *Friedland* continued to correspond with Napoleon to find a peaceful settlement (cf. *AML*,224).

326   Reportedly Napoleon, who personally led the *Ad'A* in the nearby Jena theatre, initially could not believe that Davout had routed the Prussian main corps in the Auerstedt theatre, admonishing the messenger who brought the news to "tell your Marshal he is seeing double." Having eventually accepted the news, within an hour Napoleon crushed the Prussian units at Jena. The swift destruction of the famed Prussian army buttressed Napoleon's aura of invincibility and reverberated across Europe: was there any residual doubt that *Austerlitz* inaugurated a new era, *Jena-Auerstedt* cleared it.

327   Sloterdijk, *Sphären II*, 673: "Wo Sein und Zeichen eine gemeinsame Menge bilden, dort geht es um die Macht des Ganzen, in Zeichen imposant da zu sein. Seinszeichen sind Machtzeichen, weil sie nicht nur meinen, was sie vertreten, sondern sind, was sie darstellen." No doubt Ingres' *Napoleon I on the Imperial Throne* is based on Johann Adam Delsenbach's c.1725 engraving *Statue des Zeus in Olympia*, which may well have defined the modern Europeans' (idealised) image of Zeus/Jupiter (Delsenbach's engraving may in turn have drawn on Philippe Galle's 1572 engraving of the same motif, itself based on an earlier drawing by Maarten van Heemskerk; all of these modern renderings ultimately drew on Pausania's detailed 2nd century description of the statue, which itself was destroyed in the 5th century by fire or earthquake). The sceptre is not a traditional symbol of power not of Greece but Egypt and Mesopotamia, which the Greeks adopted especially for Zeus to symbolise his power over the entire world. Pausanias describes Zeus with a statue of Nike in his right, and a sceptre supporting an eagle in the left, wheras Ingres shows Napoleon with two sceptres, in his

right one supporting a statuette of Charlemagne (originally made for the coronation of Charles VI), in his left one supporting the *Main de Justice* (the Judeo-Christian *Manus Dei*). Early Roman emperors such as Claudius (ruled 41-54 AD) and Nerva (ruled 96-8 AD) had themselves portrayed with Jupiter's symbols; with the rise of Christianity this became unpalatable, rendering Napoleon's chosen symbolism—deliberately—anachronistic, hybristic and confrontational: he crowns Joséphine in the Pope's presence while adorning himself with the pagan laurel; on Ingres' painting, pagan symbolism outshines the Christian. Re identifying Napoleon with Jupiter, cf. Müller to Gentz on 7th September 1805: *"Den ganzen Monat August hindurch, während der fürchterlichen Conjunctur von Mond, Mars und Venus, auch Jupiters, habe ich viel gelitten... Ich habe sonst schon der Venus nie getraut in der Zeit, wenn sie Abendstern werden will... nun gar Mars und... auch Jupiter dort! Große Explosionen waren vorauszusehen!"* (AML,124). August 1805 was the month in which Napoleon turned the British invasion force towards Austria (cf. *AML*,125), and by early September (the time of Müller's letter) the *Ad'A* was quickly moving into positions along the Rhine. Venus = venereal disease, Mars = war, and Jupiter = Napoleon: "maximum explosiveness" indeed.

328   Kleist could have taken his equation of Germany and Hellas from Varnhagen and Chamisso's Nordsternbund, which in 1804 met in Cohen's house in Berlin, frequented by Kleist at the time (cf. Schulz, *Kleist,* 281-2). In *Ph* epigram no. 25, *Musikalische Einsicht* (I:23), Hellas represents Germany or Prussia in fetters, succumbed to Napoleon's siren song; epigram no. 26, *Demosthenes, an die Griechischen Republiken,* laments the Germans' propensity to thwart rather than support each other. An anti-Roman attitude, especially in comparison with Greece, was a commonplace in classical satire, including that of Lucian, Juvenal, Horace and Martial.

329   Kleist deploys the same device in *Verlobung,* where Gustav in a decisive passage turns into *August,* a perfect anagram of *Gustav* provided "u' is spelled as Latin "v": *Avgvst, Gvstav.* An urGermanic Gustav turns into an urLatin August———and promptly murders *Borussia.*

330   Kleist explores Germany's *"Francofication"* via a culinary and cultural topography in which French *délicatesses* (*ortolan*) and *décadence* (*palais*) encroach on German *Hausmannskost* (*"Wurst mit Kohlköpf"*) and *Gemütlichkeit* (*"eine niedre Hütte"*). This movement is not one-sided: the *"palais"* is soon reduced to a *"Haus"* or *"Hütte,"* as if this edifice were only grand when Napoleon resides

in it, not when Fr. Wilh. does, and Merkur becomes partial to German *Wurst*, in allusion to Beauharnais' marriage to the Bavarian princess (Beauharnais in 1814 dies in Munich, the quintessential *Weißwurst* city). To this day Germans call the (imaginary) divide between northern and southern Germany *Weißwurstäquator*, and the Bavarians still like to refer to those to the north of this divide as *"Saupreißn,"* even though Prussia ceased to exist as a political entity at the end of WWII. The *"Saupreiß"* Kleist, who consistently condemned the Wittelsbachs' complicity with Napoleon, applies the derogatory term *"Aufgewärmt"* to Bavaria's culinary traditions with obvious glee and disdain.

331   This symbol, as well as the historical circumstances, suggest that Kleist compounded up to three actual personages in the complex and versatile figure of Merkur-Hermes: Beauharnais, Henri Gatien Bertrand, who after *Austerlitz* took over from Beauharnais as Napoleon's aide-de-camp, and in April 1807 as Napoleon's envoy offered Fr. Wilh. and Luise the separate peace they rejected, and Louis-Alexandre Berthier, Napoleon's chief of staff. All three men enjoyed Napoleon's fullest confidence.

332   Napoleon Bonaparte, "On Religions," in *The Mind of Napoleon: A Selection from His Written and Spoken Words*, ed. J. Christopher Herold (New York: Columbia University Press, 1955), 49; cf. also https://en.wikipedia.org/wiki/Siege_of_Acre_ (1799). Napoleon in his speech alludes to the Sacred Band of Thebes and the Persian Immortals, elite units, respectively, of the city of Thebes and the Achaemenid kingdom of Persia. Napoleon's own imperial guard became known as *"les immortels,"* and his mentioning the Sacred Band of Thebes could have piqued Kleist's curiosity. He also alludes to the *Battle of Issus* (333 BC), at which the great Alex. defeated the Persians decisively, and while *Austerlitz* was an epic victory that established him as "Emperor of the West," it is clear that he did not consider his victory at *Austerlitz* as historically significant as Alex.'s at *Issus*, which led to the collapse of the Persian Empire and Alex.'s being annointed "King of Kings." If the ultimate accolade Napoleon aspired to was Alex.'s "King of Kings," or the Caesars' "Emperor of the West and the East," he would have to conquer not only Vienna but also Constantinople. Napoleon had long held a fascination for the Orient: during his early career he offered his services to the Ottoman Porte, and during the *Egyptian Campaign* he considered rebuilding the ancient Canal of the Pharaohs, forerunner of the modern Suez Canal, which would have facilitated a future invasion of British India.

333   "Die Tage in Königsberg sind Tage des relativen Glücks. Luise trifft sich mit Blücher und zahlreichen andren preußischen Generalen. Engländer und Russen machen ihre Aufwartung." http://www.koenigin-luise.com/Napoleon/ 1807_-_Memel/1807_-_memel.html.

334   E.g., Michael Neumann in "Genius malignus Jupiter oder Alkmenes Descartes-Krise," in Hans Joachim Kreutzer (Ed.), *KjB* (Stuttgart: J.B. Metzler, 1994), 144.

335   According to one source, Saxony contributed 15,000 men, compared to Prussia's 53,000 (cf. https://www.meinanzeiger.de/jena/c-politik/jena-am-14-oktober-1806_a63868). All allied commanders were Prussian, and Kleist can perhaps be excused for ridiculing the Saxon contribution. His depicting Fr. Aug. as traitor is not entirely fair: retreating after *Jena-Auerstedt*, the Prussians left Saxony at her own devices, and the defenseless Dresden at the mercy of the advancing *Ad'A*, giving the Elector no choice but to bid for peace. Kleist did not relent: his portrayal of the Saxon Elector in *Kohlhaas* is every bit as stinging as in *Amphitryon*.

336   Magdeburg, the most important of Prussia's fortresses, was commanded by Kleist's relative General Franz Kasimir von Kleist, whose capitulation without a fight and subsequent death sentence before a court martial remained a stain on the Kleist family name—a stain Kleist is promptly reminded of in 1809 by the Austrian military police he encounters on the battlefield of Aspern (cf. *LS*,316).

337   Kleist was not the first to relocate the story's setting: his friend Joh. Daniel Falk situated his 1804 *Amphitruon* in Vienna, demonstrating that Kleist's relocations were not as idiosyncratic it may seem.

338   For Kleist ass and horse will have been as fire and water ever since he and Ulrike, en route to Paris, had a road accident when a donkey scared their horses and their carriage toppled (cf. II:666; 669),

339   Tyndarus' case is one of (exceedingly rare) double heteropaternal superfecundation, in which a mother carries twins sired by different fathers; Amphitryon's, in classical myth, is one of simple heteropaternal superfecundation, still a rare event (but hey, says Kleist, we are dealing with a "god").

340   Of Jupiter Burkert writes (*Greek Religion*, 128): "The host of children sired by Zeus is astonishing both in quantity and in quality"; in this regard, Jupiter is clearly *not* a suitable avatar for Napoleon. Herkules (Heracles), although he initially killed his own children when driven mad by Hera's wrath, by accomplishing the twelve labours purified himself of the crime and achieved immortality. With his four wives and numerous female lovers he produced many sons, and established the dynasty of the *Herakleidai* that supplied numerous kings and heroes. Burkert notes (*Greek Religion*, 127) that Herakles represented a potential risk for Jupiter: "The fact that Zeus overthrew his own father [Kronos] always looms ominously in the background. Every usurper is threatened with the same fate. Zeus, too, is imperiled by women destined to bear a son who is greater than his father." By entrusting guardianship of his son to Amphitryon-Fr. Wilh., Jupiter-Napoleon risks that Herakles will grow up to be loyal to the Hohenzollerns, not the Bonapartes. *Marquise*'s ending also plays with this ambiguity: Napoleon may produce or acquire successors, but their allegiance to him could be doubtful.

341   Khufu, whose father Sneferu established the 4th Dynasty, became its second pharaoh and ruled Egypt for 23 years, a period considered the Old Kingdom's "golden age." Khufu was succeeded by his son Djedefre, who ruled for 8 years and was succeeded by another of Khufu's sons, Khafre, who ruled for 26 years, and finally a grandson, Menkaure, who ruled for 29 years; taken together the rule of these three dynastic generations spanned a period of 86 years, during which the three great pyramids of Gizeh (Khufu's, Khafre's and Menkaure's) and the Sphinx (whose head is believed to represent Khafre's) were built. According to anecdote, Napoleon after visiting the King's chamber of the *Great Pyramid* (which the great Alex. is also said to have visited) emerged visibly shaken; purportedly he later recalled that in the chamber he had had a vision of his destiny. If Napoleon did have such a vision, it would plausibly have been that of *dynastic empire*: within weeks of his return from the aborted *Oriental Campaign* he overthrew the *Directorat* in the coup d'état of *18 Brumaire* (9th November 1799) and established himself as First Consul. Kleist may well have associated the story of Napoleon's vision in Gizeh with his turn from charismatic general into despotic dictator and dynastic emperor, and his faible for the lavish, extravagant and exotic with his bend towards the despotic: Kleist's orientalisms (to adopt Edward Said's term) systematically allude to Napoleon. Perhaps Kleist had already researched the history of the *Oriental Campaign* when working on *Guiskard*, whose geographic setting and topos of the plague suggest as much. Kleist in 1809

would apply the pyramid imagery to the future German community he envisioned—with an essential difference: whereas Napoleon's "pyramid" is dynastic and "top-down," the German is broad-based and "bottom-up." Seen in this light, Kleistian passages labled "fanatic" by some seem rather reasonable: *"Eine Pyramide bauen / Laßt uns, in des Himmels Auen, / Krönen mit dem Gipfelstein: / Oder unser Grabmal sein!"* (Germania an ihre Kinder; I:27); *"Eine Gemeinschaft gilt es, deren Wurzeln tausendästig, einer Eiche gleich, in den Boden der Zeit eingreifen; deren Wipfel, Tugend und Sittlichkeit überschattend, an den silbernen Saum der Wolken rührt"* (*Was gilt es in diesem Kriege?*; II:378).

342   Cf. https://en.wikipedia.org/wiki/Ortolan_bunting. In E. A. Poe's satire "The Duc De L'Omelette" (*Stories*, 432-4), the Duc expires before the plucked ortolan he is about to consume; three days later he finds himself in hell, where Satan requests him to strip naked, so that he may consume him in the same manner (the Duc challenges Satan to a game of cards, wins, and safely returns to the surface; whether his ortolan still awaits him is unclear).

343   In Poe's satire "Lionizing" (*ibid*, 446-50), a "nose" contest takes place, whose contestants sport illustrious names such as Count Capricornutti, Don Stiletto, Prince de Grenouille (frogs are known for oversised genitals), and Elector of Bluddennuff. One contestant cuts off Bluddennuff's "nose," whereupon the latter is pronounced the winner, because his endowment is now beyond comparison. Kleist plays on a similar idea, namely that any comparison between man and god involves complete incommensurability. Just as Poe's people of Fum-Fudge do Bluddennuff, Kleist's people of Thebes after Jupiter's departure celebrate the castrated Amphitryon as the victor.

344   Kleist may have been inspired to the "tiara" by Josef Maria Grassi's 1804 portrait of the young Luise wearing a tiara set with gems. In Plautus' version the gift is a cup, in Molière's a diamond ornament.

345   It has been pointed out that by shifting the comma, this sentence can be made to imply that Amphitryon prepares to hang himself. Kleist may well have intended this ambiguity, but more importantly, his *"anzuknüpfen"* (not *"aufzuknüpfen"*) indicates attachment to a Mesmerian bucket. Kleist may have fantasised about the combined impact of machinic sensual stimulation (cf. Russel

Hoban's pleasure chamber in *Fremder*) and psychedelic hallucination (cf. Aldous Huxley's or Ken Kesey's mescaline or LSD "trips"). The hyphen at the beginning of Kleist's sentence symbolises the Deleuzean *agencement* of the *baquet*'s string tied to Amphitryon's penis.

346   Ilse Graham (*Kleist*, 85), amazingly, considers Amphitryon's psychedelic fantasy (V.1683-6) "Kleist's poetic answer to Kant's epistemology." From Würzburg, Kleist reports in September 1800: *"Auch hier erninnert das Läuten der Glocken unaufhörlich an die katholische Religion, wie das Geklirr der Ketten den Gefangenen an die Sklaverei"* (II:563). The French are *ante portas* and Kleist anticipates Würzburg's citizens will soon slide from one form of enslavement, Catholicism, into another, *"Francofication."*

347   Kleist repeatedly invokes the setting of a BDSM dungeon, and the "tiara" and "bells" or "carillon" may belong to a set of BDSMesque devices deployed during orgiastic banquets, possibly in conjunction with eclectic practices such as electroshock, flagellation, hypnosis, entrancement, somnambulism, and induced hallucination. Toni in *Verlobung* has a rope hanging from her wall, which she uses to spreadeagle Gustav; Elvire in *Findling* keeps a whip handy, which she may be using for self-flaggelation; the knacker in *Kohlhaas* has a whip strung over his back; Adam and Ruprecht in *Krug* use, respectively, a wig and a mantle for self-flaggelation. Kleist's "carillon" may also refer to the ancient Roman *tintinnabulum*, a wind chime or assembly of bells often in a phallic or poly-phallic shape (representing the *fascinum*, the embodiment of the divine phallus). E.A. Poe refers to the *tintinnabulum* in the first, or "silver bell," section of his poem *The Bells*, which arguably celebrates a man's youthful, homosexual life phase, later followed by the "golden bell" phase of wedded life, the "brazen bell" stage of syphiliac suffering, and the "iron bell" stage of death.

348   Charis, in her account of the previous nights' proceedings, alludes to a triadic *"FFF"* constellation when she evokes *"Apollon, Hermes, oder Ganymed"* (V.1589): Apollo = *dmōs*, Hermes = *erastēs*; Ganymede = *erômenos* (the role for which he, the most beautiful of mortal youths, is archetypical: the term "catamite" is derived from his Latin name). Merkur being stretched across a pillow anticipates Gustav being spread-eagled on the bed.

349   Aristophanes discusses this practice in his *Clouds* (line 1083), which will have been among the comedian's works Kleist borrowed from the Dresden public library in 1803; Lucian in his 2nd Cent. AD satire *The Death of Peregrinus* reports that the cynic philosopher Peregrinus Proteus was punished in this manner for adultery (Lucian also accuses Peregrinus of pederasty).

350   The relationship between Jupiter and Alkmene recalls that between Sir Stephen and O in Pauline Réage's *Histoire d'O*: Alkmene is constantly available for Jupiter, who as omnipresent god may appear to her at any time, while remaining strictly off-limits for anyone else, including her husband: like O's boyfriend René, Amphitryon is relegated to a role of bystander.

351   Alkmene's *"wenn im wilden Treffen / Der Pfeil auf diesn teurn Busen zielt"* (V.435-6), alluding to Eros' arrows, anticipates an entire metaphorical complex surrounding the term *"treffen"* in *Marquise*. The verb *"treffen"* means "to hit a target" and the noun *"Treffen"* denotes "a get-together"; Kleist's *"Treffen"* here is one at which many arrows *"treffen"*—in other words, it entails an orgy.

352   Cf. Burkert, *Greek Religion*, 157. Amphitryon calls Merkur "devil" (V.1723), and Merkur confirms the validity of this epithet when he swears by Styx, one of the rivers that lead into Hades (cf. V.101; 1700). Lucian, in *Gespräche der Götter und der Meeresgötter*, VII. (trans. Chr. M. Wieland), offers a poignant portrait of the infant prodigious Hermes: thieving, scheming, pert, eloquent, musical. Kleist might well have recognised some of his own genius in this figure.

353   Gerhard Kurz, in "'alter Vater Jupiter.' Zu Kleists Drama *Amphitryon*," in: Christine Lubkoll and Günter Oesterle (Eds.), *Gewagte Experimente und kühne Konstellationen. Kleists Werk zwischen Klassizismus und Romantik* (Würzburg: Königshausen & Neumann, 2001), 178-9, notes the ominous double "*es*," but fails to offer a satisfactory explanation for it.

354   Again the parallels with *Marquise* are obvious: in the *"Einrichtung"* reached in the novella's conclusion Napoleon is married into the Hohenzollern family without retaining any rights; he shall be considered the legal father to the sons—*"eine ganze Reihe von jungen Russen"*— the Marquise produces following their legal union, irrespectively of whether he fathered them biologically. However, since for one year

following their official wedding Napoleon is not permitted to consummate their marriage, circulating instead as object of desire among the various family members while the Marquise's chambers remain open to various German lovers, her first-born to whom Napoleon shall be the legal father will be certain *not* to have Bonapartean blood. Bäumler reports (*Amors vergifteter Pfeil*, 76) that Katharina II the Great deployed a "committee" of six court ladies as *"épeuvres"* ("validators"), whose taks was to "test" the health of the Empress' lovers; Kleist could have had the Empress in mind when he has other German royals "test" Count F-Napoleon's "health" before letting him loose on the Marquise-Luise.

355   In *Marquise* the first lover to enter the "room" at the appointed time on the "dreaded Third" is not Count F but Leopardo the hunter, a figure every bit as sly and stealthy as Merkur.

356   When Jupiter terms Merkur *"Der Hintergangene,"* he may be hinting to Alkmene that Merkur took her from behind (*"Hintern"* = "rear side"; *"hinter gehen"* = "to go behind," unlike *"hintergehen"* = "to cheat," "to betray") and thus did not impregnate her. The prefix *"Ab-"* ("off-") in Jupiter's *"Abgott"* ("idol") literally marks Merkur as his "off-spring," as if Jupiter feels the need to re-assert his authority and to remind Alkmene that it is he who is the mightiest of gods, no matter how speedy and cunning Merkur may be.

357   *Marquise* features an equivalent *"ménage à trois à Tilsit,"* involving Count F, the Marquise and the "dog." Plausibly Jupiter's *"Schlamm"* and Count F's *"Kot,"* which *syphilitically* denote infection, *satirically* imply impregnation. Kleist's father-and-son double act may parody the Catholic *filioque*, i.e., the credo of the Holy Spirit proceeding from the Father *and* the Son; if so, *Guiskard*'s, in which Robert depends on Guiskard in overcoming him, may caricature the Orthodox *per filium*, i.e., the credo of the Holy Spirit proceeding from the Father *via* the Son): I noted in *Awakening Child* and *Emigrant* that Kleist repeatedly parodies the Christian *Trinity*; even the *"FFF"* constellation can be read in this light.

358   That Merkur's *kērykeion* in Kleist's day was linked to magnetic healing is suggested by the cover art for *Joh. Lorenz Böckmann*'s 1787 compendium on magnetism, *Archiv für Magnetismus und Somnambulismus*—the image can be accessed at https://reader.digitale-sammlungen.de/de/fs1/object/display/bsb10285686_00005.html.

359   Kleist's ambivalent symbolism suggests that "immaculate" lovers include not only those free of disease but also those already infected but not yet exhibiting symptoms (or no longer doing so, having undergone treatment so that their symptoms have temporarily been suppressed): below its white feathers the swan's skin is black, the dove may be grey rather than whte, the angel can fall, and the oil beetle is not only black but also anything but harmless: it secretes a potent venom.

360   A *hermai* (herm) is an icon typically featuring Hermes' bust and genitals and erected next to entrance doors or alongside roads to bring fortune and ward off evil spirits. When she claims (cf. V.1456-7) that she is no longer able to worship before a "plain wall of marble," only before the *hermai*'s "face" ("*Antlitz*") or "features" ("*Züge*'), Alkmene may *satirically* be alluding to her "*Francofication*": used to praying before a featureless Protestant altar, Luise is now worshipping before an iconographic Catholic altar. Gerhard Kurz ("*alter Vater Jupiter*," 178) has counted 13 instances of the term "*Zug*"in the drama. Assuming that *satyrically* "*Zug*" = "male genitals," this frequency is unsurprising. *Marionettentheater*'s term "*Pantomimik*" (II:339) is equivalent to *Amphitryon*'s "*Antlitz*" and "*Zug.*" Already in *Krug* (cf. V.86-90) Kleist equates facial and male genital features, and his women (as *erômenoi*) are usually *phallus*-worshippers: Alkmene's "prostrations" before Merkur's "altar" anticipate Elvire's "worshipping" before Colino's image in *Findling* and Toni's "foot washing" of Gustav in *Verlobung*. The topos of Luise's or *Borussia*'s "conversion" to Catholicism (i.e., her "*Francofication*") also recurs in Kleist's works, most notably in *Cäcilie*. Already from Dresden in May 1801 Kleist had written, having experienced the "power of music" in a Catholic church, *"Ach, nur ein Tropfen Vergessenheit, und mit Wollust würde ich katholisch werden"* (II:651). Burkert notes (*Greek Religion*, 72) that altars on which blood sacrifices were performed were often white-chalked, maximising the contrast of the sacrificial blood whose stains were left on the altar after the ceremony, but I prefer to assume that Kleist's "plain wall of marble" *satirically* refers to the Protestant, not the ancient, altar, and perhaps *syphilitically* also to the whitewashed or tiled walls of a syphilis hospital.

733

361   Solvable mercury compounds commonly used as anti-syphilitics were Mercury I chloride (*calomel*) and Mercury II chloride (*mercuric chloride*), both white crystalline powders. The *"Meierei"* ("dairy farm") which in *Kohlhaas* is the venue of a major orgy, in which much milky *cum* ist spilled, could also refer to a syphilis hospital; in *Marquise* both Count F and the Marquise use therapeutic or prophylactic

means: the former inundates the "enflamed" fortress with "water" before going on his erotic rampage, while the latter on the "dreaded Third" inundates the family with holy water before joining them in an orgy. Kleist's fictional orgies so often entail ritual of "purification" that it is palpable that the members of his "brotherhood" regularly self-medicated and group-therapied as part of their *symposiac* get-togethers, the *banquet* (orgy) also functioning as, or being accompanied by, a *baquet* (group therapy session) involving a range of prophylactic, therapeutic or palliative strategies (electro-magnetism, mercury applications, baths and steam baths, consumption of opium and alcohol, etc.). This erotico-medico-agonistic complex renders the *symposiac* banquet-room akin to a cultic temple-cum-alchemical lab or therapeutic clinic, which furthermore encompasses its own social conventions, hierarchy, language, symbolism, rites and mannerisms. Kleist's "fictional" scenes are probably not fictional at all, but poetically rendered documentaries of real events.

362   Mary Dobson, *Murderous Contagion: A Human History of Disease*. London, Quercus, 2015. Cf. also Ernst Bäumler reporting the reformer Ulrich von Hutten's 1519 reminiscenses (*Amors vergifteter Pfeil*, 47): "Die Kranken wurden in eine Hitzstube eingeschlossen, die ununterbrochen und sehr stark geheizt wurde, die einen zwanzig, die anderen dreißig Tage hindurch, einige auch noch länger." When Brüggemann identifies (*Die Magie*, 42) the image of Colino before which Elvire worships as that of *Mercurius* (Hermes played an important role in alchemy, and mercury was one of the base metals from which alchemists sought to produce gold), his analysis is impeccable and only its evaluation misguided: the god Hermes whom Elvire (and Alkmene) worships represents not the alchemical *magnum opus* and its promise of wealth and wisdom, but the treatment with mercury and its promise of relief (the alchemical process, if Kleist represents it at all, is merely cypher for the medical one he cares about). Eberhard Siebert, in a Brüggemannian reading of *Zweikampf*, points out that Trota appears in "*Federhut und Mantel*," which he associates with Mercurius/Hermes, but although the association is correct, he fails to see that in Kleist, "feather" = member and "coat" = condom, and that it is in the end *The Satyrical* and *The Syphilitical* that motivates Kleist, not "The Alchemical"—cf. Siebert, 'Schuldig, Überwiesen, Verworfen…,' in: Günter Emig et al (Eds.), *Ach, Kleist!* Vol. 1, Niederstetten: Günter Emigs Literatur-Betrieb, 2019, 34.

363   Regarding the internal application of mercury, Gerhard van Swieten in the 1760s introduced the internal use of corrosive sublimate, mercuric chloride,

or *liquor Swietenii*, which remained in use as treatment for syphilis for many years. In the course of the 19th century calomel (mercurous chloride) came to be used as unction, tablets and injection (cf. John Frith, "Syphilis," in *JMVH*, Vol. 20, No. 4). Regarding ointment, Burkert (*Greek Religion*, 78, 80) reports of ancient purification rituals whereby earth, clay, bran or blood is smeared on an initiand's face and body and then wiped off, so that "By its contrast to the artificial defilement, the subsequent purity appears all the more impressive."

364   *Krug* MS (in the book version: V.1047-51); quoted in Bernhard Greiner, *Eine Art Wahnsinn. Dichtung im Horizont Kants: Studien zu Goethe und Kleist*. Philologische Studien (PhSt) Vol. 131 (1994), 139. Apart from their *syphilitical* aspect, such passages may also have a *po(i)etical* one: Kant in *Zum Ewigen* Frieden deplores the *"Schlangenwendungen einer unmoralischen Klugheitslehre."* Kleist's "Kant-crisis" marks precisely his wrenching himself from such serpentine movements and embraces.

365   In Edgar Allan Poe's satire "Some Words with a Mummy" (*Complete Stories and Poems*, 450-62) a revitalised mummy—"Readjusting the battery, we now applied the fluid to the bisected nerves"— reports that in the process of embalmment "in my time we [the ancient Egyptians] employed scarcely any thing else than the Bichloride of Mercury," and that "Galvanism... was a common thing among us in the old days"; furthermore, that "the leading principle of embalmment consisted, with us, in the immediately arresting, and holding in perpetual *abeyance*, all the animal functions subjected to the process. To be brief, in whatever condition the individual was, at the period of embalmment, in that condition he remained," and that "After the discovery of the embalming principle... it occurred to our philosophers that a laudable curiosity might be gratified... by living this [a man's] natural term in instalments... An historian, for example,... would... get himself carefully embalmed; leaving instructions to his executors *pro tem.*, that they should cause him to be revivified after the lapse of a certain period... Resuming existence at the expiration of his time, he would invariably find his great work converted into... a kind of literary arena for the conflicting guesses, riddles, and personal squabbles of whole herds of exasperated commentators." The syphiliac mummy, in other words, was artificially kept alive in suspended animation by a permanent embalmment with Mercury II chloride, periodically being revivified with the help of electroshock, before being put back into its slumber. Poe's satire is a rather dystopian response to Kleist's utopian

faith in metempsychosis: the soul may live eternally, but without becoming detached from its disease-ridden body, which is preserved in an undead, zombiesque state. Poe's embalmment therapy-cult also anticipates the cryonics movement of the early 21st century.

366   Bäumler reports (*Amors vergifteter Pfeil*, 101) that in a 1837/8 treatise on syphilis, Philippe Ricord erroneously considered the secondary stage of syphilis noninfectious.

367   In the context of *Schroffenstein* I pointed out that conscious injection of contaminated ejaculate is wielded as a murder weapon; cf. also the Prussian tambour's request, in *Anekdote aus dem Letzten Kriege* (II:268), to be executed by a "shot" into his rear: he evidently believes that the French soldiers are highly contagious "baslilisks," and that their sodomising him will be fatal to him.

368   Most Kleistian works draw on rich "genealogies of texts"; *Krug* is unusual in that it draws on a "genealogy" not of "texts" but of "images," encompassing the topos of the *cruche cassée* going back to at least Greuse. In the case of *Amphitryon*, the "genealogy" relevant to Kleist also included Zschokke's preoccupation with Molière in 1802, and Falk's in c.1804: it is a "genealogy" not only of "texts" but also of a "praxis" of accessing, reviewing, translating, recasting, transforming pre-existing materials.

369   Thomas Mann terms Kleist *"sondergleichen," "völlig einmalig, aus aller Hergebrachtheit und Ordnung fallend"* (KH,241). Kleist himself, in *Brief eines Dichters an einen Anderen*, rejects the notion that he adheres to any particular "school" (cf. II:347), and already in 1812 Arnim notes, *"daß er keine Schule anerkannt"* (NR,251), possibly in response to Adam Müller's placing Kleist in Wieland's "school," as opposed to the Schlegels'. In the same essay Kleist admits his debt to Shakespeare, especially with respect to key themes; I argued earlier that in terms of his overall objectives and approach, the precedessor Kleist adhered to most closely is Aristophanes. Molière's immensely funny sarcasm will have intrigued Kleist, but the French master's biggest "asset," in Kleist's eyes, will have been his canonical Frenchness. Kleist scholars generally acknowledge Kleist's being *sui generis*, but still fail to read him as such, e.g., by paralleling his works with others', unsurprisingly usually with meagre insights and more questions raised than answered. No man is an island, not even Kleist, but it is most important to trace intertextualities within his œuvre, not to conjure external ones where few exist.

370   Kleist's 1811 trans. from the French of the essay *Über den Zustand der Schwarzen in Amerika* adopts the *pescheräic* principle in its purest form, in that without any change to the original content, the very act of trans. and re-publication in German in itself is *pescheräic*, turning the French version's intention and meaning on its head. Intriguingly, the French version itself was a trans. from an English original, and the French translator already deployed the text *pescheräically*. Kleist thus created a *pescherä* of a *pescherä*, a *simulacrum* of a *simulacrum*. Kleist's *Amphitryon*, in that sense, is a sixth-order simulacrum of Hesiod-Sophocles-Plautus-Rotrou-Molière (or a seventh-order simulacrum of Hesiod-Sophocles-Plautus-Rotrou-Molière-Falk). Among early critics, Kleist's *Amphitryon* was treated largely as a trans., or a mere "attempt": a critic in the *Miszellen* (1808) considered Zschokke's adaptations of Molière "more appropriate…, because [Zschokke] offers more free imitation than translation [in comparison with Kleist]" (*LS*,181); Schütz in 1817 still considered Kleist's version a trans. (cf. *LS*,148), Rahmer in 1909 may have omitted *Amphitryon* from Kleist's dramas for similar reasons, and as recently as 2003 Lose maintains (*Kleist*, 225) that Kleist with *Amphitryon*, "sich aus dem bloß nachgestalteten Vollzug lösen [will], den Übersetzer in sich überwinden und ein eigenständiges Stück schaffen." Surely there never was a "translator lodged in him" which Kleist would have needed to "overcome": instead, Kleist is the quintessential "anti-translator" in that anything he adopts, he not translates but transforms.

371   Adam Müller probably received the MS from Rühle, Marie or Körner, and not Kleist, for in May 1807 he remained convinced that Kleist was still retained at Joux, rather than Châlons (cf. *LS*,172a).

372   Cf. https://de.wikipedia.org/wiki/Vierter_Koalitionskrieg.

373   In January 1945 the author's grandparents, alongside many East Prussians, fled before the Red Army from Wormditt, 50km south-west of Königsberg, westwards to Berlin, taking with them only what they could carry, mostly documents and items of value, among them the grandfather's collection of postage stamps, hastily ripped from stamp-albums and bagged in small plastic bags, still in the author's possession today; his father, aged 17, as part of Hitler's *"Letztes Aufgebot"* was wounded not far from his hometown, taken to Russia as PoW and freed two years later. Kleist was not only fleeing from an advancing enemy but also looking to orchestrate the resistance;

during the *Evacuation of East Prussia*, in contrast, there was no thought of resistance, only of naked survival.

374   Cf. A. Müller's note to Joh. von Müller on 8th January 1806, after relocating to Dresden: "*Sie verlangen Aufklärung über diese Veränderung meines Wohnorts... Ich hatte Gründe: Nähe des Kriegstheaters, größere Leichtigkeit der Correspondenz mit Wiener und Berliner Fruenden*" (*AML*,148).

375   Kleist's requesting a French dictionary from the Joux authorities is suggestive, though not conclusive proof that he continued to work on *Amphitryon*: he could have used the dictionary, say, to work on *Penthesilea*, among whose sources will have been Claude Marie Guyon's *Histoire des Amazones* (1740), and on *Marquise*, for which he may have drawn on Rousseau's *La nouvelle Héloïse* (1761), Montaigne's *Essaies* (1588) and Cervantes' *Novelas ejemplares* (1603), German translations of which would not have been available to him in the French Jura. On the other hand, his French was probably sufficiently fluent for reading French sources, whereas for his subtle adaptation of Molière he evidently could not do without dictionary.

376   Cf. http://www.koenigin-luise.com/Napoleon/1807_-_Memel/1807_-_memel.html: "*Napoleon schlug einen abgewandelten Friedensplan vor, der auf eine Zerstörung des preußisch-russischen Bündnisses hinauslief, ohne jedoch eine Parteinahme Preußens gegen Rußland zu fordern. Der französische Abgesandte Bertrand erklärte, von Napoleon den Auftrag zu haben, sich nach dem Befinden der Königin zu erkundigen, mit der Bemerkung, er hoffe, daß sie mit ihm Frieden schließen werde. Worauf Luise schlagfertig erwiderte: "Sie wissen, daß Frauen nicht Krieg führen und sich nicht um Politik kümmern." Nie wäre ihr ein Sonderfrieden auf Kosten Rußlands zur Rettung Preußens in den Sinn gekommen. Der König verharrte bei seinem ursprünglichen Entschluß, kein Sonderfrieden mit Napoleon. Friedrich Wilhelm III., Luise und Hardenberg waren sich hierin einig. - Der harte Winter nahm kein Ende, und die trübsinnige Stimmung des Königs lähmte jede Entwicklung. Als Zar Alexander I. am 2. April 1807 in Memel eintraf, änderte sich das Bild. "Unser Retter, unsere Stütze, unsere Hoffnung" hieß es. Unter Hinzuziehung Hardenbergs, der zu Alexander I. gute Beziehungen pflegte, wurden endlich wichtige Entschlüsse getroffen. Hardenberg wurde erster Kabinettsminister. Am 26. April wurde zwischen Preußen und Rußland ein Vertrag geschlossen, der die Zurückdrängung Frankreichs über den Rhein, die Wiederherstellung Preußens und die Unabhängigkeit Deutschlands vorsah. Preußen und Rußland sollten die Waffen nur gemeinsam niederlegen.*"

377   The Coalition army mainly comprised Russian units and fought under Russian fField Marshal Benningsen's supreme command, but a last-minute intervention by L'Estocq's Prussian corps proved decisive in avoiding defeat. Kleist's depicting the battle as a duel between Jupiter-Napoleon and Alkmene-*Borussia* is thus not entirely unhistorical, though as usual he all but ignores the Russian contribution. Kleist's pattern of underestimating or ignoring Alex. and Russia was perhaps not entirely irrational: after *Austerlitz* Alex. had withdrawn from the battlefield without further ado. *Bartenstein* suggests that Fr. Wilh. saw this differently, but *Friedland* and *Tilsit* proved Kleist partially right: neither were the Russians a match for the French, nor was Alex. bent on saving anyone's skin but his own, no matter what agreements he had struck. Still, it may have been Alex. who at *Tilsit* convinced Napoleon not to annihilate Prussia, if only to preserve a buffer between the two empires.

378   Already on 6th December 1806 Kleist tells Ulrike that he hopes to visit her in Schorin "as soon as possible" (II:774), so his departure for Pomerania from Königsberg was not as precipitate as it seems. By 6th December Napoleon had reached Warsaw, and the writing was on the wall that he would soon close in on Königsberg. In January 1807 Britain and Sweden entered into negotiations with Prussia for a possible invasion, probably tin the area of Swedish-controlled Western Pomerania and Stettin, which the Prussian contingents in Kolberg and elsewhere in Farther Pomerania could have supported. In response, Napoleon ordered the occupation of Danzig. Had Kleist stayed in Königsberg any longer than he did, his only remaiing route to Berlin would have been cut off by the French push towards Danzig.

379   After *Tilsit*, Königsberg, rather than Berlin, became the centre of Prussian reforms; the King returned there from Memel and gathered ministers and technocrats there. As of early January 1807, however, with Napoleon rapidly closing in on the city, the odds will have been 10:1 in favour of Königsberg becoming French-occupied, so Kleist's predictions and moves were perfectly rational at the time. When Blamberger (*Kleist*, 244) opines that *"Kleist jetzt, in Preußens bitterster Stunde, um der patriotischen Pflicht willen ein zeitweiliges Opfer bringen… an seinen Schreibtisch zu den Reformern in der Kammer [hätte] zurückgehen müssen,"* apart from discounting the prospect of the *"noch unbesetzte"* Königsberg soon becoming enclosed by French troops, he fundamentally misjudges Kleist's intentions: Kleist would have far more impact by rallying the remaining Prussian pockets of resistance into a broader insurrection then by assisting Altenberg in drafting decrees (this is the same logic as that which

compelled Kleist to quit the army: neither a middle ranked civil servant nor a middle ranked officer can rival a national bard and leading propagandist in terms of impact during wartime. Prussia's greatest patriotic poet, Blamberger implies, in her darkest hour, should have thown poetry into the wind and served his country as an office clerk; he might as well suggest that Einstein, instead of writing the SRT (1905), should have prioritised his job as "technical expert, 3rd class" at the Basel patent office, or that Nietzsche, instead of producing his GT (1872), UB (1874-6) and MA (1878), should have focused on teaching Philology 101 at Basel university.

380   Pfuel's leaving the group shortly before it Berlin to meet Fouqué at Nennhausen suggests the hypothesis that he and Kleist (and perhaps Gauvin and Ehrenberg as well) were indeed plotting to establish resistance cells across northern Germany: Pfuel, say, with Fouqué in the Havelland (the ancient heartland of Brandenburg), Kleist, say, with other patriots in Berlin or Dresden. This remains speculative, but what would actually happen in 1808/9, during the *War of the Fifth Coalition*, puts a spotlight on what *could have* happened in 1807: in 1808/9 Prague would become the hub of an axis of resistance made up of patriotic bureaucrats, diplomats, generals and writers, a movement in which Kleist would seek to play a role; by analogy, on the eve of 1807 he may have expected a similar axis to form, with Berlin and/or Dresden as hubs. The French were clever enough to police Berlin tightly and to draw Dresden into their realm, and Napoleon at *Friedland* put a quick end to residual hopes (fanned by Gneisenau's successful defence of Kohlberg) of a Prussian counterstrike. Kleist's own fate, locked up in Joux, mirrored his King's at Memel and Gneisenau's at Kolberg: the few remaining potential pockets of Prussian resistance in the Spring of 1807 were bottled up by the French and neutralised. The question of whether Kleist was apprehended unjustly answers itself: even if he was not a spy, he was certainly plotting something against the French, and under the circumstances apprehending him was not only not unjust but also, from the point of view of the French, *wise*.

381   Kleist may be referring to the *Penthesilea* MS in June 1807 in a letter to Ulrike: "*Ich habe deren* [MSS] *noch in diesem Augenblick zwei fertig*" (II:781)—the first MS would have to be *Krug*, the second could be *Penthesilea* (it could also be *Marquise*). It is at least possible that Kleist completed a first version of *Penthesilea* already in Châlons, and continued working on it in Dresden; it is also at least possible that he already had a concept or draft on him when captured (cf. *LS*,169; 172a).

382   Among Kleist's sources for *Penthesilea*, in addition to Claude Marie Guyon's *Histoire des Amazones* (1740), will have been Benjamin Hederich's *Gründliches mythologisches Lexikon* (revised 1770), in which the entries "Penthesilea" and "Pentheus" follow upon each other (cf. Blamberger, *Kleist*, 326-8), of which the former will have informed *Penthesilea*, the latter both *Penthesilea* and *Amphitryon*: Pentheus, King of Thebes, when seeking to undermine the Dionysiac cult adhered to by the women of Thebes, is rent to pieces by the *Maenads*. Kleist indeed "plundered" (Blamberger) Hederich for suitable materials and images, and deployed them across both dramas. He could have brought Hederich's book with him from Königsberg or acquired it in Berlin before his arrest.

383   Cf. Deleuze and Guattari, *Thousand Plateaus*, 355: "In Penthesilea… the war machine has passed over to the Amazons, a State-less woman-people whose justice, religion, and loves are organised uniquely in a war-mode. Descendants of the Scythians, the Amazons spring forth like lightning, "between" the two States, the Greek and the Trojan. They sweep everything in their path."

384   In the medieval epic *Nibelungenlied*, Siegfried's bath in a pool of the slayed dragon's blood has the same effect as Achilles' in the river Styx; a heart-shaped spot on Siegfried's shoulder, onto which a leaf had fallen during his bath, remains unprotected, a vulnerability that becomes his "Achille's heel."

385   Castrated priests are attested in the cult of Artemis-Upis at Ephesos, a sanctuary purportedly founded by Amazons (cf. Burkert, *Greek Religion*, 97). Epigrams were a popular genre for guests' contributions at symposiums and thus had a strongly performative character; they also encouraged proliferation, one epigram "breeding" another, creating entire "families" of variations on a theme. All of these characteristics, of course, suited Kleist greatly.

386   Stellar collision was first theorized by Charles Messier in 1764. Kleist could also have been alluding to Shakespeare's *Romeo and Juliet*: "A pair of star-cross'd lovers take their life" (*Prologue*, V.6). The image of two heavenly bodies smashing into each other resembles that of the comet flairing up in the Sun's embrace, both encompassing fusion.

387 In Lucian's *A True History* (Book 2) the travelers reach the Isles of the Blest, where they are apprehended by the guards and bound with rose-garlands. Dirk Grathoff parallels (*Kleist: Geschichte*, 128-9) Penthesilea's tearing Achilles apart with Schiller's critique of the French Revolution in *Das Lied von der Glocke*: "Da werden Weiber zu Hyänen / Und treiben mit Entsetzen Scherz, / Noch zuckend, mit des Panthers Zähnen, / Zerreissen sie des Feindes Herz." For all its gruesomeness, colloquial expressions such as "bugger me!" and "kiss my arse" suggest that Achilles' death entails a final act of defiance of Penthesilea's authority—cf. also Sloterdijk (*Kritik*, 283): *"Als Repräsentant des kynischen Prinzips schlechthin... läßt sich der Arsch kaum verstaatlichen."*

388 According to ancient myths, Achilles was reared by the *centaur* Chiron (*"Hand"*), which may explain or facilitate his and the *"Kentaurin"* Penthesilea's mutual attraction.

389 In Lucian's *A True History* (Book 2) the travelers reach the Isles of the Blest, where they are apprehended by the guards and bound with rose-garlands. In ancient Greece garlands were used in sacrificial rites; in Rome, soldiers during the festival of the *rosalia* adorned their military standards with garlands. Hephaestus forged Aphrodite a saltire-shaped "girdle" that accentuates the breasts, making her even more irresistible to men: "Father Zeus... himself... later succumbs to the magic of Aphrodite's embroidered girdle: 'in it is love, yearning, fond discourse, and beguilement' [*Ilias*]" (Burkert, *Greek Religion*, 154). Penthesilea's gesture of putting some such garment or accessory on Achilles casts her in the masculine, Achilles in the feminine or effeminate role. In ancient myth a golden girdle plays a prominent part in the stories not of Penthesilea but of the Amazon queen Hippolyta, which Kleist would have had no qualms "borrowing"; Hippolyta's golden girdle signifies her authority as Amazon queen and becomes the object of Heracles' ninth labour, in some myths she marries Theseus, becoming the only Amazon to marry, perhaps another strand Kleist borrowed, his Penthesilea's final union with Achilles mirroring nuptials, Amazon style. Joachim Pfeiffer's contention in "Die Konstruktion der Geschlechter in Kleists *Penthesilea*," in Lubkoll and Oesterle (Ed.), *Experimente*, 197, that *"es den Frauen in Themyscira kaum möglich sein dürfte, die Männer sexuell zu vergewaltigen"* is untenable: in *Verlobung* Toni spread-eagles Gustav onto her bed, and the Amazons in Just Jaeckin's 1984 sexploitation pic *Gwendoline* spread-eagle their male prisoner onto an altar, where the "bride" lowers herself onto him. Ulrich Port traces (*KH*,53)

the term *"Rosenfest"* to a bucolic festival in the Picardie, but overlooks two far more Kleistian associations: with the sexual orgy or symposium (*Rose* being an anagram of *Eros*) and with Christ's passion (the thorny rose garlands corresponding to the crown of thorns). When Penthesilea admonishes those around her, *"Dem ist ein Pfeil / Geschärft des Todes, der sein Haupt, was sag ich! / Der seine Locken eine mir berührt!"* (V.853-5), she means that Achilles' genitals are not to be touched by them (head = glans; locks = pubic hair), in a gesture mirroring Jupiters' admonishing Amphitryon: *"doch laß sie ruhn."*

390   The swansong (cf. V.1829) aniticipates their deaths as in *Erdbeben* the nightingale's does Jeronimo Rugera's and Josephe Asteron's (cf. II:150). I note in passing that "Rugera" is an anagram of "guerra" ("war"—cf. Staengle, *Kleist. Sein Leben*, 161), and "Asteron" a partial one of "eros," denoting the lovers as embodying the very dialectic that propels Kleist's works: *Agôn* and *Erôs*. I offered in *Emigrant* that Jeronimo and Josephe represent Fr. Wilh. III and Luise, the initial letters of their names, "*J & J*," entailing a one-letter shift from "*K & K*," "*König & Königin*," as does Arthur C. Clarke's "HAL" from "IBM" (Clarke denied that this was the origin of his computer's name).

391   Burkert maintains (*Greek Religion*, 96) that ancient priesthoods were often hereditary and could almost equal hereditary kingships in status. Wolf Kittler notes (*Geburt*, 187) that the entry *"Tanaïs"* in Hederich's lexicon refers to a male figure, "an enemy of the female gender" who "rejected marriage" and whom Venus punished by having him fall in love with his own mother. Kleist will have been fascinated by this figure, and his re-casting Tanaïs as an Amazon without changing her name is in keeping with his practice of allocating masculine names to female characters who enact effeminate male lovers. Kittler's contention that Kleist aimed for *"die restlose Verschmelzung des Mannes mit der Frau oder besser: des Sohnes mit der Mutter"* (ibid, 189) is incomplete: Kleist aimed for *separation* (*"Scheidung"*) of the (homo-) erotic and reproductive functions, followed later, in death, by a final *fusion* between comet-lover (son) and Sun (which could be a mother-figure or a "brother").

392   Anthony Stephens notes in "Die Änigmen der Einsicht in Kleists Penthesilea," in Yixu Lü et al (Eds.), *Wissensfiguren*, 98-106, that in Euripides' *Hippolytos* Artemis and Aphrodite are embroiled in an incommensurable rivalry in which Aphrodite eventually prevails, at the expense of a human victim, Theseus.

Kleist in the summer of 1803 borrowed several works by Euripides (in Fr. Heinr. Bothe's trans.) from the Dresden library, and Stephens shows that Kleist may have gleaned passages or ideas from *Hippolytos* (e.g., "*mit schnellen Doggen*") and from *Bacchen*. He also points out that Kleist's "eudemonical image" of Ares' and Artemis' "complementarity" as guarantors of the Amazon state (*ibid*. 96-7) has no basis in ancient myths.

393   Cf. Martin Heidegger, *Parmenides*. Trans. A. Schuwer and R. Rojcewicz (Bloomington: Indiana UP, 1992), 111: "we are thinking the essence of the Greek gods… if we call them the attuning ones."

394   Bernard Greiner is so convinced that the Amazons free their prisoners after the *Rosenfest* and that the "myth" of Mars had "become mythology," that for him Penthesilea's contention that the Amazons are conceived by Mars constitutes "inauthentic ("*uneigentlich*") speech." He shapes Kleist's text to fit his theory instead of the reverse.

395   As Achilles' corpse has been hollowed out by Penthesilea's assault, and his soul has escaped into the either, his steely skin has become a perfectly fitted sarcophagus for a body it no longer contains, recalling the taxidermied bird Kleist observed in Würzburg.

396   Kleist's famous dyad "*Bisse/Küsse*" paraphrases a passage from an Anacreonic ode by Joh. Wilh. L. Gleim, "*Tod, warum entführst Du mir mein Mädchen?... Was willst Du mit ihr machen? Kannst du doch mit Zähnen ohne Lippen, wohl die Mädchen beißen, doch nicht küssen—,*" whose recitation, Gleim told Kleist in 1801, once saved Ewald von Kleist's life (cf. II:657). Penthesilea's biting Achilles, then, reveals her as an avatar of death, and her bite, as a "kiss of death."

397   The *Kleist-Forschung* overlooks several of Kleist's most insidious and wicked villains—e.g., *Penthesilea*'s High Priestess, who actively drives Penthesilea into suicide, *Schroffenstein*'s Agnes, who murders Ottokar, *Guiskard*'s Robert, who infects his father in order to usurp his position, *Krug*'s Licht, who frames Adam for the same purpose.

398   Greiner (*Kleists Dramen*, 162) mistakenly believes that Tanaïs dropped the bow. Kittler (*Geburt*, 184) recognises that it was the High Priestess who did so, but

believes that she did it accidentally, which is possible but not Kleistian (the same of course applies to Penthesilea's dropping the bow).

399   In most instances Kleist appears to use the Greeks as a cypher for the Germans overall, rather than the Prussians only—cf., e.g., *Ph* epigrams No. 25 and 26 (I:23). In the latter, Kleist refers to the rivalry between the Habsburgs and Hohenzollerns and posits himself as latter-day Demosthenes, i.e., a great political orator.

400   In late November 1805, as Napoleon closes in on the allied HQ at Olmütz, where Franz and Alex are both located, Gentz (in Olmütz) and Müller (in Dresden) resort to "weather code" to camouflage their discussion of the military situation—cf. Müller's *"Wissen Sie, daß ich diese Nordwest- (eigentlich und richtiger Nordnordwest) Wolken in den letzten Tagen des September sehr gut kenne"* (*AML*,134), which presumably conveys his intelligence of the ongoing mobilisation of Prussian troops in Silesia that could reinforce the 40,000 Russian troops under Fr. von Buxhöwden's command stationed near Olmütz.

401   That Kleist's *dramatis personae* represent historical personages does not prevent them from being modeled on Kleist's personal acquaintances: the Amazonian Ulrike could have served as model for Penthesilea, and the athletic Pfuel for Achilles, in the same manner as, say, Kleist and his brother Leopold for Kohlhaas' sons (who, I argued in *Emigrant, satirically* represent Fr. Wilh.'s two oldest sons), Julie Kunze for Käthchen (who could also have been modeled on Gmelin's female patients), and Dora Stock for Kunigunde. Kleistian characters may *represent* a VIP, while *resembling* an acquaintance.

402   Cf. G.W.F. Hegel to Fr. Imm. Niethammeer, 13th October 1806, quoted in Dirk Grathoff, "Heinrich von Kleist und Napoleon Bonaparte, der Furor Teutonicus und die ferne Revolution," in Gerhard Neumann (Ed.), *Kriegsfall,* 38.

403   Amazons are sometimes referred to as *"Pferdebändigerinnen,"* and frequently depicted on horseback—cf. e.g., Goethe, *Achilleis,* quoted e.g. in Paul Kluckhon, "Penthesilea," in Walter Müller-Seidel (Ed.), *Kleist*, 35, and Wichmann, *Kleist*, 129. Jacques-Louis David's idealised image shows Napoleon mounted on on Marengo crossing the Alps en route to the June 1800 *Battle of Marengo* in northern Italy, in whose remembrance he presumably (re-)named his mount. Vernet's

paintaing, showing a different mount, reminds us that Napoleon used numerous horses, yet Marengo was his favourite one, to which he entrustred himself in several important battles.

404   The personfications of Prussia and of Germany are frequently depicted clad in armour. Ulrich Port notes (*KH*,55-6) that Achilles is depicted with feminine traits and physiognomy.

405   *"Dämel"* is a corruption of *"Dame"* ("lady") or *"Damsel"* ("maiden"), whose irreverence is further exacerbated by its being near homophone with *"dämlich"* ("foolish"). *"Männer sind männlich, Damen sind dämlich"* is an evergreen *Kalauer* that corrupts grammar—the adjective of *Dame* is not *dämlich* but *damenhaft*—and whose effect, if a silly one, hinges on the rhyme the corruption creates.

406   Hence the horrendous losses on both sides. Much larger numbers of cannons were deployed in sea battles, the ships being veritable swimming fortresses: at the *Battle of Trafalgar* (1805) Britain and France/Spain between them deployed c.4,800 canons. However, numbers of personnel deployed in sea battles were significantly lower than in land battles—c.42,000 sailors in total at *Trafalgar*, compared with c.150,000 soldiers at *Eylau*, and so were fatality rates—c.4000, or one in twelve, at *Trafalgar*, compared with c.20,000, or one in seven or eight, at *Eylau*.

407   Kleist practitioners sometimes appear to be more attuned to Kleist than Kleist theoreticians, even if their understanding of Kleist's concerns remains scrappy. Hans-Jürgen Syberberg (whose family, like Kleist's, hails from Pomerania) states in an interview that "what [Kleist] shows in the Person of Penthesilea is the sacrifice of Prussia," which is directionally correct, except that Achilles, not Penthesilea, embodies the "sacrifice of Prussia" (cf. http://www.a-e-m-gmbh.com/andremuller/ interview%20mit%20hans-juergen%20syberberg.html). Syberberg, in his 1989 film *Marquise von O… 'vom Süden in den Norden verlegt"* correctly relocates the action back "from the south to the north"—to Prussia—, but does not also shift the figure of Count F "from the east to the west"—i.e., he fails to identify Count F with Napoleon. Hans Neuenfels, in his 1981 adaption of *Penthesilea* at Berlin's Schiller-Theater, correctly puts the Greeks into Prussian uniforms, but fails to also put the Amazons into French ones, and the Trojans into Austrian ones (cf. Kanzog, *Kleist,* 267). On the

other hand, Roger Vontobel in his 2007 adaption of *Schroffenstein* drops the character Ursula outright, eliminating a key aspect of Kleist's *satirical* "thread" (cf. Kanzog, *ibid*, 269-70; 295).

408   In no way did Kleist consider the pedophily prevalent in Catholic church institutions he here derides equivalent to the ancient pagan custom of pederasty, which he admired and perhaps practiced.

409   Combining Prussia's white and black with Austria's yellow and black produces a less "colourful" result than combining them with the blue, white and red of France's *tricolore*.

410   Late in the battle's second day L'Estocq's Prussian corps appeared on Davout's exposed right flank; the Russians were holding his left flank, but were about to yield to his centre.

411   In classical mythology Antilochus was among Helen's suitors, which corresponds to Kleist's *satirical* context since the Wettin was among the potential claimants of the *HRR*'s imperial dignity. Since Asteria appears on stage only after Antilochus-Fr. Aug. evaculates the stage, the same actor can be cast; only his crown or insignia have to be changed to signify his elevation and turncoating. Napoleon, in a decree of 17 May 1809 directed against the Pope, referred to Charlemagne as his "august predecessor"; Kleist sets *Cäcilie* in the city of Aachen, Charlemagne's main residence. Tanaïs, according to one account, was a male river god of Scythia; the city of Tanaïs at the mouth of the river Don was a Greek, not Scythian, settlement, although Scythian and other settlements may have existed on the same site before it; Tanaïs' thus straddling two cultural realms makes her/him a suitable avatar of Charlemagne.

412   Gerhard Kaiser argues along similar lines in *Wandrer und Idylle* (Göttingen, Vandenhoek & Ruprecht, 1977), 209-10, and so does Walter Müller-Seidel in "'Penthesilea' im Kontext der deutschen Klassik," in Walter Hinderer (Ed.), *Kleists Dramen. Neue Interpretationen* (Stuttgart: Reclam, 1981), 147.

413   Cf. Gérard Raulet, *Der opake Punkt*, 350-1: "*Insofern bildet zweifelsohne die Erfahrung der Französischen Revolution den Hintergrund seiner Tragödie... Denn wie aufgeklärt der Amazonenstaat auch ist, lastet auf dieser errungenen politischen*

Freiheit der Fluch eines Geburtsfehlers. Man kann zwar das Männliche hier als Emblem der Herrschaft schlechthin bagatellisieren, aber man wird unmöglich den Umstand wegreden, daß dieser Staat auf Ausschließung beruht und daß diese Ausschließung als Verstümmelung dargestellt wird. Die Staatsbürgerinnen sind frei. Um diese Freiheit zu erringen, haben sie aber nicht nur ihre "Individualität" aufgeben müssen, sondern auch das, was integraler Teil, wenn nicht der Kern dieser Individualität ist, nämlich ihre geschlechtliche Identität." The RF may be said to have suffered the equivalent congenital defect: Marie Antoinette's execution was followed by Napoleon's patriarchal dynastic régime, and the Republic's female representations, La République and Marianne, became mere window-dressing in a militaristic, male-dominated hierarchy.

414   Columbina is the perky maid, Pulcinella the cunning servant in *commedia dell'arte*. By inadvertently comparing Napoleon (Penthesilea) with the former and Luise (Achilles) with the latter, if anything Goethe makes a fool of himself, not Kleist. When Zschokke and Wieland laugh at *Schroffenstein*'s final scene, they do so out of *amusement*, for they understand what Kleist is up to, whereas when Goethe laughs at the above passage in *Penthesilea*, he does so out of *embarrassment*, for he does not. For Goethe, *Penthesilea* is in part monstrous, in part ridiculous, and so is its author.

415   Such *"Heiratspolitk"* (Sloterdijk: *"Sippenaußenpolitik"*) was of course widespread among European noble houses, and especially practiced by the Habsburgs, whose motto *"Bella gerant alii – tu, felix Austria, nube!"* became a winged word, but was delicate with respect to Napoleon, for at least two reasons: one, he was a parvenu and did not descend from a family of high nobility; two, the Habsburg-French rivalry that for over 300 years shaped European power politics had emerged from precisely such *"Heiratspolitik"*: the Habsburg archduke and future Holy Roman Emperor Max. I's marriage in 1477 to Mary of Burgundy.

416   E.g.,

- *"Des einen Zahn im Schlund des anderen.—"* (V.11);
- *"Und dicht zur Mauer drängen wir die Spieße"* (V.42);
- *"Achill und ich— [...] / An ihrer Jungfraun Spitze aufgepflanzt"* (V.59);
- *"Wie ein / Gewitter, zwischen waldgekrönter Felsen Gipfeln / Geklemmt"* (V.142-4);
- *"Die Schlacht [...] / Schlug sie mit Donnerkrachen eben ein"* (V.141, 5);
- *"Das Schwert ihm wetterstrahlend in den Hals"* (V.184);
- *"In das Geweih des Hirsches fällt: der Jäger"* (V.214);
- *"verbissen in des Prachttiers Nacken"* (V.216);

- *"Durchbohrt mit einem Pfeilschuß, ihn"* (V.221);
- *"Laßt uns vereint [...] / [...] keilförmig [...] / [...] setzten. / Du wirst, [...] / Den Riß schon [...] zu finden wissen. / [...] so will ich ihn / [...] nehmen, [...] einem Klotzt gleich"* (V.229-36);
- *"er rollt / Von eines Hügels Spitze scheu herab / Auf uns kehrt plötzlich sich sein Lauf, wir [...] / Aufjauchzend"* (V.257-60);
- *"sein Viergespann [...] / Vor einem Abgrund [...] / In grause Tiefen [...] niederschaut. [...] in der er Meister ist, / Des Isthmus ganze vielgeübte Kunst"* (V.262-5);
- *"Sprengt schon die Königin [...] / ins Geklüft"* (V.279-80);
- *"Sie hemmt, Staub rings umqualmt sie, / Des Zelters flüchtgen Lauf, und hoch zum Gipfel / Das Angesicht, das funkelnde, gekehrt, / Mißt sie [...] die Wand: Der Helmbusch selbst, [...] / Reißt [...] sie nach hinten"* (V.282-7);
- *"Sie drängt mit sanfter Macht von beiden Seiten / Die Frauen [...] / im unruhigen Trabe / An dem Geklüfte auf und nieder streifend, / [...] ob nicht ein schmaler Pfad sich biete / Empor sie an des Felsens Wände klimmen, / Jetzt hier, in glühender Begier, jetzt dort [...] Jetzt hat sie jeden sanften Riß versucht, [...] / Schwingt sich des Gipfels höchstem Rande näher / Um einer Orme Höh [...] / Stürzt sie urplötzlich / [...] schmetternd / [...] zurück, / Und bricht den Hals sich nicht"* (V.301-29);
- *"Rasch einen Blick den Pfad schickt sie hinan; / Und dem gestreckten / Parder gleich, folgt sie / Dem Blick"* (V345-7).

417   E.g.,
- *"Geschürzt, der Helmbusch wallt ihr von der Scheitel, / Und seine Gold- und Purpurtroddeln"* (V.60-1);
- *"Die Rüstung wieder bis zum Gurt sich färbend"* (V.98);
- *"Mit eines Waldstroms wütendem Erguß"* (V.120);
- *"den Lorbeer, / Mit ihren jungen, schönen Leibern groß, / [...] düngend"* (V.150-2);
- *"Deiphobus [...] / [...] auf der Jungfrau Seite hingestellt"* (V.176);
- *"Ein neuer Anfall, heiß, wie Wetterstrahl, /Schmolz [...] / Auf uns, wie Wassersturz, hernieder"* (V.246-9);
- *"umstarrt von Spießen"* (V.256);
- *"Automedon, des Fahrzeugs rüstger Lenker, [...] / Er hilft dem Viergekoppel wieder auf"* (V.274-6);
- *"Das Fahrzeug steht [...] geordnet—"* (V.333);

418   Joachim Pfeiffer's objection (*Geschlechter*, 192) that it is the *male* nightingale that emits the mating call overlooks that all of Kleist's actors *are male*, that his young "maidens" enact *erômenoi*, his mature "mothers," *erastai*. Katrin Pahl's intuition in "'Geliebte, sprich!'—wenn Frauen sich haben," in Rüdiger Campe (Ed.), *Penthesileas Versprechen*, 165, that the conflict between Penthesilea and Achilles is "quasi-homosexual," is correct in so far as Achilles is androgynous or hermaphrodite: male in "battle," female in reproduction; she also eports (*ibid*, 173) that according to Hederich's collection of myths, Achilles at age nine began to wear girl's clothes (cf. Chr. Moser, leaning on Jürgen Manthey, in "Politische Körper—kannibalische Körper" (*ibid*, 287), terming Achilles "*ein[en] ausgesprochene[n] Muttersohn*"). Although she does not unravel Kleist's *satyrical* subtleties, Pahl's reading is refreshing.

419   Kleist tells Marie that *Penthesilea* is "calculated towards Pfuel's bellicose disposition" (II:796). Wichmann offers (*Kleist*, 112) that in Dresden Kleist, Pfuel, Rühle and Müller formed a tightly-knit "quartet"—he means this *socially*, but of course it functioned *erotically*, and Kleist may be depicting this "quartet" here: say, Kleist = Penthesilea, Pfuel = Achilles, Rühle = the Trojan, Müller = horse.

420   Gudrun Debriacher (*Rede*, 73) helpfully explains Penthesilea's destruction of Achilles in the context of Wünsch's *Kosmologische Unterhaltungen*: "*Nur deshalb kann Penthesilea ihren Geliebten so grausam zerfleischen, ist sie doch im Augenblick der Tat aufgeladen wie eine elektrische Batterie: "Diese Batterien sind im übrigen unter allen elektrischen Geräthschaften die wichtigsten, aber auch die furchtbarsten. Denn wenn sie groß genug sind: so krachen sie bei der Entladung wie ein starkes Geschütz, und ihr Schlag ist so heftig, daß er ziemlich große Thiere fordert, Metalle schmelzt.*" Debriacher quotes Wünsch, *Kosmologische Unterhaltungen*, 2nd Vol., 2nd Ed., (Leipzig, 1794), 676-7.

421   When the ends of two electrified metal rods come into close vicinity, an "electric arc effect," first described in 1802, may occur, whereby the current discharges into the air (or an equivalent medium) between the two ends, forming an electric arc. This effect occurs naturally as thunderbolts and can be artificially created in labs and applications such as arc lamps. The German word for "arc," "arch," and "bow "is the same, "*Bogen*."

422   Cf. Adam's incidental *"Ich will von ungespaltenem Leibe sein"* (V.1233) in *Krug*, suggesting a longing for a primordial state prior to his *Fall* and Walter's *Einfall* (invasion); satirically, he is of course thinking of the earstwhile undivided HRR. Aristophanes considered the descendents of the primordial male wholes—i.e., gay men—most suitable for leadership positions (cf. Plato's *Symposion*, 192a); many members of Kleist's "brotherhood" indeed later held high offices. In *A True History* (Book 1) Lucian's space traveler visits the moon, of whose inhabitants, the Selenites, he relates, in apparent reference to Aristophanes: "Firstly, they are not born of women but of men: they marry men, and they don't even have a word for woman. Up to the age of 25 each acts as a wife, and after that as a husband. They carry their babies not in the belly but in the calf of the leg" (trans. C.D.N. Costa).

423   Instead of via *gender change*, in *Käthchen* Napoleon's *cherchez la femme* is achieved with the help of a *character change* (Käthchen replacing Kunigunde), both comprising versions of Kleist's *ur*-dynamic of *Kleidertausch*, a dialectic that propels *Schroffenstein*, *Guiskard* (the back-to-back usurpations first by, then of Guiskard), *Penthesilea* and *Käthchen*. Unlike the Fichtean or Hegelian dialectic, the Kleistian culminates not in synthesis or sublimation but in abeyance: nothing is resolved (even in *Käthchen*: Napoleon does get his bride, but in the moment he marries her she has become pure soulless body—like Achilles, a taxidermied bird).

424   Mary Shelley did not specify the life force that animates her creation; only in later film adoptions is this force shown as electricity. Yet galvanism was "in the air," in the realms of science, medicine and literature. Galvani's set-up included a friction machine for the generation of current and several Leyden jars as condensators; Aldini's used bow-shaped metal electrodes whose gap was closed by a human body or body parts to allow electricity to circulate. Not only Kleist was fascinated by advances in electromagnetism, but so was Napoleon: in 1801 he had Allessandro Volta demonstrate the "voltaic pile" to him, the first battery that allowed for a continuous electrical current, developed by Volta in response to Galvani's "frog battery." I consider it highly likely that Kleist himself underwent electo-therapy, quite possibly with Wedekind during the "lost months" of 1804; it is easy enough to picture Kleist and Wedekind, who shared a fascination for innovations in the field of medicine, huddling together in the latter's lab at the University of Mainz, recreating Galvanis's or Aldini's set ups, with the minimal difference that their lab rat was Kleist, whose body was not dead and twitching, but alive and kicking. In the age

before systematic clinical trials, would not someone suffering mortal illness and unbearable pain happily volunteer his body for experimentation with novel therapeutic techniques?

425   It was believed that in Galvanian "frog batteries" the animals' lower thighs generated most of the electricity because they sustained the greatest injuries, a phenomenon that became known as "injury potential" (cf. https://en.wikipedia.org/wiki/Frog_battery); conceivably when Penthesilea penetrates him with her "Franklin rod," Achille's steely skin amplifies the ensuing Kleistian shock that electrocutes and roasts him, burning away the soft tissues encased by his steely skin as if by a brazen Sicilian bull.

426   Napoleon in 1812, during his return from the *Invasion of Russia*, reportedly rested under a 500-year old oak tree on the river Oder in Silesia (this "*Napoleoneiche*" burned down in 2010—due to arson, not lightning or storm).

427   Buzanzy, it so happens, is only c.90km, i.e., one day's journey, from Chalôns, and one wonders whether Kleist could have seized the opportunity to visit Puységur and seek treatment with him. Kleist was allowed to move relatively freely, under certain covenants. *Penthesilea*, on which he will have worked extensively during that period, is so overflowing of *syphilitical* therapeutic imagery, including some not seen in earlier works, that one cannot help thinking that Kleist took advantage of his enforced sojourn there, of approx. three months, to explore novel methods. Buzancy apart, the major city of Reims is only 40km from Chalôns and Kleist would have found opportunities there.

428   Cf. George Bataille, *Die Erotik*. Trans. Gerd Bergfleth (Munich: Matthes & Seitz, 1994), 140, my trans. The bull was considered the most noble of sacrificial animals, and was one of the symbols of Zeus as well as of Ares (Mars) and Dionysos—notes Joseph Campbell: "The sacrifice of the bull is symbolic of the sacrifice of that mortal part in us which leads to the release of the eternal" (*Thou Art That*, Novato, CA: New World Library, 2001, 89).

429   Cf. Burkert, *Greek Religion*, 63-4. Burkert notes (*ibid*, 65): "Again and again, myth relates how an animal sacrifice takes the place of a human sacrifice or, conversely, how an animal sacrifice is transformed into a human sacrifice."

430   The passage *"Das Haupt ganz unter Wasser, Liebe! So! / Und wieder! So, so! Wie ein junger Schwan!—"* anticipates the famous Thinka scene in *Marquise*, the "defiled" Marquise, like Penthesilea, bathing either her body or her member in mercury solution; a gesture also evoked by Achilles' bath in the Styx and Siegried's in dragon's blood.

431   Ancient accounts situate Themiscyra in a verdant plain of fruit orchards and fields—indeed an enchanted garden or *Elysium*, corresponding to *Erdbeben*'s verdant valley and *satirically* referring to the intermezzos between battles or artillery poundings, *satyrically* to *symphosia* or *orgies*, and *syphilitically* to interludes between outbreaks symptoms; the nymphs, virgins, maidens, angels, doves, etc. populating Kleist's idylls are immaculate lovers, rendering Kleist's version of paradise not dissimilar to Mohammed's. Chr. Moser notes (*KH*,201-2) that Kleist turns the traditional triadic model of historic development—"golden era" => "upheaval" => "new golden era"—on its head: "catastrophe" => "idyll" => "another catastrophe."

432   Is this a veiled cue that Kleist considered his and Brockes' friend Alex. zur Lippe the source of their syphilis infection? In the case of Brockes (assuming he was syphiliac), this would seem plausible; in the case of Kleist, less so, as it would not square well with my hypothesis that Kleist became infected during the Potsdam years, precipitating his departure from the army, his sojourns to the spas of the Riesengebirge in 1799 and Rügen in 1800, and his Würzburg journey. Having said this, Lippe hailed from Muskau in the Oberlausitz (cf. Rahmer, *Kleist,* 61), a mere 35km south of the Kleist's Guben estate and a similarly short distance south-east of the "Lausitz Clan's" estates clustered around Cottbus, so that it is not out of the question that the Lippe and Kleist families were acquainted and that Kleist met Lippe *before* Brockes. Rahmer reports (*Kleist,* 62) that Lippe in his final years, in the 1830s, ended up in a private health clinic in Freiburg, which is suggestive though not conclusive.

433   Voltaire's *Candide* features a syphiliac beggar with an eroded tip of the nose. This deformity was so common among syphilis sufferers that "no nose clubs" sprung up in London in the 19th century. On 18th February 1874 the *Star* reported: "an eccentric gentleman... invited every one thus afflicted... to dine on a certain day at a tavern, where he formed them into a brotherhood." http://thechirurgeonsapprentice.com/2013/02/14/syphilis-a-love-story/. My associating the Sphinx with this deformity need not be at the expense of other plausible associations: Anthony Stephens points

out (*Änigmen*, 94) that in Benjamin Hedrich's *Gründliches mythologisches Lexikon* the Sphinx is said to have "seized, torn apart and devoured" those who failed to answer her riddles, and Kleist, in referring to the Sphinx, could at once refer to mysteriousness, voraciousness and noselessness.

434   George Steiner, in *The Death of Tragedy*, 227-8, quoted in Anthony Stephens, *Kleist. The Dramas*, 125 n.29, critiques that "Like much of German romantic art, [*Penthesilea*] carries too far the conceit that love and death are kindred." Yet for Kleist the connexion of love and death was not an effect of romanticising but of material life experience. The idea that disease can be attractive is neither new nor has it gone away—cf. Lady Gaga's 2009 song *Bad Romance*: "I want your ugly / I want your disease / I want your everything."

435   J. Sintelaer, *The Scourge of Venus and Mercury*, reprinted in James Johnson (Ed.), *The Medico-Chirurgica Review*, Vol. 2, Chp. X, "On Syphilis, Pseudo-Syphilis, and Mercury" (December 1821), 599.

436   Sufferers of *tabes dorsalis* (degeneration of the spinal cord), a possible effect of late-stage syphilis, report instances of sharp pain that they compared with being stabbed by a red-hot iron or dagger (cf. Bäumler, *Amors vergifteter Pfeil*, 207); Kleist's image may thus refer to both the disease's advanced symptoms and its treatment's side-effects. The imagery of a descent into a mine appears already appears in *Amphitryon*, "*Steigst du nicht in des Herzens Schacht hinab / Und betest deinen Götzen an?*" (V.1433-4), and presumably reflects Kleist's experience, in 1801 en route to Paris, of descending into the Rammelberg mine near Goslar, which he likened to a descent into hell or a cyclop's blacksmith shop (cff. II:657). Re Penthesilea's rhythmic "*So! So! So! So!*," Bettine Menke, in "Intertextualität, Aussetzung der Darstellung und Formeln der Passion," in Rüdiger Campe (Ed.), *Penthesileas Versprechen*, 249, notes the "*allenfalls ikonische Lesbarkeit des Buchstaben 'o' und des zustoßenden Ausrufezeichens,*" without realising that it belongs into the same metaphorical field as O/F, +/-, keyhole/key, ring/arrow, etc.

437   The poisonous metal accumulates especially in the body's lower parts and tissues—palate, bowels, pelvic floor, feet—, as well as in the brain and liver (cf. Paul Ridder's discussion of Kleist's autopsy report, https://bilddetek.hypotheses.org/498). In *Zweikampf*, Rotbart's agonising death a syphilis patient's slowly being destroyed

by mercury poisoning. Cf. Bettine Menke's essay, "Penthesilea—Das Bild des Körpers und seine Zerfällung," in Günther Emig (Ed.), *Erotik und Sexualität*, 118-19.

438 Cf. Jean Baudrillard, "Requiem for the Twin Towers," in *The Spirit of Terrorism*. Trans. Chris Turner (London: Verso, 2002), 37-52.

439 Chr. M. Wieland called Adam Müller a "philosophical Pulcinella" and a "pitchman"—cf. Blamberger, *Kleist*, 315. For a different view, cf. Hans-Jochen Marquardt (*AML,IX*): "*Müller trat [dafür] ein…, die Vereinseitigung des überkommenden Literaturerbes durch Mischung der Wirkungsweisen verschiedener Gattungen und Genres zu synthetisieren. Unzweifelhaft betrachtete Müller Kleists 'Penthesilea' als einen solchen Versuch.*"

440 The three maidens strewing flowers before Phoebus Apollo's quadriga are typically identified as *Horai* (cf., e.g., Schulz, *Kleist*, 342). *Horai* appear in different numbers—three, four, nine, ten or twelve—, of which three is most common, representing the three seasons relevant to the Greeks or the triad of Eunomia (good governance), Dike (moral justice), and Eirene (peace); however, they do not normally appear in conjunction with Apollo, and if they indeed meant these figures to represent *Horai*, Kleist and his fellow editors may have sought to signify that Schiller's *Horen* had paved the way for *Ph*. Alternatively, instead of the *Horai*, the maidens could represent the *Charites* or three of the *Muses* typically associated with Apollo. Another possibility is that Kleist wished to introduce a displacement into the frontispiece corresponding to one in his *Prolog*: the *Horai* typically appear in conjunction not with Apollo but Dionysos (cf. Burkert, *Greek Religion*, 185), and Kleist may deploy them to hint at the Dionysiac element in *Ph*, thinly veiled by an Apollonian veneer; as such they could represent members of Dionysiac retinues, e.g., the *tragodia* (raving maenads) or *kōmos* (reveling satyrs). Lastly, they may not represent maidens at all, but handsome youths associated with Apollo, such as *epheboi* or *kouroi*. The three maidens could also be included to complete a representation of the numerology of the Pythagorean triangle that may be contained in the frontispiece: 4 horses, 3 maidens, 2 wheels (not visible), 1 chariot. Marital refers to "Phoebus and the learned sisters" in a context that clearly alludes to male homosexual "brothers" (cf. *Epigrams*, 1.70).

441 Kreutzer (*Dichterische Entwicklung*, 224) links *Penthesilea* with Goethe's epic fragment *Achilleis* (1805-8), which Rühle in early January 1808 sought to solicit for *Ph* (cf. *LS*,201).

442   *Faust. Ein Fragment* was first published in 1790 and subject to reviews, e.g., in the *Allgemeinen Literatur-Zeitung* of 15th June 1805 (cf. Sembdner, *In Sachen Kleist*, 35); A. Müller referred to it in his lectures in 1806—cf. Baxa's notes to *AML*,317). The publication of *Faust. Eine Tragödie* in 1808 will have been feverishly anticipate, and Kleist must have been aware of this literary event; Gentz mentions it to Müller in early 1808—cf. *AML*,317).

443   Does not Penthesilea also represent Goethe, that other giant destined, like Napoleon, to buckle under the weight of his own gravitas and collapse in the storm of Kleist's poetry? Christa Wolf has previously touched on this possibility.

444   Around this time Kleist made the acquaintance of a colourful figure nicknamed "fat Bose," who appears to have been in the habit of mimicking Diogenes, for Bülow reports: "*Rittmeister von Bose, eine Art Falstaff, Zyniker, der nachts oft auf der Elbbrücke schlief und bei Tage meist dasaß, um Neuigkeiten anzupassen*" (*LS*,232b).

445   My usage of the term "suicide bomber" is in part inspired by Jeremy Fernando's *The Suicide Bomber; and her Gift of Death* (New York: Atropos, 2010); cf. also L. Rubiner, "Der Dichter als Sprengmeister," in *Der Dichter greift in die Politik* (Leipzig: Reclam, 1976, 251ff.), and Sloterdijk, *Kritik*, 431: "*Im Nahkampf mit der Arroganz eines Nero... blieb dem ironischen selbstwewußten Patrizier [Petronius]... am Ende kein anderer Ausweg als der, bewußt zu sterben. Dieses* savoir mourir, *das den eigenen Tod bewußt kalkuliert als möglichen letzten Preis der Freiheit, verbindet das entmachtete, jedoch stolze römische Patriziat mit dem Christentum... ein Bewußtsein von existentieller Souveränität.*"

446   Animals can be enacted by human actors with suitable costumes and masks. The drama's sense of character "overload" is heightened by a vast supporting cast of heroes, gods, and mythical creatures that are mentioned or alluded to but do not appear on stage: Priam, Agamemnon, Helena and Hector, Ares, Artemis, Aphrodite, Zeus (also alluded to by his symbols: thunderbolt, eagle, bull, oak), Dionysos (lioness, panther, tiger, maenads), Hades (Styx, Orcus), Apollo, Helios, Hecate and Persephone, not to mention anachronistic allusions to YHWH and Christ. Peter Staengle in *Kleist. Sein Leben*, 110, also points to the excessive complexity of Kleist's characters and stage machinery.

447   Sembdner (*In Sachen Kleist*, 258; 288) relates attempts by earlier directors and theatre companies—notably Kleist's contemporary Franz von Holbein (who depoyed E.T.A. Hoffmann to paint a stage set for *Käthchen*) and the famous late-19th century Meininger Theatergesellschaft—to bring Kleist's spectacles to the stage. Most of *Penthesilea*'s scenes strictly speaking require no more than three actors on stage, provided the minors and extras are members of the chorus, and more recently some directors have radically cut down the number of actors: Michael Thalheimer, in his *Penthesilea* at the *Schauspiel Frankfurt* (premièred 4th December 2015), cast but three actors, and Hans-Jürgen Syberberg, in his 1989 film, cast but a single actresss, collapsing Kleist's polyphony into a monologue.

448   Cf. Schmidt, *Kleist*, 113-15. Eybl (*Kleist-Lektüren*, 144) has four sections.

449   Gabriele Brandstetter ('Inszenierte Karthasis in Kleists *Penthesilea*,' in: Lubkoll and Oesterle (Ed.), *Experimente*, 231) and Anthony Stephens (*Kleist, The Dramas*, 100) note *Penthesilea*'s "filmic" quality. Cf. also Deleuze and Guattari, *Thousand Plateaus*, 381: "Immobility and speed, catatonia and rush, a 'stationary process', station as process—these traits of Kleist's are eminently those of the nomad." Wildbrant characterises (*Kleist*, 263) the drama as "epic" and "of frequently exaggerated plasticity."

450   Already a 1899 stage adaption of Lew Wallace's novel *Ben-Hur* featured a live chariot race (with real horses running on treadmills and secured with steel cables) against the backdrop of a vast cyclorama (a panorama inside of a cylindrical platform) rotating in the opposite direction of the horses' gallop, creating the illusion of speed.

451   During the Würzburg journey Kleist compares (cf. II:549) the rapidly changing landscapes he observes from his carriage with the pictures visible inside a *Guckkasten*. A *Guckkasten* (zograscope) is a box in which images (paintings, engravings or drawings, typically of city- or landscapes) are arranged such that when viewed through a lens, an illusion of depth and three-deminsionality is created, aided by devices and techniques such as perspectival painting, depth cues, visual angles, lighting, horizontal disparities, and overlay of several semi-transparent images. *Guckkästen* became popular attractions on markets, kermises, and funfairs from the 1750s onwards. Blamberger (*Kleist*, 340) notes that the impact of Kleist's syntax and rhythm, which is maintained for the reader or listener of a declamation, is lost in the observation of a stage performance.

452   Walter Müller-Seidel's claim (*Penthesilea*, 152) that *"Alle Kampfhandlungen... sind nur Mittel zur Darstellung seelischer Vorgänge, damit sich an ihnen und durch sie Unberechenbares im Seelenleben des Menschen zeigen kann"* is misguided: Kleist's action scenes represent physical, historical events.

453   Kleist probably composed *Das Letzte Lied* in late April or early May 1809, in the wake of Fr. Wilh.'s refusal to join the *War of the Fifth Coalition* and Napoleon's routing the Austrian army in the *Landshut Maneuvre* and subsequent march on Vienna. Michalzik notes (*Kleist*, 360) that the Kleist reception, having for a long time located this poem in the aftermath of *Wagram*, more recently put it into April 1809, following Rudolf Loch's pointing (*Kleist*, 328-9) to Austria's defeat at the *Battle of Regensburg* (18th-22nd April) as possible context. The poem's content supports Loch's hypothesis: it describes a war that, far from having ended, has only just begun (*"Die Blitze zucken schon"*), and it mourns not a military defeat but the HRR's demise (*"Der alten Staaten graues Prachtgebäude"*) in lockstep with the Bonapartean dynasty's rise (*"ein Geschlecht, von düsterm Haar umflogen"*); it marks an instant not of death but of *silence*: the instant in which the bard's song—*Hermannsschlacht*—has become irrelevant because his King has shown himself to be deaf to it. The poem reiterates Kleist's conviction that only a unified Germany can defeat Napoleon, and that, consequently, Fr. Wilh.'s refusal to join the war already precipitates Germany's defeat.

454   Karl Aug. Böttiger claims (cf. *LS*,268) that Kleist found the legend of Käthchen on a leaflet purchased on a fair during his military campaign. While Kleist's unit did not reach Swabia, it passed close-by; Kleist also could have reached Heilbronn during the 1800 Würzburg journey, although this is conjecture, and may have passed through Swabia in late 1802 en route from Thun to Oßmannstedt. Sembdner uncovered (cf. *In Sachen Kleist*, 284-5) a folk ballade that could have been the basis for Kleist's story.

455   Fr. Carl v Savigny in 1804 married Clemens Brentano's sister Kunigunde, and Kleist will have first met the Savignys in Berlin in 1810 (cf. Michalzik, *Kleist*, 386) if not earlier, and it is therefore possible that he modeled his character Kunigunde in part on Savigny's wife, who as a young woman spent two years in the Ursuline monastery at Fritzlar, a biographical detail that could have provided a reference for Kleist's plot (Kleist will have passed through Fritzlar, halfway between Kassel and Marburg en route to Frankfurt/Main, on several occasions). It has been speculated

in the *Kleist-Forschung* that Kleist modelled Käthchen and Kunigunde on women he encountered in Dresden, Julie Kunze, believed to have charmed him greatly, and Dora Stock, who perhaps charmed him less (cf. Bülow, *Kleist*, 53; Blamberger, *Kleist*, 307). While plausible, for it was efficient for Kleist to model characters on actual persons, this is ultimately immaterial for our evaluation of the drama. Gotthilf Heinr. Schubert's recurse to Gmelin's case studies of somnambulant patients, in particular the 12-year old Liesette Kornacher of Heilbronn, could also have informed Kleist's Käthchen figure (cf. Schede, *Kleist*, 95-6).

456   The Kleist reception's *communis opinio* attributes Käthchen's speechlessness either to her "purity" or her having come under the Count's spell—not a magic spell that is, but psychological suggestion (*"Tout est dans la suggestion"*: Joseph Breuer and Sigmund Freud, *Studien über Hysterie*, 1st Ed. (Leipzig/Wien: Deuticke, 1895, 86).

457   Cf. Chris Cullens and Dorothea von Mücke, "Das Käthchen von Heilbronn," in: Walter Hinderer (Ed.), *Interpretationen*, 122-3: *"Käthchen wäre das Weib, mit dem sich ein neues Geschlecht, ein Herrschergeschlecht zeugen ließe! Direkt formuliert, sieht Strahl in Käthchen eine ideale Stammutter, bestens zur Zucht von Nachkommen geeignet.*" Cullens and Mücke, perceptive as they are, overlook that while the vigorously healthy Käthchen may be an ideal *mother*, she is not in the first instance Strahl's ideal *bride*. Queen Luise, whom Käthchen at least in part represents, in the course of 15 years produced ten children, of which seven survived, and was *the* model-mom of Kleist's day. The historical Charlemagne, to whom Strahl alludes, was married at least four times, usually to princesses from allied families, though never one from the imperial family in Constantinople (though his eldest daughter was at one point engaged to Constantine VI). Charlemagne sought legitimacy by being crowned by the Catholic Pople (a gesture Napoleon mimicked), not by marrying into the imperial dynasty (the Isaurian dynasty was then on its last leg, the Empress Irene being unable to prevent the Byzantine throne from passing to the short-lived Nikephorian dynasty in AD 802). Napoleon sought both, the blessing of the Catholic church and marriage into an ancient imperial dynasty.

458   Cf. Diogenes Laertius (*Lives*, Book 6, Chapter 40): "Plato had defined the human being as an animal, biped and featherless, and was applauded. Diogenes plucked a fowl and brought it into the lecture-room with the words, 'Here is Plato's human being.' In consequence of which there was added to the definition, 'having

broad nails."' Already in *Schroffenstein*'s scene of Ursula-Napoleon throwing the emasculated little finger (penis) amidst the German princes, Kleist re-stages Diogenes' performance; and even earlier, in a letter to Ulrike dated 25th November 1800, he adopts Diogenes' famous demand to the Great Alex., to step out of the Sun: *"Wenn man [die Künste und Wissenschaften] in ihrem Gange nur nicht stört, das ist alles, was sie von den Königen begehren"* (II:602; cf. Schulz, *Kleist,* 199). In *Ph* epigram no. 2, *"die Penthesilea, / Hundekomödie"* (I:20), Kleist denotes his drama explicitly as *kynical* comedy. Sloterdijk lists (*Kritik*, 295) the following VIPs or literary figures for his *kynical/cynical* "hall of fame": Diogenes; Lucian; (Goethe's) Mephisto; (Dostoevsky's) Great Inquisitor; Rabelais; Machiavelli; Eulenspiegel; (Diderot's) Rameau's newphew; Fr. II of Prussia; de Sade; Napoleon; Heinrich Heine; Nietzsche. *Erdbeben*'s cobbler and *Kohlhaas*' knacker, who show both *kynical* and *cynical* behaviour, and both of whom represent Napoleon, perhaps highlight the generals' progression (in Kleist's view: retardation) from popular fighter who *defies* the establishment to haughty ruler who himself *is* the establishment (for Sloterdijk's distinction of the *kynical* and the *cynical*, cf. *ibid*, 366 and 399-401). In Lucian's dialogue *Death of Peregrinus* the protagonist travels to Egypt to train with cynics there, which involves undertaking "indifferent acts" such as masturbating in the middle of a large crowd; Kleist's scene in *Kohlhaas* in which the knacker relieves himself on the Dresden *Schloßplatz* is clearly derivative of this cynical practice, irrespective of whether he in fact pees, masturbates or sodomises the "cart" (cf. II:59).

459   Voltaire already commented on the *HRR* using a term at least as ironic as Kleist's "mosaic," namely *"corps"* ("body," or "corpse"): *"Ce corps qui s'appelait et qui s'appelle encore le saint empire romain n'était en aucune manière ni saint, ni romain, ni empire"* (*Essai sur l'histoire générale et sur les mœurs et l'esprit des nations*, Chapter 70, 1756). The "mosaic" Kunigunde accurately depicts the four corners of the *HRR*: Munich (Bavaria and Tyrol) in the south, the French-occupied Rhineland in the west, Habsburg Hungary in the east, Swedish Pomerania in the north, and Kleist's eclectic description succinctly states how compromised her boundaries had become by c.1810: the Rhineland was now French, Bavaria and Tyrol French vassal territories, Western Pomerania still Swedish, and Hungary altogether outside her boundaries. Aug. Heinr. Hoffmann von Fallersleben, in the first strophe of Germany's national anthem, *Das Lied der Deutschen* (1841)— *"Von der Maas bis an die Memel, / Von der Etsch bis an den Belt"*—mimicks Kleist (who in turn mimicks Walther von der Vogelweide, who already used a similar device in c.1198); but whereas Fallersleben celebrates or

evokes Germany's unity, Kleist deplores her dismemberment. Fallersleben's putative German boundaries are more "expansive" than are Kleist's, though not unrealistic if the German language area were taken as basis for its delineation: the river Maas lies to the west of the Rhine, the Etsch (in South-Tyrol) lies to the south of Munich, the Belt, a strait in the Baltic Sea between Germany and Denmark, lies to the north of Pomerania, and most of the course of the river Memel lies further to east than the buik of Hungary. In the event, Germany would never again reach Kleist's or Fallersleben's boundaries fully: the Deutscher Bund (1815-66) did not include East Prussia, the subsequent Deutsches Reich (1871-1945) did not include Austria or Limburg, and even Hitler's *Grossdeutsches Reich* did not extend to the Maas or the Etsch. Germany's dismemberment Kleist laments in this passage would thus prove to be permanent. Kleist's "three kingdoms of nature" refer to the animal, plant and mineral kingdoms— cf. Lessing's 1747 poem "*Die drey Reiche der Natur*." Concerning his depiction of the dishevelled and artificial Kunigunde, Kleist may be drawing on Martial (*Epigrams* 9.37, trans. Gideon Nisbet): "You may be at home, Galla, but your hair is out—out being done in the heart of Subura. You put away your teeth at night, same as you do your imported skills, and you lie tucked away in a hundred little jars; your face doesn't share your bed. That eyebrow you bat, they delivered this morning; and you feel no reverence for your grey-haired cunt…" (Subura was a red-light district in Rome).

460   The motif of the *HRR*'s double-headed eagle persists throughout Kleist's œuvre: in *Erdbeben* as Don F's (Franz II/I) two sons, one of whom is destroyed in the "lynching," representing the *HRR*, while the other one survives, representing Austria; in *Kohlhaas* as the the two blacks that are everyone's object of desire (cf. *Emigrant*); in *Verlobung* as Congo Hoango's (Napoleon's) two sons, Nappy and Seppy (the former name implying a Bonapartean, the latter a Habsburgian lineage); in *Schroffenstein* as the rivals' faces turned away from each other as they shake hands; in *Krug* as Adam's two legs, one of which has a prosthesis (*HRR*) that he leaves leaning against a tree, keeping only its bloody leg stump (*Rheinbund*), the other one sporting a club foot (Austria); in *Penthesilea* as the two female breasts, one of which is burned off in *Käthchen* as the mosaic Kunigunde left with only one feather in her hat. Dahlmann's hopeful statement, "once Prussia rises again from its lethargy between being and not being, the remainder of Germany will follow the united eagles of Austria and Prussia" (*LS*,316), while referring to a pan-German military alliance also contains the idea of the *HRR*'s rehabilitation.

461   Published as fairy-tale #24 in Vol. 1 of *Kinder-und Hausmärchen* by Reimer who also published Kleist's *Käthchen* and *Erzählungen*. According to the Aarne & Thompson classification system for fairy-tales, *Frau Holle* is classified as "Type 480, The Kind and the Unkind Girls." The 1812 ed. of the Grimms' *Kinder-und Hausmärchen* contained Kleist's BA anecdote from 13. November 1810, "Wie Kinder Schlachtens mit einander gespielt haben," so that the influence was clearly mutual.

462   While Schulz is convinced (*Kleist*, 413) that "*Die Kaiserstadt hat Kleist… nie betreten*," the precision with which Kleist depicts the Hofburg appears to suggest otherwise. Loch (*Kleist*, 330) notes that Austrian envoy Joseph Baron von Buol envisioned deploying Kleist as war correspondent in Vienna, which is plausible: decommissioned officers signed an oath that they would not join foreign military services, and if they decided to do so anyways, they would often do so in the guise of a non-military role—Rühle, for example, in 1809 worked as war correspondent and military adviser under the cover of a commission as war painter (his subsequently published report on the 1809 became a bestseller—cf. Schulz, *Kleist*, 409). When Kleist and Dahlmann visit the Aspern battlefield on 25th May 1809 (cf. II:826) they are apprehended by Austrian military police and escorted to the Austrian HQ, whence they return to Prague, which they reach on 31st May, so that on this occasion they can not have entered Vienna; their diplomatic passport (*Gesandtschaftspass*) issued by Buol (cf. Müller-Salget, *Kleist*, 101) will have been valid only in unoccupied Austrian territories and will not have afforded them entry into occupied Vienna until the peace, or at least the truce of 12th July, was signed. However, since Kleist and Dahlmann left Prague for Saxony only on 31st October (cf. Loch, *Kleist*, 338), i.e., a full six months after being returned there by the Austrian authorities, it is eminently possible that Kleist visited Vienna during his mysterious Prague hiatus. In the absence of further evidence we cannot decide this question, and it is not necessary for my argument that *Käthchen*'s final scene takes place at the Hofburg, for images of the type I reproduce in the main text would have been readily available to Kleist in Prague. Nevertheless, Kleist on several occasions (1800, 1802, 1808, 1811) planned to visit Vienna, and the opportunity clearly existed in the autumn of 1808. It would be oh-so-Kleistian if instead of being tied to the sick-bed in Prague during those months, he spent at least a portion of that time on a mission to Vienna. His portrait of the "wedding at Vienna" being so vivid, he could even have been present in Vienna when *Schönbrunn* was signed (in which case it is even possible that he observed Napoleon in person). On 23rd November 1809, having rushed to Frankfurt/O. to secure his

share of the value of the family home, Kleist mentions to Ulrike (cf. II:829) that he is preparing to return to Austria (perhaps to complete *Käthchen* in situ); probably he goes to Berlin instead, to observe the return of his King, and to Frankfurt/M. for treatment. One factor that speaks against his having been in Vienna in 1809 is that Napoleon in 1809 had the Burgtor, as well as several bastions and ravelins, dynamited (two extant base-maps of Vienna's fortifications, one of 1773 and the one I am using, from 1858, show the evolution—cf. https://de.wikipedia.org/wiki/Wiener_Glacis), so that as of 1810, when Kleist completed *Käthchen*, *there was no gate at the location he indicates* (the gate shown on the right-hand painting, which still stands and is today known as Äußeres Burgtor, was constructed in 1818), and if he had been in Vienna in 1809, he *presumably would have known that*: the grounds to the south-west of the Hofburg, where he locates the wedding scene, in the summer and autumn of 1809 would have been akin to a moonscape, full of rubble and ruins from the dynamited structures, unsightly and quite unsuitable for a stately ceremony. On the other hand, perhaps he *did* know all of this—and expected his audiences to know it, too, certainly the Viennese audiences—, and it was all part of his scenario: he has Napoleon and Marie-Louise's wedding take place among the rubble and ruins of the *HRR*'s former capital, conquered and rampaged by the usurper. The scene, rather than halcyonian, is apocalyptic. For an image of the old Burgtor, cf. https://www.geschichtewiki.wien.gv.at/Altes_Äußeres_Burgtor.

463   Cf. http://www.habsburger.net/de/kapitel/kaiser-franz-ii-und-napoleon

464   Cf. Richard Samuel: "*Kleist und seine Freunde fielen Metternichs geschichtlicher Kehrtwendung ebenso zum Opfer wie der Freiherr vom Stein,*" quoted by Horst Häker, *Beiträge* 1997, 201.

465   The forthcoming wedding will have beent the talk of the town, including among the intellectuals assembled in Wolfart's house: Brentano, Arnim, Müller, Kleist, Loeben, Eichendorff (cf. *LS*,319).

466   Napoleon sat on the Throne of Dagobert in 1804 when he created the Légion d'Honneur. His faible for this classical design seems to elude today's Kleist readers, who tend to discuss the curule seat (usually citing a passage from *Homburg*, not *Käthchen*) in the context of juridical sway, specifically of Lucius Junius Brutus' condemnation of his own sons, or in relation to a picture showing Goethe seated on

such a chair. Kleist's contemporaries, however, would no doubt have understood the connexion with Napoleon: well into the 1830s and 1840s, as part of *Le style Empire*, the design was copied all over Europe, including for Ludwig II's birth bed in Munich's Schloss Nymphenburg.

467   Kleist likely chose the name of the presiding judge, Otto, in reference to Emperor Otto I (AD 912-73) and the Ottonian (originally: Liudolfinger) dynasty that furbished the first Holy Roman emperors.

468   Alternatively, these characters could represent Napoleon's top envoys, e.g., Louis, comte de Narbonne-Lara, Jean-Baptiste de Nompère de Champagny, or Charles Maurice de Talleyrand-Périgord. In Paris in the autumn of 1803 Kleist requested the Prussian envoy Lucchesini to encourage Alexandre Berthier, Napoleon's war minister, to enroll him in the British invasion army. Berthier rejected; Fr. Wilh., whom Luccesini informed of the request, was not amused. It is Flammberg who advises Strahl to "step out the Greek firesparks" (V.753), i.e., to extinguish any remaining pockets of German resistance.

469   Nicolas Gosse's painting shows the Austrian envoy Karl Freiherr von Vincent submitting Franz's letter to Napoleon. Napoleon dismissed him with a rebuke similar to one he had previously given to Metternich: "Well then, it is war you seek; I have prepared for it, and I will be terrible" (Quoted in John H. Gill, *1809: Thunder on the Danube*, Vol. 1; London: Frontline Books, 2014, 389). Aristophanes' play *Acharnians* features a chorus of charcoal burners.

470   Kleist in the same *Ph* issue published the poem *Katharina von Frankreich*, which covers the same topic (*"der schwarze Prinz"* = Napoleon; cf. I:14).

471   Kleist's denoting Kunigunde as *"vom Stamm der alten sächsischen Kaiser"* (V.1378; i.e., the Liudolfinger), while not literally correct, is not inappropriate for a member of the House of Holstein-Gottorp-Romanov, whose ancestral Gottorf Castle was in Schleswig, at the northern edge of the medieval Duchy of Saxony, and which comprised a branch of the House of Oldenburg, whose ancestral Aldenburg Castle was also located within the Duchy of Saxony.

472   It is eminently plausible that the down-to-earth Mme Mère de l'Empereur showed skepticism regarding her son's marriage plans, concerning Katharina, Marie-Louise, or other contenders.

473   Käthchen's *"Kreuzweg* (V.1388), like Josephe's *"Scheideweg"* (II:149), marks a moment of decision. In both cases Kleist's protagonist chooses the path of doom: Josephine that to her death, via the valley of the pines/penises and the encounter with Don F, Käthchen that to her submission, via Heilbronn into Strahl's embrace. *Satirically* torn between Franz I and Napoleon, Käthchen *satyrically* oscillates between the immaculate Maria and two youthful angels (V.1388-9).

474   Anthony Stevens' footnote (*Kleist*, 131, n.10), "As a final discouragement for readers concerned with making things add up, a monastery of the Augustinians in Act II, Scene 1 (I:478) turns Dominican in Act III, Scene 4 (I:484)," overlooks that Kleist deliberately deploys such displacements to indicate a shift in storyline or characters—cf. the timid *Gustav* in *Verlobung* momentarily turning into the trigger-happy *August*. As a working assumption it is safest to assume that *everything* in Kleist "adds up." Here, if the "Augustine" Hatto in III/4 has become a "Dominican" (aka "*Domini canes*" because of their doggedness in combating heresy), Kleist may be alluding to the fact that Cardinal Fesch's relationship with Napoleon soured when the latter in May 1808 annexed the remains of the Papal States.

475   Bernard Greiner denotes (*Kleists Dramen*, 192) the Emperor's tryst as rape, as if Europe's (at least nominally) most powerful man would necessariily have to resort to rape if he was resolved to seduce a young commoner in a moonlit night. Since he cannot fathom that a woman may simply give herself to a man, a highly desirable one at that, Greiner, to whom Kleist's women are always chaste and innocent victims of male violence, insists that the man (be he even the Emperor) must necessarily be a rapist. Even on the *satyrical* level Greiner's contention does not hold: in so far as Käthchen is the product of the union of Habsburg Austria (*Der Kaiser*) and Hohenzollern Prussia (*die unbekannte Frau*), Kleist is here arguably referring to the *War of the First Coalition*, which the two German powers pursued in voluntary if fragile cohabitation. If anyone could be accused of rape, it would have to be *Borussia* (*die unbekannte Frau*), who with the *Treaty of Basel* unilaterally left *Austria* (*Der Kaiser*) in the lurch.

476   The French deployment of the reconnaissance ballon *l'Entreprenant*, depicted on the painting hovering above the horizon, is considered the first military use of an aircraft that influenced the result of a battle. Kleist was fascinated by military technology, and this event could well have inspired his imagery of "Jupiter rising in the East."

477   Napoleon was not personally involved in the *Battle of Fleurus* or the *Flanders Campaign*: in 1794 he was seconded to the *Armée d'Italie* in the Maritime and Ligurian Alps, where he inspected coastal fortifications, organized the artillery, and devised battle plans against Austria and Sardinia. After rising to prominence in 1795 with his decisive action to protect the *National Convention* against the royalist rebellion of 13 *Vendémiaire An* IV (5th October 1794), he took control of the *Armée d'Italie* and decisively contributed to France's ultimate success in the *War of the First Coalition*. In putting down the 1794 rebellion, his deployment of large cannons in the streets around the Tuileries—"with a whiff of grapeshot," as historian Thomas Carlyle puts it in his 1837 *The French Revolution: A History*—proved decisive and buttressed his fame as artillery general.

478   Quoted in Andrew Roberts, *Napoleon the Great* (London: Allen Lane, 2014).

479   Pope Pius VII rejected Napoleon's bid to divorce and re-marriage, and the Catholic church never anulled Napoleon's marriage with Joséphine. Napoleon in response kept the Pope under house arrest while seeking support from other members of the Catholic hierarchy. When thirteen Cardinals snubbed his wedding ceremony, he vehemently pursued these "Black Cardinals," forcing them into exile or impoverishing them. Stein, following his dismissal by Fr. Wilh. in November 1808, sought exile in Bohemia, whence he continued influencing German politics; the stage direction, *"der Kaiser und Theobald, welche in Mänteln gehüllt, im Hintergrunde"* (V.2527), suggests not only *satyrical* but also *satirical* cabal; Stein will have been among the marriage's vocal critics.

480   In completing (P), apart from striking substantial passages from (Ph II) no longer relevant to him, Kleist also adds carefully crafted insertions to ensure that later parts of the storyline link seamlessly with earlier ones, especially with respect to Käthchen and Kunigunde's transformation. Most notably, he inserts a half-sentence into Freiburg's speech in scene II/6, *"wo ich nichts tun will, als ihr das*

Halstuch abnehmen: das soll meine ganze Rache sein!" (V.938-9), which establishes the reddish mark on the imperial princess' neck—*"ein Mal... rötlich auf dem Nacken"*—as a critical nexus, conjuring the possibility of the mark being discovered not on Kunigunde's but on Käthchen's neck. This insertion he complements with the revised section II/9, in which Kunigunde confirms that she is *not* of imperial stock, and elaborates the relevance of the mark (cf. V.1230-1), a relevance to which Freiburg earlier obliquely refers when he threatens revenge (a revenge that presumably entails unveiling the fact that she does *not* bear the mark). Kleist's *Kalenderbetrachtungen* are always instructive: Theobald reports that Käthchen turned 15 at the recent feast day of Easter (cf. V.64), and if Kleist's reference point were Easter 1808—(Ph I) appeared in the April/May *Phöbus* issue—, then Käthchen was born on Easter 1793, which coincides with the *Siege of Mainz* and thus with Kleist's "innitiation." Perhaps he earlier conceived of the figure Käthchen as representing German unity, still intact during the siege, whereas now, as of 1808, he has *Der Kaiser* (Franz) claim her as his offspring, produced with the help of a woman from Swabia (by that time a French dependency). *Der Kaiser's* recalling that Jupiter rose above the eastern horizon while he sired Käthchen (cf. V.2409-10), may indicate that Käthchen's birth from the beginning stood under a "bad star"—i.e., Napoleon's. Easter Sunday in 1793 fell on the 31st March, i.e, if my conjecture were correct that Kleist's initiation took place on 27th or 28th March, when Michalzik's source suggests his unit camped at Biebrich (cf. my discussion above), his initiation could have fallen on the day before Good Friday, or, if Michalzik's source were somewhat imprecise, even on the very day of Good Friday. Did Jupiter rise in the east during the evening of Good Friday 1793? The astronomers among Kleist's readers may want to find out.

481   Like (P), the first volume of *Erzählungen* went to the printers within weeks of Luise's death, and Kleist used *Kohlhaas*, as the last one of the four novellas contained in that volume he completed, to account for this unexpected event, incorporating an eleventh-hour twist in which the protagonist's murdered wife returns as a gypsy revenant (Luise's spirit) to secure their sons' elevation. I offered in *Emigrant* that *Kohlhaas'* ending comprises Kleist's elegy to the deceased Queen, and it seems plausible that Kunigunde's unexected rising again in *Käthchen*'s final scene fulfills the same purpose.

482   Kleist's in February 1808 in *Ph* publishing *Marquise*, whose scenario encompasses Luise's (*Borussia*'s) union with Count F-Napoleon, was possible only

because in the sceanario the Count initially marries not the Marquise but her family (the "family" of the German dynasties), their "marriage" taking place in Vienna's Augustinerkirche, under the auspices of the Habsburgs, and entailing year-long political congress and negotiation, rather than a wedding ceremony proper, in which Count F foraits his imperial ambitions, following which he is finally permitted to commensurate his marriage with the Marquise-*Borussia* (Friederike?). Whereas (Ph I), published two or three months after *Marquise*, excludes the possibility of Strahl entering into a *royal* marriage, *Marquise* explores the possibility of Count F being incorporated into a *royal* dynasty by forfaiting his *imperial* ambitions.

483   Gerhard Schulz notes (*Kleist*, 385): "*Das Stück scheint Kleist bereits im Sommer 1808 abgeschlossen zu haben, wenn man Tieck glauben kann, der es damals, als er für kurze Zeit in Dresden war, gelesen und kommentiert haben will.*" Tieck in the summer of 1808 could have seen an earlier version of the stage adaptation Kleist sent to Collin in October, which would have been substantially different from (P), though it could already have contained elements of (Ph II).

484   Käthchen's *satyrical* terminology is typical—*phallus*: lamp, bar, sword, dagger, pike, magic staff, tails, well, column, feathers, thunderbolt, face (*Antlitz*), hand, lash, trunks, crown of the head, sceptre, lantern, torches, fire hooks, forehead, oaks, sting, head (*Haupt*); *anal orifice*: gate, portal, bowl, stables, door, grotto, dungeons, pigsty; *condom*: helmet, hat, glove, envelope, sheath (*Futteral*); *codpiece* or *dildo-harness*: visor, cloth, bodice (*Leibchen*), harness, gag, scarf, sash (*Schärpe*); *ejaculate*: dust, water, blood, tears, night dew, March snow, gush (*Erguss*).

485   Cf. Gentz's retelling, in *AML*, 82, of the divine "endless night" in Dresden, which evidently involved three male lovers and a female prostitute.

486   Wolf Kittler's pertinent observations regarding the *satirical* Kleist are again put into sharp relief by his misguided reading (*Geburt*, 192) of the *satyrical* Kleist: "*Infolgedessen geht sie [Käthchen] wie alle Kleistschen Frauen aus der Inquisition um ihre jungfräuliche Reinheit mit Glanz und Glorie hervor.*" Scooping up water from a well may have been "code" for intercourse long before Kleist: an early biographer of Ulrich von Hutten notes that the reformer contracted syphilis in Italy "because there he perhaps savored water from an impure well" (cf. Bäumler, *Amors vergifteter Pfeil*, 51).

487 Herminio Schmidt, who analyses the electro-magnetical references in Käthchen, perceptively identifies Kunigunde herself as Kleistian jar and the silver tablet in the workshop as electrical conductor (cf. Heinz Schoot, *Erotik*, 160-1). While I do not necessarily agree with his exact associations, his attempt at making sense of this complex is remarkable and anticipates my own.

488 Cf. Schulz (*Kleist*, 380): "*Kleist... verlegte das auf der Bühne nicht Zeigbare in eine Szenenbemerkung, wie sein Theater überhaupt oft die Tendenz hat, episches, erzählendes Theater zu sein.*" Kleist's technique of telling the *satyrical* story via stage directions could have been inspired, e.g., by Schiller's *Don Karlos* (III/7): "*Der KÖNIG kommt angekleidet heraus. DIE VORIGEN. Alle nehmen die Hüte ab... KÖNIG (den ganzen Kreis flüchtig durchschauend). / Bedeckt Euch!... (Don Karlos und der Prinz von Parma... küssen dem König die Hand...)... FERIA (ein Knie vor dem König beugend)... (Er winkt Alba zu sich, welcher sich vor ihm auf ein Knie niederlässt,..)... MEDINA SIDONIA (nähert sich wankend, und kniet vor dem Könige nieder, mit gesenktem Haupt). (Nach langem Stillschweigen)... (Er reicht ihm die Hand zum Kusse)... (Er gibt ihm einen Wink aufzustehen und sich zu bedecken—dann wendet er sich gegen die andern.)...(Der Herzog geht ab. Der König ruft Feria... Er geht ab.)*" Schiller's scene in the audience chamber can be read as an orgiastic symposium involving the king—dressed for the occasion, as the stage direction emphasises—and his courtiers, and while what for Kleist was constitutive of his textual fabric, for Schiller was perhaps mere playful *Schelmerei*, it is clear that Kleist was not the first to deploy this *po(i)etical* technique, though pushed it to its limits.

489 Jürgen Barkhoff terms Strahl's and Käthchen's relationship "sado-masochistic"—cf. Schoot, *Erotik*, 162.

490 Kleist's hilarious "mercury party" anticipates our contemporary "BYO" ("bring your own") and "potlatch" parties. It may well be that patients at syphilis clinics brought their own supply of anti-syphiliacs and pooled or swapped them.

491 "Pox" in Kleist's day was a common term for syphilis. This passage confirms that Kleist considered ejaculate ("night dew," "March snow") a vehicle for its transmission, which explains why he repeatedly equates it with poison (as well as with an antidote, provided it is "pure").

492   Cf. Dirk Grathoff (*Kleist: Geschichte*, 152): "Der Holunderstrauch war der 'joint' des Mittelalters."

493   It is sometimes held in the Kleist reception that Kleist injected an extra dose of Catholicism into *Käthchen* to please A. Müller. While not implausible (Müller himself implies as much to Gentz—cf. *AML*,292), apart from its *overtly* medieval setting demanding Catholic imagery, the work is not unusually "Catholic": *Erdbeben* is as much so, *Cäcilie* more so. Still, *Käthchen* is indeed a story of transformations couched as "conversions": Käthchen's "conversion" from Protestant plaything into Catholic bride, Kunigunde's "conversion" from Catholic (or at one point, Orthodox) bride into Protestant warrioress.

494   Kleist's "Da quillt es wieder..." anticipates Melville: "Whale. * * * ... from the Dut. and Ger. *Wallen*." (*Moby-Dick*. Ed. Hershel Parker, Harrison Hayford. New York: Norton, 2002, 7), à propos of which Sloterdijk notes (*Spären II*, 938-9): "Durch seine 'wallende' Gestalt wirkt der Wal... als Inbegriff einer Macht, die sich in unheimlichen Meerestiefen ausschließlich in sich selber dreht."

495   Dreams serve a variety of functions in Kleist's works: Adam's dream in *Krug*, in which he anticipates the drama's outcome, is *predictive* (mimicking the chorus' songs in his earlier dramas); the gipsy's self-fulfilling divination in *Kohlhaas*, which determines the Wettin (or Habsburg) dynasty's fate, is *proscriptive*; Käthchen's entranced vision, in which she reminisces about the Franco-German relationship of the past fifteen years, is *retrospective*. Strahl and Käthchen's much discussed parallel (or shared) dream, on the other hand, is above all *structural*: it renders possible—even inevitable—the resolution of the drama's constitutive dilemma expressed in Strahl's (Ph I) soliloquy. Had only one of them had the dream, Käthchen's eligibility would have been merely a contingent *possibility*, and it is the dream's *duplication* that turns the possibility into a structural *necessity*.

496   Kleist's contention, in epigram no. 23, that the feminine is "twofold," does not refer to the difference between Käthchen and Kunigunde—the latter only appears in (Ph II)—, but between Käthchen and Penthesilea, making the epigram part of the same discursive field to which the quoted letter passages belong. If Käthchen (initially) represents Luise, by maintaining that she "is as powerful through utter submissiveness as [Penthesilea] is through action," Kleist posits (as

he does repeatedly in his œuvre) that Luise's *Kniefall* (and Fr. Wilh.'s tarrying, and the Germans' discord) has been as important a cause of Germany's misery as has Napoleon's relentlessness and military prowess.

497   Cf. Deleuze and Guattari, *Thousand Plateaus*, 378 (à propos of *Über die allmähliche Verfertigung*): "this, Kleist says, is the thought of the *Gemüt*, which proceeds like a general in a war machine should, or like a body charged with electricity, with pure intensity."

498   Kleist's "code" mirrors genetic code in so far as genes comprise *potentialities* whose actualisation hinges on contingent environmental factors. The *po(i)etical* mechanics he elaborates in *Gesetze* (linking the hero's fate to his character strength), *Über die allmähliche Verfertigung* (tracing the dynamics of the three electrical states, +, -, and 0), and *Marionettentheater* (exploring the physics of gravity and friction) help Kleist avoid becoming lost in a space of infinite possibilities and pure contingencies. Nothing in his works is accidental, least of all the "accidents."

499   Hence Kleist's need for Lose and subsequently *"Mädeli"* at his Thun hideaway, in addition to Wilhelmine. Strahl's rehearsal recalls a passage in *Die Beiden Tauben* in which the cock is no longer tempted by the phallic "towers" he passes, and stoically seeks a hen in order to reproduce.

500   In 1802 *"ein abscheulicher Volksaufstand"* prevented Kleist from settling in Switzerland (cf. II:726), perhaps the first time he personally experienced the effect of a people's insurrection. Now such an "abominable" force had to be mobilsised against Napoleon.

501   Dahlmann will have been an important and worthy sparring partner for Kleist's *po(i)etical*, *satirical* and *satyrical* concerns (cf. *NR*,335) whose role appears to have been underappreciated in the Kleist reception. It was Dahlmann with whom Kleist planned the *Germania* project—had the project taken off, Dahlmann in 1809 could well have become his side-kick in the manner Müller was for *Ph*. Michalzik has 5 entries on Dahlmann vs. 32 on Pfuel, 28 on Rühle and 22 on Müller; for Schulz the corresponding figures are 3, 26, 26 and 32, for Blamberger, 2, 24, 18 and 17. While this discrepancy may be explained by their relationship having lasted less than a year—it apparently commenced in early 1809 in Dresden (cf. *LS*,317) and withered

in late 1809 with Kleist's return to Frankfurt/O. and Dahlmann's immatriculation in Wittenberg, where in 1810 he is awarded his PhD for a dissertation on Ottokar II of Bohemia (1232-78, the first ruler to unite the Austrian and Bohemian lands)—Dahlmann's comments on Kleist and his works are among the most insightful offered by any of Kleist's contemporaries. Since Kleist left Prague in October 1809 together with Dahlmann (cf. Michalzik, *Kleist*, 384), we can assume that they had remained close—and perhaps cohabitated—during Kleist's "disappearance" in Prague, making Dahlmann key to understanding that mysterious interlude. Dahlmann's 1849 reminiscences of their journey through Bohemia in April/May 1809 as "*Reise-Siamesen*" (*LS*,316), tied to each other "like a married couple" (*LS*,317) by their joint passport, their shared desire to shape history, and—I presume—their mutual erotic desire. The original "Siamese twins," who became world-famous in the early 1830s, were conjoined at the sternum and abdominal area, and Dahlmann in his reminiscences may have been implying, *satyrically*, that he and Kleist had been "conjoined in the lower parts" throughout the journey. His reference to their "circle" in which "Pfuel also consorted" (*LS*,317b;318) could be a rather Kleistian hint at a *ménage à trois* they formed during part of the journey and sojourn in Prague. A propos decommissioned Prussian officers and *Freikorps* volunteers they encountered in Prague, Dahlmann reflects: "*Denn wenn ich schmerzlich davon durchdrungen war, daß die Politik Preußens seit des großen Friedrichs Tode niedere Bahnen suche, auf welchen weder die Rettung Deutschlands, noch das Sonderheil von Preußen zu finden sei, so ertrugen diese schwer jede Kundgebung solcher Art, sie betrachteten sich noch immer als die alte Phalanx des unsterblichen Königs, der der Sieg nicht fehlen gekonnt, wenn nur diese oder jene Mißbräuche und Mißgriffe nicht im Wege gestanden hätten... man mußte sich sagen, hier sei jenes Selbstgefühl in vollem Maße vorhanden, welches politische Größen baut... [und] durch dessen Absterben das deutsche Reich zu Grunde gegangen ist*" (*LS*,316). Dahlmann's full autobiography, which unfortuantely I have not been able to obtain, could be revealing if read in accordance with Kleistian registers. That Dahlmann's reminiscenses coincide with the 40th anniversary of the Bohemian journey may be coincidental; that they coincide with the peak of the *Revolution von 1848/49* may not be: on 3rd April 1849 King Fr. Wilh. IV declines the imperial crown offered to him by the National Assembly, of which Dahlmann was a leading member, in doing so undermining the *Frankfurt* Constitution and its call for German unification. Kleist, Dahlmann may be highlighting implicitly, already in 1809 had urged German to unify under Fr. Wilh. III.

502 Cf. Walter Müller-Seidel, *Versehen und Erkennen* (Köln: Böhlau, 1961), 52-3. Anthony Stephens notes (*Kleist. The Dramas*, 158) that "the palimpsest of the text [*Hermannsschlacht*] contains something beneath the surface." Indeed it does, but so do all of Kleist's works, and what is surprising is that Kleist readers have not extrapolated this insights to other Kleistian dramas, *Homburg* excepted. Possibly the error of categorising *Hermannsschlacht* as an "outlier" has caused the sequential error of failing to generalise intertextually any insights gained from it.

503 Barbara Vinken, who in *Bestien, Kleist und die Deutschen* (Berlin: Merve, 2011), 22, juxtaposes *Hermannsschlacht* and Nazi propaganda, distinguishes between an outright "*call for* mobilisation for total war" and "instructions for *how to* mobilise for total war" (my italics). Yet Kleist arguably practiced both, and although, unlike Goebbels, he had no electronic media at his disposal to reach the masses, if he had had them, he would surely have used them: in *Hermannsschlacht* he advises his King to use all means for mass-communication available to him; likely already *Germania*, and certainly *BA*, are conceived as mass media. According to Wikipedia.com (entry "Rocket Mail"), Kleist was the first person ever to suggest (in his *BA* entry *Entwurf zu einer Bombenpost*) the delivery of mail by missile (in *Hermannsschlacht*, attached to arrows, in line with the *overt* context, though cannons are obvsiouly meant); cf. also Sloterdijk (*Kritik*, 647): "*Es lassen sich reizvolle Verbindungen denken zwischen Ballistik, Verwaltungskunde, Diplomatie, Kurierwesen (Vorläufer der Post), Buchdruck: Telekausale Funktionen, die ein neues Ego formen.*" No doubt Kleist would have been intrigued by the galvanising effect of Orson Welles' 1938 radio broadcast of H.G. Wells' *The War of the Worlds*. The real difference between him and Goebbels lies not in their means but in their *ends*: the latter's *"totaler Krieg"* aimed at *changing*, the former's *"fesselloser Krieg"* at *restoring*, the status quo ante, the latter at perpetuating, the former at resolving, a "state of exception."

504 Anthony Stephens (and Eybl: *Kleist-Lektüren*, 218) is misguided in claiming (*Sprache und Gewalt*, 236), "*daß die Instanz der Wahrheit in diesem Drama unbesetzt bleibt*": Hermann's furor represents the "truth" *kat' exochen* for the Germans in their state of disunity, for only furor can save Europe now.

505 The chorus once again relates the story *in nuce*—in *Guiskard* and *Schroffenstein* this takes place in the opening scene, in *Hermannsschlacht* in the the final act (V.2236-43; 2260-7). The chorus clarifies the unique situation in

which the Germans find themselves and calls for Hermann to act in accordance with it; Dahlmann's reminisces in 1859 (cf. II:945) that Kleist read the chorus' verses *"mit einem so unwiderstehlichen Herzklange der Stimme, daß sie mir noch immer in den Ohren tönt."*

506   In 1814, with victory against Napoleon on the horizon, Kleist received belated endorsement from Gentz in a letter to Metternich: "*Wir haben es zum Glück mit einem Feinde zu tun, gegen welchen man in der jetzigen Meinung der Welt nie im Unrecht sein kann. Die Welt denkt und sagt wie Kleist im Jahr 1809: Schlagt ihn tot!— Das Weltgerich / Fragt euch nach den Gründen nicht.*" Schulz notes (*Kleist*, 420) that at leaset one Kleist reader, Ruth Klüger, recognised Hermann as *"Revolutionär... der... einen Krieg um der Menschenrechte willen kämpft, in dem prinzipielle Menschenrechte gerade suspendiert sind."* Despite these earlier endorsements, Kleist's Hermann has suffered considerable "bad press" in the Kleist reception, and although discussions of this eminently Kleistian figure have recently become more nuanced (cf., e.g., Klaus-Müller Salget's entry in *KH*,76-9), Hermann remains among the least-loved of Kleist's major characters, alongside the likes of Kunigunde and Nicolo. Kleist's conceptualisation of this figure is traceable to much earlier passages in his writing: in late November 1801 he tells Adolphine, *"Wohl dem Arminius, daß er einen großen Augenblick fand. Denn was bliebe ihm heut zu Tage übrig, als etwa Lieutenant zu werden in einem preußischen Regiment?"* (II:700; Adolphine evidently just returned from the *"Arminiusberg,"* i.e., the Teutoburger Wald, which Kleist himself had passed by as a soldier in 1795, and which in the early 1800s had become a focal point for congregation of German patriots). Kleist vents his frustration at the contrast between the situation of 8 AD, when Arminius seized a *kairotic* moment to change the course of history, and the "orderly" world of 1801 ("ordered" not least by *Basel* and *Tilsit*) in which a reincarnated Arminius—say, a Kleist—is relegated to the irrelevance of a lieutenant, and in which even the King himself behaves like one. Hermann (Fr. Wilh.) now faces a *kairotic* moment as historically important as that faced by Arminius and by those other "great men" Kleist enumerates in his 1799 *Aufsatz* (cf. II:314)—Christ, Socrates, Leonidas, Regulus—, and like them, must seize the moment—with Kleist's help: his drama is *"mehr, als irgend ein anderes, für den Augenblick berechnet"* (II:821; 824) because this *kairotic* window is bound to shut quickly.

507   A propos of Schulz's note (*Kleist*, 418), *"heißt es von Hermann: "Er lacht und geht ab"* (V.2539)... *In der Hermannsschlacht... erreicht Kleist hinsichtlich des*

Lachens die exremste Position, tief ins Dunkle, Inhumane hinein," I maintain that Hermann's "inhuman" laughter is above all *kynical* in Sloterdijk's sense (cf. *Kritik,* 213-14; 275-6; 556), and thereby marks Hermann-Fr. Wilh. as being up to the task of challenging Augustus-Napoleon in the manner Diogenes challenged the great Alex.: Kleistian figures that most obviously demonstrate *kynical/cynical* behavior— *Schroffenstein's* witch, *Erdbeben's* cobbler, *Kohlhaas'* knacker—are usually avatars of Napoleon, so that ascribing a similar stance to Hermann levels the playing field.

508   Lawrence Ryan is among those who misread this: *"dem "Latier"—sprich: dem Franzosen";* cf. Ryan, "Die Hermannsschlacht," in Walter Hinderer (Ed.), *Neue Interpretationen,* 195. Among those who discern Kleist's subtle deliminatinos are Jochen Schmidt *(Kleist,* 153), "Bonaparte, den 'Latier'" and Rudolf Loch *(Kleist,* 488, n.17): *"Es ging ihm weder um die Ausrottung noch um die Unterdrückung der französischen Nation, sondern umd das Verjagen jener, die sich...als Unterdrücker anderer Völker mißbrauchen lassen: 'Napoleon, und so lange er ihr Kaiser ist, die Franzosen.' (Kleist: 'Katechismus der Deutschen,')."* My own terminology, "Francofication" and "French disease," is imprecise in this respect, for Kleist means in the first instance "Bonapartisation" and "Napoleonic disease" (I shall not change my terminology, but ask my reader to keep this important distinction in mind). It has been pointed out in the Kleist reception, with evident consternation, that the first speech of any of the drama's Germanic leaders—Wolf, in the third line—refers to a *Mediterranean* feature, the Colossus of Rhodes, seemingly thoroughly out of place in a conversation among Germanic chieftains (the symbolism of the Colossus itself is interesting: erected in 280 BC in honour of Helios (!) following the city's success in repelling an invading Macedonian army, it collapsed during an earthquake (!) a mere 54 years later; not only is Helios is frequently identified with Phoebus and may thus allude to the rapid collapse of Kleist's magazine, but also Kleist may *satirically* be hinting that Greece soon after fell to the Romans not least because of their perennial disunity. The pattern of Romanisations expressing Germany's ambient "Francofication" prevails throughout the drama: Jupiter is invoked more frequently than Wodan/Odin by Germans who are increasingly "hybridised" (Stefan Börnchen, in his stimulating essay "Translatio imperii. Politische Formen und hybride Metaphern in Heinrich von Kleists 'Hermannsschlacht," in *KJb* 2005, 275) and corrupted by the foreign régime. Only in Hermann's case do his personal reference points remain Germanic—e.g., Wodan's oak—, the Oriental symbols Kleist associates with him—tiger skins, the dervish, Persian chess—being evidently superficial, as if part of a deliberate ruse on

his part to overtly conveying his "Francofication" while covertly remaining eminently German. I pointed out in *Emigrant* that in *Cäcilie* the German (Gregorian) calendar is superseded by the French Revolutionary Calendar—even time itself has become "francofied"—, and this process is already under way in *Hermannsschlacht*, in which both Germanic and Roman calendar days appear (*Nornentag, Iden*). In the vanishing point of the *line of flight* of a hegemony that penetrates every nook and cranny of German identity, Kleist warns, "Germany" as such ceases to exist, as political as well as cultural entity.

509 Well into medieval times, the term "Franks" was used synonymously with "Western Europeans," for example by the people of the Levante during the Crusades. A possible objection that it was not uncommon in Germany, in Kleist's day, to refer to the French as *"Franken,"* and that Kleist simply adopted current conventions, rather than making a deliberate distinction, I cannot refute, though it is my firm conviction that Kleist never adopted conventions unthinkingly.

510 *"Diese Franken"* Gratfhof refers to appear in *Germania an Ihre Kinder*, where the chorus urges: *"So verlaßt, voran der Kaiser, / Eure Hütten, eure Häuser; / Schäumt, ein uferloses Meer, / Über diese Franken her!"* (I:26). Kleist, I maintain, in this passage calls on Franz to lead the German people to destroy not the French nation but the dynastic régimes afflicted by the twin German and French diseases—the Bonapartes, but also, say, the Wittelsbachs and Wettins—and acting against the welfare of the people, German *and* French. Kleist confronts Franz with the stark choice of either siding with the people (*"uferloses Meer"*) or seeing his Habsburg dynasty flushed away by their insurrection. What is at stake for Kleist is not only Germany as political and cultural entity, but also monarchy as legitimate system of goverance: Kleist is on monarchy's side, but recognises that as a system of governance it can (and should) only survive if it genuinely serves the people it governs; the Revolution showed that in the absence of legitimate and wise leadership, the people succumb to the spell of dictators and tyrants.

511 Cf. Schmidt, *Kleist*, 143-54; Michalzik, *Kleist*, 338-70; Jeffrey L. Sammons, "Rethinking Kleist's Hermannsschlacht," in Alexej Ugrinksy (Ed.), *Heinrich von Kleist Studien* (Berlin 1980), 36, cited in Ricarda Schmidt, "Sparagmos, Weiblichkeit und Staat," in Ricarda Schmidt et al (Ed.), *Gewalt*, 169. Schmidt insists that *Penthesilea* is "wholly apolitical" (p.151) and considers it "understandable" that for decades after

1945 *Hermannschlacht* was "taboo" (p.150). Michalzik believes (*Kleist*, 349) that "*Seit den Furchtbarkeiten des Nationalsozialismus aber kann man sich Herrmann nicht mehr als positiv besetzte Figur vorstellen*," while acknowledging that *Hermannschlacht* is not an outlier in Kleist's work: "*Das Drama seht alles andere als fremd im Werk Kleists*" (*ibid*; cf. also 350). Sammons, with far greater precision than Samuel or Kittler, recognises Kleist's drama as a manifesto to his King. Klaus Kanzog (*Kleist*, 281-2), reflecting on their 1983 discussion published in *KjB* 1984 (pp.137-46), endorses Joachim Kreutzer's terming the drama a "*Handlungsanweisung*" and Claus Peymann's terming it a "*Modell eines Befreiungskrieges*." Barbara Vinken's dismissal (*Bestien*, 11) of the idea that Kleist was aiming at political effect, "*Es mag die Verliebtheit in die politische Wirkungmacht von Dichtung sein, die viele Interpreten geblendet hat: endlich ein Stück, das nicht bloß Literatur war, sondern die Wirklichkeit verändern wollte. Gelesen wurde es nicht zum bloßen Vergnügen von ohnmächtigen Frauen und Mädchen, sondern von Entscheidern, die an der Macht waren: von Gneisenau, vielleicht von vom Stein, von Hardenberg von Scharnhorst. Radikal zielt es auf eine—man ist versucht zu sagen, ganz und gar männliche Weise—unmittelbare, miltärisch-politische Wirkung,*" is entirely misguided, although her skepticism vis-à-vis Samuel and Kittler's contention that Kleist was addressing himself primarily to the Prussian reformers is appropriate: these comprised at most Kleist's secondary audience.

512   *Nibelungenlied*'s Siegfried the dragon slayer has occasionally been identified with the historical Arminius, the dragon representing the Roman legions, whose cohorts' military standard was the *draco*, the dragon or serpent (the military standard of a legion, consisting of several cohorts, was the eagle). Like Siegfried under cover of his *Tarnkappe*, Arminius remained eerily stealthy while preparing to strike the enemy, a feature that made him a particularly suitable model in the context of the irregular guerrilla warfare Kleist sought to inspire. That the Arminius legend in the wake of Klopstock's *Hermanns Schlacht* of 1769 and Fichte's *Reden an die deutsche Nation* of 1808 became a veritable "foundational myth of the German nation" (Hansjörg Bay, "Evidenz und Exzess in Kleists Herrmannsschlacht," in Yixu Lü et al (Eds.), *Wissensfiguren*, 119) should not be held against Kleist, whose usage of the legend is more pragmatic than ideological: although he hitches onto the nationalistic fervour it transports, he above all draws on its "technical" aspects, which he turns into the "algorithm" powering his simulation.

513   First published in *JdS* V, 1961, 64-101; I quote from the 1967 reprint, Richard Samuel, "Kleists 'Hermannsschlacht' und der Freiherr vom Stein," in: Walter Müller Seidel (Ed.), *Kleist, Aufsätze und Essays*, 412-58.

514   Wolf Kittler in *Geburt*, 222-9, shows convincingly that Kleist by no means depended on Stein's intercepted letter for his political views: Gneisenau and Scharnhorst in their late summer 1808 memoranda already covered much the same ground.

515   Cf. also Michalzik (*Kleist*, 355): *"Man muss sich also vorstellen, dass zwischen Wien, Prag, Teplitz [Töplitz], Dresden und Berlin die Nachrichten, Einsichten und Gerüchte hin und her jagten. Es war ein reger und aufregender Austausch… Von einer "Kette der Intriganten" sprach der französische Botschafter Bourgoing (der Kleist im Übrigen schätzte) in einem Brief an Napoleon."* Dahlmann notes in 1840 (*LS*,319), "*Damals verstand jeder Beziehungen, […] wer die wären, die durch Wichtigtun und Botenschicken das Vaterland zu retten meinten*"; and in 1858 (*LS*,317), "*Mit den Leuten, welche Briefe schreiben und geheime Boten schicken, um das Vaterland zu retten, war von dem ungeduldigen Dichter [Kleist] der Tugendbund gemeint.*" Dahlmann's *"Wichtigtuer"* and *"Botenschicker"* clearly correspond to Kleist's *"Mißvergügte" "Schwätzer" "die schreiben, Deutschland zu befreien."* The *Tugendbund* may have had 300-400 members, by no means all of whom would have been active participants in the resistance movement, let alone any conspiracy against the King (Rühle mentions Stein, Fr. Carl Ferdinand von Müffling, and himself as members; cf. *LS*,312a). Napoleon with *Tilsit* created a veritable army of decommissioned Prussian officers, many of whom found their way to Prague in these months, among them Rühle, Pfuel and probably Müffling, and a sub-set of whom officially joined the Austrian army: e.g., Varnhagen, Clausewitz, Röder, Karl L. von Kleist (cf. Loch, *Kleist*, 490, n.69); Eugen von der Knesebrick believed (*LS*,317a) that Kleist himself was among those considering to do so. Rudolf Loch reports (*Kleist*, 490) that Stein and the Prussian envoy Fr. von dem Knesebeck circulated between Prague, Töplitz and Brünn, and Dahlmann notes (*LS*,316) that in Prague he and Kleist encountered members of Wilh. I von Hessen's *Freikorps* and Fr. Wilh. von Braunschweig's *Schwarze Schar* (*"Totenköpfe"*). Loch's conclusion (*Kleist*, 338) that for all their efforts "the patriots gathered in Prague became isolated and politically irrelevant" rings true. Kleist's sarcasm concerning those *"Mißvergügte" "Schwätzer" "die schreiben, Deutschland zu befreien"* may seem disingenuous, given that he might as well have counted himself among them; yet Sloterdijk's comment (*Kritik*, 326) on the satirist Lucian, *"Lukian*

[ist] *der Verächter der Verächter, der Moralist der Moralisten*," may be applied to Kleist, if in an inverted manner: whereas Lucian saritises *kynics* such as Peregrine for their *excessive* disdain of the world, Kleist satirises reformers such as Hardenberg or Stein for their *lack of excess*: their memoranda fall short, not necessarily in *appropriateness* of their propositions offered, but certainly in *urgency* of their language deployed: in contrast to their polite memoranda, Kleist's *Hermannsschlacht* is dynamite.

516   Among the conspirators may have been the likes of Arndt, Reimer, Schleiermacher and Gneisenau (cf. Michalzik, *Kleist*, 387), as well as other reformers or members of the *Tugendbund*. Häker deviates from Samuel in that he only acknowledges, in *Heinrich von Kleist, 'Prinz Friedrich von Homburg' und 'Die Verlobung in St. Domingo'*, Heilbronn: Kleist Achiv Sembdner, 2012, 94-5, that a "rumour" of a conspiracy led by Scharnhorst circulated at the time; my own analysis suggests that Kleist believed this conspiracy to be real and imminent, and for his work to "fall in the middle of time" he had to anticipate and even pre-empt possible moves he considered detrimental to Prussia's and Germany's welfare. Kleist's positively singling out the character Wolf suggests that he had reasons to believe that Gneisenau was not among the conspirators. Had the conspiracy gone ahead and Fr. Wilh. been replaced by Prince Wilh., Kleist's wargame would have remained a valid blueprint for the new King. What it was not designed to accommodate, however, was the case of *no* Prussian leader taking part in the war: in the moment this case materialised, the drama became obsolete instantaneously.

517   A closer study of the *Germania* project is called for, perhaps in juxtaposition with the 19th century project of German unification, whose milestones included the creation of the *Erfurter Union* of 1850 and of the *Norddeutscher Bund* in 1866. Kleist evidently favoured what would later become known as "*Grossdeutsche Lösung,*" under Hohenzollern leadership, but might have accepted a "*Kleindeutsche Lösung*" as more realistic, for the Habsburgs could be expected to refuse playing second fiddle within a unified German Empire (Merbod's bending his knee before Hermann is possible only because of the latter's charisma, and overly optimistic on Kleist's part). Dahlmann, who like Kleist advocated that the German imperial crown be proffered to the Prussian King, would in 1848 emerge as a leading proponent of the "*Kleindeutsche Lösung*"–cf. https://www.britannica.com/biography/Friedrich-Dahlmann; https://de.wikipedia.org/wiki/Friedrich_Christoph_Dahlmann.

518   Barbara Vinken deems excessive Samuel's and Kittler's focus on irregular warfare and blames Schmitt for having called the drama the *"größte Partisanendichtung aller Zeiten"*; yet her investing Kleist's drama with a concern for the "terrain of the family, the space of the *patria potestas*" (*Bestien*, 18), and with a question of "how far the strategic, sexual functionalisation of women, girls and children by husbands, fathers, princes should be allowed to go" (*ibid*, 16), is far less Kleistian than is Samuel and Kitter's topos. Her locating Kleist's drama's movens *"in der Metapher des männlichen Eindringens in den—weiblichen—Körper"* (*ibid*, 50) is misguided: Kleist, as I have shown, is interested, as it were, *"in dem Akt des männlichem Eindringens in den—männlichen—Körper."*

519   Cf. Peter Sloterdijk (*Kritik*, 134): "*Seit Uhrzeiten wissen die Angehörigen der Aristokratie, daß sie 'die Besten' sind. Ihre soziale und politische Stellung beruht auf einer offenen, demonstrativen und selbstgenießerischen Beziehung zwischen Macht und Selbstachtung. Der politische Narzißmus der Aristokratie lebt von dieser schlichten, machterfüllten Anmaßung. Sie durfte glauben, sie sei in jeder existentiell wesentlichen Hinsicht bevorzugt und zur Vortrefflichkeit berufen.*" Kleist's relationship with his aristocratic lineage was complicated: on the one hand he enjoyed and exploited the privileges that came with it, such as access to King, court, and public service jobs; on the other hand he did not consider it essential: for quite a while he dropped the *"von"* from his name. He took his aristocratic *filial* responsibility seriously, but disdained its *familial* constraints (such as conventional aristocratic career expectations). A commonor like A. Müller may have aspired to nobility—two years before his death, with Metternich's endorsement, he was knighted Ritter von Nitterdorf—; a Kleist took it for granted. On the other hand, a landed aristocrat like Fr. Aug. L. von der Marwitz, among the most ardent defenders of ancient aristocratic privileges, grew up on his family's ancient Friedersdorf Castle; a landless one like Kleist, in an ordinary bourgeois house.

520   Cf. similarly Gerhard Schulz (*Kleist*, 415),"*denn realen historischen Figuren entsprachen die Gestalten des Dramas gewiß nicht,*" and (*ibid*, 429), "*Schlüsselliteratur hat Kleist nie geschrieben,*" and Horst Häker (*Homburg und Verlobung*, 98), "*eines Dichters..., der nicht ein 'Schlüsselwerk' verfassen will.*"

521   Wilbrandt offers (*Kleist*, 327) that Kleist's Hermann acts perfectly in line with prevailing views in Germany at the time: "*Denn man sah den Kaiser [Napoleon]*

nicht wie einen mit den andern Fürsten gleichstehenden Herrscher an, sondern wie einen Räuber und Bösewicht, einen Vogelfreien, der alle Freiheit und alles Recht und Gesetz verrathen habe."

522   Vinken notes (*Bestien*, 9) that in the original version "Hermann" is spelled "Herrmann," with double "r," an unusual or anachronistic spelling; Sembdner "corrects," *MA* recovers it. "*Herr*" = "master," so that "*Herr-Mann*" = (literally) "master-man"; the ultimate "master-man" is, of course, the King.

523   The functional value of the club's *double* weight is analogous to that of the *second* Twin Tower's destruction during the "9/11" 2001 attacks in New York: according to Jean Baudrillard it is precisely in its doubling that the attack actualises its terroristic effect. Kleist put this "*basic law of terror*" into poetic practice 190 years before Baudrillard theorised it, and 90 years before Joseph Conrad had his dying character Kurtz cry out in *Heart of Darkness*: "Don't you hear them?... The horror! the horror!"

524   Kleist is referring to the two oldest Hohenzollern princes, who comprise a valuable pledge indeed: they would later be crowned, respectively, King Fr. Wilh. IV of Prussia and Emperor Wilh. I of Germany, no less. Elsewhere in the drama they are referred to as "eagle's brood"; they appear in *Kohlhaas*' final scene, where they are knighted (i.e., elevated from their royal to an imperial rank) and inherit the two blacks (i.e., the double-headed imperial eagle). In 1871, Kleist's virtual offering would indeed actualise, at which point Luise's spirit, for once, may have granted a smile to her clairvoyant bard's.

525   In 1800 the Habsburg Empire's population was c.23m, the *HRR*'s c.24m (a significant part of the former lay outside of the latter's borders), France's 38m, Russia's 35m, and Great Britain's 10m (excluding her colonies)—cf. https://en.wikipedia.org/wiki/List_of_countries_by_population_in_1800. In the *War of the Fifth Coalition* Franz was able to field 340,000 troops, compared with Napoleon's 275,000—cf. https://en.wikipedia.org/wiki/War_of_the_Fifth_Coalition. Marbod-Franz's suggestion that the Holy Roman dignity in ancient times was associated with Hermann-Fr. Wilh.'s clan (cf. V.2582-3) has triggered doubts in the Kleist reception regarding Hermann's identification with Fr. Wilh., since no Hohenzollern was emperor prior to 1871. However, this apparent discrepancy may be explained by the fact that until Fr.

Wilh. IV in 1854 commissioned a scientific study of the genealogy of the House of Hohenzollern, it was widely held that the first Hohenzollern was a Count Tassilo, who flourished at Charlemagne's court and was related to the ancient House of the Welfs (Guelphs), from which the Emperor Otto IV and Fr. Barbarossa's mother hailed.

526   http://www.koenigin-luise.com/Reformen/Hardenberg/hardenberg.html.

527   Cf. Michalzik, *Kleist*, 394. Kleist's enacting the battle in the form of Ventidius' laceration transposes it from the *satirical* into the *satyrical* realm. In 1801 he told Adolphine, *"In dem Antlitz eines einzigen Raphaels liegen mehr Gedanken, als in allen Tableaus der französischen Schule zusammengenommen, und während man kalt vor den Schlachtstücken, deren Anordnung das Auge kaum fassen kann, vorübergeht, steht man still vor einem Antlitz und denkt.—"* (II:701-2), and with the agonised Ventidius confronting the enraged she-bear Kleist enacts this insight on stage, evolving a technique he already deploys in *Penthesilea* (V.172-92), where he represents a tripartite battle of the Greek, Trojan and Amazon armies metonymically as hand-to-hand combat of their respective lead warriors—Achilles, Dheibobus and Penthesilea—, in both instances furthermore rendering the action teichoscopically.

528   *Hermannsschlacht*'s bear-keeper Childerich could have been inspired by Childerich III, the last Merovingian king, in 751 dethroned by Pope Zachary, tonsured—his long hair symbolising his Frankish dynastic heritage and royal prerogative—, and placed in the monestary of Saint-Bertin in Saint-Omer (which Kleist in 1803 would have seen, as it was then still completely erect in the centre of town).

529   The Brandenburg Elector Fr. III in 1701 elevated himself, *Deo Destinata*, to Fr. I, King of Prussia, and Kleist sniffs at the Wittelsbachs, Wettins and Württembergs' depending on a foreign despot's grace to obtain royal status. Samuel (*Kleists 'Hermannsschlacht'*, 444; *Beiträge* 1997, 198) has the Ubii represent the Württembergians, the Aedulii the Bavarians, and Aristan Fr. I. von Württemberg, without providing a rationale for his attribution. Samuel is unlikely to be correct, as Kleist would have considered Fr. I the least important of the three *Rheinbund* kings, and would not have assigned the important figure Aristan to him. Samuel also suggests that Aristan could represent multiple characters, *"Dalberg und der Herzog von Nassau, im Grunde genommen alle, die bei ihrer pronapoleonischen Haltung blieben"* (*ibid*), but such a generic representation is equally unlikely, not least given

Dahlmann's insistence that *"Damals verstand jeder die Beziehungen, wer der Fürst Aristan sei"* (*LS*,319), an assertion the author of the first dissertation on Kleist, S.F. Aug. Stjernstedt confirms when he writes: *"Die drei deutschen Fürsten, die mit den Römdern zusammenarbeiteten, entsprachen den Königen des Rheinbundes"* ("Über Heinrich von Kleist und seine Poesie," trans. Antje Helbing and Karin Hoff, Upsala: Edquist & Berglund, 1869, reprinted in Gunther Nickel (Ed.), *Kleists Rezeption*, Heilbronn: Kleist-Archiv Sembdner, 2013, 211). Given Kleist's faible for crafting names by rearranging letters, I offer that both *Fust* and *Aristan* are contractions of the names of the respective historical figures they represent: the first letter of Fr. August's first name, *F*, and the last three letters of the second name, *ust*, together produce *Fust*, while a combination of letters from the Bavarian's full name, Max. I. Maria Michael Joh. Baptist Franz de Paula Joseph Kaspar Ignatius Nepomuk, renders *Aristan*: *ari* from Maria, *st* from Baptist and *an* from Maximilian.

530   At Bayonne, Napoleon in May 1808 arm-twisted King Karl IV of Spain and his son Ferdinand into abdicating the Spanish crown and passing it to Napoleon's brother.

531   In *Brief eines politischen Pescherä* (cf. II:373) Kleist bitterly recalls a Bavarian corps in April 1809 having been the first to cut through the Austrian lines. To be fair to the Bavarians, they had initially joined the *War of the Second Coalition* (1798-1802) on Austria's side, and only following the Coalition's devastating defeat in the *Battle of Hohenlinden* (December 1800) broke ranks with the other German powers. At the outset of the *War of the Third Coalition* in 1805, Max. Joseph initially sought to remain neutral, but finding himself between the rock of Napoleon's ultimatum that he declare allegiance to France or be considered an enemy, and the hard place of Franz's pressurising him to join the Coalition (Austrian Field Marshall Schwarzenberg even threatened to occupy Munich's Nymphenburg Castle with 200 husars), on 25th August 1805 entered the secret *Treaty of Bogenhausen* that established Bavaria's alliance with Napoleon, inadvertently laying the foundation for the *Rheinbund* and the *HRR*'s dissolution. Bavaria was repeatedly under threat of being gobbled up by Austria, most recently in the *War of the Bavarian Succession* of 1778-9, and an alliance with France provided some insurance. Alas, Kleist's credo was *"Vertrauen auf uns, Einigkeit unter uns"* (cf. his bridal gift to Wilhelmine), and he would not have accepted Bavaria's precarious situation as valid excuse for what he considered treason against Germany (his unbending disdain for Max. Joseph may

have been exacerbated by Prussia's loss to Bavaria of her Frankish provinces). From today's vantage point it may be fair to say that the Wittelsbachs (and the Wettins and the Württembergs) acted no differently than the Hohenzollerns and the Habsburgs, in putting the interests of their own dynasty and principality before that of the *HRR* and German nation, and that the difference in their respective strategies was only a matter of circumstance: the former three principalities were of modest size and at risk of being annexed by more powerful neighbours, and for them it was a logical option to seek shelter under France's wings, whereas the latter two were major powers in their own right, and could only lose by accommodating France. Prussia, as the weakest of the five major powers, was situated in the middle of this continuum, a fact Napoleon well recognised, who repeatedly attempted to draw her to his side—unsuccessfully: while Prussia's resources were limited, her spirit remained unbending, and whatever may have been Fr. Wilh.'s faults, giving in to Napoleon's lure was not one of them.

532   Kleist's admiration may have been *satyrical* as well as *satirical*. Wolf Kittler evaluates (*Geburt*, 244-5) Kleist's stance thus: *"Kleists Hermann aber spricht davon, daß die Verfassungsfrage "in der gesamten Fürsten Rat" entschieden werden müsse. Er optiert also eindeutig gegen eine allgemeine Konstitution und für eine ständische Verfassung, wie sie von dem Vertreter des altpreußischen Adels, Ludwig von der Marwitz, gefordert wurde, als dessen "Schildträger" Kleist Freund Adam Müller... galt... Gneisenau war politisch radikal. Er forderte nicht nur eine freie Konstitution für die preußischen Staaten, sondern auch die Abschaffung des Geburtsadels und die Einführung einer gesellschaftlichen Rangordnung nach dem Verdienst. Der Freiherr vom Stein dagegen... stand einer ständischen Verfassung sehr viel näher, weshalb er auch zunächst durchaus Affinitäten zu der extreme konservativen Haltung eines Ludwig von der Marwitz zeigte... In militärischer Hinsicht ist [Kleist] mindestens so radikal wie die radikalsten preußischen Offiziere, wenn nicht radikaler. In politischer Hinsicht aber vertritt er eher eine conservative, nämlich ständische Position und steht insofern dem Freiherrn vom Stein näher."* To read into the passage he quotes (V.2591) a preference on Kleist's part for a *"ständische,"* as opposed to *"allgemeine,"* constitution is misguided, for the passage is concerned solely with the election of the "German King" (from 962 onwards normally as Holy Roman Emperor), which from AD 911 onwards was the prerogative of the *Kurfürsten* (Prince Electors), and what Kleist is suggesting here is that instead of merely rubber-stamping a Habsburgian dynastic succession, the Prince Electors should properly nominate and elect the future Emperor from among several candidates, as had been the original idea of this electoral college,

although it frequently waved through dynastic successors without considering other candidates (such a genuine election, Kleist may have thought, would naturally favour a Hohenzollern candidate). It is Gneisenau, not Stein, with whom Kleist in the late summer and autumn of 1811 meets and shares "essays" (cf. II:878), although it is possible that he met Stein during his Prague "disappearance." Neither Kleist's fondness for Müller, nor for wargaming with Marwitz (cf. II:880), necessarily imply alignment with their political views.

533   For an articulation of Gneisenau's views, cf. the extracts from his 14th August 1808 memorandum quoted in Kittler, *Geburt*, 222-3.

534   Kleist's perspectives regarding the liberation of Germany and Europe seem to have evolved in three phases, *Hermannsschlacht* falling into the middle phase: in the first phase, ranging from before *Austerlitz* and *Jena Auerstedt* till the aftermath of *Tilsit*, Kleist believed that Napoleon would either die, be overcome, or be tied into a new order (cf. *Guiskard, Krug, Marquise, Penthesilea*); in the middle phase, ranging from *Paris* till the early summer of 1811, he became increasingly disillusioned, but continued to harbour hopes that the Bonapartean hegemony would be overcome, if only by later generations (cf. *Hermannsschlacht, Kohlhaas, Findling, Cäcilie*); in the third phase, ranging from the King's refusal in the late summer of 1811 to declare war till Kleist's suicide, he gave up all hope of liberation, resigning himself to Prussia's perpetual submission (cf. *Zweikampf, Homburg*).

535   Kleist was personally familiar with Hermann's territory: following the *Palatine Campaign*, his regiment in 1795 crossed the Lippe at Paderborn en route to their camp at Kommende Lage, and while archaeological evidence of the historical battle was virtually non-existent in Kleist's time, the view that it took place near the Teutoburg Forest and the river Lippe was widely-held (today Kalkriese is deemed the battle's most likely location, which incidentally is a mere 10km from the Kommende Lage). Vinken points out (*Bestien*, 49) that the *Grand Duchy of Berg*, which Napoleon gave to his brother-in-law Joachim Murat, and which incorporated the formerly Prussian-held *Duchy of Cleves* where Stein had held senior government positions, straddled the Lippe. This small but strategically important "*Landstrich*" gave Napoleon a beachhead on the Rhine's right bank, including several Rhine bridges and the the wealthy city of Düsseldorf, whose eastern border straddled those of the *Kingdom of Westphalia*, ruled by Napoleon's younger brother Jérôme, which in

turn bordered on Prussia. Via these territories the *Ad'A* would be able at any time to march unobstructedly from the Rhine to France's most important German fortress, Magdeburg, and thence straight into Prussian territory (Berlin is a mere 130km east of Magdeburg; it had been above all Magdeburg that Luise in her kneefall at Tilsit begged Napoleon to restore to Prussia) or, via the territory of France's vassals Saxony or Bavaria, straight into Austrian territory. The Prussians and Austrians thus had no geographic buffer against the French and were utterly exposed to the *Ad'A* in case of war, while the French fully controlled strategic marching grounds on the Rhine's east bank and an efficient west-east transport corridor along the Lippe into the heart of Germany. "*Germanen und Römer, beides Wölfe, beide dieselben, streiten sich um dasselbe: an der Lippe um die Wolle*," writes Vinken (*ibid*, 52), though the "wool" the two "wolves" were quarreling over in AD 9, as much as in 1809, were not the German womens' blonde locks, as Vinken implies, but control of these critical marching and supply routes across the Westphalian basin (in terms of the logistics of war, little had changed in 1800 years). The various shades of violet in the right-hand image depict territories under direct Bonapartean control: the Grand Duchy of Berg, ruled by Murat, the Kingdom of Westphalia, ruled by Jérôme, and the Kingdom of Holland, ruled by Louis. Between Magedburg in the west, the three Prussian fortresses occupied by France further east—Stettin, Küstrin and Glogau, and vassal territories to the south (Saxony) and east of Prussia (Duchy of Warsaw), Berlin was literally straightjacketed. The extremely precarious strategic position in which Prussia, but also Austria, found themselves explains the need for such elaborate plans: Kleist's sought to *undermine* the French encirclement by triggering an insurrection in northern Germany (only part of which French-controlled), whereas Scharnhorst hoped to *reverse* it by luring the *Ad'A* into the Duchy of Warsaw where it would find itself encircled by Prusso-Austrian forces from Silesia, West- and East Prussia, Bohemia and Galicia. I note in passing that the city of Krefeld on the Rhine's left bank, in which I grew up, owes its main west-east axis, the *Uerdinger Strasse*, that as a high-school student I biked up and down on a daily basis and that connects the city's centre to its Rhine harbour at Uerdingen, to Napoleon's need to facilitate transport of troops and matériel from the left bank's hinterland for shipment across the Rhine.

536 Both plans are plausible, but operate under partially different assumptions: Kleist's simulation, completed after *Paris*, assumed that the remaining Prussian regular forces would be insufficient and that only a broad-based people's insurrection, bolstered by the Austrian regular army, had any chance of success; Scharnhorst's plan,

prepared before *Paris*, assumed that the Prussian regular forces would complement the Austrian forces (in both designs the far stronger Austrian army executes the decicive thrust against the enemy centre). In Kleist's simulation, the most promising strategy was to *trigger an insurrection* in the northern German plains, whose forests and marshes were ideally suited for guerrilla warfare, and where a large number of German insurrectionists could be mobilised to tie down the enemy till the Austrian regular forces arrived to finish them off; in Scharnhorst's plan, it was to *draw the enemy forces* deep into the eastern Prussian and Polish plains, where the enemy supply lines would become stretched, isolating their main corps and making it vulnerable to Coalition attacks. Wolf Kittler (*Geburt*, 233-4) provides an intriguing account of the "tellurian character" of partisan war and its relationship to the topography of Brandenburg, a relationship that Rühle would later elaborate in a treatise and that will have been subject of his discussions with Kleist (Rühle will generally have been Kleist's most important interlocutor on matters of military operations, strategy and tactic).

537   Germanic tribes sacked the city of Rome in AD 410 and 455, and Holy Roman Emperor Karl V's soldiers did so in 1527's infamous *sacco di Roma*. Kleist would not have endorsed any such acts of barbarism, against Paris or Rome. The Palais des Tuileries in 1871 was indeed burned to the ground, not by German soldiers but by French revolutionaries, whose commander Jules Bergeret stated before the *Committee of Public Safety*: "The last vestiges of royalty have just disappeared." Kleist wished Napoleon's standard to give way to the restored Bourbon one, as would indeed be the case in 1814.

538   Phallus: *Pfeil, Strich, Horn, Donnerkeil, Nacken, Pinie, Strahl, Hand, Glieder, Pergamentrolle, Dolch, Demantengriffel, Arm, geschnittner Stein, Szepterstab, Federbusch, Schwert, Fackeln, Füße, Waffen, Keule, Spieß, Keil, Krücke, Stamm, Borste, Schlüssel, Werkzeug*; glans: *Wipfel, Eiche, Scheitel, Schädel, kahler Kopf, Platte, Haupt, Laterne*; anus or bottom: *offene Straße, Gruft, Eingang, Pforte, Park, persischer Marmor, Elysium, kreuzet*; pubic hair: *Locke, Haar*; ejaculate: *Wasser, Strom, Staub, Wein*; condom: *Becher, verschleiert, Schild*; sex toys or clothing: *Gürtel, Diadem, ein kleines Rüstzeug Kupidos, Tag und Nacht, / Damit geschirrt*. Varus' member, "Hart zwischen Nichts und Nichts!" (V.1979), in oscillating between the two orifices, like Buridan's ass manages to consume neither. Barbara Vinken notes (*Bestien*, 34) that "*diabolisch wird Homosexuelles mit Kernsätzen Luthers versetzt*," and that in Klopstock's 1769 poem on

the samae historical event the Romans are depicted as effeminate and possibly gay (cf. ibid, 37), but draws no inferences for Kleist's text from her astute observations.

539   "*Den Strich am Lippgestade überlasse*" (V.65); "*laß den Strich.../ Ruhn, an der Lippe*" (V.69-70); "*bis zur Lippe vorgerückt*" (V.188); "*dir nur... / ...dein Lippgestad verbindlich schenken*" (V.250-1); "*am Strom der Lippe stehn*" (V.402); "*von deiner Lippe...die Nacht*" (V.534-5); "*dein süßer Mund*" (V.552); "*an meine Lippe heiß gedrückt*" (V.576); "*und drückt sie leidenschaftlich an seine Lippe*" (V.599-600); "*Drückt' er sie, glühend vor Entzücken, and die Lippen*" (V.636); "*wenn ihn dein schöner Mund / Um einen Dienst ersucht, er tut ihn dir*" (V.681-2); "*nach Norden, an den Lippstrom*" (V.1843); "*den Lippstrom überschifft*" (V.2021); "*die Lispelfrage: wo?*" (V.2355). While the river Lippe is indeed a key topographical feature in relation to the original battle, as well as *satirically* a convenient marker for the earstwhile Prussian Duchy of Cleves and *satirically* a plastic term for bodily topographies, the frequency of its occurance in the drama points to further references—cf. my previous note regarding Kleist and Brockes' mutual friend Alex. zur Lippe, and the cue in *Penthesilea* suggesting a *syphilitical* connection in relation to him. When producing *Hermannsschlacht* Kleist was probably still in contact with Alex. zur Lippe, and the drama could have been a homage to that lover, in which case Kleist's relationship with Lippe is significantly underappreciated in the Kleist reception.

540   In a similar vein as Vinken (cf. *Bestien*, 18), Ricarda Schmidt maintains that Thusnelda is a "mere marionette of her husband's strategies," and "flirts" with Ventidius only "on her husband's request"—cf. Schmidt, "Sparagmos, Weiblichkeit und Staat," in Ricarda Schmidt et al (Ed.), *Gewalt*, 172, 163, and 164 n 26—; yet it could just as well be the other way around, namely that Thusnelda and Ventidius fall for each other, and the opportunistic Hermann takes advantage of it; his nickname for his wife, "*Tuschen*," may suggest as much: "*Tussi*" means "bimbo." It is irrelevant for the efficacy of his scheme whether Hermann proactively faked Ventidius' letter, or reactively capitalises on its interception.

541   Cf. Anthony Stephens, *Kleist. Sprache und Gewalt* (Freiburg i.Br.: Rombach, 1999), 244.

542   A depiction of the "*Taktische Kriegsspiel*" developed in 1812 by Georg Leopold von Reiswitz (Sr.) for Fr. Wilh., cf. https://jaxenter.com/new-column-

war-game-understanding-complex-application-development-127447.html. Wargames already existed since the 1760s; according to Hans-Christian von Herrmann (*KH*,259) they were derived from chess and incorporated elements such as variable terrains and chance (via the throwing of dice). That wargaming was a Kleistian passion is clear: *LS*,317b; 318; 507a; *NR*,84; *KH*,259-60. Herrmann F. Weiss notes, in *Funde und Studien zu Heinrich von Kleist* (Tübingen: Niemeyer, 1984), 329, that Pfuel in 1809 developed an improved wargame, which could have been the (portable) version Dahlmann and Kleist used when the *Battle of Aspern* commenced; L. von der Marwitz at his estate could have had a version of Reiswitz's table-top game (cf. II:880).

543 Voodoo priests manipulate people represented by dolls; Orson Scott Card's Ender manipulates entire armies via computer simulation; Stanislav Lem's "Players" manipulate the entire world via mind games ("The New Cosmogony," in *Solaris/The Chain of Chance/A Perfect Vacuum*, Hammondsworth: Penguin, 1981, 516-43). The syncretic religion of Voodoo (Fr.: *Vodou*) in Kleist's day was practiced chiefly in Haiti, and he could have come across its practices when researching *Verlobung*. An iconic *Vodou* ceremony took place in 1791 on the eve of the Haitan Revolution; predicatably, later legends had it that it was *Vodou* that had made the Haitians invincible and allowed them to expel the French.

544 When Stephens in the context of this drama speaks of Kleist's "*Geschichtspessimismus*" (quoted in Franz M. Eybl, *Kleist-Lektüren*, 218), he is on the wrong track, for *Hermannsschlacht* ist one of Kleist's most optimistic works. Kleist was a priori neither optimist nor pessimist but realist; when a given situation appeared promising, or he intended to generate enthusiastm, he extrapolated it into an *utopian*, if it appeared unpromising, or he intended to scare, into a *dystopian* scenario. His *prognoses* must be read in conjunction with his *diagnoses* at the time of writing (hence the necessity of tracing every work's genesis and evaluating it within its context).

545 This being Kleist, the violated "maiden" is probably best thought of as a male youth; the Teutonic name Hally means "strong in war," hardly a girl's name. Ilse Graham (*Word into Flesh*, 209) is convinced that Hally is a "raped virgin," but Kleist's references to this figure, of whom the bystanders only ever see the "feet" (i.e., male genitalia—by which Teuthold identifies her/him: V.1565), remain ambiguous: Hally is initially referred to as "*Ein Mensch*" (V.1533), "*Ein Mann? Ein Weib?*" (V.1548),

and, twice, "*die Person*" (V.1549; 1564), and only after Hermann appears on the scene does s/he come to be referred to as "*Die junge Hally*" (V.1588), "*Teutholds... Tochter*" (V.1589), and "*Die Jungfrau, die geschändete*" (V.1609). By this time Hermann's instrumentalisation of this sacrificial victim is in full swing, and his declaring it a "violated virgin" is *performative*: it does not *reflect* but *produce* "truth." Hermann turns what is probably the corpse of a youth who succumbed to syphilis (cf. the young madman in the Julius-Hospital) into what best serves his propagandistic purpose: a German virgin violated by Romans. The fact that Hally "*erkrankte*" "*auf der offnen Straß*" (V.1533) implies that anyone, Roman or German, could have violated and infected him/her; DER ZWEITE CHERUSKER's assertion that Hally was subjected to gang rape by a group of Romans (cf. V.1583-4) is not corroborated by anyone, but eagerly taken up and propagated by Hermann.

546   Cf. Sloterdijk, *Sphären II*, 703: "*denn für das Reich bedeutet Sein soviel wie zusammenhängen, und zusammenhängen meint soviel wie durch Zeichentransporte vom Zentrum aus den Rand erreichen und die zum Zentrum strebenden Botschaften sammeln können. Das Reich ist seine semiosphärische Kohärenz. Die Zeichen des Reiches verbinden die Mitte mit der Peripherie.*" The dissecting and dispatching of Hally's dismembered body references a passage in the *Book of Judges*: "When he entered his house, he took a knife and laid hold of his concubine and cut her in twelve pieces, limb by limb, and sent her throughout the territory of Israel" (*Judges* 19:29). The episode this passage is taken from, *Judges* 19:20-20:48, tells of an old man who offers a Levite and his concubine shelter and, when a gang of men of Gibeah arrive at his house and demand that he hand over his guest, so that they may sodomise him, offers them his virgin daughter instead. When the men do not accept the offer, the Levite seizes his concubine and delivers her to the men of Gibeah, who ravish her all night. When the following morning the Levite finds his lifeless concubine in the house's doorway, her hands on the house's threshold, he cuts her body in twelve pieces and sends them to the tribes of Isreal. The sons of Isreal congregate and demand punishment on the men of Gibeah, requesting the sons of Benjamin, in whose territory the town of Gibeah lies, to hand them over. When the sons of Benjamin refuse, the sons of Israel defeat them in battle and burn Gibeah to the ground. Vinken notes (*Bestien*, 67) that Hally is violated by *three* (Romans) and subsequently finished off by *three* (Germans), but lacks a framework for explaining this numerical pattern. Apart from evidently invoking the *"FFF"* constellation, these two triads may entail a *satirical* representation: it could be said that three Frenchmen "violated" the *HRR*—François Barthélemy,

who negotiated the *Treaty of Basel* on France's behalf, Jean Moreau, whose victory at Hohenlinden effectively ended the *War of the Second Coalition*, and Napoleon, whose victory at *Austerlitz* ended the *War of the Third Coalition*—, while three German men "finished it off": Hardenberg and Max. Joseph, who by signing, respectively, *Basel* and *Bogenhausen* precipitated the *HRR*'s dissolution (the two "cousins"), and Franz II (the "father"), who completed it.

547   Medea, fleeing with Jason and the Golden Fleece, kills and dismembers her brother Absyrtus and throws his body parts into the water to distract their father Aeëtes; the Peliades kill their father Pelias, cut him into pieces and boil him in a pot in the hope to rejuvenate him; Judith brings the head of Holofernes to the people of Bethulia to encourage their resistance to the Assyrian conquerors.

548   Cf. Michalzik (*Kleist*, 355): "*Einen Eindruck der anspielungsreichen Atmosphäre geben auch einige Briefe, die Gentz und Müller schon 1807 wechselten. Sie sprachen immer wieder über einen Kometen. Dabei ging es nicht um einen Himmelskörper, sondern die Übermittlung geheimer Botschaften. Diese Art der Anspielung—da war Kleist in seinem Element.*" Comets were *du jour* in Kleist's day: Kleist's favourite professor at the Viadrina, Chr. Ernst Wünsch, constructed and operated comet planetariums after he in 1769 observed the famous comet *Messier*, whose sightings generated much public interest across Europe (one of Wünsch's theories was that the Christian religion had derived from the Egyptian, which in turn had originated in the observation of astronomical phenomena—cf. Michalzik, *Kleist*, 94-5). Many leading scientists in Kleist's day occupied themselves with comets and calculated their periodic appearance (cf. *AML*,275), among them Lalande, Lagrange, Cassini, Euler, Legrendre, and Bessel, some of whom Kleist could have met in Paris in 1801; he likely met Joseph Lalande, director of the Paris observatory, who provided an improved calculation of the return of Halley's comet (cf. II:721). Gentz and A. Müller discuss the sightings of the Great Comet of 1807 (C/1807 R1)—cf. *AML*,244-247).

549   Hitler's "*Volkssturm*" was in part modelled on the Prussian "*Landsturm*," with which Fr. Wilh. in 1813-15 belatedly created that force that Kleist in 1808-11 had tirelessly advocated.

550   Dirk Grathoff (*Kleist und Napoleon*, 51) considers Kleist's "*Vision der Landkartenveränderung durch die Umlenkung des Rheins*" a "*Schreckensvision.*" In so far as Kleist considered himself something of a latter-day Orpheus (cf. "*The Orphic*" below), it bears mentioning that one of the arts ascribed to Orpheus was that of *redirecting rivers*; Kleist's fantastic imagery thus had a mythical forebear. Apart from redirecting the Rhine, the only other means of reconciling the competing territorial claims would have been expelling all Germans residing west of the Rhine—an act that nowadays would presumably be termed "ethnic cleaning." It is curious that readers continue to be upset at Kleist's imagery when the alternative was far worse.

551   Cf. similarly Gentz: "*Noch aber ist zu keiner Bourbonischen Unternehmung Zeit und Stunde. Bonaparte muß erst geschlagen, gebeugt, in die alten Grenzen Frankreichs zurückgeführt, ganz mürbe gemacht werden*" (*AML*,128).

552   In a letter of December 1801 Kleist notes passing through "*das französische Elsaß*" (II:708) en route to Switzerland. The discussed passage in *Ode* confirms that for him it remained evident that the Alsace properly belonged to France. It is ironic that his works of the 1808/9 period in the 1870s and the 1930s would be mis-appropriated by nationalists who vigorously pursued Alsace's annexation into Germany. Had they come across this letter passage, they would surely have passed over it eyes wide shut. While this is purely speculative, one element in Prussia's 1815 territorial gains (cf. the regions in blue in the right-hand map) that Kleist might have objected to was her gaining control of most of the Rhineland, whereas the restitution of the status quo ante would have required only the return of the Duchy of Cleves and other minor pre-1807 Prussian possessions in western Germany. For the first time in her history, Prussia came to border directly on France, as well as shifting her economic centre westwards, to where within a few decades the Ruhr valley would emerge as the world's premier industrial region (which as of 1815 could not be *known*, but perhaps *anticipated*, industrialisation of the Ruhr valley commencing just around this time). This westward shift of Prussia's centre of gravity, with which Prussia replaced Austria as France's main rival on the Continent, arguably precipitated the *Franco-German War* of 1871, and consequently WWI and WWII. Had Kleist been present at the *Congress of Vienna*, he might have advocated more moderate Prussian demands in the Rhineland—and had he for once been heard, with just a bit of a stretch of imagination, could have prevented two world wars.

553   When Fr. Wilh. decided not to join the Coalition, he necessarily had to call off his return to Berlin, for Napoleon would have treated it as tantamount to a declaration of war. Kleist laments not so much his King's failure to return as his decision to abstain from the war.

554   In late 1808 Fr. Wilh. and Prince Wilh. met the Tsar in St. Petersburg; the result of the conversation must have been sobering and may have been decisive in Fr. Wilh.'s decision not to join the war—cf. https://de.wikipedia.org/wiki/Wilhelm_von_Preußen_(1783-1851). In 1792 the first semaphore messages were successfully sent between Paris and Lille. In 1794 the semaphore line informed Parisians of the capture of the fortress Condé-sur-l'Escaut from the Austrians less than an hour after it occurred. Other lines were built, including a line from Paris to Toulon. The system was widely copied by other European states—cf. https://en.wikipedia.org/wiki/Claude_Chappe. Napoleon saw the military advantage in being able to transmit information between locations, and carried a portable semaphore with his HQ. This allowed him to coordinate forces and logistics over longer distances than any other army of his time—cf. https://en.wikipedia.org/wiki/Semaphore_telegraph#Development. Prussia does not appear to have installed a national telegraph system until the 1830s, but German allies of Napoleon such as Bavaria and Saxony may have done so earlier. Homing pigeons were widely used in war—cf. https://en.wikipedia.org/wiki/War_pigeon.

555   We could do worse than take Dahlmann's account of their plans, and his comments on Kleist's drama, seriously: *"so wanderten wir zusammen aus Dresden fort [on 29th April 1809], der böhmischen Grenze zu. Wir wollten nicht bei den Sachsen bleiben, die unter Bernadotte gegen Deutschland zogen, Deutschland, das wir um so tiefer im Herzen trugen, je weniger es draußen zu finden war. Unser Vorsatz war, von Böhmen aus nach allen Kräften dahin zu wirken, daß aus dem österreichischen Kriege ein deutscher werde. Nicht daß wir uns mit der Hoffnung auf augenblickliche Erfolge getäuscht hätten; wir verlangten von Österreich nur Ausharren trotz der Niederlagen, und glaubten an der Haltung der Gebrüder Stadion zu erkennen, daß der Staat entschlossen sei, diesmal seinen letzten Kampf zu kämpfen; wenn dem aber so sei, so werde auch Preußen sich aufraffen aus seinem schmählichen Schwanken zwischen Sein und Nichtsein, das übrige Deutschland aber werde den vereinigten Adlern Österreichs und Preußens folgen. In welchem Lichte Kleist die Stimmung des anfangs schwachen, allein im wachsenden Drucke erstarkenden deutschen Volkes*

betrachtete, zeigt eine Stelle seiner damals vollendeten Hermannsschlacht, die ein treues, wenn auch manchmal grelles Bild der Zeiten anstellt" (*LS*,316; Dahlmann continues by quoting V.2236-30). Kleist's drama, if "occasionally strident," in Dahlmann's view "truthfully" reflected the general mood among the Germans. As late as Apri 1809 he and Kleist evidently were still hopeful that Prussia would join the war and that northern Germany would rise provided Austria could hold out against the *Ad'A*, which suggests that *Hermannschlacht* potentially remained pertinent and that Kleist remained ready to pull it out of the drawer if needed.

556   For a comprehensive overview of Kleist's plausible sources and use thereof, cf. Horst Häker, *Homburg und Verlobung*, 17-48. Michalzik terms *Homburg* a sequel to *Hermannsschlacht*—cf. *Kleist*, 370. Kleist likely conceived of *Die Zerstörung Jerusalems* around the same time, and in the same context, as *Homburg*—cf. my below *Notes on Projects Not Executed or Not Extant*.

557   Richard Samuel surmises that no private staging took place—cf. "A Final Word regarding the Manuscripts of 'Prinz Friedrich von Homburg," in: *German Life and Letters. A Quarterly Review.* Vol. XXXIII, October 1979, 23-4 (cited in Horst Häker, *Homburg und Verlobung*, 65); Häker concurs (*ibid*, 305). Interestingly, Kleist evidently anticipated that it *might* take place, which suggests that in March 1810 he had an early version under his pen for which the timing was pertinent. Since March 1810 saw Napoleon's wedding with Marie-Louise, and no other major events, Kleist may have been looking to tweak such a version into a sequel not of *Hermannsschlacht* but *Käthchen*: with the wedding, and the Franco-Austrian alliance it buttressed, Prussia risked being isolated between an unsatiable Napoleon and an Alex. I increasingly at odds with him, and a 1810 *Homburg* version could have explored the title character's being pulled to-and-fro between these two powers. A widely-held assumption in the Kleist reception, based on Kleist's 19th March 1810 note to Ulrike, that the drama as we know it was largely completed by the spring of 1810—cf., e.g., Jochen Schmidt (*Kleist*, 155); Bernard Greiner (*Kleists Dramen*, 272); Wolfgang Nehring (*Kleist Prinz*, 165)—would then be not entirely baseless: the *terminus post quem* for the drama's final version must be the King's first raising the possibility of an alliance with France, and it is not impossible that this event took place well before Count Harzberg's official offer of an alliance to Napoleon of 14th May 1811—possibly already in 1810. Häker concurs with Samuel that a 1810 version existed, but believes that it will have been significantly different from the extant

1811 version (cf. *Homburg und Verlobung*, 13; 62-5); he terms these two versions, respectively, "*Luisenfassung*" and "*Natalienfassung*," and surmises that Natalie would have had no, or a very different, role in the former version (cf. *ibid*, 13-14; 69; 81-9). Häker grounds his analysis in a firm belief in the work's close connection to its political context (including Luise's death) and highlights "*Kleists bis zur Esoterik reichende Kunst der Verschlüsselung*" (*ibid*, 15). I already expressed my appreciation for Häker's pioneering work in *Emigrant*—his observations (*ibid*, 237-8; cf. *Emigrant* n.487) resonate with my own, his insights regarding the embeddedness of Kleist's works in their historical and biographical context (cf. *ibid*, 13), their profound intertextuality (cf. *ibid*, 14), their nature as (in my terms) "code" or "encryption" (cf. his Novalis quote and his term *"entschlüsseln,"* *ibid*, 15), and their purpose of "influencing the real world" (cf. *ibid*, 81), especially the court (cf. his denoting the drama as "*höfisches Stück*", *ibid*, 82) and even explicitly the King himself (cf. *ibid*, 238), are groundbreaking and anticipate my own findings, and I wholeheartedly concur with his conclusion (*ibid*, 80), "*Es heißt daher den Dichter Kleist gründlich mißverstehen, wenn ihm die Forschung an so mancher zunächst noch undeutbaren Stelle seiner Werke "Erfindung" oder "Willkür" attestiert, anstatt daß energisch nach der vermutlich darin steckenden Anspielung oder Beziehung gesucht wird,*" which we may want to call the "first law of Kleist readership." Yet Häker is not nearly as "*gewagt*" (*ibid*, 15) as he purports to be: although he discerns the dual nature of Kleist's The Elector as "illustrious ruler" and as "enslaving despot" (*ibid*, 154-5), he fails to discern Kleist's most "daring" move, of this figure representing not a Prussian but a French *Übervater*. For all his exploration of intertextualities between *Homburg* and *Verlobung*, he fails to extend his insights to Kleist's œuvre: "*Der 'Homburg' ist bei strenger Betrachtung sogar Kleists einziges Bühnenwerk, das 'in die Mitte der Zeit' hineinfiel*" (*ibid*, 91). *Pas du tous*.

558   Since Fr. Wilh. absented himself from the war, Kleist, in one of his characteristic sleights-of-hand, in *Verlobung* forgrounds the Hohenzollerns' (enacted by Gustav and Toni) *satyrical-syphilitical* relationship while backgrounding the war between Napoleon (Congo Hoango) and Franz (Strömli). Horst Häker discerns re Congo Hoango and Strömli, "*Beide Männer sind, cum grano salis, die Führer ihrer Völker im Kampf und in der Verhandlung*" (*Homburg und Verlobung*, 159), and had he only looked past his unhelpful caveat *"cum grano salis,"* could have discerned their identity.

559   Fouqué also spend the winter of 1809/10 in Berlin before returning to Nennhausen (cf. Sembdner, *In Sachen Kleist*, 207-8). Sembdner soberly reports the facts and does not speculate about the reasons, but I do: the event of the Royals' return will have created an atmosphere of excitement and a spirit of optimism that drew many patriots to Berlin, including the likes of Eichendorff, Fouqué and Kleist; A. Müller, already in Berlin, composed a widely lauded pamphlet on the occasion (cf. Jakob Baxa's notes to *AML*,403). Among the Kleist biographers, Loch, Michalzik and Blamberger largely or entirely skip the four months between Kleist's leaving Prague in October 1809 and his settling into Berlin in February 1810 (Loch misplaces Eichendorff's diary entry into the period after 4th February—cf. *Kleist*, 343; *LS*,340), and only Schulz (*Kleist*, 441) notes the possibility of Kleist's sojourn in Berlin in December, but fails to follow up on Eichendorff and Arndt's notes—e.g., he fails to seek to establish whether or not there could indeed have been another "Major von Kleist" frequenting Müller's house during this time. That the return of the King is vital in conjunction with Kleist's late works (and his decision to settle in Berlin), his biographers all but overlook.

560   The distance by road Berlin-Frankfurt/M is c.580 km, of which Berlin-Gotha c.255 km, Gotha-Frankfurt/M, c.225 km. Had Kleist left Berlin, say, on 25th December, he could have arrived in Frankfurt/M. on 31st December; and could have eft Frankfurt/M to return to Berlin, with a stop-over in Gotha on 28th January (cf. II:831), as late as 25th January—i.e., he had up to three and a half weeks in Frankfurt/M. If he travelled this far to see his *magnétiseur*, Kleist must have been desperate, magnetic therapy his last straw, and Neufville his last hope. Did he also go to Mainz, less than 40 km from Frankfurt/M., to seek out Wedekind? Or was Wedekind too expensive? Upon leaving Prague Kleist was "more indepted than ever" (Loch, *Kleist*, 339). Or was Kleist unable to obtain a passport for French territory? In his letter to Ulrike of 23rd November 1809, Kleist cedes to her any excess capital raised by the impending sale of the Frankfurt/O. family house, withholding the reason for his gesture—"*Die Veranlassung dazu ist nicht gemacht, Dir in einem Briefe mitgeteilt zu werden*" (II:829)—, and shares his intention to return to Austria. These two pieces of information could suggest that during the Prague sojourn he had found a partner *willing to die with him*: already on 3rd May, and again on 17th July 1809, he expresses *Todessehnsucht* to Ulrike (cf. II:825-6; 828), and Michalzik notes perceptively (*Kleist*, 384) that with his 23rd November letter Kleist "*agierte wie jemand, der seine letzten Angelegenheiten ordnet.*" What, then, compelled Kleist to

travel to Frankfurt/M. *in order to live*, instead of back to Prague *in order to die*? The most plausible answer, I believe, is that within days of posting his letter to Ulrike the news broke of the King's imminent return, which gave Kleist a new lease of life: he *must* be present in Berlin in December, and settle there therafter; therefore he is unable to undergo therapy there, lest *tout le monde* would know; thus he goes as far away as possible for it: Frankfurt/M. Michalzik (*Kleist*, 384) once more offers a helpful insight without exploiting it: "*Mehr als ein Drittel der schriftlichen Spuren, die er in seinem 34-jährigen Leben hinterlassen hat, stammen aus den 22 Monaten, die er jetzt in Berlin verbrachte.*" Why does Kleist, perhaps on the brink of death, now enter the most productive period of his life? Because, I offer, the King's return re-animates him, and Berlin becomes his "last stand."

561   Kleist's contemporaries and biographies note Berlin's revival: "*Hier wimmelt die Stadt von Poeten. Neulich war ich auf einem Mittagessen, da Hitzig dem Fouquet zu Ehren angestellt hatte, mit dreißigen... Nach [Fouquet] ist Kleist angekommen*" (Arndt, *LS*,347). "*Berlin war inzwischen zu einem Sammelbecken verschiedener Strömungen einer patriotisch sich gebenden künstlerischen Intelligenz geworden. Entsprechend groß war Kleists Bekanntenkreis... Altenstein... Gruner... Staegemann... Reimer... Arndt*" (Loch, *Kleist*, 363). "*König, Königin, Politiker, Staatsbeamte und eine Reihe von Denkern und Dichtern, denen er sich selbst mit Fug und Recht zuzählen durfte: die wichtigsten dramatis personae für das letzte Kapitel im Leben Heinrich von Kleists scheinen im Moment seiner Rückkehr nach Berlin bereits beisammen zu sein*" (Schulz, *Kleist*, 443). "*Berlin wurde geistreicher, doppeldeutiger und verspielter. Immer mehr Künstler fühlten sich von der Stadt angezogen, von der bevorstehenden Rückkehr des Königlichen Hofes aus Königsberg, der Aufgabe, diese Stadt neu zu ordnen, und der Gründung der Universität. "Hier wimmelt die Stadt von Poeten," schrieb Achim von Arnim. In den letzten Monaten waren hier mehrere Männer frisch angekommen: Fichte, Arnim, Wilh. von Humboldt, Fr. Schleiermacher, A. Müller und Clemens Brentano... Es steckte Kraft in dieser jüngsten europäischen Großstadt*" (Michalzik, *Kleist*, 383; Kleist had met Wilh. von Humboldt in Paris in 1801; in Berlin he likely met Fichte, a member of the *Tugendbund* and the *Deutsche Tischgesellschaft*, with both of which Kleist was loosely associated, and possibly Schleiermacher—cf. *ibid*, 387; 447).

562   The production of the poem's three extant versions probably spanned more than a year (cf. I:915), suggesting that Kleist wrote the 1st version for the Queen's

32nd birthday in March 1809, at a time when he was desperately holding on to his hope that the Royals would return from exile to join Austria's war, before putting it into the drawer when the return did not take place, the 2nd version later during that year, possibly during his "disappearance" in Prague and in anticipation of the Royals' return following *Schönbrunn*, and the 3rd version shortly before the Queen's 33rd birthday, perhaps after it became clear that a staging of *Homburg* at that occasion was not in the cards (so that as of March 1810 the poem was a proxy for a drama not ready or not acceptable to the Queen's courtiers). For all the differences between the three versions, the poem's central verse, "Wie du das Unglück, mit der Grazie Tritt / Auf jungen Schultern herrlich hast getragen," in which, I argue in *Emigrant* (pp.145-6), Kleist accuses Luise of facilitating the propagation of the "French disease," remains essentially unaltered.

563   Cf. my discussion of *Cäcilie* in *Emigrant*. The *Salve Regina* is an antiphon traditionally associated with the first Crusade (1095-9), whose principal leader, Adhemar of Le Puy, purportedly composed it as the Crusaders' anthem. The first Crusade provides the *overt* setting for Kleist's project *Peter der Einsiedler*.

564   Such reversals pervade Kleist's œuvre: in *Verlobung*, Congo Hoango, said to have rebelled against colonial hegemony as a young man, represents not, as might be expected, a German prince resisting Napoleon, but none other than the Corsican-revoluzzer-turned-despot himself; in *Findling*, the characters whom readers frequently associate, respectively, with evil and paternal care, Nicolo and Piachi, represent not Napoleon and Fr. Wilh., but *vice versa*. Fascinatingly, Kleist appears to have been able to model his character Congo Hoango on two real persons he had encountered in Frankfurt/O.: a black tambour by the name of Cambo and a freed slave from the Kingdom of Loango—Horst Häker argues convincingly (cf. *Beiträge* 1999, 124-5; 133) that the phonetic similarity between Cambo Loango and Congo Hoango is too great to be coincidental, and Kleist will have adapted the actual names such that they came to represent two mighty rivers (Africa's Congo and China's Hoango) without losing their characteristic sound. Siebert demonstrates (*Kleistiana Collecta*, 144-6) that Kleist could have known of the river Hoango through an article in Berlin's *Spenersche Zeitung* of 18th September 1800, a paper that could also have furbished him with inspirations for *Marquise* (5th September) and *Verlobung* (16th September). Kleist was in Würzburg during this time, but could have read the issues upon his return to Berlin, or borrowed them from someone in Würzburg who had them mailed there.

Most interestingly, the article from the 18th reports that following extensive rains "the great river Hoango has burst its banks and wreaked unspeakable havoc"—what better metaphor for Napoleon's destructive wars? I argued in *Emigrant* that in *Verlobung* the two rivers *satirically* refer to the Rhône (in the south, like Africa) and Rhine (in the east, like China), over whose extent Napoleon in 1809 rules, and Kleist's double name for his villain laments that France and Germany are now entirely under his sway.

565   Gerhard Schulz's remark (*Kleist*, 499), "Fehrbellin besaß kein Schloß und mithin existierte keine Rampe…‚" is remarkable not because Schulz overlooks Schloss Wustrau's existence—it barely counts as a castle, is located at several kilometres from Fehrbellin proper, and is furthermore anachronistic relative to the battle—, but because the idea that Kleist could be thinking of another, much more prominent, castle does not appear to him at all. In this Schulz has a prominent predecessor: Theodor Fontane already expressed irritation at this and other purported inaccuracies in Kleist's drama (cf. *NR*,575). Kleist could well have visited Fehrbellin, be it en route to or from Rügen with Ulrike in the summer of 1800, or be it en route to or from Koblentz to pick up Brockes a few months later. Kleist could also have passed by Fontainebleau, e.g., in 1803 en route from Lyon to Paris.

566   Häker (*Homburg und Verlobung*, 44) makes much of the apparent parallel between the historical Homburg's silvern leg prosthesis and the wooden leg in *Marionettentheater*, but fails to explain satisfactorily why Kleist omitted this fascinating detail in his portrait of his drama's title character. Häker offers that Kleist sought to depict the middle-aged Homburg as a vigorous young man, as Carl Kretschmar had previously done on his well-known painting of Homburg and the Elector, but this explanation only begs another question: why depict him as a young, unblemished man? For which Häker offers no answer. I offer that the silver prosthesis does not suit Kleist because the prosthesis would mark Homburg as castrated from the beginning, which would undermine his plot of Homburg's becoming-castrated, his becoming-enslaved.

567   Franz was indeed a trained gardener (!) and encouraged the cultivation of exotic plants in his gardens, including at Schönbrunn's Schlosspark and the Hofburg's Hofgarten. In *Verlobung*'s final passages, Strömli-Franz retires to the Habsburgs' ancestral lands in Switzerland to tend his garden. The *Hofgarten* (today's *Burggarten*) is situated where until 1809 parts of Vienna's city fortifications had been located,

dynamited by the French during the city's occupation. In 1810/11, when Kleist completed his drama, the garden did not yet exist, though soon after Napoleon's departure Franz began ordering spaces opened up by the extensive blastings to be built up or turned into parks, and plans for the Hofgarten could well have been designed at the same time as Kleist's drama (it was not, however, properly laid out till 1818, and not "in the old French style").

568   Franz M. Eybl notes (*Kleist-Lektüren*, 224) the wreath *and* the chain,, "*Die Prinzessin steht mit erhobenem Kranz, umwunden mit der Kette des Königs*" [paragraph break] "*Ruhm und Schlacht, Lorbeer und Befehl*," but reads the latter merely as symbolising the King's (sic) "*order*," which misses the crux of the matter: that the chain symbolises specifically The Elector's *hegemony* over Homburg, i.e., the latter's enslavement. Blamberger offers, similarly generically (*Kleist*, 381), that the chain symbolises "*power.*" Dagmar Ottmann writes an entire essay on the symbolism of *Homburg*'s props ('Das Stumme Zeichen,' in Lubkoll and Oesterle (Eds.), *Gewagte Experimente*, 259-60), without paying attention to the Elector's chain, which she notes merely in passing. Häker considers the chain (*Homburg und Verlobung*, 121), but misinterprets it: "*Die Verleihung der goldnen Kette besiegelt die künftige Gleichwertigkeit des Kurfürsten und des Prinzen*." Eybl goes out of his way to stress the difficulties of interpreting Kleist's drama (*ibid*, 223), quoting and endorsing Helmut Arntzen, "*Einem so häufig interpretierten Drama wie diesem kann Respekt nur dadurch erwiesen werden, daß man zunächst und vor allem die Schwierigkeit, es angemessen zu verstehen, aufzeigt*," to which he adds (*ibid*, 234) that "*Die besseren der Interpretationen halten bewusst, wie brüchig, widersprüchlich und vertrackt der Text bei genauerem Hinsehen ist, wie sich Kleist Drama der Eindeutigkeit immer wieder entzieht,*" but engrossed as he appears to be in his sophistry, fails to notice that Kleist repeatedly—five, six, seven times—and consistently highlights the connexion between wreath and chain. The conventional symbolism of the wreath is so seductive that it misleads readers into overlooking that of the chain (cf. Poe's purloined letter). Arntzen in 'Prinz Friedrich von Homburg'—Drama der Bewußtseinsstufen," in Walter Hinderer (Ed.), *Neue Interpretationen*, 215-22 (from which Eybl quotes) elaborates a tableau of purported inconsistencies or contradictions in *Homburg* and, instead of seeking to resolve them, declares them unresolvable and even constitutive of the work, whose unity derives, or so he argues (*ibid*, 222-35), only from its formal integration. Alas, all the micro-level inconsistencies he highlights disappear on the macro-level of Kleist's *plane of consistency*.

569   Cf. Horst Häker, *Homburg und Verlobung*, 64. The blindfold marks Fortuna, who appears earlier in the drama (cf. V.355-7), and complements the *agencement* of laurel and chain, signaling that Homburg's fate is neither elevation nor death, but the *limbo* of perennial enslavement; the dialectic between illusory victory and actual enchainment is quasi *aufgehoben* in a time that is no longer *chronological, aionic* or *kairotic* but *messianic* (Agamben: the time left to us till *Parousia*; pure potentiality) and *ecstatic* (Heidegger: the time of primordial "thrownness"), as Homburg is no longer on a Homeric odyssey (whose hero eventually returns home) but arrested in a state of indeterminate suspension: a zombie, vampire, wandering Jew or flying Dutchman (vampires first appear in European literature in 1659; the Haitian-French term *zombi* in 1697; Kleist could have come across the latter in conjunction with the Haitian *voudou* cult when researching *Verlobung*).

570   Natalie's hand is as exchangeable as Littegarde's bed of straw; The Elector's offering it to the Swedish (i.e., Russian) monarch comprises Kleist's ironic reversal of Napoleon's 1808 quest for the hand of Alex.'s younger sister Katharina. The Elector's aloofness, and his delegating the "dirty work" to Natalie and Hohenzollern, mirrors the Brandenburg Elector's behaviour in in *Kohlhaas*. Kleist made his own experiences with such aloofness, e.g., in 1804 when court protocol and the King's intransigence force him to negotiate his re-entry into Prussian services with a phalanx of courtiers, and in 1810 when during the BA stand-off Hardenberg leaves it to his underling Raumer to wear Kleist down.

571   Kleist was evidently fascinated even more by the story of *Abélard et Héloïse*, whose urn he visited in Paris, than by that of *Romeo and Juliet* or *Pyramus et Thisbe*. The motif of *"Kinderkauf"* (Horst Häker) already appears in *Marquise*, where Count F parts with much of his fortune in exchange for social fatherhood to the Marquise's offspring. Homburg's *"einen Knaben, blondgelockt"* (V.1046) invokes a desireable *erômenos* just as much as it does an adorable infant.

572   Berthold Brecht already in 1939 recognised that Kleist's Homburg is forced into submission: *"Sein Degen ist noch neben ihm: in Stücken. / Tot ist er nicht, doch liegt er auf dem Rücken: / Mit allen Feinden Brandenburgs im Staub"* (NR,595). Some Kleist scholars (e.g., Schede, *Kleist*, 88; Siebert, *Kleistiana Collecta*, 113-30) surmise that Homburg is modelled on Prince Louis Ferd., prominent leader of Prussia's "War Party," and—thanks to his rash actions at the *Battle of Saalfeld*—among

the first fallen soldiers of *War of the Fourth Coalition*. Kleist could have met Louis Ferd. at the Prussian HQ at Marienborn during the *Siege of Mainz* (cf. Siebert, *ibid*, 118), and at various other occasions.

573   Cf. G. W. F. Hegel, *Phänomenologie des Geistes*, Ed. Georg Lasson (Paderborn: Voltmedia, 1807/1905-44), 159-64. Hegel's term is "*Herrschaft und Knechtschaft*," literally "lordship and bondage," but the term "master-slave dialectic" has found wider currency in English texts.

574   *Homburg* also parallels the extended *Cäcilie*, which Kleist produced more or less concurrently with *Zweikampf* and *Homburg*, in that Homburg's enslavement also entails a *conversion*: like *Cäcilie*'s Brothers and Mother, Homburg is converted from The Elector's *rival* into his ardent *disciple*. The road to *Fehrbellin* is Homburg's *road to Damascus*—his initiation, baptism, rite of passage, and *Reifeprüfung*. His transformation's completion is announced by the thunder of cannons and his fellow converts' "*Heil! Heil! Heil!,*" and perhaps recalls the scene of Kleist's initiation near Biebrich: "*Kanonenschüsse. Ein Marsch. Das Schloß erleuchtet sich*" (V.1853). consists in the progression of his syphilitic infection and mental and physical corruption. Alex. von Bormann sees in *Homburg* a drama of initiation (*Drama der Adoleszenz*, 298-302), Jochen Schmidt one of education (*Kleist*, 166), and Homburg's "*Bildung*" may entail a parody of Werther's.

575   Fr. Nietzsche, *Jenseits von Gut und Böse*, §146 (Frankfurt: Insel, 1984), 82.

576   Ilse Graham notes (*Word into Flesh*, 181) that *Homburg*'s "beginning and end meet to interlock in a perfect circle," and Günter Blamberger observes (*Kleist*, 384-5), leaning on Dagmar Ottmann, the symmetry of the drama's constellation and circulations—which he calls, quite appositely, its "framing." Wolfgang Nehring points out ("Kleists Prinz von Homburg," in Walter Müller-Seidel (Ed.), *Kleists Aktualität*, 153), that for all their parallels, the initial scene depicts a *private*, the final scene a *public* event. Satyrically the "figure 8" recalls the movement from (a...)hole to (a...)hole Kleist alludes to in letters, e.g., when comparing his mind (and body) to a "salacious butterfly's fluttering from one honey-flavoured flower to another" (cf. II:673), depicting his Paris journey as "akin to wanderings of the olden knights, from castle to castle" (cf. II:656), and recalling youths in the Tharandt valley "jumping from rock to rock, rejoicing" (cf. II:545). Zschokke in his 1842 memoirs uses similar

"code" when referring to their party's (Kleist, L. Wieland, himself) ramble from Bern to Aarau in March 1802 as *"Umherschwärmen von Schmetterlingen... von jeder Blume gelockt, von keiner gehalten"* (LS,75a).

577   In *Marionettentheater*, the I-narrator asks Herrn C. whether a *Maschinist* (puppeteer) himself has to be a "dancer" to reign his "puppets," to which Herr C. responds that in the "marionette dance" most "puppets" (lovers) make the appropriate movements spontaneously, without intervention from the *Maschinist*, but in case a "puppet" enters the "mysterious" "path of the soul," the *Maschinist* may need to engage his "centre of gravity" and join the "dance" (cf. II:340). *Satyrically,* during the symposium or orgiastic séance, the *erastês* can let himself be sodomised by *dmotes* without any effort on his part, but before an *erômenos*, he must himself erect and engage; *satirically,* in spreading political propaganda, the editor can manipulate most readers without paying special attention to them, but to manipulate the key leaders, he must penetrate their hearts and minds with finely-crafted, tailored messages. Cf. Sloterkijk (*Kritik,* 290): *"Genitalien... sind die Genies unter den Organen der unteren Körperhälfte... Sie gleichen den Drahtziehern im Dunkeln, von denen das Haifischlied in der* Dreigroschenoper *sagt, daß man sie nicht sieht. Doch bei ihnen laufen letztlich alle Fäden zusammen."*

578   Comparing Napoleon with oriental tyrants was conventional in Kleist's day—cf. Gentz to Müller, 23rd October 1802 (*AML*,32): *"seit einem Jahre, seitdem sich der regierende Sultan auf seinem Throne befestigt glaubte... die Tyrannei der willkürlichen Impositionen,"* and so was referring to him as "enchainer"—cf. A. Müller to Gentz in February 1808: *"Bonaparte'sche Ketten drücken"* (*AML*,292); the reference to the "Mameluks" will also have been current.

579   Dirk Grathoff's dismissal (*Kleist: Geschichte,* 192) of Katharina Mommsen's proposition, based on a 1800 drawing by Fr. Bury showing Goethe seated on a curule chair, that Kleist's *sella curulis* references Goethe, even if Kleist did have a painting of Brutus in mind, or Voltaire's stage adaption of his story, detracts from what is most interesting about Mommsen's suggestion, namely that Kleist's figure refers to an actual personage. No doubt that The Elector in the first instance represents Napoleon, but this does not exclude the possibility that he also represents Goethe: for Kleist, Napoleon and Goethe had much in common, and it will not have surprised him that the two men at *Erfurt* showed great respect for each other as top dogs in their

respective domains. Grathoff, when he notes (*ibid*, 195-7) that The Elector deploys a *French* logic and that Homburg is being "refined in a French manner" (i.e., in my term, he is being "francofied"), *"Der Kurfürst von Brandenburg beugt also den Filius mit den Mitteln des Gegners unter dessen Gesetz. So darf ein—gewissermaßen französisch geläuterter—Prinz von Homburg am Ende überleben, denn er liegt ja wörtlich da, wo Kleist ihn liegen läßt:* 'In Staub mit allen Feinden Brandenburgs!'," comes close to decoding *Homburg's* satirical thread. So does Dagmar Ottmann when she muses (*Das Stumme Zeichen*, 272): "*Bleibt vom Prinzen ein zerstörter Mensch am Ende übrig, über den der Despotismus seinen Sieg errungen hat, der zu einer Larve wurde, die nur noch marionettenhaft auf ein Heroentum verweist, das schon längst abgedankt hat...?*" She could have asked "*whose* despotism?" is being negotiated her, but for her, as for Grathoff, revaluing The Elector's conventional *identity* is one step too far.

580   The *"mehr noch der fremden Pflanzen"* Franz cultivates in the "garden" may refer to further *sons* to be produced by Marie-Louise and to further *lands* to be conquered by Napoleon. Kleist already in *Marquise* anticipates the dynastic scenario that plays out in 1810/11, except with inverted algebraical signs: whereas in the utopian *Marquise* Kleist puts the Marquise-Luise in the driver's seat, with Count F-Napoleon relegated to acting as her plaything, in the dystopian *Homburg* he has Napoleon clearly in charge (as *erastai*), with Franz (the gardener) relegated to tending the garden's rear (as *dmōs*) and a blindfolded, powerless Fr. Wilh. (Homburg) seduced and enchained as *erōmenos*.

581   L. Robert, quoted in Grathoff, *Kleist: Geschichte*, 169-70. The Elector is perhaps the most misunderstood of Kleistian characters: Gernot Müller opines (*Gemälde*, 244), "[Kleist] scheint... den Großen Kurfürsten zum göttlichen Antipoden des Dämons Napoleon verzeichnen zu wollen," and the drama's first publisher, L. Tieck, hails Kleist's "excellent portrait" of the Great Elector—cf. Alex. von Bormann, "Kleists *Prinz Friedrich von Homburg*—Drama der Adoleszenz," in Lubkoll and Oesterle (Eds.), *Gewagte Experimente*, 282. Cf. also *NR*,548; 554d; 579; and Grathoff, *Kleist: Geschichte*, 166.

582   By the time of *Hermannsschlacht*'s completition, in late 1808, Kleist remains reluctant to support a coup to replace Fr. Wilh. with his younger brother; by that of *Kohlhaas*', in the summer of 1810, he has come to accept that the King is dispensible and may be replaced by one of his sons, if not his brother; by that of

Homburg's, in September 1811, he may be prepared to throw in his lot with Prince Wilh.; yet by that of his suicide, ten weeks later clearly, his nod is to Fr. Wilh. and not any other Prussian leader (cf. my later section on *The Familial*). Fr. Wilh., on this part, had a feeling that something didn't square: in 1828, after three stagings in Berlin, he banned Kleist's drama from the Prussian stage (cf. *NR*,556).

583   Cf. Kittler, "Die Revolution der Revolution," in Gerhard Neumann (Ed.), *Kriegsfall*, 77-8. Because of Homburg's hasty intervention, the Brandenburgian (French) victory is incomplete: had he followed instructions, the enemy could have been not just repulsed but vanquished. Kleist may be indicating that a *combination* of Napoleonic decision autonomy and Frederician discipline is most effective.

584   Cf. Sloterdijk, *Sphären II*, 740: *"souverän ist, wer Gnade vor Recht ergehen lassen kann."* Napoleon in fact ruled like an absolute monarch, and on occasion did pardon commanders, e.g., Louis Thomas Villaret de Joyeuse, who fell into disfavour following the British *Invasion of Martinique*.

585   Cf. Häker, *Homburg and Verlobung*, 85; cf. by way of contrast Wolf Kittler, *Geburt*, 264. That Kleist borrowed the rare name Natalie from Goethe's *Wilhelm Meister*, in whose Natalie already Novalis discerned as "inadvertent portrait of the Queen" (quoted in Häker, *ibid*), is plausible. Even Häker is not immune to a blind faith in Kleist's admiration for and loyalty to the Queen: *"die von ihm unzweifelbar verehrte Königin"* (ibid, 84); *"eines schmerzlichen Prozesses der Gewöhnung"* (ibid, 87).

586   Scheuer links Kleist's equine *tinctures* to medieval tournaments, yet Kleist's interest was firmly in the "here and now," i.e., 1811. If his symbolism is "backward compatible" with medieval uses, then this is so because the rules, grammar and syntax of blazonry remain largely unchanged.

587   *"Sie kommt aus einem guten Stall"* means "she hails from a respectable family," "she is of good stock"; representing Franz as *"Stallmeister"* ("equerry") is deliciously apt, his daughter Marie-Louise hailing from the most illustrious of European "stables." According to legend, Froben in the battle exchanged his horse for the Great Elector's and was promptly killed by a bullet targetting his master, suggesting in Kleist's context that the Habsburg "dies" as Holy Roman Emperor to make way for Napoleon. Kleist's transformations, alchemical or otherwise, are always

intriguing, and often subtle. For example, Michael Ott's contention (*KH*,310) that a passage in *Kohlhaas*, "*als der Knecht... wenige Momente nachdem der Schuppen hinter ihm zusammenstürzte, mit den Pferden, die er an der Hand hielt, daraus hervortrat*" (II:33), indicates "negligence" on Kleist's part because "correctly" it should read 'before,' not 'after,'" is easily refuted: Kleist alludes to Franz II's proclaiming himself Franz I, Emperor of Austria, thereby de facto collapsing the *HRR* (the "shed"), and his de jure abdication as Holy Roman emperor taking place two years *after* he adopts the Austrian one; the "shed's" collapse and the "servant's" "taking the horses by the hand" marks one precise historical date, 11th August 1804, his stepping out of the "shed" with the—now emaciated—horses to another, namely 6th August 1806. It is thus not a matter of "negligence," but of precise causality that Kleist's "servant" Franz I exits the "shed" *after* its collapse: he *causes* the Empire's collapse while formally remaining inside, before two years later nonchalantly exiting its ruin, still holding the reigns of the—now ruffled—double-headed eagle. Ott reads Kleist's texts literally but not metaphorically, taking the "shed" as a mere shed, the "collapsed shed" as a mere collapsed shed, while Kleist's "shed" represents a *HRR* which, rather like Schroedinger's cat, is at once dead (as de facto enity) and alive (as de jure entity), and whose "*Stallmeister*" can be inside of it when it collapses, as well as exit it later unscathed (if ruffled): Franz dwells in this edifice as Franz II, and exits its ruins as Franz I (cf. the analogous symbolism of Adam's legs). This passage can also be read *satyrically*: if one takes "servant" to represent a lover's member, "shed" another lover's orifice, the "two blacks," testicles, "burning," passion, and "collapse," orgasm, then Kleist's causal chain is once again perfectly apt. When Ott suggests that "such, indeed frequent, 'errors' have been taken in recent decades as evidence of the fragility and defectiveness (*Brüchigkeit*) of Kleistian storytelling," he inadvertently points to an "error" the *Kleist-Forschung* has been prone to, namely designating as systematic errors unexplained individual incidences. Consider one of Ott's central statements: "*Insofern ist im Fall Kleists nicht nur (wie grundsätzlich) jeder Gleichsetzung der Erzählperspektive mit der des Autors zu misstrauen; die Erzählfigur der Texte ist, will man denn überhaupt eine solche "Figur" konstatieren, generell "unzuverlässig," verfährt mit wechselnder Distanz und zweifelhaften Wertungen... die diese Referenz grundsätzlich in Frage stellt.*" If one concurs with Ott, as I do, that Kleistian narrators cannot be equated with the author, in some cases remain absent, and in others are unreliable, then one can draw only one pragmatic conclusion: *to trust the author.*

588   Kleist's juxtaposing the power of music with Goethe's *Farbentheorie* provides further context for *Homburg*'s metamorphoses: colour change is merely the *visual echo* of a far greater *auditory force* (the cannons' thundering); colour is merely *reflective*, music, *performative*. Häker notes that Homburg's horse is referred to first as black (V.380), subsequently as golden chestnut (V.744) and concludes this this to be an error on Kleist's part (cf. *Homburg und Verlobung*, 47; 122). Yet not only does Kleist virtually never make such errors, but also are metamorphoses among his standard techniques. Häker elaborates, "*Die absolute Macht des Kurfürsten... manifestiert sich im Gebrauch des Goldes*" (ibid, 115-6), noting that The Elector's "*grey*"was bought with much "gold" in London, but offers no explanation for the symbolism, although he mentions the Continental System (ibid, 126), one key real-political link between Napoleon's military prowess and London's financial one; there is another: Napoleon's relentless wars entailed the flight of Continenal capital to London that turned the city into the world's financial capital (cf., e.g., the Rothschild banking dynasty's handling the wealth of the exiled Wilh. of Hessen-Kassel). In doing so, Napoleon inadvertely helped London accumulate the bullion needed to fund Britain's and her allies' war efforts; Napoleon's war horse (war machine) is indeed "bought" with gold transferred to London. Häker offers a thoughtful study of Kleist's attitude towards Fr. II, noting that he is not among the great king's most ardent fans—"*Kleists ambivalente Haltung dem großen Friedrich gegenüber*" (ibid, 59), but fails to notice that Kleist's critique of Fredericianism already appears in *Schroffenstein* and his 1799 letter to Martini, and although he notes that it was Fr. II who, in 1740, marched into Austrian Silesia (ibid, 54), fails to appreciate that in Kleist's view it may have been the loss of Silesia that for the Habsburgs became the most important bone of contention that poisoned their relationship with the Hohenzollerns, fatally weakening Germany as a whole. Häker points out that among the sources of Kleist's evaluation of Fr. II would have been A. Müller's 1808-12 lectures (ibid, 52; 65-8), and that Kleist's 1809 exhortation "*Was gilt es in diesem Kriege?*" entails a sustained critique of Fredricianism (and Josephinism), but since this criticism is already prevalent in *Schroffenstein*, it is at least as plausible that Kleist inspired Müller as it is that Müller inspired him.

589   Count H appears in the drama as frequently as Natalie, and only slightly less frequently than Homburg: I count 20 stage appearances for Homburg, 16 each for Natalie and Count H, 10 for the Elector, 9 for Kottwitz. Anthony Stephens refers to Homburg's *Duzfreund* as his "worst enemy and best friend," and his "at times malevolent alter ego"; Walter Hinderer calls him Homburg's "alleged friend"; Hans-

Jakob Wilhelm refers to him as "Machiavellian" "statesman and diplomat," and as "Homburg's personal doctor" who is "everywhere mediating"; William C. Reeve, who produces the most compelling account of this character, calls him the drama's "unsung villain." In contrast, Horst Häker considers Count H to be a benign or moderating figure. Count H is the only figure to call Homburg by his middle name Arthur—a name that indeed entails Kleist's *"Hommage à Wellington"* (Horst Häker), but with an important qualification: in the spring of 1811 Arthur Wellesley, Duke of Wellington, successfully engages Masséna, Soult and Marmont along the Portuguese border in the *Peninsula Wars*, tying up significant French troops; yet after several indecicive battles the confrontation reaches a stand-still when Wellington lifts the *Siege of Badajoz* on 10th June, allowing a 60,000-strong French army to retreat from Spain—in other words, whereas the news from Spain in mid-1809 was euphoric, in mid-1811 it was sobering for Kleist, which no doubt contributes to his pessimistic *Homburg* scenario (Wellington takes Bandajoz in April 1812 and opens up an allied corridor into French-controlled Spain, but his comes too late for Kleist), and Count H's repeatedly calling Homburg "Arthur" in the earlier scenes, and his stopping to do so in later scenes, signifies that Kleist, after initial hopes that Wellington would durably tie the French down in Iberia, as of mid-June no longer expect succour from the British, anticipating (correctly) that in a direct confrontation between Napoleon and Alex., Britain would remain sidelined. Kleist's frequent references to Britain in *BA* (cf. Häker, *Homburg und Verlobung*, 250-1, n.24) suggest that in 1810 and early 1811 he expected her to become a key player on the Continent; by the time he completed *Homburg* and veered towards suicide, this hope had abated.

590   Horst Häker associates (*Homburg und Verlobung*, 92) Gneisenau with Kleist's Kottwitz on the grounds that Gneisenau's wife was a born Kottwitz, caveating that Kottwitz could also represent Blücher (Klaus Kanzog also associates Kleist's Kottwitz with Blücher—cf. *Kleist*, 136).

591   Napoleon's annexing the Duchy of Oldenburg in December 1810 further aggrieved Alex. I, the Duke of Oldenburg being his uncle. That Kleist took a renewed interest in the northern German port cities already earlier in 1810, after the former Electorate Hannover had been annexed by Jérôme Bonaparte's Kingdom, is suggested by two articles he evidently submitted for publication in Hamburg's *Gemeinnützige Unterhaltungs-Blätter* (cf. Sembdner, *In Sachen Kleist*, 316-7; 324-54). Possibly Kleist during this period hoped for a British naval intervention on the North Sea coast and

prepared to relocate to Hamburg in case it took place (cf. also his December 1810 BA article on Helgoland, which artfully hides his pointing out this British-controlled island's strategic location underneath a hilariously pedantic description of the insignificance of its geographic features—cf. II:396-8).

592   Rudolf Loch, in discussing Kleist's resignation in the face of Fr. Wilh.'s appeasement policy, *"Auf eine Erhebung Preußens... ist für absehbare Zeit nicht mehr zu denken. Im Gegenteil, Preußen wird eine Hilfsmacht des Feindes (und neuen Verbündeten) werden"* (Kleist, 406), puts in a nutshell *Homburg*'s entire *satirical* plot, evidently without realising it, before adding the following important observations (*ibid*, 409): "Mit der Enttäuschung über das nationale Versagen steht Kleist in einer Reihe mit rund dreihundert preußischen Offizieren, unter ihnen Scharnhorst, Gneisenau, Boyen, Clausewitz, Knesebeck. Sie, die Elite des nationalen Widerstandes, verläßt, noch bevor Anfang 1812 die Allianz mit Frankreich unterzeichnet wird, demonstrative Preußen, um nicht gegen die Heimat in die Pflicht genommen zu werden. Sie sagen sich in einer Ende 1811 von Clausewitz verfaßten Denkschrift 'von dieser Meinung und Stimmung, womit man sich bei uns schmückt, als sei sie von reinem Gefühl für das Wohl Aller entprungen [...] feierlich los.' In österreichischen oder russischen Diensten suchen und finden die meisten von ihnen Gelegenheit, weiter für die 'Freiheit und Würde des Vaterlands' zu wirken. Dem in aufreibenden Existenzkämpfen zermürbten Künstler fehlte es an Kraft es ihnen gleichzutun. So faßt er den Entschluß zu sterben." In view of Clausewitz's memorandum, it is a distinct possibility that Kleist missed the "window of opportunity" for recovering his bearings by only a few weeks. Had Ulrike not rejected him so vehemently, Marie not been absent, or Henriette not appeared on the scene "just in time," Kleist might well have carried on. No wonder Ulrike and Marie were so bitter about his death: they both knew that it could have been otherwise. Had he lived to see Napoleon's débâcle in Russia in 1812, Kleist would surely have lived to see *Leipzig, Waterloo* and *Vienna* as well, and probably produced many more dramas to help propel the Coalition to victory, the Germans to unification, and the Hohenzollerns to the imperial throne.

593   Wolf Kittler analyses (*Geburt*, 268-82) parallels and differences between Kleist's depiction of *Fehrbellin* and eyewitness accounts of *Jena-Auerstedt*. While Kleist may well have drawn on details from *Jena-Auerstedt* to flesh out his fictional *Fehrbellin*, Kittler's analysis remains a red herring: Kleist by the time of *Homburg* was no longer concerned with *Jena-Auerstedt* as such.

594 In 1811 Russian staff indeed developed a plan for an offensive war, assuming a Russian assault on Warsaw and on Danzig—cf. https://en.wikipedia.org/wiki/French_invasion_of_Russia.

595 The *Grande Armée*'s main arsenals and depots for provisions and grain supply were in Danzig, Marienburg, Breslau, as well as in several Polish cities along the Vistula river: Thorn, Plock, Wyszogrod, Warsaw; its artillery (1,400 guns) was gathered in the French-controlled fortresses of Magdeburg, Danzig, Stettin, Küstrin and Glogau, all of which in or near Prussian territory, further underlining Prussia's importance in the invasion's logistics. Napoleon's Intendant General Gauillaume-Mathieu Dumas organised five supply rotes from the Rhine to the Vistula, which my yellow arrows indicate.

596 The Neman river indeed empties into the Baltic Sea (cf. V.1559), whereas the Rhyn, via the Havel and Elbe, empties into the North Sea. Kleist's deliberate "error" (i.e., clue) has gone unnoticed in the Kleist reception; is easy enough to wrongly assume that the Rhyn *does* empty into the Baltic Sea, and without consulting a detailed map of the Brandenburgian river system (nowadays made easy by Wikipedia), one would not realise the discrepancy unless one was familiar with the terrain—which Kleist's contemporaries would have been, but not today's readers. Kleist's "Rhyn" (e.g., V.9) and "Rhein" (e.g., V.349; 1030) may refer to the same—the Neman—, as location of past events (Rhein) and as that of the impending future battle (Rhyn). The Elector's reprimand to Homburg, *"Du hast am Ufer, weißt du, mir des Rheins / Zwei Siege jünst verscherzt"* (V.349-50), may then refer to *Tilsit*, where in 1807 Napoleon and Alex. signed their peace treaty on a boat midriver on the Neman/Memel river, while Napoleon and Fr. Wih. signed theirs, three days later, on the river's bank. When Homburg-Fr. Wilh abnegates Nathalie-Borussia (cf. V.1022-9) and offers to "retire to my estate on the Rhine" (cf. V.1030), he may refer not to the formerly Prussian enclave of Cleves on the Rhine (now firmly under French control), but to the city of Memel, on the estuary of Memel river, where in 1807-10 he and his family lived in exile. In other words, The Elector-Napoleon considers Homburg-Fr. Wilh. a mere nuisance, whom he should have eliminated four years prior, and from whom he expects nothing but that he not become a nuisance again in the confrontation with Alex.; meanwhile Homburg-Fr. Wilh. offers to leave *Borussia* (Natalie) to Napoleon and exile himself to the remotest corner of his ancestral lands (cf. Strömli-Franz I at the end of *Verlobung*). It is none other than the machiavellian Count H-Hardenberg

who encourages Homburg-Fr. Wilh. to go into exile, with the next "postal carriage to East Prussa" (cf. V.201); Homburg initially hesitates, dimly recalling that the "glove" left behind stemmed from Natalie-*Borussia*'s "hand" (Count H attempts to dissuade him from this thought by bringing into play various other maidens), but upon learning—again from Count H—that Natalie promised herself to the Swedish King-Alex. I (cf. V.922), abnegates her and readies himself for exile (cf. V.1030).

597   Napoleon did know the logistical challenges posed by the vastness and difficulty of Russia's territory, and in 1812 expected to trap and destroy the Russian army either soon after crossing the Neman, or before Smolensk on the Dnieper river, two-thirds of the way to Moscow. His supplies were not calculated to reach beyond the Dnieper: he expected to occupy and fortify Smolensk and Minsk, set up winter camps in Vilnius, and negotiate a peace treaty over the winter, or resume the campaign in the spring. In Europe, the Russian Empire's 35m population was second only to the French Empire's 43m (c.1811). Despite the enormous logistical preparations, Napoleon's army depended on foraging, which the Russians undermined by a systematic scorched-earth retreat tactics. *Rasputitsa* ("mud season"), "General Mud," refers to periods in autumn and spring during which rain or thawing snow turns unpaved roads into impassable mires and may have saved Moscow from German occupation during WWII's *Battle of Moscow*. King Fr. Wilh. himself, via his envoy Karl Fr. von dem Knesebeck, had advised Zar Alex. to draw Napoleon deep into Russia and to reject any peace deal until the French armies had been decimated in her infinite reaches (cf. https://de.wikipedia.org/wiki/Karl_Friedrich_von_dem_Knesebeck). When Kleist reported to Marie that the King had both "heart and mind" (II:879), he could have been referring to such strategic stratagems the King could have shared with him in their private conversation—in which case it would be even less understandable why he put so little trust in the Zar.

598   Horst Häker reads (*Homburg und Verlobung*, 126) The Elector's "*Geschlecht von Siegen*" (V.1569) as positing *Fehrbellin* as the first in a series of future battles that will make Prussia great. But since The Elector = Napoleon, the French victory against the Russians that Kleist anticipates belongs to a series whose "law" is already established: Napoleon's taking control, orchestrating every movement, and excluding any interference by Lady Luck, by the contingent and accidental— including uncontrolled actions by an erratic vasall such as Homburg-Fr. Wilh. Häker could have discerned that the grammatical subject of Kleist's sentence's second sub-

clause is *"Gesetz,"* not *"Geschlecht,"* and that the "genealogy of victories" generated by this "law" extends from the past into the future.

599   For Kleist, as former member of the *Regiment Garde*, the Prussian Kings' equivalent of Napoleon's *Garde Impériale*, portraying his King as joining Napoleon's personal guard implies that he has given up on him for good. Kleist's gesture anticipates George Lucas' Jedi knight Anakin Skywalker turning into the Sith Lord's loyal apprentice: the line *"Lord Vader… rise!"* is Lucas' equivalent of Kleist's *"Nun, o Unsterblichkeit…"* Did Lucas read *Homburg*? In *Star Wars*, it could be said, *Homburg* meets *Faust*: like Darth Vader, the historical Homburg, with his leg prosthesis, was a cyborg. Gernot Müller discerns the contradictions in the drama's final tableau, *"Der Monlog macht zwar das Gesetz (Todesurteil) zum gelassenen Akt der Freiheit. Der panoramische Szenenraum dagegen hebt als Unnatur (altfranzösicher Stil) und Gefängnis ("Gittertür"; "Offiziere mit Wache") den Spechakt in seinem Vollzug schon auf, setzt so Homburgs letztem "Anspruch" simultan den "Abbruch" entgegen,"* and comes close to recognising that the ending is not what it pertains to be, but lacks a *satirical* framework to make sense of the incommensurabilities he observes. He fails to pay attention to the Elector's chain around Homburg's neck, to which the visual pointers he highlights are subsidiary, being so caught up in his excellent analysis of the scene's panoramic imagery that he fails to recall that other elements of symbolic or functional value matter also—such as the *props* circulating on stage (not to mention the characters' actions and speeches)—, confirming a general rule that uni-modal, one-dimensional analyses of Kleist's works, though they may generate interesting insights, do not generate comprehensive understanding of patterns, which requires intertextual analysis as well as the unravelling of individual threads. Parallels with *Wilhelm Meister* have been pointed out in the Kleist reception; especially Homburg's three monologues (V.355ff; 1286ff; 1830ff) do relate the protagonist's coming of age as if in a *Bildungsroman*: in the first monologue, Homburg appeals to, even challenges, Fortuna; in the second, he finds himself suspended between life and death, uncertain where fate will pull him; in the third, he perceives himself on the threshold of a new life, overlooking that it entails enslavement, not liberation.

600   Ilse Graham traces (*Word into Flesh*, 183-4; 191-2), but does not explain, the flower symbolism in *Homburg,* apparently without noticing that it culminates in death (the cut flowers). J.M. Ellis in *Kleist's 'Prinz Friedrich von Homburg'* (Berkeley: UC Press, 1970), and Mary Garland in *Kleist's 'Prinz Friedrich von Homburg': An*

Interpretation through Word Pattern (The Hague: Mouton, 1968), already note the flower symbolism; cf. also Helbling, *Major Works*, 237.

601   Kleist's final four scenarios, in the summer of 1811, range from optimistic (*Findling*) to pessimistic (*Cäcilie*) to resigned (*Zweikampf, Homburg*): in *Findling*, the German insurrectionists ("the people of the house") bring down Napoleon (Piachi), forfaiting Fr. Wilh.'s (Nicolo's) life; in *Cäcilie*, they (the iconoclasts) are halted by the force of Napoleon's sway (the "power of music") and "francofied" (converted); in *Zweikampf*, Franz (Rotbart) and Fr. Wilh. (Trota) castrate (dismarm) each other, with Franz perishing, Fr. Wilh. being enslaved by the Emperor (Napoleon), and Littegarde (*Borussia, Germania*) becoming his mistress; in *Homburg*, Franz transfers his imperial legitimacy (his daughter = the sorrel) to Napoleon while Fr. Wilh. becomes his submissive instrument in Russia's defeat.

602   For the key events of early September 1811, cf. Michalzik, *Kleist*, 453, and Sembdner, *In Sachen Kleist*, 181-6; the latter plausibly puts Kleist's audience with the King on 11th September.

603   Reuß and Staengle date the letter early October (cf. *MA* II:988), in line with Richard Samuel, who dates it 5th October (cf. Kittler, *Geburt*, 368). I believe that Sembdner's date of 17th September is more plausible: this is precisely the kind of letter Kleist could have written Marie on the morning of the day on which he travels to Frankfurt/O. to personally deliver Ulrike the ostensible *good news* of his quasi-employment (more correctly: of his in-principle employabililty) and to ask her, with this "trump card" in hand, for financial support. In fact, he has just learned that the King is favouring an alliance with France, and Kleist has no interest whatsoever in fighting for Napoleon! Kleist implies to Marie that the funds he plans to ask from Ulrike (cf. II:878) will go not towards buying his equipage, but towards travelling to Vienna. Reuß and Staengle also redate the letter to Ulrike, dated 18th September by Sembdner, to late September (cf. *MA* II:987), but again I find Sembdner's dating more plausible: it fits the following sequence of events which I conjecture and take to be most plausible:

- In the morning of 17th September, having just found out that an alliance with France is seriously in the cards, Kleist, from a Berlin posting house, posts his letter to Marie, as he sets off for Frankfurt/O. by stage-coach;

813

- He arrives in Frankfurt/O.'s posting house in the morning of the 18th, writes the note to Ulrike in which he announces that he will swing by for lunch in half an hour (cf. II:880) and has it hand-delivered to her home; he tells her of the equipage, not of a relocation to Vienna; ("equipage" for Kleist meant the equivalent of "travelling"—cf. II:637, so that by asking for funding for it, he covertly did ask for funding for his trip to Vienna);
- the ensuing lunch famously turns disastrous as Ulrike, Auguste and *"die alte Wackern"* gang up against him; Ulrike refuses to give him money;
- Kleist leaves frustrated and empty-handed, and by late afternoon stops over at the Marwitzes' estate, where he plays the wargame and stays overnight;
- On the 19th he is back in Berlin and, having been rebuffed by Ulrike and perhaps on Marwitz's recommendation, posts his request to Hardenberg for funding (cf. II:881-2).

Reuß and Staengle insist that Kleist wrote to Hardenberg first, asking Ulrike only after receiving no response from him (cf. *MA* III:691-2), but I consider it more likely that it was the other way around: Kleist had no qualms asking Ulrike for money—asking Hardenberg was another matter. Their letter redatings require Reuß and Staengle to side with Klaus Müller-Salget's proposition (quoted in Loch, *Kleist*, 501, n.24) that Kleist travelled to Frankfurt/O. one more time in late October, at which occasion the disastrous get-together with Ulrike ostensibly took place, yet in my proposed chronology such an unsubstantiated crutch is unnecessary (it conforms to Occam's razor); cf. also my later footnote on this.

604   Wolf Kittler's note (*Geburt,* 367), "*bei Ludwig von der Marwitz, wo er eine äußerst pessimistische Prognose über den bevorstehenden Krieg hinterließ*," betrays a thorough misunderstanding of Kleist's *satirical* agenda: for Kleist Fr. Wilh.'s declaration of war and sacrifice in battle is not a pessimistic but an optimistic scenario. All of Kleist's works completed in 1810 or 1811 entail one of two scenaric outcomes for Fr. Wilh., neither of which would have been palatable to Marwitz: the King is either sacrificed (*Verlobung, Kohlhaas, Bettelweib, Findling*) or enslaved (*Cäcilie, Zweikampf, Homburg*).

605   The Marwitzes expected the King's "forever tarrying" to prevail (II:880-1), which it did. Kleist's assumption that Napoleon would force Fr. Wilh. into a situation in which tarrying was no longer an option, in which he would

be forced to make a move, turned out to be misguided: Napoleon allowed the explosiveness of the situation to difuse and diplomacy to take its course.

606   For this and the following paragraphs, I draw extensively on Wolf Kittler, *Geburt*, 366-9, who himself draws on Samuel ('Heinrich von Kleist und Neidhardt von Gneisenau,' in *JdS* 7, 1963, 352-70).

607   Cf. also Blamberger's note (*Kleist*, 388) in the context of the King's return to Berlin: "*Großen Handlungsspielraum hatte er [Fr. Wilh.] nicht, die Franzosen hatten ihre Truppen in Magdeburg und konnten Berlin jederzeit schnell wieder besetzen.*"

608   On 5th March 2012 in the *Treaty of Paris* Fr. Wilh. and Napoleon would indeed enter an alliance against Russia, and on 24th June 2012 Prussia would join the French *Invasion of Russia*.

609   Tchaikovsky's final symphony, No. 6, *Pathéthique*, which tapers off into a slow *adagio lamentoso* and a final *morendo*, has been discussed to prefigure the composer's suicide (it is not certain that Tchaikovsky committed suicide at all; he may have died of the effects of cholera), and one can reasonably ask whether Kleist's *Homburg* functions in that way. I argue that there is no clear indication that Kleist in late August or early September 1811 was making concrete preparations for his suicide. Kleist's avatar Homburg dreams of life under another star, but recoils from the death that is its prerequisite. A posteriori Kleist's last completed extant works, *Homburg* and *Zweikampf*, may appear as his testaments, but had in September and October 1811 the dice fallen differently—had the King heeded Gneisenau and confronted Napoleon, had Ulrike shown more emphaty, had Henriette not edged him on—these "final" works could just as well have marked the beginning of another period of intense production—cf. my discussions below of the lost novel, the drama project *Jerusalem*, and the musical project. Perhaps in the autumn of 1811, mentally and physically exhausted, Kleist delivered himself to lady Fortuna, and like the soldiers who in *Leopold*'s opening scene repeatedly throw the dice, he was bound to throw the fatal number sooner or later. His suicide is intelligible but was not inevitable; its concrete timing was contingent and circumstantial, and the *kairotic* moment for its exceution could easily have passed and not returned.

610   Brentano married in 1804 and again in 1806, and became weary of Kleist; Arnim married Bettine Brentano in 1811, in the spring of which year Alex. zur Lippe left Berlin (cf. Rahmer, *Kleist*, 61); Beckedorff, whom Kleist perhaps have "missed" (Michalzik, *Kleist*, 450) less as contributor to *BA* than as medical doctor and perhaps a lover, moved away in late June 1811 (cf. Sembdner, *Geschichte*, 426, n.388; Jakob Baxa's notes to *AML*,509); Fouqué, since 1803 married for the second time, yet perhaps happily "bi-," was still in Berlin, but his relationship with Kleist was complicated by their rivalry over the *Fehrbellin* material; Gleißenberg in 1804 married Kleist's cousin Caroline von Pannwitz, himself becoming something of a member of the "Lausitz Clan"; Zschokke married in 1805 and went on to produce 12 sons; Rühle married in 1808 and so did Pfuel, who fathered four surviving sons; Brockes in 1815 was about to marry Cecilie von Werthern when he suddenly passed away. (Rahmer, *Kleist*, 74) Rühle and Pfuel took to pursuing their own "circles" that Kleist was not part of, perhaps to put some distance between themselves and temptation after marrying: Rahmer reports (*Kleist*, 42) that Pfuel the second half of 1810 spent extensive periods in Töplitz, where he frequented Goethe's circle together with the likes of the Duke of Weimar, Gentz, Marwitz and Rühle, and in Prague, where had regular contact with Stein.

611   Neurosphilis may encompass impotence—cf. Bäumler, *Amors vergifteter Pfeil*, 208.

612   The "sword together with belt" could refer to a strap-on dildo or prosthesis, implying that both the officer and the prince are castrated or debilitated by disease; Homburg's handing over his "weapon" to the officer may suggests that such implements were passed around during symposiac orgies.

613   Either only lovers deemed "pure" were permitted to partake in this gathering, or it was believed that infected ejaculate could be neutralised or purified in an (al-)chemical operation of mingling it with healthy ejaculate. In the latter case, a diseased lover's purification by means of gathered ejaculate that included his own, corresponds to auto-inoculation (conceptually, a precursor of today's stemcell-therapy). Blood-transfusion from healthy mammals (usually fatal to both donor and recipient because, we today know, all species of mammals have different blood groups that are not compatible) was still practiced in Kleist's day and may have informed his therapeutic explorations.

614   Torch/tomb of course belong into Kleist's long list of phallo-anal digital (I/0) symbolism: cannon/loophole, key/keyhole, F/O, arrow/ring, - /+, double-edged sword/back-gate to paradise, etc.

615   Cf. also Arthur Henkel, "*Wenige Dichter meinten so mit ihren Phantasiegestalten sich selbst wie Kleist*" ("Traum und Gesetz im Prinzen von Homburg," in Walter Müller-Seidel, *Kleist*, 578), and Günter Blamberger: "*Kleists Homburg ist ein Vexierbild, in dem sich auch der Autor versteckt*" (*Kleist*, 577).

616   Cf. Sloterdijk, *Sphären II*, 86-8: "*Für Parmenides bedeutet die Kugel-Theorie nicht anderes als freie Umsicht im Inneren eines offenen, von sich selbst her Aufschluß über sich gebenden Seienden. Für ihn kommt darum der Gedanke an einen Standort außerhalb nie in Betracht. Wenn er... verkünden läßt, daß Denken und Sein— noeín und eínai, ein und dasselbe seien, so ist mit diesem Spruch der Tiegersprung des Gedankens in die offene Mitte der Welt vollzogen. Von nirgendwo anders als von innen her, immanent, internbleibend, läßt sich die Kugel des Seienden anschauend in Gekanken fassen... Mit einem mal nur wird das Ganzfeld des Umgebenen hell... Das Ganze leuchtet auf im Flutlicht einer simultanen Umsicht, die das Ringsum im Nu erschließt... Diese allseitige Synchronsicht in das eine Ganze... wird von der Göttin als die allein wahre Ansicht angemacht... Sie... bezeichnet... einen ekstatischen Grenzwert der naturwüchsigen Weltauffassung aus der Grundstellung des In-der-Welt-Seins. Die große Schau ins Einhellige, Offene, Ringsum-Ganze wird von den gewöhnlichen Sterblichen so gut wie nie versucht, weil sie immer am aktuell Zuständlichen und am nächstbesten Begegneten haften und inmitten der Kugel Kugelblinde sind.*" A. Müller develops a "Theory of Spheres" of which only fragments are extant, one of which reads: "*Globularform aller Wissenschaft. Alle Wissenschaften... haben Form, Maaß, Bewegung des Planeten auf dem sie ersonnen worden; haben ihre Sonne, wie er die seine. Nach Polen, Äquatoren, Meridianen und Breiten werden sie geordnet; durch Schiefe der Ecliptik, durch bestimmten wankenden Accent erhalten sie in sich jenes Wechselleben, wodurch im Laufe der Zeit alle ihre Theile gleichmäßig der Sonne zugekehrt und abgekehrt werden, jeder Punkt zum Lebenspol, jeder größte Kreis zum Lebensäquator wird. Um die Sonne die der Mensch in seinem Herzen trägt, aus jenen beyden Sonnen in ewiger Vermittlung gebildet, müssen diese Wissenschaftskugeln laufen, durch sie und in sich selbst bewegt, wenn Leben in ihnen seyn soll. Der alte Atlas der mit Mühe und Schmerz, unter ihr gebeugt, die Erdkugel trägt, und das Kind Jesus—welches erhaben darüber diese Erdkugel spielend in seinen Händen hält, sind herrliche Symbole des*

Griechisch-Römischen Heidenthums und des Christentums" (*AML*,435, notes; cf. also Sloterdijk, *Sphären II*, 60-72 and 102-9). A. Müller to Gentz: *"Mich befremdet, daß Sie unter den Meßartikeln der Runge'schen Farbenkugel und der Goethe'schen Farbenlehre nicht gedenken. Ich glaube, ich habe Ihnen schon in ganz frühen Zeiten, 1802 in Dresden oder 1805 in Wien, von meiner Überzeugung gesprochen, daß die Sphäre der einzelnen Sinne, ebensowohl wie die der Totalität aller Sinne oder des Menschen, nur nach den Gesetzen der Kugel construirt werden könne; auch müssen Sie sich des Wortes: Farbenkugel, aus unsern Gesprächen erinnern."* (*AML*,435). Müller's thought lacks Paramenides' precision; but its eclecticism (*"er...bröckt... alle Welt und Systeme untereinander"*—*AML*,502) may have suited Kleist, himself a great eclecticist.

617 Although I do not owe anything substantial to his analysis, having come across his treatise only in the editing stage of this book, I acknowledge that Gernot Müller (*Gemälde*, passim) previously discussed Kleist's panoramic technique. Gernot Müller offers a fascinating elaboration of how techniques or concepts such as *"Verzeichnen"* (a polysemic term meaning denotement or registration, and distortion or rendering falsely), *"Physiognomie des Augenblicks,"* and *"Panorama"* shape Kleist's aesthetics (cf. *ibid*, 327-8), though focusing on the *formal* functioning of these techniques, thus not heeding Kleist's advice, in *Brief eines Dichters an einen anderen*, to focus on the *content* of his poetry. Gernot Müller maintains that Kleist's interest in painting was kindled during his second visit to the Dresden *Gemäldegalerie* in 1801, but conceivably it was triggered much earlier, during his visit to the Kassel *Gemäldegalerie* in 1795. Cf. also Sloterdijk (*Kritik*, 268-9): *"der physiognomische Sinn [liefert] einen Schlüssel zu all dem, was die Nähe zur Umwelt verrät. Sein Geheimnis ist Intimität,... konvivales Wissen,... Intuition,... Einfühlung,... esprit de finesse,... Ästhetik... Erotik... libidinöse Weltnähe"*

618 Cf. Nietzsche, *Jenseits von Gut und Böse*, §150, on Parmenides: *"Um den Helden herum wird Alles zur Tragödie, um den Halbgott herum, Alles zum Satyrspiel; und um Gott herum wird Alles—wie? Vielleicht zur 'Welt'?—.* Re the Shield of Achilles, cf. Sloterdijk, *Sphären II*, 215-18: *"Homers Darstellung dieses Artifiziums... leistet... Tribut an den morphologischen Imperativ des wohlgerundeten und gutbegrenzten Bildes... das Ganze dieser vom Schildrand umgriffenen Welt... und in deren Mitte, kreisbildend durch die Macht der Stimme, ein göttlicher Sänger."*

619   Observing a landscape from the moving postal carriage is somewhat akin to observing an image inside a *Guckkasten* only if the observer is sitting inside the carriage and occasionally looks out through the window, which frames the landscape into "snapshots." Within three decades of Kleist's impression, the first technologies for displaying moving images would be designed—Joseph Plateau's *Phenakistoscope* (1832), Simon von Stampfer's *Stroboscope* (1833), William Horner's *Dædalum* (1834), Eadward Mybridge's *Zoopraxiscope* (1879), the Lumière brothers' *Cinématographe* (1890s). Cave paintings may be considered the first man-made panoramas, painted into a cave's concavity. To this day Kleist's conception of the perfect panorama has not been fully realised. The interior of Rome's Pantheon is designed such that a perfect sphere could fit inside, symbolising the cosmos; it is still not a "perfect" panorama in so far as the observer stands at the bottom, not the centre, of that sphere. Even early 21st century 360° panoramas, like Yadegar Asisi's, remain cylindrical, not spherical. Geodesic domes such as La Géode in Paris, Spaceship Earth at EPCOT in Florida, and various planetariums, come closest to Kleist's conception, but audience management imposes constraints: inside La Géode the audience is seated on an inclined plane which cross-sects the spherical structure and leaves an inclined semi-sphere for screen, and inside Spaceship Earth (a dark ride attraction) the observer moves through a series of installed scenes on a conveyor system, her field of vision remaining limited at any moment. Already in Kleist's day revolutionary architects had conceived perfect spheres, and although none of these projects were realised, prints of their designs circulated widely: Etienne-Louis Boulleé's *Cénotaphe à Newton* (1784) and *Déuxieme project pour la Bibliothéque du Roi* (1785, a tube-like structure); Claude Nicolas Ledoux's *Maison de gardes agricoles* (1804). Fictional near-"perfect" panoramas or immersive VRs include, in literature, Dante's *Inferno*, the *cyberspace* in William Gibson's 1984 novel *Neuromancer* and the digital "realm of infinite possibilities" produced inside a disused hangar in Michel Houellebecq's 2005 *La Possibilité d'une Île*, in film, the eponymous VR simulation in the Wachowskis' 1999 *The Matrix*. In philosophy, immersive realms or points of view include Plato's and Plotin's *kósmos noētós* (cf. *Rep.*, 508c; *Phaed.*, 247c-e; *Tim.*, 30-d; *Enn. I*, 7,1,23; *Enn. V*, 84,4), Leibniz's *monad*, and Jorge Luis Borges' *aleph* (cf. *The Aleph*, 1949). Re Dante's *Inferno*, cf. Sloterdijk, *Sphären II*, 609 and 617-8: "*Dante macht bei seinem Durchgang durch das Gegenreich eine formalontologische Entdeckung von großer Reichweite: Jeder Verdammte steckt in seinem eigenen Um, das sich aus penetranten Vereinigungen formt... Deswegen behalten die Delinquenten ihre Körper, sofern diese die Voraussetzungen sind für die Fixierung einer Seele an eine Tortur... Die Mitte der*

Hölle ist der Punkt in der Welt, von dem aus die Unerreichbarkeit der Welt für den, der dort ist, angeschaut werden kann. Der Satan besitzt die volle Rundumsicht, die ihm das Ausmaß des Weltverlustes enthüllt; ihm ist das parmenideische Raumauge gegeben...; seine Amphiskopie erfaßt das ganze Panorama des Verlorenen." In H.P. Lovecraft's short story *At the Mountains of Madness* the travellers experience a flight across an Antarctic landscape: "On cloudy days we had considerable trouble in flying, owing to the tendency of snowy earth and sky to merge into one mystical opalescent void with no visible horizon to mark the junction of the two."

620 Upon climbing the Wartburg near Eisenach, Kleist dismisses the castle's ruins as insignificant (an understatement), while calling the views incredible (a slight hyperbole): *"die Aussicht aber die man hier genießt kann man sich unmöglich denken"* (II:465). Already in this early reminiscence the panoramic effect and not the castle at its centre (famous as it is: Luther translated the Bible here) is what interests Kleist. His reminiscences of the cannonades of Mainz show that his idea of the perfect panorama encompassed visual as well as auditory, olfactory and tactile impressions: fire and smoke, thundering cannons and screaming people, vibrating air and shaking grounds.

621 I had the pleasure to experience, in the summer of 2017, all these panoramas when tracing Kleist's footsteps. It perhaps is and is not a coincidence that the world's oldest surviving panorama, the Thun Panorama erected in 1809-14, is located in the Schadaupark, the very spot by Lake Thun from which Kleist in 1802 enjoyed this stunning natural panorama (cf. https://de.wikipedia.org/wiki/Thun-Panorama). That Kleist's choice of a house on the tip of the Inseli was governed its exquisite panoramic views is corroborated by the fact that he also considered a house in Gwatt, a few km south of Scherzligen, whose promenade (today's Bonstettenpark) offered similar vistas. Kleist's house on the tip of the Inseli, jutting into the Aare's effluence, offered yet another feature: it recalled Rousseau's famous eremitage on the St. Petersinsel, a narrow peninsula jutting into the Bielersee. Kleist was deliberate indeed in his selection of his Arcadia: to further her education, Wilhelmine was not only to read Rousseau's works, but also to live in an eremitage mimicking his. In 1803 Kleist would enjoy panoramas in several Alpine location: Bellevue above the Rhône glacier, Madonna del Monte above Varese, possibly Madonna del Sasso above Locarno castle (the vista the novella's famous opening, enjoyed when coming down from the St. Gotthard pass, may be that of Bellinzona's three castles).

622   [late March 1793/28th July 1801] "*Wir standen damals in* Bieberich *in Kantoniersquartieren. Vor mir blühte der Lustgarten der Natur—eine konkave Wölbung, wie von der Hand der Gottheit eingedrückt. Durch ihre Mitte fließt der Rhein, zwei Paradiese aus einem zu machen. In der Tiefe liegt Mainz, wie der Schauplatz in der Mitte eines Amphitheaters... Die Terassen der umschließenden Berge dienten statt der Logen, Wesen aller Art blickten als Zuschauer voll Freude herab, und sangen und sprachen Beifall—Oben in der Himmelsloge stand Gott. Hoch an dem Gewölbe des großen Schauspielhauses strahlte die Girandole der Frühlingssonne, die entzückende Vorstellung zu beleuchten. Holde Düfte steigen, wie Dämpfe aus Opferschalen, aus den Kelchen der Blumen und Kräuter empor. Ein blauer Schleier, wie in Italien gewebt, umhüllte die Gegend, und es war, als ob der Himmel selbst hernieder gesunken wäre auf die Erde—*" (II:673-4; cf. also II:579-80). On the one hand Kleist depicts a stylised spherical panorama: at the bottom a concave hemisphere formed by the valley, on top an inverted concave hemisphere formed by the arch of the sky, both held together by a horizontal band of vine terraces—a veritable paradise *en miniature*: at the bottom the fertile Earth, encompassing human bodies, movements and sensuality; on top the blue sky of the eternal Heaven, the Sun (*girandole*) at its centre; and between Heaven and Earth the sweeping vineyards of Dionysos, representing *enthousiasmos*, *ekstasis*, and *mania*; the air filled with fragrant scents and charming voices. Kleist may have had an image of a grand theatre in his mind, as well as the landscapes of the Rhine near Mainz, Biebrich, Oppenheim and Nierstein. On the other hand he allegorically depicts his lover's anatomy: *konkave Wölbung* = lower back; *Rhein* = Crena ani; *Schauplatz in der Mitte eines Amphitheaters* = anus; *Gott* = erâstes; *Girandole* = phallus; *hernieder gesunken* = penetration.

623   [Spring 1793/19th September 1800] "*So entsinne ich mich besonders einmal als Knabe vor 9 Jahren, als ich gegen den Rhein und gegen den Abendwind zugleich hinaufging, und so die Wellen der Luft und des Wassers zugleich mich umtönten, ein schmelzendes Adagio gehört habe, mit allem Zauber der Musik, mit allen melodischen Wendungen und der ganzen begleitenden Harmonie... ich glaube sogar, daß alles was die Weisen Griechenlands von der Harmonie der Sphären dichteten, nichts Weicheres, Schöneres, Himmlischeres gewesen sei, als diese seltsame Träumerei... aber so bald ein Gedanke daran sich regt, gleich ist alles fort, wie weggezaubert durch das magische: disparois! Melodie, Harmonie, Klang, kurz die ganze Sphärenmusik*" (II:569). Kleist could scarcely have been on the Rhine nine years prior to the letter, i.e., September 1791, unless he had undertaken a trip there that we know nothing of, which is possible

but unlikely. Either his reminiscence is to the Rhyn or Oder, to be located in 1793, when he repeatedly crossed the Rhine and camped on its shores. He may deliberately put "9 years" instead of "7 years" to dissimulate the context and to make his revelation sound more innocent than it perhaps was. Among Kleist's contemporaries, the likes of Wilh. Heinr. Wackenroder and L. Tieck proposed the existence of a transcendental, "pure," "perfect" music that elevates humans above the merely human, and Kleist may have been influenced by their romantic concepts. E.T.A. Hoffman, in his 1810 review of Beethoven's 5th symphony, confers on such music the first rank among the arts, and holds that it represents "pure romanticism"; Joh. Gottfried Herder previously singled out music as the highest of the arts, on account of it's spirituality. Concepts of "spherical music" were thus "in the air."

624 [Summer 1797/early 1799] *"Wie wenig beglückend der Standpunkt auf großen außerordentlichen Höhen ist, habe ich recht innig auf dem Brocken empfunden. Lächeln Sie nicht, mein Freund, es waltet ein gleiches Gesetz über die moralische wie über die physische Welt. Die Temperatur auf der Höhe des Thrones ist so rauh, so empfindlich und der Natur des Menschen so wenig angemessen, wie der Gipfel des Blocksbergs* [Brocken], *und die Aussicht von dem einen so wenig beglückend wie von dem andern, weil der Standpunkt auf beidem zu hoch, und das Schöne und Reizende um beides zu tief liegt. Mit weit mehrerem Vergnügen gedenke ich dagegen der Aussicht auf der mittleren und mäßigen Höhe des Regensteins* [a 300m hill at the northern slope of the Harz], *wo kein trüber Schleier die Landschaft verdeckte, und der schöne Teppich im ganzen, wie das unendlich Mannifgaltige desselben im einzelnen klar vor meinen Augen lag. Die Luft war mäßig, nicht warm und nicht kalt, grade so wie sie nötig ist, um frei und leicht zu atmen"* (II:308). Cf. along similar lines E. A. Poe in *The Domain of Arnheim*: "This panorama [comparable with that from Mt. Etna] is indeed glorious, and I should rejoice in it but for the excess of its glory… Grandeur in any of its moods, but especially in that of extent, startles, excites—and then fatigues, depresses… In looking from the summit of a mountain we cannot help feeling *abroad* in the world." C.D. Friedrich's *Mönch* for Kleist conveys a similar sentiment; the topos of "right measure or proportion" appears in *Ph's Prolog* (cf. also Gentz to Müller, 23rd October 1802; *AML*,32: "*Es gibt gar kein Maß, keine Proportion, keine Regel in den Forderungen* [Napoleons] *mehr*"). The "height of the throne" may refer to Fr. Wilh. III, whose ascend to the Prussian throne in November 1797 raised expectations among young Prussians (presumably including Kleist) for a more assertive politics vis-à-vis France, expectations that already by 1798/9 begain giving way to disappointment.

625 [21st August 1800] *"Ich fand in der Nähe von Coblentz weite Wiesen, mit Graben durchschnitten, umgeben mit großen reinlich gehaltenen Wäldern... ein Johanniterkreuz auf jedem Dache, auf jedem Pfahle... Als ich vor das Schloß fuhr, fand ich, von außen... Im Hause kam mir die alte würdige Gräfin freundlich entgegen. Der Graf war nicht zu Hause"* (II:530). Kleist frequently frames his panoramas by features that induce a conventional *"Rahmenschau"* (Gernot Müller points to this in Kleist's earlier landscape descriptions)—for example, a Saxon landscape by "dark fir trees": *"Wir sahen von einem hohen Berge herab, rechts und links dungle Tannen, ganz wie ein gewählter Vordergrund; zwischen durch eine Gegend, ganz wie ein geschloßnes Gemälde"* (II:550), and a landscape near Coblenz by surrounding forests; the latter landscape is furthermore organised by a grid constituted by canals, akin to a painter's guidelines sketched on the canvas. In contrast to such artfully arranged landscapes, unbound panoramas such as the hazy view from the Brocken or the vanishing horizon in Friedrich's *Mönch* irritated Kleist. The Coblentz panorama's ithyphallic "Maltese crosses" surrounding an empty "castle," like *Penthesilea*'s "grove of oak trees" protecting "Diana's sanctuary" and *Erdbeben*'s "pines" framing the "dark valley," is a "landscape-allegorical" version of Kleist's pervasive "I/O" imagery. "Junvenal, in *Satire III* (17, trans. Peter Green), has the narrator recount: "From here we strolled down to Egeria's valley, its grotto."

626 [5th September 1800] *"Der höchste Berg in der Mitte... da stand ich. Die Aussicht über den See ist die schönste. Die andern beiden* [vistas] *sind hier versteckt"* (II:550).

627 [11th October 1800]. *"Vorgestern ging ich aus, einen andern Berg von der Nordseite zu besteigen. Es war ein Weinberg* [the Steinberg] *und ein enger Pfad führte durch gesegnete Rebenstangen auf seinen Gipfel... sie hatten aus den Weinbergen alle Steine rechts und links in diesen Weg geworfen, das Ersteigen zu erschweren——grade wie das Schicksal oder die Menschen mir auf den Weg zu dem Ziele, das ich nun doch erreicht habe. Ich lachte über diese auffallende Ähnlichkeit—liebes Mädchen,... Damals* [in Berlin, Dresden, Bayreuth] *ärgerte ich mich ebenso über die Steine, die mir in den Weg geworfen wurden,... aber erreichte doch, wie vorgestern* [on the evening before the "most important day"], *das Ziel. Das Ersteigen der Berge, wie der Weg zur Tugend, ist besonders wegen der Aussicht, die man eben vor sich hat, beschwerlich...——aber man muß an die Aussicht denken, wenn man den Gipfel erstiegen hat. O wie herrlich war der Anblick des Maintales von dieser Höhe!"* (II:580). The vinepoles recall the phallic

towers in *Die beiden Tauben* and the Prussian army's punitive practice of running the gauntlet. The wine symbolism is evidently Dionysian; the entwined poles also recall Mercury's staff.

628   [5th February 1801] *"Ach, es gibt eine traurige Klarheit, mit welcher die Natur viele Menschen, die an dem Dinge nur die Oberfläche sehen, zu ihrem Glücke verschont hat. Sie nennt mir zu jeder Miene den Gedanken, zu jedem Worte den Sinn, zu jeder Handlung den Grund—sie zeigt mir alles, was mich umgibt, und mich selbst in seiner ganzen armseligen Blöße, und dem Herzen ekelt zuletzt vor dieser Nacktheit"* (II:628). Cf. Sloterdijk, *Sphären II*, 586: *"Auf dem Grund seiner Exzentrik wirkt bei dem Tollen Menschen* [cf. Nietzsche] *also nicht Verwirrung; ihn treibt die unerträgliche Luzidität dessen, der die Fähigkeit verloren hat, an den gesund genannten Selbsttäuschungen der anderen teilzunehmen. Er ist verrückt durch ein Zuviel an Sehkraft; es gelingt ihm nicht mehr, sich und die Welt in Ordnung zu lügen."*

629   [16th December 1801] *"Es war eine finstre Nacht als ich in das neue Vaterland trat. Ein stiller Landregen fiel überall nieder. Ich suchte Sterne in den Wolken und dachte mancherlei. Denn Nahes und Fernes, alles war so dunkel. Mir wars, wie ein Eintritt in ein anderes Leben"* (II:708).

630   [1st May 1802] *"wir schiffen uns über, sie geht in die Kirche nach Thun, ich besteige das Schreckhorn, und nach der Andacht kehren wir beide zurück"* (II:724). Kleist drops his lover at Scherzligen church, sips a coffee in today's Schadaupark, and observes the glorious panorama of the Bernese Oberland peaks. Loch (Kleist, 159) reproduces a similar view by Daniel Simon Lafound, dated 1792 (Sembdner, *In Sachen Kleist*, 14, has an etching based on Lafound's aquarel); Michalzik includes an etching of Thun of c.1800 (cf. plate facing p.257) that foregrounds the area of today's Schadaupark, with the Scherzligen church and townsfolk promenading precisely on spot from which Kleist would have "scaled the Schreckhorn," with Kleist's "Inseli" on the far right, its southern tip, on which his house is located, just off the picture.

631   *"Penthesilea. Dritter Auftritt. Der Hauptmann. Eine Schar von Griechen, welche während dessen einen Hügel bestiegen haben. / EIN MYMIDONIER in die Gegend schauend. / Seht! Steigt dort über jenes Berges Rücken, / Ein Haupt nicht, ein bewaffnetes, empor? / Ein Helm, von Federbüschen überschattet? / Der Nacken schon, der mächtige, der es trägt? / Die Schultern auch, die Arme, stahlumglänzt? / Das ganze*

Brustgebild, o seht doch, Freunde, / Bis wo den Leib der golde Gurt umschließt? [...] */ Jetzt, auf dem Horizonte, steht das ganze / Kriegsfahrzeug da! So geht die Sonne prachtvoll / An einem heitern Frühlingstage auf! / DIE GRIECHEN. / Triumph! Achilleus ists! Der Göttersohn!"* (V.356-70). The Greeks scale a hill from which they scan the panoramic landscape; soon they perceive a feathered helmet appearing above the mountain ridge comprising their visual horizon, followed by, bit by bit and verse by verse, a neck, shoulders, arms, chest, etc., each verse being akin to a film's individual frame. The combination of the Greeks' horizontal scanning and Achilles' vertical rise on the horizon creates an illusion of depth that mimicks the artful arrangements in a *Guckkasten* or on a theatre stage. Gernot Müller (*Gemälde*, 146-7) points out that this scene corresponds to *Prolog*'s "scout" or "lookout" on the watchtower observing Phoebus' appearance (who, we might add, also anticipates Kleist's "sad and uneasy," all-seeing and all-suffering, observer in his *BA* essay on C.D. Friedrich's *Mönch*, as well as Homburg in his third monologue: *"Und jetzt liegt Nebel alles unter mir"*). Compared with teichoscopy, Kleist's panorama is highly immersive: the Greeks are not just watching from the sidelines, but all of a sudden find themselves right amidst Achilles' onslaught. A. Müller, in his *Ph* essay *Noch etwas über den Unterschied des antiken und modernen Theaters*, contributes theoretical underpinnings (or overlay, assuming Kleist's praxis came first) for Kleist's panoramic immersions: *"Das alte Theater zeigt uns das Plastische in der Bewegung; in den kleinsten Raum wird die größte Handlung zusammengedrängt; das neue Theater ist durchaus malerischer Natur, ein unendliches Panorama in der Bewegung: die Zuschauer in Ruhe, die Bühne im zauberhaften Wechsel des reichsten, bewegtesten Lebens."*

632   *"Käthchen. Szene: Schloßplatz, zur Rechteen, im Vordergrund, ein Portal. Zur Linken, mehr in der Tiefe, das Schloß, mit einer Rampe. Im Hintergrund die Kirche. / Dreizehnter Auftritt. Marsch. Ein Aufzug... In der Mitte des Schloßplatzes stehen der Kaiser, der Graf vom Strahl, Theobald,... Unter dem Portal, rechts Fräulein Kunidunde... Im Hintergrunde Volk"* (V.2645).

633   [20th April 1809] *"Ich wollte, ich hätte eine Stimme von Erz, und könnte sie [patriotic poems], vom Harz herab, den Deutschen absingen"* (II:824). Cf. Matthew 5:1-2: "Seeing the crowds, [Jesus] went up on the mountain, and when he sat down, his disciples came to him. And he opened his mouth and taught them" (*NT*). Cf. also Fr. Nietzsche, "Zarathustras Vorrede": *"Als Zarathustra dreißig Jahre alt war, verließ er seine Heimat und den See seiner Heimat und ging in das Gebirge... eines Morgens stand*

er mit der Morgenröte auf, trat vor die Sonne hin und sprach zu ihr also: 'Du großes Gestirn! Was wäre dein Glück, wenn du nicht die hättest, welchen du leuchtest!... Ich muß, gleich dir, untergehen, wie die Menschen es nennen, zu denen ich hinab will." (Also sprach Zarathustra, Stuttgart: Reclam, 1989, 3).

634   [BA, 1st October 1810] "Gott mein Vater im Himmel! Du hast dem Menschen ein so freies, herrliches und üppiges Leben bestimmt... Gleichwohl, von unsichtbaren Geistern überwältigt, liegt er, auf verwundernswürdige und unbegreifliche Weise, in Ketten und Banden; das Höchste, von Irrtum geblendet, läßt er zur Seite liegen, und wandelt, wie mit Blindheit geschlagen, unter Jämmerlichkeiten und Nichtigkeiten umher... Nun lässest du es, von Zeit zu Zeit, niederfallen, wie Schuppen, von dem Auge eines deiner Knechte, den du dir erwählt, daß er die Torheiten und Irrtümer seiner Gattung überschaue; ihn rüstest du mit dem Köcher der Rede, daß er, furchtlos und liebreich, mitten unter sie trete, und mit Pfeilen, bald schärfer, bald leiser, aus der wunderlichen Schlafsucht, in welcher sie befangen liegen, wecke. Auch mich, o Herr, hast du, in deiner Weisheit, mich wenig Würdigen, zu diesem Geschäft erkoren; und ich schicke mich zu meinem Beruf an" (II:325-6). Eight days later, in BA's Betrachtungen über den Weltlauf, Kleist bemoans, in a response to Schiller's Weltalter, the Prussians' and Germans' degeneration from earstwhile heroic ideals. Helmut Sembdner, in Die Abendblätter Heinrich von Kleists (Heilbronn, Kleist-Archiv Sembdner, 2001), 66-7, plausibly shows that Kleist may have read German trans. and commentaries on the Zend-Avesta accessible at Berlin's Werckmeistersches Lese-Institut. Zoroastrianisms' teachings—immanence of the supreme being; an eschatology of good overcoming evil; rejection of predestination in favour of free will, and of asceticism in favour of an active experience of the pleasures of life; practice of purification rituals involving fire and water; conceptualisation of a soul that precedes and survives a man's physical existence by decoupling from his guardian spirit at birth and reuniting with it upon death—would no doubt have fascinated Kleist, especially the 8th century Khurramite (Persian "Khurram" = "happy," "cheerful") sect, which rebelled against the hegemoniac Abbasid Caliphate and whose followers believed in metempsychosis as the only possible afterlife and practiced purification and free sex.

635   [BA, 1st and 2nd October 1810] "Ein anderer... kündigte... eine Grammatik in Form eines Panoramas an. Die inneren Wände nämlich dieser Grammatik (die Konkavität) waren überall, von oben bis unten, mit Regeln beschrieben; und da man demnach außer einem kleinen Luftloch, nichts sah, als Syntax und Prosodie, so rühmte

er sich, daß wer drei Tage und drei Nächte, bei mäßiger Kost, darin zubrächte, am vierten Tage die Sprache... inne hätte" (II:385). Kleist's observations on the hegemoniac capital mix disdain and admiration: intense competition drives irrational behaviours as well as innovation. In joking about inventors of a panoramic grammar and a poetic algebra, he is joking not least about himself, his writing being panoramic as well as algebraic (as a semiotic praxis of manipulating linguistic symbols).

636   [*BA*, 11th October 1810] *"Das Bettelweib von Locarno. Am Fuße der Alpen, bei Locarno im oberen Italien, befand sich ein altes, einem Marchese gehöriges Schloß, das man jetzt, wenn man vom St. Gottard kommt, in Schutt und Trümmern liegen sieht"* (II:196).

637   [*BA*, 13th October 1810] *"Herrlich ist es, in einer unendlichen Einsamkeit am Meeresufer, unter trübem Himmel, auf eine unbegrenzte Wasserwüste, hinauszuschauen... Dazu gehört ein Anspruch, den das Herz macht, und ein Abbruch, um mich so auszudrücken, den einem die Natur tut. Dies aber ist vor dem Bilde unmöglich, und das, was ich in dem Bilde selbst finden sollte, fand ich erst zwischen mir und dem Bilde, nämlich einen Anspruch, den mein Herz an das Bild machte, und einen Abbruch, den mir das Bild tat; und so ward ich selbst der Kapuziner, das Bild ward die Düne, das aber, wo hinaus ich mit Sehnsucht blicken sollte, die See, fehlte ganz. Nichts kann trauriger und unbehaglicher sein, als diese Stellung in der Welt: der einzige Lebensfunke im weiten Reiche des Todes, der einsame Mittelpunkt im einsamen Kreis. Das Bild... liegt... wie die Apokalypse da..., und da es, in seiner Einförmigkeit und Uferlosigkeit, nichts, als den Rahm, zum Vordergrund hat, so ist es, wenn man es betrachtet, als ob einem die Augenlieder weggeschnitten wären"* (II:327). The initial four sentences are Brentano's, the rest, Kleist's; the sentences he adopted from Brentano should still be considered Kleist's, in the same manner as his verbatim translations from Molière, because by his act of selecting them he makes them his own. Brentano's essay evidently shifted the focus from the painting to the audience, notably the cacophony of voices in the gallery; Kleist's shifts the focus back to the image and its immersive pull.

638   [*BA*, 12th-15th December 1810] *"Wir sehen, daß in dem Maße, als, in der organischen Welt, die Reflexion dunkler und schwächer wird, die Grazie darin immer strahlender und herrschender hervortritt.— Doch so, wie sich der Durchschnitt zweier Linien, auf der einen Seite eines Punkts, nach dem Durchgang durch das Unendliche,*

plötzlich wieder auf der andern Seite einfindet, oder das Bild des Hohlspiegels, nachdem es sich in das Unendliche entfernt hat, plötzlich wieder dicht vor uns tritt: so findet sich auch, wenn die Erkenntnis gleichsam durch ein Unendliches gegangen ist, die Grazie wieder ein; so daß sie, zu gleicher Zeit, in demjenigen menschlichen Körperbau am reinsten erscheint, der entweder gar keins, oder ein unendliches Bewußtsein hat, d.h., in dem Gliedermann, oder in dem Gott" (II:345). In the context of Kleist's principle of the general equivalence of the physical (bodily) and moral (mental, psychological) worlds, unconscious "grace" is inverse proportionally to concious "reflection": the less consciously one reflects on one's own body (say, before a mirror), the more "graceful" one remains or becomes; before the "angelic" Count, the Marquise becomes "graceful"—i.e., devoid of coyness, open—by swooning, i.e., by becoming unconscious. The novella's famous *hyphen*, in *"Hier—traf er"* (II:106), corresponds to the *line* that in *Marionettentheater* is said to pass through eternity (cf. II:345), on whose other side "grace" is found or restored.

639   [May or summer 1811] *"Das Leben, das vor mir ganz öde liegt, gewinnt mit einemmal eine wunderbar herrliche Aussicht, und es regen sich Kräfte in mir, die ich ganz erstorben glaubte"* (II:874; MAII:969).

640   *"Homburg. Erster Akt. Szene: Fehrbellin. Ein Garten im altfranzösischen Stil. Im Hintergrunde ein Schloß,vvon welchem eine Rampe herabführt.—Es ist Nacht. / Erster Auftritt. Der Prinz von Homburg sitzt mit bloßem Haupt und offner Brust, halb wachend halb schlafend, unter einer Eiche und windet sich einen Kranz.—Der Kurfürst, seine Gemahlin, Prinzessin Natalie, der Graf von Hohenzollern, Rittmeister Golz und andere treten heimlich aus dem Schloß, und schauen, vom Geländer der Rampe, auf ihn nieder.—Pagen mit Fackeln. [...] / Fünfter Akt. Szene: Schloß, mit der Rampe, die in den Garten hinabführt; wie im ersten Akt.—Es ist wieder Nacht. / Zehnter Auftritt. Der Prinz von Homburg wird vom Rittmeister Stranz mit verbundenen Augen durch das untere Gartengitter aufgeführt. Offizier mit Wache.—In der Ferne hört man Trommeln des Totenmarsches. / DER PRINZ VON HOMBURG. / Nun, o Unsterblichkeit, bist du ganz mein! / Du strahlst mir, durch die Binde meiner Augen, / Mir Glanz der tausendfachen Sonne zu! / Es wachsen Flügel mir an beiden Schultern, / Durch stille Ätherräume schwingt mein Geist; / Und wie ein Schiff, vom Hauch des Winds entführt, / Die muntre Hafenstadt versinken sieht, / So geht mir dämmernd alles Leben unter: / Jetzt unterscheid ich Farben noch und Formen, / Und jetzt liegt Nebel alles unter mir. [...] / Eilfter Auftritt. Der Kurfürst mit dem Lorbeerkranz, um welchen die golden Kette*

geschlungen ist, Kurfürstin, Prinzessin Natalie... und Fackeln erscheinen auf der Rampe des Schlosses.— / DER PRINZ VON HOMBURG. / Lieber, was für ein Glanz verbreitet sich?" (V.1; 1830-48). The drama's final tableau reproduces the first; the audience has completed, ouroborotically, a 360^0 scan of Kleist's panorama and observed all tableaux narrating Homburg's "journey around the world." When he arrives at the "rear entrance to paradise" (the "tomb"), instead of entering, he returns to his starting point where, still on this Earth, he is enchained with a golden chain arresting the soul's progression (cf. the *Aurea Catena Homeri, Iliad*, VIII, 18-26).

641 [20th November 1811] *"Der Himmel weiß, meine liebe, treffliche Freundin, was für sonderbare Gefühle, halb wehmütig, halb ausgelassen, uns bewegen, in dieser Stunde, da unsere Seelen sich, wie zwei fröhliche Luftschiffer, über die Welt erheben... Wir, unsererseits, wollen nichts von den Freuden dieser Welt wissen und träumen lauter himmlische Fluren und Sonnen, in deren Schimmer wir, mit langen Flügeln an den Schultern, umherwandeln werden. Adieu!"* (II:885-6). Jean-François Pilâtre de Rozier and the Marquis d'Arlandes performed the first untethered manned flight on 21st November 1783 (cf. II:591). The horizon had been discovered only in the 18th century—cf. Stephan Oettermann, *Das Panorama. Die Geschichte eines Massenmediums* (Frankfurt/M.: Syndikat, 1980), 17—, and only with the first balloon flights became a fully panoramic experience possible; Kleist himself never enjoyed this experience, but imagined it, his interest in aeronautics being *Orphical* (cf. below) and practical. Already the 2nd cent. AD Greek satirist Lucian phantasised about human flight and the birds-eye views of the world it would afford the observer: cf. his dialogues *Charon or the Observers* and *Icaromenippus or High Above the Clouds* and his short novel *A True History*.

642 Seers appear repeatedly in Kleist's œuvre: Apollo, Pythagoras, Zoroaster, Christ, Tiresias (the blind man in *Schroffenstein*), John the Baptist (Johann, *ibid*), a Pythia-type figure (the clairvoyant gypsy in *Kohlhaas*), the sibylline Alraune in *Hermannsschlacht*. The "gravedigger's widow" Ursula appears to perform necromancy, a practice that presumes the continued existence of the soul after death.

643 Already before the Würzburg Journey Kleist will have observed architecture approximating the characteristics of an amphitheatre, e.g., the *Viadrina*'s auditorium and Berlin's and Potsdam's theatres. The configuration adopted by Kosegarten's audiences at Cape Arkona, located on the cliffs above

him or in boats along the shore while he preached his sermons standing on an erratic rock on the beach, approximated that of an amphitheatre. Cf. Lucian, *Nigrinus* (trans. C.D.N. Costa): "I seat myself as it were right at the top of a theatre full of thousands and observe the scene before me."

644   Cf. Hans-Jochen Marquart (*AML*,VII): *"In seiner Vorlesung 'Noch etwas über den Unterschied des antiken und des modernen Theaters' (... im 8. Stück des 'Phöbus') wies Müller implizit auf die für ihn unübersehbare Gefahr hin, dass das durch Kunst zu bewirkende active Verhältnis des Menschen zur Welt und zu sich selbst in neuerer Zeit verlorengehen könnte, und er veranschaulichte das anhand eines Gleichnisses...: 'Um den ganzen höchst wesentlichen Unterschied der alten und neuen Kunst mit völliger Bestimmtheit aufzufassen, muß ich einladen, sich zwei gleich große Räume zu denken: in den Mittelpunkt des einen Raums denke man sich eine antike Statue; auf den andern Raum hin versetze man eines von jenen runden Gebäuden ganz neuer Erfindung, in deren Mittelpunkt sich der Zuschauer hinbegibt und nun durch die Malerei der Wände und den Lichteffekt gerade den Eindruck erhält, als befände er sich im Mittelpunkt einer reichen und schönen Gegend; ein* Panorama *meine ich.— Vergleichen wir nun die beiden Räume miteinander, so finden wir folgenden höchst charakteristischen Unterschied: im ersten Raum steht das Kunstwerk, die Statue im Mittelpunkt, und der Beschauer bewegt sich darum her; er muß es von allen Seiten umhergehend betrachten, wenn er es verstehen will; mit anderen Worten, das Kunstwerk ist die Sonne, der Zuschauer hingegen der Planet. Im Panorama andrerseits kehrt sich das ganze Verhältnis des Betrachters und des Kunstwerks um: hier steht der Zuschauer im Mittelpunkt, und das Kunstwerk läuft um ihn herum; der Betrachter ist hier die Sonne, und das Kunstwerk ist der Planet'... Statue und Panorama erzeugen demnach völlig unterschiedliche, ja entgegengesetzte Bedingungen der Rezeption, wie sie zugleich selbst deren Resultate sind. Die Statue, selbst Kunstausdruck der Konzentration, symbolisiert die auf das Objekt gerichtete* Konzentration *des Subjekts, welches hier den beweglichen Pol darstellt. Das Panorama, selbst Kunstausdruck der Zerstreuung, symbolisiert die auf das Subjekt gerichtete* Zerstreuung *des Objekts, welches, umgekehrt, hier den bewegten Pol darstellt."* Müller's theory clearly owes a debt to Kleist's practice (his statue is equivalent to Kleist's stage), while turning into a risk the deception that for the latter entails an opportunity. Kleist's self-image as "comet" may come into play: the artist begins his development by orbiting the Sun (Müller's statue), but with each orbit approaches the centre until at the climax fusing into it and thereby itself becoming the centre (viewed from which the Solar system is a panorama). Whereas

for Müller, in Marquart's interpretation (*AML*,VIII), the illusion of being his own centre puts modern man at risk of becoming entirely externalised, decentred or exterritorialised ("*ganz außer sich*"), for Kleist, the soul, by becoming (part of the) Sun, no longer merely observes but radiates, thereby *shaping the world*. Marquart in his foreword to *AML* understandably emphasises Müller's influence on Kleist, but in doing so underplays Kleist's on Müller: that his claim (*AML*,XI), "*Für den Einfluss Kleists auf Müller lässt sich nur feststellen, dass sich dieser durch das Werk Kleists in seinen ästhetischen Auffassungen bestätigt sah, zu einem Zeitpunkt, als sie bereits ausgereift vorlagen*," is untenable is demonstrated by the fact that the very device of the 'panorama' that he highlights among Müller's "esthetic concepts" is evidently derived from Kleist. His interpretation, the risk of "deception" in the context of modern arts, is Müller's own, but the concept as such is evidently not "present in a matured form" before he comes into contact with Kleist and his works.

645   Re the modern sports arena, cf. Sloterdijk, *Sphären II*, 960: "*die typischen Höchstformen makrosphärologisch engagierter Baukunst: die katholische Kathedrale und die neu-heidnische säkulare Sportarena.*" In the 2005 film *Return of the Jedi*, the Galactic Senates Chamber comprises a hemi-spherical amphitheatre within which the speaker hovers on a platform in the structure's focal point.

646   Cf. Sloterdijk, *Sphären II*, 100: "*ich schaue von einem epizentrischen Punkt aus in die Welt und sehe daher nichts bleibendes Ganzes, sondern nur den farbigen Abglanz einer unsichtbaren Totalität. Durch den Schleier der Meinungen, Bilder, Situationen hindurch erfasse ich immer nur Fragmente und Teilansichten… Die Menschen sind, sofern sie nicht den Ausnahmezustand der philosophisch-gottähnlichen Amphiskopie Erlangen,… zum Dasein auf halbblinden epizentrischen Standpunkten verurteilt. Sie sind… die Aus-dem-Zentrum-Gerückten, die in die Umstände Verschlagenen, die Randwesen, die situativ Benommenen.*" The ex-centric, de-centred emigrant Kleist, then, persists in a permanent *struggle for the centre*, a struggle to position himself near the centre or at an advantageous epicentric point, from which clear, perspectival, observation and communication are possible: in *satyrical* situations, the *erâstes*', in *satirical*, the war reporter's or spy's, in *po(i)etical*, the editor's.

647   Partial analogues of Kleist's metaphorical *Hohlspiegel* include the semaphore, telegraph and his own *Kanonenpost* (cf. II:385). Among the first experiments with electrical telegraphy were Samuel Thomas von Sömmering's in

1809, though Kleist does not mention him and may not have been aware of his efforts. The deflection of light by a planet's atmosphere, or a star's gravitational field, may be said to comprise a natural analogue of a *Hohlspiegel*. In Houellebecq's *La Possibilité d'une Île*, Daniel25 immerses his body in a puddle of saline water on the seabed of the dried-out Atlantic Ocean, where it slowly dissolves under the relentless sun; does not the concave seabed act as a giant *Hohlspiegel* that transports his ephemeral soul to heaven? The "transporter" that in the TV series *Star Treck* teleports people or objects across great distances is a futuristic analogue of Kleist's "cannon post" device. Are not our planets, our planetary system's asteroid belt and circumstellar discs, and, on at cosmic scale, our galaxies natural accelerators—of satellites, comets, asteroids, planets, stars?

648 C.D. Friedrich's painting is framed, of course, but apart from its frame offers nothing that bounds or structures the landscape, which makes it so unsettling for the observer. Sloterdijk, in discussing Georg Simmel's *Der Bilderahmen* (1902), writes (*Sphären II*, 217), *"Um das Werk zu einer selbstbezüglich Insel zu Machen, müsse der Rahmen eine 'in sich schließende Strömung' um das Bild herumführen und es mit den stärksten möglichen 'Abschlußmitteln' aus seinem Milieu ausschließen,"* in view of which we might say that Friedrich's painting precisely lacks that Simmelian "closure device," which is what Kleist means when he says that it lacks *"Abbruch."* Cf. also Sloterdijk (*Sphären III*, 528): *"Während die traditionelle Kunstausstellung überwiegend gerahmte... Objekte zeigte, präsentiert [Ilya Kabakovs] Installation [Die Toilette, 1992] das Eingebettete und das Einbettende zugleich: das Objekt und sein Ort werden mit demselben Griff vorgestellt; sie schafft damit eine Situation, die nur durch Eintreten des Beobachters ins Einbettende und eo ipso durch die Auflösung des Rahmens... rezipiert werden kann."*

649 Gernot Müller, in *Gemälde*, 250, already notes this important detail. The promegranate tree under which Jeronimo's family rests in *Erdbeben* fulfils the same function, in addition to marking the entrance to the underworld. Klaus Kanzog, in *Kleist,*76, links *Homburg*'s first scene to Friedrich's *Mönch* (not discerning it as *panoramic* but as *traumatic*).

650 Apart from the works covered here, there are an early poem mentioned by Wilhelmine, *Ariadne auf Naxos* (cf. *NR*,167), a diary of which Kleist tells Wilhelmine on 21st August 1800, his "Kantian paper" (cf. II:514), his notes for Wieland's biography

(cf. II:729); the "essays" he shares with Gneisenau in 1811 (Marie: "military essays"; cf. II:878; *NR*,91); there will also have been significant variants no longer extant whose (perhaps fragmentary) existence can be inferred, e.g., an 1810 version of *Homburg*.

651   Peter Michalzik (*Kleist,* 488, n.71) offers a sensible analysis and concludes that Hottinger's scene in itself is too incidental to be memorable for Pfuel, and that Hottinger may have borrowed it from Kleist, e.g., via Zschokke. Has the *Kleist-Forschung* scouted Hottinger's estate for traces of *Leopold?* Kleist in late 1802 planned visiting Vienna, presumably to access sources, and Wilbrandt (*Kleist,* 153) points out that with *Schroffenstein* completed, this planned journey could have been related to *Leopold.*

652   Historical references were en vogue in Kleist's day. Napoleon harked back to the symbolism of the Roman Emperors and Charlemagne; German patriots "rediscovered" the medieval *Nibelungenlied* epos and *Kyffhäuser* legend, and Classicists and Romantics harked back to the past to make sense of their present, aesthetically or politically. Kleist had an acute antenna for historical connections and was well-read, and thanks to a clear framework was able to identify relevant connections with uncanny aplomb.

653   Quoted in Joh. von Müller, *Allgemeine Aussicht über die Bundesrepublik im Schweizerland.* Ed. Doris und Peter Walser-Wilhelm (Zürich: Ammann, 1991). According to legend, Joh. Jakob Hottinger's hero Arnold von Winkelried blew the breach into the Habsburg army that allowed the Swiss to conquer the Austrian standard and kill Leopold; plausibly this figure could have featured in Kleist's drama as well, possibly even as the Napoleon figure. The theme of succumbing in a duel or battle when being encumbered by one's own equipment certainly (re-)appears in Kleist, with Trota stumbling over his own spores and Achilles being hampered by his unwieldy steely body.

654   "German dualism"—the Prusso-Austrian or Hohenzollern-Habsburg rivalry—dominated Fr. Wilh. II's and his minister Ewald Fr. Graf von Hartzberg's foreign policy in his first years on the throne, 1786-90, until the French Revolution forced an entente with Austria. For Kleist these will have been formative years, into which his poetic competition with Leopold falls—cf. my discussion below.

655   Peter appears to have played no role in the actual conquest, although in 1098 he was in Jerusalem and helped defend the city against Muslim attempts to reconquer it. In late 1099 he sailed for France; his further career is obscure, and he may have died there in 1131. Kleist could have ended his drama with the conquest of Jerusalem.

656   Kleist could have drawn on a "genealogy of texts" (Eybl) that included accounts by several Roman historians as well as Cervantes' adaption of the events in his tragedy *La Numancia*.

657   In the wake of France's victory in the *War of the Second Coalition* and her territorial gains confirmed by the *Treaty of Lunéville*, Kleist may have doubted that even jointly Prussia and Austria could be a match for Napoleon, and instead envisioned a grand alliance of all German princes and peoples.

658   In Cervantes' tragedy the Numantians vow to commit mass suicide so that none of them shall fall into the Romans' hands alive. When in the final act they fulfill their vow, the hybristic Scipio, who refused to resolve the stand-off by negotiation and to let the citizens evacuate the city, looks like the drama's loser, for with their voluntary deaths the Hispanics have defied his power, and he returns to Rome empty-handed, having captured no prisoners to lead through Rome's streets in triumph. In a side-plot involving two Numantian youths, Cervantes contrasts Hispanic love and Roman lust.

659   Michaelis' 1770/1 treatise *Mosaisches Recht* was inspired by Montesquieu's influential 1748 treatise *De l'esprit des loix*, in which he argues that geography and climate interact with culture to produce a people's unique spirit and political and social institutions. Michaelis prepared a survey of the sociology of religion of the Near East, aimed at investigating the historical basis of the Biblical stories and the traditional roots of Mosaic laws, whose findings Carsten Niebuhr published in 1767 and Michaelis used for his treatise. Kleist will have found there a wealth of details about Jewish customs and institutions for fleshing out his drama, which explains why he kept the first vol. for six weeks, the second vol. for another four (cf. *LS*,307). Bernd Hamacher (*KH*,81) discusses Kleist's reading the Hohenzollern and Jewish histories in parallel, noting that both entail cases of insubordination, and that Titus could represent a "historical substrate" of The Elector. Wilbrandt notes Kleist's penchant for siege stories and cites the two *Sieges of Zaragossa* (December 1808; February 1809),

as possible inspirations. Kreutzer (*Dichterische Entwicklung*, 24-5) explores Torquato Tasso's *Gerusalemme liberta*'s influence on *Peter*.

660   The Roman general Sulla in 87 BC destroyed Athens as thoroughly as Titus in AD 70 did Jerusalem. Michalzik (*Kleist*, 448-9; 477) posits that Kleist parallels the Prussians of 1809 with the Jews of AD 70, which he discusses in terms of not Kleist's political concerns but his purported membership in Arnim's 1811 *Deutsche Tischgesellschaft*, which he terms an "anti-Semitic association," in a discussion which I find misleading because, firstly, this club in the first instance will have been a "pro-German patriotic association" (Jews were excluded, and targets of parody and vulgar witticism, but so were women and so-called *"Philister,"* stuffy "kill-joys" or "upright citizens"), secondly, because Kleist will scarcely have been an active member, not only because he was unable to afford the 1 RT contribution per session on any regular basis, as Michalzik himself suggests (*Kleist*, 446), but also because as cosmopolitan *Reichspatriot* and close friend of several Jewish fellow citizens he would scarcely have appreciated the cheap and xenophobic rants offered there (Michalzik admits that Kleist himself never gave a talk at the club). He may have been drawn to it because of his personal—not least *erotic*—interest in some of the club's members; apart from this, he preferred to frequent the salons run by *women*, such as the *Jewess* Rahel Levin. Kleist apparently had no anti-Semitic streak, but A. Müller may have: cf. *NR*,50.

661   The design for the quadriga (*"char de triomph"*) was fixed on 3rd March 1789 at a meeting involving Langhans, Schadow and the coppersmith Emanuel Jury, but Schadow may well have produced sketches already in 1788: since January 1788 he had been retained by Fr. Wilh. II to design of the tomb for Alex. von der Mark, the King's illegitimate son, and this very personal commission will have brought them into close contact. The recorded fact that the sculpture was meant to represent Victoria and not Nike (despite the King's insistence that the Brandenburg Gate was to celebrate peace, not victory) would have intrigued the young Kleist: his King evidently mastered the art of ambiguity and double entendre that would come to form the basis for his own *pescheräic* method.

662   Cf. Blamberger, *Kleist*, 30; Schulz, *Kleist*, 48-51; Loch, *Kleist*, 23; Michalzik, *Kleist*, 70-73. In the *BA* anecdote *Mutwille des Himmels* of 10th October 1810 (Kleist's birthday; cf. II:265-6) the officer dying after "protracted illness" and whose last wish—to be laid to his final rest exactly in the condition in which he passed away, unshaven

and in pyjamas—is only half carried out (the barber shaves off half his beard before the preacher stops him and buries the corpse half-shaven) could represent Kleist's father. Had not Joh. Fr. von Kleist's final wish been that his family should be treated by the authorities as if he was still alive, so as to safeguard its welfare? To whom might the Father have communicated his wish? Possibly to the preacher Catel, whom he hoped would complete Kleist's private education. When the King four days his death refused the mother a pension, and failed to intervene on her behalf in the question of the faulty testament, the Father's wish remained unfulfilled. If in the anecdote he laments his education having been cut in half by Fr. Wilh. II's ungraciousness (representd by the barber who holds the father's corpse by the nose), Kleist may be insinuating that he now considers himself treated ungraciously by Fr. Wilh. III, who thus continues a pattern of ingratitude towards Kleist's line that spans three Hohenzollern Kings—Fr. II, who denied the Father further promotions after being displeased at him during an inspection, Fr. Wilh. II, who denied the Mother a pension and his support in the matter of the testament, and Fr. Wilh. III , who is denying him, Kleist, support for his patriotic projects. Placing this anecdote into BA on his birthday strongly suggests that it is own his own account, and that it encapsulates a sentiment that has led him, on various occasions, to caricature Fr. II's for estimating his dogs more highly than his subjects, castigate Fr. Wilh II for giving away German unity and territory at *Basel* (castrating and drowning him in return), and crash-land a hapless Fr. Wilh. III (as Achilles) in a ravine with his quadriga before having Napoleon return it to him (as Hermann) as a bribe. *Satirically*, Kleist's half-shaven corpse may allude to Franz I, one of whose two Roman numerals "I" was shaven off (the barber would then be Napoleon). Lucian reports that the *kynic* Peregrinus Proteus during a journey to Egypt shaved half his head to stir commotion.

663   Regarding the issue of Kleist's private education, cf. Loch, *Kleist*, 23: "Man kann vermuten, daß er nach dem Tode des Vaters von Berlin nach Frankfurt zurückgeholt wurde, um hier eine kostengünstigere Ausbildung zu erhalten; womöglich bei Martini"; similarly Loch, *Beiträge*, 114 n.33.

664   Blamberger is probably precisely wrong when he suggests (*Kleist*, 25) that Kleist lost the poetic constest because *"Heinrich scheint ähnliches Apokalyptisches* [in reference to Leopold's final lines] *in diesem Alter noch nicht zustande gebracht zu haben."* The opposite will have been the case: whereas Leopold's barn celebrated a Prussian glory that he anticipated could only end, in the distant future, in a

spectacular conflagration, Kleist's may have pilloried a Prussian decay, decadence and hybris, entailed in its very design, that he felt was already taking place under Fr. Wilh. II's reign.

665   Reuß and Staengle (*MA*II:483) put the entry "between 1788 and 1791" while Sembdner puts it into 1791, with a question mark (II:43). My *satyrical* reading points towards the later date. Kleist needed to look no further than Juvenal's *Satires* for inspiration of this I/O symbolism: In *Satire II* Juvenal has, e.g., "lances" and "well-smoothed passages" (12-13); "spear" and "helmet" (129-30); "trident" and "arena" (143-4). The latter pair Kleist renders as "girandole" and "amphitheatre" (cf. II:673). Phallic symbolism is as ambient in classical satire as it is in Kleist: Juvenal, in his *Satires*, has "limb," "forearm," "swelling spindle," "lance," "spear," "horn," "trumpet," "trident," etc.; Martial, in his *Epigrams*, has, e.g., "Pharos," "club of oak," "sickle," "sparrow," "pan-pipes," "lamp," and extensive references to Priapos. The same is true for anal symbolism: Martial has, e.g., "reception halls" with "scornful thresholds" and "doors thrown wide open" (1,70). Lucian, in the dialogue *Timon the Misanthrope* (trans. C.D.N. Costa), has Zeus nurse his overused organ: "And as to those flatterers..., I'll be seeing to them... as soon as I've had my thunderbolt repaired. Its two biggest prongs go broken and blunted the other day, when I was a bit too energetic in firing a shot at the sophist Anaxagoras... I missed him... and the bolt glanced off onto the Anaceum [the temple of the youthful twins Castor and Pollux], set that on fire, and almost shattered itself on the rock." Cf. Kleist: *"Die Frau, da sie sich erhob, glitschte mit der Krücke auf dem glatten Boden aus, und beschädigte sich, auf eine gefährliche Weise, das Kreuz"* (II:196); *"Die Puppen brauchen den Boden nur, wie die Elfen, um ihn zu streifen, und den Schwung der Glieder, durch die augenblickliche Hemmung neu zu beleben"* (II:342). Later in the same dialogue Zeus assuages Wealth regarding Timon: "Unless his loins are totally impervious to pain, his digging will have taught him a clear lesson... you find fault with Timon now because he opened his doors to you and let you wander around freely." In Lucian's *Demonax* the protagonist equates anus and ring: "Off with you, laddie, and take care of your own ring: this one isn't yours!" (trans. C.D.N. Costa).

666   Kleist biographers disagree whether Carl killed himself on 10th October, Kleist's assumed birthday, or on the eve of 18th October, Kleist's registered birthday (cf. my earlier note). At any rate it could have been a signal to Kleist, and probably it was. Rahmer (*Kleist*, 22-3) discerns a veritable "suicide mania" surrounding Kleist:

in addition to Carl he enumerates Hartmann von Schlotheim, Marie's brother Peter von Gualteri, and Otto von Kleist. Rahmer's idea is that these suicides in his circle of family and friends could have bolstered Kleist's suicidal leanings; the inverse possibility does not occur to him.

667 My conjecture that Kleist and Carl again spent time together in Frankfurt/O. after the Father's death is not necessarily inconsistent with Carl Eduard Albanus' view, passed to Tieck of 12th April 1832 (*LS*,5a, drawing on conversations with Martini), that Kleist and Carl "never met again in person" after jointly being educated by Martini in Frankfurt, for Albanus provides no dates and could have been referring to their being jointly educated not only before, but also after the father's death; Horst Häker could be wrong when he implicitly assumes (in seeking to demonstrate a different point), that Albanus' note necessarily refers to the period before the father's death (cf. *KJb* 1988/89, 449).

668 Schede (*Kleist*, 17) dates the centre-left image c.1792 (as does www.pastellists.org), which appears unlikely, for its presumed painter Jacob Wilh. Mechau in 1790 moved from Dresden to Italy and did not return for several years. If the portrait does depict Kleist, it would have been painted no later than 1790, when Kleist was 12 or 13. Since only the painting at c.24 is widely recognised as attributable and authenticated, the notion of Kleist's feminine features must rest on it alone—and it can.

669 Cf. Blamberger (http://www.heinrich-von-kleist.org/index.php?id=398&L=1); cf. also Loch, *Kleist*, 424. Blamberger, in his *KH* entry "Death" (*KH*,369ff.), fails to link his conjecture regarding Carl's suicide to Kleist's own. He also misquotes a revealing phrase: *"Der Tod ist in Kleists Leben und Werk eine zenrale Denkfigur von der Kindheit an, bedenkt man... die Erlebnisse des 'Kindersoldaten'... als einer Zeit, in der "wir hier so unmoralisch tödten"* (*KH*,369). Kleist did not write of, as Blamberger makes us believe, a *"Zeit, in der wir... töten,"* but of a *"Zeit, die wir... töten"* (II:471): it is unequivocally *time*, and not *people*, Kleist says he and his comrades "killed"—as in: "killing time"—; specifically, which he says they "killed immorally," i.e., which they spent in the pursuit of immoral activities. Hans-Günther Thalheim (cf. *Beiträge*, 1999, 17) similarly misquotes Kleist, while Loch (*Kleist*, 28) quotes him correctly but misinterprets the quote as kleist saying that war (killing people) is immoral. Such misreadings are far from trivial: in this particular case, not only do they veil Kleist's "immoral" experiences during the months of idleness in his unit's

winter quarters in Eschborn, but also do they put into circulation a false meme of a peace-loving, death-abhorring Kleist, thereby in turn rendering his martial language during the *Germania* period all the more "shocking." I already offered in a previous note that Kleist's reminiscence of how he and like-minded comrades were killing time immorally may coincide with the period in which his doubts about his military career first emerged, not leat thanks to Fr. Wilh. II's and Hardenberg's entertaining a separate peace with France. The "immoral activities" Kleist and his comrades engaged in will have included the usual pastimes in the life of a soldier—drinking, gambling, whoring—, as well as sodomy, as Carl's father had anticipated.

670   Albanus recalls (*LS*,5a) that Kleist and Carl entered the "suicide pact" in writing after last meeting in person; yet such a pact would scarcely be entered solely in writing: more likely they had already done so verbally and reconfirmed it in writng. The idea could inadvertently have been spurred on by Martini, an ardent student of the theologician Josias Fr. Chr. Löffler, who taught that men like Socrates and Jesus willingly died for their convictions (cf. Loch, *Kleist*, 17); Kleist himself refers to Socrates and Christ (cf. II:495). Socrates was condemned to death for being a "godless seducer of youths" (Bäumler, *Amors vergifteter Pfeil*, 36) and Christ for rallying his followers in an anti-establishment movement, and Kleist may well have considered both of them company: he, too, was looking to rally the German youths in resistance to the established power, and was willing to die in the pursuit of his cause; the "great men" Kleist enumerates in his 1799 *Aufsatz* (cf. II:314) alongside Christ and Socrates, Leonidas and the Roman Consul Regulus, died in heroic, selfless resistance to a superior enemy.

671   The "*große Schrift*" Kleist evidently sent to Rühle in c.May 1801 (cf. II:656) could well have been that biographical work, so that Rühle would be the most likely owner (and perhaps destroyer) of a MS. Kleist's legendary biography already excited the imagination of Tieck and early Kleist scholars, who could still hope that it might resurface (cf. *NR*,134; 155; 183; 223; 454), and continues to inspire Kleist readers to this day—cf. Roman Bösch's 2007 novel *Geschichte meiner Seele*, Raphael Graefe's 2010 novel by the same title, and already in 1938 Walter von Molo's novel *Geschichte einer Seele*.

672   Cf. also Kreutzer, *Dichterische Entwicklung*, 80. One could perhaps term Kleist a "neutral monist" or a proponent of "embodied cognition": the soul, while

separable from the body in death, needs a "host" body to interface with the sensual, material world, and the body needs a "resident" soul to access the immaterial and infinite—hence his insistence as to the "equivalence of the physical and moral world." Cf. also L. Wittgenstein's utterance, *"Der menschliche Körper ist das beste Bild der menschlichen Seele,"* in "Philosophische Untersuchungen," Werksausgabe, Vol 1 (Frankfurt/Main: Suhrkamp, 1984), 496. Gudrun Debriacher's term *commercium corporis et animae* is apt, and her treatise *Die Rede der Seele über den Körper. Das commercium corporis et animae bei Heinrich von Kleist* (Wien: Praesens, 2007), is a source of inspiration. Klaus Kanzog, in a discussion of *Marionettentheater* (*Kleist*, 188-9), links Kleist's *Anmut* and *Grazie* not only to Schiller's essays on aesthetics but also his medical dissertation of 1780, *Versuch über den Zusammenhang der thierischen Natur des Menschen mit seiner Geistigen*, in which Schiller states (§18): *"der Mensch ist nicht Seele und Körper, der Mensch ist innigste Vermischung dieser beiden Substanzen."* The question whether Kleist in his famous line says *"Schmutz"* or *"Schmerz"* ought to be considered conclusively and unequivocally answered: it can only be *"Schmutz,"* i.e., "blemish," "stain," "abjectedness," "darkness," in juxtaposition with *"Glanz,"* i.e., "excellence," "brilliance," "splendor," "brightness"; cf. also Sembdner, *In Sachen Kleist*,76-87.

673   Cf. already Kreutzer (*Dichterische Entwicklung*, 65-7): *"Somit gelangen wir... zum konkreten Kern der Überzeugungen Kleists.... Tod als eine Geburt 'zu einem künftigen Lebenszustande'... Damit ist die 'von Kleist selbst gegebene Prämisse' der Erschütterung von 1801 genannt..., nämlich der Palingenesiegedanke... Diese mit der Unsterblichkeitsfrage zusammenhängende und nicht nur eine Prämisse für die Kantkrise darstellende Überzeugung meinte Kleist in Wahrheit, wenn er von 'meiner Religion' sprach...Diese 'Religion' schloß...auch den Gedanken von einer Stufenleiter der Wesen ein, die nach jedem ihrer Tode auf immer anderen Sternen eine fortschreitende Höherentwicklung durchlaufen."* Kreutzer explores references to metempsychosis in the works of Wieland, Herder, Jean Paul and Novalis; re the latter, Jürg Amann in his novella "Hardenberg" (in *Nachgerufen*, München: Piper, 1987, 53-109) writes: *"Plötzlich kam ihm, während der Beschäftigung mit Goethe, aus einem nicht bestimmbaren Grund dessen 'Faust' in den Sinn, von da kam er auf die Alchemie, er holte Papiere und Bücher hervor, die er darüber besaß, und verlor sich endlich ganz in Spekulationen über die Welt und ihre Zusammenhänge, über ihre Beziehung zu anderen Welten, die hinter ihr lagen, und über die Beziehungen der Menschen auf dieser Welt untereinander und zu der anderen Welt und zu den anderen Menschen, die auf dieser Welt nicht mehr sichtbar*

anwesend waren." Philosophical speculation about metempsychosis was widespread in Kleist's day—e.g., by Kant (*Allgemeine Naturgeschichte und Theorie des Himmels*, 1755), Moses Mendelssohn (*Phädon oder über die Unsterblichkeit der Seele*, 1767), Joh. Georg Schlosser (*Über die Seelenwanderung*, 1781), Lessing (*Die Erziehung des Menschengeschlechts*, 1782), Herder (*Drei Gespräche über Seelenwanderung*, 1784) and Fichte (*Die Bestimmung des Menschen*, 1800). Georg Wedekind, with whom Kleist may have spent more time than with any other of his doctors, was a prominent proponent of reincarnation, which he later covered extensively in *Über die Bestimmung des Menschen* (1828). Sembdner (cf. I:45) seems to put Kleist's dedication for Adolphine, written into a copy of Moses Mendelssohn's *Phädon*, between August 1804 and May 1808, but also links it to his *"Jugendbriefe"* (cf. I:916-17), which suggests that he remains unsure re its dating. Reuß and Staengle put it in the Potsdam period, mid-1795 to early 1799 (cf. *MAIII*,597). Both datings are possible, the latter perhaps more plausible, as it fits with Kleist's reading patterns at the time (the dating of the entry is not necessarily indicative of when Kleist himself read the book, though it suggests that he did read it at some point).

674   The 15-year old orphan Kleist in 1793, en route to war, visited Löffler at Gotha (cf. Loch, *Kleist*, 18), the only known personal visit he made during the two-year campaign. Löffler's letter to Massow of March 1793, in which he speaks fondly of the young Kleist (cf. Loch, *Kleist*, 422 n.20), essentially coincided with Kleist's letter to her of 13th March 1793, posted upon reaching Frankfurt/M. Kleist's and Carl's reconfirmation of their suicide pact via letters could have fallen into this time, when both of them were facing war, Kleist at the French and Carl at the Polish front. Credit is due to Rudolf Loch and Wolfgang Barthel for paving the way for a re-appraisal of Löffler's importance to Kleist.

675   Quoted in Michalzik, *Kleist*, 135. Hans-Jürgen Schrader notes (*KJb* 1988/9, 165): *"Die Vorstellungen der sympathetischen Attraktion verwandter Seelen, das Planetenbild von der exzentrischen Bahn einiger Seelen, das zentrale Begriffsinventar der Bestimmung und Vervollkommnung hatte Kleist in diesem Werk vorgeprägt finden können."* Not in his poetic style, but in his outlook on life Kleist could indeed be termed a disciple of "the Wielandian school," as Fouqué put it (cf. *LS*,105). For the Pythagorean concept of metempsychosis, cf. Burkert, *Greek Religion*, 300. For the Aristophanesian concept of spiritual kinship, cf. Plato's *Symposion*. Kreutzer notes (*Dichterische Entwicklung*, 227-8) that Kleist could have encountered the motif of "love of the other half" in Wieland's *Sympathien*.

676   Cf. my discussion in *Emigrant*, 44-6 of Brentano's critique, in his novel *Godwi*, of the Schlegelian concept of radical translatability, a critque I suggested Kleist would have largely agreed with (Kleist, I might add, was more concerned with radical transmutability).

677   Cf. already Kreutzer (*Dichterische Entwicklung*, 89): "*Die Kantkrise… trug zum guten Teil nur durch den Abbau bestehender Überzeugungen dazu bei, den Weg [für die Dichtung] zu bahnen.*" The "Kant-crisis," one could say, entails Kleist's "Marx-moment"—"*Die Philosophen haben die Welt nur verschieden interpretiert; es kommt aber darauf an, sie zu verändern*"—, his "kynical turn": "*Auf kynische Weise von seiner Intelligenz Gebrauch machen bedeutet… eher eine Theorie zu parodieren, als eine Theorie aufzustellen… Die erste fröhliche Wissenschaft ist satirische Intelligenz; sie gleicht darin mehr der Literatur als der Episteme… Vater der Fröhlichen Wissenschaft…* [ist] *der denkfähige Satyr… Das satirische Verfahren… besteht… darin, daß man die Dinge 'umkehrt'*" (Sloterdijk, *Kritik*, 527-9), and even his "Platonic turn," in relation to Burkert's exploration of "philosophical religion" (*Greek Religion*, 322-3): "Plato's Socrates stands in contrast to the sophists in that instead of parading pretended knowledge he persists with more searching and more fundamental questions… Plato builds on this foundation… Mathematics provides a model of absolutely certain knowledge. This knowledge, however, does not arise from experience… True knowledge of this kind is placed in the soul from the beginning; its object exists outside the empirical sphere. What holds for concepts such as equality must also hold for…what is truly and absolutely just, beautiful, and good… It is the soul of man which is capable of the knowledge of being. It carries in it a knowledge which it has not won in this life: knowledge is recollection, *anamnesis*. With this the knowing soul rises above existence as stretched between birth and death… if there are two kinds of being, the unchangeable, true being and that which comes to be and passes away and never truly is, then the soul clearly stands on the side of the higher, permanent sphere. Death affects only the body; the soul is immortal… the soul can no longer be abandoned by the gods: on the contrary, it is called on to ascend. The ascent of the soul to cognition is not a cool acknowledgement of fact. Plato portrays this path as a passionate undertaking which seizes the whole man, an act of love, *eros* rising up to madness, *mania*. It is the beautiful which points the way. It touches the soul and excites it to a loving approach; yet ascent begins only with the insight that the beautiful appears in many bodies, one and the same in manifold impressions. From physical beauty cognition leads to the beauty of the soul, from there to the beauty of

knowledge itself, until finally a man 'moving towards the goal of the erotic suddenly glimpses a "beautiful" which is of wondrous essence, precisely that for which he had previously given such pains,' the pure being, imperishable and divine, the 'idea of the beautiful." When Michalzik highlights (*Kleist*, 96) *"Die Heftigkeit mit der [Kleist] sich im September 1800* [cf. II:315-18] *gegen ein Denken in Hinblick auf die Ewigkeit stellte,"* he is quite mistaken: Kleist does not reject "thought in relation to eternity"—in fact he reiterates the *"frohe Ewigkeit, die meiner wartet"* (II:317)—, but his concept of eternity differs from Christianity's eternal damnation attenuated by God's grace, and so do its implications for conduct in life: actions in this life that a Protestant may hope will improve their future life (say, prayer and sacrament) are useless; only achievements in this life that ennoble the immortal soul are valuable. Kleist illustrates the contingent conventionalism of a sacrament such as the Christian Communion by equating it with Aztec human sacrifice (cf. II:316-7; 683). He appeals to Wilhelmine to fulfil her duty—*"erfülle Deine Pflicht"* is the pivotal demand of his essay—as mother of his children (*"Mutter zu werden, und der Erde tugendhafte Menschen zu erziehen"*; II:318), which he ensures her will ennoble her soul.

678   Kreutzer (*Dichterische Entwicklung*, 55; 68-9) notes that Lawrence Ryan traced this same imagery in Hölderlin's 1797/9 novel *Hyperion*, and that Chr. Ernst Wünsch in *Kosmologische Unterhaltungen* discusses the idea of metempsychosis explicitly in the context of comets, referencing Abraham Gotthelf Kästner's 1781/3 *Philosophisches Gedicht von dem Kometen*, Leibniz, Pope (*Essay on Man*), Albrecht von Haller, and Kant. The "glacial erratic" (*"Findling"*) is equivalent to the "comet" in so far as both are subject to a play of physical forces beyond their control (the poetical equivalent in Kleist's *Gesetze* is *fate*). They differ in so far as the comet's orbit or "law of motion" is more regular and predictable than the glacial erratic's movement, and the comet's fate is combustion, the glacial erratic's slow erosion. Cf. also Sloterdijk, *Kritik*, 689-90: *"Was sich Dialektik nennt, ist in Wahrheit eine Rhythmik oder Polaritätsphilosophie. Rein betrachtend versucht diese, das Leben und den Kosmos zu begreifen als unermüdlichen Wechsel von Phasen und Zuständen des Seins, die im Kommen und Gehen sind—wie Ebbe und Flut, die Zyklen der Gestirne, Freude und Trauer, Leben und Tod. Diese große Rhythmik versteht alle Phänomene ausnahmslos als Pulsierungen, Phasen, Takte. Sie erkennt in ihnen nichts als das Hin und Her des Einen, des kosmologischen Prinzips… Die heraklitische 'Dialektik'—die erste und wohl auch die einzige europäische, die reine Polaritätsphilosophie ist, ohne Polemik zu werden… entspricht vollkommen diesem Typus von Weisheitslehre."* Re

Kleist's "Sun," cf. his half-joking, half-jealous admonition to Rühle, occasioned by the latter's becoming engaged: *"Liebe, mein Herzensjunge, so lange Du lebst; doch liebe nicht, wie der Mohr die Sonne, daß Du schwarz wirst!"*—"Don't love woman to the point where you burn yourself."

679   Cf. Douglas Adams' Arthur Dent hitchhiking his way through the galaxy: Kleist's sojourns parallel Dent's stop-overs, his "life plan" the "hitchhiker's guide," his postal carriages the Vogon shuttles on which Dent hitches his rides. Like a troubadour Kleist traverses romantic Saxon landscapes with his side-kick or *"jongleur"* Brockes— at times, like Dent, facing monstrous worlds inhabited by paranoid aliens: courtiers and technocrats in Berlin, surgeons and madmen at Julius-Hospital, military police at the gates of Berlin or the battlefield of Aspern, etc.

680   Cf. Horst Häker, *Homburg und Verlobung*, 165-206. Fouqué clearly seeks to position as Kleist's equal by highlighting that already in their youth they swapped "songs"—" *unsere Lieder / Einander... / Entgegen sendend"*—, a pattern of mediocrity's jealousy in the face of genius Häker traces in Fouqué's poetical career till at least 1830 (cf. *ibid*, 203).

681   Today only Kleist's hand-written writer's copy dedicated to Princess Amalie survives, reportedly not the basis for Tieck's publication (cf. Klaus Kanzog, *Kleist*, 18-19; 26); presumably few copies ever came into circulation, so that the *"fixfingrige"* Fouqué did not necessarily have to actively withdraw (even destroy) copies: his own work was safe from Kleist's competition as long as the latter's product did not pop up, and Princess Amalie evidently kepts hers under lock. Marie or her son may have burned her MS together with most of Kleist's letters (cf. Sembdner, *In Sachen Kleist*, 193). We came very close to knowing as much about *Homburg* as about *Jerusalem*.

682   Häker is likely wrong when he maintains (cf. *Homburg und Verlobung*, 177) that Kleist "broke into [Fouqué's] domain probably entirely unsuspectingly"; he quotes Kleist's *"mit Ihnen in die Schranken treten"* (*ibid*, 166) without evaluating it further. Fouqué spent his formative years (age 11-16) and later several summers on the Lentzke estate in Fehrbellin, and since 1803 lived in Schloss Nennhausen, a mere 20km from Fehrbellin, and will have been exposed to the *Fehrbellin* story before Kleist. When he and Pfuel united at Nennhausen during the hight of Prussia's catastrophe in early 1807, perhaps to hatch ideas and gather materials

to kindle Prussia's resistance, Fouqué may have shared the story, and Pfuel may subsequently have related it to Kleist—Siebert correctly notes (*Kleistiana Collecta*, 137) that Kleist may have known the history of *Fehrbellin* before borrowing the Krause book (I add that it could well have been part of the standard curriculum for Prussian officer cadets); he also reports (*ibid*, 131) that on 18th June 1800 a memorial to *Fehrbellin* was erected at the site of the battle, close to the road today known as Deutsche Alleenstraße (it connects Rügen with Wittenberg), which suggests that Kleist and Ulrike could have passed by the battlefield en route to or en retour from Rügen in June/July 1800, and even been present at the memorial's inauguration. The Mesmerian therapist Karl Chr. Wolfart, with whom Kleist was in contact in Berlin, in 1810 also published a play entitled *Herrmann*. Re the topos of poetic rivalry and jealousy, cf. Martial, *Epigrams*, 12.94 (trans. Gideon Nisbet): "I tried to write an epic once. You started writing one; so I stopped, so my poetry wouldn't compete with yours. Then my Muse redirected herself to the thigh-boots of Tragedy. You tried on the trailing robe yourself... I dare Satire; you throw yourself into becoming Lucilius. I unwind with some light elegies; you copy me and unwind just the same."

683   Like Kleist, Fouqué in his poetry processed his dilemma of having to reconcile homosexual love- and heterosexual family-life; unlike Kleist, he achieved a manageable "*Einrichtung*," being apparently happily married to Caroline von Rochow while maintaining his engagement in the "brotherhood." His mysterious figure Undine—eminently "amphibian" (in Kleist's term), exceedingly desirable, and fated to remain soulless lest she marry and produce children, at the expense of her ethereal sensuality—is a perfect avatar of Kleist, while the amorous yet conventional knight Huldbrand, who veers between the erotically supercharged Undine and his wife Bertalda, is a similarly perfect avatar of Fouqué. If he wrote *Undine* in 1809, Fouqué could have shared the tale with friends and presented it at Berlin salons around the same time when Kleist pulled *Käthchen*'s out of drawer to complete it. Fouqué published *Undine* in his own journal *Jahreszeiten* in June 1811, which gage him full editorial control of the timing of its publication, so that its publication could easily have encompassed a targeted swipe at Kleist.

684   Sembdner (*In Sachen Kleist*, 200-1) considers Ferd. Grimm an unreliable source and doubts that the novel's MS reached Reimer, if it even existed.

685   Abbé Prévost, *Manon Lescaut*. Trans. Angela Scholar (Oxford: Oxford UP, 2008), 14.

686   If Kleist completed the novel, he would have made at least one clean copy. If the novel were ever to resurface, then perhaps among Müller's or Fouqué's legacy. Ferd. Grimm could have heard of the novel from Reimer, for whom he worked (cf. *NR*,130a) and who knew of it (as work in progress), or from Kleist directly (cf. II:872); the question remains who that person was of whom Grimm says that he *read* it; this would have been Reimer or one of his editors, or someone who was in close contact with him, which at that time more likely Fouqué than Müller.

687   Fr. de la Motte Fouqué, *Undine* (München: DTV, 2005), 121-2. Quite possibly this dedication is precisely that *"Abschiedsgedicht"* Fouqué says (cf. *NR*,252) he wrote on 27th November when he learned of Kleist's death in the newspaper (cf. Sembdner, *In Sachen Kleist,* 209). In addition to his 1811 dedication, Fouqué's 1812 reminiscence, *"jünglingshell,-- / ...mein Heinrich, / So standen wir, nun fest im Männerbund / Die treue Hand uns drückend, unsere Lieder / Einander... / Entgegen sendend in die freud'ge Brust"* (*NR*,252), suggests that whatever *po(i)etical* rivalry between them he perceived or conjured, he valued and honoured their joint *satyrical* experiences. Sembdner offers (*ibid,* 210) that Fouqué's correspondence of this period with Hitzig, Pfuel, Varnhagen, and others "conveys [Fouqué's] deep and honest shock."

688   A duodrama is a theatrical melodrama for two actors or singers in which the spoken voice is accompanied by music for heightened dramatic effect—cf. https://en.wikipedia.org/wiki/Duodrama. Popularised by Georg Anton Benda since the 1760s, and influential on Mozart and Beethoven, the duodrama in the English literature is considered a form of *theatrical melodrama,* in the German, of *musical melodrama.* Rousseau's *Pygmalion* is considered a principal example (which Kleist certainly knew). As a form of *Sprechmusik,* it has affinities with Kleist's *"Sprechtheater,"* and hip hop and rap are perhaps its closest equivalents todays. Kreutzer notes, in *Dichterische Entwicklung,* 28, that Kleist may be considered a "precursor of the modern [e.g., Wagnerian] musical drama." The poems Kleist prepared in 1809 for *Germania* can be thought of as patriotic songs or Kriegslieder: "Ich *wollte, ich hätte eine Stimme von Erz, und könnte sie, vom Harz herab, den Deutschen absingen"* (I:913; cf. also II:824). Declamation, chant, play and spectacle for Kleist were merely varying means to the end of stirring his audiences into action.

689   While the *Kleist-Forschung* generally deems the duodrama (cf., e.g., Sembdner, *In Sachen Kleist,* 312), I consider it eminently Kleistian and have no doubt

that it belongs in the Kleistian canon. Kreutzer notes (*Dichterische Entwicklung*, 106) that Bülow ascribed it to Kleist with reservations, and that alhough Sembdner did not include it in his compendium, he remained undecided as to its authenticity (*ibid*, 109 n.12); Kreutzer himself also leaves the matter undecided, accepting that it could hail from Kleist's early years (which I consider unlikely, cf. my discussion in the main text). UnKleistian terms such as *"Freude"* could have been contributed by Henriette. Venus' depiction as a white body (the Heaven) topped by a golden diadem (the Sun) and girdled with a blue belt (the Earth) aligns with many of Kleist's panoramic depictions: the Mainz "amphitheatre" with its chandelier (cf. II:673-4), the "spherical music" ecstasy in which Kleist uses the term *"Agadio"* (cf. II:569), Achilles' appearance on the horizon (cf. V.356-70), the two aeoronauts in the letter to Sophie Müller (cf. II:885).

690   Kleist will have spent significant time in Wieland's Oßmannstedt estate here depicted—it will likely have been in this very room that he declamed the lines from *Guiskard* that so impressed Wieland; as Henriette's house does not appear to be extant, Wieland's salon may serve as proxy for the setting. Paul Valery, in the dialogue *Eupalinos*, assessed the principles of immersion, or inclusion-in-the-work, in relation to two art forms: architecture and music; of these he wrote (quoted in Sloterdijk, *Sphären III*, 530): *"Im Werke eines Menschen zu sein wie Fische in der Welle, vollständig in ihm zu baden, in ihm zu leben, ihm zu gehören."* It appears that Kleist, with his final project, sought precisely this kind of complete and ultimate immersion in a cosmos into which his soul would soon be released.

691   The award of the 2016 Nobel Prize for Literature to the singer/songwriter Bob Dylan may reflect a revived recognition of the artistic potential of the "convergence" of poetry and music.

692   Kreutzer speculates (*Dichterische Entwicklung*, 240-1) that the "songbook" could have been an 18th century Huguenot "songbooks" and links it to the *"Todeslitanei."* Medieval troubadours indeed used simple songbooks, in addition to bound *chansonniers*.

693   In Könisberg Kleist invented signs indicating the voice's lifting, carrying, relenting, etc. (cf. *LS*,145), aimed at facilitating his works' declamation and enhancing its effect on the audience.

694   For Dionysiac initiation rites, cf. Burkert, *Greek Religion*, 259. Caves, peak, tree and house sanctuaries, temples and graves were common cult places in ancient Greece (cf. *ibid*, 24ff).

695   Chr. Ernst Wünsch, in the prologue to the second edition of *Kosmologische Unterhaltungen* (Vol. 1; 1791), defends the usefulness of tracing the "mythical origin" of "most peoples' religions" (which he does in his 15th and 16th Conversations), arguing that to the philosopher the "seed of error and folly" is as interesting as is the "ground of truth and wisdom." One cannot avoid the impression that Christianity for him is merely one among many such "religions" whose "origin" is "mythical" and whose "seed," therefore, is "error and folly," though he avoids saying so outright. One need not look further than Wünsch for a source for Kleist's religious skepticism.

696   In addition to the *Orphica*, the *Book of the Death*, and hermetical texts, among Kleist's sources for his imagery "between Heaven and Earth" could have been: Plato's *Phaedrus* (246a-247c), in which the soul is likened to a charioteer one of whose two winged horses pulls his chariot upwards towards the gods, the other downwards towards the Earth; the myth of Persephone, forever oscillating between Hades and the surface; and Gotthilf Heinr. Schubert concept of the dream as a state of suspension between illusion and reality (cf. Zimmermann, *Kleist*, 338).

697   Blamberger (*Kleist*, 407-8) considers Kleist's agenda espoused in *Zarathustra* "questionable," maintains that Kleist "dissembles" "coherence" and "compels" readers to search for a "hidden plan" in an infinite "loop," and makes fun of "well-behaved specialists in German studies" who "obey and *a posteriori* read, e.g., all (*BA*) entries as camouflaged articles in the struggle with Napoleon." The only "well-behaved specialist in German studies" Blamberger exposes here, is himself.

698   Michalzik, *Kleist*, 397-9. For the Grimm quote, cf. Blamberger, *Kleist*, 391.

699   Already Sembdner sees *BA* as a platform for anti-Napoleonic propaganda within the same genealogy as the *Germania* materials and *Hermannsschlacht*—cf. Sembdner, *Die Berliner Abendblätter Heinrich von Kleists, ihre Quellen und ihre Redaction* (Berlin: Weidmann, 1939); cf. also Kreutzer, *Dichterische Entwicklung*, 20. Horst Häker (*Homburg und Verlobung*, 143-4) offers a compelling *satirical* reading of a 28th November *BA* entry by Armin concerning a German sea captain, pointing

out that the article portrays German sailors as being recruited to fight on the (so Häker) "wrong side." Häker assesses this *BA* entry in a context that is unKleistian (the Great Elector's attempt, in the 1680s, to participate in the West African slave trade), and misses how intimately it is connected with *Homburg*, whose entire plot is about a German captain (the Prussian King) being recruited to fight on the "wrong side." Six weeks before Kleist's 12th/15th January 1811 publication of *Über den Zustand...*, Achim's article may have marked the moment when Kleist pulled his *Homburg* drafts out of the drawer and began putting them into their final form.

700   An earlier school of thought had it that Kleist was not responsible for A. Müller's damaging *BA* articles, and perhaps not even fully aware them (cf., Rahmer, *Kleist*, 87; 117; Wilbrandt, *Kleist*, 389). In view of all we know about Kleist's production processes, this view is untenable. Mistakes can happen, but we are on safest ground assuming that every single line printed in *BA* had passed Kleist's scrutiny. Rahmer (*ibid*, 191, 197, 203) crafts a sophistical argument according to which Müller was playing a double game, being in the Prussian government's pay while enacting a pseudoi-opposition; while Rahmer's idea is not necessarily wrong, it is somewhat beside the point: Kleist was playing his own game, creating an open space for polemic views, not least as a means of driving sales and captivating a wide audience. This explains why he never blamed Müller for *BA*'s demise (cf. Jakob Baxa's note to *AML*, 1682; the quarrel over *Ph* was quite different, in that Müller had evidently acted behind his back, which to Kleist signified a breech of trust). That Kleist himself launched this polemic campaign can be seen in his reportage on Claudius' balloon flight (cf. II:388-94), which arguably comprises its opening shot, in which he questions Hardenberg's (Claudius) and Raumer's (Reichard) competence in applying the mechanics, and understanding the implications, of their rigid fiscal interventions, and advocates a more organic economic model (the entry can also be read *satyrically*, as advocating the "balloon's" natural, rather than artful, *"direction"* within its "medium," and since in *Marionettentheater* Kleist privileges the use of mechanical, inorganic *member*, taken together the two entries promote the use of dildos "directed" organically within their "medium," accommodating the latter's natural movements and resistances). Kleist's miscalculation may have been that the fiscal debate's focus soon shifted from Hardenberg's tax reforms, which he could expect a wide readership to disfavour, to the abolishment of privileges of the noble estate, which only a vocal minority (especially the *Junkers* themselves, such as Marwitz) would object to—cf. *AML*, 444-6; 451; 454 notes; 455; 459 notes; 463; also 379). There is something of a

tradition among Kleist's friends and biographers to cast A. Müller in the role of Kleist's evil *daimon*, on account of his selling *Ph*, his risky *BA* articles, and his coupling Kleist with Henriette Vogel—cf. e.g., Wibrandt, *Kleist*, 266, who nevertheless provides a balanced account of Müller, though Jakob Baxa in his notes to *AML*,1682 accuses him of *"geschichtsfälschende Darstellung"*; Dora Stock considered Müller a "bad influence" on Kleist (*LS*,261), and so did Varnhagen (*LS*,446d). Yet it is all too easily forgotten that Kleist on his part instrumentalised Müller, and that when Wilbrandt terms their friendship "dangerous" (*Kleist*, 288), he appropriately means this both ways; Kleist himself shortly before his death admitted to Marie that it had been "in several ways dangerous" to be associated with him (II:883), probably alluding to, among other things, Müller's forced departure. If Müller at times became a drag, he at other times was a boon for Kleist: he had *Amphitryon* published, introduced Kleist to his Dresden and Berlin circles (being far better networked than Kleist), and helped get *Ph* off the ground. Kleist himself was no innocent lamb: Pfuel's family, for example, may well have had Kleist in mind when they warned their scion against "bad influences" (cf. Rahmer, *Kleist*, 14).

701 For Hardenberg, Müller was the "softer target" compared with Kleist, and he never gave up his efforts to turn this vain and swayable, but eloquent and popular, figure into a mouthpiece for his own policies. Müller on his part was desperately pursuing job opportunities with the Prussian authorities, while demanding the extension of a government stipend Hardenberg's precedessor Altenstein granted him (on Kleist's instigation). Hardenberg left him dangling, neither outright declining or accepting his requests (cf. Jakob Baxa's note to *AML*,496), and eventually, having half "converted" him, without trusting him fully, Hardenberg exiled Müller to Vienna, where he could do little damage while potentially becoming a useful informer.

702 Typical examples quoted by Schulz (*Kleist*, 468) and Blamberger (*Kleist*, 392): "*Auf dem Neuen Markt ist ein abgenutztes Gefäß zerschlagen*"; "*Ein Weinhändler ist gestern früh in seinem Keller erhenkt aufgefunden*"; "*Der Posamentier-Meister Martin Friedrich Krüger...hat sich gestern, aus Melancholie, an seinem Arbeitsstuhl erhenkt*"; ein "*brodtloser Buchhalter*" hat sich "*mit einem Terzerol am Kopfe tödlich verundet.*" Blamberger (*Kleist*, 408) likens Kleist's "love of the catastrophic" to Orson Welles' famous 1938 radio drama based on H.G. Wells' *War of the Words*. Kleist aimed not merely to scare but to stoke resistance, and his "space invader" hailed not from Mars but from the Champ de Mars.

703   Quoted in Michalzik, *Kleist*, 399-400.

704   On this account Kleist's message came three months too late: Marie-Louise in June or July became pregnant with Napoléon Franz. The only remaining (hypothetical) option would have been to abduct Marie-Louise and have her deliver her son in the Hofburg rather than the Tuileries, which Kleist may have toyed with in *Verlobung*, whose Nappy ("little Napoléon") may represent a son of Napoleon's born in the Tuileries, and Seppy ("little Joseph") one born in the Hofburg.

705   Quoted in Blamberger, *Kleist*, 391-2.

706   C.1800 Berlin city maps show eight of the city's Vauban-style citadels still standing, so that Kleist's ironic doubling of the metaphorical "four corners" may have had a material basis.

707   Although *BA* is focused on *satirical* concerns, *satyrical* and *syphilitical* themes occur. For example, the anecdote *Der Griffel Gottes* (*BA*, 5th October), which in *Emigrant* I read as *satirical* parody of the recently deceased Queen Luise's mythification, can be read *syphilitically* as the *erastēs'* phallus ("*Griffel*") infecting the *erōmenos'* rear orifice ("*Gottesacker*"), leaving in its wake molten mercury and the lover's decaying corpse, his spirit forever enshrined in his adorers' tales. In *OT* (*Exod*. 31:18; *Deut*. 9:10), "Finger of God" denotes how the Ten Commandments are written onto the tablets of stone Moses brings down from Mount Sinai.

708   Cf. also Sibylle Peters' contextual and intertextual analysis of *BA* in *KH*,166-72. Already Kleist's *BA* collaborator L. Freiherr von Ompteda reckoned that Kleist deliberately placed certain articles concerning political figures in "undignified neighborhoods" (*LS*,434a). Martial, in his *Epigrams*, also put great care into juxtaposition and sequencing (cf. *Epigrams*, trans. Gideon Nisbet, Oxford: OUP, 2015, xxv).

709   Cf. Michalzik, *Kleist*, 410ff; *LS*,457. Sibylle Peters (cf. *KH*,170), leaning on Alex. Weigel, rightly observes in *BA* a "*Zusammenhang zwischen Nationaltheater und Nationalregierung.*" Iffland, following a barrage of humiliations in *BA*, offered Hardenberg his resignation (cf. *LS*,36c), but provided he was sure of Hardenberg's support, this may have been a tactical feint in his duel with Kleist. Re Armin's

contention that Hardenberg and Iffland "hung together like wheel and cart grease," compare Juvenal (*Satire II*, 47): "queers stick together like glue" (trans.: Peter Green).

710   Pfuel apparently claimed that Hardenberg actively undermined efforts by Kleist's friends to secure him financial support from the state (cf. *LS*520b; Sembdner, *In Sachen Kleist*, 188). Michalzik's evaluation is based on a fundamental misunderstanding of Kleist that mars his biography (not only his), illustrated, for example, by his statement (*Kleist*, 440): "*die grundsätzliche Einstellung Kleist, die auch im "Homburg" deutlich wurde. Kleist versuchte sich um fast jeden Preis zu integrieren*"; his misreading *Homburg* filiters into his misreading the *BA* episode.

711   The (extant) reports Müller sent to Hardenberg (cf. *AML*,516; 531) do not seem very insightful or charged, and one gets the impression that Hardenberg had simply needed a pretence for exiling Müller, for laying this troublesome but ultimately unsubstantial egg into the Habsburgs' nest. Re Hardenberg's attitude towards Kleist, a comment of his to Raumer in the context of the *BA* affair deserves our attention: "*Lassen Sie sich mit dem armen Menschen [Kleist] nicht weiter ein! Kleist hat ja einige Monate in der Kreis-Irrenanstalt zu Bayreuth gesessen.*" While this could have been a lie of convenience on Hardenberg's part, he would scarcely have invented such a far-fetched story without any basis. In light of Kleist's "disappearances" in Mainz and Prague, and other gaps in his biography, Hardenberg's insinuation cannot be rejected out of hand. Bayreuth, where Hardenberg had once been minister and may have retained loyal informers, is located only 240km from Prague, and after *Znaim* the now Bavarian city would again have been accessible to Kleist. To denigrate Kleist, Hardenberg may have systematically solicited damaging information about him, and an informer in Bayreuth could have provided him this information. However solid or shaky the basis for Hardenberg's statement, it tells us something about how Kleist was perceived in Prussia's upper echelons.

712   Cf. Sloterdijk, *Kritik*, 623-4: "*Der sexuelle Trieb wurde [mit der Aufklärung] zum qualvollen 'Stachel im Fleisch'... Sexualität erschien... als eine riesige Gefahrenzone...: die Katastrophe ungewollter Schwangerschaften; die Schande unzeitiger Verführung; das Elend tückischer Infektionen, did dich das Leben lang zerfressen; die Demütigung durch verfrühten, aussichtslosen, einsamen Trieb; das Risiko, sich als Monster zu entdecken, das homosexuelle oder perverse Tendenzen in seinen Eingeweiden mit sich trägt... etc.*"

713   Cf. https://de.wikipedia.org/wiki/Dornauszieher.

714   "In articulatory phonetics, a consonant is a speech sound that is articulated with complete or partial closure of the vocal tract"—cf. https://en.wikipedia.org/wiki/Consonant.

715   *The Fool*, depicting a young man with a stick and a white rose (symbolising innocence) walking unknowingly toward the brink of a precipice, who is the protagonist of the "Fools Journey," i.e., the path through the mysteries of life, is the first card in the cycle of the "Major Arcana"—cf. https://en.wikipedia.org/wiki/The_Fool_(Tarot_card).

716   Family connections can be boon or bane. Marie's brother Pierre Guilteri offered to employ Kleist as Prussian attaché in Spain (the opportunity came to naught), and her brother-in-law Chr. von Massenbach's brother Fr. introduced Kleist to Altenstein and Hardenberg, eventually landing him a job. Yet for Kleist these *"Connexionen"* remained a double-edged sword: secretly he may have detested being offered opportunities he could not turn down because family members were invested in them. In early 1800, commencing with his first extant letter to Wilhelmine, Kleist dropped the aristocratic *"von"* from his name, signing as Heinrich Kleist or H.K., perhaps hoping that posing as a commoner he would be at more liberty to pursue unconventional avenues with respect to family and career. By early 1805, commencing with a letter to his friend Pfuel, he reverted back to signing with his proper family name—Heinrich von Kleist, Heinrich v. Kleist, or H v. K.

717   Werben was the main estate of Joh. Heinr. Ernst von Schönfeldt's family, Gulben that of Karl Wilh. von Pannwitz's. In *Guiskard* Kleist uses the term *Sippschaft* (clan) to denote the hero's extended family, in *Krug*, Huisum's complex of citizens related to each other by marriage, in doing so implying nepotism, cronyism, and favouritism. Her mistress of the robes Countess Voß, like Kleist's mother a née von Pannwitz, and Marie von Kleist were the Queen's closest confidantes, and Fr. Count Kleist von Nollendorf was King Fr. Wilh.'s adjutant general at *Jena-Auerstedt*, illustrating how deep tightly connected with the Hohenzollerns were these ancient *Junker* families which, in the course of the German *Ostsiedlung* since the 12th century (and till the end of WWII), came to monopolise ownership of agricultural lands east of the Elbe river, until industrialisation constituting the main economic basis of

the Prussian state and the Hohenzollern monarchy (as well as supplying many of its senior army officers and civil servants). Not always did the Kleists serve their royal family well: Franz Kasimir von Kleist, commander of Prussia's Magdeburg fortress, infamously handed it over to the French without a fight, and without orders to do so (sentenced to death by a war court, he died before the verdict could be executed). Among the main knighly estates associated with the "Lausitz Clan," Tzschernowitz (Guben), Falkenhagen (Mark), Gulben, Gurthwo, Werben, Müschen, and Wormlage were located in Brandenburg, and Zützen in Saxony. King Fr. II was recorded as having been so annoyed at Karl Wilh. von Kleist's buying an estate in Saxony's Zützen (where Kleist built a splendid baroque palace), that he refused to grant him a visit when passing by. Kleist's Kohlhaas' owning estates in both Brandenburg and Saxony (cf. II:13), and thus owing allegiance to both the Brandenburg and the Saxon Elector, may reflect the "Lausitz clan's" distribution. The Pomeranian line of von Kleists centred on the knightly estates of Schmenzin, Zeblin, Dubberow and Tychow, and closely linked by marriages to the von Stojentins (first documented in 1341), on whose Schorin estate Ulrike—and briefly Kleist—in 1807 stayed. When Kleist in 1801, en route to Paris, belatedly (5 months after his departure) sends a farewell letter to his family (cf. II:655), he addresses it to a member of the family's Pomeranian line, not one of the "Lausitz Clan." The poet Franz Alex. von Kleist during 1793-6 lived at Falkenhagen Castle near Frankfurt/O., but since Kleist was away on military duty, he may not have met him (unless Franz Alex. attended Kleist's mother's funeral in 1793); Franz Alex.'s works were popular during his lifetime, and had he not died prematurely in 1797, aged 28, he could have served as Kleist's role model.

718   Rudolf Loch portrays Kleist's mother Juliane Ulrike von Kleist, née von Pannwitz, as a warm, caring and understanding woman with a "noble heart" (cf. *Beiträge*, 94-5), contrasting her with Aunt Massow, who took over the reigns after her death and already during her lifetime may have sought to influence the children, "*Waren Onkel und Tante bei einigen Kindern mit ihrem Einfluß doch dominanter geworden? Offenbar bestanden hier, womöglich im gleichen Haushalt, zwei Lebensauffassungen nebeneinander, mit denen sich die Kinder auseinandersetzen mußten,*" adding with well-placed irony, "*Die selbst kinderlose Majorswitwe v. Massow meinte offenbar, besser als die leiblichen Mütter zu wissen, wie man (im Falle der Frankfurter auch vaterlose) Kinder zu erziehen habe.*" By no means is Kleist's letter to Aunty innocent: I already noted that "*Ein steiler Fußweg zeigte mir die Öffnung zum Schloß*" (II:465) entails an early example of his (I/O) symbolism.

719   Not that this was unusual: the Pfuel family, for example, felt the same regarding Pfuel's escapades (cf. Rahmer, *Kleist*, 14). Nor was Kleist's family necessarily unusually stringent or imposing—they may merely have been typical—; Kleist may just have been unusually sensitive and excentric. Rahmer reports (*Kleist*, 61) that Alex. zur Lippe was similarly ill-disposed towards taking office, and that Brockes found it difficult to sustain himself in any office he held—it appears that Kleist found soulmates in them in this as well as other respects. Kleist himself was fully aware of the Zenges' reservations regarding his plans for their daughter (cf. II:643). Samuel Richardson's popular 1748 novel *Clarissa*, which Kleist and L. Wieland read together in 1802 (cf. *LS*,91), narrates a young woman of independent character's confrontations with an unyielding family, whose intransigence eventually drives her into death. Nor does the present author's personal experience suggest that much has changed in this respect in two hundred years: regarding what counts as "proper" "life plan," notably the pursuit of a *"Broterwerb,"* Germany's middle class in the 1980s still adhered to essentially the same mental model as Prussia's landless nobility in the 1790s. Re seed financing, to this day so-called "three F funding" ("friends, family and fools") remains the default source of initial funding for start-ups. The prospective "angel investors" Pannwitz and Stojentin may have felt that, while they *were* family, they decidedly *were not* fools.

855

720   Loch notes (*Beiträge* 1997, 116 n.40) that the memory of Kleist's father having come into conflict with the authorities and been refused promotion, and his widow having been refused a pension, will have lingered on. The extended family's disdain at Kleist's escapades—quitting the Prussian military, seeking to join a foreign army, quitting the civil service, being held as spy, etc.—is easily explained, if not necessarily excused: in their experience such excentricities would only spell misery and dishonor, which, since Kleist remains Kleist, could extend to the wider family (the flip side of family cohesion).

721   In George Lucas' *Star Wars* the Lords of the Sith Order seek to "convert" the Knights of the Jedi Order to the "dark side." Family relations and succession play a major role in Lucas' space saga, not least because "the Force" is passed on genetically, as well as being refined via apprenticeship. Correlations between Kleist and Lucas may be spurious: they may have taken similar leaves out of, e.g., Shakespeare's and Goethe's works.

722   This version of Kleist's repeated paraphrases of this traditional bonmot reflects Joh. Wilh. Gleim's affirmation to him that Ewald von Kleist produced a "beautiful work" and a "great deed" (cf. II:656-7).

723   In my "trans.": "In the buttock's groove is suspended the narrow and simple opening I long for. The coccyx secures it, perianal hair shades it, and ejaculate cools it. Further up the groove, the vulvic zone is ghastly, but towards the buttocks, the landscape is fair. A small bridge, the perineum, separates the rest of the body from this orifice. Yes it may seem that it will get crowded during intercourse, but for two lovers and their members there is sufficient room. I lost myself in reveries. I checked out that ghastly orifice in which I would have to dwell (for the purpose of impregnation), the other, where my fellow male lover would dwell, and the third, in which we would both dwell. I imagined you as mother with our *erômenos* at your breast, sitting on my lap, while in my rear youths would cling to my buttocks, rejoicing in their orgasms." Earlier the same day en route from Grimma to Waldheim Kleist reminisces of a lover whose "house's" (body's) "windows" (orifices) on both "levels" (upper and lower) are expectantly "lit up" (cf. II:540), reiterating a similar description, three days earlier, of Luise von Linckersdorf's "house" (cf. II:535). Cf. also Kleist's repeated references to Wilhelmine's "bower" (e.g., II:545; 548).

724   With apologies for my pseudo-Greek. Cf. Burkert (*Greek Religion*, 301): "the distinctive, strict way of life, *bios*, is generally regarded as characteristic of the Orphics and the Phythagoreans: there is a *bios Orphikos* as well as a *bios Phythagoreios*." Kleist's concept of "*Scheidung*" aims at *parallel processing*, not *sequencing*: his letter to Wilhelmine in which he first uses the term (cf. II:576) makes this clear, referring to a chemo-metallurgical process in which gold is extracted from lesser minerals or dross. Already his reminiscence of his departure from Frankfurt/O. in August 1800—"*Der Wagen rollte weiter, indessen mein Auge immer noch mit rückwärtsgewandtem Körper an das geliebte Haus hing*" (II:515)—anticipates the contortions "*Scheidung*" may entail, a theme that recurs in *Marquise*'s "*Hier—traf er, da*" and *Prolog*'s "*Hier jetzt lenke, jetzt dort.*" Kleist's *familial* design was 200 years ahead of time: only recently, with social, technological and legal innovations such as reconstituted families, gay marriages, coparenting and adoption rights for gay couples, donor insemination, reciprocal IVF, and surrogacy have Kleist's ideas finally become acceptable as well as practicable, at least in some countries.

725   Only in this context does the apparent skittishness of Kleist's references to Raphael's painting become intelligible: during his first visit to Dresden's Gemäldegalerie, in September 1800, the painting *offends* him—*"so gafft man so etwas an, wie Kinder eine Puppe"* (II:543)—, for at the peak of his "men's health" crisis, its perfection hits him in the face (cf., by way of contrast, how already a few days later, in the "delightful valley of Tharandt," he reproduces this vision with delight); during his second visit, in May 1801, it *delights* him—*"vor jener Mutter Gottes... mit Umrissen, die mich zugleich an zwei geliebte Wesen erinnerten"* (II:650-1); *"Ach, in Dresden war eine Gestalt, die mich wie eine geliebtes, angebetetes Wesen in der Galerie fesselte"* (II:701)—, for he is now well on his way towards realising his dream of an alternative family model; during his third visit, in 1803, it *frustrates* him—according to Falk he calls the Christ figure "malicious" (cf. *KH*,252)—, because his *familial* aspiration has been frustrated: he has broken up with Wilhelmine and no replacement is in sight. That these episodes confirm is that Kleist did not look at an image independently of his own personal context: his evaluation of a work of art (be it Raphael's, Teniers', C.D. Friedrich's or what not), just like his evaluations of landscapes, events, and other things, is always already autobiographic. Hilda M. Brown's contention, in "'Zwischen Himmel und Erde'. Kleist and the Visual Arts, with Special Reference to Caspar David Friedrich," in *German Life and Letters* XXXI/No. 2 (1978), 157ff., that the young Kleist's appreciation of art was "straightforward and conservative," and revolved around "idealised womanhood (as represented by the Sistine Madonna), that is woman in her mainly passive and selfless role, and secondly, idealised manhood, as represented by the dynamic and heroic Archangel figures," while not wrong, is naïve and requires explication: Kleist did indeed have a highly idealised view on both womanhood and manhood, but one that was extremely idiosyncratic and whose essence is not captured by Brown's generic statement.

726   Leonardo's Mary's sitting on Anne's lap may evoke a lesbian setting, although Anne's masculine facial features could also suggest that she represents the Father. Like Raphael, Leonardo deploys a prominent garment: while Mary's headscarf in Raphael's work indicates the Father's presence, her drapery in Leonardo's may convey the painter's awe of feminine mystique and life-giving power, and perhaps his latent homosexuality, as Freud speculated. Like Raphael, Leonardo indicates the Father's presence, in his case through Mary's prominent phallic arm, which appears to fertilise her while bringing forth, and perhaps sodomising, Jesus (Jesus' arm replicates this gesture to the lamb, thereby serialising it). Like Raphael's, Leonardo's work could

have inspired Kleist's ideas of *"Scheidung"* and three-somes (cf. *Erdbeben*'s tableau of Jeronimo, Josephe and Philipp under the pomegranate tree), but lacking the puttos, does not offer a complete blueprint for his alternative *familial* model.

727   My "trans." of the passage from the 1st September letter (cf. II:537): "*Brockes* and *I* were both searching, and we both did find… he, what was his, I, what was mine. We were not bothered by the delicate ejaculate gently spraying our faces from above. Eventually I could not hold back any longer and pulled the condom over my glans. There erected the lovely shape…, with all its contours and colours in the dark hole before me. I… imagined you [Wilhelmine] in this moment very vividly, and I am convinced that in this vision nothing was amiss, nothing of you, nothing of your leather harness, not the golden cross of your anus, and its location, not your butt plug that so frequently annoyed me." The "cross" anticipates the one Gustav in *Verlobung* transfers from Mariane to Toni, demanding her body's openness (Kleist's cross anticipates Réage's O-ring). My "trans." of the letter's postscript in which Kleist offers Wilhelmine a run-through of the type of "fantasies which imagination produces according to its most liberal license" (cf. II:538): "in the morning I enter your rear, in the afternoon your frontal orifice, in the evening again the former, and at midnight again the latter, which I have only once visited before, so that my imagination envisions it with utmost capriciousness." Kleist did not expect Wilhelmine to fully grasp his innuendos, but could have explain them to her later in the privacy of her bower: "*Warum… spreche ich ich so geheimnisreiche Gedanken halb aus, die ich doch nicht ganz sagen will? Warum rede ich von Dingen, die Du nicht vesthen kannst und sollst?... Wenn ich so etwas schreibe, so denke ich immer zwei Monate alter. Wenn wir dann einmal, in der Gartenlaube, einsam, diese Briefe durchblättern werden, und ich Dir solche dunkeln Äußerungen erklären werde, und Du mit dem Ausruf des Erstaunens: ja so, so war das gemeint——*" (II:548). Kleist in his Würzburg letters *rehearses* his message and induces Wilhelmine's maieutic *allmähliche Verfertigung der Gedanken beim Lesen*.

728   Clarinett/mouthpiece and lips/mouth obviously belong into the (I/O) symbolic field. Kleist's story from Potsdam may allude to his liaison with Luise von Linckersdorf (cf. below). *"Musikus Baer,"* who introduced him to the use of wooden dildos, anticipates the fabricant Benjamin Cohen, from whose "splendid cabinet of physical instruments" in Berlin he is permitted to avail himself (cf. II:628), and *Marionettentheater*'s *"englischen Künstler"* (II:341), a master craftsman of mechanical

dildos. After meeting Baer, Kleist himself refines the craft of shaping wooden dildos to perfectly fit his anatomy.

729   In *Amphitryon* Jupiter requests of Alkmene, *"Du bist, du Heilige, vor jedem Zutritt / Mit diamantnem Gürtel angetan"* (V.1259-60). Kleist's schemes might have been more acceptable among aristocrats of ancient Greece, which explains why he was enamoured of their codes of conduct and alienated from those of his own day, in which aristocratic values rapidly gave way to bourgeois ones. If Nietzsche added a *Dionysiac* dimension to Winckelmann's *Apollonian* vision of ancient Greece, Kleist contributed a *satyrical* one that overlaps, but is not coextensive with, the *Dionysiac*.

730   Kleist pays tribute to Brockes for always "accepting the most inconvenient position" (cf. II:622), for leaving the "juiciest fruit" to him (cf. II:623), and for "never entering [Kleist's] chamber" uninvitedly—in other words, for accepting the role of *erômenos* even though he was older, as well as for serving him, "condom thrown over," as *dmōs* (cf. *ibid*). When people close to Kleist, including Wilhelmine, repeatedly emphasise his *"Sittlichkeit"* (cf. *LS*,21;30;38), they may be availing themselves of the same "code" that encompassed terms such as *"Tugend"* ("virtue"), *"Vortrefflichkeit"* ("excellence"), and *"Ziererei"* ("coyness"). Wilhelmine, in seeking to comply with Kleist's scheme, may even have gone so far as to procure herself a lesbian partner—a "female Brockes" (II:632)—with whom she could practice "openness" and "overcoming coyness" in preparation for her reunion with Kleist.

731   Instead of book-knowledge and quizzes, Kleist now sends Wilhelmine travel reports and reflections in preparation for her journey to their joint Arcadia (cf. also Michalzik, *Kleist*, 165).

732   Kleist may have modelled *"Mme C..."* on a well-known procuress plying her trade in Berlin during his sojourn there in 1804 (cf. Michalzik, *Kleist*, 239). Michalzik (*ibid*) quotes Eduard Vehse's depiction of 1800 Berlin's upper society, *"Die Weiber sind so verdorben, daß selbst vornehme adlige Damen... sich zu Kupplerinnen herabwürdigen, junge Weiber und Mädchen von Stande an sich ziehen, um sie zu verführen,"* without noting that Kleist's own Berlin circles belonged to the very social strata he depicts, and evidently without the faintest suspicion that Kleist himself could have procured the services of a procuress in his quest for a bride, or of prostitutes for his heterosexual "rehearsals."

733   The main *dramatis personae* who compelled Kleist to settle near Bern will have been Zschokke, a long-time friend, expert in Habsburg history, and public figure who could provide access to national achives and other sources, and who could potentially be an alternative to Lose in his *familial* scheme, and the prominent Bernese doctor Wyttenbach, whom Brockes may have recommended to him (cf. Rahmer, *Kleist*, 77). The search for a "Third" lover is a recurring theme in Kleist's works, be it in a *chercher la femme* or a *chercher l'homme*, be it to complete an *"FFO"/"FOF"* or an *"FFF"* "Triad." Kleist's story of "Mädeli" (evidently a lad, not a maiden) is no less congruent than that of his "scaling" the peaks of the Bernese Oberland; I do not doubt that he is referring to a real person, perhaps his landlord's son, whom he cast in the role of *erômenos*, whose *"Schwyzertracht"* (traditional Swiss costume) will have consisted in the Swiss equivalent of *Lederhosen* (not Dirndl), whose admonishment to economise (*"sie solle sparen"*; II:724) will have referred not to money but ejaculate, i.e., to avoid coming prematurely, and whose tasks will have encompassed, in addition to household and garden work, entertaining Kleist and completing the "Triad." Burkert reports (*Greek Religion*, 261) a custom from Dorian Crete whereby "a man from the men's hall would carry off a beautiful boy, as Zeus carried off Ganymede. For the chosen lad this actually meant a distinction. The man made known his intention in advance, and the boy's relatives arranged for a mock pursuit that ended at the men's hall. Presents were then distributed, and the man with his boy... retired to some place in the countryside for two months," and Kleist may have "acquired" his "Jüngli" in a similar manner.

734   Réage's O in Sir Stephen's Samois estate submits herself to the most rigorous régime, including being branded on her buttocks and having rings pierced through her labia. I am not suggesting that Kleist necessarily envisioned anything of that kind for Wilhelmine, but that he expected her to condone and partake in his symposiac orgies while raising their children and running his household. Michalzik's naïvité concerning Kleist's erotic life never fails to amuse: *"Er wollte [Wilhelmine] unbedingt dazu bewegen, ihm als Bäuerin in die Schweiz zu folgen... Er sehnte sich nach dem Glück der reinen, natürlichen Liebe... Sie könnten in der neuen Einsamkeit immer füreinander da sein"* (*Kleist*, 181). Ha ha: Kleist's "countrywoman" Wilhelmine was to be a bondaged "bottom" in black leather gear and dildo harness, engaging with him and his male lover(s) in "pure, natural" orgies, keeping herself permanently open to them in the "new isolation" of his dungeon (a Rousseauian Arcadia with a decidedly Réagean twist). *Ach!*—this is the trouble with Kleist biographies: they tell his story

from all the wrong angles. In terms of making a living, Kleist was looking to become not exactly a farmer but perhaps a small-scale *Landjunker* or esquire, and may have hoped that the combined revenues from the estate and from his publications would suffice to sustain a family and a small farm with a few hired hands (Sir Stephen is evidently independently wealthy; many a great man in antiquity withdrew to a country estate for part of his life, as Kleist notes, if not without irony—cf. II:694—, and many an educated emigrant in Kleist's day led a fulfilled life in the countryside of his adopted country—cf. Bülow, *Kleist*, 23). Kleist evidently planned and pursued his projects very systmatically: he defined a clear objective, scope and approach (*"Lebensplan"*, *"Scheidung"*), set a timeline (initially 5, extended to 6, then 10 years), orchestrated partners (Wilhelmine, with Ulrike and Mme C… as proxies; Brockes, Lose, aspirationally Zschokke, finally Mädeli as fall-back) and resources (funding from Ulrike; his inheritance), selected a suitable location as test-bed and pilot site (first Berlin, then Paris, finally Thun's Inseli), commenced the experiment, monitored progress and revised input parameters as needed; if a project became infeasible, he let go and started afresh—an approach which he consistently applied to his *po(i)etical* projects (*Guiskard, Ph, Germania, BA*, etc.) as much as the *satyrical* and *familial* ones.

735   *KJb* 2005, 44. Kleist's authorship of *Wissen, Schaffen, Zerstören, Erhalten* (*BA*, February 2011) is uncertain. Even if he was not its author, as Sembdner suggests, he included the essay in *BA* and will have edited it; at any rate, in my view the essay's content is eminently Kleistian: it begins with a sketch of *"Scheidekunst"* (i.e., chemistry or alchemy), specifically of the "artificial synthesis of gold," before exploring the "artificial creation of an organic, even living body" and "the mechanical or chemical production even of humans," thus not only anticipating, as Walter Hinderer suggests, gene- and clone-technologies (cf. *KJb* 2005, 42), but also expanding on *Marionettentheater*'s *"Gliedermann"* and anticipating E.T.A. Hoffmann's 1816 figure Olimpia. Cf. also Günter Blamberger's discussion in *KH*,370.

736   This sheds a fresh light on Kleist's comedy: from the point of view of *The Familial* and *The Filial*, Adam may *want* to be granted legal fatherhood to Eve's son, in which case his ominous performance in court would be but a charade. Such a scenario would explain why his shenanigans get him into ever deeper water, why he must backmail Eve and Ruprecht (who may remember what took place in said night), and why so any "clues" pop up that implicate him: he planted them himself, to frame himself. Only Walter's appearance throws a spanner in Adam's works. Kleist repeats

variations on this theme in several works of 1805-7: in *Erdbeben*, the people of St. Iago assign responsibility to Jeronimo for Josephe's illegitimate child, which Don F (probably the biological father) after Jeronimo's sacrifice adopts, thereby legalising his own illegitimate child; in *Amphitryon*, the citizens of Thebes grant the eponymous hero the legal right to the divine son (whose biological father—Jupiter or Merkur—is devine and hence excluded from the mortals' concept of legal fatherhood); in *Marquise*, the family sells the "legal rights" to the Marquise's offspring to Count F for an astronomical fee (the biological father to the son the Marquise is currently pregnant with may be the last "dog," who has been executed for ravishing her).

737   Compare Burkert's portrait of Heracles (*Greek Religion*, 205; 208)—"no god is a hero, and no hero becomes a god; only Dionysos and Heracles are able to defy this principle. [...] A number of figures in cult and myth... reach with equal ease into the heroic-chthonic domain and the domain of the gods, and it is this which gives them their special powers: they penetrate below and above... The most popular of these figures is Heracles"—with Kleist's image of an "ideal" youth born of an idyllic encounter: *"derjenige, der, in einer heiteren Sommernacht, ein Mädchen, ohne weitern Gedanken, küßt, zweifelsohne einen Jungen zur Welt bringt, der nachher, auf rüstige Weise, zwischen Erde und Himmel herumklettert, und den Philosophen zu schaffen gibt"* (II:329).

738   In *Krug*, Eve's "cured butter" parallels the "seed" Adam collects from Marthe (which *satirically* may signify Franz's extracting the Habsburg lands—the "seed" of the Austrian Empire—from the *HRR*). In Homer's *Odyssey*, Odysseus conjures the dead by pouring libations of honey, wine and water; in Aeschylus' *Persians*, the queen brings milk, honey, water, wine and oil to the grave of the dead king; and in Sophocles' *Oedipus at Colonus*, participants in a libation ritual fetch water from a freshly flowing spring, fill cauldrons with water and honey, and tip them over (cf. Burkert, *Greek Religion*, 71-3; Burkert concludes that "the fundamental sense of libation" consists in "raising hope through serene wastefulness"). Yet Kleist's "libations" with ejaculate entail not only the promise of purification but also the risk of renewed pollution. Cyropreservation only became a functional technique in the 20th century, but already in Kleist's day Lazzaro Spallanzani had made important discoveries with respect to the preservation of organic matter: in 1768 he refuted Buffon and Needham's *theory of spontaneous generation* by showing that boiling killed off any residue of life in a solution, thus anticipating Pasteur's discoveries a century later, and in 1776 he

showed that tardigrades, water-dwelling micro-animals that withstand extreme living conditions such as near absolute-zero temperatures, undergo cyclomorphosis and reproduce by parthenogenesis. In 1780 Spallanzani performed the first successful artificial insemination of a viviparous animal (a dog); he also performed the first in vitro fertilisation (on a frog). Spallanazani became a celebrity across Europe and was received by Emperor Joseph II; his influence prevailed well into the 19th century. Although Kleist does not mention him by name, many of the scientists he met in Paris and elsewhere could have been influenced by Spallanazani, whose theories and discoveries could have influenced Kleist, directly or indirectly, as much as those of the likes of Galvani, Volta, Aldini, Mesmer, Puységur, Gmelin, Brown, Hufeland and Wedekind. Spallanzani refuted the widely-held *preformation theory*, according to which organisms develop from a miniature version of themselves (in the case of humans, a *homunculus*), in favour of a *theory of epigenesis*, according to which the form of living things comes into existence from an undifferentiated mass in a process of genesis. As such, the idea that sperms contain the perfect "image" of a fully developed person in Kleist's day was on the verge of becoming outdated, though it was not fully refuted until 19th century advancements in microscopy and *cell theory*, and Kleist's notion of Strahl's spermata corresponding to his "image" may have remained scientifically up-to-date at time of writing. Just as he kept his *satirical* plots up to date vis-à-vis political developments, Kleist strove to keep his *po(i)etical* devices up to date vis-à-vis scientific developments. The *theory of spermism*, according to which fathers contribute the essential characteristics of their offspring, while mothers contribute the material substrate, first proposed by Pythagoras, and via Aristotle transmitted to modern Europe, remained unrefuted until the laws of Mendelian inheritance and chromosome theory established modern genetics in the course of the 19th century. Kleist's aristocratic convention that only sons, in particular the eldest, propagate family lineage, may have been buttressed by a scientific adherence to *spermism*: his Würzburg letters to Wilhelmine and his interest in the imagery of the Madonna suggest as much (Maria being a mere vessel, Jesus the product of "divine spermism"). Gottfried Wilh. Leibniz, whose teachings remained influential in Kleist's day, supported *panspermism*, according to which wasted spermata scatter and generate life wherever they find a suitable host—which implies that sperm had to be transportable, durable and resistant, bolstering Kleist's topos of the gathering and storing of ejaculate in condoms for use as *phamakon*—and perhaps also for impregnating women?

739   Natalie's "glove" fulfils the same function as Strahl's "case." In this context an obscure passage in a letter to Wilhelmine of September 1800 becomes intelligible: "*Mit welchen Vorgefühlen werde ich das Kuvert betrachten, das* kleine *Gefäß das so vieles in sich schließt! Ach Wilhelmine, in sechs Worten kann alles liegen, was ich zu meiner Ruhe bedarf… ich bin gesund; ich liebe Dich,—und ich will weiter nichts mehr*" (II:564). While *overtly* referring to Wilhelmine's envelopes, *syphilitically* Kleist may be alluding to his reproductive health, telling her that following his successful treatment he shall gather and store his ejaculate in a condom or "small receptacle" (to be used later for Wilhelmine's fertilization?).

740   When in spring 1806 she moved to Stolp in Farther Pomerania, Ulrike expressed the hope that Kleist would soon join her. Kleist was in Prussian employment, and when in Feburary 1806 Prussia was forced to relinquish her Frankish provinces to Bavaria, nullifying Kleist's posting to Ansbach, she may have hoped that he could be allocated an equivalent posting in Stolp (as Kleist's younger brother Leopold indeed would in 1811), whereas in October 1807 Kleist had left his employment. Ulrike, for all her patience with his eccentricities, like the rest of her family always expected him to take a "proper job."

741   Kleist on 25th September announces a trip to Dresden, of which Sembdner doubts (*In Sachen Kleist*, 367) that it took place. I do not know better, but I offer that it is plausible that Kleist (possibly with Henriette) planned such a trip, to survey the precise location for their suicide in the Spreewald, en route to Dresden from Berlin (the destination Dresden could have been a decoy, as he may have wished to hide that he was planning to spend time in the neighbourhood of the family's estates).

742   The third marked text, Klopstock's *Rotschilds Gräber*, may have aimed at Fr. Wilh.: Klopstock composed it as a hymn to his royal patron Fr. V of Denmark on the occasion of the latter's premature death in 1766, aged 42. Fr. Wilh. would turn 42 in August 1812, and since in his wargame with Marwitz Kleist anticipated Fr. Wilh.'s death in mid-October 1811 (cf. II:880), marking Klopstock's royal obituary amounted to a reiteration of his scenario, shifted by one year. Kleist's final message to Fr. Wilh. is two-fold: if Fr. Wilh. in 1812 were to die in heroic resistance to Napoleon, he shall deserve a hymn every bit as celebratory as Klopstock's; conversely, if not, he shall deserve the same fate that befell Fr. V: the Danish King is presumed to have died from syphilis (cf. Bäumler, *Amors vergifteter Pfeil*, 79).

743   For commentary on this event, cf. Wilbrandt (*Kleist*, 259); cf. also Loch (*Beiträge* 1997, 106-8; *Kleist*, 503 n.36). Sembdner fails to identify that third person present (cf. II:1103, entry *Wackern*). Loch simply refers to her as "stranger"; his idea that the sisters' behaviour could have galled Kleist even more in her presence is unconvincing: Kleist did not generally care about the opinion of strangers. "*Die alte Wackern*" may have been Kleist's derogatory reference, akin to "*die alte Wachtel*" ("old maid," "spinster"), to a family member or neighbor. A *Wackerstein*, a bolder deposited on an open field by running water, is curiously similar to a *Findling*, a bolder deposited on an open field by a glacier; in the Grimmian fairy tale *Der Wolf und die sieben Geißlein*, in allusion to the figure of speech "*einem schwer im Magen liegen*," "to sit heavily in one's stomach", the goats fill the sleeping wolf's tummy with heavy, undigestible *Wackersteine* so that when he leans over the edge of a well to drink he is pulled down by their weight and drowns.

744   Klaus Müller-Salget (quoted in Loch, *Kleist*, 501, n.24) seeks to resolve the apparent incongruency between Kleist's generally positive mood at that time and the evidently devastating family get-together by positing that Kleist travelled to Frankfurt/O. one more time in late October, after his hopes for imminent re-employment in the military had been shattered, by which time, Müller-Salget argues, his sisters' reproaches would have been more fitting. His argument is predicated on the crucial letter to Marie being dated early October (MAIII:692) rather than 17th September (II:877), for which I, however, see no reason. What Marie told the King was highly "crafted"and "tailored": she may have purported Kleist's good spirits in late September *precisely* because she wanted to defray any notion that his suicide was closely linked to the King's political decisions of mid-September and after.

745   *The Hanged Man*, depicting a man suspended by one foot from a gallows, is the 12th card of the "Major Arcana"; it represents life in suspension, duty and self-sacrifice, deep entrancement, and the relation between the Divine and the Universe—a suspension between Heaven and Earth—cf. https://en.wikipedia.org/wiki/The_Hanged_Man_(Tarot_card).

746   Cf. Loch's discussion, in *Beiträge* 1997, 79, of Karl Wilh. von Pannwitz's equivalent situation. As of October 1801, upon reaching maturity, Kleist notionally headed a family encompassing the recently divorced Minette (financially independent following her divorce), the unmarried Ulrike (financially independent due to her

inheritance from her mother's side), Auguste (soon to marry Wilh. von Pannwitz), Leopold (then adjujant in Kleist's former Regiment Garde No. 15b), and Juliane. Only the latter had reached neither maturity nor financial independence, though she could live for free in the family's house in Frankfurt/O. or on any of the family's estates. Although his family members thus did not depend on Kleist financially, they will have expected that he appropriately represent the family, perpetuate its name, and pursue a suitable career.

747   I include Henriette Hendel-Schütz despite arguing that Kleist would not have been drawn to her; she may exemplify that despite the increasing urgency of his *filial* aspiration (if not to say: his desperation) Kleist remained choiceful. I do not reproduce the following images: Julie Kunze (e.g., Michalzik, 304ff, Schede, 98), Luise Wieland (e.g., Loch, 165, Schulz, 251), Henriette von Schlieben (e.g., Schede, 70), Sophie Müller (Schulz, 331). I could not find images of Luise von Linckersdorf, Caroline von Schlieben and Sophie Sander. "Kleist's "filial" issue was, of course, an ancient one. Juvenal notes regarding gay men or "pansies" (*Satire II*,137-8, trans. Peter Green): "But still they have one large painful problem: they can't hang on to their 'husbands' by producing babies."

748   The 6th century BC lyrical poetress Sappho has come to represent female homosexuality (the term *lesbian* derives from the name of her home island of Lesbos), but in Old Comedy and later Attic comedy she is frequently caricatured as a promiscuous *heterosexual* woman—she may have been, with Kleist, "amphibian." Sappho is held to have performed her poetry in a circle of female friends and to have been a teacher or cult-leader for them; she may have been a lover of the lyric poet Alcaeus (Alkaios), exiled to Lesbos and like Sappho considered one of ancient Greece's nine canonical lyrical poets, with whom she may have collaborated on poetry (they are repeatedly depicted in artwork performing poetry together). Sappho was later exiled to Sicily, where she may have committed suicide by jumping off a cliff. Franz Alex. von Kleist published a dramatic poem, *Sappho*, and Kleist's teacher Samuel Heinr. Catel trans. Sappho's works (of which only one complete poem, *Ode to Aphrodite*, and fragments are extant). Kleist quotes from the former's poem (a dialogue on virtue involving Sappho and Alcaeus) in *Aufsatz* (Kreutzer's verdict, in *Dichterische Entwicklung*, 49; 110, that Kleist overlooked or willfully neglected the passage's "panerotic" atmosphere, is outlandish).

749   Ulrike was the only family member to whom Kleist may have been (almost) entirely open; in May 1799 he writes her: *"Du bist die einzige die mich hier ganz versteht... Deine Mitwissenschaft meiner ganzen Eempfindungsweise, Deine Kenntnis meiner Natur schützt sie um so mehr vor ihrer Ausartung"* (II:487; the term *"Ausartung"* is suggestive).

750   Rudolf Loch unearthes a telling entry by Ulrike into Ernst von Schönfeld's album, dated 17th November 1794, encompassing the caption *"Erinnerungen der wichtigsten Scenen unsers Lebens"* and, on the facing page, an ink drawing of a young man before a litter or sedan chair, a money belt in hand, and four young women lined up before the entrance of a house, the first two reaching out to the man (cf. *Beiträge* 1997,96). Of the five girls in Kleist's immediate family—Wilhelmine (Minette), Ulrike, Friederike (Fritz), Auguste (Gustel) and Juliane (Julchen)—, as of 1794 Minette had married Ernst von Loeschbrand and the other four remained unmarried, so that plausibly the four maidens receiving the man represent Kleist's unmarried sisters, lined up by age (Ulrike first, followed by Fritz, Gustel and Julchen). The man's arrival signifies that one of them is about to be married, yet the important detail is that not only the first in line, Ulrike, reaches for him, but also the second in line, Fritz, who indeed in 1794 married Philipp von Stojentin. In short, Ulrike's album entry depicts how she *is passed over for marriage* as her younger sister Fritz marries the man arriving before their house. As the caption suggests, this was a defining moment in Ulrike's life: passed over for marriage at her prime marriable age, her guardians, Uncle Pannwitz and Aunt Massow (represented by the house), permitting this to happen, and her remaining two younger stisters already lining up next to her, this inconspicuous drawing puts in a nutshell the moment in which Ulrike turned her back on married life.

751   Helma Sanders-Brahms in her 1977 film *Heinrich* depicts Kleist and Ulrike in an incestuous relationship. Prevailing incest laws in Germany prohibited marriage between half-siblings; in ancient Athens, whose conventions were closer to Kleist's heart, marriage among half-siblings was legal if they had different mothers, as is the case with him and Ulrike. Re Apollo and Artemis, Burkert notes in *Greek Religion*, 219: "As a brother-sister pair free from sexual tensions—though these are hinted at in an apocryphal myth [*Orphicorum Fragmenta*]—Apollo and Artemis are particularly closely associated in the Greek mind... as the archetype of adolescent youth." They are, respectively, master and mistress of bow and arrow, representatives *par excellence*

of Kleist's favourite accolade *"vortrefflich,"* i.e., excellent in hitting a target (and in avoiding the tragic error—*harmatia*—of missing the target). Apollo signifies both healing and plague; the inviolable virgin Artemis is both protectress of childbirth and she who threatens with her arrows every girl that fulfills her womanly destiny (cf. Burkert, *ibid*, 151). Kleist and Ulrike in 1801 in Paris saw Abélard and Héloïse's urn at the Musée des monuments français (today L'École nationale supérieure des beaux-arts, cf. II:703; it was since transferred to Père Lachèse—had he been able to see their tomb there, erected in 1817, Kleist might have been amused by its depiction of the castrated Abélard and the female Héloïse pressing their hands together in prayer before their abdomen such that they can scarcely fail to evoke an observer's Freudian fantasy of erect *phalloi*).

752   There is a tradition in the *Kleist-Forschung*, since Tieck and Bülow, of blaming those closest to Kleist for withholding information; Ulrike, Marie, Rühle and Pfuel are usually named the chief culprits; Rahmer also notes (*Kleist*, 128) that Fouqué in his autobiography is "surprisingly reticent and cool about this phase of his life." The old Pfuel, whom Bülow interviewed in person for his 1848 Kleist biography, is furthermore declared unreliable. Yet the reasons for their silence, recitence or apparent unreliability should be obvious: they *knew too much* about Kleist—as it were, *den ganzen Schmutz zugleich und Glanz*—, and they were *themselves implicated in* his exploits. That Kleist's best friends remained loyal to him till the very end merely proves that they *truly were* his best friends. When Pfuel, in a swipe at A. Müller and others, in the aftermath of Kleist's suicide told Caroline de la Motte Fouqué (cf. *NR*,63) that some of Kleist's friends had been Christians firstly, friends secondly, whereas he himself remained Kleist's friend firstly, Christian secondly, he could just as well have said that he remained Kleist's friend firstly, contributor to the *Kleist-Forschung* secondly. If he indeed spread "fake news" about Kleist (it is not actually clear to me that he did), he may have done so not due to his senility but as deliberate camouflage. Naturally, we tend to mourn what has been lost, but we ought to celebrate what has been saved, and close-knit friendships with "brothers" and "sisters" having been integral to Kleist's life and work, ought to appreciate that if we had everything he wrote to his closest friends at our fingertips, our situation would no longer be "Kleistian" but "Goethean" (of Goethe, it appears, we practically know what he had for breakfast every day). Mystery is the wellspring of fascination; and were there not such gaps, this book would not exist, for it would not have been needed.

753　　Judging by a portrait of her provided by her great-nice Helene von Hülsen, Adolphine could have been Kleist's "kinda girl": *"Ungewöhnliche Schärfe des Verstandes, Güte des Herzens, eigenartige Lebensverhältnisse und Schicksale hatten diesen Charaktere so originell und scharf ausgeprägt, daß er der Mehrzahl der Fernerstehenden ein unlösbares Problem blieb, und selbst in ihrem engeren Familienkreise oft nicht verstanden wurde. In den Kreisen des Hofes ihres oft beißenden Witzes halber mehr gefürchtet als geliebt und bewundert, zeigte Adolfine von dem Knesebeck ihr warmes, für alle, die sie liebte, so opferfähiges Herz nur wenigen in seinem ganzen Reichtume."* (cf. https://de.wikipedia.org/wiki/Adolphine_von_Klitzing).

754　　We are indebted to Rudolf Loch, who more than other Kleist biographers shed light on the *"terra incognita"* (Loch) of Kleist's family context and youth. His excellent detective work is not always matched by soundness of interpretation: he claims that Kleist's album entry for Luise von Linckersdorf expresses "high moral standards" (*Kleist*, 432, n.72), which is evidently misguided: Kleist's objective is to get Luise to permit him to sodomise her, and possibly to agree to sodomise him with a dildo.

869

755　　A passage in her letter to Kleist of April 1802 (which he left unopened), *"ob Du noch unter den Sterblichen wandlest oder vielleicht auch schon die engen Kleider dieser Welt mit bessern vertauscht habest"* (II:721), suggests that Wilhelmine appreciated, and perhaps shared, his *orphical* outlook.

756　　Cf. Rahmer, *Kleist*, 51: *"Karl von Zenge war in Berlin in den ersten Jahren von Kleists Anwesenheit der vertrauteste und tägliche Umgang mit Kleist; das beweisen zahlreiche Andeutungen in den Briefen an seine Braut, und dafür spricht die Tatsache, daß Kleist, wie aus dem Briefe vom 11. Januar 1801 zweifellos hervorgeht, mit Zenge sein Zimmer gemeinsam innehatte. Karl v. Zenge starb ganz plötzlich am 30. Januar 1802, und Wilhelmine teilte Kleist den Tod am 10. April nach der Schweiz mit."*

757　　Cf. Rahmer, *Kleist*, 74. Rahmer suggests (*Kleist*, 76) that the two travelers picked the nondescript Saxon town of Öderan for a stop-over en route to Würzburg because Brockes was to secretly meet Cäcilie von Werthern there.

758   Reuß and Staengle exclude this letter, presumably because they do not accept its attribution to Kleist; I side with Sembdner, whose notes on the matter strike me as eminently plausible.

759   Kleist was obsessed with "handicraft," as I pointed out in *Emigrant* re passages in *Marquise* and *Findling*. A *BA* article (cf. II:398-9) about handicraft productions at a Christmas market, *"Es hat etwas Rührendes, das man nicht beschreiben kann, wenn man in diese Zimmer tritt; Scham, Armut und Fleiß haben hier, in durchwachten Nächten, beim Schein der Lampe, die Wände mit allem was prächtig oder zierlich oder nützlich sein mag, für die Bedürfnisse der Begüterten, ausgeschmückt. Es ist, als sähe man die vielen tausend kleinen niedlichen Hände sich regen,"* may entail a homage to the Schlieben sisters.

760   Cf. Sloterdijk (*Kritik*, 316-17): *"Der Kyniker kündigt also die landläufige Gängelung durch die tief eingefleischten Schamgebote... Das politische Tier durchbricht die Politik der Schamhaftigkeit... Mit seiner öffentlichen Onanie beging [Diogenes] eine Schamlosigkeit, mit der er sich in Opposition brachte zu den politischen Tugenddressuren aller Systeme"* [Sloterdijk in a footnote refers to Diogenes' formula *"die Münze umprägen"* and Nietzsche's *"Umwertung aller Werte"*]. When Sloterdijk notes (*ibid*) that Diogenes' public masturbation was "a frontal attack against all family politics" and that "sexual independence remains one of the premier conditions for emancipation," he inadvertently hits on Kleist's limits as *kynic*: his family values *were* traditional, and his sexual dependencies, e.g. on Müller, *did* restrain him—cf. the *BA* affair.

761   While it is *possible* that the Schlieben sisters were specimens of Michalzik's "well-behaved, virtuous type of woman" (*Kleist*, 222), *probable* it is not. Michalzik says the same of Wilhelmine (*ibid*), who was evidently *not* of that type, and we had better not trust his judgment in such matters. Many Kleist scholars stubbornly assume that all the women Kleist came across, as well as all the female characters appearing in his works, were invariably innocent wallflowers. Of course, we should not assume with similar automatism the opposite to necessarily be true, but we ought to allow that the "women around Kleist" (Sembdner) must have had a penchant for the extraordinary, by virtue of their sticking "around" this weirdo. Sembdner's list (*LS*, p.10) is incomplete, though he deserves credit for discerning the pattern; my own list is bound to be incomplete as well: Kleist, after all, *was* a master of camouflage, and so were many of these women. A *Social History of Camouflage*, it seems, is still to be

written—if one day it is, Kleist and the "women [and men] around Kleist" deserve a central section.

762   Lose was evidently more important to Kleist than Caroline—cf. his note to Lose appended to a letter by Caroline of April 1803 (II:731-2). His chosen form of transmission forced Kleist to heavily camouflage his message; as aid to Lose, who may not have been as familiar with Kleist's techniques as a Brockes, Rühle or Pfuel, the bracketed *"Du verstehst mich"* marks the "navel" from which he is to unravel Kleist's meaning: "if you believe it to be condusive to your wholehearted commitment to our love affair (*"mit freier Bewegung Deiner Kräfte wenigstens Dir allein..."*) to let go of Caroline, please do." The original "Siamese twins" Chang and Eng Bunker in 1843 married sisters; the two couples shared a bed built for four and between them produced 22 or 23 children. Had the Schlieben girls joined Kleist and Lose in Switzerland, Kleist might have sent notice to Wilhelmine that she need not come.

763   Müller in early 1805, when both men lived near each other in Dresden, seeing each other regularly, instigated Gentz to a similar gift exchange: *"Da ich meine eigene Tabakdose verloren habe, werden Sie wohl die Freundschaft haben, mich mit der Ihrigen hierbei erfolgenden, angefüllt zurückzugebenen, zu unterstützen, auf acht Tage etwa"* (AML,94); in my "trans.": "after eight days [in which I cannot see you], please return to me the enclosed condom filled with your daily *cum* [so that I can be sure that you did not waste it on anyone else]."

764   Wieland's letter of 24th June 1804, in which he gives Kleist solace (cf. II:739), is not extant, but we imagine that it was similarly encouraging as that of July 1803 (II:733-4). I do not concur with Sembdner that Wieland "unequivocally abandoned" Kleist, a contention based primarily on Wieland's remark to Falk concerning Ph No.3 (cf. LS,264), to the effect that of this issue's content all that is *true* is already known, and all that is *new* is trite. The issue contains four items, of which two were already known—Kleist's *Krug* and Fouqué's *Pelegrin* fragment—, thus fall into the "true but known" category; the other two, Kleist's two fables and Müller's lecture on the beautiful, then, make up the "new but trite" category. Especially in light of the powerful *Guiskard* recitation he had witnessed at Oßmannstedt, Wieland can be forgiven for not getting overly excited about Kleist's clever but vindictive veiled attacks, in his fables, on critics such as K.A. Böttiger; nevertheless, as much as the old-fashioned, straight-line Wieland may have disdained these childish games, he will

not have discounted Kleist's genius merely on the basis of a few lines of spite. And what he was given to read and see of *Krug*—Wieland presumably was present at the failed performance under Goethe's directorship, cf. *LS*,246—may not have matched what he heard of *Guiskard*, but nevertheless he put *Krug* into the "true but known" category—reflecting perhaps no rousing endorsement, but no "abandonment" either. Wieland clearly considers *Ph* a bad idea, or a good idea badly executed, but he does not mention Kleist by name, and the primary target of his cricitism is the "morosphic" "philosophical Pulcinella" A. Müller. After Kleist's death, Wieland would refer to him as *"eines der genievollsten und edelsten Sterblichen"* (*NR*,85a), and we have no reason to doubt that he meant it. I maintain, therefore, that Wieland did not "abandon" Kleist, but perhaps neglected him, and upon his death came to regret that he had not paid more attention to him when he needed it most. It may in fact be closer to the truth to say that Kleist "abandoned" Wieland, especially after Wieland, together with Goethe, met Napoleon at *Erfurt* and received, from the Emperor's hand, the *Chevalier de la Légion d'Honneur*.

765   Michalzik takes note of Bülow's report without exploring it further; Loch, Schulz and Blamberger ignore it. As an aside, in *Emigrant* (pp.43-9) I speculated (on the basis of parallels between Brentano's novel *Godwi* and Kleist's letters of that period) that Kleist during the Würzburg journey could have met Clemens Brentano at Savigny's Trages estate near Hanau. If so, he could even have met Karoline there as well, as she regularly spent time at Trages during that period (to this day the small house on the estate in which she used to stay is called Karoline-von-Günderrode Haus).

766   In 1801 Karoline writes Kunigunde Brentano: "*Nur das Wilde, Große, Glänzende gefällt mir. Es ist ein unseliges, aber unverbesserliches Mißverhältnis in meiner Seele; und es wird und muß so bleiben, denn ich bin ein Weib und habe Begierden wie ein Mann, ohne Männerkraft. Darum bin ich so wechselnd und uneins mit mir*" (https://de.wikipedia.org/wiki/Karoline_von_Günderrode). Creuzer was perhaps unprepared to divorce his wife not least because he could not imagine Karoline fitting into married life and a professorial household; at one point he explored a *ménage à trois*, though it would scarcely have been reconcilable with his staid public persona in Heidelberg: "[Creuzer] *spielte mit dem Gedanken an eine* ménage à trois: *'Meine Frau sollte bei uns zu bleiben wünschen – als Mutter, als Führerin unseres Hauswesens. Frei und poetisch sollte Ihr Leben sein,' schlug er Karoline vor. Es war die Zeit neuer Entwürfe*

des Zusammenlebens. So steht Creuzers Utopie in Beziehung zu den revolutionären Vorstellungen, wie sie zur gleichen Zeit in Frankreich Henri de Saint-Simon und sein Freundeskreis zu leben versuchten. Von einigen Kennern der Zeit wird sie gleichwohl als Charakterschwäche eingestuft – der kränkliche Friedrich Creuzer hatte nicht den Mut, sich von seiner Frau zu trennen" (ibid).

767   Karoline's book will have been published either at Frankfurt/M.'s 1804 spring or autumn book fair; if the former, her putative meeting with Kleist could have been coloured by this event. Savigny's wedding will have been announced, and she will have been aware of his engagement in May 1803. Kleist had reasons for leaving Mainz and traveling homewards: his brother Leopold was set to marry on 20th June, and he had to present himself, sooner or later, before the authorities in Berlin to redeem himself (and his family name) following his Saint-Omer adventure, which he did, from 22nd June onwards. However, there is no known reason for him to leave Mainz already in April. Since we know that he was apt to change tack suddenly, it is not out of the question that Karoline's falling for Creuzer triggered his departure. The end of the Enghien affair and the announcement of Napoleon's coronation may have been *satirical* triggers, and Karoline is not a *necessary* factor in his departure, but a plausible one.

768   Fictional accounts of Kleist's and Karoline's acquaintance have been offered in Christa Wolf's 1979 tale *Kein Ort. Nirgens* and in Rainer Rubbert's and Tanja Langer's 2008 opera *Kleist*; in the former, the two meet in 1804 at a tea party in Winkel, at which Bettine Brentano is also present and which they excape for a long walk together; in the latter, they meet in 1806 at Bettine's salon, where they discuss death (Karoline already carries the dagger under her dress with which she will soon kill herself).

769   Cf. this quote of Karoline's: "Wer irgendeine Art von Religion zur Stütze seiner Sittlichkeit bedarf, dessen Moralität ist nicht rein, denn diese muss ihrer Natur nach in sich selbst bestehen" (https://hpd.de/node/3802).

770   Rahmer maintains (*Kleist*, 33-4) that Emma was "Pfuel's girl." There clearly was extensive jockeying for positions in the Körner household, among the "brothers" as well as "sisters."

771 In *Cäcilie* a gang of male foxes ("iconoclasts"), high on testosterone and alcohol, seeks to wreak havoc in a nearby henhouse ("convent") but is overwhelmed by the hens' ("nuns'") powerful audio-visual orgiastic "performance," orchestrated and directed by the irresistible "Antonia." Picture *that*!

772 Rahmer believes (*Kleist*, 369) that Kleist demanded that Julie correspond with him without her parents' knowledge, and when she hesitated, broke up with her. While possible, it is perhaps more likely that Kleist demanded that she have unorthodox sex with him, and she refused. Rahmer also offers (*ibid*, 370) that two "mean" (his term) *Ph* epigrams, nos. 30 & 31, refer to Julie, which is more plausible in the case of the former than the latter: if no. 30 refers to Julie, Kleist makes with it makes it clear that it was he who broke their (quasi-) engagement; no. 31 may plausibly refer to another "hen" in the Körner household—say, Emma—, for by the time the June issue was distributed, Julie was already married, so that the epigram, if it referred to her, would have been outdated and hence for Kleist no longer publishable (unless Julie's marriage was arranged secretly and Kleist was unaware).

773 Kleist's trans./rewriting of Lafontaine's fable *Die Beiden Tauben* falls into the Dresden period. Kleist turns Lafontaine's two cock pigeons into a cock and a squab, and relates how the cock (presumably Kleist himself) repeatedly passes over *male lovers* ("ignoring all towers") in his quest for a *female mate* ("the other grotto"), yet consistently fails in his attempts and ultimately despairs. While the first of the "squabs" Kleist reminisces about may well have represented Wilhelmine, as her husband Krug intuited, the others presumably allude to Kleist's other exploits during this period.

774 Goethe visited Körner's house during this period and took note of the divorce (cf. *LS*,308b). Loch (*Kleist*, 485) considers Ulrike's claim that Kleist sought to prevent the divorce "highly questionable," but it made sense if he was loath to lose A. Müller; what is clear is that Kleist would not have travelled all the way to the Hazas' family estate at Lewitz, near Posen, out of pure disinterested kindness. Kleist's trip to Lewitz is sufficiently mysterious to encourage us to consider other plausible purposes: for example, if Kleist had completed *Herrmannsschlacht*, he may have circulated it to select addressees to test its insurrectionary potential, while evading the Dresden censors' radar screen by going to the remote Prussian province for a while, sitting out and monitoring initial reactions at a safe distance.

775   Rahmer notes (*Kleist*, 34) that Pfuel frequented the Haza household during this period; since in March 1808 he had married Caroline von Byern, he would likely not have been a rival for Sophie.

776   The letter to Sophie (cf. II:885-6) is friendly, but writing it made Kleist feel "singular." The BA anecdote *Der Griffel Gottes* could entail a prophecy that Sophie's bringing down his "brotherhood" (by taking Müller from him) would one day be revealed. Kleist may have immortalised Sophie von Haza in two of his figures: in the irresistible Antonia in *Cäcilie* (Antonia = *"die den Ton angibt,"* "she who calls the tune") whose "somnambulistic surety" as a "organist" becomes the bane of the "brotherhood" (the iconoclasts), and in the no less irresistible *femme fatale* Littegarde in *Zweikampf*, who is the bone of contention in Rotbart's and Trota's contest, poisons (I argue in *Emigrant*) Rotbart by infecting the tip of Trota's "sword," and precipitates Trota's enslavement. Rotbart = Kleist; Trota = Müller; Littegarde = Sophie: could this be the autobiographical constellation depicted in Kleist's final novella?

777   Cf. Rahel to Varnhagen in 1812 (*NR*,52d): *"Ich kenne nichts Elenderes, als so bis Sechzig hinan zu warten; mit Hoffnung... Freunde lassen es geschehen. Erschöss' ich mich: wunderten sie sich, wie über Kleist."* Rahel died in 1833, aged 62, of a natural death. According to Hannah Arendt, who wrote her habilitation about Rahel's life, Rahel sought to escape her Jewishness by assimilation, not least by getting off with non-Jewish men, in particular aristocratic ones—among them Karl von Finckenstein, Gentz and Varnhagen. And, one wonders, Kleist? It certainly suited Kleist if a prospective bride had her own agenda for a liaison with him, such as the desire to "go legit"—be it as a lesbian or, in Rahel's case, a Jewess. Kleist may have been awkward, gay, ill and poor, but he was still a Prussian aristocrat with an impeccable family name—no small asset in the marketplace for weddable women.

778   The late 18th/early 19th century salons could be said to have marked the beginnings in Germany of what we today term "open society": modelled on Parisian precursors and often hosted by highly educated women for the purpose of networking, education and high-brow entertainment, these remarkable institutions were a product of a time in which women's roles were still largely confined to the household, but in which highly educated ones began to assert themselves and widen their social role by inviting outsiders into their household. Salons were crossroads at which aristocrats and commoners, men and women, Christians and Jews met, transcending traditional

classes and gender roles. Leading salonières in Vienna, Berlin and Dresden would continue to exert significant influence on the intellectual life of their respective cities into the early 20th century.

779   Cf. *"Bekannte Habitués,"* https://de.wikipedia.org/wiki/Elisabeth_von_Staegemann.

780   Hedwrig von Olfers, née Staegemann, *Ein Lebenslauf*—cf. https://de.wikipedia.org/wiki/Friedrich_August_von_Staegemann.

781   Cf. *LS*,427b. Among Cäcilie's godfathers and mothers were Arnim, Pfuel, Kleist, Beckedorff, Buol, Kunigunde von Savigny, Wilhelmina von Sommerfeldt, Johanna von Peguilhen, and others.

782   Cf. II:862; cf. also II:860 and *LS*,489a-e. In 1814 Henriette H.-S. would give another performance of *Penthesilea* (cf. *NR*,601;601a). Kleist may have been lukewarm about his drama being performed as pantomime: as *"Sprechtheater"* or *"Lesedrama,"* it depended on the spoken word to get his messages (and poetic genius) across. Kleist disdained actors who replaced declamatory skill with gesticulation—cf. his satire of Iffland's "hands." Rahmer offers (*Kleist*, 374) that Kleist and Henriette H.-S. could have met already in Dresden in 1807/8, and that certain letters of his, whose addressee is uncertain, could have been to her; I consider it unlikely that Kleist wasted time on her, in Dresden or Berlin.

783   Kleist's headless flight to Peguilhen's house may have informed episoded in *Verlobung*, where Gustav makes a beeline for a friend's house across the Rhine after precipitating Mariane's execution, and *Findling*, where Piachi seeks refuge in Valerio's bed after killing Nicolo.

784   Rahmer notes (*Kleist*, 341) that emancipated and domineering women repelled Kleist—a category into which Henriette H.-S. evidently belonged. Kleist's disdain at the actress' self-indulgence shines through in his acerbic response to her invitation to meet her in person before the performance (cf. II:860); to her "offer" to "educate" him in certain "arts" he sarcastically retorts that it shall be his pleasure to "trace her footprints in the sand."

785   During this period in Berlin Kleist lived in Fr. von Massenbach's house at Markgrafenstraße 61 and the Vogels lived virtually next door (cf. Häker, *Beiträge*, 130).

786   Whether Henriette suffered from cervical or vaginal cancer remains unclear: the reports from her doctors are inconclusive and contradictory, and the autopsy report unreliable, for it was commissioned to make the medical facts fit the King's official statement. What mattered most in this respect is that Henriette evidently *made Kleist believe* that she could no longer become mother to his son, otherwise he might have deferred the double suicide. It is, then, indeed possible that Henriette contributed to his death by deliberately misleading him about her health.

787   Piattoli refers to a Marquis', Chodowiecka to a famous engraver's widow. And the third woman mentioned by Körner?—Marie? Elisabeth? another? Re the rumours of their love affair, cf. *NR*,2; 2a; 2d; 3; 4b; 4e; 5a; 5b; 14; 15; 16a; 58. Re the widely held perception of their "mysticism," cf. *NR*,3; 5c; 7b; 19; 19a; 19b; 20a; 24).

788   Rahmer points out (*Kleist*, 144) that in Kleist's circles divorces featured as prominently as suicides. He asks in how far these occurances may have influenced Kleist, but fails to ask, conversely, in how far Kleist was drawn to such situations or even fostered them. In the cases of Aug. Ferd. Bernardi and the von Hazas, Kleist is known to have assisted in the divorce proceedings, be that because he had an interest in fostering, or in preventing, the divorce.

789   In Robert Löhr's 2007 novel *Das Erlkönig-Manöver*, Bettine (not Karoline) is the female protagonist in a fictional 1805 plot pursued by several German writers—Goethe, Schiller, Kleist, A. von Humboldt, Arnim—to free the Dauphin from a Mainz prison and re-install him to the French throne. Bettine in 1810 together with the Savignys undertook extensive travels to Vienna and Prague, which may explain why she does not appear more prominently in Kleist's biography. Kleist in October 1810 ruffled Brentano and Arnim's feathers (the former's more than the latter's) by effectively hijacking their *BA* article on Friedrich's *Mönch* (cf. II:839: "*Machen Sie doch den Brentano wieder gut, lieber Arnim*").

790   Kleist could have targeted other married couples for his scheme—say, Müller and Sophie von Haza, Fouqué and Caroline von Rochow—; I have not seen evidence that would suggest that these married ladies would have been so inclined, but I have not explored this in detail.

791   *The Sun*, featuring a young boy with a red flag riding a white horse before an anthropomorphised sun (in some decks depicted as Apollo), represents attained knowledge, accomplishment, renewal and optimism—cf. https://en.wikipedia.org/wiki/The_Sun_(Tarot_card).

792   Blamberger's conclusion (*Kleist*, 461), "*Kleists Todesbereitschaft ist... keine Jenseits-, sondern eine Diesseitsfeier. Von religiösem Trost angesichts des Todes kann bei Kleist keine Rede sein*," contradicts the evidence, and his assertion (*ibid*, 463), "*Freitod wird uns als Ausdruck eines destruktiven Characters begreiflich..., der Freiheit als einen Akt begreift, der die eigene Selbsterhaltung notwendig verletzten muss. Wobei der destruktive Akt zugleich ein schöpferischer Akt ist*," leaves us, with Goethe's Faust, "*so klug als wie zuvor*."

793   Kreutzer is quoted by Siebert, *Kleistiana Collecta*, 166. Ilse Graham, in a reading of Kleist heavily coloured by her own Christian faith, concludes (*Word into Flesh*, 2): "I have a picture [of Kleist] of stressful greatness and a power of assault deriving, precisely, from unspirituality and dogged immanence." Her "green glasses" make it nigh impossible for her to consider that Kleist could have possessed a spirituality and transcendence that was not Christian. Fouqué, who will have known better, terms Kleist "*nicht ohne Ahnung von Religion*" (NR,55b).

794   Re the latter point, cf. Sembdner, *In Sachen Kleist*, 147. Sembdner (*ibid*) calls Homburg's "*Todeserlebnis*" the drama's "*Brennpunkt*" and takes note of other metaphors of metempsychosis in Kleist's works, e.g., "*einen der Millionen Tode, die wir schon gestorben sind*," "*aus einem Zimmer in das andere*." Parabolic mirror, rear gate, tree of knowledge, threshold between rooms are all metaphors of the threshold between life on Earth and life on another planet, as are *Schroffenstein*'s grotto, *Erdbeben*'s pomegranate tree, *Käthchen*'s ordeal by fire, *Zweikampf*'s duel, *Homburg*'s gaping tomb. From the perspective of Kleist's faith in metempsychosis, Ottokar and Agnes, Jeronimo and Josephe, and Rotbart are the lucky ones—they die and their souls are freed—, whereas Käthchen, Trota and Homburg are the unlucky ones— they are condemned to eternal suspension. In the rare instances in which characters representing Napoleon die—Guiskard (about to), the Marchese, Piachi—, they appear to be exempted from metempsychosis: of Guiskard it is said that his bones will be unearthed by his successor, and of the Marchese that his bones are scattered around the castle, both images suggesting that their soul remains restless; of Piachi it is said that he rots in hell.

795 Cf. Michalzik, *Kleist*, 76; 96. Loch (*Kleist*, 50) quotes from Wünsch's 1791/4 treatise *Kosmologische Unterhaltungen*, which underpinned his lectures: "*Durch wissenschaftliche Beschäftigung, so lehrte er—und er faßte diese als sittlich bildende 'erhabene Betrachung[en]' auf—, begreife der 'nach göttlichem Bilde geschaffene Geist des Menschen' in der 'ewig unveränderlichen und schönen Harmonie' der Natur, welche die Gottheit nach ihren Gesetzen leite, deren 'gütiges Wesen* [...] *als eine[r] durch allmächtiges Wollen hervorgebrachte[n] und zusammengeordnete[n] Schöpfung', und er sei angehalten, diese 'immer näher zu durchforschen, zu bewundern und anzubeten.*" Wünsch also authored the notorious *Horus*, anonymously published in Leipzig in 1783, seized by the authorities and publicly burned, in which he seeks to explain Jesus Christ's miracles scientifically (cf. Loch, *Kleist*, 437, n.18; Horus, hero of the *Osiris Myth*, was integral to Egyptian and Greek conceptions of kingship, succession and the afterlife—cf. Plutarch, *De Iside et Osiride*). Neither Kleist nor Ulrike appear to have adhered strictly to their family's Protestant faith; nor were they drawn to Catholicism, as were A. Müller and other prominent Romantics (Kleist was fascinated by Catholicism's magnetic force, less by its doctrines). In May 1799 Kleist tells Ulrike: "*Etwas muß dem Menschen heilig sein. Uns beide, denen es die Zeremonien der Religion und die Vorschriften des konventionellen Wohlstandes nicht sind, müssen um so mehr die Gesetze der Vernunft heilig sein*" (II:491).

796 Cf. Schulz, *Kleist*, 560, n.169. Stephens is responding to Schulz's inquiry, who notes that Kleist's utterance is situated in the context of *Guiskard*, in which Ulrike, as his financier, indeed had a "stake." Kleist could well have been intrigued by Melpomene, mother of several Sirens, and Thalia, Muse of Comedy and Idyllic Poetry and mother of the *Corybantes*, self-castrated dancers who performed at the annual Spartan *gymnopaidiai*, the "Feast of the naked (or unarmed) youths," itself linked to pederast symposia, though in both cases not primarily in the context of his "religion."

797 Gernot Müller suggests that *Prolog* "represents a distorted contrafactum to Schiller's poem '*Die Künstler*' in which Urania... occupies the place of Kleist's thundering God of the arts" (*Gemälde*, 145). Kleist may well have expected his audiences to discern a *covert* Urania veiled by the *overt* Phoebus; the frontispiece's partial zodiac points to Urania (Muse of Astronomy) rather than Phoebus. According to some sources, Urania and Apollo together produced Linus, the master of eloquent speech.

798 In *Die Liebe und die Freude* Venus Urania concludes that spiritual and sensual love comprise a single entity: "*Ist nur ein einzig, euch unnennbar Wesen, / ... Wir Götter flieh'n euch nicht, denn Lieb' und Freude / Ruht überall, wenn euer Herz nur hört*" (quoted in Bülow, *Kleist*, 256-9). The term "Uranian," denoting a person of a third sex, specifically someone with "a female psyche in a male body" and sexually attracted to men, appeared in publication only in the 1860s, but could have been current before; the epithet Aphrodite Urania refers to Aphrodite's having been created out of Uranus' testicles. Basilius von Ramdohr in 1798 published a work in three vols. entitled *Venus Urania*.

799 Of the Catholic convert A. Müller Gentz in January 1803 notes in his diary: "*Unter anderem sagte ich ihm in einer nächtlichen Unterredung über die Unsterblichkeit der Seele, sein System habe an mir den Tod überwunden*" (*AML*,42; cf. also Gentz to Brinkmann: "*je me sentais véritablement* avoir vaincu la mort," *AML*,82, and Zimmermann, *Kleist*, 272). Karl Chr. Fr. Krause developed a universal utopian humanism ("*Krausismo*") that encompassed not only the residents of Earth but also those of other planets (cf. Jakob Baxa's note to *AML*,240; cf. also II:421); Fr. Schlegel, in *Von der Philosophie* (1799), elaborates a "*System der Seelenwanderung und Emanation*", which A. Müller refers to in a letter to Fr. Gentz of May 1808 (cf. *AML*,318 and Jakob Baxa's notes thereto); Kleist appears to first have met Schlegel in 1801, via Adolphine's mediation (cf. II:679). Zimmermann (*Kleist*, 258) quotes Schubert's memoir, *Der Erwerb aus einem vergangenen und die Erwartungen von einem zukünftigen Leben*, in which Schubert recalls that among A. Müller's circle, Kleist was most fascinated by his deliberations (*NR* misses this quote). Mesmerism may have intrigued Kleist not only as therapeutic method but also as a technique for simulating metempsychosis: the connection between the mesmerised state and the experience of metempsychosis is explored by E.A. Poe in the 1849 short story "Mesmeric Revelation" (*Complete Stories and Poems*, 505-13), in which a Mr Vankirk, suffering from tuberculosis for many years, is mesmerised by his doctor "P" (Poe?), and before he expires, in mesmeric trance, anticipates his soul's transformation from "rudimental, primitive, organic, mortal life" on Earth to "ultimate, complete, inorganic, unorganised, immortal life" detached from an existence on Earth and the suffering it entails; "P," by his bedside, is left wondering whether he just witnessed metempsychosis (one of Poe's metaphors occuring this story, of "the worm and the butterfly," anticipates Deleuze's "larval and actualised subject"). Poe's report would have suited Kleist: "[mesmerism's] startling *facts* are now almost universally admitted... that man, by mere exercise of will, can so

impress his fellow, as to cast him into an abnormal condition, in which the phenomena resemble very closely those of *death*...; that while in this state, the person so impressed employs only with effort, and then feebly, the external organs of sense, yet perceives, with keenly refined perception, and through channels supposed unknown, matters beyond the scope of the physical organs; that, moreover, his intellectual faculties are sonderfully exalted and invigorated; that his sympathies with the person so impressed him are profound... pleasure, in all cases, is but the contrast of pain. *Positive* pleasure is a mere idea. To be happy at any one pont we must have suffered at the same. Never to suffer would have been never to have been blessed. But... in the inorganic life, pain cannot be; thus the necessity for the organic. The pain of the primitive life of Earth, is the sole basis of the bliss of the ultimate life of Heaven." Syphilis is among several plausible causes for Poe's premature death at 40 considered in the literature.

800   Kleist refers to Phythagoras repeatedly: in his *satyrical* recourse to the "Pythagorean rule" in *Krug* (V.1530-3); in his allusion to a passage in *As You Like It* (Act 4), in which Shakespeare relates Pythagoras' admonition that the soul of the poulty about to be slaughtered could be one's aunt's (*BA*, 16th October 1810; cf. II:328; perhaps Kleist here gleefully imagined that the poultry about to be slaughtered hosted Aunt Massow's); in his report from Paris concerning a poetic Pythagorean mathematics in the *BA*'s *Fragment eines Schreibens aus Paris*: *"An Louvre fand ich letzthin eine Mathematik in zwölf Gesängen angekündigt. Der Verfasser hatte die algebraischen Formeln und Gleichungen gereimt; als z.B.: "Donc le quarré de cinq est égal, à la fois, / A la somme de ceux de quatre et de trois"* (i.e., $5^2 = 4^2 + 3^2$); in his reference to "the wise men of Greece" who teach spherical harmony, i.e., Pythagoras' school (II:569); perhaps in *Amphiitryon*'s Thebes: forced to flee from Croton, Southern Italy, in c.501 BC, the Pythagoreans based themselves in that city—cf. Quigley, *Evolution*, 299; 312: "The critics and enemies of democracy and of the whole Athenian way of life... especially the Pythagoreans, the defenders of nobility, of oligarchy, and of the state's authority, the admirers of Sparta, and the enemies of science... the nucleus of this revived oligarchic movement came from the Pythagorean refugees in Thebes." Phythagoreanism overlapped with astrology, "from the late Hellenistic period onwards a dominant spiritual force as a new kind of divination with scientific appeal" (Burkert, *Greek Religion*, 329), and influenced Gnosticism (directly or via Middle Platonism) and Hermeticism (esoteric teachings of Hermes Trismegistus that influenced early Christians and medieval alchemists), which may explain why Brüggemann identifies frequent alchemical connotations in Kleist's works: they are

indicative of Kleist's interest in various esoteric trends, including those associated with Phythagorean, Orphic, Dionysiac and Hermetic teachings, and with Alchemy and Masonry. In Kleist's era, pseudo-science increasingly gave way to modern science (cf. his interest in gravity, electricity, magnetism, optics, etc.), but still influenced discourse and poetry; the classical subjects of theology, philosophy, mathematics and physics Kleist hoped to study at Göttingen University (cf. II:483) were precisely the subjects pursued by Pythagoras' disciples. Pythagoreanism comprised a syncretism of religious credos, mathematics, esoteric teachings and (emerging) science: "that an Ionian of the sixth century should assimilate elements of Babylonian mathematics, Iranian religion, and even Indian metempsychosis doctrine is intrinsically possible" (Burkert, *Greek Religion*, 299). Cf. also Sloterdijk (*Sphären II*, 362): "Was Diongenes in seinem berüchtigten píthos, dem Wohn-Faß, vorgemacht hat, das gilt im nächsten Jahrtausend und länger für alle authentischen Vertreter der Zunft: Sie wohnen nicht mehr in der empirischen Stadt, sondern in einer luminosen Tonne, dem Kosmos."

801   This classification is based on E. Cobham Brewer, *Dictionary of Phrase and Fable* (1894), cf. https://en.wikipedia.org/wiki/Pythagoras, n.28. Burkert enumerates (*Greek Religion*) several related doctrines: "According to Pindar there are three paths in the other world... Whoever has led a pious and just life finds a festive existence in the underworld... The soul thereafter returns to the upper world where its fate is determined by its previous deeds, whoever stands the test thrice enters the Island of the Blessed forever... [For] Herodotus... the soul must wander through every domain of the cosmos, being drawn in with the breath of a newly born living creature. According to Empedocles the wandering through all of the elements is atonement for a blood guilt incurred in the divine world; the goal is return to the gods, apotheosis... Aristotle... writes that it was stated 'in the so-called Orphic poems' that the soul, being borne by the winds from out of the universe, enters a living creature with its first breath; but he also knew Phythagorean myths according to which 'any soul can enter any body'... Xenophanes, our earliest witness of Phythagoras, ascribes to him the belief that a human soul, indeed the soul of a friend, could be present in a whipped dog... [T]he opposition between Olympian and Chthonic constitutes a polarity in which one pole cannot exist without the other and in which each pole only receives its full meaning from the other. Above and below, heaven and earth together form the universe (201-2)... The idea finally that the soul is some light, heavenly substance and that man's soul will therefore eventually ascend to heaven set the stage for a momentous synthesis of cosmology

and salvation religion (300)... The association of soul and heaven... could easily be combined with this: soul is heavenly matter. At death, the body falls to the earth, earth to earth; the *psyche*, however, returns to the *aither*" (319-20).

802   Kleist's assertion "that one can lift oneself above fate, indeed, that in a proper sense it be even possible to direct fate" (cf. II:488) is consistent with Pythagoras' concept of the tripartite soul, according to which one can influence the transitions of the soul's luminous and terrestrial vehicles. This faith that the poet can influence the fate of actors comprises the very core of Kleist's *po(i)etical* project. Kleist's imagery of the comet that flares up in the Sun's "embrace" informs *Homburg*'s third monologue: Napoleon has become the Fr. Wilh.'s Sun, to which he is now so close that her glare is thousandfold increased (cf. V.1832), and into which his body is about to fuse, releasing his soul (cf. V.1833-4). When in the 11th scene he awakens from his somnambulant state, he finds his body alive and his soul's departure illusory. Kleist will have been fascinated by this image not least because of the utter annihilation it entails: nothing remains of the comet but its name and history (for lesser comets, not even that). Kleist wished his own soul to be freed absolutely, freed from any Earthly "baggage": *"Nachruhm!... O über den Irrtum, der die Menschen um zwei Leben betrügt, der sie selbst nach dem Tode noch äfft"* (to Wilhelmine, 15th August 1801); when he burned his MSS, it was to destroy all traces of his previous life, so that his next life would be unencumbered by them. Cf. Sloterdijk (*Sphären II*, 423): *"Darum hatte schon das ominöse Wort vom Kosmopolitismus, das Diogenes von Sinope in die antike Debatte geworfen haben soll, einen sarkastischen Unterton, auch wenn die Stoiker später sich bemühten, es ohne Ironie zu gebrauchen: In der Stadt namens Welt kommt für den Weisen alles darauf an, keinesfalls in der heruntergekommenen Innenstadt, der Erde, zu wohnen, sondern in den vornehmen Außenbezirken, wo die besseren Äther-Kreise ihre Villen haben."*

803   In his BA satire *Entwurf einer Bombenpost*, Kleist proposes to complement Samuel Thomas von Soemmering's recent (1809) invention of an electrical telegraph with an "artillery post" capable of transporting massy items across great distances. While comprising a *satirical* dig at that master of the *"Grande batterie"* Napoleon, whose cannons transport no useful goods (whose régime entails only destruction), Kleist's fantasy can also be read in an *orphic* vein, by equating the incorporeal "laconic messages" instantenously transported by Soemmering's telegraph with the human soul, and the parcels to be transported by Kleist's "artillery post" with the human body.

The soul is inherently and infinitely transmissible, while the body is not: one cannot transport the latter to another planet and must therefore dispose of it on Earth. Kleist may have known Gottfried August Bürger's 1786 fantasy of Baron Münchhausen riding on a cannonball (*Käthchen* is sometimes linked to Bürger's ballad *Lenore*), and would have been delighted by Jules Verne's 1865 novel *De la terre à la lune*, in which space travellers are shot to the moon with a giant space cannon (and by E.A. Poe's 1835 short story *The Unpralleled Adventure of One Hans Pfaal*, in which an aeronaut reaches the moon by balloon).

804   https://www.britannica.com/science/Pythagoreanism. The characteristics l list are also compiled from *ibid*.

805   Cf. Bertrand Russel (*History of Western Philosophy*, London: George Allen & Unwin, 1947, 37): "The Orphics were an ascetic sect; wine, to them, was only a symbol, as, later, in the Christian sacrament. The intoxication that they sought was that of "enthusiasm," of union with the god. They believed themselves, in this way, to acquire mystic knowledge not obtainable by ordinary means. This mystical element entered into Greek philosophy with Pythagoras, who was a reformer of Orphism as Orpheus was a reformer of the religion of Dionysus. From Pythagoras Orphic elements entered into the philosophy of Plato, and from Plato into most later philosophy..." Cf. Burkert (*Greek Religion*): "In that late Hellenistic compilation of *Orphica* known as the *Rhapsodies* anthropogony was connected with metempsychosis. This is a speculative doctrine more characteristic of India... which... appears in the fifth century in varying forms in the works of Pindar, Empedocles, and Herodotus and later in Plato's myths (298)... Bacchic, Orphic, and Pythagorean are circles each of which has its own centre, and while these circles have areas that coincide, each preserves its own sphere... Within the sphere of *Orphica*, two schools may perhaps be distinguished, an Athenian-Eleusinian school which concentrated on... the Demeter myth and the Eleusinian mysteries, and an Italian, Pythagorean school... with the doctrine of the transmigration of souls" (300); he adds that Plato attributed to Orphism the doctrine that the soul must "suffer punishment" in this life "until it has paid what is due" (302).

806   The caption on Albrecht Dürer's 1494 drawing *The Death of Orpheus* reads "Orpheus, the first pederast." In how far the semi-mythical Spartan lawgiver Lycurgus's laws of c.820 BC were influenced by Orphism remains unclear.

807   The comet became conspicuous in the evening sky in late summer, reached its brightest aspect on 6th October, with an exceptionally large coma, perhaps 50% larger than the Sun, and an unprecedented 25°-long tail, and was still sighted on 18th December. It later became known as "Napoleon's Comet," as it was popularly thought to have portended Napoleon's *Invasion of Russia*, and appears in Tolstoy's *War and Peace* (cf. https://en.wikipedia.org/wiki/Great_Comet_of_1811). In November 1805, Gentz takes a meteor sighting in Wesel as a good omen (cf. *AML*,132).

808   Bäumler (*Amors vergifteter Pfeil*, 205) notes that paralysis typically sets in at age 30-50. Today it is known that only about 5% of syphiliacs develop paralysis (cf. Bäumler, *Amors vergifteter Pfeil*, 368), still a large number in absolute terms: during the 19th century, paralysis patients may have accounted for 10-20% of all patients admitted to mental asylums (cf. https://de.wikipedia.org/wiki/Neurolues). Kleist could have had a heightened fear of this fate after observing the madmen in the Julius-Hospital, and may have self-diagnosed, or been diagnosed with, early signs of paralysis or *tabes dorsalis*. In so far as *Homburg* is considered by some to be his most accomplished work, like Nietzsche, Kleist may have produced his "best" output at the very onset of madness. Although Kleist and those close to him remain guarded concerning his health, there are signs that it was deteriorating fast: to Ulrike he writes on 18th September: *"Da Du Dich aber... bei meinem Anblick so ungeheuer erschrocken hast, ein Umstand, der mich... auf das allertiefste erschütterte"* (II:880); to Rahel, on 24th October: *"Obwohl ich das Fieber nicht hatte"* (II:882), which suggests that he is regularly plagued by fever; Wilhelmine von Zenge reports that Kleist in his final period was physically ill (cf. *NR*,87). As much as his official autopsy report exaggerates evidence of melancholy and mental troubles, it downplays physical symptoms: no one involved had any interest in reporting symptoms of a communicable and socially frowned-upon disease. The hardening of Kleist's brain substance noted in the autopsy report, which Paul Ridder links to mercury deposits, could be a sign of paralysis, which leads to brain atrophy. Since syphilis typically destroys bone matter, the only possible means today to obtain hard evidence that Kleist was syphiliac would be to exhume his remains.

885

809   Ernst Fr. Peguilhen, who found the corpses, describes Henriette's aspect thus (*NR*,39): *"Halb sitzend, halb liegend, die Hände gefalten, den freundlichen Blick wie im Leben zum Himmel gerichtet, lag sie da."* Michalzik (*Kleist*, 465) is among those to note the parallel with Vouet's painting. Since the double suicide by (phallic) bullets

combines the twin movements of impregnation and (self-) sodomy, it also comprises Kleist's ultimate enactment of his elusive project of *"Scheidung."*

810   Burkert notes (*Greek Religion*, 328;331) that according to Heraclitus, "the daimon's purpose is 'to direct us upward from earth to kinship with heaven,'" and that in Plato's *Symposion* (202e-203a) *daimones* "stand in the middle between gods and men, they are 'interpreters and ferrymen' who communicate the messages and gifts from men to gods and from gods to men."

811   Kleist's letter to Marie of 10th November 1811 could mark this shift: having let off steam regarding the catastrophic get-together in Frankfurt/O., Kleist towards the end of the letter shifts gear (indicated by one of his notorious hyphens) and voices his desperation at the King: "—Die Allianz, die der König jetzt mit den Franzosen schließt, ist auch nicht eben gemacht, mich am Leben festzuhalten" (II:884). Horst Häker takes this letter as proof that Kleist *"stand bis zu seinem Ende (vgl. den Brief an Marie vom 10. November 1811) in der Tradition des preußischen Adels, der all sein Tun auf die Person des (von Gottes Gnaden regierenden) Königs ausrichtete und nur über ihn das Wohl des Staates zu fördern trachtete"* (*Homburg und Verlobung*, 250, n.9), but does not link it with Kleist's death by the Potsdamer Chaussee 11 days later; to Häker's *"nur über ihn"* we might add: *", oder über seine Leiche..."*

812   Rudolf Loch (*Kleist*, 503, n.36; 37) discusses the symbolism of the Spreewald and Kl. Wannsee locations. In 1801 Kleist, Rühle and Pfuel, upon passing the bridge at the Kl. Wannsee, debated that the surest way to commit suicide would be to take a boat out to a deep spot on the lake, fill one's pockets with stones, and sit on the boat's edge as one pulled the trigger, so that even if the bullet failed to be deadly, one would fall backwards into the water and drown (cf. *LS*,53; in 1811 Kleist evidently considers this "boat-trick" unsuitable, be that because it does not correspond to Vouet's constellation or because he wants his body to be found; a direct shot at Henriette's heart followed by one in his mouth for the trained soldier was as sure as any method). Reportedly an August 1811 letter by Kleist reached Fouqué at Stimmings Krug during a get-together with Berlin literary figures, and plausibly Kleist's choice was a sign to a Berlin literary scene from which he became increasingly isolated, and to Fouqué in particular.

813   *The World* (aka *The Universe*), featuring a *Sophia* (wisdom) figure dancing above the Earth, surrounded by a wreath (or *ourobouros*) and the symbols of the four Evangelists, is the final card in the cycle (No. XXI) of the "Major Arcana," representing a cycle of life's ending, a pause before the next cycle begins, cosmic consciousness, and the possibility of union with the universe—cf. https://en.wikipedia.org/wiki/The_World_(Tarot_card).

814   As does Plato's, Kleist's *symposion* features seven symposiasts, if one assumes that alongside the two speakers the four rustic lovers and the *Maschinist* are present. Kleist previously rehearsed symposiac dialogues in *Amphitryon* (Jupiter and Alkmene as speakers, others in the background) and in *Krug*'s court scene. It goes without saying that there could be many plausible "trans." of this essay, of which I am offering but one, focused on *The Satyrico-Syphilitical* ("puppets" = rustic peasants = gay lovers). Other plausible "trans." could focus on, e.g., *The Satirical* ("puppets" = kings, emperors, courtiers), *The Familial* ("puppets" = aunts and uncles, siblings and cousins), *The Filial* ("puppets" = eligible brides, rival suitors), or *The Po(i)etical* ("puppets" = Hardenberg, Iffland, etc.; in French usage *"paradis"* denotes a theatre's gallery from which commoners view a play, often responding to it boisterously, and in so far as the essay entails Kleist's critique of the Berlin theatre scene, the Cherub of the flaming sword who guards access to it could be Hardenberg or Iffland). Any "trans." must address in how far the *Maschinist* partakes in the action on stage or remains behind or above the stage, pulling the strings. *Satyrically*, in order to experience maximum jouissance, the master *erâstes* must immerse himself physically into the action; *filially*, the answer depends on whether the procreator seeks to produce a biological son or to socially legitimize a suitable heir; *satirically*, the bard may remain backgrounded, using the stage as his communication channel, but at times may have to come forth to obtain first-hand information: he must go to Saint-Omer, Kolberg, Aspern, Wagram. By investing his self into a "puppet," the *Maschinist* immerses himself into the movements and actions on stage. *Marionettentheater* has been a key target for Kleist readers seeking a "key" or "formula" for Kleist's œuvre—cf., e.g., Klaus Kanzog in "Heinrich von Kleists *Über Das Marionettentheater*—Wirklich eine Poetic?" (*Kleist*, 182-96); I sought to show that such "keys" can be found anywhere and everywhere in Kleist's works, so that the essay is not unique, although it is perhaps paradigmatic, and may be considered Kleist's theoretical condensation of past works as well as his test-bed for forthcoming works, notably *Homburg*.

815 My "trans." seeks to convey that the two speakers' exchange is as much physical as it is discursive, and uses technical terms borrowed from magnetism: "passes" are the movements of a *magnétiseur*'s "hand" (Kleist: penis) across the medium's "body" (Kleist: buttocks); "fluid" or "fluidum" are a medium's bodily flows (Kleist: ejaculate) or intensities (Kleist: orgasm) generated by the *magnétiseur*'s "passes"; "stoppage points" are a medium's bodily resistances that block its "fluidum" (Kleist: physical constriction and mental coyness during intercourse) but may be released by the "passes."

816 Two worthy successors of Kleist's in the department of *satirical* poetry, René Coscinny and Albert Uderzo, never failed to acknowledge the bard's ultimate powerlessness: in their *Astérix* comics the bard Cacofonix at the end of each episode is invariably strung up or tied to a tree and gagged, thus prevented from singing, in a humorous but also humble gesture of self-irony on the part of the authors, for the bard of course represents them. Kleist was, evidently, less humble. Kleist's faith, that any logically and consistently encrypted message always *can*, and eventually *will*, be decrypted, anticipates A.E. Poe's, who in *The Gold Bug* seeks to demonstrate as much.

www.ingramcontent.com/pod-product-compliance
Lightning Source LLC
Chambersburg PA
CBHW071351300426
44114CB00016B/2024